T0180243

Lecture Notes in Computer Science 10964

Commenced Publication in 1973
Founding and Former Series Editors:
Gerhard Goos, Juris Hartmanis, and Jan van Leeuwen

Editorial Board

More information about this series at http://www.springer.com/series/7407

Osvaldo Gervasi · Beniamino Murgante
Sanjay Misra · Elena Stankova
Carmelo M. Torre · Ana Maria A. C. Rocha
David Taniar · Bernady O. Apduhan
Eufemia Tarantino · Yeonseung Ryu (Eds.)

Computational Science and Its Applications – ICCSA 2018

18th International Conference
Melbourne, VIC, Australia, July 2–5, 2018
Proceedings, Part V

 Springer

Editors
Osvaldo Gervasi ⓘ
University of Perugia
Perugia, Italy

Beniamino Murgante ⓘ
University of Basilicata
Potenza, Italy

Sanjay Misra ⓘ
Covenant University
Ota, Nigeria

Elena Stankova ⓘ
Saint Petersburg State University
Saint Petersburg, Russia

Carmelo M. Torre ⓘ
Polytechnic University of Bari
Bari, Italy

Ana Maria A. C. Rocha ⓘ
University of Minho
Braga, Portugal

David Taniar ⓘ
Monash University
Clayton, VIC, Australia

Bernady O. Apduhan
Kyushu Sangyo University
Fukuoka shi, Fukuoka, Japan

Eufemia Tarantino ⓘ
Politecnico di Bari
Bari, Italy

Yeonseung Ryu ⓘ
Myongji University
Yongin, Korea (Republic of)

ISSN 0302-9743　　　　　ISSN 1611-3349　(electronic)
Lecture Notes in Computer Science
ISBN 978-3-319-95173-7　　　ISBN 978-3-319-95174-4　(eBook)
https://doi.org/10.1007/978-3-319-95174-4

Library of Congress Control Number: 2018947453

LNCS Sublibrary: SL1 – Theoretical Computer Science and General Issues

Printed on acid-free paper

This Springer imprint is published by the registered company Springer International Publishing AG
part of Springer Nature
The registered company address is: Gewerbestrasse 11, 6330 Cham, Switzerland

Preface

These multiple volumes (LNCS volumes 10960–10964) consist of the peer-reviewed papers presented at the 2018 International Conference on Computational Science and Its Applications (ICCSA 2018) held in Melbourne, Australia, during July 2–5, 2018.

ICCSA 2018 was a successful event in the International Conferences on Computational Science and Its Applications (ICCSA) conference series, previously held in Trieste, Italy (2017), Beijing, China (2016), Banff, Canada (2015), Guimaraes, Portugal (2014), Ho Chi Minh City, Vietnam (2013), Salvador, Brazil (2012), Santander, Spain (2011), Fukuoka, Japan (2010), Suwon, South Korea (2009), Perugia, Italy (2008), Kuala Lumpur, Malaysia (2007), Glasgow, UK (2006), Singapore (2005), Assisi, Italy (2004), Montreal, Canada (2003), and (as ICCS) Amsterdam, The Netherlands (2002) and San Francisco, USA (2001).

Computational science is a main pillar of most current research and industrial and commercial activities and it plays a unique role in exploiting ICT innovative technologies. The ICCSA conference series has been providing a venue to researchers and industry practitioners to discuss new ideas, to share complex problems and their solutions, and to shape new trends in computational science.

Apart from the general tracks, ICCSA 2018 also included 33 international workshops, in various areas of computational sciences, ranging from computational science technologies, to specific areas of computational sciences, such as computer graphics and virtual reality. The program also featured three keynote speeches.

The success of the ICCSA conference series, in general, and ICCSA 2018, in particular, is due to the support of many people: authors, presenters, participants, keynote speakers, session chairs, Organizing Committee members, student volunteers, Program Committee members, International Advisory Committee members, International Liaison chairs, and people in other various roles. We would like to thank them all.

We would also like to thank Springer for their continuous support in publishing the ICCSA conference proceedings and for sponsoring some of the paper awards.

July 2018

David Taniar
Bernady O. Apduhan
Osvaldo Gervasi
Beniamino Murgante
Ana Maria A. C. Rocha

Welcome to Melbourne

Welcome to "The Most Liveable City"[1], Melbourne, Australia. ICCSA 2018 was held at Monash University, Caulfield Campus, during July 2–5, 2018.

Melbourne is the state capital of Victoria, and is currently the second most populous city in Australia, behind Sydney. There are lots of things to do and experience while in Melbourne. Here is an incomplete list:

– Visit and experience Melbourne's best coffee shops
– Discover Melbourne's hidden laneways and rooftops
– Walk along the Yarra River
– Eat your favourite food (Chinese, Vietnamese, Malaysian, Italian, Greek, anything, … you name it)
– Buy souvenirs at the Queen Victoria Market
– Go up to the Eureka, the tallest building in Melbourne
– Visit Melbourne's museums
– Walk and enjoy Melbourne's gardens and parks
– Visit the heart-shape lake, Albert Park Lake, the home of the F1 Grand Prix
– Simply walk in the city to enjoy Melbourne experience
– Try Melbourne's gelato ice cream

Basically, it is easy to live in and to explore Melbourne, and I do hope that you will have time to explore the city of Melbourne.

The venue of ICCSA 2018 was in Monash University. Monash University is a member of Go8, which is considered the top eight universities in Australia. Monash University has a number of campuses and centers. The two main campuses in Melbourne are Clayton and Caulfield. ICCSA 2018 was held on Caulfield Campus, which is only 12 minutes away from Melbourne CBD by train.

The Faculty of Information Technology is one of the ten faculties at Monash University. The faculty has more than 100 full-time academic staff (equivalent to the rank of Assistant Professor, Associate Professor, and Professor).

I do hope that you will enjoy not only the conference, but also Melbourne.

David Taniar

---

[1] The Global Liveability Report 2017, https://www.cnbc.com/2017/08/17/the-worlds-top-10-most-livable-cities.html

Organization

ICCSA 2018 was organized by Monash University (Australia), University of Perugia (Italy), Kyushu Sangyo University (Japan), University of Basilicata (Italy), and University of Minho, (Portugal).

Honorary General Chairs

Antonio Laganà	University of Perugia, Italy
Norio Shiratori	Tohoku University, Japan
Kenneth C. J. Tan	Sardina Systems, Estonia

General Chairs

David Taniar	Monash University, Australia
Bernady O. Apduhan	Kyushu Sangyo University, Japan

Program Committee Chairs

Osvaldo Gervasi	University of Perugia, Italy
Beniamino Murgante	University of Basilicata, Italy
Ana Maria A. C. Rocha	University of Minho, Portugal

International Advisory Committee

Jemal Abawajy	Deakin University, Australia
Dharma P. Agrawal	University of Cincinnati, USA
Marina L. Gavrilova	University of Calgary, Canada
Claudia Bauzer Medeiros	University of Campinas, Brazil
Manfred M. Fisher	Vienna University of Economics and Business, Austria
Yee Leung	Chinese University of Hong Kong, SAR China

International Liaison Chairs

Ana Carla P. Bitencourt	Universidade Federal do Reconcavo da Bahia, Brazil
Giuseppe Borruso	University of Trieste, Italy
Alfredo Cuzzocrea	University of Trieste, Italy
Maria Irene Falcão	University of Minho, Portugal
Robert C. H. Hsu	Chung Hua University,Taiwan
Tai-Hoon Kim	Hannam University, South Korea
Sanjay Misra	Covenant University, Nigeria
Takashi Naka	Kyushu Sangyo University, Japan

| Rafael D. C. Santos | National Institute for Space Research, Brazil |
| Maribel Yasmina Santos | University of Minho, Portugal |

Workshop and Session Organizing Chairs

Beniamino Murgante	University of Basilicata, Italy
Sanjay Misra	Covenant University, Nigeria
Jorge Gustavo Rocha	University of Minho, Portugal

Award Chair

| Wenny Rahayu | La Trobe University, Australia |

Web Chair

| A. S. M. Kayes | La Trobe University, Australia |

Publicity Committee Chairs

Elmer Dadios	De La Salle University, Philippines
Hong Quang Nguyen	International University (VNU-HCM), Vietnam
Daisuke Takahashi	Tsukuba University, Japan
Shangwang Wang	Beijing University of Posts and Telecommunications, China

Workshop Organizers

Advanced Methods in Fractals and Data Mining for Applications (AMFDMA 2018)

Yeliz Karaca	IEEE
Carlo Cattani	Tuscia University, Italy
Majaz Moonis	University of Massachusettes Medical School, USA

Advances in Information Systems and Technologies for Emergency Management, Risk Assessment and Mitigation Based on Resilience Concepts (ASTER 2018)

Maurizio Pollino	ENEA, Italy
Marco Vona	University of Basilicata, Italy
Beniamino Murgante	University of Basilicata, Italy
Grazia Fattoruso	ENEA, Italy

Advances in Web-Based Learning (AWBL 2018)

| Mustafa Murat Inceoglu | Ege University, Turkey |
| Birol Ciloglugil | Ege University, Turkey |

Bio- and Neuro-inspired Computing and Applications (BIONCA 2018)

Nadia Nedjah   State University of Rio de Janeiro, Brazil
Luiza de Macedo Mourell   State University of Rio de Janeiro, Brazil

Computer-Aided Modeling, Simulation, and Analysis (CAMSA 2018)

Jie Shen   University of Michigan, USA
Hao Chen   Shanghai University of Engineering Science, China
Youguo He   Jiangsu University, China

Computational and Applied Statistics (CAS 2018)

Ana Cristina Braga   University of Minho, Portugal

Computational Geometry and Security Applications (CGSA 2018)

Marina L. Gavrilova   University of Calgary, Canada

Computational Movement Analysis (CMA 2018)

Farid Karimipour   University of Tehran, Iran

Computational Mathematics, Statistics and Information Management (CMSIM 2018)

M. Filomena Teodoro   Lisbon University and Portuguese Naval Academy,
                        Portugal

Computational Optimization and Applications (COA 2018)

Ana Maria Rocha   University of Minho, Portugal
Humberto Rocha   University of Coimbra, Portugal

Computational Astrochemistry (CompAstro 2018)

Marzio Rosi   University of Perugia, Italy
Dimitrios Skouteris   Scuola Normale Superiore di Pisa, Italy
Albert Rimola   Universitat Autònoma de Barcelona, Spain

Cities, Technologies, and Planning (CTP 2018)

Giuseppe Borruso   University of Trieste, Italy
Beniamino Murgante   University of Basilicata, Italy

Defense Technology and Security (DTS 2018)

Yeonseung Ryu   Myongji University, South Korea

Econometrics and Multidimensional Evaluation in the Urban Environment (EMEUE 2018)

Carmelo M. Torre	Polytechnic of Bari, Italy
Maria Cerreta	University of Naples Federico II, Italy
Pierluigi Morano	Polytechnic of Bari, Italy
Paola Perchinunno	University of Bari, Italy

Future Computing Systems, Technologies, and Applications (FISTA 2018)

Bernady O. Apduhan	Kyushu Sangyo University, Japan
Rafael Santos	National Institute for Space Research, Brazil
Shangguang Wang	Beijing University of Posts and Telecommunications, China
Kazuaki Tanaka	Kyushu Institute of Technology, Japan

Geographical Analysis, Urban Modeling, Spatial Statistics (GEO-AND-MOD 2018)

Giuseppe Borruso	University of Trieste, Italy
Beniamino Murgante	University of Basilicata, Italy
Hartmut Asche	University of Potsdam, Germany

Geomatics for Resource Monitoring and Control (GRMC 2018)

Eufemia Tarantino	Polytechnic of Bari, Italy
Umberto Fratino	Polytechnic of Bari, Italy
Benedetto Figorito	ARPA Puglia, Italy
Antonio Novelli	Polytechnic of Bari, Italy
Rosa Lasaponara	Italian Research Council, IMAA-CNR, Italy

International Symposium on Software Quality (ISSQ 2018)

Sanjay Misra	Covenant University, Nigeria

Web-Based Collective Evolutionary Systems: Models, Measures, Applications (IWCES 2018)

Alfredo Milani	University of Perugia, Italy
Clement Leung	United International College, Zhouhai, China
Valentina Franzoni	University of Rome La Sapienza, Italy
Valentina Poggioni	University of Perugia, Italy

Large-Scale Computational Physics (LSCP 2018)

Elise de Doncker	Western Michigan University, USA
Fukuko Yuasa	High Energy Accelerator Research Organization, KEK, Japan
Hideo Matsufuru	High Energy Accelerator Research Organization, KEK, Japan

Land Use Monitoring for Soil Consumption Reduction (LUMS 2018)

Carmelo M. Torre	Polytechnic of Bari, Italy
Alessandro Bonifazi	Polytechnic of Bari, Italy
Pasquale Balena	Polytechnic of Bari, Italy
Beniamino Murgante	University of Basilicata , Italy
Eufemia Tarantino	Polytechnic of Bari, Italy

Mobile Communications (MC 2018)

Hyunseung Choo   Sungkyunkwan University, South Korea

Scientific Computing Infrastructure (SCI 2018)

Elena Stankova	Saint-Petersburg State University, Russia
Vladimir Korkhov	Saint-Petersburg State University, Russia

International Symposium on Software Engineering Processes and Applications (SEPA 2018)

Sanjay Misra   Covenant University, Nigeria

Smart Factory Convergence (SFC 2018)

Jongpil Jeong   Sungkyunkwan University, South Korea

Is a Smart City Really Smart? Models, Solutions, Proposals for an Effective Urban and Social Development (Smart_Cities 2018)

Giuseppe Borruso	University of Trieste, Italy
Chiara Garau	University of Cagliari, Italy
Ginevra Balletto	University of Cagliari, Italy
Beniamino Murgante	University of Basilicata, Italy
Paola Zamberlin	University of Florence, Italy

Sustainability Performance Assessment: Models, Approaches and Applications Toward Interdisciplinary and Integrated Solutions (SPA 2018)

Francesco Scorza	University of Basilicata, Italy
Valentin Grecu	Lucia Blaga University on Sibiu, Romania
Jolanta Dvarioniene	Kaunas University, Lithuania
Sabrina Lai	Cagliari University, Italy

Advances in Spatio-Temporal Analytics (ST-Analytics 2018)

Rafael Santos	Brazilian Space Research Agency, Brazil
Karine Reis Ferreira	Brazilian Space Research Agency, Brazil
Joao Moura Pires	New University of Lisbon, Portugal
Maribel Yasmina Santos	University of Minho, Portugal

Theoretical and Computational Chemistry and Its Applications (TCCA 2018)

M. Noelia Faginas Lago	University of Perugia, Italy
Andrea Lombardi	University of Perugia, Italy

Tools and Techniques in Software Development Processes (TTSDP 2018)

Sanjay Misra   Covenant University, Nigeria

Challenges, Trends and Innovations in VGI (VGI 2018)

Beniamino Murgante   University of Basilicata, Italy
Rodrigo Tapia-McClung   Centro de Investigación en Geografia y Geomática Ing
                               Jorge L. Tamay, Mexico
Claudia Ceppi   Polytechnic of Bari, Italy
Jorge Gustavo Rocha   University of Minho, Portugal

Virtual Reality and Applications (VRA 2018)

Osvaldo Gervasi   University of Perugia, Italy
Sergio Tasso   University of Perugia, Italy

International Workshop on Parallel and Distributed Data Mining (WPDM 2018)

Massimo Cafaro   University of Salento, Italy
Italo Epicoco   University of Salento, Italy
Marco Pulimeno   University of Salento, Italy
Giovanni Aloisio   University of Salento, Italy

Program Committee

Kenny Adamson   University of Ulster, UK
Vera Afreixo   University of Aveiro, Portugal
Filipe Alvelos   University of Minho, Portugal
Hartmut Asche   University of Potsdam, Germany
Michela Bertolotto   University College Dublin, Ireland
Sandro Bimonte   CEMAGREF, TSCF, France
Rod Blais   University of Calgary, Canada
Ivan Blečić   University of Sassari, Italy
Giuseppe Borruso   University of Trieste, Italy
Ana Cristina Braga   University of Minho, Portugal
Yves Caniou   Lyon University, France
José A. Cardoso e Cunha   Universidade Nova de Lisboa, Portugal
Rui Cardoso   University of Beira Interior, Portugal
Leocadio G. Casado   University of Almeria, Spain
Carlo Cattani   University of Salerno, Italy
Mete Celik   Erciyes University, Turkey
Alexander Chemeris   National Technical University of Ukraine KPI, Ukraine
Min Young Chung   Sungkyunkwan University, South Korea

Florbela Maria da Cruz Domingues Correia	Polytechnic Institute of Viana do Castelo, Portugal
Gilberto Corso Pereira	Federal University of Bahia, Brazil
Carla Dal Sasso Freitas	Universidade Federal do Rio Grande do Sul, Brazil
Pradesh Debba	The Council for Scientific and Industrial Research (CSIR), South Africa
Hendrik Decker	Instituto Tecnológico de Informática, Spain
Frank Devai	London South Bank University, UK
Rodolphe Devillers	Memorial University of Newfoundland, Canada
Joana Matos Dias	University of Coimbra, Portugal
Paolino Di Felice	University of L'Aquila, Italy
Prabu Dorairaj	NetApp, India/USA
M. Irene Falcao	University of Minho, Portugal
Cherry Liu Fang	U.S. DOE Ames Laboratory, USA
Florbela P. Fernandes	Polytechnic Institute of Bragança, Portugal
Jose-Jesus Fernandez	National Centre for Biotechnology, CSIS, Spain
Paula Odete Fernandes	Polytechnic Institute of Bragança, Portugal
Adelaide de Fátima Baptista Valente Freitas	University of Aveiro, Portugal
Manuel Carlos Figueiredo	University of Minho, Portugal
Maria Antonia Forjaz	University of Minho, Portugal
Maria Celia Furtado Rocha	PRODEB–PósCultura/UFBA, Brazil
Paulino Jose Garcia Nieto	University of Oviedo, Spain
Jerome Gensel	LSR-IMAG, France
Maria Giaoutzi	National Technical University, Athens, Greece
Arminda Manuela Andrade Pereira Gonçalves	University of Minho, Portugal
Andrzej M. Goscinski	Deakin University, Australia
Sevin Gmïgmï	Izmir University of Economics, Turkey
Alex Hagen-Zanker	University of Cambridge, UK
Malgorzata Hanzl	Technical University of Lodz, Poland
Shanmugasundaram Hariharan	B.S. Abdur Rahman University, India
Eligius M. T. Hendrix	University of Malaga/Wageningen University, Spain/The Netherlands
Tutut Herawan	Universitas Teknologi Yogyakarta, Indonesia
Hisamoto Hiyoshi	Gunma University, Japan
Fermin Huarte	University of Barcelona, Spain
Mustafa Inceoglu	EGE University, Turkey
Peter Jimack	University of Leeds, UK
Qun Jin	Waseda University, Japan
A. S. M. Kayes	La Trobe University, Australia
Farid Karimipour	Vienna University of Technology, Austria
Baris Kazar	Oracle Corp., USA
Maulana Adhinugraha Kiki	Telkom University, Indonesia
DongSeong Kim	University of Canterbury, New Zealand

Taihoon Kim   Hannam University, South Korea
Ivana Kolingerova   University of West Bohemia, Czech Republic
Rosa Lasaponara   National Research Council, Italy
Maurizio Lazzari   National Research Council, Italy
Cheng Siong Lee   Monash University, Australia
Sangyoun Lee   Yonsei University, South Korea
Jongchan Lee   Kunsan National University, South Korea
Clement Leung   Hong Kong Baptist University, Hong Kong, SAR
                           China
Chendong Li   University of Connecticut, USA
Gang Li   Deakin University, Australia
Ming Li   East China Normal University, China
Fang Liu   AMES Laboratories, USA
Xin Liu   University of Calgary, Canada
Savino Longo   University of Bari, Italy
Tinghuai Ma   NanJing University of Information Science
                           and Technology, China
Luca Mancinelli   Trinity College Dublin, Ireland
Ernesto Marcheggiani   Katholieke Universiteit Leuven, Belgium
Antonino Marvuglia   Research Centre Henri Tudor, Luxembourg
Nicola Masini   National Research Council, Italy
Eric Medvet   University of Trieste, Italy
Nirvana Meratnia   University of Twente, The Netherlands
Alfredo Milani   University of Perugia, Italy
Giuseppe Modica   University of Reggio Calabria, Italy
Josè Luis Montaña   University of Cantabria, Spain
Maria Filipa Mourão   IP from Viana do Castelo, Portugal
Laszlo Neumann   University of Girona, Spain
Kok-Leong Ong   Deakin University, Australia
Belen Palop   Universidad de Valladolid, Spain
Marcin Paprzycki   Polish Academy of Sciences, Poland
Eric Pardede   La Trobe University, Australia
Kwangjin Park   Wonkwang University, South Korea
Ana Isabel Pereira   Polytechnic Institute of Bragança, Portugal
Maurizio Pollino   Italian National Agency for New Technologies, Energy
                           and Sustainable Economic Development, Italy
Alenka Poplin   University of Hamburg, Germany
Vidyasagar Potdar   Curtin University of Technology, Australia
David C. Prosperi   Florida Atlantic University, USA
Wenny Rahayu   La Trobe University, Australia
Jerzy Respondek   Silesian University of Technology, Poland
Humberto Rocha   INESC-Coimbra, Portugal
Alexey Rodionov   Institute of Computational Mathematics
                           and Mathematical Geophysics, Russia

Jon Rokne	University of Calgary, Canada
Octavio Roncero	CSIC, Spain
Maytham Safar	Kuwait University, Kuwait
Chiara Saracino	A.O. Ospedale Niguarda Ca' Granda - Milano, Italy
Haiduke Sarafian	The Pennsylvania State University, USA
Marco Paulo Seabra dos Reis	University of Coimbra, Portugal
Jie Shen	University of Michigan, USA
Qi Shi	Liverpool John Moores University, UK
Dale Shires	U.S. Army Research Laboratory, USA
Inês Soares	University of Coimbra, Portugal
Takuo Suganuma	Tohoku University, Japan
Sergio Tasso	University of Perugia, Italy
Ana Paula Teixeira	University of Trás-os-Montes and Alto Douro, Portugal
Senhorinha Teixeira	University of Minho, Portugal
Parimala Thulasiraman	University of Manitoba, Canada
Carmelo Torre	Polytechnic of Bari, Italy
Javier Martinez Torres	Centro Universitario de la Defensa Zaragoza, Spain
Giuseppe A. Trunfio	University of Sassari, Italy
Toshihiro Uchibayashi	Kyushu Sangyo University, Japan
Pablo Vanegas	University of Cuenca, Ecuador
Marco Vizzari	University of Perugia, Italy
Varun Vohra	Merck Inc., USA
Koichi Wada	University of Tsukuba, Japan
Krzysztof Walkowiak	Wroclaw University of Technology, Poland
Zequn Wang	Intelligent Automation Inc., USA
Robert Weibel	University of Zurich, Switzerland
Frank Westad	Norwegian University of Science and Technology, Norway
Roland Wismüller	Universität Siegen, Germany
Mudasser Wyne	SOET National University, USA
Chung-Huang Yang	National Kaohsiung Normal University, Taiwan
Xin-She Yang	National Physical Laboratory, UK
Salim Zabir	France Telecom Japan Co., Japan
Haifeng Zhao	University of California, Davis, USA
Kewen Zhao	University of Qiongzhou, China
Fabiana Zollo	University of Venice Cà Foscari, Italy
Albert Y. Zomaya	University of Sydney, Australia

Reviewers

Afreixo Vera	University of Aveiro, Portugal
Ahmad Rashid	Microwave and Antenna Lab, School of Engineering, Korea
Aguilar José Alfonso	Universidad Autónoma de Sinaloa, Mexico
Albanese Valentina	Università di Bologna, Italy
Alvelos Filipe	University of Minho, Portugal
Amato Federico	University of Basilicata, Italy
Andrianov Serge	Institute for Informatics of Tatarstan Academy of Sciences, Russia
Antunes Marília	University Nova de Lisboa, Portugal
Apduhan Bernady	Kyushu Sangyo University, Japan
Aquilanti Vincenzo	University of Perugia, Italy
Asche Hartmut	Potsdam University, Germany
Aslan Zafer	Istanbul Aydin University, Turkey
Aytaç Vecdi	Ege University, Turkey
Azevedo Ana	Instituto Superior de Engenharia do Porto, Portugal
Azzari Margherita	Universitá degli Studi di Firenze, Italy
Bae Ihn-Han	Catholic University of Daegu, South Korea
Balci Birim	Celal Bayar Üniversitesi, Turkey
Balena Pasquale	Politecnico di Bari, Italy
Balucani Nadia	University of Perugia, Italy
Barroca Filho Itamir	Instituto Metrópole Digital da UFRN (IMD-UFRN), Brazil
Bayrak §sengül	Haliç University, Turkey
Behera Ranjan Kumar	Indian Institute of Technology Patna, India
Bimonte Sandro	IRSTEA, France
Bogdanov Alexander	Saint-Petersburg State University, Russia
Bonifazi Alessandro	Polytechnic of Bari, Italy
Borruso Giuseppe	University of Trieste, Italy
Braga Ana Cristina	University of Minho, Portugal
Cafaro Massimo	University of Salento, Italy
Canora Filomena	University of Basilicata, Italy
Cao Yuanlong	University of Saskatchewan, Canada
Caradonna Grazia	Polytechnic of Bari, Italy
Cardoso Rui	Institute of Telecommunications, Portugal
Carolina Tripp Barba	Universidad Autónoma de Sinaloa, Mexico
Caroti Gabriella	University of Pisa, Italy
Ceccarello Matteo	University of Padova, Italy
Cefalo Raffaela	University of Trieste, Italy
Cerreta Maria	University Federico II of Naples, Italy
Challa Rajesh	Sungkyunkwan University, Korea
Chamundeswari Arumugam	SSN College of Engineering, India
Chaturvedi Krishna Kumar	Patil Group of Industries, India
Cho Chulhee	Seoul Guarantee Insurance Company Ltd., Korea

Choi Jae-Young	Sungkyunkwan University, Korea
Choi Kwangnam	Korea Institute of Science and Technology Information, Korea
Choi Seonho	Seoul National University, Korea
Chung Min Young	Sungkyunkwan University, Korea
Ciloglugil Birol	Ege University, Turkey
Coletti Cecilia	University of Chieti, Italy
Congiu Tanja	Università degli Studi di Sassari, Italy
Correia Anacleto	Base Naval de Lisboa, Portugal
Correia Elisete	University of Trás-Os-Montes e Alto Douro, Portugal
Correia Florbela Maria da Cruz Domingues	Instituto Politécnico de Viana do Castelo, Portugal
Costa e Silva Eliana	Polytechnic of Porto, Portugal
Cugurullo Federico	Trinity College Dublin, Ireland
Damas Bruno	LARSyS, Instituto Superior Técnico, Univ. Lisboa, Portugal
Dang Thien Binh	Sungkyunkwan University, Korea
Daniele Bartoli	University of Perugia, Italy
de Doncker Elise	Western Michigan University, USA
Degtyarev Alexander	Saint-Petersburg State University, Russia
Demyanov Vasily	Heriot-Watt University, UK
Devai Frank	London South Bank University, UK
Di Fatta Giuseppe	University of Reading, UK
Dias Joana	University of Coimbra, Portugal
Dilo Arta	University of Twente, The Netherlands
El-Zawawy Mohamed A.	Cairo University, Egypt
Epicoco Italo	Università del Salento, Italy
Escalona Maria-Jose	University of Seville, Spain
Falcinelli Stefano	University of Perugia, Italy
Faginas-Lago M. Noelia	University of Perugia, Italy
Falcão M. Irene	University of Minho, Portugal
Famiano Michael	Western Michigan University, USA
Fattoruso Grazia	ENEA, Italy
Fernandes Florbela	Escola Superior de Tecnologia e Gestão de Braganca, Portugal
Fernandes Paula	Escola Superior de Tecnologia e Gestão, Portugal
Ferraro Petrillo Umberto	University of Rome "La Sapienza", Italy
Ferreira Fernanda	Escola Superior de Estudos Industriais e de Gestão, Portugal
Ferrão Maria	Universidade da Beira Interior, Portugal
Figueiredo Manuel Carlos	Universidade do Minho, Portugal
Fiorini Lorena	Università degli Studi dell'Aquila, Italy
Florez Hector	Universidad Distrital Francisco Jose de Caldas, Colombia
Franzoni Valentina	University of Perugia, Italy

Freitau Adelaide de Fátima Baptista Valente	University of Aveiro, Portugal
Gabrani Goldie	Bml Munjal University, India
Garau Chiara	University of Cagliari, Italy
Garcia Ernesto	University of the Basque Country, Spain
Gavrilova Marina	University of Calgary, Canada
Gervasi Osvaldo	University of Perugia, Italy
Gioia Andrea	University of Bari, Italy
Giorgi Giacomo	University of Perugia, Italy
Giuliani Felice	Università degli Studi di Parma, Italy
Goel Rajat	University of Southern California, USA
Gonçalves Arminda Manuela	University of Minho, Portugal
Gorbachev Yuriy	Geolink Technologies, Russia
Gordon-Ross Ann	University of Florida, USA
Goyal Rinkaj	Guru Gobind Singh Indraprastha University, India
Grilli Luca	University of Perugia, Italy
Goyal Rinkaj	GGS Indraprastha University, India
Guerra Eduardo	National Institute for Space Research, Brazil
Gumgum Sevin	İzmir Ekonomi Üniversitesi, Turkey
Gülen Kemal Güven	Istanbul Ticaret University, Turkey
Hacızade Ulviye	Haliç Üniversitesi Uluslararas, Turkey
Han Longzhe	Nanchang Institute of Technology, Korea
Hanzl Malgorzata	University of Lodz, Poland
Hayashi Masaki	University of Calgary, Canada
He Youguo	Jiangsu University, China
Hegedus Peter	University of Szeged, Hungary
Herawan Tutut	Universiti Malaysia Pahang, Malaysia
Ignaccolo Matteo	University of Catania, Italy
Imakura Akira	University of Tsukuba, Japan
Inceoglu Mustafa	Ege University, Turkey
Jagwani Priti	Indian Institute of Technology Delhi, India
Jang Jeongsook	Brown University, Korea
Jeong Jongpil	Sungkyunkwan University, Korea
Jin Hyunwook	Konkuk University, Korea
Jorge Ana Maria, Kapenga John	Western Michigan University, USA
Kawana Kojiro	University of Tokio, Japan
Kayes Abu S. M.	La Trobe University, Australia
Kim JeongAh	George Fox University, USA
Korkhov Vladimir	St. Petersburg State University, Russia
Kulabukhova Nataliia	Saint-Peterburg State University, Russia
Kumar Pawan	Expert Software Consultants Ltd., India
Laccetti Giuliano	Università degli Studi di Napoli, Italy
Laganà Antonio	Master-up srl, Italy
Lai Sabrina	University of Cagliari, Italy

Laricchiuta Annarita	CNR-IMIP, Italy
Lazzari Maurizio	CNR IBAM, Italy
Lee Soojin	Cyber Security Lab, Korea
Leon Marcelo	Universidad Estatal Península de Santa Elena – UPSE, Ecuador
Lim Ilkyun	Sungkyunkwan University, Korea
Lourenço Vanda Marisa	University Nova de Lisboa, Portugal
Mancinelli Luca	University of Dublin, Ireland
Mangiameli Michele	University of Catania, Italy
Markov Krassimiri	Institute for Information Theories and Applications, Bulgaria
Marques Jorge	Universidade de Coimbra, Portugal
Marvuglia Antonino	Public Research Centre Henri Tudor, Luxembourg
Mateos Cristian	Universidad Nacional del Centro, Argentina
Matsufuru Hideo	High Energy Accelerator Research, Japan
Maurizio Crispini	Politecnico di Milano, Italy
Medvet Eric	University of Trieste, Italy
Mengoni Paolo	Università degli Studi di Firenze, Italy
Mesiti Marco	Università degli studi di Milano, Italy
Millham Richard	Durban University of Technology, South Africa
Misra Sanjay	Covenant University, Nigeria
Mishra Anurag	Helmholtz Zentrum München, Germany
Mishra Biswajeeban	University of Szeged, Hungary
Moscato Pablo	University of Newcastle, Australia
Moura Pires Joao	Universidade Nova de Lisboa, Portugal
Moura Ricardo	Universidade Nova de Lisboa, Portugal
Mourao Maria	Universidade do Minho, Portugal
Mukhopadhyay Asish	University of Windsor, Canada
Murgante Beniamino	University of Basilicata, Italy
Nakasato Naohito	University of Aizu, Japan
Nguyen Tien Dzung	Sungkyunkwan University, South Korea
Nicolosi Vittorio	University of Rome Tor Vergata, Italy
Ogihara Mitsunori	University of Miami, USA
Oh Sangyoon	Ajou University, Korea
Oliveira Irene	University of Trás-Os-Montes e Alto Douro, Portugal
Oluranti Jonathan	Covenant University, Nigeria
Ozturk Savas	The Scientific and Technological Research Council of Turkey, Turkey
P. Costa M. Fernanda	University of Minho, Portugal
Paek Yunheung	Seoul National University, Korea
Pancham Jay	Durban University of Technology, South Africa
Pantazis Dimos	Technological Educational Institute of Athens, Greek
Paolucci Michela	Università degli Studi di Firenze, Italy
Pardede Eric	La Trobe University, Australia
Park Hyun Kyoo	Petabi Corp, Korea
Passaro Tommaso	University of Bari, Italy

Pereira Ana	Instituto Politécnico de Bragança, Portugal
Peschechera Giuseppe	University of Bari, Italy
Petri Massimiliano	Università di Pisa, Italy
Pham Quoc Trung	Ho Chi Minh City University of Technology, Vietnam
Piemonte Andrea	Università di Pisa, Italy
Pinna Francesco	Università degli Studi di Cagliari, Italy
Pinto Telmo	University of Minho, Portugal
Pollino Maurizio	ENEA, Italy
Pulimeno Marco	University of Salento, Italy
Rahayu Wenny	La Trobe University, Australia
Rao S. V.	Duke Clinical Research, USA
Raza Syed Muhammad	Sungkyunkwan University, South Korea
Reis Ferreira Gomes Karine	National Institute for Space Research, Brazil
Reis Marco	Universidade de Coimbra, Portugal
Rimola Albert	Autonomous University of Barcelona, Spain
Rocha Ana Maria	University of Minho, Portugal
Rocha Humberto	University of Coimbra, Portugal
Rodriguez Daniel	The University of Queensland, Australia
Ryu Yeonseung	Myongji University, South Korea
Sahni Himantikka	CRISIL Global Research and Analytics, India
Sahoo Kshira Sagar	C. V. Raman College of Engineering, India
Santos Maribel Yasmina	University of Minho, Portugal
Santos Rafael	KU Leuven, Belgium
Saponaro Mirko	Politecnico di Bari, Italy
Scorza Francesco	Università della Basilicata, Italy
Sdao Francesco	Università della Basilicata, Italy
Shen Jie	University of Southampton, UK
Shintani Takahiko	University of Electro-Communications, Japan
Shoaib Muhammad	Sungkyunkwan University, South Korea
Silva-Fortes Carina	ESTeSL-IPL, Portugal
Singh V. B.	University of Delhi, India
Skouteris Dimitrios	SNS, Italy
Soares Inês	INESCC and IPATIMUP, Portugal
Sosnin Petr	Ulyanovsk State Technical University, Russia
Souza Erica	Universidade Nova de Lisboa, Portugal
Stankova Elena	Saint-Petersburg State University, Russia
Sumida Yasuaki	Kyushu Sangyo University, Japan
Tanaka Kazuaki	Kyushu Institute of Technology, Japan
Tapia-McClung Rodrigo	CentroGeo, Mexico
Tarantino Eufemia	Politecnico di Bari, Italy
Tasso Sergio	University of Perugia, Italy
Teixeira Ana Paula	Universidade Católica Portuguesa, Portugal
Tengku Adil	La Trobe University, Australia
Teodoro M. Filomena	Lisbon University, Portugal
Tiwari Sunita	King George's Medical University, India
Torre Carmelo Maria	Polytechnic of Bari, Italy

Torrisi Vincenza	University of Catania, Italy
Totaro Vincenzo	Politecnico di Bari, Italy
Tran Manh Hung	Institute for Research and Executive Education, Vietnam
Tripathi Aprna	GLA University, India
Trunfio Giuseppe A.	University of Sassari, Italy
Tóth Zoltán	Hungarian Academy of Sciences, Hungary
Uchibayashi Toshihiro	Kyushu Sangyo University, Japan
Ugliengo Piero	University of Torino, Italy
Ullman Holly	University of Delaware, USA
Vallverdu Jordi	Autonomous University of Barcelona, Spain
Valuev Ilya	Russian Academy of Sciences, Russia
Vasyunin Dmitry	University of Amsterdam, The Netherlands
Vohra Varun	University of Electro-Communications, Japan
Voit Nikolay	Ulyanovsk State Technical University, Russia
Wale Azeez Nurayhn	University of Lagos, Nigeria
Walkowiak Krzysztof	Wroclaw University of Technology, Poland
Wallace Richard J.	Univeristy of Texas, USA
Waluyo Agustinus Borgy	Monash University, Australia
Westad Frank	CAMO Software AS, USA
Wole Adewumi	Covenant University, Nigeria
Xie Y. H.	Bell Laboratories, USA
Yamauchi Toshihiro	Okayama University, Japan
Yamazaki Takeshi	University of Tokyo, Japan
Yao Fenghui	Tennessee State University, USA
Yoki Karl	Catholic University of Daegu, South Korea
Yoshiura Noriaki	Saitama University, Japan
Yuasa Fukuko	High Energy Accelerator Research Organization, Korea
Zamperlin Paola	University of Florence, Italy
Zollo Fabiana	University of Venice "Cà Foscari", Italy
Zullo Francesco	University of L'Aquila, Italy
Zivkovic Ljiljana	Republic Agency for Spatial Planning, Belgrade

Sponsoring Organizations

ICCSA 2018 would not have been possible without the tremendous support of many organizations and institutions, for which all organizers and participants of ICCSA 2018 express their sincere gratitude:

Springer International Publishing AG, Germany
(http://www.springer.com)

Monash University, Australia
(http://monash.edu)

University of Perugia, Italy
(http://www.unipg.it)

University of Basilicata, Italy
(http://www.unibas.it)

Kyushu Sangyo University, Japan
(www.kyusan-u.ac.jp)

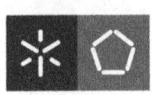

Universidade do Minho, Portugal
(http://www.uminho.pt)

Keynote Speakers

New Frontiers in Cloud Computing for Big Data and Internet-of-Things (IoT) Applications

Rajkumar Buyya[1,2]

[1] Cloud Computing and Distributed Systems (CLOUDS) Lab,
The University of Melbourne, Australia
[2] Manjrasoft Pvt Ltd., Melbourne, Australia

Abstract. Computing is being transformed to a model consisting of services that are commoditised and delivered in a manner similar to utilities such as water, electricity, gas, and telephony. Several computing paradigms have promised to deliver this utility computing vision. Cloud computing has emerged as one of the buzzwords in the IT industry and turned the vision of "computing utilities" into a reality.

Clouds deliver infrastructure, platform, and software (application) as services, which are made available as subscription-based services in a pay-as-you-go model to consumers. Cloud application platforms need to offer

1. APIs and tools for rapid creation of elastic applications and
2. a runtime system for deployment of applications on geographically distributed computing infrastructure in a seamless manner.

The Internet of Things (IoT) paradigm enables seamless integration of cyber-and-physical worlds and opening up opportunities for creating newclass of applications for domains such as smart cities. The emerging Fog computing is extending Cloud computing paradigm to edge resources for latency sensitive IoT applications.

This keynote presentation will cover:

a. 21st century vision of computing and identifies various IT paradigms promising to deliver the vision of computing utilities;
b. opportunities and challenges for utility and market-oriented Cloud computing,
c. innovative architecture for creating market-oriented and elastic Clouds by harnessing virtualisation technologies;
d. Aneka, a Cloud Application Platform, for rapid development of Cloud/Big Data applications and their deployment on private/public Clouds with resource provisioning driven by SLAs;
e. experimental results on deploying Cloud and Big Data/Internet-of-Things (IoT) applications in engineering, and health care, satellite image processing, and smart cities on elastic Clouds;

f. directions for delivering our 21st century vision along with pathways for future research in Cloud and Fog computing.

Short Bio Dr. Rajkumar Buyya is a Redmond Barry Distinguished Professor and Director of the Cloud Computing and Distributed Systems (CLOUDS) Laboratory at the University of Melbourne, Australia. He is also serving as the founding CEO of Manjrasoft, a spin-off company of the University, commercializing its innovations in Cloud Computing. He served as a Future Fellow of the Australian Research Council during 2012-2016. He has authored over 625 publications and seven text books including "Mastering Cloud Computing" published by McGraw Hill, China Machine Press, and Morgan Kaufmann for Indian, Chinese and international markets respectively. He also edited several books including "Cloud Computing: Principles and Paradigms" (Wiley Press, USA, Feb 2011).

He is one of the highly cited authors in computer science and software engineering worldwide (h-index = 117, g-index = 255, 70,500 + citations). Dr. Buyya is recognized as a "Web of Science Highly Cited Researcher" in both 2016 and 2017 by Thomson Reuters, a Fellow of IEEE, and Scopus Researcher of the Year 2017 with Excellence in Innovative Research Award by Elsevier for his outstanding contributions to Cloud computing.

Software technologies for Grid and Cloud computing developed under Dr. Buyya's leadership have gained rapid acceptance and are in use at several academic institutions and commercial enterprises in 40 countries around the world. Dr. Buyya has led the establishment and development of key community activities, including serving as foundation Chair of the IEEE Technical Committee on Scalable Computing and five IEEE/ACM conferences. These contributions and international research leadership of Dr. Buyya are recognized through the award of "2009 IEEE Medal for Excellence in Scalable Computing" from the IEEE Computer Society TCSC.

Manjrasoft's Aneka Cloud technology developed under his leadership has received "2010 Frost & Sullivan New Product Innovation Award". He served as the founding Editor-in-Chief of the IEEE Transactions on Cloud Computing. He is currently serving as Co-Editor-in-Chief of Journal of Software: Practice and Experience, which was established over 45 years ago. For further information on Dr. Buyya, please visit his cyberhome: www.buyya.com.

Approximation Problems for Digital Image Processing and Applications

Gianluca Vinti

Department of Mathematics and Computer Science,
University of Perugia, Italy

Abstract. In this talk, some approximation problems are discussed with applications to reconstruction and to digital image processing. We will also show some applications to concrete problems in the medical and engineering fields. Regarding the first, a procedure will be presented, based on approaches of approximation theory and on algorithms of digital image processing for the diagnosis of aneurysmal diseases; in particular we discuss the extraction of the pervious lumen of the artery starting from CT image without contrast medium. As concerns the engineering field, thermographic images are analyzed for the study of thermal bridges and for the structural and dynamic analysis of buildings, working therefore in the field of energy analysis and seismic vulnerability of buildings, respectively.

Short Bio Gianluca Vinti is Full Professor of Mathematical Analysis at the Department of Mathematics and Computer Science of the University of Perugia. He is Director of the Department since 2014 and member of the Academic Senate of the University. Member of the Board of the Italian Mathematical Union since 2006, member of the "Scientific Council of the GNAMPA-INdAM "(National Group for the Mathematical Analysis, the Probability and their Applications) since 2013, Referent for the Mathematics of the Educational Center of the "Accademia Nazionale dei Lincei" at Perugia since 2013 and Member of the Academic Board of the Ph.D. in Mathematics, Computer Science, Statistics organized in consortium (C.I.A.F.M.) among the University of Perugia (Italy), University of Florence (Italy) and the INdAM (National Institute of High Mathematics).

He is and has been coordinator of several research projects and he coordinates a research team who deals with Real Analysis, Theory of Integral Operators, Approximation Theory and its Applications to Signal Reconstruction and Images Processing.

He has been invited to give more than 50 plenary lectures at conferences at various Universities and Research Centers. Moreover he is author of more than 115 publications on international journals and one scientific monography on "Nonlinear Integral Operators and Applications" edited by W. de Gruyter. Finally he is member of the Editorial Board of the following international scientific journals: Sampling Theory in Signal and Image Processing (STSIP), Journal of Function Spaces and Applications, Open Mathematics, and others and he holds a patent entitled: "Device for obtaining informations on blood vessels and other bodily-cave parts".

Contents – Part V

Workshop Defense Technology and Security (DTS 2018)

Workshop Geomatics for Resource Monitoring and Control (GRMC 2018)

8th International Symposium on Software Quality (ISSQ 2018)

Workshop Smart Factory Convergence (SFC 2018)

Workshop Theoretical and Computational Chemistry and Its Applications (TCCA 2018)

Workshop Parallel and Distributed Data Mining (WPDM 2018)

Workshop Sustainability Performance Assessment: Models, Approaches and Applications Toward Interdisciplinary and Integrated Solutions (SPA 2018)

Workshop Cities, Technologies and Planning (CTP 2018)

Spatial Data Analysis and Evaluation by Urban Planners of a PPGIS Experiment Performed in Porto Alegre, Brazil

Geisa Bugs[✉]

Centro Universitário Ritter dos Reis - UniRitter, Porto Alegre, Brazil
geisa.bugs@uniritter.com.br

Abstract. We analyze spatial data on the public perception collected in a Public Participation Geographic Information System (PPGIS) experiment performed in Porto Alegre, Brazil. Aiming to verify PPGIS capability to access inhabitants local knowledge and facilitate its incorporation into urban planning, using an exploratory analysis in the form of heat maps, we describe the spatial distribution of our variables and identify patterns. In addition, PPGIS was evaluated by urban planners in order to assess expert's openness to the method. The results indicate that by collecting public perceptions in an automated, geo-referenced manner, PPGIS enables these data to be analyzed together with other information layers necessary for urban planning. Moreover, local knowledge collected with PPSIG can help improve the content quality of urban plans and/or projects in the opinion of the urban planner's consulted. However, it is necessary to expand technical knowledge so that the data collected can be analyzed and incorporated in urban planning in a consistent way.

Keywords: Spatial analysis · Public perception · Urban planners

1 Introduction

Cities are complex organizations. The production, use, and exchange of spatial knowledge in various forms are essential processes for city planning and management. It is from the confrontation between inhabitant's local knowledge and the technical expert's knowledge that a better understanding of a given territory arises [1].

Local knowledge is acquired through life experience, cultural tradition, and is based on individual experiences and perceptions. Local knowledge, while being subjective and difficult to generalize, adds unique information regarding local configurations, specific knowledge of circumstances, events, and spatiotemporal relationships Expert knowledge, on the other hand, objective and abstract, stems from the practice developed by professionals in their work contexts, is collected by methods and tools, and tested through peer review [1, 2].

In general, expert knowledge is dominant in urban planning because planners have the power to choose which knowledge to use and how to use it. This choice is nearly always based on the professional values of these experts [2]. Thus, urban planning remains primarily based on the technical approach that emphasizes accurate,

© Springer International Publishing AG, part of Springer Nature 2018
O. Gervasi et al. (Eds.): ICCSA 2018, LNCS 10964, pp. 3–18, 2018.
https://doi.org/10.1007/978-3-319-95174-4_1

unambiguous information. According to [3], aggregated statistics from official data represent the only means to take public into account into urban planning.

Knowing how to consistently analyze and use inhabitant knowledge in urban planning is a crucial issue [4]. Such knowledge integration reflects an aspiration for deeper, more impactful participatory planning. However, thus far, planners have generally failed to consistently address the public perspective in urban planning [3, 5].

The growing importance attached to public participation pushes planners to find new ways of combining their technical knowledge with the knowledge that only the inhabitants possess. Distinguished authors advocate the need to reformulate urban planning using technologies that facilitate more interactive, emancipatory, and collaborative methods [6–8]. That is, urban planning must improve its understanding of the knowledge hidden in the everyday individual's experiences and develop the skills and methods required to use that knowledge.

Recent studies suggest that Public Participation Geographic Information System (PPGIS) have the potential to efficiently collect public perceptions and thus provide a better understanding of the inhabitant's experiences in a given territory [9–11]. As the name suggests, PPGIS uses GIS tools for public participation, connecting the GIS technical capacity to local knowledge [12]. The public participates by producing maps and spatial data that represent their perceptions of the urban space in question.

1.1 Public Participation Geographic Information System

PPGIS emerged in the 1990s from reflections on the interface of GIS and society. During the early 2000s, the approach was considered an evolution of classical participation methods [13]. However, the initial enthusiasm began to decline in approximately 2005 [10], when several problems were noted, such as the recognition that terms and concepts, such as "participation" and "empowerment", were used uncritically [14]. Soon thereafter, so-called map mash-ups (i.e., the mixture of different types of software and data) and voluntary mapping emerged in the Web 2.0. Projects soon emerged that took advantage of interactive online maps and the increased knowledge of geographic information by the public (e.g. [14]). These projects demonstrate an increasing interest in using online mapping participation tools [10], and subsequently the interest in PPGIS was renewed.

However, with few exceptions, PPGIS remains relatively uninvestigated from the urban planner's perspective. Most of the experiments that have been performed were developed by geographers, with a focus on producing participatory mapping, or by information-technology professionals, with a focus on technological development. Examples of the use of PPGIS as an integral part of planning practice are still scarcer[1], particularly in contexts like the Brazilian.

As highlighted by [15], optimal conditions for performing PPGIS projects emerged with the advent of the Web 2.0 and its bidirectional approach based on user-generated

---

[1] In Finland, the mainstreaming of PPGIS has already occurred. For example, PPGIS was used in Helsinki's master planning process as a tool for participatory planning, and a large-scale dataset was collected from nearly 4,000 participants (see [25]).

content, usability, and interoperability. This context presupposes innovations in PPGIS applications. Thus, to extend existing empirical knowledge regarding the method and its possible benefits for urban planning, we propose to analyze the spatial data collected in a PPGIS experiment performed in Porto Alegre, Brazil, to evaluate the ability of the approach to collect public perceptions and facilitate their incorporation into urban planning practices. The authors follow Brandt's (as cited in [16]) guidelines for PPGIS evaluation: the value of the results lies in their ability to provide useful, proper, and timely information that civil and governmental organizations can use.

Additionally, we investigate how urban planners evaluate alternative methods, such as PPGIS. An information overlay exercise, which aims to show relationships between different variables and interpretations of the issue at hand, is a fundamental analysis tool for urban planning. However, such an exercise is not simple to produce [4]. The geo-visualization and interpretation of the data collected with PPGIS require theoretical and practical improvement. Different to analyze the data commonly used in urban planning (i.e., physical territorial, socioeconomic and cadastral data), studies on how to represent and analyze the subjective and qualitative nature of the attributes mapped by the public are not known. Similarly, the professional's view of the usefulness of such data is unknown.

In short, this paper analyzes spatial data on the public perceptions collected in a PPGIS experiment performed in Porto Alegre/Brazil and evaluates urban planner's perspective on the method. The objectives are two: (1) evaluate PPSIG capacity to access local knowledge and facilitate its incorporation into urban planning, and (2) evaluate expert's opinion of new approaches usage in urban planning, such as PPSIG. Thereby, we aim to expand the empirical knowledge about the PPGIS usage in the Brazilian urban planning context, and contribute to the PPSIG debate by approaching the urban planner's perspective.

First, we contextualize and present the PPSIG experiment in Sect. 2, along with the performed urban planners PPGIS assessment. Section 3 presents the results from the spatial data analysis, through heat maps, and the urban planner's answers to the PPGIS evaluation questionnaire. Finally, Sect. 4 ends with conclusions and research directions within the research domain and practice.

2 Method

2.1 PPGIS Experiment

Developed at Aalto University, SoftGIS is a PPGIS method that facilitates the study of inhabitants' location-based experiences [17]. Here, "soft" refers to the qualitative and subjective nature of the attributes mapped by participants in contrast to the "hard" geospatial data layers generally associated with GIS. The method has been previously applied in more than twenty cities in different countries (for a list, see [18]). The method consists of an online questionnaire with an interactive map interface. Respondents answer predefined questions by marking points, lines, or polygons on the map. Thus, the answers refer to locations and can be transferred into table formats and shapefiles.

Thanks to its do-it-yourself interface, SoftGIS was easily customized for the experiment performed in Porto Alegre, here referred to as PPGIS Guaíba Waterfront. This type of interface enables anyone, even those without programming skills, to build a web application.

Porto Alegre is the capital of Brazil's southernmost state, Rio Grande do Sul and has approximately 1.4 million inhabitants. The city is recognized for being a pioneer in participative budgeting (1989) and for hosting the first meetings of the World Social Forum (2001, 2002 and 2003). The city lies on the eastern bank of Guaíba Lake (also referred to as a river) (Fig. 1).

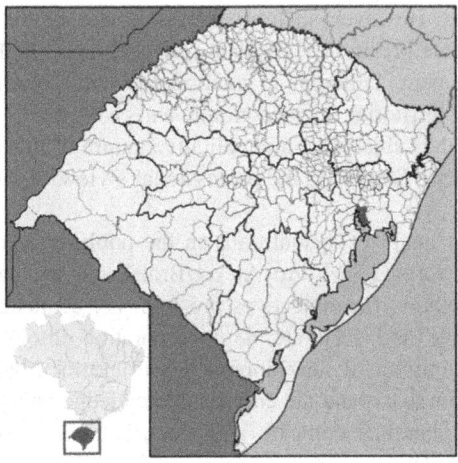

Fig. 1. Rio Grande do Sul location in Brazil and Porto Alegre location in the state.

The revitalization of the Guaíba Waterfront represents a long-held desire. The Porto Alegre master plan considers the waterfront a special area that must be revitalized. With this intent, the Municipal Planning Department has already produced three studies: Guidelines for the Guaíba Waterfront [19]; the Guaíba Report: Current Conditions, Possibilities and Instruments for the Qualification and Rescue of the Porto Alegre Waterfront; and Urban Design Guidelines for the Central Waterfront [20].

However, there is no record of public participation in these studies. Thus, we can state that public perceptions regarding this urban space, which is highly significant for the inhabitants, were not considered. The controversial repercussions of a revitalization project in 2013 [21] indicate that the city's inhabitants wish to participate in the development of revitalization proposals for the area. Such urban issue fits well the experiment requirement of attracting the attention of different interest groups.

Thus, the objective of the PPGIS Guaíba Waterfront experiment was to collect information on inhabitant perceptions regarding the quality of the waterfront, given the desire and need to revitalize this urban space and the lack of established knowledge regarding such perceptions. The online questionnaire based on the PPGIS's interactive map contained twelve questions that required marking locations on the map (e.g., "Which locations should have exclusive pedestrian access?") and that addressed four themes: preferences, future use, accessibility and improvements.

The PPGIS Guaíba Waterfront had nine pages (i.e., interfaces). The first page presented the tool and invited the respondent to participate. The second page contained questions regarding the respondents' personal information. The next five pages presented the questions that involved the use of the interactive online map. The penultimate page contained a PPGIS evaluation questionnaire, and the last page presented a closing comment and a thank you.

PPGIS Guaíba Waterfront was announced on Porto Alegre social networks and online discussion groups. Being an online, voluntary participation tool, we expected that the link to access it would be shared in a "snowball" effect, as occurs with much Internet content today. Therefore, one can describe the respondent data as a random respondent's sample, without control. There was no way to establish a return rate. The only restrictions reported in the PPGIS presentation were that the respondent should be at least 16 years old (i.e., electoral majority) and have resided in Porto Alegre for at least one year.

2.2   PPGIS Evaluation by Urban Planners

The PPGIS method was evaluated by urban planners via a questionnaire that was distributed to architects and urban planners involved in urban planning in Rio Grande do Sul state. More specifically from city halls, universities and private companies that develop urban plans and/or projects. Although professionals from different areas perform urban planning, we determined to only work with architects and urban planners for greater access feasibility. In addition, generally, architects and urban planners are the professionals who are most closely identified with the activity of urban planning because only they are qualified to assume technical responsibility for a master plan in Brazil.

In total, we distributed 100 questionnaires by e-mail and obtained a 42% rate of return (i.e., 42 of 100). Of the returned questionnaires, only 19 respondents (45.2% - 19 of 42) stated that they had prior knowledge of the PPGIS method. Therefore, these respondents were the ones considered in this evaluation. The respondents evaluated (i.e., completely agree, agree, neither agree or disagree, disagree or completely disagree) statements adopted from literature review and provided comments on them.

3   Results

3.1   Spatial Data Analysis

In total, 156 respondents used the interactive online map from the PPGIS Guaíba Waterfront, marking 3,366 locations on the map. The minimum time of tool use was 4 min, the maximum time was 53 min, and the average time was 14.6 min. The tool was available online during December 2013.

In sum, the respondents were aged between 26 and 40 years (59.8%), had an income from 5 to 10 minimum wages (34.9%) and university education (96.3%). Notably, 5 respondents (4.6%) were over 60 years old. This profile is similar to that of the samples from other studies performed in the area (e.g., [10, 11]). Regarding Internet access, nearly all respondents (99.1%) access the Internet daily. Regarding familiarity with interactive online maps, such as Google Maps, again, nearly all (99.1%) claim to be familiar with such maps, facilitating usability.

We spatially manipulated, analyzed and represented the collected spatial data in GIS software. The purpose of this spatial analysis was to measure properties and relationships, while considering the spatial location of the studied phenomenon. The procedures included exploratory analysis and data geo-visualization through the creation of thematic maps. This approach enabled us to describe the distribution of the study variables and to identify patterns in the spatial distribution.

The data take the form of points, lines or polygons. In the case of point pattern analysis, the object of interest is proper event location [22]. When the point is used, we assumed that each point represents a polygonal area with an unknown shape and size [11]. For example, one participant may refer to a spatial area the size of a football field, while another may refer to a spatial area as large as a neighborhood. Thus, the data analysis uses the spatial aggregation of points to create heat maps that delineate areas of concentration. In response to certain questions, the respondents drew lines. In these cases, the analysis consisted of the overlapping of the various answers to arrive at a synthesis of the areas delimited by the respondents.

Next, we present the maps generated using the data collected for each of the four PPGIS Guaíba Waterfront themes: preferences, future use, accessibility, and improvements.

Preferences. The first PPGIS Guaíba Waterfront theme was addressed by asking the respondents which location "I like most" and "I like less" within a delimited waterfront section and the main reasons why they preferred (or did not prefer) it. Figure 2 shows the marked points and an interpolation between them, which provides an idea of continuity between the points. This "double" visualization was adopted to enable quick visual communication of the points marked as locations that "I like most" (red) and that "I like less" (green). That is, in this way, concentrations of similar responses are more clearly perceived.

The map's visual analysis facilitates highlighting as areas that "I like most" those areas near the following reference points/landmarks: Gasômetro Power Plant (former), Maurício Sirotsky Sobrinho Park, Marinha do Brasil Park, Iberê Camargo Museum, Veleiros do Sul (yacht club), and the State Auditors Association (a recreational club). Similarly, the areas that "I like less" are found close to the following reference points/landmarks: Sunset Amphitheater, International Sport Club (soccer), Só Shipyard, and Fisherman Village.

The main reasons for liking each location were as follows[2]: Gasômetro Power Plant - visual contemplation (21% - 62 of 295); Maurício Sirotsky Sobrinho

---

[2] Each respondent could mark up to three points per question. Neither marking a point nor selecting a reason were mandatory. Thus, there are different numbers of responses per question.

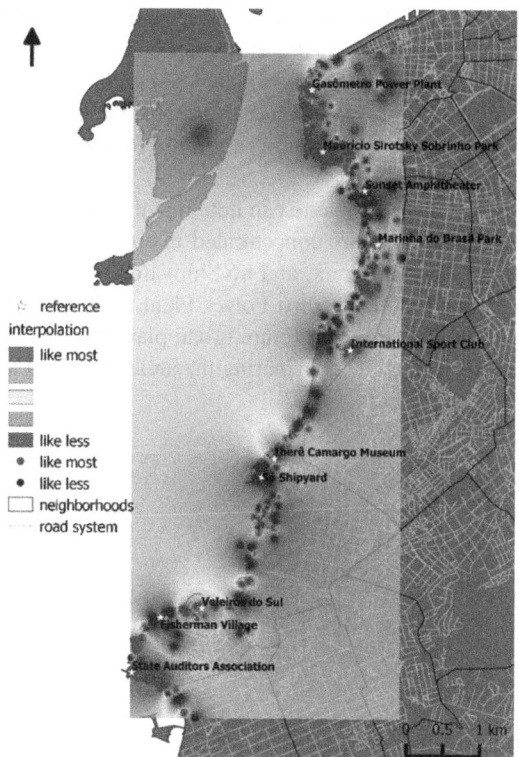

Fig. 2. Locations "I like most" and "I like less". Note: "Double" representation (points and interpolated surface). (Color figure online)

Park - visual contemplation (19.5% - 24 of 123); Marinha do Brasil Park - visual contemplation and contact with nature (15% - 23 of 151, each); Iberê Camargo Museum - visual contemplation (31% - 32 of 104) and cultural space visitation (25% - 26 of 104); Veleiros do Sul - visual contemplation (23.5% - 8 of 34) and contact with nature (18% - 6 of 34); and the State Auditors Association - visual contemplation (27% - 19 of 71) and the positive appearance of open space (18% - 13 of 71). The reason most often provided for liking a location was visual contemplation (21.6% - 168 of 778), which makes evident what the respondents most like to do on this part of the waterfront.

The main reasons respondents provided for not liking a location were as follows (see footnote 2): Sunset Amphitheater - negative appearance of open space (24% - 35 of 144) and trash (24% - 35 of 144); International Sport Club – negative appearance of open space (16% - 10 of 61) and lack of maintenance (16% - 10 of 61); Só Shipyard - negative appearance of open space (21.5% - 33 of 153) and lack of maintenance (18% - 27 of 153); and Fisherman Village – negative appearance of open space (23% - 10 of 43) and traffic insecurity (23% - 10 of 43). The most often cited reason for not liking a location was the negative appearance of open space, with 21.9% (88 of 401) clearly indicating a desire for the renovation of these spaces.

Future Use. The second PPGIS Guaíba Waterfront theme addressed the desired uses for the area in the future. The most cited uses were visual contemplation (12.4% - 173 de 1,391), sports (11.7% - 163 de 1,391), bars and restaurants (10.9% - 151 de 1,391), and recreation (10.4% - 144 de 1,391). Figure 3 presents the heat map (used to identify areas in which there is a high concentration of points) for each of the four future uses that were most often cited.

Through the map visual analysis, one can note that the points marked for the future use of visual contemplation (left) are concentrated in areas close to Gasômetro Power Plant, Maurício Sirotsky Sobrinho Park, and Só Shipyard. The points marked for sports use (right) are concentrated at Gasômetro Power Plant, Sunset Amphitheater, and Só Shipyard. Thus, one may conclude that future urban planning should encourage visual contemplation and sports use, while considering the areas indicated by the respondents.

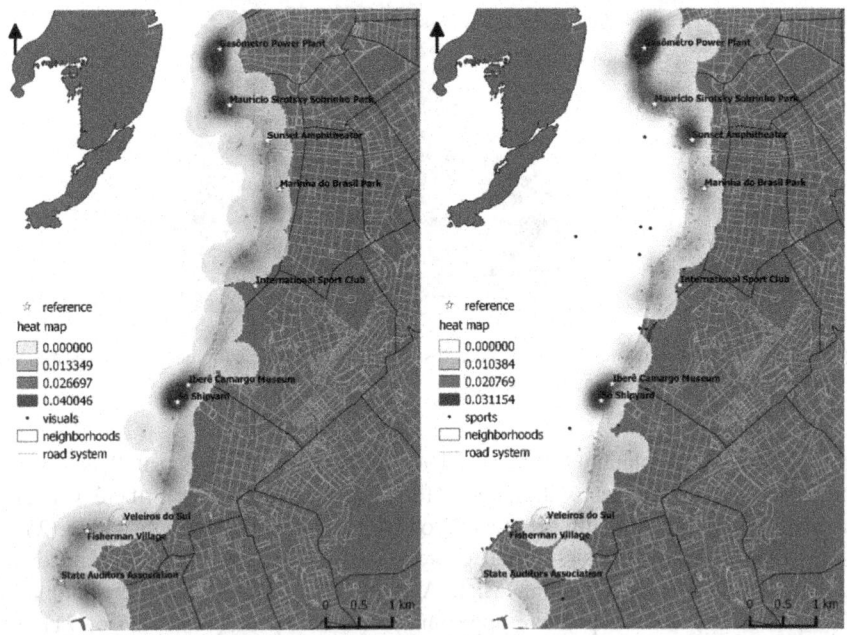

Fig. 3. Future uses that were most often cited. Note: The value is higher in the point location and decreases with increasing distance, which can reach zero. That is, larger values represent a higher density of the phenomenon. (Color figure online)

Accessibility. The third PPGIS Guaíba Waterfront theme was accessibility. We asked which locations should have exclusive pedestrian access, which should provide pedestrian paths, which should have bicycle lanes, and which should provide contin-uous vehicular traffic routes along the border.

The points marked for exclusive pedestrian access are concentrated near Gasômetro Power Plant, between the Maurício Sirotsky Sobrinho Park and the Sunset Amphitheater, at Marinha do Brasil Park, and at Só Shipyard. Thus, according to the respondents, in these locations, access by motor vehicles, which is currently permitted at nearly all of the locations, should be prohibited allowed, as it is currently the case in almost all of them.

In turn, pedestrian paths should be included throughout the waterfront area. Figure 4 - left presents in the background the layer of existing bicycle paths, in dark blue, according to the Cycle Map of Open Street Maps. One can note that the bicycle paths drawn by the respondents (pink) overlap the existing paths (blue) and extend throughout the waterfront and the adjacent streets. Therefore, one can affirm that there is a wide demand for bicycle path expansion.

The map for the continuous circulation of vehicles (Fig. 4 - right) shows Open Street Maps as a background. One can note that the lines marked by the respondents generally correspond exactly to the current avenues. Therefore, there is no significant demand for future modification of the existing road system.

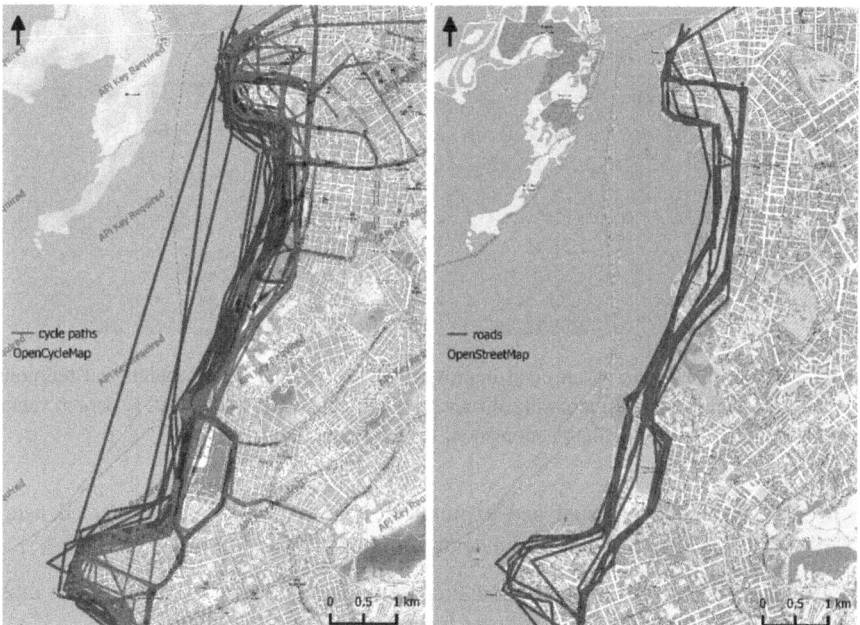

Fig. 4. Mosaic of maps regarding the accessibility theme. Note: The value is higher at the point location and decreases with increasing distance, which can reach zero. That is, larger values represent a higher density of the phenomenon. (Color figure online)

Improvements. The final PPGIS Guaíba Waterfront theme addressed the main improvements required to renovate the waterfront area's border in the respondents' opinion. The most cited improvements were lighting (20.6% - 207 of 1,007), cleaning/maintenance (15.8% - 159 of 1,007), public toilets (15.5% - 156 of 1,007), and furniture (13.4% - 135 of 1,007). The points marked for the four improvements are concentrated at Gasômetro Power Plant, Sunset Amphitheater and Só Shipyard (Fig. 5:

lighting – left and cleaning – right). Therefore, in the opinion of the respondents, the Guaíba Waterfront is unsatisfactory in terms of public space quality, given that there are demands for minimum urban amenities even in well-frequented locations, such as those cited.

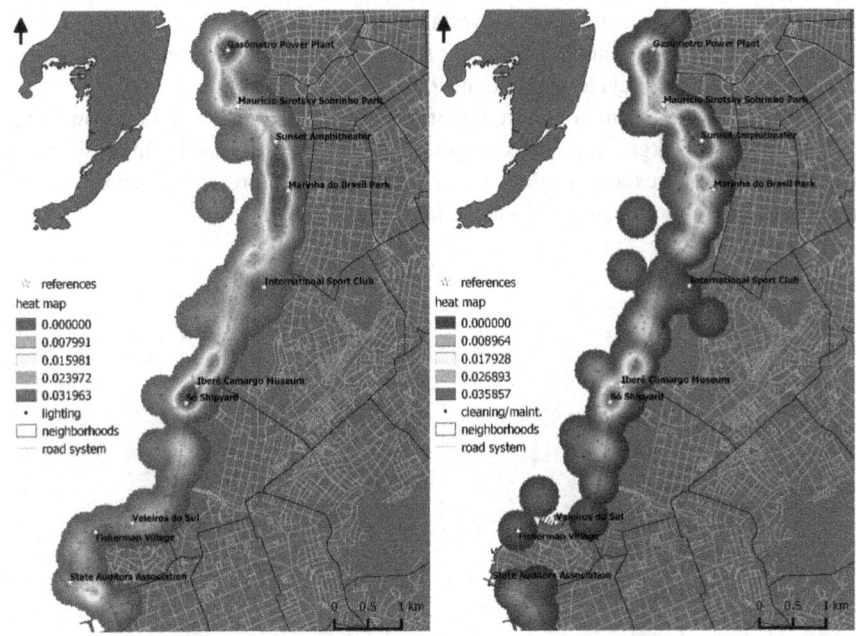

Fig. 5. Mosaic of the most often cited improvements. Note: The value is higher at the point location and decreases with increasing distance, which can reach zero. That is, larger values represent a higher density of the phenomenon. (Color figure online)

In sum, through the visual and exploratory analysis of the data collected using PPGIS Guaíba Waterfront, the respondents' opinions are as follows:

- Maintenance and prevalence of visual contemplation conditions – the reason most often cited to like a location and the future use more often cited;
- Improving the appearance of spaces as a whole - the most often cited reason for not liking locations;
- Future use predominantly for visual contemplation, sports, recreation and bars and restaurants;
- Exclusive pedestrian access at points where access to vehicles is currently allowed, such as: Sunset Amphitheater and Maurício Sirotsky Sobrinho Park;
- Extension of pedestrian paths and exclusive bicycle paths along the entire waterfront; and
- Improvements, primarily lighting, cleaning/maintenance, public toilets and urban furniture.

In principle, each urban intervention proposal should consider the perceptions of local inhabitants. In this way, it becomes possible to incorporate resident wishes in the design of future proposals, plans and/or projects, thus facilitating their acceptance, and not only to hold public hearings and/or public consultations that are exclusively based on expert knowledge. Importantly, the tendency has been for residents to oppose projects regarding which they have not been consulted or formally informed [3, 23].

Here is an opportune moment to observe that the general guidelines for the Guaíba Waterfront described in the studies produced by [19, 20] were solely elaborated from the view of technicians/experts and were more generic than the information generated by the analysis of the spatial data collected using PPGIS Guaíba Waterfront.

3.2   PPGIS Assessment by Urban Planners

All of the urban planners completely agreed (52.6% - 10 of 19) or agreed (47.4% - 9 of 19) with the statement "PPSIG makes it possible to systematically include local knowledge in a spatial database that can feed a decision support system" [4] (Table 1).

Table 1. PPSIG makes it possible to systematically include local knowledge in a spatial

	PPSIG makes it possible to include local knowledge systematically in a spatial database that can feed a decision support system	
	N°	%
Totally agree	10	52.6
Agree	9	47.4
Neither agree nor disagree	0	0
Disagree	0	0
Totally disagree	0	0
Total	19	100

In the comments, one respondent highlighted the need to transform the collected data into useful information: *"local knowledge is fundamental, but if it is not properly structured (if the data is not converted into useful information), it may end up not contributing to an efficient decision support system"*. Similarly, another respondent drew attention to the need to possess adequate technical knowledge to analyze the data consistently: *"This depends very much on how this 'qualitative' data is inserted... or one can easily incur false correlations."*

Regarding the assertion "With the PPSIG method, individually significant quality factors (e.g., levels of satisfaction with urban spaces) can be easily analyzed in relation to other layers of information (e.g., census data)" [11], a clear majority of respondents (89.4% - 17 of 19) completely agree (36.8% - 7 of 19) or agreed (52.6% - 10 of 19) (Table 2).

Table 2. Individually significant quality factors can be easily analyzed, and the information collected with PPSIG may lead to different solutions

	With the PPSIG method individually significant quality factors can be easily analyzed in relation to other layers of information		The information collected with PPSIG may lead to different solutions from those that would have been achieved using only official data sources and expert knowledge	
	N°	%	N°	%
TA[a]	7	36.8	7	36.8
A	10	52.6	9	47.4
NAD	2	10.5	2	10.5
D	0	0	0	0
TD	0	0	1	5.3
Total	19	100	19	100

[a]Legend: TA – Totally agree; A – Agree; NAD - Neither agree nor disagree; D – Disagree; and TD – Totally disagree.

A significant majority of respondents (84.2% - 16 of 19) also completely agreed (36.8% - 7 of 19) or agreed (47.4% - 9 of 19) with the statement "the information collected with PPSIG may lead to different solutions from those that would have been achieved only using official data sources and expert knowledge" [13] (Table 2).

However, in the comments, several urban planners expressed reservations: *"I would not argue that there would be a duality between locals and specialized information"* and *"Yes, but I think it's important to know which audience you're actually attending."* In any case, the literature (e.g. [4, 26]) indicates that planners will inevitably need to improve their understanding of the knowledge hidden in the everyday experiences of individuals and develop skills to address such knowledge. This statement implies the need to reconsider ways of working and the methods, by which planning information is created, distributed, processed and used [26].

Regarding the assertion "the information collected with PPSIG may make the urban planning task even more difficult because it adds a layer of information: public opinion" [3], the majority of respondents (73.7% - 14 of 19) disagreed (31.6% - 6 out of 19) or completely disagreed (42.1% - 8 out of 19) (Table 3).

Notably, according to the comments, although the urban planners recognize that including public opinion adds complexity to urban planning, this information is welcome because it contributes detail to urban planning discussions and tends to make results more effective. In this sense, the use of the information collected with PSIG would translate into efficiency gains in urban management through a greater social acceptance of the proposals, according to [3].

Similarly, the majority of the urban planners completely disagreed (26.3% - 5 of 19) or disagreed (36.8% - 7 of 19) with the statement "the information collected with PPSIG is difficult to interpret because it is vague [27]" (Table 3). Several comments explain that depends on how the tool is elaborated, for example: *"It depends on how the platform will be. It can point to specific questions, or it can be extremely open for comments (this will require comments grouping by theme)."*

Table 3. The information collected with PPSIG may make the urban planning task even more difficult, and the information collected with PPSIG is difficult to interpret because it is vague.

| | The information collected with PPSIG may make the urban planning task even more difficult, because it adds an extra layer of information: public opinion | | The information collected with PPSIG is difficult to interpret because it is vague | |
	N° de AU	%	N° de AU	%
TA[a]	0	0	0	0
A	2	10.5	3	15.8
NAD	3	15.8	4	21.1
D	6	31.6	7	36.8
TD	8	42.1	5	26.3
Total	19	100	19	100

[a]Legend: TA – Totally agree; A – Agree; NAD - Neither agree nor disagree; D – Disagree; and TD – Totally disagree.

The following comments should also be noted: *"In fact, they are difficult to interpret but not because they are vague; they may be very accurate, but they fail to include the wealth of face-to-face discussions or the depth of advanced spatial analysis"*; *"If the population is not qualified and if the method used is not very objective, very vague information may emerge. The same is true with information collected through traditional (face-to-face) methods"*; and *"Information contains, in addition to the user's response, the spatialized variable, which is fundamental in the urban planning process."*

While the first comment focuses on the quality of public opinion to face-to-face methods, the second believes that if the public is not trained to participate, any method may be flawed. The first comment implies that the use of various participatory techniques is ideal because online participation does not replace face-to-face discussion but complements it, as [28] affirm. The second comment illustrates that despite being in the minority certain professionals continue to regard the public as lacking relevant knowledge, as discussed by [5]. Finally, the third comment values an important difference of the PPSIG method, also noted by [10]: the convenience of having the data collected in an automated and geo-referenced form, which (unlike in face-to-face meetings) aggregates valuable information to public opinion, i.e., location, which considerably facilitates the interpretation and analysis of data and their subsequent incorporation into urban planning.

4 Conclusions

In sum, the visual and exploratory analysis of the data collected in the PPGIS Guaíba Waterfront experiment facilitated the identification of patterns of behavior and opinions that are highly pertinent for urban planning. In addition, having these data mapped enables planners to view a variety of complex information together while making such information more accessible to colleagues, decision-makers, and the public. Therefore, in agreement with [24], one can affirm that maps, such as those presented, have the potential to support public debate on urban planning.

In addition, because most of the information necessary for the formulation of public policies contains a spatial component, the usefulness of the collected information is not restricted to the urban planning sector [12]. From this specified knowledge of the local reality, which was inaccessible through official data sources, it was possible to obtain highly specific guidelines, in accordance with [13].

This outcome was possible primarily because the data collected using PPGIS store the exact spatial locations of the answers. The convenience of collecting data via an automated, geo-referenced form optimizes and extends the capabilities of analysis, as highlighted by [10]. The data are suitable for manipulation in a GIS environment and can be processed along with the other information layers that comprise an urban planning database. Therefore, it confirms the possibility of connecting hard data (i.e., physical-territorial data, socioeconomic data, and cadastral data) and soft data (i.e., knowledge based on inhabitant experiences), as advocated by [4], thus forming a fourth dimension in urban-planning spatial databases.

The representation of public perceptions in a spatial data layer facilitates the incorporation of those perceptions during the beginning phases of planning and design for urban projects. The early incorporation of public perceptions facilitates public acceptance of proposals, thus preventing subsequent opposition to projects, as often occurs in cases in which residents have not been consulted in advance or officially informed, as [3, 23] discuss.

Regarding the evaluation of the PPGIS by urban planners, the results indicate a consensus among the respondents that the method facilitates accessing and incorporating local knowledge into urban planning in a systematic way. In addition, because this knowledge is a unique source of up-to-date information, it can help improve the content quality of urban plans and/or projects. However, for this outcome to occur, it is necessary to expand our technical knowledge so that the data collected using PPGIS can be analyzed and subsequently incorporated in urban planning in a consistent way.

In the future, we would like to have a research project that follow all the stages of a participatory process with the PPSIG tool. Thus, in addition to verifying that PPSIG is effective in accessing and incorporating local knowledge into urban planning, it would be possible to verify if and how this information is assimilated in the formulation of proposals, plans and/or urban planning projects, given that so far there is little evidence that the PPSIG method has influenced practical decisions.

In addition, the map is the type of representation most frequently used to visualize and transmit geographic information. Thus, improving this format is important to better represent the reality in question and for the expansion of the communication capacity of the conveyed information. It is important to expand the technique to improve the geo-visualization and interpretation of geospatial information in GIS environments, making analysis results increasingly intelligible and useful for urban planning.

Finally, we understand that the approach presented in this research represents the possibility of establishing a permanent system of collecting public perceptions about urban space, which is essential for urban planning.

References

1. Pfeffer, K., Baud, I., Denis, E., Scott, D., Sydenstricker-Neto, J.: Participatory spatial knowledge management tools: empowerment and upscaling or exclusion? Inf. Commun. Soc. **16**(2), 258–285 (2013)
2. Rantanen, H., Kahila, M.: The SoftGIS approach to local knowledge. J. Environ. Manag. **90** (6), 1981–1990 (2009)
3. Friedmann, J.: A spatial framework for urban policy: new directions, new challenges. In: OECD International Conference: What Policies for Globalizing Cities? Rethinking the Urban Policy Agenda, Madrid, pp. 74–93 (2007)
4. Kahila, M., Kyttä, M.: SoftGIS as a bridge-builder in collaborative urban planning. In: Geertman, S., Stillwell, J. (eds.) Planning Support Systems Best Practice and New Methods. The GeoJournal Library, vol. 95, pp. 389–411. Springer, Dordrecht (2009). https://doi.org/ 10.1007/978-1-4020-8952-7_19
5. Corburn, J.: Bringing local knowledge into environmental decision making improving urban planning for communities at risk. J. Plan. Educ. Res. **22**(4), 420–433 (2003)
6. Hansen, H.S., Reinau, K.H.: The citizens in e-participation. In: Wimmer, M.A., Scholl, H.J., Grönlund, Å., Andersen, K.V. (eds.) EGOV 2006. LNCS, vol. 4084, pp. 70–82. Springer, Heidelberg (2006). https://doi.org/10.1007/11823100_7
7. Yigitcanlar, T.: Australian local governments' practice and prospects with online planning. URISA J. **18**(2), 7–17 (2006)
8. Horelli, L., Jarenko, K., Kuoppa, J., Saad-Sulonen, J., Wallin, S.: New approaches to urban planning: insights from participatory communities. Aalto University (2013)
9. Kingston, R.: Online public participation GIS for spatial planning. In: Nyerges, T. et al. (eds.) The SAGE Handbook of GIS and Society, pp. 361–380 (2011)
10. Poplin, A.: Web-based PPGIS for Wilhelmsburg, Germany: na integration of interactive GIS-based maps with an online questionnaire. URISA J. **24**(2), 75–88 (2012)
11. Brown, G.: Public Participation GIS (PPGIS) for regional and environmental planning: reflections on a decade of empirical research. URISA J. **24**(2), 7–18 (2012)
12. Sieber, R.: Public participation geographic information systems: a literature review and framework. Ann. Assoc. Am. Geogr. **96**(3), 491–507 (2006)
13. Carver, S.: Participation and geographical information: a position paper. In: ESF-NSF Workshop, Spoleto, Italy (2001)
14. Hall, G.B., Chipeniuk, R., Feick, R.D., Leahy, M.G., Deparday, V.: Community-based production of geographic information using open source software and Web 2.0. Int. J. Geogr. Inf. Sci. **24**(5), 761–781 (2010)
15. Brovelli, M.A., Minghini, M., Zamboni, G.: Public participation GIS: a FOSS architecture enabling field-data collection. Int. J. Digit. Earth **8**(5), 345–363 (2015)
16. Dunn, C.E.: Participatory GIS—a people's GIS? Prog. Hum. Geogr. **31**(5), 616–637 (2007)
17. Kyttä, M., Broberg, A., Tzoulas, T., Snabb, K.: Towards contextually sensitive urban densification: location-based softGIS knowledge revealing perceived residential environmental quality. Landscape Urban Plan. **113**, 30–46 (2013)
18. Brown, G., Kyttä, M.: Key issues and research priorities for public participation GIS (PPGIS): a synthesis based on empirical research. Appl. Geogr. **46**, 122–136 (2014)
19. PMPA. Diretrizes urbanísticas para a Orla do Guaíba no Município de Porto Alegre. http:// lproweb.procempa.com.br/pmpa/prefpoa/spm/usu_doc/projeto_orla7.pdf. Accessed 29 May 2014
20. PMPA. Qualificação Urbana da Orla. http://www2.portoalegre.rs.gov.br/spm/default.php?p_ secao=151. Accessed 29 May 2014

21. Revitalização da orla do Guaíba, em Porto Alegre, volta à mesa de discussão. http://zh. clicrbs.com.br/rs/noticias/noticia/2013/10/revitalizacao-da-orla-doguaiba-em-porto-alegre-volta-a-mesa-de-discussao-4301362.html. Accessed 29 May 2014

22. Câmara, G., Monteiro, A.M., Fucks, S.D., Carvalho, M.S.: Análise espacial e geoprocessamento. Análise espacial de dados geográficos, v. 2 (2002)

23. Stern, E., Gudes, O., Svoray, T.: Web-based and traditional public participation in comprehensive planning: a comparative study. Environ. Plan. B: Plan. Des. 36(6), 1067–1085 (2009)

24. Van Herzele, A., Van Woerkum, C.: On the argumentative work of mapbased visualisation. Landscape Urban Plan. 100(4), 396–399 (2011)

25. Kahila, M., Broberg, A., Kyttä, M., Tyger, T.: Let the citizens map—public participation GIS as a planning support system in the Helsinki Master Plan Process. Plan. Pract. Res. 31 (2), 195–214 (2016)

26. Staffans, A., Rantanen, H., Nummi, P.: Online environments shake up urban planning. In: Wallin, S., Horelli, L., Saad-Sulonen (ed.) Digital Tools in Participatory Planning, pp. 37–57. Centre for Urban and Regional Studies Publications, Espoo (2010)

27. Jankowski, P., Nyerges, T.: GIS for Group Decision Making. Taylor & Francis, New York (2003)

28. Rojas, H., Puig-i-Abril, E.: Mobilizers mobilized Information expression mobilization and participation in the digital age. J. Comput.-Mediat. Commun. 14(4), 902–927 (2009)

A GIS-Based Method to Assess the Pedestrian Accessibility to the Railway Stations

Gabriele D'Orso and Marco Migliore[✉]

Department of Civil Environmental Aeronautics and Materials Engineering,
Transport Research Group, University of Palermo, Viale delle Scienze Building 8,
90128 Palermo, Italy
{gabriele.dorso,marco.migliore}@unipa.it

Abstract. Modern cities, affected by congestion, atmospheric and acoustic pollution, land consumption, should change and return to being on a human scale, rather than designed for cars. Proper land-use planning, infrastructure improvement and implementation of targeted interventions have to ensure that there is a rapprochement of citizens about the public transport, in order to reduce these problems. An important aspect of modal choice by users of the public transport system is, however, linked to the quality of the pedestrian routes. In fact, every journey made by public transport begins and finishes on foot. Therefore, studying pedestrian accessibility to transit stations and the walkability of the pedestrian environment is really important, in order to understand how they influence the user's choices. So, in this paper, a GIS-based method, useful for the assessment of the quality of pedestrian paths and accessibility to stations, is proposed. The measurement of the quality of road segments is useful for the redesign of the spaces, the planning of interventions on the pedestrian routes and the setting of the intervention priorities, developing a decision support system. Different indicators, linked to the pleasantness of the route, to practicability and to safety, which have a different influence on the user's choice, have been chosen for the quality of the pedestrian routes. As a case study, some stations of the railway link of Palermo (Belgio, Francia and San Lorenzo) have been chosen, in order to identify solutions to be proposed to the municipal administration.

Keywords: GIS · Walkability · Pedestrian mobility · Pedestrian catchment area
Decision support system

1 Introduction

Urban diffusion, a phenomenon that has characterized the growth of our cities in recent years, is certainly the cause of many problems afflicting modern cities. They have developed, in fact, in an asymmetric way, with residential areas increasingly peripheral, disconnected and far from the activities and the city center; this development creates automobile dependency, generating costs that can't be considered sustainable, neither from an economic point of view, nor from a social or environmental one. The excessive use of the car causes, in fact, congestion, atmospheric and acoustic pollution, land consumption and accidents. These problems should at least be mitigated by incentive

© Springer International Publishing AG, part of Springer Nature 2018
O. Gervasi et al. (Eds.): ICCSA 2018, LNCS 10964, pp. 19–30, 2018.
https://doi.org/10.1007/978-3-319-95174-4_2

policies for public transport and by policies that encourage pedestrian mobility, improving pedestrian accessibility to the stations and the walkability of the areas where they arise.

Therefore, new attention must be paid to pedestrian mobility in the planning of the urban environment. Cities must be reorganized in such a way that there are different types of activity concentrated and reachable from the residences within a small walking distance. Neighborhoods must be more walkable and their development must be a Transit Oriented Development (TOD), ensuring high levels of accessibility, sustainability and livability of urban areas [33]. Even the center of our cities, however, often reveal an insufficient care for urban furniture, maintenance of sidewalks, the construction of separate and safe paths for pedestrians. On the other hand, walking is the most vital mode of transport, that mode of transport on which all social activities depend: by walking, you may come into contact with all the commercial and cultural activities in the area, you may have interactions with other people and with nature, and you may experience all those colors, sounds and smells that make the city alive. As a means of transport, walking has predictable travel times, continuous availability, easily maintained routes and non-emission of pollutants, and it offers a relaxing and healthy exercise.

Health is, in fact, one of the main reasons why administrations should pay more attention to walking. Physical activity is recognized as an important element of a healthy lifestyle, since it reduces the risk of illness and premature death. The modern lifestyle, with a wide use of the car in our travel, the presence of sedentary activities and the automation of some activities at home and at the workplace, has led to a spread of obesity, depression and cardiovascular diseases. Therefore, the design of the city has effects on the inactivity of the population - the World Health Organization also affirms it - and having more walkable neighborhoods means putting the citizen in a position to practice physical activity [1, 38]. For many people, in fact, the most acceptable form of physical activity is the one embodied in everyday life, such as walking or cycling, instead of using the car. Therefore, in order to counteract inactivity and decrease the health costs that derive from it, the administrations, which until now have underestimated the problem and have not considered it in their decision-making processes, should make interventions that promote walking and make it a safe, convenient and attractive way to do our daily errands.

Another important aspect is related to safety. The lack of accessibility or the poor quality of the footpaths is very often caused by the conflict that is generated when different functions are attributed to the same road and by the danger that arises when the road is traveled by different categories of users. In Europe, many experiences have shown, however, how the redesign of the roads, through a different distribution of spaces, can make the different functions of the road, such as the movement of vehicles, the movement of pedestrians, resting or shopping, compatible and, at the same time, increase the safety of all users, reducing the severity and the number of accidents.

Nowadays urban planners and engineers are starting to pay more attention to the role that walking has to play in urban mobility. This can be seen in the adoption, by many cities, of Sustainable Urban Mobility Plans, which include pedestrianizations, downsizing of roadways in favor of pedestrian space, limitations of vehicle speeds and introduction of 30 km/h zones, or in the construction of new infrastructures dedicated to bicycles and pedestrians [25]. But attention is also paid to the weakest pedestrians: children, the elderly and disabled people; it is therefore seen in the creation of safe routes to school, in the organization of walking school buses, in interventions that try to adapt urban spaces to the needs of people with reduced mobility [11]. New attention is also evident in the diffusion and success of many applications for smartphones that seek to encourage walking and promote an active lifestyle through the reward mechanism.

For these reasons, a method for assessing the pedestrian accessibility to the stations and the quality of the pedestrian paths that can be traveled around them, is useful in order to easily identify the actions that the public administrations must put in place in order to encourage pedestrian mobility and sustainable mobility with urban public transport and counteracting the excessive use of cars in urban areas [5, 7, 27]. Therefore the aim of this paper is the development of a method that evaluates the quality of pedestrian routes and includes all the factors affecting it. After the review of the literature, the developed method will be described and it will be applied to the case study of three Palermo railway stations to verify how little attention is currently given to walkability.

2 Background

The themes of pedestrian accessibility, the quality of pedestrian paths and the walkability of urban spaces are strongly linked to each other and there is a vast amount of literature on them. The walkability of an urban area is defined as the measure of how much that area is suitable for walking. To be walkable, an urban space must first be accessible.

A first assessment of the walkability of a neighborhood or of an area around a station is, in fact, represented by the evaluation of the Pedestrian Catchment Area, which represents pedestrian accessibility with respect to a specific destination, and is calculated as the ratio between the effective pedestrian area determined on the basis of the existing pedestrian network and an ideal pedestrian area calculated on the basis of the Euclidean distance as the crow flies [35]. Moreover, a global measure of the walkability of a neighborhood is also provided by Walk Score™ [8], which considers pedestrian accessibility to a series of different activities (schools, parks, shops, restaurants, cinemas, etc.).

Accessibility is linked to the measure of the ease of access to a set of destinations in an area, starting from a given origin, in relation to the characteristics of the area itself. The concept of accessibility is also closely linked to mobility, since "the real meaning of mobility or the true goal of transport is access" [26, 37]. To better understand what accessibility is, we can also introduce the concept of generalized transport cost, consisting of an economic cost, time, physical energy, psychic energy, cost of risk, comfort and transport reliability [6]. All these factors can make a decisive contribution to making a place accessible or inaccessible to a certain category of users.

Pedestrian accessibility to transit stations [13], which is a measure of the opportunity for using the public transport system [30], is strongly linked to bus ridership [19], and this means that if a transit station exists within a walking distance the probability that residents use the system increases. Characteristics favouring pedestrian access to a station are the absence of barriers [31, 39], a grid street pattern with many pedestrian links [16, 19, 24, 39], higher densities, land use mix [14, 19, 24, 39], a small number of parking spaces at the station [24], safety [14, 32, 36], and an attractive and reliable transit service [36]. In terms of stops and stations, the number of lines at the station [21, 39] increases the willingness to walk, while long waiting times [22, 32] and many transfers during a trip to reach the destination [2] decrease access walking distances. Finally also temperature, rain, humidity and wind have effects on the accessibility [21, 22].

Furthermore, a poor quality of the footpaths around the stations actually worsens their accessibility. Empirical studies have shown how a real urban transformation of an area can be carried out and how an area can be made accessible increasing the quality of the pedestrian paths, their linearity and continuity with the urban fabric [34].

The Highway Capacity Manual (HCM) primarily analyzes the quality of a pedestrian space by calculating the Level of Service (LOS) of pedestrian facilities [15, 18]. The pedestrian LOS depends on the space available for the pedestrian, the flow and the average speed at which pedestrians can walk. But this definition of quality of a pedestrian path, while considering important elements such as the width of the sidewalk and the presence of obstacles, is certainly limited, since there are many additional factors that must be considered and which influence the mode choice or the route choice of the user. There are many studies in which the walkability and the quality of a pedestrian path are, in fact, assessed on the basis of interviews given to pedestrians who have chosen to follow that path and these studies highlight the influence of various factors [20].

The pedestrian will choose to follow the path perceived as shorter, faster, safer and more pleasant, and the one that better follows his lines of desire [28]. The primary consideration when choosing a route is, in fact, to minimize time and distance [36]. Planners who want to encourage journeys on foot must ensure that pedestrians can have direct routes to reach their destinations. Therefore, grid street patterns are a good choice, although the width of the blocks should be limited. Secondly, the other fundamental factors that influence the choice of whether or not a walking route is made are the safety, the attractiveness of the route, the quality of the sidewalk and the absence of long waiting times at traffic lights. This suggests to engineers and planners to pay particular attention, firstly, to the sense of safety of pedestrians, especially at pedestrian crossings, limiting the speed of vehicular traffic and by introducing appropriately traffic lights and traffic control devices.

Some researchers [23] have devised methods that quantify the perception of safety and comfort of pedestrians traveling along an urban road as a function of physical elements that characterize the pedestrian path, taking into account the presence of barriers and separation from the space dedicated to vehicles. Other researchers have considered as quality indicators for pedestrian routes lighting and visibility at night, which is part of the safety aspects [29].

The sense of security that the urban environment transmits to the pedestrian is also very important. The presence of illegal graffiti, abandoned buildings, litter and construction sites can, in fact, make the environment perceive as hostile [4]. The presence of green spaces, a pleasant architectural context, sites of particular historical or social interest, the presence of shops and the presence of street furniture, such as benches, baskets, shelters for protection from the rain or trees for protection from the sun [17] are, instead, factors that stimulate walking and make it pleasant.

Another factor to consider is the state of maintenance of the sidewalk, an aspect that involves comfort of walking and, above all, the safety of the elderly. Although it is difficult to quantify, the number of elderly who injure themselves due to holes in the sidewalks of the Italian cities is significant [3].

3   The Method

The aim of this study is to develop a methodology that can evaluate the quality of the pedestrian paths, facilitate the identification of the interventions that the pedestrian infrastructure needs and determine the intervention priorities. The method has been developed in a GIS environment, since it is useful for associating data of all types with geographical data and, moreover, since it allows the creation of thematic maps, which show more immediately the features of the pedestrian network on which to intervene. On the basis of the literature and of the influence that each of the factors has on the route choice and the mode choice by the user, it has been decided to consider as indicators of the quality of a pedestrian route those shown in Table 1.

Table 1. The indicators of the quality of the pedestrian path

Practicability	Sidewalk slope
	Pedestrian LOS (presence of obstacles and sidewalk width)
	Surface degradation
Pleasantness	Street furniture (benches, baskets, shelter from rain and sun)
	Green spaces
	Shops
	Building context, land use mix and urban design
Safety	Lighting
	Traffic volume and vehicle speed
	Barriers for pedestrian protection from vehicles
	Traffic control signal at intersections
	Driveways

For each arch of the pedestrian network, the method provides for the assignment of a score for each individual indicator, based on the presence or absence of the elements considered or on the basis of objective evaluations on them. Therefore the method involves carrying out inspections and collecting data arc by arc, building a database.

The indicators considered were grouped into three factors:

- Practicability: it concerns the comfort that the pedestrian perceives when traveling along the pedestrian infrastructure, therefore the available space, the slope, the presence of holes, dips, obstacles, like cars parked on the sidewalk;
- Pleasantness: it concerns the pleasantness of the path perceived by the pedestrian, therefore the presence of trees and green spaces, of shop windows and commercial activities, of places of social and cultural interest, the presence of street furniture or urban decay;

- Safety: it concerns the sense of safety that the pedestrian has when walking on the sidewalk or crossing the pedestrian crossings, thus the congestion of the road, noise and air pollution, the presence of traffic signals, the presence of driveways or the presence of barriers for pedestrian protection.

Since these aspects do not affect the pedestrian's perception of the quality of the route in the same way, weights have been assigned (0.3 for practicability, 0.3 for pleasure and 0.4 for safety). By adding the scores obtained for each indicator, the scores for the factors can be determined. Multiplying these by the relative weights and adding them, the quality index is obtained for each arc. By reporting the data in QGIS - a GIS software - it is possible to easily obtain a map of the quality of the pedestrian arcs and determine which are the arcs that need more interventions. It is also possible for each arc to see which indicators are insufficient and to determine which specific type of intervention should be put in place in order to improve the overall quality of the arc itself.

4   Case Study

The method was applied to Palermo as case study. In particular, the accessibility to the stations Belgio, Francia and San Lorenzo of the railway link was studied. These three stations were involved in the works concerning the doubling of the railway link, which included the construction of new stations, like Belgio station, and the modernization of the existing stations, like Francia and San Lorenzo. The works have not yet been completed and the stations are not yet in service. Therefore this study concerns the future scenario that will be created when the works will be completed [12].

Francia and Belgio stations are located in densely populated residential areas, with several schools, kindergartens, public offices, gyms and small shops. Nearby there is, for example, Viale Strasburgo, one of the shopping streets of Palermo. Instead, San Lorenzo station is located in a different context, near a more industrial area (Via Ugo La Malfa), with several large shopping centers, large offices and technical centers. The presence of numerous activities and services in these areas means that the stations have a high Walk Score™ (81 San Lorenzo, 85 France, 94 Belgium), since several travel attractor poles are reachable with short distances on foot.

In order to determine the accessibility, firstly, the places where the stations will arise have been precisely located and the ideal service areas, calculated as circular areas with a radius of 500 m around the stations, are evaluated. Then, the pedestrian network within the ideal service area has been designed with the help of the QAD plugin, which allows to use CAD functions in QGIS. The pedestrian network has been designed with precision, considering every sidewalk and every pedestrian crossing as an arc and positioning a node at each intersection point between them. Furthermore, the travel attractor poles (schools, kindergartens, shopping centers, gyms, public offices and company offices) have been identified within the ideal catchment area (Fig. 1).

After the construction of the pedestrian network, it was possible to evaluate the Pedestrian Catchment Area for each station, determining the actual service area. It is interesting to note that the presence of Viale della Regione Siciliana, a urban freeway which links north and south of the city, near the three stations, strongly influences the effective service

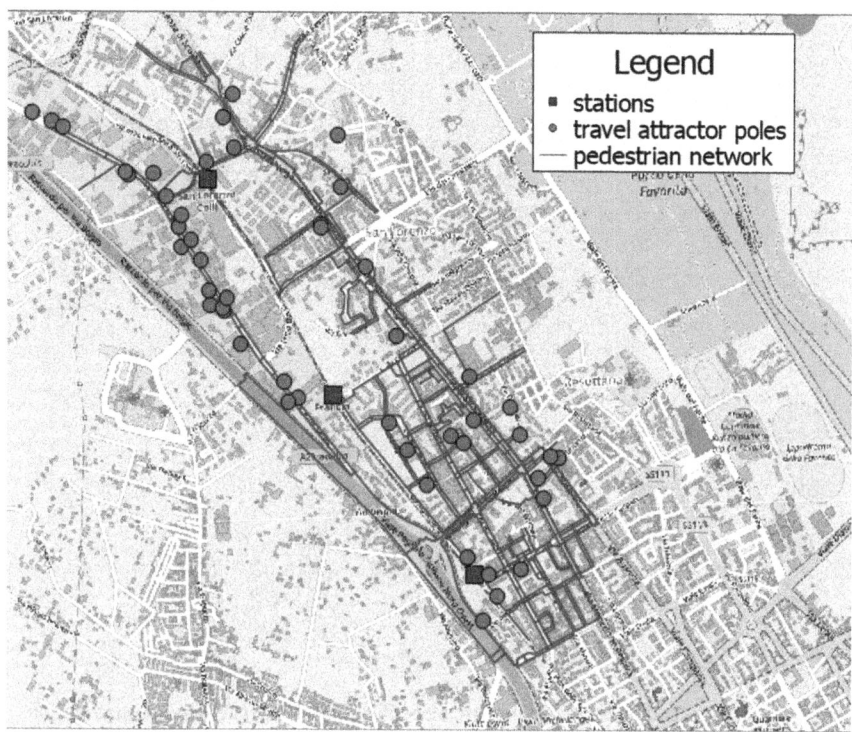

Fig. 1. Pedestrian network, stations and travel attractor poles in QGIS

areas, reducing them by more than 50%, as shown in Fig. 2. In fact, PCA is equal to 0.29 for Belgium station, 0.18 for France and 0.39 for San Lorenzo. Viale Regione is, therefore, a real barrier for pedestrians, strongly limiting pedestrian accessibility to the stations. Moreover, some of the identified travel attractor poles are outside the effective service area of the stations, thus being inaccessible within 500 m on foot.

Once the accessibility to the stations has been globally determined, the quality of the pedestrian arcs has been assessed. The research team followed the methodology by assigning to each arc the scores for each considered indicator, on the basis of surveys or with the help of Google Street View. The score for each of the three factors (practicability, pleasure and safety) was then evaluated and, by applying the established weights, the quality index of each arc was obtained. The scores of each indicator and the quality index were assigned in an Excel table, in which the identification codes of each arc were reported, and then entered on PostgreSQL, a relational database management system. Subsequently, through a union of tables in PostgreSQL, these data were joined to the geographical data of each arc and it was possible to build in QGIS a thematic map concerning the quality of the arcs of the pedestrian network, in which each color is associated with a range of quality index values. The result is presented in Fig. 3.

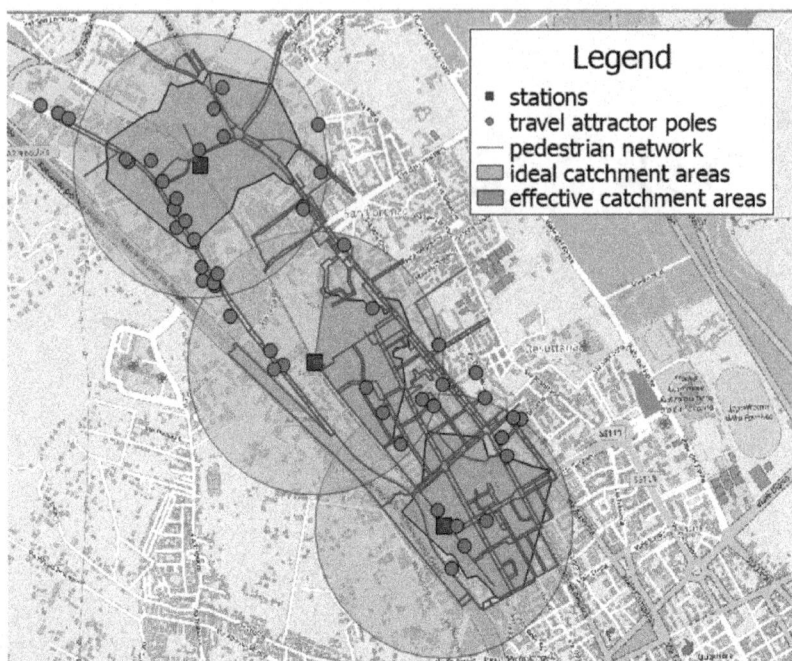

Fig. 2. The ideal and effective catchment areas of Belgio, Francia e San Lorenzo stations

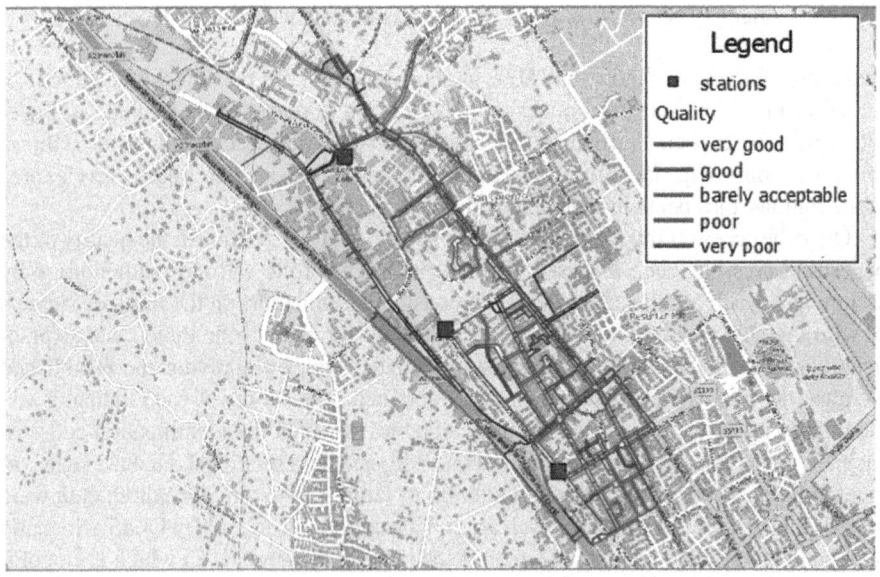

Fig. 3. The quality of the footpaths

Therefore, the quality of the pedestrian network of this area of Palermo is very poor. The sidewalks are in many places dirty or uneven, with holes and depressions, mainly caused by the roots of the trees. In many pedestrian arcs it was found the absence of street furniture, such as benches for resting or baskets, and the presence of real obstacles for pedestrians, as cars parked on the sidewalk, which is unfortunately a widespread habit. Pedestrian crossings are also critical points because often the road markings are not visible or missing. Even lighting in many road is insufficient or missing. Moreover, there are many lawsuits filed against the City of Palermo by citizens, especially the elderly, who fell due to uneven sidewalks, and in recent times many pedestrians have been invested in these areas due to poor visibility at night. The area around San Lorenzo station appears to be poorly walkable and serious, above all, is the situation of Via Ugo La Malfa, shown in Fig. 4, in which it can see the accentuated deterioration of the paving, the lack of cleanliness and the presence of cars on the sidewalk, which force pedestrians to walk on the roadway putting at risk their own safety.

Fig. 4. Uneven sidewalk in Via Ugo La Malfa

5   Conclusion

In order to encourage the use of public transport and pedestrian mobility in urban areas, administrations need to pay greater attention to pedestrian traffic and the quality of pedestrian routes, since accessibility to the stations and the effective use of public transport depend on them. The developed method is an effective tool for the classification of the arcs of the pedestrian network on the basis of their quality and the planning of the various types of intervention. The GIS environment allows the data to be treated with relative simplicity and allows an immediate visualization of the results. In addition, it allows you to be able to update the data if necessary, as well as to see how the situation will change after an intervention has been carried out. In particular, for the city of Palermo, the method could be used to underline the need for redesign of pedestrian spaces as part of the completion of the modernization works of the stations.

Future research could be aimed at improving the system of scores to be attributed to the indicators that determine the overall quality of each arc. Therefore, surveys and audits with a wider sample of citizens who could walk along some of the analyzed streets could be carried out. This could lead to better understand how each indicator actually affects the pedestrian mobility of the inhabitants of Palermo and make the method of evaluating the quality index of the pedestrian routes more precise.

Future work will focus on establishing the priorities for interventions. Once the quality of each single arc of the pedestrian network has been assessed, the importance of the arc in terms of pedestrian flow could be determined for this purpose. In fact, we will intervene primarily in those arcs that serve a large demand. To do this, the travel attractor poles in the service areas of the stations could be identified and the attractiveness of each of them could be assessed considering the number of employees or the number of daily attendance. Estimated the share of passengers that uses each station, considering the station as the origin of the movement and the travel attractor poles as destinations, the pedestrian flow could be distributed on the network through an All-or-Nothing assignment: the pedestrian flow will be assigned only to those arcs that are part of the minimum cost paths between the Origin-Destination pairs and each arc will have as a flow the sum of the flows of the paths that include it. With the help of QGIS, it is easy to determine the minimum cost paths, where the cost is the travel time, through the application of the Dijkstra algorithm [9]. It is therefore possible to assign pedestrian flows and to determine those arcs which have a high number of users, but an insufficient quality. The methodology, developed in the GIS environment, is therefore a powerful tool for decision support [10] in the evaluation of the interventions to be carried out on pedestrian infrastructures and in determining the priorities to be attributed to them. Finally, it could also be interesting for a new research path, starting from the quality index, to develop an arc cost, as function of quality and travel time, with which to calculate the minimum cost routes and the flows of the arcs, in order to study which can actually be the route choices made by the users.

References

1. Adams, M.A., Frank, L.D., Schipperijn, J., Smith, G., Chapman, J., Christiansen, L.B., Sallis, J.F.: International variation in neighborhood walkability, transit, and recreation environments using geographic information systems: the IPEN adult study. Int. J. Health Geogr. **13**, 43 (2014)
2. Alshalalfah, B., Shalaby, A.: Case study: relationship of walk access distance to transit with service, travel, and personal characteristics. J. Urban Plann. Dev. **133**(2), 114–118 (2007)

3. Amoroso, S., Caruso, L., Castelluccio, F.: Road safety for the elderly pedestrians in urban contexts. Vivere e Camminare in Città 2011-Living and Walking in Cities 2011, EGAF (2011)
4. Amoroso, S., Castelluccio, F., Maritano, L.: Indicators for sustainable pedestrian mobility. Urban Transport XVIII: Urban Transport and the Environment in the 21st Century. Southampton: WIT Press (2012)
5. Amoroso, S., Migliore, M., Catalano, M., Galatioto, F.: The interaction between rail stations and urban area in medium-sized towns. A case study for Trapani. Ingegneria Ferroviaria **11**, 923–941 (2012)
6. Amoroso, S., Migliore, M., Catalano, M., Castelluccio, F.: Vertical take-off and landing air transport to provide tourist mobility. J. Air Transp. Manag. **24**, 49–53 (2012)
7. Amoroso, S., Migliore, M., Catalano, M., Galatioto, F.: A demand-based methodology for planning the bus network of a small or medium town. Eur. Transp. - Trasporti Europei **44**, 41–56 (2010)
8. Carr, J.L., Dunsiger, S.I., Marcus, B.H.: Walk score as a global estimate of neighborhood walkability. Am. J. Prev. Med. **39**, 460–463 (2010)
9. Castelluccio, F., D'Orso, G., Migliore, M., Scianna, A.: GIS infomobility for travellers. In: Gervasi, O., Murgante, B., Misra, S., Rocha, A.M.A.C., Torre, C., Taniar, D., Apduhan, Bernady O., Stankova, E., Wang, S. (eds.) ICCSA 2016. LNCS, vol. 9788, pp. 519–529. Springer, Cham (2016). https://doi.org/10.1007/978-3-319-42111-7_41
10. Catalano, M., Migliore, M.: A Stackelberg-game approach to support the design of logistic terminals. J. Transp. Geogr. **41**, 63–73 (2014)
11. Davis, A.: Value for money: an economic assessment of investment in walking and cycling. United Kingdom (2010)
12. D'Orso, G., Migliore, M.: A GIS-based methodology to estimate the potential demand of an integrated transport system. In: Gervasi, O., et al. (eds.) ICCSA 2017. LNCS, vol. 10407, pp. 525–540. Springer, Cham (2017). https://doi.org/10.1007/978-3-319-62401-3_38
13. El-Geneidy, A., Grimsrud, M., Wasfi, R., Tetreault, P., Surprenant-Legault, J.: New evidence on walking distances to transit stops: Identifying redundancies and gaps using variable service areas. Transportation **41**(1), 193–210 (2014)
14. Fitzpatrick, K., Perkinson, D., Hall, K.: Findings from a survey on bus stop design. J. Public Transp. **1**(3), 17–27 (1997)
15. Fruin, J.J.: Designing for pedestrians: a level-of-service concept. 1–15 Highway Research Record, Number 355, Pedestrians, Highway Research Board. Washington, D.C. (1971)
16. Fruin, J.J.: Designing for pedestrians. Public Transportation USA (1992)
17. Galanis, A., Eliou, N.: Evaluation of the pedestrian infrastructure using walkability indicators. WSEAS Trans. Environ. Dev. **7**(12), 385–394 (2011)
18. Highway Capacity Manual, TRB of the National Academes (2010)
19. Hsiao, S., Lu, J., Sterling, J., Weatherford, M.: Use of geographic information system for analysis of transit pedestrian access. Transp. Res. Rec. **1604**, 50–59 (1997)
20. Kelly, C.E., Tight, M.R., Hodgson, F.C., Page, M.W.: A comparison of three methods for assessing the walkability of the pedestrian environment. J. Transp. Geogr. **19**, 1500–1508 (2011)
21. Kuby, M., Barranda, A., Upchurch, C.: Factors influencing light rail station boardings in the United States. Transp. Res. Part A **38**, 223–247 (2004)
22. Lam, W., Morrall, J.: Bus passenger walking distances and waiting times: a summer-winter comparison. Transp. Q. **36**(3), 407–421 (1982)
23. Landis, B.W., Vattikuti, V.R., Ottenberg R.M., McLeod, D.S., Guttenplan, M.: Modeling the Roadside Walking Environment: A Pedestrian Level of Service, Transportation Research Record 1773, Transportation Research Board, Washington, D.C. (2001)

24. Loutzenheiser, D.: Pedestrian access to transit: modeling of walk trips and their design and urban form determination around bay area rapid transit stations. Transp. Res. Rec. **1604**, 40–49 (1997)
25. Migliore, M., Burgio, A.L., Di Giovanna, M.: Parking pricing for a sustainable transport system. Transp. Res. Procedia **3**, 403–412 (2014)
26. Migliore, M., Burgio, A.L., Maritano, L., Catalano, M., Zangara, A.: Modelling the accessibility to public local transport to increase the efficiency and effectiveness of the service: the case study of the Roccella area in Palermo. WIT Trans. Built Environ. **130**, 163–173 (2013)
27. Migliore, M., Catalano, M.: Urban public transport optimization by bus ways: a neural network-based methodology. WIT Trans. Built Environ. **96**, 347–356 (2007)
28. Migliore, M., Catalano, M., Lo Burgio, A., Maritano, L.: The analysis of urban travellers' latent preferences to explain their mode choice behavior. WIT Trans. Ecol. Environ. **162**, 193–203 (2012)
29. Moayedi, F., Zakaria, R., Bigah, Y., Mushairry, M., Che Puan, O., Safitri Zin, I., Klufallah, M.A.: Conceptualising the indicators of walkability for sustainable transportation. J. Teknologi Sci. Eng. **65**, 3 (2013)
30. Murray, A., Davis, R., Stimson, R., Ferreira, L.: Public transportation access. Transp. Res. Part D **3**(5), 319–328 (1998)
31. O'Neill, W., Ramsey, D., Chou, J.: Analysis of transit service areas using geographic information systems. Transp. Res. Rec. **1364**, 131–139 (1992)
32. O'Sullivan, S., Morrall, J.: Walking distance to and from light-rail transit stations. Transp. Res. Rec. **1538**, 19–26 (1996)
33. Papa, E., Bertolini, L.: Accessibility and transit-oriented development in European metropolitan areas. J. Transp. Geogr. **47**, 70–83 (2015)
34. Pucci, P.: I nodi infrastrutturali: luoghi e non luoghi metropolitani. Franco Angeli, Milano (1996)
35. Schlossberg, M., Brown, N.: Comparing transit-oriented development sites by walkability indicators. Transp. Res. Rec. **1887**, 34–42 (2004)
36. Schlossberg, M., Weinstein Agrawal, A., Irvin, K., Bekkouche, V.L.: How far, by which route, and why? A spatial analysis of pedestrian preference. Mineta Transportation Institute Report, June 2007 (2007)
37. Tolley, R.S., Turton, B.J.: Transport System, Policy and Planning: A Geographical Approach. Longman Scientific & Technical, Harlow (1995)
38. Wasfi, R.A., Dasgupta, K., Eluru, N., Ross, N.A.: Exposure to walkable neighbourhoods in urban areas increases utilitarian walking: longitudinal study of Canadians. J. Transp. Health **3**(4), 440–447 (2015)
39. Zhao, F., Chow, L., Li, M., Ubaka, I., Gan, A.: Forecasting transit walk accessibility: regression model alternative to buffer. Transp. Res. Rec. **1835**, 34–41 (2003)

Urban Regeneration for a Sustainable and Resilient City: An Experimentation in Matera

Piergiuseppe Pontrandolfi[1] and Benedetto Manganelli[2]

[1] Department of European and Mediterranean Cultures, University of Basilicata,
Via San Rocco, 3, 75100 Matera, Italy
piegiuseppe.pontrandolfi@unibas.it
[2] School of Engineering, University of Basilicata, Viale dell'Ateneo Lucano, 85100 Potenza, Italy
benedetto.manganelli@unibas.it

Abstract. In urban policies, Italian and European, the urban regeneration of residential districts, especially suburbs built in post-war urban expansions, has been a crucial question since the 1990s. An integrated approach is now essential for effective urban redevelopment programs, which consider not only architectural and urban, but also social, economic, naturalistic-environmental and cultural aspects, in order to return dignity, identity and centrality to the marginal areas that today express tangible and intangible forms of urban unease. The development in recent decades of innovative tools such as complex programs, social housing, therefore, marks the transition to a new way of urban planning, characterized by a different approach to urban and territorial policies, aimed at integrating a plurality of functions and typologies of intervention and that contemplates the possibility to involve private operators and private financial resources for the realization of public works. The paper presents a case study as a best practice approach to urban regeneration.

Keywords: Urban regeneration · Sustainability · Resiliency · Housing market
Profitability of the investment

1 Introduction

The great urban expansion in the years of the post-war boom has generated in many cities a building product that today is characterized by a serious situation of urban blight. This condition is often accompanied by socio-economic decay, which to some extent can be considered an effect and cause of the former. The answer to the post-World War II housing demand, determined primarily by population growth, was mainly quantitative, with little attention to the quality aspect of the building. This has generated mostly peripheral built areas without adequate urbanization works and essential services. Moreover, the majority of those buildings were built in reinforced concrete with the use of materials and techniques that currently, even for the changed awareness of the risks, would not be eligible and that make the building stock, in the areas prone to seismic risk, very vulnerable. This is compounded by the degradation of many of these buildings caused by the absence of normal maintenance, which has amplified the effects of time on poor projects and poor quality materials.

© Springer International Publishing AG, part of Springer Nature 2018
O. Gervasi et al. (Eds.): ICCSA 2018, LNCS 10964, pp. 31–43, 2018.
https://doi.org/10.1007/978-3-319-95174-4_3

It is known, both in Italy and in Europe, the existence of a considerable percentage of residential buildings that has now exceeded the performance efficiency limit, both due to the widespread obsolescence and the lack of maintenance interventions, necessary to fight the unstoppable degradation process. The 15th General Census of Population and Housing (ISTAT 2011) highlights that 70% of residential buildings are older than 30 years, while 55%, over 40 years of life, the limit beyond which substantial interventions of maintenance are indispensable.

This is a patrimony of about ten million homes, which does not respect the technological qualities required today for a building and that, due to its advanced aging, risks losing part of its economic value. Many of those suburban residential districts built in post-war urban expansions are today characterized by building obsolescence, physical and psychological isolation from the city, abandonment and degradation of the spaces outside the houses, single-function (dormitory).

The described constructive and urban characteristics that regulated the construction of residential real estate, from the post-war period to the early 80s, today characterized by physical degradation and obsolescence often accompanied by socio-economic depression, have imposed a reflection on the opportunity to intervene on the built, with redevelopment strategies adapted to real needs.

Urban regeneration has become a crucial question in current Italian and European urban policies [1]. A new approach to tackling the issue is fundamental, capable of developing both physical (construction or urban) and social and economic actions.

Another fundamental factor that generates a growing concern both in Italy and in other European countries and that decisively pushes planning towards forms of urban regeneration is the consumption of soil. For example, Germany has set the goal of reducing to 75% the current land consumption by 2020; the United Kingdom has implemented a series of actions ranging from the establishment of *green belts*, to the priority recovery of *brownfields*, to the adoption of minimum density limits for areas of new urban growth.

The second paragraph describes the principles that underlie a correct and sustainable approach to urban regeneration. In the third part with reference to a case study, a simulation of a process of urban regeneration was carried out to verify the feasibility and sustainability of complex interventions through the partial demolition and reconstruction of the existing obsolete building stock of which energy retrofit and the structural and functional renovation is not convenient.

2 Model of Sustainable Approach to Urban Regeneration

There is a strong link between urban regeneration and sustainable development. Some researchers have tried to measure the sustainability of urban regeneration processes [2–5]. In literature, there are many attempts to conceptualize urban regeneration sustainability in different contexts [6–8]. Respect for the criteria of environmental, social and economic sustainability is fundamental to regeneration processes. Urban regeneration is a comprehensive integration of vision and action aimed at resolving the multi-faceted problems of deprived urban areas to improve their economic, social, and environmental conditions [9]. In fact, an effective urban regeneration process is based on compliance with the criteria of environmental, social and economic sustainability. Environmental sustainability must be pursued through strategies that can act on the transformation of urban spaces, reducing land consumption, increasing the resilience of existing real estate assets or reducing their vulnerability to natural events or environmental changes. The notion of resilience is rapidly gaining ground in the urban sustainability literature [10, 11]. The urban resilience has been defined as "the degree to which cities are able to tolerate alteration before reorganizing around a new set of structures and processes" [12]. The natural disasters that hit the cities of central Italy in the last decade and the consequent awareness of the vulnerability of human settlements make resilience a fundamental question in the planning for future of urban lands.

Social sustainability [13] can instead be fostered by actions that aim at social inclusion, that is, the coexistence of social classes of different economic capacities, through a mix of properties sold and leased with financial contributions to families [14], avoiding recognizable differences between buildings made by private companies and public buildings.

Finally, economic sustainability can be achieved through the planning and execution of urban regeneration based on concertation and partnership forms [15–17]. The spread of negotiation practices through the involvement of private investors in the implementation of social housing projects and in the renewal/redevelopment of existing assets and the use of specific financial and fiscal instruments [18, 19], can guarantee the success of urban regeneration processes.

The introduction of a reward system, financial incentives and tax relief tools has triggered a growing participation of private individuals in the complex transformation processes of the cities: real estate investors, banking and insurance institutions, non-profit companies, social sector operators. These subjects actively cooperate through forms of partnerships often activated from below, aimed at the construction of shared paths of physical, social and economic development. Please note that tools and policies aimed at involving private capital are essential to respond to the current housing disadvantage that often invests families belonging to the so-called "grey belt", whose income is too high to access public housing policies, financed exclusively with the use of now very limited public resources.

In order to achieve sustainable development, public-private partnerships need to move beyond the realm of narrowly defined economic development to encompass social and environmental aspects that eventually have impact on economic development.

In cases where the expectations regarding the increase on value of land deriving from forms of urban regeneration that include demolition and reconstruction interventions are not able to generate a surplus with respect to the existing real estate, the hypothesis of the city's destruction seems unlikely [20]. Instead, an intervention, more selective, aimed at enhancing the existing building capital is feasible. The value of the existing city, linked to its still unexpressed development or to the residue of what is still contained in the buildings, becomes crucial in order that the sustainability of urban development to be transformed into sustainable economic processes. Otherwise, the abandonment of obsolete urban lands and the exploitation of new lands is a rational choice in the absence of economically sustainable alternatives [21].

The implementation of urban regeneration also deals with operational problems that often cannot be overcome. For example, those neighborhoods built in the post-war years, which today have reached an important level of obsolescence, have fractional properties that are not homogeneous in terms of intentions and strategies, whose recomposition must certainly be considered complex and financially burdensome. Even when a developer were to purchase the property of a plurality of owners, he should bear all the costs related to recomposition of properties. In the case study this problem, for reasons of simplicity, was not considered but obviously significantly affects the conditions of legal and managerial feasibility of reconversion processes of areas of the existing city.

3 Case Study

3.1 Area Description

In order to assess the feasibility of urban regeneration that also includes interventions for the replacement and reconstruction of the existing building, research[1] has been carried out with reference to the concrete situation of an urban area of Matera in Basilicata.

This urban area considered (Fig. 1) is in the southern outskirts of the city and includes the neighborhoods of "Cappuccini", "Agna", "La Specchia", "Agna Le Piane" and "San Francesco". The total population settles amounts to about 6,000 units. The experimentation started with a cognitive analysis aimed at getting to know the structure and conditions of the territory and related social problems. The field analysis highlighted the presence of poorly exploited places and empty urban spaces, within a settlement often characterized by urban, building and social decay.

Fig. 1. Area under study

---

[1] The research started from the study developed by Alessandra Patti as part of the degree thesis in Building Engineering-Architecture at the University of Basilicata.

The urban environment under examination (Fig. 2) has developed since the Second World War, based on different interventions. First - at the turn of the '40s and '50s - an intervention of "spontaneous urban planning" with the construction of the Cappuccini district and then with the semi-rural village of the Agna district, built in the 60s, as part of the rehabilitation of the Sassi, and characterized by isolated single and two-family house with backwaters.

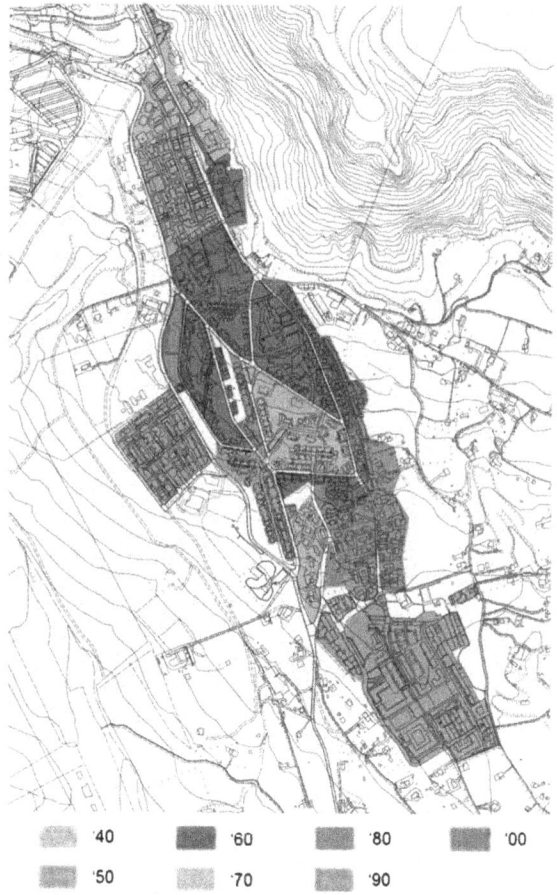

Fig. 2. Stages of growth of the Agna-Le Piane settlement in Matera

In the '80s and '90s, the urban area, in implementation of the Land-use Plan of 1975, was expanded with the construction of a public housing project – which partially densified the existing residential fabric with the construction of aligned buildings or with courtyards, inserted in the wide meshes of pre-existing semi-rural gardens – and with the construction of a new church and annexed buildings.

In the '90s, in Agna Le Piane, a new district of public housing was built, characterized by an aligned buildings system, distributed around large condominium courtyards that gravitate on a large central public space, today still poorly equipped. At the same time a private parceling out was created in the San Francesco district, on the edge of the Montescaglioso road, with multifamily residential buildings and without any provision of public facilities and spaces.

The extra-urban space has great environmental value characterized by the presence of a rocky and spontaneous vegetation; the southwestern margin was partly affected by the proposal of the "Integrated Program" (IP) called "Housing città dei Sassi". The area covered by the IP, of about 53 hectares and whose perimeter is implemented by the new Town Planning Regulations not yet adopted, includes the suburban agricultural area, now abandoned, owned by the Matera '90 company, and degraded urban areas or underutilized public property (Fig. 3).

Fig. 3. Area involved in the Integrated Program called "Housing città dei Sassi"

The IP aims to improve the urban-building quality of the southern outskirts of the city by increasing the housing offer of the district and strengthening the endowment of essential services and infrastructures in order to guarantee a high level of mix functional to an area that, for the position, is strategic for the regeneration of the entire city. The IP takes advantage offered by the "Piano Casa", approved by the Basilicata Region, and transforms the social and private housing project into an opportunity to promote a more rational urban structure of the southern suburbs of the city, through the creation of new infrastructures and services, both on a neighborhood level and on an urban-territorial level. A fundamental element of the program is the public-private partnership, which sees the cooperation between the Matera '90 srl, as private investor and owner of most of the areas involved, and the Matera Health Authority (MHA) as public subject.

The contents of the IP are divided into five lines: (1) infrastructure and parking, (2) public and/or public services and commercial functions, (3) sports equipment and green spaces, (4) social housing (Fig. 4), (5) private residential construction. Moreover, in the southwestern edge of the area, the enhancement of the Jazzo Gattini and the Masseria San Francesco and the construction of a large public park, called "Parco San Francesco", are proposed.

Fig. 4. Rendering of the social housing project planned by Integrated Program

At present, the restoration of the Masseria San Francesco is completed, which is an important element of attraction, welcoming and promoting local tourism. In 2015, the construction work for the social housing was started, while the next planned intervention is the construction of a House for the Elderly.

3.2 Problems Highlighted

Despite the quality of the numerous design choices, the IP presents a great limitation: it deals only with areas owned by the Matera '90 srl. There has not been the will and the ability of the municipal administration to develop a reflection on the entire urban area south of the city to promote a more general process of urban regeneration of this part of the territory. The surveys and analyzes conducted for the entire urban area have highlighted, in fact, the presence of an urban structure characterized by the lack of infrastructure, public and private services and public aggregation spaces, as well as by a non-homogeneous urban pattern resulting from disjointed summation of uneven urban episodes. The work of preliminary knowledge, also supported by the administration of questionnaires to a significant sample of the residents, represented the basis for developing a process of interpretation and evaluation of the context after which the main problems and, therefore, the objectives and the strategies to pursue to start a widespread process of urban regeneration were identified. Problem framing in urban regeneration is pivotal to understand urban regeneration strategies [22].

3.3 Solution Proposed

The vision proposed in this research is the development of a process of urban regeneration characterized by a building and urban planning operation of composition and completion of the different parts of the settlement system. The project proposal - starting from the redefinition of some choices of the Integrated Program approved but not fully implemented – aims to outline an organic urban planning configuration, including, in addition to the areas covered by the Integrated Program, also the areas not yet transformed indicated and regulated by the Urban Planning Regulations, currently being approved.

The proposal, in addition to the completion of the settlement system (involving some transformation areas provided for by town planning instruments), also provides for the demolition and reconstruction of the most degraded buildings in the Cappuccini district. Some previous experiences have shown that positive benefits can be extended from regeneration areas to contiguous relevant portions of the city, and that even a limited number of regeneration areas can produce relevant benefits [23].

This last intervention, in fact, is achievable thanks to the possibility of creating new surfaces fact, on the transformation areas and in addition to those already programmed by the Planning Regulations, with design solutions that respect environmental and urban sustainability. The additional surfaces and adjacent lots will be in the availability of the public administration in exchange for the recognition of building rights to the current landowners to the extent already provided for by planning instruments.

The proposal also concerns some land currently included in the suburban area, already subject to assessments in the past regarding the possibility of partial building transformations; also for these lands – on which there are, however, new limits to the extensive settlement based on a restrained index of conventional building recognized to the owners – through an equalization mechanism, the construction of new buildings to replace the existing ones will be balanced by the free transfer to the Municipality of areas for equipment (in particular, in order to relocate the sanitary equipment already provided for by the IP, and to increase in the urban park).

The urban regeneration proposal reinterprets some design choices of the Integrated Program "Housing Città dei Sassi", in the light of the opportunity to involve other areas not yet used in the process of transformation and completion of the settlement. The goal is to develop a more rational and functional urban design and, at the same time, respecting the environmental characteristics of the territory. In particular, by distributing the volumes, envisaged by the IP, on a wider territory, significant results can be obtained in terms of lesser impact of the buildings with respect to the landscape features, as well as significant expansions of the urban park planned at the edge of the area.

Likewise, by developing a reflection on the entire urban context under examination, the conditions could create to imagine credible proposals for redevelopment of the urban pattern of the Cappuccini district, with demolition and partial reconstruction and the transfer, in public adjoining areas, of building rights necessary to make cost-effective the replacement of the existing building stock, as shown below.

The Cappuccini district, which covers an area of about 7.2 ha, has developed since the post-World War II years, in an area surrounded by arable land, vegetable gardens and orchards, through unplanned and spontaneous interventions, consisting mainly of private residential buildings, made of tuff bricks. Over the years, the quality of life in the entire district has undergone considerable deterioration, due to a widespread state of abandonment of buildings and the surrounding urban environment.

The lack of a unitary urban project, in fact, has produced a chaotic development of the district that, today, presents several critical issues both at urban and building level. The lack of services makes this part of the city a simple aggregate of residential buildings, moreover, with questionable characteristics from an aesthetic and compositional point of view, rather than an organized place of common interests and social identity.

The interventions provided for by the Planning Regulations for the Cappuccini district are aimed at reorganizing, improving and/or completing the morphological/ functional characteristics of the settlement, in order to give greater identity to the organization of the space through the increase of the services and the green space equipped, the improvement of accessibility and of vehicular and pedestrian mobility, the qualification of public spaces and building. In light of these indications, the demolition and reconstruction of a part of the Cappuccini district was proposed, through interventions aimed at improving the urban fabric, for the most part obsolete and of low value, at redefining accessibility, at increasing of parking areas and open spaces for social gathering.

The project proposal provides for the redevelopment of the existing urban fabric through the demolition of some degraded buildings that present greater criticality in terms of architecture, energy and structure (Fig. 5).

Fig. 5. Plan with indication of the buildings to be demolished in the Cappuccini district (red). (Color figure online)

In the area previously occupied by the demolished buildings, the construction of a new system of aligned residential buildings is provided for, characterized by a new distribution, in order to create an urban fabric with lower building density in favor of open-air social gathering spaces, green areas, currently non-existent (Fig. 6).

Fig. 6. Plan of the new intervention proposed in the Cappuccini district.

The realization of a multi-storey underground garage for public and private use under the buildings and public spaces is also planned.

In addition to the intervention on the building fabric, the urban regeneration proposal also provides for the redefinition of the road and infrastructural system in order to reduce the traffic that crosses the district and to improve pedestrian mobility.

Regarding the social and economic sustainability of the proposal, a simulation was carried out which, starting from the evaluation of the demand expressed by many families currently resident. It assumes that a private entrepreneur, to be selected on the basis of a public announcement, proposes to private owners of the buildings, to be demolished and rebuilt, the exchange with a smaller housing unit, but built with new construction technologies and therefore of equal value or higher than the demolished one. To promote this operation, the private investor will have to build a larger amount of residential properties to be sold in the free market, within two areas subject to new construction and completion (which will be acquired by the Municipality, as compensatory areas, within the equalization district), consistent with the provisions of the Urban Planning Regulations.

In this way, the investor can recover the construction costs of the properties to be sold in exchange for the building to be demolished through the revenues obtained from the sale of the new housing units. In the simulation an algorithm has been defined that allows, once the percentage of building to give to the original owners has been preliminarily fixed, to calculate the amount of surface that the investor must realize and, consequently, the housing units that will be sold in the free market.

Finally, the Internal Rate of Return (14%) was calculated in order to determine the profitability of the investment. The assessment is therefore performed on behalf of the private investor. This is a summary evaluation which, however, takes into account all the possible elements useful for verifying the economic sustainability of potential private operators. The future development of research is the measuring of the economic viability of the operation on behalf of the community through the discount cash flow analysis of all social benefits and costs.

Given the complexity of the proposed transaction, the hypothesis is that an Urban Transformation Company conducts the operation, in which one or more private entrepreneurs, together with other public subjects (the municipality certainly) and private (for example the owners of lands to be transformed), will implement the urban regeneration project.

The Matera '90 company will have an interest in accepting the proposed changes compared to the original approved Integrated Program, and will take care of the implementation of the interventions already defined in the signed Program Agreement. Within the territorial dominion, the private owners of the areas will carry out the interventions relative to their share of housing units and will cede the lands for services and for social housing to the Municipal Administration. The Municipality will take care of all the urbanizations that are not charged to private operators.

The selection of the private operator who will carry out the demolition and reconstruction of part of the Cappuccini district and the new residential volumes, to be sold, on the lands that the Municipality will acquire for free as a compensatory surface, will take place in a public tender.

4   Conclusion

The assessment of the social costs related to land consumption and settlement dispersion are the premise for policies that promote the redevelopment of the already urbanized parts of our territory through the reuse of public and private parts [24].

An important issue concerns the ways in which economic operators look to re-use as an investment opportunity and, in particular, if such opportunities for performance can derive from demolition and reconstruction or only from more or less significant transformations of existing buildings [25].

The simulation made in the case study can be a useful example of how to intervene in the existing city, where there are no conditions and economic advantages for the redevelopment and recovery of existing buildings. This case has shown how demolition and reconstruction of existing buildings can become convenient if placed within an urban regeneration program that involves larger urban spaces than those directly affected, including public property, and a volumetric reward system.

The case study proposes a simulation that, unlike previous experiences, tries to verify the concrete sustainability (social, economic and environmental) of the operation, involving a wider area than the one occupied by the existing buildings to be demolished and rebuilt, limiting the impact of the increase in existing volumes aimed at making urban transformation economically sustainable. The interests and needs that the simulation has tried to balance are of:

(1) the private owners of the properties to be demolished, which will have to accept as compensation new housing units whose surfaces are equivalent to those resulting from the relationship between the market value of original buildings and the unit price of the new ones;
(2) the investors who will have to obtain a financial advantage from additional volumes that can be placed on the market;
(3) the community that from the whole process of urban regeneration can obtain economic benefits (recovery of dignity, identity and centrality of the places) able to balance the social costs (land consumption).

Due to its particular complexity, the proposed operation can be achieved thanks to the collaboration between different subjects that, organized within an Urban Transformation Company, could guarantee, through public and private funding, the feasibility of urban regeneration.

The promotion of an Urban Transformation Company would allow the Municipality to maintain the political control of the initiative and, at the same time, entrust to a public-private entity the direction of all the operations, from the acquisition of the properties to the marketing of the same after transformation.

References

1. Saaty, T.L., De Paola, P.: Rethinking design and urban planning for the cities of the future. Buildings 7(3), 76 (2017)
2. Hunt, D.V., Lombardi, D.R., Rogers, C.D., Jefferson, I.: Application of sustainability indicators in decision-making processes for urban regeneration projects. Eng. Sustain. 161, 77–91 (2008)
3. Hemphill, L., Berry, J., McGreal, S.: An indicator-based approach to measuring sustainable urban regeneration performance. Part 1: conceptual foundations and methodological framework. Urban Stud. 41(4), 725–755 (2004)
4. Laprise, M., Lufkin, S., Rey, E.: An indicator system for the assessment of sustainability integrated into the project dynamics of regeneration of disused urban areas. Build. Environ. 86, 29–38 (2015)
5. Peng, Y., Lai, Y., Li, X., Zhang, X.: An alternative model for measuring the sustainability of urban regeneration: the way forward. J. Clean. Prod. 109, 76–83 (2015)
6. Zheng, H.W., Shen, G.Q.P., Wang, H.: A review of recent studies on sustainable urban renewal. Habitat Int. 41, 272–279 (2014)

7. Lombardi, D.R., Porter, L., Barber, A., Rogers, C.D.F.: Conceptualising sustainability in UK urban regeneration: a discursive formation. Urban Studies **48**(2), 273–296 (2011)
8. Lorr, M.J.: Defining urban sustainability in the context of North American cities. Nat. Cult. **7**(1), 16–30 (2012)
9. Ercan, M.A.: Challenges and conflicts in achieving sustainable communities in historic neighbourhoods of Istanbul. Habitat Int. **35**(2), 295–306 (2011)
10. Meerow, S., Newell, J.P., Stults, M.: Defining urban resilience: a review. Landsc. Urban Plan. **147**, 38–49 (2016)
11. Sharifi, A., Yamagata, Y.: Resilient urban planning: major principles and criteria. Energy Proc. **61**, 1491–1495 (2014)
12. Alberti, M., Marzluff, J.M., Shulenberger, E., Gordon, B., Ryan, C., Zumbrunnen, C.: Integrating humans into ecology: opportunities and challenges for studying urban ecosystems. Bioscience **53**(12), 1169–1179 (2013)
13. Yiftachel, O., Hedgcock, D.: Urban social sustainability: the planning of an Australian city. Cities **10**(2), 139–157 (1993)
14. Roberts, M.: Sharing space: urban design and social mixing in mixed income new communities. Plan. Theory Pract. **8**(2), 183–204 (2007)
15. Calabrò, F., Della Spina, L.: The public-private partnerships in buildings regeneration: a model appraisal of the benefits and for land value capture. Adv. Mater. Res. **931–932**, 555–559 (2014)
16. Pontrandolfi, P., Scorza, F.: Making urban regeneration feasible: tools and procedures to integrate urban agenda and UE cohesion regional programs. In: Gervasi, O., et al. (eds.) ICCSA 2017. LNCS, vol. 10409, pp. 564–572. Springer, Cham (2017). https://doi.org/10.1007/978-3-319-62407-5_40
17. Pontrandolfi, P., Scorza, F.: Sustainable urban regeneration policy making: inclusive participation practice. In: Gervasi, O., et al. (eds.) ICCSA 2016. LNCS, vol. 9788, pp. 552–560. Springer, Cham (2016). https://doi.org/10.1007/978-3-319-42111-7_44
18. Morano, P., Tajani, F., Manganelli, B.: An application of real option analysis for the assessment of operative flexibility in the urban redevelopment. WSEAS Trans. Bus. Econ. **11**(1), 465–476 (2014)
19. Manganelli, B.: Real Estate Investing: Market Analysis, Valuation Techniques, and Risk Management. Springer, Cham (2015). https://doi.org/10.1007/978-3-319-06397-3
20. Morano, P., Tajani, F.: Saving soil and financial feasibility. A model to support public-private partnerships in the regeneration of abandoned areas. Land Use Policy **73**, 40–48 (2018)
21. Dragotto, M., India, G. (eds.): La città da rottamare. Dal dismesso al dismettibile nella città del dopoguerra. Cicero, Venezia (2007)
22. Tan, X., Altrock, U.: Struggling for an adaptive strategy? Discourse analysis of urban regeneration processes – a case study of Enning Road in Guangzhou City. Habitat Int. **56**, 245–257 (2016)
23. La Rosa, D., Privitera, R., Barbarossa, L., La Greca, P.: Assessing spatial benefits of urban regeneration programs in a highly vulnerable urban context: a case study in Catania, Italy. Landsc. Urban Plan. **157**, 180–192 (2017)
24. Micelli, E.: L'eccezione e la regola. Le forme della riqualificazione della città esistente tra demolizione e ricostruzione e interventi di riuso. Valori e Valutazioni **12**, 11–20 (2014)
25. Vona, M., Mastroberti, M., Manganelli, B.: Novel models and tools to evaluate the economic feasibility of retrofitting intervention. In: Papadrakakis, M., Fragiadakis, M. (eds.) COMPDYN 2017, Proceedings of the 6th International Conference on Computational Methods in Structural Dynamics and Earthquake Engineering, vol. 2, pp. 3213–3224. National Technical University of Athens (2017)

Internal Areas and Smart Tourism. Promoting Territories in Sardinia Island

Silvia Battino[1], Ginevra Balletto[2], Giuseppe Borruso[3(✉)], and Carlo Donato[1]

[1] DISEA – Economics and Business, University of Sassari, Via Muroni, 25, Sassari, Italy
{sbattino,cadonato}@uniss.it
[2] DICAAR – Department of Civil and Environmental Engineering and Architecture,
University of Cagliari, Via Marengo, 2, Cagliari, Italy
balletto@unica.it
[3] DEAMS – Department of Economic, Business, Mathematic and Statistical Sciences "Bruno de Finetti", University of Trieste, Via A. Valerio, 4/1, 34127 Trieste, Italy
giuseppe.borruso@deams.units.it

Abstract. The paper tackle the issue related to the promotion of internal areas of Sardinia, considered the contrast existing between a strong, peak coastal tourism and a lower development in the internal areas. Considered the vast amount of cultural and environmental goods present in the territory, particularly in internal areas, in this paper we promote a mixed qualitative – quantitative method for highlighting more promising areas for targeting ad hoc policies of development. We start with a hot spot analysis of cultural and environmental goods in Sardinia Region, with particular reference to the internal areas. We then proceed with highlighting the municipalities or aggregation of municipalities presenting the highest concentrations of such goods. Then we qualitatively evaluate those events or sites generally more renown and appreciated, observing if local – municipal or regional – policies have been activated for their promotion. Observed that, we suggest possible interventions to enhance the touristic offer of such part of the Sardinia island.

Keywords: Smart tourism · Internal areas · GIS · Sardinia island

1 Introduction

The sustainability, the safeguarding of heritage and biodiversity, the concentration of the population in the cities and the fight climate change are just some of the issues studied and explored starting from the Second World War and in particular, with more attention and rigor in the last two decades. Specifically, the many different scientific studies have focused on the significant territorial imbalances between urban and rural geographical

This research is developed in the context of "PRIN Progetto 73. PI Maria PREZIOSO - 20155NXJ8T - SH3 - Territorial Impact Assessment of territorial cohesion of Italian regions". A Model on the basis place evidence for the evaluation of policies aimed at the development of the green economy in internal and inner areas.

© Springer International Publishing AG, part of Springer Nature 2018
O. Gervasi et al. (Eds.): ICCSA 2018, LNCS 10964, pp. 44–57, 2018.
https://doi.org/10.1007/978-3-319-95174-4_4

regions, which are often defined as peripheral, weak or marginal. A gap is increasing because of the continuous and significant transfer of people from the countryside to the cities: the first mostly lacking in job opportunities, and the second real driving force of economy and places able to offer more opportunities for cultural growth. Thus, the excessive concentration of the population in higher-ranking centres and the depopulation of rural areas prompted the European Union to develop restyling strategies able to renew the attractiveness of marginal areas and improving their competitive potential as a whole of localized assets (natural, human, relational and organizational). The "Europe 2020 Strategy" aims at an inclusive, sustainable and intelligent growth of European regions, to be achieved through the reduction of territorial gaps, the enhancement of diversity and the propensity towards a development of the entire European space [1–3].

In such sense, all the most important national and international debates - Biennal exhibition of Venice 2018, Chile 2017 – are to-date oriented to read and understand the diversity among strong and weak areas, in order to avoid useless runs towards homologation, to prefer a tourist appreciation coherent with habitats and places, making of differences the distinctive and promotional force, by means of the vast collective material and immaterial heritage.

The interest of cohesion policies in Italy, in the wake of European spatial planning, is therefore aimed at reorganizing the territory, rethinking those spaces that live a condition of peripherality so-called "internal areas". A peripherality understood as a marginal socio-economic conditions related to distance from the centres and that also finds expression in the problems of social exclusion due to the difficulty in accessing some significant social and economic opportunities. So we can define the internal areas at such a distance from the closest and most important centre to cause their disadvantage in terms of accessibility to basic and/or essential services, of competitiveness and social inclusion [8–13]. In recognizing an internal region of the Italian polycentric territory, it was fundamental to consider together the geographic and relational components that were well highlighted by the research group that worked to develop the Project "National Strategy for Internal Areas" (SNAI) launched in September 2012, within the framework of the regional cohesion policy for the 2014–2020 cycle. There are more than 4.000 municipalities (internal areas) identified according to the reference centres and at the presence of some factors such as mobility (a railway station with category Silver), Health (hospital with DEA headquarters – 1st level i.e. emergency centres and First aid), education (the presence of a secondary school institution) and Internet access. The availability of these essential services guarantees a fundamental precondition for development, but their absence or scarcity does not always imply that the areas concerned are marginal. In most cases they are small municipalities that have lost in time their economic and social "attractiveness", due also to the often inadequate capacity to networking [16–18]. This disadvantage, which has a strong impact on their ability to be resilient to the thrust of economic growth set on traditional incremental pathways, could otherwise represent a strength to outline a new sustainable development of territory. These territories have long been in a situation of degradation and abandonment, but thanks to the presence of a rich and variegated landscape, could be understood not only as places to "use" but to "draw". In these areas the heritage represents not only a remedy for the "recovery" of history, but a real resource for economic and social development and a real possibility to increase the quality of life. This last is an indicator that is based on economic values and also considers the environmental sustainability, the health and well-being of the communities and the functionality of social networks [19, 20].

The study of the Snai, then, highlights how sustainable tourism is an excellent element of attraction of residents and tourists, and of activation of local development processes [21, 22]. The "rural" tourism activity, in order to represent an opportunity for the territory, must necessarily be started together with other elements characterizing the place (cultural heritage, food and wine, local renewable energy etc.). This start must follow a "participatory" project with precise purposes and means able to help the local communities without losing the traditional identities [5, 7, 23, 24]. The valorization of the natural and cultural heritage is therefore a primary role for the revival of an internal area and its fruition becomes the main objective in order to be able to converge towards a new and diversified sustainable offer. In doing this, the local planning policies must follow a resource based approach that considers the cultural system, not as a "museum object" to be protected from aesthetic, artistic and social fruition, but as an "investment" value generator and memories able to communicate with the specificity and the identity of the place [18]. This goal aims to transform the condition of peripherality of the internal areas making them emerge as "niche" destinations often flanked by consolidated tourist destinations at regional, national and international level [25].

Competing in a global market, therefore, is the conditio sine qua non to come out of isolation by developing a smart tourist industry where technological innovation and environmental sustainability are the two fundamental pillars. Smart tourism, Smart and IoT (Internet of Things), is based on the diffusion of ICT (Information and Communication Technology), a multimedia technology useful to create integrated development training platforms. A technology able to promote, share and extend the usability of territorial resources beyond the traditional channels, where they become the absolute protagonists and tourists play an active role in the cultural experience. In the wake of the concept of smart city one could rethink the internal territories, where there is an insignificant technological diffusion, like the smart region. Here the enhancement of the communication networks can guarantee the availability of essential services improving the indigenous quality of life.

This alternative approach of rethinking the tourist spaces moves public and private operators minds of different rural regions including the Sardinian internal areas that for more time tries to bring the holidaymakers of the 3s - sun, sea, sand - typical of the mass tourism model, to that of the 3L – Landscape, Leisure, Learning – Linked to the sustainability and enhancement of the local heritage.

2   The Selection of Sardinian Internal Areas

As we have stated, the internal areas of the national territory have been identified by the distance from the main essential service centres (secondary schools, health structures of DEA of II level, railway stations of type at least "silver"). On the basis, therefore, of an indicator of accessibility, calculated in terms of travel minutes compared to the nearest pole, the Italian municipalities were classified in 4 peripherality zones: peri-urban areas;

intermediate areas; peripheral areas and ultra-peripheral areas. In Sardinia on 377 municipalities 318 were classified as "internal areas": of which 93 "intermediate areas" and 225 "peripheral and ultra-peripheral areas" with a population, at 2011, of 856,897 units, 52.27% of the total residents. This territorial division is determined by the situations of disadvantage and obstacle to the obtaining of rights and opportunities that the inhabitants of the internal areas bear, differently to those who live and work in the urban contexts or "belt" to the latter. There are many municipalities that, although they are located along the coastal area, are classified as internal (intermediate, peripheral, ultra-peripheral), as this requirement is not linked to the geographic position, but rather to the functional one, revealing a demographic, socio-economic and spatial marginality [29].

This first national analysis was redesigned in a second moment by the Sardinia Region (SRAI) on the basis of its territorial characteristics. The regional study, at first, applied rigorously the criterion of compresence and completeness of the services used by the national method that has led to the identification of only the poles of Sassari, Cagliari, Oristano, Nuoro, Carbonia and Iglesias. In a second phase of the analysis, the three SNAI indicators were revised considering the territorial structure and in particular the inadequate distribution of the settlements and the disadvantages of railway services. This has allowed bringing out as pole the city of Olbia that while being the seat of hospital (DEA) and having a railway station "Silver" presents a poor secondary school offer. In addition small centres have emerged (inter-municipal poles) of Alghero, Tortolì and Lanusei, which carry out service functions for the sub-regional reference areas (Fig. 1). After locating the main agglomerations, the internal areas were classified using the SNAI criterion of the distance from the poles measured in journey times. After locating the main agglomerations, the internal areas were classified using the SNAI criterion of the distance from the poles measured in journey times and taking into consideration further municipal discriminating identified on the basis of the social material deprivation indexes, in relation to the composite indicator of state of demographic malaise and on the assessment of the conditions of viability of the regional territory or better on the discomfort of access to services-DAS [31].

The use of new variables and other indicators allowed to highlight a different municipal nomenclature (Fig. 1), compared to the previous one analyzed at national level. On a total of 377 municipalities were, thus, detected 6 "Poles", 4 "Intermunicipal Poles", 52 centres of "belt" and 315 municipalities of which 172 "peripheral and outlying" for a total of 824,054 inhabitants [33].

In the continuation of the work, it was also considered advisable to exclude from the calculation of the internal areas the 72 municipalities belonging to the coastal strip, because they were largely interested in an important bathing tourist activity, from highly seasonal characters.

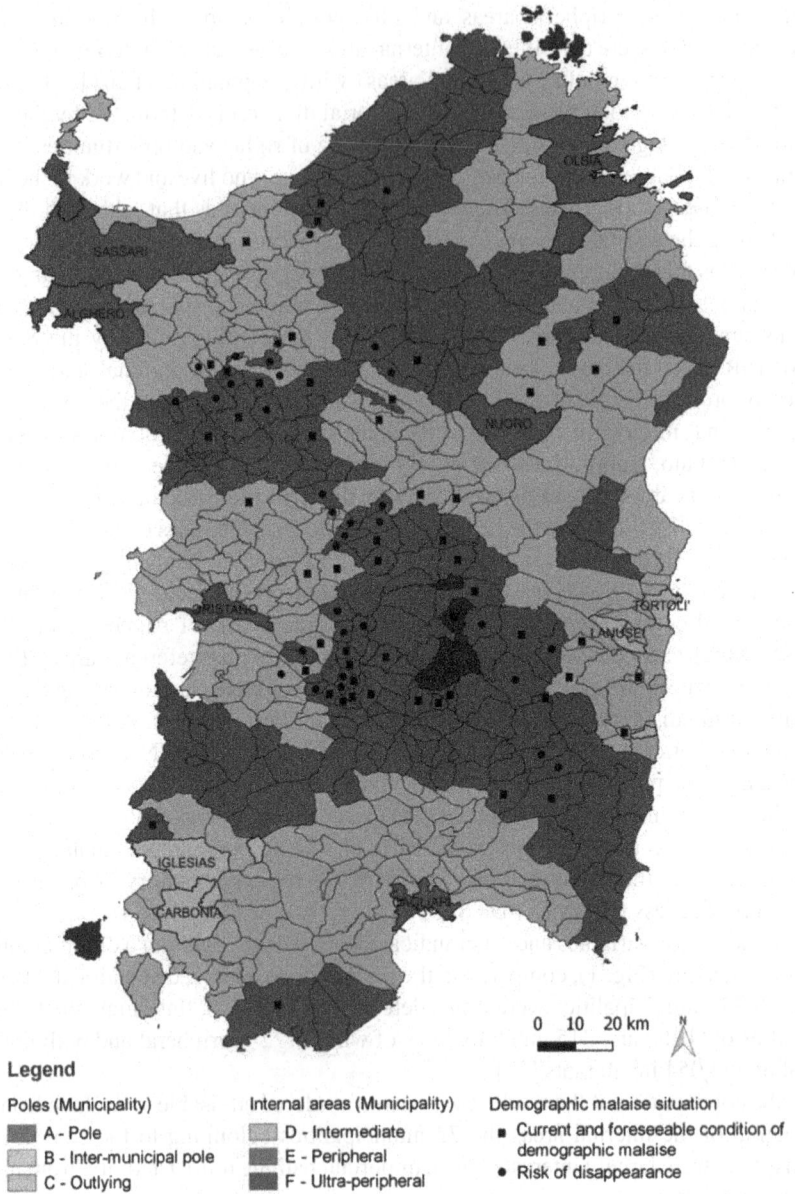

Fig. 1. Classification of municipalities according to the remodulation of Sardinia Region. Common with demographic malaise situation. Source: Our elaboration on Gis data from Opendata Sardegna [45]

3   Sardinia Inner and Non-coastal Areas

Inner areas, although understandable as weak in the economical and social meanings, are characterized by strong peculiarities, also because of their peripherality, as gradually the relations of living have been weakened in favour of other places. The same abandonment of places is fueling this peculiarity [47]. In most of the cases such places are resources exploited in a very limited way, that can be elements of attraction for residents, tourists and private operators that can be recalled to revitalize such places. In such sense the Sardinia Region, in characterizing SNAI approved and founded 4 Projects of Territorial Development (PST) involving 38 municipalities in total: such projects deal with different elements as (1) "Parte Montis – Culture, Handicraft, History, Agri-food sector"; (2) "The city of Villages of Gallura"; (3) "Marghine al centro – Tourism, Sport, Culture and Nature"; (4) "Ogliastra, Long-life trials". Each of these projects is characterized by a model of governance aims at promoting inner areas starting from the exploitation of the existing territorial capital, involving actively all the local operators [34]. The 'less important' places of culture are able to attract more and more tourists, aiming at short-time travels and in search for a quality holiday [35]. Sardinian natural environment and cultural heritage represent therefore the most important attractiveness for tourism. Cultural heritage are source of dynamic and active sources of income, not related to climate changes or seasonality and therefore enjoyable in every period of the year [36, 37].

Sardinian territory is full of culture, represented by basic resources as the tangible, real estate, religious goods – churches, monasteries, temples – monuments bridges, castles, palaces, houses, squares – and historical ones – streets, historical centres, archeological sites; to these categories we have to add the mobile goods as dialects, food, events and feasts [38, 39] (http://whc.unesco.org). Such an heritage has been the object of a catalogue by the Autonomous Region that, together with the Italian Ministry of Cultural Heritage and Tourism, realizes and updates constantly the database of cultural heritage, containing 4 sections: Landscape, Identity, Cultural Architectural and Cultural Archaeological heritage. This database contains 9,566 items involving 322 municipalities of the total 377,66% of which lay in the territorial areas of the 305 non coastal municipalities (Fig. 2 – http://www.sardegnaterritorio.it).

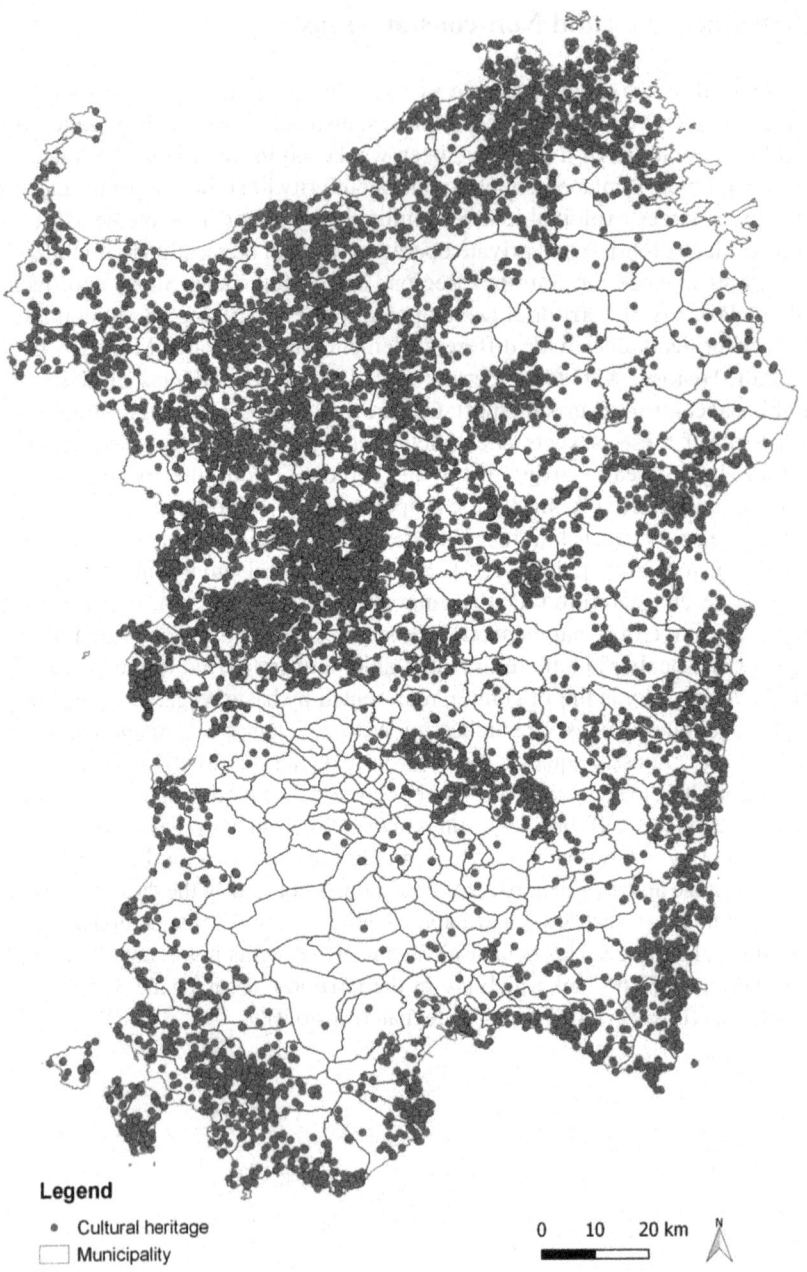

Fig. 2. Spatial distribution of cultural heritage in Sardinia. Source: Our elaboration on GIS data from Opendata Sardegna [45]

4   The Main Areas of Concentrations of Cultural Elements

The elaboration of a density map (Fig. 3) allows to highlight the areas where more numerous and intense is the presence of a cultural heritage.

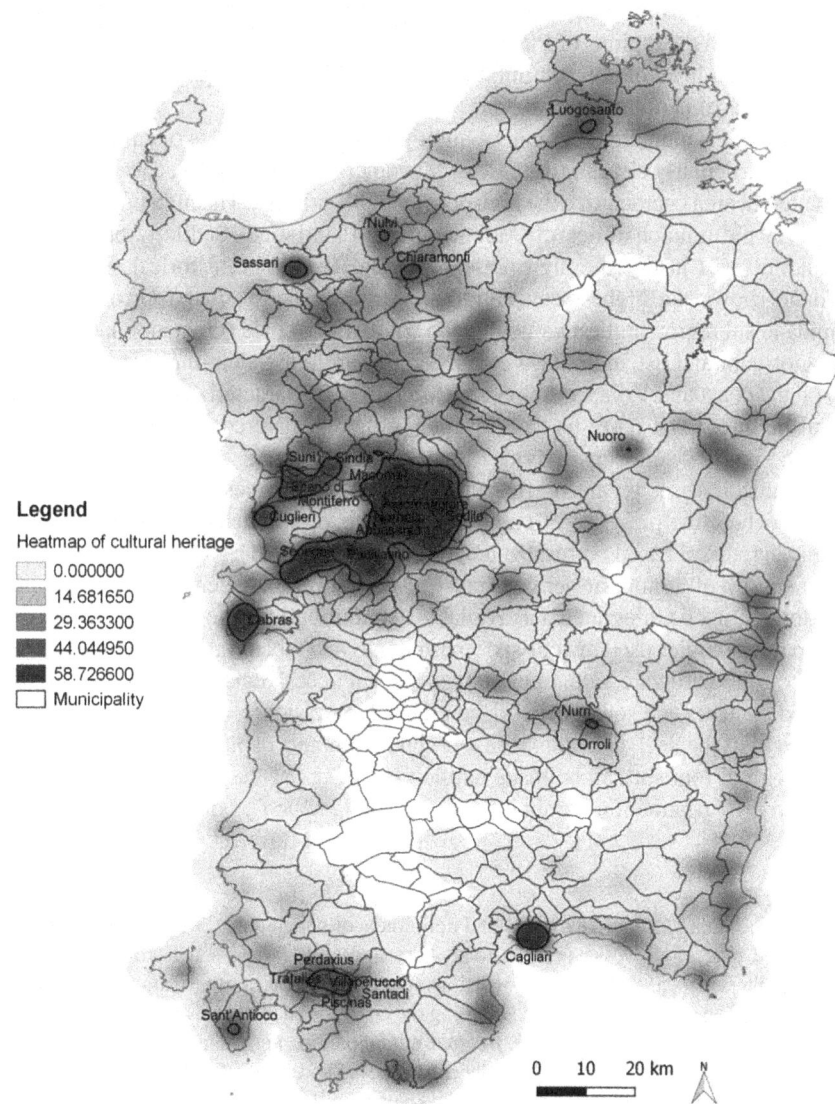

Fig. 3. Heatmap of Cultural Heritage. Source: Our elaboration on Gis data from Opendata Sardegna [45]

The analysis was performed using a heat map function in QGIS and using the cultural heritage database of Sardinia Region.

In the North of Sardinia the historical sub-regions of Alta Gallura and Anglona can be highlighted. Luogosanto is the main place for cultural heritage in Alta Gallura, while Anglona hosts Chiaramonti and Nulvi. Sassari presents the higher concentration in the internal area, in the old units of Romangia and Coros. Heading South, Nuoro can be highlighted, with the regions of Planargia, Marghine, Montiferru and Barigadu. Within Planargia a high level of concentration can be found in Tresnuraghes on the coast and Flussio and Sagama in the internal area.

In Marghine 8 municipalities can be highlighted for the presence of cultural heritage and this is particularly clear for the case of Macomer. Cuglieri on the coast and Seneghe in the internal area characterize the high density of Montiferru. The high number of such heritage in the municipalities of Aidomaggiore, Paulilatino, Sedilo, Abbasanta and surrounding ones justify the high presence in Barigadu. The historical subregion of Sarcidano shows the highest concentration in places as Nurri and Orroli, while in Campidano subregion highest values can be spotted in Cabras (Oristano) and Cagliari, the Region capital. Last, in South Western part of Sardinia, Sulcis-Inglesiente Sant'Antioco on the coast and Villaperuccio in the internal part characterize for the presence of cultural heritage. The inner part of Sardinia, although favored by a rich and unique cultural heritage, is suffering in terms of tourist infrastructure[1].

From this, it arises the need to incentive the competitiveness of such territories, in particular where the presence of cultural heritage is more intense, actuating forms of sustainable tourism based on rural and cultural characters [41].

The supply of a cultural heritage must respond to the challenges of the web 4.0, where these must be integrated and available also through the most advanced and now standard technologies used by tourists: smartphones and tablets, also integrated with 3D viewers on the hardware side, open data and open access data and information, user generated contents and social networks on the software side[2].

The tourists themselves become the users and promoters of places. Such link between real and virtual tourism can be made explicit by means of the bloggers, able of story telling a tourist destination. Among them, "Sardinia Mood", born in 2016, promotes

---

[1] In 2016, Sardinia hosted 4,787 hotels and non-hotels of which only 25% in the internal area, where bed places – 209,896 units in total – are limited to 7% (www.istat.it). Non coastal municipalities present mainly little dimensions structures - B&B, agritourism – with an average value of "beds per structure" (pl/es) 13. Along the coastline such value is higher (54 pl/es) and sets up at 44 pl/es at regional level. Internal municipalities are characterized by the 6% of arriving tourists and 3% of regional presences (2,879,495 and 13,485,744). The average staying time in the internal municipalities is 2.2 days versus 4.9 in the coast. This count does not consider second houses that are generally present mainly in the coastal area. This kind of hospitality determines a higher demand than those officially registered by regional institutions [42].

[2] A project can be cited in this sense as the "Homogeneous System of Visual Identity - Cultural Heritage Sardinia" that led to installing in museums 117 information points with video, photos and 3D reconstructions of the cultural and identity heritage of the island.

territories and offers suggestions useful for visits also on social networks and media platforms [27, 43] (https://sardiniamood.com).

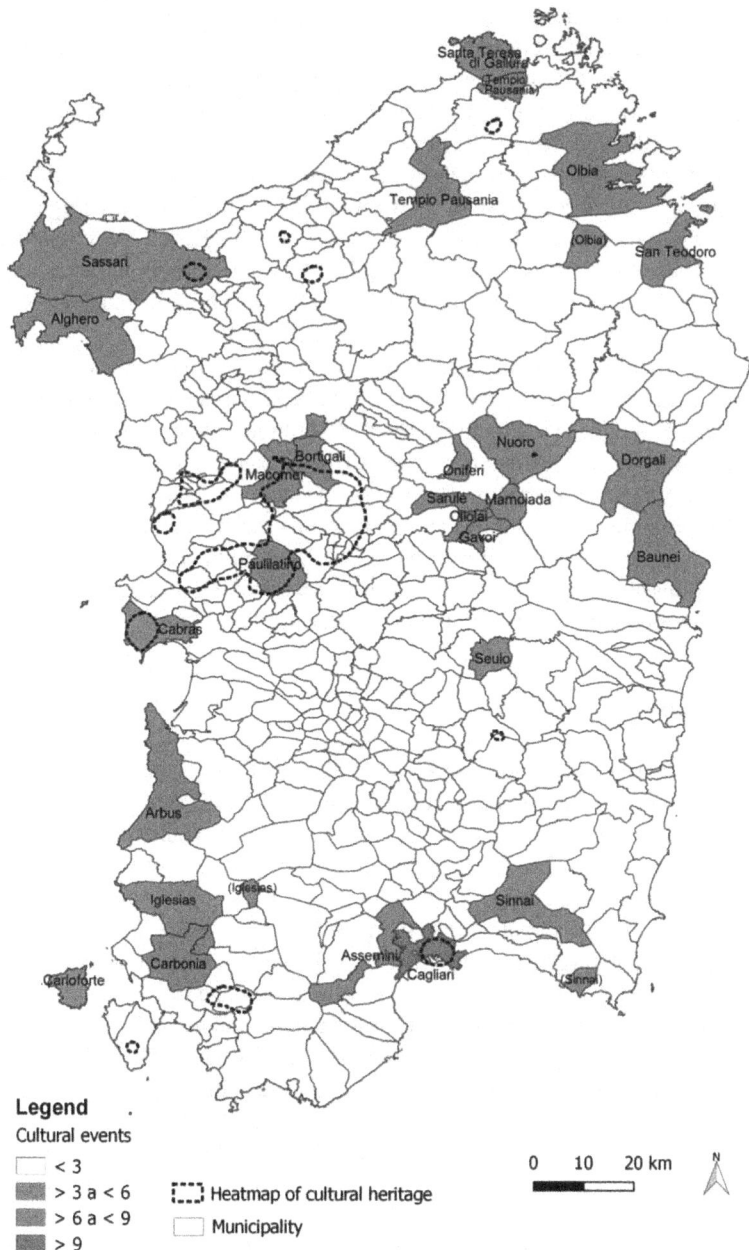

Fig. 4. Distribution of cultural events. Source: Our elaboration from www.sardegnacultura.it, www.sardegnainfesta.com, www.sardegnagrandieventi.it

Such rich 'internal' heritage is promoted also by the organization of small and medium cultural events stimulating the curiosity of 'soft tourism' lovers, aimed at increasing the visibility of the territory on a large scale. Religious feasts, carnivals, art exhibitions, literature festivals and food events are some of the examples for attracting new travelers. This can be related to the initiatives of active tourism promoted for the first time by Sardinia Region, aimed at putting together sport, cultural heritage and traditional and not traditional events. (https://www.regione.sardegna.it/j/v/2611? s=1&v=9&c=7106&na=1&n=10&va=2%20).

The Internet hosts several webpages dedicated to promotion and development of such events, as "Sardegna Cultura", (www.sardegnacultura.it), "Sardegna Grandi Eventi" (www.sardegnagrandieventi.it) e "Sardegna in Festa" (www.sardegnain-festa.com). These three websites host 550 cultural events. In internal areas names as Bortigali, Gavoi, Macomer, Mamoiada, Nuoro, Ollolai, Oniferi, Paulilatino, Sarule, Seulo and Tempio Pausania for a total of 51 events (Fig. 4).

These and other inner municipalities adhere to different initiatives and thematic itineraries to discover territories and their landscape values. We can remind here "Primavera nel cuore della Sardegna" (Spring in the heart of Sardinia) involving from April to June 20 municipalities from the historical regions of Marghine, Ogliastra and Baronia; "Autunno in Barbagia" (Autumn in Barbagia), a project followed by nearly 30 municipalities that promote their traditions and productions. Lastly the project "Open Monuments" (Monumenti Aperti), born in 1997 in Cagliari, and to-date involving more than 50 municipalities and 15 thousands students that, for two days, promote their territories. Around 600 monuments are open to the public during such event.

5   Conclusions

From the territorial reading and analysis it emerges that inner areas, for their constant weak socio-economic face, several cultural elements have been considered which, possibly, would have been lost in case the coastal - location would have been furtherly implemented. These elements represent a cultural heritage that is older if compared to the coastal one, these latter areas being traditionally more accessible and therefore easier to have access to cultural and artistic contaminations.

A first question arising deals with the reasons behind the little choices expressed by tourists for internal areas, so rich in terms of cultural heritage.

A first reply deals with the fact that most of these municipalities are considered internal areas (Fig. 1) and as such show serious difficulties within the regional mobility, being nearly isolated from coastal and more accessible centres and logistic nes. Inner regions present critical demographic situations that seem putting difficulties also to cohesion policies set up by the Region and aimed at fostering local development. The touristic supply however does not seem yet present and widespread, still concentrated on few municipalities.

Quantity (Fig. 2) and concentration (Fig. 3) of Sardinian cultural heritage do not appear yet able to determine a significant number of cultural events (Fig. 4). This is to be found partly in the above mentioned problems, but also on the "quality" and "attractiveness" of the cultural goods themselves. A question arises therefore on the activity of recovery, restoration and renewed accessibility of such cultural heritage and on its capacity of igniting the interest of the potential visitor. However, reinforcing a 'smart' tourism can favour the knowledge and evaluation, also from a socioeconomic point of view, of the internal regions. The dynamics of to-date international scenario, in fact, impose Sardinia region to follow the path of competitiveness that must adopt innovative approaches involving all the possible stakeholders. Setting up a system of integrated players, enhancing the image of Sardinia also in terms of internal areas, invest time and money in ICT are the directions to be consolidated. Also, Web 2.0 and 4.0, virtual marketing and social networks are only some of the possible ICT applications able to supply on-line information by means of fitted for purpose apps for smartphones and tablets. The physical channels of communications must be however maintained and enhanced, particularly in rural areas where the supply of cultural heritage is localized. There is also the need for a vision for Sardinia, half a way between local and global, important to break a the logic of a touristic system highly seasonal and coast-located.

References

1. Mozzoni, I.: Geografia della politica di coesione europea. Aracne editrice, Roma (2012)
2. Scanu, G., Lampreu, S.: Osservazioni sui riflessi territoriali delle politiche di coesione dell'Unione Europea in Sardegna. In: Marconi, M., Sellari, P. (a cura di): Verso un nuovo paradigma geopolitico. Raccolta di scritti in onore di Gianfranco Lizza, Tomo I – Tomo II, pp. 493–596. Aracne Editrice, Roma (2015)
3. Comitato Europeo Delle Regioni: Il futuro della politica di coesione dopo il 2020. Per una politica europea di coesione forte ed efficace dopo il 2020, 123a sessione plenaria dell'11 e 12 maggio 2017 (2017)
4. Angelini, A., Bruno, A.: Place-based. Sviluppo locale e programmazione 2014–2020. Milano, Franco Angeli (2016)
5. Prezioso, M.: Confronto tra Strategia Europe 2020 e obiettivi nazionali/regionali in Green economy e capitale territoriale. Dalla ricerca geografico economica proposta di metodi, indicatori, strumenti, Bologna, Patron Editore, pp. 55–57 (2016)
6. Montrone, S., Perchinunno, P., Rotondo, F., Selicato, F.: Internal areas strategies: from statistical methods to planning policies. In: Gervasi, O., et al. (eds.) ICCSA 2015. LNCS, vol. 9157, pp. 658–672. Springer, Cham (2015). https://doi.org/10.1007/978-3-319-21470-2_48
7. Coronato, M.: Gli strumenti europei a servizio delle aree interne. Bollettino AIC **157**, 53–59 (2016)
8. European Union. Cities of tomorrow Challenges, visions, ways forward, Bruxelles (2011)
9. http://ec.europa.eu/regional_policy/sources/docgener/studies/pdf/citiesoftomorrow/ citiesoftomorrow_final.pdf
10. Conti Pourger, A., Napolitano, P.: Studio per una caratterizzazione del policentrismo tra prossimità fisica e attributi relazionali in alcune aree urbane italiane. Memorie Geografiche. Oltre la Globalizzazione Prossimità/Proximity, Firenze, Società di Studi Geografici (2013)

11. Dematteis, G.: La Montagna nella strategia per le Aree interne 2014–2020. Agriregionieuropa **IX**(34), 1–6 (2013)

12. Prezioso, M.: Quali investimenti urbani di breve periodo per un futuro europeo di lunga durata. In: Cappellin, R., Baravelli, M., Bellandi, M., Camagni, R., Ciciotti, E., Marelli, E. (a cura di): Investimenti, innovazione e città. Una nuova politica industriale per la crescita, pp. 389–397. Studi&Ricerche Egea, Milano (2015)

13. Copus, A., Noguera, J.: Le 'periferie interne'. Che cosa sono e di quali politiche necessitano? Agriregionieuropa **12**(45), 1–6 (2016)

14. Neumeier, S.: Accessibility to services in rural areas. The example of petrol service provision in Germany. disP – Plan. Rev. **52**(3), 32–49 (2016)

15. RAS – Regione Autonoma della Sardegna: La Strategia nazionale per le aree interne. Processo programmatico e nota metodologica per l'individuazione delle aree interne per la Regione Sardegna, Assessorato della Programmazione, Bilancio, Credito e Assetto del Territorio Centro Regionale di Programmazione, Cagliari (2014)

16. Monaco, F., Tortorella, W. (a cura di): I comuni della Strategia Nazionale Aree interne. Prima edizione – 2015. Studi e Ricerche, Fondazione IFEL (2015)

17. Pezzi, M.G., Punziano, G.: La categoria di "distanza" come proxy delle questioni ruralità, pericificità e sviluppo locale nella Strategia nazionale per le aree interne. Sociologia e Politiche Sociali **20**(3), 167–192 (2017)

18. Lucatelli, S.: Strategia Nazionale per le Aree Interne: un punto a due anni dal lancio della Strategia. Agriregionieuropa **12**(45), 4–10 (2016)

19. Battino, S., Lampreu, S.: Strategie di valorizzazione e promozione in chiave turistica del patrimonio culturale nelle aree interne. Un caso in Sardegna. Annali del Turismo, vol. VI, pp. 83–105 (2017)

20. Bertolini, P., Pagliacci, F.: Territorial unbalances in quality of life. A focus on Italian inner and rural areas. In: DEMB Working Paper Series, vol. 87, pp. 1–25 (2016)

21. Campolo, D.: L'uso sostenibile delle aree interne attraverso il paesaggio culturale e le cultural routes. LaborEst **12**, 80–84 (2016)

22. Battaglia, F.: Turismo rurale: l'albergo diffuso per la conservazione del paesaggio. Il caso della Carnia. In Donato, C. (a cura di): Turismo rurale, agriturismo ecoturismo quali esperienze di un percorso sostenibile. Trieste, EUT Edizioni, pp. 108–122 (2007)

23. Grumo, R.: Le strade del vino e il binomio agricoltura-turismo: tipicità, qualità e appeal del territorio. Annali del turismo, 1, Novara, Geoprogress Edizioni, pp. 193–208 (2012)

24. Salvatore, R., Chiodo, E.: Aree interne e "tourism transition": nuove pratiche turistiche e riorganizzazione dell'offerta in funzione della rivitalizzazione. Agriregionieuropa **12**(45), 69–78 (2016)

25. Salvatore, R., Chiodo, E. (eds.): Non più e non ancora. Le aree fragili tra conservazione ambientale, cambiamento sociale e sviluppo turistico. Franco Angeli, Milano (2017)

26. Salvatore, R.: Networking e destinazioni turistiche: nuove forme di sviluppo locale per il rilancio delle aree interne. Rivista trim. di Scienza dell'Amministrazione **2**, 51–61 (2013)

27. Smith, V.L.: Indigenous tourism: the four h's. In: Butler, R., Hinch, T. (eds.) Tourism and indigenouspeoples. International Thomson Business Press, London (1996)

28. Ercole, E.: Smart tourism: il ruolo dell'informazione social. Annali del turismo **II**, 35–48 (2013)

29. Buhalis, D., Amaranggana, A.: Smart tourism destinations. In: Xiang, Z., Tussyadiah, I. (eds.) Information and Communication Technologies in Tourism 2014, pp. 553–564. Springer, Cham (2013). https://doi.org/10.1007/978-3-319-03973-2_40

30. Dematteis, G.: La Montagna nella strategia per le aree interne 2014–2020. Agriregionieuropa **9**(34), 1–6 (2013). https://agriregionieuropa.univpm.it/it/content/article/31/34/la-montagna-nella-strategia-le-aree-interne-2014-2020#footnote1_pzuex3u

31. Marchetti, M., Panunzi, S., Pazzagli, R.: Aree interne. Per una rinascita dei territori rurali e montani. Soveria Mannelli (CZ), Rubettino editore (2017)

32. RAS – Regione Autonoma della Sardegna: Indice di Deprivazione Multipla della Sardegna, Assessorato della Programmazione, Bilancio, Credito e Assetto del Territorio, Cagliari (2012)

33. RAS – Regione Autonoma della Sardegna: Comuni in estinzione. Gli scenari dello spopolamento in Sardegna, Centro Regionale di Programmazione, Cagliari (2013)

34. RAS – Regione Autonoma della Sardegna: La Strategia Nazionale per le aree interne. Processo programmatico e nota metodologica per l'individuazione delle aree interne per la Regione Sardegna, Cagliari (2014). http://www.galmarmilla.it/media/228820/Documento-Definizione-Aree-Interne-finale-26052014.pdf

35. Cannas, I., Curreli, S., Ruggeri, D.: La Sardegna nella Strategia Nazionale per le aree interne. XXXVIII Conferenza Italiana di Scienze Regionali 20–22 settembre Cagliari (2017)

36. Martelloni, R.: Nuovi territori. Riflessioni e azioni per lo sviluppo e la comunicazione del turismo culturale. Franco Angeli, Milano (2007)

37. Muscarà, C.: Gli spazi del turismo. Per una geografia del turismo in Italia. Patron editore, Bologna (1983)

38. Ugolini, G. M.: Turismo, valori ambientali e organizzazione del territorio: il caso della Liguria, Univ. di Genova, Collana di Studi dell'Ist. di Geogr. Economica e di Economia dei Trasporti (1996)

39. Montero Muradas, I., Oreja Rodrìguez, J.R.: La disponibilidad de los recursos tangibile de la oferta de produco de turismo cultural de las Islas Canarias. Aplicaciòn del modelo probabilistico de Rasch. Cuadernos de turismo **16**, 135–151 (2005)

40. Logan, W., Craith, M.N., Kockel, U. (eds.): A Companion to Heritage Studies. Wiley Blackwell, Oxford (2016)

41. Borruso, G.: Il ruolo della cartografia nella definizione del Central Business District. Prime note per un approccio metodologico. Bollettino A.I.C., 126-127-128, pp. 271–287 (2006)

42. Battino, S.: Turismo sostenibile in Gallura: prospettiva vincente o modello illusorio? I principali caratteri distintivi del cuore turistico della Sardegna. Patron editore, Bologna (2014)

43. Battino, S.: Stime quantitative ed un primo studio cartografico delle seconde residenze nel processo di litoralizzazione della fascia costiera del Nord-Est della Sardegna. Bollettino A.I.C., 150, pp. 4–19 (2014)

44. Ejarque, J.: Content destination strategy. Destin. Tour. **13**, 2–7 (2012)

45. Coni, M.: Le prospettive di sviluppo del sistema viario della Sardegna, relazione presentata all'incontro presso l'Università di Cagliari (20 Aprile 2007) "Le infrastrutture di trasporto in Sardegna oggi e domani. Verso un nuovo piano di investimenti 2007–2013", Cagliari, RAS (2007)

46. Opendata Sardegna. http://dati.regione.sardegna.it

47. Teti, V.: Quel che resta: l'Italia dei paesi, tra abbandoni e ritorni. Donzelli editore, Roma (2017)

Gentrification and Sport. Football Stadiums and Changes in the Urban Rent

Ginevra Balletto[1], Giuseppe Borruso[2(✉)], Francesco Tajani[3],
and Carmelo M. Torre[3]

[1] DICAAR – Department of Civil and Environmental Engineering
and Architecture, University of Cagliari, Via Marengo, 2, Cagliari, Italy
balletto@unica.it
[2] DEAMS – Department of Economic, Business, Mathematic and Statistical
Sciences "Bruno de Finetti", University of Trieste, Via A. Valerio,
4/1, 34127 Trieste, Italy
giuseppe.borruso@deams.units.it
[3] MITO Lab, Department of Civil Engineering Science and Architecture,
Polytechnic University of Bari, Via Edoardo Orabona, 4, 70125 Bari, Italy
francescotajani@yahoo.it, carmelomaria.torre@poliba.it

Abstract. In this paper we examine the changes in terms of urban rent and urban planning occurring after the introduction on the Italian law of 21 June 2017, n. 96 on Football stadiums property and management. Such law is actually paving the way to a set of new and still unexplored consequences on urban rents and urban renewal processes and real estate markets, as well as in terms of new patterns of urban behaviors. In detail, changes deal with the times strictly related to sport events, well scheduled in time (peak events), and those related to the ordinary life of the area (off peak events) as retail, transport and leisure/residential activities, often now coupled with the presence of such sport facilities. We briefly analyze some few Italian cases of football stadiums renewals, especially looking at those settled in cities hosting premier league clubs. We looked also at consequences they had in terms of urban rent, urban services. After, we started considering the possible implications that such investments can have on the cities that are likely to host such renewal processes in the near future, trying to highlight some possible changes in the "hedonic price" asset, and suggestions in terms of policy aimed at igniting a 'good' gentrification process.

Keywords: Gentrification · Urban planning · Real estate appraisal
Football stadiums · Cities · Sport

The paper derives from the joint reflections of the four authors. Ginevra Balletto realized Sects. 1, 2.2 and 4.1, Giuseppe Borruso wrote the 'Abstract' and Sect. 3.1. Francesco Tajani wrote Sect. 2.1 and Carmelo Torre Sects. 3.2, 3.3 and 4.2.

The paper is part of a wider research on the relations between sports and cities involving researchers from the universities of Bari, Cagliari and Trieste.

O. Gervasi et al. (Eds.): ICCSA 2018, LNCS 10964, pp. 58–74, 2018.
https://doi.org/10.1007/978-3-319-95174-4_5

1   Introduction

Sport and stadiums have been always connected each other in a double thread. Sport - understood as educator and instrument of population control - has been a used since ancient times propaganda and as a currency of exchange, both for freeing and amplifying the differences between ethnic groups. From pitches in the suburbs, to the "premier league" fields, from stadium stands to television, sport has been the true mass phenomenon that unifies the entire world population. Sport can be considered a religion, a belief that accepts practice and support, representing an is expression of urban customs and urban society [1, 2].

While sport fulfills tasks related to the recreational, educational and social spheres, the stadiums perform the task of spectacularization the city. Born as a sporting event, on the other the impulse of the population's affection for sport, supported by a progress of sponsors [3]. The stadium, since ancient times, is one of the devices in which the public city is celebrated [4], whose origin is closely linked to the dawn of the city, through the political and urban link, which has always provided the most remote urban procedures and relative of the social structure up to the present day.

2   Sport and Competitiveness of Urban Areas

2.1   Determinants of Economic and Urban Dimension of Sport Districts and Sport Facilities

Sport has always been an element of promotion of economic activities: the so-called "Great sporting events" have always been an occasion for the reconfiguration of cities and neighborhoods. Sport has a public and a private dimension. On an international scale, the Olympics, the world championships of various disciplines have been occasions for the renewal of parts of the city.

In sports there are also periodic and cyclical practices, acting as weekly catalysts. Cities become the cradles of large-scale periodic events, whose venues were decided with the support of international negotiations, with protocols for the evaluation of applications, and at the same time were the sites of more frequent practices, of less important scale, but which frequently involve urban areas. On the one hand four-year competitions occur, as the Olympics or the World Cup, athletics; on the other hand national sports championships - such as soccer, football basket, etc. - are repeated throughout the year every week in the same cities.

For the first category of sporting events, international and multi-annual frequency, the venues are selected through nominations, by international committees, and following protocols that evaluate the economic, logistic, advertising, and urban aspects. For the second, the periodic and weekly, the role and importance of competitions depends essentially on the successes of the teams, who can play in the national or local championships, and therefore depending on the success obtained, can be protagonists of events of national importance, or of minor importance. Some activities presuppose "de facto" the reconfiguration or the creation of new neighborhoods - such as the "Olympic cities" - in which not only the large buildings for the practice of sport are located, but also the services for spectators and for commercial activities and business. In other events, as cycling or marathons, on the contrary the urban impacts are not "long term ones", as they do not need to transform parts of the settlement, but happens through the realization of a complex logistics suitable for events extremely episodic.

The construction of neighborhoods dedicated to the performance of service activities to sporting events, normally corresponds to a gentrification phase of an area, as for Olympic Games [5]. It is therefore important to evaluate the impact on the economic fabric of a city, the presence of mass sports activities. We can therefore say that the effects determined by the realization of a large sports structure are in two different scales of the phenomenon: "sports districts", as large urban areas with a complex urban framework and several mixed activities; "sports facilities", more focused on local aspects. The birth of an "urban district for sports" has different consequences after the start-up, that can be considered at both international (Table 1) and national (Table 2) levels.

Table 1. Urban effects of sport districts (international).

Physical settlements	Social impact	Real estate market
- a permanent transformation of the urban fabric that can take place through a redevelopment intervention, or through a new settlement [6] - the inclusion of volumes that can be adapted to future urban uses - a new system of connections for the new pole [7] - any physical remediation and redevelopment [8]	- a Gentrification process [9] - the birth of a new centrality [10, 11] - the increase of commercial economic activities - the increase in services - the potential "expulsion" of residents who do not have sufficient economic capacity [12] - environmental impacts of various kinds	- a transformation linked both to public intervention (infrastructures and services) and to private intervention (services, infrastructures, offices, etc.) [13] - an increase in the real estate offer - a new soil regime [14] - an increase in the attractiveness of investors - an anticipation of significant expenditure

Table 2. Urban effects of sport facilities (national).

Physical settlements	Social impact	Real estate market
- a permanent transformation of the urban fabric - a new system of connections for the new pole - any physical remediation and redevelopment [15] - various kinds of environmental impacts [13]	- the birth of a new centrality - the increase of commercial economic activities - the increase in services	- a transformation mainly linked to public intervention (infrastructure and services) - a change in the real estate regime [17] - a smaller anticipation of expenses

The consequences of such changes in a given area/district can generate both negative and positive effects, and can interest several social components and stakeholders. It is evident that also the urban context welcoming such sports activities changes according to type of event and reason for which the structures are realized. In the case of major events, the number of potentially interesting urban contexts is generally limited to large metropolitan areas. The realization or the renewal of sports facilities for a more ordinary use, instead, may regard frequently smaller urban contexts.

The assessment procedures that can describe all the effects of the construction of sports facilities and areas are numerous, given the large number of aspects that may be involved. The short-term effects must also be separated from the long-term effects. In the short term, the transformation of territories creates situations of shock, problems related to the interference between site works and the daily life of involved areas in urban changes. The gravitational effect of the pole shaped starts after the completion of works. This effect can occur either in positive terms – i.e., due to the presence of "leisure areas" - or negative - i.e., weekend traffic during sporting events. In addition, the assessment involves several entities, and therefore the "Community impacts" should be considered. This is a typical case of "conflicting estimate", [16] with positive and negative components that sum up, which therefore make the application of an overall form of impact assessment very uncertain [18]. Generally speaking, when we want to evaluate the effect of the inclusion of sport activity content on the "quality of life" of residents and users of the surrounding areas, it becomes immediately evident the difficulty of reaching a one-dimensional, general or summary indicator of the effect on real estate [19]. Expressing a simple positive or negative judgment, linked to a multi-dimensionality of aspects, induces to refer to models with several variables [20]. In this regard, it may appear useful to recall the most well-known forms of synthetic evaluation of urban quality, with the attempt to build a tool to support the decision on the location of new sports areas equipped in a territorial context [21].

The traditional model for evaluating hedonic prices emerges from the urban economic literature. As is known, the hedonic price measures the increase or decrease of the quality of an area, depending on the characteristics of the context, suffering from the principle that the demand for residential properties on the market is higher in contexts in which the services (including those social, cultural and environmental) is greater. In this approach, the synthetic indicator of the quality of life in the analyzed area is given by the hedonic price, i.e., the incidence of context factors on the market price of real estate assets. Traditionally, the hedonic price is linked to the multiple (frequently linear) regression models, in which each component (called Amenity) represents the "marginal contribution" to the increase/decrease in the real estate value.

The main advantage of the model is its conceptual simplicity: the greater the number of positive factors in an area, the more one is willing to pay to live in that area. The limitation is given by the difficulty in parameterizing these factors and the definition of the area of influence of the factors themselves. For example, some studies have shown that the contribution of factors of quality of life in American cities, expressed in terms of marginal price, are often related with the demographic size of the city, rather than the characters of the context close to the analyzed area [21]. Some more studies, on the other hand, inspired by traditional models of the distance-to-distance ratio, have attempted to evaluate the area of influence exercised by a given Amenity, on real estate market prices.

A further approach, instead, is the Community Impact Evaluation [22], which analyzes the impact considering the articulation of the social components, starting from the assumption that the advantage/discomfort is distributed in a diversified way among subjects who have different lives and needs. In the case of the stadiums, for example, the green areas surrounding them generate positive effects, while the flows of fans generate disturbing effects. The evaluation in this case may have more general or more detailed levels of identification of needs and advantages for the various social components. For example, the most general classification can identify a few simple categories, such as the "users" groups, the "residents" groups and the "promoters" groups. Obviously, the distinction of the categories can be extended, considering for example traders, residents, sports enthusiasts, young people, the elderly, workers in the sector [23]. A further approach - that is borrowed from the logical framework of environmental impact assessment - suggests a specific assessment for each phase of works: an evaluation in the regime phase, and an assessment in the eventually phase of disposal or reuse of some structures for different purposes from the initial ones - i.e., using stadiums for concerts or social events. This latter approach plays a very important role when it is necessary to identify groups of cities, in sports events that affect an entire national territory - such as the World Championships of certain types of sports, such as football, or the Olympic Games, which do not take place in a single metropolitan area.

2.2 Sports as Urban Rent Catalysts, After the Italian Law on Stadiums

The wide debate on the modern and contemporary public city [24] has fueled the tracing of the integration between parts of cities and societies [25], increasingly global and always hyper-connected [26], in connection with everyday life and urban sports events [27]. In this framework the recent interpretations on the 'public city' are seen and understood as a 'common space' of public use [28]. The origin of such role of sport structures dates back to modern cities, in its multiple declinations, inertias and contradictions today received, but which at the same time helped to outline a new interpretation of the 'public city' now markedly oriented towards all that can be intended as 'the common interest', thus modifying form and substance of the 'public city' [29]. In this sense, open spaces are places where a fundamental role in the articulation of physical form has been always played [30], even in the presence of constraints due to converging socioeconomic relations with the shaping of the sense of community from local to global [31].

The role of open spaces in the process of transformation and/or urban regeneration is under the eyes and is understandable by everyone, even by non-lovers of the city [32]. In fact, open spaces are given a fundamental role in the regeneration of the public city, understood in the sense of the mediation that originates from the innumerable quantum approaches typical of the use of urban planning standards, the poverty of the typological design vocabulary, the modest attention domestic-common-public space, etc. [33]. In the open spaces and more generally in the spaces of the game and the sport, multiple functions are inserted. The game of football through the many highly characterized events, often as a real 'branding city' [34], but opening up different and new problems such as the re-employment after game typical of the famous phenomenon of 'Olympic City' [35].

It is no coincidence that the UEFA (Union of European Football Associations) guide for the realization of quality stadiums [36] is a fundamental reference to address the quality of the same not unrelated from the city of afference, reinforcing the historic bond that unites them [37], not only in terms of architecture, but also ideologically [38], as well as with the most recent links with the industrialization of free time [39]. More in detail, the industrialization of free time finds in private management of large facilities such as stadiums the full legitimacy in the Law Decree n.50/2017 as confirmed by the Law 96/2017. Urban changes due to the renewal of real estate, give place to new assets in the hands of the football clubs, according to an already outlined trend that started in other countries, in order to accommodate a wide mix of functions - commercial, conference, accommodation - setting in motion new processes of urban regeneration and thus affecting urban policies and choices [40].

3 Some Experiences

3.1 The Experience of Stadiums According to the New Italian Laws. Cases

The reason for investigating the case studies accompanies the possibility of counterbalancing the regime of urban rents, that usually in a metropolitan area, or in generic urban/territorial spaces is characterized as containing a centrality.

In the rest of the paragraph a brief description of the case studies is provided. The aim is to discover the influence on land-use rent and estate value are affected by the presence of sport structure or district. For this reason, the newest stadiums will be analyzed, looking at the effect of prepositive actions by private entrepreneurs can have a social effect on neighbors. For this scope a brief illustration of the history of recent reconstruction/refurbishment of old stadiums in Turin, Udine and Cagliari can show some effect on the real estate assets, even if the intervention are very recent, and effects maybe can be only germinal. The last case is related with the project of a sports and commerce district, in the quarter of "Tor di Valle", in Rome. This latter case regards a project proposal, instead of a reconstruction of an existing structure. Therefore, the rent is to be depicted in some way, anticipating the future development of the neighborhood of "Tor di Valle".

3.2 Turin, Udine, Cagliari and Rome: Combining Urban Development with Stadiums

Juventus-Allianz Stadium, Turin. The "Juventus Stadium" (named "Allianz Stadium" in 2017) is the first football facility in Turin. The Stadium is owned by "Juventus Football Club" and is hosting the matches of the team since the 2011–2012 season.

Starting from the 1st of July 2017, the sport structure assumed the commercial name of "Allianz Stadium" after the transfer of the "naming rights" from Juventus club to the "Allianz" Company. "Allianz Stadium" is the sixth larger Italian stadium, with 41,507 seats; the structure rises on the same area of the now demolished, "Stadium of the Alps", and reuse some pieces of the previously existing structures. The stadium is the first Italian football structure completely welcoming people with limited mobility, and the world's "first environmentally friendly" sport facility, is one of the four Italian stadiums belonging to the "level 4" of UEFA classification, that corresponds with the highest technical level. It is also the first modern facility owned by a club in the country. [7] Allianz Stadium is not only considered among the most advanced plants in the world, but as well as, one of the architectural symbols of contemporary.

Turin, and among the major tourist attraction poles in the city, the Stadium was awarded the Stadium Innovation Trophy Global Sports Forum 2012 as the most innovative sports scenario in Europe. The structure is located between the residential neighbors of Vallette and Lucento, and the area of Continassa, in the north-western area of the city, on the border with the Municipalities of Venaria Reale and Cologno. The influence of the King's Castle of Venaria is reduced by the main ring-road that "cuts" the connections of Venaria with Turin (Fig. 1).

Fig. 1. The Allianz Stadium, owned by the Juventus Football Society in the center of an inhomogeneous crown of surroundings

Dacia Arena (Friuli Stadium), Udine. "Friuli" Stadium is the football facility in the city of Udine. The structure welcomes 25,132 spectators for football matches. The Stadium is the largest urban arena in terms of number of seats, and the second regional largest structure in Friuli-Venezia Giulia. It is primary used by "Udinese" football club, the main in the city and also in the Friuli Venezia Giulia Region (Fig. 2).

Fig. 2. The new "Friuli Stadium, in Udine

The Stadium is placed 4 km from the center of Udine, in the so-called neighborhood "Rizzi". The permission of use, after the construction, was celebrated officially in 1976. The name "Friuli" was chosen to commemorate the Region, hit by the severe Earthquake in 1976. The Friuli Stadium, in fact, was inaugurated in substitution of the Moretti stadium, demolished after the earthquake and an urban park was realized in its place.

The structure was renovated several times, but the main change was carried out in the period 2013–2016. After the last intervention, the stadium is hosting only football matches, due to the elimination of the athletic ring around the playing field. At the same time as the last restructuring was launched, in 2013 it was conceived by the Municipality exclusively to the Udinese Football Club for 99 years, one of the most ancient football club of Italy. The concession of use to the football club, was the second in Italy, regarding a modern sport facility after the Juventus Stadium.

Sant'Elia Stadium, Cagliari. The Sant'Elia stadium was a sports facility in the Italian city of Cagliari. Open in 1970 in the homonymous quarter of the city, taking the place of the "Amsicora Stadium", the Structure represented the largest urban and regional open arena in terms of number of seats (around 50,000), built honoring the Championship of the Italian Football League that was conquered by the Cagliari Team in the same period. As regard the functional point of view, the new structure was a multi-function stadium, equipped with an athletics track.

The main activity was anyway represented by football, serving for the internal matches of "Cagliari" football club. Even if refurbished in view of the 1990 World Cup, after 1999 Sant'Elia Stadium suffered for a quick structural decline. The physically degradation initially caused the need of limiting the capacity of welcoming seats, and then (since 2002) the need of closing large portions of the terraces, replaced by prefabricated structures in the interior circle of the old basin, after the elimination of the athletic track. Despite the intervention, the continuing increase of the stadium's obsolescence caused, in a first step the declaration of inability, and, at the final, the dismissing of the structure. In 2017, a project for the demolition and reconstruction of the structure was started, and now the area of Sant'Elia aspires to represent a leisure and sport area in the nearest southern area of Cagliari.

Fig. 3. The area of the new Sant'Elia Stadium in Cagliari

The Project of Tor di Valle Stadium Rome. The most recent Italian attempt of gentrification thanks to the demand for Sports Districts is coming from the proposal of building a new Stadium in the city of Rome: in detail, in the neighbor named "Tor di Valle", where some dismissed sport facilities are standing in a state of degradation.

The proposal was object of a debate, during the transition from the former Municipal Council to the new one. The masterplan of the area of new Stadium, proposes a group of skyscrapers in commercial and business center, interventions of land reclamation and new infrastructure connection. The project was defining a sort of mega-structure of aggregation, socialization, commerce, more and more recipients of ICT, a sort of journey into the future, from "augmented reality" to "bit-coin", while maintaining the attention with their relationship with the landscape and the place, sometimes integrations techno-grains and sometimes as real landmark [21] (Fig. 4).

Fig. 4. The project of the "new sport district" (left) and the current state of Tor di Valle (right)

3.3   Facts and Data

The interplay between urban rents and new sports districts: through such cases we start investigating the effects due to the reallocation of sports facilities in the urban context. In the first step we can register some similarities among the four cases.

Even if the episodes are quite recent and there is a small possibility of forecasting the long term issues of the new project, the evident common line is the new stadiums arise from the rehabilitation or the demolition of existing structures and/or the reuse of the existing areas devoted to the old sport activities. All four cases in fact, see the birth of new stadiums as replacement of the older ones. In all cases, as well, the rebirth of the sport district is accompanied by the hope of an increase of urban rent in the area. The rent effect anyway is readable through some issues, that are "similar" but not "homogeneous" from a case to another. Data are referring to the Observatory of Property Market (OMI) provided by the Italian Tax Agency. OMI reviews periodically the market values for various typologies of real estate in the urban market, subdivided by zone. In the cases of Udine and Turin, we can observe a faster, even small, increase of real estate value, respect to the surroundings. As regards Udine, the real estate values in the area of Friuli Stadium seems to decrease until the 2017 (year of the reconstruction), starting with a weak increase (Fig. 5).

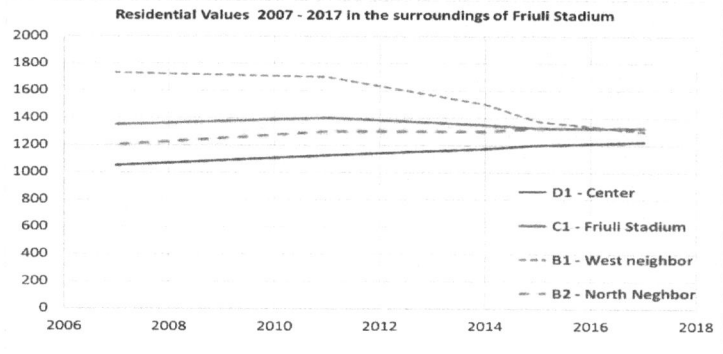

Fig. 5. Trend of residential estate values near to the Friuli Stadium in Udine

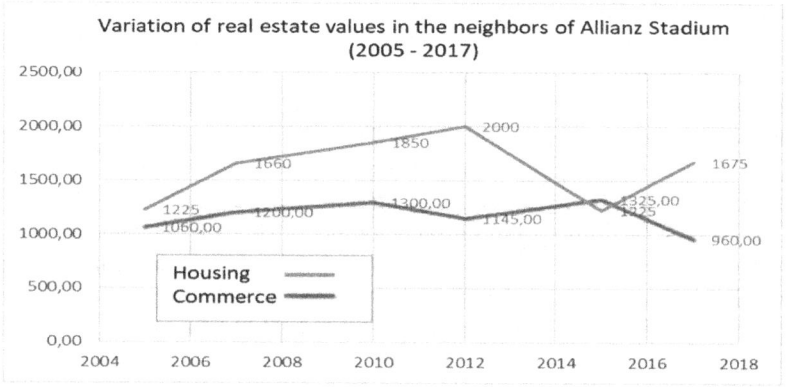

Fig. 6. Trend of commercial and residential estate near the Allianz Stadium, Turin

Table 3. Real estate values in the area of Allianz Stadium: look competitive for housing

Nearest neighbors	Allianz stadium	Turin municipality	Venaria municipality	Collegno municipality
(OMI Zones)	D13 €/m^2	D10 €/m^2	C1 €/m^2	D2 €/m^2
Housing	1675	1325	1500	1250
Commerce	960	825	1495	680
Offices	815	1030	1020	940
Car boxes	1145	1145	980	

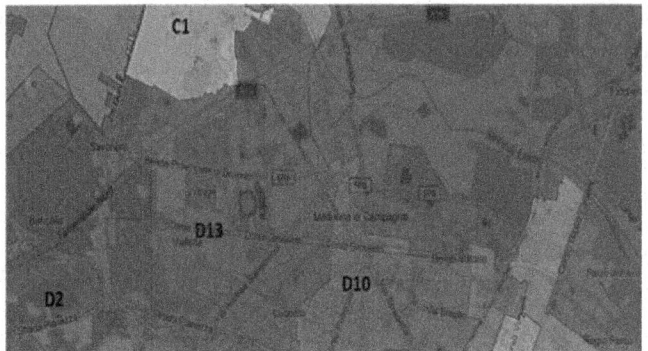

Fig. 7. Classification of neighbors according the OMI observatory of real estate market around the Allianz Stadium of Turin

The same appears for the area of Juventus-Allianz Stadium, but the increase regards only the real estate value of the residential stock. Despite this the value of commercial activities is still decreasing. The reason could be identified with the increase of presence of general stores reducing the competitiveness of shops and small commerce (See Fig. 6 and Table 3). The positive effect of reconstruction is clear enough in the case of Turin, since the reconstruction was carried out in 2012. The new Friuli Stadium instead dates back to less than one year (Fig. 7).

As regards the future of "Tor di Valle", the area and the project seem to be related by different dynamics respect to Udine and Turin. The probability of a strong gentrification in the area is very high. Private investors will be interested to the creation of the district, just because of the current small rent of soils in the middle of several built areas. Looking at land-use in the surrounding of Tor di Valle, the area appears as a point of transition among urban mono-functional areas (commercial, manufacturing, residential) where leisure and sports can be offered, also accompanied by commerce and advanced tertiary activities (not so far from the Institutional seats of the EUR Quarter) (Fig. 8 and Table 4).

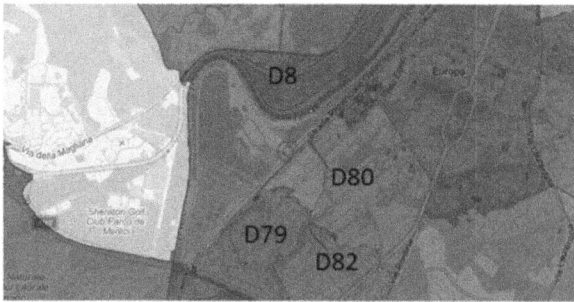

Fig. 8. Estate sectors (letter and number of OMI zones) surrounding Tor di Valle (in green) (Color figure online)

Table 4. Real estate value in surroundings of Tor di Valle

Tor di valle nearest neighbors (OMI zones)	D79 €/m²	D8 €/m²	D80 €/m²	D82 €/m²
Housing	2950	2400	3225	2800
Commerce	2800	2000	2600	2450
Offices	2800	2250	2900	2650

Sant'Elia in Cagliari appears as a more complex case. The reason of the intervention is related with the need to put on safety the structures and the area of the Stadium, with a public intervention. The plan for rehabilitation becomes the occasion to think about a new pole, thinking to realize fast connection to the area, that become a gravitational center for free-time and public activities. It is difficult to forecast the impact on property values, and to understand the economic dimension of social effects of the new stadium, since the works of rehabilitation started in 2017. What makes the difference between the works on Sant'Elia, respect to the previous three cases is the

Fig. 9. The area of Sant'Elia in 1996

Fig. 10. The subdivision of real estate zones around Sant'Elia.

Table 5. Real estate values for different categories of property, according to the observatory of real estate market in 2017 (€/m²)

Type of property	B2 (near city center)	C4 (intermediate)	D3 (north limit of Sant'Elia)	D4 (east limit of Sant'Elia)
Housing	2075	2450	2250	2325
Commerce	2300	2250	2000	1900
Offices and tertiary	2000	2150	2000	2000

dimension and the willingness of public bodies (firstly Municipality, but also County Council etc.) to create a "social value" [22]. At the end of the interventions, it will be possible to identify indirect benefits also for private property market.

Observing Fig. 9 we can compare the area in 1996 with 2018 (Fig. 3) Even the possibility of comparing the time change of real estate values of neighbors is quite difficult, due to the changes of delimitation of Real Estate Zones of Cagliari in 2014, that gives the possibility of comparing only the period 2014–2017, without the possibility of a diachronic study on property trends, as in the previous examples, in the middle-long period. The only possible comparison is between different activities related to property (Housing, commerce, business) (Fig. 10 and Table 5).

4   Concluding Remarks

4.1   General Remarks

The paper can host a first set of general and specific remarks. We can observe as stadiums moved from elements containing functions related only to sport and competition, to multi-function places spanning from sport events to commerce. It is a new model based on collective emotional intelligence, translated into an overall sense of exhilaration of single persons into a group, from the spectacularization of sport.

Stadiums can be considered as new urban generators, de facto playing the same multi-functional role once played by waterfronts and shopping malls, but based on aspects related to emotional and social distances. Stadiums can be seen as elements playing a role at different scales of distances. Relations among people and between people and places occur actually at different scales of distances. During a match a prossemic distance is expressed varying from intimate (0–50 cm) to social (1–4 m). A bigger scale is considered when we think about the 300–500 m buffer drawn around stadiums, where the sport plant's manager can work as a retail monopolist.

Longer distances are considered if we think about the catchment areas of stadiums, being the metropolitan scale or even national/international ones (for major matches). Smaller classes of distance are possible at intermediate scales, these being possible in case stadiums are permeable and allow being crossed by people, actually allowing different and better levels of accessibility and livability. The 'time' variable is therefore oriented towards the internal accessibility, that of the sport structures' layouts and it is directly proportional to its overall dimension. Their success, in fact, is tightly related to accessibility, from and to the main urban access – bus and tram stations, railway stations, airport – but also from the capacity of attracting daily users. In such sense, periurban and urban stadiums present major elements of coherence, with respect to extra urban, urban and periurban ones without a podium, caused by the effect of new concepts and functions introduced by a mix of 'Over Mix' and 'Over Time'. The deregulation introducing the law on stadiums is actually – as it is – characterized by loosening the urbanistic indexes, in order to insert football as a phenomenon into an urban dimension. This is nothing new if compared to games in ancient Rome, where sport gave momentum to urban development and architecture in the city, as the Coliseum and Circus Maximus.

4.2 Local Remarks

When moving to the case studies analyzed, the case of Turin and Udine put on evidence the possibility of private investors to get profit by modernize stadium structures, having as further advantage the increase of quality of public facilities. Such improvements often arise inside the old perimeters, welcoming the birth of more functional and technologically advanced arenas. The case of "Sant'Elia" in Cagliari and "Tor di Valle" show the wish of accompanying the refurbishment of sport structures by the creation of new additional built environments hosting sports activities, but not only. The two last cases anyway show some relevant difference.

The project of "Tor di Valle" produces a pay-off for the costs of the new sports district, compensated by the real estate values of the additional settlement represented by the skyscrapers. The urban make-up of the surroundings of Sant'Elia, instead, is addicted to host green spaces, public leisure and services, with the attempt to create a public central place with a public policy, taking the chance from the intervention on the Stadium. This central place could create a pole, inverting - or at least compensating - the variation of the rent between the city center and peripheries, in a traditional model of polycentric rent variation. From the social point of view, the project of Sant'Elia emphasizes the public dimension of gentrification, "making places more gently" for people; the project of Tor di Valle, instead sees the Stadium as a "pass partout" to create a new Business District where sports activities represent an accessory, an adjunct to the context.

Even if it could be useful to have more data for a more appropriate study on urban dynamics born from the rehabilitation of great structures, some aspect are clearly on evidence: the first aspect concerns the public dimension of rehabilitation, even though provided by private or public funding; the second aspects concerns the connection between new poles and urban tissues, as an occasion for qualifying neighbors. Finally, the last aspect - maybe more feasible in the nearest future - concerns the possibility to read the birth of new social centralities outside the inner urban areas, as element of a social equity, analyzing real estate values.

References

1. Watt, P.: 'It's not for us': regeneration, the 2012 Olympics and the gentrification of East London. City **17**(1), 99–118 (2013)
2. Kool, R.: Football stadiums and urban development. Do they provide more for the city than just the classical 'bread and circuses'? A study into the impact of football stadiums in the Dutch context (2017). http://theses.ubn.ru.nl/bitstream/handle/123456789/5374/Kool%2c_Rowan_1.pdf?sequence=1
3. Eddy, T., Dwyer, B., Slavich, M.: The impact of team outcomes, brand connection, and game attendance on the corporate image of a stadium naming rights sponsor. JAMT **7**(1), 1–17 (2017)
4. Cottino, P.: Competenze possibili. Sfera pubblica e potenziali sociali nella città, vol. 865. Editoriale Jaca Book, Milano (2009)
5. Ritchie, B.W., Shipway, R., Cleeve, B.: Resident perceptions of mega-sporting events: a non-host city perspective of the 2012 London Olympic games. J. Sport Tour. **14**(2–3), 143–167 (2009)
6. Huggins, R., Clifton, N.: Competitiveness, creativity, and place-based development. Environ. Plan. A **43**(6), 1341–1362 (2011)
7. Hoch, I., Waddel, P.: Apartment rents: another challenge to the monocentric model. Geogr. Anal. **25**(1), 20–34 (1993)
8. Perchinunno, P., Rotondo, F., Torre, C.M.: A multivariate fuzzy analysis for the regeneration of urban poverty areas. In: Gervasi, O., et al. (eds.) ICCSA 2008. LNCS, vol. 5072, pp. 137–152. Springer, Heidelberg (2008). https://doi.org/10.1007/978-3-540-69839-5_11
9. London, B.: Gentrification as urban reinvasion. In: Laska, S., Spain, D. (eds.) Back to the City: Issues in Neighborhood Renovation, pp. 77–92. Pergamon Press, New York (1980)
10. Battaglia, F., Borruso, G., Porceddu, A.: Real estate values, urban centrality, economic activities. A GIS analysis on the city of Swindon (UK). In: Taniar, D., Gervasi, O., Murgante, B., Pardede, E., Apduhan, B.O. (eds.) ICCSA 2010. LNCS, vol. 6016, pp. 1–16. Springer, Heidelberg (2010). https://doi.org/10.1007/978-3-642-12156-2_1
11. Montrone, S., Perchinunno, P., Torre, C.M.: Analysis of positional aspects in the variation of real estate values in an Italian southern metropolitan area. In: Taniar, D., Gervasi, O., Murgante, B., Pardede, E., Apduhan, B.O. (eds.) ICCSA 2010. LNCS, vol. 6016, pp. 17–31. Springer, Heidelberg (2010). https://doi.org/10.1007/978-3-642-12156-2_2

12. Castells, M.: Crisis, planning, and the quality of life: managing the new historical relationships between space and society. Environ. Plan. D: Soc. Space **1**, 3–21 (1983)
13. Allen, I.: The ideology of dense neighborhood redevelopment. Urban Aff. Q. **15**, 409–428 (1980)
14. Tajani, F., Morano, P., Locurcio, M., Torre, C.M.: Data-driven techniques for mass appraisals. Applications to the residential market of the city of Bari (Italy). Int. J. Bus. Intell. Data Min. **11**(2), 109–129 (2016)
15. Morano, P., Tajani, F.: Saving soil and financial feasibility. A model to support public-private partnerships in the regeneration of abandoned areas. Land Use Policy **73**, 40–48 (2018)
16. Torre, C.M., Morano, P., Tajani, F.: Saving soil for sustainable land use. Sustainability **9**(3), 350 (2016)
17. Smith, N.: The New Urban Frontier. Gentrification and the Revanchist City. Routledge, London (1997)
18. Cerreta, M., Inglese, P., Malangone, V., Panaro, S.: Complex values-based approach for multidimensional evaluation of landscape. In: Murgante, B., et al. (eds.) ICCSA 2014. LNCS, vol. 8581, pp. 382–397. Springer, Cham (2014). https://doi.org/10.1007/978-3-319-09150-1_28
19. Cerreta, M., De Toro, P.: Urbanization suitability maps: a dynamic spatial decision support system for sustainable land use. Earth Syst. Dyn. **3**(2), 157–171 (2012)
20. Borruso, G.: Network density and the delimitation of urban areas. Trans. GIS **7**(2), 177–191 (2003)
21. Blomquist, G.C., Berger, M.C., Hoehn, J.P.: New estimates of quality of life in urban areas. Am. Econ. Rev. **78**, 89–107 (1988)
22. Lichfield, N.: Community Impact Evaluation: Principles And Practice. UCL Press, London (1996)
23. Stover, M.E., Leven, C.L.: Methodological issues in the determination of the quality of life in urban areas. Urban Stud. **29**(5), 737–754 (1992)
24. Bello, M.E.: Spazi moderni nella città contemporanea: Trasformazioni di quartieri di edilizia pubblica. Franco Angeli, Milano (2018)
25. Merlini, C.: Luigi Piccinato. Una professione per la città e la società. In: Di Biagi, P., Gabellini, P. (eds.) Urbanisti italiani. Piccinato, Marconi, Samonà, Quaroni, De Carlo, Astengo, Campos Venuti, Laterza, Bari, pp. 23–95 (1992)
26. Denicolai, L.: Mediantropi. Introduzione alla quotidianità dell'uomo tecnologico. Scienze della Formazione - Università degli Studi di Torino (2018)
27. Van Den Berg, L., Braun, E.: Sports and City Marketing in European Cities. Routledge, London (2017)
28. Basso, S.: Ripensare la prossimità nella città pubblica. Strumenti per la ricomposizione degli spazi, oltre l'alloggio. Territorio. **72**, 75–82 (2015)
29. Balducci, A., Fedeli, V., De Leonardis, O.: Terzo Rapporto sulle Città. Mind the gap. Il distacco tra politiche e città. Il Mulino, Bologna (2018)
30. Levi, M.A.: La città antica: morfologia e biografia della aggregazione urbana nell'antichità, vol. 12. L'Erma di Bretschneider (1989)
31. Sassen, S.: The global city: strategic site, new frontier. In: Ferro, L., et al. (eds.) Moving Cities – Contested Views on Urban Life, pp. 11–28. Springer, Wiesbaden (2018). https://doi.org/10.1007/978-3-658-18462-9_2
32. Giordano, F.: La rigenerazione di beni e spazi urbani: il nuovo volume a cura di Francesca Di Lascio e Fabio Giglioni. LABSUS, pp. 1–3 (2018)

33. Rossi, U.: La strada come spazio collettivo della città. Spazio pubblico e approccio interdisciplinare al progetto. L'architettura delle città - The Journal of the Scientific Society Ludovico Quaroni, **10**, pp. 131–158 (2017)
34. Vanolo, A.: City Branding. The Ghostly Politics of Representation in Globalising Cities. Routledge Research in Planning, London (2017)
35. Weinstein, A.: Evanescent Event: Using the Olympic City as a catalyst for change in post-industrial cities (Doctoral dissertation) (2018)
36. http://www.figc.it/other/UEFA_Stadium_Guide_ITA_Web_1.pdf
37. Valavanis, P.: Games and Sanctuaries in Ancient Greece: Olympia, Delphi, Isthmia, Nemea, Athens. Getty Publications, Los Angeles (2006)
38. Bolognini, M.: Spazio urbano e potere: politica e ideologia della città: crisi urbana e decentramento infracomunale. Franco Angeli. Milano (1981)
39. Codeluppi, V.: Metropoli e luoghi del consumo. Mimesis, Milano (2014)
40. Gastaldi, F., Traverso, M.: Stadi di proprietà in Italia: una questione aperta, EyesReg. Giornale di scienze regionali **8**, 2 (2018)

ALARP Approach for Risk Assessment of Civil Engineering Projects

Gianluigi De Mare[1] ⓘ, Antonio Nesticò[1](✉) ⓘ, Renato Benintendi[2],
and Gabriella Maselli[1] ⓘ

[1] Department of Civil Engineering, University of Salerno, Fisciano, SA, Italy
{gdemare,anestico,gmaselli}@unisa.it
[2] Megaris Ltd, Reading, UK
renato.benintendi@megaris.co.uk

Abstract. Risk assessment is essential to express judgments of economic convenience on investment initiatives. This certainly applies to civil engineering projects, where the risk components are not only economic, but also environmental, social and cultural. Thus, the aim of the paper is to delineate a risk analysis model in the economic evaluation of investments through the development of algorithms where the Cost-Benefit Analysis (CBA) logic is integrated with the ALARP principle. The latter provides operative tools ensuring that risk is tolerable if it is "As Low As Reasonably Practicable". The study shows that the ALARP logic, widely applied in sectors such as nuclear, energy and oil & gas, but less implemented in civil engineering, can instead become an important investigative tool if used jointly with the CBA precisely in the evaluation economic of civil projects, contributing to the characterization of efficient forecast protocols.

In the first paragraph of the paper, the steps necessary to manage the risk connected to a project initiative are described and the ALARP logic is analysed. The second paragraph presents the risk analysis approaches traditionally used in the economic evaluation of projects. In the third section the logical scheme of an innovative protocol for the management of project risk is defined, by integrating the ALARP principles in the procedural scheme of the CBA. In conclusion, prospects for future research are outlined.

Keywords: Economic evaluation of projects · Risk analysis · Urban planning
Cost-Benefit Analysis · ALARP logics

1 ALARP Criteria: Definition and Introductory Issues

The ALARP logic, as defined by the Health and Safety Executive (HSE), provides a guide for the acceptance of the residual risk connected to an investment. Generally applied in high-risk sectors, this logics allows to accept a residual risk, if this is As Low

---

The contribution to this paper is the result of the joint work of the four authors, to which the paper has to be attributed in equal parts.

© Springer International Publishing AG, part of Springer Nature 2018
O. Gervasi et al. (Eds.): ICCSA 2018, LNCS 10964, pp. 75–86, 2018.
https://doi.org/10.1007/978-3-319-95174-4_6

As Reasonably Practicable (ALARP), in order to achieve a triangular balance between risks, mitigation costs and related benefits [1–6].

Based on that premise, in this paragraph the meaning of "residual risk" shall be identified in order to clarify in which phase of the risk management process the ALARP principle intervenes. Then we analyse the meaning of "As Low As Reasonably Practicable", define the criteria for considering a as tolerable risk and identify the fields in which ALARP logic is used.

In order to verify the applicability of the ALARP criteria to the Cost-Benefit Analysis of civil engineering projects, the approach to analysing investment risks is described in Sect. 2. In Sect. 3, a protocol for the management of the project risk is outlined by implementing the ALARP principle in the CBA schemes. In the last paragraph, the conclusions of the work and future research perspectives are stated.

1.1 The Risk Management Process

The definitions associated with the concept of "risk" are different: on one hand, the qualitative one, according to which risk is intended as the possible occurrence of an adverse event or the potential unwanted consequences generated by an event [6, 7]; on the other, the quantitative one, according to which the risk is the probability that an event that can generate a certain effect will occur [8].

In the corporate environment, risks are related to events that hinder the pursuit of the enterprise mission. On the other hand, business opportunities coincide with those episodes that allow the achievement of strategic objectives, facilitating the production of wealth. Management of events, in terms of their dual risk/opportunity profile, is the primary task of the management and, consequently, represents the cornerstone of corporate governance. Every company that decides to adopt a risk management system shall define its own risk profile, identifying the possible risky events that it intends to measure and govern [7, 9]. In this regard, the Committee of Sponsoring Organizations of the Treadway Commission (COSO) issued in 2004 a framework relating to Enterprise Risk Management (ERM), a document that establishes the operational tools to define an effective and integrated system of analysis, assessment and management of business risks.

As shown in Fig. 1, the risk management process is divided into six steps [6, 10–12]:

1. definition of the risk management goals and of the criteria to be followed;
2. identification of the hazards/threats/opportunities that may influence the detected objectives. Many methods have been developed for this task, including checklists, HAZOP and FMEA, HAZard and OPerability analysis (HAZOP); Failure Mode and Effects Analysis (FMEA);
3. analysis of the causes and consequences arising from the risky events, implementing techniques such as *fault tree analysis, event tree analysis, Bayesian networks*;
4. risk characterization, expressing judgments on the probability of occurrence of the events considered risky. In this phase, the risk is expressed in terms of probability and impact;

5. quantitative assessment or measurement of risk. This is necessary to define actions for the risk management;
6. risk treatment, through diversified strategies such as *risk avoidance*, *risk reduction*, *risk transfer*, *risk sharing*.

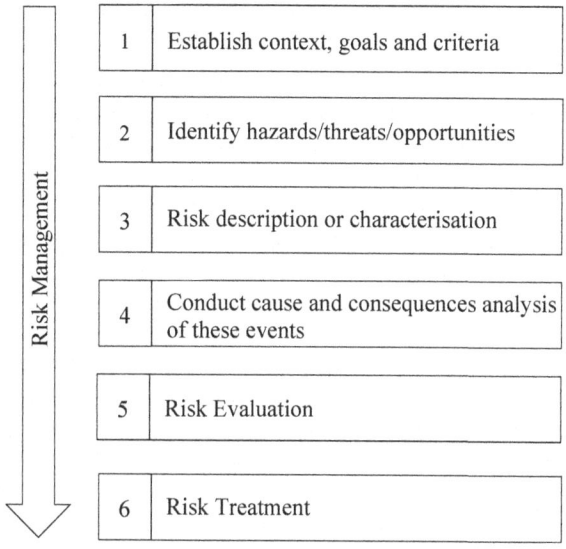

Fig. 1. The risk management process

Is worth noting that in the risk management process it is important to evaluate the effectiveness of the planned mitigation actions. This aims to establish whether or not is the "residual risk", which is the one that remains despite the treatment strategy chosen, tolerable and therefore acceptable, thus using the terminology typical of the ALARP logic reported in Sect. 1.2.

1.2 The ALARP Decision Making

The ALARP principle, currently used above all in decision-making processes concerning safety and health, requires that the responsible for work activities reduce the risks to levels which can be considered as low as reasonably practicable, after which a further reduction in risk would be excessively expensive [2, 4]. Already exposed in the regulations of the Health and Safety Executive, this logic has distant origin in time, already appearing in English documents such as the Salmon Fishery Act of 1861, the Self-acting Mules Regulations of 1905 or still the Electricity Regulations of 1908 [13–16].

Since the 1950s, the concept of ALAP (As Low As Practicable) has been introduced in the United States in the field of radiation protection, which prescribed the containment of radiation exposure within certain limits. In 1979 the acronym ALAP is replaced with ALARA (As Low As Reasonably Achievable). The difference between the two concepts lies in the distinct meaning of "Practicable" and "Achievable": an intervention can be defined as "practicable" as long as its technical feasibility is demonstrated; on the other hand, the "feasibility" implicitly assumes that an intervention is always possible, even if it its actual practical execution has not been demonstrated. The meaning of the term "reasonable" is also substantial. To understand its significance, reference is made to "Best Available Technology" (BAT) in a specific sector regardless of costs. In the mitigation interventions the BAT allow to reduce the risk to ALAP ("As Low As Practicable"), but not necessarily they are the "reasonably practicable" techniques. Indeed, "reasonableness" implies the necessity to consider also extra-monetary aspects such as social, cultural and environmental. In other words, any ALARP risk reduction interventions must be "reasonably" feasible and sustainable in a broad sense [5]. It is precisely with this meaning that in Health and Safety at Work etc. Act 1974 (HSWA), the British statute that regulates and protects safety at work, it is required that the risk is reduced to "as long as it is reasonably practicable" (So Far As is Reasonably Practicable, SFAIRP). It should be noted that the concepts of SFAIRP and ALARP are interchangeable, with the difference that the former is mostly used in health and safety regulations, while risk specialists mainly use the latter [15]. While the HSWA does not offer any prescriptions on how the acceptability threshold should be determined, the HSE defines – precisely through the ALARP principle – a guide to address the decision-making process on risk tolerance known as «the will to live with a risk in order to guarantee some benefits» [13, 17].

The HSE summarizes the ALARP principle using a triangular graph, represented in Fig. 2, which identifies three risk regions:

1. the lower, where risk is "broadly acceptable" without requiring any reduction;
2. the central one, which is the "tolerable region" or the ALARP region, where risk is tolerable only if it is impossible to reduce it further or if costs to mitigate it are disproportionate;
3. the upper, "unacceptable region" in which risk must be mitigated, making it at least ALARP.

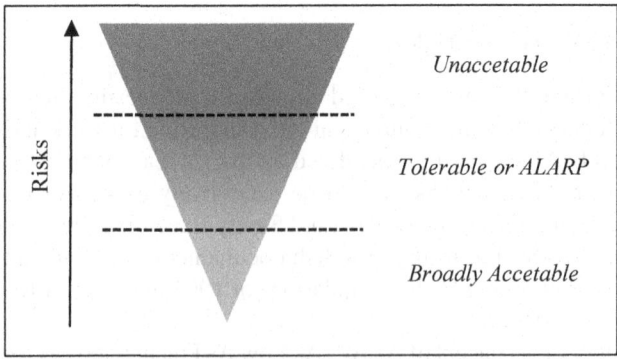

Fig. 2. HSE framework for the tolerability of risk

The border lines between the three regions has been established by the HSE on statistical data [13]. As regards the extremes of the diagram, given by the base and the inverted triangle vertex in Fig. 2, the first represents a negligible rather than null risk; while the second does not define a catastrophic risk, but more generally an unacceptable limit.

In light of the above, some important aspects are highlighted:

– ALARP principle recognizes that zero risk is not a viable option. Therefore, to ensure that risks are reduced to ALARP does not mean that no harmful events will occur, but that the specific risk is tolerable within certain limits;
– ALARP does not necessarily imply that risk mitigation measures shall be taken. In fact, the latter must not involve disproportionate costs;
– the core of ALARP logic is the concept of tolerable risk, namely that risk in the absence of benefits is not acceptable;
– implementing the ALARP principles, evaluation risk cannot be separated from social, cultural and environmental issues.

These aspects make it possible to glimpse how the ALARP logic can be integrated with Cost-Benefit Analysis (CBA) criteria, typical of the economic-evaluation disciplines, in order to manage the investment risk. The contents of the following paragraphs how to implement ALARP principles in the applications of CBA.

2 Mentions About Traditional Approaches for Risk Analysis of Investment Projects

Risk is an intrinsic feature of investments. Therefore, the analysis and evaluation of the multiple risk components related to the project through probabilistic representations is fundamental [18, 19]. This makes to identify actions to reduce risk possible since the planning phase, which can be done either by varying the investment initiative structure or by using suitable measures to mitigate the effects.

As to the approaches traditionally used for the risk analysis of investment projects, it is necessary to mention: probabilistic tools such as Monte Carlo simulation model, frequently used in practice; the Decision Tree Analysis, valid above all for really complex investments; the so-called Mean-Variance statistical approach, in which a probability distribution is associated to Cash Flows (CF) and a judgment of economic convenience is expressed on the basis of the value assumed by the dispersion indices. However, the project risk may be taken into account acting directly on the profitability indicators, in particular on the Net Present Value (NPV), which expresses the sum of the CF discounted through the discount rate. In fact, the logic of risk analysis can be based on the transformation of risky CF into lower certainty equivalent CF, leaving the discount rate unchanged; or, with antithetical criteria, discounting the expected flows at a rate that includes, in addition to the *risk free rate*, a risk premium according to formulations *Consumption-based Capital Asset Pricing Model*, CCAPM [20–22]. In order to define a model for acceptance of residual risks related to investment projects, the Monte Carlo probabilistic method is useful. In fact, this technique can be applied to support the

Cost-Benefit Analysis (CBA), which makes possible to express judgments of economic convenience on the execution of projects also using the probabilistic analysis, namely taking into account the riskiness of the investment if the cash flows of the initiative are treated as random variables.

The CBA consists of: forecast of the costs and benefits that the project generates during the analysis period; in the subsequent discounting of Cash Flows (CF); therefore in the estimation of the performance indicators, traditionally the Net Present Value (NPV), the Internal Rate of Return (IRR), the Benefits/Costs ratio, the Payback Period. The study can be integrated with the sensitivity analysis to identify the sensitive variables of the system, namely those that significantly influence the success/failure of the project. These variables can be described in probabilistic terms. Thus proceeding, with the implementation of the Monte Carlo method, it is possible to estimate the probability distribution of the evaluation indicator. In summary, the project risk analysis can take place through the following steps:

1. definition of the input, i.e. the probability distributions to be associated with the sensitive variables;
2. through the Monte Carlo logic, generation of the output i.e. the cumulative probability distribution of the economic performance indicator of the project.

The reading of the frequency distribution of the evaluation indicator provides information of extreme importance as regards the riskiness of the investment project.

3   On the Implementation of the ALARP Criteria in the CBA Models

Aspects of considerable logical operating interest characterise the ALARP criteria and the CBA principles. Nonetheless, they show limits in the terms described below in points 3.1 and 3.2 respectively. This leads to useful reflections for the characterization of an innovative protocol of investment risk analysis, as in point 3.3.

3.1. The ALARP provides the tools useful to define tolerable a risk as low as reasonably practicable namely that enables to establish if a risk mitigation intervention has disproportionate costs compared to the benefits obtained:

$$\frac{\text{Costs}}{\text{Benefits}} > D_F \tag{1}$$

with D_F = Disproportionality Factor of costs with respect to the benefits obtained.

In accordance with the ALARP logic the first term of (1) translates into the estimate of the Implied Cost of Averting one Fatality (ICAF). This indicator, which represents the cost to save an additional life, is the ratio between the cost of the investment made and the decrease in the expected number of fatalities due to the mitigation action:

$$\text{ICAF} = \frac{\text{Cost of mitigation measure}}{\text{Reduction in Potential Loss of Life}} \tag{2}$$

Therefore, the ICAF is the cost of achieving an increment of risk reduction for life safety. For example, the ICAF to reduce the risk of fatality for 1 in 10,000 individuals each year at an annual cost of $ 1,000 is $ 10,000,000:

$$ICAF = \frac{\$1,000}{\dfrac{1}{10,000}} = \$10,000,000 \tag{3}$$

The ICAF estimated for the proposed option is then compared with specific ICAF values according to the sectors considered. This is to verify if the costs risk mitigation are disproportionate in relation to the benefits. In this case, the risk is tolerable if it falls in the ALARP area, because additional costs to bring the risk to the acceptability threshold would be excessive.

The main difficulty of the analysis is to estimate the monetary value of human life, also known as Value of a Statistical Life (VOSL) or also Cost of Statistical Life saved (CSL). In fact, according to some Authors it is difficult, if not impossible, to attribute a monetary appreciation to human life [2, 5]. Moreover, the ICAF reference values are very diversified, both depending on the chosen estimation method, and according to the country in which the assessment is conducted. For example, a method to estimate the ICAF is to approximate it to willingness to pay to save a life.

A further limitation is qualitative and holistic principles are the basis of ALARP processes. This can lead to different decisions, even in similar contexts, which cause uncertainty and unpredictability in decision-making [2, 5, 23].

3.2. The Cost-Benefit Analysis is a technique to evaluate both the economic feasibility of a specified intervention and the best alternative among different possible ones based on the greatest economic advantage [24]. In the CBA the flow of costs and benefits generated over time by the investment is expressed in monetary terms. If the evaluation criterion is the Net Present Value (NPV), then a project is economically convenient when the sum of the discounted Cash Flows is positive and sufficiently large:

$$NPV = \sum_{t=0}^{n} \frac{B_t - C_t}{(1 + r)^t} > 0 \tag{4}$$

where B_t e C_t are the benefits and costs generated by the project over time and r is the discount rate.

The CBA requires that all the benefits and costs of the investment be converted into monetary terms in order to make them comparable to each other and to provide results through a single index. However, this is the main limitation of the evaluation tool. It does not unable to consider those impacts that cannot be well expressed in quantitative terms such as the socio-cultural impacts or the environmental damages/benefits. In essence, the CBA limits consist in the heterogeneity of the project effects and in the uniqueness of the evaluation criterion [2].

3.3. In light of the limits set out, it is considered that the ALARP qualitative logic and the quantitative principles of the CBA can be used in a complementary way in the decision-making processes on investments, also in the civil engineering sectors. This by structuring a model that traces the logical process set out in the following steps:

1. *definition of the goals of the risk management activity.* This concerns the management of the project risk in order to avoid failure or in order to find positive values of the economic performance indicators regarding the intervention;

2. *identification of risk components* that may affect the pursuit of the objectives defined in step 1. This translates into an estimate of the costs and benefits deriving from the project and the identification of the sensitive variables of the system, i.e. those that can influence more the economic advantage of the investment;

3. *risk analysis,* which consists in generating the cumulative frequency distribution of the performance indicator, for example the NPV (output), starting from the estimation of the probability distribution related to the risk variables (input);

4. *risk assessment,* by comparing the risk of project failure, which can be read from the cumulative frequency distribution of the output (for example the NPV) estimated in step 3, and the thresholds of acceptability (A_T) and tolerability (T_T) as defined by the ALARP logics. Therefore, if the risk falls: (a) in the area below the acceptability threshold, then the intervention is feasible; (b) in the area above the tolerability threshold, then the risk is considered too high and therefore the investment is to be avoided; (c) in the central region, then it can only be considered tolerable if ALARP, i.e. only if any mitigation options are not disproportionate to the benefits obtained;

5. *definition of risk mitigation measures*;

6. *evaluation of the effects of risk mitigation actions.* It is necessary to repeat the operations in steps (3) and (4) to evaluate R_2, i.e. the risk of failure considering the costs related to the risk reduction interventions. The aim is therefore to assess whether the costs incurred are disproportionate to the benefits achieved. This is possible by comparing a coefficient C, based on the logic of the ICAF, with a reference coefficient D_F that is a disproportionality factor of costs with respect to the benefits obtained. The C coefficient is a function of the risk mitigation costs C_m, of the R_1 risk of failure preceding the mitigation intervention, of the R_2 risk of failure following the mitigation intervention. The coefficient D_F can be understood as the maximum cost that one is willing to support to bring the risk from the tolerability threshold T_T and to the acceptability threshold A_T. In summary:

   - if C = f (C_m, R_1, R_2) < D_F, then mitigation measures have an acceptable cost compared to the benefits obtained;

   - if C = f (C_m, R_1, R_2) > D_F, then the mitigation measures have a disproportionate cost compared to the benefits achieved. In this case, if A_T < R_1 < T_T, then the risk R_1 is tolerable as ALARP. This means that further interventions would entail excessive costs in relation to the induced mitigation effects.

7. *monitoring of the risk mitigation effects.*

Figure 3 shows the procedure to be followed to implement the model for acceptance of the residual risk in the economic evaluation activities of the investment projects. Thus, the use of ALARP principles in Cost-Benefit Analysis for investment projects in the civil engineering sectors opens up new research and innovative applications in fields different from those of traditional employment.

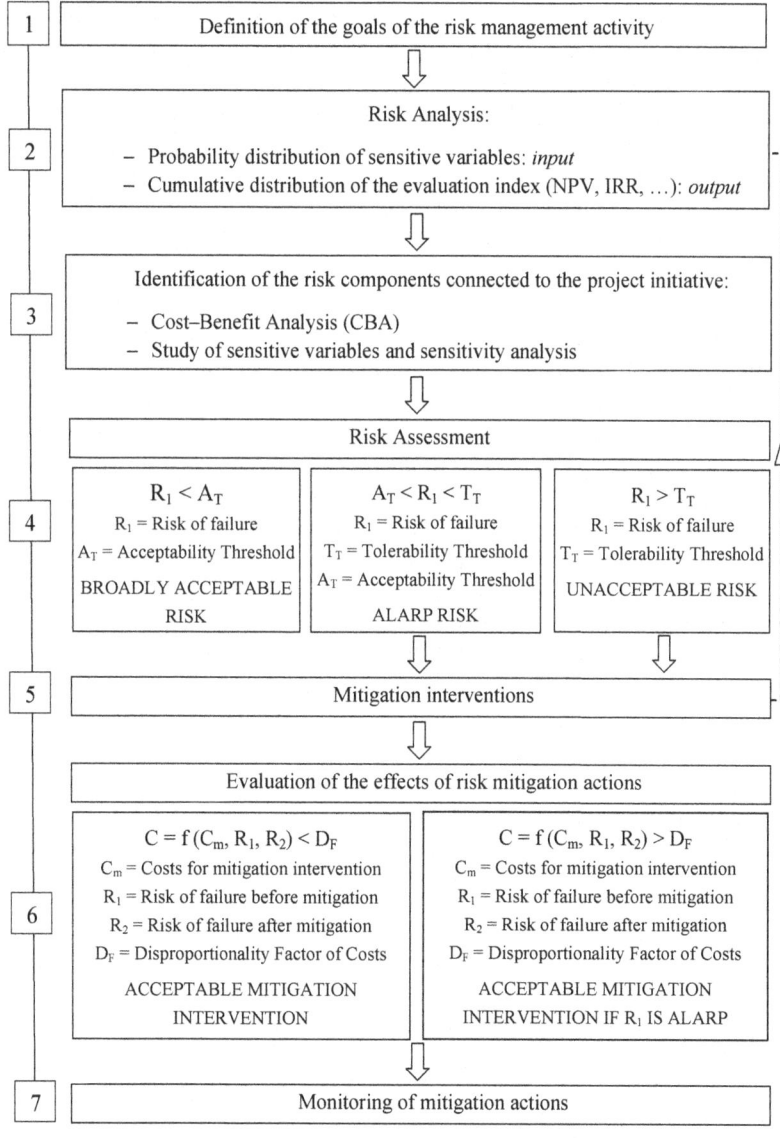

Fig. 3. Model of risk acceptance for investment projects

4   Conclusions

Investment projects are characterized by intrinsic risk, which influences their feasibility [25, 26]. Accordingly, risk analysis and assessment are essential in decision-making processes that regard the allocation of resources, both public and private. This also applies to civil engineering projects, characterized by profiles of complexity that arise from multiple interrelations with rural areas and urban spaces. These interrelations are not only technical-functional, but they are also economic, so covering financial, social, cultural and environmental issues [27–30]. Risk analysis carried out according to the procedural schemes of the Cost-Benefit Analysis has the limit to include in the evaluations only those contributions expressed in monetary terms, often reducing the acceptability of an intervention to a question of simple financial profitability. The purpose of the paper is to outline an innovative risk analysis model for the economic evaluation of investment projects in the civil field that will make up for this limit.

The idea is to jointly use the traditional CBA techniques for the economic evaluation of projects with the ALARP logic, used in highly risky sectors such as nuclear, energy, oil & gas. In particular, the ALARP principle leads to determine if a risk mitigation intervention has disproportionate costs compared to the benefits obtained.

The proposed protocol, schematized in the logical-operative phases of Fig. 2, shows the possibility to determine a function for the estimation of a C coefficient, according to the principles of the ICAF, to express a judgment on the acceptability of the residual risk investment in relation to the cost of interventions for mitigating the risk itself. This taking into account the different risk components that connote the project initiative, including the extra-financial ones that are rarely considered in economic studies.

The paper demonstrates that the evaluation of interventions in the civil sector, which already has the support of CBA techniques, can find theoretical advantages and practical utility from the implementation of ALARP logics. So as to reconcile multiple effects, both monetary and cultural, social and environmental.

Innovative research ideas emerge with regard to the characterization of the acceptability and tolerability thresholds of the individual residual risk rates also attributable to extra-financial effects. In order to estimate these thresholds, the ALARP probabilistic criteria can be followed. This is based on the logic that compares the financial sum of the benefits arising from risk mitigation and of the financial sum of costs for mitigation interventions.

References

1. Melchers, R.: On the ALARP approach to risk management. Reliab. Eng. Syst. Saf. **71**(2), 201–208 (2001)
2. French, S., Bedford, T., Atherton, E.: Supporting ALARP decision making by cost benefit analysis and multiattribute utility theory. J. Risk Res. **8**(3), 207–223 (2007)
3. Aven, T., Abrahamsen, E.B.: On the use of cost-benefit analysis in ALARP processes. Int. J. Perform. Eng. **3**, 345–353 (2007)
4. Jones-Lee, M., Aven, T.: ALARP – what does it really mean? Reliab. Eng. Syst. Saf. **96**, 877–882 (2011)

5. Ale, B.J.M., Hartford, D.N.D., Slater, D.: ALARP and CBA all in the same game. Saf. Sci. **76**, 90–100 (2015)
6. Aven, T.: Risk assessment and risk management: review of recent advances on their foundation. Eur. J. Oper. Res. **253**, 1–13 (2016)
7. Borghesi, A., La gestione dei rischi di azienda: Economia e Organizzazione, Teoria e Pratica. CEDAM, Padova (1985)
8. Knight, F.H.: Risk, Uncertainty and Profit. The London School of Economics and Political Science, London (1921)
9. Floreani, A.: Enterprise Risk Management. I rischi aziendali e il processo di risk management, I.S.U. – Università Cattolica, Milano (2004)
10. Aven, T.: Risk Analysis, 2nd edn. Wiley, Chichester (2015)
11. Meyer, T., Reniers, G.: Engineering Risk Management: De Gruyter Graduate, Berlin (2013)
12. Zio, E.: An Introduction to the Basics of Reliability and Risk Analysis. World Scientific Publishing, Singapore (2007)
13. HSE: Reducing risks, protecting people: HSE's decision-making. London: HSE Books (2001)
14. HSE (2014a). http://www.hse.gov.uk/risk/theory/alarpglance.htm
15. HSE: Principles and Guidelines to Assist HSE in its Judgements that Dutyholders have Reduced Risk as Low as Reasonably Practicable (2014b). http://www.hse.gov.uk/risk/theory/alarp1.htm
16. HSE (2014c). http://www.hse.gov.uk/risk/theory/alarpcba.htm
17. Ale, B.J.M.: Tolerable or acceptable, a comparison of risk regulation in the UK and in the Netherlands. Risk Anal. **25**(2), 231–241 (2005)
18. D'Alpaos, C., Marella, G.: Urban planning and option values. Appl. Math. Sci. **8**(157–160), 7845–7864 (2014). https://doi.org/10.12988/ams.2014.49744
19. Ferretti, V., Bottero, M., Mondini, G.: A spatial decision support tool to study risks and opportunities of complex environmental systems. J. Environ. Acc. Manag. **3**(2), 197–212 (2015). https://doi.org/10.5890/JEAM.2015.06.008
20. Lucas, R.: Asset prices in an exchange economy. Econometrica **46**, 1429–1446 (1978)
21. Harrison, M.: Valuing the future: the social discount rate in cost-benefit analysis. Visiting Researcher Paper, Productivity Commission, Canberra (2010)
22. Gollier, C.: Pricing the Future: The Economics of Discounting and Sustainable Development. Princeton University Press, Princeton (2011)
23. Yasseri, S.: The ALARP argument. Safe Sight Technology, UK (2013)
24. Bezzi, C.: Cos'è la valutazione: Un'introduzione ai concetti, le parole chiave e i problemi metodologici. Franco Angeli, Milano (2006)
25. Bertelli, R., Linguanti E.: Analisi finanziaria e gestione di portafoglio. Valutazione del rischio, tecniche di asset allocation, strumenti di analisi tecnica e fondamentale. Franco Angeli, Milano (2005)
26. Barotta, P.: IL Rischio. Aspetti tecnici, sociali, etici. Armando Editore, Roma (2012)
27. Nesticò, A., De Mare, G.: Government tools for urban regeneration: the cities plan in Italy. A critical analysis of the results and the proposed alternative. In: Murgante, B., et al. (eds.) ICCSA 2014. LNCS, vol. 8580, pp. 547–562. Springer, Cham (2014). https://doi.org/10.1007/978-3-319-09129-7_40
28. De Mare, G., Granata, M.F., Nesticò, A.: Weak and strong compensation for the prioritization of public investments: multidimensional analysis for pools. Sustainability (Switzerland) **7**(12), 16022–16038 (2015). https://doi.org/10.3390/su71215798

29. Morano, P., Locurcio, M., Tajani, F., Guarini, M.R.: Fuzzy logic and coherence control in multi-criteria evaluation of urban redevelopment projects. Int. J. Bus. Intell. Data Min. **10**(1), 73–93 (2015). https://doi.org/10.1504/IJBIDM.2015.069041
30. Nesticò, A., Pipolo, O.: A protocol for sustainable building interventions: financial analysis and environmental effects. Int. J. Bus. Intell. Data Min. **10**(3), 199–212 (2015). https://doi.org/10.1504/IJBIDM.2015.071325

Smart Block EAN: Ten Scalable Initiatives for a Smart City

Alix E. Rojas$^{(\boxtimes)}$ ⓘ, Camilo Mejía-Moncayo ⓘ,
and Leonardo Rodríguez-Urrego ⓘ

Universidad EAN, Bogotá, Colombia
{aerojash,cmejiam,lrodriguezu}@universidadean.edu.co

Abstract. The accelerated urbanization is a global problem and smart cities are at the center of the debate on sustainability and urban development around the world. Transforming current cities into smart cities is a great challenge, since it requires, among other things, transcendental changes in public administration and in the social conscience of citizens. We propose a scale solution in which we apply the concept of Smart city to a smart block. This article presents the conception of the Smart Block EAN project and the development of its ten phases. Finally, we show the progress of the ten projects that make up the Smart Block EAN project and provide conclusions.

1 Introduction

The economy activities of countries around the world are concentrated in urban areas. Millions of people live together in cities, and more than half of the worlds population already occupies these urban sites and it will reach two thirds by 2030 [27]. This growing urbanization brings challenges, as the cities and the population that inhabits them grow, the needs and demands of people must be satisfied in a sustainable manner without affecting the environment [3].

Smart cities strongly address current global challenges, such as climate change and scarce resources. Their claim is also to ensure their economic competitiveness and quality of life for urban populations in constant increase. Smart cities are futuristic, progressive and efficient in terms of resources, while providing a high quality of life [31]. They promote social and technological innovations and link existing infrastructures [16]. They incorporate new concepts of energy, traffic, and transportation that are easy for the environment. With the development of new technological innovations -mainly Information and Communication Technologies (ICT) - the concept of the Smart City emerges as a means to achieve more efficient and sustainable cities [6, 26].

2 An Initiative at Scale: A Smart Block at Bogotá

Smart cities are at the center of the debate on sustainability and urban development worldwide [15, 16, 24]. Colombia has given priority to the construction

O. Gervasi et al. (Eds.): ICCSA 2018, LNCS 10964, pp. 87–99, 2018.
https://doi.org/10.1007/978-3-319-95174-4_7

of a framework for the development of cities that encourage technology, citizen participation and open Governments to promote the quality of life and wellbeing of the inhabitants. These advances are evident in the transversal strategy of the green growth of the current national Development Plan 2014–2018 *"Todos por un Nuevo país"*, and in the "National policy to consolidate the system of cities in Colombia", which was submitted for consideration of the National Council of Economic and Social policy [9].

Our country shows advances in regulatory matters that will allow the development of new technologies in the fields of renewable energies, telecommunications, virtual reality, unmanned aerial vehicles, among others [21]. This is enabling Colombia to be in the sights of investors from around the world interested in technological development. According to the report *"La ruta de las smart cities"* [5] from Inter-American Development Bank-IADB, a smart and sustainable city is an innovative city that uses information and communication technologies (ICT) and other means to improve their decision making, the efficiency of their operations, the provision of urban services and their competitiveness. At the same time, it seeks to meet the needs of current and future generations in relation to the economic, social and environmental aspects. It is also attractive to citizens, entrepreneurs and workers because it generates a safer space, with better services and an innovation environment that encourages creative solutions, generates jobs and reduces inequalities. Thus, smart cities promote a virtuous cycle that produces not only economic and social well-being, but also the sustainable use of their resources with a view to raising the quality of life in the long term [14].

In 2012, in a study that was co-financed by COLCIENCIAS, the Information Technology and Communications Research and Development Center (CINTEL by its abbreviation in Spanish) developed a model to define and identify the principles that make up the idea of a Smart City in Colombia. This model sought to be a guide for the national government, territorial entities and private entities on the subject of smart cities. In addition, it was intended that, based on the region's own needs, policies that would allow the harmonious development of the economic activity and the exploitation of natural resources could be established, integrating the service systems in cities through a unifying system, by means of the intensive use of technology. This proposal of harmonious development is presented in the document: "SMART CITIES: opportunities to generate sustainable solutions". CINTEL define Smart City as one that is characterized by the intensive use of ICT in the creation and improvement of the systems that make up the city. Likewise, CINTEL adds that a city is called intelligent when it successfully adopts these intensive ICT systems, and develops the capacity to create, collect, process, and transform information to optimize its processes and services. This initiative of the Colombian government and the IADB report, as well as the improvement of the block on 79th Street for the construction of the new building "EAN Legacy", encouraged the implementation of the project Smart Block EAN, main objective of this paper.

The EAN Smart Block seeks to be a prototype of an smart and sustainable block that, inspired by a Smart City, models and emulates, through the functions and relations typical of University life, the processes and decision-making of an urban center (Fig. 1).

Fig. 1. Smart Block EAN project logo

This initiative is based on a block in Bogotá city. Located between the 11th and 12th Avenues and between the 78th and 79th streets, where the Nogal Headquarters of the EAN University are currently located. This block will have an intervention for the adaptation and construction of a new building called EAN Legacy, which will impact the physical facilities of the EAN University due to its magnitude, and will also impact the sector due to its relevance in the sustainable construction policy linked to the Cradle to Cradle methodology [18].

The University took advantage of the intervention in this block in order to make a smart city model that not only interacts with the university community, but that also establishes links with the surrounding neighborhood, strengthening crowd sourcing or community collaboration environments. The Smart Block EAN is an infrastructure that guarantees the improvement of the quality of life of its citizens. This proposal seeks to add value to the existing infrastructure. In the same way the EAN University already has research works, such as the book "Urban Environment of the Headquarters of the EAN University" [19]. This research identifies the development and urban conditions of the surroundings of the University's venues and represents them in architectural technical sheets. Its starting point is adopting a sustainable city model and the principles that are stipulated in the Institutional Educational Project (PEI by its abbreviation in Spanish), on Sustainability. Essentially a desirable image of the University and its surroundings towards the future clearly, in front of the model "inclusive city".

Likewise, it explores the environment and the possibilities of participating and becoming involved in the transformation and urban impact, and the appropriation and daily use of the University. Through the EAN Smart Block, the Nogal Campus can become a model of Smart City, where the objectives of sustainable development, "quality of life" of the community, correct use of resources and active citizen participation, bring and strengthen the academy with innovative ways of delivering knowledge to the urban, social and business development of future generations. In this way, the Campus will become a "laboratory" that comes to life through the actions of students, professors, administrative staff, allies, and others involved in the operation of the University.

The main objective of the Smart Block EAN is to design and implement a smart city model in the physical infrastructure of the *Nogal* Headquarters of the EAN University by 2021, aligned with the Development Strategy of the Higher Purpose. In order to carry out this great project, ten initiatives were designed to provide benefits and opportunities based on ICT. The first of these initiatives is called Drone Guide, which entails the acquisition and training of drone driving, and the development of an application that reserves drones for University visitors.

3   A Progress Project

Although the block project was defined from the ten initiatives described in Sect. 3, these projects did not start at the same time. Partly because the ten projects have different dynamics, and not all of them require an investor. Figure 2 shows a consolidated status of the ten projects by phase.

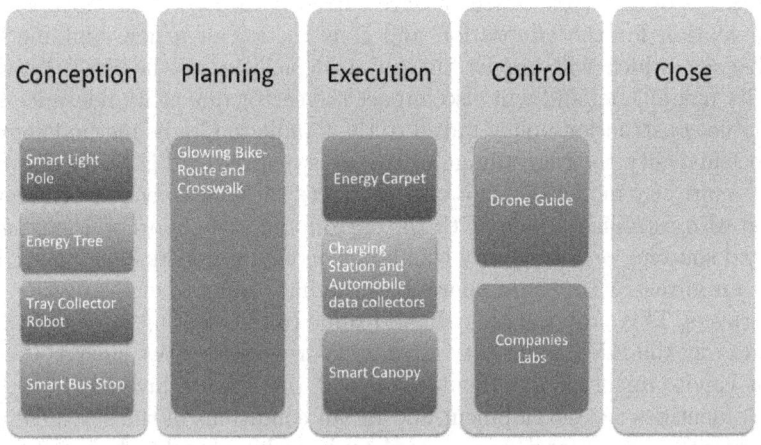

Fig. 2. Progress of the Smart Block EAN project

Likewise, Fig. 3 shows a timeline for the implementation of the project, where the main projects carried out during the current, past, and future execution are previewed. The Smart Block EAN project will end in 2021 with the inauguration of the EAN Legacy building.

4   Smart Block EAN

The basis of this project is a dynamic technology transfer model in which skills, knowledge, technologies, manufacturing methods, and samples are transferred between the EAN University and private companies, in order to ensure that

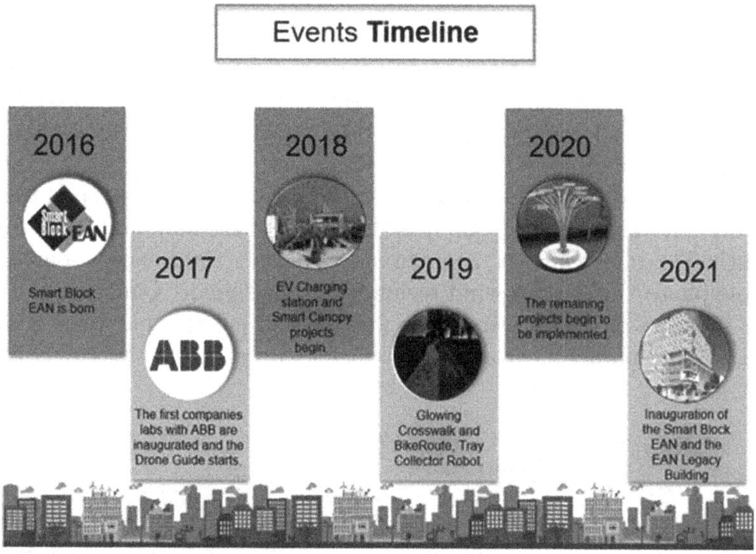

Fig. 3. Project timeline

scientific and technological advances are accessible to a greater number of users who can develop and exploit these technologies even more in new products and thus create value, processes, new applications, and services. This project uses information and communication technologies (ICT) to create dynamic collaboration groups among the University, the research centers and the companies. The objective of these collaborations for technology transfer is to promote the development and growth of the different sectors of society through the access to the knowledge and experience of the research, innovation, and development (RiD groups).

This Project Aims to:

- Transfer knowledge and skills between the EAN University and different industries in order to stimulate the economy.
- Promote formation and training activities for members of the different organizations and institutions.
- Increase interest in research activities and academic training in students and industries.
- Generate products and activities that can be exploited from the commercial point of view, derived from technological innovation.
- Generate new investment spaces for the private sector in the ICT field.
- Create spaces for collaboration among the different entities involved.

In the following sections, we will define the ten points that make up the project at the University's scale conductive to turn this construction into an intelligent block.

4.1 Smart Canopy

Canopy is a space that is set with the typical flora of our region, which fulfills the functions of air quality improvement, organic farm and shop, rainwater collection, and clean energy production under renewable energy technologies. In addition, Smart Canopy serves as a refuge and a place to visit for different species of birds and bees. It is a place designed for nature at the top of the EAN *Nogal* and EAN Legacy buildings. It is the cradle of the flora and fauna and the lungs of the Smart Block EAN, apart from serving as a clean energy source under renewable photo-voltaic and wind technologies [21]. Smart Canopy is a laboratory for students of the University, as well as a social example for neighboring buildings by promoting environmental technologies and clean energy (Fig. 4).

Fig. 4. Urban Canopy EAN University (original image)

4.2 Companies Labs

These are laboratories of technology and innovation that allow students and society in general to be trained in new technologies that will efficiently change the industry and the cities. These laboratories are supported by national and multinational companies becoming the effective synergy between industry and academia [8]. This laboratory aims at seeking research alliances in new technologies with national and multinational companies, as well as training students, entrepreneurs and ordinary citizens in future technologies. LabEnergy with ABB will be an example of University Business Alliance with an initial focus on technologies for energy efficiency in industries (Figs. 5 and 6).

4.3 Charging Station and Automobile Data Collectors

This project has two phases: the first consisting of a fast charging station for electric vehicles of different brands, bicycles and motorcycles of the electric type, with a free service for people of the University and external to it. The station will have a mobile application to book the service in advance. This charging station

Fig. 5. ABB laboratories - 74th Street headquarters

Fig. 6. (Left) Location charging station. (Right) App for booking electric cars)

will promote the use of sustainable means of transport based on electric charge. Likewise, it will serve as an impetus in this type of urban mobility for one of the nerve sectors of the city. The promotion and use of this type of vehicles will be the main objective of the project, as well as offering the neighboring community a free electric charging service. The second phase is about an approximation of urban sense that consists of the acquisition of electric vehicles equipped with different types of sensors for collecting data in cities like Bogotá: its habitants and environment. The cars are driven by students, professors, and other workers of the University.

4.4 Energy Carpet

The objective of this project is to extract the kinetic energy from the footsteps of hundreds of students and visitors who walk into the EAN University every day, store it in batteries and then use it for lighting purposes at the entrance and reception of the University. The purpose of this initiative is to integrate university students in the efficient use of energy, to impact visitors with energy produced from their own footsteps, be energy efficient, and make EAN University's entrance and reception electrically autonomous (Fig. 7).

Fig. 7. (Left) Power Generator Carpet-Pilot test May 2015. (Right) EAN University entrance (modified image)

4.5   Smart LightPole

The Smart LightPole is an efficient lighting system for the platform of the EAN University. This system is based on a LED technology luminary, a photo-voltaic energy production system and a storage system to deliver energy at night. This system contemplates the possibility of having Internet, security cameras and sensors for environmental measures. Smart LightPole is used to enable strategic lighting, communication, security, and environmental measures at a strategic point. In Smart Block EAN, it serves to show that although it is one of the technologies that is mostly used in the cities nowadays, it is obsolete and only needs to strengthen its functionalities (Fig. 8).

Fig. 8. Public luminaire. Source: carmanah.com

4.6   Energy Tree

The Energy Tree is a tree of solar panels that allows charging a battery to offer electrical connectivity to mobile devices such as cell phones, tablets, etc. It will also allow the connection of some AC devices such as laptops and will offer lighting at night. This tree will have a base in its trunk so that users can sit there and rest, and has been conceived as the central symbol of the EAN University platform. This tree will serve as an icon of the EAN University square valuing the harmony among nature, energy, relaxation, light, work, tranquility and the pleasantness of a talk in one of the busiest places in the world college. It will integrate efficient technologies of energy production and storage, lighting and design (Fig. 9).

Fig. 9. Energy tree in the central square (modified image)

4.7   Robotic Tray Collector

This robot will have the capacity to follow a certain path between the tables in the cafeteria to search for empty trays. When a user touches it. It will stop for a few minutes so that the user can place the tray in its arms before continuing its path. When the robot reaches the maximum number of trays programmed. It will return its starting point. The robotic tray collector will have the task of making the collection of trays in the cafeteria effective, reducing the tray collection time, preventing pigeons from perching on trays and encouraging robotic culture in public places. Likewise, "Robotic Tray Collector" will promote technologies based on electronic control and sensorization.

4.8   Glowing Bike-Route and Crosswalk

The illuminated crosswalk is a normal zebra crossing in its design, but with a layer of phosphorus-based paint, which charges during the day and reflects the light at night. And the illuminated bike route is an ordinary bike lane for the transit of cyclists that is charged with solar radiation during the day and illuminates at night. It also uses phosphor-based technology that allows it to adhere to simple routes by demarcating specific locations according to the appropriate use. That is the union of Smart Block EAN with the community, it is the way of integrating the local society to the project foundering this type of applications that give the pedestrian crossing characteristics of respect, security, lighting, trust and protection, always bearing in mind its simple use of indicating to the vehicles that it is a crosswalk (Fig. 10).

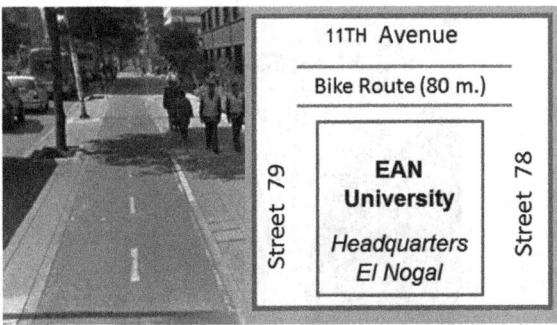

Fig. 10. Energy tree in the central square (modified image)

4.9   Smart Bus Stop

It is like any bus stop, a place to wait for public transport. However, it allows the community to access services such as energy, Internet, route information in real time without ignoring an environment of nature that inspires tranquility. The intelligent bus stop is an alternative to improve the quality of public transport in the area, and to lower the concept of the Urban Canopy but at the disposal of society. This bus stop provides information of the routes using artificial vision, and has a bio-stable vegetation layer on the cover to capture CO_2. It works energetically with renewable technology, offers lighting, security and promotes technologies in all engineering.

4.10   Drone Guide

It is an alternative to guide visitors to the interior of the EAN University by means of a drone-controlled UAV robot remotely controlled by a First-Person View (FPV). The Drone Guide has a software platform for booking and using the Drone. Ore than a robot, the Drone Guide is a guide that helps the University visitors to get to their meeting destination faster. On the other hand, the

Drone Guide can work to generate confidence and security in the users. Besides closeness to a novel and simple technology. In addition, it will promote robotic and computer technologies and will dazzle every visitor and every stakeholder interested in the University.

The four projects, which at this moment are in the conception phase, have already defined scope and work team, as well as stakeholders and sponsors of the project. When the projects reach the planning phase, the will require the budget approval.

The Energy Carpet project is in the process of design purchase of the materials needed for the installation of the carpet at the entrance of the University. About the charging station and the Automobile Data Collectors: the University is already in the possession of two electric vehicles donated by Mitsubishi Motors and the Android Application to book the use of the cars. Currently, it is in the process of conditioning the vehicles with sensors. The Drone Guide project already counts with both the drones and the booking software, as groups of systems engineering students developed the Android Application and the reservation software as a classroom project. Now we are looking for practitioners to proof test the drones.

The two projects in control phase are in the test mode. The Energy laboratory equipped by ABB is already installed in the laboratory headquarters of the University. It will soon be ready for use by the students and professors of the University.

5   Conclusions

The aim of the document was to present the ten initiatives that make up the smart block EAN project. These ten initiatives are projects that together with the construction of the EAN Legacy building, are the strategy to transform the campus of the University into the first Scale Smart City in Colombia and Latin America. This is a sample of a flexible model of Smart City for Bogotá that considers leadership, innovation, and sustainable, fundamental elements in the generation of better opportunities for citizens.

The general policy in this project has been zero outgoings, minimum investment, and maximum agreements, to the extent that mutually beneficial agreements are established, in which large companies such as ABB, Enel Group and Mitsubishi Motors invest in the universities, and the University returns the investment with new knowledge and technological development.

References

1. Al Nuaimi, E., Al Neyadi, H., Mohamed, N., Al-Jaroodi, J.: Applications of big data to smart cities. J. Internet Serv. Appl. 6(1), 25 (2015)
2. Allwinkle, S., Cruickshank, P.: Creating smart-er cities: an overview. J. Urban Technol. 18(2), 1–16 (2011)

3. Batty, M., Axhausen, K.W., Giannotti, F., Pozdnoukhov, A., Bazzani, A., Wachowicz, M., Ouzounis, G., Portugali, Y.: Smart cities of the future. Eur. Phys. J. Spec. Top. **214**(1), 481–518 (2012). https://doi.org/10.1140/epjst/e2012-01703-3
4. Banco Interamericano de Desarrollo - BID: CES Implementacin del enfoque del programa ciudades emergentes y sostenibles (2017). http://webpoc.iadb.org/es/temas/ciudades-emergentes-y-sostenibles/implementacion-del-enfoque-del-programa-ciudades-emergentes-y-sostenibles,7641.html
5. Bouskela, M., Casseb, M., Bassi, S., DeLuca, C., Facchina, M.: La ruta hacia las Smart Cities: Migrando de una gestin tradicional a la ciudad inteligente. Monograph from the Inter-American Development Bank (IADB) (2016). https://doi.org/10.18235/0000377
6. Caragliu, A., Del Bo, C., Nijkamp, P.: Smart Cities in Europe. Research Memoranda Series 0048 (VU University Amsterdam, Faculty of Economics, Business Administration and Econometrics). CRC Press, Boca Raton (2009)
7. CONNECT: Informe de gestin. CONNECT, Bogot (2016)
8. Consejo Empresarial Colombiano para el Desarrollo Sostenible CECODES: Primer laboratorio de eficiencia energtica en Colombia (2017). http://www.cecodes.org.co/site/primer-laboratorio-de-eficiencia-energetica-en-bogota/. Accessed 05 Apr 2017
9. Departamento Nacional de Planeacin - DNP: Concepto sobre las bases del Plan Nacional de Desarrollo 2014–2018 "Todos por un nuevo pas". Departamento Nacional de Planeacin, Bogot D.C (2015)
10. Enerlis, E., Young, F.: Madrid Network: Libro Blanco Smart Cities. Imprintia, Madrid (2012)
11. Evans, D.: Internet de las cosas Cómo la próxima evolución de Internet lo cambia todo. CISCO, Informe Técnico, pp. 1–12 (2011). https://www.cisco.com/c/dam/global/es-mx/solutions/executive/assets/pdf/internet-of-things-iot-ibsg.pdf
12. Gartner: Hype Cycle for Big Data (2012). https://www.gartner.com/doc/2100215/hype-cycle-big-data
13. GhaffarianHoseini, A., Dahlan, N.D., Berardi, U., GhaffarianHoseini, A., Makaremi, N., GhaffarianHoseini, M.: Sustainable energy performances of green buildings: a review of current theories, implementations and challenges. Renew. Sustain. Energy Rev. **25**, 1–17 (2013)
14. Glasmeier, A., Christopherson, S.: Thinking about smart cities. Camb. J. Reg. Econ. Soc. **8**(1), 3–12 (2015)
15. Komeily, A., Srinivasan, R.: Sustainability in smart cities: balancing social, economic, environmental, and institutional aspects of urban life. In: Smart Cities: Foundations, Principles, and Applications, pp. 503–534. Wiley, Hoboken (2017)
16. Murgante, B., Borruso, G.: Smart cities in a smart world. In: Rassia, S.T., Pardalos, P.M. (eds.) Future City Architecture for Optimal Living. SOIA, vol. 102, pp. 13–35. Springer, Cham (2015). https://doi.org/10.1007/978-3-319-15030-7_2
17. Letaifa, S.B.: How to strategize smart cities: revealing the SMART model. J. Bus. Res. **68**(7), 1414–1419 (2015)
18. McDonough, W., Braungart, M.: Cradle to cradle = de la cuna a la cuna: rediseando la forma en que hacemos las cosas. McGraw-Hill/Interamericana de Espaa, Madrid (2005)
19. Ocampo, D.R.: Entorno Urbano de las Sedes de la Universidad EAN. Universidad EAN, Bogota (2017)
20. Ohlson, C.: The Best Commercial Drones. Buy the Best Drone (2016)
21. Rodrguez-Urrego, D., Rodrguez-Urrego, L.: Photovoltaic energy in Colombia: current status, inventory, policies and future prospects. Renew. Sustain. Energy Rev. **92**, 160–170 (2018). https://doi.org/10.1016/j.rser.2018.04.065. ISSN 1364-0321

22. Rubin, K.S.: Essential Scrum: A Practical Guide to the Most Popular Agile Process. Addison Wesley, Boston (2012)
23. Schwaber, K., Sutherland, J.: The Scrum Guide (2017). https://www.scrumguides. org/docs/scrumguide/v2017/2017-Scrum-Guide-US.pdf
24. Shahrokni, H., Solacolu, A.: Real-time ethics—A technology enabled paradigm of everyday ethics in smart cities: shifting sustainability responsibilities through citizen empowerment. In: IEEE International Symposium on Technology and Society, ISTAS, pp. 1–5. IEEE, November 2015
25. Trejo, A.: Open Smart Cities: Tecnologas de fuentes abiertas para ciudades inteligentes. CENATIC - Centro Nacional de Referencia de Aplicacin de las TIC basadas en Fuentes Abiertas (2013). https://es.slideshare.net/anatrejo/open-smart-cities-tecnologas-de-fuentes-abiertas-para-ciudades-inteligentes
26. United Nations Conference on Trade and Development - UNCTAD: Science, technology and innovation for sustainable urbanization. United Nations Publication, New York, Geneva (2015)
27. United Nations, Department of Economic and Social Affairs/Population Division: World Urbanization Prospects: The 2014 Revision (2014). http://esa.un.org/unpd/ wup/Publications/Files/WUP2014-Report.pdf
28. United Nations, Economic and Social Council: Smart cities and infrastructure. Report of the Secretary-General (2016). http://unctad.org/meetings/en/ SessionalDocuments/ecn162016d2-en.pdf
29. West, G.: Drone On. In Foreign Affairs (2015). https://www.foreignaffairs.com/ articles/2015-05-01/drone
30. Winters, J.V.: Why are smart cities growing? Who moves and who stays. J. Reg. Sci. **51**(2), 253–270 (2011)
31. Zubizarreta, I., Seravalli, A., Arrizabalaga, S.: Smart city concept: what it is and what it should be. J. Urban Plan. Dev. **142**(1), 8 (2015)

Spatial Indicators to Evaluate Urban Fragmentation in Basilicata Region

Lucia Saganeiti[1], Angela Pilogallo[1], Francesco Scorza[1] (ID),
Giovanni Mussuto[2], and Beniamino Murgante[1,2(✉)] (ID)

[1] School of Engineering, University of Basilicata, Viale dell'Ateneo Lucano 10,
85100 Potenza, Italy
{lucia.saganeiti, francesco.scorza, beniamino.murgante}
@unibas.it, angela.pilogallo@libero.it
[2] Environmental Observatory Foundation of Basilicata Region (FARBAS),
Corso Vittorio Emanuele II n. 3, 85052 Marsico Nuovo, (PZ), Italy
giovanni.mussuto@farbas.it

Abstract. The increase of artificial land use represents a relevant indicator in land management policies and practices. It is a useful tool in assessing the quality of settlement processes and the protection and enhancement policies in rural and natural areas. Over time land take processes have been caused by different phenomena: urban or industrial expansion, realization of infrastructures, the development or the productive exploitation of territorial areas characterized by the presence of specific resources (natural, mining, etc.). This phenomenon is no longer a direct consequence of a real need of new expansion areas throughout Italian national territory. In the past the phenomenon was mainly due to residential, productive or tertiary sector needs, and it was generated by demographic growth and the consequent urbanization process. In the last two decades land take is more and more related to a weak territorial governance, generally linked to an inefficiency of urban and territorial planning instruments and sometimes of speculative real estate initiatives. In this paper a spatial analysis procedure oriented to calculate indicators of urban fragmentation for Basilicata Region has been presented. Such indicators could drive to the identification of two phenomena: urban-sprawl and urban-sprinkling according to the literature classification proposed in several researches by Romano et al. The results represent a useful contribution in order to improve regional normative system concerning urban development. The research is part of a wider project on environmental and territorial indicators (INDICARE) promoted by FARBAS (Environmental Observatory Foundation of Basilicata Region) in collaboration with the University of Basilicata.

Keywords: Fragmentation · Urban sprawl · Basilicata region
Land take

© Springer International Publishing AG, part of Springer Nature 2018
O. Gervasi et al. (Eds.): ICCSA 2018, LNCS 10964, pp. 100–112, 2018.
https://doi.org/10.1007/978-3-319-95174-4_8

1 Introduction

In the last decades, in Europe, urban fabric is developing according to the sprawl model [1–4]. Among the main impacts of this model of territorial development the destructuring of settlement fabric, urban fragmentation, insulation, natural landscape degradation can be certainly included.

In particular, the fragmentation process of natural landscape can be divided in two main components: one relates to the disappearance of natural environments and reduction of their surface; the other one concerns the progressive insularization and redistribution of residual environments in the space. The continuous expansion of the anthropized areas transforms agricultural and natural soil in new residential areas, often characterized by low residential density. This constantly growing trend determines not negligible environmental and social effects, leading to the formation of medium-small urban centres, geographically decentralized with respect to the main poles [5, 6]. Among other effects, land cover dynamics influence the spatio-temporal evolution of RUI (Rural Urban Interface), which are the areas most prone to human-caused forest fires [7]. In 2015, the wooded and non-wooded areas of Basilicata Region crossed by fire were 1.6 m^2 over 1000 km^2 [8].

Scattered settlements generate an increase the demand of infrastructure and transport services, producing an increase of costs which goes over sustainable thresholds [9, 10, 24]. Italian settlement models show non-negligible differences compared to the European ones, thus justifying the use of the term *sprinkling* [11].

This work aims at the evaluation of spatial fragmentation indicators allowing to characterize current urban development processes, as sprawl or sprinkling [12]. It is part of a larger research project, called "INDICARE", which deals with the indexing of regional environmental critical issues (of Basilicata Region) in several environmental fields. The operational approach proposed by the research project is based on the construction of a methodology linking knowledge to actions, information and participation. Through advanced tools and techniques, useful results for regulatory and procedural innovation in the field of territorial governance and monitoring of dynamics under way have been achieved.

Among the main components characterizing the wider research, great importance has been given to the evaluation of urban growth and its effects in terms of territorial fragmentation and degradation of natural-environmental system. More in particular, it is oriented to obtain qualitative and quantitative assessment framework defining territorial exposure to stress factors considered in spatial and temporal dimensions. The proposed indicators are configured as a decision support tool for the construction of territorial management models considering the mitigation of impacts as a priority. This study will be also finalized to enrich the spatial database already available on the RSDI[1] [13] platform of Basilicata Region.

---

[1] RSDI: acronym for Regional Spatial Data Infrastructure. Is an infrastructure for the Territorial Information, aligned with the indications of the European INSPIRE directive, open to the participation of local authorities and local companies interested in territorial information systems, according to the logic of data sharing and cooperation and geographic services. All data are open.

The paper starts from the description of the study area, discusses the methodology used and presents the main results. Conclusions concern reflections on obtained data and any future developments.

2 Materials and Methods

In this paper the evolution of settlement system according to information coming from three official sources will be analysed: geo-topographic regional database (RSDI Basilicata Region); ortho-photos from the national geo-portal of the Ministry of the Environment and IGM (Military Geographic Institute) cartography. Concerning temporal dimension of the analysis, selected sources allow us to identify five time phases: 1950 – 1989 – 1998 – 2006 – 2013 according to which we calculated territorial fragmentation. Furthermore, we compared such results with census data.

2.1 Study Area

The study area includes the whole territory of Basilicata region in southern Italy (Fig. 2), which covers about 10.000 km², and has a population of 570.365 inhabitants (ISTAT [14], 2016) with a density of 57.93 inhabitants/Km².

Table 1 shows the statistical data relative to the two provinces. The population of the region has been continuously decreasing since 1980s, this trend is completely in contrast with urban settlement development which actually increased during the same period (Fig. 1).

No correspondences could be found between population growth and new housing demand. This means that urban growth is mainly due to a lack in urban regulation and in the implementation of planning tools at municipal and regional level. All this has led, in most cases, to a high fragmentation.

2.2 Data Acquisition

In order to build the spatial datasets describing settlement evolution of the study area, several sources of information were considered: the main reference is the regional cartography (scale 1:5000) of Basilicata Region at 2013. This spatial dataset is available as open data on the RSDI website. Such information has been used as a starting point to extract buildings. Starting from the buildings at 2013, the date of the last photogrammetric survey, we proceeded backwards: analysing [1] the ortho-photos available as *wms* service on National Geoportal of the Ministry of the Environment and Protection of Land and Sea [15] and considering different dates of photogrammetric flights at 2006, 98/2000 and 1988/89. Comparing the current regional cartography with previous ortho-photos several backwards maps have been constructed.

In order to identify a source of information after the Second World War, corresponding to the greatest urban growth in Italy, maps at 1: 25000 scale, realized by the Military Geographical Institute (IGM) in 1950 have been used. Despite they are not very detailed maps, they represent the oldest reliable technical representation of Basilicata Region, allowing to recognize single buildings.

Table 1. Distribution of population (2016, date of the last census – ISTAT), territorial surface, Population density and number of municipalities in the two Provinces of Basilicata Region.

Territorial area	Population (inhabitants)	Territorial surface (Km²)	Population density (inhab/Km²)	Municipality (number)
Province of Potenza	370.680	6.541	57.68	100
Province of Matera	199.685	3.443	58.42	31
Basilicata region	**570.365**	**9.984**	**57.93**	**131**

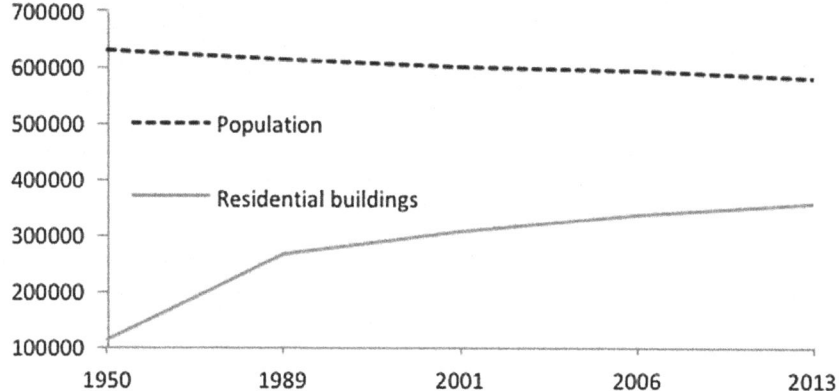

Fig. 1. Comparison between settlement evolution concerning residential buildings and population evolution from 1950 to 2013.

Concerning demographic data, Italian National Institute of Statistics (ISTAT) databases have been used.

Data at municipalities aggregation have been analysed, considering the population at different years: 1950 – 1989 – 1998 – 2006 – 2013, in order to compare population and urban growth. In addition, data on demographic projections at provincial and regional level were analysed.

2.3 Methodology

The regional technical map, provided by RSDI, contains the representation of the built environment dated 2013 for the whole region. In particular, the shape file of the 'volumetric units' was used. The information included in the file allowed us to derive area and volume for each building.

From the comparison between the shape file of the volumetric units and the ortho-photos from National geo-portal and IGM maps, five shape files have been created representing the built environment at different dates:

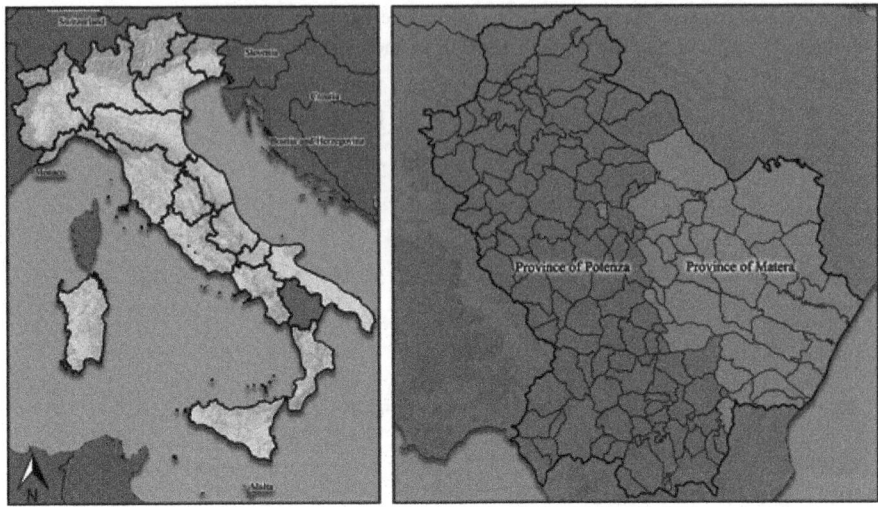

Fig. 2. The location of Basilicata region in Italy on the left and the location of the Provinces of Potenza and Matera with their relative municipalities on the right.

- Volumetric units in 2013: directly from the regional technical map of the Basilicata region.
- Volumetric units in 2006: from digital colour ortho-photos of the Italian territory with a resolution of 1:10000 and viewable only at scales above 1: 100000 in *wms* service.
- Volumetric units in 2000: from digital color ortho-photos of the Italian territory with a resolution of 1:10000 and viewable only at scales above 1: 100000 in *wms* service. The dates of the photogrammetric flights vary according to the area from 1998 to 2000.
- Volumetric units in 1989: from black and white ortho-photos of the Italian territory with a resolution of 1:10000 and viewable only at scales above 1: 100000 in *wms* service. The dates of the photogrammetric flights vary according to the area from 1988 to 1989.
- Volumetric units in 1950: from the topographic map of Italy to scale 1: 25000 (IGM).

For each temporal phase, data about resident population, buildings number and volumes were reported.

Since the regional technical map does not contain information on the use of buildings, a crosscheck with data collected during the residential buildings census realized by ISTAT at 2011 was performed.

2.3.1   Aggregates Formation

Once the historical evolution of buildings was completed, the aggregates were formed. The advantage of studying urban aggregates is to understand in detail the path of settlement evolution. It is important to underline that the increase of buildings may correspond to an increase in the number of aggregates or, alternatively, to an increase of the aggregate area, which is explained by a growth in buildings around pre-existing urban areas. Aggregates are orthogonal polygons constructed starting from a distance between single original elements, in this case buildings, which can be, from time to time, modified. Aggregation occurs only when two polygon limits are within the specified aggregation distance. The aggregation can take place with orthogonal or not orthogonal features (Fig. 3).

It is necessary to specify that the urban aggregates do not contain perimeters of built up centres. In fact, the built-up centre is delimited, for each inhabited nucleus or inhabited centre, by an uninterrupted perimeter including all areas built with continuity and interclused lots. In this context we simply refer to a new strategy representative of groups of buildings clustered together within an urbanized area.

2.3.2 DA Index

A fragmentation index has been adopted for the assessment of the fragmentation degree of the territory. More in detail, the Density index of Aggregates DA [16] index has been used. DA (1) allows to analyse the variation in the number of aggregates and their areas in order to evaluate the degree of fragmentation of each municipality of Basilicata Region.

$$DA = \frac{\Delta NA}{\Delta A_{Average}} \qquad (1)$$

Where:

- ΔNA represents the variation in the number of aggregates present in every municipality of Basilicata in the considered historical phase.
- $\Delta A_{Average}$ represents the variation in average of the areas of all the aggregates present in every municipality of the regional territory. The area of the larger aggregate, generally represented by the main urban centre, will be subtracted from this value.

The bigger the DA absolute value will be, the greater the degree of fragmentation of a territory will be [17]. alues very close to zero will correspond to an almost null degree of fragmentation, while higher values will correspond to a medium-high fragmentation degree. For the assessment of the index, the absolute value will be considered. The negativity of index is depending on:

- $\Delta NA < 0$: the number of aggregates between two historical phases decreases i.e., existing aggregates are merged. Such a phenomenon does not cause an increase in fragmentation. An example is shown in Fig. 4.
- $\Delta A_{Average} < 0$: between one historical phase and another the average of the areas of all the aggregates decreases. This corresponds to the formation of new small aggregates, a phenomenon that negatively affects the degree of territorial fragmentation.

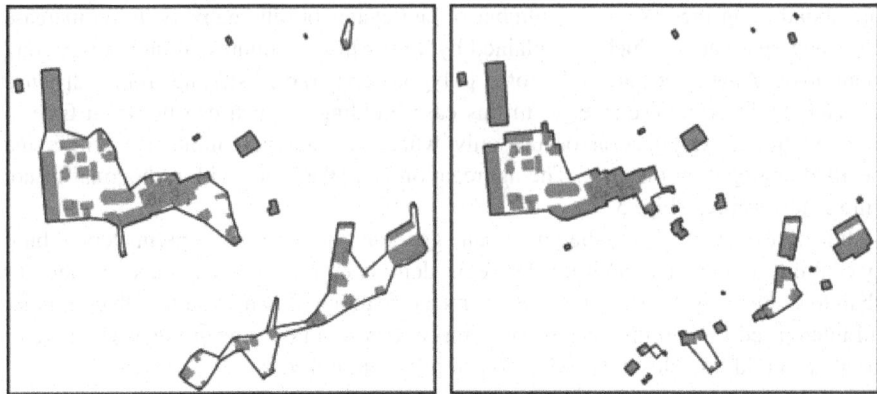

Fig. 3. Aggregations of buildings: with not orthogonal features on the left and with orthogonal features on the right.

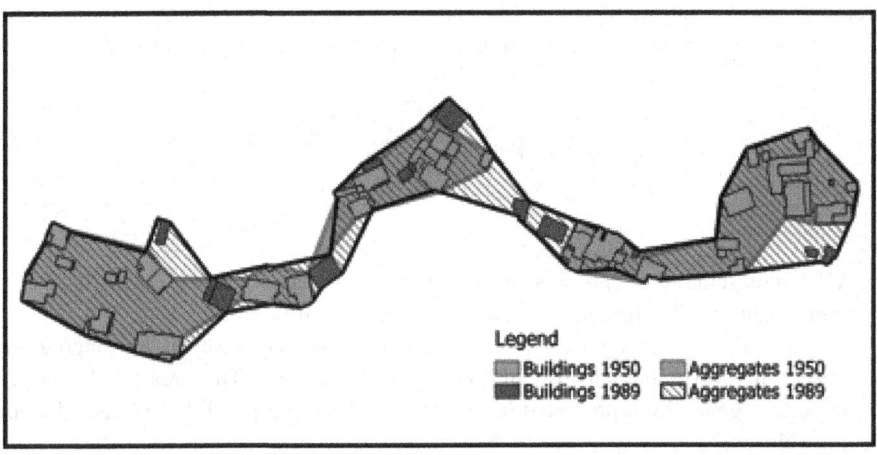

Fig. 4. Example of negative variation of aggregates number.

In order to identify the degree of fragmentation of each single municipality of the region brought about by the constructions that took place during certain years, the DA index will be calculated on the variation of the data between 1950 and 1989 and between 1989 and 2013.

3 Results and Discussion

The analysis of the historical evolution of the building was carried out on the regional territory, obtaining results for all the 131 municipalities. Table 2 shows the results grouped for the entire region for each considered phase. It can already be seen from this first analysis how the population decreased and the number of buildings increased from 1950s up to nowadays (Fig. 1).

Table 2. Variation of population and buildings in Basilicata region over time.

Years	Pop (inhab)	Building (n)	Volume (m³)	m³/inhab	Building/inhab	m²/inhab
1950	627.586	113.479	90.974.952	144.96	0.18	48.32
1989	610186	266.409	223.249.429	365.87	0.44	121.96
1998	597.468	307.649	263.237.360	440.59	0.51	146.86
2006	591.338	335431	291.679.901	493.25	0.57	164.42
2013	578.391	356785	304.459.018	526.39	0.62	175.46

Table 3. Variation of number of aggregates and their surface, variation of urban density (DU) and population density.

Years		Basilicata Region	Province of Potenza	Province of Matera
1950	N. of aggregates	27.062	20.712	6.350
	Surf. of aggregates *(Km²)*	34.06	26.19	7.87
	DU *(%)*	0.34	0.40	0.23
	Dp *(inhab/km²)*	62.85	68.06	52.98
1989	N. of aggregates	56.958	37.981	18.977
	Surf. of aggregates *(Km²)*	106.93	74.72	32.21
	DU *(%)*	1.07	1.14	0.94
	Dp *(inhab/km²)*	61.12	61.39	60.70
1998	N. of aggregates	62.818	42.518	20.300
	Surf. of aggregates *(Km²)*	130.52	93.63	36.89
	DU *(%)*	1.31	1.43	1.07
	Dp *(inhab/km²)*	59.84	60.11	59.34
2006	N. of aggregates	66.127	45.161	20.966
	Surf. of aggregates *(Km²)*	148.40	106.34	42.06
	DU *(%)*	1.49	1.63	1.22
	Dp *(inhab/km²)*	59.22	59.29	59.11
2013	N. of aggregates	68.941	47.126	21.815
	Surf. of aggregates *(Km²)*	160.56	115.19	45.37
	DU *(%)*	1.61	1.76	1.32
	Dp *(inhab/km²)*	57.93	57.67	58.42

Buildings inhabitants were 0.62 in 2013 over 0.18 buildings inhabitants in 1950. The datum is very high if we consider that we are not talking about rooms but of whole buildings. The rate regarding the surface available for each inhabitant, calculated assuming an inter-floor space of 3 m, is also vertiginously increasing.

For each of the five phases of settlement evolution, buildings have been aggregated with a methodology explained in Sect. 2.3.1, by the non-orthogonal features and considering a minimum distance of 50 ms. Such distance was the most appropriate to represent the aggregation of buildings in Basilicata Region. The 50 m aggregation was chosen among the various aggregates obtained with distances set at 50, 100 and 200 m and has allowed the perimetration of urban aggregates for each temporal phase. This analysis allows a preliminary assessment of number of urban aggregates variation, their area and urban density (DU). DU, the urban density index is expressed as a percentage and it is calculated as the ratio between the surface of all aggregates and the whole surface of the municipality. The results are summarized in Table 3, grouped at Provincial and Regional level. In Table 3 it is reported also the Dp (Density Population) index measured as inhabitants/Km^2. It has been calculated for the five temporal phases, for each municipality of Basilicata Region, as the ratio between the population (number of inhabitants) and the territorial surface (Km^2) (cfr. Table 2) [18].

Table 4. Degree of urban fragmentation according to the value of DA.

Fragmentation	DA
Not fragmented	$DA = 0$
Little fragmented	$0 < DA < 1$
Fragmented	$1 \leq DA < 10$
Highly fragmented	$DA \geq 10$

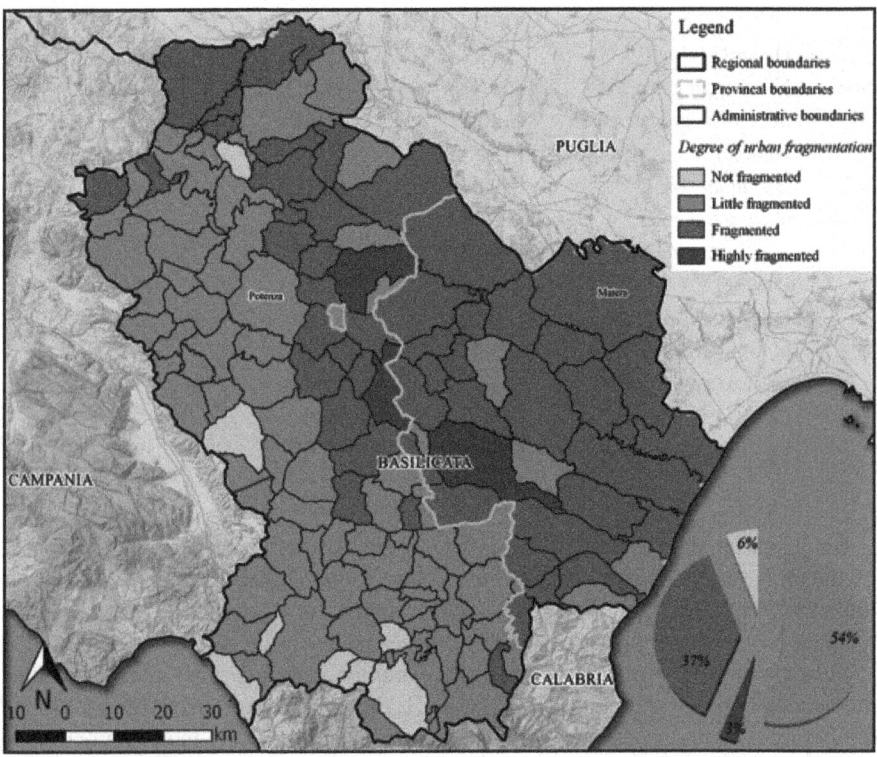

Fig. 5. Degree of urban fragmentation of 131 municipalities of Basilicata region. 1950–1989.

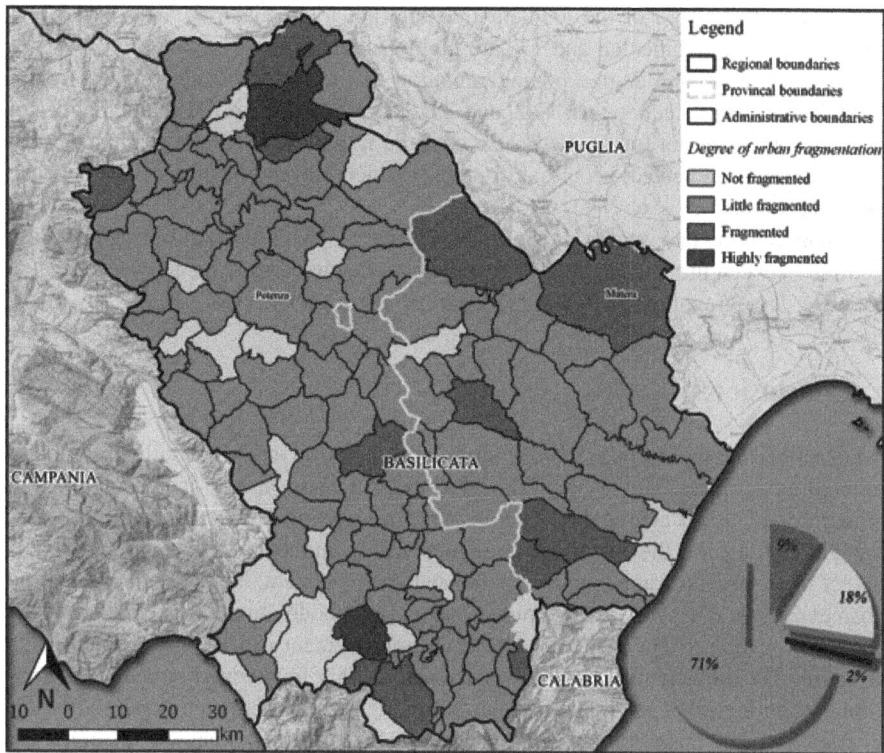

Fig. 6. Degree of urban fragmentation of 131 municipalities of Basilicata region. 1989–2013.

The DA (1) index was calculated, for each municipality, based on the variation of the number of aggregates and their surfaces between 1950 and 1989 and between 1989 and 2013. It can assume values varying between $-\infty$ and $+\infty$, depending on reference territorial extent with respect to which the index is calculated. In our case, the values obtained oscillated in a range between -20 and $+20$. As anticipated in Sect. 2.3.2 the DA index is considered as absolute value and values very close to zero will correspond to an almost zero degree of fragmentation, while higher values willl represent degrees of medium-high fragmentation. A schematization is shown in Table 4.

A little rate of fragmentation represents a little variation in the number of aggregates and an increase in the average of aggregates surface. This means that the aggregates expand and incorporate the existing ones, as shown in Fig. 4.

A highly rate of fragmentation represents an increase in number of aggregates and in average of their surfaces. This means that the buildings evolution variation occurred in a given period has led to the birth of numerous big aggregates far from the existing ones.

Figure 5 shows the degree of fragmentation of each municipality according to building development that took place between 1950 and 1989. Figure 5 highlights a degree of medium-high fragmentation in most of municipalities of Matera province and a low degree of fragmentation in large part of municipalities in Potenza province. In the whole Region only 6% of the municipalities are not fragmented, 54% are little fragmented, 37% are fragmented and 3% are highly fragmented.

Figure 6 shows the degree of fragmentation of the territory following the recent urban development, i.e. between 1989 and 2013. Considering the 131 municipalities of Basilicata, 18% are not fragmented, 71% are little fragmented, 9% are fragmented and 2% are highly fragmented, according to the settlement development occurred between 1989 and 2013.

Comparing the two images, it is possible to observe that great part of fragmentation occurred between the '50s and the '80s, a period when housing demand was correlated to a huge demographic growth and great part of urban growth was governed by plans.

4 Conclusions

The described analyses aim to provide spatial and temporal indices of soil consumption for building purposes. The results, from 1950 to 2013, show an ever increasing trend in the number of urban aggregates. This involves on one side a decrease of aggregates average area and on the other side their increase in number. The whole territory is subject to a growing fragmentation of the settlement system. Throughout the region, urban expansion takes place with a pulverized growth model, to the disadvantage of the urban aggregation that would have led to an improvement in land management, also improving the infrastructural system organization. This fragmented structure of territorial system increases land take and has a significant environmental impact [19–22].

Although the main Italian law (n. 1150/1942) on urban planning is quite old Basilicata Region has always shown delays. The region approved his first territorial government law only in 1999 and since then this law has not been implemented at all. Before 1968 no municipality had an approved plan, between 1968 and 1978 only 15 municipalities had a plan and in 1985 only 26 municipalities approved a plan [23]. This means that in the greatest expansion period only a few municipalities adequately managed this phenomenon. This justifies the high degree of fragmentation generated by the urban expansion that took place between 1950 and 1989, without adequate planning tools. Another aspect that characterizes Basilicata region is the huge decrease of population, especially in small municipalities, which generates abandonment of housing.

A particularly useful future development of this paper could be the monetary quantification of fragmentation, based on the distance between the scattered settlements and the compact centre calculating all extra costs related to all the infrastructural and transport networks. The monetization of the index makes it possible to give greater importance to the analysed phenomenon making it comparable with other quantities.

Acknowledgements. This research has been supported by the Environmental Observatory Foundation of Basilicata Region (FARBAS).

References

1. Di Palma, F., Amato, F., Nolè, G., Martellozzo, F., Murgante, B.: A SMAP supervised classification of landsat images for urban sprawl evaluation. ISPRS Int. J. Geo-Inf. **5**(7), 109 (2016). https://doi.org/10.3390/ijgi5070109
2. Brueckner, J.K.: Urban sprawl: diagnosis and remedies. Int. Reg. Sci. Rev. **23**(2), 160–171 (2000). https://doi.org/10.1177/016001700761012710
3. Zanganeh Shahraki, S., Sauri, D., Serra, P., Modugno, S., Seifolddini, F., Pourahmad, A.: Urban sprawl pattern and land-use change detection in Yazd. Iran. Habitat. Int. **35**(4), 521–528 (2011). https://doi.org/10.1016/J.HABITATINT.2011.02.004
4. Amato, F., Pontrandolfi, P., Murgante, B.: Using spatiotemporal analysis in urban sprawl assessment and prediction. In: Murgante, B., et al. (eds.) ICCSA 2014. LNCS, vol. 8580, pp. 758–773. Springer, Cham (2014). https://doi.org/10.1007/978-3-319-09129-7_55
5. Foley, J.A., DeFries, R., Asner, G.P., et al.: Global consequences of land use. Science **309** (5734), 570–574 (2005). https://doi.org/10.1126/science.1111772
6. Hennig, E.I., Schwick, C., Soukup, T., Orlitová, E., Kienast, F., Jaeger, J.A.G.: Multi-scale analysis of urban sprawl in Europe: towards a European de-sprawling strategy. Land Use Policy **49**, 483–498 (2015). https://doi.org/10.1016/J.LANDUSEPOL.2015.08.001
7. Amato, F., Tonini, M., Murgante, B., Kanevski, M.: Fuzzy definition of Rural Urban Interface: an application based on land use change scenarios in Portugal. Environ. Model Softw. **104**, 171–187 (2018). https://doi.org/10.1016/J.ENVSOFT.2018.03.016
8. Istituto Nazionale di Statistica. il benessere equo e sostenibile in Italia (2017). https://www.istat.it/it/files//2017/12/Bes_2017.pdf. Accessed 14 Mar 2018
9. Martellozzo, F., Amato, F., Murgante, B., Clarke, K.C.: Modelling the impact of urban growth on agriculture and natural land in Italy to 2030. Appl. Geogr. **91**, 156–167 (2018). https://doi.org/10.1016/J.APGEOG.2017.12.004
10. Marchetti, M., Marino, D., De Toni, A., et al.: Consumo di suolo, dinamiche territoriali e servizi ecosistemici. Edizione 2017 (2017). https://iris.unimol.it/handle/11695/65538#. WvXKbJfYWUl. Accessed 11 Mar 2018
11. Romano, B., Fiorini, L., Zullo, F., Marucci, A.: Urban growth control DSS techniques for de-sprinkling process in Italy. Sustainability **9**(10), 1852 (2017). https://doi.org/10.3390/su9101852
12. Antrop, M.: Landscape change and the urbanization process in Europe. Landsc. Urban Plan. **67**(1–4), 9–26 (2004). https://doi.org/10.1016/S0169-2046(03)00026-4
13. RSDI – Geoportale Basilicata. https://rsdi.regione.basilicata.it/. Accessed 6 Mar 2018
14. Istat.it. https://www.istat.it/. Accessed 5 Apr 2018
15. Home - Geoportale Nazionale. http://www.pcn.minambiente.it/mattm/. Accessed 10 Feb 2018
16. Irwin, E.G., Bockstael, N.E.: The evolution of urban sprawl: evidence of spatial heterogeneity and increasing land fragmentation. Proc. Natl. Acad. Sci. U.S.A. **104**(52), 20672–20677 (2007). https://doi.org/10.1073/pnas.0705527105
17. Romano, B., Zullo, F.: The urban transformation of Italy's Adriatic coastal strip: fifty years of unsustainability. Land Use Policy **38**, 26–36 (2014). https://doi.org/10.1016/J.LANDUSEPOL.2013.10.001
18. Kew, B., Lee, B.: Measuring sprawl across the urban rural continuum using an amalgamated sprawl index. Sustainability **5**(5), 1806–1828 (2013). https://doi.org/10.3390/su5051806
19. Amato, F., Maimone, B., Martellozzo, F., Nolè, G., Murgante, B.: The effects of urban policies on the development of urban areas. Sustainability **8**(4), 297 (2016). https://doi.org/10.3390/su8040297

20. Amato, F., Nolè, G., Martellozzo, F., Murgante, B.: Preserving cultural heritage by supporting landscape planning with quantitative predictions of soil consumption. J. Cultural Heritage Elsevier **23**, 44–54 (2017). https://doi.org/10.1016/j.culher.2015.12.009
21. Murgante, B., Salmani, M., Molaei Qelichi, M., Hajilo, M.: a multiple criteria decision-making approach to evaluate the sustainability indicators in the villagers' lives in Iran with emphasis on earthquake hazard: a case study. Sustainability **9**, 1491 (2017)
22. Amato, F., Pontrandolfi, P., Murgante, B.: Supporting planning activities with the assessment and the prediction of urban sprawl using spatio-temporal analysis. Ecol. Inf. **30**, 365–378 (2015). https://doi.org/10.1016/j.ecoinf.2015.07.004
23. Cozzi, M.: La Carta Regionale dei Suoli della Basilicata: modelli interpretativi degli areali agricoli e ambientali. CeSET **XXXV**(35), 1000–1021 (2005). https://doi.org/10.1400/56173
24. Del Giudice, V., De Paola, P., Manganelli, B., Forte, F.: The monetary valuation of environmental externalities through the analysis of real estate prices. Sustainability **9**, 229 (2017)

Increasing the Walkability Level
Through a Participation Process

Raffaella Carbone, Lucia Saganeiti, Francesco Scorza (iD), and Beniamino Murgante (✉) (iD)

School of Engineering, University of Basilicata, Viale dell'Ateneo Lucano 10,
85100 Potenza, Italy
rafcar88@gmail.com,
{lucia.saganeiti,francesco.scorza,beniamino.murgante}@unibas.it

Abstract. The paper analyses the theme of walkability in the western part of Potenza municipality. It is based on participatory process developed in Active Citizenship for Sustainable Development of the Territory (CAST) project. During this experience a cognitive framework has been defined both adopting traditional approaches, and, in order to increase the participation, using new information technologies and social networks. The data that emerged were revised and evaluated for the definition of possible strategies for the improvement of walkability, accessibility to the services and equipment and, more generally, the neighbourhood liveability.

Keywords: Walkability · Liveable city · Citizens participation
Urban regeneration · Pedestrian mobility

1 Introduction

Nowadays the regeneration of cities requires a particular attention to the theme of walkability: reducing the use of private cars, increasing the number of people walking or cycling, using public transport are the conditions for transforming cities and improving the people quality of life. The contemporary city is suitable for motorists, because of the centrality given to cars. Consequently, urban spaces, squares and streets are designed on the needs of private mobility. The possibility of walking is often denied culturally and materially because of the hypertrophy of the urban areas, urban and planning deficiencies, with serious consequences on the quality of life and health.

Walkability, therefore, must be conceived as the possibility of citizens to move on foot. Consequently, it is fundamental for people to have a modal choice in moving, and therefore to choose whether to move on foot or not. It is important to consider walking as a valid alternative to motorized vehicles, and not, as often happens, a limitation. In fact, the possibility of moving on foot is often reserved for a few categories of users, or worse for a few areas.

Therefore, the concept of walkability [21–28] goes beyond the accessibility to urban services, but it implies a discussion on spatial quality and on the ability to accommodate and promote pedestrian mobility in urban areas. With reference to theories of the capability [12–15], approach and the right to the city [11, 16–20], walkability must be understood as one of the main factors of urban capacities. The quality of urban life doesn't represent the quality of life of individuals living in a certain geographical limit, but the quality of the urban environment that influences the development and the possibilities of choice and action, according to the individual needs and desires. In fact, the characteristics of the environment influence and are influenced by the spatial behaviour of individuals. In this framework, we have to consider the walkability not only as a goal to be pursued to improve the quality of life of people who live in the city, but also as a tool that urban planners and architects can use to orient the methods of assessing the quality of the urban life and to innovate urban policies and projects, especially those that benefit the most marginal areas of the city and the groups of the most disadvantaged individuals [1, 2]. The walkability level can be improved by means of a participatory process, where citizens can express needs, opinions, preferences, etc. in order to improve the urban quality of life.

The theme of walkability was tackled during the participatory process carried out in the city of Potenza (Fig. 1) in the contest of the Cast project.

Fig. 1. The location of Potenza municipality and Basilicata region in Italy.

Potenza is the main city of the Basilicata region, located in the mountains (900 above sea level) in southern Italy, has approximately seventy thousand inhabitants. In this place, and in its surrounding area several participatory activities have been developed, in great part of cases based on direct citizens' initiative with a bottom-up approach [35–40], and in other cases promoted by local authorities [3, 34].

2   The CAST Project

The CAST Project (Active Citizenship for Sustainable Development of Territory) is an experimentation of a participatory process for the definition of an urban regeneration program in Potenza municipality. It has been selected within a call for application for the development of innovative and creative activities launched by Basilicata Region [3, 4].

One of the first activities of the project was the experimentation of a Participatory Planning Workshop about urban regeneration in a neighbourhood in the western part of the city that involved citizens, some decision makers and technical staff of the municipality, cultural associations and volunteers. The area of CAST Project includes (Fig. 2) the neighbourhood of Poggio Tre Galli, the G area, defined in this way by master-plan, and the district called "Study-Centre" [5].

Fig. 2. Location of the area of CAST project: the neighbourhood of Poggio Tre Galli, the G area and the district called "Study-Centre".

The Participatory Planning Workshop was supported by evolved ICT tools which has generated a wide interest of the local community and public administration, and which has contributed to the implementation of forms of Inclusive Smart Planning [4, 6, 29–33, 41–43].

2.1   The Implementation Context of the Workshop

The urban area involved in the process includes the neighbourhood of Poggio Tre Galli, the G area and the district called "Study-Centre" (Fig. 2).

Poggio Tre Galli and the G area are predominantly residential neighbourhoods with high settlement density, instead in the Study-Centre district there are several high and primary school institutes and a lot of not built areas.

The neighbourhood of Poggio Tre Galli and the district of the "Study-Centre" were built between the '70 s and '80 s on the basis of two plans whose implementation has never been satisfied. In recent years the original planning forecasts have been changed leading to a transformation of the urban structure.

The G area was built in more recent years and is currently lacking in public services and equipment.

According to the Italian National Institute of Statistics (ISTAT) demographic data, at 2011 the neighbourhood of Poggio Tre Galli has a population of 4357 inhabitants, while the G area has 1919 inhabitants. In both cases, in the last decades an increase of population over the age of 50 and a reduction of younger people occurred. This is also confirmed by the increase of the old age index in the decade 2001–2011.

In these neighbourhoods there are a lot of green areas and some services of territorial interest like the regional bureaus. There are also potential areas that could be used to promote a comprehensive urban regeneration of the neighbourhood, but this is connected to potential risks related to some provisions of Planning Rules that instead could represent elements of degradation of the neighbourhood.

2.2 The Methodological Approach and the Adopted Techniques

Workshop activities have been development with two different approaches: the first, more traditional (Fig. 3), based on the work of a small group of people (experts, neighbourhood representatives, organizations, and associations) and the second, more innovative, centred on a dialogue with a wider audience through the use of new information technologies and social networks (Fig. 4).

Fig. 3. Traditional approach of public participation based on public meeting in C.A.S.T. project.

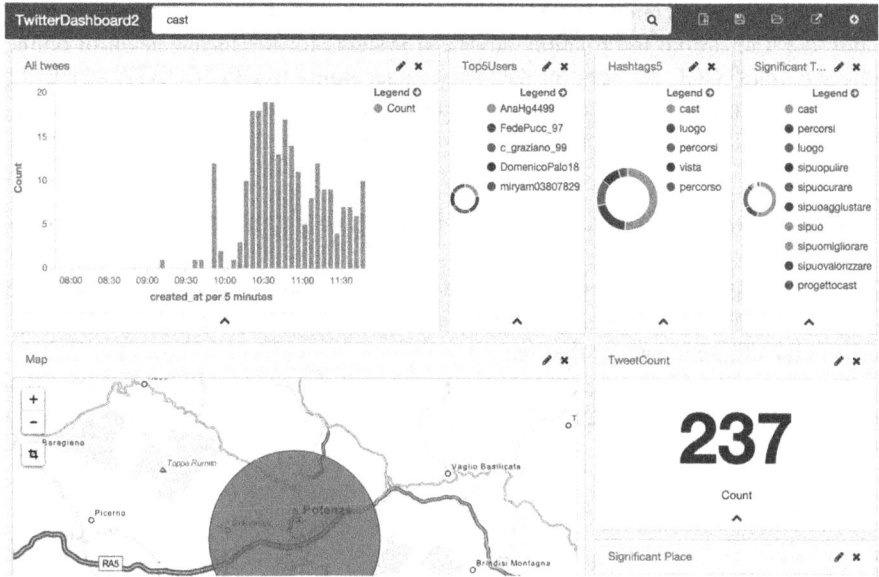

Fig. 4. ICT platform C.A.S.T. project.

At the beginning of the workshop, great attention has been paid to territorial knowledge as collective and shared construction according to the interaction between different actors [5].

In this phase, a cognitive framework was elaborated on the basis of the existing urban planning instruments, site inspections, photographic take-over and qualitative thematic cards (traditional methodology), but also by means of twitter that allowed to different users to report positive and negative elements of the area, and online questionnaires (innovative methodology).

The collected data were processed in thematic maps and used for definition of problem tree and objective tree that were discussed in the workshop to define some strategies about urban regeneration, according to the Logical Framework Approach procedure [7–10].

2.3   The Support of ICT

The Project C.A.S.T. was supported by a technological component based on an online ICT platform (Fig. 4), which integrates open-source tools and frameworks in order to have a high level of interaction among users [3, 5].

The use of ICT has enabled the involvement of a large number of citizens, giving them the opportunity to participate to workshop activities even after time and space from the scheduled meetings, making the dissemination of information fast and the participatory process more transparent.

Information and communication technologies allowed analysis of urban realities and communication between various social actors enabling access and use of information.

The system used combines CMS features (Content Management System), a Geo-portal to get territorial information, advanced systems for the management of online polls and votes, OGC services for data sharing according to OPEN DATA standards, the integration of social networks and the management of spatial social alerts for partic-ipation and collaborative mapping [3].

3   Results of the Workshop: The Cognitive Framework

Walkability was one of the topics discussed in the workshop. This activity highlighted significant criticalities that negatively affect the accessibility and the connections between the different parts of the area.

The analyses carried out and shared during the workshop, highlighted a discontin-uous and lacking pedestrian network from quantitatively and qualitatively point of view (Fig. 5).

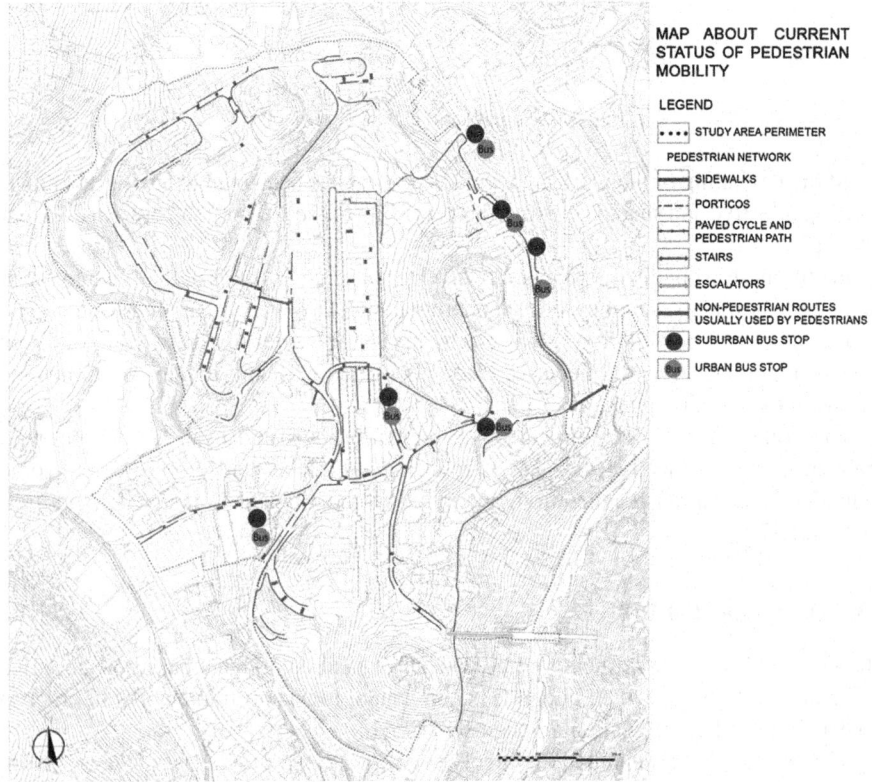

Fig. 5. Map of current status of pedestrian mobility.

The pedestrian mobility has different problems:

- The presence of architectural barriers, in particular along the sidewalks, which do not allow to everyone the usability of the routes;
- The discontinuity of the sidewalks, absent in some stretches where there is a connection between vehicular and pedestrian traffic;
- Insufficient section of the paths: in some cases they are too narrow, in others the section is restricted by the presence of elements such as trees and benches;
- Absence of security measures (parapets), especially along the sidewalks adjacent to the most traffic driveways;
- Presence of dangerous pedestrian crossings;
- Presence of not much used paths in a state of neglect and decay;
- Poor maintenance and cleaning;
- Absence of cycle paths.

These problems do not allow a full use of the network to all categories of users, limiting pedestrian access to the equipment and services.

Based on these considerations, it can be said that pedestrian mobility in this part of the city is lacking and unsafe.

This is particularly important in the Study-Centre district because there aren't adequate and safe connections for a lot of students who walk through the area.

In the Study-Centre district there is no efficient pedestrian network linking the various schools to each other and with the services present in the remaining part of the area. The main effect is the presence of disconnected schools, which in some cases are not connected with the Study-Centre district and are isolated.

It was possible to analyse all these aspects in different way, with the surveys carried out on the territory, using social media and examining the results of questionnaires submitted to the inhabitants of the area.

With the online questionnaires, the point of view of different types of users was identified: residents, students and users of services located in the neighbourhoods.

About walkability, many users have said to move on foot in the district even if this is not considered safe and comfortable: vehicular traffic, the slope of roads, the presence of stray and domestic dogs, the poor path maintenance are elements that discourage cycle and pedestrian mobility. Access to the area with public transport is also negatively assessed.

The same considerations also emerge from the questionnaires addressed to the students who expressed the desire for alternative pedestrian paths to car traffic along which to find spaces of relationship immersed in the green, multifunctional spaces equipped for leisure and other services.

3.1 The Strategies Proposed in the Workshop

The overall vision for the proposal and intervention strategies developed in the participatory workshop refers to an urban regeneration project based on the promotion of sustainable mobility and the development of pedestrian mobility.

More particularly, an effective construction of a network system of green infrastructure, services and open spaces for the community of citizens have been considered as a fundamental cornerstone for the promotion of a sustainable city. The proposal is to develop an urban structure based on green, pedestrian zones and integrated services [5] (Fig. 6).

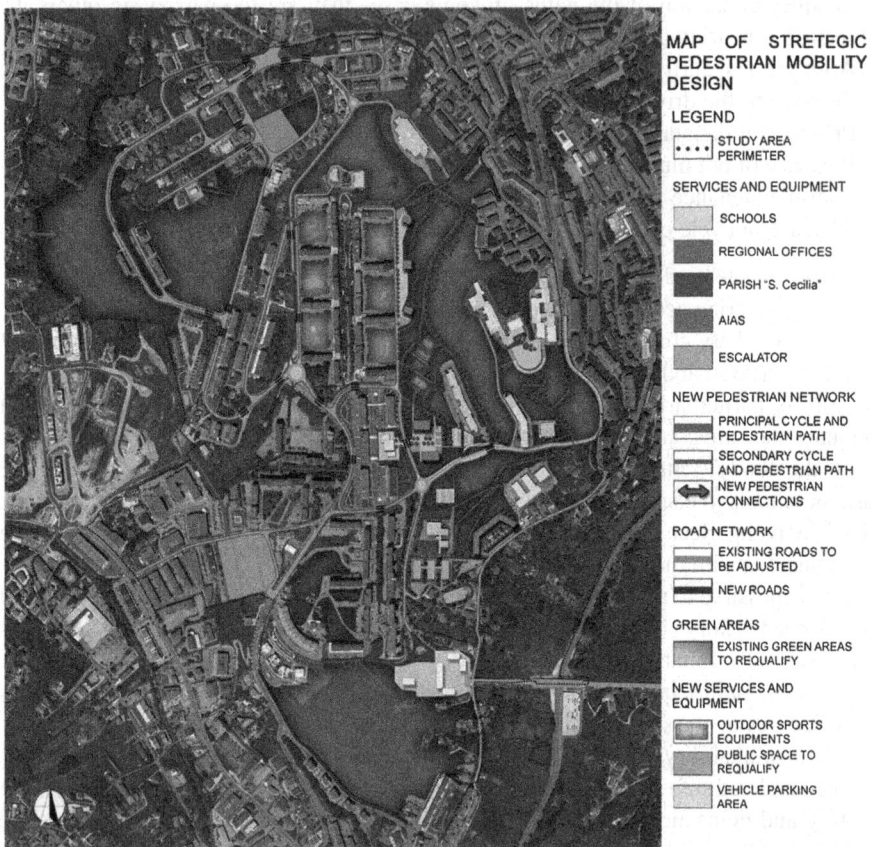

Fig. 6. Degree of urban fragmentation of 131 municipalities of Basilicata region 1989–2013.

About walkability, this proposal aims to promote sustainable mobility and to improve technology networks. This strategy generally based on the improvement of driveways, public transport system and pedestrian mobility, can be summarized in the following points:

– The functional improvement of the sections of the main road infrastructures;
– Traffic calming interventions.
– The construction of a network of pedestrian paths for reconnecting the different parts of the area.

- The adaptation of the rainwater disposal networks along the main road and in the stretches at risk of flooding.
- Through the improvement of the public lighting network (especially in the G area).

More particularly, in the workshop the following interventions have been identified:

- The improvement of the characteristics and maintenance status of the sidewalks (especially in the G area).
- The construction of secure pedestrian crossings.
- The construction of a protected pedestrian path able to connect the most popular areas.
- The functional reorganization of some streets in order to create pedestrian spaces.

4   Conclusions

The experience of the workshop described in this paper shows how it could be possible to analyse a theme and to arrive at shared choices that take into account different points of view. In particular, it demonstrates how the use of social networks, and more generally of electronic participation tools, represents a fast and solid approach through which to define a shared knowledge framework with citizens.

The urban regeneration proposal that derives from this experience gives great importance to the theme of pedestrian mobility, because its improvement would help to solve many problems exposed by the citizens who took part in the workshop, in a sustainable way.

Improving pedestrian mobility means creating the conditions for a re-appropriation of spaces. Creating an efficient pedestrian network would allow greater accessibility to green areas, to equipment and services, favouring the rehabilitation of disconnected urban areas and problems related to vehicular traffic congestion. Creating a valid alternative to the use of the private vehicle can lead to an improvement in the quality of life.

Acknowledgements. This research has been supported by the University of Basilicata, more particularly the activities developed by Raffaella Carbone are part of Smart Basilicata Project (Bando "Smart Cities and Communities and Social Innovation" Avviso MIUR n. 84/Ric2012, PON 2007 – 2013 del 2 marzo 2012) Educational Objective Three (OF3) "Smart Mobility and Urban Services".

References

1. Arras, F., et al.: Perché e come promuovere la camminabilitá urbana a partire dalle esigenze degli abitanti piú svantaggiati: il progetto "Extrapedestri. Lasciati conquistare dalla mobilità aliena!". In: International Conference Virtual City and Territory. 9° Congresso Città e Territorio Virtuale, Roma, 2, 3 e 4 ottobre 2013, pp. 185–196. Università degli Studi Roma Tre, Roma (2014)
2. Blecic, I., Cecchini, A., Fancello, G., Talu, V., Trunfio, G.: Camminabilità e capacità urbane: valutazione e supporto alla decisione e alla pianificazione urbanistica. In: Territorio Italia 2015, pp. 49–65 (2015)

3. Scorza, F., Pontrandolfi, P.: Citizen participation and technologies: the C.A.S.T. architecture. In: Gervasi, O., Murgante, B., Misra, S., Gavrilova, M.L., Rocha, A.M.A.C., Torre, C., Taniar, D., Apduhan, B.O. (eds.) ICCSA 2015. LNCS, vol. 9156, pp. 747–755. Springer, Cham (2015). https://doi.org/10.1007/978-3-319-21407-8_53

4. Pontrandolfi, P., Scorza, F.: Making urban regeneration feasible: tools and procedures to integrate urban agenda and UE cohesion regional programs. In: Gervasi, O., Murgante, B., Misra, S., Borruso, G., Torre, C.M., Rocha, A.M.A.C., Taniar, D., Apduhan, B.O., Stankova, E., Cuzzocrea, A. (eds.) ICCSA 2017. LNCS, vol. 10409, pp. 564–572. Springer, Cham (2017). https://doi.org/10.1007/978-3-319-62407-5_40

5. Pontrandolfi, P., Scorza, F.: Sustainable urban regeneration policy making: inclusive participation practice. In: Gervasi, O., Murgante, B., Misra, S., Rocha, A.M.A.C., Torre, C., Taniar, D., Apduhan, B.O., Stankova, E., Wang, S. (eds.) ICCSA 2016. LNCS, vol. 9788, pp. 552–560. Springer, Cham (2016). https://doi.org/10.1007/978-3-319-42111-7_44

6. Lanza, V., Prosperi, D.: Collaborative E-Governance: Describing and Pre-Calibrating the Digital Milieu in Urban and Regional Planning. Taylor and Francis, London (2009)

7. Las Casas, G.B., Scorza, F.: Un approccio "context-based" e "valutazione integrata" per il futuro della programmazione operativa regionale in Europa". In: Lo Sviluppo Territoriale Nell'economia Della Conoscenza: Teorie, Attori Strategie, Collana Scienze Regionali, vol. 41 (2009)

8. Las Casas, G.B., Scorza, F.: Sustainable planning: a methodological toolkit. In: Gervasi, O., et al. (eds.) ICCSA 2016. LNCS, vol. 9786, pp. 627–635. Springer, Cham (2016). https://doi.org/10.1007/978-3-319-42085-1_53

9. Gasper, D.: Evaluating the 'logical framework approach' towards learning-oriented development evaluation. Publ. Adm. Dev. **20**(1), 17 (2000)

10. Aune, J.B.: Logical framework approach. Dev. Methods Approaches, 214 (2000)

11. Harvey, D.: The right to the city. New Left Rev. **53**, 23–40 (2008)

12. Sen, A.: Commodities and Capabilities. Elsevier Science Publishers B.V, Amsterdam (1985)

13. Sen, A.: Inequality Reexamined. Oxford University Press, Oxford (1992)

14. Sen, A.: Development as Freedom. Oxford University Press, Oxford (1999)

15. Sen, A.: Capability and well-being. In: Nussbaum, M., Sen, A. (eds.) The Quality of Life, pp. 30–53. Clarendon Press, Oxford (1993)

16. Lefebvre, H.: Critica della vita quotidiana. Dedalo, Bari (1993)

17. Lefebvre, H.: Le droit à la Ville. Anthropos, Paris (1968)

18. McCann, E.J.: Space, citizenship, and the right to the city: a brief overview. Geo J. **58**, 77–79 (2002)

19. Purcell, M.: Possible worlds: henri lefebvre and the right to the city. J. Urban Aff. **36**(1), 141–154 (2014)

20. Marcuse, P.: Whose right(s) to what city. In: Brenner, N., Marcuse, P., Mayer, M. (eds.) Cities for People, Not for Profit; Critical Urban Theory and the Right to the City, pp. 24–41 (2012)

21. Cervero, R., Duncan, M.: Walking, bicycling, and urban landscapes: evidence from the San Francisco bay area. Am. J. Public Health **93**(9), 1478–1483 (2003). https://doi.org/10.2105/AJPH.93.9.1478

22. Blečić, I., Cecchini, A., Congiu, T., Fancello, G., Trunfio, G.A.: Evaluating walkability: a capability-wise planning and design support system. Int. J. Geogr. Inf. Sci. **29**(8), 1350–1374 (2015). https://doi.org/10.1080/13658816.2015.1026824

23. Carr, L., Dunsiger, S., Marcus, B.: Walk score as a global estimate of neighborhood walkability. Am. J. Prev. Med. **39**(5), 460–463 (2010). https://doi.org/10.1016/j.amepre.2010.07.007

24. Speck, J.: Walkable city. Farrar, Straus and Giroux, New York (2012)

25. Blečić, I., Canu, D., Cecchini, A., Congiu, T., Fancello, G.: Factors of perceived walkability: a pilot empirical study. In: Gervasi, O., et al. (eds.) ICCSA 2016. LNCS, vol. 9789, pp. 125–137. Springer, Cham (2016). https://doi.org/10.1007/978-3-319-42089-9_9

26. During, A.T.: The Car and the City: 24 Steps to Safe Streets and Healthy Communities. Northwest Environment Watch, Seattle (1996). No. 3

27. Ewing, R., Handy, S.: Measuring the unmeasurable: urban design qualities related to walkability. J. Urban Des. **14**(1), 65–84 (2009). https://doi.org/10.1080/13574800802451155

28. Blecic, I., Canu, D., Cecchini, A., Congiu, T., Fancello, G.: Walkability and street intersections in rural-urban fringes: a decision aiding evaluation procedure. Sustainability **9**, 883 (2017)

29. Murgante, B., Borruso, G.: Smart cities in a smart world. In: Rassia, S.T., Pardalos, P.M. (eds.) Future City Architecture for Optimal Living. SOIA, vol. 102, pp. 13–35. Springer, Cham (2015). https://doi.org/10.1007/978-3-319-15030-7_2. ISBN 978-3-319-15029-1

30. Soligno, R., Scorza, F., Amato, F., Casas, G.L., Murgante, B.: Citizens participation in improving rural communities quality of life. In: Gervasi, O., Murgante, B., Misra, S., Gavrilova, M.L., Rocha, A.M.A.C., Torre, C., Taniar, D., Apduhan, B.O. (eds.) ICCSA 2015. LNCS, vol. 9156, pp. 731–746. Springer, Cham (2015). https://doi.org/10.1007/978-3-319-21407-8_52

31. Murgante, B., Borruso, G.: Smart city or smurfs city. In: Murgante, B., et al. (eds.) ICCSA 2014. LNCS, vol. 8580, pp. 738–749. Springer, Cham (2014). https://doi.org/10.1007/978-3-319-09129-7_53

32. Pantazis, D.N., Moussas, V.C., Murgante, B., Daverona, A.C., Stratakis, P., Vlissidis, N., Kavadias, A., Economou, D., Santimpantakis, K., Karathanasis, B., Kyriakopoulou, V., Gadolou, E.: Smart sustainable Islands vs smart sustainable cities. ISPRS Ann. Photogram. Remote Sens. Spat. Inf. Sci. **3**, 45–53 (2017). https://doi.org/10.5194/isprs-annals-iv-4-w3-45-2017

33. Murgante, B., Borruso, G.: Cities and smartness: a critical analysis of opportunities and risks. In: Murgante, B., Misra, S., Carlini, M., Torre, C.M., Nguyen, H.-Q., Taniar, D., Apduhan, B.O., Gervasi, O. (eds.) ICCSA 2013. LNCS, vol. 7973, pp. 630–642. Springer, Heidelberg (2013). https://doi.org/10.1007/978-3-642-39646-5_46

34. Murgante, B., Tilio, L., Lanza, V., Scorza, F.: Using participative GIS and e-tools for involving citizens of Marmo Platano – Melandro area in European programming activities. J. Balkans Near East. Stud. **13**(1), 97–115 (2011). https://doi.org/10.1080/19448953.2011.550809. ISSN 1944-8953

35. Murgante, B.: Wiki-Planning: the experience of Basento Park in Potenza (Italy). In: Borruso, G., Bertazzon, S., Favretto, A., Murgante, B., Torre, C. (eds.) Geographic Information Analysis for Sustainable Development and Economic Planning: New Technologies, pp. 345–359. Information Science Reference IGI Global, Hershey (2012). https://doi.org/10.4018/978-1-4666-1924-1.ch023

36. Lorusso, S., Scioscia, M., Sassano, G., Graziadei, A., Passannante, P., Bellarosa, S., Scaringi, F., Murgante, B.: Involving citizens in public space regeneration: the experience of "garden in motion". In: Murgante, B., et al. (eds.) ICCSA 2014. LNCS, vol. 8580, pp. 723–737. Springer, Cham (2014). https://doi.org/10.1007/978-3-319-09129-7_52

37. Amato, F., et al.: "Serpentone Reload" an Experience of Citizens Involvement in Regeneration of Peripheral Urban Spaces. In: Gervasi, O., Murgante, B., Misra, S., Gavrilova, M.L., Rocha, A.M.A.C., Torre, C., Taniar, D., Apduhan, B.O. (eds.) ICCSA 2015. LNCS, vol. 9156, pp. 698–713. Springer, Cham (2015). https://doi.org/10.1007/978-3-319-21407-8_50

38. Rocha, M.C.F., Pereira, G.C., Murgante, B.: City visions: concepts, conflicts and participation analysed from digital network interactions. In: Gervasi, O., Murgante, B., Misra, S., Gavrilova, M.L., Rocha, A.M.A.C., Torre, C., Taniar, D., Apduhan, B.O. (eds.) ICCSA 2015. LNCS, vol. 9156, pp. 714–730. Springer, Cham (2015). https://doi.org/10.1007/978-3-319-21407-8_51
39. Rocha, M.C.F., Pereira, G.C., Loiola, E., Murgante, B.: Conversation about the city: urban commons and connected citizenship. In: Gervasi, O., et al. (eds.) ICCSA 2016. LNCS, vol. 9790, pp. 608–623. Springer, Cham (2016). https://doi.org/10.1007/978-3-319-42092-9_46
40. Sassano, G., Graziadei, A., Amato, F., Murgante, B.: Involving citizens in the reuse and regeneration of urban peripheral spaces. In: Nunes Silva, C., Buček, J. (eds.) Local Government and Urban Governance in Europe. TUBS, pp. 193–206. Springer, Cham (2017). https://doi.org/10.1007/978-3-319-43979-2_10
41. Forte, F., Girard, L.F., Nijkamp, P.: Smart policy, creative strategy and urban development - studies in regional. Science 35(4), 947–963 (2005)
42. Forte, F., Fusco Girard, L.: Creativity and new architectural assets: the complex value of beauty. Int. J. Sustain. Dev. 12, 160–191 (2009)
43. Forte, F., Russo, Y.: Evaluation of user satisfaction in public residential housing - a case study in the outskirts of Naples, Italy. IOP Conf. Ser. Mater. Sci. Eng. 245, 052063 (2017). https://doi.org/10.1088/1757-899X/245/5/052063

Workshop Defense Technology and Security (DTS 2018)

VM-CFI: Control-Flow Integrity for Virtual Machine Kernel Using Intel PT

Donghyun Kwon, Jiwon Seo, Sehyun Baek, Giyeol Kim,
Sunwoo Ahn, and Yunheung Paek$^{(\boxtimes)}$

Department of Electrical and Computer Engineering, Seoul National University,
Seoul, South Korea
{dhkwon, jwseo, shbaek, gykim, swahn}@sor.snu.ac.kr,
ypaek@snu.ac.kr

Abstract. Nowadays cloud computing technology is used for a variety of services, such as the internet of things and artificial intelligence. However, as more data is being processed in the cloud, there is growing concern about security issues in the cloud computing environment. To solve this concern, many studies have been conducted to ensure the integrity of virtual machines in a cloud computing environment. However, in the case of the control-flow integrity for the virtual machine, existing studies are not only necessary to modify the kernel code, but also cannot protect it efficiently. In this paper, we propose VM-CFI which efficiently protects the control-flow integrity of VM kernel without modification of VM kernel in cloud computing environment. For this purpose, VM-CFI utilizes Processor Trace (PT), a hardware feature that is recently supported by Intel architecture. According to the experimental results, VM-CFI incurs on average 4.2% overhead.

Keywords: Control-flow integrity · Intel Processor Trace · Cloud computing

1 Introduction

Today, through cloud computing environments, many services are being offered to people from artificial intelligence services such as speech recognition technology to internet of things services such as a smart home. As the number of such services increases, much sensitive information is processed in the cloud environment, which is causing concern about security problems in the cloud computing environment [1]. Therefore, as a way to enhance security in cloud computing environment, a cloud administrator has to ensure the integrity of the kernel of a VM in which individual cloud users execute her application. To verify memory integrity of the kernel, previous studies have examined either the hardware events occurring in the VM through virtualization, or the information which extracted when kernel executes instrumented code [2, 3].

However, existing works do not guarantee Control-Flow Integrity (CFI) of the guest OS efficiently. CFI is to check whether the target program is executed as a legitimate control-flow. CFI studies [4–6] for kernels have modified the kernel code or binary to verify the control-flow of the kernel. However, there are two reasons why this approach is difficult to use in a cloud environment. First, there is a problem that it is difficult to apply to all types of guest OS supported in a cloud environment. In the cloud computing environment, cloud administrators support a variety of vendors' kernels, and even multiple versions of each kernel. Therefore, the approach based on kernel modifications is not practical because it requires the cloud administrator to modify the kernel code or binary each time a new kernel is introduced or the kernel is patched. Next, it may also be a problem in terms of Quality of Service (QoS) guarantee of cloud users. Cloud users contract with the cloud administrator to determine the hardware resources used in the virtual machine. And while the cloud user is using it, the cloud administrator must provide a certain QoS to the cloud user according to the contract. However, if the kernel code is modified for CFI, this can cause unpredictable performance overhead and it would be difficult to guarantee QoS.

In this paper, we propose VM-CFI which protects the control-flow integrity for existing guest OS efficiently, without modification of guest OS. For this purpose, VM-CFI use a Processor Trace (PT) provided by Intel architecture. PT provides the control-flow information of the currently executed processor as a stream of the packet through the hardware, so that VM-CFI can obtain the control-flow information without modifying the kernel code of a virtual machine. In addition, since the CFI verification of VM-CFI is independently operated with the monitored virtual machine, VM-CFI imposes small performance overhead on the monitored virtual machine.

VM-CFI makes the following contributions:

(1) **No kernel modification.** We enforce control-flow integrity on guest OS without guest OS modification, so user don't need to rewrite the source code of kernel to update it.
(2) **Low overhead.** We implement VM-CFI which has low overhead by using hardware features in the Intel processor called Intel PT.

2 Background

2.1 Intel Processor Trace

Intel PT is a hardware feature provided to enable the extraction of performance flow information of Intel processors with low overhead. Intel PT stores control-flow information in a memory buffer in the form of several packets. Table 1 summarizes the packets to be used for analyzing the control-flow of the virtual machine among these packets. Intel PT also provides packet-related settings and filter-related functions depending on the purpose of use. The details of this are described in the related manual [7].

2.2 Privilege Levels on Intel Architecture

Intel architecture has a privilege level called Ring. Ring 0 is the kernel privilege and Ring 3 is the privilege that the user application is running on. Ring 0 has higher privilege than Ring 3, so the various system configuration registers can be changed only in Ring 0.

Table 1. Intel PT packets analyzed by VM-CFI

Packet name	Packet description
Paging Information Packet (PIP)	This is a packet that occurs whenever there is a change in the CR3 register that contains the current paging information. In particular, it includes non-root (NR) bits that distinguish between execution of the guest OS and execution of the host kernel
Target IP Packet (TIP)	It is a packet that records the destination address when indirect branch, exceptions, and interrupts occur
Flow Update Packets (FUP)	It is a packet that records the source address when an interrupt and exception occurs

In addition to these ring-based privileges, the virtualization extension VT-x, which is provided by Intel architecture, has a separate CPU operating mode called root/non-root. Therefore, the application of the virtual machine (Ring 3) and the kernel of the virtual machine (Ring 0) is executed in the non-root mode, and the host application (Ring 3) and the host kernel including the virtual machine manager (VMM) (Ring 0) are executed in the root mode. Switching between these root and non-root modes will result in VM entry and VM exit events. Figure 1 is an abstracted figure summarizing these terms.

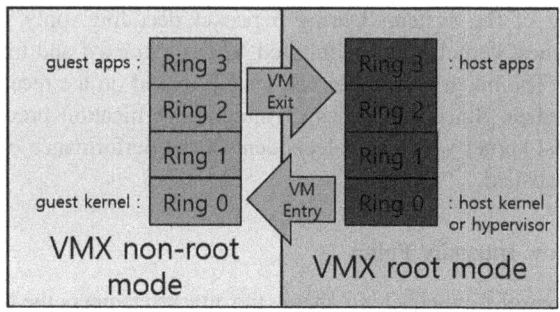

Fig. 1. Privilege levels on Intel architecture

3   Threat Model

In this paper, we assume that a remote attacker who attacks the victim's guest OS through a network connection, or a malicious user who attacks the guest OS to attack the cloud computing environment. Such an attacker does not have the right to modify the guest OS, but can perform a control-flow hijacking attack using a vulnerability existing in the guest OS.

VM-CFI, on the other hand, does not consider internal attacks which caused by a malicious cloud provider. Also, in order to protect the code integrity of existing guest OS, it is assumed that existing solutions are already adopted in the cloud environment [8], and VM-CFI only is designed to ensure CFI of the guest OS.

4 Design

4.1 Design Principles

(P1) Minimize Modification to Existing Software. A cloud provider supports various versions of the kernel for users in the cloud environment. If she need to modify the kernel to guarantee CFI, she have to revise it every time the kernel version is updated, which will result in less practicality of VM-CFI.

(P2) Minimize the Performance Overhead of Monitored Virtual Machines. Cloud users must be assured of the QoS they have contracted with the cloud provider. Therefore, if substantial performance overhead occurs in a cloud user's virtual machine to guarantee CFI, this may cause problems in terms of the QoS.

4.2 Design Overview

As shown in Fig. 2, the overall operation of VM-CFI can be divided into (1) offline binary analysis and (2) runtime integrity enforcement. In the offline binary analysis, the binary analyzer analyzes the guest kernel binary to generate the control-flow metadata to be used for the integrity verification before the monitored VM runs. In this control-flow metadata, information for each basic blocks existing in the guest kernel code is stored. At this time, as a binary of the guest OS is not modified, we can satisfy P1. Then, while the monitored VM is running, VM-CFI uses Intel PT to extract the control-flow trace of the system. During a packet decoding, only the trace corresponding to the guest kernel of the monitored VM is extracted and transmitted to the integrity checker. The integrity checker verifies CFI based on the received trace using control-flow metadata. Since this series of integrity verification process works as a process of the host kernel which is independent of the performance of the monitored VM, P2 can be satisfied.

4.3 Control-Flow Integrity Policy

In the case of a control-flow hijacking attack, the attacker tampers the control-flow and attempts to execute the malicious code. To do this, the attacker have to use a control transfer instruction. The control transfer instruction can be divided into two types. First, the direct control transfer instruction is an instruction in which the control transfer target address is stored in the code. So to exploit this instruction, an attacker should modify code memory region. However, it is well known that this code manipulating behavior can be easily defended through the existing W^X policy [8]. On the other hand, in the case of an indirect control transfer instruction, the control transfer target address is determined by the general purpose registers. Therefore, an attacker can manipulate the control-flow without modifying the code. To protect this, in VM-CFI, it is always enforced to jump to the basic block entry for the indirect control transfer instruction executed by the guest kernel.

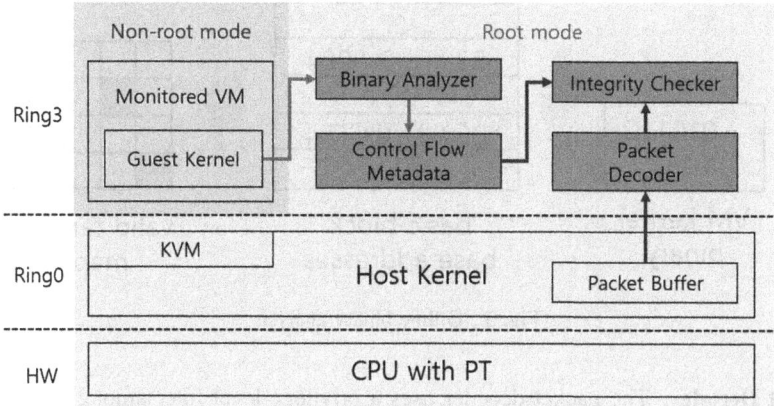

Fig. 2. System overview of VM-CFI. Modules marked with gray boxes correspond to VM-CFI, and red arrows indicate the operation of offline binary analysis. A blue arrow indicates the runtime integrity enforcement process. (Color figure online)

Since VM-CFI monitors CFI of the guest OS, in addition to branch behavior of such indirect control transfer instructions, branch behavior caused by interrupt and exception should be handled. This is because the control-flow is changed due to these events during the kernel execution, and the attacker can manipulate the control-flow in the guest OS by using this system events. For this purpose, we also have verified the return address of a handler code in hypervisor.

4.4   Offline Binary Analysis

In order to guarantee the CFI policy described above, it is necessary to know information about the start address of basic blocks existing in the guest OS code. Offline binary analysis is the process for doing this. We use *objdump* tool to disassemble the guest OS binary first, then extract the start addresses of all basic blocks in the binary. As shown in Fig. 3, we generate a valid target map that shows the valid indirect branch target address as 1 bit for each byte address of each code.

4.5   Runtime Integrity Enforcement

In VM-CFI, we used Intel PT to extract the indirect branch target address that occurred during execution of the guest kernel for integrity verification. At this time, we implemented a packet decoder to extract and analyze only the packets required for integrity verification among various kinds of packets coming from Intel PT. And the integrity checker verifies the integrity with the indirect branch target address extracted by the packet decoder.

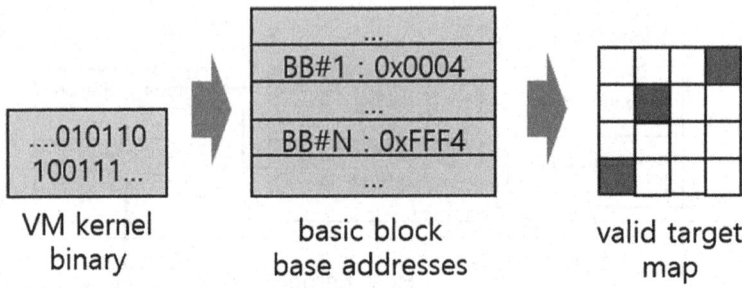

Fig. 3. Offline binary analysis

Packet Decoder. The packet decoder uses a privilege-level filter among the various filter functions provided by Intel PT. In VM-CFI, packets of guest or host user applications (programs executed in Ring 3) can be excluded. In addition, timing information and power events, which are not related to integrity verification, are set so that packets are not generated.

For the extracted packets, the packet decoder implements two functions to select only the information needed for integrity verification. First, the packet decoder distinguishes packets for the host kernel and the guest kernel. Fortunately, Intel PT knows the root/non-root mode through the PIP packet at the VM-entry/VM-exit, so that the packet decoder can distinguish it. Besides this method, there is a alternative method to enable trace packet generation in virtual machine only by using MSR load list in VM entry and VM exit respectively. However, VM-CFI does not use this method because it can only use Intel PT in non-root mode. Therefore, in VM-CFI, we design the packet decoder to identify the packet of the guest kernel. Next, in the packet decoder, only the TIP packet containing the target address information of the indirect branch among the control-flow related packets and the FUP containing the source address information are extracted and hand over to the integrity checker.

Integrity Checker. The Integrity Checker verified the integrity through the control information delivered by the packet decoder as shown in Fig. 4. We want VM-CFI to check two things: whether (1) the target address is in the valid target map (2) the address which the interrupt handler jumps from is the same as the address returned from interrupt hadler. First, if the packet transmitted by the packet decoder is a FUP packet (not a TIP packet), the corresponding source address is pushed onto the async-event stack, and the next packet is processed. If the packet is a TIP packet, check the corresponding bit of the valid target map for the target address to determine whether or not the base address of the basic block is valid. If the bit value is 1, the next packet is processed since it is a branch of the normal control-flow. If the bit value is 0, it confirms whether the control-flow branch is caused by the asynchronous event. That is, compare the top element of the async-event stack with the target address. To deal with the case where the target address points to the next instruction of the address indicated by the top element, the case is treated as a normal case when the difference is within 0xf, and then the corresponding value is popped on the stack before the next packet is processed. If it does not correspond to the top element, it is regarded as an attack.

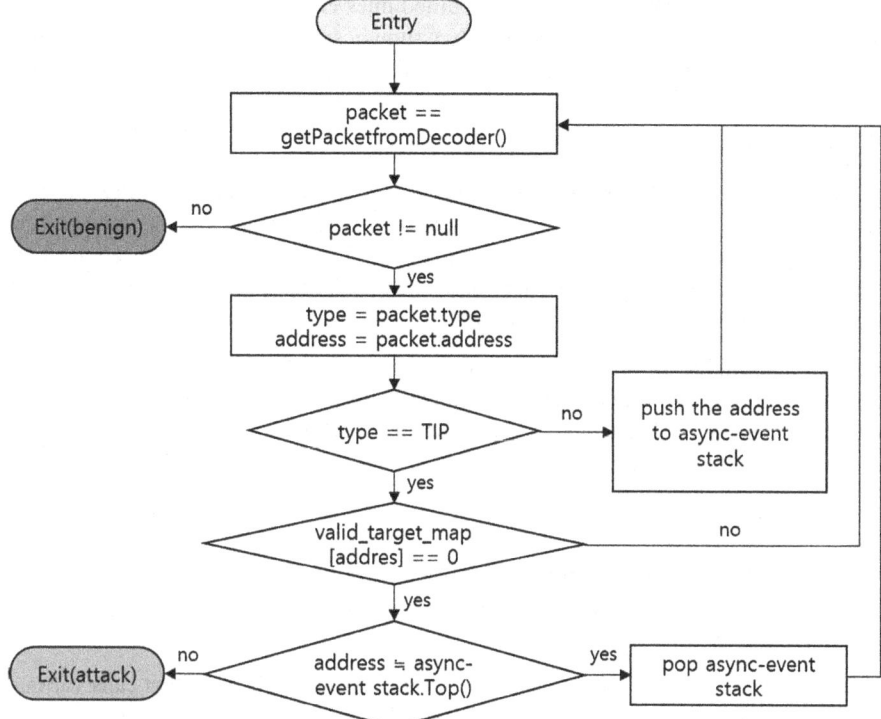

Fig. 4. Work flow of integrity checker

5   Evaluation

In this chapter, we will evaluate performance overhead due to VM-CFI and whether it can detect control-flow hijacking attacks targeting guest OS.

5.1   Experiment Environment

We have implemented a prototype of VM-CFI in real physical machine. The used machine has specifications of 4 Intel Core i5-6600 CPU @ 3.30 GHz and 4 GB RAM, and both the host kernel and the guest kernel use version 4.8.0 of linux. We used KVM as the hypervisor.

5.2   Prototype Implementation

As previously mentioned in the design, VM-CFI is implemented in the host kernel application without modifying the kernel. The binary analyzer is implemented by parsing the output file obtained by dumping the kernel binary with objdump, and implemented with 98 SLoC. The packet decoder and integrity checker are implemented by modifying the perf tool, which is provided for performance measurement and debugging in linux, and the number of modified lines is 244 SLoC. As such, VM-CFI guarantees virtual machine integrity by only writing a small amount of code in the user application without modification of the host and guest kernels.

5.3   Performance Evaluation

In order to measure the performance overhead of VM-CFI, we conducted two experiments. First, we measured the execution time of VM-CFI to analyze the control-flow of the virtual machine and to verify the integrity. Next we conduct an application benchmark experiment to conform that there is no performance overhead of the virtual machine despite the operation of VM-CFI.

Micro-benchmarks. In order to measure the time taken for VM-CFI to analyze the control-flow information and verify the integrity of the virtual machine during the execution of the virtual machine, we conducted a performance measurement experiment for the following cases.

- async-event-only: Validate only the async-event through the virtual machine's control-flow packet
- decode-only: Parse the control-flow packets of the virtual machine in VM-CFI
- vm-cfi: Parse the control-flow packet of the virtual machine through VM-CFI and verify integrity.

In the experiment, the virtual machine executes a user application that calls various system calls, and analyzes the resulting packets. As a result, it is confirmed that it takes about 10 s to process the packet of 20 MB in Fig. 5.

Application-Benchmarks. The following experiment was designed to measure the performance overhead on the virtual machine by VM-CFI. First, the virtual machine to be monitored is executed in core 0, and VM-CFI is executed in core 1. (This assumption is identical to the one used in previous Intel PT-based studies [9, 10].) Table 2 compares the performance of VM-CFI with the performance of Unixbench in the virtual machine, and summarizes the performance overhead. The result was an average performance overhead of 4.2%. This overhead is caused by memory virtualization during VM-CFI operation because memory is a computing resource used by VM-CFI and virtual machine simultaneously.

5.4   Security Evaluation

VM-CFI is designed to guarantee CFI of the guest OS. In this chapter, we have actually launched a rootkit attack which manipulate control-flow of guest OS. The rootkit attack modifies the data structure related to the virtual file system (VFS) managed by the guest OS. Specifically it modifies the function pointer associated with the file operation of the specific file. When the function pointer used later, the attack code injected by the attacker is executed instead of the normal file operation function. As a result, VM-CFI analyzes the indirect call packet generated at the moment when the attack code is executed by referring the manipulated function pointer, and confirms that it is not in the valid target map.

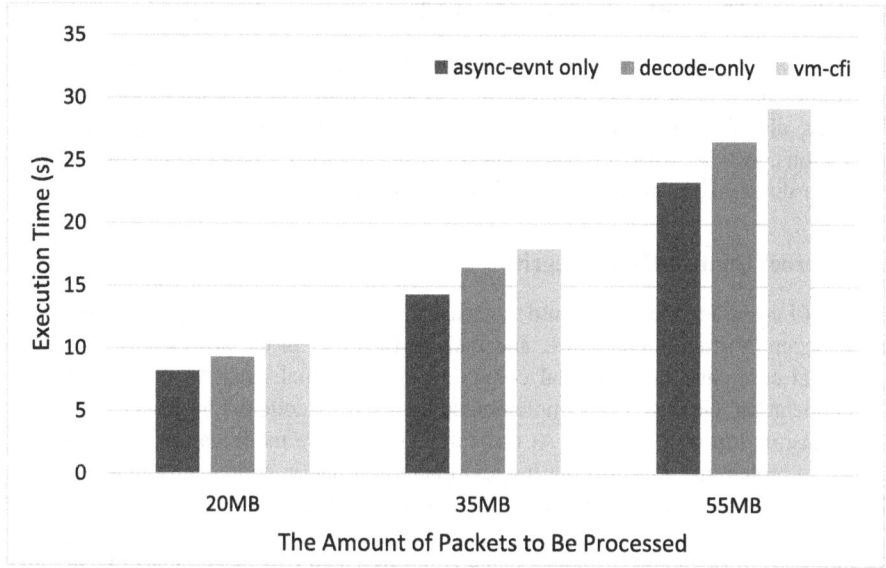

Fig. 5. Micro-benchmark experimental results. The horizontal axis indicates the amount of packets to be processed, and the vertical axis indicates the execution time (s).

Table 2. Unixbench performance overhead of virtual machines

Benchmark	Performance overhead
hanoi	2.5%
arith	2.5%
int	2.7%
syscall	7.8%
dhry	5.8%
context1	2.6%
spawn	5.4%
average	4.2%

6 Related Work

6.1 Virtual Machine Introspection

VMI researches have been examined to verify the state of each virtual machine in the cloud environment [2, 3]. These studies basically use virtualization technology or binary modification technology to monitor the hardware resources used by the virtual machine, or extract information about various events that occur when the virtual machine is running. However, there are no studies to efficiently extract the control-flow information of the guest OS. VM-CFI efficiently extracts and processes this information using Intel PT to ensure CFI for the guest OS.

6.2   Control-Flow Integrity Using Intel PT

Recently, Intel PT has been able to efficiently extract new execution flow information, and studies have been made to maintain execution flow integrity by using it [9–11]. However, all of these studies are different from run-time integrity studies for user applications, in that VM-CFI targets guest OS in the cloud environment. Specifically, there is a difference in processing Intel PT packets due to asynchronous events.

6.3   Kernel Control-Flow Integrity

KCoFI [4] compiles the kernel into a virtual instruction in a virtualized environment called Secure Virtual Architecture, and then verifies CFI in the process of converting the virtual command to the actual command in the virtual machine manager during kernel operation. Ge et al. [5] is implemented by inserting code that verifies CFI of each branch instruction of the kernel. At this time, kernel code modification is also implemented to protect the table storing the legitimate destination address from the attacker. On the other hand, krx [6] blocked the kernel code from being readable and defended against the Just-In-Time Code Reuse Attack for the kernel by arbitrarily randomizing the addresses of the codes. There is also a study to verify CFI of the guest OS in units of memory pages [12]. Although the previous technique has something in common in that it verifies CFI for the kernel, there is a limitation in practically applying all of the kernel code to recompile or modify a lot of parts. However, VM-CFI ensures CFI for the guest OS without these modifications.

7   Future Work

Our concern about VM-CFI is that the packet buffer could become full before integrity checks executed by VM-CFI are done. In this case, VM-CFI can only either protect guest OS in real time, or check all the packets generated by Intel PT. Even though this case did not occur in our experiment, the possibility still remains. We expect this problem to be solved by using multi-processor or GPU in decoding packets and integrity check, and it remains as the future work.

8   Conclusion

VM-CFI is a Control-Flow Integrity study for guest OS. Compared to kernel CFI studies with modifications to existing kernel code, VM-CFI uses hardware features called Intel PT to verify CFI of the virtual machine with a 4.2% lower overhead without modifying kernel code.

Acknowledgements. We thank anonymous reviewers for the support and insightful remarks that improved the paper. This work was supported by Institute for Information & communications Technology Promotion (IITP) grant funded by the Korea government (MSIP) (No. 2016-0-00078, Cloud based Security Intelligence Technology Development for the Customized Security Service Provisioning) and by the National Research Foundation of Korea

(NRF) grant funded by the Korea government (MSIP) (NRF-2017R1A2A1A17069478). This research was also supported by the MSIT (Ministry of Science and ICT), Korea, under the ITRC (Information Technology Research Center) support program (IITP-2017-2015-0-00403) supervised by the IITP (Institute for Information & communications Technology Promotion).

References

1. Samarati, P., di Vimercati, S.D.C., Murugesan, S., Bojanova, I.: Cloud security: issues and concerns. Encycl. Cloud Comput. 1–14 (2016)
2. Zeng, J., Fu, Y., Lin, Z.: Pemu: a pin highly compatible out-of-vm dynamic binary instrumentation framework. In: ACM SIGPLAN Notices, vol. 50, pp. 147–160. ACM (2015)
3. Xiong, H., Liu, Z., Xu, W., Jiao, S.: Libvmi: a library for bridging the semantic gap between guest os and VMM. In: 2012 IEEE 12th International Conference on Computer and Information Technology (CIT), pp. 549–556. IEEE (2012)
4. Criswell, J., Dautenhahn, N., Adve, V.: KCoFI: complete control-flow integrity for commodity operating system kernels. In: 2014 IEEE Symposium on Security and Privacy (SP), pp. 292–307. IEEE (2014)
5. Ge, X., Talele, N., Payer, M., Jaeger, T.: Fine-grained control-flow integrity for kernel software. In: 2016 IEEE European Symposium on Security and Privacy (EuroS&P), pp. 179–194. IEEE (2016)
6. Pomonis, M., Petsios, T., Keromytis, A.D., Polychronakis, M., Kemerlis, V.P.: kR^ X: comprehensive kernel protection against just-in-time code reuse. In: Proceedings of the Twelfth European Conference on Computer Systems, pp. 420–436. ACM (2017)
7. Seshadri, A., Luk, M., Qu, N., Perrig, A.: SecVisor: a tiny hypervisor to provide lifetime kernel code integrity for commodity OSes. In: ACM SIGOPS Operating Systems Review, vol. 41, pp. 335–350. ACM (2007)
8. Guide, P.: Intel® 64 and IA-32 Architectures Software Developer's Manual. Volume 3B: System programming Guide, Part 2 (2011)
9. Ge, X., Cui, W., Jaeger, T.: GRIFFIN: guarding control flows using intel processor trace. In: Proceedings of the Twenty-Second International Conference on Architectural Support for Programming Languages and Operating Systems, pp. 585–598. ACM (2017)
10. Gu, Y., Zhao, Q., Zhang, Y., Lin, Z.: PT-CFI: transparent backward-edge control flow violation detection using intel processor trace. In: Proceedings of the Seventh ACM on Conference on Data and Application Security and Privacy, pp. 173–184. ACM (2017)
11. Liu, Y., Shi, P., Wang, X., Chen, H., Zang, B., Guan, H.: Transparent and efficient CFI enforcement with intel processor trace. In: 2017 IEEE International Symposium on High Performance Computer Architecture (HPCA), pp. 529–540. IEEE (2017)
12. Zhan, D., Ye, L., Fang, B., Zhang, H., Du, X.: Checking virtual machine kernel control-flow integrity using a page-level dynamic tracing approach. Soft Comput. 1–11 (2017)

Study on Classification of Defense Scientific and Technical Information in Korea

Ara Hur and Yeonseung Ryu[⊠]

Department of Security Management Engineering, Myongji University, Yongin,
Gyeonggi-do, Korea
ara7494@gmail.com, ysryu@mju.ac.kr

Abstract. The Korean government enacted the Defense Industrial Technology Security Act in 2015 and announced the list of defense industrial technologies to be protected for national security. Accordingly, defense industry companies should establish the defense technology protection system and protect the defense industrial technology information designated by law. Currently the Korean government is trying to develop the classification system of defense scientific and technical information. In this paper, we study a classification system of defense scientific and technical information. To do this, we analyze the directives currently operated by the Ministry of National Defense of Korea and the classification system of scientific and technical information of the US Department of Defense. Then, we propose a classification system which is based on Korean system and adopts the US system to supplement the shortcomings.

Keywords: Defense industry · Defense scientific and technical information
Classification · National security · Protection

1 Introduction

National defense science and technology is defined as the science and technology used in weapon systems and fighting power support systems to build and maintain defense capabilities [1]. In the past few decades, Korea has sought to raise the level of defense science and technology. As a key strategy for the promotion of defense science and technology, Korea has pursued expansion of defense research and development base, activation of civil and military technical cooperation, strengthening international competitiveness of defense science and technology and so on. Accordingly, the level of defense science and technology of Korea is highly evaluated and ranked ninth in the world in 2015 [2].

With the development of technology and the increasing risks of leakage of defense technology information, the Korea government enacted the "Defense Industrial Technology Security Act" in 2015 and designated 141 items of defense industrial technology in December 2016 [3, 4]. However, designated institutions such as defense companies have difficulty in identifying their defense industrial technologies and establishing the protection system. Besides identification of the defense industrial technologies, it is necessary to establish the method of assigning importance level for defense industrial technical information.

© Springer International Publishing AG, part of Springer Nature 2018
O. Gervasi et al. (Eds.): ICCSA 2018, LNCS 10964, pp. 138–147, 2018.
https://doi.org/10.1007/978-3-319-95174-4_11

Before enacting the Defense Industrial Technology Security Act, the defense companies have protected the classified information such as military secrets and defense industrial classified information according to the Ministry of National Defense order named "Order for Defense Industrial Security Duties". This order instructs procedures about document security, personnel security, facility security, information communication security, and so on. Furthermore, the order explains the classification of military secrets. The order instructs which classification level is applied to defense industrial classified information. Among defense industrial classified information, some technical information must be classified as military secret. For example, integrated blueprint of critical parts of submarine should be classified as secret. However, when technical information is about designated defense industrial technology but is not classified as military secret by the Order for Defense Industrial Security Duties, there is not any classification system that deals with how to classify it.

In this paper, we propose a classification system of defense scientific and technical information in Korea. To do this, we first analysis the science and technology management directives currently operated by the Ministry of National Defense of Korea and the classification system of scientific and technical information of the US Department of Defense. Then, we propose a classification system which is based on Korean system and partly adopts the US system to supplement the current shortcomings. The proposed classification system of defense scientific and technical information can be used by both defense agencies and defense companies in order to protect the designated defense industrial technology appropriately.

The rest of this paper is organized as follows. In Sect. 2, we introduce the background of defense scientific and technical information classification system. We also explain the classification system of Korea and the United States. In Sect. 3, we propose a classification system of defense scientific and technical information that can be used by defense companies in Korea. Finally, Sect. 4 describes conclusion.

2 Background of Defense Scientific and Technical Information Classification

2.1 Classification System of Defense Scientific and Technical Information in Korea

The Korean government has enacted the Presidential Order "Security Operational Regulation" to safeguard the confidential information produced by the executive departments and agencies. Each department should establish own regulation in accordance with the Presidential Order. The Ministry of National Defense has also established the regulation named "Order for Defense Security Duties". This order prescribes a system for classifying, safeguarding, and declassifying the military secret. According to the Order for Defense Security Duties, military secret is classified into three levels as shown in Table 1.

Table 1. Classification levels of military secret

Level	Definition
Top secret (TS)	Information that lead to exceptionally grave damage if leaked
Secret (S)	Information that cause serious damage to national security if leaked
Confidential (C)	Information that cause damage to national security if leaked

In Korea, the defense science and technology is basically owned by government. In other words, the Ministry of National Defense and its affiliated organizations such as the Defense Acquisition Program Administration (DAPA) and the Defense Agency for Technology and Quality (DTAQ) own the defense science and technology. The defense industry company receives the R&D project grants from the DAPA and develops the defense materials including weapons systems. The result of research and development, defense technology, will be delivered to the DAPA and ownership will be attributed to the government. Currently, the Korean government has designated about 100 defense industry companies for the stable production of defense materials.

In order to manage the defense scientific and technical information systematically, DAPA has established a guideline named "Guideline for Defense Scientific and Technical Information Management". According to the guideline, the technology-owned institutions register the defense scientific and technical information in DTiMS[1]. When providing technical information to DTiMS, they shall assign the protection class to it according to the release range after security review. As shown in Table 2, there are four protection classes and their release ranges. The protection class is given to limit the scope of disclosure per DTiMS user according to the importance of technical information.

The Ministry of National Defense has established an order named "Order for Defense Industrial Security Duties" in order to provide a guideline to defense companies. The defense companies must obey this order to protect the classified information such as military secrets and defense industrial classified information. This order instructs procedures about document security, personnel security, facility security, information communication security, and so on. Furthermore, the order explains the classification of military secret, which follows the Order for Defense Security Duties.

The Order for Defense Industrial Security Duties instructs which classification level is applied to defense industrial classified information. Among defense industrial classified information, some defense technical information must be classified as military secret. For example, integrated blueprint of critical parts of submarine should be classified as Secret level military secret and software related to electronic warfare equipment also should be classified as secret level.

---

[1] Defense Technology Information Management System: Integrated information service system for the latest defense technology and weapons system technology information operated by the Defense Agency for Technology and Quality (DTAQ).

Table 2. Protection classes of defense scientific and technical information [1]

Protection class	Release range	Classification criteria (some)	Examples
Defense network limited information	Technology holding organizations (information generating organizations) and program related organizations (departments)	• It is necessary to limit the scope of disclosure of defense technical information not classified as secret or confidential because it is sensitive to disclosure outside organizations	i. Information that restricts the disclosure of defense agencies due to contracts ii. Information requested by the technology holding organization to be classified as limited information on the defense network
Defense network general information	Defense related organizations (agencies that can use defense network)	• In the event that leak age of data to the outside of the defense organization may cause damage to the performance of the work	i. General information of Defense R&D projects ii. Among the technical data acquired through the purchase of weapons systems, information that can be disclosed to defense related organizations iii. Defense standard related information like specification, drawings, etc.
Internet network limited information	Defense related organizations and registrars/companies	• It does not include the performance and specific technologies of the weapon system, and can be released by the inspection procedure to the registrars/companies other than the defense organizations for the purpose of R&D recycling	i. Information on munitions and standard/commercial items that can be released to restricted users for the private procurement ii. Configuration information such as standard drawings, for which a decision is made to open the Internet to limited users
Internet network general information	Public	• It can be opened without any restriction in order to expand private sector utilization of defense science and technology	i. Public information about defense research and development program (excluding weapon system R&D program and ADD-directed development program) ii. Technical information that can be transferred to private company iii. Information about industrial property rights (patent) and academic papers iv. List of technical data acquired through offset program

2.2 Classification System of Defense Scientific and Technical Information in the US

2.2.1 Classification System of the US National Information

In the United States, the Presidential Executive Order 13526, Classified National Security Information, prescribes a uniform system for classifying, safeguarding, and declassifying national security information, including information relating to defense against transnational terrorism [5, 6, 9]. Typically, Executive Order 13526 defined:

- who in the federal government may classify information,
- what levels of classification and classification markings (e.g., "top secret") may be used,
- who may access classified information, and
- how and when classified information is to be declassified.

According to the Executive Order 13526, information may be classified at one of the following three levels (Table 3):

Table 3. Classification levels of classified information

Level	Definition
Top secret	Information that lead to exceptionally grave damage if leaked
Secret	Information that cause serious damage to national security if leaked
Confidential	Information that cause damage to national security if leaked

Further, the order limits classification to information that pertains to:

- military planning, weapons systems, military operations
- foreign government information
- intelligence activity, intelligent sources or methods, or cryptology
- foreign relations or foreign activities of the United States, including confidential source
- scientific, technological, or economic matters relating to the national security
- United States Government programs for safeguarding nuclear materials or facilities
- vulnerabilities or capabilities of systems, installations, infrastructures, projects, plans, or protection services relating to the national security
- the development, production, or use of weapons of mass destruction

Therefore, the scientific and technical information related to national security should be classified as shown in Table 4.

The Presidential Executive Order 13556, Controlled Unclassified Information, specifies controlled unclassified information (CUI) [7]. This order establishes an open and uniform program for managing information that requires safeguarding or dissemination controls pursuant to and consistent with law, regulations, and Government-wide policies, excluding information that is classified under Executive Order 13526.

Table 4. Classification levels of scientific and technological information

Level	Examples
Top secret	R&D information or engineering · scientific · technical information that would result in strategic disruption if leaked
Secret	R&D information or engineering · scientific · technical information that would result in loss of cutting-edge technology or operational efficiency reduction of cutting-edge system if leaked
Confidential	R&D information or engineering · scientific · technical information that would threat the capability to perform war if leaked

Prior to 2010, more than 2,200 government agencies in the United States had become increasingly confused as they managed various forms of CUI [8]. Each executive departments and agencies apply their own ad-hoc policies and markings to unclassified information that requires safeguarding or dissemination controls, resulting in inconsistent marking and safeguarding of documents, unclear or unnecessarily restrictive dissemination policies, and impediments to authorized information sharing. Accordingly, in November 2010, the Presidential Executive Order 13556 was enacted to manage the unified CUI at the national level. This order establishes a program for managing information, described as controlled unclassified information, that emphasizes the openness and uniformity of Government-wide practice. CUI office collects CUI from executive governments and agencies, and makes standard for category and subcategory of CUI. The CUI information is registered in the CUI registry at https://www.archives.gov/cui.

Among the categories, there is "Controlled Technical Information (CTI)" category in "Procurement and Acquisition" organizational index group. Controlled Technical Information means technical information with military or space application that is subject to controls on the access, use, reproduction, modification, performance, display, release, disclosure, or dissemination. Examples of technical information include research and engineering data, engineering drawings, and associated lists, specifications, standards, process sheets, manuals, technical reports, technical orders, catalog-item identifications, data sets, studies and analyses and related information, and computer software executable code and source code.

According to these two executive orders (13526 and 13556), we can summarize that the United States categorizes the national information handled by government agencies into three types: (i) classified information, (ii) controlled unclassified information (CUI), and (iii) unclassified information as shown in Fig. 1.

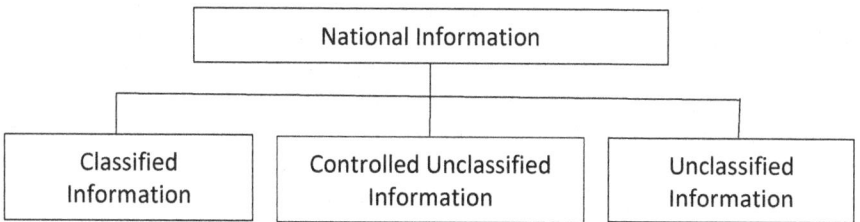

Fig. 1. Classification of US national information

2.2.2 Classification System of Defense Scientific and Technical Information

The US Department of Defense (DoD) prescribes directives for management and protection of classified information and CUI, which is DoD Manual 5200.01, DoD Information Security Program. This manual consists of a total of 4 volumes, volumes 1, 2, and 3 deals with the management and protection of classified information, and volume 4 covers the management, protection, and distribution of CUI (Table 5).

Table 5. DoD Manual 5200.01

Volume	Title
Volume 1	DoD information security program: overview, classification and declassification
Volume 2	DoD information security program: marking of classified information
Volume 3	DoD information security program: protection of classified information
Volume 4	DoD information security program: controlled unclassified information

The US DoD defines the scientific and technical information acquired through research and development program as "STI (Scientific and Technical Information)" and operates directives, instructions and manuals as shown in Table 6.

Table 6. DoD Instructions related to scientific and technical information management

Number	Title
DoDI 3200.12	DoD scientific and technical information program (STIP)
DoDM 3200.14, volume 1	principles and operational parameters of the dod scientific and technical information program (STIP): general processes
DoDM 3200.14, volume 2	Principles and operational parameters of the dod scientific and technical information program (STIP): information analysis center
DoDI 5230.24	Distribution statements on technical documents
DoDD 5105.73	Defense technical information center (DTIC)
DoDD 5230.25	Withholding of unclassified technical data from public disclosure

In DoDI 3200.12, STI is defined as findings and technological innovations resulting from R&E efforts and science and technology work of scientists, researchers, and engineers, whether contractor, grantee, or federal staff. STI also conveys the results of demonstration and commercial application activities as well as experiments, observations, simulations, studies, and analyses. STI is found in many forms and formats including textual, graphical, numeric, multimedia, and digital data, technical reports, scientific and technical conference papers and presentations, theses and dissertations, scientific and technical computer software, journal articles, workshop reports, program documents, patents, and other forms or formats of technical data.

STI may be classified, controlled unclassified information (including export controlled or personally identifiable information), or unclassified publically releasable. DoD components have the responsibility to ensure that STI is marked in accordance with DoDI 5230.24 and DoDM 5200.01. STI must be protected in the interest of national security, in accordance with Executive Order 13526 as described in 2.2.1. All DoD components generating or responsible for technical documents shall determine their distribution availability and mark them appropriately before primary distribution. Distribution statements shall be used in addition to applicable classification and dissemination control markings specified in volume 2 of DoDI 5200.01.

STI may disclose information registered at the Technology Defense Information Center (DTIC). DTIC should keep all documents and records created by the Department of Defense internal and external science and technology aid projects. Distribution statements assigned to technical documents by the controlling DoD office that sponsored the work are used to control the secondary distribution of those documents through use of the DoD-wide "Registration System for Scientific and Technical Information," administered by DTIC, in accordance with DoDM 3200.14. All newly created, revised, or previously unmarked classified and unclassified DoD technical documents shall be assigned Distribution Statement A, B, C, D, E, or F as shown in Table 7.

Table 7. Distribution statement of STI

Distribution statement	Meaning
A	Public release
B	Distributed to US Government agencies
C	Distributed to US Government agencies and their contractors
D	Distributed to the US department of Defense and its contractors
E	Distribution only to DoD components
F	Further dissemination only as directed by or higher DoD authority

3 Proposed Classification of Defense Scientific and Technical Information

In this section, we propose a classification system of defense scientific and technical information in Korea. As explained in 2.2, some defense technical information must be classified as military secret according to the Order for Defense Industrial Security Duties. For example, integrated blueprint of critical parts of submarine and software related to electronic warfare equipment should be classified as Secret level military secret. However, when technical information is about the defense industrial technology designated by Defense Industrial Technology Security Act but is not classified as military secret by the Order for Defense Industrial Security Duties, there is not any classification system that deals with how to classify it.

Prior to the enforcement of the Defense Industrial Technology Security Act, defense scientific and technical information is classified into two classes: military secret and general information. Military secret is classified into three levels as shown in Table 1. Since June 2016, however, if general information is identified as defense industrial technical information, it should be protected by Defense Industrial

Technology Security Act. Currently, the Guideline for Defense Scientific and Technical Information Management prescribes four protection classes of defense scientific and technical information as shown in Table 2.

In this work, we synthesis the classification levels of the Order for Defense Industrial Security Duties and the protection classes of the Guideline for defense scientific and technical information management [10]. And we propose a classification system for Korea's defense scientific and technical information as shown in Table 8. We define three classes of information: secret information, controlled technical information and public information. The secret information class has two levels, II and III, which correspond with Secret and Confidential level of military secret, respectively. The controlled technical information is information that is not secret, but must be protected according to its importance. It has two levels, A and B, which correspond with 'defense network limited information' and 'defense network general information' protection class in Table 2. The public information can be opened without any restriction.

Table 8. Proposed classification classes and levels for defense scientific and technical information

Class level		Classification criteria
Secret information	II	• Follow the classification criteria of order for defense industrial security duties
	III	
Controlled technical information	A	• If it is not classified as secret, but it is sensitive to disclosure outside related organizations
	B	• In the event that leakage of data to the outside of the defense organization may cause damage to the performance of the work • When public information is limited by request from foreign government/company
Public information		• It can be opened without any restriction

Figure 2 shows the proposed classification system of defense scientific and technical information. This is very similar to that of the United States (see Fig. 1). The United States has established the Controlled Unclassified Information (CUI) system since 2010 in accordance with the Presidential Executive Order 13556. However, Korea does not yet have such a government-wide information classification system and thus defense agencies also do not have a classification system for classifying, safeguarding, and declassifying the unclassified but need-to-protect information. The proposal of this work can contribute to build the basis of such information classification system in Korea.

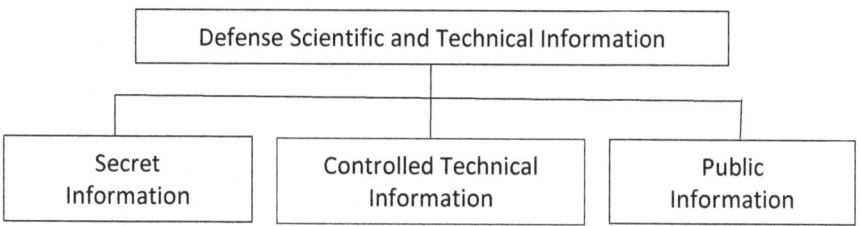

Fig. 2. Classification of defense scientific and technical information

4   Conclusion

With the development of defense technology, the Korea government enacted the Defense Industrial Technology Security Act in 2015. However, there is not yet any classification system for defense scientific and technical information which is unclassified but is need-to-protect.

In this paper, we analyze the related regulations currently operated by Korea and the United States. Then, we propose a classification system which partly adopts the US system to make up for the weakness of the Korean system. This study can contribute not only to establishing the classification system of defense information but also to building the basis of information classification system in Korea.

References

1. Guideline for Defense Scientific and Technical Information Management, Korea Defense Acquisition Program Administration Established Rule No. 356 (2017)
2. Defense Science and Technology Level Survey, Korea Defense Science and Technology Quality Agency (2015)
3. Defense Industrial Technology Security Act, Korea Ministry of National Defense (2015)
4. Study on Identification of Defense Industrial Technology, Korea Defense Acquisition Program Administration Research Report (2014)
5. Barack, H.O.: Classified National Security Information, Executive Order 13526 (2009)
6. Wolsoo, J.: National secret classification system of the United States. Korea Defense Issue Anal. **1638**, 16–41 (2016)
7. Barack, H.O.: Controlled Unclassified Information, Executive Order 13556 (2010)
8. Knezo, J.: Sensitive but unclassified and other federal security controls on scientific and technical information: history and current controversy. Defense Technical Information Center. http://www.dtic.mil/docs/citations/ADA437391. Accessed 30 Apr (2018)
9. Raymond, S.: Identification and protection of critical program information (CPI). In: 18th Annual NDIA Systems Engineering Conference (2016)
10. Ara, H.: A study on the classification system of technical information in the defense industry. MS thesis, Department of Security Management Engineering. Myongji University, Yongin, Korea (2018)

A FPGA-Based Scheme for Protecting Weapon System Software Technology

Minhae Jang[1], Yeonseung Ryu[1(✉)], and Hyunkyoo Park[2]

[1] Department of Security Management Engineering, Myongji University,
Yongin, Gyeonggi-Do, Korea
jully6363@naver.com, ysryu@mju.ac.kr
[2] Petabi Korea, Seoul, Korea
hyunkyupark@petabi.com

Abstract. Recently the Korean government has established a law to protect the defense industrial technology for the sake of national security and is trying to apply the anti-tamper methodology to weapon systems acquisition programs. The anti-tamper refers to the system engineering activity to protect critical information in systems from tampering and reverse engineering. Adversary's malicious tampering can weaken our military advantage, shorten the expected combat life of our system, and erode our defense industrial technological competitiveness. In this paper, we introduce the overview of the anti-tampering techniques and suggest a software protection technique using FPGA which can be efficiently used for weapon systems.

Keywords: Weapon systems · Anti-tamper · FPGA · Software protection

1 Introduction

The Korean government has invested about tens of billions of dollars every year in developing the weapon systems and technologies. According to the Korea National Defense Science and Technology Survey, the Korea's defense technology level is about 81% of the United States, which is the most advanced country, and the ranking is ranked ninth in the world in 2015. In recent years, the export of military goods such as battle ships, training fighter and self-propelled guns has increased and the number of exporting countries has also increased significantly. Besides, Korea imports a large number of weapons from many countries including the United States and is required to have a security system that protects the technologies implemented in imported weapon systems. If importing countries tamper with weapon systems to acquire military technologies, military advantage of exporting country can be weaken and the expected combat life of weapon systems can be shorten. Therefore, since 1999 the United States applies anti-tamper technology to ensure that importing countries do not reverse the weapon technology when exporting their weapon systems [1–4].

In the 1970s, the United States was friendly with Iran and sold the Iranians 80 F-14 Tomcats. The United States also provided flight training to Iranian pilots and support crew training in conjunction with the sale. Overall, an estimated $4 billion dollars of

© Springer International Publishing AG, part of Springer Nature 2018
O. Gervasi et al. (Eds.): ICCSA 2018, LNCS 10964, pp. 148–157, 2018.
https://doi.org/10.1007/978-3-319-95174-4_12

hardware was purchased by Iran in order to upgrade their Air Force. However, in the late 1970s, the Islamic Revolution occurred, which led to a hostile regime change. Now the United States made F-14s in hostile regime's possession. There was no anti-tamper technology in place to counter the exploitation of weapon system and critical technologies. The weapon systems and technologies can be exposed to the risk of compromise when they are exported, stolen, lost during combat, or damaged during routine missions. When weapon technologies are compromised, it can weaken military advantage, shorten the expected combat life of a system, and erode the industrial base's technological competitiveness in the international marketplace. In an effort to protect weapons and technologies from exploitation, the United States established a policy in 1999 to implement anti-tamper techniques, which include software and hardware protective devices, when technologies are determined to be critical and vulnerable to exploitation [1].

Recently Korean government established a law to protect the defense industrial technology for national security and is making an effort to apply the anti-tamper methodology to weapon systems acquisition program. Further Korean government will invest in the development of anti-tamper technology. The weapon system is becoming the embedded system consisting of hardware and software, and thus critical technology to be protected is implemented by hardware or software. Some anti-tamper technologies include software encryption, integrated circuit protection coating, and hardware access denied systems. Use of anti-tamper protection technologies must be refined according to the technologies to be protected. For example, the latest technology in critical characteristics usually requires more sophisticated anti-tamper applications.

In this paper, we study a software protection technique using Field Programmable Gate Array (FPGA) which can be efficiently used for weapon systems. A FPGA is a semiconductor device that includes a programmable logic element and a programmable internal line [5, 6]. The logic devices can be programmed by replicating the functions of basic logic gates, and more complex decoders or combinations of computational functions. When critical technology is implemented by software code, it is inherently easy to reverse engineer. Even though the software is decoded using source-level or binary-level obfuscation techniques, it can be cracked. However, it is difficult to reverse engineer if the critical technology is implemented as a hardware circuit such as FPGA. Using this property, we propose an anti-tamper technology to protect weapons and technologies from exploitation. The proposed method isolates the parts of the source code that contain the critical technology. The code is converted to HDL and then converted to bitstream of specific FPGA circuit. When the system runs, the machine code of the target system and the code of the FPGA are executed in an integrated way.

The rest of this paper is organized as follows. In Sect. 2, we introduce the anti-tamper techniques briefly. Section 3 describes the details of FPGA-based software protection scheme and related products. Finally, Sect. 4 describes conclusion and future work.

2   Background

2.1   Anti-tamper Techniques

In military domain, anti-tamper means the system engineering activity to prevent or delay the outflow of critical technologies from the weapon system [7]. Enemies want critical information from the weapon system in order to weaken military advantage, shorten the expected combat life of weapon system, and erode the industrial technological competitiveness. Weapon system consists of hardware and software components. Attacks can be performed on weapon system by means of two type attacks: passive or active. Passive attacks include a side channel analysis to determine the timing, dynamic power consumption, or secrets from an electromagnetic leak, as well as probe circuitry or imaging components. Active attacks include not only physical intrusion and hardware modification, but also failure induction through signal corruption, protocol attack, or malicious software.

Figure 1 shows that the anti-tamper techniques are composed of hardware and software techniques [8]. Each technique can be categorized by three techniques: prevention, detection and response.

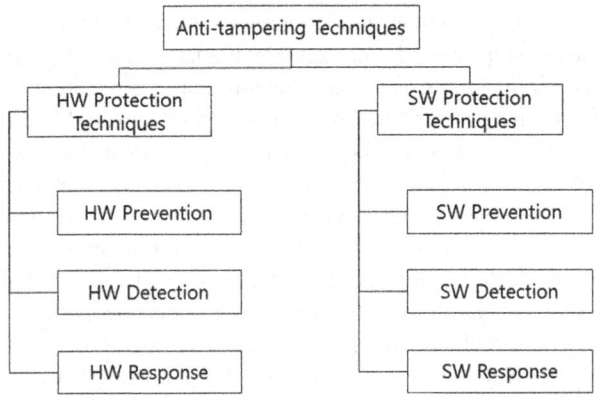

Fig. 1. Category of anti-tamper techniques

Prevention Techniques
The tamper protection techniques can prevent tampering attacks. However, when the threat of an attack is more severe than the protective strategy, it delays the collection of the least important information and makes it no longer usable. Examples of preventive safety measures for this are shielding, encapsulation, obfuscation, and encryption. The hardware protective coatings make it difficult to extract or dissect components without damaging the system. The software encryption scrambles software instructions to make them unintelligible without being reprocessed through a deciphering technique.

Detection Techniques

Tamper detection techniques may block tampering, either actively or passively, after detecting threats. Protection interlocks and low-power or non-power modulation sensors can detect and alert intrusions, and silicon's physically interruptible function (PUF) can uniquely identify a device for verification.

Response Techniques

Once tampering attack is detected, the weapon system can respond by destroying its own critical components to protect critical information. Disabling memory resources, disabling the communication interface, clearing out encryption keys, and causing explosive or high current corruption are examples of tamper response techniques (Table 1).

Table 1. Well-known 13 techniques for anti-tamper

1	Tamper indicating devices: seal and labels
2	Uniquely shaped screw heads
3	Locks for removable covers and doors
4	Coating: encapsulation materials
5	Mechanical mechanisms
6	Protective sensor mesh wall
7	Use of brittle components
8	Sensors
9	Zeroisations circuitry
10	Encryption wrappers
11	Code obfuscation
12	Guarding
13	Watermarking/fingerprinting

2.2 Weapon System Program Protection of the United States

In 1999, the United States DoD issued a policy memorandum for implementing anti-tamper protection in acquisition programs [1]. In 2000, DoD issued a policy memorandum stating that technologies should be routinely assessed during the acquisition process to determine if they are critical and if anti-tamper techniques are needed to protect these technologies [3]. In 2001, DoD designated the Air Force as the AntiTamper Executive Agent. The executive agent's office is responsible for implementing DOD's anti-tamper policy and managing anti-tamper technology development through the Air Force Research Laboratory. Acquisition program managers are responsible for ensuring anti-tamper protection is incorporated on any weapon system with critical technologies that need protection. Since it is not feasible to protect every technology, program managers are to conduct an assessment to determine if anti-tamper protection is needed.

The anti-tamper decision process is illustrated in Fig. 2 [9–14]. When assessing if anti-tamper protection is needed, program managers make several key decisions regarding the identification of critical technologies, assessment of threats and vulnerabilities, and determination of anti-tamper techniques or solutions. The process begins with determining whether or not their system's critical program information includes any critical technologies. If it is determined that the system has no critical technologies, program managers are to document the decision and request concurrence from either the office within their component that is designated with anti-tamper responsibilities or the Anti-Tamper Executive Agent. For systems that are determined to have critical technologies, the next key steps are to identify potential threats and vulnerabilities and select anti-tamper techniques to protect those technologies. Techniques are ultimately verified and validated by a team composed of representatives from the DOD components. The program manager documents decisions in an annex of the program protection plan.

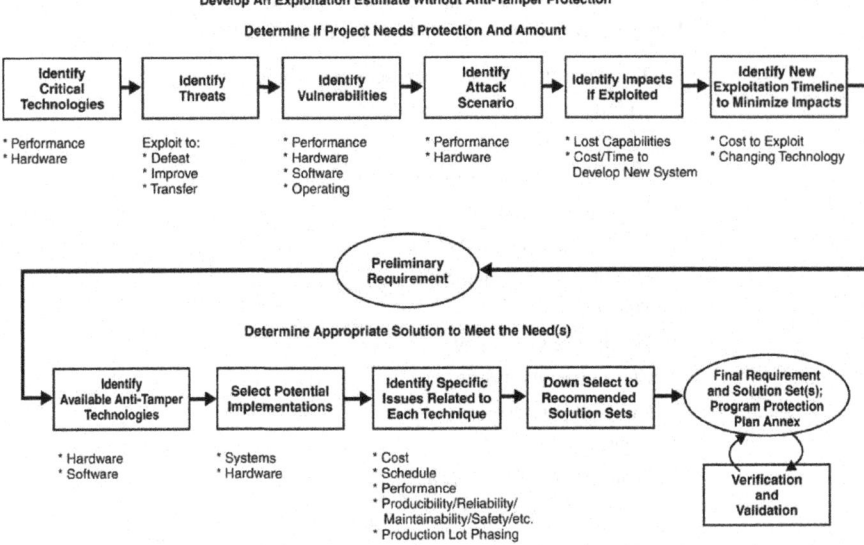

Fig. 2. US DOD's anti-tamper decision process [7]

DoD issued "Program Protection Plan Outline & Guidance" in 2011 that provides an outline, content, and formatting guidance for the Program Protection Plan (PPP) required by DoD Instruction 5000.02 and DoD Instruction 5200.39.

3   FPGA-Based Software Protection

3.1   FPGA Overview

An FPGA (Field Programmable Gate Array) is a logic device that includes a typical logic cell in a two-dimensional array and a programmable switch. Figure 3 shows the conceptual structure of the FPGA device [6]. Logical cells can be configured (programmable) to perform simple functions and programmable switches can be customized to provide interconnection between logical cells. A custom design can be implemented by specifying the functions of each logical cell and optionally setting up connections for each programmable switch. Once designed and synthesized, a simple adapter cable can be used to change the desired logic cell to the FPGA device and obtain the custom circuitry. Because this process can be performed on site, it is known that the device enables field programming.

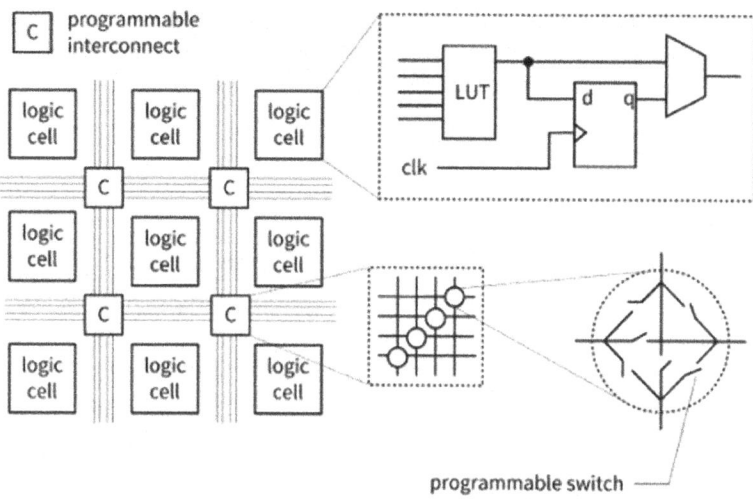

Fig. 3. Conceptual structure of a FPGA device [6]

LUT-based logic cells usually have a small configurable combination circuit with D FF (D type flip-flop). The most common method of implementing a configurable combination circuit is the LUT (lookup table). N Input LUTs can be considered small 2×1 memory. Using LUTs, n input combination functions can be implemented if memory contents are properly written. A schematic of the input LUT-based logic cell is shown in the upper right corner of Fig. 3. The LUT output can be directly used or stored on DFF. The latter can be used to implement sequential circuits.

In a macro cell, most FPGA devices contain a particular macro cell or macro block. They are designed and produced at the transistor level, which complements the common logic cells. Common macrophages include memory blocks, combination multiplier, clock management circuits, and I/O interface circuits. Advanced FPGA devices may also contain one or more pre-built processor cores.

3.2   Transformation Software Code into FPGA Code

When weapon technology is implemented by software, it is inherently easy to reverse engineering. However, it is difficult to reverse engineering if the critical technology is implemented as a hardware circuit such as FPGA. Recently some tools have been developed to translate the high-level source code into FPGA hardware circuit. Using these tools we can protect some software code by implementing as FPGA-level hardware circuit.

Figure 4 shows overall process of the proposed software protection techniques using FPGA. First of all, we identify and isolate the parts of the source code that contain the critical technology. The rest of the code is compiled in the normal way and made into the machine language of the target system. But, the code that needs to be protected is converted to HDL and then converted to bitstream to make the FPGA circuit. When the code is executed, the machine code of the target system and the code of the FPGA must be integrated and executed together. To do this, we need a well-defined call interface between the code in the target system and the code in the FPGA.

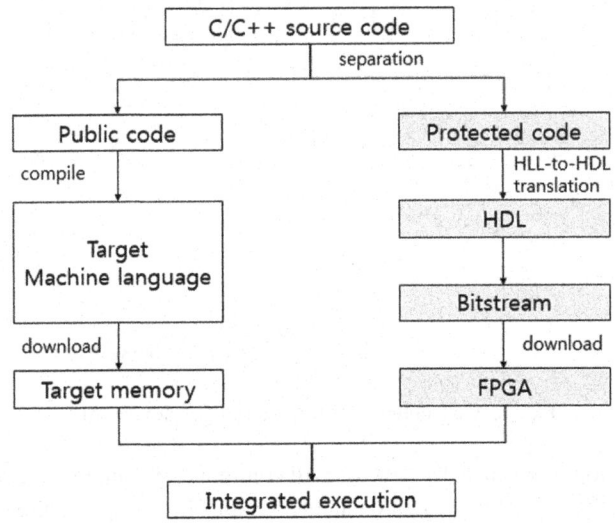

Fig. 4.   Process for software code protection using FPGA

3.3   Existing Technologies

In this subsection, we introduce some products which can be used in our proposed software protection method.

Impulse C
Impulse C from Impulse Accelerate Technologies is a C-based development system for programmable hardware targets, including mixed processors and FPGA platforms [15]. This technique is based on the impulse C compiler, the related tools and the Impulse application programmer interface (API). Impulse C can process the C code block with either a Verilog Hardware Description Language (VHDL) or a Verilog Hardware Description. Impulse technique provides several FPGA platform packages which allow us to simplify C-to-hardware compilation for specific FPGA-based platform. The Impulse C compiler and optimizer supports automatic scheduling of C doors for loop growth and for the automation such as parallelism, loop pipe lining and frozen rolling, and for semi-automatic optimization. The interactive tools that come with the compilers

allow the designer to continually analyze and experiment with alternative hardware pipeline strategies.

Mitrion-C

Mitrion-C from Mitrionics provides software programmability for FPGA [16]. Further, the virtual processor is introduced as a large parallel processor for the FPGA, which runs software written in the Mitrion-C programming language. The processor architecture follows the cluster model, which places all processing nodes within the FPGA. The Mitrion-C compiler and processor unit uses the Mitrion-C source code to create processing nodes and ad-hoc network-on-a-chip.

Unlike standard C, Mitrion-C provides a fully parallel programming language to complement the fine parallel processing of the processor. In Standard C, the programmers explain the order in which programs run. This order forces a specific sequential order to run, and is therefore not suitable for parallel running. The processing model of Mitrion-C is based on data dependency and is much more appropriate for parallel processing (Fig. 5).

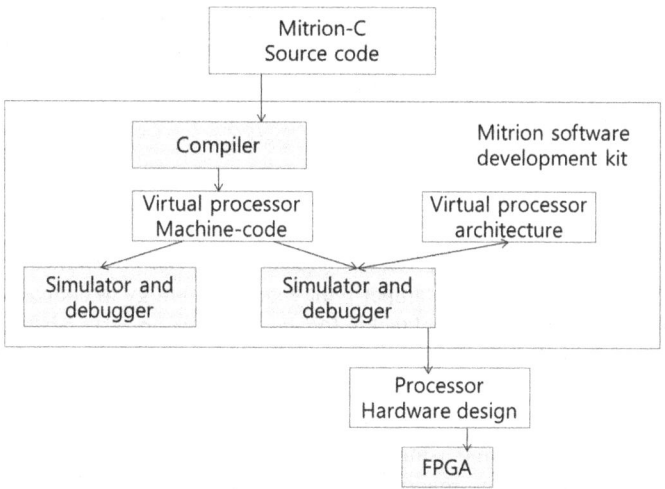

Fig. 5. Mitrion-C architecture

Carte

Carte from SRC Computers is development tools which support traditional programming development environment [17]. It allow us to write code in advanced programming languages such as C and Fortran until the implementation of the appropriate program runs correctly in a microprocessor environment. And then we can recompile the source code into the final FPGA chip configuration bitstream. Carte also provides the parallelism capability by pipelining loops, scheduling memory references, and supporting parallel code blocks and streams.

Handel-C

Handel-C from Celoxica also consolidates high-level user codes into the FPGA [18]. Handel-C was originally developed by Oxford University Computing Laboratory. By replacing the algorithm loop in the original Fortran, C, or C++ source code with API calls, the Handel-C user can derive the source code to be compiled with the FPGA. The FPGA C compiler has a runtime part to establish interactions with the hardware environment. Programmers can define the parallel process using extensions that instruct the compiler to write parallel hardware. The compiler converts the input Handel-C code into an abstract syntax tree and then optimizes the high-level netlist and then compiles it into the FPGA bitstream. Handel-C also supports a development tool that includes a GUI environment, code editing, and source-level debugging.

Trident

Trident also synthesizes circuits from a high-level language source code [19]. Unlike other products, it provides an open framework for mapping the C program's floating-point operations to hardware floating-point modules and automatically allocating floating-point arrays to off-chip memory banks. Users are free to select floating-point operators from a variety of standard libraries. It also supports various hardware platforms by defining new interface description files and producing the code to tie the design to the description interface. Unlike other products, compiler's open source code is available (http://trident.sf.net).

4   Conclusion

As defense technology level of Korea is increasing, Korean government has plan to invest in the development of anti-tamper policy and technology to counter the exploitation of weapon system and critical technologies. The weapon system is becoming the embedded system consisting of hardware and software, and thus most critical technologies to be protected are implemented by hardware or software.

In this paper, we introduce the overview of the anti-tamper techniques and propose a software protection technique using FPGA which can be efficiently used for weapon systems. Since it is difficult to reverse engineering the software code which is implemented as a hardware circuit such as FPGA, we can efficiently protect the critical technology of weapon systems. We found that there are already some products similar to the proposed techniques. For the future work, we will implement the proposed technique and validate its effectiveness.

References

1. US DoD Memorandum: Implementation of Anti-tamper (AT) Techniques in Acquisition Programs (1999)
2. Huber, I.I., Arthur, F., Scott, J.M.: The role and nature of anti-tamper techniques in U.S. defense acquisition (1999)
3. US USD (A&T) Memorandum: Guidelines for Implementation of Anti-tamper Techniques in Weapon System Acquisition Programs (2000)

4. US USD (A&T) Memorandum: Implementing Anti-Tamper (2001)
5. Pong, C.: FPGA Prototyping by VHDL Examples: Xilinx Microblaze MCS SoC, 2nd edn. Wiley, Hoboken (2017)
6. Underwood, K.: FPGAs vs. CPUs: trends in peak floating-point performance. In: 12th ACM International Symposium on Field-Programmable Gate Arrays (FPGA 2004), pp. 171–180. ACM Press (2004)
7. US General Accounting Office Report GAO-04-302: Defense acquisitions: DoD needs to better support program manager's implementation of anti-tamper protection (2004)
8. Abaco Systems White Paper: Anti-tamper technology: safeguarding today's COTS platforms (2016)
9. US DoD Directive 5000.01: The Defense Acquisition System (2003)
10. US DoD Instruction 5000.02: Operation of the Defense Acquisition System (2015)
11. US DoD Instruction 5200.39: Critical Program Information (CPI) Identification and Protection Within Research, Development, Test, and Evaluation (RDT&E) (2015)
12. US DoD Directive 5200.47E: Anti-Tamper (2015)
13. US DoD DASD: Program protection plan outline & guidance, Version 1.0 (2011)
14. Raymond, S.: Identification and protection of critical program information (CPI). In: 18th Annual NDIA Systems Engineering Conference (2016)
15. Impulse C Homepage. http://www.Impulsec.com
16. Mitrion-C Homepage. http://www.mitrionics.com
17. CARTE Homepage. http://www.src-labs.com
18. Handel-C Homepage. http://www.mentor.com
19. Justin, T., Maya, G., Kristopher, P.: Trident: from high-level language to hardware circuitry. IEEE Comput. **40**(3), 28–37 (2007)

Conceptualization of Defense Industrial Security in Relation to Protecting Defense Technologies

Heungsoon Park$^{(\boxtimes)}$ (iD), Heejae Go, and Jonghyeon Hwang

Office of Defense Industrial Security, Defense Security Institute, Seoul, South Korea
heungsoon.park@gmail.com

Abstract. In order to protect the advancement of defense technology that has a tremendous effect on both the national security and the economy, the Republic of Korea established the Defense Technology Security Act in 2015. As the new enactment brought changes to the landscape of the defense industry and defense industrial security, a new examination of the concept of the defense industrial security now became necessary. Even after taking in a consideration of the undisclosed nature of defense industrial security research, and the fact that only the limited number of firms participates in the subject matter, scientific researches related to the topic have not been active. However, with the new enactment of the Defense Technology Security Act, it is necessary to expand the scope of security and to redefine the concept of defense industrial security. In this paper, we analyzed the research works on related technology protection policies and our environment of the defense industry in order to conceptualize defense industrial security. It is expected that the established concepts could provide a systematic way to protect the confidential and defense technology.

Keywords: Defense industrial security · Defense technology · Defense industry
Defense acquisition program · National security · National interest

1 Introduction

The volume of defense industry in the Republic of Korea export has reached 262 billion dollars in 2005, 2.35 trillion dollars in 2012, and up to 3.612 trillion dollars in 2014 [1]. During the growth over the year, primary exports have shifted from the fundamental necessities such as munitions and equipment parts to high-technology-based products like KM-SAM and T-50 supersonic jet. The defense industry in the Republic of Korea has evolved to the point where it is capable of developing a world-class weapons system independently. Furthermore, target markets for the defense industry exports have been expanding not just towards North America and the Middle East, but also throughout Latin America, Africa, and Asia. The advancement level of defense technology of the Republic of Korea has reached up to 80% that of the United States and marked the 9th in the global rankings [2]. Embarking on the 40th year anniversary of the Project Yulgok, the defense industry of the Republic of Korea is about to face a new era of full production on high-tech-based aircrafts, submarines, and other high-value equipment.

© Springer International Publishing AG, part of Springer Nature 2018
O. Gervasi et al. (Eds.): ICCSA 2018, LNCS 10964, pp. 158–169, 2018.
https://doi.org/10.1007/978-3-319-95174-4_13

Entering the 40th year of self-reliable and independent national defense of the Republic of Korea (ROK), the enactment of the Defense Technology Security Act has brought in a number of big shifts to its sector in 2015. A shifting landscape of the defense industry sector and related industrial security require a new transformation accordingly. However, this has not been the case under the reason of protecting military confidential as higher priority [3].

There are some problems below to handle in this paper. The first problem is an ambiguous definition of defense industrial security. The current legal definition of defense industrial security has led to the general concept of security measures only for the defense contractors designated by the government. It causes to reduce the significant amount of size of the defense industry. In addition, it is the ambiguity concerning what to protect. While the existing security policy has focused on the military confidential [4], it should include a variety of defense companies with defense technologies as well as designated defense contractors after the Defense Technology Security Act enacted. The ambiguous definition makes it difficult to determine security policies and to study academic researches. Second, the concepts of defense industrial security and defense technology security have been considered as two different entities, which further leads to the lack of synergy between them on the issues when it comes to the government supports, public policies, and ongoing researches.

The recent defense industry has advanced technologies high enough to affect national security and national interest so that the defense firms must conduct their own security tasks. From this perspective, it is necessary to establish a clear concept of defense industrial security in advance for proper research and policy establishment in security for the defense industry although there are very few studies on academic approaches. Accordingly, the purpose of this study is to analyze the problems associated with existing works related to establishing the concept of defense industrial security and to redefine the concept in accordance with the current environment of the ROK defense industry.

The rest of the paper is organized as follows. Section 2 provides background with respect to the history of the ROK defense industry, the term 'defense industry' in relation to the defense acquisition program, the concept of security, and defense technology security. Section 3 develops the concept of defense industrial security using a series of conceptual specifications for the security policy.

2   Related Works

2.1   History of Defense Industrial Security in the Republic of Korea

Defense industrial security measures have been continuing along with the independent national defense capability of the Republic of Korea. During the early years, the national defense has been dependent on the United States Army Military Government in Korea (USAMGIK) after independence from Japanese occupation in 1945. After the incidence of Blue House Raid in 1968, the declaration of Nixon Doctrine in 1969, and a possibility of U.S. Armed Forces withdrawal from the Korean peninsula became an issue, developing independent weapons system has become the high priority project. In the year 1977, a former president Park, Chung-hee opened up a discussion to promote a research and development of the defense industry. He stated that the defense industry requires private sector firms to put great effort on research & development and for the Ministry of National Defense to put counter security measures on the firms for the facility access control. After the executive order has been issued under the title, Enforcement Rule of the Defense Industrial Security Service for the defense firms, the legislation has been put in practice to protect the military confidential and weapon manufacturing facilities. At that time, defense industrial security has been established in the Republic of Korea.

2.2 Defense Industry in Relation to the Defense Acquisition Program

The term 'Defense Industrial Security' can be interpreted in various ways, depending on how it defines the defense industry in terms of a combination of the two words 'defense industry' and 'security'. First, the term 'Defense Industry' has two meanings in relation to a point of view. From the narrow perspective, the defense industry is defined in the Defense Acquisition Program Act as an industry that produces or develops government-designated defense supplies. The Defense Acquisition Program Administration (DAPA) uses it to incentivize specific firms in terms of stable procurement and the guaranteed supply of weapons systems in any circumstances. In a broad sense, 'Defense Industry' could be defined as an industry that contributes to the production and development of supplies required in military for the national defense.

Security studies should have a clear definition of the defense industry being targeted, but recent studies have rarely found it [5–8]. As checked the concept of the defense industry in these papers, only Woo [5] applied the definition of a narrow perspective. Other than that, none of the articles [6–8] clearly defined the defense industry in terms of perspectives and have not applied them further in the context.

In case of the United States, a leading nation in the defense industry, it has defined the term as an industry that is composed of key contractors, subcontractors and part suppliers who provide the systems of the army, navy, and air force by operating both the government and private owned facilities, which has the ability to expand the supply system during wartime or national emergencies. In Europe, the term of defense industry has the legal meaning that all the firms and institutes which are participating in military goods research, development, production, analysis, and maintenance. As shown above, the examples of leading nations in the field have defined the legal term from a broad perspective, rather than a narrow point of view [9].

The concept of the defense industry can also be seen in relation to the defense acquisition program. The general meaning of the defense acquisition program is an acquisition, development, and manufacturing of military equipment, goods, and services to ensure national security and to protect the lives and properties of citizens. Applying the context of the Republic of Korea to the sentence, the party that acquires the weapons system is the DAPA, and the parties that develop and manufacture it are the firms in the defense industry. After all, the concept of defense industry is a derivative of the defense acquisition program. As shown from Fig. 1, there are a variety of defense firms such as defense contractors, general enterprises, and munitions suppliers [10].

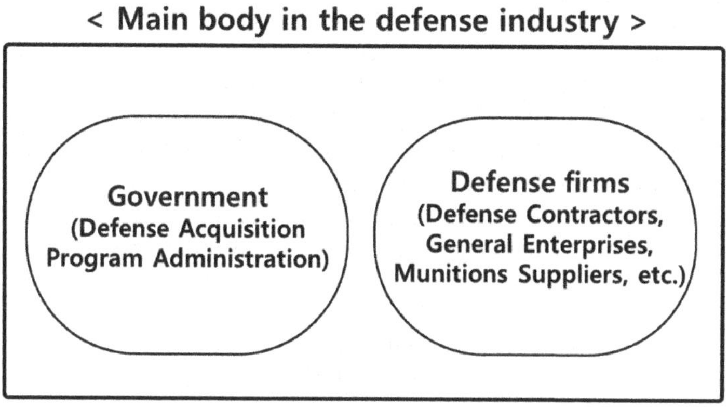

< Main body in the defense industry >

Fig. 1. Main body in the defense industry of the Republic of Korea

2.3 The Concept of Security

The term 'security' is commonly used as a daily language, but it is not an easy word to conceptualize clearly. It is used in widespread fields with different levels, from the highest level such as 'national security' to the lower level like 'door security'. The dictionary definition of 'security' is 'freedom from risk or danger; safety' in the American Heritage Dictionary and Webster's College Dictionary. The Collins English Dictionary calls it as 'the state of being secure'. On the Korean Language Dictionary of the National Institute of Korean Language, it is defined as 'maintaining safety' and 'maintaining peace and order of society'.

The term 'security' has a negative connotation as it went along with political organizations to maintain specific political power in the history of the Republic of Korea. However, in recent years, the term 'security' has been widely used to protect the privacy and assets, including industrial security, cybersecurity, and information security, and so on. A number of security firms and the magnitude of security industry have grown amongst the lives of people.

As shown above, the term 'security' was defined differently, and related studies were conducted on the definition or concept of security. Baldwin [11] provides a variety of approaches to the conceptualization of security, and Zedner [12] examines various meanings by comparative analysis: as negative or positive presence, as a material or symbolic good, as a public good or private service, and external versus internal security. In this paper, we analyze the defense industrial security for the rationality of security policy by the specifications introduced in [11].

2.4 Defense Technology Characteristics and Protection

Every year, countries around the world are attempting to penetrate the security system to acquire advanced technologies from other countries' companies. As a result, possible economic damages are spreading to the national level, not just businesses. Accordingly, technologically advanced nations are promoting various policies to protect their technologies as the innovation competition accelerates.

Recognizing the importance of such defense technologies, the Korean government enacted the Defense Technology Security Act in December 2015 and enforced it in June 2016. As shown in Fig. 2, the 'defense technology' is a technology that should be protected for national security, among the 'National Defense Science and Technologies' [13] related to the defense industry. It is also required to be designated and publicly announced by the ROK Defense Acquisition Program Administration.

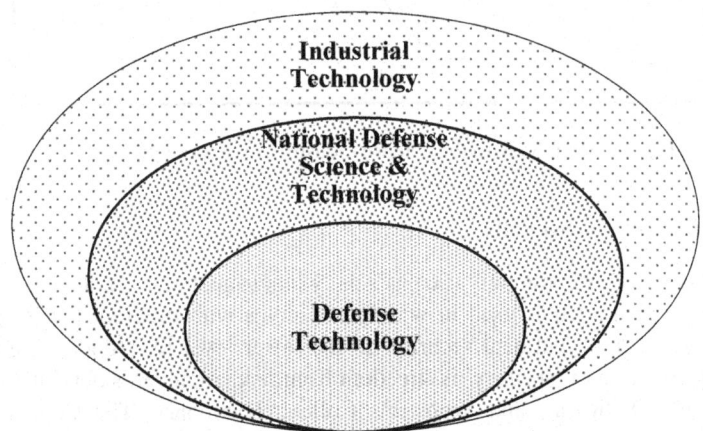

Fig. 2. This diagram shows the relationship between the defense technology and other technologies. The defense technology means technologies requiring protection for national security among the national defense science and technologies related to the defense industry. The national defense science and technology means engineering techniques that perform technical investigations, research, development and testing on weapons systems (weapons, equipment and materials) and automation systems (tactical computer systems and software) for national defense. And those two technologies are also part of industrial technology, which means engineering and manufacturing technologies to make production more efficient in this paper.

Defense technologies have their own characteristics, which are different from common industrial technologies. First, the defense technologies are a combined form of various high-technologies. In history, the latest technologies were applied to the weapon development at the time of the war, which could lead to victory in the battlefield. Second, it is necessary to apply the security measures from the initial stage of research and development. It is because it takes a longer than the general product development, and the leakage of defense technology into the enemy directly affects to national security.

Third, it contributes to the national economy as a high value-added technology. In recent, the effects on the export of aircrafts and naval vessels are estimated to generate billions of dollars in domestic industry and tens of thousands of jobs in the Republic of Korea.

The Defense Technology Security Act stipulates that 'target institutions' with defense technologies should establish 'defense technology security systems', comprised of four entities: the system for identifying and managing technologies, access control, facility protection, and information security system [14]. The target institutions are government agencies, the armed forces, defense companies, research institutes, universities, and other corporations which own defense technologies or conduct research and development project related to defense technologies. It expanded existing target parties from only designated defense contractors to all organizations having the defense technologies. The Defense Technology Security Act, compared with the conventional defense industrial security policies [15], features additional functions of defense technology management and enhanced information security systems. The information security systems include a variety of security solutions in order to prevent and respond to cyber threats. This is because the aspects of technology management were highlighted while the existing security target was military secrets, and recently the products related to technology are usually managed by digital information. The following Table 1 shows a comparison between the defense technology protections and existing defense industrial security in the Republic of Korea. The problem arises from the difference between the legal and policy departments' perspective, which it is difficult to enforce consistent policies since the security targets and related rules are different. In the future, combined security polices from a single leading policy department is crucial, and therefore, would be required.

Table 1. Comparison between the defense technology protection and existing defense industrial security in the Republic of Korea

	Defense technology protection	Conventional defense industrial security
Law	Defense Technology Security Act	Defense Acquisition Program Act, Military Secret Protection Act
Target party	All organizations handling defense technology	Designated defense contractors
Assets to protect	Defense technologies designated by government	Military secrets (mainly)
Policy department	Defense Acquisition Program Administration	Defense Intelligence Agency

3   Conceptualization of Defense Industrial Security

In this section, we propose to establish the systematic concepts of defense industrial security based on our previous background knowledge. In order to make the defense industrial security useful scientifically, we make an analysis framework by setting up some specifications. Next, we diagnose the current environment of defense industrial security and present the goals of security for the future policy establishment.

3.1 Analytical Specifications for Conceptualization

According to Wolfers, the term 'security' can be a vague concept if it is used without any specifications [16]. Considering that the purpose of defining the concept of defense industrial security is to establish the related security policies, it makes sense. This section identifies some specifications for defining the security policy, in reference to Wolfers' specifications. The security policy can be defined in terms of the specifications as follows.

First specification is *the actors of security*. The security actors can be the individual, the group, the organization, or the system, etc. The selection should be determined in accordance with the characteristics of the particular security area. The target organizations for the defense industrial security could be the defense firms and related organizations such as research institutes or government agencies.

Second one is *the assets to protect*. Defining what to protect is the beginning of the security policy. The assets to protect should be identified for both tangible and intangible properties, considering the value of the assets and the effects of being leaked out or disrupted. If the detailed steps are considered, the form of the assets must be classified since the security measures need to be taken for each type of assets. Conventional concept of defense industrial security has focused on protecting assets designated as the military confidential, but it is necessary to expand its scope.

Third, the security must be defined *for which values*. Individual, groups, organizations, and countries have a lot of values. The level of the individual could include physical safety, psychological stability, financial affluence, welfare, etc. On the other hand, national security contains political independence and protection of territory. For the defense industrial security, it may include the national security and the economic values.

The fourth is *the degree of security*. Some people, such as traditional security policymakers, may be critical of the idea of security as a matter of degree. They claim that the security is a condition which cannot be qualified. It implies an absolute condition with top-down approaches which is either secure or insecure. Intuitively, however, the status of absolute security is not attainable. Then, we have to determine how much of scarce resources are to be allocated for the security condition that is not absolute.

Fifth, the security policymaker has to identify all possible *threats*. They usually establish specific countermeasures by each threat. In addition, security policies that already have been established once should be re-established according to newly identified threats. For example, if bank security systems focused on robbers in the past, it would now consider cyberattacks. The concept of security, considering the 'safety', may need to be expanded to include unintended threats or natural disaster such as fire, earthquakes, or power outages.

The sixth is *the means* which are directly related to threats. The security policies comprise a wide variety of means. Furthermore, the means are updated in response to threats and selected by the policymakers. In recent, it needs state-of-the-art technology system resolving the complex threats. In the example above, the bank security systems would adopt cameras and security guard for robbers and now establish an AI-based information security system for cyber hacking.

Seventh, *costs* always matter. In terms of target institutions' perspective, it takes money to implement policies and establish measures. However, the actors of security, like a group or a nation, have limited resources and are willing to allocate these resources efficiently for the goals of the organization as a whole. Therefore, the decision-makers do not tend to look at the degree of security as an 'absolute' condition to avoid spending unnecessary costs.

The last one is *the time period*. As a perspective of time to expect the effects of a policy, there are short-term and long-term ways. Mostly, the short-term policies for security may differ from the ways in the long-term. The short-term usually focuses on a direct approach to eliminating threats, which is easy to apply, conspicuous, and cheaper. But in the long run, it may be relatively difficult to apply and requires the system improvement with a large amount of financial support.

So far, the specifications for the concept of security have been reviewed. But, the specifications mentioned above are not exactly suitable for the security policy establishment. Not all of the items need to be described all the time, and each of the items can be explained in broad or narrow views.

3.2 Problems on the Previously Established Concepts of Defense Industrial Security

There are few research works on defense industrial security since the study has the characteristics of not being actively engaged in academic research in terms of its closed nature and only being carried out by specific vendors despite having a long history in the Republic of Korea. This section, therefore, tries to identify the problems as a result of changes in the defense industry environment and related policies, rather than the problems from the existing studies of defense industrial security.

First problem comes from the small scope of target institution. Existing defense industrial security measures were controlled by the government with the only designated defense contractor. As a result, the companies (general enterprises, subcontractors, etc.) that work in cooperation with the defense contractors are vulnerable because they are not covered by the government's security policies. The government usually delegates responsibility for establishing security measures to prime defense contractors. On the other hand, in the United States, the industrial security policies with the National Industrial Security Program Operating Manual are implemented for all contractors to prevent leakage of confidential information during the entire contract process [17].

As for the assets that need protection, conventional security policy has focused primarily on the leakage of the military confidential, including defense technology recently. Nonetheless, some information related to defense materials not applicable to them is difficult to be protected. The defense firms need to be willing to protect some technologies or information that are not designated by the government.

Even the dualized policy department is also a problem. Although the existing defense industrial security has been carried out by the Defense Intelligence Agency with the Enforcement Rule of the Defense Industrial Security Service, the defense technology is protected by the policies of the Defense Acquisition Program Administration with the Defense Technology Security Act. From the defense firms' perspective, the same security measures can be established for a particular threat, but dual policies can make redundant efforts. Thus, it needs to set up an integrated concept of the defense industrial security with a unified policy department.

3.3 Newly Establishing the Concept of Defense Industrial Security

This section redefines the concept of defense industrial security based on previous discussions by the dimensions of specifications. In terms of the value of security, particularly for the Republic of Korea, security of defense industry is crucial in maintaining the nation's safety. As technology-intensiveness becomes more advanced, the defense industry evolves to produce more sophisticated and high-tech weapons system. The defense technology today has gone over the realm of national security matter to be recognized as the source for creating added values for the national industry and economy. In particular, defense technologies leaked to North Korea, IS and other terrorist groups have caused massive economic losses but also serves as a great threat to the whole world, thereby becoming an increasingly relevant issue in terms of global security. In conclusion, the values concerned include national security, national interest and heightening national credibility.

With respect to the assets to protect, as discussed in the previous section, it should cover all forms of information related to the whole process of the defense acquisition program, as well as designated military confidential and defense technologies. It requires efforts by the government and defense firms together to identify the information that becomes protected assets from the start of the defense acquisition program.

The actors of security are strongly tied to the assets to protect. Therefore, it is also necessary to expand the area of actors to all organizations that hold the information of the whole process of the defense acquisition program. The organizations include defense contractors, general enterprises, munitions suppliers, laboratories, public institutions, and so on.

In conventional industrial security, the threats mainly focused on intended risks such as theft, espionage, terrorists, hostile countries, insiders, and so on for the leakage of information on the defense firms. It only emphasized security policies in terms of confidentiality and integrity. In recent days, cyber threats have been increasing as assets are digitized, and as security measures become more sophisticated, threats have changed in multiple ways. On the other hand, in terms of loss of availability, it is necessary to contain unintended actions or natural phenomena such as fire, floods, earthquake, and power outage.

Today, the means of protection is diverse as threats are hard to predict. Typically, security measures have been sector-based solutions such as personnel, facilities, information security, etc. in order to cope with such threats. However, deploying a sector-specific solution has limitations in responding to unpredictable threats. Therefore, it requires the security convergence which integrates the sector-based controls and a partnership with related organizations. In addition, in terms of loss of availability, it will be necessary to develop the concept of preventing and recovering the spread of damage in the event of an infringement. The government needs to work with other countries or defense firms to set conditions and share information to prevent the threat. Recently, information sharing communities have been activated mainly by developed countries for critical infrastructures. The DIB ISAC [18] in the United States is a good example of information sharing community for the defense industry in order to jointly respond to threats.

When it comes to the degree of security, the traditional security officer has criticized the opinion that the security can be qualified. Typically, the government-led security policies are also intended to seek the highest-class security by applying them to all organizations in an absolute manner. However, how much security is enough? No one will be able to answer this question. From the private sector's perspective, security measures are needed to take into consideration the company's system environment and workflow. Ultimately, optimized user-centric security policies are required to achieve cost-effectiveness with limited resources.

In terms of the costs, the concept of security is strongly associated with the degree of security. In the defense industry environment of the Republic of Korea, defense companies invest the costs of security in their own money early in the project because most of their assets are private. Thus, defense firms with low security awareness tend to make a relatively small investment to security measures. However, since the defense industry has strong characteristics of public goods, government financial support is required for the common efforts across the organizations. Furthermore, it is necessary to induce voluntary participation by defense companies with government incentives.

For the time period, short-run and solution-based security policies have a relatively small impact on threats because of the rapidly changing security environment. Considering the economic losses of countries and defense firms as well as national security when the defense information is leaked, long-term security policies are required, such

Table 2. Summary of the conceptualization for defense industrial security by specifications

Specification	As-Is	To-Be
Values concerned	National security	National security, National interest, National credibility
Assets to protect	Military confidential, Designated defense technologies, Relevant facilities	All the information for the defense acquisition program, Relevant facilities
Actors	Designated defense firms, Public organizations	All organizations that handle the information related to defense acquisition program
Threats	Theft, Espionage, Competitors, Insiders, Cyber terrorists, etc.	All threats, including natural disasters
Means	Sector-based solutions, (personnel, facilities, IT system, etc.)	Security convergence, Partnership with other agencies
Degree of security	Absolute	Optimum
Costs	Company's own budget	Government financial support needed
Time period	Solution-driven, short-run policies	Additional long-term policies required to improve awareness

as one that encourages voluntary participation in the security polices by improving security awareness.

So far, improvements for defense industrial security by specification have been reviewed. Table 2 shows a summary of them. For the new definition of the defense industrial security, this paper selects only the core specifications (values, assets, actors, and threats) since it is too detailed to use all the specifications. We suggest that the redefined concept of defense industrial security is 'Activities to protect all tangible or intangible assets, associated with the defense acquisition program, of all organizations to produce, develop or manage the defense materials for national security and national interest against a variety of threats.'

4   Conclusion

The defense technology in the Republic of Korea has developed to a world-class level, and defense industrial security has a long history since the year of 1945. However, so far, it has not been interested in setting up the concept of the term 'defense industrial security.' Conventional defense industrial security is primarily addressed in terms of the leakage of military confidential. Although the discussion on the defense technology protection has been activated with the related act, the concepts of security policies are still insufficient. The lack of academic researches and the closed defense industry environment also have made it difficult to establish the concept of security.

This paper provides the conceptualization of defense industrial security using the methodology by specifications. The redefined concept of defense industrial security will contribute to the development of defense industrial security policies by promoting academic research activities and providing the direction for partnership with the relevant organizations as well as government financial support. In the future, studies for the integrated security system at the government level are needed to protect all the information systematically.

References

1. ROK Defense Acquisition Program Administration: Defense Acquisition Program Statistical Yearbook (2016)
2. Jang, W.: The present status and development strategies of defense industry in South Korea. Sci. Technol. Policy 27(11), 38–45 (2017)
3. ROK Ministry of National Defense: Military Secret Protection Act (2015)
4. Kim, Y.: A study on the criminal laws of security in the defense industry of South Korea. Korean J. Ind. Secur. 2(2), 49–90 (2011)
5. Woo, K.: Research trend and conceptualization of defense industry security from convergence security perspective. J. Inf. Secur. 15(6), 69–78 (2015)
6. Cho, W.: Industrial policies enhancing the level of security of the defense industry. Master's thesis, The University of Suwon, South Korea (2015)
7. Lee, J.: Legal restrictions on the industrial secret outflow: concentrated on the defense industry. Master's thesis, Seoul School of Integrated Sciences and Technologies (2013)

8. Shin, H.: A study on the analysis and countermeasure of the real condition for defense industry secrecy-spillage. Master's thesis, Dongguk University, South Korea (2008)
9. Dussauge, P., Cornu, C.: L' industrie Francaise de l'armement. Economica (1998). (in French)
10. ROK Ministry of National Defense: Defense Acquisition Program Act (2017)
11. Baldwin, D.A.: The concept of security. Rev. Int. Stud. **23**, 5–26 (1997)
12. Zedner, L.: The concept of security: an agenda for comparative analysis. Leg. Stud. **23**(1), 153–175 (2003)
13. ROK Defense Agency for Technology and Quality: Dictionary of National Defense Science and Technology Terms (2017)
14. ROK Ministry of National Defense: Defense Technology Security Act (2017)
15. ROK Ministry of National Defense: Directive, Defense Industrial Security Service (2017)
16. Wolfers, A.: "National Security" as an ambiguous symbol. Polit. Sci. Q. **67**(4), 481–502 (1952)
17. U.S. Department of Defense: (DoD) 5220.22-M, National Industrial Security Program Operating Manual (2006)
18. Defense Industrial Base Information Sharing and Analysis Center. http://www.dibisac.net

Secure Cluster-Wise Time Synchronization in IEEE802.15.4e Networks

Wei Yang$^{(\boxtimes)}$, Zhixiang Lai, JuanJuan Zheng, Yugen Yi,
and Yuanlong Cao

School of Software, Jiangxi Normal University, Nanchang, China
yw@jxnu.edu.cn

Abstract. In IEEE802.15.4e networks, all nodes need to keep high-precision synchronization, which can enable highly reliable and low-power wireless networks. Cluster-wise time synchronization is usually necessary in IEEE802.15.4e networks, which provide a common time among a cluster of nodes. However, it cannot survive malicious attacks in hostile environments. We propose a secure cluster-wise time synchronization for IEEE802.15.4e networks. This paper makes three contributions: First, we provide an in-depth security analysis of cluster-wise time synchronization in IEEE802.15.4e networks. Second, we propose a security countermeasure which includes an improved µTESLA broadcast authentication protocol and fault-tolerant time synchronization algorithm. The improved µTESLA broadcast authentication protocol adopts a packet-based key chain mechanism to resolve the conflict between the delay of disclosed keys and the length of key chain in the original µTESLA. The fault-tolerant time synchronization algorithm adopts a cluster-wise time synchronization model to guarantee an upper bound of time difference between normal nodes in a cluster. Finally, theoretical analysis and real experiment results validate the effectiveness and feasibility of the security countermeasure.

Keywords: Secure · Time synchronization · Cluster-wise · IEEE802.15.4e

1 Introduction

As industrial wireless applications have critical requirements on reliability, low-power and real-time, the historical medium access control (MAC) protocol of IEEE802.15.4-2006 standard has suffered from many flaws. IEEE802.15.4e [1] is the new MAC standard for the industrial Internet of things (IIoT), which enables highly reliable and low power wireless networking through time-synchronized channel hopping (TSCH) technique. Currently, IEEE802.15.4e is the fundamental of the industrial wireless standards, such as ISA100.11a [2], and WirelessHART [3].

IEEE802.15.4e [1] well supports Start networks topology. Start network usually consists of a cluster head node and many child nodes. In order to make the nodes in a cluster cooperate with each other to complete the task, these nodes need to share the same local time. For example, nodes in a cluster go to sleep and wake up at same time to reduce energy consumption. Cluster-wise time synchronization allows cluster nodes

© Springer International Publishing AG, part of Springer Nature 2018
O. Gervasi et al. (Eds.): ICCSA 2018, LNCS 10964, pp. 170–182, 2018.
https://doi.org/10.1007/978-3-319-95174-4_14

and cluster heads to keep time synchronization. The IEEE802.15.4e standard supports two methods to implement cluster-wise time synchronization: one is Keep-alive (KA)-based mode, and the other is Advertisement (ADV)-based mode. Figure 1 shows two ways of cluster-wise time synchronization in IEEE802.15.4e. Research shows that ADV-based synchronization consumes less energy and is more suitable for low power consumption industrial wireless network. Therefore, our paper mainly focuses on ADV-based cluster-wise time synchronization. In the process of ADV-based cluster-wise time synchronization, cluster head nodes broadcast the EB packets periodically, and the cluster-wise nodes receive the EB packets for time synchronization. However, ADV-based cluster-wise time synchronization faces some security challenges. For example, if an attacker forges a wrong time synchronization packet, all legitimate nodes in the cluster may calculate the wrong time because these nodes do not authenticate the source of the broadcast synchronization packet. In the IEEE802.15.4e network, a wrong time offset can result in packet loss, energy consumption, and communication latency, significantly reducing network performance. Therefore, it is very necessary to design a security countermeasure.

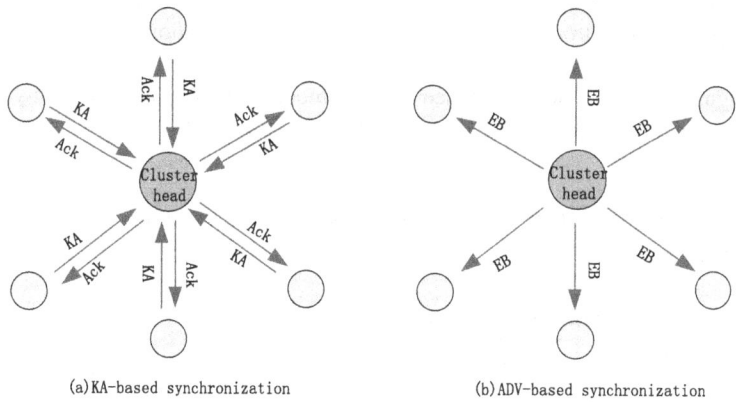

(a) KA-based synchronization   (b) ADV-based synchronization

Fig. 1. Two ways of cluster-wise time synchronization in IEEE802.15.4e networks.

There are mainly two methods for authenticating broadcast packets in WSN: digital signature based on asymmetric cryptography [4, 5] and μTESLA protocol based on symmetric cryptography [6]. Although the digital signature method can be implemented on most WSN platforms, it has high computational complexity and is not suitable for sensor networks with limited resources. In addition, when the digital signature method suffers DOS attacks, a lot of energy will be wasted in nodes' operation of authentication of signature. μTESLA authentication protocol is based on a symmetric encryption method with relatively low computational complexity and high security, so it is very suitable for resource-constrained sensor networks. However, the original μTESLA authentication protocol cannot be directly applied to the IEEE802.15.4e cluster-wise time synchronization, whose key announcement delay conflicts with key chain length. This paper presents an improved μTESLA authentication protocol, using a packet-based key chain mechanism. In addition, fault-tolerant time synchronization algorithms [7] are often used in distributed networks to defend against internal attacks. However, these algorithms have some problems such as too large computational overhead and communication overhead, which are not suitable for resource-constrained WSNs.

Our paper proposes secure cluster-wise time synchronization protocol, which can effectively guarantee secure time synchronization between cluster-wise child nodes and cluster heads. During each round of cluster-wise time synchronization, all nodes in the cluster are elected as a cluster head in sequence. The cluster head should periodically broadcast the time synchronization packets and use the authentication protocol to authenticate the broadcast packets. After receiving the broadcast time synchronization packet, the child node needs to authenticate the broadcast packet. We adopt the μTESLA authentication protocol based on symmetric cryptography to authenticate the broadcast packets, avoiding the use of digital signature algorithms with high computational cost. In addition, a fault-tolerant algorithm based on cluster-wise time synchronization model is used. When the number of captured nodes is less than one third of the total number of nodes in a cluster, this algorithm guarantees that there is an upper limit on the synchronization error between any two legitimate nodes.

This paper first introduces cluster-wise time synchronization protocol and points out its security challenges. Then, it proposes a cluster-wise time synchronization model and designs a security scheme based on the model. Finally, the feasibility of this security countermeasure is verified by theory and experiment.

2   Cluster-Wise Time Synchronization and Security Challenges

2.1   Cluster-Wise Time Synchronization Protocol

Cluster-wise time synchronization allows cluster nodes and cluster heads to keep time synchronized. IEEE802.15.4e standard supports two methods for cluster-wise time synchronization: one is the Keep-alive (KA)-based mode, and the other is the Advertisement (ADV)-based mode. During KA-based time synchronization, each cluster node needs to send a KA request packet to the cluster head, and then the cluster head returns the synchronization error to the corresponding cluster node through the Ack method. In the ADV-based time synchronization process, the cluster head periodically broadcasts the EB packets, and the cluster nodes receive the EB packets for time synchronization. However, IEEE802.15.4e standard does not define how to select a cluster head, and the cluster head can be pre-configured or chosen dynamically. Research shows that ADV-based synchronization consumes less energy and is more suitable for low power consumption industrial wireless network. Therefore, our paper mainly focuses on ADV-based cluster-wise time synchronization. Figure 2 depicts the process of ADV-based cluster-wise time synchronization in IEEE802.15.4e networks. The cluster head sends an EB packet at certain time slot TsTxoffset ms. The receiver records the current time immediately after receiving the preamble of the EB packet.

The time error is then calculated from Eq. (1) and the synchronization with the cluster head is achieved by compensating for the slot length.

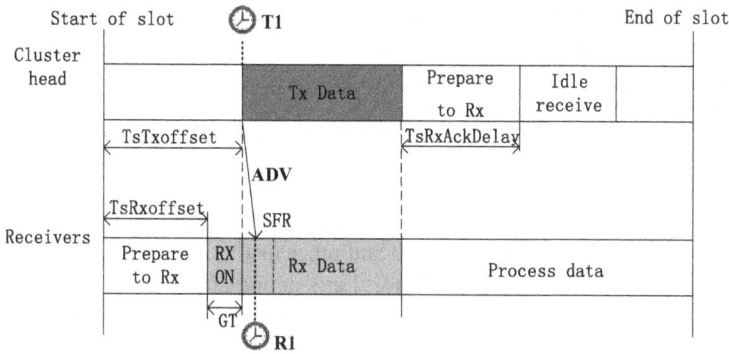

Fig. 2. ADV-based cluster-wise time synchronization in IEEE802.15.4e networks.

$$offset = timeReceived - TsTxoffset \tag{1}$$

2.2 Security Challenges

In the process of cluster-wise time synchronization, the cluster head makes all nodes in the cluster share time through broadcasting time synchronization packet. Because the cluster-wise time synchronization protocol in IEEE802.15.4e networks does not authenticate the source of broadcast synchronization packet, the malicious node easily forges a broadcast synchronization package which can lead the legitimate nodes receive an incorrect clock offset. In addition, when some legitimate nodes in a cluster are compromised, they become internal attack nodes, which may be elected as a cluster head during cluster head rotation. Once an internal attack node is elected as a cluster head, it can use a variety of ways to destroy the normal cluster-wise time synchronization, such as the use of directional antenna to send a wrong time synchronization packet to a legitimate node. In the IEEE802.15.4e network, all nodes need to maintain high synchronization accuracy to communicate normally. An incorrect time offset can result in packet loss, energy consumption and communication latency, significantly deteriorating the performance of network.

3 Time Synchronization Model

In this section, we present a cluster-wise time synchronization model which is similar to [8]. The following Table 1 defines the notation used in the cluster-wise time synchronization.

Table 1. Notation in time synchronization model.

Symbol	Definition
ρ	Maximum value of clock drift rate
ε	Maximum clock read error
t_{beg}^f	The real time of the earliest start of the f-th synchronization
t_{end}^f	The real time of the latest start of the f-th synchronization
δ	Maximum time deviation between two legitimate nodes in $[t_{beg}^f, t_{end}^f]$

Nodes in industrial WSNs are usually clocked by inexpensive crystals. Due to the operating temperature, voltage, technique and other factors, drift phenomenon exists in the actual operation of the crystal oscillator. Let's define ρ(where $\rho > 0$) the maximum value of clock drift rate of a legitimate node, which satisfies Eq. (2) for any real time $t1$ and $t2$ (where $t1 < t2$) and the maximum time drift rate between any two legitimate nodes can be deduced $\lambda = (1 + \rho) - \frac{1}{1+\rho} = \rho(2 + \rho)/(1 + \rho)$, where $\lambda < 2\rho$.

$$\frac{1}{1+\rho} < \frac{C(t2) - C(t1)}{t2 - t1} < (1 + \rho) \tag{2}$$

Due to the drift phenomenon of the crystal oscillator, there is a time deviation between nodes after a period of time. In order to align the time between the nodes, the time synchronization needs to be periodically performed. Assuming that the synchronization between nodes takes place every same time T, and the real time of the earliest and the latest start of the f-th synchronization in the legitimate nodes are t_{beg}^f and t_{end}^f, respectively, it can be deduced that the maximum time deviation between two legitimate nodes in $[t_{beg}^f, t_{end}^f]$ is δ.

$$\delta = 2\rho(t_{end}^{f+1} - t_{end}^f) \tag{3}$$

4   Security Cluster-Wise Time Synchronization

4.1   Basic Approach

In IEEE802.15.4e standard cluster-wise time synchronization, the cluster head periodically broadcasts time synchronization packets while child nodes perform time alignment after receiving time synchronization packets. In order to improve energy utilization and network lifetime, cluster head is generally dynamically chosen. In this paper, we select the cluster head by round. Assuming the total number of nodes in the cluster is n, each node can be elected as cluster head in turn, and the initial order can be based on the order in which the nodes join the network; in IEEE802.15.4e network, when the cluster-wise synchronization period T is determined, each node can calculate when it will be elected as a cluster head again.

IEEE802.15.4e cluster-wise time synchronization protocol mainly faced with two major types of attacks: fake broadcast synchronization packets and compromise attacks. Aiming at fake broadcast synchronization packet attack, an improved μTESLA broadcast authentication protocol is proposed. The child nodes authenticate the broadcast synchronization packet and filter fake broadcast synchronization packets. For the situation of compromised nodes in the cluster, the programs running on compromised nodes may be tampered with. Because the cluster head is elected by round, the captured node may be elected as the cluster head, at which point, it broadcasts wrong time synchronization packet and cluster-wise child nodes will calculate the wrong time offset. In order to defend against compromised attack, a fault-tolerant cluster-wise time synchronization algorithm is proposed. When the number of malicious nodes is less than 1/3 of the total number of nodes in a cluster, the cluster-wise nodes can perform cluster-wise time synchronization normally, and the synchronization error between any two legitimate nodes can be guaranteed.

4.2   The Improved μTESLA Authentication Protocol

The original μTESLA authentication protocol cannot be applied directly to IEEE802.15.4e cluster-wise time synchronization, whose key announcement delay conflicts with key chain length. In the original μTESLA authentication protocol, the key K_i needs to be assigned to each time slot i, the length of the time slot T_{int} is defined, and the receiver must wait for $N * T_{int}$ $(N > 1)$ to receive the disclosed key. If the slot length T_{int} is set to a relatively small value, a large number of keys will be consumed in a period of time, and the sender of the broadcast must also store a very long key chain. This is impractical for resource-constrained sensor nodes, and many time slots may be wasted due to the absence of broadcast packets. In addition, in industrial applications such as industrial process control and factory automation, data acquisition is usually periodic in nature and has relatively large intervals. In order to save energy, the node can be dormant most of the time, so μTESLA authentication protocol whose T_{int} is smaller is obviously not suitable for IEEE802.15.4e network. If the slot length T_{int} is set to a relatively large value, the receiver needs to wait for a long time to receive the disclosed key. This is not suitable for a time synchronization scenario and is subject to DOS attacks.

In order to avoid the above conflict, an improved μTESLA authentication protocol is proposed in this paper, which adopts the packet-based key chain mechanism to replace the previous time-based key chain mechanism. Figure 3 shows the improved μTESLA authentication protocol applied to IEEE802.15.4e cluster-wise time synchronization protocol. A typical IEEE802.15.4e network superframe contains 101 time slots, each with a slot size of 10 ms. When the broadcast synchronization packet Pi is generated, the cluster head generate the MIC_i using the key K_i. Then it sends the authentication broadcast packet. The receivers buffer the received broadcast packet first. When the key K_i is released, it uses key K_i authentication buffer to broadcast packets. Only after the authentication is successful can the time synchronization be performed. As for the attacker, it cannot forge a legitimate broadcast packet, because it cannot forge the correct message authentication code MIC_i before the key K_i is released. In the IEEE802.15.4e network, the cluster head usually only needs to send broadcast packets every 30 s to maintain time synchronization among the nodes in the cluster. Therefore, the improved μTESLA authentication protocol consumes an authentication key for about 30 s, which can greatly reduce the length of the key chain. In addition, according to the resource scheduling algorithm, the delay of the key is about several slot lengths. Therefore, the improved μTESLA authentication protocol can balance the key chain length and key announcement delay well.

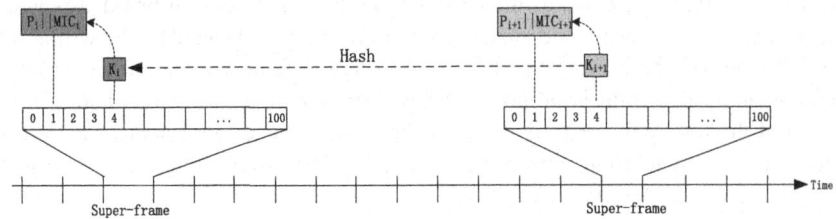

Fig. 3. The improved μTESLA authentication protocol.

4.3   Fault-Tolerant Time Synchronization Algorithm

In order to defend against compromise attacks, a fault-tolerant cluster-wise time synchronization algorithm is proposed which is shown in Algorithm 1. Due to the operating temperature, voltage, technique and other factors, drift phenomenon exists in the actual operation of the crystal oscillator. Cluster nodes need to periodically perform cluster-wise time synchronization. In addition, cluster nodes are elected as cluster heads by the round robin method. This is necessary for battery-powered sensor nodes to avoid a node always acting as a cluster head, causing the battery to run out. Assuming the period of the node's performing cluster-wise time synchronization is T and the initial f-value of each node is 1, then after each cluster-wise time synchronization, the f-value of each node should be increased.

Algorithm 1 describes the steps to be performed by the cluster head and cluster-wise child nodes in a fault-tolerant cluster-wise time synchronization process. The cluster heads and the cluster-wise child nodes negotiate the key chain first, and the initial key can be distributed during the single-hop pair-wise time synchronization process. Assuming that node H is elected as a cluster head, it broadcasts the time synchronization packet "M, NA, MIC (K_f, H, M, N_A)", where N_A is a random number that can be used to defend against replay attack, and generates message authentication code using key K_f. After some time slots, the cluster head will disclose the key K_f. Assuming that node B is a child node in the cluster, when it receives the preamble of the broadcast time synchronization packet, it records the current time R_b and buffers the broadcast time synchronization packet. After some time slots, the node B will receive the key K_f, and it can use the previous key K_{f-1} to verify the validity of the current key K_f. If the result of Hash function is equal, it receives the key K_f, and then use key K_f to verify the legitimacy of buffered broadcast time synchronization packet. Otherwise, the broadcast time synchronization packet will be discarded. The synchronization error offset is continuously calculated. Because IEEE802.15.4e sets the GT threshold, the clock offset will be discarded if it exceeds the threshold. If the synchronization error offset is within the interval $[k\Delta, GT]$, $k\Delta$ is used to replace the offset, and then adjust the synchronization period of the node. In the following, we will verify the effective of the fault-tolerant cluster-wise time synchronization algorithm.

Algorithm 1 Fault-tolerant cluster-wise time synchronization

---

1 Nodes periodically do cluster-wise time synchronization and cluster head is

elected by order; set f=1; $k = \dfrac{n - \dfrac{\varepsilon(1+4\rho)}{\delta+\varepsilon(1+4\rho)}m}{n-3m}$; $\Delta = \delta + \varepsilon(1+4\rho)$

2 Cluster head H broadcast synchronization packet to the children nodes :

3        $H\rightarrow *$: H, M, N_A, MIC(K_f, H, M, N_A) ;

4   Wait for some timeslots, H broadcast the key K_f ; f++ ;

5 Child node B receive the broadcast synchronization message:

6   Record the receiving time R_b , buffer the message M and MIC1;

7   Wait for some timeslots, B receive the disclosed key K_f;

8   Check K_{f-1} ==Hash(K_f) and MIC(K_f, H, M, N_A)== MIC1;

9   if success

10   offset= R_b-TsTxoffset;

11   if $offset \geq GT \parallel offset \leq -GT$ drop the message ;

12   else if $k\Delta \leq offset \leq GT$ $offset = k\Delta$;

13   else if $-GT \leq offset \leq -k\Delta$ $offset = -k\Delta$

14   newPeriod=newPeriod+offset; f++ ;

15   else drop the message ; f++ ;

Lemma 1. If a legitimate child node i synchronizes a legitimate cluster head h at time t_i^f, where $t_{beg}^f \leq t_i^f \leq t_{end}^f$, for any time $t \in [t_i^f, t_{end}^f], -2\rho\varepsilon < C_h(t) - Ci(t) < (1 + 2\rho)\varepsilon$.

Proof. (1) prove the left part, according to Eq. (2), we have

$$|(Ci(t) - \hat{C}i(t_i^f)) - (C_h(t) - C_h(t_i^f))| \leq 2\rho(t - t_i^f),$$

When $t \in [t_i^f, t_{end}^f]$, we have $2\rho(t - t_i^f) < 2\rho\varepsilon$,
so $Ci(t) - C_h(t) < 2\rho\varepsilon + (\hat{C}i(t_i^f) - C_h(t_i^f)) < 2\rho\varepsilon$.
(2) first prove the right part, we have

$$C_h(t) - Ci(t) < |C_h(t_i^f) - \hat{C}i(t_i^f)| + 2\rho(t - t_i^f),$$

we have $|C_h(t_i^f) - \hat{C}i(t_i^f)| < \varepsilon$, so $C_h(t) - Ci(t) < (1 + 2\rho)\varepsilon$.
Together, we have $-2\rho\varepsilon < C_h(t) - Ci(t) < (1 + 2\rho)\varepsilon$.

Theorem 1. When all nodes are legitimate, all nodes in the cluster perform a fault-tolerant cluster-wise time synchronization algorithm. Assuming that for any node i and j, the initial state satisfies $|Ci(t_{end}^0) - Cj(t_{end}^0)| < \varepsilon(1 + 4\rho)$, for any time $t > t_{end}^0$, synchronization error between any node i and j satisfy: $|Ci(t) - Cj(t)| < \delta + \varepsilon(1 + 6\rho)$.

Proof. Using mathematical induction to prove that, for $f \geq 0$, $|Ci(t_{end}^f) - Cj(t_{end}^f)| < \varepsilon(1 + 4\rho)$.

(1) For $f = 0$, $|Ci(t_{end}^0) - Cj(t_{end}^0)| < \varepsilon(1 + 4\rho)$ is true.
(2) Assuming $f = k$, then $|Ci(t_{end}^k) - Cj(t_{end}^k)| < \varepsilon(1 + 4\rho)$.

In the next step, when deriving $f = k + 1$, $|Ci(t_{end}^{k+1}) - Cj(t_{end}^{k+1})| < \varepsilon(1 + 4\rho)$.
Suppose the cluster head in the $k + 1$ round is h, and node i and j are synchronized at the time t_i^{k+1} and t_j^{k+1}, Set $t_{beg}^{k+1} < t_i^{k+1} < t_j^{k+1} < t_{end}^{k+1}$.
When $t \in [t_{beg}^k, t_i^{k+1}]$, according to the Eq. (2), it can be deduced $|Ci(t) - Cj(t)| < |Ci(t_{end}^k) - Cj(t_{end}^k)| + 2\rho(t - t_{end}^k) < \varepsilon(1 + 4\rho) + \delta$.
When $t \in [t_i^{k+1}, t_j^{k+1}]$, according to the Lemma 1, it can be deduced $0 < C_h(t) - Cj(t) < |C_h(t_{end}^k) - Cj(t_{end}^k)| + 2\rho(t - t_{end}^k) < \varepsilon(1 + 4\rho) + \delta$.
Together, we have $|Ci(t_{end}^f) - Cj(t_{end}^f)| < \varepsilon(1 + 4\rho)$.

5   Security Analysis

In the secure cluster-wise time synchronization protocol, an improved μTESLA authentication protocol is proposed, which uses the symmetric cryptography and Hash mechanism to authenticate the broadcast packets. And messages integrity authentication based on symmetric cryptography can effectively defend against information tampering or forgery attacks with low computational cost. The key delay announcement mode is adopted to authenticate the broadcast source. Prior to the announcement of a new key, an attacker could not forge the correct message authentication code because of the irreversibility of the Hash function and the inability to push a new key from the published key.

In addition, aiming at the problem of internal attack nodes among cluster nodes, a fault-tolerant time synchronization algorithm is proposed. To avoid a node has been a cluster head node and lead to depletion of power, the cluster nodes elected as cluster heads by round. When the internal attack node is selected as the cluster head, the legitimate nodes in the cluster will calculate an incorrect clock offset. In order to resist such attacks, the fault-tolerant intra-cluster time synchronization algorithm can detect excessive synchronization errors and fit out the synchronization messages.

6 Experiment

6.1 Settings

In order to verify the effectiveness of the secure cluster-wise time synchronization, OpenMoteSTM hardware node and OpenWSN software platform [9] are used to build up a real experiment. Figure 4 shows the scenario of cluster-wise time synchronization in IEEE802.15.4e networks. The cluster head node periodically broadcasts the time synchronization packet and uses the improved μTESLA authentication protocol to authenticate the integrity of the broadcast packet. After receiving the broadcast time synchronization packet, the child node needs to authenticate it. In order to avoid a node has been a cluster head node and lead to waste energy power, the cluster nodes in a sequential manner elected as cluster head. An attacker may personate the cluster head node to broadcast the wrong time synchronization packet. If the legitimate sub-node in the cluster does not adopt any security countermeasure, the legitimate nodes may synchronize to the attacker and obtain an incorrect time. In the process of cluster-wise time synchronization, the network time slot set to 15 ms, the key length set to 16 bytes and the key chain update period set to 1 min, each super-frame period produces two broadcast synchronization packages.

6.2 Result

An improved μTESLA authentication protocol is proposed for the secure cluster-wise time synchronization. In the improved μTESLA authentication protocol, symmetric cryptography and reverse Hash mechanism are adopted for synchronization packet authentication. Before the key disclose, attackers cannot forge the correct message authentication code MIC. In addition, the improved μTESLA authentication protocol uses a packet-based key chain mechanism and a low-delay resource schedule algorithm, which can well balance the key chain length and the delay of key disclosed. To evaluate the performance of the proposed countermeasure, we mainly consider two metrics: the length of key chain and the delay of key disclosed.

In resource-constrained WSN, storage size is an important metric. In both authentication protocols, a large number of authentication operations require a longer

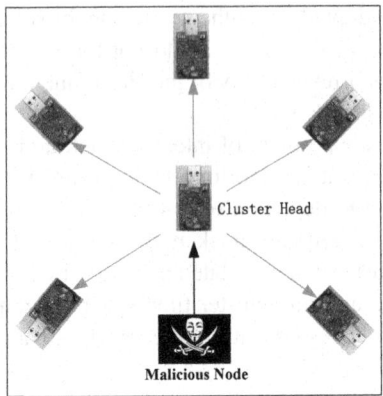

Fig. 4. The scenario of cluster-wise time synchronization in IEEE802.15.4e networks.

keychain. Figure 5 shows that the key chain lengths of the two solutions vary with the length of the time slot. As can be seen, the key chain length under the original µTESLA authentication protocol is much longer than the improved µTESLA authentication protocol. When the length of the time slot is T_{int} = 100 ms, the key chain length of the original µTESLA authentication protocol reaches 9600 bytes, but the improved µTESLA authentication protocol requires only 1920 bytes of storage key. It mostly reduce about 80% key chain length.

In the IEEE802.15.4e cluster time synchronization protocol, the delay of key disclosed is a very important metric. The IEEE 802.15.4e network has a slot size of 15 ms.

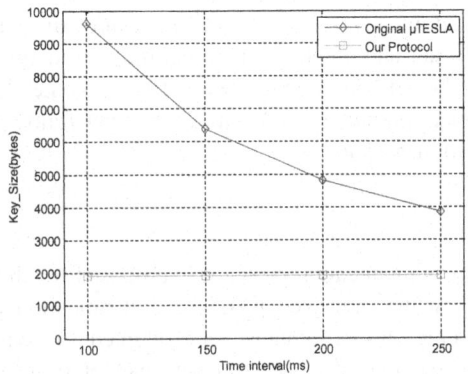

Fig. 5. The key_size vary with time interval.

With the low-delay resource scheduling algorithm, the key of the improved µTESLA authentication protocol can be delayed by 3 time slots. Figure 6 shows the key announcement delay of the two schemes varies with the length of the time slot. When the time slot length T_{int} = 250 ms, the key announcement delay of the original μTESLA authentication protocol is 250 ms, and the key delay of the improved μTESLA authentication protocol is only 45 ms, the key announcement delay is greatly reduced. In summary, the improved μTESLA authentication protocol uses a packet-based key chain mechanism and a low-delay resource schedule algorithm, which can reduce the key chain length and the delay of key disclosed.

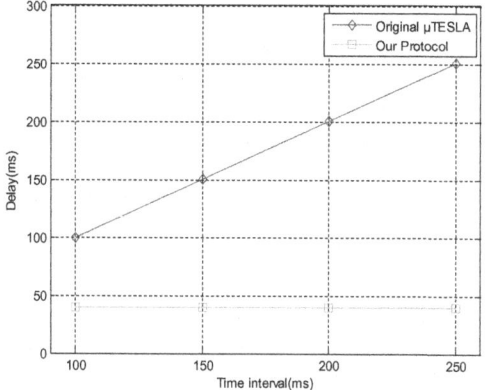

Fig. 6. The delay of the disclosed key vary with time interval.

7 Conclusion

Time synchronization is a fundamental requirement for the IEEE802.15.4e-based industrial wireless sensor networks. Cluster-wise time synchronization can provide a common time among a cluster of nodes. But it usually subjects to forge broadcast synchronization packet attack and compromise attack. Our paper proposes a security countermeasure which includes an improved μTESLA broadcast authentication protocol and fault-tolerant time synchronization algorithm. The improved μTESLA broadcast authentication protocol adopts a packet-based key chain mechanism to resolve the conflict between the delay of disclosed keys and the length of key chain in the original μTESLA. And the security analysis proves it can defend against forge broadcast synchronization packet attack. The fault-tolerant algorithm based on time synchronization model can guarantee the upper limit of the synchronization error between any two legal nodes when the number of captured nodes is less than 1/3 of the total number of nodes in a cluster. It can successfully defend against compromise attack. Finally, the real experiment results validate the effectiveness and feasibility of the security countermeasure.

Acknowledgment. This work is supported by the National Natural Science Foundation of China under Grants 61741125.

References

1. IEEE Standard for Local and Metropolitan Area Networks-Part 15.4: Low-rate wireless personal area networks (LR-WPANs) amendment 1: MAC Sublayer, IEEE Standard 802.15.4e-2012 (2012)
2. HART Communication Foundation: WirelessHART Specification 75: TDMA Data-Link Layer (2008)
3. International Society of Automation (ISA): ISA-100.11a-2011: Wireless systems for industrial automation: process control and related applications (2011)
4. Murthy, S., D'Souza, R.J., Varaprasad, G.: Digital signature-based secure node disjoint multipath routing protocol for wireless sensor networks. IEEE Sens. J. **12**(10), 2941–2949 (2012)
5. Das, M.L.: Two-factor user authentication in wireless sensor networks. IEEE Trans. Wirel. Commun. **8**(3), 1086–1090 (2009)
6. Ruan, N., Hori, Y.: DoS attack-tolerant TESLA-based broadcast authentication protocol in Internet of Things. In: 5th International Conference on Selected Topics in Mobile and Wireless Networking, pp. 60–65. IEEE, Avignon (2012)
7. Short, M., Pont, M.J.: Fault-tolerant time-triggered communication using CAN. IEEE Trans. Ind. Inf. **3**(2), 131–142 (2007)
8. Sun, K., Ning, P., Wang, C.: Fault-tolerant cluster-wise clock synchronization for wireless sensor networks. IEEE Trans. Dependable Secur. Comput. **2**(3), 177–189 (2005)
9. Watteyne, T., Vilajosana, X., Kerkez, B., et al.: OpenWSN: a standards - based low - power wireless development environment. Trans. Emerg. Telecommun. Technol. **23**(5), 480–493 (2012)

Defense Technology Security Education Status

Hyoung-ryoul Cho[(✉)]

Information Support Team, Korea Defense Industry Association, Seoul, Korea
palpadac@kdia.or.kr

Abstract. Since Defense Technology Security Act was conducted on June 30, 2016, target organization having defense industry technology should have the organization and build a technical security system necessary for protection and management of defense technology, and educate their employee regarding to the law and how to protect their defense industry technology. Defense technology security education is conducted to raise awareness of defense technology security and nurture defense technology security experts. The defense industry allows employees to share the importance of defense technology and to feel the need for security. However, training on defense technology security experts is still in its infancy and needs improvement. This paper emphasizes the necessity of new security education by recognizing the problem of current defense technology security education and analyzing similar education. Also, it suggests improvement directions of defense technology security education through on-line education system and advanced curriculum presentation.

Keywords: Defense Technology Security Act
Defense technology security education · Awareness improvement
Technology protection

1 Introduction

Korea's defense industry has increased about 14 times from US$2.5 billion in 2006, achieving export of US$3.6 billion in 2014 through rapid development. Export items are diversified into high-tech products such as components, ammunition, light aircraft, escort, and logistics support. Target countries such as the US, the Middle East, Central and South America, Asia, Europe, and Africa also diversify export destinations from 45 countries in 2006 to 87 countries in 2014 [1].

The proportion of arms procurement costs in the world's defense budget is expected to grow steadily from $340 billion in 2010 to $440 billion in 2019. This means that the military shifts from a labor-intensive organization to an equipment-centered organization, and the defense industry is transformed into a capital-intensive industry in line with the development of science and technology. As the importance of developing advanced and advanced new weapons has increased, and the battlefield has been expanded to four-dimensional space including space and cyberspace, inorganic weapons systems are gradually aiming at unmanned, guided precision, and smartiza-tion, of the total population is gradually expanding.

In order to adapt to such changes in the environment, developed countries are focusing on defense research and development by developing their own core

© Springer International Publishing AG, part of Springer Nature 2018
O. Gervasi et al. (Eds.): ICCSA 2018, LNCS 10964, pp. 183–192, 2018.
https://doi.org/10.1007/978-3-319-95174-4_15

technologies and are strengthening export control to protect core technologies. The defense industry is also increasingly aware of the importance of critical technologies, and the need to protect technology is also emerging. We are competing fiercely for securing and maintaining technical superiority in the defense industry globally, and we are using various infringement techniques to secure important technologies of other countries. In order to protect its technology from various kinds of infringement techniques that are gradually becoming more intelligent and advanced, many efforts are being made not only to develop and secure the technology but also to protect it [2].

Defense Technology Security Act was conducted in Korea on June 30, 2016. The target organization (Defense Acquisition Program Administration (DAPA), Agency for Defense Development (ADD), each Military, Defense Agency for Technology and Quality, Defense Industries, research institutes, etc.) having defense industry technology should have the organization and build a technical security system necessary for protection and management of defense technology, and educate their employee regarding to the law and how to protect their defense industry technology [3]. This paper introduces the current state of defense technology security education. It is focusing on raising the awareness of the employees of the defense technology security organization. And training the professional manpower to strengthen the security capability of the defense industry technology.

2 Defense Technology Security Education

2.1 Overview

The Defense Technology Security Act provides defense technology security training for employees of the organization to raise awareness of the target organization's staff and improve technical security and report the results to the Defense Acquisition Program Administration (DAPA). The contents of the education should include relevant laws and regulations, security guidelines, defense industry technology leakage status, countermeasures such as countermeasures, and other matters that are recognized as necessary for security of defense technology. Target organization have to report the education result to DAPA at least once a year [4, 5].

The Defense Technology Security Act requires the target organization to conduct its own training, but many professional educators can not provide education. Therefore, Defense Acquisition Program Administration (DAPA) provides diverse educators and manpower training courses for defense technology security awareness.

2.2 Education Status

Defense technology Security education can be divided into awareness raising and capacity building education for professional manpower training. The awareness raising education is to educate all employees of the target organization about the importance of protection of defense industry technology, contents of related laws and guidelines, leakage and countermeasures. According to data released by the Defense Acquisition Program Administration, the figure increased by about 5.5 times in 2017 compared to 2012 (Table 1).

Table 1. Participation in defense technology security education

Year	2012	2013	2014	2015	2016	2017
Persons	548	1,174	1,368	1,869	2,170	3,000

Raising awareness education was provided through private instructors, visiting education, and various programs. Training was conducted through local and on-site training. The Defense Acquisition Program Administration (DAPA) Training Center, Defense Security Command (DSC), and community joint education provided training for awareness raising. Also, Defense Acquisition Program Administration (DAPA) visited the Agency for Defense Development (ADD), Defense Agency for Technology and Quality, defense industries to conduct education to raise awareness of defense technology security. This is an increase of 38% compared to 2016 and 3,000 people have completed education. In the case of employees who can't participate in education, Company posted DAPA's e-learning and instructional videos, to the company website or groupware so that employees can receive training [6].

The Korea Defense Industry Association (KDIA) is running the 'Defense Technology Security Manpower Education Program' project from 2016. This education consists of a basic course, specialized course, top professional course, and top executive special education. In 2017, a new researcher course was created to emphasize the importance of defense technology security to researchers.

The basic course was held in four regions to improve security awareness through training for security practitioners, operators and researchers. The contents of education include the importance of protection of defense industry technology and policy direction, defense export policy, construction of defense technology security system, case of technology leakage. So that employees' awareness was improved and security awareness level was improved.

The specialized course was held twice in each region to contribute to the formation of a policy consensus on professional education and defense technology security for defense technical security officers and import/export personnel. It is a two-day course. On the first day, the contents of defense technology security education consist of introduction of defense technology, infrastructure protection plan, information security enhancement plan, legal leakage policy and countermeasures against infringement and establishment of technical security system. On the second day, the import and export licensing education consist of the contents of defense export licensing system, import procedures, trade secret protection, strategic technology export control system, and intangible transfer control method of defense science and technology. Participants in this course will learn defense industry technology security expertise and will be able to train other employees in the company. This is the most important purpose of this education.

The researcher course was conducted twice for researchers, engineers, and technical security officers for the purpose of technology security, technology asset management, research developer security and ethical awareness between R & D and business promotion. The education was carried out with defense technology security techniques, national R & D security management plan, and technology leakage cases to protect defense technology security and defense technology output. This course focuses on recognizing the importance of preventing the leakage of defense technology and the security of technology for researchers, which may occur in the R & D stage.

The best professional course was educated to provide technical security with technical skills for security education, discussion training and demonstration training so that they could upgrade to defense technology security experts. Education was conducted through a two-day education. The main contents were conducted with information protection management system for security of defense technology, digital forensics, and countermeasures against cyber infringement of defense technology. In addition, the education participants were given time to discuss technical security of defense technology, so that they could share information on technology security of other companies. Participants in this course will learn defense industry technology security expertise and will be able to train security beginners and operator in the company.

The CEO special education was held twice in order to raise awareness and consensus of defense technology security to management, in defense technology security meeting. The main purpose of this course is to educate the importance of defense technology security and introduction of major policy directions to induce security management for defense technology security.

In 2016, 713 employees from 212 companies and 589 employees from 153 companies in 2017 completed training in defense technology specialist training [7, 8] (Table 2).

Table 2. Participation in defense technology security manpower education (KDIA)

	Basic	Specialized	Top professional	CEO special education	Researcher	Total
2016Y	322P	290P	16P	85P	–	713P
2017Y	232P	159P	26P	92P	80P	589P

In the table above, you can see that the participants in the Basic and Professional courses have been greatly reduced. In the case of basic courses, self-education is increasing through e-learning and educational videos, and the number of educational attendees is decreasing as more companies request visiting education. Overall, however, the number of awareness-raising trainees increased by 830 compared to 2016. This is because of the increase in the number of trainees who completed the education through visiting education. In the case of specialized courses, most training attendees are security experts, reducing the number of people applying for import and export licensing procedures. In addition, the number of applicants decreased due to the lack of overlapping participation because the content of education was similar to the previous year. The new researcher course was attended by 80 researchers who actively participated. This is because the necessary training courses were held in a timely manner.

According to the results of the questionnaire survey for two years, the overall satisfaction of education was about 83%. Prior to the implementation of the Defense Technology Security Act, education on awareness raising was the most common. There has been little training in the technology security practitioners of enterprises to cultivate their abilities. There are other existing security education programs, but there is no training on policies and systems for defense technology security. Therefore, the satisfaction level of education conducted from 2016 is high (Table 3).

Table 3. Questionnaire survey in defense technology security manpower education (KDIA)

	Education operations	Education contents	Total
2016Y	87%	80%	84%
2017Y	85%	79%	82%

In 2018, the curriculum has changed based on two years of education. The basic course has been changed to be carried out through visits to training for awareness of technology security. Visit the application company to educate employees on the importance of defense technology security, regulations and policy direction. More people will be able to participate in education, and the company will feel more efficient in improving employee awareness. Specialized courses are offered separately. Defense technology security course, defense import and export license course. Training time has been changed to 4 h per day.

The defense technology security course teaches the identification of the technologies requiring protection, manpower management, and operation of information security systems. The defense industry import and export course teaches defense export license regulations, strategic export control systems, and export control systems. A new information security system course has been launched to enable information security officers to participate. This education covers information security system construction and operation, cyber infringement incident response, and the latest information security trends and development. The education focuses on the cyber intrusion and information security mentioned in recent press. It is a detailed education in each field rather than education conducted in the past two years.

2.3   Comparison of Industrial Technology Outflow Prevention and Protection Education and Defense Technology Security Education

The industrial technology outflow prevention and protection law was implemented nine years before the Defense Technical Security Act. This law has been implemented to enhance the competitiveness of domestic industries by preventing illegal leakage of industrial technology, protecting industrial technology, ensuring national security and economic development, and is said to be the birthplace of the Defense Technology Security Act. The Industrial Technology Security Act stipulates that education on prevention and protection of industrial technology leakage, the status of industrial technology spill, and countermeasures against industrial technology leakage must be conducted at least twice a year. This can be said to be similar to the Defense Technology Security Act, which provides education on related laws, protection guidelines, leakage of defense industry technology and countermeasures.

Industrial Technology Security education conducted by Korea Association Industrial Technology Security (KAITS) [9] consists of 4 processes in total (Table 4).

Table 4. Comparison of industrial technology outflow prevention and protection education and defense technology security education

Defense technology security education	Industrial technology outflow prevention and protection education	Comparison
Visiting education	Visiting education	Curriculum-like
CEO special education	CEO technology security education	
Defense technology security course	CSO training course	Defense technology education is more fragmented
Import and export license course		
Researcher course		
Information security system course		
Top professional course (2 days)	CEO technology security education (5 days)	Industrial technology education conducted in more detail

Visiting education is conducted to raise the raising awareness of employees. In accordance with the request of the employees of the company, they visit the association directly to support the education service for the awareness of industrial security.

CEO technology security Education is conducted to raise awareness of technology protection through technology protection education for executives and to induce interest and investment in technology protection.

Third, there is a CSO training course to train the next-generation Chief Security Officer (CSO) with sufficient knowledge of practical skills. The contents of this training are industrial security related laws, legal countermeasures in case of technology leakage, technical security management plan, and digital forensics.

Finally, CEO technology security education is to educate industry security professionals to prevent, manage, and respond to internal security threats and external threats to corporate security professionals. This is similar to 'top professional course' in defense technology security education.

Visiting education and CEO technology security education are is similar to the 2018 education of defense technology security, but the rest of the process is somewhat different.

The two trainings both provide visiting education to raise awareness. It is judged to be more efficient because it is less regulated in time and place than education in past convening education. In the case of the personnel who could not participate in the training and invitation education, the training of the employees was carried out through the educational contents. This is because employees can receive education by posting e-learning and educational videos distributed by the Defense Acquisition Program Administration (DAPA) on the company's website or groupware.

Defense technology security education is more subdivided than industrial technology outflow prevention and protection education. Industrial technology outflow prevention and protection education. Defense technology security education's Defense technology security, defense import and export license, researcher, information security system courses are more subdivided than CSO training course. Defense technology security education is structured so that education subject can be divided into education, such as technology protection, import and export, researcher, information system manager.

CEO technology security education course is conducted in five days in the areas of industrial security education, management, physical and technical security, security incident response, and industrial security knowledge management, providing more detailed training.

3   Suggestion

3.1   Reconstruction of Defense Technology Security Education

The target audience can be divided into all employees, managers, technology protection practitioners, researchers, import and export personnel and technical protection officers. This is illustrated in the Defense Technical Security Guidelines [10]. This includes a detailed list of the training required for each subject (Table 5).

Basic education contents are involved understanding of the importance and general knowledge of defense technology security. This is similar to the content of awareness-raising education.

CEO special education's object is executives. This education contents are 'Role as supervisor role', 'Improved identification of violation of regulations', 'Raising awareness of technical security'.

Researcher, defense import and export license, defense technology security courses is similar to 'Defense Technology Security Manpower Education Program's contents.

Defense technology security educator education is a curriculum for employees training.

Defense technology security education should be done in the same way as industrial technology protection education. This is because it is believed that professional course includes training for awareness raising, which can cause confusion among training participants and that most employers are aware of the importance of defense technology security. Therefore, education for awareness raising should be conducted separately from the professional course.

Visiting education and CEO special education are excluded from defense technology security manpower education. Because, visiting education will invites professional instructors to train employees or conducts self-teaching through e-learning and training videos.

Table 5. Main contents of training by education target (defense technology security guideline)

Course	Object	Education contents
Basic education	Employee	• Understand the importance and general knowledge of defense technology security - Defense technology security laws and guidelines - Defense technology leakage situation, case, countermeasure - Raising awareness of technical security and What is considered necessary
CEO special education	Executives	• Role as supervisor role • Improved identification of violation of regulations • Raising awareness of technical security
Researcher	Researchers and technicians	• Step-by-step research achievement protection • Technology security and management plan between research • Knowledge required for other research work
Defense import and export license	Overseas sales & Imports	• Understanding the defense import and export license system • Strategic material management system and import and export procedure • International arms trade treaty and international technology protection trend
Defense technology security	Defense technology security director	• Ability to recognize discrimination against breach of defense technology security laws • Construction and operation of defense technology security system • Raising the ability to educate employees on new transfers and retirees
Defense technology security educator	Education manager	• Introduction to Defense Technology Security • Understanding the defense import and export license system • Acquire professional lecturers and design educational programs

The CEO special education is conducted at defense technology security meeting. This method is more effective in terms of time and cost. And it is judged that it is more efficient to cultivate specialists by carrying out the process of professional manpower education in the field of practical training of the practitioner and the best expert course (Table 6).

Table 6. Reconstruction of defense technology security education

	Course	Object	Education contents
Raising awareness	Visiting education	Employee	• Professional instructors inviting education • e-learning and training videos
	CEO special education	Executives	• At technology security meeting
Professional manpower	Manager course	Field manager	• Defense technology security, defense import and export, information security system, researcher course
	Top professional course	Technology security director	• Defense technology security further education

4 Conclusion

Defense technology security education is still in its infancy. Many awareness raising sessions have been held since the implementation of the Defense Technology Security Act. Most employees will recognize the importance and necessity of defense technology security. However, current education has limitations in maintaining and improving the perception level of defense technology security. There are not enough professional trainers and the technical security officer is still lacking. Therefore, we need to introduce an online education system so that many people can receive education. Online education offers convenience to many people. This helps maintain defense technical security levels.

Professional training should be provided to train defense experts. In other words, it is important to improve defense technology security by improving the education curriculum that will spread throughout the defense industry. It is believed that physical factors such as information protection systems for defense technology security can be achieved through investment. However, in order to increase the level of defense technology security, it is essential to improve the level of human security through education. Therefore, a special education system should be constructed for defense technology security to enhance the quality of the defense industry.

References

1. Korea Defense Acquisition Program Administration (DAPA): Defense Acquisition Program Administration White Paper, 85–98 (2015)
2. Korea Defense Acquisition Program Administration (DAPA): Research on technical security competence (2015)
3. Defense Industry Technology Protection Act, Law No. 15052, implemented on 28 November 2017
4. Enforcement Decree of the Defense Industry Technology Protection Act, Presidential Decree No. 28211, 27 July 2017

5. Defense Industry Technical Protection Act Enforcement Regulations, Ministry of Defense Decree No. 898, 30 June 2016 (2016, enforced)
6. Korea Defense Acquisition Program Administration (DAPA): 2018 Defense Technology Security Implementation Plan (2017)
7. Korea Defense Industry Association: 2016 Business Report (2016)
8. Korea Defense Industry Association: 2017 Business Report (2017)
9. KAITS Homepage. http://www.kaits.or.kr
10. Korea Defense Acquisition Program Administration (DAPA): Defense technology security guideline (2017)

Multi-lateral Cybersecurity Cooperation for Military Forces in the Digital Transformation Era

Hyun Kyoo Park[1]([✉]), Wootack Lee[2], Zinkyung Ha[2], and Namhee Park[2]

[1] Petabi Corp., Seoul, Republic of Korea
hyunkyoopark@petabi.com
[2] Ministry of National Defense, Seoul, Republic of Korea
{tack123, namhee}@mnd.go.kr, hazin@korea.kr

Abstract. Most organizations including armed forces continuously invested on security solutions such as security information and event management, next generation firewall and intrusion prevention systems to improve their cybersecurity capabilities. Even though most legacy monitoring tools can detect cyber threats, the warfighting and business information systems remain vulnerable to modified or unknown threats since those are evolved continuously in a covert manner.

At the Seoul Defense Dialogue (SDD) Cyber Working Group (CWG) 2017, we discussed several agendas related to the civil-military cooperative effort those can improve cybersecurity capabilities with high-risk/high-payoff research in the digital transformation era. The essence is granting the cyber workforces access to appropriate data from various sources needed to assure mission completeness based on the current technological achievement.

In various situations, military operations must be synchronized with kinetic forces by appropriate cyber information. For this purpose, the cyber situational awareness (SA) provides the risk mitigation and the resilience capability for the mission completeness. To improve SA capabilities, it is important to share data with big data and machine learning technology among civil-military and international cooperation especially for defensive cyber operations.

In this paper we described the lessons learned from SDD CWG to improve the state of the cybersecurity and the cognitive technology for the improved cyber situational awareness.

Keywords: Cybersecurity · Seoul Defense Dialogue · Cognitive technology
Digital transformation · Cyber situational awareness

1 Introduction

By the rapid advancement in computer and communication technologies, today's information and communication environment has become more prevalent and attacks have moved from static to dynamic. It is generally accepted that cybersecurity could be started from removing potential vulnerabilities that are susceptible to exploitation and then established security systems. However, the complete protection of information systems at the boundary of internal network is hardly achievable. Attackers utilize multiple vectors to accomplish their objectives, hence it requires a change in the way of understanding and the strategy about cybersecurity.

In the military, as tightening the correlation between the cyber and kinetic operations, military forces are very dependent on cyber capabilities for their mission completeness. The cyberspace is one of the operational space and the cybersecurity is considered as an essential factor of military activities even in the peace time. The connectivity expansion of weapon systems and business systems incurs hardships of preventing adversary attacks and internal threats. Furthermore activists, nation states and cyber terrorists are increasing with a little modification of easily available exploitation toolkits as a persuading method of their requirements with the same or similar hacking tools.

Hence, most countries have been trying to expand the civil-military cooperation for the mitigation of cyber threat not only in the war-time and in the peace time. Whenever new malware is shown up, government agencies and companies share the signature information to make detection rules or develop defense methods with new technologies. The cyber situational awareness (CSA) can help detecting initial breach in parallel with understanding comprehensive operational environments to share information with kinetic activities.

In spite of previous efforts, the cyber threat detection in real time is still remained as a big challenge. In practice, military forces build security operation centers (SOC) for conducting cyber operations in a complex global security environment. For this purpose, we have studied technologies related to an enhanced CSA and discussed in a partial effort of the Seoul Defense Dialogue (SDD).

In this article, we presented three main objectives of our research as a partial effort of SDD.

- Share knowledge and experiences on the cybersecurity research and development based on civil-military cooperation.
- Ensure survivability and resilience capability based on cognitive technology with open source platforms.
- Enhance CSA capability for prevention, mitigation and recovery of military information systems from adversarial attacks.

The rest of this article is organized as follows. Section 2 places our research into the field of related work. Section 3 discusses the background of security issues for military operations and the international cooperative work for cybersecurity. Section 4 provides our research on technological achievement for cybersecurity. Our conclusion is shown in Sect. 5 with future work.

2   Research Background

2.1   Cybersecurity in Military Operations

In the military, most warfighting and business information systems are becoming more complex to being monitored and protected by commercially available anti-virus and anti-APT (Advanced Persistent Threat) solutions those acclaim more than 99% malware detection. Security professionals have challenges of constantly evolving current information and network environments that of the emergence of the Internet of Things (IoT), the transition to software defined networks (SDN) and the proliferation of embedded mobile devices with the spread of cloud services [1, 2].

The operational environment is the composite of the conditions, circumstances, and influences that affect the employment of capabilities and bear on the decisions of the commander [3]. It encompasses cyberspace of networks, systems and information to provide current and predictive knowledge of operational environments including all factors affecting friendly and adversary forces. In the defensive cyber operations, for both military operations and the public safety, the situational awareness (SA) must be maximized so operational risks may be mitigated, managed, or resolved prior to a mission or during operations but it is very time consuming and costly [4].

The Endsley's definition of SA is that it denotes a person's "perception of the elements in the environment within a volume of time and space, the comprehension of their meaning and the projection of their status in the near future [5]." To detect, analyze and correlate intrusion events through the network and application monitoring, the capability of performing strategic and tactical analysis should be improved based on the collected threat information in real time.

There are several perspectives on cyber capabilities depending on the specific situation of countries and requirements for the military forces. In spite of each circumstances, the more commercial information technology is adopted into military systems rapidly.

2.2   Cooperative Effort to Mitigate Cyber Threat

In the year of 2012, the deputy minister-level and civil experts on security affairs participated an international dialogue that was held in Seoul for the purpose of interchanging opinions in the region of Asia-Pacific named Seoul Defense Dialogue (SDD). In the SDD, participants had consensus about the importance of cybersecurity and settled a working group on the cybersecurity continuously named the Cyber Working Group (CWG).

Since 2014, Korean Ministry of National Defense has hosted the SDD CWG to play a consultative body to foster multi-lateral cooperative effort of responding to growing cybersecurity effectively. In the year of 2017, the SDD CWG was an opportunity for the participants came from twenty-one countries and two international organizations to build trust, and to get one step closer to cooperation in matters of cyber defense and cybersecurity.

Information technology has generated much faster tempo in modern military operations and has changed the reactive posture into the proactive defensive operations, persuasion and more generally achievement of the competitive information advantage in the battle space. In the public society, exaggerated fears of cybersecurity even with a little harm may cause huge economical damage [4]. A futuristic direction would include methods for establishing cooperative relationship between elements of the defense force and the public. The diplomatic effort with neighbor countries to share cyber threat information and a comprehensive global norm is important as like an enhancement of domestic technical capability. However, effective collaboration is difficult in the domain of cybersecurity.

In the SDD CWG, participants discussed two objectives 'Deployment of cyber security technology developed through civil-military cooperation' and 'Confidence building for global cybersecurity' in the era of digital transformation age. The delegations showed a special interest in a role for civil-military collaboration of the state-of-the-art cybersecurity technology [6].

2.3   Cognitive Technology in the Cybersecurity

Traditionally the cybersecurity service has been provided by on-premise infrastructures with well-known concepts. In cyber operations, strategic cybersecurity capability process must show connectivity in the information environment and help navigate that environment. Digital transformation urges technological innovation to fill the gap between offensive and defensive posture.

Cyber situational awareness models provide a new paradigm to view the platform-based ICT environment such as weapon systems, internet services and business systems. A platform constitutes a set of the network traffics to be connected friendly forces and adversaries.

Security intelligence comes from the experiences of cyberattacks. However, it is more challenging to detect malicious codes in today's complex network environments while cyberattacks taking instantaneous effect in a privileged position against adversaries. In the defensive perspective, the detection of cyber threats and information leakage must be achieved in real time and defenders need to rethink the effectiveness of indicators of compromises (IoC) (Fig. 1).

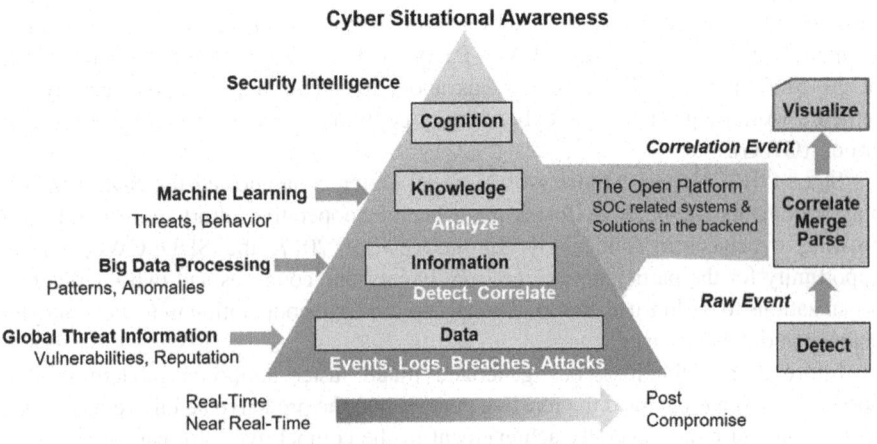

Fig. 1. A conceptual view for cyber situational awareness with related cognitive technology and required information.

3 International Cooperative Cybersecurity

3.1 Lessons Learned from the Seoul Defense Dialogue Cyber Working Group

The Seoul Defense Dialogue (SDD) 2017 contributed to establishing "a culture of multilateral defense dialogue" thorough an active and diversified defense exchange and cooperation under the main theme of "Visions for Security Cooperation in an Age of Uncertainty [6]." There are number of international agreements or treaties are existed for cyber cooperation among countries in a shape of bilateral or multi-lateral. In this perspective, the SDD CWG is an opportunity for the delegates to build trust and cooperation in matters of cybersecurity.

In today, policymakers in Korea as well as western countries often portray North Korea as posing an organizational hacking group. North Korean officials described cyberspace as a highly asymmetric and decisive domain of warfare as like the western countries define it a domain of battlespaces [3]. But usually there is little evidence of skill or subtlety by North Korean military forces regardless of overt damage like destroying data or causing information leakage.

The secrecy regarding the cyber capabilities and activities between South and North Korea creates difficulty in estimating the relative balance of cyber power in Asia-Pacific region. That is the reason why the SDD announced that the main theme of "Visions for Security Cooperation in an Age of Uncertainty [6]." Working group members representing their countries and organizations presented their views on confidence-building measures together with their cyber policies.

Previously, the US and the NATO countries have thrived the Tallinn Manual for more than decade as an international norm. In spite of previous effort, there is no solid international treaty concerning on cyber operations.

In the panel discussion, many participants and invited presenters talked especially on security solutions powered by artificial intelligence (AI) and big data technologies in an era of the digital transformation age. They shared their opinions about various strategies for deploying AI-based cybersecurity technology in the defense sector. In the next session, they discussed on the topic of "Confidence-building for global cybersecurity."

Even though AI has a potential, security professionals must aware of gaps between the technology and appropriate information. Those are very expensive and another challenging issue that will be discussed continuously in the SDD CWG. However, the scientific intricacies of cyber technology and bureaucratic issues sometimes prohibit civil-military cooperative research and investigation. Policymakers may depend on ideas and opinions from experts especially for technology dependent areas.

3.2 A Strategy to Counter Cyber Threat

The information systems generate huge amounts of log data difficult to be analyzed in real time. The existing techniques for predictive protection take input as some pre-processed or mined data that becomes time consuming. Hence most organizations continue to invest in prevention-only strategies since enterprise systems are under continuous attack and are compromised with limited visibility in advanced attacks.

The cyber operational environment is rapidly evolving and CSA models do not support uncertainty appropriately that leaves us exposed to dangerous influences without proper defenses. It is critical to regard the cyber domain not as a separate warfighting space, but rather an integral component of each of the traditional battle spaces. The operational environment can be characterized by technical features against various attacks that typically take advantage of security vulnerabilities. It thrives the weaponization of information.

A desirable starting point for research direction would be changing mindset shift from existing blocking and prevention capabilities to a new approach of enterprise security immune systems. Many global security companies use their next-generation solutions with AI technology and one of participants in SDD CWG showed the current status of security intelligence [6, 7].

In order to enhance the performance of predictive analysis, the cybersecurity system encompasses event correlation technique within the data processing phase. In addition to correlation of security alerts, we require valid and proper predictive log analysis to track the adversarial tactics, techniques and procedures (TTP). Such a resource ideally isn't achievable by one country or organization based on their isolated experience, though. Instead, it should focus on cooperation between different organizations to be capable of quickly adapting to new cyber-attacks.

COGSEC uses intelligent technologies to be resilience over time, learning with each interaction and getting better at preventing threats proactively. It is basically based on rule-based approach for processing real-time events and produces attack classes as output for multistage attack detection [8]. The security intelligence gives military forces an information superiority because it helps security professionals know what enemies might do in the future, offering indicators of potential compromises. This approach is a big challenge, allowing information superiority in the cyberspace. A COGSEC architecture uses a security operation center (SOC) that supports continuous detection and protection with security intelligence. Security professionals need to understand how to improve threat detection, monitoring and incident response capabilities especially for freedom of maneuver in cyberspace.

COGSEC services leverage advanced threat defense, along with security analytics, which can be expensive, difficult to obtain and hard to sustain for many organizations, but is vital in defending and fighting through cyberspace in order to assure the security interests and systems. Because enterprise systems produce a lot of data, and it would be impractical to take on the burden of collecting and analyzing it in real time.

That's why IT security industries are dedicated to collecting up-to-date threat intelligence together and offering it as actionable business intelligence for security service providers. Event processing typically acts upon log files or network messages like SNMP. In the perspective of networks, detecting the exploit is essential since every phase after that can be encrypted by the attacker [10, 11]. Hence the security event monitoring in many organizations is focused on internet and network perimeter, ingress-egress traffics, rather than lateral (east-west) movement, once an attacker is inside the organization [9].

4 Cognitive Technology for Cyber Situational Awareness

Cognitive security (COGSEC) is a next generation cybersecurity concept to mitigate cyber threats, and managing escalation and hardening cybersecurity capability against cyberattacks. The COGSEC can empower the CSA to harness the intelligent analytics within tremendous volume of datasets [12, 13].

What is needed for COGSEC is a security operation center (SOC) to develop and apply relevant tools those are integrated into legacy cybersecurity systems. Open platforms for a cyber security operation center (SOC) have already begun to emerge [14]. Those are fundamental infrastructures of our ever-changing information environment and to defend us in that environment both in the military and private sectors (Fig. 2).

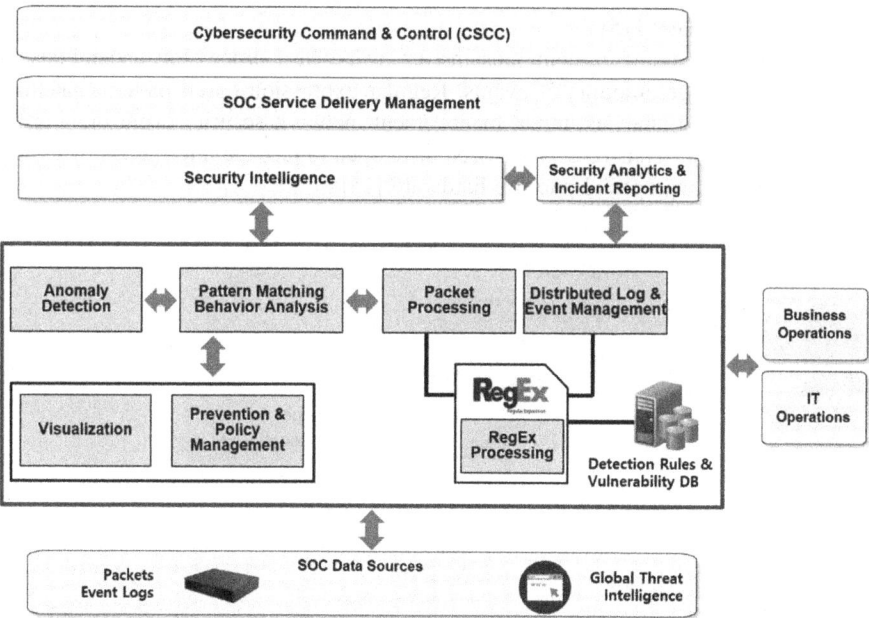

Fig. 2. A conceptual view of SOC and COGSEC architecture proposed by Petabi Corp.

Unstructured data such as video, audio and application specific data have to be translated to an universal language for effective analysis and information sharing. Regular expressions offer a more expressive method for representing patterns over fixed binary strings. Several commercial and open source tools adopted it and several high-performance regular expression matching libraries can increase the throughput performance of intrusion detection systems such as Hyperscan, Snort, Bro and Suricata in an effective way but it does not support full PCRE features.

Since PCRE has become a de facto standard in regular expression matching, it is important to provide full PCRE features for detecting malicious codes and their variants. Petabi's regular expression matching software library REmatch utilizes parallelism that is already available in various CPUs for high-speed matching in capable of providing full PCRE features as shown in [1].

4.1   Event Correlation Based on Regular Expressions

The two pillars of cognitive technology are data sets and algorithms. The primary data source is network packets and log data, but heterogeneous security devices produce threat information, vulnerabilities and configurations in various formats. In the previous research, we developed PERL compatible regular expression processing toolkit, names REmatch, in real time [1]. In addition, we have developed an event enumeration and correlation tool, called REconverge, that can read these events and automatically condense the events into smaller, but more meaningful events, that can be propagated further into the system [15].

The event processing system must assure worst-case processing capabilities in order to handle large amounts of events. Regular expression based pattern matching performance for log analysis, threat management, network security event monitoring and user behavior analysis (UBA) has been developed to provide line-speed processing without incorporating special purpose hardware [15].

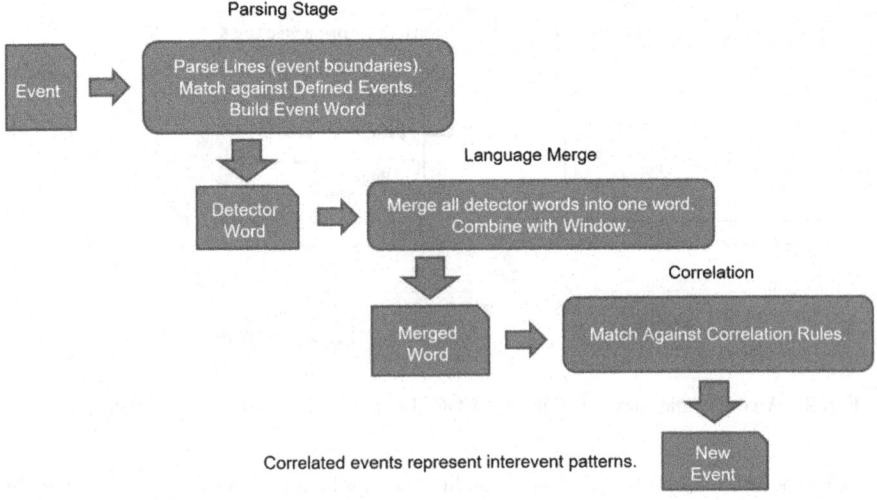

Fig. 3. Event correlator workflow

Transforming events into regular expressions can provide identification of threats through analysis of frequent signatures from massive datasets for effective anticipation of the environment at the edge of network segments. We have studied these shared patterns for automatic analysis and propose a framework for clustering and classifying malware based on regular expressions. A schematic overview of our analysis frame-work is depicted in Fig. 3. It provides semi-supervised classification of 'Base Events' with a regular expression processing method rather than text based event log processing.

For this particular evaluation, 4 million randomly generated events were processed by a single Universal Translator with only a single Detector and with the number of events. All tests were performed in a single-threaded process on a MacBook Pro with 2.9 Ghz i5 CPU and 16 GB RAM.

An event system must have good worst-case processing capabilities in order to handle large bursts of events. We have implemented our event processing using high-speed regular expression matching to ensure no bottlenecks from that crucial aspect of this work. Non-optimized regular expression matching ran at speeds 100 times slower than the worst-case processing times. Regardless, we further optimized the critical path to minimize any extraneous processing.

Table 1 illustrates the statistics concerning the training sets employed and the resultant number of clusters. It correlations across a diverse set of data formats with universal language and in small latency. Our approach can reduce processing overhead and leads to low utilization of memory. It makes use of such highly processed data for future attack prediction which makes the system more efficient.

Table 1. Number of events and derived clusters with training data.

Data	Total events	Total clusters
Nginx access log	1,240,874	216
Nginx error log	562,244	80
Auth.log	8,555	39

4.2 Cognitive Security with Open Platforms

We have studied regular expressions and COGSEC technologies, open platform and CSA framework while emphasizing formality and quantitative measurement, as distinct from the more conceptual discussions. For the speed and scalability, compatibility and quality in the cybersecurity of military operations, the overall achievement of this study can be used for security professionals and enterprise security systems for enhancing CSA. It usually supports decision makers in relation to knowing about the state of an operating environment and relevant entities within the complications relating to cyber defense and problems of strategic instability.

Figure 4 shows the conceptual architecture of our methodology and software toolkits. Many organizations install firewalls or IPS's as initial response systems to cyber threats. In this paper, we recognize that any detector, be it a logging system, a sensor, a Network Intrusion Detection System (NIDS), or an event message from a router, will speak a language. We further recognize that these languages can be translated into an Universal Language that can be shared among detectors. Further, we note that each detector language will demonstrate common cases that can be used to classify and define that language. This simple, powerful, transformation provides the groundwork for comparison of events across time and space.

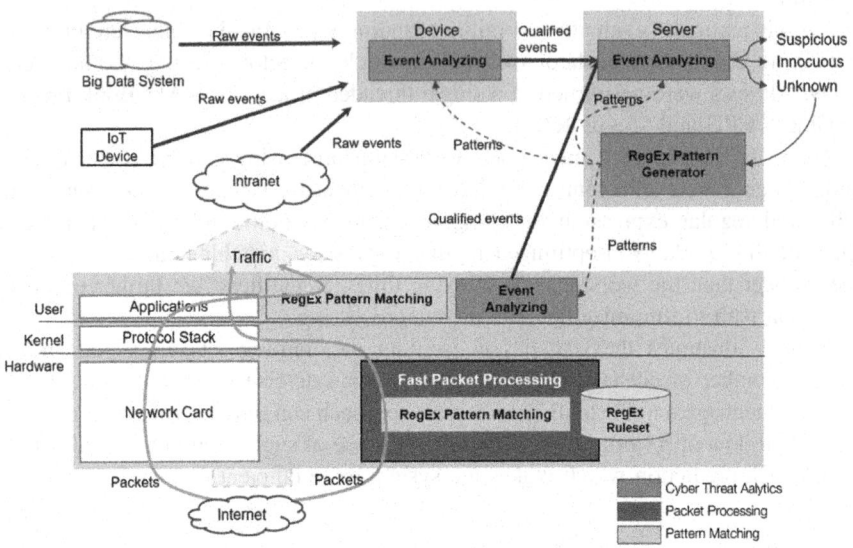

Fig. 4. An architectural view of network packet and event correlation processing based on regular expressions in real time.

Advanced analytics and other software tools help security analysts detect anomalies and determine high-risk threats, but the volume of information combined with the rate and sophistication of attacks has made it nearly impossible for any single analyst to keep up. Our toolkits need to be able to recognize patterns involving events. First, integrating cognitive technologies into military operations is necessary both for developing effective policies and for enhancing the cyber situational awareness.

The main contribution of the research effort can be transferring the previous cooperative work to a mission-oriented integrated security management. In the past, network packets and event logs from various devices treated and processed by security professionals in a batch mode as an incident response.

By taking COGSEC with our regular expression based analytics technology, cybersecurity professionals can be more mission-oriented with relevant data to understand cyber operational environment. Consequently, it can enhance the CSA capability with an information superiority.

5   Conclusive Remarks

The current military operational environment is putting new requirements on cyber operations. Although the cybersecurity has not fundamentally altered the nature of war, it nevertheless has consequences for important issues of new normal including non-military threats and the ability of hacktivists, criminals to influence both international and private sectors. One of intrinsic characteristics of cybersecurity is the dependency between military and civil technology. Hence there are various strategies for possibility of adopting civil technologies into military information systems.

The civil-military cooperative work is unlikely to the traditional criterion of research because cyberweapons are not overtly, and malware is characterized by covert and diverse behavior in various forms of simple modifications of previous malicious codes or a new method. It is reasonable that the artificial intelligence technology can be regarded as a future direction of cybersecurity research.

In the Seoul Defense Dialogue Cyber Working Group, we acknowledged a consensus on the civil-military cooperation for the end-to-end protection and workforce trainings. Those issues are main topics of the SDD CWG for the future of collaboration and acceleration progress both technology and policy. It is generally accepted that it is almost impossible to prevent all cyber threats at the edge of networks.

This article has described the CSA and its related technological research achievement in the perspective of defensive operations. The changing requirements coupled with technological advancements have triggered a paradigm shift in the design and establishment of a SOC that is a core infrastructure of the CSA.

In the future, the research and development plan will proceed as demonstrating the generality and applicability of this approach in a practical way and implementing feedback from both in the simulation and real environments. Also, the SDD CWG will be held at Seoul from 12 September for 3 days and productive discussion related cybersecurity enhancement is expecting.

Acknowledgement. This work was supported by Defense Acquisition Program Administration and Agency for Defense Development under the contract. (UD060048AD).

References

1. Park, H.K., Kim, M.S., Park, M., Lee, K.: Cyber situational awareness enhancement with regular expressions and an evaluation methodology. In: IEEE MILCOM Conference 2017, October 2017
2. Cisco, I.: Cisco visual networking index: forecast and methodology (2014–2019), Cisco white paper, May 2015
3. United States Army War College Strategic Cyberspace Operations Guide, June 2016
4. Matthews, E.D., Arata III, H.J., Hale, B.L.: Cyber situational awareness. Army Cyber Institute, West Point (2016)
5. Endsley, M.: Toward a theory of situation awareness in dynamic systems. Hum. Factors **37** (1), 32–64 (1995)
6. Ministry of National Defense, Republic of Korea, Seoul Defense Dialogue 2017, Book Chapter 10, September 2017
7. Dheap, V., Hale, V.: Applied cognitive security complementing the security analyst. In: RSA Conference 2017, February 2017
8. Vaarandi, R., Kont, M., Pihelgas, M.: Event log analysis with the LogCluster tool. In: IEEE MILCOM Conference, November 2016

9. Crowly, C.: Future SOC: SANS 2017 Security Operations Center Survey. SANS Institute InfoSec Reading Room, May 2017
10. Schales, D., Hu, X., Jang, J., Sailer, R., Stoecklin, M., Wang, T.: FCCE: highly scalable distributed feature collection and correlation engine for low latency big data analytics. In: Proceedings of ICDE, pp. 1316–1327, April 2015
11. Krizak, P.: Log analysis and event correlation using variable temporal event correlator (VTEC). In: 24th LISA Conference, November 2010
12. Rieck, K., Trinius, P., Willems, C., Holz, T.: Automatic analysis of malware behavior using machine learning. J. Comput. Secur. **19**(4), 639–668 (2011)
13. NIST, SP 800-92 Guide to Computer Security Log Management, NIST CSRC, September 2006
14. OSSEC: Open Source Host Intrusion Detection Security. https://ossec.github.io
15. Valgenti, V.C., Lin, Y.W., Suzuki, A., Kim, A.S.: Simulating exploits for the creation and refinement of detection signatures. In: IEEE MASCOTS (2017)

A Study on the Weapon System Software Reliability Prediction and Estimation Process at the Software Development Phase

In Soo Ryu$^{(\boxtimes)}$ and Suk Jae Jeong

The Graduate School Kwangwoon University, Seoul, Korea
youinsure@hanmail.net, sjjeong@kw.ac.kr

Abstract. The proportion of software in the weapon system gradually increases and the embedded software in weapon system is becoming an important factor in determining the performance of the weapon system. The defect in the software of the weapon system are those that are not found at the development phase. To minimize the cost of software defect correction, systematic software quality control is required from the development phase. To increase the reliability of the software, reliability prediction and reliability estimation should be performed in the software development phase. This paper suggests the process of software reliability and the result of comparison on the software quality metrics of the project that applied the reliability prediction and estimation model are presented. It will contribute to improving the quality of software by minimizing potential defects in the software development phase.

Keywords: Software reliability · Reliability estimation · Reliability prediction
Software quality

1 Introduction

Technology related to the Fourth Industrial Revolution has been applying to weapon systems, the functions of weapon systems have improved, and the software included in the weapon systems has become the time to determine the performance of weapon systems.

The defects in the software that are found in the operational phase of the weapon system are defects that are not found during the development phase. Therefore, systematic software quality management is required from the development phase to minimize the cost due to the defect correction of the weapon system software. Reliability should be predicted and estimated using quantitative data of software development phase and testing phase.

This paper suggests the process of software reliability and the result of comparison on the software quality metrics of the project that applied the reliability prediction and estimation model.

© Springer International Publishing AG, part of Springer Nature 2018
O. Gervasi et al. (Eds.): ICCSA 2018, LNCS 10964, pp. 205–217, 2018.
https://doi.org/10.1007/978-3-319-95174-4_17

2 Current Regulation and Improvement Direction

To improve the quality of the weapon system software, systematic development management and activities are required, and the quality of the technical documents and the source code generated in the development phase are needed.

The software quality requirements of Korea Defense Acquisition Program Administration (DAPA)'s "Weapon System Software Development and Management Manual" are carried out with a focus on reviewing software documentation [1].

Therefore, there is a possibility that the opinions of the reviewers are different from each other according to the level of job knowledge of the reviewers. In addition to the product quality review of the document review, an objective assessment of the reliability of the software Product quality are required.

3 Software Quality Evaluation Activities Process

3.1 Software Reliability

Software reliability is defined in IEEE 982.1-1988 as "a software reliability optimization procedure that emphasizes the use of Metrics, error detection and prevention of software defects to maximize reliability in view of limited resources, schedule and performance of the project" [2].

3.2 Purpose of Software Reliability Evaluation

Software failures are caused by remaining faults. Software reliability can be quantitatively measured when the number of potential defects can be accurately estimated at the test phase [3]. Continuous testing improves software quality but leads to substantially increased time and cost. The purpose of software reliability evaluation is to predict the number of latent defects inherent in improving the quality of software being developed and then to determine the optimal software release time point considering the costs incurred in the event of a failure and the cost of testing up to the time of release.

3.3 Software Reliability Evaluation Process

Lyu's software reliability engineering process overview [4] is shown in Fig. 1. This process can estimate the software reliability using the test data that can be extracted from the test phase.

This is does not include the software reliability prediction from the software development planning phase to the implementation phase. Therefore, it is necessary to study a process that can be applied in the software development process from the software development planning phase to the test completion.

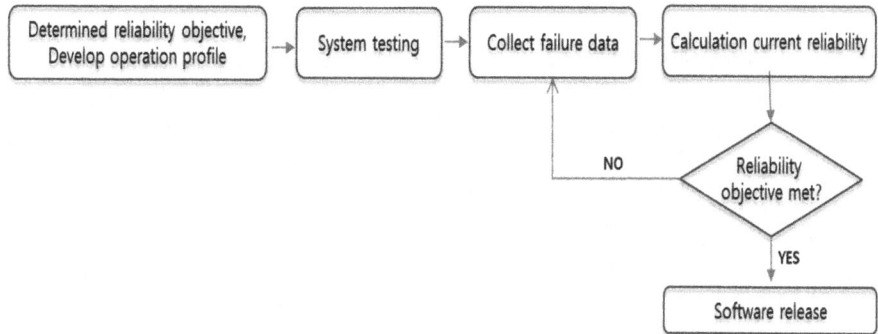

Fig. 1. SW reliability engineering process overview

Weapon system software is usually developed through the process of requirements analysis, design, coding, unit testing, and integration testing using V-model [1]. In this study, the reliability prediction and estimation process in accordance with the V-model process is shown in Fig. 2.

Existing studies use one model of prediction and estimation to predict and estimate reliability, but in this paper, the use of five models to predict reliability and the additional reliability improvement activity can makes the better quality of the software.

Applying this process, we will be able to shorten the software test period (static analysis and dynamic testing), and it will also improve the testability, maintainability-related quality metrics. This will be presented as a result in Sect. 4 case studies. In the step of establishing and assigning the goal value of reliability, it is the process of setting the reliability goal value of the software part throughout the system and assigning the reliability to the subsystem. What is available as a software reliability goal value is availability among hardware reliability goal value. This is the most relevant of software [5]. What the software reliability goal value means the potential defect rate that may remain at the time of releasing the software.

The software reliability goal value is determined by setting the software goal value based on the reliability of the system, allocating the reliability goal value according to the importance of the software configuration item (CSCI). And checking whether the reliability goal value is achieved in the development phase.

In the reliability analysis model selection phase, the reliability prediction from the software development planning phase to the coding phase and the reliability estimation model to be used in the test phase are selected. The model for measuring the software reliability is classified into a prediction model and an estimation model. As shown in Fig. 3, the prediction model is a model that analyzes software reliability from the requirements analysis to the coding phase, and the estimation model is the software reliability after the coding phase.

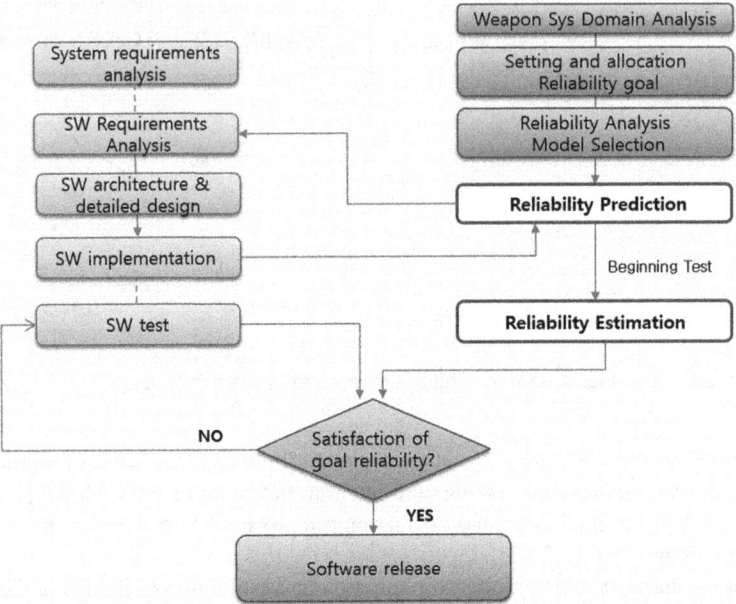

Fig. 2. Software reliability prediction and estimation analysis process

In the reliability prediction phase, the defect density and the number of defects is predicted from the software development environment and the experience data using the selected reliability prediction model.

In the reliability estimation step, the software test result data are used to evaluate whether the reliability goal value is achieved.

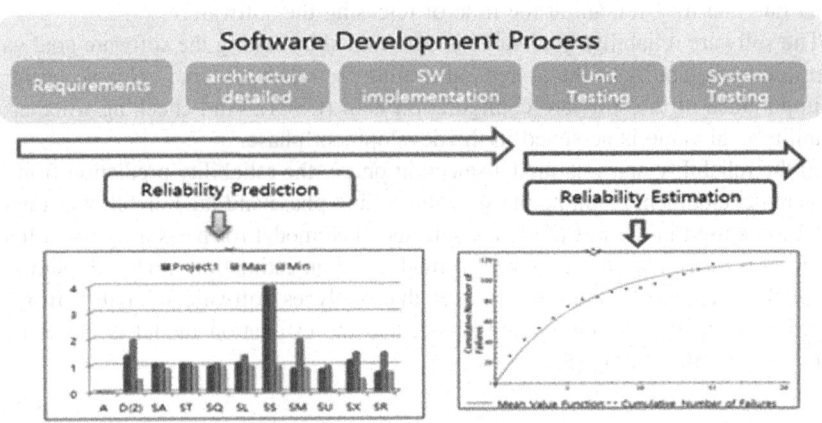

Fig. 3. Predicting and estimating reliability in software development phase

The reliability estimation can determine the current reliability based on the defect data obtained during the test [6], compare the reliability goal value to the satisfaction level, determine the test suspension, and calculate the time required for the test to be additionally performed to achieve the reliability goal.

3.4 Software Reliability Prediction

The appropriate model for weapon system software reliability prediction is RADC (RL-TR-92-15) model, Industry/Application type model and Shortcut model. Software Reliability Prediction and Reliability Improvement Process is suggested in Fig. 4.

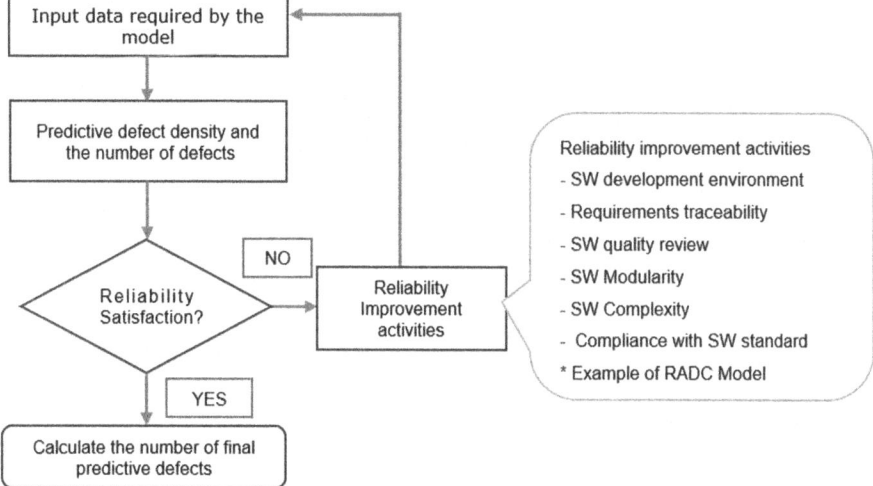

Fig. 4. SW reliability prediction and reliability improvement process

3.4.1 Reliability Prediction Using RADC(RL-TR-92-15) Model
This model calculates software defect density for each development phase and predicts the number of defects based on reliable quantitative measures in software development process [6]. The software defect density and the number of defects can be predicted from the early phase of software development as shown in Fig. 5.

3.4.2 Reliability Prediction Using Industry/Application Type Models
This model predicts the defect density through the ratio of the application type of the system to be developed. The defect density and the number of defects in the test step and the operation step can be predicted as shown in Fig. 6.

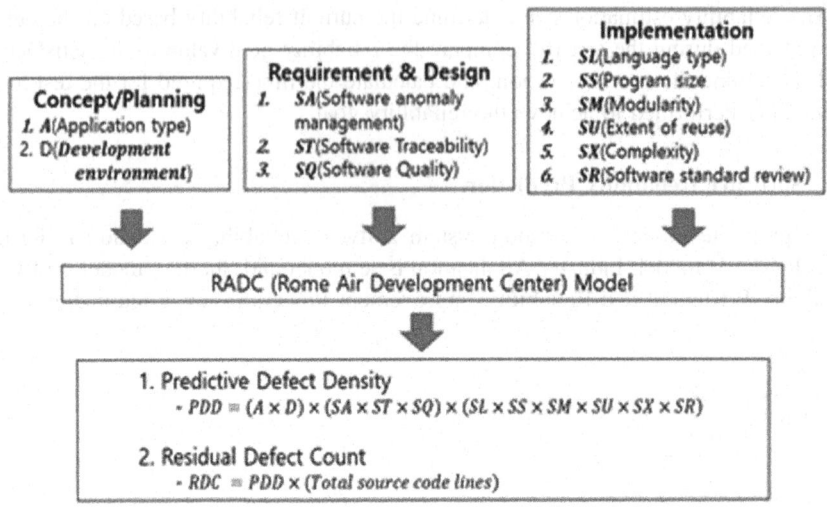

Fig. 5. RADC model reliability prediction

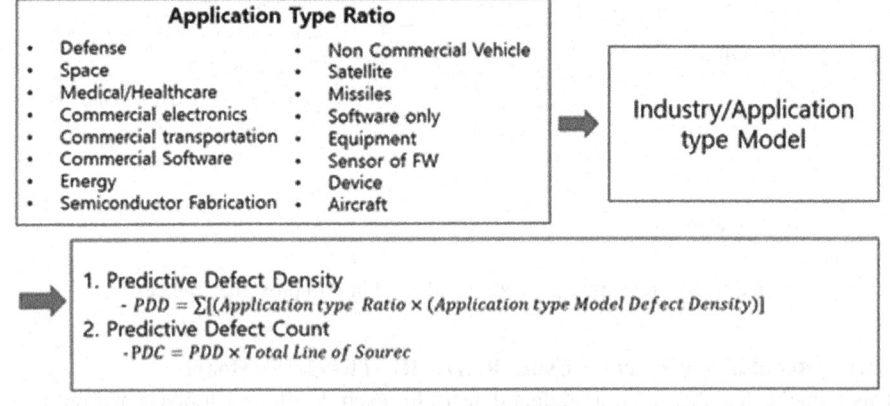

Fig. 6. Industry/application type model reliability prediction

Calculate the defect rate by assigning weights according to the industry/application type ratio of the divided items [6]. (Multiply by 'Application rate of system' and 'Testing defect density' for each level, then add all together, where percentage is divided by 100 to a value between 0 and 1).

3.4.3   Reliability Prediction Using Shortcut Model

This model predicts the defect density in the test phase and the operation phase by evaluating 15 strong points and 7 risk factors according to the software development environment and development method with a checklist [6]. The defect density and the number of defects are predicted as shown in Table 1.

① Prepare a checklist for Strengths and Risks.
② Yes is 1 point and Somewhat is 0.5, and Strength and Risk are added.
③ Subtract the risks from the sum of strengths.
④ Calculate the defect density according to the range of the following table.

Table 1. Calculation of shortcut model

Range	Testing defect density	Operational defect density
③ result >= 4.0	0.001015	0.000110
③ result <= 0.5	0.002252	0.000647
0.5 < ③ result < 4.0	0.001846	0.000239

3.5   Software Reliability Estimation

3.5.1   Reliability Estimation Process

The process of estimating the current reliability and future reliability based on defect data or coverage data in the software testing phase is suggested in Fig. 7.

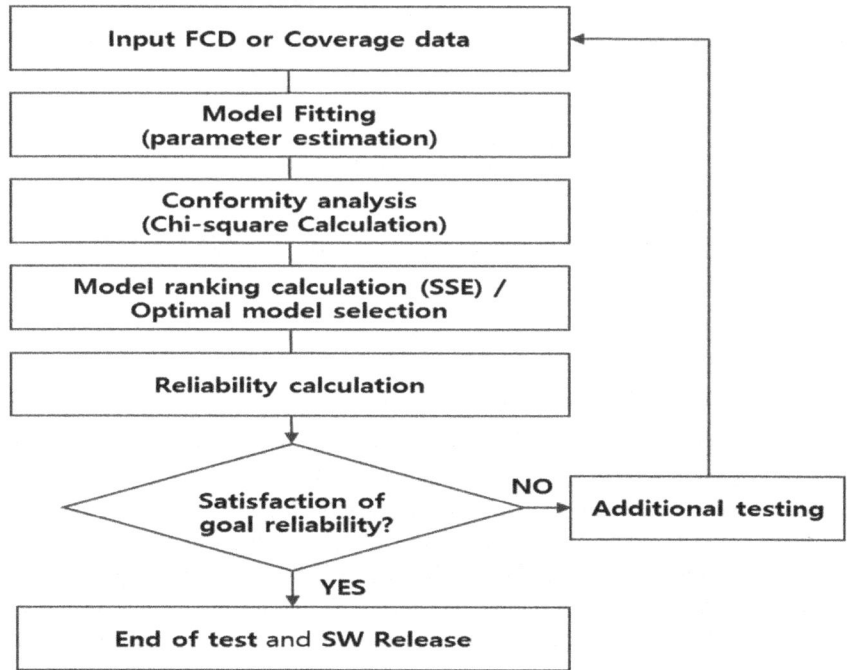

Fig. 7. Reliability estimation process

Estimate the current reliability and future reliability by selecting one model with a minimum SSE value, which is calculated with five reliability estimation models.

3.5.2   Reliability Measurement Using Estimation Model

Reliability measurement method is suggested as a method of estimating the current reliability and future reliability based on the defect data in the software testing phase. We can calculation when to achieve the software reliability goal value (for example, 0.95) and stop testing are shown in Fig. 8 as example.

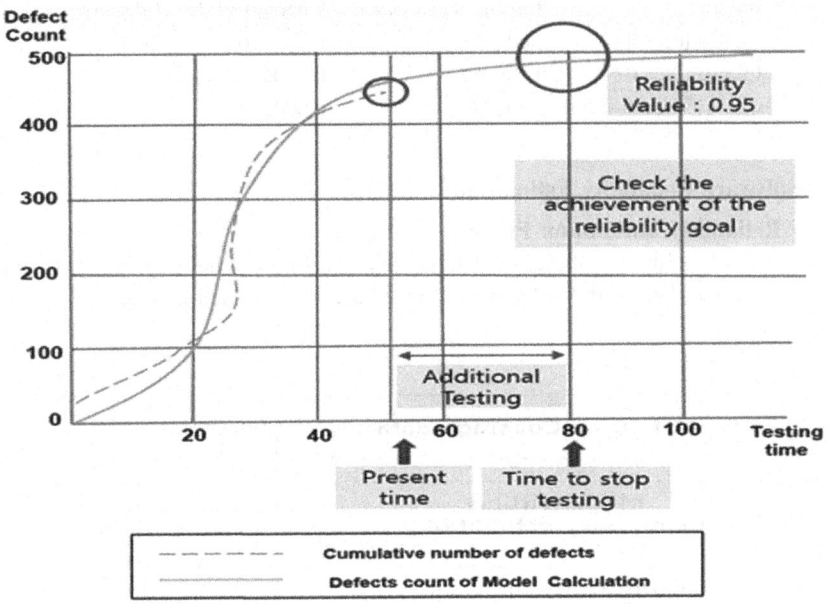

Fig. 8. Software reliability measurement by estimation model

4   Case Studies

4.1   Case Studies of Prediction Model

Project 1 applied RADC model, Application Type model, and Shortcut model. The results of the three models presented in the IEEE 1633 recommended practice on Software reliability were applied to one project, resulting in different defect densities in the RADDC model, industry/Application type model, and shortcut model.

This is because of reliability of prediction model is different between the primitive data used by each model and the empirical data. Therefore, it is desirable to use several models to calculate the defect density and use it as a reference indicator for reliability improvement activities.

Cases for calculating defect densities by applying RADC models, application type models, and Shortcut models to Project 1 are presented in Sects. 4.1.1, 4.1.2, and 4.1.3.

4.1.1 RADC Prediction Model

We predicted software reliability for projects developed by M company by considering software type, development environment, exception management, traceability, quality, development language, standards compliance, modules and complexity. It is shown in Table 2.

Table 2. Calculation results of RADC model

	Concept Phase	Requirement / Design Phase	Implementation Phase
Primitive Data	System type Development environment	Anomaly management Traceability Quality Review	language Type Program size Modularity Reusability Complexity Standard Compliance
Defect Density	0.003983	0.005415	0.004195
Number of defects (DD*SLOC)			0.004195*25,353 =106.35 (Initial defect count)

4.1.2 Industry/Application Type Model

This model assumes that software defect density is directly related to the application type or industry [6]. This project consists of Defense 50%, Commercial software 40%, Equipment 10%.

The defect density is calculated from this.
Defense (50%) 0.5 * 1.116 = 0.558
Commercial software (40%) 0.4 * 0.095 = 0.038
Equipment (10%) 0.1 * 1.451 = 0.1451
Defect density: 0.558 + 0.038 + 0.1451 = 0.7411
Therefore, Defect density of this project is 0.7411(EKSLOC)

4.1.3 Shortcut Model

Shortcut model assumes that the defect density is a function of the number of risks versus strengths regarding this release of the software [6]. The 15 strengths and 7 risks of software development are used to Calculate defect density.

This project has derived strengths 11 and weaknesses 3. The defect density is calculated from this.

ⓐ strength-risk: 11-3=8

ⓑ if ⓐ >= 0.4, the defect density is 0.11

ⓒ if ⓑ <=0.5, the defect density is 0.647

Therefore, the defect density of this project is 0.11(EKSLOC)

4.1.4 Comparison of Applied Case and None-Applied Case

The software quality metrics were compared by LDRA to calculate the software quality metrics for projects that applied the processes presented in the paper and those that did not apply.

The results show that the applied case from all metrics related to testability, maintainability metrics and clarity metrics showed superior quality metrics. The projects are presented in Table 3.

Table 3. Comparison of two projects

	Applied case	Non-applied case
Project name	Project 1: SIRIUS reliability evaluation module	Project 2: fatigue test tool
Quality metrics measure tool	LDRA testbed/TBvision	

We measured the key quality metrics using the quality metrics measurement tool of the LDRA company.

Using LDRA's Quality measurement tool, Projects that have a Prediction model applied, Projects that do not have a Prediction model applied. The result of measuring key quality metrics using the LDRA's Quality measurement tool is Table 4.

Table 4. Results of measuring key quality metrics

	Prediction model applied projects	Projects that do not applied prediction model
Clarity	90	69
Maintainability	93	67
Testability	92	77

Key quality metrics are follows;

Clarity: Executable ref. Lines, Total Comments, Comments in Headers, Comments in Declarations, Comments in Executable Code, Blank Lines, Total Comments/Exe. Lines, Declaration Comments/Exe. Lines, Code Comments/Exe. Lines, Average Length of Basic Blocks, Unique Operands, Total LCSAJs, Depth of Loop Nesting, Expansion Factor.

Maintainability: Essential Knots, Essential Cyclomatic Complexity, Knots, Cyclomatic Complexity, Vocabulary, Number of Procedures, Total LCSAJs, Unreachable LCSAJs, Maximum LCSAJ Density, Unreachable Lines, Unreachable Branches.

Testability: Knots, Cyclomatic Complexity, Executable reformatted Lines, Number of Basic Blocks, Total Operands, Number of Loops, Procedure Exit Points, Number of Procedures, Total LCSAJs, Unreachable LCSAJs, Maximum LCSAJ Density, Unreachable Lines, Unreachable Branches, File Fan in, Fan Out.

Using LDRA tool, measurements of quality metrics of project that applied prediction model (Table 5) and project that do not applied prediction model (Table 6) are presented.

Table 5 Results of prediction model applied projects

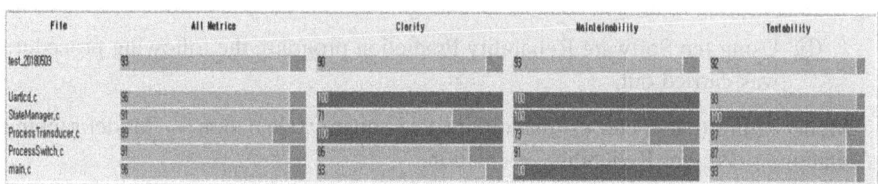

Table 6 Results of non-applied project

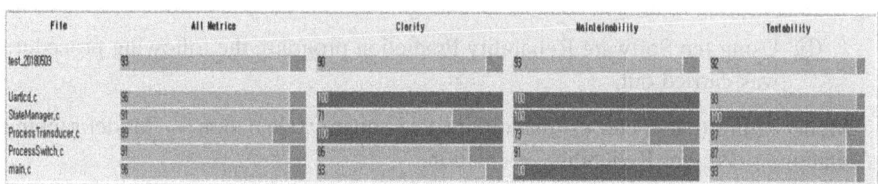

By comparing the quality metrics of the two projects, we can see that the quality metrics of the projects with the quality metrics are very well. In conclusion, the software quality of the project that managed the software quality by calculating the defect density and the number of defects using the prediction model was good.

4.2 Estimation Model Applied Cases

4.2.1 Reliability Estimation Using Failure Count Data

ⓐ Input Failure Count Data of software testing

We can Estimate the time to reach the software current reliability and goal reliability by utilizing the defect data found in the testing phase since the software was coded.

Table 7. Failure count data

Date	1	2	3	4	5	6	7	8	9	10
FCD	5	5	5	5	6	8	2	7	4	2
Date	11	12	13	14	15	16	17	18	19	20
FCD	31	4	24	49	14	12	8	9	4	7
Date	21	22	23	24	25	26	27	28	29	30
FCD	6	9	4	4	2	4	3	9	2	5
Date	31	32	33	34	35	36	37	38	39	40
FCD	4	1	4	3	6	13	19	15	7	15
Date	41	42	43	44	45	46	47	48	49	50
FCD	21	8	6	20	10	3	3	8	5	1

Defect unit time is one day, and the defect data found for 50 days is showed Table 7.

ⓑ Using the Software Reliability Prediction program, the following procedure was carried out.

Model fitting (parameter estimation) → Chi-square Calculation → Model ranking calculation → Present Reliability calculation.

ⓒ Calculate additional test time to reach goal reliability (95%)

The 50-hour-tested results current reliability is 0.9012. It takes 10 h to reach the goal reliability of 0.95, and We will be able to release the software thereafter.

ⓓ Calculating the number of defects remaining

Total number of predicted defects are 454. The current cumulative number of defects is 431. The total number of defects remaining is 23 (Fig. 9).

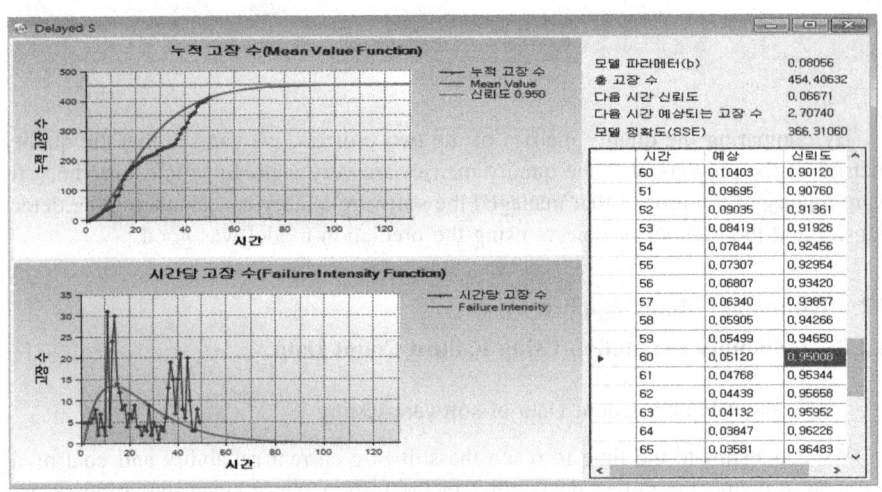

Fig. 9. Software reliability measurement by estimation model

4.3   Benefits of Software Quality Improvement Activities Processes

The benefits of applying Software Quality improvement activities processes were derived as follows:

First, the reliability prediction model can be used in the software development phase to improve reliability. Software developers are usually pressed by time, and software quality management is neglected. The result is large number of bugs that were not found during the development phase, wasting much time and effort in the test phase. Applying the software quality improvement activities processes presented in this paper, we can improve the quality and save time of software development.

Second, the reliability prediction model can be used to lower complexity and modularity, thereby static analysis and dynamic testing can be easy.

Third, the software testing phase can accurately estimate the software release time, such as the current reliability, future reliability, and additional time measurements to reach the goal reliability, which allows for the accurate estimation of the timing of releasing the software to the market when it can be predicted.

5   Conclusion

Potential defects that are not found during the development phase can lead to serious failure in the Operating phase. Therefore, quality management in software development phase is very important, so software quality management is needed in R&D of software weapons system.

In this study, the process of software reliability prediction and estimation was suggested. We presented the result of Comparison on the software quality metrics of the project that applied the reliability prediction and estimation model. A comparison of software quality metrics in a project that applied the reliability prediction model has been evaluated with excellent metrics on the quality of the project that applied the process presented in this paper.

It can be improved the quality of software by minimizing potential defects at the phase of software development. We think that it will contribute to the development of weapon system software. And additional study is needed to analyze and compare effects such as shortening the test period and reducing the effort.

References

1. Weapon System Software Development and Management Manual Korea Defense Acquisition Program Administration (2017)
2. IEEE Standard Dictionary of Measures to Produce Reliable Software. IEEE Std 982.1(1988)
3. Guide to the Software Engineering Body of Knowledge. IEEE SWEBOK (2004)
4. Lyu, M.R.: Handbook of Software Reliability Engineering. IEEE Computer Society Press, Washington, D.C. (1996)
5. Ryu, I.S.: A study on the applying method for the life cycle sustainment plan of weapon system software. Kunguk University (2014)
6. IEEE Recommended Practice on Software Reliability. IEEE Std 1633 (2016)

Decentralized Message Broker Federation Architecture with Multiple DHT Rings for High Survivability

Minsub Kim[1], Minho Bae[1], Sangho Yeo[1], Gyudong Park[2], and Sangyoon Oh[1(✉)]

[1] Department of Computer Engineering, Ajou University,
Suwon, Gyeonggi-do, Republic of Korea
{skms8622,minkkang,soboru963,syoh}@ajou.ac.kr
[2] Agency for Defense Development, Seoul, Republic of Korea
iobject@add.re.kr

Abstract. A message broker is an essential component of messaging services that connect information providers and consumers, message service clients, to enable the integrated message network. To support large scale message clients with the contracted service level, multiple brokers have to collaborate and form a federated broker cluster in many cases. For example, Kafka is one of the most popular messaging systems that allows multiple brokers co-working together. ZooKeeper, the distributed cluster coordinator, manages cluster nodes and stores metadata of messages for Kafka. Even though ZooKeeper does the coordination job well in a simple way, its half-centralized coordinating methods make the overall system less capable in survivability. In some domains such as military warfare and embedded sensor networks, we may lose the primary coordinator or lose more than a half of the coordinator machines. In these cases, we cannot support the minimum survivability to maintain the message network. To address this limited survivability problem, we propose a decentralized message broker federation architecture with distributed hash table. In our proposed architecture design, the decentralized coordinator supports the DHT exchanges between brokers to manage metadata of distributed message partitions. We built a prototype of a message broker federation based on our proposed decentralized metadata coordinator design to show the feasibility in terms of practical application.

Keywords: Coordination scheme · Distributed hash table
Message broker federation

1 Introduction

Connecting distributed software components and delivering messages between them is one of most essential requirements to achieve "the distributed system in collaboration." For a small-scale system with a few participating components, a synchronous and direct connection between two works efficiently. However, the complexity of many communication systems is quite big and the communication overhead caused by the complexity becomes unbearable in large scale systems. The publish/subscribe

© Springer International Publishing AG, part of Springer Nature 2018
O. Gervasi et al. (Eds.): ICCSA 2018, LNCS 10964, pp. 218–226, 2018.
https://doi.org/10.1007/978-3-319-95174-4_18

communication paradigm that decouples data pipelines (between a sender and a receiver) is a better choice of the communication paradigm for large scale distributed systems. To deliver messages between message subscribers (i.e., message consumers) and publishers (i.e., message producers) who are unaware of the existence of each other, many distributed systems use a broker architecture. A broker sits in between the subscriber and the publisher delivering the messages based on their interest. Thus, the overall complexity and the performance of the distributed system can be improved.

To achieve higher scalability and availability, a messaging system for a large-scale distributed system (e.g., Kafka [1]) tends to be designed to enable the collaboration between brokers in the form of a federation. Because a broker federation is a cluster of nodes that are disparately located, it needs a coordinator or coordination service. Two major roles of the coordinator are (1) managing cluster nodes through monitoring their status and (2) managing metadata of messages (i.e., sharing information). Kafka, currently the most popular message brokerage system, delegates the coordination task to Zookeeper [2]. Zookeeper is a software platform that enables a distributed coordination service through a simple shared namespace like a file system. Zookeeper is designed to be simple and high performance. Also, it is designed to be reliable by applying a replication scheme (i.e., primary-backup).

Even though Zookeeper is simple and reliable, it doesn't fit to all environments. Since its critical component Zookeeper atomic broadcast (Zab) [3] requires a consensus of a quorum, it cannot continue to serve its task if it loses more than a half of its servers and it takes a significant amount of time to recover from the failure of the leader with a large-scale ensemble. Covering these fault cases is very critical to a certain domain of software where the loss of servers is common such as a military combat situation. For example, the messaging service is used to integrate C4I (Command, Control, Communication, Computer and Information) software systems in the NCW (Net-Centric Warfare) environment [4]. When it uses a distributed coordination service with primary-backup scheme such as Zookeeper, a broker federation for a company that consists of an individual broker for a platoon will not be in operation if it loses the majority of its broker nodes. For this case, a more resilient and fault-tolerant coordination service is required.

In this paper, we propose a DHT (distributed hash table) based distributed coordination service for a broker federation with high survivability. The coordination service such as Zookeeper provides a shared namespace service through managing a metadata of messages. For this role of managing message metadata, we introduce a novel DHT based lookup algorithm. In our proposed algorithm, an individual DHT ring is assigned for each messaging topic to reduce the lookup time. Our multi-ring approach gives the message broker federation the advantage in message lookup performance when the number of participating nodes in the federation is large and messages can be classified into different categories such as topics. In addition, because we leverage the structure of a DHT based lookup algorithm, higher level of survivability compared to existing half-centralized services is achieved.

To evaluate the efficiency of our proposed scheme, we build a prototype based on our scheme and compare its performance with Chord, a popular distributed lookup algorithm. The experiment result shows that the number of hops for traversing the key space can be reduced with our proposal compare to Chord.

2 Related Work

2.1 Apache ZooKeeper

Apache ZooKeeper is a widely used distributed coordination service that allows multiple loosely-coupled processes to manage shared namespaces in a consistent manner. For instance, in case of Apache Kafka, the partitioned topic-based messages that reside across multiple brokers need to be located by the Kafka clients. The responsibility of managing the metadata is delegated to an external coordination service, Apache ZooKeeper, so that the multiple distributed Kafka brokers provide correct and consistent data locations to client requests.

In order to guarantee the consistency of the shared data, ZooKeeper uses Zab (ZooKeeper atomic broadcast algorithm) that implements a primary-backup scheme. In a primary-backup scheme, a single primary process executes client requests and then informs backup processes of the incremental state changes of the shared data, through the Zab protocol. In other words, Zab relies on the primary process to synchronize with all the backup processes. With this perspective in mind, Giraffe [5] tackles the scalability issue of ZooKeeper, by showing that the primary process becomes the bottleneck in large scale systems. Through experiments, they showed that the increase in the size of an ensemble causes the recovery time to grow linearly, when a leader fails. Furthermore, because Zab relies on a consensus of a quorum, it requires that a majority of the servers have not crashed, in order to provide a consistent view of the shared data.

Although a leader failure and over-half of the servers crashing may not be a frequent occasion in systems that are deployed in relatively stable conditions such as Kafka, Hadoop [6] and Spark [7], it may not be the same for message systems that are used in harsh conditions such as military warfare. In such conditions, rather frequent crash of the coordination leader and the crash of the majority has to be taken into consideration. Therefore, ZooKeeper, which heavily relies on the primary process may not be a one-size-fits-all solution.

2.2 Chord

Chord [8] is a decentralized lookup protocol based on distributed hash tables that maps keys to nodes. It uses a variant of consistent hashing in order to achieve load balance by assigning roughly the same number of keys to each node. Each of the nodes (i.e., peers) maintains routing information so that without a centralized coordinator a peer is able to locate a node with the requested key, by sequentially traversing the key space in a clockwise manner. To accelerate the process of traversing the key space without visiting every succeeding node, each node maintains an additional routing information called a finger table, where an ith entry of the table contains the identity of the node that succeeds it by at least 2^{i-1} on the identifier circle. This scheme can improve a lookup time complexity $O(\log N)$ from $O(N)$ that is the case without a finger table where N is the number of peers participating in the Chord ring. Figure 1 depicts a Chord ring with finger tables. Figure 1 shows an example where the number of bits in the identifier is three and the total number of identifiers is eight ($2^3 = 8$). There are three nodes with identifier 4, 5 and 7. Because 7 is the first clockwise identifier from node 6, the node with the identifier 7 is the successor of the identifier 6. Likewise, the node with identifier 4 is the successor of node 3. The node with the identifier 5 itself is the successor of its own identifier, 5.

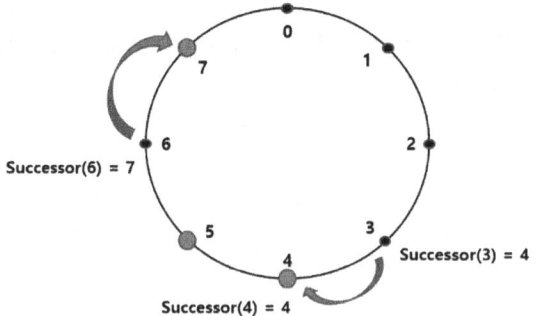

Fig. 1. A Chord ring (m = 3) example with nodes 4, 5, and 7.

Peers in the Chord key space are able to maintain a correct list of successors and a predecessor through Chord's stabilize protocol. Every peer in the key space runs stabilize protocol periodically. The protocol is as follows. A peer asks its successor for the successor's predecessor p, and decides if its successor should be updated to the peer p, which is the case if p has recently joined the network. The protocol also lets the peer to inform the successor of its existence in the network, giving the chance for a successor to update its predecessor. Figure 2 shows the pseudo-code for the stabilization protocol. For an example, suppose that a peer n joins the network, and its hashed ID is between that of peers n_p and n_s. n will have n_s as its successor. Peer n_s will update its predecessor when it is notified by the newly joined peer n. Now when n_p runs the stabilize protocol, it will ask n_s for a predecessor, and n_s will reply that n is its predecessor. Thus, n_p updates its successor to n, instead of the previous n_s.

```
n.join (n')
    predecessor = nil;
    successor = n'.find_successor(n)

// periodically verify n's successor,
// and tell the successor about n.
n.stabilize ()
    x = successor.predecessor;
    if ( x ∈ (n,successor) )
        successor = x;
    successor.notify(n);

n.notify (n')
    if ( predecessor is nil or n' ∈ (predecessor, n) )
        predecessor = n';
```

Fig. 2. Pseudo-code for Chord's stabilize protocol

Additionally, n_p will notify n, and n will now update its predecessor to n_p, completing the stabilizing process. This process is run periodically in order to correctly maintain the list of successors and a predecessor, even when there are frequent joins and leaves of peers.

3   Multi-ring DHT Scheme of Message Broker Federation for Higher Survivability

3.1   Overview

To achieve higher scalability, message brokers may be clustered and form a message broker federation. A coordination service such as Zookeeper is responsible for managing the metadata of messages maintained by the broker federation. However, a coordination service that manages metadata in a half-centralized way such as the primary-backup scheme does not suit well for harsh conditions where many of the participating nodes (coordinators) come and go frequently. It causes a significant amount of time to recover from a loss a primary process with a large ensemble size. During the recovery, the coordination service is unavailable, which is unacceptable in circumstances such as military combats. Instead, lookup algorithms used for peer-to-peer systems provide better survivability.

Chord, a popular lookup algorithm that utilizes distributed hash tables enables the lookup by letting each peer maintain a list of successors. Upon a failure of a peer, the lookup can traverse through the next successor, thus providing high survivability even with many arrivals and leaves. Furthermore, it uses consistent hashing so that the keys are evenly distributed over the peers, achieving load balance, and it does not impose any constraint on the structure of keys that the lookup performs on.

However, the key drawback of the algorithm is that the key lookup must traverse around the Chord ring in a sequential manner for every requested key lookup. Even though the finger table maintained by each peer accelerates the process from $O(N)$ to $O(\log N)$, the large number of peers in the ring still causes a significant overhead. Particularly, the search process involves multiple hops between peers that may be redundant if the extent of the metadata to which a peer is interested in is actually a subset of the original key space. Thus, to reduce the redundancy of the traversal while leveraging the existing advantages of the Chord lookup algorithm, we introduce a multi-ring DHT scheme that utilizes multiple Chord rings based on topics of messages. Figure 3 shows the overview of our proposed multi-ring scheme. In the figure, message brokers 1 and 2 are participating in the original key space whereas the clients request one of the brokers to locate the broker that they need to communicate with. Topic-based rings A and B have additionally been constructed so that the key lookup process can be done within a relevant key space.

3.2   Multi-ring DHT Scheme for Efficient Lookup

As previously mentioned, the time complexity of a key lookup, $O(\log N)$, is a large cost of the Chord lookup algorithm. In order to minimize the number of hops among

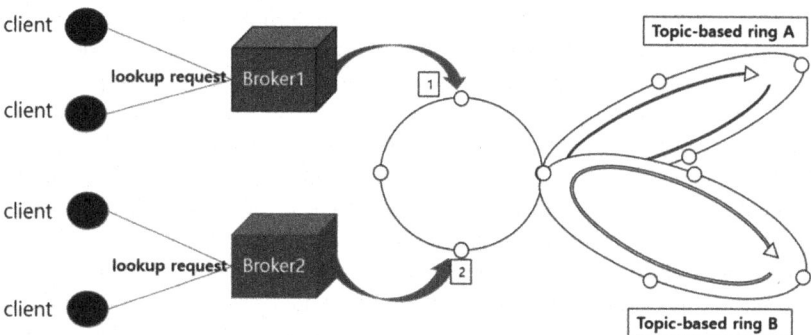

Fig. 3. Overview of our proposed scheme

the peers involved in the lookup process, it is important to make the number of peers small. In our proposed scheme, this is achieved by multiple topic rings. We construct multiple rings based on the contents of messages (i.e., topics) by having each peer participate in a key space that is relevant to itself.

In our modified scheme based on Chord, the relevance of a peer to a topic is determined based on a subscription vote made. In the conventional vote scheme, every peer in the network constantly makes a vote during its participation. However, the scheme causes larger communication overhead than the benefits of reducing the number of hops, which is our objective. Hence, in our multi-ring DHT scheme, a voting procedure is initiated by only a limited set of peers along a single trip, while the initiation condition is given as a threshold of lookup response latency.

Our scheme operates as follows; a subscription vote to a topic is initiated when two conditions are met. The first condition is that the latency of any lookup is larger than the predefined threshold. If this condition is met, it means that the number of peers participating in the network is too large (i.e., increasing the latency of lookup requests). Thus, it is needed to decrease the number of participants (i.e., peers). For the second condition, a new join of a peer will initiate the vote along with the first condition. Because the lookup latency in general tends to increase with the number of peers in the key space, a new join of a peer becomes a trigger for a vote. However, if every peer in the network gathers votes from other peers, there will be unnecessary network traffic to handle duplicate and redundant votes. Therefore, we specify the list of successors in the newly joined peer's predecessor, as the peers that initiate a vote and call them *initiators*.

Along with the periodic stabilize protocol of Chord algorithm, each peer that have received the set of votes from its predecessor concatenates its vote for topics. When the concatenated votes return to any of the initiators, some of them might have voluntarily left the ring, or have failed to operate. Any initiator who receives the returned vote notifies to its succeeding initiators that the vote has returned, and makes a decision based on the number of votes for each topic whether to construct a new ring for a topic.

If the number of votes for a certain topic is at a pre-specified threshold, the initiators construct a new Chord ring for each of the topics that have the number of votes higher than the specified level. The reason for having the threshold is that a peer in a ring with only a small number of peers is likely to be over-loaded. That is, that peer has to process much more lookup requests than a peer in a ring with large size. Therefore, the number of votes should be determined while considering both the lookup latency and the load balance between peers.

After the construction, the initiators sequentially notify the peers similar to the voting procedure so that the peers that made a valid vote can now join the newly constructed ring. In the new ring, only the peers voted for the topic exist, thus minimizing the number of redundant peers in the new key space.

While the multi-ring scheme brings reduction in the number of search hops, the maintenance costs of the proposed scheme must be addressed. Among them the most significant is the network traffic caused by the voting procedure. The size of the vote message passed between peers during a voting procedure is equal to the number of topics multiplied by the size of an integer. If the number of topics is small, the overhead will be negligible. If it is large, the overhead may be non-negligible and thus the voting messages have to be passed in a compressed form. Thus, in the multi-ring approach, there is a trade-off between the reduction in the number of hops and the network traffic overhead. We intend to study the trade-off in more detail in our follow-up work. On the other hand, the parameters used in the ring construction include the lookup response latency and the minimum number of votes. Based on the conditions of environments, the best suited parameter values may vary from an environment to another. We leave a sophisticated study of the parameters as our future work.

The proposed scheme requires parameters to construct a new ring such as the lookup response latency and the number of votes. Based on the conditions of environments, the best suited parameter values vary from an environment to another. We leave a sophisticated study on the parameters as our future work.

4 Experiment

4.1 Objective and Specification

To evaluate the efficiency of our scheme, we compare our proposed multi-ring scheme with the original Chord algorithm. We perform empirical experiments with respect to the number of hops to locate a successor of a randomly given key. The number of keys in the identifier space is two to the power of 23 (2^{32}). The number of peers in the original Chord algorithm is fixed to 250. The number of topic rings created for our proposed scheme varies from 1 to 5, assuming that the rings are evenly sized and each peer subscribes only to one of the given topics. For instance, with two topics given, the number of peers in each ring is 125. For each number of topics, 500 random lookup requests were given and the average number of hops was calculated. The original Chord algorithm and the proposed scheme were implemented in Java language (OpenJDK 1.7), and the experiment was conducted on the machine with Intel Core I7-5930K and 16 GB of memory.

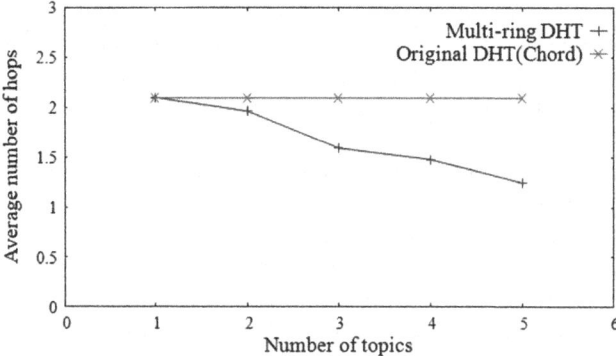

Fig. 4. The number of hops for a key lookup.

4.2 Experiment Results

Figure 4 shows the average number of hops during key lookup traversals. The points in the graph represent the average number of hops during a lookup based on the original Chord algorithm and our proposed multi-ring approach during a traversal. The downward tendency shows that our multi-ring approach results in a fewer number of hops for lookup requests compared to the original Chord algorithm. This is because the size of the ring gets smaller as new rings are constructed, thereby decreasing the possibility of longer traversal for a key lookup.

The limitations of the experiment are as follows. First, in the experiment we assumed that the peers in the original key space subscribe to only one of the given set of topics. Second, the overhead caused by the voting procedure before ring construction is not measured, which must be considered when determining if a new ring should be constructed. Third, larger number of peers should be involved in order to account for a realistic use of message systems. We will conduct more experiments for the future work to have results without these three limitations.

5   Conclusion

We present our novel coordination scheme for multi-broker messaging system. Our proposed coordination scheme with multiple DHT ring provides higher scalability than the popular coordination service, Chord as well as higher survivability than half-centralized services like Zookeeper. Our multiple ring DHT scheme leverages the inherent fault-recovery capability from the regular DHT based coordination service. However, we enhanced the scalability by introducing multiple rings in the system that reduces the number of peer participants in a ring. Since the frequent and large amount of subscription votes (i.e., naïve voting) among large number of peers may cause severe overheads, we also introduce a voting procedure only initiated by the limited set of peers along a single trip. The initiation condition is given as a thresh-old of lookup response latency.

Our proposed coordination scheme inherits the survivability advantage of the DHT-based lookup algorithm, Chord. In order to reduce the higher lookup latency than the half-centralized lookup services such as ZooKeeper, we introduce a multi-ring scheme. The multi-ring scheme constructs additional key spaces so that redundant search process is reduced.

Since our proposed coordination scheme provides high scalability as well as high fault recovery capability, it suits well to the message broker federation in the harsh conditions such as military combat situation that requires survivability (i.e., the system should endure the effects of external events such as messaging peers leaving frequently). Our proposed multi-ring approach to form a decentralized message broker federation targets survivability while decreasing the overhead caused by de-centralized lookup.

Acknowledgement. This research is supported by C2 integrating and interfacing technologies laboratory of Agency for Defense Development (UD180010ED).

References

1. Kreps, J., Narkhede, N., Rao, J.: Kafka: a distributed messaging system for log processing. In: Proceedings of the NetDB (2011)
2. Hunt, P., et al.: ZooKeeper: wait-free coordination for internet-scale systems. In: USENIX Annual Technical Conference, vol. 8. no. 9 (2010)
3. Junqueira, F.P., Reed, B.C., Serafini, M.: Zab: High-performance broadcast for primary-backup systems. In: 2011 IEEE/IFIP 41st International Conference on Dependable Systems and Networks, DSN. IEEE (2011)
4. Wilson, C.: Network centric warfare: background and oversight issues for Congress. Library of Congress Washington DC Congressional Research Service (2004)
5. Shi, X., et al.: Giraffe: a scalable distributed coordination service for large-scale systems. In: 2014 IEEE International Conference on Cluster Computing (CLUSTER). IEEE (2014)
6. Apache Hadoop. http://hadoop.apache.org/
7. Apache Spark. https://spark.apache.org/
8. Stoica, I., et al.: Chord: a scalable peer-to-peer lookup protocol for internet applications. IEEE/ACM Trans. Netw. (TON) **11**(1), 17–32 (2003)

Method to Judge the Coupling State of the Resonator in the Q-Factor Measurement

Hai Zhang[1,2,3](✉)

[1] School of Information Engineering, Nanchang Institute of Technology,
Nanchang 330099, China
worklab_cst@163.com
[2] Jiangxi Province Key Laboratory of Water Information Cooperative Sensing and
Intelligent Processing, Nanchang Institute of Technology, Nanchang 330099, China
[3] Research Laboratory of Cooperative Sensing and Advanced Computing Techniques,
Nanchang Institute of Technology, Nanchang, China

Abstract. The judgement of the coupling state of the cavity is the key of
the Q-factor measurement in the microwave devices and communication
system. A simple and real-time method to determine the coupling state of
resonators has been proposed. The coupling states are determined by the
graphical relationship between the resonance circles and the match point
in Smith chart. The extraction of the coupling coefficient and unloaded
quality factor can be performed directly and timely. The procedure is
validated with experimental measurements of manufactured cavities. The
proposed method could provide an effective way to solve parameters
extraction problem for resonators.

Keywords: Coupling · Cavity · Q-factor

1 Introduction

The high quality resonator is an important component in the acoustical, optical, electromagnetic systems and so forth. It plays more and more important
role in various kinds of sensors and electronic device such as filters, antennas,
coupler, dielectric resonators, etc. Especially in the field of microwave measurement, such as coaxial cavity that is used to perform broadband measurement on
liquid properties [1] and also circular cylindrical cavity resonator that is used to
characterise isotropic homogenous nonmagnetic dielectric materials [2]. The Q
factor determines the accuracy of the sensor and measurement [3–10].

Especially in electromagnetic properties measurement, by measuring the
change in resonant frequency and Q factor, the electromagnetic information of
the material can be calculated. There has been increasing demand for material

Supported by the Science and Technology Research Project of Jiangxi Provincial
Education Department (Grant No. GJJ151115).

© Springer International Publishing AG, part of Springer Nature 2018
O. Gervasi et al. (Eds.): ICCSA 2018, LNCS 10964, pp. 227–235, 2018.
https://doi.org/10.1007/978-3-319-95174-4_19

electromagnetic properties measurement, as many physical and chemical properties can be related to a material's electromagnetic properties. Knowledge of dielectric properties is essential in the design and control of Electromagnetic systems.

The perturbation theory of high Q factor cavities is more accurate and has been widely used to study the dielectric and magnetic properties of materials especially for the low-loss material. In this method, the real part of relative complex permittivity is calculated from the change of the resonant frequency, and the imaginary part is done from the change of Q-factor. The accurate determinations of resonance frequency and Q-factor of the microwave resonators are required.

The precise characterization of resonators is crucial to microwave measurement. The basic parameters of the resonator are the resonance frequency, unloaded quality factor and coupling coefficient. The coupling coefficient representing the ratio of the power dissipated in the external circuit to the power dissipated in the unloaded resonator can be defined as

$$\beta = Q_0/Q_e \tag{1}$$

where Q_0 and Q_e represent the unloaded and the external quality factors. If $\beta < 1$, the resonator is said to be undercoupled, whereas if $\beta > 1$ the resonator is overcoupled. The match condition is referred to as critical coupled when $\beta = 1$ [11]. Figure 1 describes the S_{11} circles in Smith chart for three coupling conditions.

The universal instrument for measuring the Q factor is the automatic VNA (vector network analyzer). For the case of loaded Q-factor measurement of microwave resonators, it employs measurement of the transmitted or reflected power as a function of frequency. And then the unloaded Q factor can be calculated by the loaded quality factors and the coupling coefficient.

The key to get the unloaded quality factor is the coupling state determination of the resonance system. Hence, we proposed a method to determine the coupling state of the system, which is adapted to VNA measurement techniques. The procedure described here uses the data measured directly from the VNA. A one-port cavity for quality factor estimation of a metallic resonator is presented. The method is validated by fitting it to a one-port cavity measurement data of dielectric constants, permittivity determination of materials. The proposed method provides an effective way of determining the coupling state situation of resonators.

2   Method and Results

The measurement of quality factor is important for applications in which the resonator is used. The measurement and the influence of the quality factor in the presence of coupling are well described in [12–16]. The coupling coefficient is a measure of the degree of the coupling between the cavity and the input feed

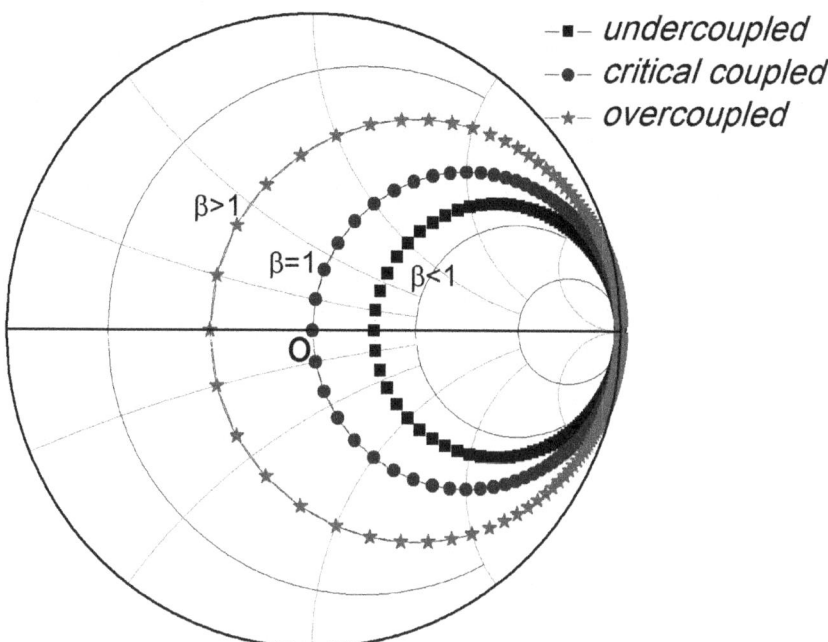

Fig. 1. Smith chart for coupling states.

line. In order to obtain the quality factor, the coupling state of the system should be determined firstly.

$$Q_0 = (1 + \beta)Q_l \begin{cases} (1 + 1/\rho)Q_l, & \text{undercoupled;} \\ 2Q_l, & \text{critical coupled;} \\ (1 + \rho)Q_l, & \text{overcoupled.} \end{cases} \tag{2}$$

Q_l and ρ represent the loaded quality factor and VSWR (voltage standing wave ratio) both directly measured by the VNA. Hence Q_0 can be calculated from (2), as long as the coupling state of the system has been determined. There are several methods to determine the coupling state of the resonator [11]. Ginzton describes in detail the analysis of measured resonant circles on the Smith chart in order to deduce the values of quality factor and coupling coefficient [17].

Several techniques for obtaining unloaded quality factor are described in [18–26]. These methods require the creation of an equivalent circuit to accurately extract quality factor. The traditional processing method is relatively more complex. In the reference [22], to obtain the Q_0 value, the following steps are needed: 1. rotate the resonance circle into the standard series circuit position; 2. draw the Q curve in the graph; 3. find the special point, then the quality factor can be calculated. Even taking no account of the coupling loss, finishing these steps is complicated in Smith chart.

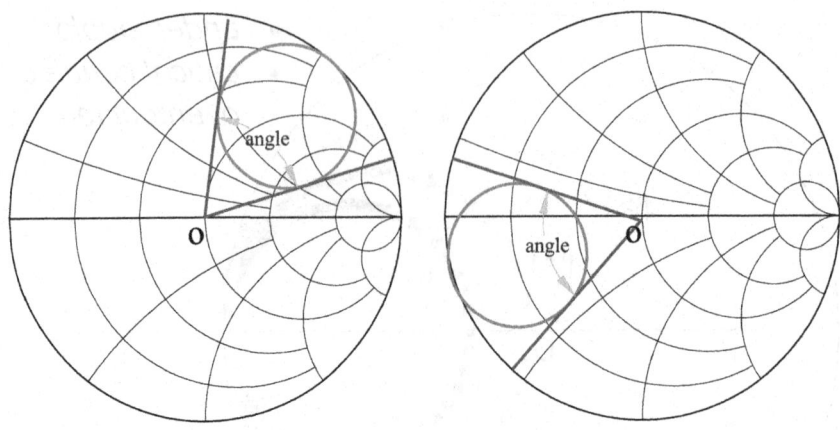

(a) undercoupled, the circle in the upper complex plane

(b) undercoupled, the circle in the down complex plane

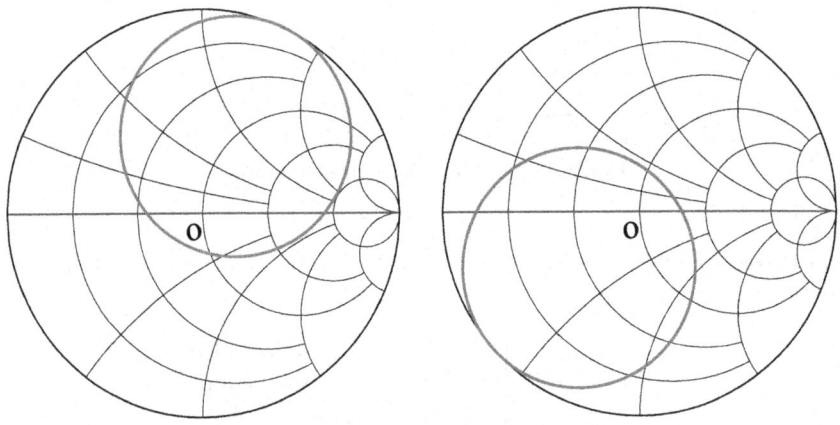

(c) overcoupled, the circle in the upper complex plane

(d) overcoupled, the circle in the down complex plane

Fig. 2. Phase change for coupling states

From the measurements point of view, the measurement should be real-time and simple. Once the coupling state is known, the coupling coefficient can be acquired by the VSWR; by observing the power decay profile of S_{11} the loaded quality factor can be computed. Then the unloaded quality factor can be calculated through the VSWR and loaded quality factor. A graphical method to accurately determine the coupling state is presented here. It is inspired by the phase relationship between the closed contour and the origin point in complex variable function theory [27]. We can use the relationship between the resonance circles and match point O to determine the coupling state.

As shown in Fig. 1, in the overcoupled state, notice that the matching point O is always on the left side, if one walks along the curve anti-clockwise. The S_{11} resonance curve enclose the match point O. The phase changes by 2π across the point O. On the other hand, for under coupled condition the position relationship between the matching point position and the walker will be changed. The undercoupled resonance demonstrates a relatively small phase variation. The resonator circle locates itself in the sector zone from point O, and the change of the phase is less than π.

As shown in Fig. 2(a) we can directly obtain the maximum and minimum of the phase array of the resonance curves. The phase array can be directly get from the VNA, then the phase variation is

$$angle = max - min \tag{3}$$

However it will be more complex in practical operation. As shown in Fig. 2(b), the actual phase difference should be the angle. But the maximum and minimum of the phase array are π and $-\pi$ respectively, because the phase range of the VNA is $(-\pi, \pi)$. It will lead to wrong judgments. On the other hand, the other two cases are relatively simple as shown in Fig. 2(c) and (d). When the resonator is overcoupled, the angle is 2π, no matter what the resonance circle locates in any position in Smith chart.

According to the above problem, the following method based on graphical relationship and real-time measurement data from VNA, has been obtained as shown in Fig. 3. If angle $< \pi$, we directly judge that the coupling state of the resonator is undercoupled; If angle $> \pi$, the phase array will be transformed as follows: the positive phases remain the same; the negative phases are added by 2π, in order to transform the phase interval from $(-\pi, \pi)$ to $(0, 2\pi)$. Then we search the maximum and minimum again, get the new angle. At this time, if angle $< \pi$, the coupling state is undercoupled; if angle $> \pi$, the coupling state is overcoupled. The described measurement procedure is automatically completed by the computer, and needn't any human judgment. The most important thing is that it avoids the complex operation in Smith chart, compared with the traditional methods.

In order to verify this method, a one-port cavity system [28, 29] has been realized, which is based on the reflected power technique. Test system mainly consists of two parts: cylinder cavity and VNA (CETC AV3620, 30 kHz 6 GHz). The cavity radius is 230 mm, and its height is 328 mm. The method has been applied in the permittivity measurement system as shown in Fig. 4. The measurement is based on perturbation theory. The system consists of an coupler, an upper end plate, a cavity and a VNA, etc. The radius of the circular cylindrical cavity is 230 mm. A coaxial line is connected between the type-N connector and the VNA. First of all the coupling state of the cavity should been determined by the above method as shown in Fig. 3. Then the unloaded Q factor can be obtained by (2). Hence, the real part of complex permittivity is calculated from the change of the resonant frequency, and the imaginary part is done from Q factor [30].

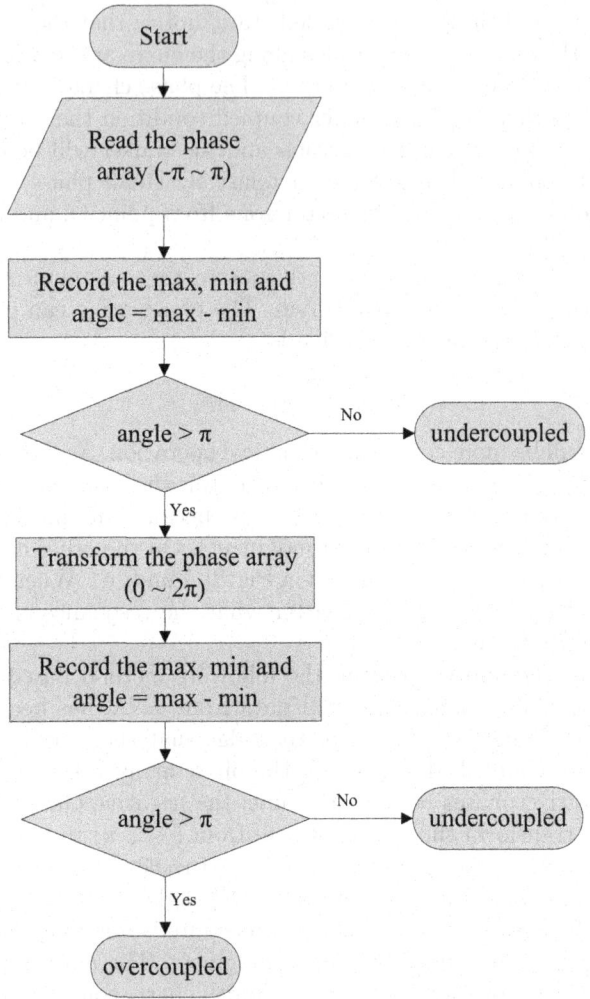

Fig. 3. Flow chart for determining the coupling state.

$$\epsilon' - 1 = \frac{2}{\eta} \frac{f_c - f_s}{f_s} \tag{4}$$

$$\epsilon'' = \frac{1}{\eta} \left(\frac{1}{Q_s} - \frac{1}{Q_c} \right) \tag{5}$$

where f_c and Q_c are the resonant frequency and unloaded quality factor of the empty cavity, respectively, f_s and Q_s are the corresponding quantities in the presence of the dielectric sample. η is the filling factor. Teflon Measurements are repeated for times, and results are averaged to reduce random errors due to uncertainty in the determination of the resonant parameters. To avoid signal aliasing, the VNA was set to its maximum number of points.

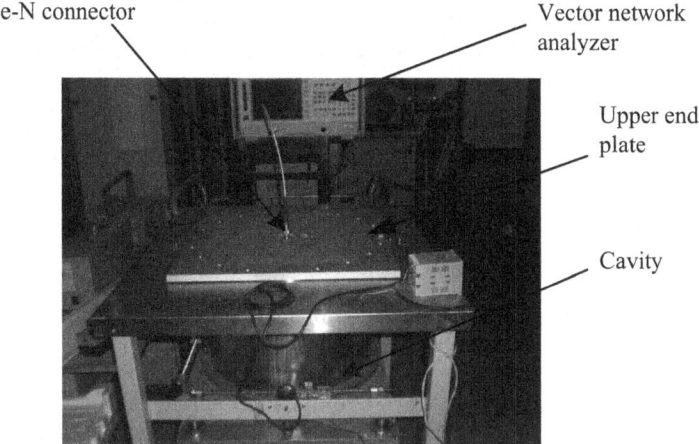

Fig. 4. Manufactured cavity for permittivity measurement.

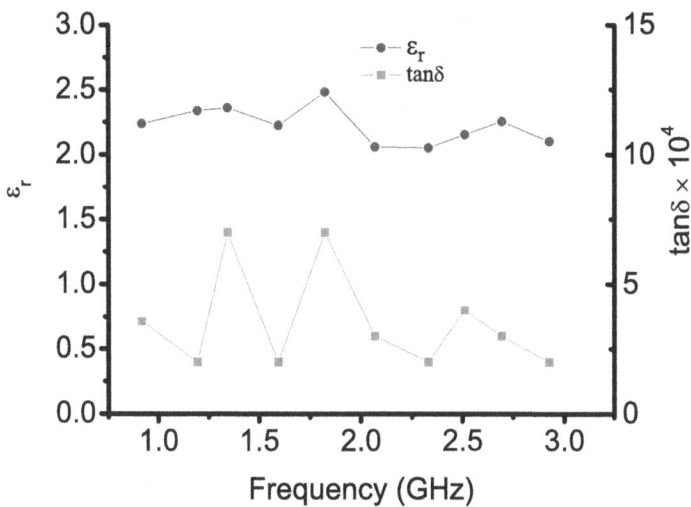

Fig. 5. Method applied in Teflon permittivity measurement.

Measurements results are in good agreement with the published works [31–34], as shown in Fig. 5.

3   Conclusion

A method to determine the coupling state of the resonator has been proposed. Based on the geometric relationship between the resonance circles and the match point in the Smith chart, the coupling state can be determined. This method has the advantages of real-time and complete automation. The procedure is validated with experimental measurements of manufactured cavities. Measurements results indicate that this method is consistent with the published works, and it is commonly used for cavities or other kinds of resonators. The proposed method offered an effective way to obtain quality factor of resonators.

References

1. Raveendranath, U., Bijukumar, S., Mathew, K.T.: Broadband coaxial cavity resonator for complex permittivity measurements of liquids. IEEE Trans. Instrum. Meas. **49**(6), 1305–1312 (2000)
2. Kilc, E., Siart, U., Faz, O.W.U., Ramakrishnan, R., Saal, P., Eibert, T.F.: Cavity resonator measurement of dielectric materials accounting for wall losses and a filling hole. IEEE Trans. Instrum. Meas. **62**(2), 401–407 (2013)
3. Kadirloglu, F., Hasar, U.C.: A highly accurate microwave method for permittivity determination using corrected scattering parameter measurements. J. Electromagn. Wave Appl. **24**(16), 2179–2189 (2010)
4. Xu, S., Yang, L., Huang, L., Chen, H.S.: Experimental measurement method to determine the permittivity of extra thin materials using resonant metamaterials. Prog. Electromagn. Res. **120**, 327–337 (2011)
5. Deshpande, M.D., Reddy, C.J., Tiemsin, P.I., Cravey, R.: A new approach to estimate complex permittivity of dielectric materials at microwave frequencies using waveguide measurements. IEEE Trans. Microw. Theory Tech. **45**, 359–366 (1997)
6. Bethe, H.A., Schwinger, J.: Perturbation theory for cavities, NDRC Report, D 1117 (1943)
7. Condon, E.: Forced oscillations in cavity resonators. J. Appl. Phys. **12**, 129–132 (1941)
8. Carter, R.: Accuracy of microwave cavity perturbation measurements. IEEE Trans. Microw. Theory Tech. **49**, 918–923 (2001)
9. Galani, Z., Bianchini, M.J., Waterman, R.C., Dibiase, R., Laton, R.W., Cole, J.B.: Analysis and design of a single resonator GaAs FET oscillator with noise generation. IEEE Trans. Microw. Theory Tech. **32**, 1556–1565 (1984)
10. Hasar, U.C.: Unique permittivity determination of low-loss dielectric materials from transmission measurements at microwave frequencies. Prog. Electromagn. Res. **107**, 31–46 (2010)
11. Pozar, D.M.: Microwave Engineering, 3rd edn, pp. 292–294. Addission-Wesley Publishing Company, Beijing (2006)
12. Kajfez, D., Hwan, E.J.: Q-factor measurement with network analyser. IEEE Trans. Microw. Theory Tech. **32**(7), 666–670 (1984)
13. Sun, E.-Y., Chao, S.-H.: Unloaded Q measurement - the critical points method. IEEE Trans. Microw. Theory Tech. **43**(8), 1983–1986 (1995)
14. Barannik, A.A., Cherpak, N.T., Chuyko, D.E.: Q-Factor measurement of quasi-optical dielectric resonators under conditions of the whispering gallery mode degeneration removal. IEEE Trans. Instrum. Meas. **55**(1), 70–73 (2006)
15. Isagawa, S.: Measurements of the Q of a loosely coupled cavity by the decrement method. IEEE Trans. Instrum. Meas. **26**(4), 329–330 (1977)
16. Chua, L.H., Mirshekar-Syahkal, D.: Accurate and direct characterization of high-Q microwave resonators using one-port measurement. IEEE Trans. Microw. Theory Tech. **51**(3), 978–985 (2003)

17. Fang, X., Linton, D.: A tunable split resonator method for nondestructive permittivity characterization. IEEE Trans. Instrum. Meas. **53**, 1473–1478 (2004)
18. Drozd, J.M., Joines, W.T.: Determining Q using S parameter data. IEEE Trans. Microw. Theory Tech. **44**(11), 2123–2127 (1996)
19. Rezaee, P., Tayarani, M., Knochel, R.: Active learning method for the determination of coupling factor and external Q in microstrip filter design. Prog. Electromagn. Res. **120**, 426–432 (2011)
20. Lee, J., Hong, Y.-K., Yun, C., Lee, W., Park, J.-H., Bae, S.: Ferrite magnetic - anisotropy field effects on inductance and quality factor of planar GHz inductors. Prog. Electromagn. Res. **156**, 25–35 (2016)
21. Ruby, R.: Method of fitting Q-circles of measured mechanical resonators, 2010 IEEE International Ultrasonics Symposium, pp. 427–430 (2010)
22. Montgomery, C.G. (ed.): Techniques Of Microwave Measurement - 1947, 1st edn, p. 337. McGraw-Hill Book Company, New York/London (1947)
23. Chang, K.: Encyclopedia of RF and Microwave Engineering, p. 3943. Wiley, Hoboken (2005)
24. Shahid, S., Ball, J.A.R., Wells, C.G., Wen, P.: Reflection type Q-factor measurement using standard least squares methods. IET Microw. Antennas Propag. **5**(4), 426–432 (2011)
25. Nyberg, D., Kildal, P.-S., Carlsson, J.: Effects of intrinsic radiation Q on mismatch factor of three types of small antennas: single-resonance, gradual-transition and cascaded-resonance types. IET Microw. Antennas Propag. **4**(1), 83–90 (2010)
26. Goussetis, G., Lopez-Villarroya, R., Doumanis, E., Arowolo, O.S., Hong, J.-S.: Quality factor of E-plane periodically loaded waveguide resonators and filter applications. IET Microw. Antennas Propag. **5**(7), 818–822 (2011)
27. Riley, K.F., Hobson, M.P., Bence, S.J.: Mathematical Methods for Physics and Engineering, pp. 721–722. Cambridge University Press, Cambridge (2006)
28. Zhang, H., Zeng, B., Ao, L., Zhang, W., Li, N., Guo, J.: Printed four arcs coupler in cylindrical cavity for permittivity measurement. Electron. Lett. **48**(23), 1460–1462 (2012)
29. Zhang, H., Ao, L., Fang, Y., Rao, W., Liu, B.: Printed arc coupler in a circular cylindrical measurement cavity for suppressing degenerate modes. IET Sci. Meas. Technol. **10**(3), 215–220 (2016)
30. Altschuler, H.M., Sucher, M., Fox, J. (eds.): Handbook of Microwave Measurement, vol. 2, p. 530. Brooklyn Polytechnic Press, NewYork (1963)
31. Harrington, R.F.: Time-Harmonic Electromagnetic Fields, pp. 452–455. McGraw-Hill Book Company, INC., New York/Toronto/London (1961)
32. Afsar, M.N., Ding, H.: A novel open-resonator system for precise measurement of permittivity and loss-tangent. IEEE Trans. Instrum. Meas. **50**(2), 402–405 (2001)
33. Dube, D.C., Natarajan, R.: Measurement of the permittivity of films at microwave frequencies. J. Phys. E: Sci. Instrum. **7**(4), 256 (1974)
34. Ghodgaonkar, D.K., Varadan, V.V., Varadan, V.K.: A free-space method for measurement of dielectric constants and loss tangents at microwave frequencies. IEEE Trans. Instrum. Meas. **38**(3), 789–793 (1989)

An Efficient Transmission Approach for Information-Centric Based Wireless Body Area Networks

Longzhe Han[1(✉)], Yi Bu[2], Xin Song[3], and Jia Zhao[1]

[1] Jiangxi Province Key Laboratory of Water Information Cooperative Sensing and Intelligent Processing, Nanchang Institute of Technology, Nanchang 330099, Jiangxi, China
lzhan@nit.edu.cn
[2] National Computer Network and Information Security Administration Center Hainan Center, Haikou 570206, Hainan, China
[3] China Telecom Jilin Corporation, Changchun 130033, Jilin, China

Abstract. Wireless body area networks (WBANs) are the promising network infrastructure to achieve ubiquitous personal health management services. In WBANs, the biological sensors are attached to the human body to obtain health related information and the communication gateway sends the sensed data to the health data server periodically. The health service providers can use the data to provide specific treatment for each individual according to her personal condition. Despite many advantages, the TCP/IP protocols used by WBANs incur efficiency issue of the data transmission. In TCP/IP, the data and their storage location are coupled, which greatly affects data transmission performance of WBANs. Moreover, additional security layer is required to support data privacy and security in WBANs. In this paper, an Efficient Transmission Approach for Information-Centric based Wireless Body Area Network (ETA-ICWBAN) is proposed. The proposed ETA-ICWBAN classifies the data into different priorities (high, normal, low) and the communication gateway buffers the data in the designated queue. We design a hybrid queue management algorithm to balance the different priority data transmission with various network conditions. Simulation results show that the proposed approach is able to improve the data transmission performance for WBANs.

Keywords: Information Centric Network · Wireless Body Area Network
Wearable computing · Wireless communications

1 Introduction

In the advance of wireless sensing and communication technology, wireless body area networks (WBANs) have become the key network platform to provide ubiquitous personal health management services [1–5]. WBANs consist of self-organized biological sensors and wireless communication gateway. Biological sensors can be implanted into wearable devices such as clothes, glasses, watch, shoes, etc., to collect the body condition information constantly [1]. The collected information is periodically sent to

© Springer International Publishing AG, part of Springer Nature 2018
O. Gervasi et al. (Eds.): ICCSA 2018, LNCS 10964, pp. 236–245, 2018.
https://doi.org/10.1007/978-3-319-95174-4_20

the health data server through the wireless communication gateway. The health service providers are able to analyze individual health data to customize health management program. The convergence of biological sensors, wireless communications and bioinformatics enable the new opportunities to build an augmented platform for ubiquitous personal health management services [2].

Recently, many different types of biological sensors have been designed to monitor the body conditions conveniently. The attachable body sensors are contacted to human bodies to monitor health-related information, for example, blood pressure, body temperature and heartbeat rate [3]. The implantable sensors can be implanted under the skin to observe the internal body conditions, for instance, inflammation, blood sugar level, and nitric oxide [4]. With the development of nanotechnology, nano-scale body sensors can be used to detect cancerous cells [5]. The communication gateway such as tablet PC or smart phone collects the sensed data. Depending on different applications, the communication gateway could store the data locally or send to the central data server of the health management system [3].

Connecting heterogeneous body sensors, ensuring personal information privacy and responding emergent situation pose challenges on the design of communication mechanism for the health management system [6]. Currently, the most of proposed solutions are based on TCP/IP protocols. The goal of TCP/IP protocols is to interconnect two end hosts through multiple packet-switching networks. The underlying communication paradigm is end-to-end (or conversation) model. The network applications usually adopt the client/server architecture. In order to exchange data, two end hosts need to establish a connection and then transfer their required data. In this way, the data is tightly coupled with its storage location and the host IP address. Despite its successful application in the Internet, TCP/IP protocols may have problems for wearable health care services. Because of the routine activity and movement, the health-related information collected by body sensors can be stored in different devices at different locations. With the increasing number of wearable sensors and personal mobile devices, the data management, configuration and synchronization become complex by using TCP/IP's end-to-end model. In addition, the TCP/IP security model is to ensure the connection between the hosts instead of the exchanged data.

To overcome the limitations of TCP/IP protocols, we propose an Efficient Transmission Approach for Information-Centric based Wireless Body Area Networks (ETA-ICWBANs). Information-Centric Network (ICN) is novel network architecture to replace TCP/IP protocols [7]. The main difference between ICN and TCP/IP is that the named data is the core communication element in ICN. Instead of IP address, the name of the data is the key identifier. Our proposed system follows the ICN architecture. In order to support efficient data transmission, sensed data are classified into three priorities (high, normal, low). The communication gateway associates a separated transmission queue to each priority. A hybrid queue management algorithm has been proposed to consider both importance of the data and the network condition. In addition, security scheme is discussed to support secure data transmission.

The remainder of this paper is organized as follows. Section 2 discusses background and related work. Section 3 presents our proposed ETA-ICWBANs. Section 4 describes the simulation settings used in our experiments and analyzes the experimental results. Finally, Sect. 5 summarizes our work and concludes this paper.

2 Related Work

The traditional TCP/IP protocols were designed to transfer packets between to two end nodes through the packet switching networks. The IP addresses are the most important information to mark the node and used to route the packets. In this way, the data is bonded with the nodes where it is stored. When retrieving any data, the requesting nodes have to contact the data hosting nodes and retrieve the data. This is called end-to-end conversation model. However, with the advance of personal computer, wireless communications and mobile networks, the main functions of the Internet have been changed from data transmission to content sharing. The traditional TCP/IP protocols are not suitable for the emerging network applications. For example, in the case of the video streaming system, all video data are stored at the video streaming server and sent to the video streaming clients from the server. The workload of the server is proportional to the number of clients, which is inefficient scheme for the large scale video streaming system [8].

In order to solve the problem, many researchers have been working on the future Internet research. ICN proposed by V. Jacobson is regarded as the potential architecture for the next generation Internet. In ICN, the content is the most important item and associated a unique name. Two types of packets, interest packet and data packet, are used for the transmission [9]. A typical transmission path consists of multiple content consumers, intermediate nodes and one content provider. ICN adopts the receiver-driven scheme as shown in Fig. 1. If the content consumers plan to acquire some content, an interest packet is broadcasted into ICN as a data request. For each interest packet, a unique name is associated to identify the content. Every ICN node has three main data structures, Pending Interest Table (PIT), Content Store (CS), and Forwarding Information Base (FIB) [10].

When an intermediate node receives an interest packet, it firstly searches the PIT. If the corresponding record is found, this means that the node has already forwarded the interest packet and waited for the return of the data packet. Then, the node will mark the reception network link of the interest packet at the corresponding record and drop the interest packet. The CS is used to buffer the data packets. If the corresponding record is not found in the PIT, the intermediate node searches the CS. If there is a match, the data packet is sent back to the content consumer without further forwarding. If there is no match, the intermediate node forwards the interest packet to the next node according the routing information in the FIB. The ICN protocols specify the management mechanism of PIT, CS and FIB.

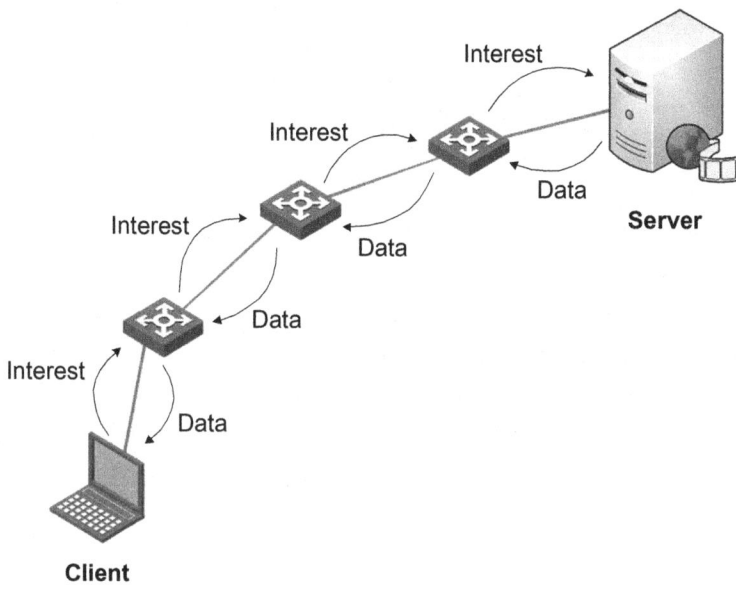

Fig. 1. Receiver-driven model of the ICN

3 Efficient Data Transmission for Information-Centric Based Wireless Body Area Networks

3.1 Network Architecture for the Wireless Body Area Network

Our proposed communications scheme is based on ICN architecture. In ICN, the wearable health care system does not require the central data server. The health-related data can be stored in any personal devices, such as desktop computer, mobile phone, and tablet. The name based routing approach enables that the data requester does not need to know where the data is stored. Figure 2 presents the network architecture of the proposed scheme.

The body sensors continuously sense the health conditions and the sensed data are transferred to personal communication gateway. In order to reduce the energy consumption, the body sensors adopt a low-power and wireless transmission protocol. After receiving the data, the personal communication gateway classifies them according their categories, size and priority. Because some data have small size, for example blood pressure and body temperature, multiple data records are encapsulated into one data packet. The personal communication gateway assigns a unique name to the data packet. Due to the limited storage of the mobile devices, the personal communication gateway sends the received data to a data repository periodically. When users try to check their body conditions, they just simply send an interest packet for requesting the sensed data to the Information-Centric Wireless Body Area Networks (ICWBANs). Regardless of where the data are stored, the corresponding data packets will send back to the users.

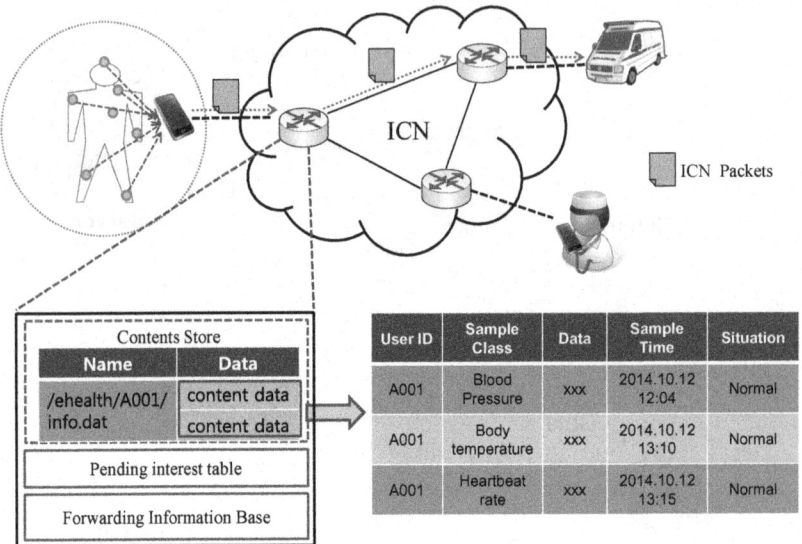

Fig. 2. The ICN network architecture for the wearable health care system

Thus, our proposed scheme provides a seamless and transparent data communication platform. This unified platform enables ubiquitous wearable health care services.

3.2 The Naming Structure and Security

In order to separate the storage location and support information-centric model, ICN uses the name to define the exclusive identifier for the content. In addition, the rules of packet routing and forwarding are also based on the name. The network application can decide any forms for naming the content: simple text, encrypted code and binary encodings. However, ICN protocols require that names follow the hierarchical structure. The uniform resource locator (URL) based naming structure is recommended. As a result, a name consists of one or multiple components. The first component is a "DNS name" as the root of the name tree. The rest components build the branch nodes and leaf nodes of the tree. Choosing DNS names as first component reduces the chance of duplicated names and name spaces. Figure 3 shows the example of content name and its hierarchical structure.

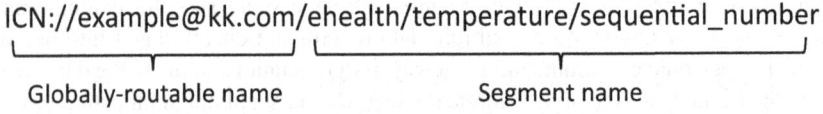

Fig. 3. Example of content name

The health-related information is very sensitive. To protect the privacy, the content is encrypted by using the private key. The digital signature is embedded into the data packet for identification. The segment name of the content can also be encoded to binary code. Therefore, the interest packets and data packets might travel through untrusted network links, only designated hosts can understand the content.

3.3 Efficient Data Transmission for Information-Centric Based Wireless Body Area Networks

As mentioned in Sect. 2, the ICN is based on the receiver-driven scheme. The receiver initiate the communication session by sending an interest packet into the network. The content holder, any ICN routers or the data source, can serve the request with returning the corresponding data packet. In ETA-ICWBAN, we classify the data into different priorities for the efficient data transmission.

The wearable devices constantly sense the vital signals, such as blood pressure, body temperature and heartbeat rate. After collecting the sensed data from the devices, the personal communication gateway estimates the personal health conditions. Usually, the users can set the range of each vital signal. If all signal values are within the given ranges, then the health condition is considered as normal. In this case, the sensed data could be stored at any personal devices. When the user wants to see the records, an interest packet will send to the network. No matter where it is stored, the ICN is able to locate the data packet and deliver to the user's device. The user's device is the initiator of the communication and the data transmission delay is not a major factor.

However, if any signal value is out of the given ranges, the health condition is considered as abnormal. For the cases like heart attack, timely treatment is extremely important. The proposed ETA-ICWBAN uses emergent mode to handle this critical situation. The eHealth service providers should register the name list of relevant agencies, for instance hospitals, first-aid centers, and guardians etc., on the personal communication gateway. The personal communication gateway initiates the communication by broadcast a special interest packet, called notification packet, to the network. The purpose of notification packet is different with general interest packet, which is for data request. The notification packet is to timely report the emergency to relevant agencies.

Because of the in-network caching capability of ICN nodes, the interest packets may not reach the data resource. In order to guarantee that the relevant agencies can receive the notification packet, we define a new naming structure as shown in Fig. 4. The urgent code field presents the type and level of the emergent situation. The Universally Unique Identifier (UUID) is to assure no corresponding data packet exists in the network. Thus, the notification packets can travel to the designated destinations. When the relevant agencies receive the notification packet, they can carry out the emergency processing procedure.

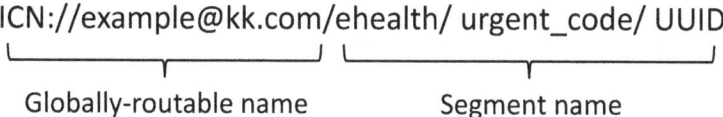

Fig. 4. Notification packet naming structure

When the emergent situation occurs, the notification packet and health related information should be delivered as soon as possible. The personal communication gateway usually connects to the central health data server through wireless link for convenience. Due to physical characteristics of the wireless channel, data transmission can be failed by wireless signal fading, hidden terminal and signal interference. The notification and health data packets may suffer the packet loss during the wireless transmission. In addition, mobile devices such as mobile phone and tablet PC are generally used as the personal communication gateway. Besides health data, other applications (video streaming, voice chatting, mobile gaming and web surfing) also constantly transmit huge amount of data through the personal communication gateway. The emergent packets mixed up with other applications' packets could cause severe delay.

In order to solve the problem, we propose an efficient data transmission for ICWBANs. The ETA-ICWBAN firstly performs classification of the packets in the personal communication gateway. Three priorities, high, normal, and low are marked to each packet. The emergent packets have the high priority, delay sensitive application packets have the normal priority and delay non-sensitive application packets have the low priority. The personal communication gateway assigns the marked packets to corresponding queues. When there is an opportunity for transmission, the packets in the high priority queue are always selected. If the high priority queue is empty, the personal communication gateway randomly select packets from normal and low priority queues with different probabilities. If the loss of notification packet is detected, the packet will be directly retransmitted without further delay. The detail process of our proposed approach is presented in Table 1.

Table 1. Efficient transmission approach for ICWBANs

```
 1: if high-priority-queue is not empty then
 2:     pkt = high-priority-queue.get_packet( );
 3:     send_packet(pkt);
 4:     result = mac_trans_result(pkt);
 5:     if result == lost then
 6:         send_packet(pkt);
 7:         goto step 3;
 8:     end if
 9: else
10:     prob = len(normal-priority-queue) /
11:         len(normal-priority-queue) + len (low-priority-queue);
12:     if random() < prob then
13:         pkt = normal -priority-queue.get_packet( );
14:     else
15:         pkt = low -priority-queue.get_packet( );
16:     end if
17:     send_packet(pkt);
18: end if
```

4   Experiment and Result Analysis

The Network Simulator 2 is used to perform the experiment and evaluate the performance of our proposed ETA-ICWBAN. In the experiment, the personal communication gateway connects to the ICWBANs with IEEE 802.11 link. The data rate of IEEE 802.11 link is 50 Mbit/s. When emergent situation is detected, the personal communication gateway continuously sends the notification packets until the confirmation message is received. The experiments were carried out with three traffic flows: health data traffic, HTTP traffic and FTP traffic with different network loss rates. The proposed ETA-ICWBAN was compared to the default ICN approach.

Figure 5 shows the average end-to-end delay of emergent packets under various packet loss rates. Because the proposed ETA-ICWBAN gives high priority to the emergent packets and early detects the packet losses, it can transmit the emergent packets to the destination much faster than the default ICN approach.

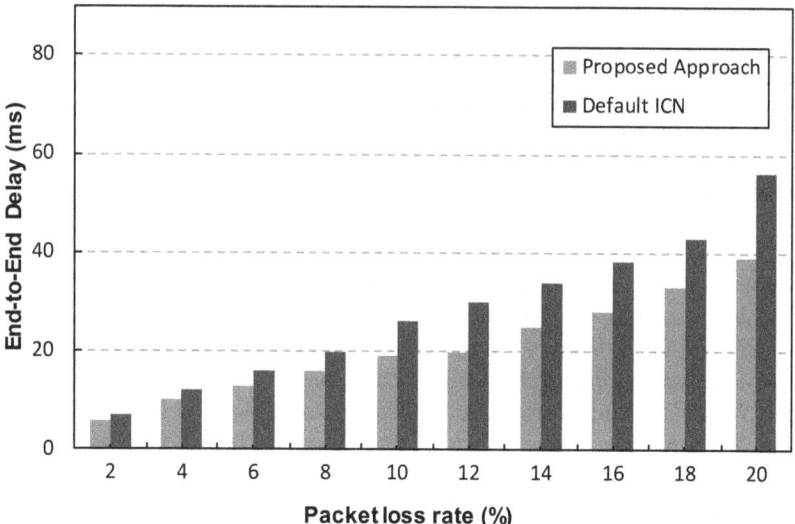

Fig. 5. Average delay of emergent packets under various packet loss rates

In the emergent situation, it is expected that relevant agencies should receive the notification packets fast. The Fig. 6 depicts the notification packet arrival rate with in 100 ms. Due to the rising packet errors, many packets required retransmission, which caused increasing of the end-to-end delay. Because the proposed ETA-ICWBAN is able to detect the packet losses at the MAC layer, the arrival rate is higher than the default ICN approach. By rapidly transmitting multiple notification packets, it ensures that the packets can arrive at the destination.

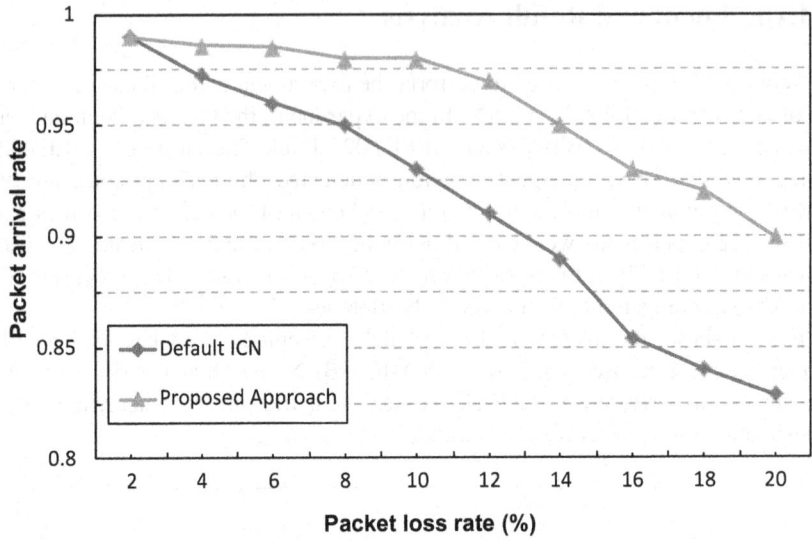

Fig. 6. Notification packet arrival rate under different packet error rates

5 Conclusion

In wireless body area networks, the mobile phones or tablet PC are usually adopted as the personal communication gateway to transfer health condition information. Because the personal communication gateway also transmits data from other applications, it incurs the end-to-end delay of emergent data. In this paper, we propose an Efficient Transmission Approach for Information-Centric based Wireless Body Area Network (ETA-ICWBAN) for future wearable health care services. According the importance, the ETA-ICWBAN categorizes the data to three priorities: high, normal and low. Based on the network conditions, the ETA-ICWBAN dynamically adjusts the data transmission. From the simulation results, the proposed ETA-ICWBAN achieves low transmission delay and high arrival rate than default ICN approach. For the future work, we plan to develop the queuing model of the ETA-ICWBAN and analyze its performance under complex network environments.

Acknowledgment. The research by the National Natural Science Foundation of China (No. 61561035, No. 51669014, No. 61663029) by the Scientific Research Foundation for the Returned Overseas Chinese Scholars, State Education Ministry, and Natural Science Foundation of Jiangxi, China (No. 20151BAB207039).

References

1. Movassaghi, S., Abolhasan, M., Lipman, J., Smith, D., Jamalipour, A.: Wireless body area networks: a survey. IEEE Commun. Surv. Tutor. **16**(3), 1658–1686 (2014)
2. Cavallari, R., Martelli, F., Rosini, R., Buratti, C., Verdone, R.: A survey on wireless body area networks: technologies and design challenges. IEEE Commun. Surv. Tutor. **16**(3), 1635–1657 (2014)
3. Rasheed, M.B., Javaid, N., Imran, M., Khan, Z.A., Qasim, U., Vasilakos, A.: Delay and energy consumption analysis of priority guaranteed MAC protocol for wireless body area networks. Wirel. Netw. **23**(4), 1249–1266 (2017)
4. Liu, B., Yan, Z., Chen, C.W.: Medium access control for wireless body area networks with QoS provisioning and energy efficient design. IEEE Trans. Mob. Comput. **16**(2), 422–434 (2017)
5. He, D., Zeadally, S., Kumar, N., Lee, J.H.: Anonymous authentication for wireless body area networks with provable security. IEEE Syst. J. **11**(4), 2590–2601 (2017)
6. Liu, H., Chen, Z., Tian, X., Wang, X., Tao, M.: On content-centric wireless delivery networks. IEEE Wirel. Commun. **21**(6), 118–125 (2014)
7. Xylomenos, G., Ververidis, C.N., Siris, V.A., Fotiou, N., Tsilopoulos, C., Vasilakos, X., Polyzos, G.C.: A survey of information-centric networking research. IEEE Commun. Surv. Tutor. **16**(2), 1024–1049 (2014)
8. Tourani, R., Misra, S., Mick, T., Panwar, G.: Security, privacy, and access control in information-centric networking: a survey. IEEE Commun. Surv. Tutor. (2017)
9. Amadeo, M., Campolo, C., Molinaro, A.: A novel hybrid forwarding strategy for content delivery in wireless information-centric networks. Comput. Commun. **109**, 104–116 (2017)
10. Liu, X., Li, Z., Yang, P., Dong, Y.: Information-centric mobile ad hoc networks and content routing: a survey. Ad Hoc Netw. **58**, 255–268 (2017)

Efficiencies in Binary Elliptic Curves

Scott T. E. Hirschfeld$^{(\boxtimes)}$, Lynn M. Batten [ID],
and Mohammed K. I. Amain

Deakin University, Geelong, VIC 3216, Australia
{scott.hirschfeld, lmbatten, mkamain}@deakin.edu.au

Abstract. This paper discusses the choices of elliptic curve models available to the would-be implementer, and assists the decision as to which model to use by examining the links between security and efficiency. In early public key cryptography schemes, such as ElGamal and RSA, the use of finite fields over large prime numbers was prevalent, thus preventing the need for difficult and expensive computations over extension fields. Thus, with the introduction of elliptic curve models, the same computational infrastructure using prime fields was inevitably used. As it became clear that elliptic curve models were more efficient than their public key competitors, they acquired a great deal of attention. In more recent times, and with the onset of the Internet of Things, the cryptography community is faced with the challenge of improving the efficiency of cryptography even further, resulting in many papers dealing with improvements of computational efficiencies. This search, along with improvements in both software and hardware dealing with characteristic two fields has instigated the analysis of elliptic curve constructions over binary extension fields. In particular, the ability to identify an object in the field with a bit string aids computation for binary elliptic curves. These circumstances account for our focus on binary elliptic curve fields in this paper in which we present an in-depth discussion on their efficiency and security properties along with other relevant features of various binary elliptic curve models.

Keywords: Elliptic curve · Binary extension field · Internet of Things

1 Motivation and Aims

Elliptic curves have been studied for many years, but only recently have evolved into cryptographic systems as proposed independently by Koblitz in [1] and Miller in [2]. In 1987, Lenstra discovered a method of using elliptic curve addition for the factoring of integers [3]. Since that period, cryptographic implementations were formalised and standardised by various regulating agencies. Such standards were designed to enable secure communications between businesses and governments using insecure communication channels.

The wide range of properties now available which improve the security and efficiency for elliptic curve cryptosystems (ECCs) came from research that focused on: the types of attacks against elliptic curve cryptosystems (examples of relevant papers can be found in the survey papers [4, 5]), optimising point arithmetic algorithms (examples of relevant papers include [6, 7] and their references), and developing better hardware

© Springer International Publishing AG, part of Springer Nature 2018
O. Gervasi et al. (Eds.): ICCSA 2018, LNCS 10964, pp. 246–260, 2018.
https://doi.org/10.1007/978-3-319-95174-4_21

or software for implementations of elliptic curves by authors of papers such as [8, 9]. As a direct result of several practical attacks against elliptic curves, the authors Joye and Yen in [7] and Joye in [10] developed elliptic curve algorithms based on the papers [11, 12] by Montgomery, to introduce what has come to be known as the 'Montgomery powering ladder', that they argued is simultaneously secure and efficient.

Overall, research focusing on implementations of elliptic curves, has allowed for a greater understanding of their security and efficiency, driven and directed the current standards and hardware, and will continue to direct research into future generations of elliptic curves.

The aim of this paper is to *derive an understanding of what binary elliptic curves are in use today, and what their role is likely to be in future generations of cryptographic systems, as well as what research needs to take place to improve their use in future applications.*

In Sect. 2, we examine factors that have affected the efficiency and security of implementations of elliptic curves. Because this examination leads to discussion of hardware and software improvements, many of which give rise to faster implementations with byte forms, we are forced to discuss ECC over binary fields. Therefore, Sect. 3 considers current models for ECC over binary fields; these are compared, in our Table 1, on the basis of addition and doubling formula operation counts. We also point out at the end of that section, that research has shown that endomorphisms can reduce these counts in all cases.

We move, in Sect. 4 to the reasons for interest in binary ECC in the future; these reasons include the exponential move to Internet of Things devices which will need authentication to each other, and the fact that recent research has shown that binary-based processors can be faster and more energy efficient than prime field based processors. In addition, new hardware compatible with binary field processing has been produced by Intel.

Finally, in Sect. 5, we give examples of a point doubling computation based on two different regular algorithms which are resistant to side-channel attacks. The curve chosen is over $GF(2^8)$. Section 6 presents a summary of our conclusions.

2 Factors Affecting Recent Advances in ECC Efficiency and Security

Threats to the security of elliptic curve algorithms and their implementations have led to research into ways that efficiency and security could be improved. In this section, we consider the three most productive approaches. The arithmetic of elliptic curves defined over fields of characteristic 2, can be found in Sect. 13.3 of [13].

2.1 Optimisation of Point Arithmetic Algorithms

In the papers [11, 12], Peter Montgomery introduced ideas for speeding known methods of factorization; the focus was on efficiency. His principal context was finite fields with a multiplicative operation, but he also considered the elliptic curve case with an additive operation in the later paper. Since those papers were published, many authors have developed from them efficient algorithms for point addition in the elliptic curve case, and these have been determined to be resistant to a number of modern day side channel attacks. What has come to be known as the 'Montgomery powering ladder' has been studied extensively by Joye and Yen in [7] and by Joye in [10] and is used and referred to in numerous papers.

Computations on an elliptic curve can be performed in affine or projective coordinates. Using projective coordinates has the advantage that field inversions in point operations are simplified by the introduction of the additional coordinate. However, the authors of [14] claim that points should be converted from projective back to affine before outputting the result as this saves the cost of transferring a coordinate; not transferring back to affine coordinates before output also provides an adversary with the opportunity of capturing some side-channel information from the projection as has been shown in [15]. An examination of choice of coordinates and methods of speeding point additions is described well in Sect. 13.3 of [13].

In 2007, Edwards [16] introduced complete addition formulas for elliptic curves over algebraic number fields, pointing out that "every elliptic curve is equivalent – in an appropriate sense" to one in his Theorem 3.1. The formulas given in that theorem appear to be the first in the literature to be usable for the addition of any two points P and Q on the curve without the usual exceptions of $P \neq Q$ or $- Q$, explaining the term 'complete'. The following year, Bernstein et al. introduced a characteristic two version of Edwards' curves and analogous complete addition formulas [17]. They also show in their Sect. 4, that for n at least 3 every ordinary elliptic curve over $GF(2^n)$ is birationally equivalent to a complete binary Edwards curve. They explain that, while their formulas give speed improvements when evaluating doubling and differential addition formulas, they are not as fast as standard Weierstrass in evaluating general addition with incomplete formulas.

By devising a novel coordinate system, the authors of [18] improved the efficiency of the point doubling, mixed addition and the projective point addition for Weierstrass form curves; however, their formulas are not complete. In 2014, motivated by the fast computations in binary of [17] and of the improvements in speed of [18] (though with non-complete formulas), the authors of [19] were able to speed up the complete formulas for the binary Edwards curve arithmetic of [17] to obtain the fastest ones then known on the curves. Significant improvements were obtained in both affine and (standard) projective coordinates.

Note that the authors of [17] define unified scalar multiplication formulas as those for which the same formulas are used to perform the addition and doubling of points; usually, exceptional formulas are needed for situations when adding a point to its negative. They also define complete scalar multiplication formulas as those for which the same formulas are used to perform the addition and doubling of points without exception.

2.2 Improvements in Hardware Implementations

In [4], the authors offer an overview of the implementation attacks and countermeasures on ECC which existed at that time. Their useful Table 1 suggests countermeasures for various passive and active attacks. For instance, to prevent a differential attack, they suggest the use of both a point validity check and a coherence check. Two years later, Fan and Verbauwhede in [5] update this 2010 paper re-organizing the attacks and adding 4 possible countermeasures.

Passive attacks (also known as side-channel attacks) observe outputs and inputs of parameters without interfering in the elliptic curve protocol [4, 19]. Examples of such attacks include Simple Power Analysis (SPA) which identifies patterns in the power traces correlated to operations on a device performing an execution of an elliptic curve protocol as well as a second technique, known as Differential Power Analysis (DPA) using statistical methods to reveal the secret scalar from measurements made [5]. This same paper points out that typical countermeasures for SPA include the use of dummy operations, indistinguishable point formulas, double-and-add-always formulas, point validations and Montgomery ladders; the use of unified formulas is also a countermeasure against SPA and DPA.

In the paper [20], the author provides a detailed review of hardware elliptic curve implementation designs, based on Field Programmable Gate Array (FPGA) and Application Specific Integrated Circuit (ASIC) concepts, with detailed descriptions of both of these platforms. In his Sect. 6, he pays equal attention to binary elliptic curves and to elliptic curves over other prime fields. The author points out, in particular, that addition and doubling over $GF(2^m)$ can easily be implemented by XOR gates in hardware. His Subsects. 6.1.1 and 6.2.1 describe FPGA and ASIC implementations respectively of binary elliptic curves. His Table 1 shows the area, power and time needed for FPGA implementations of various binary Weierstrass curves. We summarize some of the recommendations of his paper in our Conclusion Sect. 6.

2.3 Improvements in Software Implementations

In 2009, Bernstein [21; p. 317] asked 'Which curves should one choose for elliptic curve cryptography?' And answered that the first choice is between curves over prime fields and curves over binary extension fields. In that paper, he introduces new software to demonstrate that elliptic curves over binary extension fields can be just as fast and just as secure as those over prime fields. As Bernstein also points out in his paper, "Multiplication in the polynomial ring $F_2[t]$ is … just like multiplication in Z but skips all the carries. Furthermore, squaring in $F_2[t]$ is simply a relabeling of exponents. One might therefore guess that curves over binary fields are considerably faster than curves over large-characteristic fields." This insight motivates him to show that, at least in the case of binary Edwards curves, speed limits of the prime curves can be exceeded. This work on binary Edwards curves follows on some of the author's previous papers, such as [17] in which the first complete addition formulas are given for binary curves.

The work of Bernstein, Lange and Farashahi was quickly followed by that of Devigne and Joye [22] describing differential and unified point addition laws for binary Huff curves indicating their ability to offer both security and speed. Devigne and Joye claim that, apart from some exceptional cases, their formulas result in binary Huff curves that can perform better than binary Edwards curves.

3 Common Types of Elliptic Curve Models Over Binary Fields

This section describes the six binary elliptic curve models considered in this paper, explains why some are equivalent, and compares them based on the cost of addition and doubling operations. We use Sect. 13.3 of [13] as our guide to the required arithmetical operations on elliptic curves.

3.1 Short Weierstrass Curves

Over a characteristic 2 field, the general Weierstrass equation $a_0 y^2 + a_1 xy + a_3 y = x^3 + a_2 x^2 + a_4 x + a_6$ for elliptic curves as in [23], can be transformed into the 'short curve' equation

$$y^2 + xy = x^3 + ax^2 + b \tag{1}$$

where coefficients a and b come from the field. In binary form, these curves are considered in two modes, one being the pseudo-random binary elliptic curve from the ANSI X9.62 standard [24; p. 40] and the other being the λ-coordinates projective version as defined in [25]. The short Weierstrass curves are used with the addition and doubling formulas that can be found in [23].

3.2 Binary Montgomery Curves

In the late 1980s, Montgomery developed a revised form of (1) to speed up elliptic curve factorisation methods [12, 26, 27]. The generic version of these Montgomery curves for prime order fields of characteristic greater than 2 in affine form is given by:

$$By^2 = x^3 + Ax^2 + x \tag{2}$$

where A and B are elements of the underlying field. As argued in [28; p. 293], if $A^2 - 4$ is not 0, then (2) can be considered of general Weierstrass form as in [23], even in the case of characteristic 2.

As pointed out by Hamburg in [29], over fields of prime characteristic congruent to 3 modulo 4, the curve in (2) is equivalent to one with $B \equiv 1$, whereas this is not the case for fields of prime characteristic congruent to 1 modulo 4. The same Eq. (2) over a field of prime order congruent to 3 modulo 4, can be transformed into a Montgomery curve with $B \equiv 1$, in which case, the curve is referred to as 'untwisted'.

3.3 Binary Edwards Curves

These were discussed in Sect. 2. The binary Edwards curve with coefficients d_1 and d_2 from the underlying field is the affine curve

$$d_1(x + y) + d_2(x + y) = xy + xy(x + y) + x^2 y^2.$$

In Sect. 4.3.5 of [28], the authors prove that Montgomery curves and twisted Edwards curves cover the same set of elliptic curves by demonstrating that a birational equivalence, and hence a group isomorphism exists, between the two sets.

3.4 Binary Huff Curves

A binary Huff curve is the set of projective points $(X : Y : Z)$ in $P^2(GF(2^m))$ that satisfies

$$aX(Y^2 + YZ + Z^2) = bY(X^2 + XZ + Z^2)$$

where $a, b \in GF(2^m)$ and $a \neq b$. See Sect. 2 of [22] in which the authors point out that these curves are birationally equivalent to Weierstrass curves, and where this equivalence is used to produce point doubling and addition formulas based on (but different from) those for Weierstrass equations. These differences are reflected in our Table 1 below.

3.5 Binary Hessian Curves

Some unified formulas for binary Hessian curves are complete under certain conditions [30]. The efficiency of the group law for binary Hessian curves has proven to be very competitive against other binary elliptic curve models for its additions, doublings and complete formulas. Thus binary Hessian curves are among the better binary curve options for the implementer. The binary Hessian curve is represented by the equation below ([30]; pp. 245–246), where $d \neq 27$:

$$x^3 + y^3 + 1 = dxy.$$

3.6 Binary Koblitz Curves

A Koblitz curve is a short Weierstrass curve as in (1) with $b = 1$ and $a = 0$ or 1. Details and examples of Koblitz curve arithmetic can be found in [31]. In a later paper [32], the authors focus on computations on the Koblitz curve NIST-K283 over the binary field 2^{283}. By employing time-memory trade-offs for computing fixed powers of 2, their aim is to show that Koblitz curves are the fastest choice for deploying curve-based cryptography if sufficient native support for binary field arithmetic is available in the target platform.

Our comparative Table 1 displays the cost of one addition and one doubling using affine, projective and mixed formulas. The relevant references are noted by the model used. Since Montgomery and Koblitz curves can be represented in short Weierstrass form, their efficiencies are the same when used with the same addition and doubling formulas. Hence we do not include these curves separately in Table 1.

Table 1. Comparison of addition and doubling formulas operation count

Model	Addition formulas			Doubling formulas	
	Affine	Projective	Mixed	Affine	Projective
Short Weierstrass:					
pseudo-random [24]	12.2M	13.8M	9M	12.2M	4.8M
λ-coordinates [25]	24.4M	11.4M	8.4M	10.2M	5.8M
Binary Edwards [17, 21]	31.4M	19.4M	15.4M	14.8M	6M
Binary Huff [22]	29M	15.4M	–	30.2M	9.2M
Binary Hessian [30]	18.8M	12M	11.6M	15.6M	7.6M

In the table, M stands for the cost of one multiplication, and in calculating these figures, we took the cost of field squaring as $0.2M$ and the cost of inversion to be $10M$ as in [33]. Clear differences arise depending on the format of the operation. However, the table does show that projective addition formulas are generally more efficient than affine versions. For doubling formulas, this efficiency is apparent in all models. This table assists those choosing between affine and projective coordinates.

In Subsect. 6.1.1 of [20], the author describes FPGA implementations of binary Edwards, binary Huff and generalized Hessian curves. His Table 7 in Subsect. 6.2.1 gives the area, time and power consumption of ASIC implementations of various binary elliptic curves.

3.7   Galbraith-Lin-Scott Point Multiplication over Binary Curves

In [34], the authors demonstrated how the use of endomorphisms can accelerate point multiplication on certain elliptic curves over finite fields of characteristic greater than 3; in the literature, this method is referred to as the GLV technique. In 2008, Galbraith et al. [35] developed efficiently-computable endomorphisms suitable for the purposes of elliptic curve point multiplications. The authors show that their method reduces the times of the previous best methods by approximately 20–25% on general curves.

Hankerson et al. in [36] give the background of the above work and extend it by showing that the general method also works in the case of binary fields. Specifically, the authors show there is a large class of elliptic curves over binary fields for which the GLV technique is particularly effective in speeding up point multiplication by about the same amount as for curves over fields of characteristic greater than 3. In their Sect. 6.2, they are careful to state that comparisons vary depending on several factors, including the method used (doubling- versus halving-based, the efficiency of the programming, and the processor used.) Serendipitously, this technique has been introduced at a time when Intel Corporation is providing new processors which incorporate characteristic 2 multipliers on 64-bit operands [37].

From the work of [36], we can estimate that use of the GLV method would improve all the times in our Table 1 by about 20%. It remains to be seen how much additional improvement will result from the use of the new Intel processors.

4 Reasons for Recent and Future Interest in Binary Elliptic Curves

4.1 The Internet of Things and Cryptography

The Internet of Things (IoT) is comprised of many users and many devices in addition to numerous services. As stated by the authors of [38], "The IoT paradigm integrates all networked everyday objects and services into the same network platform, today namely the Internet". While registration for a service in the IoT may be with a 'remote' server and require cryptographic authentication, in many situations, authentication or identification between devices which supply and use the service will occur locally making end-to-end authentication a critical requirement for many IoT scenarios as noted in [39] and consequently requiring efficiency as a high priority. In consequence of this, the authors of [39] propose an end-to-end authentication based on ECC and demonstrate its efficiency based on elliptic twisted Edwards curves.

The authors of [40] instantiate an example of an IoT network as a privacy-preserving smart parking system based on binary field ECC. They study the performance of their system in outdoor IoT testbeds and analyze the execution time and network overhead for each of the hardware platforms Contiki, TinyOS, iSenseOS, ScatterWeb and Arduino. The main challenge they faced was the implementation of zero-knowledge protocols in low-end devices. Based on the resource limitations and restrictions imposed by low power wireless communication protocols (e.g. IEEE 802.15.4) for such devices, they applied the ECC approach, transforming well established zero-knowledge protocols based on the discrete logarithm problem, into protocols involving the elliptic curve discrete logarithm problem. They state that (page 176) "this transformation step was the key for implementing such heavy protocols, in terms of computation and communication, on constrained environments, due to the fact that ECC offers similar levels of security with other cryptosystems (e.g. RSA) using smaller keys."

4.2 Efficient Hardware Implementations

Wenger and Hutter in [41], investigate whether binary fields or prime fields are better (in terms of area, speed, power and energy) when executing multi-precision arithmetic. To perform the comparison, they first build two custom designed 16-bit processors and compare results on running the elliptic curve digital signature algorithm (ECDSA). Their findings were mixed (see the Conclusion of their paper), however, overall, the binary-based processor was shown to be faster and more energy efficient than the prime field based processor.

More recently, using the Gaussian normal form representation of a characteristic 2 finite field, the authors of [42] demonstrate what is so far the most efficient hardware implementation of point addition over Koblitz elliptic curves; using application-specific integrated circuit (ASIC) hardware platforms as a prototype using a 65-nm CMOS technology, their comparison (Table 3 of their paper) with other implementations over the smallest NIST field, $GF(2^{163})$, confirms their claim of lower energy consumption and fewer clock cycles than needed in previous implementations of binary curves over

$GF(2^{163})$; this confirms their claim to have found an implementation suitable for extremely constrained devices.

Finally in this subsection, we refer to a 2016 work, [43], in which the authors review ECC coprocessors which vary critically depending on whether a binary field or prime field is being used. They state that "over binary fields $GF(2^m)$... the carry-free arithmetic often leads to a more efficient hardware architecture ... however elliptic curves over prime fields $GF(p)$ are often preferred due to standards in Europe and the US." They conclude by saying that, despite the fact that software implementations of ECC give most flexibility with least cost, dedicated hardware implementations must be introduced to deal with the future needs of the finance industry, the IoT and of post-quantum cryptography.

4.3 New Hardware

With the aim of increasing performance and security in future IA processors, Intel has recently developed 'Galois Counter Mode' (GCM), a block cipher mode of operation based on AES symmetric encryption (whose useage depends on polynomial arithmetic over binary fields) and hashing over a binary field [44]. Performance of GCM mode is improved by use of algorithms run in parallel, optimized polynomial multiplication methods, and both architecture and implementation improvements. Intel aimed at improving IPSec, SSH, 802.1AE MACSec and SSL/TLS protocols. Such processors are also expected to speed up computations of cryptographic protocols based on characteristic 2 finite fields. NIST approved the GCM specifications in 2007, but Intel has continued to develop it since then.

5   Examples of Weierstrass Curve Point Doubling over Binary Fields

The underlying mathematics of ECC is securely based on the difficulty of solving the Discrete Logarithm Problem [45]. However, implementing ECC on devices has proven to be susceptible to non-mathematical attacks (referred to as 'side-channel attacks') which include power, timing and safe error attacks. (Descriptions of these can be found in [46–48] for example).

Such attacks have led to the development of improved algorithms for point addition which try to hide differences between key operations. Such algorithms are referred to as 'regular'. There is now a broad set of point addition ECC regular algorithms available, which are considered to be resistant to power, timing, and safe error attacks. Examples can be found in [5, 7, 10, 49].

To illustrate the choice of algorithms for elliptic curve addition, we choose two left-to-right algorithms and use an AES field of characteristic 2. In order to keep computations simple, we use a Weierstrass elliptic curve where the relevant point addition formulas are given in [23; pp. 37–38]. Because these additions formulas for the characteristic 2 case have not been commonly used, we reproduce them here directly as in the previous reference:

Given two points, $P_1 = (x_1, y_1)$ and $P_2 = (x_2, y_2)$, on a Weierstrass curve over a field of characteristic two, whether the points are identical or not, the same formulas can be used to determine their sum $P_3 = (x_3, y_3)$ Since we are only interested in the case of doubling, we have $x_1 = x_2$. If these are not zero, letting $\lambda = (x_1^2 + y_1) * x_1^{-1}$ and $\mu = x_1^2$, then $x_3 = \lambda^2 + \lambda + a_2 + x_1 + x_2$ and $y_3 = (x_1 + x_3)\lambda + x_3 + y_1$. (Here, a_2 is the coefficient of x^2 on the curve, and for the curve we choose, Eq. (3), this is 0.)

Example 1. We choose a Weierstrass elliptic curve over the extension field $GF(2^8)$ of $GF(2)$ using a solution w of the irreducible polynomial $x^8 + x^4 + x^3 + x + 1$ over $GF(2)$ (as in AES). The curve is:

$$y^2 + xy = x^3 + \left(w^4 + w + 1\right) \tag{3}$$

where the coefficients are polynomials in $GF(2^8)$. Based on points in affine form, we choose the point $P = (w, w^2 + 1)$, value $k = 2$, and by using Algorithm 1, compute $Q = kP$. We use Maple software [50] for the basic computations, but need to do by-hand polynomial computations as our Maple software is not designed to handle it. (The reason for choosing such a small value of k is that most of the polynomial arithmetic for this algorithm has to be done by hand.)

We first use point addition algorithm – the Left-to-Right Montgomery Powering Ladder, taken from [7; Fig. 7], to compute the multiple of P. It is shown as Fig. 1. (Fig. 16 of Subsect. 6.1.1 of [20] describes the hardware implementation of this algorithm.) So that we do not have to implement extensive by-hand polynomial computations, we simply double P; however, we do need to derive it manually in Step 2.

Algorithm 1. The Left-to-Right Montgomery Powering Ladder

INPUT: $k \equiv (k_t, k_{t-1}, \dots, k_1)_2$, $P \in E(F_q)$.

OUTPUT: $k*P$.

1. $R(0) \longleftarrow O$, $R(1) \longleftarrow P$.

2. For i from t down to 1 do

    2.1 $R(\neg k_i) \longleftarrow R(0) + R(1)$.

    2.2 $R(k_i) \longleftarrow 2R(k_i)$.

End for

3. Return $R(0)$.

Fig. 1. The left-to-right Montgomery powering ladder

In this case, $t = 2, k_2 = 1$ and $k_1 = 0$.

Step 1
>R(0)= O=[inf, inf];
>R(1)= P=[w, w^2 +1];
Step 2 (COMMENT: The variable i will go from 2 down to 1)
> i=2;
Iteration 1
R(¬k$_2$)=R(0)=R(0)+R(1)= O+P= P =[w, w^2 +1];
COMMENT: The value of 2P must be computed by hand during the algorithm.
R(k$_2$)=R(1)=2R(1) = 2P = [w^6+w^2+w, w^6+w^5+1];
i=i-1=1;
Iteration 2
Since i ≥ 1, continue;
Since k$_1$ =0 then
R(¬k$_2$)=R(1)=R(0)+R(1)= P+2P= 3P;
COMMENT: We did not compute 3P as we will not need it.
R(k$_2$)=R(0)=2R(0)=2(P)= 2P = [w^6+w^2+w, w^6+w^5+1];
i=i-1=0;
Iteration 2
Since i <1, END FOR
Step 4
Return Q=R(0) =2P = [w^6+w^2+w, w^6+w^5+1];

Example 2. For this example, we use the same elliptic curve set-up, but use a different point addition algorithm to which we refer as the Left-to-Right Joye-Yen algorithm; it is in fact the Left-to-Right Montgomery Powering Ladder, modified by Joye and Yen to avoid a safe-error attack, and is taken from [7; Fig. 9] where it is presented in multiplicative form. Algorithm 2 describes the method of scalar multiplication beginning the point additions from the left-most bit. Again, so that we do not have to implement by-hand polynomial computations, we simply derive 2P; we need to derive it manually in Step 2 here. The algorithm is shown in Fig. 2.

In binary form, k is 10, and so $t = 2$ and $k_1 = 0$. To use the algorithm, we need to compute 2P by hand in Step 2.2. Using $w^8 = w^4 + w^3 + w + 1$, we compute 2P using the addition formulas in III.3.2 of [23] for the cases the same non-zero x-coordinate. We obtain $2P = \left(w^6 + w^2 + w, w^6 + w^5 + 1\right)$.

Algorithm 2. The Left-to-Right Joye-Yen Algorithm

INPUT: $k \equiv (1, k_{t-1}, \ldots, k_1)_2$, $P \in E(F_q)$.

OUTPUT: $k*P$.

1. $R(0) \longleftarrow O$, $R(1) \longleftarrow P$.

2. For i from t down to 1 do

    2.1 $R(\neg k_i) \longleftarrow R(0)+R(1)$.

    2.2 $R(k_i) \longleftarrow 2R(k_i)$.

End for

3. Return $R(0)$.

Fig. 2. The left-to-right Joye-Yen algorithm

Step 1
$>R(0)= P=[\ w,\ w^2 +1]$;
Step 2
$>R(1)=2P=[w^6+w^2+w,\ w^6+w^5+1]$;
Step 3
$>$Set i = 1;
Iteration 1
Since $i \geq 1$, continue;
Since $k_1 = 0$ then
$R(\neg k_1)=R(1)=R(0)+R(1)= P+2P= 3P$;
COMMENT: We did not compute 3P as we will not need it.
$R(k_1)=R(0)=2R(0) =2P = [w^6+w^2+w,\ w^6+w^5+1]$;
$i=i-1=0$;
Iteration 2
Since $i <1$, iterations end.
Step 4
Return $Q=R(0) =2P = [w^6+w^2+w,\ w^6+w^5+1]$;

Both algorithms give us the correct answer for 2P.

6 Conclusion

Our paper has reviewed the many improvements to ECC point addition algorithms which have appeared over the last 20 years in order to withstand attacks on implementations. Nevertheless, with the development of new micro-processor type, cheap hardware produced en masse specifically for use in the IoT of the future, it is likely that variations of current algorithms will be needed to resist attacks such as DDOS.

As part of his conclusions in [20], Rashidi indicates that further work should also be developed on 'implementation of ECC on microprocessors', 'new scheduling methods of hardware implementation of binary Edwards curves', 'new scheduling methods for generalized Hessian curves' and, since (p. 47) "field addition and multiplication operations in $GF(3^m)$ are comparable in performance to a space equivalent characteristic two alternative" hardware implementation of ECC over characteristic 3 fields require further investigation.

References

1. Koblitz, N.: Elliptic curve cryptosystems. Math. Comput. **48**(177), 203–209 (1987)
2. Miller, V.S.: Use of elliptic curves in cryptography. In: Williams, H.C. (ed.) CRYPTO 1985. LNCS, vol. 218, pp. 417–426. Springer, Heidelberg (1986). https://doi.org/10.1007/3-540-39799-X_31
3. Lenstra Jr., H.W.: Factoring integers with elliptic curves. Ann. Math. **126**(3), 649–673 (1987)
4. Fan, J., Guo, X., De Mulder, E., Schaumont, P., Preneel, B. and Verbauwhede, I.: State-of-the-art of secure ECC implementations: a survey on known side-channel attacks and countermeasures. In: 2010 IEEE International Symposium on Hardware-Oriented Security and Trust (HOST), pp. 76–87. IEEE, June 2010
5. Fan, J., Verbauwhede, I.: An updated survey on secure ECC implementations: attacks, countermeasures and cost. In: Naccache, D. (ed.) Cryptography and Security: From Theory to Applications. LNCS, vol. 6805, pp. 265–282. Springer, Heidelberg (2012). https://doi.org/10.1007/978-3-642-28368-0_18
6. De Win, E., Mister, S., Preneel, B., Wiener, M.: On the performance of signature schemes based on elliptic curves. In: Buhler, J.P. (ed.) ANTS 1998. LNCS, vol. 1423, pp. 252–266. Springer, Heidelberg (1998). https://doi.org/10.1007/BFb0054867
7. Joye, M., Yen, S.-M.: The Montgomery powering ladder. In: Kaliski, B.S., Koç, K., Paar, C. (eds.) CHES 2002. LNCS, vol. 2523, pp. 291–302. Springer, Heidelberg (2003). https://doi.org/10.1007/3-540-36400-5_22
8. Marzouqi, H., Al-Qutayri, M., Salah, K.: Review of elliptic curve cryptography processor designs. Microprocess. Microsyst. **39**(2), 97–112 (2015)
9. Belgarric, P., Fouque, P.-A., Macario-Rat, G., Tibouchi, M.: Side-channel analysis of Weierstrass and Koblitz curve ECDSA on android smartphones. In: Sako, K. (ed.) CT-RSA 2016. LNCS, vol. 9610, pp. 236–252. Springer, Cham (2016). https://doi.org/10.1007/978-3-319-29485-8_14
10. Joye, M.: Highly regular right-to-left algorithms for scalar multiplication. In: Paillier, P., Verbauwhede, I. (eds.) CHES 2007. LNCS, vol. 4727, pp. 135–147. Springer, Heidelberg (2007). https://doi.org/10.1007/978-3-540-74735-2_10
11. Montgomery, P.L.: Modular multiplication without trial division. Math. Comput. **44**, 519–521 (1985)
12. Montgomery, P.L.: Speeding the Pollard and elliptic curve methods of factorization. Math. Comput. **48**, 243–264 (1987)
13. Cohen, H., Frey, G., Avanzi, R., Doche, C., Lange, T., Nguyen, K., Vercauteren, F.: Handbook of Elliptic and Hyperelliptic Curve Cryptography. Chapman and Hall, CRC Press, Boca Raton (2006)
14. Karaklajić, D., Fan, J., Schmidt, J.M., Verbauwhede, I.: Low-cost fault detection method for ECC using Montgomery powering ladder. In: Proceedings of 2011 Design, Automation & Test in Europe, pp. 1–6. IEEE (2011)

15. Naccache, D., Smart, N.P., Stern, J.: Projective coordinates leak. In: Cachin, C., Camenisch, J.L. (eds.) EUROCRYPT 2004. LNCS, vol. 3027, pp. 257–267. Springer, Heidelberg (2004). https://doi.org/10.1007/978-3-540-24676-3_16
16. Edwards, H.: A normal form for elliptic curves. Bull. Am. Math. Soc. **44**(3), 393–422 (2007)
17. Bernstein, D.J., Lange, T., Rezaeian Farashahi, R.: Binary edwards curves. In: Oswald, E., Rohatgi, P. (eds.) CHES 2008. LNCS, vol. 5154, pp. 244–265. Springer, Heidelberg (2008). https://doi.org/10.1007/978-3-540-85053-3_16
18. Oliveira, T., López, J., Aranha, D.F., Rodríguez-Henríquez, F.: Lambda coordinates for binary elliptic curves. In: Bertoni, G., Coron, J.-S. (eds.) CHES 2013. LNCS, vol. 8086, pp. 311–330. Springer, Heidelberg (2013). https://doi.org/10.1007/978-3-642-40349-1_18
19. Kim, K.H., Lee, C.O., Negre, C.: Binary edwards curves revisited. In: Meier, W., Mukhopadhyay, D. (eds.) INDOCRYPT 2014. LNCS, vol. 8885, pp. 393–408. Springer, Cham (2014). https://doi.org/10.1007/978-3-319-13039-2_23
20. Rashidi, B.: A Survey on Hardware Implementations of Elliptic Curve Cryptosystems. arXiv preprint arXiv:1710.08336 (2017)
21. Bernstein, D.J.: Batch binary Edwards. In: Halevi, S. (ed.) CRYPTO 2009. LNCS, vol. 5677, pp. 317–336. Springer, Heidelberg (2009). https://doi.org/10.1007/978-3-642-03356-8_19
22. Devigne, J., Joye, M.: Binary Huff curves. In: Kiayias, A. (ed.) CT-RSA 2011. LNCS, vol. 6558, pp. 340–355. Springer, Heidelberg (2011). https://doi.org/10.1007/978-3-642-19074-2_22
23. Blake, I.F., Seroussi, G., Smart, N.: Elliptic curves in cryptography. In: London Mathematical Society Lecture Notes, vol. 265. Cambridge University Press, Cambridge (1999)
24. [X9.62.1999] Accredited Standards Committee X9. American national standard x9.62-1999, public key cryptography for the financial services industry: The elliptic curve digital signature algorithm (ECDSA). Draft at http://grouper.ieee.org/groups/1363/Research/Other. html
25. Oliveira, T., López, J., Aranha, D.F., Rodríguez-Henríquez, F.: Two is the fastest prime: lambda coordinates for binary elliptic curves. J. Cryptogr. Eng. **4**(1), 3–17 (2014)
26. Costello, C., Smith, B.: Montgomery curves and their arithmetic: the case of large characteristic fields. IACR Cryptology ePrint Archive, vol. 2017, p. 212 (2017)
27. Oliveira, T., López, J., Rodríguez-Henríquez, F.: The Montgomery ladder on binary elliptic curves. J. Cryptogr. Eng. 1–18 (2017). https://doi.org/10.1007/s13389-017-0163-8
28. Bernstein, D.J., Lange, T.: Montgomery curves and the Montgomery ladder. IACR Cryptology ePrint Archive (2017)
29. Hamburg, M.: Decaf: eliminating cofactors through point compression. In: Gennaro, R., Robshaw, M. (eds.) CRYPTO 2015. LNCS, vol. 9215, pp. 705–723. Springer, Heidelberg (2015). https://doi.org/10.1007/978-3-662-47989-6_34
30. Farashahi, R.R., Joye, M.: Efficient arithmetic on Hessian curves. In: Nguyen, P.Q., Pointcheval, D. (eds.) PKC 2010. LNCS, vol. 6056, pp. 243–260. Springer, Heidelberg (2010). https://doi.org/10.1007/978-3-642-13013-7_15
31. Solinas, J.A.: Efficient arithmetic on Koblitz curves. In: Koblitz, N. (ed.) Towards a Quarter-Century of Public Key Cryptography, pp. 125–179. Springer, Boston (2000). https://doi.org/10.1007/978-1-4757-6856-5_6
32. Aranha, D.F., Faz-Hernández, A., López, J., Rodríguez-Henríquez, F.: Faster implementation of scalar multiplication on Koblitz curves. In: Hevia, A., Neven, G. (eds.) LATINCRYPT 2012. LNCS, vol. 7533, pp. 177–193. Springer, Heidelberg (2012). https://doi.org/10.1007/978-3-642-33481-8_10

33. Bernstein, D., Lange, T.: Explicit-Formulas Database (2014). http://hyperelliptic.org/EFD/. Accessed 2 Apr 2017
34. Gallant, R.P., Lambert, R.J., Vanstone, S.A.: Faster point multiplication on elliptic curves with efficient endomorphisms. In: Kilian, J. (ed.) CRYPTO 2001. LNCS, vol. 2139, pp. 190–200. Springer, Heidelberg (2001). https://doi.org/10.1007/3-540-44647-8_11
35. Galbraith, S.D., Lin, X., Scott, M.: Endomorphisms for faster elliptic curve cryptography on a large class of curves. In: Joux, A. (ed.) EUROCRYPT 2009. LNCS, vol. 5479, pp. 518–535. Springer, Heidelberg (2009). https://doi.org/10.1007/978-3-642-01001-9_30
36. Hankerson, D., Karabina, K., Menezes, A.: Analyzing the Galbraith-Lin-Scott point multiplication method for elliptic curves over binary fields. IEEE Trans. Comput. **58**(10), 1411–1420 (2009)
37. Gueron, S.: AES-GCM for efficient authenticated encryption–ending the reign of HMAC-SHA-1. Real-World Cryptography (2013)
38. Alcaide, A., Palomar, E., Montero-Castillo, J., Ribagorda, A.: Anonymous authentication for privacy-preserving IoT target-driven applications. Comput. Secur. **37**, 111–123 (2013)
39. Markmann, T., Schmidt, T.C., Wählisch, M.: Federated end-to-end authentication for the constrained internet of things using IBC and ECC. ACM SIGCOMM Comput. Commun. Rev. **45**(4), 603–604 (2015)
40. Chatzigiannakis, I., Vitaletti, A., Pyrgelis, A.: A privacy-preserving smart parking system using an IoT elliptic curve based security platform. Comput. Commun. **89**, 165–177 (2016)
41. Wenger, E., Hutter, M.: Exploring the design space of prime field vs. binary field ECC-hardware implementations. In: Laud, P. (ed.) NordSec 2011. LNCS, vol. 7161, pp. 256–271. Springer, Heidelberg (2012). https://doi.org/10.1007/978-3-642-29615-4_18
42. Azarderakhsh, R., Jarvinen, K.U., Mozaffari-Kermani, M.: Efficient algorithm and architecture for elliptic curve cryptography for extremely constrained secure applications. IEEE Trans. Circ. Syst. I Regul. Pap. **61**(4), 1144–1155 (2014)
43. Halak, B., Waizi, S.S., Islam, A.: A Survey of Hardware Implementations of Elliptic Curve Cryptographic Systems (2016). https://eprint.iacr.org/2016/712.pdf
44. Ozturk, E., Gopal, V.: Enabling High-performance Galois-counter mode on Intel architecture processors. Intel white paper (2012)
45. Galbraith, S.D., Gaudry, P.: Recent progress on the elliptic curve discrete logarithm problem. Des. Codes Crypt. **78**(1), 51–72 (2016)
46. Feix, B., Roussellet, M., Venelli, A.: Side-channel analysis on blinded regular scalar multiplications. In: Meier, W., Mukhopadhyay, D. (eds.) INDOCRYPT 2014. LNCS, vol. 8885, pp. 3–20. Springer, Cham (2014). https://doi.org/10.1007/978-3-319-13039-2_1
47. Chen, C.: FPGA implementation for elliptic curve cryptography over binary extension field. M.A.Sc., University of Windsor, 10 December 2017, Electronic Theses and Dissertations (2017)
48. Lalonde, D.R.: Private and public-key side-channel threats against hardware accelerated cryptosystems. M.A.Sc., University of Windsor, 13 December 2017, Electronic Theses and Dissertations (2017)
49. Coron, J.-S.: Resistance against differential power analysis for elliptic curve cryptosystems. In: Koç, Ç.K., Paar, C. (eds.) CHES 1999. LNCS, vol. 1717, pp. 292–302. Springer, Heidelberg (1999). https://doi.org/10.1007/3-540-48059-5_25
50. Maplesoft. User Manual (2015). http://www.maplesoft.com/documentation_center/

Workshop Geomatics for Resource Monitoring and Control (GRMC 2018)

A Low Cost Methodology for Multispectral Image Classification

Michele Mangiameli[✉], Giuseppe Mussumeci, and Alessio Candiano

Dipartimento di Ingegneria Civile ed Architettura, University of Catania, Catania, Italy
mmangiam@dica.unict.it

Abstract. Multispectral and hyperspectral remote sensing have significantly improved territorial surveys and mapping. However aerial images are often expensive being acquired through aircraft and satellite sensors. Furthermore, the processing and classification of these images need commercial software that increases the entire cost of the analysis. For these reasons, we propose an approach of data acquisition and analysis based on supervised classification to obtain accurately maps of the area of interest in reduced time. The images have been acquired through 3-channels Tetracam ADC-Lite camera, and processed with free and open source software, PixelWrench2 and QGIS. The results obtained demonstrate that the approach can compete with traditional acquisition and classification methods, due to simple operational procedures, low operational costs, and high accuracy of supervised classification. This approach provides promising results that encourage its development and optimization of these technologies for other purposes, such as the mapping of asbestos-cement (AC) roof coverings.

Keywords: Remote sensing · Free and open source software · GIS technology

1 Introduction

Remote sensing is a technology aimed at studying phenomena occurring on the Earth's surface, as well as at detecting and acquiring properties of objects present on it. This is conducted by means of a spectral analysis of solar radiation, which is reflected in different ways by different natural and anthropic surfaces, using multi and hyperspectral sensors able to acquire information on large areas hardly detectable in the same time by terrestrial surveying [1].

Nowadays remote sensing represents a valid alternative to traditional methods of territory investigation [1–4] especially in those cases where it is difficult to reach the investigation site or there is the presence of hazardous materials to human health [5–7]. An important application of remote sensing in recent years is the detection and mapping of asbestos roofing, which is one of the most hazardous substances for human health in the modern era [8, 9]. For these reasons the remote sensing can be an excellent method of investigation, especially with hyperspectral airborne sensors with high geometric and spectral resolution [10–12] or multi-channels satellite sensors [13, 15].

© Springer International Publishing AG, part of Springer Nature 2018
O. Gervasi et al. (Eds.): ICCSA 2018, LNCS 10964, pp. 263–280, 2018.
https://doi.org/10.1007/978-3-319-95174-4_22

These experiences shows that:

i.   to perform an accurate classification it's fundamental that the initial data must have high geometric and radiometric resolutions [10–12]; these characteristics clearly require high costs for the acquisition phase, both from airborne sensors and satellite; a further increase in costs is related to operational difficulties due to the weight of the sensor and to the platforms, which must be suitably equipped [15, 16];

ii.   the acquired data often need to be pre-proceed and processed by one or more commercial and closed source software [15];

iii. the thematic maps, which can reach a high accuracy, are georeferenced and integrated as additional data layers in GIS software [10–12].

GIS technology is a valid support to manage the spatial data [17–19]. Here the GIS desktop platform is used to process the remote sensing data.

The research in the field of remote sensing is geared towards more economical and low-cost methods for the acquisition of multispectral images [15, 16] and towards free and open-source software for processing these images.

Here we propose a procedure which exploits free and low-cost methodologies to acquire multispectral images and to classified them using open source software. In particular, the images, acquired using a multispectral camera ADC-Lite, were pre-processed through Pixel Wrench2 and successively classified with QGIS.

The procedure proposed has allowed to obtain georeferenced thematic maps with a high information content. Indeed, although the limited spectral resolution (only three bands), we were able to distinguish and classify different objects present in the scenes with a high accuracy.

2   Materials and Methods

2.1   Multispectral Camera

The acquisition of images was performed using a multispectral low-cost camera Tetracam ADC-lite model (see Fig. 1). This multispectral camera weights 200 g and is equipped with a 3.2-megapixel CMOS sensor (2048 * 1536 pixels), a remote power and display features for optimized placement on UAV platforms. The primary use of this product is to record vegetation canopy reflectance; the resulting image is suitable for derivation of several vegetation indices (NDVI, Soil Adjusted Vegetation Index, canopy segmentation and Near Infrared/Green ratios). Images are recorded in the visible red, green and near infrared (NIR) spectrum with nominal wavelengths of 520–600, 630–690, and 760–900 nm.

Fig. 1. Tetracam ADC-Lite.

2.2 Multispectral Imaging Editing Software

The software used for the editing and processing of multispectral data is Tetracam PixelWrench2, which is a proprietary application supplied to users of Tetracam cameras. PixelWrench2 is a simple powerful image editing program incorporating a specialized set of tools for working with multi-spectral images, including a full interface to Tetracam cameras (Fig. 2). The program provides controls for opening and manipulating several images on the desktop. Editing features include, tone, contrast, gamma, scaling, rotation, sharpen, blur etc. In addition PixelWrench2 allows image translation, cloning, optical distortion correction and several other more specialized features.

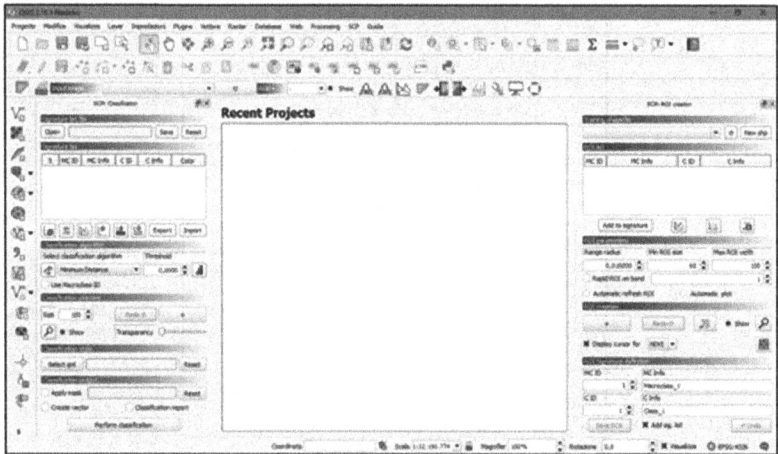

Fig. 2. Layout of QGIS and semi-automatic classification plugin.

QGIS (Quantum GIS) is a software based on GIS technology, which provides functionalities commonly available into commercial GIS packages. Since it's distributed as open source package, the QGIS source code is freely available for the developers and can therefore be downloaded and modified. to meet specific needs.

In addition, in order to increase the functionality and compatibility, plugins can be compiled, that are small extensions loaded at the time of program launch. For our procedure we particularly used the Semi-Automatic Classification Plugin (see Fig. 2), which is a free open source plugin for QGIS allowing semi-automatic classification (also known as "supervised classification") of remote sensing images using the following classification algorithms: *Minimum Distance, Maximum Likelihood,* and *Spectral Angle Mapping.*

2.3   Framework of the Adopted Methodology

The procedure proposed in the present work and described in Fig. 3, can be summarized mainly in two major phases: the phase of calibration and preprocessing of images using the PixelWrench2 software; the phase of image classification and assessment of the accuracy of the classifications obtained by the software QuatumGIS.

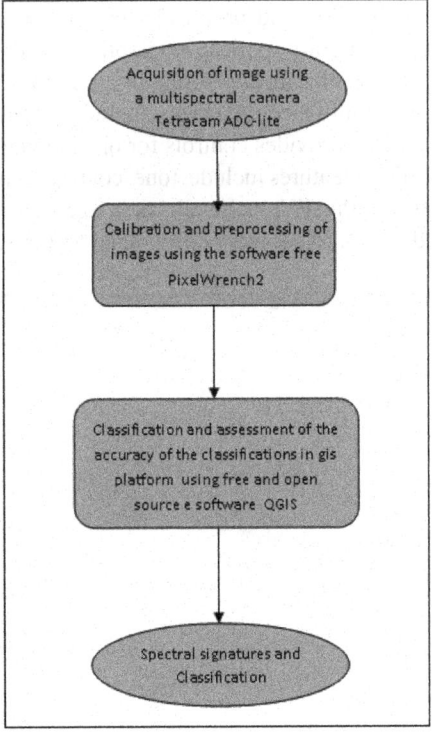

Fig. 3.   Workflow of the methodology.

In order to test the sensor, we chose a scene with heterogeneity of materials (elements of vegetation, soil types, concrete constructions) acquired during the summer period and the middle hours of the day to obtain the maximum reflectance (being the Sun fairly high on the horizon). Only 3 bands of the sensor were used to distinguish the materials from the scene. As example of a photo taken during the survey campaign is reported in Fig. 4.

Fig. 4. Example of image taken through Tetracam ADC-Lite.

2.4 Image Preprocessing with PixelWrench2

The preprocessing phase consists in the calibration and false color processing of the images. The software also offers the possibility to perform editing images and exporting for later processing.

Calibration of the Images. The PixelWrench2 software can be calibrated to determine the spectral balance of the daily light and to refine the selected index calculation. A fully occupied image of the calibration plate equipped with the camera is taken under the same light conditions, visualized through the software, selected and calibrated (Fig. 5).

Fig. 5. Image of the calibration plate.

Color Processing. Before using images taken with the ADC-Lite camera they must be processed in false colors to be displayed on the monitor, representing images for additive synthesis of RGB bands. To this purpose a color matrix is needed to select, derive the DN relating to different bands (Nir, Red and Green) and to obtain an image in false colors. Figure 6 shows the image of Fig. 4 after the color processing phase. The vegetation appears magenta being obtained by the sum of channel Nir (shown red) and of the Green channel (shown blue).

Fig. 6. Color processing on the taken image through Tetracam ADC-Lite. (Color figure online)

Image Editing. The PixelWrench2 software also allows editing images using the tools contained within the EditTools module of the View menu (Fig. 7). The EditTools module, consisting of the tabs Basic, HSV, ApplyCurve, Text/Drwg, allows to make changes just on one color plane, or on all three (as seen at the bottom you can select the color plane in which to make the changes) with the exception of operations such as rotation, scaling or cutting the image that act on all the color planes. Editing operations can be also performed on the entire image or just a portion of it, depending on the selection.

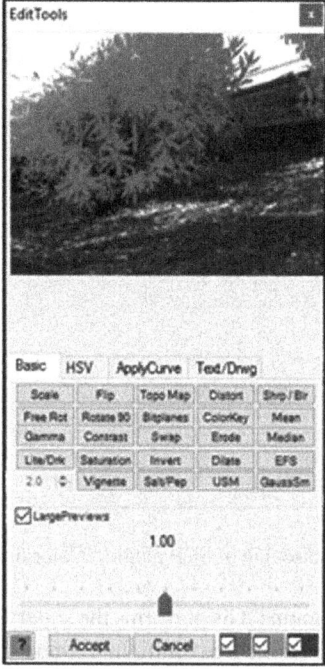

Fig. 7. The EditTools module.

2.5   Image Processing with SCP Plugin in QGIS Platform

The processing phase, performed using the SCP plugin of QGIS, consists in the definition of the bands of the taken images and in the ROI creation, that is necessary to the
supervised classification. Once the ROIs are defined, the spectral signatures can be
viewed to evaluate the spectral separability, and the classification can be run through
the chosen algorithm. Finally the accuracy of the obtained classifications is assessed to
evaluate the results obtained with different spectral signatures, and with different algorithms.

Bands Definition.   Once the picture is loaded, the next step was the definition of the
different bands, through the Band set tab of SCP plugin (Fig. 8); in this case the band
centers detectable through Tetracam ADC-Lite were inserted in the tab: 560 nm (Green
band center), 660 nm (Red band center) and 830 nm (Nir band center).

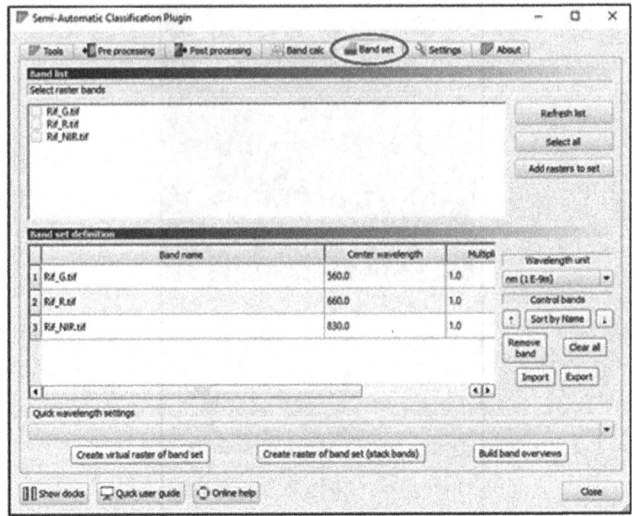

Fig. 8. Band set tab of SCP plugin. (Color figure online)

ROIs Creation. The SCP plugin QGis performs the supervised classification of remote sensing images. The supervised methods initially require the definition of the number and nature of the classes by means of a series of pixels of training (called Training Areas or ROIs (Regions Of Interest), to create a spectral signature that is characteristic and distinctive for each considered class.

For the ROI creation we used the SCP: ROI creation panel of SCP plugin (Fig. 9).

ROIs are polygons that can be created automatically using a region growing algorithm with a click on a pixel of the image (i.e. the polygon ROI is segmented around a pixel seed); in this way the created ROIs include pixels spectrally homogeneous. Alternatively, the ROIs can be created manually by drawing a polygon manually. In particular, for each ROI, the average spectral signature and the standard deviation are calculated for each band of the raster. If the result is good, the ROI can be saved in the ROI shapefile.

An example of scatter-plot of the ROIs is shown in Fig. 10.

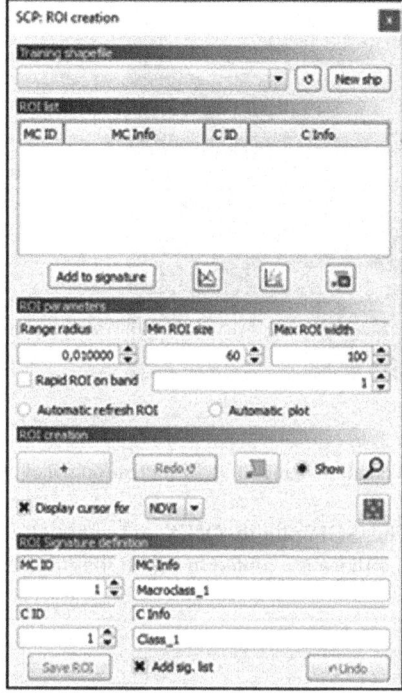

Fig. 9. SCP: ROI creation panel of SCP plugin.

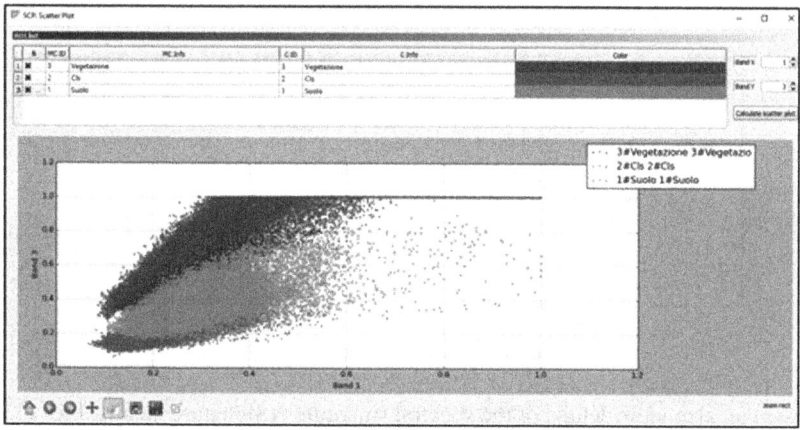

Fig. 10. Scatter-plot of the ROIs.

For the images taken with the Tetracam ADC-Lite, the ROIs have been defined manually, Fig. 11, since the classes were easy to find; in particular three classes have been identified: concrete, soil and vegetation.

Fig. 11. ROIs creation using SCP: ROI creation panel of SCP plugin.

Spectral Signatures. The SCP plugin QGIS automatically calculates the spectral signatures of the ROI once these are added to the Signature list (Fig. 12).

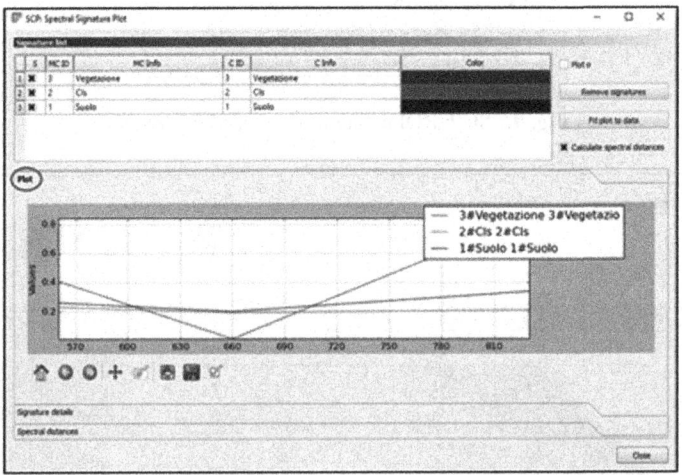

Fig. 12. Spectral signature plot.

User can also view details of the spectral signatures (Signature details, Fig. 13) and the spectral distances (Spectral distances, Fig. 14) between the spectral signatures for evaluating the spectral separability.

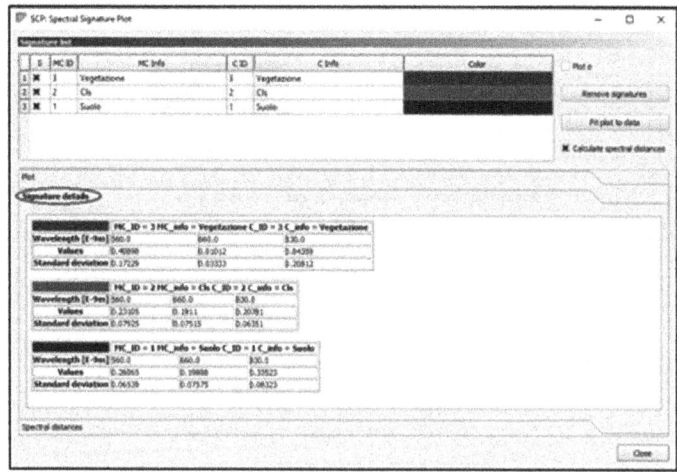

Fig. 13. Signature details of Spectral signature plot.

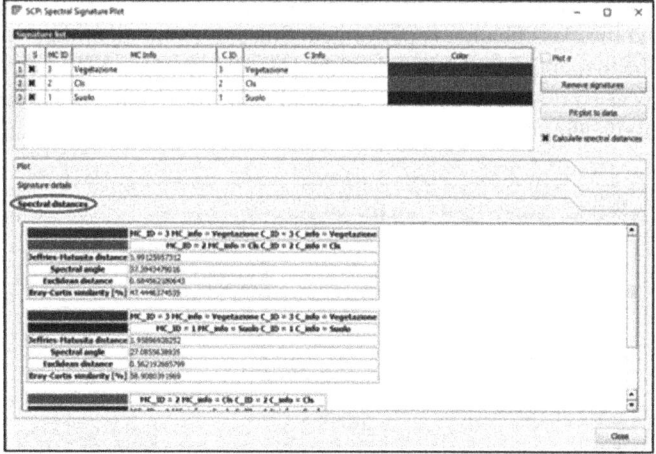

Fig. 14. Spectral distances of Spectral signature plot.

Moreover it is possible to import or export spectral signatures from external sources, or to download the spectral signature from USGS spectral library by means specific tools. Using this tool it has been verified the reliability of the spectral signatures calculated on ROI comparing them with the UGS signatures.

For example the spectral signature of the concrete was obtained by comparing the one obtained in the ROI of the image with the USGS spectral library (Fig. 15).

The two spectral signatures of the concrete are very similar, indicating that the approach provides good results. The similar comparison for soil and vegetation was not performed because in the USGS literature libraries does not exist a perfectly coincident signing with the elements present in the scanned image.

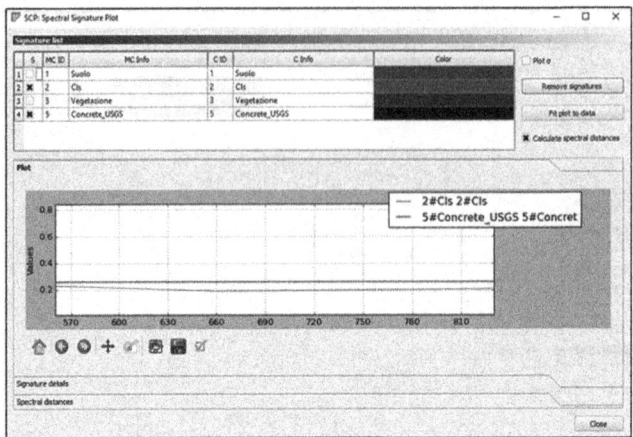

Fig. 15. Comparison between the concrete spectral signature of ROI with the same spectral signature from USGS.

Classification Through SCP Plugin. After ROIs definition the spectral signatures are calculated and the classification is performed. Since different algorithms are available in the SCP, the first option is the choice of the algorithm preferred for the classification (Fig. 16). It is also possible to define a threshold value (also different for each class) to refine the classification.

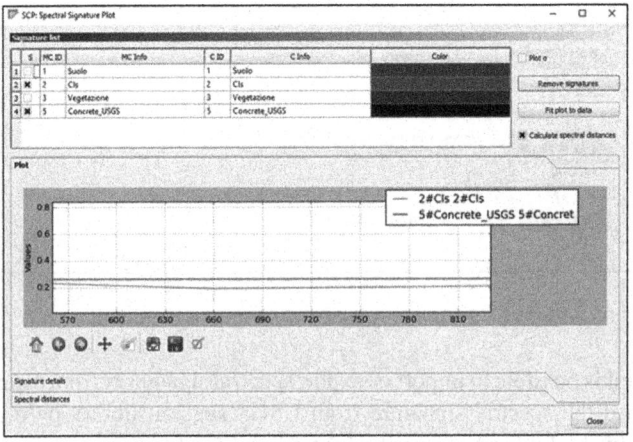

Fig. 16. SCP: Classification panel of SCP plugin.

Accuracy Evaluation of Classification. The classified images must be subjected to a rigorous statistical evaluation of accuracy. Following a classification process, in fact, some errors can be introduced, like the assignment of a pixel to a wrong class.

In particular, the accuracy assessment was performed according to site-specific technique using the confusion or error matrix, which contains all the information from the comparison between the pixels of the classified image and the pixels of the reference one, considered as ground truth. The calculation of the error matrix and of its parameters was made through the post-processing tab of the plugin SCP.

3 Results and Discussion

3.1 Classification

In order to perform a comparison, we report the results obtained using different algorithms for the classification (Figs. 17, 18 and 19).

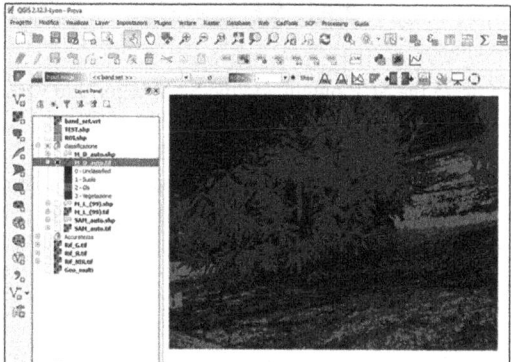

Fig. 17. Classification using the SCP plugin and the Minimum Distance algorithm with automatic threshold values.

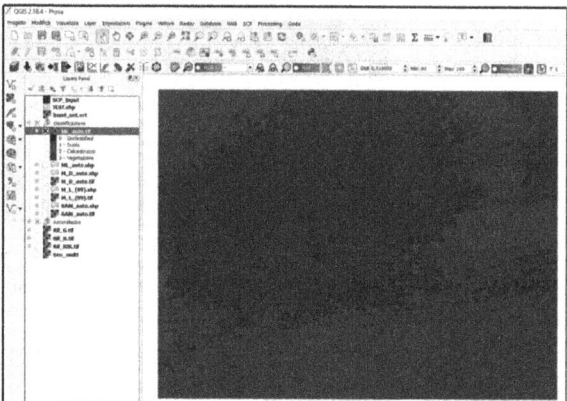

Fig. 18. Classification using the SCP plugin and the Maximum Likelihood algorithm with automatic threshold values.

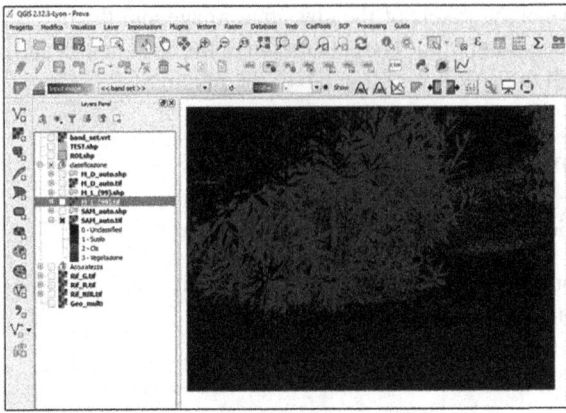

Fig. 19. Classification using the SCP plugin and the SAM algorithm with automatic threshold values.

Moreover, we imported the spectral signature of the concrete from the USGS spectral library to carry out additional classification tests, which can be compared with those obtained considering only the ROIs (Fig. 20).

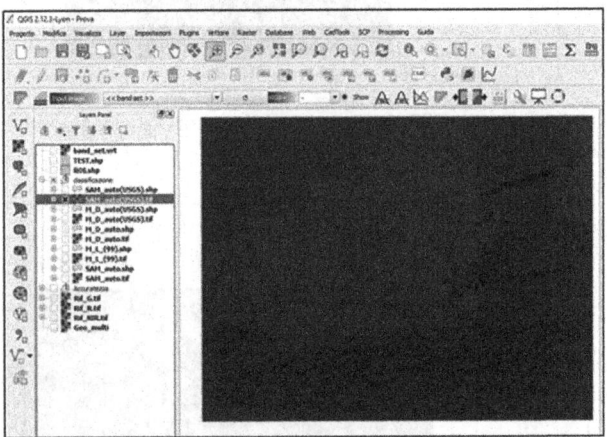

Fig. 20. Classification using the SCP plugin and the SAM algorithm with automatic threshold values, using the spectral signature of concrete from USGS spectral library.

3.2 Accuracy Evaluation of Classification

The SCP plugin allows the calculation of the error matrix through the Post-processing tab of the SCP-plugin. Ideally, this process should be applied to the entire image. However, due to its complexity, we applied it just to some test samples that must not be absolutely coincident with the training areas (ROIs), because it would mean assessing the classification through the information used to produce it. Therefore the first operation is to define three new test areas (Fig. 21), apply the algorithms to classify and calculate the error matrices for each of the classifications in order to assess the accuracy.

Fig. 21. Test areas used for the calculation of the error matrix through the accuracy tab of SCP plug-in.

Analyzing the results (Figs. 22, 23 and 24) by the error matrices, it appears evident that the best classification is made by the algorithm of Maximum Likelihood with an overall *accuracy* of 96% and a *Kappa Cohen value,* that is a parameter that provides an

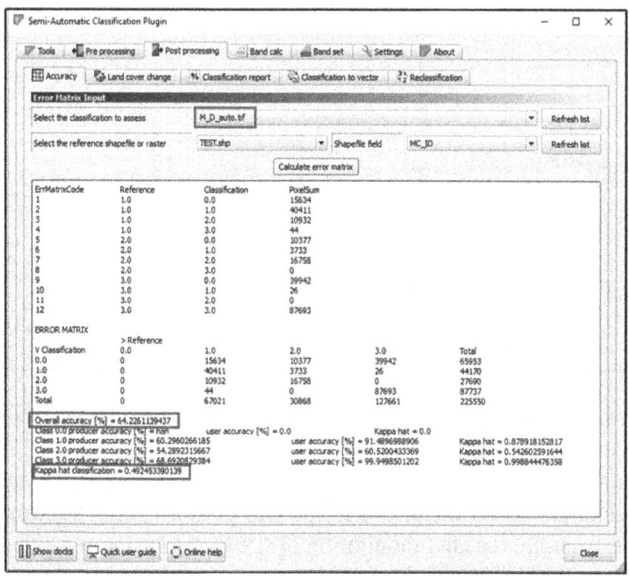

Fig. 22. Error matrix of the obtained classification through Minimum Distance algorithm.

estimate of the accuracy of the classification, is 0,94; considering that the maximum K value is 1. So, the best algorithm for the classification is Maximum Likelihood.

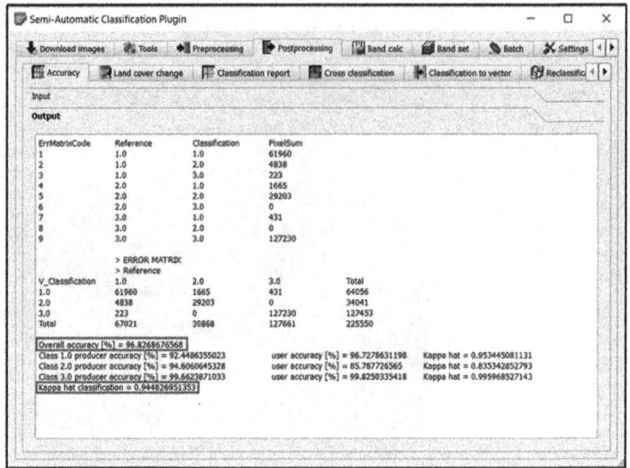

Fig. 23. Error matrix of the obtained classification through Maximum Likelihood algorithm.

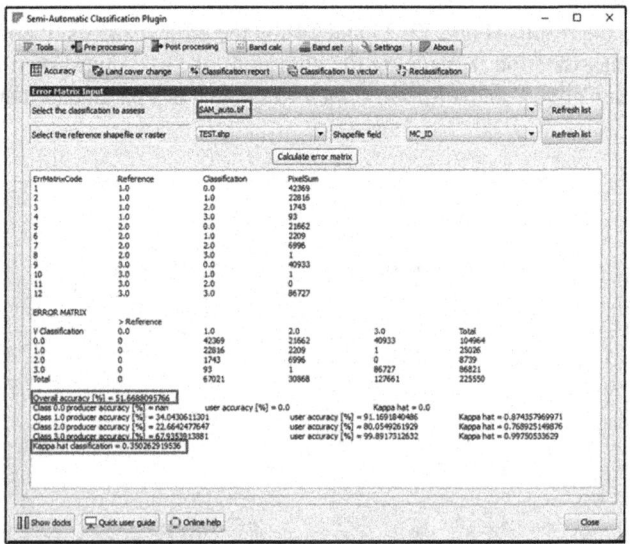

Fig. 24. Error matrix of the obtained classification through SAM algorithm.

The information in output from the classification process can be managed in the GIS platform as vector and raster thematisms. The GIS platform, both desktop and webgis, is suitable, for example, for land monitoring [18, 19], also using sensors and real-time data coming from UAVs [16, 19, 21–25].

4 Conclusions

We propose an approach of multispectral image analysis based on supervised classification, which provides different advantages. The images have been acquired by the multispectral camera ADC-Lite, mainly used for the calculation of vegetation indices, and processed to perform supervised classification. In this context, the camera may be a viable low-cost alternative to satellite multispectral sensors, because the camera may be installed on UAV drones to capture images of good geometric resolution. Moreover the processing and classification can be done with free and open source software, such as PixelWrench2 and QGIS. The results obtained show that, although only three bands (limited spectral resolution) were available, we were able to distinguish between different objects in the scene shooted with excellent results and high accuracy of the classification. In particular, we found that the best algorithm for the classification is the Maximum Likelihood, allowing to reach an overall accuracy of 96% and a Kappa Cohen value of 0.94.

One of the most interesting prospects surely consists in the use of this approach for determining the asbestos roofing, which are currently difficult to detect with the traditional approaches, because they are expensive or operatively difficult to realize.

The outlook for the future is therefore that new low-cost methodological approaches to remote sensing, such the one here proposed, could be developed and spread more and more.

References

1. Borengasser, M., Hungate, W.S., Watkins, R.: Hyperspectral Remote Sensing: Principles and Applications, 13 December 2007. https://www.crcpress.com/Hyperspectral-Remote-Sensing-Principles-and-Applications/Borengasser-Hungate-Watkins/p/book/9781566706544
2. Traore, B.B., Foguem, B.K., Tangara, F.: Data mining techniques on satellite images for discovery of risk areas. Expert Syst. Appl. **72**, 443–456 (2017)
3. Caprioli, M., Tarantino, E.: Identification of land cover alterations in the Alta Murgia National Park (Italy) with VHR satellite imagery. Int. J. Sustain. Dev. Plan. **1**(3), 261–270 (2006)
4. Crocetto, N., Tarantino, E.: A class-oriented strategy for features extraction from multidate ASTER imagery. Remote Sens. **1**(4), 1171–1189 (2009)
5. Totaro, V., Gioia, A., Novelli, A., Caradonna, G.: The use of geomorphological descriptors and landsat-8 spectral indices data for flood areas evaluation: a case study of Lato river basin. In: Gervasi, O., et al. (eds.) ICCSA 2017. LNCS, vol. 10407, pp. 30–44. Springer, Cham (2017). https://doi.org/10.1007/978-3-319-62401-3_3
6. Olang, L.O., Kundu, P., Bauer, T., Furst, J.: Analysis of spatio-temporal land cover changes for hydrological impact assessment within the Nyando River Basin of Kenya". Env. Monit. Assess. **179**(1), 389–401 (2011)
7. Pattison, I., Lane, S.N.: The link between land-use management and fluvial flood risk: a chaotic conception? Prog. Phys. Geogr.: Earth Environ. **36**(1), 72–92 (2011)
8. Ferrante, D., Bertolotti, M., Todesco, A., Mirabelli, D., Terracini, B., Magnani, C.: Cancer mortality and incidence of mesothelioma in a cohort of wives of asbestos workers in Casale Monferrato, Italy. Environ. Health Perspect. **115**, 1401–1405 (2007)
9. Stato dell'arte e prospettive in materia di contrasto alle patologie asbesto-correlate. Quaderni del Ministero della salute, no. 15 (2015)

10. Cilia, C., Panigada, C., Rossini, M., Candiani, G., Pepe, M., Colombo, R.: Mapping of asbestos cement roofs and their weathering status using hyperspectral aerial images. Int. J. Geo-Inf. **4**, 928–941 (2015). https://doi.org/10.3390/ijgi4020928

11. Fiumi, L., Atturo, C., Fontinovo, G.: Mapping of the asbestos-cement by remote sensing and GIS. In: Proceedings on Asbestos Monitoring and Analytical Method (AMAM) (2005)

12. Fiumi, L., Congedo, L., Meoni, C.: Developing expeditious methodology for mapping asbestos-cement roof coverings over the territory of Lazio Region. Appl. Geomat. **6**, 37–48 (2014)

13. Kux, H.J.H., Souza, U.D.V.: Object based image analysis of WorldView2 satellite data for the classification of mangrove areas in the city of Sao Luis, Maranhao state, Brazil. ISPRS Ann. Photogram. Remote Sens. Spat. Inf. Sci. **4**, 95–100 (2012)

14. Katarzyna, O.S., Ostrowski, W.: Use of satellite and ALS data for classification of roofing materials on the example of asbestos roof tile identification. Tech. Sci. **18**(4), 283–298 (2015)

15. Matese, A., Toscano, P., Di Gennaro, S.F., Genesio, L., Vaccari, F.P., Primicerio, J., Belli, C., Zaldei, A., Bianconi, R., Gioli, B.: Intercomparison of UAV, aircraft and satellite remote sensing platforms for precision viticulture. Remote Sens. **7**, 2971–2990 (2015)

16. Primicerio, J., Di Gennaro, S.F., Fiorillo, E., Genesio, L., Lugato, E., Matese, A.: A flexible unmanned aerial vehicle for precision agriculture. Precis. Agric. **13**(4), 517–523 (2012)

17. Mangiameli, M., Mussumeci, G.: Real time integrating of field data into a GIS platform for the management of hydrological emergencies. In: International Archives of the Photogrammetry, Remote Sensing and Spatial Information Sciences - ISPRS Archives, vol. 40, pp. 153–158, February 2013

18. Mangiameli, M., Mussumeci, G.: GIS approach for preventive evaluation of roads loss of efficiency in hydrogeological emergencies. In: International Archives of the Photogrammetry, Remote Sensing and Spatial Information Sciences - ISPRS Archives, vol. 40, pp. 79–87 February 2013

19. Famoso, D., Mangiameli, M., Roccaro, P., Mussumeci, G., Vagliasindi, F.G.A.: Asbestiform fibers in the Biancavilla site of national interest (Sicily, Italy): review of environmental data via GIS platforms. Rev. Environ. Sci. Bio/Technol. **11**(4), 417–427 (2012). https://doi.org/10.1007/s11157-012-9284-9. ISSN 1569-1705

20. Mangiameli, M., Mussumeci, G.: Real time transferring of field data into a spatial DBMS for management of emergencies with a dedicated GIS platform. In: AIP Conference Proceedings, pp. 780012_1–780012_4 (2015)

21. Cantelli, L., Mangiameli, M., Melita, C.D., Muscato, G.: UAV/UGV cooperation for surveying operations in humanitarian demining. In: 2013 IEEE International Symposium on Safety, Security, and Rescue Robotics, SSRR 2013 (2013)

22. Mangiameli, M., Muscato, G., Mussumeci, G.: Road network modeling in open source GIS to manage the navigation of autonomous robots. In: AIP Conference Proceedings, pp. 1224–1227 (2013)

23. Cafiso, S., Condorelli, A., Mussumeci, G.: Functional analysis of the urban road network in seismic emergencies: a GIS application on Catania city. WIT Trans. State Art Sci. Eng. **8** (2005). ISSN 1755-8336

24. Maugeri, M., Motta, E., Mussumeci, G., Raciti, E.: Lifeline seismic hazards: a GIS application. Earthq. Resistant Eng. Struct. VII. WIT Trans. Built Environ. **VII**, 381–392 (2009)

25. Cafiso, S., Condorelli, A., Cutrona, G., Mussumeci, G.: A seisismic network reliability evaluation on GIS environment. A case of study on Catania province. Risk Anal. IV. WIT Trans. Ecol. Environ. 131–140

Low-Altitude UAV-Borne Remote Sensing in Dunes Environment: Shoreline Monitoring and Coastal Resilience

Gabriella Caroti⑩, Andrea Piemonte⑩, and Yari Pieracci$^{(\boxtimes)}$

Dipartimento di Ingegneria Civile e Industriale – Sezione Vie,
Trasporti e Geomatica, Università di Pisa, Pisa, Italy
`yari.pieracci@ing.unipi.it`

Abstract. UAV systems, fitted with either active or passive surveying sensors, can provide land-related measures and quantitative information with low costs and high resolution in both space and time. Such surveying systems can be quite valuable in defining geometrical and descriptive parameters in coastal systems, especially dune ecosystems. The present work is based on a survey of the dune system at the mouth of the Fiume Morto Nuovo in the San Rossore Estate (Pisa) and focuses on comparing LiDAR with UAV- and airplane-borne photogrammetry, as well as the respective 2D and 3D cartographic output, in order to assess topography changes along a stretch of coastline and to check their possible use in defining some ecological resilience features on coastal dune systems. Processing of survey data generates a Digital Surface Model (DSM) or Digital Terrain Model (DTM) and an orthophotograph, checked for accuracy and image resolution. Comparison of these products against those available in public access cartographical databases highlights differences and respective strengths.

Keywords: UAV · Photogrammetry · Coastal environment
Dunes, Resilience

1 Introduction

In recent years, the increasingly frequent occurrence of disasters has prompted the development of approaches based on climate change, resilience, sustainability and disaster management in order to achieve more effective emergency management and quicker recovery, thus reducing risks for the community [1–3].

Although these concepts have not yet been uniquely defined, they take on some different nuances, depending on Authors [4]. However, each definition shares some common topics, such as the identification of actions to be taken after a failure, in order to recover a previous performance state, and the requirement for monitoring activity of environmental data [2, 5].

The assessment of resilience indicators, as well as periodic monitoring, are important topics in coastal zones [6–8], but they are very complex due to issues related to shoreline shifts and difficulties in evaluating features of rare disruption events.

© Springer International Publishing AG, part of Springer Nature 2018
O. Gervasi et al. (Eds.): ICCSA 2018, LNCS 10964, pp. 281–293, 2018.
https://doi.org/10.1007/978-3-319-95174-4_23

Along the coasts with high anthropic pressure, like across all Mediterranean, one factor that considerably influences coastal resilience is the shoreline course [9].

The variations of tide levels and the anthropic activity (e.g. disruption in solid transport and dredging activities), in long-term, and storms, in short-term, are the main causes of shoreline changes [10], especially in coastal dune ecosystems.

According to the Climate Change National Adaptation Plan of 2017 [2], monitoring is needed both before each environmental investigation, in order to collect qualitative and quantitative preparatory data, and after a significant disruption event, to correlate its features to changes induced on the environment [11, 12].

In fact, due to climate change and to low statistical knowledge of rare events (e.g. storms, floods or hurricanes), intensities and recurrence intervals are complex to assess, due to the scarcity of historical data to perform statistical analyses [11].

Monitoring can be carried out by means of several sensors (remote sensing, aerial mapping, LiDAR, UAV-borne photogrammetry, etc.). Each one has a different cost-effectiveness ratio in relation to efforts, processing costs and survey extension. These methods can collect a wide array of environment information and features, which are also useful in multidisciplinary studies (e.g. vegetation types, geomorphological conditions, etc.) [13–15].

Technological advancements in remote sensing have provided several methodologies enabling land survey and monitoring at both large and small scale, by exploiting active and/or passive sensors for collecting high-density data.

Remote sensing from medium-resolution (1pixel = 10 ÷ 30 m) satellite images (passive sensor) features a favorable cost-to-effectiveness ratio for monitoring of large spatial expanses, though spatial and/or temporal resolution of data can often be quite coarse, limiting its usability for small restitution scales [16, 17].

High-resolution (1pixel <10 m) satellite images are suitable for localized maps, such as Ikonos, GeoEye, Quickbird, whose pixel coverage ranges from 0.5 m to 4 m, but can be quite expensive for large areas. While offering a low-cost alternative, Google Earth images have variable resolution, in both spatial and temporal terms; updated, high-resolution images do not provide full land coverage.

The use of satellite images in surveying poses some additional problems: each satellite collects images at a given time for any area, and end users can only choose from images available in the archive database (for example, images relative to a specific investigation can show a cloud cover preventing any processing).

Airborne mapping imagery provides high spatial resolution (pixel coverage even <0.1 m), in relation to camera-lens features and flight elevation. These surveys entail difficult and costly campaign organization efforts.

LiDAR (Light Detection And Ranging) methodology uses active sensors to store data as 3D coordinates, and is capable of efficient and reasonably accurate characterization of the terrain morphology, with high spatial [18–20] but poor temporal resolution. High costs, strict logistics requirements and the introduction of Unmanned Aerial Vehicles (UAVs) in Geomatics, limited the application of LiDAR in morphology analysis.

For terrain surveying and monitoring, the use of UAVs with imaging sensors is quite common in large scale applications [21], providing high-resolution data at much lower costs than airborne LiDAR.

The disadvantages of UAV include range (limiting their use to small areas), low payload capabilities and wind susceptibility. Thanks to the ability to provide relevant data and information with adequate precision compared to classic survey methodologies, with fewer resource requirements [22, 23], they opened the way to new uses of Geomatics in outstanding application domains of Geosciences and in hazardous situations [24–27].

Several Authors [28–31] recognize that UAV-borne photogrammetry is potentially a major breakthrough in the study and monitoring of morphological changes induced by coastal dynamics [32–34].

Low-altitude photogrammetric surveys, thanks to the massive data sets provided, the high-resolution of collected data and the short-term survey repeatability with reduced costs compared to traditional surveying methodologies, can offer information for direct assessment of some indicators of resilience [35–37].

The present work focused on comparing LiDAR with UAV- and airplane-borne photogrammetry, along with the respective 2D and 3D cartographic outputs. In order to assess the topographic changes along a stretch of coastline, available historical maps and LiDAR data were overlaid in a GIS (Geographic Information System) environment with those obtained by means of the UAV-borne survey.

Finally, some articles about coastal resilience were identified [10, 38, 39], highlighting the valuable support of UAVs (by means of DSMs and orthophotographs) in the assessment of some resilience-related parameters.

2 Materials and Methods

2.1 Experimental Site and Previous Studies

The test area for this investigation is the coast adjacent to the estuary of Fiume Morto Nuovo. The area is in the North section of the Pisa coastline with reference to the Arno estuary, and is included in the Natural Park of Migliarino, San Rossore, Massaciuccoli. The coastline is suffering an ongoing erosion, started around the half of the 19th century, endangering the existence of the coastal dunes-wetlands environment.

This area has been a study subject for several Authors, among which Bini, Casarosa and Ribolini [39] have studied shoreline changes of the whole Pisa coast for years 1938 to 2004, and have quantitatively assessed the corresponding beach area variations. Their work was addressed for the analysis and georeferencing of more than 340 photograms, which provided the raw material for the creation of 18 photomosaics, each for a different year, and in order to extend the temporal scope of the investigation, they used 1:10000 Regional Technical Maps issued in 1997and two 1:25000 historical maps of the Military Geographic Institute (I.G.M.) issued in 1878 and 1928 (Table 1).

Analysis of each photomosaic allowed to detect shoreline position for each year and to assess area variations.

Table 1. Input data in 2008 coastal evolution study.

Aerial image

Year	Owner	Film	Year	Owner	Film
1938	I.G.M.	B&W	1990	I.G.M.	Infrared
1944	Royal air force	B&W	1991	Tuscany region	B&W
1954	I.G.M.	B&W	1994	Tuscany region	B&W
1965	I.G.M.	B&W	1995	Tuscany region	B&W
1975	Tuscany region	B&W	1996	I.G.M.	B&W
1982	Tuscany region	colour	2000	Tuscany region	B&W
1982	I.G.M.	B&W	2002	Tuscany region	B&W
1984	Tuscany region	B&W	2003	Tuscany region	B&W
1986	I.G.M.	B&W	2004	Tuscany region	Colour
1987	Tuscany region	B&W			

Cartography

Year	Owner	Scale
1878	I.G.M.	1:25000
1928	I.G.M.	1:25000
1997	Tuscany region	1:10000

2.2   Historical Reference Data

The present work aimed at extending coastline analysis up to the current situation. For this purpose, necessary cartography was found on the available public platforms. In particular, historic data come from the Cartography Bureau of the Tuscany Region (http://www502.regione.toscana.it/geoscopio/cartoteca.html), the Italian National Geoportal (http://www.pcn.minambiente.it/mattm/) and from Google Earth images (https://www.google.it/intl/it/earth/).

Subject data coming from Tuscany Region include:

- 1:5000 technical map (issued 1976), coordinate system Gauss-Boaga Roma40.
- 1:10000 Tuscany Region technical map (issued 1995), coordinate system Gauss-Boaga Roma40.
- 1:2000 orthophotograph (issued 2013), coordinate system Gauss-Boaga Roma40.
- DTM and DSM from LiDAR – 2x2 resolution, flight year 2008.
- DTM and DSM from LiDAR – 1x1 resolution, flight year 2006.
- Physical coastline, year 2010.

These data are already georeferenced and stored along the metadata for datum and reference system.

The National Geoportal provided the following data:

- Colour orthophotograph, years 2000 and 2006 Geoportal – spatial resolution 1:10000 equivalent, UTM-WGS84.
- Grayscale orthophotograph, years 1988 and 1994 Geoportal – spatial resolution 1:10000 equivalent, UTM-WGS84.

Georeferencing metadata are not directly available for the Geoportal; orthophotographs have been collected as plain images and georeferenced in GIS environment thanks to the numerous control points (CPs), detectable in the study area at an adequate resolution and fixed through time.

Google Earth provided the images in Table 2 and data have been downloaded as raw images, which have been subsequently georeferenced in a GIS environment as for the Geoportal. In particular, GIS management was performed by means of ESRI's ArcGIS software with the standard Arctoolbox packages for georeferencing maps and the additional Profiler tools for interpolating section points from DSMs.

Table 2. Google earth images

Google earth images		
March 11, 2017 (digital globe)	August 11, 2013	July 2, 2010
August 8, 2016	March 27, 2012	August 16 2004
August 28, 2015	April 8, 2011	January 31, 2004

2.3 Unmanned Aerial Vehicle (UAV) Measurements

Data investigated in this work included both historical sources and a 2016 UAV-borne photogrammetry survey. As part of a standing collaboration, Leica Geosystems provided the Aibotix Aibot X6V2 system for surveying. This is a midrange-to-high-end hexarotor UAV, with a payload of about 2.5 kg and a stabilized gimbal. During the survey, the UAV carried an Olympus E-PL5 Kit 1442 Silver camera, with a 4:3 LiveMos 16MPixel sensor and a 14–42 mm variable focus lens.

The survey area is about 400 m by 300 m; complete covering has required 8 strips, with a theoretical end lap of 70% and side lap of 60% (Fig. 1). By locking the lens focus at 14 mm and keeping a mean flight altitude of 60 m above ground, the Ground Sample Distance (GSD) was about 1.6 cm.The UAV speed was about 5 m/s, so, in order to ensure the required forward overlap, the shooting timer was set at 3 s. Shooting time was set at 1/800 s in time priority mode. Under these operating conditions, the drag effect was about 0.6 pixels; accuracy computations, using the "normal case" formulas, assess the theoretical error of 3D restitution in each component as $\sigma_X = 0.023$ m, $\sigma_Y = 0.029$ m and $\sigma_Z = 0.046$ m [39]. The survey included measuring of 17 control points, suitably marked by means of ground-fixed targets, as well as of 3 additional points belonging to networks set up by external Authorities and marked with specific studs. Two of these are part of a network set up by the Pisa Soil Protection Authority as #55 and #56, respectively, in an April 2005 survey. The third point belongs to a GNSS (Global Navigation Satellite System) network set up by the Pisa Bureau for Rivers and Ditches, as #0034 in a June 2002 survey.

The survey of ground points coordinates relied on GNSS measures with Stop&Go differential technique, using the corrections broadcast by the ItalPos network of Leica Geosystems. GNSS coordinates were subsequently transformed in the Gauss Boagacartography reference system and orthometric height by means of IGMI's (Istituto Geografico Militare Italiano) Verto software and related grids.

Fig. 1. Flight plan and position of GCPs and CPs overlaid to the UAV survey area.

Processing of 145 images collected by means of Agisoft's Photoscan 1.1.3 software defined internal and external orientation parameters, by using points GS0002, GS0003B and GD0007 as Ground Control Points (GCPs) for rototranslation with scale factor, and the remaining points as CPs. The resulting photogrammetry model is correctly oriented, with a mean error of 0.48 pixels on Tie Points and 0.046 m on CPs. Table 3 shows the deviation values for each coordinate of the CPs. Results are in line with default theoretical precision.

This model yielded a dense cloud and mesh surface rendering, as well as an orthophotograph at the highest resolution possible with the working image set. The orthophotograph and the model allowed digitizing 2D fault lines and 3D break lines for use in subsequent computation of regular mesh digital models. Processing of the dense cloud by means of Kriging algorithms and interpolation yielded a 1 m × 1 m DSM.

Figures 2 and 3 show two DSMs of the same area relating to different years. Both are 1 × 1 m DSMs: the first is obtained by classic photogrammetry in 2006 for the compilation of the Technical Regional Map; the other is obtained in 2016 from UAV-borne photogrammetry. Sectioning of these models along the same cutting plane resulted in the profiles shown in Fig. 4.

Both profiles are almost coinciding in zones unaffected by erosion, allowing to check for the presence of dune fronts and to measure dune height and slope.

Figure 5 shows shoreline changes as per the analysis of the full historical series of available data, from 1988 to the 2016 UAV-borne photogrammetry survey.

Orthophotographs derived from classic photogrammetry for compilation of Technical Regional Maps, as well as those available on the Google Earth platform only allow to tell apart vegetated from bare areas, while identification of plant types is in no way possible (Fig. 6, right). Figure 6 (left), on the other hand, clearly shows that such identification is possible for trained operators working with orthophotographic maps derived from UAV-borne photogrammetry, due to definitely lower flight altitudes.

Table 3. Study CPs deviation values for X, Y, Z coordinates.

CPs	X_error [m]	Y_error [m]	Z_error [m]
GS0005	0.000	0.020	0.020
GS0006	0.027	0.029	0.019
GS0003	0.004	0.006	0.016
GS0004	0.007	0.034	0.033
BONIF34	0.006	−0.004	−0.003
GD0001	−0.008	0.038	0.029
GD0004	0.003	0.010	0.017
GD0005	−0.013	0.014	0.035
GD0006	−0.012	0.024	0.069
GD0008	0.026	0.027	0.065
GS0002	0.015	0.011	−0.016
GS0008	0.006	0.017	0.025
GS0009	0.035	−0.009	0.027
Gd009b	−0.033	0.061	0.063
Gd010b	−0.013	0.006	0.027
PROV55	0.024	0.005	−0.034
PROV56	−0.027	0.002	0.005
Mean [m]	**0.003**	**0.017**	**0.023**
St. dev. [m]	**0.019**	**0.017**	**0.027**
RMSE [m]	**0.019**	**0.024**	**0.036**

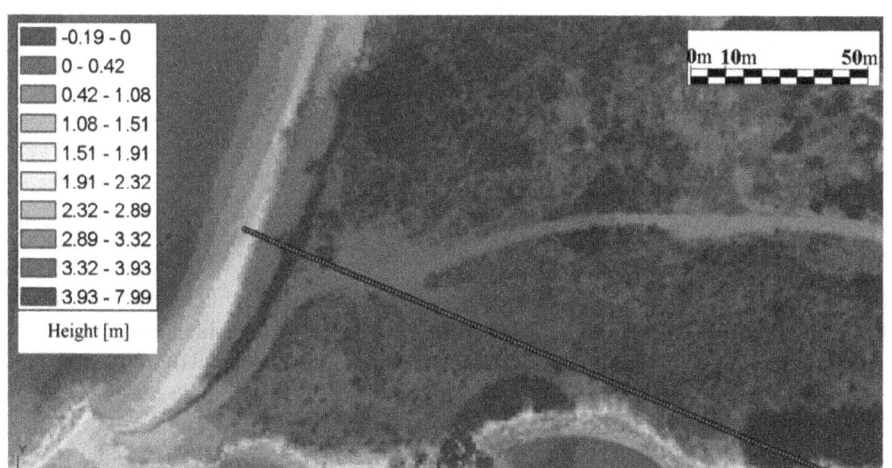

Fig. 2. 1 × 1 DSM - classic photogrammetry, 2006.

Fig. 3. 1 × 1 DSM - UAV-borne photogrammetry, 2016.

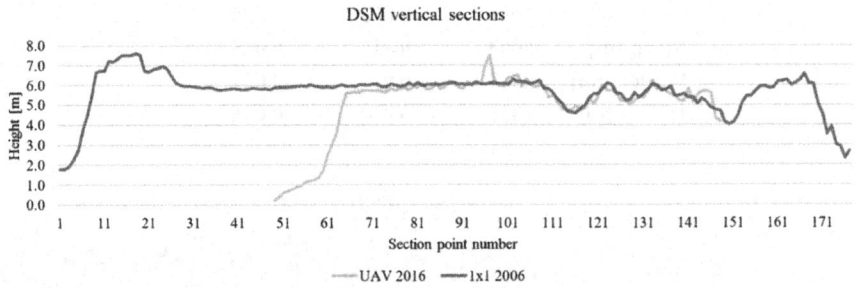

Fig. 4. Reference section comparison: 2006 1 × 1 DSM from classic photogrammetry (orange), 2016 1 × 1 UAV-based DSM (blue). (Color figure online)

2.4 Studies Based on Resilience

Resilience in coastal environments involves several indexes as highlighted in the study of Bini, Casarosa and Ribolini [39]. Apart from shoreline course, resilience involves geomorphology, coastal dynamics and anthropic pressure. The main goal of this study is the definition of Mediterranean Dune Vulnerability Index (MDVI) for dune coasts, based on Dune Vulnerability Index (DVI) suggested by García-Mora, Gallego-Fernández, Williams e García-Novo in [15] for Ocean coasts and then adapting it to Mediterranean coasts by means of some corrective factors.

The index is computed for coastal dune systems on peninsular and continental Italian territories referring to Tuscany. The investigation included 11 coastal sites belonging to Migliarino, San Rossore, Massaciuccoli (MSRM) Natural Park and Maremma Regional Park. Authors suggest an index based on the following main factor groups:

Fig. 5. Shore line progression from 1988 to 2016.

Fig. 6. Geometric and radiometric resolution: Google earth image (right) and UAV-borne image (left).

Geomorphological Conditions of the Dune Systems (GCD), Marine Influence (MI), Aeolian Effect (AE), Vegetation Condition (VC) and Human Effects (HE).

Computation of MDVI parameters requires supporting topographic documentation, as well as on-site inspections by qualified personnel.

In particular, definition of the Geomorphological Condition of the Dune System (GCD) requires knowledge of the length of homogeneous active dune system, the average height of frontal and secondary dunes, the foredune, the slope steepness and the relative areas of the wet slacks. All these values are easily definable by analysis of a 3D land model, providing sections and 2D information on position and distance. Definition of the Marine Influence (MI) parameter requires analysis of shoreline variations in time. This is possible by comparing historical series of available 2D representations (maps, orthophotographs, coast line thematic databases). For the assessment of the Vegetation Condition (VC) parameter, UAV-based surveys do not provide directly the information, but high-resolution orthophotographs can be used by qualified personnel for ground operations, such as the evaluation of plant type, the percentage of covered surface on the beach, on the dune front and along the transect.

The interpretation of orthophotographs can directly provide other parameters [39]; the% of seaward dune vegetated for Aeolian Effect (AE) and the Path network as percent of the frontal dune, the Relative surface (%) forested in the system and the Relative surface (%) of agriculture in the system for the Human Effect (HE) variable.

The study by Brooks et al. [10] links landward retreat to the features of the storm of 5 December 2013 in three sites along the North Norfolk coast in United Kingdom.

Since the recovery time between two consecutive storms affects coastal resilience, one monitoring survey of the shoreline was scheduled twice per year. These have been performed by means of LiDAR since 1992 to 2015, and by Real Time Kinematic (RTK) survey since 2013 to date. In this case, UAV-borne photogrammetry could provide the relevant advantage of cost reduction compared to previously used methods. In fact, UAV-borne surveys are a suitable solution for monitoring at short time intervals, such as in emergencies. It allows the direct adaptation of effective mitigation actions to protect the environment [27].

Pajares, in a review of the state-of-art of remote-sensing applications based on UAV-borne sensors [14], reported that some Authors ([28, 38]) obtained high-resolution surfaces by low-altitude UAV-borne surveys in coastal environments. For example, Mancini [28] used an hexacopter equipped with a camera, and tested the use of SfM (Structure from Motion) to build the DSM of a dune system in Marina di Ravenna (Italy) starting from low-altitude images. Delacourt [43] highlighted as remote-sensing images resolution is not sufficient for coastal monitoring. He built a system capable to extract a DEM and high spatial resolution orthorectified images (<5 cm), which was tested on the beach of Porsmill in (French Brittany) to assess the transport of sediments in coastal domains, analysing submersed areas in shallow waters [14].

3   Conclusions

Following the availability and the development of digital sensors and effective image processing algorithms, photogrammetry has become, over the last two decades, an essential surveying tool in the Geosciences field.

Besides, the availability of small-to-medium sized remotely piloted aircrafts has allowed low-cost photogrammetry campaigns, for the compilation of large- to very large-scale cartography.

The present work shows how the combination of these two methodologies, thanks to precision levels comparable with LiDAR surveys, is quite useful in the assessment of coastal systems resilience, with particular reference to endangered dune systems.

The very large representation scale, together with the low costs and therefore the frequent repeatability of the surveys, provides useful information for the definition of indexes and parameters typical of these ecosystems, planning of erosion management, *a posteriori* effectiveness assessment and performing analysis and studies to link disruption and environment damage.

Acknowledgements. The authors would like to thank Leica Geosystems for carrying out the photogrammetric survey by means of the Aibotix multirotor.

The research was developed within the project "PRA_2017_60: Sicurezza e resilienza delle infrastrutture civili" financed by the University of Pisa.

References

1. Faturechi, R., Miller-Hooks, E.: Measuring the performance of transportation infrastructure systems in disasters: a comprehensive review. J. infrastruct. syst., **21**(1), article no. 04014025 (2015). https://doi.org/10.1061/(asce)is.1943-555x.0000212
2. Supporto tecnico-scientifico per il Ministero dell'Ambiente e della Tutela del Territorio e del Mare (MATTM): Piano Nazionale di Adattamento ai Cambiamenti Climatici (2017). http://www.minambiente.it/sites/default/files/archivio_immagini/adattamenti_climatici/documento_pnacc_luglio_2017.pdf. Accessed 27 Feb 2018
3. UNISDR (United Nations International Strategy for Risk Reduction): UNISDR terminology on Disaster Risk Reduction (2009). https://www.unisdr.org/files/7817_UNISDRTerminologyEnglish.pdf. Accessed 27 Feb 2018
4. Hagelsteen M., Becker P.: A great babylonian confusion: terminological ambiguity in capacity development for disaster risk reduction in the international community. In: 5th International Disaster and Risk Conference: Integrative Risk Management - The Role of Science, Technology and Practice, IDRC Davos 2014, Code 110967, pp. 295–297 (2014)
5. Bruneau, M., et al.: A framework to quantitatively assess and enhance the seismic resilience of communities. Earthq. Spectra **19**(4), 733–752 (2003). https://doi.org/10.1193/1.1623497
6. Dunkin, L., Reif, M., Altman, S., Swannack, T.: A spatially explicit, multi-criteria decision support model for loggerhead sea turtle nesting habitat suitability: a remote sensing-based approach. Remote Sens., **8**(7), article no. 573 (2016). https://doi.org/10.3390/rs8070573
7. Meng, X., Zhang, X., Silva, R., Li, C., Wang, L.: Impact of high-resolution topographic mapping on beach morphological analyses based on terrestrial LiDAR and object-oriented beach evolution. ISPRS Int. J. Geo-Inf., **6**(5), article no. 147 (2017). https://doi.org/10.3390/ijgi6050147
8. Monge, J.A., Stallins, J.A.: Properties of dune topographic state space for six barrier islands of the U.S. southeastern Atlantic coast. Phys. Geography **37**(6), 452–475 (2016). https://doi.org/10.1080/02723646.2016.1230041
9. Martinez, M.L., Taramelli, A., Silva, R.: Resistance and resilience: facing the multidimensional challenges in coastal areas. J. Coast. Res. **77**, 1–6 (2017). https://doi.org/10.2112/si77-001.1
10. Brooks, S.M., Spencer, T., Christie, E.K.: Storm impacts and shoreline recovery: mechanisms and controls in the southern North Sea. Geomorphology **283**(15), 48–60 (2017). https://doi.org/10.1016/j.geomorph.2017.01.007
11. Park, J., Seager, T.P., Rao, P.S.C., Convertino, M., Linkov, I.: Integrating risk and resilience approaches to catastrophe management in engineering system. Risk Anal. **33**(3), 356–367 (2013). https://doi.org/10.1111/j.1539-6924.2012.01885.x

12. Comes, T., Van de Walle, B.: Measuring disaster resilience: the impact of hurricane sandy on critical infrastructure systems. In: 11th International Conference on Information Systems for Crisis Response and Management (ISCRAM 2014), pp. 195–204 (2014). ISBN 978-069221194-6

13. Kroon, A., et al.: Application of remote sensing video systems to coastline management problems. Coast. Eng. **54**(6–7), 493–505 (2007). https://doi.org/10.1016/j.coastaleng.2007.01.004

14. Pajares, G.: Overview and current status of remote sensing applications based on unmanned aerial vehicles (UAVs). Photogramm. Eng. Remote Sens. **81**(4), 281–329 (2015). https://doi.org/10.14358/PERS.81.4.281

15. García-Mora, M.R., Gallego-Fernández, J.B., Williams, A.T., García-Novo, F.: A coastal dune vulnerability classification. a case study of the SW Iberian Peninsula. J. Coast. Res. **17**(4), 802–811 (2001). ISSN 07490208

16. Hedley, J.D., et al.: Remote sensing of coral reefs for monitoring and management: a review. Remote Sens. **8**(2), article no. 118 (2016). https://doi.org/10.3390/rs8020118

17. Aquilino, M., Tarantino, E., Fratino, U.: Multi-temporal land use analysis of AN ephemeral river area using an artificial neural network approach on landsat imagery. ISPRS-Int. Arch. Photogram. Remote Sens. Spat. Inf. Sci. **1**, 167–173 (2013). https://doi.org/10.5194/isprsarchives-xl-5-w3-167-2013

18. Caroti, G., Piemonte, A., Redini, M.: The elevation net for the saltwater intrusion phenomenon analysis in the coastal plain of Pisa. Int. Arch. Photogram. Remote Sens. Spat. Inf. Sci. **XL-5/W3**, 99–105 (2013). https://doi.org/10.5194/isprsarchives-xl-5-w3-99-2013

19. Caroti, G., Camiciottoli, F., Piemonte, A., Redini, M.: The accuracy analysis of Lidar-derived elevation data for the geometric description of cross-sections of a riverbed. Int. Arch. Photogram. Remote Sens. Spat. Inf. Sci. **XL-5/W3**, 51–57 (2013). https://doi.org/10.5194/isprsarchives-xl-5-w3-51-2013

20. Caroti, G., Piemonte, A., Redini, M.: Geomatics monitoring and models of the insalination of the freshwaters phenomenon along the Pisan coastline. Appl. Geomat. **7**(4), 243–253 (2015). https://doi.org/10.1007/s12518-015-0155-2

21. Caroti, G., Piemonte, A., Nespoli, R.: UAV-Borne photogrammetry: a low cost 3D surveying methodology for cartographic update. In: International Conference on Advances in Sustainable Construction Materials and Civil Engineering Systems (ASCMCES-17), United Arab Emirates, MATEC Web of Conferences., vol. 120, article no. 09005 (2017). https://doi.org/10.1051/matecconf/201712009005

22. Cheng, J., Wang, P., Guo, Q.: Measuring beach profiles along a low-wave energy microtidal coast, West-Central Florida, USA. Geosciences **6**(4), article no. 44 (2016). https://doi.org/10.3390/geosciences6040044

23. Cosanti, B., Squeglia, N., Lo Presti, D.C.F.: Analysis of existing levee systems: the Serchio river case. Riv. Ital. di Geotecnica **48**(4), 49–67 (2014). ISSN 05571405

24. Giordan, D., Manconi, A., Remondino, F., Nex, F.: Use of unmanned aerial vehicles in monitoring application and management of natural hazards. Geomat. Nat. Hazards Risk **8**(1), 1–4 (2017). https://doi.org/10.1080/19475705.2017.1315619

25. Gindraux, S., Boesch, R., Farinotti, D.: Accuracy assessment of digital surface models from unmanned aerial vehicles' imagery on glaciers. Remote Sens. **9**(2), article no. 186 (2017). https://doi.org/10.3390/rs9020186

26. Martínez-Espejo Zaragoza, I., Caroti, G., Piemonte, A., Riedel, B., Tengen, D., Niemeier, W.: Structure from Motion (SFM) processing of UAV images and combination with terrestrial laser scanning, applied for a 3D-documentation in a hazardous situation. Geomat. Nat. Hazards Risk **8**(2), 1492–1504 (2017). https://doi.org/10.1080/19475705.2017.1345796

27. Caroti, G., Piemonte, A., Pieracci, Y.: UAV-borne photogrammetric survey as USAR firefighter teams support. In: Gervasi, O., et al. (eds.) ICCSA 2017. LNCS, vol. 10407, pp. 3–15. Springer, Cham (2017). https://doi.org/10.1007/978-3-319-62401-3_1
28. Mancini, F., Dubbini, M., Gattelli, M., Stecchi, F., Fabbri, S., Gabbianelli, G.: Using unmanned aerial vehicles (UAV) for high-resolution reconstruction of topography: the structure from motion approach on coastal environments. Remote Sens. **5**(12), 6880–6898 (2013). https://doi.org/10.3390/rs5126880
29. Casella, E., Rovere, A., Pedroncini, A., Stark, C.P., Casella, M., Ferrari, M., Firpo, M.: Drones as tools for monitoring beach topography changes in the Ligurian Sea (NW Mediterranean). Geo-Mar. Lett. **36**(2), 151–163 (2016). https://doi.org/10.1007/s00367-016-0435-9
30. Ballari, D., Orellana, D., Acosta, E., Espinoza, A., Morocho, V.: UAV monitoring for environmental management in Galapagos islands. ISPRS – Int. Arch. Photogram. Remote Sens. Spat. Inf. Sci. **XLI-B1**, 1105–1111 (2016). https://doi.org/10.5194/isprs-archives-xli-b1-1105-2016
31. Eltner, A., Kaiser, A., Castillo, C., Rock, G., Neugirg, F., Abellán, A.: Image-based surface reconstruction in geomorphometry-merits, limits and developments. Earth Surf. Dyn. **4**, 359–389 (2016). https://doi.org/10.5194/esurf-4-359-2016
32. Papakonstantinou, A., Topouzelis, K., Pavlogeorgatos, G.: Coastline zones identification and 3D coastal mapping using UAV spatial data. ISPRS Int. J. Geo-Inf. **5**(6), article no. 75 (2016). https://doi.org/10.3390/ijgi5060075
33. Long, N., Millescamps, B., Guillot, B., Pouget, F., Bertin, X.: Monitoring the topography of a dynamic tidal inlet using UAV imagery. Remote Sens. **8**(5), article no. 387 (2016). https://doi.org/10.3390/rs8050387
34. Guillot, B., Pouget, F.: UAV application in coastal environment, example of the oleron island for dunes and dikes survey. ISPRS – Int. Arch. Photogram. Remote Sens. Spat. Inf. Sci. **XL-3/W3**, 321–326 (2015). https://doi.org/10.5194/isprsarchives-xl-3-w3-321-2015
35. Li, Z., Xu, D., Guo, X.: Remote sensing of ecosystem health: opportunities, challenges, and future perspectives. Sensors **14**(11), 21117–21139 (2014). https://doi.org/10.3390/s141121117
36. Scheffer, M., Carpenter, S.R., Dakos, V., Van Nes, E.H.: Generic indicators of ecological resilience: inferring the chance of a critical transition. Ann. Rev. Ecol. Evol. Syst. **46**, 145–167 (2015). https://doi.org/10.1146/annurev-ecolsys-112414-054242
37. Clark, A.: Small unmanned aerial systems comparative analysis for the application to coastal erosion monitoring. GeoResJ **13**, 175–185 (2017). https://doi.org/10.1016/j.grj.2017.05.001
38. Delacourt, C., Allemand, P., Jaud, M., Grandjean, P., Deschamps, A., Ammann, J., Cuq, V., Suanez, S.: DRELIO: an unmanned helicopter for imaging coastal areas. J. Coast. Res. **2**(56), 1489–1493 (2009). ISSN 0749-0258
39. Bini, M., Casarosa, N., Ribolini, A.: L'evoluzione diacronica della linea di riva del litorale pisano (1938–2004) sulla base del confronto di immagini aeree georeferenziate [Diachron-icevolution of Pisa shore line (1938–2004) based on the comparison of georeferenced airborne images]. Atti Soc. Tosc. Sci. Nat. Mem. Serie A **113**, 1–12 (2008)
40. Caroti, G., Martínez-Espejo Zaragoza, I., Piemonte, A.: Accuracy assessment in structure from motion 3D reconstruction from UAV-born images: the influence of the data processing methods. Int. Arch. Photogramm. Remote Sens. Spat. Inf. Sci. **4**, 103–109 (2015). https://doi.org/10.5194/isprsarchives-XL-1-W4-103-2015

Calibration of CLAIR Model by Means of Sentinel-2 LAI Data for Analysing Wheat Crops Through Landsat-8 Surface Reflectance Data

Giuseppe Peschechera and Umberto Fratino[(✉)]

DICATECh – Politecnico di Bari, Via Orabona 4, Bari, Italy
{giuseppe.peschechera, umberto.fratino}@poliba.it

Abstract. This study proposes a method to calibrate the semi-empirical CLAIR model, a simplified reflectance model used to estimate the Leaf Area Index (LAI) from optical data, using Landsat-8 Operational Land Imager Surface Reflectance (OLISR) data over wheat cultivation areas.

The procedure can be applied lacking both LAI field measurements and surface reflectance (SR) data by exploiting free of charge data, as the novel high-level Landsat8 OLISR and the Sentinel-2 LAI (S2 LAI) products. This last dataset was used as LAI reference at field size scale. Once calibrated, the model generates LAI information from OLISR data consistent with the S2 LAI. In this way it is possible merge the two products to obtain a finer temporal resolution LAI estimation during all the crop seasons.

The method was tested and statistically assessed on three different wheat test fields located in the Capitanata area (Apulia region, Italy).

Keywords: Leaf area index · CLAIR model · Landsat-8 · Sentinel-2 SNAP

1 Introduction

Leaf Area Index (LAI) is a dimensionless variable defined as the one half of the total leaf area per unit ground area [1]. Mapping, quantifying and monitoring changes in LAI over large areas is essential to understand the dynamics of vegetation cover in different climate, ecological and agricultural applications [2]. LAI is essential in agronomic studies since it regulates the interaction between the vegetation and the atmosphere. For this reason, it is used as input parameter in many biophysical models for calculating vegetation parameters as evapotranspiration (e.g. [3, 4]) and net primary production [5].

Direct field measurements of LAI require continuous updates and can be extremely time-consuming and not cost-effective [6]. This is especially true over large areas with heterogeneous and fragmentated landscapes [7]. Therefore, Remote Sensing (RS), and especially passive remotely sensed observations covering the spectral region from the visible to shortwave infrared (SWIR), is a valid alternative to provide a rapid and non-destructive LAI estimation from regional to global scale [8]. Several algorithms

© Springer International Publishing AG, part of Springer Nature 2018
O. Gervasi et al. (Eds.): ICCSA 2018, LNCS 10964, pp. 294–304, 2018.
https://doi.org/10.1007/978-3-319-95174-4_24

were developed to estimate LAI from optical, SAR and LIDAR sensors. A recent review by Verrelst [9] classifies the procedures in four groups: parametric regressions (which estimate LAI by means of vegetation index retrieved from SR data), non-parametric regressions, physical based approaches and hybrid methods. In this study was selected the semi-empirical CLAIR model (Clevers leaf area index by reflectance) [10]. For its easy conception, it is utilized in many studies (e.g. [11–14]) also for the wheat crop [15]. It is a parametric method to estimate LAI of green canopy (vegetative stage) using an empirical logarithmic relationship between observed LAI and the Weighted Difference Vegetation Index (WDVI) [16]. Due to the WDVI, the model can compensate the errors related to soil background reflectance [17]. For the estimation of LAI using the CLAIR model it is necessary identify the soil-line slope (a) value (needed for calculating the WVDI) and estimate its parameters: the asymptotic value of WDVI (WDVI∞) and the extinction and scattering coefficient (α). Although these parameters have a physical nature, they are usually estimated empirically from a set of SR and LAI simultaneous field measures [4, 8, 18, 19], even if this calibration procedure is not cost-effective. Moreover, technical aspects as the consistence in ground-based LAI measurements, protocols and methods for spatial scaling from ground plot to pixel, require special attention. When LAI and SR field measurements are not available, it is possible to retrieve the model parameters from dataset of previous CLAIR model applications retrieved in literature. However, this solution is hardly applicable because the number of possible soil and crop types is larger than the number of studies conducted. Thus, image-based calibration can be a useful alternative to extend the range of CLAIR model application.

The main goal of this work was to calibrate the CLAIR model at field scale for wheat crops and L8 OLISR data using as reference the Sentinel-2 LAI data product. In this way, it is possible to estimate LAI without expensive in-situ measurements and using only free of charge satellite data. The proposed procedure generates reliable LAI information from Landsat 8 OLISR data consistent with the Sentinel 2 LAI. As result, temporal resolution of LAI data, useful for crop growing monitoring and management, can be improved.

The procedure was tested and statistically assessed over three wheat fields located in the north of the Apulia Region, one of the larger area of wheat cultivation in Italy.

2 Study Area and Data

The study area (Fig. 1) falls within the Tavoliere, a large cultivated area located in the North of the Apulia Region (Italy). It is characterized by a heterogeneous crop mixing with the presence of cereals, vineyards, olive trees and orchards. The climate is the typically Mediterranean one with strong seasonal and inter-annual variability: winter is moderately rainy whereas summer is hot and dry.

Inside the selected study area were retrieved three different crop wheat plots, used as test site for the calibration. They were selected using the crop map provided by the "Capitanata" Reclamation and Irrigation Consortium which manage the area. The characteristics and location of test-plots are summarized in Table 1.

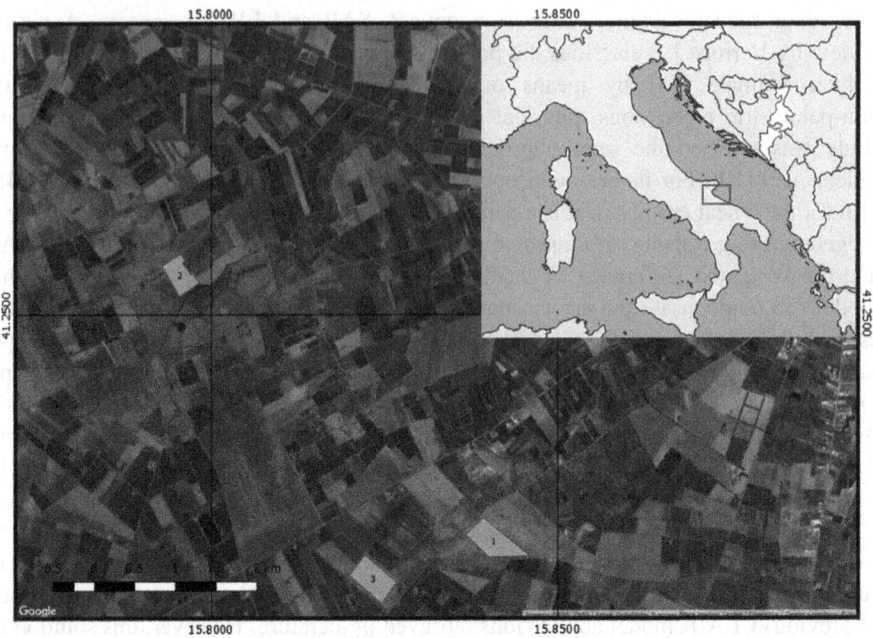

Fig. 1. The selected study area (Google earth image - reference system WGS 84).

Table 1. Extension and location of the three wheat fields used as test sites.

	Extension [m²]	Coordinate (reference system WGS 84)
Plot 1	167.878	15.84028, 41.22676
Plot 2	107.889	15.79597, 41.25426
Plot 3	152.562	15.82330, 41.22230
Total	428.329	

For the purpose of the study, were selected the cloud-free pairs of SR images (Landsat 8 OLISR and Sentinel 2 MSI) acquired during the 2016–2017 crop season over the selected study area. Moreover, to assume a constant value of LAI between the two SR acquisitions, where selected only the pairs of images acquired with a temporal shift in acquisition smaller than 4 days. Only three pairs of images satisfied these requirements. The complete scene list utilized is reported in the Table 2.

Landsat-8 OLISR data are developed for supporting land surface change studies. OLISR products include: original input products (Level-1 data), Top of Atmosphere reflectance, surface reflectance, brightness temperature products and SR-based Spectral Indices (NDVI, NDMI, NBR, SAVI, EVI). These data are obtained with the Landsat 8 Surface Reflectance Code (LaSRC), a new algorithm that should be considered provisional, also if first test carried out showed as it is able to perform better than previous LEDAPS code (Landsat Ecosystem Disturbance Adaptive Processing System) [20]. This result was achieved by using the coastal aerosol band and auxiliary climate data from MODIS. Landsat 8 OLISR products are generated every 16 days with a spatial resolution of 30 m [21]. Further details (e.g. data type, data range, etc.) can be found in the "Provisional Landsat 8 surface reflectance code (LASRC)" product guide. For the proposed CLAIR model calibration procedure were used the Red (Band 4) and Near Infrared (NIR - Band 5) SR bands.

Sentinel-2 (S-2) SR images were used for estimating LAI values. S-2 is a polar-orbiting, multispectral high-resolution imaging mission for environment monitoring developed into the European Commission's Copernicus program. It offers continuity and expands the French Spot and US Landsat missions [22] and is based on a constellation of two identical satellites (S-2A and S-2B) in the same orbit, 180° apart for optimal coverage and data delivery to cover all Earth's land surfaces every five days at the equator. S-2 carries an innovative wide swath high-resolution Multi Spectral Instrument (MSI) with 13 spectral bands, from the visible (VIS) and the near infrared (NIR) to the shortwave infrared (SWIR) at different spatial resolutions ranging from 10 to 60 m. It is the first optical Earth observation mission and includes three bands in the 'red edge' which, combinate with the high resolution and frequent revisit times, can provide key information for vegetation health and growth monitoring from regional to global scale. Moreover, it makes possible to distinguish between different crop types as well as data essential for monitoring the plant growth (e.g. LAI, leaf chlorophyll content and leaf water content).

In detail, three S-2 TOA reflectance images (Level-1C), acquired in the crop season and selected for their low cloud contamination were used. Level-1C products are radiometric and geometric corrected and available free of charge from the Copernicus Open Access Hub (https://scihub.copernicus.eu/dhus/#/home). The atmospheric correction was performed using the European Space Agency's (ESA) Sen2Cor processor [23] provided in the ESA's Sentinel Application Platform (SNAP). It performs the atmospheric, terrain and cirrus correction of the Level-1C input data and creates the Bottom-Of-Atmosphere (BoA) corrected reflectance images (Level-2A). In addition, it provides the Aerosol Optical Thickness, the Water Vapor, Quality Indicators and the Scene Classification Maps. This last product (L2A_SceneClass) was used in the preliminary cloud removal phase to identify and exclude cloud-covered and cloud-shadowed areas; it was made possible by masking pixels flagged as "no data", "saturated", "dark features/shadows" and "cloud covered". Sen2Cor output is resampled and generated with an equal spatial resolution for all bands, based on the requested resolution (20 m in the present work).

From the Level-2A product, it is possible to create value-added products (Level-2B) with a special focus on agricultural vegetation monitoring, as the LAI, using the Biophysical Processor tool (L2B). The L2B processor uses a neural network algorithm, tailored for S-2 and trained by means of radiative transfer simulations from PROSAIL radiative transfer models [24]. The algorithm provides the biophysical variable product (FVC and LAI) values and the relative input/output quality flag, for excluding out of range or bad quality pixels.

Table 2. Available Landsat 8 OLIS and S2 scenes in the 2016/2017 crop season.

Landsat 8 OLISR			MSI Sentinel 2	
Date	DOY	WRS-2	Date	DOY
02/23/2017	54	188 – 031	02/27/2017	58
04/12/2017	103	189 – 031	04/08/2017	99
05/14/2017	135	189 – 031	05/18/2017	139

3   Method

The semi-empirical model CLAIR is a simplified reflectance model based on an empirical relationship between LAI and WDVI (Eq. 1) [16]:

$$\text{LAI} = -\frac{1}{\alpha}\log\left(1 - \frac{\text{WDVI}}{\text{WDVI}_\infty}\right) \tag{1}$$

where WDVI is a vegetation index that takes into account the soil background reflectance [17]. It is defined (Eq. 2) as a weighted difference between the measured NIR and Red reflectance (respectively ρ_{NIR} and ρ_{Red}), where a (Eq. 3) is the "soil-line slope" defined as the ratio between NIR and red reflectance of bare soil ($\rho_{NIR,s}$, $\rho_{Red,s}$):

$$\text{WDVI} = \rho_{NIR} - (a \times \rho_{Red}) \tag{2}$$

$$a = \frac{\rho_{NIR,s}}{\rho_{Red,s}} \tag{3}$$

The image-based procedure used for retrieving the soil-line slope (a) and the parameters of the model (WDVI$_\infty$ and α) are wisely described in the following.

3.1   Identification of the Soil-Line Slope (α)

The soil-line slope is a key parameter used to estimate soil surface status and vegetation biophysical parameters. Literature shows as it can be easily retrieved also from the scatter plot between Red and NIR SR [25]. According to Eq. (3), the value of soil-line slope was assumed equal to the angular coefficient of the fitting line of the scatter plot.

Following the assumption of the model CLAIR, the soil-line slope is not dependent by the soil water content and thus can be used a unique value for the entire crop season. For the selected study area, it was estimated by Peschechera et al. [26] using the image-based procedure and the OLISR L8 SR data. Its value was in the range 1.22–1.38 with an average value of 1.31, that was applied in the present work.

3.2   Estimation of WDVI$_\infty$ and of Extinction Coefficient (α)

WDVI$_\infty$ and α are the two parameters of the CLAIR model. They are crop specific and are usually estimated empirically from a set of simultaneous SR and LAI field measures [19]. Image-based calibration is an alternative solution when field measurements are not available.

Table 3. Maximum WDVI, $WDVI_{\infty}$ and extinction coefficient (a) values retrieved for each satellite image in the study area using the proposed image-based method.

		$WDVI_{MAX}$	$WDVI_{\infty}$	α
Plot 1	Dataset 1	0.179	0.535	0.365
	Dataset 2	0.398	0.514	0.353
	Dataset 3	0.285	0.560	0.462
Plot 2	Dataset 1	0.398	0.582	0.368
	Dataset 2	0.398	0.527	0.284
	Dataset 3	0.215	0.389	0.653
Plot 3	Dataset 1	0.304	0.652	0.255
	Dataset 2	0.467	0.494	0.385
	Dataset 3	0.322	0.403	0.793

Table 4. Maximum WDVI, $WDVI_{\infty}$ and extinction coefficient values (a) retrieved during the whole crop season estimated for each plot and from the entire study area using the proposed image-based method.

	$WDVI_{MAX}$	$WDVI_{\infty}$	α
Plot 1	0.398	0.514	0.353
Plot 2	0.398	0.454	0.451
Plot 3	0.467	0.473	0.449
Plot 1 + 2 + 3	0.467	0.472	0.438

The image-based estimation of $WDVI_{\infty}$ is usually performed assuming it as the maximum WDVI value for vegetated areas within the image (e.g. [2, 8, 18, 26]). However, it is necessary to increase the maximum retrieved value of WDVI [20] because LAI can be estimated by Eq. (1) only if the logarithm's argument is greater than zero. Moreover, the model shows problem of saturation of LAI, when WDVI value tends to $WDVI_{\infty}$.

The extinction coefficient describes the canopy architecture and depends on the crop type and on the corresponding Leaf Angle Distribution (LAD) value [8]. Hence its estimation requires crop specific calibration with LAI field measurements, Vuolo et al. [18] tested a procedure able to calculate site-specific values of α and $WDVI_{\infty}$. In a previous work [27] a simple image-based procedure was adopted to retrieve LAI from Landsat SR using MODIS LAI products as reference following the procedure proposed by Gao et al. [28].

In the present work, the $WDVI_{\infty}$ and the extinction coefficient values were retrieved for each dataset by a regression analysis between S2 LAI and Landsat8 OLISR WDVI without setting a $WDVI_{\infty}$ and α values range. The limited temporal shift between the S2 and L8 acquisition, considered in the selection of the satellite data, allows to suppose a near-simultaneous satellite acquisition. In addition, to compare the two different datasets, it was necessary a resampling of the WDVI map to the finer resolution of the S2 LAI product. All the calculations were carried out through R software platform.

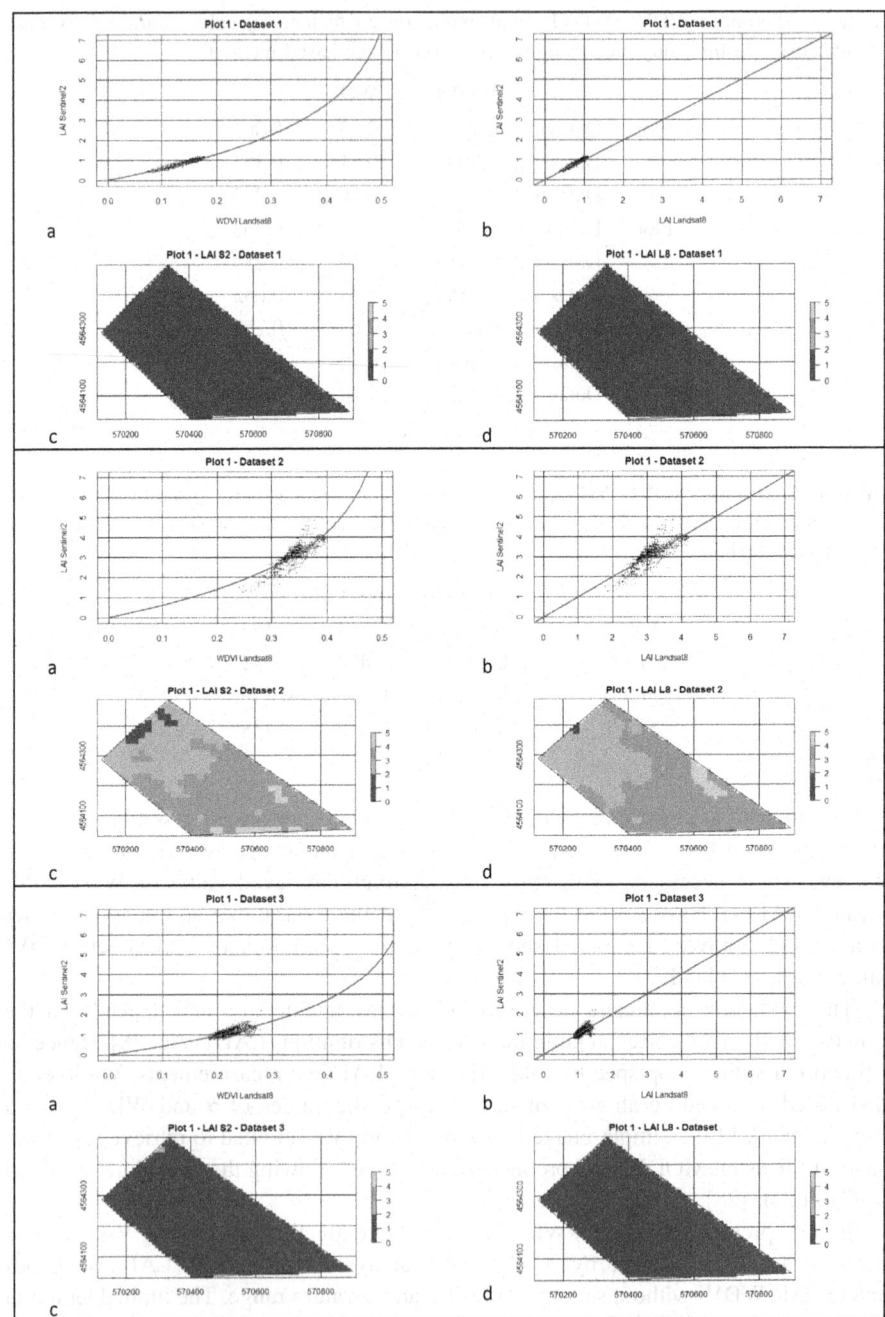

Fig. 2. Relationship between L8 WDVI and S2 LAI (a) used for the model calibration, scatter plot between reference LAI (S2 LAI) and estimated LAI (L8 LAI) (b), reference (c) and retrieved (d) LAI maps for the "plot 1" for each dataset.

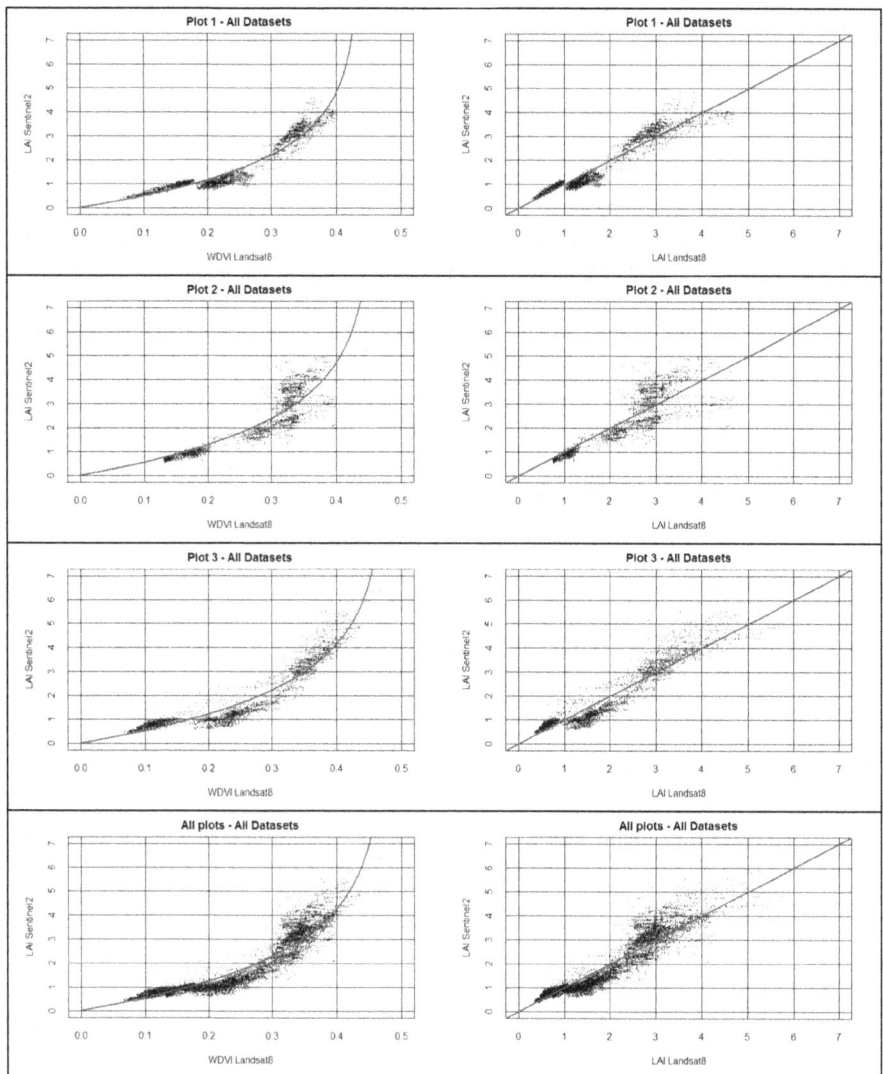

Fig. 3. On the left column are reported the empirical relationship between Landsat8 WDVI and Sentinel2 LAI used for the model Clair calibration. On the right column are showed the scatter plots between LAI Landsat retrieved using the calibrated model CLAIR and the Sentinel 2 LAI product. Graphs are evaluated for the entire crop season and are reported for each plot and for the entire study area.

4   Results and Discussion

The model CLAIR parameters for each image were retrieved following the described procedure. Table 3 summarizes the calibration results retrieved for each plot and for each pairs of S-2 LAI – L8 OLISR WDVI datasets. In this way it is possible to define the parameters during the different vegetative stages. Moreover, the entire calibration procedure was applied to each plot and for the entire study area by merging the three datasets (Table 4). Hence it was possible estimate the parameters valid for the entire crop season. In both cases, the calibration results are in line with the literature values as summarized in Peschechera et al. [27].

The calibration procedure was conducted without setting a $WDVI_\infty$ and α values range. It is worth to mention as the estimated $WDVI_\infty$ values were similar to the corresponding maximum value of WDVI retrieved for each image. Therefore, the results were consistent also with the $WDVI_\infty$ image-based estimation methods previously described.

For a better comparison, Fig. 2 shows the WDVI-LAI fitting, the scatter plots between reference S2 and the corresponding Landsat8 LAI for each dataset and the relative comparison among the reference S2 LAI map and the estimated L8 OLISR LAI as retrieved with the CLAIR model. The same WDVI-LAI fitting and scatter plots for the entire crop season, obtained merging the three datasets, estimated for each plot and for the entire study area were reported in Fig. 3.

5   Conclusions

This study proposes an image-based method for the calibration of the CLAIR model for wheat crop for Landsat 8 SR data using as reference the S2 SR and LAI products. The proposed procedure can be applied in case of lacking both LAI and SR field measurements, representing a valid solution to extend the field of application of the model CLAIR. It generates reliable LAI information from OLISR consistent with the S2 LAI. In this way, it looks possible to merge the LAI maps retrieved from both the satellites in order to generate LAI maps with a higher temporal resolution useful for a better crop growth monitoring and management.

References

1. Chen, J.M., Black, T.A.: Defining leaf area index for non-flat leaves. Plant, Cell Environ. **15**(4), 421–429 (1992)
2. Balacco, G., Figorito, B., Tarantino, E., Gioia, A., Iacobellis, V.: Space–time LAI variability in Northern Puglia (Italy) from SPOT VGT data. Environ. Monit. Assess. **187**, 1–15 (2015)
3. Duchemin, B., Hadria, R., Erraki, S., Boulet, G., Maisongrande, P., Chehbouni, A., Escadafal, R., Ezzahar, J., Hoedjes, J.C.B., Kharrou, M.H.: Monitoring wheat phenology and irrigation in Central Morocco: on the use of relationships between evapotranspiration, crops coefficients, leaf area index and remotely-sensed vegetation indices. Agric. Water Manag. **79**(1), 1–27 (2006)
4. Vanino, S., Nino, P., De Michele, C., Bolognesi, S.F., Pulighe, G.: Earth observation for improving irrigation water management: a case-study from Apulia Region in Italy. Agric. Agric. Sci. Procedia **4**, 99–107 (2015)
5. Trombetta, A., Iacobellis, V., Tarantino, E., Gentile, F.: Calibration of the AquaCrop model for winter wheat using MODIS LAI images. Agric. Water Manag. **164**(2), 304–316 (2016)

6. Bréda, N.J.J.: Ground-based measurements of leaf area index: a review of methods, instruments and current controversies. J. Exp. Bot. **54**(392), 2403–2417 (2003)
7. Martinez, B., Cassiraga, E., Camacho, F., Garcia-Haro, J.: Geostatistics for mapping leaf area index over a cropland landscape: efficiency sampling assessment. Remote Sens. **2**(11), 2584–2606 (2010)
8. Richter, K., Vuolo, F., D'Urso, G., Dini, L.: Evaluation of different methods for the retrieval of LAI using high resolution airborne data. In: The International Society for Optical Engineering Proceedings of SPIE. Society of Photo-Optical Instrumentation Engineers (2007)
9. Verrelst, J., Rivera, J.P., Veroustraete, F., Muñoz-Marí, J., Clevers, J.G., Camps-Valls, G., Moreno, J.: Experimental sentinel-2 LAI estimation using parametric, non-parametric and physical retrieval methods–a comparison. ISPRS J. Photogram. Remote Sens. **108**, 260–272 (2015)
10. Clevers, J.G.P.W.: Application of a weighted infrared-red vegetation index for estimating leaf area index by correcting for soil moisture. Remote Sens. Environ. **29**(1), 25–37 (1989)
11. Clevers, J.G.P.W., Vonder, O.W., Jongschaap, R.E.E., Desprats, J.F., King, C., Prévot, L., Bruguier, N.: A semi-empirical approach for estimating plant parameters within the RESEDA-project. In: International Archives of Photogrammetry and Remote Sensing 33 (B7/1; PART 7), pp. 272–279 (2000)
12. Vuolo, F., Dini, L., D'Urso, G.: Assessment of LAI retrieval accuracy by inverting a RT model and a simple empirical model with multiangular and hyperspectral CHRIS/PROBA data from SPARC. In: Proceedings 3rd CHRIS/Proba Workshop (2005)
13. Akdim, N., Alfieri, S.M., Habib, A., Choukri, A., Cheruiyot, E., Labbassi, K., Menenti, M.: Monitoring of irrigation schemes by remote sensing: phenology versus retrieval of biophysical variables. Remote Sens. **6**(6), 5815 (2014)
14. Vanino, S., Pulighe, G., Nino, P., De Michele, C., Bolognesi, S.F., D'Urso, G.: Estimation of evapotranspiration and crop coefficients of tendone vineyards using multi-sensor remote sensing data in a mediterranean environment. Remote Sens. **7**(11), 14708–14730 (2015)
15. Clevers, J., Vonder, O., Jongschaap, R., Desprats, J.F., King, C., Prévot, L., Bruguier, N.: Using SPOT data for calibrating a wheat growth model under mediterranean conditions. Agronomie **22**(6), 687–694 (2002)
16. Clevers, J.G.P.W.: The derivation of a simplified reflectance model for the estimation of leaf area index. Remote Sens. Environ. **25**(1), 53–69 (1988)
17. Baret, F., Jacquemoud, S., Hanocq, J.F.: The soil line concept in remote sensing. Remote Sens. Rev. **7**(1), 65–82 (1993)
18. Vuolo, F., Neugebauer, N., Bolognesi, S.F., Atzberger, C., D'Urso, G.: Estimation of leaf area index using DEIMOS-1 data: application and transferability of a semi-empirical relationship between two agricultural areas. Remote Sens. **5**(3), 1274–1291 (2013)
19. Clevers, J.G.P.W.: Application of the WDVI in estimating LAI at the generative stage of barley. ISPRS J. Photogram. Remote Sens. **46**(1), 37–47 (1991)
20. Vermote, E., Justice, C., Claverie, M., Franch, B.: Preliminary analysis of the performance of the Landsat 8/OLI land surface reflectance product. Remote Sens. Environ. **185**, 46–56 (2016)
21. Roy, D.P., Wulder, M.A., Loveland, T.R., Woodcock, C.E., Allen, R.G., Anderson, M.C., Helder, D., Irons, J.R., Johnson, D.M., Kennedy, R.: Landsat-8: science and product vision for terrestrial global change research. Remote Sens. Environ. **145**, 154–172 (2014)
22. Drusch, M., et al.: Sentinel-2: ESA's optical high-resolution mission for GMES operational services. Remote Sens. Environ. **120**, 25–36 (2012)

23. Louis, J., Debaecker, V., Pflug, B., Main-Knorn, M., Bieniarz, J., Mueller-Wilm, U., Cadau, E., Gascon, F.: Sentinel-2 Sen2Cor: L2A processor for users. In: Proceedings Living Planet Symposium 2016, pp. 1–8. Spacebooks Online (2016)
24. Jacquemoud, S., et al.: PROSPECT + SAIL models: a review of use for vegetation characterization. Remote Sens. Environ. **113**, S56–S66 (2009)
25. Yoshioka, H., Miura, T., Demattê, J.A., Batchily, K., Huete, A.R.: Soil line influences on two-band vegetation indices and vegetation isolines: a numerical study. Remote Sens. **2**(2), 545–561 (2010)
26. Aquilino M., Novelli A., Tarantino E., Gentile F., Iacobellis V.: Evaluating the potential of GeoEye data in retrieving LAI at watershed scale. Remote Sensing for Agriculture Ecosystems and Hydrology (2014)
27. Peschechera, G., Novelli, A., Caradonna, G., Fratino, U.: Calibration of the CLAIR model by using Landsat 8 surface reflectance higher-level data and MODIS leaf area index products. In: Gervasi, O., et al. (eds.) ICCSA 2017. LNCS, vol. 10407, pp. 16–29. Springer, Cham (2017). https://doi.org/10.1007/978-3-319-62401-3_2
28. Gao, F., Anderson, M.C., Kustas, W.P., Wang, Y.: Simple method for retrieving leaf area index from Landsat using MODIS leaf area index products as reference. J. Appl. Remote Sens. **6**(1), 063554 (2012)

Multi-image 3D Reconstruction: A Photogrammetric and Structure from Motion Comparative Analysis

Grazia Caradonna[1], Eufemia Tarantino[1(✉)], Marco Scaioni[2], and Benedetto Figorito[3]

[1] DICATECh—Politecnico di Bari, Via Orabona 4, 70125 Bari, Italy
{grazia.caradonna,eufemia.tarantino}@poliba.it
[2] DABC - Politecnico di Milano, 20133 Milan, Italy
marco.scaioni@polimi.it
[3] ARPA Puglia, Via Trieste 27, 70126 Bari, Italy
b.figorito@arpa.puglia.it

Abstract. Virtual Web Reconstruction of cultural heritage is one of the most interesting and innovative tool to preserve historical, architectural and artistic memory of many sites, particularly the ones prone to disappear, as well as to promote territories and tourism development. Recently, high-resolution 3D models are realized through improved technology and integration of survey techniques such as laser scanning and photogrammetry. However, the large and complex volume of 3D data makes difficult to access and handle them for either experts and citizens. In particular, the rendering of large 3D models may influence the performance of web publication and browsing. Considering this background, the goal of this paper is the comparison between the level of accuracy and realism of 3D models optimized using two different mesh simplification.

The metric used is based on the Hausdorff distance which is a generic technique to define a distance between two nonempty sets, considering 3D scanner mesh as a reference in the measure. The "Casale di Pacciano" near Bisceglie (Apulia region, Italy), has been investigated as study case.

Keywords: Cultural heritage · Hausdorff distance · Low-cost sensors
SfM · Simplification algorithms · Terrestrial laser scanning

1 Introduction

Nowadays, Cultural Heritage (CH) safekeeping and promotion are topics of great relevance in all countries. The documentation of CH through digital archiving has now become a global goal [1].

CH and technologies are today strongly linked: the modern geomatics techniques and information and communication technologies (ICT) offer significant potential applications for documentation, representation, fruition and multimedia communication of CH [2]. In recent years several studies, projects and pieces of literature regarding the use of new technologies applied to CH have put their attention mainly to those

© Springer International Publishing AG, part of Springer Nature 2018
O. Gervasi et al. (Eds.): ICCSA 2018, LNCS 10964, pp. 305–316, 2018.
https://doi.org/10.1007/978-3-319-95174-4_25

technologies to reconstruct and narrate the complexity of the territory and CH. These include 3D reconstruction, Augmented Reality (AR) [3], and web applications [4], which allow the user to enrich the reality through the visualization of digital graphic contents overlapped to the real surveyed data [5].

The use of 3D survey technology applied to the study of historical buildings is become an established method for determining the geometry of the structures, because it provides comprehensive and accurate analysis even in complex architectures. In this way, the perception of geometrical details that are difficult to be detected with traditional representation techniques is supported. The result is a 3D database that is helpful for improving the knowledge and for the design of any intervention aimed at conservation. Furthermore, thanks to the interaction with computer techniques for visualization and online dissemination, the surveying technologies, and particularly terrestrial laser scanning and photogrammetry [6], can be used effectively for more purposes than the ones concerning experts only. For example, 3D realistic models can be used for disseminating CH, to support education in schools, to promote tourism, and the like.

Therefore, such 3D models have an added value and potential, compared to 2D models. They are more realistic, [7] even if they are more difficult to implement and the rendering of heavy objects, in terms of details and meshes, influences visualization time of the scene [8, 9].

In fact, despite of technological developments, the management of large polygonal datasets can be limited by several technical problems, mainly the long processing and editing time and some constraints in real-time visualization due to the current performances of the graphic cards. The alternative way to the increment of computing performance is offered by the reduction of the final volume of 3D models in terms of geometry and texture. From a geometric point of view, it is possible to reduce the number of vertices and optimize the geometry [10, 11]. In addition, in order to maintain a high quality visualization and not to miss geometric details that are necessary for studies and analysis purpose, normal and displacement maps can be used [12, 13]. From a radiometric point of view, it is possible to reduce and compress the high-resolution images or, if necessary, a single texture can be generated for each model. In all cases, it is necessary to find a compromise between accuracy, size and visualization of 3D models.

Considering this background, in this paper first a comparison between different 3D point cloud reconstruction methods is proposed. The adopted methods are based on the use of terrestrial laser scanning (TLS) and structure-from-motion (SfM) photogrammetry, the latter applied within different software packages. These two reconstruction techniques are used in the large majority of current projects, even though other sensors have been also tested (see, e.g. [14]).

In the following step, two different subdivision algorithms have been applied to improve and reduce the size of the meshes but preserving the high level of precision and realism. The metric used to compare the results is the Hausdorff distance [15], which represents a good technique to define a distance between two nonempty sets.

2   3D Model Reconstruction

2.1   Case Study: "Casale di Pacciano"

The "Casale di Pacciano" near Bisceglie (Apulia region, Italy) has been investigated as study case (Fig. 1). This settlement has a great historical relevance and is protected by the municipal administration. Nowadays only a few buildings have been preserved since the construction started (11ᵗʰ Century). The most relevant of them are the Church of Ognissanti and the Church of Sant'Angelo.

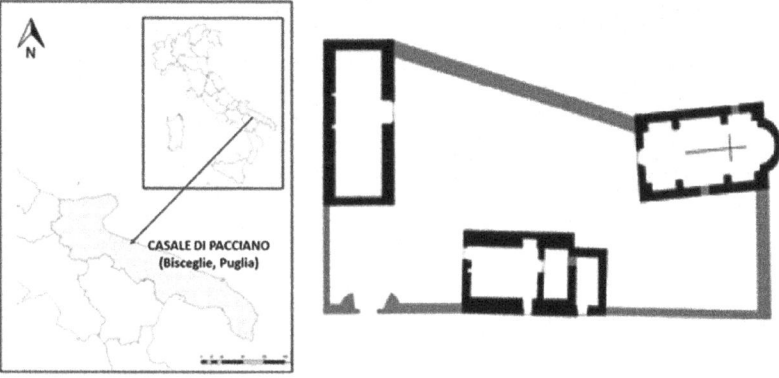

Fig. 1. Geographic location of "Casale di Pacciano" (on the left) and planimetric view (on the right), where still erected buildings are drawn in black.

The Church of Ognissanti, dating back to the 11ᵗʰ Century, is a small treasure of pre-Romanesque architecture (Fig. 2). The entire building has a single nave, barrel vaulted with a spherical dome in axis, with a transept outlined by two lateral niches, typical of buildings with a contracted cross, and a semicircular protruding apse. The restoration work has brought to light its original appearance, recovering the roof with "chiancarelle" and the fretwork that decorate the central pyramid roof.

2.2   Surveying Procedures and 3D Reconstruction

The generation of reality-based 3D models of heritage sites and objects is nowadays operated by using methodologies based on passive sensors and image data [16], active sensors and range data [17], classical surveying (e.g., total stations or GPS), or an integration of the aforementioned techniques [18]. The choice or integration depends on required accuracy, size of the target object, possible location constraints, surveying system's portability and usability, surface characteristics, working team experience, project's budget, final goal and required products, etc.

Fig. 2. The Church of Ognissanti in the "Casale di Pacciano"

2.3   Image-Based Modeling

Structure-from-Motion (SfM) Photogrammetry is based on automatic detection of key points (features) in more images. For 3D information to be extracted, images must contain sufficient overlap, generally 60%. The Scale-Invariant Feature Transform (SIFT) or similar algorithms are used to detect and describe local features in images aimed at post processing [19].

Then, a bundle adjustment procedure is performed to evaluate the image orientation.

During this stage, the estimation of camera calibration parameters (inner orientation) is also operated, when this task has not been carried out independently [20]. Since the 3D coordinates of key points are not in general sufficient to reconstruct the shape of the surveyed object, in a next stage the aim is to derive a dense points cloud on the basis of dense surface matching techniques [21]. Finally, a 3D model is obtained by converting a point cloud made up of unstructured points into a triangular or quadrangular mesh, which are composed by vertices and faces. In this final phase, the model may be also cleaned and textured. In strict sense, the term SfM should be adopted for the image orientation stage only. In practice, it is commonplace now to use the SfM for the entire automatic image-based 3D reconstruction process [22, 23] (Fig. 3).

Photogrammetric surveying operations have been carried out in two different phases: first, converging shots have been captured from camera stations around the church; secondly, a series of images have been recorded from above. A Canon EOS 600D equipped with an 18 mm lens and a sensor size 5184×3456 pixels was used for data acquisition. A total number of 207 photos have been collected in the field, but only 186 have been considered suitable for the SfM reconstruction process. The camera was independently calibrated using Agisoft Photoscan Lens® software. To accomplish this task, fourteen convergent poses have been recorded.

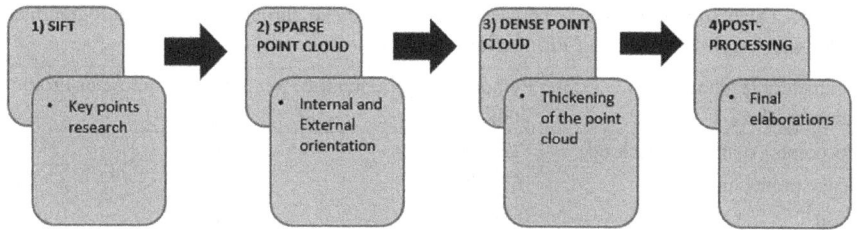

Fig. 3. 3D object reconstruction process using SfM method

Two different software packages have been tested to reconstruct a three-dimensional model of the Church of Ognissanti:

- Agisoft Photoscan Pro® (ver. 1.2.4), which is a popular low-cost commercial software package [24];
- PythonTMPhotogrammetric Toolbox (PPT), which is an open-source a free software [25].

Both software packages are able to work in fully automatic way using a SfM approach for image orientation, followed by dense image matching operated in a multi-view stereo mode [26]. A qualitative comparison between the final 3D models that have been obtained using both approaches has been carried out on the basis of the number of points in the sparse point clouds, dense point clouds and the mesh.

Agisoft Photoscan Pro® software has selected for the comparison according to and [27, 28], who demonstrated that it may provide largely reliable results among existing commercial software packages based on SfM algorithms.

Python Photogrammetric Toolbox (PPT), released under GPL v.3 license, is a FLOSS project in which instruments and knowledge are shared. It implements a pipeline to perform 3D reconstruction from a set of images. This pipeline is designed as a Python module with a High-Level API. It integrates Bundler (image orientation), CMVS and PMVS (Patch Multi View Stereo) modules into an open-source photogrammetric toolbox [29]. The result is a 3-level application: Interface, Python modules and Software. Despite the automation, the user can control the result choosing two initial parameters: the image size and feature detector. Acting on the first parameter determines a reduction of the computation time and a decreasing density of the point cloud. Acting on the feature detector influences final result: PPT can work both with SIFT (patent of the University of British Columbia - freely usable only for research purpose) and with VLFEAT (released under GPL v.2 license). The use of VLFEAT ensures a more accurate result, though it increases the time of calculation.

The points clouds made of tie points (also referred in Photoscan® environment as "sparse point cloud") and the ones obtained after dense surface matching (called "dense point cloud") from the two software packages are shown in Fig. 4. The mesh reconstructed by PPT has been chosen as input for the reduction algorithm and compared with the mesh from terrestrial laser scanning surveying (Table 1).

Table 1. Qualitative comparison between models obtained through Python Photogrammetric Toolbox and Agisoft Photoscan Pro software packages

Parameters [# number of points/meshes]	Python Photogrammetric Toolbox	Agisoft Photoscan Pro (ver. 1.2.4)
Tie points (sparse point cloud)	226,034	144,548
Dense points cloud	1672,285	1405,288
Mesh	7616,296	2832,667

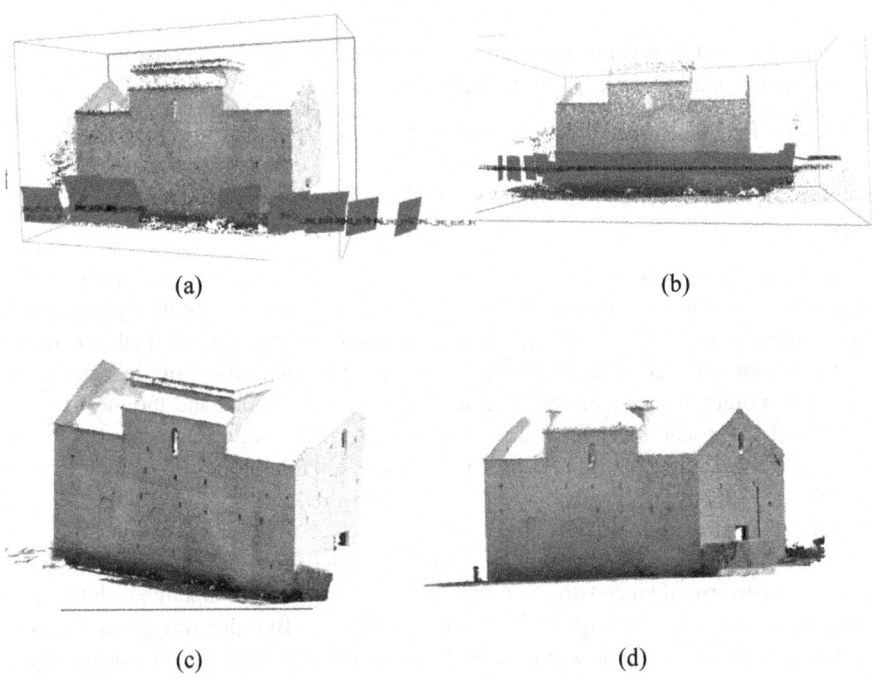

(a)   (b)

(c)   (d)

Fig. 4. (a) PPT sparse point cloud; (b) PPT dense point cloud (c); Photoscan Pro® sparse point cloud (d); Photoscan Pro® dense point cloud.

2.4 Terrestrial Laser Scanning Modeling

A terrestrial laser scanner P30 Leica Geosystems has been adopted for the surveying of the Church of Ognissanti. This choice has been motivated by its battery-driven capability, portability, and accuracy in meeting the final requirements (scanning speed of around 1,000,000 points/s and a precision in the order of ±1.2 mm). A multi-station network has been used for the terrestrial laser scanning (TLS) surveying, consisting of 11 stand-points. A set of targets has been deployed to be used as ground control points (GCPs), whose measurement has been operated using a GNSS geodetic receiver Leica GS 14.

Fig. 5. Point cloud of the Church of Ognissanti after the filtering process

Fig. 6. Visualization of the triangular mesh of the Church of Ognissanti.

The post of recorded laser scans has been done through CycloneTM v9.2 software. This stage has provided the registration of all scans through the ICP algorithm, which resulted in a unique point cloud of the church. Finally, a filtering process has been applied to the point cloud output displayed in Fig. 5.

The standard deviation of registration obtained has been estimated to be ±0.01 m. Starting from the point cloud, a surface model has been generated, through the dedicated Cyclone tools, and finally a triangular mesh has been generated, in order to obtain a surface model (Fig. 6).

3 Re-mesh and Comparison of the Simplified 3D Mesh Models

Usually two types of information are encoded in the created meshes: the geometrical information (i.e., the 3D position of its vertices in space and the normal surface) and the topological information (i.e., the mesh connectivity and the relations between faces) [30].

In recent years, with the HTML5 standard and the development of handheld mobile devices, people can use WebGL or OpenGL ES technology for achieving real-time rendering of complex three-dimensional scenes on browser or mobile device.

The size of these big data sets sometimes influences the processing chain and the visualization of the 3D model [31].

In this way, complex models are needed to be reduced with mesh simplification algorithms. Correspondingly, mesh simplification can be defined as the process of reducing the number of faces and vertices of a given input mesh while maintaining a faithful approximation to the original mesh.

The simplification algorithms can be classified according their approaches to the subject [32]:

- Subdivision rules

  1. Primal: a new vertex for every edge of the given mesh is inserted and then the new vertices are connected,
  2. Dual: each vertex is divided to create new vertices.

- Mesh type:

  1. Triangular;
  2. Quadrangular;
  3. Manifold;
  4. Non-manifold.

- Simplification Algorithms:

  1. Iterative algorithms: each mesh element (vertex, faces or edge) is removed once at a time;
  2. Single pass algorithms: the whole input mesh is processed in a single step.

Table 2. Applied simplification algorithms' properties

Algorithm	Simplification parameters	Mesh type	Mesh continuity
Butterfly [33, 34]	Interpolation	Triangular	C1
Kobbelt [35]	Interpolation	Triangular	C1

In this work, two simplification algorithms have been implemented, based on primal rule and shown in Table 2, to re-mesh and reduce the mesh.

The simplified mesh obtained have been then compared using Butterfly and Kobbelt methods. Considering both meshes and their vertices, for each vertex of the first mesh (X) the distance with respect to the closest vertex in the second mesh (Y) is evaluated using the algorithm of Hausdorff distance as implemented in Python. This type of distance is a symmetric distance [36]. In fact, in some cases the lack of symmetry of this distance leads to problems at the edges. This can either happen near to the borders of the original mesh or at parts of the mesh that resemble to the border, in the sense that the angle between adjacent triangles along a common edge is very small (Fig. 7).

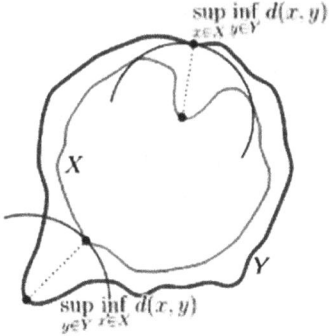

Fig. 7. Graphic representation of Hausdorff distance

The output of Hausdorff distance evaluation is given by the maximum distance found in the comparison process:

$$\sup_{x \in X} \inf_{y \in Y} d(x, y) \tag{1}$$

In general, Hausdorff distance is a symmetrical measure d(X, Y) = d(Y, X). The complete definition is given by the following equation:

$$dH(X, Y) = \max\{\sup_{x \in X} \inf_{y \in Y} d(x, y), \sup_{y \in Y} \inf_{x \in X} d(x, y)\} \tag{2}$$

The computation of the Hausdorff distance, considering 3D laser scanner mesh as reference in the measure, led to the values indicated in Table 3:

Table 3. Values of mesh simplification algorithms

Mesh simplification algorithm	Min	Max	Mean	RMS (Root Mean Square)
Butterfly	0.0 cm	34.5 cm	2.7 cm	1.0 cm
Kobbelt	0.5 cm	31.8 cm	3.9 cm	0.9 cm

The simplification algorithm resulted to be not computationally intensive (i.e. 175 ms execution times) on a system configured with a Intel® Xeon CPU E5-1650 (3.50 GHZ).

4   Results and Conclusion

The results obtained demonstrated that the two simplification algorithms have been comparable, though the Butterfly algorithm produced a better mesh improvement. In fact, the order of differences resulted around 1 cm in both cases, which is fully acceptable for the considered case study.

Future works are foreseen to test the speed of real-time rendering related to these 3D simplified model on browser.

Acknowledgement. The authors are grateful to VisualDrone (an Apulian start-up operating in the world of UAS), to Dr. Antonio Novelli for their precious collaboration in the survey campaign and to Dr. Giuseppe Troilo, president of the Physis Trekking Astrophile Association, for his availability.

References

1. Webb, C.: Guidelines for the preservation of digital heritage (2003)
2. Boehler, W., Heinz, G., Marbs, A.: The potential of non-contact close range laser scanners for cultural heritage recording. Int. Arch. Photogramm. Remote Sens. Spat. Inf. Sci. **34** (5/C7), 430–436 (2002)
3. Boehler, W., Heinz, G., Marbs, A.: The potential of non-contact close range laser scanners for cultural heritage recording. In: Proceedings of the CIPA–International Symposium, Potsdam, Germany (2001)
4. D'Agnano, F., Balletti, C., Guerra, F., Vernier, P.: Tooteko: a case study of augmented reality for an accessible cultural heritage. Digitization, 3D printing and sensors for an audio-tactile experience. Int. Arch. Photogramm. Remote Sens. Spat. Inf. Sci. **40**(5), 207 (2015)
5. Guttentag, D.A.: Virtual reality: applications and implications for tourism. Tour. Manag. **31** (5), 637–651 (2010)

6. Fritz, F., Susperregui, A., Linaza, M.T.: Enhancing cultural tourism experiences with augmented reality technologies. In: 6th International Symposium on Virtual Reality, Archaeology and Cultural Heritage, VAST (2005)
7. Balletti, C., Guerra, F., Scocca, V., Gottardi, C.: 3D integrated methodologies for the documentation and the virtual reconstruction of an archaeological site. Int. Arch. Photogramm. Remote Sens. Spat. Inf. Sci. **40**(5), 215 (2015)
8. Aita, D., Barsotti, R., Bennati, S., Caroti, G., Piemonte, A.: 3-DIMENSIONAL geometric survey and structural modelling of the dome of Pisa cathedral. ISPRS-Int. Arch. Photogramm. Remote Sens. Spat. Inf. Sci. 39–46 (2017)
9. Caradonna, G., Lionetti, S., Tarantino, E., Verdoscia, C.: A comparison of low-poly algorithms for sharing 3D models on the web. In: Cefalo, R., Zieliński, J.B., Barbarella, M. (eds.) New Advanced GNSS and 3D Spatial Techniques. LNGC, pp. 237–244. Springer, Cham (2018). https://doi.org/10.1007/978-3-319-56218-6_19
10. Noh, Z., Sunar, M.S., Pan, Z.: A review on augmented reality for virtual heritage system. In: Chang, M., Kuo, R., Kinshuk, Chen, G.D., Hirose, M. (eds.) Edutainment 2009. LNCS, vol. 5670, pp. 50–61. Springer, Heidelberg (2009). https://doi.org/10.1007/978-3-642-03364-3_7
11. Liu, T., Zhao, D., Pan, M.: An approach to 3D model fusion in GIS systems and its application in a future ECDIS. Comput. Geosci. **89**, 12–20 (2016)
12. Pecchioli, L., Pucci, M., Mohamed, F., Mazzei, B.: Browsing in the virtual museum of the sarcophagi in the Basilica of St. Silvestro at the Catacombs of Priscilla in Rome. In: 2012 18th International Conference on Virtual Systems and Multimedia, VSMM. IEEE (2012)
13. Kersten, T.P.: 3D scanning and modelling of the bismarck monument by terrestrial laser scanning for integration into a 3D city model of hamburg. In: Ioannides, M., Fellner, D., Georgopoulos, A., Hadjimitsis, D.G. (eds.) EuroMed 2010. LNCS, vol. 6436, pp. 179–192. Springer, Heidelberg (2010). https://doi.org/10.1007/978-3-642-16873-4_14
14. Altuntas, C., Yildiz, F., Scaioni, M.: Laser scanning and data integration for three-dimensional digital recording of complex historical structures: the case of mevlana museum. ISPRS Int. J. Geo-Inf. **5**(2), 18 (2016)
15. Aspert, N., Santa-Cruz, D., Ebrahimi, T.: MESH: measuring errors between surfaces using the hausdorff distance. In: Proceedings of the 2002 IEEE International Conference on Multimedia and Expo, ICME 2002. IEEE (2002)
16. Remondino, F., El-Hakim, S.: Image-based 3D modelling: a review. Photogramm. Rec. **21**(115), 269–291 (2006)
17. Blais, F.: Review of 20 years of range sensor development. J. Electron. Imag. **13**(1), 231–244 (2004)
18. El-Hakim, S.F., Beraldin, J.A., Picard, M., Godin, G.: Detailed 3D reconstruction of large-scale heritage sites with integrated techniques. IEEE Comput. Graph. Appl. **24**(3), 21–29 (2004)
19. Barazzetti, L., Forlani, G., Remondino, F., Roncella, R., Scaioni, M.: Experiences and achievements in automated image sequence orientation for close-range photogrammetric projects. In: 2011 Proceedings of International Society for Optics and Photonics, Videometrics, Range Imaging, and Applications XI, vol. 8085, p. 13, paper no. 80850F (2011)
20. Luhmann, T., Fraser, C., Maas, H.G.: Sensor modelling and camera calibration for close-range photogrammetry. ISPRS J. Photogramm. Remote Sens. **115**, 37–46 (2016)
21. Remondino, F., Spera, M.G., Nocerino, E., Menna, F., Nex, F.: State of the art in high density image matching. Photogramm. Rec. **29**(146), 144–166 (2014)
22. Fugazza, D., Scaioni, M., Corti, M., D'Agata, C., Azzoni, R.S., Cernuschi, M., Diolaiuti, G. A.: Combination of UAV and terrestrial photogrammetry to assess rapid glacier evolution and map glacier hazards. Nat. Hazards Earth Syst. Sci. **18**(4), 1055 (2018)

23. Granshaw, S.I.: Structure from motion: origins and originality. Photogramm. Rec. **33**(161), 6–10 (2018)
24. Weiss, M., Baret, F.: Using 3D point clouds derived from UAV RGB imagery to describe vineyard 3D macro-structure. Remote Sens. **9**(2), 111 (2017)
25. Moulon, P., Bezzi, A.: Python photogrammetry toolbox: a free solution for three-dimensional documentation. In: ArcheoFoss (2011)
26. Cogliati, M., Tonelli, E., Battaglia, D., Scaioni, M.: Extraction of DEMS and Orthoimages from archive aerial imagery to support project planning in civil engineering. ISPRS Ann. Photogramm. Remote Sens. Spat. Inf. Sci **4** (2017)
27. Gini, R., Pagliari, D., Passoni, D., Pinto, L., Sona, G., Dosso, P.: UAV photogrammetry: block triangulation comparisons. Int. Arch. Photogramm. Remote Sens. Spat. Inf. Sci. **1**, W2 (2013)
28. Jaud, M., Passot, S., Le Bivic, R., Delacourt, C., Grandjean, P., Le Dantec, N.: Assessing the accuracy of high resolution digital surface models computed by PhotoScan® and MicMac® in sub-optimal survey conditions. Remote Sens. **8**(6), 465 (2016)
29. Bezzi, A., Bezzi, L., Gietl, R., Pisu, N.: ArcheOS and UAVP, a free and open source platform for remote sensing: the case study of Monte S. Martino ai Campi of Riva del Garda (Italy). In: Archaeology in the Digital Era, pp. 792–799 (2013)
30. Zorin, D., Schröder, P., Sweldens, W.: Interpolating subdivision for meshes with arbitrary topology. In: Proceedings of the 23rd Annual Conference on Computer Graphics and Interactive Techniques. ACM (1996)
31. Catmull, E., Clark, J.: Recursively generated B-spline surfaces on arbitrary topological meshes. Comput.-Aided Des. **10**(6), 350–355 (1978)
32. Labsik, U., Greiner, G.: Interpolatory $\sqrt{3}$-subdivision. In: Computer Graphics Forum. Wiley Online Library (2000)
33. Zhang, J., Wang, B., Li, X.: Geometric calibration of projector imagery on curved screen based-on subdivision mesh. In: Chen, F., Jüttler, B. (eds.) GMP 2008. LNCS, vol. 4975, pp. 592–600. Springer, Heidelberg (2008). https://doi.org/10.1007/978-3-540-79246-8_52
34. Dyn, N., Levine, D., Gregory, J.A.: A butterfly subdivision scheme for surface interpolation with tension control. ACM Trans. Graph. (TOG) **9**(2), 160–169 (1990)
35. Klein, R., Liebich, G., Straßer, W.: Mesh reduction with error control. In: Proceedings of the 7th conference on Visualization 1996. IEEE Computer Society Press (1996)
36. Kobbelt, L.: $\sqrt{3}$-subdivision. In: Proceedings of the 27th Annual Conference on Computer Graphics and Interactive Techniques. ACM Press/Addison-Wesley Publishing Co. (2000)

Investigation of a Flood Event Occurred on Lama Balice, in the Context of Hazard Map Evaluation in Karstic-Ephemeral Streams

Vito Iacobellis[1], Audrey M. N. Martellotta[1], Andrea Gioia[1],
Davide Prato[2], Vincenzo Totaro[1(✉)], Rocco Bonelli[2],
Gabriella Balacco[1], and Alisa A. M. G. Esposito[2]

[1] Department of Civil, Environmental, Land, Building Engineering
and Chemistry, Politecnico di Bari, DICATECh, via Orabona 4, 70125 Bari, Italy
{vito.iacobellis,andrea.gioia,vincenzo.totaro,
gabriella.balacco}@poliba.it,
audreymartellotta@gmail.com
[2] Basin Authority of Puglia, SP62, 70010 Bari, Italy
{davide.prato,rocco.bonelli,
alisa.esposito}@adb.puglia.it

Abstract. In the context of flood risk assessment and urban territory protection, the proposed research is focused on the definition of flood hazard maps by using high-resolution Digital Terrain Models (DTMs) obtained by a Light Detection And Ranging [LiDAR], remote sensing technique. The hydrologic/hydraulic model was calibrated on a flood event occurred on June 2014 on Lama Balice, ephemeral stream located in Puglia (Southern Italy), using the water levels observed during field campaign. In particular the analysis was performed for the definition of hazard maps with return periods of 30, 200 and 500 years, exploiting a combined scheme of a mono/two dimensional flood propagation approach for the delineation of flooded areas. The conducted research gives a significant contribution for the assessment of techniques of dynamic hazard and risk evaluation, in order to support institutions (like Basin Authorities and Civil Protection agencies) and professionals, in the context of the application of recent European legislation on flood risk protection (Floods Directive 2007/60/EC) and for European programs of scientific research (as Horizon 2020) in ungauged karstic catchment.

Keywords: Hazard maps · Karstic areas · Flood propagation

1 Introduction

Among natural disasters, floods were the most frequent in the last few years, especially in urban areas; in particular in the years 1994–2013, they account for 43% of all natural events and affect 2.4 billion of persons [1]. The increasing occurrence of flood events can be due to the effects of climate and land use change on runoff generation processes; this is an important topic investigated in the recent literature (e.g. [2–4]).

© Springer International Publishing AG, part of Springer Nature 2018
O. Gervasi et al. (Eds.): ICCSA 2018, LNCS 10964, pp. 317–333, 2018.
https://doi.org/10.1007/978-3-319-95174-4_26

Different tools and models are nowadays available for practical design, useful for the evaluation of areas exposed to inundations and for proposing mitigation measures in the context of the hydraulic protection of the territory. A quickly preliminary identification of flood prone areas may be conducted by using DTM-based hydrogeomorphic methods (e.g. [5, 6]) integrated with the use of satellite images (e.g. [7, 8]), with the aim to obtain indices that can provide reliable information on flood susceptibility (e.g. [9–11]). Although these techniques lead to interesting results, they need reference flood maps for calibration, which can be obtained by using the traditional mono and two-dimensional hydraulic numerical models; this kind of approach is frequently used in practical applications for analyzing physical and natural phenomena, such as floods (e.g. [12–17]), in a territory characterized by different type of urbanizations and land use.

In this context, for a selected geographical area, the classic approach for flood hazard assessment that uses a combined scheme of hydrological (e.g. [18–25]) and hydraulic model for flood propagation (e.g. [26–29]) is needed, in order to define a reliable numerical model which, through calibration and/or validation on a real case, allows to predict the natural catastrophic events in order the provide territory protection and human lives safeguard.

These methodologies, although widely consolidated in recent literature, becomes, in ungauged catchment, difficult to be applied because of its parameterization; in fact, in order to take into account the complexity of the explored phenomena and the peculiarities of the investigated geographical area, these models are characterized by a high number of variables and, consequently, by a high degree of complexity, in order to predict the ground effects of a meteoric event with an assigned return period. In order to make these approaches easily to be used in practical applications, in the last few decades techniques able to monitor from remote sensor the spatio-temporal evolution of terrestrial phenomena have been developed, in order to obtain distributed information useful to be integrated in hydraulic/hydrological applications (e.g. [30–37]) in territories with limited availability of data directly observed in situ, such as those derived by vegetation (e.g. [38–42]) or soil moisture.

In particular new technologies for remote surface elevation observation (i.e. global positioning systems [GPS], synthetic aperture radar [SAR] interferometry, airborne laser altimetry technology LiDAR [e.g. 43]) provide the increasing availability of high-resolution topographical maps (known as digital terrain models-DTMs), that are an important and useful tool for performing exposed areas to flood inundation, because they can provide a lot of information on morphology and earth surface's characteristic.

In the proposed work in the context of risk assessment and evaluation, an application of the above-mentioned methodologies for hazard map evaluation was illustrated on a case study of a Lama Balice river basin, which is characterized by a particular morphological structure present in the Puglia Region (Southern Italy) with an ephemeral stream network. Such evaluation was carried out by performing a calibration procedure, at event scale, of an extreme meteoric event occurred on June 2014, for which it was possible to directly measure the effects and the damages occurred in particular sections located on the main stream network.

Specifically, after the illustration of the adopted hydrological and hydraulic models on the Lama Balice river, we describe a rational for hazard map evaluation in the context of the integration of the current Hydrogeological Setting Plan (PAI) of Apulia River Basin Authority.

2 Study Area

Study area is located into the municipality area of Bari, which is crossed by several ephemeral stream networks; most of them have been already analysed by the River Basin Authority of Puglia (hereafter called AdBP) and are reported on the WebGis of the Puglia Hydrogeological Setting Plan, where the areas with different hydraulic hazards and risks have been defined. Among the most significant karstic stream network of the Murgian territory, there is the Lama Balice river that rises in the Murgia Plateau (see Fig. 1) in the municipal areas of Ruvo di Puglia and Corato and, oriented in a SW-NE direction, run down to the Adriatic Sea, crossing the territories of Terlizzi and Bitonto cities.

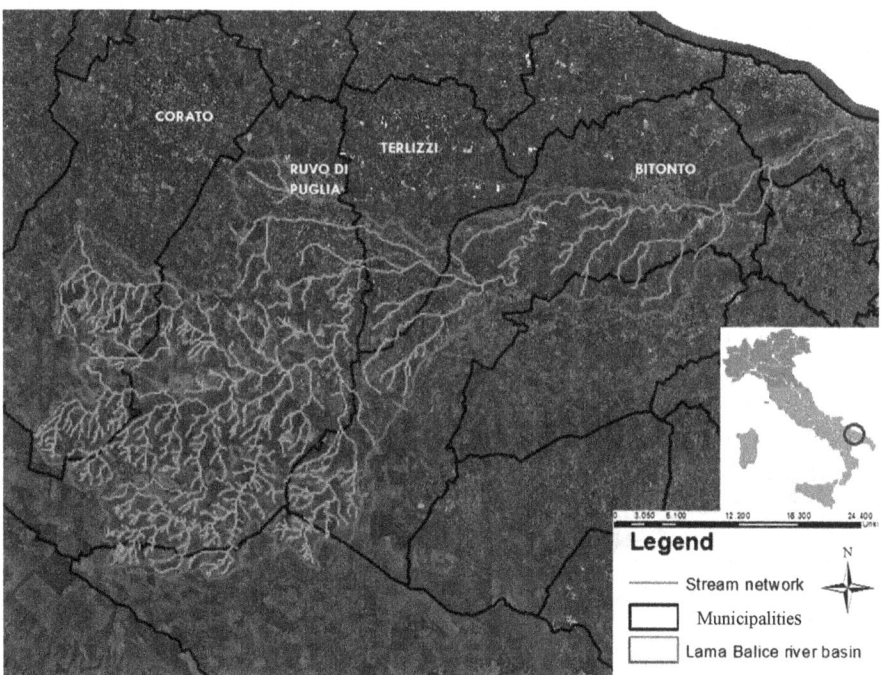

Fig. 1. Lama Balice catchment

The Lama Balice stream network has a general sub-flat morphological pattern and it, crossing the local roads and railway lines, goes through anthropogenic transformations.

A preliminary examination of the morphological depressions in Quantum GIS environment has been conducted before performing hydrological and hydraulic analysis. The evaluation was achieved on the base of the best available topographic data, represented by the LiDAR technology. Moreover, a calibration of an extreme meteoric event, occurred on June 2014, was performed by using the maximum water levels observed at some control sections located on the main stream of the investigated Lama Balice river, illustrated in Fig. 2.

Lama Balice Control sections   1.Water level at SP151 Ruvo-Altamura

2. Water level at SP22 Ruvo-Palombaio   3. Water level at Santa Teresa Bridge

4. Water level at ASI Railway Bridge   5.Water level at SS16 Bridge

Fig. 2. The maximum water levels observed at five control sections located on the main stream of the Balice river

On days 16th, 17th, 18th of June 2014 in the metropolitan area of Bari, temporal phenomena of impulsive character occurred with an intensity peak in the afternoon of June 17; locally more than 100 mm of cumulative rain were recorded, producing the reactivation of Lama Balice, with local flooding and huge damages to streets and infrastructures.

3   Materials and Methods

The purpose of this study is to delineate hydraulic hazard maps of the main stream network of Lama Balice river corresponding to return periods of 30, 200 and 500 years. With this aim the HEC-GeoHMS (e.g. [44]) hydrological model was calibrated, comparing the simulated flow data with those indirectly estimated by the observation of the flood event occurred on June 2014; the calibrated hydrological model was useful for the application of a mono-two dimensional hydraulic model, using design rainfall events with return period of 30, 200 and 500 years.

3.1   Material and Dataset

The Balice catchment surface close to its mouth and its sub-basins have been defined in Quantum GIS environment exploiting the Digital Terrain Model raster with cell of 8 m length, extracted from the topographical map, with scale 1:5000, provided by the territorial information system of Puglia Region. In particular, the basin was divided in sub-basins (see Fig. 5) with average surface of 10 km^2, characterized by outlet sections located at the intersections with the main roads and in correspondence to those sections where the maximum water depths of the event occurred on June 2014 were detected.

Morphometric parameters were extracted from the available topographical map: average slope of the basin, maximum, minimum and average altitude, exposure, flow length, longitudinal curvature, morphological surface curvature along the steepest slope, area and perimeter of the contributing basin. In Table 1 the main morphometric characteristics of the entire watershed are reported.

Table 1. Main morphometric characteristics of the entire Lama Balice basin

Physiographic characteristics of the Lama Balice basin					
Contributing area (km^2)	Average slope of the basin i_m (%)	Minimum basin height Q_{min} (m a.s.l.)	Maximum basin height Q_{max} (m a.s.l.)	Medium basin height Q_{ave} (m a.s.l.)	Length of the main stream network L_{max} (km)
339.61	4.84	0.34	635.00	316.87	61.54

The calibration of the hydrological model was performed using hourly rainfall datasets of the flood event occurred on 16–18 June 2014, obtained by Civil Protection department of Puglia; with this aim the hydrometeorological stations whose Thiessen polygons intersect the Lama Balice watershed were considered; they are: Bari Osservatorio, Castel del Monte, Corato, Grumo Appula, Masseria Modesti, Quasano and

Ruvo di Puglia (see Fig. 3). In particular, the time window between the 11 and the 18 June 2014 was selected considering some days before the occurrence of the investigated flood event, in order to take into account the antecedent soil moisture conditions for the application of the SCS-CN (Soil Conservation Service-Curve Number e.g. [45]) hydrological model.

The rainfall data show a dry condition with absence of precipitation in the days before the rainfall event, followed by low intensity rainfall on 14 and 15 June 2014. Then, from 16 to 18 June, the rainfall becomes more intense generating critical situation especially in the towns of Bari and Bitonto.

In order to evaluate hazard maps, precipitation events with return periods of 30, 200 and 500 years were considered in each sub-basin using the VAPI (e.g. [46]) Puglia regionalization methodology (i.e. an Italian research project, based on the use of Two-Component Extreme Value probabilistic model), which is useful for the estimation of hydrological variables in areas with poor availability of data. Moreover, the SCS-CN methodology was applied for the determination of the CN, which identifies the ability of soil to generate runoff events, by using lithological map extracted from the ACLA2 Project (e.g. [47]) and Corine Land Cover map (e.g. [48]) vector data.

Finally, a high-resolution topographic information (i.e. LiDAR) was exploited for the implementation of the hydraulic model.

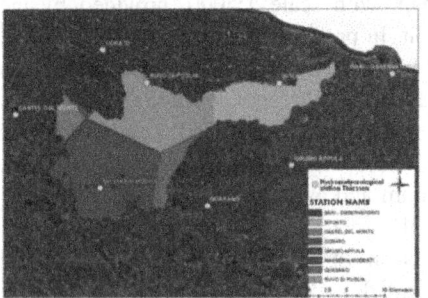

Fig. 3. Thiessen of Balice river

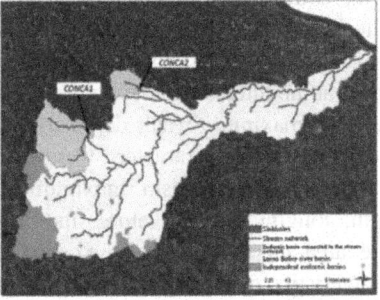

Fig. 4. Map of endoreic contributing area to Balice river

3.2 Methods

The HEC-GeoHMS hydrological model has been realized (in ESRI Arcmap 10 environment) through the discretization of the investigated basin into sub-basins, introducing hydrological parameters (lag time, CN, etc.) and cumulative rainfall, in order to estimate the discharge at the outlet of each sub-basin and at the mouth of the Balice river. HEC-GeoHMS calculates the discharge using the SCS Unit hydrograph (UH e.g. [49]) which is obtained by the SCS dimensionless hydrograph.

The Lama Balice stream network is characterized by the alternation of both morphologically very pronounced incisions and sub-flat areas; moreover, several intersections with roads, towns and productive areas are present. For this reason, a mono-dimensional approach (HEC-RAS proposed by [50]) was applied on its main stream network and, in areas characterized by particular low slope conditions, a two-dimensional flood propagation was carried out by using the SMS-TUFLOW model (e.g. [51]) in unsteady flow regime.

4   Results and Discussion

In the proposed study the calibration of the SCS-CN hydrological model was performed with reference to a flood event occurred on June 2014, in order to define a hydrological-hydraulic model able to depict flood hazard maps, corresponding to return periods of 30, 200 and 500 years. The torrential regime of the investigated karst stream network and its morphological characteristics make the calibration analysis very complex; moreover, these areas are not equipped with gauged river stations for discharge measurements, due to the ephemeral/episodic behavior of their natural incisions, called "lame", characterized by the absence of significant flows for long periods. Therefore, to perform the calibration analysis it is necessary to carry on field campaigns, where the phenomena is observed during its development and water level measurements are conducted on fixed elements internal to the stream, in order to find the relationship between rainfall data recorded at gauged stations and the consequent ground effect. The calibration analysis was performed using hourly rainfall datasets provided by the Civil Protection department of Puglia, for the period of 11–18 June 2014; the analyzed time window was selected considering some days previous to the occurrence of the investigated flood event, in order to take into account the antecedent soil moisture conditions for the application of the SCS-CN hydrological model.

The morphometric analysis and the definition of the total Balice watershed (see Fig. 4) close to its mouth and its sub-basins were performed by interpolating contour lines and soil elevation points obtained by a Digital Terrain Model with cell of 8 m length, extracted from the Puglia Region Topographic Database with scale 1:5000. In order to calculate the total contributing area of Lama Balice, the endoreic basins that contribute to the exoreic outfall, for floods event with high return periods (from 200 to 500 years) were considered; in particular two endoreic sinkholes, located in the upper zone of the watershed and named "Conca 1" and "Conca 2" (see Fig. 4), were considered and their contribution to the exoreic network was estimated as the excess volume, respect to that accumulated in the sinkhole, that overflows through a wide-threshold weir.

For the application of the HEC-GeoHMS hydrological model, the basin has been divided in sub-basins (represented as tanks in the HEC-GeoHMS schematization, see Fig. 5) and for them the morphological characteristics have been evaluated and introduced in the software, in order to calculate flood hydrographs of the investigated event. The basin has been modelled according to the following elements:

- for the investigated sub-basins, the hourly rainfall datasets were evaluated according to Thiessen polygons method;
- runoff generation was evaluated using the SCS unit hydrograph; in particular for each sub-basin, hydrological losses were estimated through the SCS-CN methodology, considering the CNII values evaluated from Corine land-use and ACLA2 lithological maps, available as vector data;

- the discharge in each outlet sub-basin section was evaluated by using the Lag Time method, where the velocity was determined according to Chézy formula under the hypothesis of steady flow;
- in the sub-basins delineation, the outlet sections have been selected considering: (1) the five calibration points [hereafter called "control sections" and reported in the following Fig. 5] where the observed maximum water level was available; (2) main streets, railways and infrastructures; (3) intersection with urbanized areas; (4) relevant changes of slope.

The model was then applied under the hypothesis of elevated antecedent soil moisture condition, providing the reconstruction of the investigated flood event, which peak discharge (occurred on 17 June at 23:05) was calculated equal to 168,4 m^3/s, at the outlet of the Lama Balice.

4.1 Hydrological Model Calibration

To evaluate the performances of the adopted HEC-GeoHMS hydrological model, the maximum observed water level, obtained by performing a field campaign on five selected "control sections", was reproduced by one-dimensional (1D) hydraulic simulation and the corresponding flow rate (then indirectly evaluated) has been compared to the ground effect (in terms of discharge) evaluated by hydrological simulation. In the following Fig. 5 the five selected "control sections" located on the main stream of the investigated river basin are indicated, where significant traces (displayed in the Fig. 1) due to the occurrence of the flood event were observed.

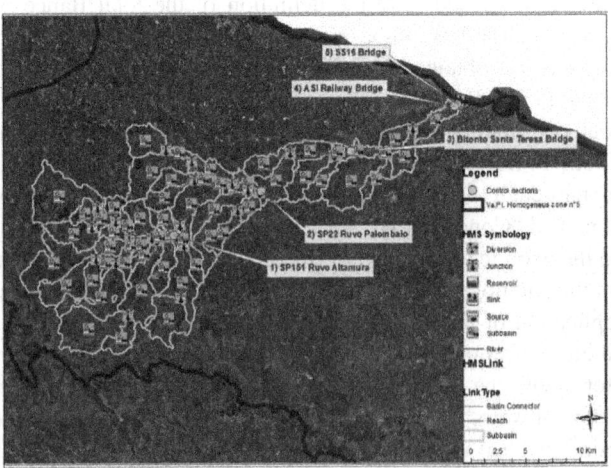

Fig. 5. Control sections used for calibration analysis

The results of a comparison between the HEC-GeoHMS simulated discharges in the five selected "control sections" and those indirectly estimated through the application of the 1D hydraulic model are resumed in the following Table 2; it is necessary to point out that at the outlet of the Lama Balice (Sect. 5, SS 16 BRIDGE), the simulated flow is sensibly overestimated in comparison with the one observed during the flood event. The 1D Model have been implemented thanks to the LiDAR laser altimetry technology.

Table 2. A comparison between simulate and observed flow values at the selected five "control sections" before and after calibration procedure

Sections		Q values at the peak [m³/s] before calibration		Q values at the peak [m³/s] after calibration		
		Observed	Simulated	Observed	Simulated	
		(Estimated through the hydraulic model HEC-RAS)	From the hydrological model HEC-HMS	(Estimated through the hydraulic model HEC-RAS)	From the hydrological model HEC-HMS	
		[m³/s]	Peak [m³/s]	[m³/s]	Peak [m³/s]	Peak time
1	SP151 Ruvo-Altamura	60	60	60	60.4	June, 17 – 19:15
2	SP22 Ruvo-Palombaio	70	85.5	70	69.7	June, 17 – 22:00
3	Bitonto Santa Teresa Bridge	85	123.2	85	85	June, 17 – 23:55
4	ASI Railway Bridge	95	168.4	95	95.5	June, 18 – 01:35
5	SS16 Bridge	95	168.4	95	95.5	June, 18 – 01:35

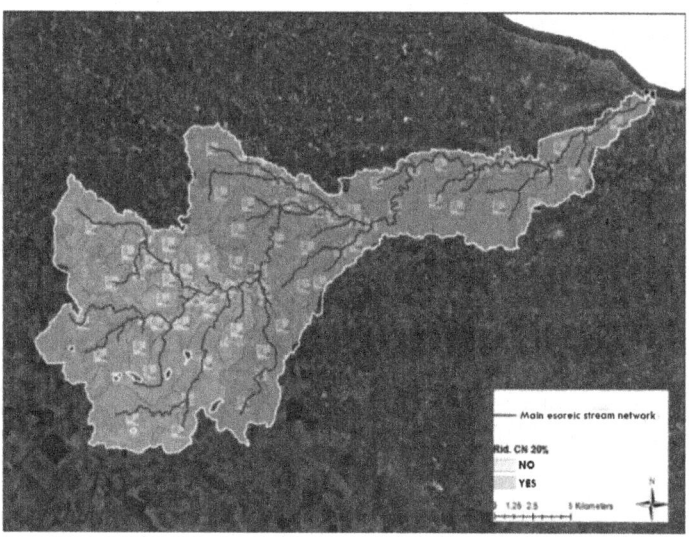

Fig. 6. Basin areas affected by the reduction of curve number

Table 3. Resulting hydrograph obtained from the calibrated hydrological model and the correspondent hydraulic sections extracted from the HEC-RAS.

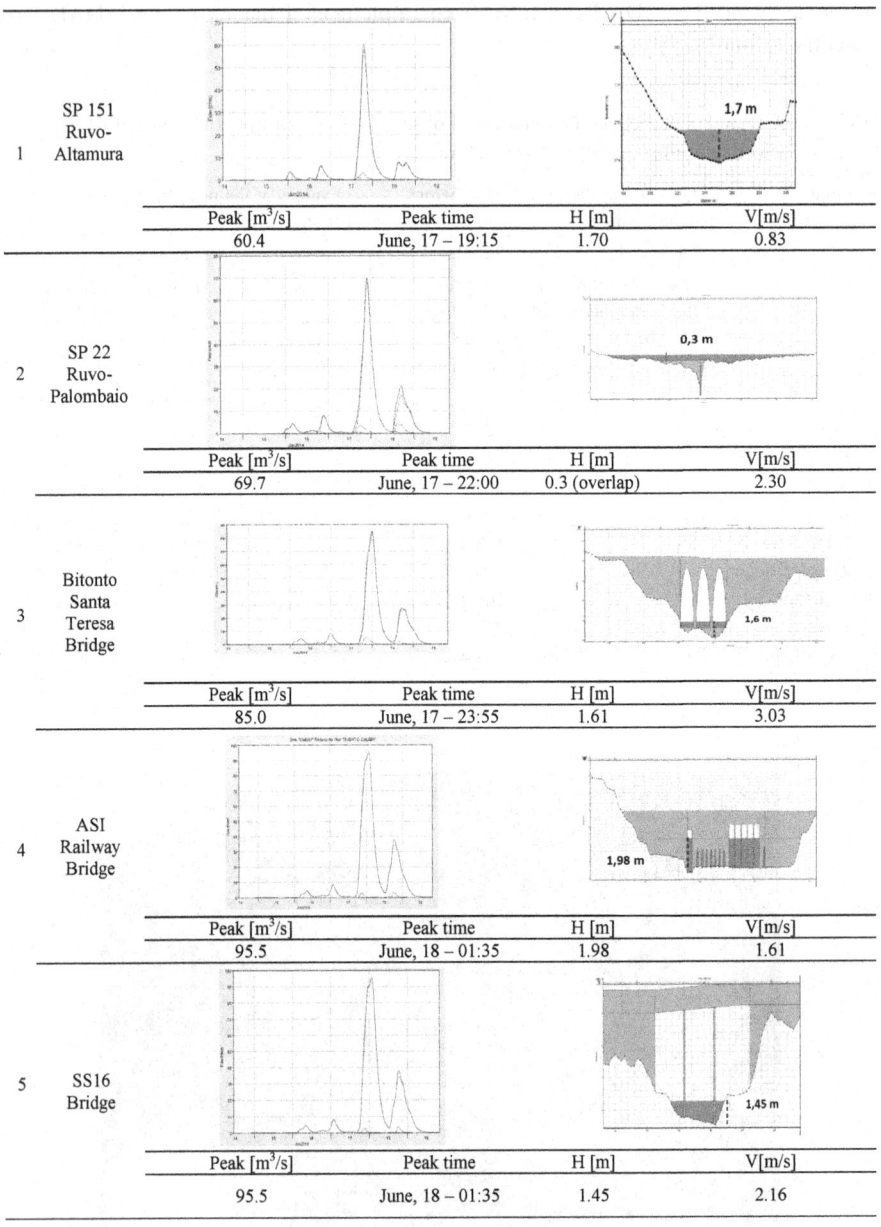

		Peak [m³/s]	Peak time	H [m]	V[m/s]
1	SP 151 Ruvo-Altamura	60.4	June, 17 – 19:15	1.70	0.83
2	SP 22 Ruvo-Palombaio	69.7	June, 17 – 22:00	0.3 (overlap)	2.30
3	Bitonto Santa Teresa Bridge	85.0	June, 17 – 23:55	1.61	3.03
4	ASI Railway Bridge	95.5	June, 18 – 01:35	1.98	1.61
5	SS16 Bridge	95.5	June, 18 – 01:35	1.45	2.16

Among the different factors that determine the difference between the observed and the simulated flow rates, the most significant is the Curve Number value that was estimated in the first instance by using literature's values, exploiting the lithological map extracted from ACLA2 Project and Corine land cover classification. After further analysis, we chose to reduce this value by 20% for the sub-basins downstream the provincial road Ruvo-Altamura (as reported in the Fig. 6) so, leaving unchanged all the other parameters, and obtaining the results reported in Table 2.

The defined model significantly represents the hydrological response to the considered event occurred on June 2014; in the following Table 3 the resulting hydrographs obtained by the application of the calibrated hydrological model and the correspondent hydraulic sections, extracted from the HEC-RAS geometry for all the control sections are reported:

4.2 Flood Hazard Evaluation

The goal of the proposed work was to define the hydraulic hazard maps, corresponding to return periods of 30, 200 and 500 years.

In this context, the performed calibration analysis allowed the definition of the hydrological model parameters, able to give a reliable response of the real functioning of the Lama Balice basin, under the occurrence of the investigated flood event. Under the hypothesis of stationarity of the statistical variables responsible for the hydrological response of the basin, the defined hydrological model can be applied to evaluate flood hydrographs generated upon the occurrence of meteoric events with return periods of 30, 200 and 500 years. To this end, we used the rainfall analysis performed by the VAPI Puglia methodology, according to which Lama Balice watershed is entirely within the homogeneous zone indicated with the number five, among the six zones defined by the regionalization of the third order statistic moment (see Fig. 5); the application of this methodology provides the estimation of the intensity duration curve for each assigned return period; hereafter in Fig. 7 the three depth duration curves for the selected return periods of 30, 200 and 500 years are reported:

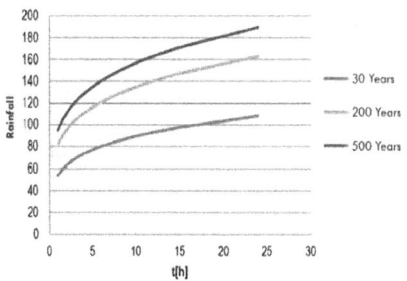

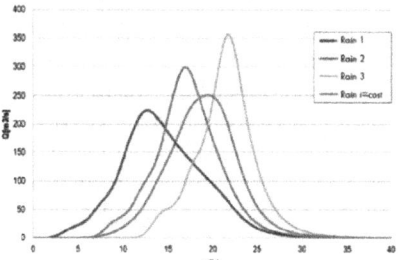

Fig. 7. Depth duration curves for the selected return periods of 30, 200 and 500 years.

Fig. 8. Hydrographs resulting from different precipitation distributions with a duration of 12 h and return period of 200 years.

The corrivation time estimation was conducted introducing a constant rainfall intensity with different durations and return period of 200 years in the HEC-GeoHMS hydrological model; the critical duration (equal to 12 h) of the entire Balice basin, was defined as the duration that maximizes the peak flow rate. So, in order to define the critical temporal distribution of the precipitation, different precipitation distributions of duration equal to 12 h and return time of 200 years have been hypothesized, using the different rainfall depths (between 1 to 12 h) extracted from the depth duration curve previously calculated and reported in Fig. 7. Then four different scenarios of precipitation have been hypothesized:

1. Meteoric event with a decreasing rainfall intensity – "Rain 1"
2. Meteoric event with an increasing and a decreasing intensity – "Rain 2"
3. Meteoric event with an increasing rainfall intensity – "Rain 3"
4. Meteoric event with a constant intensity "Rain const";

The four meteoric events were then implemented in the calibrated hydrological HEC-GeoHMS model, in order to find the one that maximizes the discharge; so, the third hypothesis was selected giving the highest peak equal to 356,1 m³/s (see Fig. 8).

Therefore, the hypothesis of a meteoric event with an increasing rainfall intensity and duration of 12 h is that used as rainfall input of the hydrological analysis, conducted to define hydraulic hazard maps corresponding to return periods of 30, 200 and 500 years. With this aim a combined scheme of a one-two dimensional flood propagation was considered, introducing as boundary conditions the flood hydrographs (corresponding to return periods of 30, 200 and 500 years) resulting from the application of the HEC-GeoHMS calibrated model; moreover a variable Manning roughness value, evaluated exploiting the Corine land-use map of Puglia, was used in the present work.

In particular, a 1D approach (HEC-RAS) was used to simulate flood propagation where only one direction may be identified (see Fig. 9), while where the hypothesis of one-directional propagation is not true, we used the SMS-TUFLOW software (see Fig. 9) based on a two-dimensional (2D) hydraulic approach. Models have been implemented thanks to the laser altimetry technology LiDAR, which provides the definition of a computation domain with square grid cells with size equal to $5 * 5$ m², while at the mouth of Lama Balice, because of the presence of the road infrastructures, the mono/two-dimensional hydraulic model has been realized with a computation domain characterized by square grids cells with size equal to $2 * 2$ m². The resolution of the 2D models was defined considering the right compromise between the high resolution of a LiDAR topographical map and the elaboration capacity of the available calculators. The spatial distribution of flow depth and velocity obtained by SMS-TUFLOW application, close to the mouth of the investigated basin, is reported in Fig. 10.

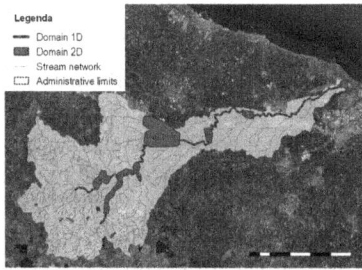

Fig. 9. Localization of the adopted mono and two-dimensional approaches.

Fig. 10. Application of a 2-D model.

The hydrological and hydraulic assessments achieved according to the above described methodology in a portion of territory crossed by the Lama Balice stream network, allow the definition of the areas with different degree of hydraulic hazard: high (T = 30 years), medium (T = 200 years) and low (T = 500 years); they have been obtained combining water depths and velocities respectively major than 0.2 m and 0.52 m/s, for each selected return period. Below, in the Fig. 11, the hazard maps corresponding to return periods of 30 (in dark cyan), 200 (in light cyan) and 500 (in grey) years are reported.

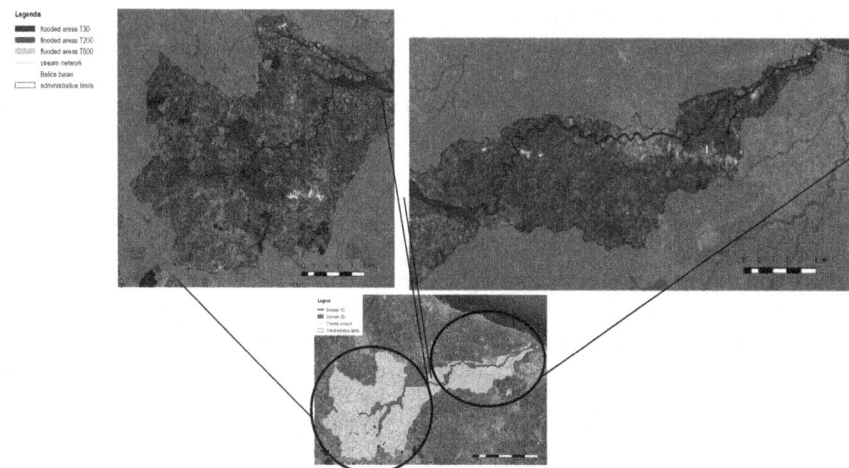

Fig. 11. Hazard maps corresponding to return periods of 30, 200 and 500 years (Color figure online)

5 Conclusions

In order to support institutions and professionals for the assessment of techniques of dynamic hazard and risk evaluation, in the proposed work a rational for the delineation of flood hazard maps is described; they were obtained using a combined scheme of a mono/two-dimensional flood propagation approach, coupled to an hydrological model for boundary conditions evaluation.

In particular hazard maps of 30, 200 and 500 years have been depicted in a portion of territory crossed by the Lama Balice stream network, by using the HEC-GeoHMS hydrological model, which calibration was performed on a flood event occurred in June 2014, using water depths observations on five important infrastructures located inside the Balice river basin.

The simulated flood hydrographs corresponding to the three selected return periods have been implemented in a mono/two-dimensional hydraulic model generated by using high-resolution Digital Terrain Models (DTMs), obtained by a LiDAR remote sensing technique.

References

1. CRED - Centre for Research on the Epidemiology of Disasters – Human cost of natural disaster: a global perspective (2015). http://emdat.be/human_cost_natdis
2. Reynard, N.S., Prudhomme, C., Crooks, S.M.: The flood characteristics of large U.K. rivers: potential effects of changing climate and land use. Clim. Change **48**(2–3), 343–359 (2001)
3. Bronstert, A., Niehoff, D., Burger, G.: Effects of climate and land-use change on storm runoff generation: present knowledge and modelling capabilities. Hydrol. Process. **16**(2), 509–529 (2002)
4. Brath, A., Montanari, A., Moretti, G.: Assessing the effect on flood frequency of land use change via hydrological simulation (with uncertainty). J. Hydrol. **324**(1–4), 141–153 (2006)
5. Jafarzadegan, K., Merwade, V.: A DEM-based approach for large-scale floodplain mapping in ungauged watersheds. J. Hydrol. **550**, 650–662 (2017)
6. Manfreda, S., Samela, C., Sole, A., Fiorentino, M.: Flood-Prone Areas Assessment Using Linear Binary Classifiers Based on Morphological Indices. Vulnerability, Uncertainty, and Risk, 2002–2011 (2014). https://doi.org/10.1061/9780784413609.201
7. Jain, S.K., Singh, R.D., Jain, M.K., Lohani, A.K.: Delineation of flood-prone areas using remote sensing techniques. Water Resour. Manag. **19**, 333–347 (2005)
8. Totaro, V., Gioia, A., Novelli, A., Caradonna, G.: The use of geomorphological descriptors and landsat-8 spectral indices data for flood areas evaluation: a case study of Lato river basin. In: Gervasi, O., et al. (eds.) ICCSA 2017. LNCS, vol. 10407, pp. 30–44. Springer, Cham (2017). https://doi.org/10.1007/978-3-319-62401-3_3
9. Van Alphen, J., Martini, F., Loat, R., Slomp, R., Passchier, R.: Flood risk mapping in Europe, experiences and best practices. J. Flood Risk Manag. **2**, 285–292 (2009)
10. De Giorgis, M., Gnecco, G., Gorni, S., Roth, G., Sanguineti, M., Taramasso, A.C.: Classifiers for the detection of flood-prone areas using remote sensed elevation data. J. Hydrol. **470–471**, 302–315 (2012)

11. Gioia, A., Totaro, V., Bonelli, R., Esposito, A.A.M.G., Balacco, G., Iacobellis, V.: Flood susceptibility evaluation on ephemeral streams of Southern Italy: a case study of Lama Balice. In: Gervasi, O., et al. (eds.) ICCSA 2018. LNCS, vol. 10964, pp. 348–362. Springer, Cham (2018)

12. Biancamaria, S., Boone, A.A., Mognard, N.: Large-scale coupled hydrologic and hydraulic modelling of an Artic river: the Ob River in Siberia. J. Hydrol. **379**, 136–150 (2009)

13. Fiorentino, M., Gioia, A., Iacobellis, V., Manfreda, S.: Regional analysis of runoff thresholds behaviour in Southern Italy based on theoretically derived distributions. Adv. Geosci. **26**, 139–144 (2011). ISSN 1680-7340

14. Leandro, J., Chen, A.S., Djordjevic, S., Savic, D.A.: Comparison of 1D/1D and 1D/2D coupled (sewer/surface) hydraulic models for urban flood simulation. J. Hydraul. Eng. **135** (6), 495–504 (2009)

15. Ghimire, S., Wilkinson, M., Donaldson-Selby, G.: Application of 1D and 2D numerical models for assessing and visualizing effectiveness of natural flood management measures. In: 11th International Conference on Hydroinformatics (2014)

16. Gioia, A., Iacobellis, V., Manfreda, S., Fiorentino, M.: Influence of infiltration and soil storage capacity on the skewness of the annual maximum flood peaks in a theoretically derived distribution. Hydrol. Earth Syst. Sci. **16**, 937–951 (2012)

17. Gioia, A., Manfreda, S., Iacobellis, V., Fiorentino, M.: Performance of a theoretical model for the description of water balance and runoff dynamics in Southern Italy. J. Hydrol. Eng. **19**(6), 1113–1123 (2014)

18. Jasper, K., Gurtz, J., Lang, H.: Advanced flood forecasting in Alpine watersheds by coupling meteorological observations and forecasts with a distributed hydrological model. J. Hydrol. **267**(1–2), 40–52 (2002)

19. Di Modugno, M., Gioia, A., Gorgoglione, A., Iacobellis, V., La Forgia, G., Piccinni, A.F., Ranieri, E.: Build-up/wash-off monitoring and assessment for sustainable management of first flush in an urban area. Sustainability (Switzerland) **7**(5), 5050–5070 (2015)

20. Fiorentino, M., Gioia, A., Iacobellis, V., Manfreda, S.: Analysis on flood generation processes by means of a continuous simulation model. Adv. Geosci. **7**, 231–236 (2006). ISSN 1680-7340

21. Grimaldi, S., Petroselli, A., Arcangeletti, E., Nardi, F.: Flood mapping in ungauged basins using fully continuous hydrologic–hydraulic modeling. J. Hydrol. **487**, 39–47 (2013)

22. Beven, K.: Rainfall-Runoff Modelling the Primer, 2nd edn. Wiley-Blackwell, Chichester (2012)

23. Cantisani, A., Giosa, L., Mancusi, L., Sole, A.: FLORA-2D: a new model to simulate the inundation in areas covered by flexible and rigid vegetation. Int. J. Eng. Innov. Technol. **3**, 179–186 (2014)

24. Gioia, A.: Reservoir routing on double-peak design flood. Water **8**, 553 (2016)

25. Gioia, A., Iacobellis, V., Manfreda, S., Fiorentino, M.: Comparison of different methods describing the peak runoff contributing areas during floods. Hydrol. Process. **31**(11), 2041–2049 (2017)

26. Cobby, D.M., Mason, D.C., Horritt, M.S., Bates, P.D.: Two-dimensional hydraulic flood modelling using a finite-element mesh decomposed according to vegetation and topographic features derived from airborne scanning laser altimetry. Hydrol. Process. **17**, 1979–2000 (2003)

27. Fluet-Chouinard, E., Lehner, B., Rebelo, L.-M.P.F., Hamilton, S.K.: Development of a global inundation map at high spatial resolution from topographic downscaling of coarse-scale remote sensing data. Remote Sens. Environ. **158**, 348–361 (2014)

28. Iacobellis, V., Castorani, A., Di Santo, A.R., Gioia, A.: Rationale for flood prediction in karst endorheic areas. J. Arid Environ. **112**(PA), 98–108 (2015)

29. Manfreda, S., Samela, C., Gioia, A., Consoli, G.G., Iacobellis, V., Giuzio, L., Cantisani, A., Sole, A.: Flood-prone areas assessment using linear binary classifiers based on flood maps obtained from 1D and 2D hydraulic models. Nat. Hazards **79**(2), 735–754 (2015)

30. Bates, P.D., Horritt, M.S., Smith, C.N., Mason, D.C.: Integrating remote sensing observations of flood hydrology and hydraulic modelling. Hydrol. Process. **11**, 1777–1795 (1997)

31. Horritt, M.S., Mason, D.C., Luckman, A.J.: Flood boundary delineation from synthetic aperture radar imagery using a statistical active contour model. Int. J. Remote. Sens. **22**(13), 2489–2507 (2001)

32. Balenzano, A., Satalino, G., Belmonte, A., D'Urso, G., Capodici, F., Iacobellis, V., Gioia, A., Rinaldi, M., Ruggieri, S., Mattia, F.: On the use of multi-temporal series of COSMO-SkyMed data for landcover classification and surface parameter retrieval over agricultural sites. In: Proceedings of the 2011 IEEE International Geoscience and Remote Sensing Symposium, Vancouver, Canada, pp. 142–145 (2011)

33. Mattia, F., Satalino, G., Balenzano, A., D'Urso, G., Capodici, F., Iacobellis, V., Milella, P., Gioia, A., Rinaldi, M., Ruggieri, S., Dini, L.: Time series of COSMO-SkyMed data for landcover classification and surface parameter retrieval over agricultural sites. In: Proceedings of the IEEE 2012 International Geoscience and Remote Sensing Symposium, IGARSS 2012, Munich, Germany (2012)

34. Balenzano, A., Satalino, G., Iacobellis, V., Gioia, A., Manfreda, S., Rinaldi, M., De Vita, P., Miglietta, F., Toscano, P., Annichiarico, G., Mattia, F.: A ground network for sar-derived soil moisture product calibration, validation and exploitation in southern Italy. In: Proceedings of the IEEE 2014 International Geoscience and Remote Sensing Symposium, IGARSS 2014, Quèbec, Canada (2014)

35. Tarantino, E., Novelli, A., Laterza, M., Gioia, A.: Testing high spatial resolution WorldView-2 imagery for retrieving the leaf area index. In: Proceedings of SPIE 9535, Third International Conference on Remote Sensing and Geoinformation of the Environment (RSCy2015) (2015)

36. Trombetta, A., Iacobellis, V., Tarantino, E., Gentile, F.: Calibration of the AquaCrop model for winter wheat using MODIS LAI images. Agric. Water Manag. **164**(Part 2), 304–316 (2016)

37. Iacobellis, V., Gioia, A., Milella, P., Satalino, G., Balenzano, A., Mattia, F.: Inter-comparison of hydrological model simulations with time series of SAR-derived soil moisture maps. Eur. J. Remote Sens. **46**(1), 739–757 (2013)

38. Olang, L.O., Kundu, P., Bauer, T., Fürst, J.: Analysis of spatio-temporal land cover changes for hydrological impact assessment within the Nyando River Basin of Kenya. Environ. Monit. Assess. **179**, 389–401 (2011)

39. Pattison, I., Lane, S.N.: The link between land-use management and fluvial flood risk: a chaotic conception? Prog. Phys. Geogr. **36**, 72–92 (2011)

40. Balacco, G., Figorito, B., Tarantino, E., Gioia, A., Iacobellis, V.: Space-time LAI variability in Northern Puglia (Italy) from SPOT VGT data. Environ. Monit. Assess. **187**, 434 (2015)

41. Caprioli, M., Tarantino, E.: Identification of land cover alterations in the Alta Murgia National Park (Italy) with VHR satellite imagery. Int. J. Sustain. Dev. Plan. **1**(3), 261–270 (2006)

42. Crocetto, N., Tarantino, E.: A class-oriented strategy for features extraction from multidate ASTER imagery. Remote Sens. **1**(4), 1171–1189 (2009)

43. Killinger, D.K.: Lidar (Light Detection and Ranging) Laser Spectroscopy for Sensing Fundamentals, Techniques and Applications, pp. 292–312 (2014)

44. Feldman, A.D.: Hydrologic Modeling System HEC-HMS. US Army Corps of Engineers, Institute for Water Resources, Hydrologic Engineering Center, USA (2000)

45. SCS (USDA Soil Conservation Service): National Engineering Handbook, Section 4: Hydrology. U.S. Department of Agriculture, Washington, DC, USA (1972)

46. Claps, P., Copertino, V.A., Ermini, R., Fiorentino, M.: Analisi regionale dei massimi annuali delle precipitazioni di diversa durata. In: Valutazione delle piene in Puglia, CNR-GNDCI, Potenza (1992)

47. Regione Puglia: Progetto Acla 2: Studio per la caratterizzazione agronomica della Regione Puglia e la classificazione del territorio in funzione della potenzialità produttiva. http://www. cartografico.puglia.it. Accessed 07 Mar 2018

48. EEA: CORINE Land Cover Project, published by Commission of the European Communities (1995)

49. USDA-SCS: National Engineering Handbook, Sec, 4 - Hydrology, Washington, D.C. (1985)

50. USACE, Hydrologic Engineering Center: River Analysis System HEC-RAS. Hydraulic Reference Manual version 3.0, January 2001. www.usace.army.mil

51. Aquaveo: Water modeling solutions. http://www.aquaveo.com/. Accessed 02 Mar 2013

Flood Susceptibility Evaluation on Ephemeral Streams of Southern Italy: A Case Study of Lama Balice

Andrea Gioia[1], Vincenzo Totaro[1(✉)], Rocco Bonelli[2],
Alisa A. M. G. Esposito[2], Gabriella Balacco[1], and Vito Iacobellis[1]

[1] DICATECh - Department of Civil, Environmental, Land, Building
Engineering and Chemistry, Politecnico di Bari, via Orabona 4, 70125 Bari, Italy
{andrea.gioia,vincenzo.totaro,gabriella.balacco,
vito.iacobellis}@poliba.it
[2] Basin Authority of Puglia, SP62, 70010 Bari, Italy
{rocco.bonelli,alisa.esposito}@adb.puglia.it

Abstract. In the proposed work areas exposed to flood risk were evaluated in a particular context of karst ephemeral streams located in Puglia region (Southern Italy). The case study of Lama Balice, characterized by a natural geomorphologic structure, was tested for the application of a DTM-based approach, aimed to the rapid identification and mapping of flood risk. The inundated areas, obtained with a 2D hydraulic model, following design rainfall events characterized by different return periods, were used as reference maps for the selection of the most appropriate geomorphological descriptor exploiting the binary classifiers test. The performance of the adopted procedure was tested by validating the selected geomorphological descriptors on a different area with respect to that used for calibration, in order to estimate the discrepancy between DTM-based flood maps and those obtained by numerical simulation.

Keywords: Geomorphological descriptors · Flooded areas
DTM-based approach

1 Introduction

"Lame" are shallow karst ephemeral/episodic streams which characterize the Puglia region located in Southern Italy. Typically, they run down from Murgia plateau to Adriatic and Ionian Seas and are mainly present both in the metropolitan area of Bari and in the Taranto province. Along the coast of Bari there are the mouths of nine "lame", running from the north-western Murgia towards the Adriatic Sea (Balice, Lamasinata, Villa Lamberti, Picone, Fitta, Valenzano, San Marco, San Giorgio and Giotta). Instead along the Ionian coast of the region, there are two important "lame", located near Palagiano municipality: the lama Lenne, which flows into the sea and the Chiàtone Lama which flows into the river Lato before reaching the Ionian Sea.

These incisions are unique geomorphologic structures, characterized by very fertile alluvial soils as opposed to the limestone and the outcroppings typical of the "Alta Murgia", a plateau located on the northwestern part of Puglia and marked by broad

© Springer International Publishing AG, part of Springer Nature 2018
O. Gervasi et al. (Eds.): ICCSA 2018, LNCS 10964, pp. 334–348, 2018.
https://doi.org/10.1007/978-3-319-95174-4_27

fractures. Instead the less elevated zone of Murgia is composed of a calcareous platform covered by a thin layer of reddish clay, rich in iron peroxide with fragments of limestone. These characteristics, together with the presence of water, had favored human settlements since the Neolithic age. This is evident from a lot of rupestrian settlements excavated into the soft limestone.

The limestone of the Murgia is characterized by high infiltration capacity, with the consequence that its drainage networks has no significant flows for long periods and is formed by numerous natural incisions (ephemeral/episodic rivers) that in some cases disappear into the ground through sinkholes. As opposed, when extreme rainfall events exceed the soil infiltration capacity, extreme floods may occur in these areas, that are often unprepared to receive these natural phenomena, which become more difficult to prevent and deal with, generating devastating effects. These latter even more evident in presence of climatic factors rapidly changing or in areas where human factors have led to the reduction of the natural water retention capacity of the soil.

This kind of floods are becoming more frequent in recent decades; for this reason, the recent European legislation on flood risk protection (Floods Directive 2007/60/EC [1]), European programs of scientific research (as Horizon 2020) and institutions (like the Basin Authorities and Civil Protection agencies) had focused their attention on the definition of dynamic hazard assessment techniques for urban territory protection.

In recent years, much effort has gone into the identification of areas exposed to flood hazard through the use of a combined scheme of hydrological and hydraulic models; the former are useful for the definition of flood events (e.g. [2–10]) and for dam and reservoir management (e.g. [11–15]); the latter are adopted for evaluating flood propagation and areas exposed to inundations (e.g. [16–22]) with different level of accuracy. These models, in more cases, are difficult to be applied because of their parameterization, that needs to be calibrated and/or validated in areas with scarce availability of hydrological/hydraulic information, due to difficult of performing adequate monitoring campaigns.

In this context, for satisfying the needs of recent legislation and the increasing requirements of end users, the challenge of the scientific community is to improve and develop new techniques able to provide a rapid identification of a flood susceptibility. This necessity is greater in areas with limited availability of hydrological information, in order to select study areas that need major insights, avoiding expensive and time-consuming analyses on the whole river basin.

In the last few decades sophisticated earth observation techniques, able to monitor from remote sensor the spatio-temporal evolution of terrestrial phenomena, provide distributed information for hydraulic/hydrological application (e.g. [23–29]) even in territories where there is limited availability of the data measured in situ, such as extensive and reliable maps of vegetation status (e.g. [30–34]) and soil moisture condition (e.g. [35]) respectively used for building datasets (e.g. [36]) and for calibration/validation of hydrological models (e.g. [37]).

In particular new technologies for the measurement of surface elevation (i.e. global positioning systems [GPS], synthetic aperture radar [SAR] interferometry, airborne laser altimetry technology [LiDAR, Light Detection And Ranging]) provide the increasing availability of high-resolution topographical data (digital terrain models-DTMs), giving strong impulse to the development of DTM-based hydrogeomorphic models (e.g. [38, 39]) that allow to obtain indices that can provide reliable information on flood susceptibility (e.g. [22, 40–43]), using only geomorphological information.

This study is focused on the Lama Balice, which has a geographic and historical importance and is one of the most significant karst phenomena of central Puglia region, in terms of both flood risk and naturalistic landscapes. Over the centuries it has periodically been used as an open urban waste dump, ignoring its environmental value.

The lama Balice preserves long stream pathway with a natural behavior, but it is possible to find areas subject to anthropic transformations, like Bitonto town and different crossings of roads and railways.

In this context, we propose a procedure for a preliminary rapid identification of areas exposed to inundations by applying a DTM-based approach, in order to demonstrate the performances of this methodology for an a-priori estimation of flood susceptibility. Specifically, different synthetic and composite descriptors, were performed to ephemeral/episodic incisions of Balice Lama, located in Puglia region - Southern Italy. The inundated areas, obtained with a 2D hydraulic model, for three design events characterized by return periods (T) of 30, 200 and 500 years were used for the selection of the most performant geomorphological basin descriptor. The achieved results are useful to support institutions and professionals for improving evaluation procedures for flood risk assessment, Civil Protection emergency plans or defining prioritary mitigation investments.

2   Case Study

The best geomorphological descriptor for the identification of floodable areas (given a design meteoric event), was derived over the Balice river basin; Fig. 1 shows in green the calibration domain located downstream the river basin and in yellow the validation domain located upstream, next to Bitonto town; moreover, flooded areas with return period of 200 years within the investigated domains are highlighted with black contours. Calibration and validation domains were selected on the base of the availability of digital terrain model with high resolution.

Lama Balice originates in the municipal areas of Ruvo di Puglia and Corato and, oriented in a SW-NE direction, slopes down towards the sea crossing the territories of Terlizzi and Bitonto cities. It has a drainage area of 339.61 km^2, average slope equal to 4.84%, mean and maximum altitude respectively equal to 316.87 and 635 m.a.s.l.; it is part of a protected area of Regional Natural Park, characterized by the highest percentage of vegetation, rich in olive trees, downy and holm oak; its mouth is covered by a forest (about 50% of rate) with plant species such as Typha, Phragmites austrialis mixed algae and a few tufts of beached Posidonia oceanica.

In the lama Balice two morphological configurations are present: one is shallower and more sinuous, while the other, where the incision increases appreciably, is characterized by steep cliffs where the stratified limestone can be observed. Moreover, there are natural occurring caves, which still retain traces of ancient prehistoric settlements and there is also abundant evidence of medieval houses, churches and farms (e.g. [44]).

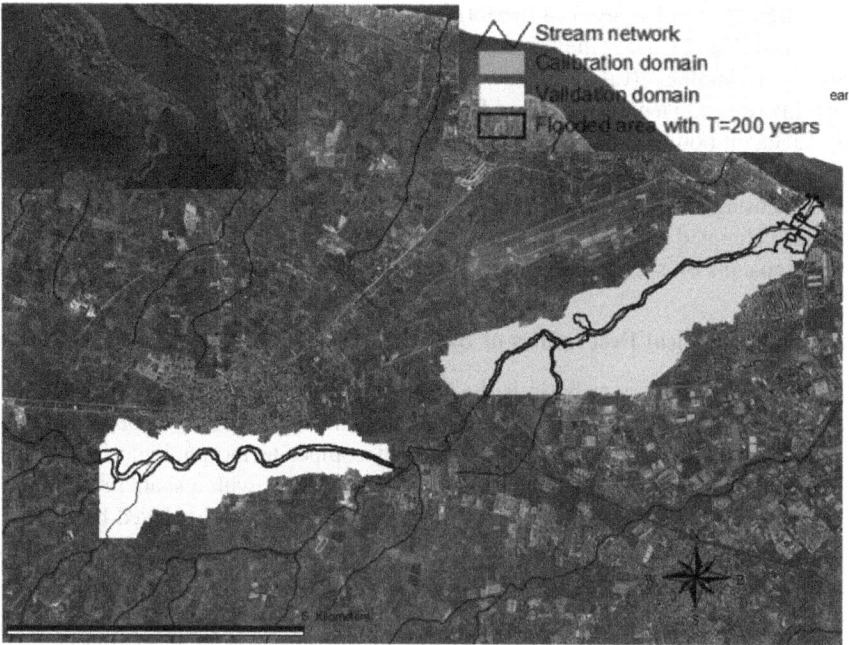

Fig. 1. Study area. Coordinate System UTM WGS 84 zone 33N. In yellow is reported the validation area and in green the calibration area; black contours delineate flooded area with T = 200 years. (Color figure online)

3 Methodologies

In the following section are illustrated: the hydrologic/hydraulic approach for the definition of the reference map of flooded area; the different geomorphological descriptors (synthetic and composite), used for the reconstruction of floodable areas and the binary classifiers method for the selection of the most appropriate basin descriptor.

3.1 Hydrologic/Hydraulic Modeling

The inundated areas of three design events characterized by return periods of 30, 200 and 500 years, were used as reference flooding maps for the selection of the most performant DTM-based basin descriptor. In particular, the reference maps (extracted from the database of the Basin Authority of Puglia e.g. http://www.adb.puglia.it/public/news.php) were determined by using a mono/two-dimensional hydraulic approach (Hec-Ras [45], FLO-2D [46]) coupled to the CN SCS hydrological model (e.g. [47]) for the estimation of flood hydrographs consequent to the selected three design events. The hydrological/hydraulic evaluation was preceded by a morphological analysis, aimed to the preliminary selection of the natural depressions in GIS environment. The rainfall analysis was performed exploiting the VAPI methodology (e.g. [48]).

Numerical simulations were performed over the selected computational domains (reported in Fig. 1), using the Digital Terrain Model (DTM) obtained by airborne laser altimetry technology (LiDAR). A valuable characteristic of this technology is the capability to derive a high-resolution DTMs from the last pulse LiDAR data by filtering the vegetation points (e.g. [49]).

Selected flood events were reproduced introducing the simulated hydrographs (obtained using the hydrological model) as boundary condition. The hydraulic modeling has been calibrated by means of a comparison with flooded areas and depth evaluated by field campaigns on site, carried out during the flood event occurred on 14 June 2017.

3.2   Morphological Descriptors of Basin

The morphology of a river basin is the basic element that allows the identification of the effects of the runoff distribution, resulting from the occurrence of a meteoric forcing as input to the basin itself. The synthetic and composite morphological descriptors analyzed in this paper were obtained from a DTM LiDAR with a spatial resolution of $2 * 2$ m. As observed in [50], an important role in this context is played by the DTM characteristics, which provides a relevant influence on results analysis. In the following, we analyzed some of the descriptors shown in [51].

Synthetic Descriptors

- *upslope contributing area, A_s [m^2]*;
- *distance from the nearest stream, D [m]:* length of path connecting present cell with that hydrologically connected on the drainage network;
- *elevation to the nearest stream, H [m]:* unlike the previous one, which evaluate path length between two defined points, this index computes their elevation difference.

It is worth noting that these descriptors take into account both the morphological structure of the basin and its hydrological characteristics (fundamental for the analysis).

Composite Descriptors

- *modified topographic index, TI_m:* proposed by [52] as a reworking of the topographic index proposed by [53], introducing an exponent $n < 1$

$$TI_m = ln\left(\frac{A_d^n}{tan(\beta)}\right) \quad (1)$$

being A_d the drainage area per unit contour length, $tan(\beta)$ the local gradient and n a dimensionless parameter with values lesser than 1.

- *downslope index, DW_i,* introduced by [54], its expression is

$$DW_i = \frac{d}{L_d} \quad (2)$$

which allows to evaluate the length (L_d) of the flow path which leads a loss of water potential energy of d(m). It is a way to estimate local hydraulic gradient. We imposed $d = 5$ m (as stated in [22]).

- $ln(hl/H)$: this index relates, in each point, water depth h_l with the synthetic descriptor H, where h_l can be defined for each basin location with the following relationship:

$$h_l \cong bA_l^n \tag{3}$$

with A_l [m^2] upslope contributing area at the considered point, b a scale factor usually set equal to 10^{-2} and n a dimensionless exponent set equal to 0.3 as stated in [50].
- *Geomorphic Flood Index (GFI)* $ln(h_r/H)$: this index is different from the previous, because the upslope contributing area A_r is evaluated on the cell belonging to the hydrographic network hydraulically nearest to the considered cell.
- *($h_r - H$)/D*: ratio between the difference of water depth h_r and H, and the distance D;
- *($h_r - H$)/DW$_i$*: ratio between the difference of water depth h_r and H, and the downslope index;
- H/D: this index is evaluated as the ratio between the single descriptors H and D.

3.3   Linear Binary Classifiers Method and ROC Curves

The reliability of these index in the evaluation of flood-prone areas has been tested using the linear binary classifiers method, proposed by [41].

The implementation of this methodology involves a preliminary processing, by scaling and normalizing the descriptor in the range [−1, 1]; to find the optimum value of the descriptor, a calibration procedure is performed using a moving threshold. Therefore, for each assigned threshold the map of the geomorphological descriptor is converted into binary type (using 0 for non-flooded cells and 1 for inundated ones) and compared with the reference map (preliminarily converted in binary type), providing the following classification:

- TP (True Positive): the classifier correctly identifies a flooded element reported on the reference map;
- FP (False Positive): the cell is inundated for the classifier, but the flood reference map doesn't identify it as an element of a flood prone area;
- TN (True Negative): the classifier correctly identifies a not flooded element;
- FN (False Negative): the cell is not inundated for the classifier, but the flood reference map identifies it as an element of a flood prone area.

Defining the *true positive rate* r_{tp} and *false positive rate* r_{fp} the following ration:

$$r_{tp} = \frac{TP}{TP + FN} \tag{4}$$

$$r_{fp} = \frac{FP}{FP + TN} \tag{5}$$

the best performing threshold can be evaluated by minimizing the following objective function:

$$OB = r_{fp} + \left(1 - r_{tp}\right) \tag{6}$$

Furthermore, other considerations can be carried out by constructing the Receiver Operating Characteristic (ROC), which relates false positive and true positive rates for each assigned threshold. The computation of the underlying area (AUC) (e.g. [55]) is an interesting tool for comparing different indices and obtaining a better comprehension of the results.

4   Results and Discussion

In this section the performances achieved by a comparison between flooding maps obtained by the application of hydrologic/hydraulic model (with reference to three selected design events with return period of 30, 200 and 500 years) with those obtained by the use of geomorphological descriptors on the Balice river basin are described. Moreover, the analysis provided the evaluation of the effects of the return period on the estimation of both the optimal value of the geomorphological descriptor and its performances in terms of flooded areas delineation. The investigation was conducted over a validation selected area, in order to assess the reliability of the proposed procedure. In particular, in the following the behavior of the different investigated descriptors is described, focusing the attention on the most performants.

4.1   Performances of Geomorphological Indices

The calibration of geomorphological descriptors has been carried out in an area close to the outlet of the river basin (see Fig. 1), by seeking the τ value of the threshold that minimized the objective function (see Tables 1 and 2) obtained by comparing geomorphological and reference hydraulic flood maps, corresponding to three selected design flood events of return periods of 30, 200 and 500 years. Figures 2 and 3 show a comparison between the aforesaid mentioned inundated areas on the calibration and validation domains. It is necessary mentioning that the 2D hydraulic model was applied on the main stream of the Balice river basin, so the minor order stream and the tributaries were not considered in the hydraulic simulation.

Looking at the Table 1, where for each selected descriptor the value of the calibrated threshold is reported together with the objective function and the corresponding AUC value (which ROC curve is reported in Fig. 4), it is possible to recognize good performances of the H (synthetic) and the $\ln(h_l/H)$ (composite) descriptors. it is surprising to observe (see Table 2) good performances of the aforesaid mentioned descriptors on the validation domain; this confirms the reliability of the proposed methodology.

In particular, considering the calibration for T = 200 years the test applied to the H synthetic descriptor, returned a minimum value (see Table 1) of the objective function equal to 0.07, leading to an overestimation of 5% (due to false positive errors) and to an underestimation of the 2.5% (due to false negative errors) of the flooded area. Instead among the composite descriptors, the test for the $\ln(h_l/H)$ descriptor returned a minimum value of the objective function equal to 0.16, leading to an overestimation of 9.9% (due to false positive errors) and to an underestimation of the 6.5% (due to false negative errors) of the flooded area. For the return periods of 30 and 500 years, the test gave similar results with a minimum value of the objective function for the H and the $\ln(h_l/H)$ descriptors.

The validation procedure for the same return period shows also good performances for H and $\ln(h_l/H)$: it is interesting to note that the results in terms of true positive and false positive rate are very similar to that obtained in the calibration phase. A small increasing in the objective function value confirms the optimal performances of the adopted descriptors. Figures 2 and 3 show a comparison between the aforesaid mentioned inundated areas on the calibration and validation domains. The reliability of the investigated methodology has been also evaluated by comparing flooding image obtained using the geomorphological descriptor with that obtained by performing

Table 1. Results of the linear binary classification test for synthetic and composite calibrated descriptors.

	Indices	τ_{norm}	τ	r_{fp}	r_{tp}	OB	AUC
30 years	A_s (km²)	−0.997	0.014	0.011	0.036	0.975	0.512
	D (m)	−0.779	420.860	0.325	0.791	0.534	0.836
	H (m)	**−0.791**	**5.511**	**0.047**	**0.975**	**0.071**	**0.987**
	DW$_i$	−0.916	0.038	0.137	0.564	0.574	0.725
	$\ln(h_r/H)$	**−0.479**	**−2.194**	**0.058**	**0.856**	**0.202**	**0.949**
	$\ln(h_l/H)$	**−0.671**	**−5.527**	**0.082**	**0.943**	**0.139**	**0.978**
	$(h_r − H)/D$	0.054	−0.009	0.073	0.618	0.435	0.783
	$(h_r − H)/DW_i$	−0.932	−65.072	0.136	0.693	0.444	0.863
200 years	A_s (km²)	−0.997	0.014	0.011	0.032	0.979	0.510
	D (m)	−0.762	453.234	0.333	0.836	0.497	0.853
	H (m)	**−0.753**	**6.513**	**0.051**	**0.975**	**0.077**	**0.989**
	DW$_i$	−0.916	0.038	0.136	0.505	0.631	0.678
	$\ln(h_r/H)$	**−0.491**	**−2.285**	**0.057**	**0.819**	**0.237**	**0.933**
	$\ln(h_l/H)$	**−0.697**	**−5.751**	**0.099**	**0.935**	**0.165**	**0.975**
	$(h_r − H)/D$	0.054	−0.009	0.070	0.550	0.520	0.729
	$(h_r − H)/DW_i$	−0.932	−65.072	0.124	0.717	0.407	0.875
500 years	A_s (km²)	−0.997	0.014	0.011	0.030	0.981	0.509
	D (m)	−0.766	445.617	0.324	0.838	0.486	0.855
	H (m)	**−0.753**	**6.513**	**0.044**	**0.967**	**0.077**	**0.990**
	DW$_i$	−0.914	0.040	0.151	0.501	0.650	0.673
	$\ln(h_r/H)$	**−0.493**	**−2.301**	**0.053**	**0.815**	**0.238**	**0.931**
	$\ln(h_l/H)$	**−0.710**	**−5.863**	**0.112**	**0.937**	**0.175**	**0.973**
	$(h_r − H)/D$	0.054	−0.009	0.069	0.519	0.551	0.722
	$(h_r − H)/DW_i$	−0.932	−65.072	0.120	0.709	0.411	0.877

Table 2. Results of the linear binary classification test for validated descriptors

	Indices	τ_{norm}	τ	r_{fp}	r_{tp}	OB
30 years	H (m)	−0.791	5.511	0.059	0.955	0.104
	ln(h_r/H)	−0.479	−2.194	0.032	0.721	0.311
	ln(h_l/H)	−0.671	−5.527	0.074	0.910	0.164
200 years	H (m)	−0.753	6.513	0.058	0.970	0.088
	ln(h_r/H)	−0.491	−2.285	0.026	0.712	0.315
	ln(h_l/H)	−0.697	−5.751	0.087	0.920	0.167
500 years	H (m)	−0.753	6.513	0.041	0.945	0.096
	ln(h_r/H)	−0.493	−2.301	0.018	0.669	0.349
	ln(h_l/H)	−0.710	−5.863	0.089	0.902	0.187

hydraulic simulation. In particular, considering the flooded areas derived by the best synthetic H descriptor reported in the Figs. 2a and 3a, it is possible to recognize how this descriptor is able to depict flooded areas also in the validation domain (see Fig. 3a). Moreover it is also necessary to highlight the ability of the composite descriptor ln(h_l/H) to delineate also the areas exposed to flood inundation (see Figs. 2b and 3b) located outside of the reference hydraulic inundated areas (reported in Figs. 2c

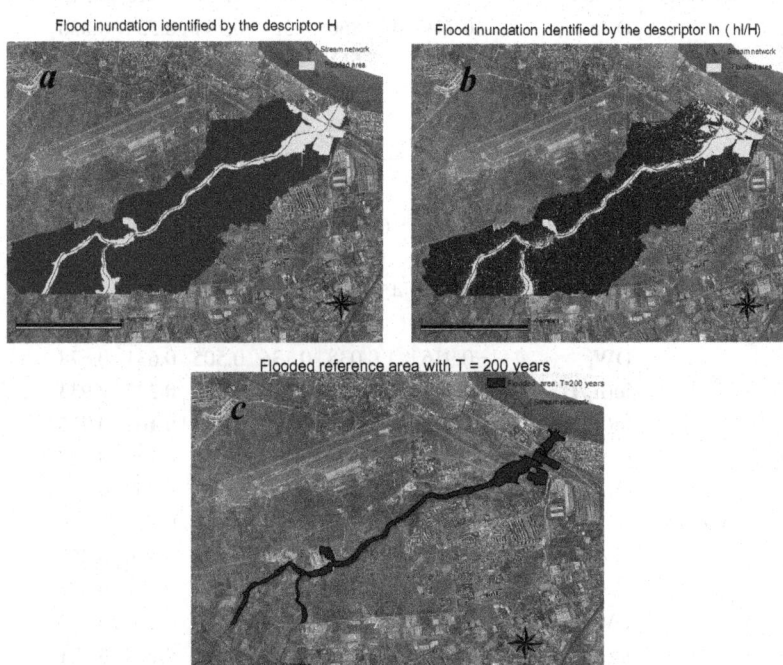

Fig. 2. Calibration: comparison between the area exposed to flood inundation identified by the descriptors H (a), the area identified by the descriptors ln(h_l/H) (b) and the reference map with flooded area (c) with T = 200 years. Reference System UTM WGS84 zone 33N.

and 3c), both in the calibration and in the validation domain; this demonstrate the usefulness of the descriptor to extend the delineation of floodable areas from small to large scale for a preliminary analysis, avoiding time consuming applications of numerical models.

Looking at Table 1, where the threshold values are reported for each return period, it is simple to recognize that the return period weakly affects the threshold identification, due to the slight difference between the selected design flooded areas belonging to the calibration and the validation domain; this effect can be reasonably related to the particular morphology of the investigated river network, consisting of incisions called "lame".

The ROC curves reported in the Fig. 4 reinforce the ability of the geomorphological descriptor to represent the effect on the ground of meteoric events corresponding to the three selected return periods. According to the results showed in Tables 1 and 2, the ROC curves confirm the H index as the best index among the synthetic descriptors, and the $\ln(h_l/H)$ index, among the composite descriptors, for all the investigated return periods.

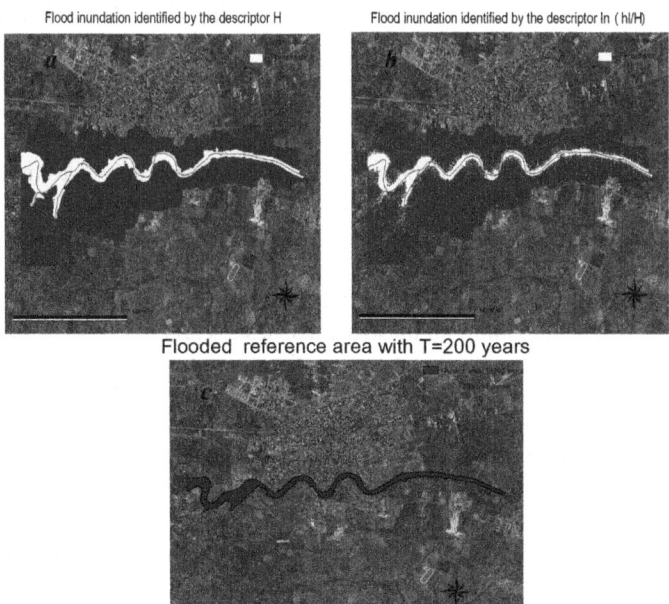

Fig. 3. Validation: comparison between the area exposed to flood inundation identified by the descriptors H (*a*), the area identified by the descriptor $\ln(h_L/H)$ (*b*) and the reference map corresponding to T = 200 years (*c*). Reference System UTM WGS84 zone 33N.

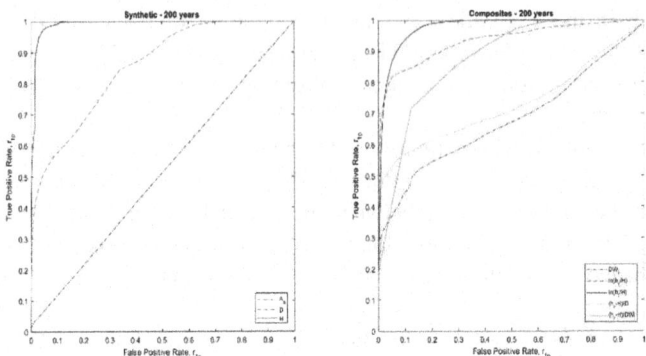

Fig. 4. Calibration: ROC curves for the three selected return periods, for synthetic and composite descriptors.

5 Conclusions

In this manuscript, the performances of DEM-based approach able to evaluate in first approximation, the flooded areas following a given design meteoric event is described, through the comparison between the areas exposed to flood inundation extracted from geomorphological descriptors and flooded areas derived by hydraulic numerical simulation, in a typical area of southern Italy characterized by ephemeral/episodic streams called "lame". The Lama Balice (located in Puglia – southern Italy) was investigated in this study, which is one of the most significant karst phenomena of central Apulia, in terms of both flood risk and naturalistic landscapes.

The performances above described in calibration and in validation phases, demonstrated the ability of the DTM based approach to reproduce flood-prone areas and confirms the high reliability of these approaches to carry out a priori estimations of the ground effect of a meteoric event, especially when it is very expensive time consuming for end users to extend numerical analysis from small to large scale. The described procedures still deserve some limitations in areas close to the outlet (as already observed by [52]) of the river basin in which the geomorphological indices fail to consider a number of human interventions.

It is interesting to remark that the aim of the proposed research is not to find the most performing index, but is to investigate the capability of the proposed approach in order to evaluate areas exposed to flood susceptibility.

Moreover, we can state that the proposed work gives a strong contribution to the scientific research in this field, showing how the described procedures may be easily applied for an priori evaluation of inundated areas for different applications for a new qualitative mapping of flooding risk on a large scale, avoiding time consuming and expensive applications of hydraulic mono/two dimensional modeling, in some cases difficult to apply due to the poor dataset availability. Finally, the investigation of different design events demonstrates similar performances of the adopted descriptors for different return periods.

References

1. Floods Directive 2007/60/EC on the assessment and management of flood risks entered into force on 26 November 2007
2. Feldman, A.D.: Hydrologic Engineering Center (U.S.), Hydrologic Modeling System HEC-HMS, US Army Corps of Engineers, Hydrologic Engineering Center (2000)
3. Rigon, R., Bertoldi, G., Over, T.M.: GEOtop: a distributed hydrological model with coupled water and energy budgets. J. Hydrom. **7**, 371–388 (2006). https://doi.org/10.1175/JHM497.1
4. Fiorentino, M., Gioia, A., Iacobellis, V., Manfreda, S.: Analysis on flood generation processes by means of a continuous simulation model. Adv. Geosci. **7**, 231–236 (2006). www.adv-geosci.net/7/231/2006/. https://doi.org/10.5194/adgeo-7-231-2006. ISSN 1680-7340
5. Merz, R., Blöschl, G.: Flood frequency hydrology: 1. Temporal, spatial, and causal expansion of information. Water Resour. Res. **44**(8) (2008). http://dx.doi.org/101029/2007WR006744
6. Fiorentino, M., Gioia, A., Iacobellis, V., Manfreda, S.: Regional analysis of runoff thresholds behaviour in Southern Italy based on theoretically derived distributions. Adv. Geosci. **26**, 139–144 (2011). www.adv-geosci.net/26/139/2011/. https://doi.org/10.5194/adgeo-26-139-2011. ISSN 1680-7340
7. Beven, K.: Rainfall-Runoff Modelling the Primer, 2nd edn. Wiley-Blackwell, Chichester (2012)
8. Gioia, A., Manfreda, S., Iacobellis, V., Fiorentino, M.: Performance of a theoretical model for the description of water balance and runoff dynamics in Southern Italy. J. Hydrol. Eng. **19**(6), 1113–1123 (2014). https://doi.org/10.1061/(ASCE)HE.1943-5584.0000879
9. Di Modugno, M., Gioia, A., Gorgoglione, A., Iacobellis, V., la Forgia, G., Piccinni, A.F., Ranieri, E.: Build-Up/wash-off monitoring and assessment for sustainable management of first flush in an urban area. Sustainability **7**, 5050–5070 (2015)
10. Gioia, A., Iacobellis, V., Manfreda, S., Fiorentino, M.: Comparison of different methods describing the peak runoff contributing areas during floods. Hydrol. Process. **31**(11), 2041–2049 (2017)
11. Mizyed, N.R., Loftis, J.C., Fontane, D.G.: Operation of large multireservoirs ystemsu singo ptimal-controlt heory. J. Water Resour. Plan. Manag. **118**(4), 371–387 (1992)
12. Crawley, P.D., Dandy, G.C.: Optimal operation of multiple reservoir system. J. Water Resour. Plan. Manag. **119**(1), 1–17 (1993)
13. Oliveira, R., Loucks, D.P.: Operating rules for multireservoir systems. Water Resour. Res. **33**(4), 839–852 (1997)
14. Gioia, A.: Reservoir routing on double-peak design flood. Water **8**, 553 (2016)
15. Sordo-Ward, A., Gabriel-Martin, I., Bianucci, P., Garrote, L.: A parametric flood control method for dams with gate-controlled spillways. Water **9**, 237 (2017). https://doi.org/10.3390/w904023
16. De Wrachien, D., Mambretti, S.: Mathematical models for flood hazard assessment. Int. J. Saf. Secur. Eng. **1**(4), 353–362 (2011). https://doi.org/10.2495/SAFE-V1-N4-353-362
17. Iacobellis, V., Castorani, A., Di Santo, A.R., Gioia, A.: Rationale for flood prediction in karst endorheic areas. J. Arid Environ. **112**(10), 98–108 (2015). https://doi.org/10.1016/j.jaridenv.2014.05.018
18. Bates, P., Anderson, M., Price, D., Hardy, R., Smith, C.: Analysis and development of hydraulic models for floodplain flows. In: Anderson, M.G., Walling, D.E., Bates, P.D. (eds.) Floodplain Processes. Wiley, New York (1996)

19. Aronica, G., Hankin, B., Beven, K.J.: Uncertainty and equifinality in calibrating distributed roughness coefficients in a flood propagation model with limited data. Adv. Water Resour. **22**(4), 349–365 (1998)

20. Jain, S.K., Singh, R.D., Jain, M.K., Lohani, A.K.: Delineation of flood-prone areas using remote sensing techniques. Water Resour. Manag. **19**, 333 (2005). https://doi.org/10.1007/s11269-005-3281-5

21. Fluet-Chouinard, E., Lehner, B., Rebelo, L.-M., Papa, F., Hamilton, S.K.: Development of a global inundation map at high spatial resolution from topographic downscaling of coarse-scale remote sensing data. Remote Sens. Environ. **158**, 348–361 (2015)

22. Manfreda, S., Samela, C., Gioia, A., Consoli, G.G., Iacobellis, V., Giuzio, L., Cantisani, A., Sole, A.: Flood-prone areas assessment using linear binary classifiers based on flood maps obtained from 1D and 2D Hydraulic models. Nat. Hazards (2015). https://doi.org/10.1007/s11069-015-1869-5

23. Bates, P.D., Horritt, M.S., Smith, C.N., Mason, D.C.: Integrating remote sensing observations of flood hydrology and hydraulic modelling. Hydrol. Process. **11**, 1777–1795 (1997)

24. Horritt, M.S., Mason, D.C., Luckman, A.J.: Flood boundary delineation from synthetic aperture radar imagery using a statistical active contour model. Int. J. Remote Sens. **22**(13), 2489–2507 (2001)

25. Mattia, F., Satalino, G., Balenzano, A., D'Urso, G., Capodici, F., Iacobellis, V., Milella, P., Gioia, A., Rinaldi, M., Ruggieri, S., Dini, L.: Time series of COSMO-SkyMed data for landcover classification and surface parameter retrieval over agricultural sites. In: Proceedings of the IEEE 2012 International Geoscience and Remote Sensing Symposium, pp. 6511–6514 (2012). ISBN 978-1-4673-1159-5

26. Balenzano, A., Satalino, G., Belmonte, A., D'Urso, G., Capodici, F., Iacobellis, V., Gioia, A., Rinaldi, M., Ruggieri, S., Mattia, F.: On the use of multi-temporal series of COSMO-SkyMed data for landcover classification and surface parameter retrieval over agricultural sites. In: Proceedings of the 2011 IEEE International Geoscience and Remote Sensing Symposium, 24–29 July, Vancouver, Canada, pp. 142–145 (2011)

27. Balenzano, A., Satalino, G., Iacobellis, V., Gioia, A., Manfreda, S., Rinaldi, M., De Vita, P., Miglietta, F., Toscano, P., Annichiarico, G., Mattia, F.: A ground network for SAR-derived soil moisture product calibration, validation and exploitation in southern Italy. In: Proceedings of the IEEE 2014 International Geoscience and Remote Sensing Symposium, IGARSS 2014 (2014)

28. Tarantino, E., Novelli, A., Laterza, M., Gioia, A.: Testing high spatial resolution WorldView-2 imagery for retrieving the leaf area index. In: Proceedings of the SPIE 9535, Third International Conference on Remote Sensing and Geoinformation of the Environment (RSCy2015) (2015). https://doi.org/10.1117/12.2192561

29. Trombetta, A., Iacobellis, V., Tarantino, E., Gentile, F.: Calibration of the AquaCrop model for winter wheat using MODIS LAI images. Agric. Water Manag. **164**(Part 2), 304–316 (2016)

30. Olang, L.O., Kundu, P., Bauer, T., Fürst, J.: Analysis of spatio-temporal land cover changes for hydrological impact assessment within the Nyando River Basin of Kenya. Environ. Monit. Assess. **179**, 389–401 (2011)

31. Pattison, I., Lane, S.N.: The link between land-use management and fluvial flood risk: a chaotic conception? Prog. Phys. Geogr. **36**, 72–92 (2011)

32. Balacco, G., Figorito, B., Tarantino, E., Gioia, A., Iacobellis, V.: Space-time LAI variability in Northern Puglia (Italy) from SPOT VGT data. Environ. Monit. Assess. **187**, 434 (2015). https://doi.org/10.1007/s10661-015-4603-6

33. Caprioli, M., Tarantino, E.: Identification of land cover alterations in the Alta Murgia National Park (Italy) with VHR satellite imagery. Int. J. Sustain. Dev. Plan. **1**(3), 261–270 (2006)
34. Crocetto, N., Tarantino, E.: A class-oriented strategy for features extraction from multidate ASTER imagery. Remote Sens. **1**(4), 1171–1189 (2009)
35. Saradjian, M.R., Hosseini, M.: Soil moisture estimation by using multipolarization SAR image. Adv. Space Res. **48**(2), 278–286 (2011)
36. Gioia, A., Iacobellis, V., Manfreda, S., Fiorentino, M.: Influence of infiltration and soil storage capacity on the skewness of the annual maximum flood peaks in a theoretically derived distribution. Hydrol. Earth Syst. Sci. **16**, 937–951 (2012). https://doi.org/10.5194/hess-16-937-2012
37. Iacobellis, V., Gioia, A., Milella, P., Satalino, G., Balenzano, A., Mattia, F.: Inter-comparison of hydrological model simulations with time series of SAR-derived soil moisture maps. Eur. J. Remote Sens. **46**(1), 739–757 (2013)
38. Nardi, F., Vivoni, E.R., Grimaldi, S.: Investigating a floodplain scaling relation using a hydrogeomorphic delineation method. Water Resour. Res. **42**(9), W09409 (2006)
39. Marks, K., Bates, P.D.: Integration of high resolution topographic data with floodplain flow models. Hydrol. Process. **14**, 2109–2122 (2000)
40. Dodov, B.A., Foufoula-Georgiou, E.: Floodplain morphometry extraction from a high-resolution digital elevation model: a simple algorithm for regional analysis studies. Geosci. Remote Sens. Lett. IEEE **3**(3), 410–413 (2006). https://doi.org/10.1109/LGRS.2006.874161
41. De Giorgis, M., Gnecco, G., Gorni, S., Roth, G., Sanguineti, M., Taramasso, A.C.: Classifiers for the detection of flood-prone areas using remote sensed elevation data. J. Hydrol. **470–471**, 302–315 (2012)
42. De Risi, R., Jalayer, F., De Paola, F., Giugni, M.: Probabilistic delineation of flood- -prone areas based on a digital elevation model and the extent of historical flooding: the case of Ouagadougou. Boletín Geológico Minero **125**, 329–340 (2014)
43. Totaro, V., Gioia, A., Novelli, A., Caradonna, G.: The use of geomorphological descriptors and landsat-8 spectral indices data for flood areas evaluation: a case study of Lato river basin. In: Gervasi, O., et al. (eds.) ICCSA 2017. LNCS, vol. 10407, pp. 30–44. Springer, Cham (2017). https://doi.org/10.1007/978-3-319-62401-3_3
44. Milone, F., Camarda, D.: Modeling knowledge in environmental analysis: a new approach to soundscape ecology. Sustainability **9**, 564 (2017). https://doi.org/10.3390/su9040564
45. US Army Corps of Hydraulic Engineers: HEC-2 User's Manual (1985). http://www.hec.usace.army.mil/publications/pubs_distrib/hec/hec2.htmlUSDA-SCS. National Engineering Handbook, Sec, 4 – Hydrology. Washington, D.C. (2001)
46. O'Brien, J.S., Julien, P.Y., Fullerton, W.T.: Two-dimensional water flood and mudflow simulation. J. Hydraul. Eng. **119**(2), 244–261 (1993). https://doi.org/10.1061/(ASCE)0733-9429
47. USDA-SCS: National Engineering Handbook, Sec, 4 - Hydrology, Washington, D.C. (1985)
48. Claps, P., Copertino, V.A., Ermini, R., Fiorentino, M.: Analisi regionale dei massimi annuali delle precipitazioni di diversa durata. In: "Valutazione delle piene in Puglia" a cura di Copertino, V., Fiorentino, M., CNR-GNDCI, Potenza (1992). (in Italian)
49. Slatton, K.C., Carter, W.E., Shrestha, R.L., Dietrich, W.E.: Airborne laser swath mapping: achieving the resolution and accuracy required for geosurficial research. Geophys. Res. Lett. **34**, L23S10 (2007). https://doi.org/10.1029/2007gl031939
50. Samela, C., Manfreda, S., Paola, F.D., Giugni, M., Sole, A., Fiorentino, M.: DEM- based approaches for the delineation of flood-prone areas in an ungauged basin in Africa. J. Hydrol. Eng. (2015). http://dx.doi.org/10.1061/(ASCE)HE.1943-5584.0001272

51. Samela, C., Troy, T.J., Manfreda, S.: Geomorphic classifiers for flood-prone areas delineation for data-scarce environments. Adv. Water Resour. **102**, 13–28 (2017). https://doi.org/10.1016/j.advwatres.2017.01.007

52. Manfreda, S., Di Leo, M., Sole, A.: Detection of flood prone areas using digital elevation models. J. Hydrol. Eng. **16**(10), 781–790 (2011). https://doi.org/10.1061/(ASCE)HE.1943-5584.0000367

53. Kirkby, M.J.: Hydrograph modelling strategies. In: Peel, R., Chisholm, R., Haggett, P. (eds.) Processes in Physical and Human Geography, pp. 69–90. Heinemann, Oxford (1975)

54. Hjerdt, K.N., McDonnell, J.J., Seibert, J., Rodhe, A.: A new topographic index to quantify downslope controls on local drainage. Water Resour. Res. **40**, W05602 (2004)

55. Fawcett, T.: An introduction to ROC analysis. Pattern Recogn. Lett. **27**, 861–874 (2006)

Static and Kinematic Surveys Using GNSS Multi-constellation Receivers and GPS, GLONASS and Galileo Data

Raffaela Cefalo[1]([✉]) [ID], Antonio Novelli[2] [ID], Tatiana Sluga[1] [ID],
Paolo Snider[1], Eufemia Tarantino[3] [ID], and Agostino Tommasi[1] [ID]

[1] GeoSNav Lab, University of Trieste, via Valerio 6/2, 34127 Trieste, Italy
{raffaela.cefalo,agostino.tommasi}@dia.units.it,
tatiana.sluga@gmail.com, snider.paolo@gmail.com
[2] Eurac Research Institute for Renewable Energy,
A.Volta Straße 13/A, Bolzano, Italy
antonio.novelli@eurac.edu
[3] AGLAB, DICATECh - Politecnico di Bari, via Orabona 4, 70125 Bari, Italy
eufemia.tarantino@poliba.it

Abstract. In this paper the results of static and kinematic surveys using GNSS multi-constellation receivers acquiring GPS, GLONASS and Galileo Open Service (OS) data are presented.

The static and kinematic GNSS data processing have been performed using the open source program package RTKLIB. The kinematic surveys have been compared with a reference trajectory computed from a Mobile Mapping System (MMS) using a high performance GNSS/INS system. As reference stations a multi-constellation Leica receiver belonging to ItalPos network and located at University of Trieste, Italy and a reference station belonging to the Friuli Venezia Giulia Region Marussi GNSS network have been used for static and kinematic surveys.

The obtained results show, even at this initial phase, good planimetric performances both in static than in kinematic applications. Two different static sessions performed in a six months period allowed the Authors to analyze the solution improvements due to the increased number of Galileo satellites.

Keywords: Kinematic · Galileo · GPS · GLONASS · Mobile Mapping System
RTKLIB

1 Introduction

The Galileo navigation satellite system is a global positioning European program designed to be fully interoperable with the analogues American GPS and Russian GLONASS positioning systems. With Galileo, the European Union aims at owning and providing an independent positioning/navigation service under civilian control [1].

The fully deployed Galileo system will consist of 30 Medium Earth Orbit (MEO) satellites, including 6 spares, in a so called Walker 24/3/1 constellation. This

© Springer International Publishing AG, part of Springer Nature 2018
O. Gervasi et al. (Eds.): ICCSA 2018, LNCS 10964, pp. 349–363, 2018.
https://doi.org/10.1007/978-3-319-95174-4_28

particular Walker configuration implies that the Galileo constellation will consist of 24 satellites homogenously distributed in three different orbital planes (A, B and C) separated in the equatorial plane by 120°.

In each orbital plane, each satellite is separated with an angular distance of 45°. The relative phase shift factor between satellites in adjacent planes is 1, leading to an offset of 15° between satellites in adjacent planes [2].

The Galileo navigation CDMA (Code Division Multiple Access) Signals are transmitted in four frequency bands. These four frequency bands are the E5a, E5b, E6 and E1 bands. They provide a wide bandwidth for the transmission of the Galileo Signals (Fig. 1). The E5a and E5b signals are part of the E5 signal in its full bandwidth. The wideband E5 signal is generated with the AltBOC (Alternate Binary Offset Carrier) modulation. E5a and E5b signals can be processed independently by the user receiver as though they are two separate QPSK (Quadrature Phase-Shift Keying) signals with a carrier frequency of 1176.45 MHz and 1207.14 MHz respectively [3].

The Galileo frequency bands have been selected in the allocated spectrum for Radio Navigation Satellite Services (RNSS) and in addition to that, E5a, E5b and E1 bands are included in the allocated spectrum for Aeronautical Radio Navigation Services (ARNS), employed by Civil-Aviation users, and allowing dedicated safety-critical applications.

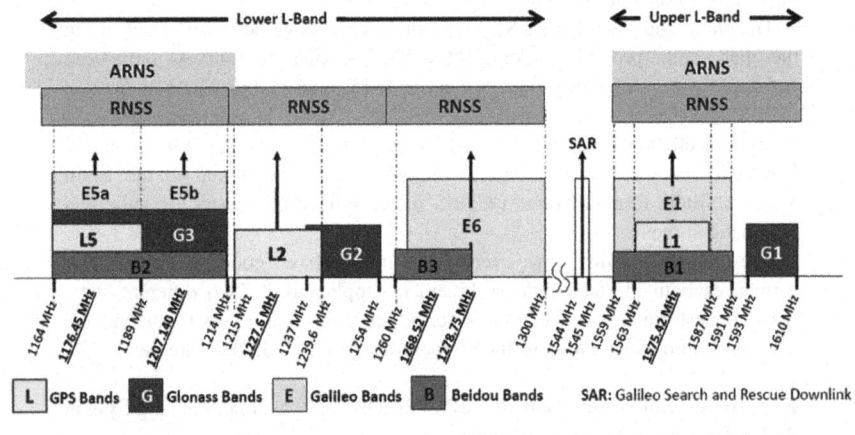

Fig. 1. Galileo and other GNSS frequency plan [4]

Galileo will provide peculiar services, also independently by others positioning systems:

Open Service (OS): is a free service for all over the world users; generally, OS applications will combine Galileo and GPS signals to improve both performances. No "integrity" information are given.

Safety of Life Service (SoL): improves OS performances, adding "integrity" information for critical navigation applications; based on EGNOS (European Geostationary Navigation Overlay Service) System.

Commercial Service (CS): devoted to applications requiring higher performances than OS provides; it will be a charge service.

Public Regulated Service (PRS): intended for security corps, requiring high service continuity and restricted access; it will be an under government control service.

Search And Rescue (SAR): this service will be comprised of two components; the former (launched on April 2017) permits to send an automatic distress alert, to identify the location of the requested rescue; the latter (expected to be added to the system by the end of 2018) will give a return link, a signal informing the person in distress that the signal has been received and localized [5].

The Galileo program has been scheduled in three different phases:

In-Orbit Validation (IOV) Phase. In this phase, at first, two test satellites, GIOVE-A and GIOVE-B were launched, respectively in December 2005 and in April 2008 in Medium-Earth Orbit (MEO), to characterize environmental conditions and evaluate signal-in-space and on board instruments performances. They were declared fully operational on the first orbital plane since April 2012. Two more Galileo satellites, completing the IOV quartet, were launched on the second orbital plane on 12 October 2012. The first "position fix" using Galileo signals was reported on 12 March 2013 by ESA's navigation laboratory in the Netherlands. In February 2014, after a wide variety of tests all over the Europe, Galileo achieved In-Orbit Validation.

Initial Operational Capability (IOC) Phase. The second phase target was a partial commissioning of the ground and space infrastructure (14 more satellites), the start of the Open Service (OS), the Search And Rescue (SAR) service and the Galileo Public Regulated Service (PRS). The 18th satellite was launched on 17 November 2016. On 15 December 2016 at 13:00 UTC, Galileo initial Open Service (OS) was formally announced by the European Commission. On April 2017 Search And Rescue service officially took launch.

Full Operational Capability (FOC) Phase. This phase will consist of 30 satellites (24 satellites and two back-up satellites for each orbital plane), control centers located in Europe and a network of sensor stations and Uplink Stations (ULS) installed all over the world.

The Full Operational Capability of Galileo should be achieved by 2020, with a phased approach from the IOC phase.

At present (March 2018) 14 Satellites are "usable", 2 under "testing" and 4 "under commissioning" [2].

For the experimental activities presented in this paper, the Galileo Open Service (OS) was used. The Galileo OS service does not require any authorization and can be used by anyone equipped with an adequate receiver. E1 Signal supports the Open Service and the Commercial Service, E5a Signal supports Galileo Open Service and overlaps in the spectrum with the GPS-L5-signal, E5b supports the Open Service and the Commercial Service, E6 Signal supports Galileo Commercial Service [3].

Aim of this paper is a preliminary analysis of the Galileo OS performances both in static then in kinematic applications, compared with the ones obtained using GPS and GLONASS GNSS Systems. The point positioning computations and derived kinematic trajectories were compared to a reference trajectory computed using a Mobile Mapping System (MMS) implementing a POS/LV (Position and Orientation System for Land Vehicles) system produced by Applanix Corporation.

2 Existing Studies

Galileo data were increasingly used to produce and validate scientific studies. In some of them, as occurred in [6–8], they were analyzed even before the IOV phase with a numerically simulated signal.

In the paper proposed by Odijk et al. [9], during the IOV phase, the observations acquired from GPS data and Galileo In-Orbit Validation Element (GIOVE) were mixed together. By combining GPS and Galileo acquisitions, in an inter-system solution, an improved instantaneous ambiguity resolution was achieved respect the one obtained using GPS only data. Galileo IOV data were used by Cai et al. [10] to analyze both the quality of the acquired signal and the positioning accuracy. They focused their attention on the quality of the transmitted orbits and demonstrated that Galileo signal features both a better signal-to-noise ratio (SNR) and multipath performance, compared with the ones related to GPS data.

The higher performance of Galileo system was also demonstrated by Gaglione et al. [11]. They focused their attention on the geometry improvements achieved with two new FOC satellites (FOC-FM1 and FOC-FM2). Lastly, in Gioia et al. [12], a whole week of IOV acquisitions was used to study Galileo IOV performance.

Some authors have already performed comparisons among GPS, GLONASS, BeiDou, Galileo, and QZSS. E.g. Precise Point Positioning (PPP) with GPS, GLO-NASS, Galileo and BeiDou data was the topic addressed in the paper proposed by Tegedor et al. [13]. The MGEX (Multi-GNSS Experiment) data were exploited by Lou et al. [14] to assess the accuracy of a multi-GNSS PPP model. Particularly, MGEX experiment has been powered by the IGS to acquire, compare and process both the existing GNSS signals (e.g. from BeiDou, Galileo, QZSS, and IRNSS, modernized GPS and GLONASS) and the Satellite Based Augmentation Systems (SBASs) [15]. Multi-GNSS PPP was also proposed in the papers of Liu et al. [16], Pan et al. [17], and Afifi et al. [18]. The zero-baseline approach was implemented by Cai et al. [19] to compare multipath and receiver noise for GPS, BeiDou, GLONASS and Galileo acquisitions. Pan et al. [20] used four constellation data to produce a Multi-GNSS accuracy assessment. Guo et al. [21] studied precise orbit and clock, for the QZSS, BeiDou and Galileo, by exploiting MGEX data.

Galileo acquisitions have been used also in real-time multi-GNSS applications. In this sense, Odijk et al. [22] implemented the IOV data in a real-time kinematic (RTK) application involving both pseudorange and carrier-phase acquisitions. Single frequency multi GNSS RTK was also the subject of the paper proposed by Odolinski et al. [23] whereas Li et al. [24] performed a precise real-time estimation of multi GNSS positioning, orbit, and clock. In [25, 26] an attitude estimation was performed with the Galileo system. Lastly, in Nicolini et al. [27] paper, Multi-GNSS time systems and reference frames were studied.

The aforementioned works have shown that Galileo data were used mainly in static surveys. The importance of testing Galileo system performances in real operative conditions and on a continuous basis is justified by a varying system configuration related to the progress in constellation implementation. The repetition of static measurement sessions on the same points and in homogeneous conditions allows to evaluate the improvements in point positioning results.

As far as regards the kinematic test presented in this paper, the Author chose a test configuration able to give a continuous and accurate reference trajectory by using a precise MMS (Mobile Mapping System) for GNSS systems comparisons and Galileo positioning performances evaluation. In particular, the Authors, in Tarantino et al. [28] coupled a Leica GS14 with a MMS equipped with a POS/LV (Position and Orientation System for Land Vehicles). The aim of their work was to propose a single frequency kinematic performance assessment of Galileo, GPS and, GLONASS data.

3 Method Case Studies

3.1 Static Sessions Using Multi-constellation Receiver

The results of two static sessions respectively performed on 18th July 2017 and 26th January 2018, are herein reported [29].

The acquisitions were performed using a multi-constellation GNSS Leica GS14 receiver, able to acquire GPS L1, L2P(Y), GLONASS L1, L2P, Galileo E1, BeiDou B1 and B2 signals.

The positioning solutions were computed by means of the Free and Open Source Software (FOSS) RTKLIB. RTKLIB is an open source program package for standard and precise positioning and consists of a portable program library and several APs (application programs). It supports: standard and precise positioning algorithms with GPS, GLONASS, Galileo, QZSS, BeiDou and SBAS; Single, DGPS/DGNSS, Kinematic, Static, Moving-Baseline, Fixed, PPP-Kinematic, PPP-Static and PPP-Fixed positioning modes with GNSS for both real-time and post-processing.

As master station a Leica GR30 multi-constellation receiver connected to a Leica AR10 geodetic antenna, located on the roof of C8 Building, University of Trieste, and belonging to Leica Geosystem SmartNet ItalPos permanent station network, has been used. The network uses ETRF2000-RDN (National Dynamic Network) frame.

In Fig. 2 is shown, in green, the location of the vertex used for the static tests, inside the main campus of University of Trieste, Italy, in front of A Building.

Trimble GNSS Planning Online software was used in order to verify Galileo satellites availability and optimize the static session schedule and duration.

In Fig. 3, the planned number of GPS, GLONASS and Galileo satellites from 11 am to 5 pm for the operation site chosen for the static tests, is reported.

Inside this interval, a measurement span time characterized by a continuous availability of 4 satellites with picks of 5 satellites was chosen. In these tests, by using RTKPOST functionality of RTKLIB and different post-processing options, many

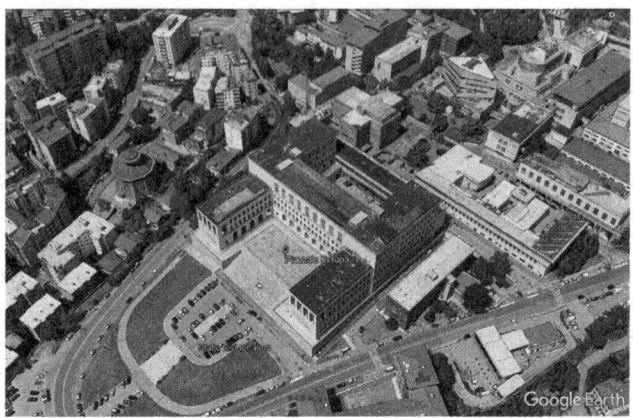

Fig. 2. The static tests location inside the main campus of University of Trieste, Italy (© Google Earth)

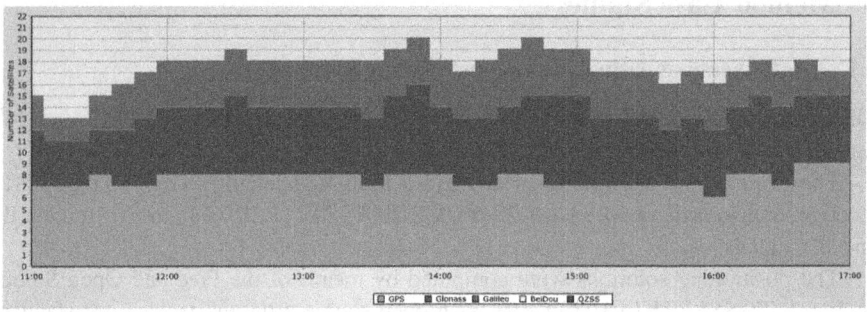

Fig. 3. Planned number of GPS (green), GLONASS (red) and Galileo (blue) satellites (https://www.trimble.com/gnssplanningonline) (Color figure online)

solutions have been obtained and compared with the point reference solution with the aim to analyze the influence of the used parameters and highlight the improvements obtained in the final solution.

The Master GNSS receiver acquired GPS L1/L2P(Y)/L2C/L5, GLONASS L1/L2P/L2C, Galileo E1/E5a/E5b/E5a+E5b AltBOC and BeiDou B1/B2 signals.

In Fig. 4 the Skyplot computed for the measuring session is shown. In particular the GLONASS R22 satellite was characterized by an high occurrence of cycle slips (indicated with red dashes in the North-East quadrant of the Skyplot).

As reference, the solution computed using GPS L1/L2, GLONASS G1/G2 data, precise ephemeris in sp3 format, downloaded from CODE Analysis Centre [30], ANTEX (ANTenna EXchange format) and IONEX (IONosphere model EXchange format) correction files, has been used. RINEX (Receiver Independent Exchange Format) 3.x observation data was used for Leica GS14 and GS30 receivers.

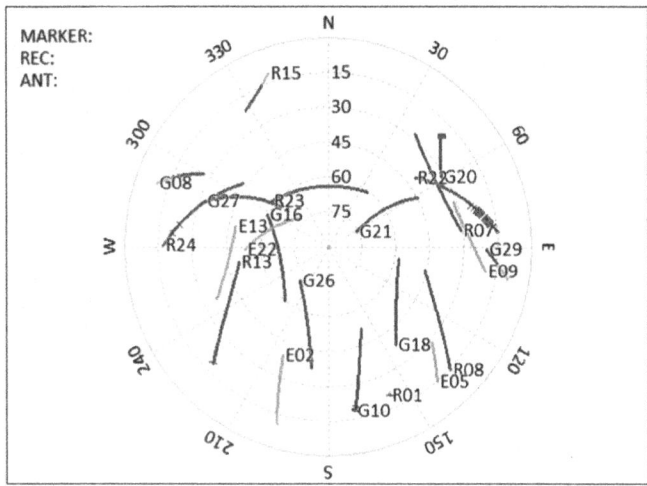

Fig. 4. The Skyplot with GPS (G), GLONASS (R) and Galileo (E) satellites (with red dashes the cycle slips occurrences are indicated, particularly evident on R22 GLONASS satellite) (Color figure online)

Klobuchar model has been used to reduce the ionospheric errors and the Saasta-moinen model for the tropospheric propagation delays.

In Fig. 5 the number of GPS satellites and related DOPs (on the left) and the number of GLONASS satellites and computed DOPs (on the right) are shown.

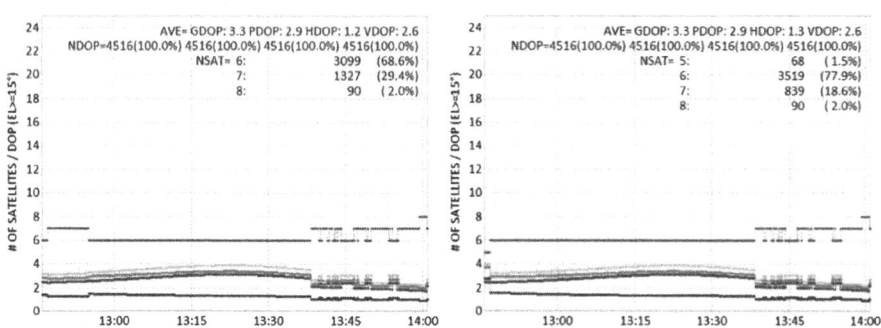

Fig. 5. Number of GPS satellites (green) with elevations higher than 15° and related DOPs (on the left) and number of GLONASS satellites (green) above 15° and DOPs (on the right) (Color figure online)

In Fig. 6 the same parameters are shown for the used Galileo constellation.

The high VDOP (Vertical DOP) values, with an average value of 8.2, are due to a not optimal distribution of the satellites in elevation, like visible in the Skyplot (Fig. 4).

In Table 1 are reported the difference in millimetres between the reference solution (computed using GPS L1/L2+GLONASS G1/G2 and precise ephemeris) and the

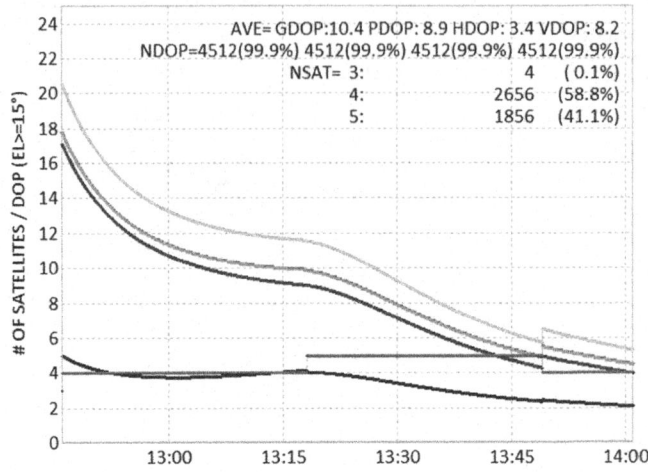

Fig. 6. Number of Galileo satellites with elevation higher than 15° and related DOPs (yellow: GDOP, purple: PDOP purple, blue: HDOP, red: VDOP) (Color figure online)

solutions computed using single GPS, GLONASS, Galileo and multi-constellations (GPS+GLONASS, GPS+GLONASS+Galileo) using broadcast ephemeris, for the 1st static session, performed on 18th July 2017.

In Table 2 the same differences have been computed for the 2nd static session, performed on the same vertex on 26th January 2018. One more Galileo satellites was operational in orbit and used for data processing.

The comparisons for Galileo data are highlighted: in particular, the comparison on Easting coordinates shows an improvement from 2.8 to 0.7 mm, the comparison on Northing coordinate is stable and the one on the height component shows a reduction from 6.3 to 5.1 mm.

The multi-constellation solution computed using GPS+GLONASS+Galileo data with broadcast ephemeris shows an improvement in the Easting comparison from 0.5 mm to 0.2 mm.

Table 1. Static session 18 July 2017 - Difference between the reference solution (GPS L1/L2 +GLONASS G1/G2 precise ephemeris) and the solutions computed using single GPS, GLONASS, Galileo and multi-constellations (GPS+GLONASS, GPS+GLONASS+Galileo)

Constellation/observables	ΔE (mm)	ΔN (mm)	ΔQ (mm)
GPS L1/L2+GLONASS G1/G2 precise eph	0.0	0.0	0.0
GPS L1/L2+GLONASS G1/G2 broadcast eph	0.0	−0.2	3.9
GPS L1 broadcast eph	0.3	−0.1	0.3
GLONASS G1 broadcast eph	−1.3	0.6	4.3
Galileo E1 broadcast eph	**2.8**	**−0.2**	**6.3**
MultiGNSS GPS+GLO+Gal broadcast eph	0.5	−0.1	3.5

Table 2. Static session 26 January 2018 - Difference in mm between the reference solution (GPS L1/L2+GLONASS G1/G2 precise ephemeris) and the solutions computed using single GPS, GLONASS, Galileo and multi-constellations (GPS+GLONASS, GPS+GLONASS +Galileo)

Constellation/observables	ΔE (mm)	ΔN (mm)	ΔQ (mm)
GPS L1/L2+GLONASS G1/G2 precise eph	0.0	0.0	0.0
GPS L1/L2+GLONASS G1/G2 broadcast eph	0.0	−0.3	3.8
GPS L1 broadcast eph	−0.6	1.3	0.7
GLONASS G1 broadcast eph	−1.1	−0.9	7.1
Galileo E1 broadcast eph	**0.7**	**−0.2**	**5.1**
MultiGNSS GPS+GLO+Gal broadcast eph	0.2	−0.3	4.0

3.2   Kinematic Experiments Using a MMS (Mobile Mapping Systems)

In this part of the paper the results of kinematic tests performed on 25th July 2017 are reported.

OS Galileo positioning data have been acquired, processed and compared with the contemporaneous GPS and GLONASS data acquired using the Leica GS14 multi-constellation receiver and with a reference GNSS/INS trajectory surveyed by a MMS (Mobile Mapping System).

The MMS, GeoSNav Lab, University of Trieste, implements a POS/LV (Position and Orientation System for Land Vehicles) produced by Applanix Corporation. It integrates the GNSS measurements acquired by two GPS geodetic receivers with an IMU (Inertial Measurement Unit) in order to guarantee continuity and higher accuracies (Fig. 7).

The epoch by epoch comparisons refer to the positions obtained using GPS L1, GLONASS G1 and Galileo E1 data. The differences between the three dimensional Easting, Northing and Height coordinates processed using single constellation data and the contemporaneous reference positions derived from GNSS/INS system, were computed.

Fig. 7. The MMS of the GeoSNav Lab, University of Trieste, and the Applanix Corpora-tion POS LV© system components mounted on board the vehicle.

The kinematic tests were carried out on 25th July 2017 at Basovizza, Trieste, Italy, along the internal viability of Sincrotrone Elettra Research Centre park.

The time interval was chosen on the basis of the visibility planning of Galileo satellites, the location was selected with the aim to maximize the satellite availability during the tests. The Sincrotrone Elettra Research Centre is located on the Karst plateau, at an average height of 375 m above msl with an open view from all the sides: the only geographical obstacle is represented by Monte Cocusso (674 m) 3.5 km away in NE direction.

The Applanix POS/LV system was used with the aim to compute a continuous and high precise reference trajectory, thanks to the integration between GPS and INS data by extended Kalman filtering. The L1/L2 GPS receiver mounted on board the vehicle is used to compute the positions and the L1 GPS receiver is used for heading determination. The high accurate INS is formed by 3 laser gyros, 3 accelerometers and an odometer mounted on the left back wheel of the vehicle for run distances measuring.

The main data produced by the system are: latitude, longitude and ellipsoidal heights, run distances, roll, pitch and yaw angles, velocities along north, east and z axis, accelerations in the vehicle frame, angular velocities, measurements rms.

All GNSS data were acquired with 1 Hz acquisition rate, while the odometer and the inertial system send data to the System CPU at a 200 Hz rate.

In Fig. 8 the computed GDOPs (Geometric Dilution of Precision) for GPS, GLONASS and Galileo satellites used for the computations are shown. Note that the GDOPs refers to the constellation actually used for data processing (see Table 3 for more details).

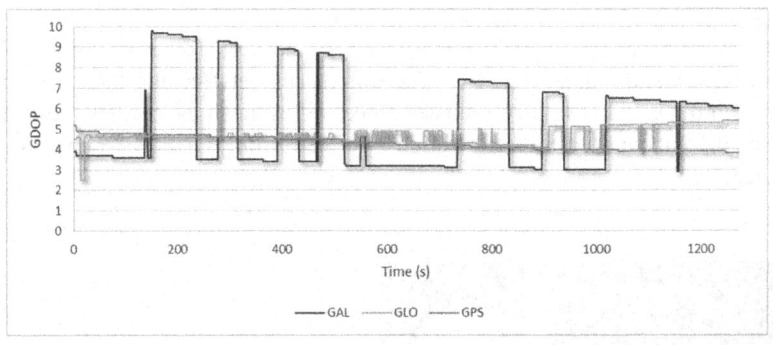

Fig. 8. Computed GDOPs for GPS, GLONASS and Galileo vs time (s)

The vehicle positioning data and the different derived trajectories were analyzed and compared. The geodetic GPS/INS MMS trajectory is characterized by a centimetric accuracy, therefore it has been assumed as reference trajectory.

In Fig. 9 the trajectories are superimposed on technical digital cartography (in blue is drawn the MMS trajectory, in red is visible the Galileo trajectory).

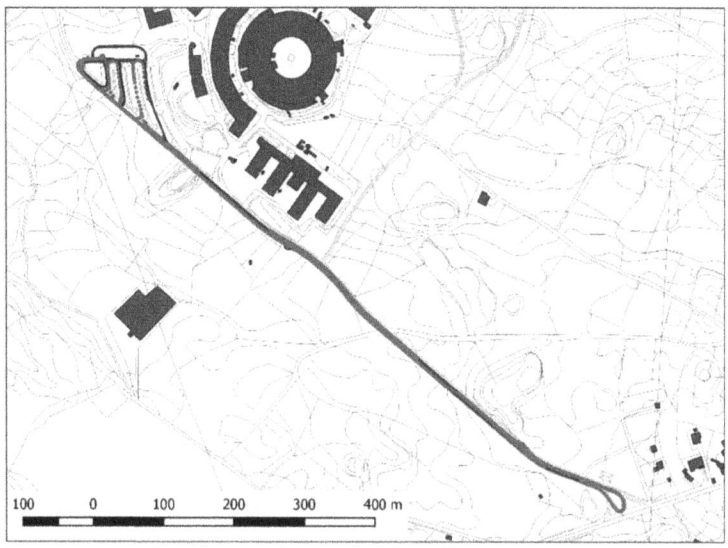

Fig. 9. MMS (blue) and Galileo (red) 3D trajectories imported into C.T.R.N. (Friuli Venezia Giulia Region digital technical cartography) - Basovizza site test, Trieste, Italy (Color figure online)

In Fig. 10 the differences between planimetric and altimetric components relative to the three trajectories (GPS, GLONASS and Galileo) respect to the reference one are reported vs time (s).

The phase antenna centre of the GS14 receiver was used as reference point for the MMS positioning data applying the level arms between the GNSS/INS reference system and the GS14 antenna position, surveyed by using a total station.

In Table 3 are reported the cut-off angles, the DOPs values (GDOP, PDOP, HDOP and VDOP), the percentage of positioning solutions computed with phase ambiguities fixed to integer values, the satellites excluded from computations, the used frequencies and the max/min number of used satellites with the correspondence percentage of epochs for Galileo, GPS and GLONASS.

E02 Galileo satellite was excluded from the computations due to its low elevation; G01, G11, G21, G26 and G32 GPS and R01, R15 and R22 GLONASS satellites were excluded from the computations in order to simulate homogeneous geometric conditions for GPS, GLONASS and Galileo used constellations. The GDOP values reported in the Table 3 are quite the same for the three constellations.

Due to a not optimal distribution in elevation for the Galileo satellites available during the kinematic tests, the VDOP values were higher than the ones computed for GPS. This justifies the worst vertical performances obtained with Galileo data.

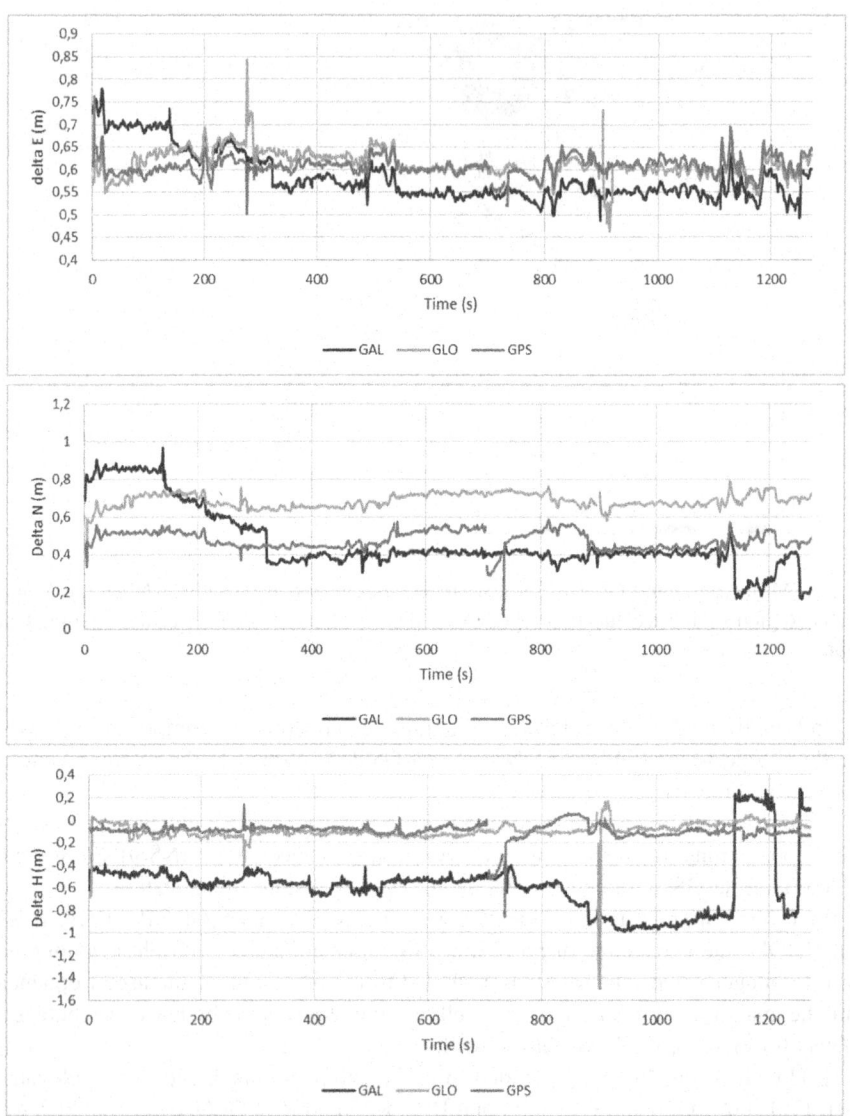

Fig. 10. Kinematic tests - computed GPS, GLONASS and Galileo positioning data differences in East, North and ellipsoidal heights to respect to the MMS reference trajectory

In Table 4 the mean delta Easting, delta Northing and delta Height values and the corresponding root mean squares are reported for Galileo, GPS and GLONASS comparisons to the reference MMS trajectory.

Table 3. Cut-off angles, DOPs values, fix percentage, satellites excluded from computations, used frequencies and max/min number of used satellites with correspondence percentage of epochs for Galileo, GPS and GLONASS data used for the kinematic test

Constellation	Galileo	GPS	GLONASS
Cut-off	10	10	10
GDOP	4.8	4.2	4.8
PDOP	4.2	3.4	4
HDOP	2	1.8	1.9
VDOP	3.7	2.9	3.6
% Fix	81.60%	77.10%	83.00%
Excluded sats	E02	G01 G11 G21 G26 G32	R01 R15 R22
Used frequencies	E1	G1	L1
N. sats max (% epochs)	5 (49.7%)	4 (99.0%)	6 (0.4%)
N. sats min (% epochs)	3 (2.2%)	3 (1.0%)	4 (50.8%)

Table 4. ΔE, ΔN and ΔH and corresponding root mean square values for Galileo, GPS and GLONASS comparisons to the reference MMS trajectory

		Galileo	GLONASS	GPS
ΔE	Mean (m)	0.584	0.614	0.607
	rms (m)	0.055	0.031	0.021
ΔN	Mean (m)	0.466	0.685	0.475
	rms (m)	0.168	0.039	0.050
ΔH	Mean (m)	0.598	0.098	0.099
	rms (m)	0.199	0.085	0.071

4 Conclusions

The aim of this paper was to compare the results of static and kinematic surveys using GNSS multi-constellation receivers acquiring GPS, GLONASS and Galileo Open Service (OS) data and test the open source program package RTKLIB functionalities and capabilities.

Two different static sessions performed in a six months period allowed the Authors to analyze the solution improvements due to the increased number of Galileo satellites.

The kinematic surveys have been performed in a quite open area using multi-constellation receiver acquiring GPS, GLONASS and Galileo data and compared to a reference trajectory computed from a Mobile Mapping System (MMS) using a high performance GPS/INS system.

The obtained results showed, the high quality of Galileo signals and, even at the actual Galileo phase - Initial Operational Capability (IOC) – characterized by a reduced availability of satellites, good planimetric performances both in static than in kinematic applications.

Acknowledgments. The authors thank Leica representatives for their availability and technical support and for giving access to SmarNet ItalPos Galileo data used for the processing and analyses presented in this paper.

References

1. ESA: Galileo Fact Sheet. http://esamultimedia.esa.int/docs/galileo/GalileoFactsheet2017.pdf. Accessed 21 Jan 2018
2. European Global Navigation European Agency - European GNSS Service Center. https://www.gsc-europa.eu/system-status/Constellation-Information. Accessed 18 Mar 2018
3. European Union. Galileo open service, signal in space interface control document (OS SIS ICD); European space agency/European GNSS supervisory authority (2016)
4. Sanz Subirana, J., Juan Zornoza, J.M., Hernández-Pajares, M.: GNSS Data Processing Volume I: Fundamentals and Algorithms, Leiden, The Netherlands: An ESA Communications Production, Publication, May 2013
5. Galileo search-and-rescue service officially launched. GPS World, 6 April 2017. http://gpsworld.com/galileo-search-and-rescue-service-officially-launched/. Accessed 15 Mar 2018
6. Ochieng, W.Y., Sauer, K., Cross, P.A., Sheridan, K.F., Iliffe, J., Lannelongue, S., Ammour, N., Petit, K.: Potential performance levels of a combined Galileo/GPS navigation system. J. Navig. **54**, 185–197 (2001)
7. O'Keefe, K., Julien, O., Cannon, M.E., Lachapelle, G.: Availability, accuracy, reliability, and carrier-phase ambiguity resolution with Galileo and GPS. Acta Astronaut. **58**, 422–434 (2006)
8. Diessongo, T.H., Schüler, T., Junker, S.: Precise position determination using a Galileo E5 single-frequency receiver. GPS Solut. **18**, 73–83 (2014)
9. Odijk, D., Teunissen, P.J., Huisman, L.: First results of mixed GPS + GIOVE single-frequency RTK in Australia. J. Spat. Sci. **57**, 3–18 (2012)
10. Cai, C., Luo, X., Liu, Z., Xiao, Q.: Galileo signal and positioning performance analysis based on four IOV satellites. J. Navig. **67**, 810–824 (2014)
11. Gaglione, S., Angrisano, A., Castaldo, G., Freda, P., Gioia, C., Innac, A., Troisi, S., Del Core, G.: The first Galileo FOC satellites: from useless to essential. In: IEEE, pp. 3667–3670 (2015)
12. Gioia, C., Borio, D., Angrisano, A., Gaglione, S., Fortuny-Guasch, J.: A Galileo IOV assessment: measurement and position domain. GPS Solut. **19**, 187–199 (2015)
13. Tegedor, J., Øvstedal, O., Vigen, E.: Precise orbit determination and point positioning using GPS, GLONASS, Galileo and BeiDou. J. Geod. Sci. **4**, 65–73 (2014)
14. Lou, Y., Zheng, F., Gu, S., Wang, C., Guo, H., Feng, Y.: Multi-GNSS precise point positioning with raw single-frequency and dual-frequency measurement models. GPS Solut. **20**, 849–862 (2016)
15. IGS MGEX. http://mgex.igs.org/IGS_MGEX_Data.php. Accessed 15 Mar 2018
16. Liu, T., Yuan, Y., Zhang, B., Wang, N., Tan, B., Chen, Y.: Multi-GNSS precise point positioning (MGPPP) using raw observations. J. Geod. **91**, 253–268 (2017)
17. Pan, L., Zhang, X., Liu, J., Li, X., Li, X.: Performance evaluation of single-frequency precise point positioning with GPS, GLONASS, BeiDou and Galileo. J. Navig. **70**, 465–482 (2017)
18. Afifi, A., El-Rabbany, A.: Single frequency GPS/Galileo precise point positioning using un-differenced and between-satellite single difference measurements. GEOMATICA **68**, 195–205 (2014)

19. Cai, C., He, C., Santerre, R., Pan, L., Cui, X., Zhu, J.: A comparative analysis of measurement noise and multipath for four constellations: GPS, BeiDou, GLONASS and Galileo. Surv. Rev. **48**, 287–295 (2016)
20. Pan, L., Cai, C., Santerre, R., Zhang, X.: Performance evaluation of single-frequency point positioning with GPS, GLONASS, BeiDou and Galileo. Surv. Rev. **49**, 197–205 (2017)
21. Guo, F., Li, X., Zhang, X., Wang, J.: Assessment of precise orbit and clock products for Galileo, BeiDou, and QZSS from IGS Multi-GNSS experiment (MGEX). GPS Solut. **21**, 279–290 (2017)
22. Odijk, D., Teunissen, P.J., Khodabandeh, A.: Galileo IOV RTK positioning: standalone and combined with GPS. Surv. Rev. **46**, 267–277 (2014)
23. Odolinski, R., Teunissen, P.J., Odijk, D.: Combined BDS, Galileo, QZSS and GPS single-frequency RTK. GPS Solut. **19**, 151–163 (2015)
24. Li, X., Ge, M., Dai, X., Ren, X., Fritsche, M., Wickert, J., Schuh, H.: Accuracy and reliability of multi-GNSS real-time precise positioning: GPS, GLONASS, BeiDou, and Galileo. J. Geod. **89**, 607–635 (2015)
25. Nadarajah, N., Teunissen, P.J.G.: Instantaneous GPS/Galileo/QZSS/SBAS attitude determination: a single-frequency (L1/E1) robustness analysis under constrained environments. Navigation **61**, 65–75 (2014)
26. Nadarajah, N., Teunissen, P.J., Raziq, N.: Instantaneous GPS–Galileo attitude determination: single-frequency performance in satellite-deprived environments. IEEE Trans. Veh. Technol. **62**, 2963–2976 (2013)
27. Nicolini, L., Caporali, A.: Investigation on reference frames and time systems in multi-GNSS. Remote Sens. **10**, 80 (2018)
28. Tarantino, E., Novelli, A., Cefalo, R., Sluga, T., Tommasi, A.: Single-frequency kinematic performance comparison between Galileo, GPS, and GLONASS satellite positioning systems using an MMS-generated trajectory as a reference: preliminary results. ISPRS Int. J. Geo-Inf. **7**(3), 122 (2018)
29. Snider, P.: Primi test statici del sistema satellitare europeo Galileo con l'utilizzo di software open source, Master Degree thesis, Università degli Studi di Trieste (2018)
30. CODE Analysis Center AIUB, Astronomical Institute University of Berne. http://www.aiub. unibe.ch/research/code___analysis_center/index_eng.html

Geometric Accuracy Evaluation of Geospatial Data Using Low-Cost Sensors on Small UAVs

Mirko Saponaro, Eufemia Tarantino$^{(\boxtimes)}$, and Umberto Fratino

Politecnico di Bari, via Orabona 4, 70125 Bari, Italy
saponaromirko@gmail.com,
{eufemia.tarantino,umberto.fratino}@poliba.it

Abstract. The recent development and proliferation of Unmanned Aircraft Systems (UASs) has made it possible to examine environmental processes and changes occurring at spatial and temporal scales that would be difficult or impossible to detect using conventional remote sensing platforms. However, new methodologies need to be codified in order to be compared with traditional photogrammetric products. This can be done by testing geometrical accuracies reached by the models when external orientations have changed. In this paper two dense point clouds, derived from the same spatial database, were compared to evaluate the discrepancies resulting from two different relative orientations: the first one based on the GPS position of each UAV frame and the second one based on GCPs, measured through GNSS positioning. The two dense point clouds presented an average offset of 3.4 cm and a standard deviation of 5 cm, proving that relative accuracy is only influenced by the matching intensity. To assign three different absolute orientations, the georeferencing procedure of the same orthomosaic was then verified based on GCPs coming from three different open geo-data sources. By evaluating the position discrepancies of some Independent Check Points (ICPs), the three open geo-data sources provided three estimates of different root-mean-square error (RMSE) positional accuracy, of which the absolute geometrical precision was the related function.

Keywords: UAV · Geometric accuracy · Low-cost sensors · VisualSfM
PMVS/CMVS · CloudCompare · PhotoScan · QGIS

1 Introduction

In last decades, the need to gather information for the management of complex environmental issues has encouraged the growth of new investigations and monitoring methods [1–3] and the development of new advanced instruments, alternative or often complementary to the existing remote sensing systems. In this context, the rise of the Unmanned Aircraft Systems (UASs), now common and very widespread in the research and industrial sectors, is probably the most striking example [4–6].

As a consequence, scientific studies using UASs have strongly increased for the management of natural hazard effects and risk identification, both before disasters and after damage occurrence [7–11]. Given their flexibility and versatility of use, they guarantee reliable and fast data collection even in inaccessible areas and can be used in

© Springer International Publishing AG, part of Springer Nature 2018
O. Gervasi et al. (Eds.): ICCSA 2018, LNCS 10964, pp. 364–374, 2018.
https://doi.org/10.1007/978-3-319-95174-4_29

various fields such as in agriculture, forestry, archaeology, architecture, traffic moni-toring, environmental safety and emergency management [7]. The limited operating costs make these systems also convenient for multi-temporal applications where it is often necessary to acquire information from an active process over time.

However, we still lack codified methodologies to validate these techniques [7] and to seek structured approaches for obtaining high geometric accuracy, enhancing them as alternative or often complementary to consolidated systems [9].

This work investigates the potentialities of a short-range UAS analysing geomet-rical accuracies attainable through different orientation methodologies of photogram-metric models, combining different software and processing techniques.

The survey was carried out at the waste water treatment plant located in the Lama San Giorgio territory (Apulia region, Italy).

Firstly, two dense point clouds, derived using the Structure from Motion (SfM) techniques from the same images database, were compared to evaluate the relative geometric accuracies resulting from two different relative orientations: the first one based on the GPS position of each UAV frame and the second one based on GCPs, measured through GNSS campaigns. To assign three different absolute orientations, the georeferencing phase of the same orthomosaic was then verified, based on GCPs coming from three different open geo-data sources. By evaluating the position dis-crepancies of some Independent Check Points (ICPs), the three open geo-data sources provided three estimates of different root-mean-square error (RMSE) positional accu-racy, of which the absolute geometrical precision was the related function.

The purpose of this work was to develop advanced strategies to produce pho-togrammetric models, that may contribute to technical improvements aimed at the optimization of accuracy.

2 Methodology

In order to validate the photogrammetric models in geometric terms with respect to traditional photogrammetric products, a comparative analysis of the geometrical accuracies achievable changing external orientations (relatives and absolutes) [12] was carried out. As proposed in Pulighe et al. [13], a model with a good relative external orientation is one that accurately represents the shape of the terrain or distance and direction between two well-defined points. Essentially, the procedure will produce a model generally conforming with reality but without any metric or geographical meaning. The absolute geometric precision, on the other hand, that introduce metric information, will depend on the quality of the applied georeferencing process and will therefore be influenced by the type and truthfulness of the support points used. In this way, through a statistical inference the root-mean-square error (RMSE) positional accuracy of the generated photogrammetric products was evaluated [13]. Both open-source (i.e. VisualSfM, PMVS/CMVS, CloudCompare, Microsoft ICE) and licensed (i.e. Agisoft PhotoScan) software platforms were used to simultaneously test the applicability of Computer Vision/Structure from Motion algorithms in the gener-ation of three-dimensional models.

2.1 The Data and the Study Area

The test flight was performed on a small test area located in the Lama San Giorgio territory, an ephemeral river area of about 13 ha, near Sammichele di Bari (see Fig. 1). At present, based on the European Water Framework Directive (2000/60), it is a place of reception of the waste water treated in the local plant. The discharge in an ephemeral river area, according to Water Protection Plan (Piano di Tutela delle Acque) issued by the Apulia Regional Government, is assimilated to a discharge on the ground which entails a more restrictive adjustment of the limits imposed to the effluents present in the wastewater and, consequently, it requires more frequent checks of the environmental conditions of the water body. The survey was performed using a fixed-wing UAV eBee SenseFly equipped with a low-cost multispectral camera Canon NIR S110 (focal length of 5.2 mm, pixel size of 1.86 μm). The UAV comes with desktop software to prepare flight plans (i.e. 3D GPS waypoints) based on the amount of overlap and camera specifications. The flight lines were optimized to minimize flight time, wind direction or topography. Flight plans were prepared to obtain 80% image overlap in flight direction and 70% side overlap. Images were taken at specific time intervals to obtain the predefined overlap: 111 images were collected in about 8 min at a flight height of 101 m Above Ground Level (AGL) with a Average Ground Sample Distance (GSD) of 0.04 m.

Fig. 1. Location of the study area.

2.2 3D Model Generation Procedure

A chain of open-source applications for three-dimensional reconstruction of dense point clouds was used in the method [14]. These software platforms guaranteed full control of the reconstruction phases allowing the careful analysis of the parameters governing all processes involved. This ensured the possibility to choose the best strategy for the production of valid and consistent models, such as the VisualSfM platform, valid for SfM techniques, and PMVS/CMVS algorithms, which were associated to the platforms retrieving useful results for dense matching.

After collecting the necessary frames for the survey, it is essential to set up a series of operations to orient the projective bundles of each image. Today these operations are automatically performed by the software platforms, although managing their parameters is necessary. This process essentially depends on the characteristics of the sensor used and therefore it represents the internal orientation phase of each frame. Being peculiarly related to the camera, the procedure is identical for all the acquired images and therefore this phase was considered as secondary for the purpose of this work.

The second step is to detect the features of each image and then find the correlations between pairs of images. In this case, VisualSfM was used to perform two operations:

- Applying the SiftGPU algorithms based on GLSL (OpenGL Shading Language), i.e. the Scale Invariant Feature Transform (SIFT) algorithms processed by the Graphics Processing Unit (GPU);
- Detecting the correlations of the features between pairs of images, using the SiftMatchGPU always based on GLSL.

Misalignments observed from visual inspections were compensated by correcting the sparse point clouds and images positions through the Bundle Block Adjustment algorithms provided by VisualSfM, rectifying the correlations of the features. In this way the relative orientation of the model was performed both through positioning data provided by the UAV integrated GPS/INS navigation systems and through external Ground Control Points (GCPs). Two models of the same workflow were then saved to develop the following steps by setting the two different relative orientations.

For the first model, the GPS data used were extrapolated from the Extended File Information (EXIF) Headers of each loaded image. At the end of the process a point cloud with relative external orientation based on GPS data was generated. The procedure assigned an absolute external orientation based on the Earth-Centred, Earth-Fixed (ECEF) coordinate system.

Simultaneously, the twin model was generated defining an absolute positioning referenced to the WGS84-ETRS89 system. The transformation function was based on GCPs acquired during a surveying campaign with GNSS equipment, i.e. Leica Viva GS14 receivers. The points were detected performing RTK measurements with sub-centimetric accuracies carrying out an NRTK positioning on stable location with known coordinates estimated with high accuracy based on the National Dynamic Network (RDN2008).

After assigning the two relative external orientations to each sparse points cloud generated by the same work path, the dense points cloud reconstruction was finally implemented through CMVS (Clustering views for Multi-View Stereo) and PMVS2 (Patch-based Multi-View Stereo software - version 2) tools provided by VisualSfM. In Fig. 2 a visual comparison between the two dense reconstructions performed by the two models is presented.

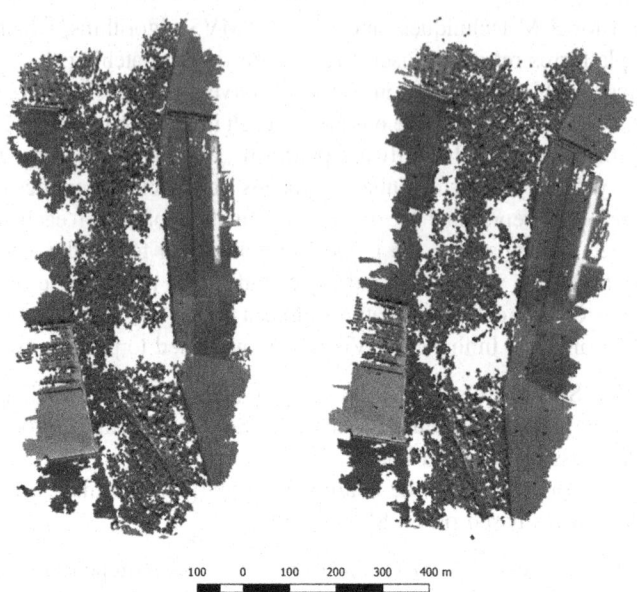

100   0   100   200   300   400 m

Fig. 2. On the left the dense point clouds reconstructed based on GCPs, on the right the reconstructed model based on the positions of GPS images. The scale reference performs approximately the metric information of the two sparse point clouds.

2.3   Comparing the Two Dense Point Clouds

The two dense point clouds models were compared by using CloudCompare open-source software.

The two models were initially not perfectly superimposed due to different scales and orientations. The direct comparison was made possible by registering the models based on absolute external orientation and in this case on the GCPs. At the end of the process both point clouds were perfectly aligned showing optimal results, i.e. a root-mean-square (RMS) of 0.007 m and a transformation Scale Factor of 0.845. With the alignment phase, a single absolute external orientation was then assigned, maintaining the relative external orientations unaltered for the two dense clouds.

For comparison purposes, the "Distances" tool provided by CloudCompare was used. For each point of the cloud compared, the nearest point in the reference cloud was searched, calculating their distance (Euclidean) by applying the 'Octree Level', i.e. the subdivision level of the Octree in which the distance calculation was performed.

The process generated four scalar fields, one for each axis, associated with the assigned point cloud, in our case the one based on GPS points. The results in absolute terms are shown in Fig. 3. The statistical distribution of Gauss that best adapts to the effective distribution of distances was related to the scalar field: the operation identified the mean value and standard deviation.

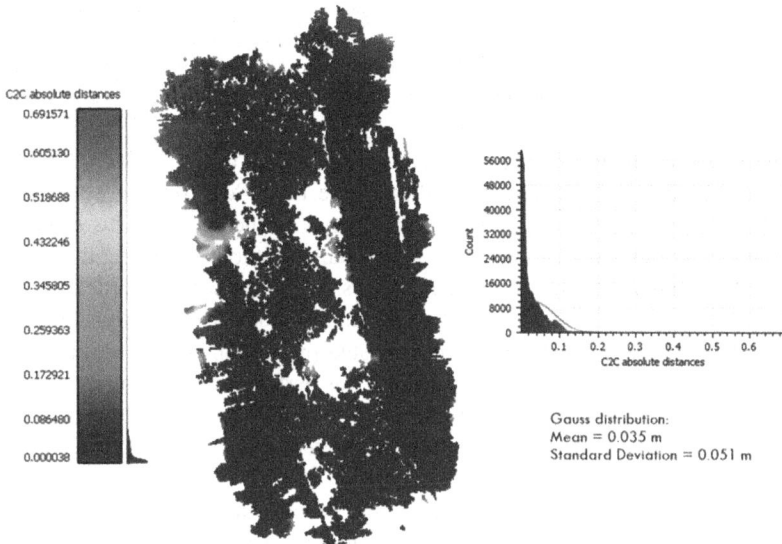

Fig. 3. Scalar field of the two dense point clouds and a plot of the best adapted statistical Gaussian distribution.

3   Assessment of Absolute Geometric Accuracies

In the context of absolute external orientation operations, 7 unknown parameters for each pair of images have to be determined to allow the adjustment of total scale and roto-translation of a whole model as a rigid body into space. To determine these parameters it is necessary to know the position of a minimum of four GCPs belonging to the object. The position of these GCPs can be determined by means of traditional topographic operations or collected from available cartographic data sources such as Google Earth, Bing Map, SIT Puglia, etc. Practically, it is always advisable to refer to a larger number of points than strictly necessary. In this way the resulted uncertainties can be mediated. Hence the quality of an absolute external orientation will be strongly influenced by the data source accuracies adopted for georeferencing. A photogrammetric model could have different absolute geometrical accuracy when the related absolute orientation varies from source to source.

In this study case, the absolute precision was measured as the error between the coordinates of some Independent Check Points (ICPs) identified by the targets on three different georeferenced orthomosaic images, each oriented through the same 10 GCPs extrapolated from different open geo-data sources, and the coordinates of the same points measured by means of a GNSS survey. It was expressed as the root-mean square error (RMSE), which is a general indicator of the cumulative result of all errors [13], i.e. both random and systematic errors related to the georeferencing process. The RMSE values were evaluated following the equations proposed by the Federal Geographic Data Committee (FGDC) [15, 16].

3.1   Orthomosaic Generation from the Agisoft Photoscan Workflow

At this stage, data were processed through the Agisoft PhotoScan platform which is characterized by a process reliability derived from the greater solidity of the algorithms operating in the orthomosaic generation.

Firstly, the working space was set, initially referring to the EPSG_4326 WGS84 reference system. Subsequently, in the first phase PhotoScan run the estimate of the internal and relative external orientation parameters of the images. This estimate was performed using the data of each image individually, without excluding the possibility that the final estimates might present some errors. High errors, not recorded in our case, could lead to non-linear deformations of the final model. The possible linear deformations of the model could however be adjusted by optimizing the estimation of the point cloud and the camera parameters, which was performed by basing the corrections on the GPS coordinates collected by the EXIF of each image. Photoscan thus minimized the sum of the errors of the camera parameters and made a re-projection of the misalignment errors of the reference coordinates.

The next phase was the construction of the dense points cloud. This cloud represents a first visualization of the three-dimensional model of the scene detected. To produce an Orthomosaic of the area it was necessary to generate a Digital Elevation Model (DEM) from the dense point clouds. Once the DEM was generated, it was possible to construct an Orthomosaic of the orthorectified images. The pixel dimensions on the ground for the production of raster files was set at a sufficient resolution for the elaborations programmed in the workflow. For this purpose, the pixel dimensions pre-calculated by the software were set to generate the orthomosaic with optimal resolution (13988 × 24244 with 3.6 cm/pix) and exported in JPEG format.

3.2   Georeferencing Orthomosaics Through GCPs Derived from Open Geo-Data

The absolute geometrical accuracy achievable on some ICPs distributed in the scene, adopting different absolute external orientations, was evaluated using the open source software platform QGIS, by identifying GCPs on geo-referenced cartographic sources. These open geo-data can be retrieved and freely consulted by means of plug-ins implemented on the QGIS platform or by using the Web Map Services (WMSs) available on the network. The satellite and aerial images of Google Maps, satellite and aerial images of Bing and the Orthoimage 2016 of the SIT Puglia were used as geo-referenced maps (see Fig. 4). The coordinates of ten ICPs were determined and compared with the coordinates values of the same points but measured by means of GNSS solutions with sub-centimeter accuracies. Following a robust statistical inference procedure, a set of parameters (Table 1) were processed to summarize the errors and the positional accuracy related to the different georeferencing operations.

Google Maps   Bing Aerial   Orthoimage 2016 - SIT Puglia

Fig. 4. Image orthomosaics georeferenced using open geo-data sources (Google maps – Bing Aerial – Orthoimage SIT Puglia).

Table 1. Statistical inference of discrepancies retrieved in 10 ICPs.

	GOOGLE MAPS		**BING AERIAL**		**ORTOPHOTO 2016 SIT PUGLIA**	
	ΔX (m)	*ΔY (m)*	*ΔX (m)*	*ΔY (m)*	*ΔX (m)*	*ΔY (m)*
Average Offset (m)	7.513	-4.537	6.502	-5.472	0.411	-0.600
Hor. Aver. Offset (m)	8.777		8.499		0.728	
Dev. St. Error (m)	8.552	6.833	1.168	3.347	0.471	2.968
Bias (m)	-7.513	4.537	-6.502	5.472	-0.411	0.600
RMSE (1D) (m)	11.058	7.913	6.596	6.327	0.607	2.879
RMSE (2D) (m)	13.597		9.140		2.943	

4   Results

Figure 3 shows the variability of the relative geometrical accuracy, presented as an average of the three axes, achieved by a different process of relative external orientation. In general, the average offset (mean) can be understood as the value of the systematic error, signalling a discrepancy that is the result of different approaches for relative orientation. However, it should be noted that the two models only deviate by 3.4 cm. Comparing the average offset value with the one derived from the standard deviation, we can observe that the latter is prevalent. The standard deviation, equal to 5 cm, can be understood as an index of the geometric stability of the image data set and is the result of random errors, which are difficult to assess. Hence, the two approaches used to assign a different relative orientation basically returned equivalent products.

This confirms the secondary role of the GCPs or of the information related to the GPS positions in the relative orientation phase. In fact, these may certainly be useful to shorten the calculation time and to determine additional pairs of collimable points on the various images. But the relative geometric accuracy will mainly be influence by the robustness of the matching estimates of the features performed by the algorithms.

Something different, however, was obtained in the subsequent phase about the absolute external orientation. In this case, the precise knowledge of some GCPs would certainly facilitate and improve absolute geometrical accuracy. The right placement in space and the assignment of a univocal scale to a photogrammetric product essentially depends on the quality of the available support points on which to set up a geo-referencing procedure. Table 1 illustrates three estimates of the positional accuracy (RMSE (2D) values) of the cartographic sources analyzed. The effect of each error on RMSE is proportional to the size of the quadratic error and this implies that the biggest errors will have a disproportionate effect, making it suitable to describe the presence of anomalous values. In the whole procedure of evaluating the same identified GCPs on different data sources, the Orthophoto 2016 available by the SIT Puglia was found to have a greater absolute positional accuracy than Google Maps and Bing open data sources. This means that every point identified as useful for georeferencing will be characterized by a positional error of about 2.943 m, and that the final photogrammetric product will necessarily be influenced by this approximation.

5   Conclusion

In this work different orientation methodologies to develop photogrammetric models were implemented in order to define advancement strategies in the generation of products from low-cost sensors on UAS.

Two dense point clouds were compared to evaluate the discrepancies resulting from two different relative orientations. To assign three different absolute orientations, the georeferencing process of the same orthomosaic was then verified based on GCPs coming from three different open geo-data sources.

Observing the results of the two dense point clouds, we can assume that to refine the accuracy of relative orientations between images, with the aim of generating products highly conforming with reality [13], it is preferable:

- to use a sensor pre-calibration to correctly and unambiguously fix the internal orientation of frames, avoiding estimation calculations by the software which may become a further source of errors;
- to provide the UAS with cameras adapted to the degree of precision commissioned, providing more distinctive points for matching processing;
- to use open source or licensed software to work with full resolution images;
- to analyse and develop a UAS flight planning by looking for an optimal flight height and a suitable overlap/sidelap degree in order to increase collimable points in the various images.

On the other hand, given the results obtained in terms of positional accuracy, the scientific usefulness of open data image archives is therefore summarily limited by the errors retrieved [17] and the coordinates extracted from these sources should only be used as approximations and not as fundamental truths. The quality of final photogrammetric products, explicitly affected by these limitations, will therefore require sources of greater accuracy to correctly orient the model. In the case where the project budget allows the detection of coordinates of different points with sub-centimetre accuracy in GNSS solution, this certainly makes the process cleaner.

Acknowledgements. The authors are grateful to VisualDrone (an Apulian start-up operating in the field of UAS) and to Dr. Antonio Novelli for their precious collaboration in the survey campaign.

References

1. Gioia, A., Iacobellis, V., Manfreda, S., Fiorentino, M.: Influence of infiltration and soil storage capacity on the skewness of the annual maximum flood peaks in a theoretically derived distribution. Hydrol. Earth Syst. Sci. **16**, 937–951 (2012)
2. Iacobellis, V., Castorani, A., Di Santo, R.A., Gioia, A.: Rationale for flood prediction in karst endorheic areas. J. Arid Environ. **112**(PA), 98–108 (2015)
3. Totaro, V., Gioia, A., Novelli, A., Caradonna, G.: The use of geomorphological descriptors and landsat-8 spectral indices data for flood areas evaluation: a case study of lato river basin. In: Gervasi, O., et al. (eds.) ICCSA 2017. LNCS, vol. 10407, pp. 30–44. Springer, Cham (2017). https://doi.org/10.1007/978-3-319-62401-3_3
4. Martínez-Espejo Zaragoza, I., Caroti, G., Piemonte, A., Riedel, B., Tengen, D., Niemeier, W.: Structure from motion (SfM) processing of UAV images and combination with terrestrial laser scanning, applied for a 3D-documentation in a hazardous situation. Geomat. Nat. Hazards Risk **8**, 13 (2017)
5. Mangiameli, M., Muscato, G., Mussumeci, G., Milazzo, C.: A GIS application for UAV flight planning. IFAC Proc. Vol. **46**, 147–151 (2013)
6. Caroti, G., Piemonte, A., Nespoli, R.: UAV-Borne photogrammetry: a low cost 3D surveying methodology for cartographic update. In: MATEC Web of Conferences, vol. 120, pp. 09005. EDP Sciences (2017)
7. Giordan, D., Hayakawa, Y., Nex, F., Remondino, F., Tarolli, P.: Review article: the use of remotely piloted aircraft systems (RPAS) for natural hazards monitoring and management. Nat. Hazards Earth Syst. Sci. Discuss. **2017**, 1–26 (2017)
8. Nakano, T., Kamiya, I., Tobita, M., Iwahashi, J., Nakajima, H.: Landform monitoring in active volcano by UAV and SFM-MVS technique. In: The International Archives of the Photogrammetry, Remote Sensing and Spatial Information Sciences, vol. XL-8, pp. 71–75 (2014)
9. Nex, F., Remondino, F.: UAV for 3D mapping applications: a review. Appl. Geomat. **6**, 1–15 (2014)
10. Remondino, F., Barazzetti, L., Nex, F., Scaioni, M., Sarazzi, D.: UAV photogrammetry for mapping and 3D modeling-current status and future perspectives. In: International Archives of the Photogrammetry, Remote Sensing and Spatial Information Sciences, vol. XXXVIII-1, p. C22 (2011)
11. Roncella, R.: Sviluppo e applicazioni di tecniche di automazione in fotogrammetria dei vicini (2018)

12. del Mar Saldana, M., Aguilar, M.A., Aguilar, F.: Generation and quality assessment of stereo-extracted DSM from GeoEye-1 and WorldView-2 imagery. IEEE Trans. Geosci. Remote Sens. **52**, 1259–1271 (2014)
13. Pulighe, G., Baiocchi, V., Lupia, F.: Horizontal accuracy assessment of very high resolution google earth images in the city of Rome, Italy. Int. J. Digit. Earth **9**, 342–362 (2016)
14. Teo, T.-A., Shih, P.T.-Y., Yu, S.-C., Tsai, F.: The use of UAS for rapid 3D mapping in geomatics education. In: The International Archives of the Photogrammetry, Remote Sensing and Spatial Information Sciences, vol. XLI-B6, pp. 95–100 (2016)
15. Congalton, R.G., Green, K.: Assessing the Accuracy of Remotely Sensed Data: Principals and Practices. Lewis Publishers, Boca Raton (2009)
16. Federal Geographic Data Committee: Geospatial Positioning Accuracy Standards - Part 3: National Standard for Spatial Data Accuracy . National Spatial Data Infrastructure (1998)
17. Potere, D.: Horizontal positional accuracy of google earth's high-resolution imagery archive. Sensors **8**, 7973 (2008)

Fire Risk Estimation at Different Scales of Observations: An Overview of Satellite Based Methods

Rosa Lasaponara[(⊠)], Angelo Aromando, Gianfranco Cardettini, and Monica Proto

Italian National Research Council, C.da Santa Loja, Tito Scalo, Potenza, Italy
Rosa.lasaponara@imaa.cnr.it

Abstract. Since the mid-1980 s satellite remote sensing data have been used in forest fire monitoring for applications related to the diverse phases of fire management as, fire prevention, danger estimation, detection of active fires, estimation of fire effects (burned area mapping, fire severity estimation, smoke plumes, biomass losses, etc), post fire recovery, fire regime characterization, etc. Today satellite technologies can fruitfully support both research and operational activities for fire monitoring and management at different temporal and spatial scales and with cost effective tools. This paper provides a short overview of satellite remote sensing for forest fire danger estimation at different scale of observations.

Keywords: Fire risk · Monitoring and management · Satellite images
Copernicus

1 Introduction

Fires are considered one of the most important causes of degradation being that they induce significant alterations not only on the vegetation cover but also on fauna, soil, atmosphere producing high direct and indirect losses including economic ones. Fire affects vegetation, landscape and environment at short as well as long-term. At short term fires induce patch homogenization and create positive feedbacks in future fire susceptibility, fuel loading, fire spreading and intensity and facilitate alien plant invasion.

At long term fires lead permanent changes in the composition of vegetation community, cause decrease in forests and loss of biodiversity, impact vegetation dynamics. Moreover, fires induce soil degradation, alteration of landscape patterns and ecosystem functioning, thus speeding desertification processes up.

This paper provides a short overview of satellite remote sensing for forest fires danger estimation. Since the mid-1980 s satellite Remote sensing data have been used for forest fire monitoring for applications in the diverse phases of fire management. Today satellite technologies can fruitfully support both research and operational activities for investigations and monitoring of fire and fire effects at different temporal and spatial scales, with cost effective tools.

O. Gervasi et al. (Eds.): ICCSA 2018, LNCS 10964, pp. 375–388, 2018.
https://doi.org/10.1007/978-3-319-95174-4_30

At global as at a local scale, remote sensing can provide suitable tools for short and long term investigations to support fire management issues for both knowledge and operational applications [1–8]. "The contribution of remote sensing (RS) to forest fires may be grouped in three categories, according to the three phases of fire management: (i) risk estimation (before fire), (ii) detection (during fire) and (iii) assessment (after fire). Relating each of these phases, wide research activities have been conducted over the years.

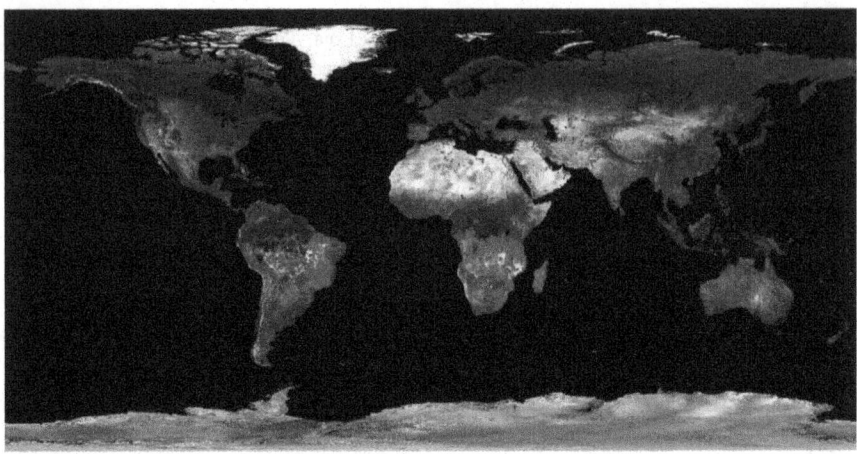

Fig. 1. Overview of fire occurrence at global scale (Nasa courtesy [9] http://www.nasa.gov/topics/earth/features/wildfires.html)

Actually up to now, significant efforts have been addressed by the major national and international space agencies, so that several products are currently made available

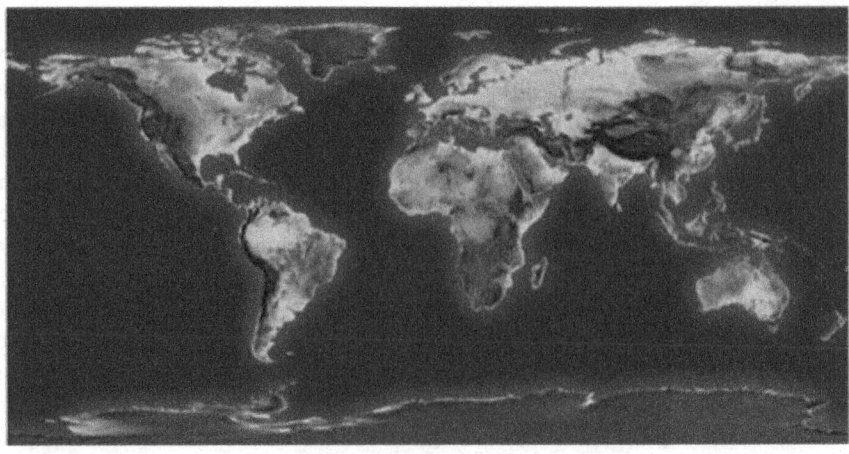

Fig. 2. Distribution of fire hotspots derived from the ATSR (ESA courtesy).

for free by NASA (see for examhttp://modis-fire.uhp) and ESA (see for example http://www.esa.int/About_Us/ESRIN/World_fire_maps_now_available_online_in_near-real_time [10]) mainly related to global active fire and burned areas. As an example, Fig. 1 provides an overview of fire occurrence at a global scale provided by NASA (Fig. 2).

Traditionally satellite based investigations on fire have been mainly based on the use of AVHRR (NOAA), MODIS (onboard TERRA and AQUA), ATRS, AATRS, MERIS, VEGETATION (onboard SPOT), TM, ASTER, due to their technical characteristics (i.e. spectral, spatial and temporal resolution). Moreover, investigations have been also approached using geostationary satellite sensors as SEVIRI as well as microwave active and passive data. Today, fire is one of the most important focal issues

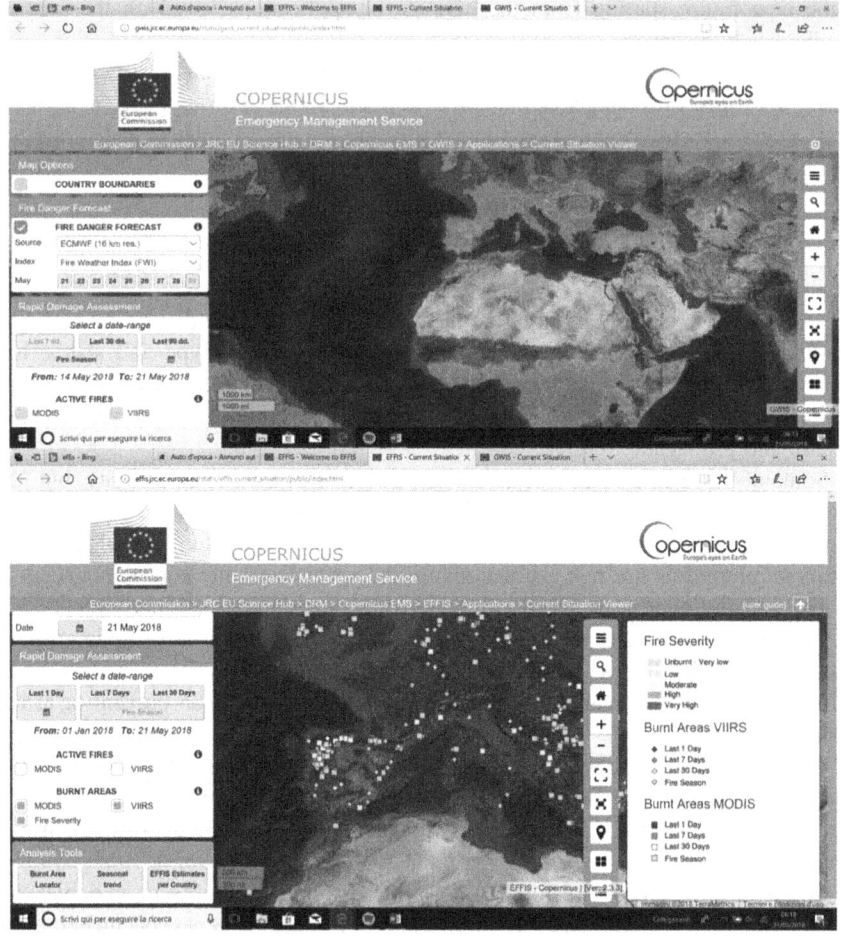

Fig. 3. Examples of Copernicus products: up: fire danger estimation at a global scale; bottom: fire severity at European scale (Copernicus courtesy, [11] see http://gwis.jrc.ec.europa.eu/static/gwis_current_situation/public/index.html).

of Copernicus in the framework of EFFIS aimed at supporting EU member states through the use of satellites for active fire mapping and rapid assessment of burnt areas (see Fig. 3).

The Sentinel sensor satellites (see [12] https://eox.at/2015/12/understanding-sentinel-2-satellite-data/) are part of Europe's ambitious program (formerly known as Global Monitoring for Environment and Security (GMES)). The overall mission is composed of five constellations of satellites, each targeting a different application domain. All the Sentinel missions release under an Open Data policy allowing free access to images in order to foster enhanced knowledge generation and support application developments.

All Sentinels were designed for supporting the management of (i) natural disaster from risk analysis to loss assessment and (ii) humanitarian aid in crisis situations. Therefore, knowledge advancements in fire management and monitoring are expected in the next future starting from the heritage of applications based on the past and existing satellite sensors.

This paper provides a short overview of the main applications of satellite remote sensing for forest fires danger estimation at different scales of observation, in particular Sects. 3 and 4 focused on a short summary of fire danger parameters at (i) long term (fuel types) and (ii) short term estimation (fuel moisture).

2 Fire Danger Estimation

Fire occurrence is induced by different factors, some of them are depending on human actions, others, such as topography, meteorology, vegetation type and status, have physical nature and are generally called "susceptible" factors see Lasaponara 1998 [14] and reference therein quoted, because they refer to conditions that can make fire ignition and propagation easier.

Some of the "susceptible" factors cannot be modified by human activity, but, they can be predicted. Fire forecasting solely based on physical factors are generally classified as fire danger estimation models, whereas the coupled use of physical and human factors is referred as fire risk estimations. In the specialized literature the concepts of fire risk and fire danger are used with these different meanings.

Fire forecasting plays an important role in the framework of programs for fire damage mitigation. It is a valuable support for designing strategies related to the use and distribution of the available fire-fighting resources, which can prevent or at least minimize fire effects.

In the context of forest fire emergencies management, decision makers require timely and effective decision support tools that must be able to provide information for large areas updated on a short term basis in which daily predictions are usually required.

The main problem of fire forecasting is the extreme variability of variables connected with fire ignition and fire propagation. In fact, changes occurring in the proneness of vegetation to fire are due to a number of factors, some of them are permanent and others dynamic and characterized by different spatial and temporal variations.

Static variable/indices, that do not vary at least during the given "fire season", are:

– Digital Terrain Model (DTM): Slope, Aspect, Elevation
– Vegetation-Fuel types/models
– Burned area mapping and severity of past fires
– Fire Regime
– Human factors: including population density, seasonal/touristic fluxes, road and accessibility, human activities,

Dynamic Variables are:

– Meteorological factors: temperature, humidity, Wind, insolation, etc.
– State of the vegetation (moisture content, stress)

Many of the above quoted static and dynamic variables can be estimated using satellite data. As, for example, the DTM that can be fruitfully obtained from active (SAR) or passive data (as ASTER, for example) and directly available for free from the NASA website, as in the case of the SRTM mission today detailed DTM at 30 m ([13] http://www2.jpl.nasa.gov/srtm/cbanddataproducts.html) (Fig. 4).

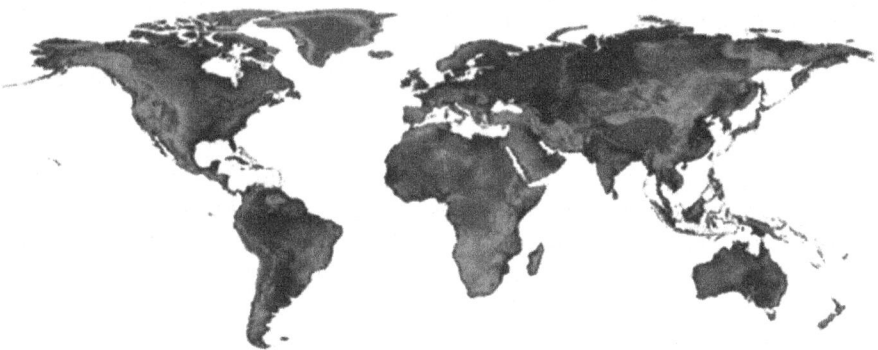

Fig. 4. Digital terrain model DTM from SRTM (NASA courtesy) In late 2014, the United States government released the highest resolution SRTM DEM to the public. This 1-arc second global digital elevation model has a spatial resolution of about 30 m. Also, it covers most of the world with absolute vertical height accuracy of less than 16 m.

Obviously, vegetation cover is considered a key factor in fire danger estimation and it is generally accounted as "fuel" (see Sect. 3) in terms of its load and flammability. The flammability depends on the species and for a most complex factors to be esti- mated because it depends on meteorological conditions and also in the case of live fuel on the evapotranspiration process and can change significantly over a period of few days.

The use of satellite images is considered very attractive for monitoring the state of vegetation due to their technical characteristics (i.e. spectral, spatial and temporal resolution) on a daily basis, by using routine and automated data processing.

Moreover, satellite data overcome the problem of the uncertain linked to the · spazialization of meteorological data with particular reference to fuel moisture. Nevertheless, today high spatial resolution meteorological forecasts are available as COSMO 2 (around 2 km) model based on ECMWF or Moloch (around 1 km) and as in the case of Copernicus can be successfully used for fire danger estimation based on meteorological parameters.

Traditionally, fire danger estimation based on satellite data has been mainly based on the use of satellite data for the estimation of both long and short term parameters. Due to their technical characteristics (i.e. spectral, spatial and temporal resolution) some satellite sensors as, AVHRR (onboard NOAA), MODIS (onboard TERRA and AQUA), VEGETATION (onboard SPOT) have been widely used for fire danger estimation. Nevertheless, some examples of SAR data are also present in the specialized literature (see Sect. 4).

3   Fuel Types from Space

Fuel types denote the categorization of vegetation on the basis of its physical parameters and spatial distribution also indicated as "fuel models" (see, for example, 2–4 and references therein quoated). More specifically, a fuel model has been defined as "an identifiable association of fuel elements of distinctive species, form, size, arrangement, and continuity that will exhibit characteristic fire behavior under defined burning conditions".

Several satellite sensors have been used in last decades, applying direct or indirect mapping strategies: (i) direct mapping strategies extract fuel classifications directly from imagery; (ii) indirect fuel mapping strategies use ecosystem characteristics as surrogates for fuels. Direct fuel mapping using remote sensing refers to the direct assignment of fuel characteristics to the results of image classification

The main advantage of the direct approach is its simplicity: by classifying fuels directly from imagery, compounding errors from biomass calculations, translation errors from vegetation classifications and image processing steps are minimized. Also the ground references are simplified. However, the main disadvantage is that it is difficult to classify all fuel characteristics in a way useful to fire management in many forested ecosystems.

Passive sensors cannot get information about understory therefore it is not possible to discriminate understory in forest areas. Moreover, a direct remote sensing mapping often distinguishes vegetation types rather than fuel attributes. An approach based on a direct fuel mapping (using remote sensing) provides high performances in grasslands and shrub-land but meets serious difficulties when used in forested ecosystems because of passive sensors are usually unable to detect understory under close canopies.

Indirect fuel mapping based on remote sensing uses ecosystem characteristics as surrogates for fuels to overcome the limitations of imagery to directly map fuel characteristics. This approach assumes that biophysical or biological properties can be accurately classified from remotely sensed imagery. These properties are often related to the vegetation and well correlate with fuel characteristics or fuel models (Fig. 5 and Table 1).

Table 1. Fuel type classification developed for Mediterranean ecosystems in the framework of Prometheus project (Prometheus Project 1999)

Fuel type class	Fuel type description in terms of percentage of cover	Fuel type description in terms of vegetation typology
1	Ground fuels (cover >50%)	Grass
2	Surface fuels (shrub cover >60%, tree cover <50%)	Grassland, shrub land (smaller than 0.3–0.6 m and with a high percentage of grassland), and clear cuts, where slash was not removed
3	Medium-height shrubs (shrub cover >60%, tree cover <50%)	Shrubs between 0.6 and 2.0 m
4	Tall shrubs (shrub cover >60%, tree cover <50%)	High shrubs (between 2.0 and 4.0 m) and young trees resulting from natural regeneration or forestation
5	Tree stands (>4 m) with a clean ground surface (shrub cover <30%)	The ground fuel was removed either by prescribed burning or by mechanical means. This situation may also occur in closed canopies in which the lack of sunlight inhibits the growth of surface vegetation
6	Tree stands (>4 m) with medium surface fuels (shrub cover >30%)	The base of the canopies is well above the surface fuel layer (>0.5 m). The fuel consists essentially of small shrubs, grass, litter, and duff (the layer of decomposing organic materials lying immediately above the mineral soil but below the litter layer of freshly fallen twigs, needles, and leaves; the fermentation layer)
7	Tree stands (>4 m) with heavy surface fuels (shrub cover >30%)	Stands with a very dense surface fuel layer and with a very small vertical gap to the canopy base (<0.5 m)

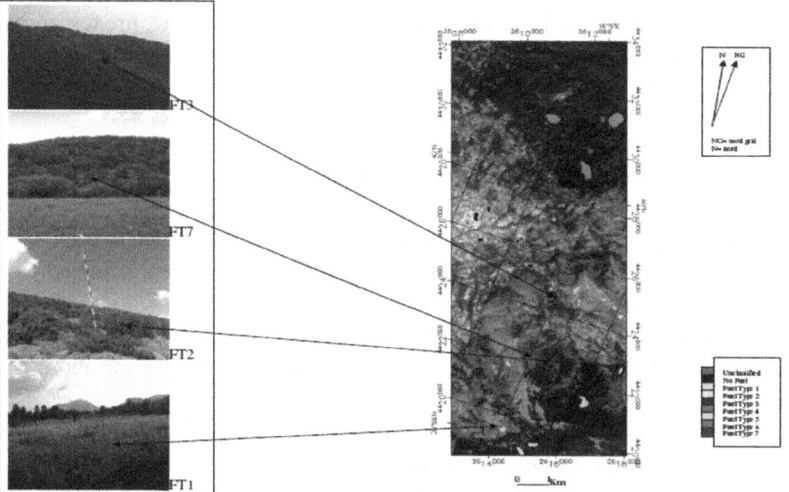

Fig. 5. Examples of fuel types as classified following Prometheous model applied to the Pollino national park and since 2015 Unesco geosite (see [1–4] and references therein quoted).

Table 2. Summary of primary use of fuel map and related spatial scale

Fuel maps	Spatial scale		
	Coarse	Mid	Fine
Primary application	Fire danger	Fire risk and hazard	Fire growth
Fire uses	Plan and allocate resources	Locate and prioritize treatment areas	Simulate fire behaviour, predict fire effects
Other possible uses	Global carbon budgets	Forest health assessment	Simulate ecosystem and fire Dynamics
Most probable mapping approach	Indirect, gradient model	Direct, indirect, gradient model	Field reconnaissance, direct, indirect, gradient model
Mapping entities	Land use types	Fuel models	Fuel models, fuel loadings
Possible pixel sizes	500 m–5 km	30–500 m	5–30 m
Imagery	A\HRR, MODIS	MODIS, MSS,TM	TM, ASTER, SPOT, AVIRIS, IKONOS, QuickBird, MIVIS, LiDAR, SAR, aerial photos

The importance of using multisensor data source to map fuel model was emphasized by many authors. Actually, the advent of new sensors with improved spatial and spectral resolutions as sentinel 2 may improve the accuracy and reduce the cost (being the data free available from ESA website). Nevertheless, up to now, fire researchers did not paid enough attention to the potentiality of using remote sensing data from different data sources (Table 2).

4   Satellite Based Fire Danger Estimation

The estimation of the vegetation proneness to fire at short term has been generally based on the time variation of several satellite derived parameters assumed as proxy indicators of vegetation moisture content.

Over the years a lot of investigations have been conducted using optical satellite images (as AVHRR, MODIS, VEGETATION, TM ASTER etc), and more recently also using satellite SAR data.

The use of optical satellite data for estimating the variations of moisture content as a proxy indicator of the proneness of vegetation to fire are generally conducted using the well-known vegetation indices (namely spectral combinations of different bands) that are traditionally used for vegetation monitoring. Among the various vegetation indices, NDVI is the most widely used. It is calculated (see Eq. 1) as function of surface reflectance of red [0.60–0.70 μm] and near infrared (NIR) [0.70–0.90 μm] spectral bands.

$$NDVI = (NIR - RED)/(NIR + RED) \tag{1}$$

The normalization of the NDVI reduces the effects of variations caused by atmospheric contaminations. High values of the vegetation index identify pixels covered by substantial proportions of healthy vegetation. NDVI is indicative of plant photosynthetic activity and has been found to be related to the green leaf area index and the fraction of photosynthetically active radiation absorbed by vegetation. Therefore, variations in NDVI values become indicative of variations in vegetation composition and dynamics. It is one of the most commonly adopted proxy indicator of vegetation status being that it is able to account for vegetation vigour, and therefore, it should be able to detect the vegetation stress and drought as well as deteriorations of pigments and leaf structure which makes the vegetation more prone to fire. Other commonly used vegetation indices for pre fire monitoring are NDII, GREENNEES, NDWI, LTS (Land Surface Temperature), RH (Relative Humidity (also obtained from Modis).

Burgan et al. (1997) used relative greenness index as an input parameter for estimating and discriminated live from dead fuel. High relative greenness values indicate that the vegetation is healthy and vigorous whereas low greenness values indicate that the vegetation is under stress, dry (possibly from drought), is behind in annual development, or dead. Burgan et al. proposed as danger indication the Relative Greenness indices, as in formula (2).

$$RGI = \frac{NDVI_{cur} - NDVI_{min}}{NDVI_{max} - NDVI_{min}} \times 100\% \tag{2}$$

where RGI is the value of relative greenness, NDVIcur is the observed NDVI for a given pixel, NDVImin and NDVImax are the minimum and maximum NDVI values for a given pixel during the study period.

Finally, on the basis of the Greenness relative index, we can estimate using formula (3) the living part of the fuel load, using formula which provides live-ratio (Burgan et al. 1998):

$$LR = GRNrel \; x(0.35 + 0.5NDVImax) \tag{3}$$

The complementary part of LR namely $(1 - LR)$ provides the estimation of the dead part of the fuel load, using formula (4)

$$DR = (1 - LR) \tag{4}$$

The combination of NIR and SWIR spectral channels is the basis of the NDWI and NDII indices that are more sensitive to variations in vegetation moisture content, and therefore, much more able to estimate the reduction of moisture availability due to drought. NDWI and NDII can be obtained using diverse SWIR channels (also available from MODIS) one of the most commonly used is NDII7, computed using formula (5):

The NDWI is a remote sensing based indicator sensitive to the change in the water content of leaves NDWI is computed using the near infrared (NIR – MODIS band 2) and the short wave infrared (SWIR – MODIS band 6 or MODIS band 7) reflectance's.

$$NDVI = (NIR - SWIR)/(NIR + SWIR) \tag{5}$$

One of the most used index obtained from both meteorological or satellite data is the Dead Fuel Moisture Index (DFMI) that is an estimation of the content of dead fuel using the

$$DFMI = 10 - 0.25\,(LST - RH) \tag{6}$$

where LST and RH cab ne obtained from meteorological stations or using the LST MODIS product also for obtaining RH using MODIS data (see [13]).

Table 3. Overview of satellite-based spectral indices and methodologies adopted for fire danger estimation

Indices	Sensor	Method	Locations	Reference
NDVI TS	AVHRR	Established relations between NDVI and TS variation for estimating different degree of fire danger.	Canada	Chuvieco et al. [14]
NDVI TS	AVHRR	Established relations between NDVI and TS variation for estimating different degree of fire danger	South of Italy	Lasaponara [15]
NDVI TS DTM		Integration of satellite estimation of fire danger with weather forecast		Lasaponara et al. [16]
NDWI	MODIS	Established relations between FMC and: (i) 8-day composite of NDWI (Stow et al. 2005); and (ii) 10-day composite of NWDI (Dennison et al. 2005). The agreements were reasonable in both of the cases, such as r2value of: (i) 0.50 in case of Stow et al. 2005; and (ii) between 0.39 to 0.80 for Dennison et al., 2005	Chaparral shrub-lands in California, USA	Sow et al. [18] Dennison et al. [19]
NDVI TS NDWI, NDII,	AVHRR MODIS	Comparison of diverse satellite based indices	South of Italy	Lasaponara [8]
NDWI NDII, GVMI MSI, SRWI	MODIS	Used 8-day composite for the index of interest and compared with the FMC and equivalent water thickness (EWT); and found good agreements in most of the cases (i.e., r2 values in the range of 0 to 0.81).	Savanna forests in Senegal, West Africa	Stow and Niphadkar [20]

(continued)

Table 3. (*continued*)

Indices	Sensor	Method	Locations	Reference
NMDI, NDWI	MODIS	Employed daily NMDI and NDWI-values in detecting forest fires. The performance was evaluated against the MODIS-based active fire spots during the fire occurrences and observed that NMDI performed better (i.e., matched with over 75% of the fire instances).	Southern Georgia, USA and mixed forests in southern Greece	Wang et al. [21, 22]
GVMI NDVI	MODIS	Employed 8-day composite to calculate the vegetation water content (VWC) using the empirical relationship of GVMI and EWT. In addition, monthly composite of NDVI were also compared with the VWC. Both of the indices indicated that their lowest values were coincided with the fire occurrences during the period of spring fires (March to May).	Inner Mongolia plateau and Song Liao plain	Jiang et al. [23]
NDWI CWC	MODIS	Compared 8-day composite of these indices with the FMC; and found to have reasonable relations (i.e., r2 values in the range of 0.26 to 0.44)	Northern Utah, USA	Qi et al. [24]
NDII6, NDII7, NDWI	MODIS	Used 16-day composite and compared with the FMC. Multiple regressions was performed during the period of 2000–2006 and found good relationships (i.e., r2 values in the range of 0.64 to 0.70).	Chaparral Shrub-lands in California, USA	Peterson et al. [25]
NDII6, NDII7, WI, NDWI EWT	AVIRIS MODIS	Employed both AVIRIS and MODIS-derived indices during the period 1994–2004 with the FMC; and found that the AVIRIS-derived indices were better correlated (i.e., r2 values in between 0.72 to 0.85) than the MODIS derived ones (i.e., r2 values in between 0.55 to 0.61)	Shrub-lands in California, USA	Roberts et al. [26]
DFMI = 10–0.25 (LST – RH)	Modis	Employed daily MODIS data to compute TS and RH and in turn to obtain DFMI-values for assessing vegetation fire susceptibility	China	Li et al. [13]

Table 3 provides an overview of both mainly used satellite based spectral indices and methodologies adopted for fire danger estimation The spectral indices, herein considered, were selected because they appear to be useful for fire danger estimation being that were already investigated for the scope. The question is to assess which parameters are more suitable and adequate for the implementation of automatic algorithms for mapping the proneness of vegetation to fire.

Related to radar-based investigations, it must be considered that the backscatter measurement depends on two main physical parameters that are moisture and roughness. The latter is not an absolute parameter but is strongly linked with the radar operating frequency. Related forest cover the backscatter measurements depend on (i) topography and surface roughness and canopy height, (ii) vegetation in terms of type, species, structure, and vegetation biomass (iii) vegetation moisture content and (iv) the presence/absence of standing water.

Studies reviewed in [27–29] conducted over boreal forests have shown positive relationships between rainfall amounts and radar backscatters from ERS-1 C-VV SAR images and with RADARSAT-1 C-VH SAR images [27–29]. Nevertheless, considering satellite SAR data only a few experimentations are available. Additional investigations are required in order to assess if as expected the encouraging results of the early studies can be improved considering the technical characteristics of the satellite SAR sensors such as the fully polarimetric X-, C- and L-band available from the diverse satellite platforms as for example Sentinel 1, ALOS-PALSAR, TerraSAR-X, Cosmo, RADARSAT-2, PALSAR 2).

5 Final Remarks: Forest Fires, Climate Change and Adaptation Strategies

Fire represents one of the main disturbances for vegetation, causing profound transformations at different temporal and spatial scales which affect ecosystems, landscapes and environments. Climate change is expected to bring increased forest fire risk by altering the water cycle at seasonal time scale, by increasing the occurrence of prolonged droughts and heat waves in the Mediterranean basin, as well as in Alpine ecosystems and boreal forests, with severe environmental and economic consequences.

The use of satellite data for fire monitoring has a "long history" as evident from a consolidated literature spanned over than 30 years with a rich variety of investigations conducted in diverse ecosystems and geographical areas. In particular, due the large availability of active and passive data at diverse temporal and spatial scales, remote sensing techniques can be considered fully operational for the estimation fire danger and fire effects (burnt areas, fire severity, smoke plumes) including the investigation post fire recovery and the impact on climate change on fire regime.

The operational applications are made possible and fully supported by the availability for free of data such as MODIS, TM, and Sentinel platforms that are systematically acquired daily, weekly or biweekly. Related the estimation of burned area and fire severity improved performances are expected from Sentinel active and passive data.

Moreover, focusing on applications linked to the diverse phases of fire management including danger estimation (pre-fire), fire detection (identification of active fires), assessment of fire effects from different point of views (fire impact on vegetation, soil, atmosphere) satellite can provide useful information at different spatial and temporal scales for developing adaptation and mitigation strategies to also face the impact of climate change on fire occurrence as well as to also investigate other impact of climate change (as on the sea [31] extract information and feature in automatic way as for example in [32].

Acknowledgment. The activities were carried out within the project SERV_FORFIRE "Integrated services and approaches for Assessing effects of climate change and extreme events for fire and post fire risk prevention". Project SERV_FORFIRE is part of ERA4CS, an ERA-NET initiated by JPI Climate, and funded by FORMAS (SE), DLR (DE), BMWFW (AT), IFD (DK), MINECO (ES), ANR (FR) with co-funding by the European Union (Grant 690462).

References

1. Chuvieco, E., Martin, M.P.: Global fire mapping and fire danger estimation using AVHRR images. Photogramm. Eng. Remote Sens. **60**(5), 563–570 (1994)
2. Lasaponara, R., Lanorte, A.: VHR QuickBird data for fuel type characterization in fragmented landscape. Ecological Modelling in press (ECOMOD845R1) 204, 79–84 (2007a)
3. Lasaponara, R., Lanorte, A.: Remotely sensed characterization of forest fuel types by using satellite ASTER data. Int. J. Appl. Earth Observations Geoinf. **9**, 225 (2007b)
4. Lasaponara, R., Lanorte, A.: Multispectral fuel type characterization based on remote sensing data and Prometheus model. For. Ecol. Manag. **234**, S226 (2006)
5. Lasaponara, R., Cuomo, V., Macchiato, M.F., Simoniello, T.: A self-adaptive algorithm based on AVHRR multitemporal data analysis for small active fire detection. Int. J. Remote Sens. **24**(8), 1723–1749 (2003)
6. Lasaponara, R.: Estimating spectral separability of satellite derived parameters for burned areas mapping in the Calabria region by using SPOT-vegetation data. Ecol. Model. **196**, 265–270 (2006)
7. Telesca, L., Lasaponara, R.: Investigating fire-induced behavioural trends in vegetation covers. Commun. Nonlinear Sci. Numer. Simul. **13**, 2018–2023 (2008)
8. Lasaponara, R.: Inter-comparison of AVHRR-based fire danger estimation methods. Int. J. Remote Sens. **26**(5), 853–870 (2005)
9. http://www.nasa.gov/topics/earth/features/wildfires.html
10. http://www.esa.int/About_Us/ESRIN/World_fire_maps_now_available_online_in_near-real_time
11. http://gwis.jrc.ec.europa.eu/static/gwis_current_situation/public/index.html
12. http://www2.jpl.nasa.gov/srtm/cbanddataproducts.html
13. Li, X., Song, W., Lanorte, A., Lasaponara, R.: Remote sensing fire danger prediction models applied to Northern China. In: Gervasi, O., et al. (eds.) ICCSA 2016. LNCS, vol. 9790, pp. 624–633. Springer, Cham (2016). https://doi.org/10.1007/978-3-319-42092-9_47
14. Chuvieco, E., Aguado, I., Cocero, D., Riano, D.: Design of an empirical index to estimate fuel moisture content from NOAA-AVHRR images in forest fire danger studies. Int. J. Remote Sens. **24**(8), 1621–1637 (2003)

15. Lasaponara, R.: AVHRR based investigation for forest fire detection and risk estimation. Ph. D. thesis, University of Florence (2008)
16. Lasaponara, R., Cuomo, V., Tramutoli, V., Pergola, N., Pietrapertosa, C.: Forest fire danger estimation based on the integration of satellite AVHRR data and topographic factors. Remote Sens. Earth Sci. Ocean Sea Ice Appl. 3868, 241–253
17. Lasaponara, R., Simoniello, T., Cuomo, V., Macchiato, M.: A review of AVHRR-based fire susceptibility estimation methods. In: Goossens, R. (ed.) Proceedings of the 23rd Symposium of the European Association of Remote Sensing Laboratories: Remote Sensing in Transition, Ghent, Belgium (2003)
18. Sow, M., Mbow, C., Hély, C., Fensholt, R., Sambou, B.: Estimation of herbaceous fuel moisture content using vegetation indices and land surface temperature from MODIS data. Remote Sens. 5, 2617–2638 (2013)
19. Dennison, P.E., Roberts, D.A., Peterson, S.H., Rechel, J.: Use of normalized difference water index for monitoring live fuel moisture. Int. J. Remote Sens. 26(5), 1035–1042 (2005)
20. Stow, D., Niphadkar, M.: Stability, normalization and accuracy of MODIS-derived estimates of live fuel moisture for southern California chaparral. Int. J. Remote Sens. 28, 5175–5182 (2007)
21. Wang, L., Zhou, Y., Zhou, W., Wang, S.: Fire danger assessment with remote sensing: a case study in Northern China. Nat. Hazards 65, 819–834 (2013)
22. Wang, L., Qu, J.J.: NMDI: A normalized multi-band drought index for monitoring soil and vegetation moisture with satellite remote sensing. Geophys. Res. Lett. 34, L20405 (2007)
23. Jiang, M., Hu, Z., Ding, D., Fang, D., Li, Y., Wei, L., Guo, M., Zhang, S.: Estimation of vegetation water content based on MODIS: application on forest fire risk assessment. In: 20th International Conference on Geoinformatics, p. 14. IEEE Conference Publications (2012)
24. Qi, Y., Dennison, P.E., Spencer, J., Riano, D.: Monitoring live fuel moisture using soil moisture and remote sensing proxies. Fire Ecol. 8(3), 71–87 (2012)
25. Peterson, S.H., Roberts, D.A., Dennison, P.E.: Mapping live fuel moisture with MODIS data: a multiple regression approach. Remote Sens. Environ. 112, 4272–4284 (2008)
26. Roberts, D.A., Dennison, P.E., Peterson, S., Sweeney, S., Rechel, J.: Evaluation of airborne visible/infrared imaging spectrometer (AVIRIS) and moderate resolution imaging spectrometer (MODIS) measures of live fuel moisture and fuel condition in a shrubland ecosystem in southern California. J. Geophys. Res. 111, 1–16 (2006)
27. Leblon, B., Kasischke, E.S., Alexander, M.E., Doyle, M., Abbott, M.: Fire danger monitoring using ERS-1 SAR images in the case of northern boreal forests. Nat. Hazards 27, 231–255 (2002)
28. Abbott, K.N., Leblon, B., Staples, G.C., Maclean, D.A., Alexander, M.E.: Fire danger monitoring using RADARSAT-1 over northern boreal forests. Int. J. Remote Sens. 28(6), 1317–1338 (2007)
29. Bourgeau-Chavez, L.L., Garwood, G., Riordann, K., Cella, B., Alden, S., Kwart, M., Murphy, K.: Improving the prediction of wildfire potential in boreal Alaska with satellite imaging radar. Polar Rec. 43(4), 321–330 (2007)
30. Crocetto, N., Tarantino, E.: A class-oriented strategy for features extraction from multidate ASTER imagery. Remote Sens. 1(4), 1171–1189 (2009)
31. Tarantino, E.: Monitoring spatial and temporal distribution of sea surface temperature with TIR sensor data. Ital. J. Remote Sens./Rivista Italiana di Telerilevamento 44(1) (2012)

8th International Symposium on Software Quality (ISSQ 2018)

Developer Focus: Lack of Impact on Maintainability

Csaba Faragó[1] and Péter Hegedűs[2(✉)]

[1] Department of Software Engineering, University of Szeged, Szeged, Hungary
farago@inf.u-szeged.hu
[2] MTA-SZTE Research Group on Artificial Intelligence, Szeged, Hungary
hpeter@inf.u-szeged.hu

Abstract. We were looking for evidence that a connection between source code quality erosion and the developer focus exists. We assumed that more focused developers, i.e. those who are concerned with a well specified part of the source code at a time are likely to commit higher quality code compared to those who are less focused, i.e. committing to various parts of the code. We estimated code quality with the ColumbusQM quality model and developer focus with structural scattering. Despite the assumption sounds quite logical, we could not find any supporting evidence.

As structural scattering assigns a measure to a set of source files/classes (i.e., how close they are to each other in the package hierarchy), we could apply it in various ways. First, we defined developer focus to be the structural scattering of the set of source files in a commit to validate if more focused changes have better impact on maintainability than less focused ones. Second, we calculated the structural scattering of all the files the developer of a commit modified in the last 3 months and assigned this measure as the developer focus to that commit. With this test we checked if more focused developers tend to commit better quality code, compared to less focused ones. We also performed this test for every developer separately, considering only the subset of the commits that were created by that particular developer.

We calculated the level of developer focus and the maintainability changes for every commit of three open-source and one proprietary software system. With the help of Wilcoxon rank test we compared the focus values of commits causing a maintainability increase with those of decreasing the maintainability. The results are non-conclusive, they do not even tend to the same direction, therefore we did not find any evidence of an existing connection between maintainability and developer focus. Therefore this is a publication of negative results.

Keywords: Developer focus · ISO/IEC 25010
Source code maintainability · Wilcoxon test · Negative results

1 Introduction

Maintenance of the software consumes big efforts, high proportion of the total amount of software development costs are spent on this activity. Source code

© Springer International Publishing AG, part of Springer Nature 2018
O. Gervasi et al. (Eds.): ICCSA 2018, LNCS 10964, pp. 391–402, 2018.
https://doi.org/10.1007/978-3-319-95174-4_31

maintainability is in direct connection with maintenance costs [2]. Our motivation in this work was to investigate the effect of the development process on the maintainability of the code. Our goal was to explore typical patterns causing similar changes in software maintainability, which could either help to avoid software erosion, or provide information about how to better allocate efforts to improve software maintainability.

We already investigated this area of research in previous works [6–11]. In article [11] we showed that a strong connection between the version control operations and the maintainability of the source code exists. In study [7] we revealed the connection between the version control operations and maintainability. We found that file additions have rather positive and file updates have negative effect on maintainability. A clear effect of file deletions was not identified. In article [6] we presented the results of a variance analysis. We found that file additions and file deletions increase the variance of the maintainability, and operation Update decreases it. In work [9] we analyzed code churn, i.e. the intensity of past modifications. We found that modifying high-churn code is more likely to decrease the overall maintainability of a software system. In study [8] we considered the developer and investigated how code ownership impacts maintainability. We concluded that common code is more likely to erode further than code with clear ownership. In article [10] we defined a few version control history metrics and checked their connection with maintainability. Our tests resulted that higher intensity of modifications, the higher number of code modifications and developers, the older code and the later last modification date have lower maintainability and higher number of post-release bugs.

Up to now we published in this area of research positive results only. But we think that publishing negative results is also very important; a negative result can also be very helpful. In this paper presents the negative results of a study performed but never published as part of our research investigating how code ownership impacts maintainability [8]. That paper was motivated by works of others [3,4,21] revealing an increased bug-prediction capability of models with some form of code ownership included as a predictor. We could confirm that clear ownership has a positive effect on code maintainability (measured by the combination of well-known source code metrics) as well. This result showed that common code is more likely to erode than code with clear ownership. This complements and generalizes bug-prediction studies on this topic. As part of this work, we wanted to show that the focus of developers also has a significant impact on software maintainability. This assumption was inspired by Di Nucci et al. [5] who investigated the impact of developer focus on post-release bugs. They found that a bug prediction model including the structural and semantic scattering metrics, which measure how close the modified code parts are structurally and conceptually overperforms the models not using these indicators.

We defined developer focus based on their definition of structural scattering [5], which is the distance between the files the developers work with at a time: the number of steps needed to take from the package of one file to another. The closest ones – having distance 0 – are those located in the same package.

The focus of a set of source files is the normalized aggregation of pairwise distances. The study of developer focus that is developer oriented (i.e., investigates the effect of what else the developer modified) would complement the code ownership study [8], which took a source code oriented approach (i.e., studies the effect of who else modified the same source code).

Formally, we investigated the following research questions:

RQ1: *Do more focused commits (i.e., commits affecting a set of source files with low scattering value) have better impact on maintainability compared to those of less focused commits?*

RQ2: *Do developers who were more focused in the past (i.e., the scattering value of the set of files they changed in the past 3 months are low) tend to commit more maintainable code, compared to less focused ones?*

To answer these questions we studied the code change history of three open-source systems and an industrial one. Our null-hypothesis was that there is no connection between developer focus and maintainability of the source code. Based on the statistical tests, unfortunately, we could not reject the null hypothesis, therefore we could not report evidence that developer focus impacts code maintainability.

All data for replicating our study is available as an online appendix at: http://www.inf.u-szeged.hu/~ferenc/papers/DeveloperFocus/.

The remaining of the paper is organized as follows. Section 2 provides a brief overview of works that are related to this research. In Sect. 3 we present how we collected the data and what kinds of tests we performed. In Sect. 4 we present the results of the statistical tests. We conclude the paper in Sect. 5.

2   Related Work

Code ownership, which is very close to the topic of this paper, is widely investigated. The results are very contradictory: some researcher find significant correlation between code ownership and code quality, which others do not.

Nordberg [18] describe in their study four types of code ownership: product specialist, subsystem ownership, chief architect and collective ownership. They discuss the advantages and disadvantages of each model.

LaToza et al. performed two surveys and eleven interviews, conducted by software developers at Microsoft, regarding software development questions, and presented the results in article [17]. Some of the questions were related to code ownership, strongly related to this study. The authors formed an interesting statement: the code ownership can also be wrong, as if a code is understood and maintained by a single developer, it makes individuals too indispensable. As an alternative of individual code ownership, they investigated the team code ownership. This topic would be interesting also for us: to somehow determine teams and define team level code ownership and team level focus instead of individual level ones.

In their work Fritz et al. [13] investigated the frequency and the elapsed time of interactions on the code by developers. They asked questions to find out if the developers can recall details about the source code: types of variables, types of parameters, method names, another method calls and methods which calls a specified method. The results supported their assumed hypothesis, the developers know their code that was modified by him/her frequently and recently better compared to foreign code. This study is strongly related to code ownership and developer focus, as a more focused developer might better recall source code elements regarding to the related code, compared to less focused developers.

Weyuker et al. [21] tried to enhance their defect prediction model by including the number of developers. They found that the achieved improvement is negligible, which is similar to the results we present in this study.

The same authors (Bell et al. [3]) tried to improve their defect prediction model considering the individual developers: they investigated whether files in a large system that are modified by an individual developer consistently contain either more or fewer faults than the average of all files in the system. They found negligible improvement: the study indicates that adding information to a model about which particular developer modified a file is not likely to improve defect predictions.

Hattori and Lanza [16] analyzed the problem of code ownership, especially finding the hidden co-authors. They considered in their model the developer interaction information as well. This could lead to a finer result also in case of developer focus.

The study by Bird et al. [4] investigated the effects of ownership on software quality. Under term of software quality they considered pre-release faults and post-release failures. They performed the analysis on binary and release level of the source code of Windows Vista and Windows 7. For a binary they defined the terms minor contributor (developers who contributed at most 5% of the total commits), major contributor (above 5%) and ownership (proportion of the commits of the highest contributor). Among others, they found that software components with many minor contributors had more failures than other software components. Moreover, the high level of ownership resulted in less defects.

Rahman and Devanbu [20] introduced a code ownership and experience based defect prediction model, but instead of just considering the modifications performed on source file itself, they introduced a fine-grained level by analyzing the contributions to code fragments. This approach could be a good direction for future investigation of developer focus as well: besides considering source code package, other source code elements like class or function could also be taken into account.

Greiler et al. [14] defined several contributor-related metrics and used those for defect predicting model. Their findings confirm the original finding by Bird et al. [4] that code ownership correlates with code quality.

On the other hand, Foucault et al. [12] performed similar study as Bird et al. [4] on open-source systems, but they found that the relationship between ownership metrics and module faults is weak. The performed an in-depth analysis to find the reason of the different results of open-source and closed-source software systems, and found that the reason is the distributions of contributions among developers and the presence of "heroes" in the open-source projects.

Di Nucci et al. [5] investigated the impact of developer focus on post-release bugs. They defined structural and semantic scattering (we implemented our developer focus value based on their structural scattering definition), and found that a bug predicting model including these metrics over performs models without these.

We also experienced these contradictory results. Our earlier model [8] considering the number of developers resulted in a not too strong but still significant result, but this study, considering developer focus did not show significant correlation at all.

3   Methodology

3.1   Overview

As we wanted to analyze the connection between developer focus and maintainability, we had to find a method to express these numerically. Neither of them are trivial concepts, and currently there are no exact definitions on how to compute them.

Considering maintainability, we performed the same calculation method that we applied in our previous studies [6–11]. We present the maintainability estimation method in detail in Sect. 3.3. The used quality model is capable of analyzing certain revisions of a system, therefore we chose to work on a per commit basis.

We calculated the developer focus values based on the definition of structural scattering by Di Nucci et al. [5]. We present the calculation details in Sect. 3.4. Section 3.5 describes the statistical tests we used to analyze the data. In Sect. 3.6, we explain our decisions made during the elaboration of the methodology.

3.2   Preliminary Steps

As first step we did some data cleaning. The analyzed software systems were all written in Java. As the used quality model considers Java source files only, we removed the non Java source files (e.g., xml files) from the input. If a commit contained non Java files only, then we also removed that one. So we worked on an input commit set that contained Java source files exclusively. Furthermore, each analyzed revision contained at least one affected Java file.

3.3   Estimation of the Maintainability Change

We used the ColumbusQM [1] probabilistic software quality model for estimating the maintainability value of every revision. It considers the following source code metrics: logical lines of code, the number of ancestors, the maximum nesting level, the coupling between object classes, clone coverage, number of parameters, McCabe's cyclomatic complexity, number of incoming invocations, number of outgoing invocations, and number of coding rule violations. The basis of this model is the fact that there is a negative correlation between these metrics and software maintainability [15]. The quality mode compares these metrics of the analyzed system with those of other systems in a benchmark, and then aggregates the results of the comparisons by utilizing weights provided by developers.

From the study's viewpoint we treat this quality model as a black box. Details of this model is described the work of Bakota et al. [1]. The authors validated the model and they also revealed the correlation between the estimated quality value and the development costs [2]. The quality model results a real number between 0 and 1; better maintainability is indicated by higher value.

For each analyzed systems we calculated the maintainability values for every revision available in their version control systems. As next step we calculated the difference of the maintainability values of subsequent revisions, and then considered the sign of the result: positive, zero, or negative, indicating if the actual commit increased, did not considerably change or decreased the maintainability of the source code, respectively.

3.4 Calculation of Developer Focus

For calculating the focus of developers, we adopted the definition of *structural scattering*, described by Di Nucci et al. (see [5], p. 243).

Let $CH_{d,p}$ be the the set of classes changed by a developer d during a time period p. The authors defined the *structural scattering* measure as:

$$StrScat_{d,p} = \frac{|CH_{d,p}|}{\binom{|CH_{d,p}|}{2}} \times \sum_{\forall c_i, c_j \in CH_{d,p}} [dist(c_i, c_j)]$$

where $dist$ is the number of steps to be taken in order to go from class c_i to class c_j. For example, the $dist$ between classes pkg.entities.User and pkg.logic.util.Convert is 3: pkg.entities $\rightarrow$ pkg $\rightarrow$ pkg.logic $\rightarrow$ pkg. logic.util. The multiplication factor at the beginning of the formula normalizes the distances between the code components and assigns a higher scattering to developers working on a higher number of code components in the given time period.

3.5 Comparison Tests

Once we had a maintainability change direction and a developer focus value for every commit in the revision history, we could check if there is any connection between the maintainability change direction and the focus of the developers. For this we performed several comparison tests, which fall into three categories: *commit-based*, *developer-based*, and *individual-based* tests. In all cases the basic setup of the tests was the same. First, we divided the commits into 3 subsets based on the sign of maintainability changes, and analyzed their calculated developer focus values. How we defined the set of source code elements to which the developer focus should be calculated is described below. We omitted the neutral maintainability changes (i.e., no change in maintainability values happened), therefore we ended up with 2 sets of numbers:

- developer focus values of the commits with positive maintainability change, i.e. code quality increase, and
- developer focus values of the commits with negative maintainability change, i.e. code quality decrease.

The null hypothesis was that there is no significant difference between these values. The alternative hypothesis was that the developer focus values related to commits with positive maintainability changes are significantly lower than those related to negative maintainability changes, meaning that more focused commits (i.e., commits with low scattering value) are more likely to increase the maintainability.

We performed the Wilcoxon rank correlation test on the data, as this one is suitable for kind data we have (e.g., it is not normally distributed, or it has outliers). This test compares all the elements of the first data set with all the elements of the other one, taking all the possible combinations into consideration. According to our null hypothesis the number of "greater" elements should be roughly the same as the number of "less" elements. The alternative hypothesis expresses that the elements of one of the sets should be significantly higher than the elements of the other.

We used the R statistical program [19] for performing the tests, using the `wilcox.test()` function. As a result, we got p-values for all software systems we performed the test on. We ran tests with 3 different setups: *(1)* for answering RQ1; *(2)* and *(3)* for answering RQ2:

Commit-Based Comparison Tests. In this case we used every commit for the developer focus calculation, and calculated the focus value considering all the files affected by that commit, as described in Sect. 3.4. As a result we got developer focus values for every commit.

Developer-Based Comparison Tests. In this case first we calculated a running developer focus value for every developer. For every commit we considered the developer who performed that commit and took all the files the developer changed in the previous 3 months. Therefore we simulated the process of forgetting. Furthermore, we omitted the commits containing more than 20 files, because that would have caused a big bias. For example, a directory rename could affect a large amount of source files, which would drastically increase the focus value of that developer for the next 3 months, but in the reality that developer has not lost the focus.

We defined the commit related focus value to be the focus value of the actual developer who performed the commit.

Individual-Based Comparison Tests. In this case we considered the version control history individually for every developer, considering commits performed only by that developer. This results in the same number of version control sub-histories as many developers contributed to the source code. We applied the methodology in every case as described in the developer-based comparison tests.

In order to avoid the non-explanatory results we excluded the developers who contributed too little, i.e. whose sub-history was too short to analyze. We considered only those developers who contributed at least 5 commits resulting a maintainability increase and at least 5 commits resulting a maintainability decrease.

3.6 Discussion

The *commit-based* comparison test is a rough approach, however our expectation was that if connection between maintainability change and developer focus existed, this could have been observed even by this method. In this case we did not consider earlier modifications of the developer, just the actual commit (i.e., we did not consider past focus).

On the other hand, *developer based* comparison tests are more fine-grained, and we thought of this as the main outcome of our study. The focus value calculation would be the same as in the commit-based case if we considered the union of all the contributions of the actual developer in the past 3 months (with the exception of huge commits). Our expectation was that considering this focus value the comparison tests would yield significant results.

In case of *individual-based* comparison tests we practically sliced the whole version control history to as many pieces as many developers contributed to that project, and kept only those that contained enough number of commits. This resulted in several tests per analyzed system (i.e., a separate test for every developer). With this test we wanted to ensure that we find per developer patterns even if we cannot find a general connection between developer focus and maintainability.

4   Results

4.1   Examined Software Systems

We executed the tests on four independent software systems. Our selection criteria for the subject systems were the following: availability of at least 1000 commits and at least 200% code increase during the analyzed period. We performed the analysis of the following 4 systems:

- **Ant** – a command line tool for building Java applications (http://ant.apache.org). All together 37 developers contributed at least once. The total number of available commits was more than 6000.
- **Gremon** – a proprietary greenhouse work-flow monitoring system (http://www.gremonsystems.com). 13 programmers took part in the development.

- **Struts 2** – a framework for creating enterprise-ready Java web applications (http://struts.apache.org/). The number of developers was 26.
- **Tomcat** – an implementation of the Java Servlet and Java Server Pages technologies (http://tomcat.apache.org). 15 developers contributed at least once.

4.2   Results of the Statistical Tests

Table 1 contains the results of the commit-based and the developer-based comparison tests. The results are very sporadic, and the only significant p-value (0.003 in case of Gremon) seems to be rather casual than valid.

Similarly, the individual tests resulted sporadic results (each p-value is related to a particular developer but we ommited user names):

- **Ant:** 0.048, 0.082, 0.256, 0.373, 0.454, 0.485, 0.516, 0.576, 0.646, 0.673, 0.722, 0.762, 0.781, 0.830, 0.853, 0.883, 0.905, 0.933, 0.949, 0.991 (17 omitted)
- **Gremon:** 0.002, 0.038, 0.199, 0.211, 0.251, 0.410, 0.765, 0.787, 0.886, 0.940 (3 omitted)
- **Struts2:** 0.030, 0.100, 0.104, 0.144, 0.409, 0.434, 0.442, 0.600, 0.618, 0.651, 0.687, 0.774, 0.920, 0.950 (14 omitted)
- **Tomcat:** 0.020, 0.855, 0.872 (12 omitted).

Table 1. Resulting p-values of the commit-based and developer-based comparison tests (bold means significant p-value)

System	Commit	Developer
Ant	0.943	0.214
Gremon	0.208	**0.003**
Struts 2	0.571	0.687
Tomcat	0.921	0.951

4.3   Discussion

According to these results not just that we could not reject the null-hypothesis, but sporadic values did not even show us another possible direction with the research. For example, if the resulting p-values would have been close to 1, then we could perform the execution of the opposite tests, meaning that the more focused commits tend to result in maintainability erosion. Although it sounds counter-intuitive a possible explanation for this could be for example, that a more focused developer might be new on that project, and a lead developer's commits affect different parts of the code. But even that was not the case.

A bug in our software could also lead to negative results. To minimize the risk of this, we added unit tests to our implementation. Furthermore, we played around with different "forgetting" intervals (instead of the actually used 3 months) and huge commit threshold values (instead of the actually used 20), without relevant change in the results.

For omitting the too little contributions we performed the individual based comparison tests only for those who contributed at least 5 commits causing maintainability increase and same number for decrease. Using another value instead of 5 just changes the number of omitted values, but the actually calculated values will not change. We did not experience any relevant changes in the distribution of the resulting p-values by modifying this threshold (i.e., there is no such threshold value that would filter out only the high p-value results).

5   Conclusions and Future Work

As we already stressed in the introduction this is a publication of negative results. According to the statistic tests we performed we could not reject any of the null-hypotheses, either that more focused developers tend to contribute better quality code, or that more focused commits tend to improve code quality.

Out of the 8 main test (commit-based and developer-based tests for 4 systems) we performed, only one turned out to be significant: the developer-based comparison for the Gremon project, which is our only closed-source subject system. It would be worthwhile to investigate this in more detail because in an industrial environment a developer typically works on one singe project at a time, while in open-source environments a developer might contribute to several projects simultaneously. Bird et al. [4] and Greiler et al. [14] investigated some of their industrial products at Microsoft, and concluded that considering focus improve their fault prediction model, while Foucault et al. [12] could not achieve significant improvement by adding developer focus to an analysis of open-source systems. Do the open versus closed-source differences cause the contradictory results? This could be a topic of further investigations, however, it is hard to obtain the whole version control history, including the source code, for industrial software systems.

Acknowledgment. This research was supported by the project "Integrated program for training new generation of scientists in the fields of computer science", no EFOP-3.6.3-VEKOP-16-2017-0002. The project has been supported by the UNKP-17-4 New National Excellence Program of the Ministry of Human Capacities, Hungary and the European Union and co-funded by the European Social Fund.

References

1. Bakota, T., Hegedűs, P., Körtvélyesi, P., Ferenc, R., Gyimóthy, T.: A probabilistic software quality model. In: 2011 27th IEEE International Conference on Software Maintenance, pp. 243–252. IEEE (2011)
2. Bakota, T., Hegedűs, P., Ladányi, G., Körtvélyesi, P., Ferenc, R., Gyimóthy, T.: A cost model based on software maintainability. In: 2012 28th IEEE International Conference on Software Maintenance (ICSM), pp. 316–325. IEEE (2012)
3. Bell, R.M., Ostrand, T.J., Weyuker, E.J.: The limited impact of individual developer data on software defect prediction. Empirical Softw. Eng. **18**(3), 478–505 (2013)

4. Bird, C., Nagappan, N., Murphy, B., Gall, H., Devanbu, P.: Don't touch my code! Examining the effects of ownership on software quality. In: Proceedings of the 19th ACM SIGSOFT Symposium and the 13th European Conference on Foundations of Software Engineering, pp. 4–14. ACM (2011)

5. Di Nucci, D., Palomba, F., Siravo, S., Bavota, G., Oliveto, R., De Lucia, A.: On the role of developer's scattered changes in bug prediction. In: 2015 IEEE International Conference on Software Maintenance and Evolution (ICSME), pp. 241–250. IEEE (2015)

6. Faragó, C.: Variance of source code quality change caused by version control operations. Acta Cybernetica **22**, 35–56 (2015)

7. Faragó, C., Hegedūs, P., Ferenc, R.: The impact of version control operations on the quality change of the source code. In: Murgante, B., et al. (eds.) ICCSA 2014. LNCS, vol. 8583, pp. 353–369. Springer, Cham (2014). https://doi.org/10.1007/978-3-319-09156-3_26

8. Faragó, C., Hegedűs, P., Ferenc, R.: Code ownership: impact on maintainability. In: Gervasi, O., et al. (eds.) ICCSA 2015. LNCS, vol. 9159, pp. 3–19. Springer, Cham (2015). https://doi.org/10.1007/978-3-319-21413-9_1

9. Faragó, C., Hegedűs, P., Ferenc, R.: Cumulative code churn: impact on maintainability. In: 15th IEEE International Working Conference on Source Code Analysis and Manipulation-SCAM 2015 (2015)

10. Faragó, C., Hegedűs, P., Ladányi, G., Ferenc, R.: Impact of version history metrics on maintainability. In: Proceedings of the 8th International Conference on Advanced Software Engineering and Its Applications (ASEA), pp. 30–35. IEEE Computer Society (2015)

11. Faragó, C., Hegedűs, P., Végh, Á.Z., Ferenc, R.: Connection between version control operations and quality change of the source code. Acta Cybernetica **21**, 585–607 (2014)

12. Foucault, M., Falleri, J.R., Blanc, X.: Code ownership in open-source software. In: Proceedings of the 18th International Conference on Evaluation and Assessment in Software Engineering, p. 39. ACM (2014)

13. Fritz, T., Murphy, G.C., Hill, E.: Does a programmer's activity indicate knowledge of code? In: Proceedings of the the the 6th Joint Meeting of the European Software Engineering Conference and the ACM SIGSOFT Symposium on the Foundations of Software Engineering, pp. 341–350. ACM (2007)

14. Greiler, M., Herzig, K., Czerwonka, J.: Code ownership and software quality: a replication study. In: Proceedings of the 12th Working Conference on Mining Software Repositories, pp. 2–12. IEEE Press (2015)

15. Gyimóthy, T., Ferenc, R., Siket, I.: Empirical validation of object-oriented metrics on open source software for fault prediction. IEEE Trans. Softw. Eng. **31**(10), 897–910 (2005)

16. Hattori, L., Lanza, M.: Mining the history of synchronous changes to refine code ownership. In: 2009 6th IEEE International Working Conference on Mining Software Repositories, MSR 2009, pp. 141–150. IEEE (2009)

17. LaToza, T.D., Venolia, G., DeLine, R.: Maintaining mental models: a study of developer work habits. In: Proceedings of the 28th International Conference on Software Engineering, pp. 492–501. ACM (2006)

18. Nordberg III, M.E.: Managing code ownership. IEEE Softw. **20**(2), 26–33 (2003)

19. R Core Team: R: A Language and Environment for Statistical Computing. R Foundation for Statistical Computing, Vienna (2015). http://www.R-project.org/

20. Rahman, F., Devanbu, P.: Ownership, experience and defects: a fine-grained study of authorship. In: Proceedings of the 33rd International Conference on Software Engineering, pp. 491–500. ACM (2011)
21. Weyuker, E.J., Ostrand, T.J., Bell, R.M.: Do too many cooks spoil the broth? Using the number of developers to enhance defect prediction models. Empirical Softw. Eng. **13**(5), 539–559 (2008)

Software Reliability Assessment Using Machine Learning Technique

Ranjan Kumar Behera[1](✉), Suyash Shukla[1], Santanu Kumar Rath[1], and Sanjay Misra[2]

[1] Department of Computer Science and Engineering,
National Institute of Technology, Rourkela, Odisha, India
jranjanb.19@gmail.com
[2] Department of Electrical and Information Engineering, Covenant University,
1023, Ota, Nigeria

Abstract. Software reliability is one of the major attributes in software quality assurance system. A large number of research works have been attempted in order to improve the reliability of the software. Research directions in improving software reliability may be defined in a three-step process i.e., software modeling, software measurement and software improvement. Each of these phases is equally important in obtaining reliable software system. It is important to achieve better accuracy in estimating reliability in order to manage the software quality. A number of metrics have been proposed in the literature to evaluating the reliability of a software. Machine learning approaches are found to be suitable ways in evaluating different parameters of software reliability. Several machine learning techniques have been evolved in order to capture the different characteristics of a software system. The machine learning algorithms like naive bayes, support vector regression, decision tree and random forest algorithms are found to be successful in classifying the bug data from data where feature sets are dependent with each other. In this paper, deep learning approach has been proposed to estimate the reliability of software. The proposed approach uses recurrent neural network for predicting the number of bugs or failure in software. Effectiveness of deep learning is extensively compared with the standard machine learning algorithms by considering the dataset collected from the literature.

Keywords: Recurrent neural network · Support Vector Machine
Software reliability · Mean time to failure

1 Introduction

Software reliability is one of the most important factor that effects system reliability. It can also be defined as the probability of software to be executed successfully for a given interval of time. A number of approaches have been proposed for assessing the reliability of software. However, there is a trade-off associated

© Springer International Publishing AG, part of Springer Nature 2018
O. Gervasi et al. (Eds.): ICCSA 2018, LNCS 10964, pp. 403–411, 2018.
https://doi.org/10.1007/978-3-319-95174-4_32

with the designing the reliable software. It is necessary to have balance between cost of effort and development time. Reliability of the software is associated with usability, functionality, maintainability, capability and documentation. All of these stages must be correctly synchronize in order to have bug-free modules in software. Software reliability growth models (SRGM) are the promising models in order to estimate the relationship between mean time to 2 Software Reliability Assessment using Deep Learning Technique failure and cumulative fault count between the interval. It is often classified as parametric and non-parametric in nature. It is found that mean value function for the models in traditional models follows exponential curve or S-shaped curve.

Neural network comes out as a possible alternative to the problem. The functionality of neural network resembles that of a human brain. To make computations quick, it is capable of organizing Neurons that are its structural elements. The architecture comprises an Input Layer: where the values are introduced to the network, a Hidden layer: responsible for processing the input values and one output Layer: the provides the final output for the network. But the mentioned architecture would not prove sufficient enough to carry out complex problems. Using a shallow network for a complex function would involve computational units in a very huge number with a large amount of time put in training. It is likely that issues like over-fitting could come up. A possible solution for this can be to introduce more hidden layers of neurons in the network but that would add to the complexity of the network even on keeping the count of neurons relatively small. An observation has been made that making some extension to the network becomes helpful in representing complex problems. Such extended networks are known as Deep Networks. In this paper, recurrent neural network (RNN) is implemented to assess the reliability of software and to evaluate the performance of RNN model comparative study has been done with various other regression models such as Naive Bayes, Decision Tree and Support Vector Machine.

The subsequent section of the paper is presented as follows: The background details of the work has been discussed in Sect. 2. Section 3 presents the machine learning techniques that have implemented to identify the fault in software system. Dataset description is presented in Sect. 4. Results is presented in Sect. 5. Section 6 conclude the paper.

2   Background Detail

2.1   Software Reliability

For improving the quality of software one important factor which is often considered is software reliability. Software reliability deals with bugs that are present in the system [11]. Generally, failure occurs in the system because of fault in the code, and sometime one fault could result many failures. Software reliability is the process of finding faults in the system and then removing those faults to increase the quality of the system. Software reliability can be measured by various analytical models called as software reliability growth models (SRGMs) [2,3].

2.2   SRGMs and Criterion to Measure Performance

To assess the reliability of software many SRGMs have been presented in the past. SRGMs are mathematical models to assess software reliability and estimating mean time to failure (MTTF). These models are based on certain assumptions. According to nature of process, SRGMs are divided into 2 categories

1. Times between failures models
2. Fault Count Models.

Thus, SRGMs are basically useful in deciding the level of reliability and when to stop testing [5]. Many SRGMs has been presented till now but the Commonly used model of software reliability models are Jelinski and Moranda model, Musa-Okumoto model, Goel and Oku-moto model, Sch model, S-Shape model. Many criterion's have been used to evaluate the performance of various models. In this paper 4 criterion are used: Average Error (AE), Normalized Root Mean Square Error (NRMSE), Root Mean Square Error (RMSE) and Mean Absolute Error (AE). Equations 1–5 are used to calculate the values of these measures to find the difference between actual and predicted value

$$Relative Error(RE_i) = \left(\left| \left(\frac{p_i(f) - a_i(f)}{p_i(f)} \right) \right| \right) * 100 \tag{1}$$

$$AE = \frac{1}{k} \sum_{i=1}^{k} RE_i \tag{2}$$

$$RMSE = \sqrt{\frac{1}{k} \sum_{i=1}^{k} (p_i(f) - a_i(f))^2} \tag{3}$$

$$NRMSE = \frac{\left[\sqrt{\sum_{i=1}^{k} (p_i(f) - a_i(f))^2} \right]}{\sum_{i=1}^{k} p_i(f)^2} \tag{4}$$

$$MAE = \frac{(\sum_{i=1}^{n} |(p_i(f) - a_i(f))|)}{n} \tag{5}$$

Where k is the number of failures, $a_i(f)$ is number of actual failures, $p_i(f)$ is number of predicted failures. For getting higher accuracy in prediction the values of above mentioned criterion should be small [6,7].

3   Methodology Used for Reliability Assessment

3.1   Naive Bayes

Given an sample S, consider a problem of predicting a value of target variable T. S consists of m attributes A_1, A_2, ..., A_m. Attributes could be numeric or nominal. If the probability density function (PDF) $p(T|S)$ of the output value is known for every sample S, then T can be choosen to minimize the error. However, $p(T|S)$ is usually unknown, and has to be calculated from dataset. Naive Bayes determines this by using Bayes theorem and assuming that attributes A_1, A_2, ..., A_m are independent given the target value T. Bayes theorem states that

$$p(T|S) = \frac{p(S,T)}{\int p(S,T)d(T)} = \frac{p(S|T)p(T)}{\int p(S|T)p(T)d(T)} \tag{6}$$

where $p(S|T)$ is the pdf of the sample S for a given target value T, and p(T) is the prior probability. According to Naive Bayes algorithm all the attributes are independent of each other. So, Eq. 6 can be written

$$p(T|S) = \frac{p(A_1|T)p(A_2|T)....p(A_m|T)p(T)}{\int p(A_1|T)p(A_2|T)....p(A_m|T)p(T)d(T)} \tag{7}$$

Here, to estimating the value of pdf $p(S|T)$, the individual pdfs $p(A_i|T)$ are estimated separately. This will reduce the dimensionality of the problem and also makes the problem easier.

3.2 Decision Tree Regression

In Decision tree, classification or regression model is build like a tree structure. It divides the dataset into many smaller subsets and parallely decision tree is developed. Finally, we will get tree which consist of leaf nodes and decision nodes. A decision node contains a condition and it has 2 or more branches. Leaf nodes represent an output value for the tested attribute. The topmost decision node is called as a root node of the tree. Decision trees can handle numerical as well as categorical data. following are the steps for decision tree algorithm:

- Calculate standard deviation for target value.
- Split the dataset into different attributes. Then, calculate standard deviation for each branch.
- Then, find the difference between current standard deviation and the standard deviation before the split. Difference of these standard deviations is called standard deviation reduction (SDR).
- Then, attribute which has highest SDR value is selected as decision node.
- Divide the dataset based on the selected attribute.
- Until all data is processed, recursively run the process on non-leaf branches.

Calculate final average value for the target when number of instances exceeds 1 at leaf node.

3.3 Support Vector Machine (SVM)

SVM can be used for both regression as well as classification. When it is used for a regression problem, it is called as support vector regression (SVR). We have set of linearly separable points of 2 classes, the aim of SVM is to find a

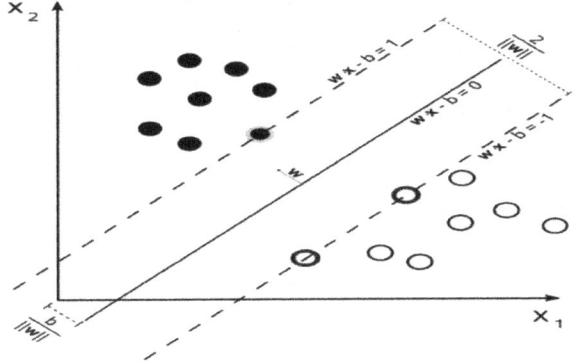

Fig. 1. Hyper-plane for separating 2 classes

hyper-plane that can separate points of these 2 classes with minimum error and maximizing the perpendicular distance between 2 nearest points from either of the 2 classes. Figure 1 is representing an hyper-plane for dividing 2 classes:

Similarly, regression problem can also be setup. Suppose set of points are there that lies on a straight line. Constraints can be set as follows:

$y_i - w.x_i - b \leq \epsilon$

$w.x_i + b - y_i \leq \epsilon$. In SVR, the aim is to minimize generalization error instead of training error. This will help to achieve generalized performance. Linear regression function is computed in a high dimensional space where the input data is mapped using non linear function. Kernel functions used by SVR:

$$Ker(P_i, P_j) = \begin{cases} P_i.P_j & Linear \\ (\gamma P_i.P_j + C)^d & Polynomial \\ exp(-\gamma |P_i - P_j|^2) & RBF \\ tanh(\gamma P_i.P_j + C) & Sigmoid \end{cases} \tag{8}$$

where $Ker(P_i, P_j) = \phi(P_i).\phi(P_j)$ is the kernel function. γ is an adjustable parameter.

3.4 Recurrent Neural Network (RNN)

RNNs are called recurrent because for every element of sequence a same task is carried out and the output of current state is dependent on previous states. These are also called memory network as they captures the result of previous computation and use them for future computations. The simple architecture for RNN is shown in Fig. 2. Following are the few steps to be followed in recurrent neural network:

- Input ($Input_t$) is supplied to the network.
- Then the calculation of current state is done on the basis of previous state and current input i.e. calculate $State_t$.

$$State_t = f(State_{t-1}, Input_t) \tag{9}$$

- For the next time step the current $State_t$ becomes $State_{t-1}$.
- According to the demand of problem go for as many time steps and then combine the information of all previous states.
- Calculate the output $Output_t$ by using final current state.

$$Output_t = W_{output} * State_t \tag{10}$$

here, W_{output} is weight at output neuron.
- Calculate error by finding the difference between actual and predicted output.
- Update the weights by back propagating the error in the network.

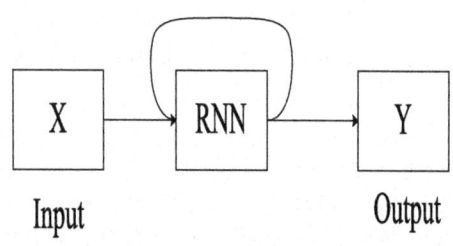

Fig. 2. Recurrent neural network

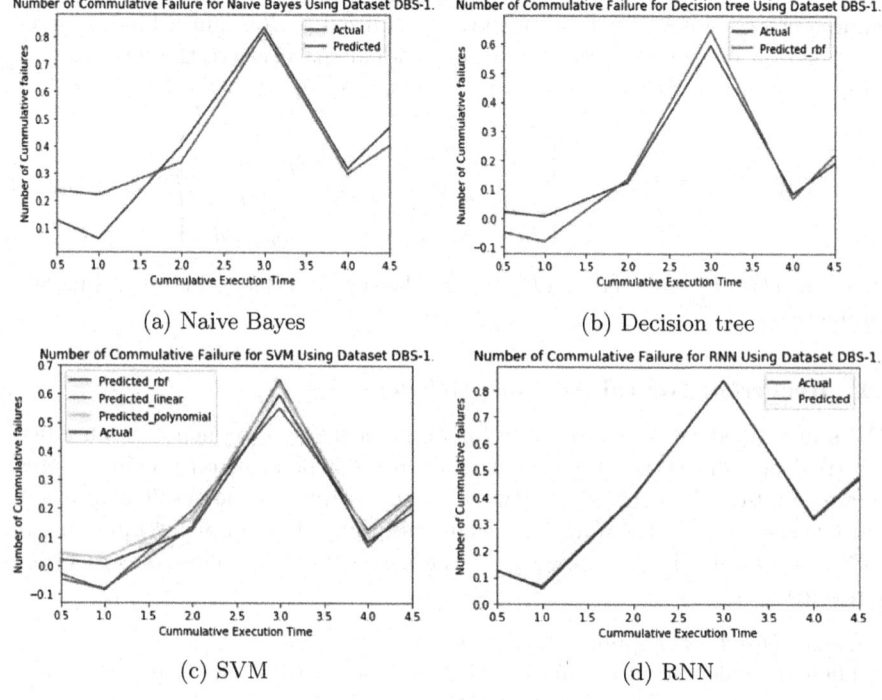

(a) Naive Bayes

(b) Decision tree

(c) SVM

(d) RNN

Fig. 3. Performance analysis for dataset DBS-1

4   Dataset

DBS-1 from Musa (1980) and DBS-2 from Iyer and Lee (1996) datasets are considered to evaluate the performance of above mentioned techniques. The actual data set consists of Failure Number, Cumulative execution time, Day of Failure. For the above mentioned techniques cumulative execution is given as input and the failure number as output. The cross-validation is done by dividing the dataset into 2 sets:

– Training dataset
– Test dataset.

70% of the data is considered for training and remaining 30% for testing. Then, the dataset and the dataset is normalized in a range of [0, 1] because the model work well for this range.

5   Results

Above mentioned techniques for software reliability assessment are developed in python 3.6. The performance of Naive bayes, Decision tree, Support vector

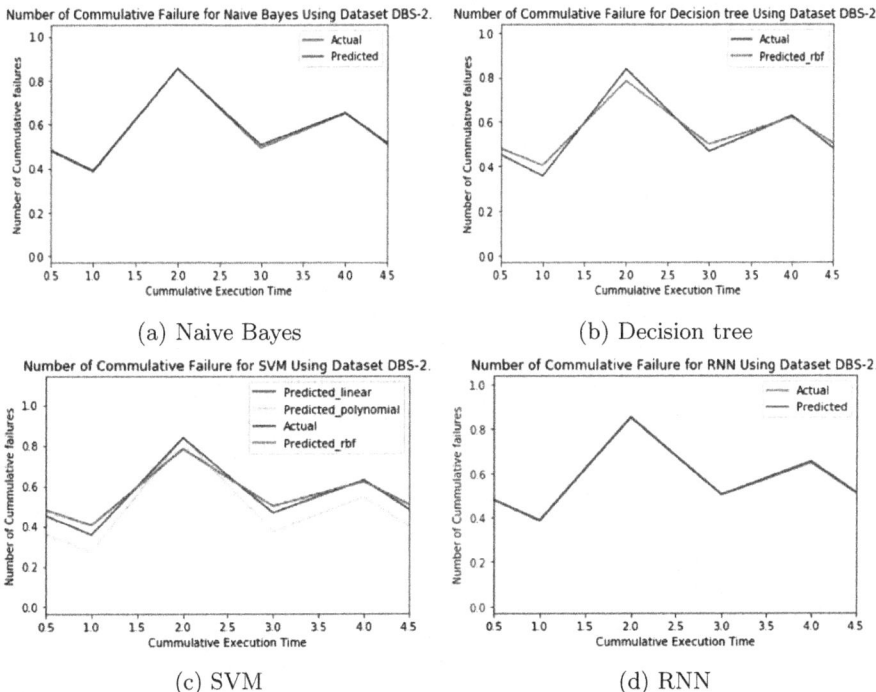

(a) Naive Bayes   (b) Decision tree

(c) SVM   (d) RNN

Fig. 4. Performance analysis for dataset DBS-2

regressor and Recurrent neural network is evaluated by using data set DBS-1 and DBS-2. AE, RMSE, NRMSE and MAE criteria's are considered to determine the difference between the target and predicted values. For getting higher accuracy in prediction the values of AE, RMSE, NRMSE, and MAE should be small. Figure 3 represents the graph between predicted cumulative number of failures and actual cummulative number of failures by using Naive bayes, Decision tree, SVR and RNN respectively for DBS-1. Similarly, Fig. 4 represents the graph between predicted cumulative number of failures and actual cumulative number of failures by using Naive bayes, Decision tree, SVR and RNN respectively for DBS-2. The values of AE, RMSE, NRMSE, MAE obtained from various machine learning techniques in DBS-1 and DBS-2 are listed in Tables 1 and 2 respectively.

Table 1. AE, RMSE, NRMSE, MAE values for DBS-1

Technique	AE	RMSE	NRMSE	MAE
Naive bayes	4.2573	0.0538	0.0997	0.0658
Decision tree	3.8277	0.0426	0.0835	0.0523
SVM (RBF)	3.3748	0.0073	0.0823	0.0397
SVM (linear)	3.4748	0.0079	0.0877	0.0413
SVM (polynomial)	3.4318	0.0077	0.0848	0.0406
RNN	3.2506	0.0051	0.0632	0.0276

Table 2. AE, RMSE, NRMSE, MAE values for DBS-2

Technique	AE	RMSE	NRMSE	MAE
Naive bayes	3.4258	0.0072	0.0871	0.0313
Decision tree	3.2256	0.0061	0.0631	0.0277
SVM (RBF)	3.1018	0.0051	0.0435	0.0297
SVM (linear)	3.3027	0.0065	0.0531	0.0323
SVM (polynomial)	3.2791	0.0060	0.0499	0.0309
RNN	2.9738	0.0039	0.0357	0.0216

6 Conclusion

In this paper, various regression techniques for software reliability prediction has been used. Based on the observations, recurrent neural network accurately predicts the software reliability. To analyze the effectiveness of these models AE, RMSE, NRMSE, and MAE criterion's are considered. Experimental evidence is been presented which is showing that recurrent neural network gives the more accurate results as compared to other models. On the basis of results we can say that the recurrent neural network based approach is computationally feasible and this will be helpful to decrease the cost of testing by accurately estimating the reliability of software.

References

1. Lyu, M.R. (ed.): Handbook of Software Reliability Engineering. IEEE Computer Society Press, Los Alamitos (1996)
2. Yamada, S.: Software Reliability Modeling: Fundamentals and Applications. Springer, Heidelberg (2014). https://doi.org/10.1007/978-4-431-54565-1
3. Almering, V., van Genuchten, M., Cloudt, G.: Using software reliability growth models in practice. IEEE Comput. Soc. **24**, 82–88 (2007)
4. Inoue, S., Yamada, S.: Two-dimensional software reliability measurement technologies. In: 2009 IEEE International Conference on Industrial Engineering and Engineering Management, IEEM 2009, pp. 223–227. IEEE, December 2009
5. Quadri, S.M., Ahmad, N., Farooq, S.U.: Software reliability growth modeling with generalized exponential testing effort and optimal software release policy. Glob. J. Comput. Sci. Technol. **11**(2), 27–42 (2011)
6. Bisi, M., Goyal, N.K.: Software reliability prediction using neural network with encoded input. Int. J. Comput. Appl. **47**(22), 46–52 (2012)
7. Wang, G., Li, W.: Research of software reliability combination model based on neural net. In: 2010 Second World Congress on Software Engineering (WCSE), vol. 2, pp. 253–256. IEEE, December 2010
8. Tamura, Y., Matsumoto, M., Yamada, S.: Software reliability model selection based on deep learning. In: Proceedings of the International Conference on Industrial Engineering, Management Science and Application 2016, Korea, 23–26 May 2016, pp. 77–81 (2016)
9. Blum, A., Lafferty, J., Rwebangira, M.R., Reddy, R.: Semi-supervised learning using randomized mincuts. In: Proceedings of the International Conference on Machine Learning, p. 113. ACM, New York (2004)
10. George, E.D., Dong, Y., Li, D., Acero, A.: Contextdependent pre-trained deep neural networks for large-vocabulary speech recognition. IEEE Trans. Audio Speech Lang. Process. **20**, 30–42 (2012)
11. Schick, G.J., Wolverton, R.W.: An analysis of competing software reliability models. IEEE Trans. Softw. Eng. **SE–4**(2), 104–120 (1978)

Quantitative Quality Assessment of Open Source Software by Considering New Features and Feature Improvements

Kamlesh Kumar Raghuvanshi[1], Meera Sharma[2], Abhishek Tandon[3], and V. B. Singh[4(✉)]

[1] Ramanujan College, University of Delhi, Delhi, India
raghukamlesh@gmail.com
[2] Swami Shraddhanand College, University of Delhi, Delhi, India
meerakaushik@gmail.com
[3] SSCBS, University of Delhi, Delhi, India
abhishektandon86@gmail.com
[4] Delhi College of Arts and Commerce, University of Delhi, Delhi, India
vbsinghdcacdu@gmail.com

Abstract. Open Source Software (OSS) evolves through active participation of users in terms of requesting for features, i.e. new features (NFs) and improvements in existing features (IMPs). Fixing of these features results in generation of further features improvements. In this paper, we have proposed a mathematical model to embody the OSS development based on the rate at which IMPs are generated as a result of fixing of features (NFs and IMPs). We have validated the model for datasets of five products, namely Avro, Pig, Hive, jUDDI and Whirr of Apache open source project. Results show that the model exhibit significant goodness of fit in terms of MSE (Mean Square Error), Bias, Variation, RMSPE (Root Mean Square Prediction Error) and R^2 performance measures.

1 Introduction

In OSS development paradigm active users/developers are located at different geographical locations and these users are requesting for NFs and IMPs to be introduced in the software. The main constituent for OSS evolution is fixing of these features by the active users. These active users may be the same who have requested for features introduction or may be different who have an interest in the development of the software. Developers review and modify the source code to introduce new features and incorporate improvements in the existing features. Fixing of these features may generate further feature improvements.

In the line of OSS development paradigm proposed in [1], we have extended it by adding requests for features, namely NFs and IMPs. Figure 1 shows that fixing of different features (NFs and IMPs) may result in further IMPs. IMPs are necessary to be incorporated so that the performance and software quality can be improved. This results in various releases of the software. In this paper, we have proposed a mathematical model by considering the rate of generation of feature improvements from fixing of

© Springer International Publishing AG, part of Springer Nature 2018
O. Gervasi et al. (Eds.): ICCSA 2018, LNCS 10964, pp. 412–423, 2018.
https://doi.org/10.1007/978-3-319-95174-4_33

different features (NFs and IMPs). The model has been validated on five products of the Apache project. Results show significant goodness of fit for different performance measures.

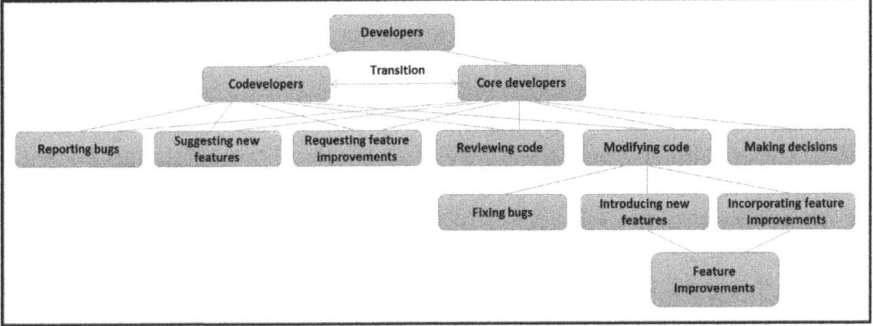

Fig. 1. Fixing of different features results in feature improvements

The rest of the paper is organized as follows: Sect. 2 of the paper describes the data collection and model building. Results have been presented in Sect. 3. Section 4 presents the related work. Threats to validity have been discussed in Sect. 5 and finally the paper is concluded in Sect. 6.

2 Data Collection and Model Building

A. Data Collection

The proposed mathematical model has been validated on issue datasets of five Apache products [2]. In the issue tracking system, different symbols have been used for different types of issues (bugs, NFs and IMPs) as shown in Fig. 2.

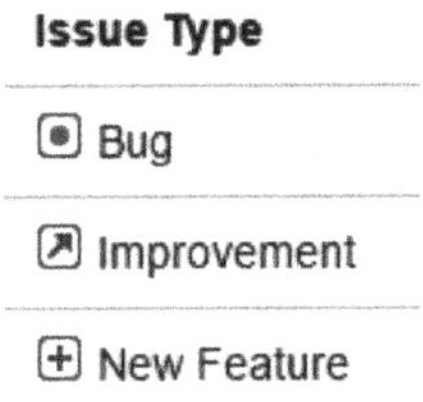

Issue Type

⊙ Bug

↗ Improvement

⊕ New Feature

Fig. 2. Apache products have different symbols for different issues

Those features (NFs and IMPs) that are not duplicate and are reproducible for others have been selected. We collected, fixed features on the monthly basis. The time period of data collection is: Avro (July 2009–July 2014), Hive (April 2009–April 2014), Pig (April 2009–October 2013), Whirr (September 2010–April 2013) and jUDDI (February 2009–February 2014).

The features of five products have been collected from [2]. Figure 3 shows sample of different feature reports for Avro project.

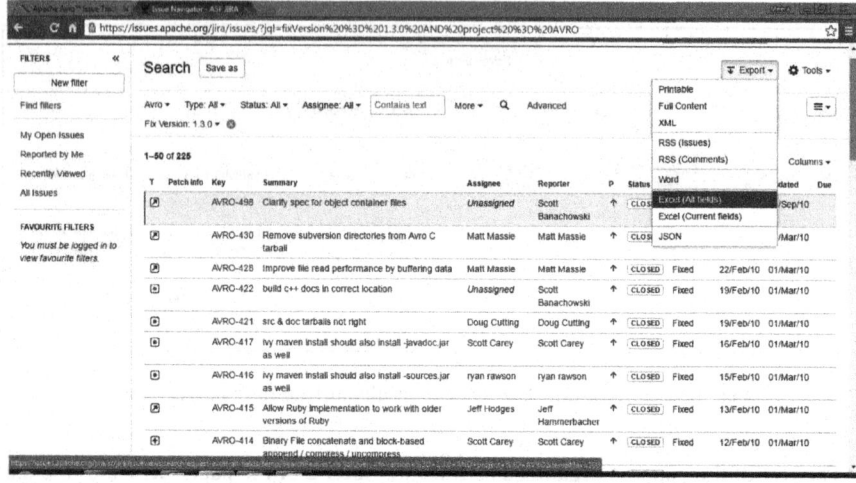

Fig. 3. Sample feature reports for Avro project

Table 1 show the monthly number of features for five Apache products which have been used to validate the proposed model.

Table 1. Monthly number of features in Apache products.

Time (months)	Avro IMPs + NFs	Pig IMPs + NFs	Hive IMPs + NFs	Whirr IMPs + NFs	jUDDI IMPs + NFs
1	8	4	15	9	3
2	4	8	11	5	0
3	15	6	14	9	0
4	16	4	32	5	2
5	30	3	23	20	0
6	13	13	16	6	3
7	53	22	11	8	1
8	26	16	13	15	0
9	20	14	13	11	0
10	8	6	23	8	1
11	5	7	25	3	1
12	8	14	15	12	0
13	8	18	12	2	0
14	20	14	8	13	0
15	9	13	19	1	0

(continued)

Table 1. (*continued*)

Time (months)	Avro IMPs + NFs	Pig IMPs + NFs	Hive IMPs + NFs	Whirr IMPs + NFs	jUDDI IMPs + NFs
16	4	25	11	1	0
17	2	25	20	7	1
18	5	11	12	11	1
19	10	1	15	7	0
20	17	2	24	0	0
21	9	8	18	2	2
22	10	10	15	0	0
23	2	8	19	2	0
24	4	17	12	10	1
25	8	17	12	4	0
26	5	8	9	3	4
27	15	4	13	2	1
28	22	12	20	0	1
29	2	15	18	1	0
30	9	7	19	2	0
31	2	5	21	7	0
32	10	12	15	2	3
33	4	9	17	-	0
34	4	12	11	-	0
35	10	9	10	-	0
36	4	8	23	-	0
37	2	9	17	-	0
38	2	15	7	-	0
39	7	11	12	-	1
40	0	4	9	-	0
41	9	5	10	-	0
42	2	13	16	-	0
43	4	9	13	-	0
44	8	10	13	-	0
45	4	5	17	-	0
46	7	7	18	-	1
47	4	6	16	-	0
48	4	14	17	-	0
49	3	6	27	-	0
50	0	7	2	-	4
51	0	4	12	-	6
52	5	6	20	-	7
53	9	4	23	-	4
54	7	9	32	-	6
55	3	5	25	-	6

(*continued*)

Table 1. (*continued*)

Time (months)	Avro IMPs + NFs	Pig IMPs + NFs	Hive IMPs + NFs	Whirr IMPs + NFs	jUDDI IMPs + NFs
56	2	-	29	-	1
57	1	-	24	-	6
58	1	-	23	-	8
59	2	-	19	-	3
60	3	-	19	-	14
61	-	-	6	-	1
62	-	-	1	-	-

Figures 4, 5, 6, 7 and 8 show the monthly distribution of features for different Apache products.

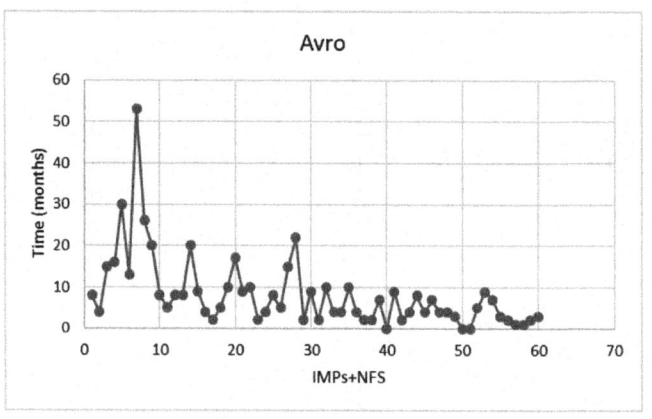

Fig. 4. Monthly feature distribution for Avro

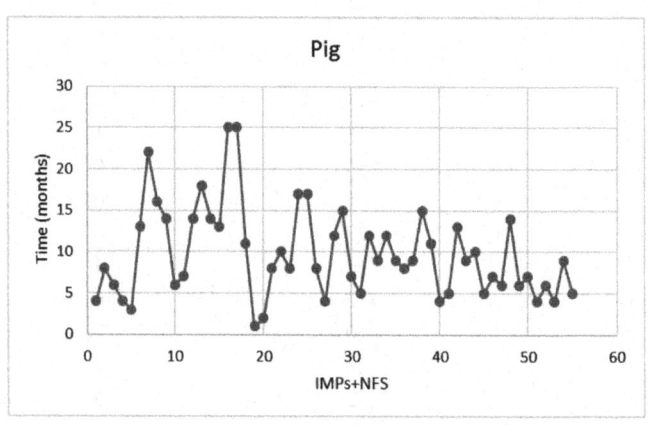

Fig. 5. Monthly feature distribution for Pig

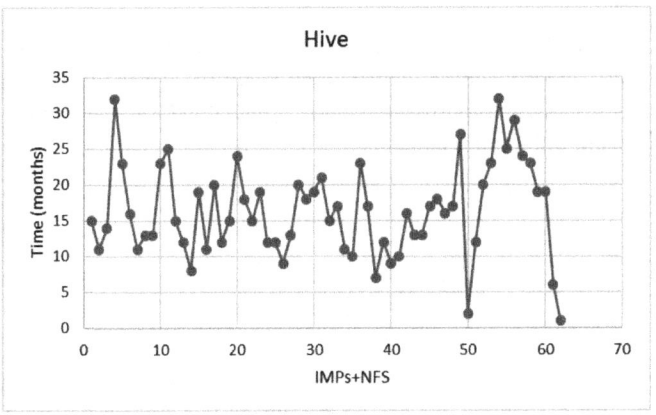

Fig. 6. Monthly feature distribution for Hive

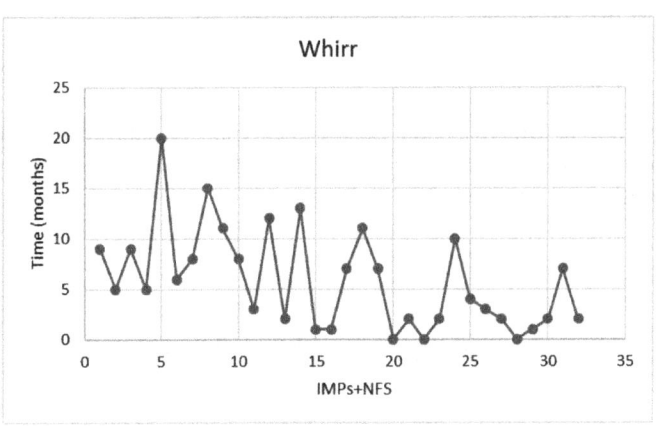

Fig. 7. Monthly feature distribution for Whirr

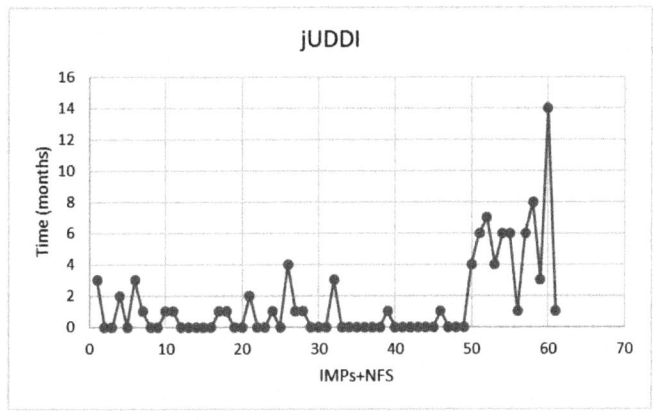

Fig. 8. Monthly feature distribution for jUDDI

B. Model building

In OSS, different features (NFs and IMPs) are requested by active users to be added into the software. Fixing of these features may result in further feature improvements. By considering this fact and following the differential equation given in [3, 14], we can write the following differential equation:

$$\frac{dm(t)}{dt} \propto (a(t) - m(t))$$

$$\frac{dm(t)}{dt} = b(a(t) - m(t)) \tag{1}$$

Here, $m(t)$ is the number of features (NFs + IMPs) introduced in a software at time t. 'a' is the number of features that can be introduced in a software over a long run. 'b' is the rate of introduction of features per remaining feature.

The value of 'a' cannot be constant as this quantity may change due to some improvements may take place for the features fixed. We have,

$$a(t) = a(1 + \alpha t) \tag{2}$$

'α' is the rate at which feature improvements are introduced in a software per feature introduction. '$a\alpha t$' is the number of feature improvements for existing features.

By using (2) in (1), we get (3) as following

$$\frac{dm(t)}{dt} = b(a(1 + \alpha t) - m(t)) \tag{3}$$

$$\text{At } t = 0, \quad m(0) = 0$$

$$m(t) = a\left(\alpha t + (1 - \frac{\alpha}{b})(1 - \exp(-bt))\right) \tag{4}$$

The above model is used to predict the number of features that can be introduced in software over a long run and the rate of generation of feature improvements from the fixing of these features. We validated the proposed model discussed above for five Apache products.

We have estimated the parameters a, b and α of the model based on Nonlinear Regression (NLR) using Statistical Package for Social Sciences (SPSS) software.

3   Results

We have estimated the number of features (NFs + IMPs) need to be fixed in a software product over long run and estimated the rate of generation of feature improvements from these fixed features. Table 2 shows the parameter estimates for features of different products. 'O' shows the observed number of features fixed in the software product. 'a' is the number of features that need to be fixed over long run. 'α' is the rate at which feature improvements are introduced in a software per feature introduction.

Table 2. Estimated parameter values for Apache products

Product	O	a	b	α
Avro	490	432	0.049	0.005
Pig	536	564	0.022	0.013
Hive	1011	1088	0.015	0.015
Whirr	188	239	0.049	0
jUDDI	93	98	0.001	0.301

The rate of generation of feature improvements is 0.005, 0.013, 0.015 and 0.301 in Avro, Pig, Hive and jUDDI respectively. In case of Whirr rate of generation of feature improvements is 0. Table 3 shows the performance measures of the proposed model for different Apache products. R^2 lies in the range of 0.825 to 0.997 across different products. Results show high goodness of fit of the proposed model in terms of MSE, Bias, Variation and RMSPE.

Table 3. Performance measures for Apache products

Product	MSE	Bias	VAR	RMSPE	R^2
Avro	134.02	−1.09	11.62	11.67	0.993
Pig	167.46	−2.58	12.67	12.94	0.994
Hive	266.27	1.67	16.36	16.44	0.997
Whirr	75.69	1.43	8.65	8.77	0.991
jUDDI	25.42	−0.88	5.04	5.04	0.825

Figures 9, 10, 11, 12 and 13 show goodness of fit curve for different Apache products. We observed that the predicted values are close to the observed values for features.

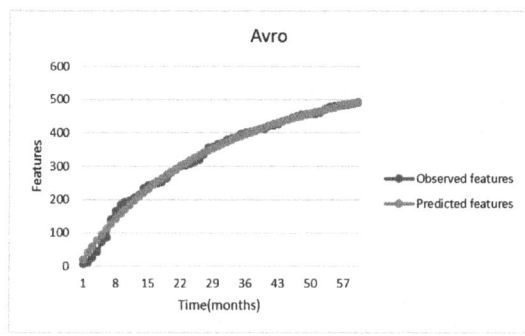

Fig. 9. Goodness of fit curves for Avro

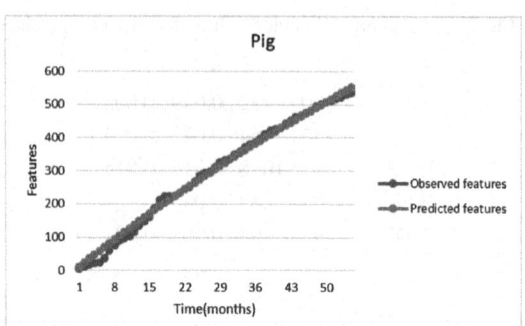

Fig. 10. Goodness of fit curves for Pig

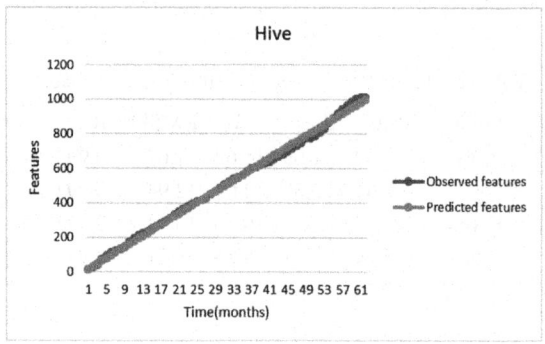

Fig. 11. Goodness of fit curves for Hive

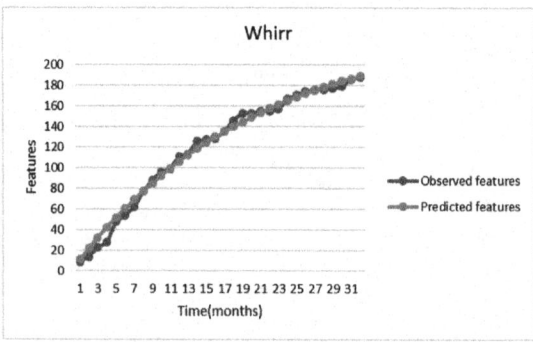

Fig. 12. Goodness of fit curves for Whirr

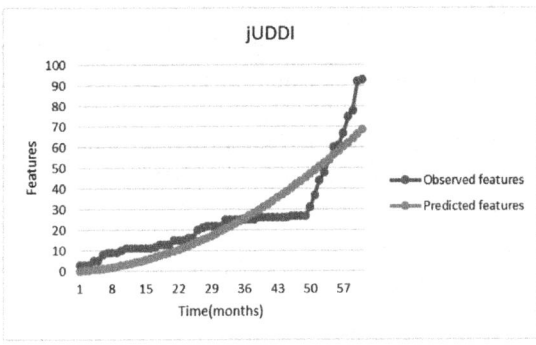

Fig. 13. Goodness of fit curves for jUDDI

4 Related Work

Mathematical models are proven to be useful in measuring the reliability growth of the software products. The development of OSS is different from the closed source software. The failure data of OSS has been modelled by applying different mathematical models to show their applicability [4]. A model has been developed for OSS using power function of testing time and change point. The model has provided a better goodness of fit [5]. In another study, bug reported data has been collected from the bug tracking system and an empirical investigation has been done. The authors found that open source reliability growth is in line with that of the closed source reliability growth [6]. The reliability assessment of OSS has been done and an effective reliability assessment method has been proposed by authors by considering the actual OSS development paradigm [7]. A modified software reliability growth model to reconsider the reliability of OSS systems has been proposed by using a power-law function of testing effort and the interdependency of multigeneration faults. The models have been validated on several real-world data [8]. In another study, defect data of twenty five releases of five OSS projects has been considered. These data sets have been modelled using eight software reliability growth models. It has been found that it is better to take the defect creation date instead of defects fixing date during quantitative quality assessment of open source software products [9]. In [10], the authors proposed reliability analysis of the projects as a three stage process, namely bug-gathering, bug-filtering and bug-analysis. It was found that Weibull distribution well fits in the reliability growth modeling of such products. A bug has different severity levels and a generalized reliability growth model has been proposed to measure the reliability growth of the OSS product [4]. A bug reported on the bug tracking system keeps an irregular state, this characteristic follows in OSS bug reporting. A model has been proposed by considering this characteristic using a stochastic differential equation [11]. Modeling of failure occurrence in OSS has been presented with reliability growth in [12]. Recently, an entropy based reliability growth model has been proposed for multi-version open source software products. A release time problem has also been proposed in [13]. It is evident from the review of the related literature that mathematical models have been widely used to measure the reliability growth of the OSS products. But, none of the work presented or exist in the literature to the best of our knowledge which deals with the development paradigm of the OSS products. In this paper, we have proposed a mathematical model which considers the open source software development paradigm where features (NFs + IMPs) are requested/fixed by the users and improvements to these features are added later on.

5 Threats to Validity

The factors that affect the validity of our study are as follows:

Internal Validity: We proposed a model based on the rate of generation of improvements in features from the fixing of features (NFs + IMPs). But, we have not empirically validated the real number of feature improvements generated from the fixing of different features.

External Validity: We have studied feature datasets of five Apache products. Our results may not generalize to all software products. More software projects need to be studied.

6 Conclusion

In this paper, we have proposed a mathematical model for feature prediction based on OSS development paradigm that fixing of different features (NFs + IMPs) generates further feature improvements. We investigated the quantitative quality assessment of the OSS products by predicting the potential number of features that need to be fixed in the software over a long run. We have used rate of generation of these feature improvements. We have validated the model by using feature datasets of five Apache products (Pig, Hive, jUDDI, Avro and Whirr). Results show a high goodness of fit of the model across different products for different performance measures, i.e. MSE, Bias, Variation, RMSPE and R^2. The value of R^2 lies in the range of 0.825 to 0.997 across different products.

In the future, we will extend the proposed work by taking other rates of feature introduction like Erlang and logistic.

References

1. Gacek, C., Arief, B.: The many meanings of open source. IEEE Softw. **21**(1), 34–40 (2004)
2. http://www.apache.org/
3. Yamada, S., Tokuno, K., Osaki, S.: Imperfect debugging models with fault introduction rate for software reliability assessment. Int. J. Syst. Sci. **23**(12), 2241–2252 (1992)
4. Singh, V.B., Singh, G.P., Kumar, R., Kapur, P.K.: A generalized reliability growth model for open source software. In: 2010 2nd International Conference on Reliability, Safety and Hazard (ICRESH), pp. 523–528. IEEE, December 2010

5. Singh, V.B., Kapur, P.K., Basirzadeh, M.: Open source software reliability growth model by considering change–point. BVICAM's Int. J. Inf. Technol. **4**(1), 405–410 (2012)
6. Zhou, Y., Davis, J.: Open source software reliability model: an empirical approach. In: ACM SIGSOFT Software Engineering Notes, vol. 30, no. 4, pp. 1–6. ACM, May 2005
7. Tamura, Y., Yamada, S.: Comparison of software reliability assessment methods for open source software. In: Proceedings of the 11th International Conference on Parallel and Distributed Systems 2005, vol. 2, pp. 488–492. IEEE, July 2005
8. Li, F., Yi, Z.L.: A new software reliability growth model: multigeneration faults and a power-law testing-effort function. Math. Probl. Eng. **2016**, 13 (2016)
9. Ullah, N., Morisio, M.: An empirical analysis of open source software defects data through software reliability growth models. In: EUROCON, 2013 IEEE, pp. 460–466. IEEE July 2013
10. Rahmani, C., Siy, H., Azadmanesh, A.: An experimental analysis of open source software reliability. Department of Defense/Air Force Office of Scientific Research (2009)
11. Singh, V.B., Kapur, P.K., Tandon, A.: Measuring reliability growth of open source software by applying stochastic differential equations. In: 2010 Second World Congress on Software Engineering (WCSE), vol. 2, pp. 115–118. IEEE, December 2010
12. Rossi, B., Russo, B., Succi, G.: Modelling failures occurrences of open source software with reliability growth. In: Ågerfalk, P., Boldyreff, C., González-Barahona, J.M., Madey, G.R., Noll, J. (eds.) OSS 2010. IAICT, vol. 319, pp. 268–280. Springer, Heidelberg (2010). https://doi.org/10.1007/978-3-642-13244-5_21
13. Singh, V.B., Sharma, M., Pham, H.: Entropy based software reliability analysis of multi-version open source software. IEEE Trans. Softw. Eng. (2017). https://doi.org/10.1109/tse.2017.2766070
14. Kapur, P.K., Verma, A.K.: Quality, Reliability and Infocom Technology: Trends and Future Directions. Narosa Publications, New Delhi (2005)

A Framework for Quality Measurement
of BPMN Process Models

Anacleto Correia[1(✉)] ⓘ, António Gonçalves[2] ⓘ, and Mário Simões-Marques[1] ⓘ

[1] CINAV, Alfeite, 2810-001 Almada, Portugal
{cortez.correia,simoes-marques}@marinha.pt
[2] INESC-ID, UL-IST, Avenida Rovisco Pais, 1, 1048-001 Lisbon, Portugal
antonio.goncalves.pt@gmail.com

Abstract. Nowadays organizations are collaborative and process-intensive. Measurement of process models have a variety of applications including process models' quality evaluation, process improvement and task planning. The objective of this work is to propose a framework for quantifying and linking different quality characteristics of process models built with a standard process modeling language: BPMN. The framework supports the derivation of measures regarding internal quality characteristics of process models, to enable measurement of the quality perceived by process models' users, at the end of the modeling process. To this aim, a measurement terminology for process modeling was set up in order to support process models' measures instantiation. This was done through the specification of a set of activities to be developed in order to derive the base measures and indirect measures for prediction of process models' quality. This work follows a product-oriented approach, by which, quality is assumed as being multi-dimensional concept, with several interrelated characteristics.

Keywords: Process modeling · BPMN · Process models · Measurement
Business process

1 Introduction

Processes are a set of coordinated activities and procedures fueled by resources, aiming to fulfill specific goals of particular stakeholders [1]. A process can be formally documented, or merely informally defined. Regardless its nature, processes exhibit features that make them suitable for usage of modeling techniques. Process modeling is the set of activities conducted for visually depicting qualitatively grounded models of organization's processes, so that the quality of processes can be analyzed, monitored and improved regarding their configuration or outcome.

The design of processes through process modeling is an activity carried out in the early stages of a process elicitation. This activity helps to identify problems in the beginning of the process development [2] and assists the design of valid process models. Moreover, a suitable analysis and verification of processes at the modeling stage would make easier the process maintenance tasks [3] by reducing its implicit costs. This is why efforts should be made to impose quality characteristics to the process models.

© Springer International Publishing AG, part of Springer Nature 2018
O. Gervasi et al. (Eds.): ICCSA 2018, LNCS 10964, pp. 424–437, 2018.
https://doi.org/10.1007/978-3-319-95174-4_34

For representing process models that could be analyzed, regarding their quality, it is important to choose a visual language. For this work it was chosen the Business Process Model and Notation (BPMN) [4] since it is nowadays the most well-equipped process modeling language [5, 6], backed up by the Object Management Group (OMG). BPMN is currently the business process notation most used among process modeling practitioners [7] and is one of the process modeling languages with more modeling tools available. Also, since the BPMN language definition is based upon a metamodel, this favors the quality validation of process models.

So, as it happens with other software requirements artifacts, to evaluate process models, the quality must be addressed as a multi-dimensional concept, given its several characteristics. The ISO/IEC 25000 series (SQuaRE) [8], is a well-known quality standard where the factors contributing to quality are grouped to constitute the basis of a quality model. A quality model often decomposes the view of quality into different levels of characteristics. The interrelationships between quality characteristics and their measures should also be documented. Eventually, the internal attributes of the artifacts are linked to its external quality attributes.

According to the taxonomy of Mylopoulos et al., regarding quality attributes in software systems [9], to deal with the formal treatment of quality in process modeling, two approaches can be followed: a process-oriented approach that focuses upon quality attributes that outputs of processes must target; and a product-oriented approach, which attempts to define methods and tools to ensure that process modeling outcomes, i.e. the process diagrams, can be evaluated to the degree to which they meet certain external quality attributes.

Therefore, in the case of process modeling, this results in a quality model with directly measurable attributes of process models diagrams (e.g. size, complexity) linked to the perceived quality by stakeholders (e.g. correctness, maintainability).

The aim of this work is to propose a framework for quantifying and linking different quality characteristics, amenable to measure and control the internal quality characteristics of process models, in order to ensure the final quality of the modeling process.

This work is structured as follow. In Sect. 2 related work regarding quality in process modeling is surveyed, both from process-oriented and a product-oriented approaches. A BPMN measurement framework for quality evaluation of process models is described in Sect. 3, by proposing a model for measurement of process models (Sect. 3.1), as well as a process for deriving process modeling measures (Sect. 3.2). Section 4 concludes the paper and suggest future work.

2 Related Work on Quality in Process Modeling

Process modeling is a design discipline that produces conceptual models (process diagrams) from processes' elicitation. By following a taxonomy of Mylopoulos et al. regarding quality attributes in software systems [9], two approaches can be considered to deal with the formal treatment of quality in process modeling: process-oriented and product-oriented approaches.

2.1 Process-Oriented Approach

The process-oriented approach to quality in process modeling focus its attention in the definition and assessment of the set of quality attributes that outputs of processes must attain. Thus, according to this approach, alongside information regarding the characteristics of outputs, the processes specification should also contain information about the quality characteristics relevant for the domain that provides the products and services (e.g. response time, availability, accuracy). The process-oriented approach is in line with the critical-realist perspective [10] by which, the design artifacts should be used to actively construct and assess the world, rather than simply describe it. Therefore, processes' models, as an outcome of process modeling, should also provide information regarding the value delivered to the stakeholders, i.e., the beneficiaries of the processes. Some of the research threads developed in-line with the process-oriented approach are the following:

- The approach of Kueng and Kawalek address the processes modeling and assessing, at a conceptual level, namely highlighting how process models can be evaluated against nonfunctional goals. However, they concluded that the assessment of processes, if carried out at model level, would be always partial [11].
- Assessment of quality properties of processes using structural measures similar to those of software [12].
- Korherr and List added a context perspective to an earlier work [13], which had considered functional, behavior, data and organizational perspectives. The extension of some business process modeling languages metamodels with business process goals and performance measures, allowed these concepts to become explicitly visible in the corresponding models. Furthermore, they propose a mapping of the performance measures in process modeling languages onto the process execution languages intended to enable the monitoring of process upon the execution environment [14–16].
- Go4flex approach [17] uses process goals to describe what is to be achieved, instead of addressing exclusively the activities that should be done, using traditional activity-oriented workflow languages. They proposed a framework that includes the five perspectives from Korherr and List, as well as concepts developed in the area of agents and multi-agent systems.
- The approach from Popova and Sharpanskykh's, coming from the areas of Artificial Intelligence (AI) and Business Engineering (BE), proposed a model of an organization that included its goals, as well as relevant Performance Indicators (PIs) (aka measures) for measurement and analysis of the organizational performance. The contribution of the approach is a framework, with formal foundations, which allows the formalization of the PI concept, the relationships among PIs, as well as the analysis and verification of temporal aspects of the represented relations, with the Temporal Trace Language (TTL) [18]
- Johannes composed the UML Schedulability, Performance, and Time (SPT) specification with the UML Activity Diagram (AD) specification to allow a language for simulation of processes execution within a process diagram [19]. A model-driven method was introduced for performance prediction of automated processes,

implemented as an orchestration of web services, based on an BPMN extension for the specification of performance properties [20].

- It was proposed to be added to BPMN symbols, new artifacts to model process models' constraints and operational conditions [21]. The method intended to assist the early discovery of non-functional requirements during systems development and a tool support for the method was made available. The same authors also presented a survey regarding modeling quality information within process diagrams [22].

2.2 Product-Oriented Approach

The product-oriented approach attempts to define methods and tools to ensure that process modeling outcomes, i.e. the process diagrams, can be evaluated to the degree to which they meet certain external quality attributes.

To evaluate the quality of process diagrams, as with the software artifacts, we must be aware that quality is a multi-dimensional concept, with several characteristics. The ISO/IEC 25000 series (Software product Quality Requirements and Evaluation – SQuaRE), the successor of ISO/IEC 9126 standard, is a well-known example where the factors contributing to quality are grouped to constitute the basis of a quality model. A quality model often decomposes the view of quality into different levels of quality characteristics. The inter-relationships between quality characteristics and their measures are also documented. Eventually, the internal attributes are linked to external quality attributes. In the case of process modeling, this results in a quality model with directly measurable attributes of process models diagrams (e.g. size, complexity) linked to the perceived quality by stakeholders (e.g. correctness, understandability, maintainability). So, since a quality model is a framework for quantifying and linking different quality characteristics, one could expect that if we are able to control the internal quality characteristics of process models, this will ensure more control over the final quality of the modeling process.

In the next section, the product-oriented approach is followed for deriving a measurement framework for quality evaluation of process models designed with BPMN.

3   A Framework for Quality Measurement of Process Models

Process models' measurement play an important role in the assessment and improvement of the quality of processes' design. Nowadays, given the process-intensive and collaborative work done in organizations, the measurement and assessment of process diagrams have a variety of applications including process models' quality prediction, business improvement, and task planning [23].

Measurement is a mechanism that can help answering several questions concerned with the activity of modeling processes:

- It helps, during the course of process design, to assess the modeling progress, to take corrective actions based on the assessment of process models' internal characteristics (e.g. process model size, entanglement, autonomy, etc.);

- It allows assessing the strengths and weaknesses of the current process models (e.g., the frequency and density of certain types of errors);
- It provides a rationale for adopting best-practice techniques (e.g., measure the impact of a certain technique on preventing errors in process models).

Being the aim of BPMN to provide a standard language for process modeling, why not to take the standardization efforts one step further in order to provide BPMN standard quality measures. This would certainly contribute to define the thresholds that good process models would aim to comply with. Furthermore, it would also facilitate the benchmarking among process models intended for the same objectives.

However, if a measure is proposed for BPMN process modeling, the researcher should demonstrate whether it is actually representative of the attribute intended to be characterized. Moreover, it is required to scrutinize the measure through a structured approach [24].

A two steps measurement process, is usually sought as the way of ensuring that a measure is accepted by the corresponding community. Through theoretical validation the researcher should use logic to formally verify whether a measure is meaningful or not. Empirical validation, on the other hand, implies using data collected from observation or derived by experimentation to support the relevancy of proposed BPMN measure [23]. As generally recognized (e.g. [23, 24]), both theoretical and empirical validations of measures are necessary and complementary. In this work we focus upon the definition of the framework for BPMN measures derivation that include those mentioned two steps.

However, the methodology for BPMN measures' derivation, is not to build from scratch. The approach consists in the adaption to the context of BPMN an existent framework for measures' validation already used in the domain of software engineering [24]. So, the framework used for derivation of BPMN measures is adapted and instantiated from the measure definition process Goal Question Metric/MEtric DEfinition Approach (GQM/MEDEA) [25], a systematic approach proposed for software measurement, with a set of guidelines for the design and definition of sound software measures. The GQM/MEDEA framework received several contributions and influences from the measurement literature, among them, from Goal Question Metric (GQM) paradigm [26] regarding the goals and models' definition through a top-down approach.

With the BPMN measurement framework presented in the following sections, it is intended to support the definition of process models' measures, preventing possible sources of threats that could hamper their validity. For elicitation of the customized framework we begin by to setting up the BPMN measurement terminology (Sect. 3.1), and then define the process (set of activities) needed for derivation of BPMN measures (Sect. 3.2).

3.1 A Model for Measurement of Process Models

In software engineering field there are no unequivocal consensus about many of the concepts and terminology regarding the measurement process [27]. The same problem arises when trying to collect the set of terms and vocabulary regarding process modeling measures.

The vocabulary concerning the measurement of quality characteristics is sometimes conflicting and inconsistent among the several sources and references that can be used by researchers and practitioners. So, there is the need to set up terms and concepts, aiming to contribute to the harmonization of the BPMN measurement terminology, even before proposing a customized BPMN measurement process for derivation the BPMN measures. The terms herein defined, are based in concepts and definitions of measurement from software engineering, as well as from the metrology vocabulary, and closely follow the approach of SMO (Software Measurement Ontology) by Garcia et al. [27].

Several contributions have enriched, during the last decades, the measurement terminology particularly in the software engineering domain. It was done an initial effort through the CMM (Capability Maturity Model for Software), later superseded by the CMMI (Capability Maturity Model Integration), and the international standard ISO/IEC 15504 (Software Process Improvement and Capability dEtermination – SPICE), derived from the standard of process life cycle ISO/IEC 12207 and from maturity models.

The industry's concerns about measurement in quality management systems was reflected in ISO 9001, and also translated to the specific case of computer software and related support services, through the ISO/IEC 9000-3 standard, which is focused in the activities of acquisition, supply, development, operation and maintenance related to computer software.

The ISO organization made an effort to harmonize the measurement terminology by delivering the international vocabulary of metrology (VIM), covering the terms and concepts related to measurement, later extensively adopted by other standards. Among the international standards that address software measurement concepts and terminology some of the major references are:

- the IEEE 610.12-1990, a glossary of Software Engineering terminology;
- the IEEE 1061-1998, regarding a software quality measures methodology;
- the ISO/IEC TR 14143-3 establishes "a framework for verifying the statements of a functional size measurement method and/or for conducting tests requested by the verification sponsor, relative to a specified set of performance properties";
- the ISO/IEC 25000 series (Software product Quality Requirements and Evaluation – SQuaRE) [ISO05b] is a set of standards that provides methods for measurement, assessment and evaluation of software product quality, and proposes a software product quality model, and measures for internal quality, external quality, and quality in use;
- the ISO/IEC 15939 defines the activities of the measurement process for System and Software Engineering and management disciplines required for adequately specify: (a) the measurement information needed, (b) the way measures and analysis results should be applied, and (c) the way of assessing the validity of results analysis;

Relevant proposals regarding software measurement came also from the research community, namely the set of proposals for defining measures of product attributes in Software Engineering [25].

From the several efforts due to researchers and practitioners, discrepancies, gaps, and terminology conflicts were revealed [27]. Terms commonly used (e.g. measure, metric, measurable attribute, measurement) raised the debate and disparate interpretations regarding their precise meaning were suggested. Eventually, terminological agreements have emerged in the more recent standards (e.g. ISO/IEC 25000 and ISO/IEC 15939 series) that chose not to use the more controversial terms, such as metric, using instead more consensual terms of measurement and measure.

Since this work of process modeling supported by BPMN, we are naturally concerned about terms regarding the definition of concepts required to establish the scope and objectives of the measurement process, as well as those related to the characterization of BPMN measures. A natural approach to achieve such purposes is by using the general accepted measurement vocabulary distilled in the above-mentioned references. Nevertheless, some alignment on terminology definitions to the process modeling field is needed. Hence, the concepts used in this work for now on, regarding BPMN measurement, and the relationships among them, is depicted in Fig. 1, and are based on the following definitions:

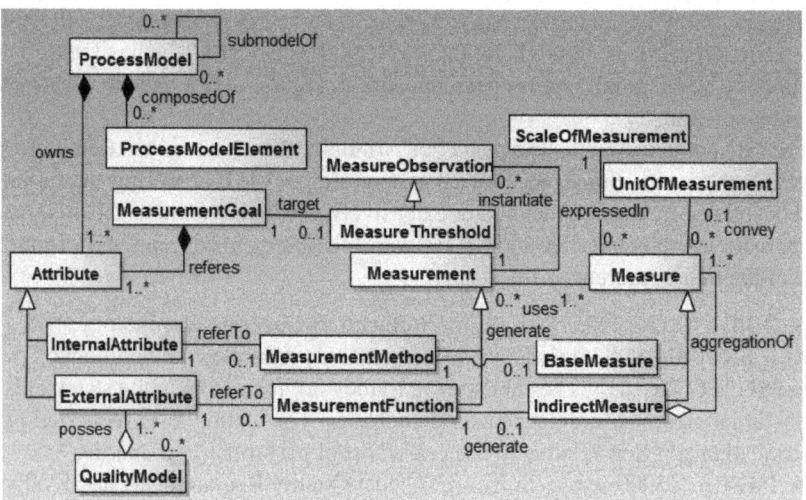

Fig. 1. Concepts regarding process modeling measurement

Process Model: A set of intertwined process elements depicted in a diagram using a specific notation (BPMN).

Sub-Model: One of the parts that make up a process model. A sub-model may be also subdivided into other sub-models. In BPMN, a sub-model may be embedded in the model as a regular process diagram external to the main model as an instance of a *CallableElement* (Fig. 2) or be depicted as an instance of *SubProcess* (Fig. 3).

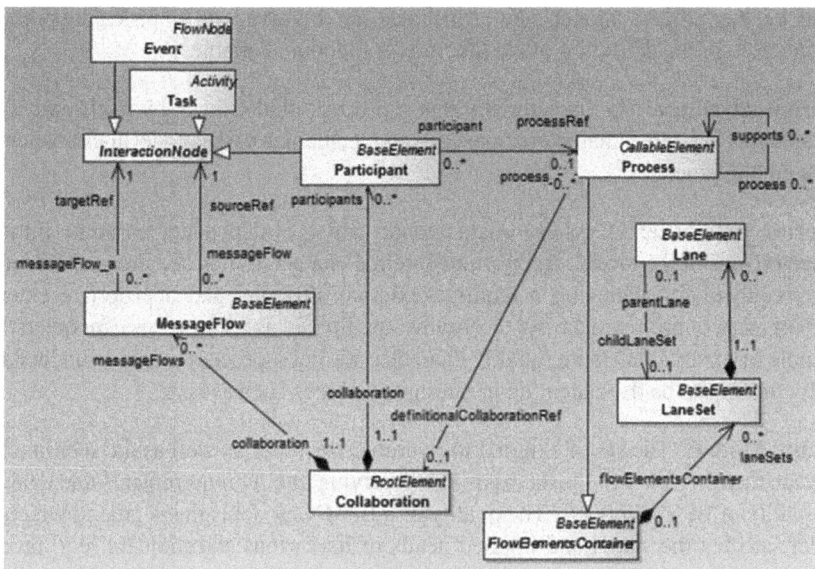

Fig. 2. Excerpt of BPMN metamodel: relationships with the metaclass process

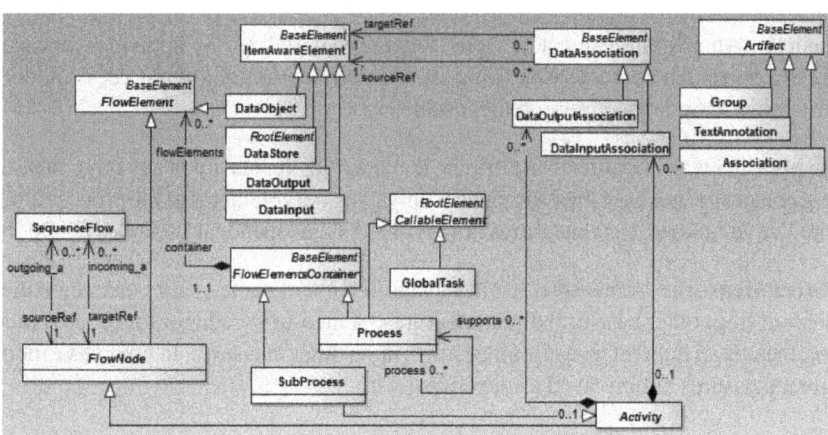

Fig. 3. Excerpt of BPMN metamodel: metaclass of the depicted elements in process models' diagrams

Process Model Element: A metaclass embodying a concept of the process modeling language which is depicted in process models. BPMN elements that can be seen depicted in diagrams are shown in Fig. 2.

Attribute: A particular characteristic of a process model. For example, in a BPMN diagram, the attribute that denotes the number of elements that constitutes the model could be the process model size. Attributes are involved in empirical hypotheses formulation, in the definition of explanatory or outcome variables.

Internal Attribute: A characteristic that a process model owns by itself and is not dependent of any other characteristic. For example, the size of the model does not depend on its entanglement.

External Attribute: A quality characteristic which is dependent on some intrinsic characteristics of the model. Appropriate internal characteristics of a process model are a pre-requisite for achieving a required external attribute, and appropriate external attributes are a pre-requisite for achieving quality in use by process modelers. An example of external attribute (quality characteristic) of a process model is understandability that could be dependent upon internal attributes such as size.

Quality Model: The set of external measurable attributes as well as the relationships between them which provide the basis for specifying quality requirements and evaluate the quality of BPMN models. The quality of a BPMN model is the degree to which the model satisfies the stated and implied needs of its various stakeholders (e.g. process analysts, process implementers), and thus provides value. A quality model categorizes model quality into external attributes (quality characteristics, which in some cases are further subdivided into sub-characteristics).

Measure: An abstract value amenable of being materialized by applying a measurement to a particular characteristic (internal or external attribute) of a process model. A measure has a predefined measurement scale.

Base Measure: A measure of an attribute that does not depend upon any other measure. The size measure is a base measure since it only considers elements of the process model. In predictive models, base measures are involved as independent variables [ISO05b].

Indirect Measure: A measure that is a quantification of some quality characteristic. It is derived from other base or indirect measures. A measure predictor for process model correctness is an indirect measure since relies upon other measures. In predictive models indirect measures are involved as dependent variables.

Measurement Scale: The nature of the relationship between measure observations regarding the specific sort of mathematical properties (e.g. equality, inequality, addition). Within measurement theory, there are different scales that a measure can take the form of, which provides a set of allowable transformations for that scale. Four main measurement scales are often used [28] by increasing the degree of accuracy and expressiveness:

- **Nominal** (aka categorical variable): if there is no implicit order or distance among the categories of a variable, to which the measured observations are assigned. The only transformation admissible to a nominal measure is equality;
- **Ordinal:** if the measured observations are discrete an can be ranked (ordered). The order of the measured observations matters but not the difference between values.

Besides the equality transformation, inequality using relational operators (e.g. >, <), is also an admissible transformation;

- **Interval:** if the continuous variable can be ranked, as in an ordinal variable, and additionally the magnitudes of the differences between two values are meaningful. Admissible transformations include equality, inequality, addition, and subtraction.
- **Ratio:** if a continuous variable beside the interval scale features has a meaningful zero value (a beginning or ending point), so that a meaningful rate between two measured observations is allowed. Admissible transformations include equality, inequality, addition, subtraction, multiplication, and division.

Unit of Measurement: A particular magnitude, defined and adopted by convention with other quantities with the same meaning are compared to express their relative magnitude. The number of activities per subprocess could be the unit of measurement of the measure modularization.

Measurement: A logical sequence of operations aiming to instantiate a particular measure for a given attribute. The resulting instance is called measure observation.

Measurement Method: A set of operations performed through an algorithm or calculation, aiming to derive a particular base measure for a given internal attribute.

Measurement Function: A set of operations performed through an algorithm or calculation, by combining base or indirect measures aiming to instantiate a particular indirect measure for a given external attribute.

Measurement Goal: The goals' specification intends to provide guidance for the validation process, and the definition of the scope for interpreting the results of the validation. The measurement goal supports the definition of targets for base and indirect measures in process modeling. The measurement goals constraint the measurements of values of internal or external attributes attained by specific measures. As an example of a measurement goal one can point out the targets for base measures of BPMN models such as size or modularity, assuming they are related with the indirect measure of correctness of BPMN models, resulting from failures in complying with the well-formedness rules of the BPMN language [26].

Measure Observation: The quantity or quality assigned as a value to an attribute of a process model through a measurement process.

Measure Threshold: A target used as pattern to determine the level of acceptance or rejection of the measure observed in a certain attribute of a process model.

3.2   The Process for Derivation of Process Modeling Measures

This process aims the specification of a set of activities to be developed in order to derive a set of measures for a prediction model in the context of BPMN. Like any methodological approach, by following and documenting a series of steps, a researcher is able to trace all design decisions made in the process as well as, justify changes and reviews made, as more logical or empirical evidence is unveiled. Besides, it will provide the basis for replications by other researchers.

For a certain measure to be generally accepted regarding its interpretation, as well as its usage in the context of the process modeling language such as BPMN, it is necessary that the measure has been derived through a well-grounded, relevant, meaningful and logically correct process [29], i.e., the measure should have been validated.

To be carried out the measurement process validation, the language abstract syntax (i.e., the BPMN metamodel) plays an important role, since it contains the elements that will be used for the measure specification and implementation. The measure definition must be provided in a clear form, backed up by a measurement method, i.e., computed by a deterministic algorithm. This is crucial for measures' validation and also important for the measure's correct reproduction so that it can be analyzed and studied by other researchers and practitioners.

To extract and analyze measure observations from actual BPMN process models, which are the sources of information for the measurement process, the measurement goals must also be formulated upon the BPMN metamodel.

In this work, we assume that measures' validation is done through a set of four coarse grained steps. The process diagram in Fig. 4 depicts the operational structure of the proposed framework and represents the dynamic view over the concepts and relationships of the static model on process modeling measurement depicted in Fig. 1.

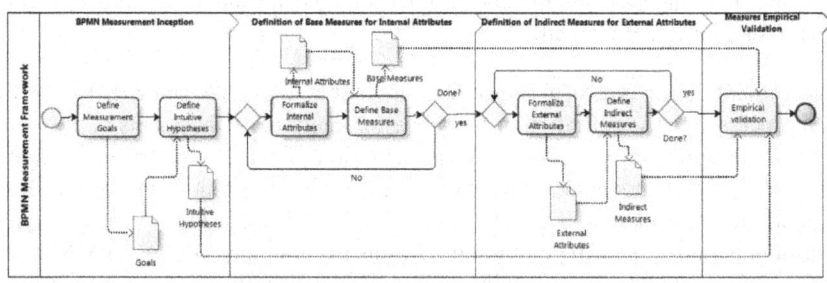

Fig. 4. Process for measures' definition and validation

BPMN Measurement Inception

The objectives of measures' designers are summarized into measurement goals, based on their knowledge about the process modeling language (BPMN) and regular usage of the notation producing process models. Driven by measurement goals, a set of intuitive hypotheses are established highlighting the qualitative relation between internal attributes of process models (independent variables candidates) to other external attributes of the same models (dependent variables candidates). For instance, starting with predicting the correctness of process models as a measurement goal, a measures' designer could possibly conjecture that could exist a positive association between the process model size and the number of errors found in the model.

Definition of Base Measures for Internal Attributes
This phase evaluates the suitability of base measures for conveying the internal attributes characteristics of process models. Internal attributes capture factors that are assumed to have a causal relationship with external attributes. Internal attributes are formalized by a set of mathematical properties (e.g. non-negativity, monotonicity). The theoretical validation of a base measure is a formal approach to assess whether the measure is valid or not, regarding the properties of internal attributes. The properties should be as generic as possible, i.e., independent of the process models' representation. Underpinned by properties, base measures are defined, as well as the measurement method that must be performed over a set of predefined process model elements. For instance, size is an internal attribute of a BPMN process model whose base measure could be defined by the number of *FlowNode* (Fig. 3) elements in the model, calculated through a specific measurement method.

Definition of Indirect Measures for External Attributes
The external attributes are quality characteristics of process models (e.g. correctness, understandability, maintainability). Those are the qualities that process models should convey when they are in use, namely by process analysts and process implementers either for documenting sake or for process enactment. During this phase it must be assessed whether the indirect measures adequately capture the external attributes of the process model.

Measures' Empirical Validation
The intuitive hypotheses give way to grounded empirical hypotheses. These, empirical hypotheses are verified using the measures defined for the internal and external attributes. The empirical hypotheses are a refinement of the intuitive hypotheses by providing a specific function for the relationship between base and indirect measures used to build the predictive model. The adequacy of the predictive model is determined by the level of significance of results.

4   Conclusions

Processes are coordinated activities aiming to fulfill specific goals. The design of process models is carried out in the early stages of a process elicitation through process modeling, a set of activities conducted for visually depicting qualitatively grounded models of processes, so that their quality can be analyzed, monitored and improved regarding their configuration or outcome. Process model quality validation helps to identify problems in the beginning of any process development and assists the design of valid process models.

In this work it was proposed a framework for quality measurement of process models built using BPMN language. The BPMN measurement framework for quality evaluation of process models is composed by a model, an ontology of process models' measurement, and the specification of a process for deriving measures regarding process modeling outcomes.

Future work will be focused on verification of results presented here, by theoretically and empirically validating the measures derived from the proposed framework.

Acknowledgment. The work was funded by the Portuguese Ministry of Defense and by the Portuguese Navy/Escola Naval/CINAV.

References

1. Melao, N., Pidd, M.: A conceptual framework for understanding business processes and business process modelling. Inf. Syst. J. **10**(2), 105–129 (2000). https://doi.org/10.1046/j.1365-2575.2000.00075.x
2. Rolón, E., Cardoso, J., García, F., Ruiz, F., Piattini, M.: Analysis and validation of control-flow complexity measures with BPMN process models. In: Halpin, T., Krogstie, J., Nurcan, S., Proper, E., Schmidt, R., Soffer, P., Ukor, R. (eds.) BPMDS/EMMSAD -2009. LNBIP, vol. 29, pp. 58–70. Springer, Heidelberg (2009). https://doi.org/10.1007/978-3-642-01862-6_6
3. Aguilar, E.R., et al.: Evaluation measures for business process models, pp. 1567–1568 (2006)
4. OMG, BPMN: Business Process Model and Notation (BPMN) (2011)
5. Recker, J.C., Indulska, M., Rosemann, M., Green, P.: Do process modelling techniques get better? A comparative ontological analysis of BPMN. In: Campbell, B., Underwood, J., Bunker, D. (eds.) 16th Australasian Conference on Information Systems, Sydney, Australia, 30 November– 2 December 2005 (2005)
6. Recker, J., Rosemann, M.: Business process modeling: a comparative analysis. J. Assoc. **10**(4), 333–363 (2009)
7. Harmon, P., Wolf, C.: Business process modeling survey, December 2011
8. I.O.f.S. ISO, ISO/IEC 25000:2005 – Software Engineering – Software product Quality Requirements and Evaluation (SQuaRE) – Guide to SQuaRE (2005)
9. Mylopoulos, J., Chung, L., Nixon, B.: Representing and using nonfunctional requirements: a process-oriented approach. IEEE Trans. Softw. Eng. **18**(6), 483–497 (1992). https://doi.org/10.1109/32.142871
10. Moody, D.L.: Theoretical and practical issues in evaluating the quality of conceptual models: current state and future directions. Data Knowl. Eng. **55**(3), 243–276 (2005)
11. Kueng, P., Kawalek, P.: Goal-based business process models: creation and evaluation. Bus. Process Manage. J. **3**(1), 17–38 (1997)
12. Phalp, K., Shepperd, M.: Quantitative analysis of static models of processes. J. Syst. Softw. **52**(2–3), 105–112 (2000). https://doi.org/10.1016/s0164-1212(99)00136-3
13. Curtis, B., et al.: Process modeling. Commun. ACM **35**(9), 75–90 (1992)
14. List, B., Korherr, B.: An evaluation of conceptual business process modelling languages. In: Proceedings of the 2006 ACM Symposium on Applied Computing - SAC 2006, pp. 1532–1532 (2006). https://doi.org/10.1145/1141277.1141633
15. Korherr, B., List, B.: Extending the EPC and the BPMN with business process goals and performance measures. In: Book Extending the EPC and the BPMN with Business Process Goals and Performance Measures, Series Extending the EPC and the BPMN with Business Process Goals and Performance Measures, pp. 287–294 (2007)
16. Korherr, B.: Business Process Modelling: Languages, Goals, and Variabilities. VDM Publishing, Saarbrücken (2008)

17. Braubach, L., Pokahr, A., Jander, K., Lamersdorf, W., Burmeister, B.: Go4Flex: goal-oriented process modelling. In: Essaaidi, M., Malgeri, M., Badica, C. (eds.) Intelligent Distributed Computing IV. Studies in Computational Intelligence, vol. 315, pp. 77–87. Springer, Heidelberg (2010). https://doi.org/10.1007/978-3-642-15211-5_9
18. Popova, V., Sharpanskykh, A.: Formal modelling of organisational goals based on performance indicators. Data Knowl. Eng. **70**(4), 335–364 (2011)
19. Johannes, J.: ATL Use Case - Model Driven Performance Engineering: From UML/SPT to AnyLogic. Book ATL, TU Dresden (2008)
20. Bocciarelli, P., Ambrogio, A.D.: Automated performance analysis of business processes. In: Proceedings of the 2012 Symposium on Theory of Modeling and Simulation-DEVS Integrative M&S Symposium. Society for Computer Simulation International (2012)
21. Pavlovski, C.J., Zou, J.: Non-functional requirements in business process modeling, vol. 79 (2008)
22. Heinrich, R., et al.: Modeling quality information within business process models. In: Proceedings of the 4th SQMB Workshop, TUM-I1104 (2011)
23. Meneely, A.: Software metrics validation criteria: a systematic literature review. North Carolina State University. Department of Computer Science (2010)
24. Briand, L., et al.: Theoretical and empirical validation of software product measures. In: International Software Engineering Research Network, Technical report ISERN-95–03 (1995)
25. Briand, L.C., et al.: An operational process for goal-driven definition of measures. IEEE Trans. Softw. Eng. **28**(12), 1106–1125 (2002)
26. Basili, V.R., et al.: The goal question metric approach. In: Marciniak, J. (ed.) Encyclopedia of Software Engineering, vol. 1, pp. 578–583 (2000)
27. García, F., et al.: Towards a consistent terminology for software measurement information and software technology. Inf. Softw. Technol. **48**(8), 631–644 (2006)
28. Fenton, N.E., Pfleeger, S.L.: Software Metrics: A Rigorous and Practical Approach. Brooks, Baltimore (1998)
29. Meneely, A.: Validating software metrics : a spectrum of philosophies. ACM Trans. Software Eng. Methodol. (TOSEM) **21**(4), 24 (2012)

Feature Level Complexity and Coupling Analysis in 4GL Systems

András Kicsi[1(✉)], Viktor Csuvik[1], László Vidács[1,2], Árpád Beszédes[1],
and Tibor Gyimóthy[1,2]

[1] Department of Software Engineering, University of Szeged, Szeged, Hungary
{akicsi,csuvikv,lac,beszedes,gyimothy}@inf.u-szeged.hu
[2] MTA-SZTE Research Group on Artificial Intelligence, University of Szeged,
Szeged, Hungary

Abstract. Product metrics are widely used in the maintenance and evolution phase of software development to advise the development team about software quality. Although most of these metrics are defined for mainstream languages, several of them were adapted to fourth generation languages (4GL) as well. Usual concepts like size, complexity and coupling need to be re-interpreted and adapted to program elements defined by these languages. In this paper we take a further step in this process to address product line development in 4GL. Adopting product line architecture is a necessary step to handle challenges of a growing number of similar product variants. The product line adoption process itself is a tedious task where features of the product variants play crucial role. Features represent a higher level of abstraction that are cross-cutting to program elements of 4GL applications. We propose a set of metrics related to features by linking existing program elements to metrics and by relating features with each other. The focus of this study is on complexity and coupling metrics. We provide a metrics based analysis of several variants of a large scale industrial product line written in the Magic XPA 4GL language.

Keywords: Product lines · SPL · Feature analysis · 4GL · Quality
Metrics · Complexity · Coupling

1 Introduction

Quality assurance tools rely heavily on the use of product metrics. Despite the great variety of metrics that are already defined for mainstream languages [1], there exists only a few solutions for fourth generations languages (4GL). The structure of these languages are closer to human thinking and part of the program logic is provided by the environment itself. Usual notions of size, complexity and coupling need to be re-interpreted in these cases. Building on previous works on metrics based quality assurance for 4GL [2,3] we take new direction to extend metrics towards product line architectures. Maintaining and releasing similar

© Springer International Publishing AG, part of Springer Nature 2018
O. Gervasi et al. (Eds.): ICCSA 2018, LNCS 10964, pp. 438–453, 2018.
https://doi.org/10.1007/978-3-319-95174-4_35

new products accumulates significant overhead over time. The natural way of handling new customer needs is the clone-and-own approach, where product variants have parallel life cycles in independent repositories. Introducing product line architecture offers a long term solution to these challenges [4]. Product line adoption is usually approached from three directions: the proactive approach starts with domain analysis and applies variability management from scratch. The reactive approach incrementally replies to the new customer needs when they arise. Finally, the extractive approach analyzes existing products to obtain feature models and build the product line architecture [5]. An advantage of the extractive approach in general is that several reverse engineering methods exist to support feature extraction and analysis [6]. Static analysis methods for obtaining structural information and dependencies and the analysis of dynamic execution traces foster feature detection and location activities [7,8].

In this paper we propose product metrics at the feature level. These metrics are extensions of usual complexity and coupling metrics linked to features. Our work is motivated by a research project where product line architecture is to be built based on an existing set of products. The subject system is a high market value logistical wholesale system, which has been adapted to various domains in the past using clone-and-own method. Product variants of this system were written in different main versions of Magic 4GL in more than 20 years. In this current work we concentrate on complexity [9] and coupling metrics. The proposed metrics play a role in the product line adoption process and can be used in the future maintenance and evolution of the product line. We provide the following contributions: (1) we propose metrics at the feature level for Magic 4GL; (2) we describe empirical experiments of 4 product variants of a large scale industrial system; and (3) we analyze 4 product variants and 10 high level features of the product line using the proposed metrics.

The paper is organized as follows. We present the background of our research in the next section by depicting the variability in systems developed by a software company using the Magic language. We introduce the proposed feature level metrics on complexity and coupling in Sect. 3. Measurements on 4 product variants and the analysis based on 10 high level features of the product line are presented in Sect. 4. Related work is discussed in Sect. 5, and we conclude the paper in the last section.

2   Background

The most important parts of a Magic application are illustrated in Fig. 1. An application written in Magic usually consists of one or more projects. These projects contain tasks which are units that handle the actual work done by the application. They can control logic units that define the background logic and make use of data stored in data objects. Tasks are the closest things we would call methods in a traditional language. A task can contain other tasks too, which defines a hierarchy. The topmost level of these tasks are called programs which can be viewed as distinguished tasks. Programs are usually small enough

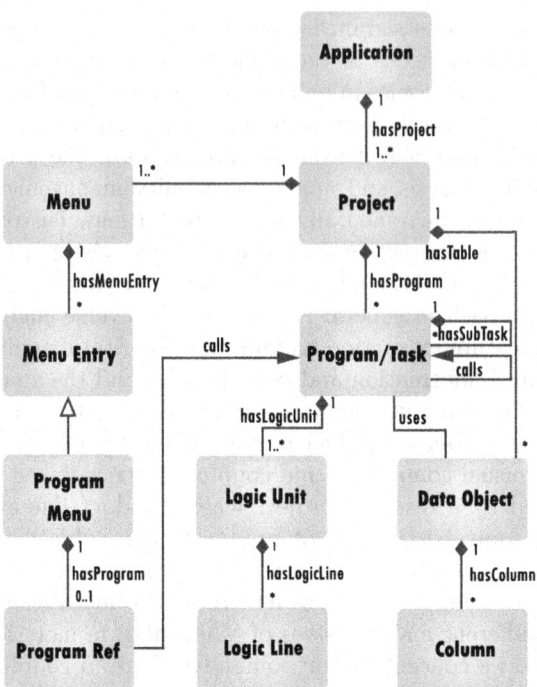

Fig. 1. An illustration of the main components of a Magic system

units that we can handle as a process working towards a single goal, which can make programs ideal units for feature extraction. Programs can also be called by elements called menus. A menu is a control unit inside the application through which calls can be initiated to perform different processes.

Software quality is a highly researched subject with properly defined quality metrics in many specific fields of software development. This also involves SPL adoption and even Magic. Software quality is not highly different in 4GL systems than in a traditional environment, most common quality metrics can be computed but there may be a need to redefine or modify some or adopt new ones. Quality can be defined to 4GL systems just as well as to any other branch of software development. Some metrics are already well defined for Magic tasks and systems too [9].

Complexity as a quality metric is also a popular field of research. Since complexity can be understood in many ways many different complexities exist even in the same domain. Undoubtedly the best complexity metrics are the ones that correlate best with the opinions of the users, in this case most frequently the developers. Scientific work has already compared several of these metrics based on user questionnaires [10] even in the 4GL domain, including Magic [9].

3   Proposed Metrics

Features represent a higher level abstraction over program code. This is the area where domain experts and developers need to interact: features provide a logical view of system functionality, while they are implemented by various parts of the program code. In previous work we provided methods for feature extraction based on textual similarity and call graphs [11,12]. Our textual similarity based extraction relies on the Latent Semantic Indexing (LSI) technique. Textual similarity is often referred to as Information Retrieval (IR) in scientific literature, we use this abbreviation in the following chapters.

We consider features as sets of Magic programs that take part in their implementation. These sets usually have overlaps since programs can be used by more than one feature. In this work we present our results computed on the topmost level of features we have been provided with by domain experts, which involves 10 high level features and represent the main functions of the system. Their size properties after extraction can be observed in Table 1 and Fig. 2 the values representing the number of programs implementing each feature, working with more than 2000 programs in total. We worked with four variants of the subject system, their properties are further defined in Sect. 4.

Table 1. The recovered number of programs for each feature of the variants with call-graph (CG) and information retrieval (IR) based extraction

Variant	CG-V1	CG-V2	CG-V3	CG-V4	IR-V1	IR-V2	IR-V3	IR-V4
Manufacturing	49	48	47	405	12	13	12	12
Interface	5	5	5	68	36	43	34	22
Access management	13	83	12	421	37	44	36	125
Quality control	152	146	146	441	60	82	60	113
Stock control	348	352	339	769	208	225	209	312
Administrator interventions	198	196	190	647	202	392	205	312
Supplier order management	156	155	156	466	206	235	201	335
Invoicing	272	267	265	602	278	299	274	394
Master file maintenance	70	68	66	467	266	299	259	374
Customer orders	294	290	288	457	193	208	190	276

In this section we define several metrics that we deemed suitable for measuring the properties of features. Some of our proposed feature level metrics are extensions of already defined metrics on program level. In many cases these can be summed up or averaged to get suitable measurements for feature level too. In other cases we define new ways that didn't exist on program level. Feature level metrics can also be utilized in the analysis of not just features but the whole system itself or the feature extraction process.

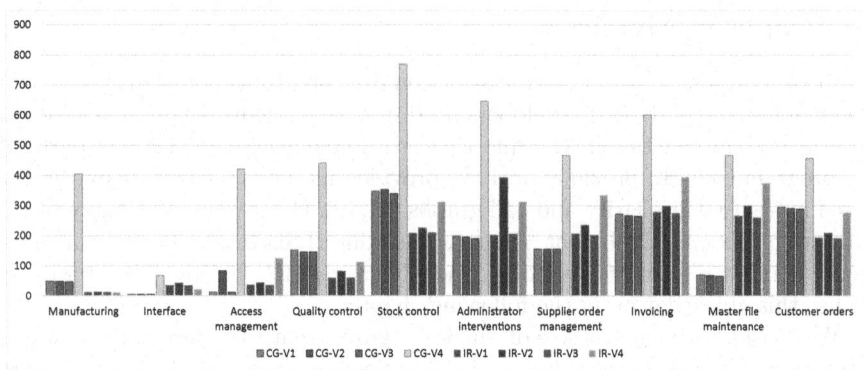

Fig. 2. Number of programs for each feature with call-graph (CG) and the information retrieval (IR) based extraction

3.1   Coupling

Coupling metrics for features represent the differences in their inner and outer references. A high number of valid outer references can possibly imply bad modular design.

Coupling Between Features (CBF): One of the most straightforward coupling metric can be the number of features a feature in question is calling. This number is computed by inspecting the programs of the features. If we imagine features as sets of programs, we can easily see that there is a call between features if there is at least one call between the set of programs of both features. Coupling between features measures only the outgoing calls from each feature. It can be viewed as a metric letting us know how many other features does a single features depend on. Being aware of dependence can be valuable for instance if we decide not to provide a feature, the other features that depend on this can potentially be crippled and if we want to provide those features we may have to bridge this gap created.

Coupling Between Programs Inside Features (CBTIF): While coupling between features measures the outgoing calls from each feature, knowing of the inside structure of a feature can be just as important. For this we can count the calls with both participating programs inside the same feature. This is coupling between programs inside a feature, which does not represent a number of features but a number of calls, thus usually higher than CBF.

Sum of Coupling Between Programs and Data Objects (SCTBDO): Feature coupling can be also viewed at the data object level. The number of used data objects is a metric that already exists for each program, it is useful for measuring the extent of data used by each program. The total of this number for each feature can give us the sum of coupling between programs and data objects, which provides information about the same thing. On feature level this can be interesting information since we can see how much each feature relies on stored data, thus getting a more complete picture of the feature itself.

Program Clarity (PC): Another piece of interesting information can be derived from the number of features a single program is connected to. If a program is only connected to a sole feature it can be more easily maintainable with less consideration of the subsequent changes in functionality because the effects of a change only affect one feature. Additionally if the customer decides not to require a specific feature, the programs of this feature can be excluded. A number indicating this condition which we called program clarity represents the percentage of programs that are unique to that single feature.

3.2   Complexity

The quantification of software complexity is a basic idea that is widely used throughout software development. Complexity can be defined in many ways, and this is the same with feature complexity. Since a feature is handled as a set of programs that aims to reach a common goal, the complexity of the feature is derived from the complexity of its programs.

As established in the paper of Nagy et al. [9] in Magic context the generally used McCabe complexity measure is not really suitable for representing the real complexity of a program. On the other hand Halstead complexity metics [13] correlated well with the opinions of the experienced developers involved. To complete Halstead complexity metrics we us the following values:

- n_1: the number of distinct operators
- n_2: the number of distinct operands
- N_1: the total number of operators
- N_2: the total number of operands.

Halstead Volume (HV): It represents the magnitude of information inside a feature, more precisely the bits required for its coding. This can be also interpreted as a measure describing the amount of information a reader of the code must attain to completely understand the feature itself. Since a feature can involve many programs this number is usually very high. As it can be seen from its formula this measure involves all operators and operands in the feature. It computes as follows:

$$HV = (N_1 + N_2) * log_2(n_1 + n_2)$$

Halstead Difficulty (HD): It can be used to measure fault sensitivity. The important factors in this property are the number of distinct operators inside a feature and the ratio of all and distinct operands. Both of these properties result in more sensitivity. It computes as follows:

$$HD = \left(\frac{n_1}{2}\right) * \left(\frac{N_2}{n_2}\right)$$

Other metrics that can relevantly measure complexity on feature level include Halstead Vocabulary which describes the sum of all distinct operators and distinct operands in a feature, Halstead Effort (HE) which describes the product of volume and effort and represents the developer effort of the code. Henry-Kafura Complexity (HKC) can also be valuable which works with the inner and outer calls of the features, practically building complexity on coupling information. It computes as:

$$HKC = (N_1 + N_2) * (\text{fan-in} * \text{fan-out})^2$$

During our work we also computed these measures.

4   Experiments and Analysis

In this section we present some of the results of the proposed metrics of four variants of our system under study and we examine their possible meanings to comparison of features and to variants also.

The four variants under study will be mentioned simply as V1, V2, V3 and V4. These are all real variants of the system that are currently under use by customers of our industrial partner. To our knowledge V4 differs from the other variants significantly, while the others share a great number of programs and support a very similar set of functions but still vary somewhat in the specifics. Table 2 displays the size and properties of these four variants. From these data it is even more clear that V4 is the largest variant although V2 has the most tasks. V1 and V3 are very similar both in our experiences and their characteristics.

Table 2. The characteristics of the variants under analysis

Variant	Logic lines	Tasks	Programs	Data objects
V1	366 328	13 365	2 001	699
V2	467 823	25 457	2 719	703
V3	355 604	13 151	2 001	697
V4	518 304	18 291	4 251	1 065

In the remaining part of the section we present a number of results and discuss the meaning of the data retrieved. Experiments were done on all top level features of all four variants on both call graph (CG) and information retrieval (IR) based feature extraction outputs. We present the results in graphic format. Due to space limitations and for the elimination of monotony we only display the results found most notable.

We can note that through all variants the IR technique seems to provide more stable numbers while the CG technique usually shows large differences between variants and even features of the same variant. This does not mean that the CG technique would be inferior in any way, and from our previous knowledge we are aware that the output of the IR based extraction contains a large amount of noise as a result of short feature names which have served as queries for Latent Semantic Indexing. The seemingly more stable results can even be a consequence of the noise itself. The CG based extraction on the other hand can produce a variable number of programs for each feature and each variant. These calls found by the call graph technique are present in the system itself and provide a less conceptual grouping. It is also important to note that with the call graph technique we find a high number of more general programs that are connected to nearly every feature. Even considering these differences we can find that the results of the metrics still move along very similar curves in case of both extraction techniques.

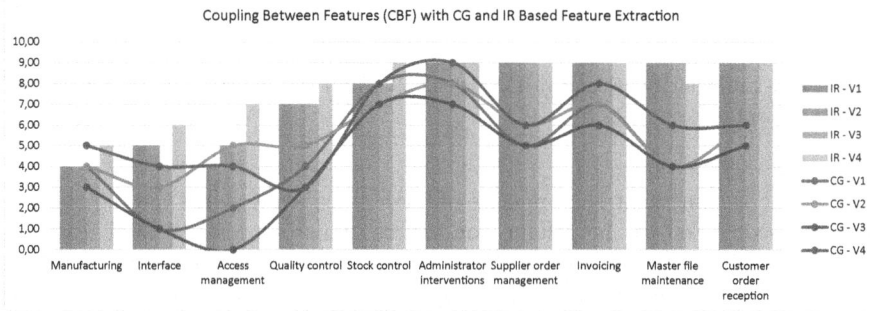

Fig. 3. Coupling Between Features at each variant with call graph and information retrieval based feature extraction

The results of the proposed Coupling Between Features metric can be seen in Fig. 3. As on the following figures, the columns represent the results of measurements done on IR based extraction while the lines represent the results of the extraction based on CG. The maximum of feature coupling is 9 since there are 10 features on top level hence this is the true maximum number of features another feature can call. As it can be seen in the case of IR based extraction many features achieve this with a minimal coupling of 4 in overall. With CG based extraction on the other hand only one feature, Administrator interventions of V4 achieves this high level while the minimal coupling is at the Access management feature of V3 which appears to be calling no other feature at all. In the IR case the high values are caused by the already mentioned noise as well as other factors like how general the concept of each feature is. It is apparent that in this case the features achieving the lower coupling values are also the same that had the lowest number of programs, but this can also be a consequence of the more specific text of the feature that the IR based extraction could benefit from. Access management seems to be the most diverse feature in both cases with different values at nearly every variant. This is probably the consequence of different customer requests and needs about user permissions. It can be also noted that though V4 is significantly larger than the other variants, its coupling values are only slightly higher. It can also be noted here that CG and IR seem to move along similar curves.

Figure 4 represents our results of Program Clarity. High clarity means that there are more programs of the feature that only contribute to that single feature.

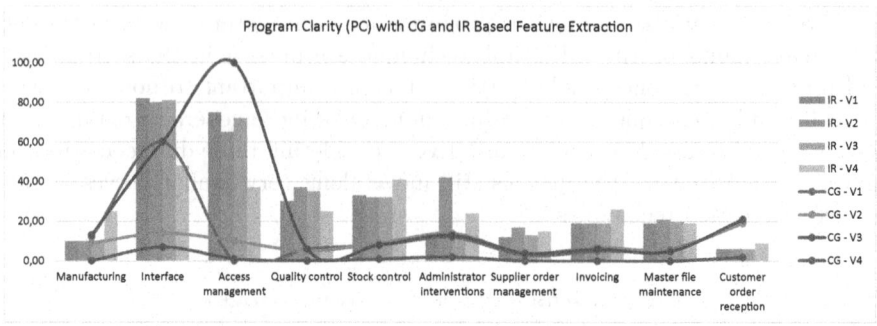

Fig. 4. Program Clarity at each variant with call graph and information retrieval based feature extraction

This metric is somewhat the opposite of CBF since it measures the self reliance of features opposed to the reliance on others. This can also be seen from the results themselves, CG-V3 achieves the greatest clarity which also had the lowest coupling, and particularly with IR we can see that the values seem to be quite on the opposite side of the scale at each feature. Still some interesting exceptions are present like the values of Quality control in the CG case which was at a medium level considering coupling and one of the lowest at clarity. The highest values are of the Access management feature of V3 and the Interface of V1 and V3. These features all consist of a low number of programs with only 12 and 5 programs at CG which can contribute to high clarity but this raises questions about the Interface feature of V2 which also contains only 5 programs but achieves a much lower value.

The results of the Sum of Coupling Between Data Objects are presented in Fig. 5. This metric is meant to measure each feature's reliance on stored data.

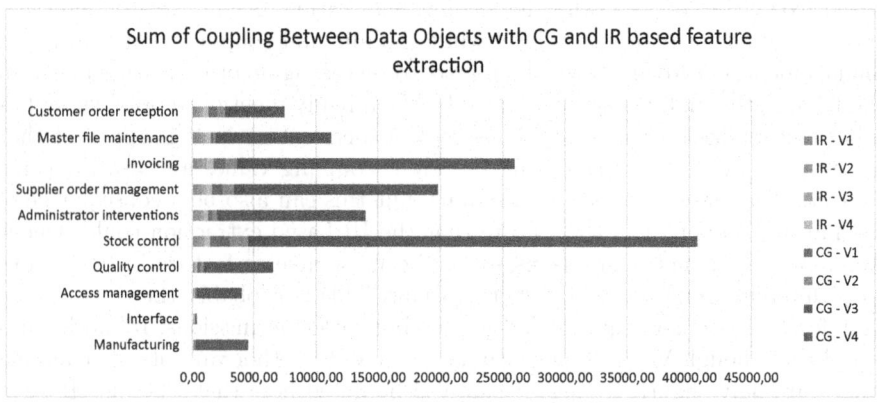

Fig. 5. Sum of Coupling Between Data Objects with CG and IR based feature extraction

Since it sums the values of programs it is logical for larger systems to achieve greater values. This is the exact case that seems to happen seeing that V4 dominates every single feature. It is interesting though that this only seems to happen in the CG case. In case of IR the highest values are also usually achieved by V4 but to a significantly less extent. It is apparent that in most cases CG achieves higher values than IR. This can stem from the fact that Magic is a highly data intensive language and there are a lot of programs that manipulate data for a feature. Since the main goal of these programs can be data object interaction there may be less text for information retrieval to build upon, hence these programs are overlooked. CG on the other hand is aware of the calls themselves which are made in case of data reliance and discovers these programs easily.

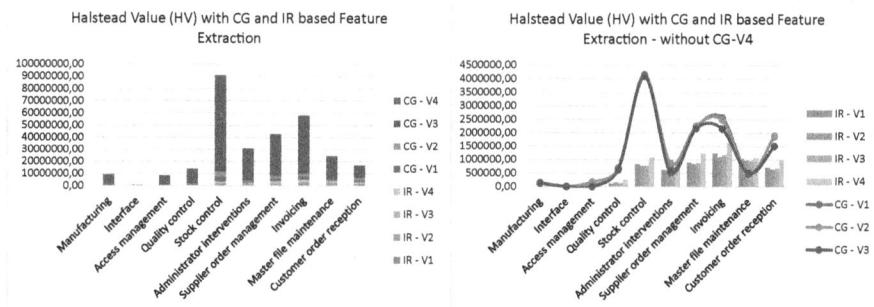

Fig. 6. Left: Halstead Value with CG and IR based feature extraction. Right: Halstead Value with CG and IR, disproportionally large values filtered out for easier analysis

Considering complexity we can see similar trends as with SCBDO, CG-V4 dominates the results in every case and seems disproportionally large on the figures. Figure 6 represents the results of Halstead Value, which measures the information value of features. On the left side we can see that CG-V4 takes up most of the space, indicating that V4 is the most complex variant of these four, having a large amount of non-trivial code and can be much harder to understand in its entirety. On the right side we filtered out CG-V4 to have a chance to get a better look at the values of the other cases. As it can be seen CG usually produces programs with higher complexity. This can also be a consequence of IR overlooking a number of programs with complex logic or data manipulation that have less lexical information value and are much more meaningful on the data or logic side. We can also note here that while IR remains relatively low in case of every feature it can be seen that IR follows CG values, just to a much lesser extent.

Figure 7 shows the results of Halstead Difficulty. This metric measures fault sensitivity. As we have already seen in the case of HV, the CG based extraction of V4 produces a set of programs with very high complexity. This can also be seen here, on the left side of the figure. Surprisingly, there is also one feature, Invoicing of CG-V2 that achieved the same magnitude of HD value. This is

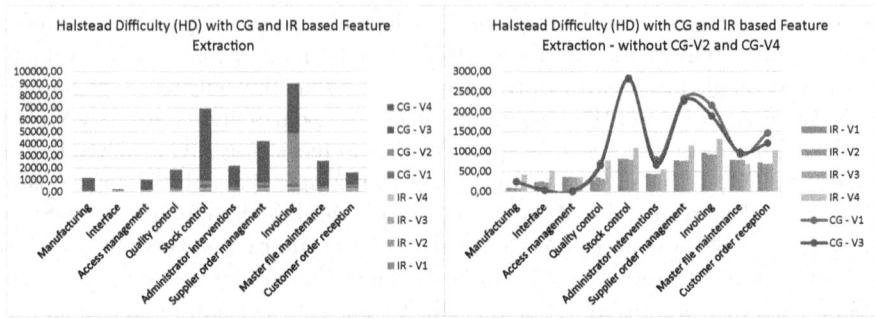

Fig. 7. Left: Halstead Difficulty with CG and IR based feature extraction. Right: Halstead Difficulty with CG and IR, disproportionally large values filtered out for easier analysis

a very interesting matter since the number of programs extracted here, 267 is very close to the values of V1 and V3 and much less than V4's 602 programs even if invoicing is usually one of the most complex methods in each case. One possible explanation for this can come from the number of tasks of the variants. As we could see from Table 2, V2 has a very high number of tasks, significantly higher than every other variant, while its number of programs falls somewhere in between. This has to mean that V2's programs contain more subtasks than the programs of other variants. Since we could see from our previous metrics that V2 nearly always achieves lower values than V4 we could wonder how this difference in program sizes failed to influence any of the metrics. The answer could be that a major part of the extra tasks inside V2 are contributing to the Invoicing feature providing more functions upon specific requests of the customer. Since HV is not exactly high in this case it can mean that while the feature did not gain much complexity, it became much more fault sensitive, thus this feature could be hard to maintain and deserves consideration of refactoring. On the right side of the figure we also filtered out CG-V4 and CG-V2 for easier glance at the rest of variants. We can see that these results usually move along the same curves as HV.

Finally, we would like to emphasize that these metrics are not only capable of revealing meaningful information about systems, features and outputs of feature extraction methods but can also be combined in several ways to attain even more understanding. Some metrics are dependent on the number of programs or tasks in a feature, which in some cases can be beneficial but in others it can hide some significant differences. To eliminate this we can divide the metric with the number of programs or tasks inside a feature. For example we could do this to any complexity metric to get the average complexity of programs or tasks of each feature or to SCBDO to get average reliance on data. These can paint a much different picture. For instance Henry-Kafura Complexity provides similar data to HV with a difference of some IR values becoming significantly higher. On the other hand if we divide it by the number of tasks we get an average HKC

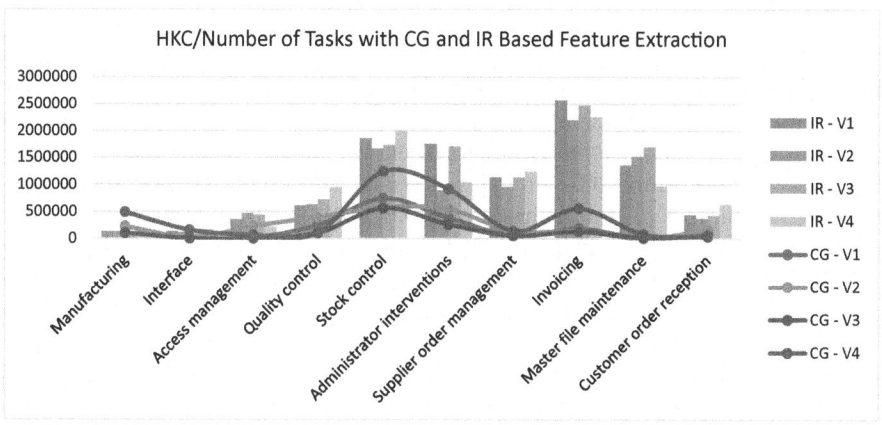

Fig. 8. Henry-Kafura Complexity in proportion to the number of programs at each variant with CG and IR based feature extraction

value of tasks in each feature, this is illustrated in Fig. 8. From this figure we can see that IR values are usually higher most probably because of the high number outer calls we have seen at the CBF metric. Even considering this it is apparent that IR and CG values move along the same lines meaning that on task level the features tend to behave the same way with both feature extraction methods.

Considering these findings our opinion is that feature level metrics are suitable for the analysis of features in variants of Magic systems. Properly utilizing these we can come to realizations that can greatly aid not just product line adoption but also ease the future maintenance of a system.

5   Related Work

By the time the 4GL paradigm arisen, most papers coped with the role of those languages in software development, including discussions demonstrating their viability. The paradigm is still successful, although only a few works are published about the automatic analysis and modeling 4GL or specifically Magic applications. The maintenance of Magic applications is supported by cost estimation and quality analysis methods [9,14,15]. Architectural analysis, reverse engineering and optimization are visible topics in the Magic community [2,3,16,17], and after some years of Magic development migration to object-oriented languages [18] as well.

Measuring the complexity of a software at source code level is approached from many directions. First, and still popular complexity measures (McCabe [19], Halstead [13], Lines of Code [20]) were surveyed by Navlakha [21]. A recent survey which sums up complexity measures was published by Yu et al. [22]. In 3GL context there are papers available to analyze the correlation between certain complexity metrics. For instance, Meulen et al. [23] showed that there are very strong connections between LOC and HCM, LOC and CCM in C/C++

programs. In 4GL environment, to our best knowledge, there were no previous researches to measure structural complexity and coupling attributes of a Magic application at feature level. For other 4GLs there are some attempts to define metrics to measure the size of a project [14,15,24]. There are also some industrial solutions to measure metrics in 4GL environment. For instance *RainCode Roadmap*[1] for Informix 4GL provides a set of predefined metrics about code complexity (number of statements, cyclomatic complexity, nesting level), about SQLs (number of SQL statements, SQL tables, etc.), and about lines (number of blank lines, code lines, etc.). In the world of Magic, there is a tool for optimization purposes too called Magic Optimizer[2] which can be used to perform static analysis of Magic applications. It does not measure metrics, but it is able to locate potential coding problems which also relates to software quality.

Software product line extraction is a time-consuming task. To speed up this activity, many semi-automatic approaches has been proposed [25–27]. Reverse engineering is a popular approach which has recently received an increased attention from the research community. With this technique missing parts can be recovered, feature models can be extracted a set of features, etc. [25,28]. Applying these approaches companies can migrate their system into a software product line. However, changing to a new development process is risky and may have unnecessary costs. The work of Krüger et al. [29] supports cost estimations for the extractive approaches and provides a basis for further research. Feature models are considered first class artifacts in variability modeling. Haslinger et al. [27] present an algorithm that reverse engineers a FM for a given SPL from feature sets which describe the characteristics each product variant provides. She et al. [30] analyze Linux kernel (which is a standard subject in variability analysis) configurations to obtain feature models. Within product line research a related aim is to make systems dynamically configurable, which is a problem known as Dynamic SPL [31–35].

In this paper we introduce novel feature level metrics for the Magic 4GL language, which topic is not directly addressed in the related literature.

6   Conclusions

In this paper we reported experiments carried out on 4 variants of a large scale logistics wholesale system. The system is implemented in the Magic 4GL language. In this context the usual product metrics need to be adapted to the unique properties of the language. We extended the state of the art methods by feature oriented metrics applicable to Magic programs. Experiments were conducted to compute metrics on these variants using high level features defined by domain experts of the developer company. We provided insights into the feature structure in two dimensions: feature coupling and complexity. We demonstrated the usability of feature oriented metric analysis in the large on variants containing 2000 to 4000 Magic programs. We have shown that the proposed feature

---

[1] http://www.raincode.com/fglroadmap.html.
[2] http://www.magic-optimizer.com/.

level metrics are suitable for highlighting previously not visible information with special value in the analysis and even the maintenance of the systems. Their appropriate utilization can highlight the properties of feature extraction and the system itself and even point out specific weak spots that deserve further attention.

Acknowledgements. The project has been supported by the European Union, co-financed by the European Social Fund (EFOP-3.6.3-VEKOP-16-2017-00002). We acknowledge the help of Magic experts of the SZEGED Software Llc.

References

1. Chidamber, S.R., Kemerer, C.F.: A metrics suite for object oriented design. IEEE Trans. Softw. Eng. **20**(6), 476–493 (1994)
2. Nagy, C., Vidács, L., Ferenc, R., Gyimóthy, T., Kocsis, F., Kovács, I.: MAGISTER: quality assurance of magic applications for software developers and end users. In: 26th IEEE International Conference on Software Maintenance, pp. 1–6. IEEE Computer Society, September 2010
3. Nagy, C., Vidács, L., Ferenc, R., Gyimóthy, T., Kocsis, F., Kovács, I.: Solutions for reverse engineering 4GL applications, recovering the design of a logistical wholesale system. In: Proceedings of CSMR 2011, 15th European Conference on Software Maintenance and Reengineering, pp. 343–346. IEEE Computer Society, March 2011
4. Clements, P., Northrop, L.: Software Product Lines: Practices and Patterns. Addison-Wesley Professional, Boston (2001)
5. Krueger, C.W.: Easing the transition to software mass customization. In: van der Linden, F. (ed.) PFE 2001. LNCS, vol. 2290, pp. 282–293. Springer, Heidelberg (2002). https://doi.org/10.1007/3-540-47833-7_25
6. Kästner, C., Dreiling, A., Ostermann, K.: Variability mining: consistent semi-automatic detection of product-line features. IEEE Trans. Softw. Eng. **40**(1), 67–82 (2014)
7. Assunção, W.K.G., Vergilio, S.R.: Feature location for software product line migration. In: Proceedings of the 18th International Software Product Line Conference on Companion Volume for Workshops, Demonstrations and Tools - SPLC 2014, pp. 52–59. ACM Press, New York (2014)
8. Eyal-Salman, H., Seriai, A.D., Dony, C., Al-msie'deen, R.: Recovering traceability links between feature models and source code of product variants. In: Proceedings of the VARiability for You Workshop on Variability Modeling Made Useful for Everyone - VARY 2012, pp. 21–25. ACM Press, New York (2012)
9. Nagy, C., et al.: Complexity measures in 4GL environment. In: Murgante, B., Gervasi, O., Iglesias, A., Taniar, D., Apduhan, B.O. (eds.) ICCSA 2011. LNCS, vol. 6786, pp. 293–309. Springer, Heidelberg (2011). https://doi.org/10.1007/978-3-642-21934-4_25
10. Katzmarski, B., Koschke, R.: Program complexity metrics and programmer opinions. In: 2012 20th IEEE International Conference on Program Comprehension (ICPC), pp. 17–26. IEEE, June 2012
11. Kicsi, A., Vidács, L., Beszédes, A., Kocsis, F., Kovács, I.: Information retrieval based feature analysis for product line adoption in 4GL systems. In: Proceedings of the 17th International Conference on Computational Science and Its Applications - ICCSA 2017, pp. 1–6. IEEE (2017)

12. Kicsi, A., et al.: Supporting product line adoption by combining syntactic and textual feature extraction. In: Capilla, R., Gallina, B., Cetina, C. (eds.) ICSR 2018. LNCS, vol. 10826, pp. 148–163. Springer, Heidelberg (2018). https://doi. org/10.1007/978-3-319-90421-4_10

13. Halstead, M.H.: Elements of Software Science. Operating and Programming Systems Series. Elsevier Science Inc., New York (1977)

14. Verner, J., Tate, G.: Estimating size and effort in fourth-generation development. IEEE Softw. **5**, 15–22 (1988)

15. Witting, G., Finnie, G.: Using artificial neural networks and function points to estimate 4GL software development effort. Australas. J. Inf. Syst. **1**(2), 87–94 (1994)

16. Harrison, J.V., Lim, W.M.: Automated reverse engineering of legacy 4GL information system applications using the ITOC workbench. In: Pernici, B., Thanos, C. (eds.) CAiSE 1998. LNCS, vol. 1413, pp. 41–57. Springer, Heidelberg (1998). https://doi.org/10.1007/BFb0054218

17. Ocean Software Solutions: Homepage of Magic Optimizer. http://www.magic-optimizer.com. Accessed Feb 2018

18. M2J Software LLC: Homepage of M2J. http://www.magic2java.com. Accessed Feb 2018

19. McCabe, T.: A complexity measure. IEEE Trans. Softw. Eng. **SE-2**(4) (1976)

20. Albrecht, A.J., Gaffney, J.E.: Software function, source lines of code, and development effort prediction: a software science validation. IEEE Trans. Softw. Eng. **9**, 639–648 (1983)

21. Navlakha, J.K.: A survey of system complexity metrics. Comput. J. **30**, 233–238 (1987)

22. Yu, S., Zhou, S.: A survey on metric of software complexity. In: Proceedings of ICIME 2010, The 2nd IEEE International Conference on Information Management and Engineering, pp. 352–356, April 2010

23. van der Meulen, M., Revilla, M.: Correlations between internal software metrics and software dependability in a large population of small C/C++ programs. In: Proceedings of ISSRE 2007, The 18th IEEE International Symposium on Software Reliability, pp. 203–208, November 2007

24. MacDonell, S.: Metrics for database systems: an empirical study. In: IEEE International Symposium on Software Metrics, pp. 99–107 (1997)

25. Valente, M.T., Borges, V., Passos, L.: A semi-automatic approach for extracting software product lines. IEEE Trans. Softw. Eng. **38**(4), 737–754 (2012)

26. Assunção, W.K.G., Lopez-Herrejon, R.E., Linsbauer, L., Vergilio, S.R., Egyed, A.: Multi-objective reverse engineering of variability-safe feature models based on code dependencies of system variants. Empir. Softw. Eng. **22**(4), 1763–1794 (2017)

27. Haslinger, E.N., Lopez-Herrejon, R.E., Egyed, A.: Reverse engineering feature models from programs' feature sets. In: 18th Working Conference on Reverse Engineering, pp. 308–312. IEEE, October 2011

28. Lima, C., Chavez, C., de Almeida, E.S.: Investigating the recovery of product line architectures: an approach proposal. In: Botterweck, G., Werner, C. (eds.) ICSR 2017. LNCS, vol. 10221, pp. 201–207. Springer, Cham (2017). https://doi.org/10. 1007/978-3-319-56856-0_15

29. Krüger, J., Fenske, W., Meinicke, J., Leich, T., Saake, G.: Extracting software product lines: a cost estimation perspective. In: Proceedings of the 20th International Systems and Software Product Line Conference on - SPLC 2016, pp. 354–361. ACM Press, New York (2016)

30. She, S., Lotufo, R., Berger, T., Wąsowski, A., Czarnecki, K.: Reverse engineering feature models. In: Proceeding of the 33rd International Conference on Software Engineering - ICSE 2011, p. 461. ACM Press, New York (2011)

31. Lee, K., Kang, K.C., Lee, J.: Concepts and guidelines of feature modeling for product line software engineering. In: Gacek, C. (ed.) ICSR 2002. LNCS, vol. 2319, pp. 62–77. Springer, Heidelberg (2002). https://doi.org/10.1007/3-540-46020-9_5

32. Baresi, L., Quinton, C.: Dynamically evolving the structural variability of dynamic software product lines. In: 10th International Symposium on Software Engineering for Adaptive and Self-Managing Systems (2015)

33. Bashari, M., Bagheri, E., Du, W.: Dynamic software product line engineering: a reference framework. Int. J. Softw. Eng. Knowl. Eng. **27**(02), 191–234 (2017)

34. Capilla, R., Bosch, J., Trinidad, P., Ruiz-Cortés, A., Hinchey, M.: An overview of dynamic software product line architectures and techniques: observations from research and industry. J. Syst. Softw. **91**(1), 3–23 (2014)

35. Uchôa, A.G., Bezerra, C.I.M., Machado, I.C., Monteiro, J.M., Andrade, R.M.C.: ReMINDER: an approach to modeling non-functional properties in dynamic software product lines. In: Botterweck, G., Werner, C. (eds.) ICSR 2017. LNCS, vol. 10221, pp. 65–73. Springer, Cham (2017). https://doi.org/10.1007/978-3-319-56856-0_5

A Case Study on Measuring the Size
of Microservices

Hulya Vural[1], Murat Koyuncu[1], and Sanjay Misra[2(✉)]

[1] Atilim University, Ankara, Turkey
hulya.vural.tr@gmail.com, mkoyuncu@atilim.edu.tr
[2] Covenant University, Ota, Nigeria
sanjay.misra@covenantuniversity.edu.ng

Abstract. In cloud computing, the microservices has become the mostly used architectural style. However, there is still an ongoing debate about how big a microservice should be. In this case study, a monolith application is measured using Common Software Measurement International Consortium (COSMIC) Function Points. The same application is divided into pieces by following the Domain Driven Design (DDD) principles. The resulting cloud friendly microservices are measured again using COSMIC Function Points and the obtained results are compared.

Keywords: Cloud computing · Web services · Microservices
COSMIC function points

1 Introduction

In the world of cloud computing, the priorities of software engineering have shifted. The decentralization and the ability to carry on dev-ops operations smoothly have become much more important than it was about two decades ago. The microservices architectural style enables the decentralization of governance and data management [1]. The change of focus resulted in a polynomial increase on the number of research papers on microservices architectural style [2].

As mentioned in [3, 4], finding the right size of a microservice is a challenge. Even though the topic about the optimal size of a microservice is quite hot, there have been only two research papers about the size of microservices [5, 6]. As of April 2018, a brief search has been carried on with the keywords "Microservice" and "COSMIC" keywords at Google Scholar and Web of Science. Neither Web of Science nor Google Scholar returned any research papers which propose a method on how to measure the size of a microservice using COSMIC function points. However, in order to make the final conclusion about the nonexistence of previous research on measuring Microservices using COSMIC function points, a detailed systematic mapping should be carried out.

Hassan and Bahsoon [5] propose to use artificial intelligence (AI) on finding the optimal size of a microservice through measuring the quality of service parameters. Aforementioned hypothetical method assumes that developers can easily make a certain service more granular and measure the quality of service parameters again. In real life, it would not be ideal to rewrite the same functionality over and over again. There is

© Springer International Publishing AG, part of Springer Nature 2018
O. Gervasi et al. (Eds.): ICCSA 2018, LNCS 10964, pp. 454–463, 2018.
https://doi.org/10.1007/978-3-319-95174-4_36

another research proposing a totally new concept on measuring the size [6], however the measurement method is new and not yet used in any real-life application yet.

There are many different methods for measuring the size of a software. Certain ones comply with the measurement standards, such as Function Points and COSMIC Function Points [7, 8]. In the current research, the main reason for choosing COSMIC Function Points over International Function Point Users' Group (IFPUG) Function Points is that the COSMIC function point manual is freely available [9].

The size debate is only one aspect of the tough challenges microservices pattern brings. Another related tough challenge is how to divide the system into microservices. Unlike the size, in this challenge there is an emerging pattern which points to the bounded contexts as explained in DDD [5, 10–13].

In the current research, a sample application [14] was chosen for evaluating as a monolith and a microservice based architecture. The application was divided into microservices by following the DDD concepts [15]. The aim of the research is proposing a method to measure a microservice using COSMIC Function Points.

In the next section the sample cloud application is explained. Then the solution is divided into DDD constructs. This process also defines each microservice in the system. Afterwards the monolith as well as the microservice based system are measured using COSMIC Function Points.

2   The Sample Application

One of the de-facto examples for cloud computing domain is chosen as the sample application – eShop (Fig. 1). The application is a cloud based online shop for selling items. The end user browses the items on the website, adds the items to a cart and checkouts. In the future studies, a real-life example should be studied as well.

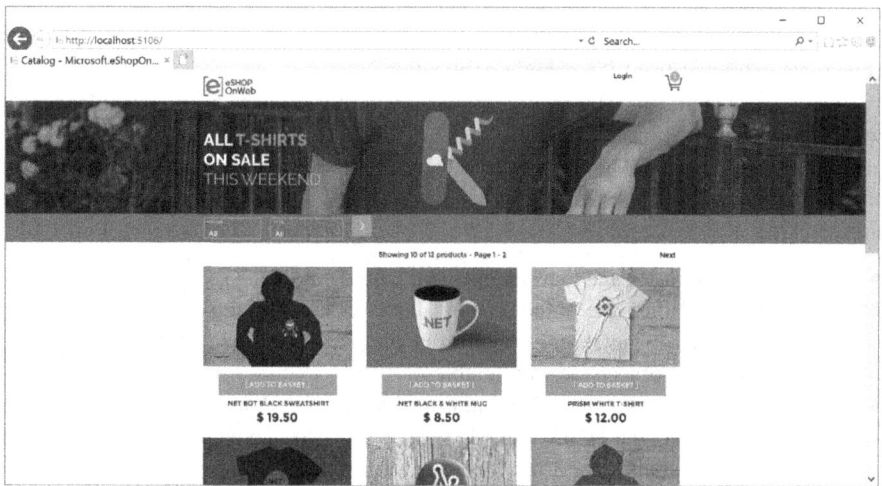

Fig. 1. A screenshot of eShop application.

The COSMIC Function Point calculation aims to measure the system at the time of planning. This size calculation can be used for effort estimation.

The COMSIC Function Point calculation starts with identifying the function points of the system. The functionalities covered in the sample application chosen - eShop - are listed in the Table 1.

Table 1. The functional user requirements of eShop application.

Function point number	Function point name
FP#1	Login
FP#2	List items for sale
FP#3	Filter based on brand
FP#4	Filter based on type
FP#5	Add item to a basket
FP#6	List items in the basket
FP#7	Update item in the basket
FP#8	Delete item from the basket
FP#9	Checkout
FP#10	Get buyer profile
FP#11	Update buyer profile
FP#12	Update buyer password
FP#13	List orders
FP#14	Get order item detail
FP#15	Logout

3   Constructing Microservices Based on DDD Bounded Context

In this section, we first explain DDD and its constructs. Then we mention the DDD constructs extracted from the sample application.

The main benefit of DDD is dividing a large software system into granular pieces with minimal interaction between them. As a result, automaticity of the cloud system can be achieved between different microservices as long as the interacting parts use the same ubiquitous language. The building blocks for the model driven design are as follows [16]:

- Entity: Objects which have an identity are called entities.
- Value Objects: When the object doesn't have an identity and it is useful only for carrying certain attributes or carrying out a calculation, then it is called a value object. The value objects are immutable.
- Domain Event: Unlike the other building blocks, the domain events were introduced after the original DDD book [15] was published. Domain event represents an event that the domain expert (end user) cares about.

- Aggregate: When certain objects are related to each other in a sense that one cannot exist without the root, then those are combined into one identity called aggregate. The main purpose of the aggregates is insulating the domain knowledge into one object so that any external method does not change it in a wrong way.
- Service: When an operation does not belong to only one entity or aggregate, then it is best to serve that functionality as a service.
- Repository: The infrastructure is responsible for carrying out the persistency operations (e.g. read from a database). The repository pattern shields the details of persistence in such a way that the aggregates can be properly encapsulated.
- Factory: There are cases when a construction of an object is so complicated that the caller may get tangled in that coupled code. In order to avoid such cases, the factories should be leveraged. Using the factory pattern frees the caller from dealing with the details of the object to be used.

In eShop application five main entities have been identified (Fig. 2.):

- Catalog Item
- Catalog Brand
- Catalog Type
- Basket
- Basket Item.

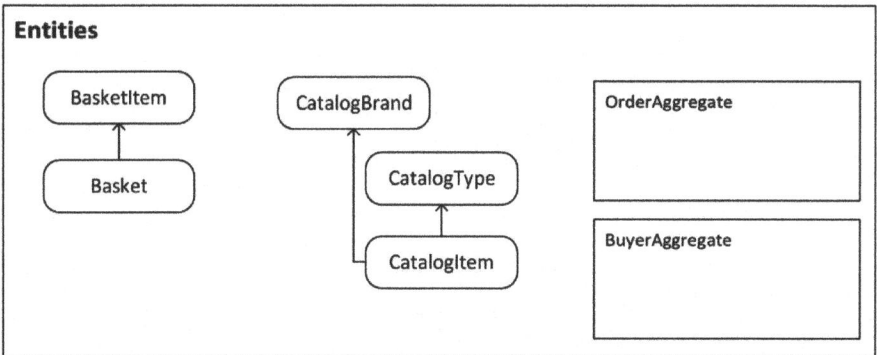

Fig. 2. Entities in eShop application.

In the application, there are two aggregates, which are the Order and Buyer aggregates as seen in Fig. 3. The Order and the Catalog Item Ordered are tightly correlated. If the program allows one to be updated without the other, the system might fall into an unsupported state.

The functionality which covers more than one entity and does not belong to an aggregate is created as a service. The services for the eShop application can be seen in Fig. 4. The Basket and the Order services need to operate on its own by using the entities and the aggregates.

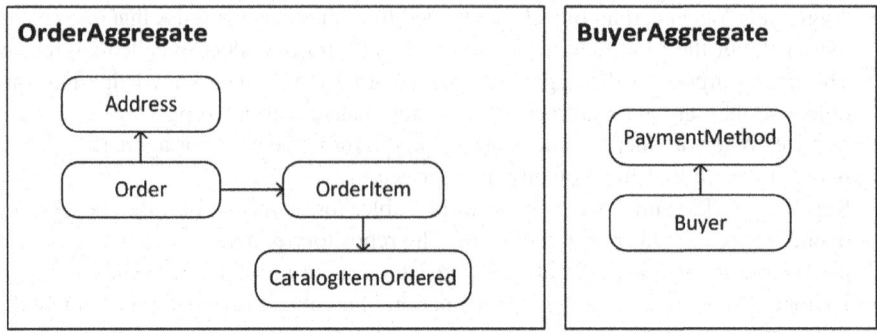

Fig. 3. Order and buyer aggregates in eShop application.

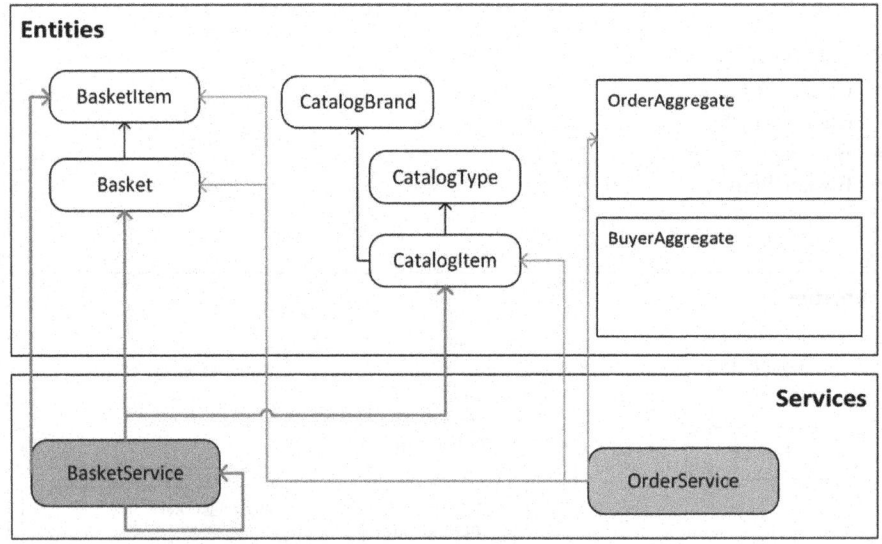

Fig. 4. Services in eShop application.

In Fig. 5, the bounded contexts were marked with different rectangles. If the bounded context is used for guiding the division of a microservice, in the eShop application, there should be three different microservices:

- Basket Microservice
- Catalog Microservice
- Order Microservice

One key point in here is that the regular service and a microservice are two different concepts. The basket microservice has a regular service (as defined in Service Oriented Architecture - SOA) and plus two entities in it.

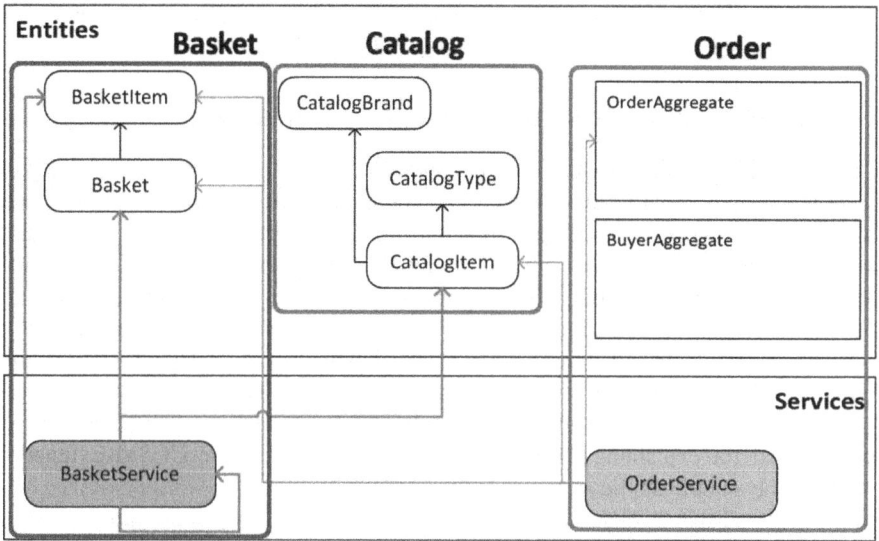

Fig. 5. Microservices in eShop application.

4 COSMIC Function Point Calculation

The COSMIC method focuses on data movements between different layers. One of the benefits of COSMIC method is that it can give a size estimation result in the planning phase based on the functional user requirements (FUR). The four main data group types are as follows [9]:

- Entry (E): An event triggers the beginning of a function process. When a data group is crossing a layer as a result of an event, then it is marked as an entry.
- Exit (X): When the result of an entry is returned, it is marked as an Exit. This shall also include the error cases if a message or notification is shown to the user. Unhandled/exceptional cases of errors do not count as an exit.
- Read (R): When data is read from a storage, it is marked as a read. The storage can be a database or cache. However, access to items kept in memory in that layer are not counted as a read.
- Write (W): When data is written to a storage, it is marked as a write. The storage can be a database or cache. However, storing an item in memory within the same layer does not count as a write.

If the eShop example mentioned above was implemented as a monolithic solution, the cost of development could have been cheaper. However, in a cloud system, the cost of releasing the product is not the real issue. The real issue is keeping the design clean with upcoming new feature requests.

In order to have an opinion about whether a monolithic solution would be cheaper to implement or not, in this study, the eShop COSMIC function points are calculated both for monolithic and DDD based microservice architecture.

In the previous section three microservices were identified. The current goal is to calculate the size of each microservice using COSMIC Function Points.

4.1 Monolithic eShop COSMIC Function Point Calculation

It is assumed that in the monolithic eShop application, the aggregate pattern defined by DDD is not used. As a result, the program can access multiple database tables freely just to realize one functional user requirement. The aggregate pattern is a natural boundary if implemented according to the DDD rules. If the boundaries are not well defined in an enterprise application, multiple groups of developers start manipulating the same tables/entities in different ways. It becomes easier to cause a regression. Certain companies, try to introduce an artificial boundary by assigning responsible individuals for each area. However, such an artificial boundary can easily be broken.

Due to the size limitation, in this paper only FP#2 and FP#9 (mentioned in Table 1) will be used for explaining the method on how to calculate the COSMIC function points of the sample application.

As seen in Table 2, FP#2 is a simple operation accessing only three entities; catalog item, catalog brand and catalog type. It has 1 entry, 3 reads and 1 exit operation. The total number of COSMIC Function Points (CFPs) for FP#2 is 5.

As seen in Table 2, the FP#9 is a rather complex operation which accesses five different entities. It has 1 entry, 3 reads, 2 writes and 1 exit operation. The total number of CFPs for FP#9 is 7.

When all the FPs mentioned in Table 1 are calculated with this approach, the total COSMIC Function Points of monolithic eShop application is 71.

Table 2. Monolithic eShop solution COSMIC function point analysis.

FUR	FP#	FP name	DM type	Data group descriptor
1	2	List items for sale	E	List catalog items request
			R	Catalog item
			R	Catalog brand
			R	Catalog type
			X	List of catalog items
1	9	Checkout	E	Checkout request
			R	Basket
			R	Basket item
			R	Buyer
			W	Order
			W	Order items
			X	Error/confirmation

4.2   DDD Based eShop COSMIC Function Point Analysis

Unlike the previous monolithic eShop application, the domain driven design-based solution uses aggregates and services extensively. In the monolithic application FP#9, there were 2 write operations: one for "order" and the other one for "order items". However, the order microservice reads the "order" along with the "order items" as part of one operation only, because the order aggregate contains order items in it as well.

Table 3. Microservices based eShop solution COSMIC function point analysis.

FUR	FP	FP name	DM type	Data group desc. in application layer	Data group desc. in domain layer	Service/application
1	2	List items for sale	E	List catalog items request		Application layer
			X	**Retrieve catalog items**		**Application layer**
			E		**Retrieve catalog items**	**Catalog service**
			R		Catalog item	Catalog service
			R		Catalog brand	Catalog service
			R		Catalog type	Catalog service
			X		**List of catalog items**	**Catalog service**
			X	List of catalog items		Application layer
1	9	Checkout	E	Checkout request		Application layer
			X	**Collect basket info**		**Application layer**
			E		**Collect basket info**	**Basket service**
			R		*Basket & basket items*	*Basket service*
			X		**Basket info**	**Basket service**
			E		**Create order**	**Order service**
			R		Buyer	Order service
			W		*Order*	*Order service*
			X		**Error/confirmation**	**Order service**
			X	Error/confirmation		Application layer

When the aggregate pattern is used, there is a possibility of reading more than the functional requirement suggests. This might cause performance degradation. Unlike the monolithic solution, no one is free to access the data they seek. There is a clear definition on who the owner is. If someone requires a data which is not in their bounded context - microservice, they have to call the responsible microservice for retrieving the data. The owner microservice will return the data in the agreed upon ubiquitous language format.

In case of using aggregates, in order to prevent the performance degradation, the microservice owners could decide to present a simplified version of the data. That is why deciding the ubiquitous language between the microservices is the key.

In Table 3, the sample CFP calculation for FP#2 and FP#9 are shown for a DDD based eShop application. When the boundaries between microservices are crossed, these are represented with an exit (X) and an entrance (E) operation.

The total CFP for FP#2 is 8 for DDD solution. The number increased by 3 (bolded in Table 3) when compared to monolith application. The increase is due to crossing the application layer and service boundaries.

As seen in Table 3, the total number of CFPs for FP#9 is also increased by 3. It was 7 for monolith application and it is 10 for the DDD based microservice solution. The interesting point is that the cost increase for a complex structure is the same for a simple one. The main reason for that is the usage of aggregates. The usage of aggregates pattern allows read or write of the data in one shot. As a result, the same R or W operation can be used for different cases.

When all the FPs mentioned in Table 1 are calculated with this approach, the total COSMIC Function Points of DDD based microservice eShop application is 103.

5 Conclusion and Future Work

In the cloud business, there is an upcoming trend in adopting microservices architectural style [2]. However, there is still no definite rules on how to achieve the optimal size of a microservice. The current research is a case study in measuring the size of microservices and comparing them to the monolith size.

As seen in Sect. 4, the usage of aggregates decreases the size by using the same data read techniques. There are cases where this might cause more than needed data to be fetched from the database. This would also cause increase in disk and memory usage. When compared to the reduced complexity of the system, this would be a small price to pay.

The total cost of the eShop application was 71 CFPs for a monolith design and 103 CFPs for a DDD based microservices design. The increase of CFPs for a simple case and a complex case were almost the same. This data can suggest that unless the application is complex enough the return of using microservices for the cost won't be reflected in the results.

Another interesting point we can see in the resulting measurements is that the number of COSMIC function points of the overall system increases when microservices are used. In the current example, the increase is about 45%. The result may suggest increased effort in development. However, the increased effort at the beginning would result in reduced cost in maintenance moving forward. After the introduction of the cloud systems, the era of shipping DVDs has come to an end. The new way is to deliver continuous functionality in live systems. The reduced cost in maintenance would be more important in a cloud system where there is constant change.

One of the drawbacks of the current research is that it is based on a hypothetical situation. It would be best to repeat the study on a real-life case study.

The current research can be a stepping stone in defining the optimal size of a microservice. The future research might use the way the microservices measured using COSMIC function points to define the optimal size.

References

1. Lewis, J., Fowler, M.: Microservices. http://martinfowler.com/articles/microservices.html. Accessed 20 Nov 2016
2. Vural, H., Koyuncu, M., Guney, S.: A systematic literature review on microservices. In: Gervasi, O., et al. (eds.) ICCSA 2017. LNCS, vol. 10409, pp. 203–217. Springer, Cham (2017). https://doi.org/10.1007/978-3-319-62407-5_14
3. Salah, T., Zemerly, M.J., Yeun, C.Y., Al-Qutayri, M., Al-Hammadi, Y.: The evolution of distributed systems towards microservices architecture. In: 11th International Conference for Internet Technology and Secured Transactions (ICITST), Barcelona (2016)
4. Thönes, J.: Microservices. IEEE Softw. **32**(1), 113–116 (2015)
5. Hassan, S., Bahsoon, R.: Microservices and their design trade-offs: a self-adaptive roadmap. In: 13th IEEE International Conference on Services Computing (SCC), San Francisco (2016)
6. Asik, T., Selcuk, Y.: Policy enforcement upon software based on microservice architecture. In: IEEE 15th International Conference on Software Engineering Research, Management and Applications (SERA), London (2017)
7. Morris, P.: COSMIC-FFP and IFPUG 4.1 Similarities and Differences. https://www.totalmetrics.com/function-point-resources/downloads/IFPUG-COSMIC-and-IFPUG—Similarities-and-Differences_2009-.pdf. Accessed 13 Jun 2017
8. Morris, P.: COSMIC-FFP and IFPUG 4.1 Similarities and Differences. https://www.totalmetrics.com/function-point-resources/downloads/COSMIC-Versus-IFPUG-Similarities-and-Differences.pdf. Accessed 13 Jun 2017
9. COSMIC: Measurement Manual 4.0.1. https://cosmic-sizing.org/publications/measurement-manual-401. Accessed 01 Jan 2018
10. Zimmermann, O.: Microservices tenets. Computer Science - Research and Development **32** (3–4), 301–310 (2016)
11. Johanson, A.N., Flögel, S., Dullo, W-C., Hasselbring, W.: OceanTEA: Exploring Ocean-Derived Climate Data Using Microservices. http://eprints.uni-kiel.de/34758/1/CI2016.pdf. Accessed 03 Feb 2018
12. Newman, S.: Building Microservices. O'Reilly Media, Inc, Sebastopol (2015)
13. Fowler, M.: BoundedContext. https://martinfowler.com/bliki/BoundedContext.html. Accessed 03 Feb 2018
14. eShopOnWeb: GitHub. https://github.com/dotnet-architecture/eShopOnWeb. Accessed 03 Feb 2018
15. Evans, E.: Domain-Driven Design. Addison-Wesley, Boston (2014)
16. Evans, E.: Domain-Driven Design Reference. Dog Ear Publishing, LLC, Indianapolis (2015)

A Hands-on OpenStack Code Refactoring Experience Report

Gábor Antal[1], Alex Szarka[1], and Péter Hegedűs[2(✉)]

[1] Department of Software Engineering, University of Szeged, Szeged, Hungary
{antal,szarka}@inf.u-szeged.hu
[2] MTA-SZTE Research Group on Artificial Intelligence,
University of Szeged, Szeged, Hungary
hpeter@inf.u-szeged.hu

Abstract. Nowadays, almost everyone uses some kind of cloud infrastructure. As clouds gaining more and more attention, it is now even more important to have stable and reliable cloud systems. Along with stability and reliability comes source code maintainability. Unfortunately, maintainability has no exact definition, there are several definitions both from users' and developers' perspective. In this paper, we analyzed two projects of OpenStack, the world's leading open-source cloud system, using QualityGate, a static software analyzer which can help to determine the maintainability of software. During the analysis we found quality issues that could be fixed by refactoring the code. We have created 47 patches in this two OpenStack projects. We have also analyzed our patches with QualityGate to see whether they increase the maintainability of the system. We found that a single refactoring has a barely noticeable effect on the maintainability of the software, what is more, it can even decrease maintainability. But if we do refactorings regularly, their cumulative effect will probably increase the quality in the mid and long-term. We also experienced that our refactoring commits were very appreciated by the open-source community.

Keywords: OpenStack · Refactoring · Quality assurance
Static analysis · Code quality

1 Introduction

Restructuring the source code of an object-oriented program without changing its observed external behavior is called refactoring. Since Opdyke's PhD dissertation [28] – where the term was introduced – and Fowler's book [16] – where refactoring is used on "bad-smells" – many researchers studied refactoring as a technique to improve the maintainability of a software system. However, there are still only few empirical evidences that would objectively prove the effects of refactoring on code maintainability.

In an earlier work [17] we analyzed the effect of code refactorings by automatically extracting refactorings using the RefFinder [21] tool from various small

© Springer International Publishing AG, part of Springer Nature 2018
O. Gervasi et al. (Eds.): ICCSA 2018, LNCS 10964, pp. 464–480, 2018.
https://doi.org/10.1007/978-3-319-95174-4_37

and mid-sized open-source projects. As a means of measuring maintainability, we used static source code metrics. We found that refactorings reduce complexity and coupling, however, code clones were affected negatively and commenting did not show any clear connection with refactoring activities. The disadvantage of this approach was the high false positive rate of RefFinder and the lack of real, certainly valid set of refactorings to analyze.

During an in-vivo industrial experiment [38], we showed that bulk-fixing coding issues found by various code linters can lead to a quality increase. The drawback of this approach was that developers tend to perform the easiest code changes, which typically were not even classical Fowler refactorings.

In this paper, we present a large-scale, open-source study on the OpenStack cloud infrastructure [33], where we contributed a large number of refactoring code modifications to the upstream code bases. For quality estimation we used the QualityGate maintainability assesment framework [6] and the SonarQube[1] technical debt measurement model [22]. We calculated the system-level maintainability of the OpenStack modules before and after the refactoring patch is being applied on the code base. This way we could analyze the direct impact of our code rafactoring activity on the OpenStack modules.

We found that often such small, local refactoring changes will not have any traceable effect on the overall level of maintainability of a large OpenStack module. This was particularly true for the Nova module, as it is very large compared to Watcher for example. In case of Watcher, the smaller module we analyzed, we found that several refactoring changes caused a quality increase and a technical debt decrease. Nonetheless, in general we can say that in most of the cases where we were able to measure the maintainability changes, refactorings had a positive effect on them. It was a slightly easier to show a decrease in the technical debt measures in SonarQube.

The rest of the paper is organized as follows. In Sect. 2, we list the related literature and compare our work with them. In Sect. 3, we introduce OpenStack, the contribution workflow, and what are the difficulties we had to face with, in order to contribute to the code. Section 5 describes how the patches were created and how we analyzed our merged patches. In Sect. 6, we present the results of the analysis. We list the possible threats of the analysis in Sect. 7 and conclude the paper in Sect. 8.

2   Related Work

Mens et al. published a survey to provide an extensive overview of existing research in the area of software refactoring [25]. Unfortunately, it is still unclear how specific quality factors are affected by the various refactoring activities.

Many researchers studied refactoring but only a few papers analyze the impact of refactoring on software quality. Sahraoui et al. [34] use quality estimation models to study whether some object-oriented metrics can be used for

---

[1] https://www.sonarqube.org/.

detecting code parts where a refactoring can be applied to improve the quality of a software system. They do not validate their findings within an large-scale experiment. Stroulia and Kapoor [37] investigate how size and coupling metrics behave after refactoring. They show that size and coupling metrics of a system decrease after refactoring; however, they only validate this in an academic environment.

Du Bois et al. [11] propose refactoring guidelines for enhancing cohesion and coupling metrics and obtain promising results by applying them on an open-source project. Simon et al. [35] follow a similar strategy, they use a couple of metrics to visualize classes and methods which help the developers to identify the candidates for refactoring. Demeyer [10] shows that refactoring can have a beneficial impact on software performance (e.g. compilers can optimize better on polymorphism than on simple if-else statements). Bois and Mens [12] develop a framework for analyzing the effects of refactoring on internal quality metrics, but again, they do not provide an experimental validation in an industrial environment.

There are abundance of studies [9,26,27,36] on OpenStack, the cloud infrastructure we used in our study. However, they do not target the analysis of code refactoring effects on software quality. Baset et al. [9], for example, analyze the evolution of OpenStack from testing and performance improvement point of view. Slipetskyy [36] analyze OpenStack from a security perspective. Musavi et al. analyze the API failures in the OpenStack ecosystem [26,27]. Advani et al. [5] extract refactoring trends from open-source systems in general.

In our paper we performed a large number of refactorings and observed their effect on the quality of the OpenStack open-source cloud infrastructure modules. These refactorings fixed different kinds of coding issues and introduced improved code structures, thus so we could investigate the system states before and after applying different types of patches. Our work was carried out in an *in vivo* open-source environment (OpenStack has a huge contributor base and is very active), which is an important difference compared to previous studies.

3   OpenStack

3.1   Overview of OpenStack

OpenStack is an open-source cloud computing software platform [13,15,29,33], mainly developed in Python. It is mostly used to provide an infrastructure-as-a-service platform, it helps their users to create private and/or public clouds. In this model, the service provider (who runs OpenStack) provides virtual machines and other resources to their customers (who pays for the resources monthly or on-demand). OpenStack is modularly developed, which means you can customize your cloud infrastructure well. You can deploy only the modules you really need, e.g. if you need a load balancer to your cloud system, you can install the specific module (Octavia) but your cloud can fully operate without it.

There are several core services which is often used together, including Nova (managing computing resources), Keystone (authentication and authorization),

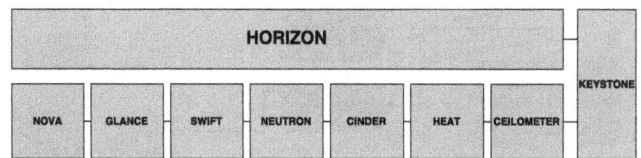

Fig. 1. Schematic structure of OpenStack

Neutron (networking), Glance (image services for virtual machine images), Horizon (dashboard). A schematic figure of the modules can be found in Fig. 1. All of the modules have their own developers, core members (who are experts of the module, and who can directly push modifications into the codebase). These teams are usually not distinct, one contributor often develops to several modules. You can find the list of OpenStack modules in [4].

OpenStack was started in 2010 as a collaboration project between Rackspace and NASA. As the project became more and more popular, other companies have joined and started working on the core modules and also on their own drivers in OpenStack, for example there are several hardware hypervisors that OpenStack can use (e.g. HyperV, VMware, Xen, Libvirt).

Nowadays, the project is handled by the OpenStack Foundation [29], which is a non-profit organization. Their goal is to provide an independent and strong home for OpenStack projects, provide resources and an entire ecosystem to build community, and help collaboration between open-source technologies. OpenStack Foundation consists of more than 500 companies (e.g. Intel, Canonical [14,32]), 82000 community members, from more than 180 countries worldwide.

The full codebase of all OpenStack modules is now consists of more than 1 million lines of code. OpenStack projects often use a six-month release cycle [30, 31] with several (typically 3) development milestones. This agile model lets the contributors to quickly land new features to OpenStack.

3.2 Contribution

As OpenStack is an open-source software, everyone can contribute to it. The developers are completely decentralized around the world, they have different coding habits. In order to contribute, some contribution guidelines [3] must be followed. The schematic view of the code developing process can be seen in Fig. 2.

The pre-requisite is to get familiar with Git, as the OpenStack community uses it as their version control system, and GitHub to host their codebase. First of all, if you want to contribute, you need to set up your local environment where you can develop, execute tests, and run the components of the OpenStack for your features (or bug fixes) on a live system. After that, you have to clone the repository you want to work on. Of course, then you have to make the modification you want to do. Then, you have to commit the changes to your local Git repository. After that, you have to send the modifications to a code review system. Code review is a manual process when people verify each others

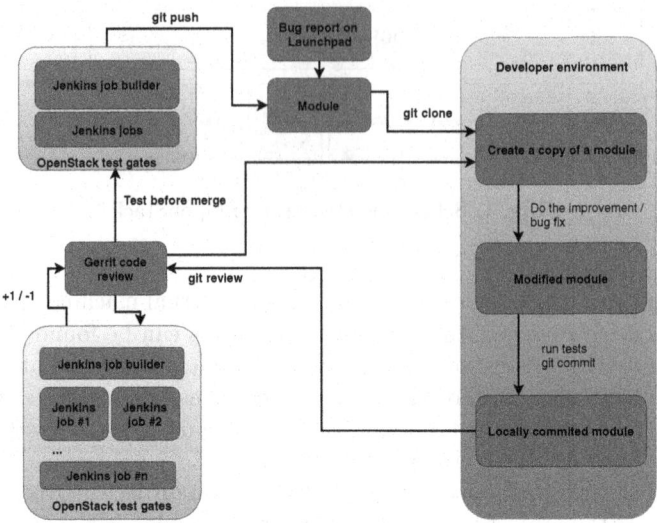

Fig. 2. OpenStack contribution flow

code by hand. This process needs to be highly automated in a worldwide open-source system.

To achieve this, the OpenStack projects use the Gerrit code review system from Google. Based on Git version controlling, Gerrit is a powerful code review system, which manages the modifications that are intended to be merged to a Git repository (to OpenStack's GitHub repository in our case). Gerrit is a great platform where developers can share their opinion on a modification, giving feedback to the authors how they can improve their patches, what are the additional tasks with a patch. They can rate patches +1 or −1 based on whether they found the patch mature enough to get merged or not.

At OpenStack, developers can get their modifications merged only via Gerrit. In Gerrit, every project has core members who are experts in that specific project. At least two of the core members need to approve the code before it can be merged. Core members can approve a patch by rating it +2 or disapprove by rating it −2. It basically means that a patch is probably not needed at that time. This process helps both developers and maintainers to have a good quality code [20, 24].

In addition to the manual approval, there are automated Jenkins[2] tests which can also approve or disapprove the code. When a Jenkins job fails, the author has to fix the code before it can be merged. These Jenkins jobs run the tests of the projects in various environments (e.g. with specific version of Python), with various settings enabled, on various hardware platforms. There are some really specific Jenkins jobs which only run on a specific code change (e.g. on

---

[2] Jenkins is an open-source continuous integration system. More details can be found at https://jenkins.io/.

specific, hardware-related driver changes). The jobs are managed by the Jenkins job builder (which is also an OpenStack project[3]). The Jenkins job builder is triggered when someone uploads a new set of modifications to the project or updates an already existing one.

When both Jenkins and the core members of the project approve a patchset (a set of modifications), the changes are getting tested once again, before being merged to a specific branch (mostly to the main branch) of an OpenStack project. If the patch still seems to be correct, an automated system merges it.

3.3 Quality Assurance

Quality assurance is one of the most important tasks in software engineering. However, it is not trivial even for a company, and also not a trivial task when the developers are all around the world, represent different companies, or they are just individuals who want to work on an open-source software system. Thus, a well-defined quality assurance model is necessary in order to have a good quality, manageable project. At OpenStack, there are 3 main aspects of quality assurance.

Manual Code Review. People can verify each others planned modifications. More details on how it works can be found in Sect. 3.2.

High Test Coverage. Having high test coverage is also a really important, continuous job in an international open-source project like OpenStack. Since everyone can contribute, it is cardinal to know whether a modification has unwanted side effects or not. To find out, we need to run the test suite provided by the project. If there is something we did but not intended to do, we can investigate the source of the problem. The OpenStack modules have quite good code coverage: Nova has a coverage of 87%, Watcher has a 86% coverage, Glance has a coverage of 72%, and Neutron has a 85% coverage.

To keep the coverage high, most of the time when a new feature is implemented, the patchset have to contain test cases for the new features. This is also a validation point when a bug fixing patch is getting merged. In general, a bug fixing patch should also contain test cases where the fixed bug would have occurred. At OpenStack, there are 3 levels of testing.

The first one is unit testing, which is needed for almost every case. Second level is the integration tests. This is only a common test level which is necessary when someone create modifications between 2 or more components. The last one is the live tests that are only required when one creates a modification, which can only be tested on a live and running OpenStack instance (tempest[4] tests). The used test coverage tool measures only the unit test coverage, and since these are functions that can be tested only with integration test, they are not taken into account while measuring coverage.

---

[3] https://github.com/openstack-infra/jenkins-job-builder.
[4] https://github.com/openstack/tempest.

All of the tests are run with the *tox* testing framework. This helps to automate and unify testing procedure across modules so that all the modules can run the tests in the same way. Tox builds virtual, separated environments where the tests can be run. The ability to change between Python versions is also an advantage of tox, as OpenStack mostly supports Python 2.7 and 3.4 in parallel.

The pep8 Jenkins Job. There are so called Jenkins test gates that test the modification from quality point of view. These jobs execute the pep8[5] tool to check if the code complies with the coding standards. In addition, these jobs run the style guide checker tool as well, which is created by the OpenStack community and called *hacking* rules. Hacking is a set of *flake8* plugins that test and enforce rules defined by [1].

There are global *hacking* rules, which must be conformed in each and every module. Additionally, every module can create its own *hacking* rules, which must be conformed only by that module. Local rules are often stricter than the global ones and usually contain rules that only make sense in the defining module.

4   Tools to Measure Code Quality

4.1   QualityGate

For the definition of software quality we refer to the ISO/IEC 9126 standard [18] and its successor the ISO/IEC 25000 [19], which defines six high-level characteristics that determine the product quality of software: *functionality, reliability, usability, efficiency, portability,* and *maintainability*. There is another related standard, the ISO/IEC 14764 that describes the quality of the maintenance process (for example, maintenance planning, execution and control, evaluation). The proposed metrics address process quality, while we wanted to study product metrics particularly as our analyzed projects already had a well-defined release and maintenance cycle [31].

Due to its direct impact on development costs [8], and being in close relation with the source code, maintainability is one of the most important quality characteristics.

To calculate the absolute maintainability values for every revision of the system we used the Columbus Quality Model, a probabilistic software quality model that is based on the quality characteristics defined by the ISO/IEC 25000 [19] standard. The computation of the high-level quality characteristics is based on a directed acyclic graph (see Fig. 3) whose nodes correspond to quality properties that can either be internal (low-level) or external (high-level). Internal quality properties characterize the software product from an internal (developer) view and are usually calculated by using source code metrics. External quality properties characterize the software product from an external (end user) view and are usually aggregated somehow by using internal and other external quality properties. The nodes representing internal quality properties are called *sensor nodes*

---

[5] https://www.python.org/dev/peps/pep-0008/.

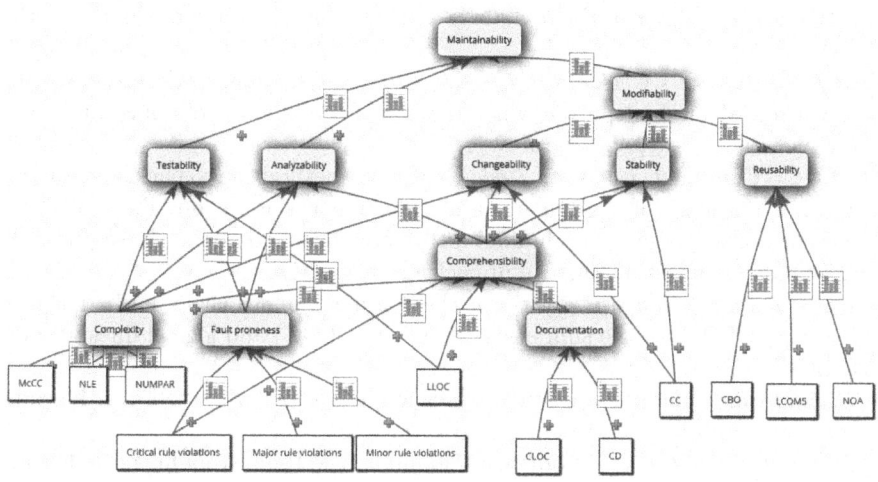

Fig. 3. Attribute dependency graph of Columbus Quality Model (Color figure online)

as they measure internal quality directly (light yellow nodes in Fig. 3). The other nodes are called *aggregate nodes* as they acquire their measures through aggregation. In addition to the aggregate nodes defined by the standard (i.e. Testability, Analyzability, Changeability, Stability, Reusability, Modifiability) we also introduce new ones (i.e. Complexity, Fault proneness, Comprehensibility, Documentation).

For the Python version of the model we used for the analysis of OpenStack before and after the refactorings, the following source code metrics apply:

- *LLOC (Logical Lines Of Code)* – the LLOC metric is the number of non-comment and non-empty lines of code.
- *NOA (Number Of Ancestors)* – NOA is the number of classes that a given class directly or indirectly inherits from.
- *NLE (Nesting Level Else-if)* – NLE for a method is the maximum of the control structure depth. Only if, **for**, and **while** instructions are taken into account and in the **if-elif-else** constructs only the **if** instruction is considered.
- *CBO (Coupling Between Object classes)* – a class is coupled to another if the class uses any method or attribute of the other class or directly inherits from it. CBO is the number of coupled classes.
- *CC (Clone Coverage)* – clone coverage is a real value between 0 and 1 that expresses what amount of the item is covered by code duplication.
- *LCOM5 (Lack of Cohesion On Methods)* – the value of the metric is the number of local methods that share at least one common attribute, call an abstract method or invoke each other, not counting constructors, getters, or setters.

- *NUMPAR (NUMber of PARameters)* – the number of parameters of the methods.
- *McCC (McCabe's Cyclomatic Complexity)* – the number of decisions within the specified method plus 1, where each if, for, while counts once and each try block with N catch counts N+1.
- *CLOC (Comment Lines of Code)* – for a method/class/package, CLOC is the number of comment and documentation code lines of the method/class/package, excluding its anonymous and local classes/nested, anonymous, and local classes/subpackages respectively.
- *CD (Comment Density)* – ratio of the comment lines of the method/class/package (CLOC) to the sum of its comment (CLOC) and logical lines of code (LLOC).
- *Critical rule violations* – Critical issues found by the Pylint tool[6] in the code that can cause bugs and unintended behaviour.
- *Major rule violations* – Major issues found by the Pylint tool in the code that can cause e.g. performance issues.
- *Minor rule violations* – Minor issues found by the Pylint tool in the code that e.g. decrease the code readability.

The edges of the graph represent dependencies between an internal and an external or two external properties. The aim is to evaluate all the external quality properties by performing an aggregation along the edges of the graph, called Attribute Dependency Graph (ADG). We calculate a so called *goodness value* (from the [0, 1] interval) for each node in the ADG that expresses how good or bad (1 is the best) the system is regarding that quality attribute. The probabilistic statistical aggregation algorithm uses a so-called benchmark as the basis of the qualification, which is a source code metric repository database with 100 open source and industrial software systems.

For further details about Columbus Quality Model [7], see work by Bakota et al. They also showed that there was a converse exponential relationship between the maintainability of a software system and the overall cost of development [8], supported by an empirical validation. The QualityGate SourceAudit tool by Bakota et al. [6] is based on this quality model.

4.2   SonarQube

SonarQube is an open-source static analyzer for continuous inspection of code quality. It is written in Java and it can work with more than 20 programming languages, including Python. It has a user-friendly web front-end where one can read the analysis reports and inspect the source code. SonarQube is able to detect various code smells, violation of coding standards, code duplications, test coverage, and security issues. SonarQube also measures some software metrics, and helps the developers with advices. On the web front-end, developers can see several figures, tables that helps the understanding of the system.

---

[6] https://www.pylint.org/.

It also integrates a high-level quality indicator called "Technical debt". Technical debt shows how many person days of effort would be needed to fix all of the found problems. The technical debt module in SonarQube is based on the SQALE model [22]. We used SonarQube for an initial investigation of the source code in order to find bad smells, which we can refactor.

We have created an own SonarQube server[7], which analyzes some of the core modules to help others in finding issues for refactoring. Along with this we have added a quality improvement plan [2]. Since then, our quality improvement plan is available in the official contribution guide [3].

5 Methodology

A schematic overview of our process can be seen in Fig. 4. First of all, we selected two of the OpenStack modules where we wanted to work on and create refactorings. We wanted to do refactoring on an mature, bigger module, and also on a smaller, younger one to see if that matters in the case of refactoring. We selected Nova and Watcher to work on. Nova is the oldest project in OpenStack that is responsible for the resource management. Watcher is a younger module, which is responsible for resource optimization in multi-tenant OpenStack clouds. Nova has 362480 lines of code, Watcher has 43866 lines of code.

We used three sources of oracles to decide where to refactor: static analyzers (results of both SonarQube and QualityGate), issue tracking system (maybe there are already detected bad smells), and manual code investigation (we searched for bad smells, code snippets which can be simplified).

We have managed to merge 47 patches in the two modules: 22 patches were merged into Nova, 25 patches were merged to Watcher, all of them contain refactoring to a specific issues, like removing code duplication, replacing orders when catching exceptions, using more specific assert methods in tests, fixing indentation, reducing code complexity. All details of the changes can be found in our online appendix[8].

Sometimes our proposed patches got merged quickly, and sometimes we had to modify them several times before core members approved them. After our patches got merged, we did some data mining from GitHub.

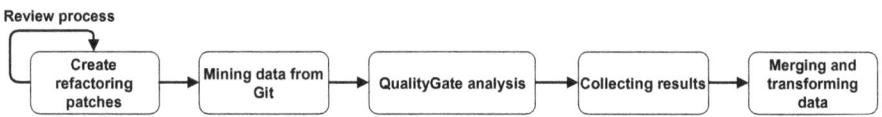

Fig. 4. Overview of the process

---

[7] http://openqa.sed.hu.

[8] http://www.inf.u-szeged.hu/~antal/pub/2018-iccsa-openstack-refactoring/.

It is obvious that if we want to examine the effect of a refactoring, we have to analyze both the version of the source code before refactoring and after refactoring. To achieve this, we collected the hashes (the unique identifier of a commit in Git) of our patches and we also collected the hash of the commit before the refactoring along with other data (date, commit message). The data mining script is also available in our online appendix (see footnote 8).

Once we finished mining, we did the analysis with QualityGate (Sect. 4.1) based on the list collected from the GitHub repository. We analyzed the patches pairwise, we used the commit before the refactoring as an initial state, and then we analyzed the commit after the refactoring. Analyzing all of the commits which were on the list took hours.

After finishing the analysis, we had to collect all the data from QualityGate. QualityGate stores its qualification data in a database, which we had to query in order to get the raw data. Then, the collected raw data had to be transformed into a more readable form where we can investigate all of the quality indicators defined in Sect. 4.1 and compute the effect of a refactoring. Furthermore, we needed some other data from the mined Git repository, so we combined all of the collected data into a big table. All of the combined data is available in our online appendix (see footnote 8).

6   Results

6.1   Overall Change of Maintainability

The effect of our submitted refactorings on the code quality can be seen in Figs. 5 and 6. In these figures, blue lines represent the succeeding commits (before and after a refactoring), and between the pairs we used dashed gray lines. The y-axis shows the value of *Maintainability* as shown in Fig. 3, the x-axis shows the number of analyzed versions.

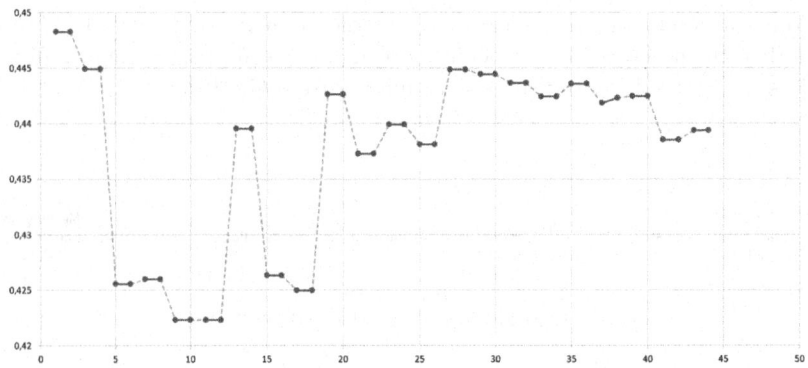

Fig. 5. Maintainability change of Nova (Color figure online)

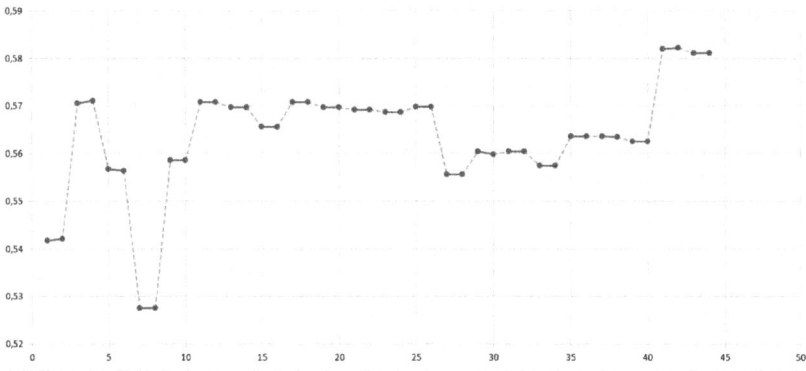

Fig. 6. Maintainability change of Watcher (Color figure online)

As it can been seen, most of the time refactorings made undetectable changes in the quality of the whole system. We consider this to be normal as the systems had lots of lines of code, thus small changes have very small impact on the module as a whole. However, in some cases QualityGate showed a change in the software's quality. Out of the 47 patches, significant change could be detected only in 8 cases – 7 out of 25 in Watcher, which is the smaller project, and 1 out of 22 case in Nova, which is the bigger project. The detected changes and impact on *Maintainability* can be seen in Fig. 7. The changes of aggregated quality nodes and sensor nodes can be seen in Tables 1 and 2, where negative numbers represents increased quality (the node had a better quality after refactoring; we subtracted the value of the quality indicator after the refactoring from the value before refactoring).

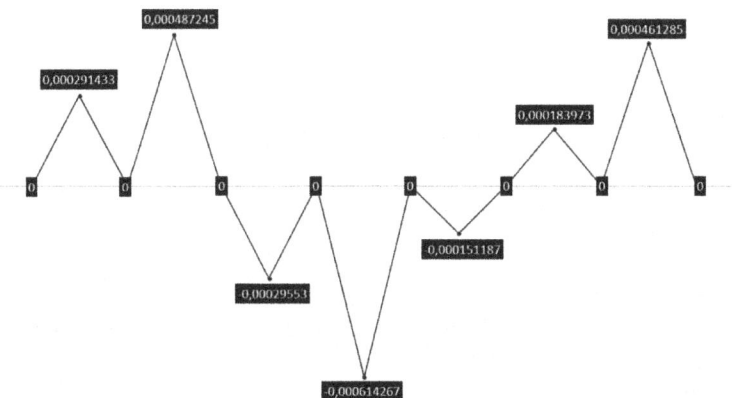

Fig. 7. Maintainability changes on patches which had any impact on quality

The significant patches caused increasing the software's *Maintainability* in 4 cases; decreasing the quality in 3 cases; and caused zero change in 1 case. The aggregate quality-indicator nodes *Analyzability*, *Stability* and *Testability* show increase in 5 out of 8 cases. It is also an interesting fact that the goodness of *Documentation* were decreased in all affected patches. All the analysis result data can be found in our online appendix.

Table 1. Changes in the aggregated quality nodes

(N)ova/(W)atcher	Analyzability	Changeability	CodeComplexity	Comprehensibility	Documentation	CodeFaultProneness	Critical rule violations	Major rule violations	Minor rule violations	Modifiability	Stability	Testability	Maintainability
N	-0.00049	-0.00043	-0.00060	-0.00063	0	0	0	0	0	-0.00028	-0.00025	-0.00070	-0.00046
W	-0.00015	0.00002	0.00049	-0.00048	0		-0.00085	-0.00143	0	-0.00019	-0.00055	-0.00067	-0.00029
W	-0.00062	-0.00046	-0.00111	-0.00014	0.00125	-0.00057	0	-0.00143	-0.00143	-0.00022	-0.00005	-0.00070	-0.00049
W	0.00104	0.00075	0.00321	-0.00006	0.00079	-0.00128	-0.00143	0.00143	0	0	-0.00088	-0.00047	0.00030
W	-0.00033	0.00055	-0.00066	-0.00010	0.00069	-0.00015	0		-0.00143	0.00058	0.00095	-0.00038	0
W	0.00066	0	0	0	0	0.00341	0.00571	0	0	0.00053	0.00145	0.00069	0.00061
W	0.00019	0.00017	0.00033	0.00015	0	0	0	0	0	0.00010	0.00006	0.00017	0.00015
W	-0.00014	-0.00012	0	-0.00035	0	0	0	0	0	-0.00010	-0.00014	-0.00038	-0.00018

Table 2. Changes in the sensor nodes quality

	CC	CD	CLOC	LLOC	McCC	NLE	NUMPAR
Nova	0	0	0	−0.00143	0	−0.00143	0
Watcher	0	0	0	−0.00286	−0.00143	0	0.00429
Watcher	0	0	0.00286	0	−0.00143	−0.00143	0
Watcher	−0.00143	0.00143	0	−0.00714	−0.00143	0.00571	0.00571
Watcher	0.00286	0	0.00143	0	0	0	−0.00286
Watcher	0	0	0	0	0	0	0
Watcher	0	0	0	0	0	0	0.00143
Watcher	0	0	0	−0.00143	0	0	0

6.2 Quality Degradation

The definition of refactoring implies that refactoring a code will increase the quality of the source code. Nonetheless, the *Maintainability* of the project decreased in 3 cases, which is almost 40% of all the cases. We investigated these cases to find out the reason of decrease.

First, we investigated the patch titled "Reduced the complexity of the execute() method".[9] In this patch, we split a large method that had a high

---

[9] https://github.com/openstack/watcher/commit/a2750c7.

cyclomatic complexity. We introduced 5 more methods, which impacted the quality; we improved the sensor nodes *McCC*, *LLOC*, *CC*, and improved the aggregated nodes *CodeFaultProneness*, *Stability*, *Testability*, *Critical rule violations*. Quality value of *Analyzability*, *Changeability*, and *NUMPAR* has decreased. These changes are consistent with the introduction of new methods. In overall, the number of methods has grown, which means that there are more methods in the code after the refactoring, there are more connections between them, so inspecting the connections between the code is harder than before.

The second patch that caused decreasing Maintainability is titled "Missing super() in API collection controllers".[10] In this case, we placed missing constructor calls to the base class. Before the refactoring, there were no connection between super and base class, which is obviously bad. After placing the super call, the connection between the base and child class is created which affects the quality in the wrong way by increasing coupling.

The third patch which decreased quality is titled "`Removed duplicated function prepare_service()`".[11] This patch contained merging of two methods since they were almost exactly the same. We needed only one copy of the merged method, thus the other occurrence was deleted. Since the file contained only the deleted method, we got rid of the file entirely. Deleting the file caused the decrease in the quality as the deleted file was simple, contained only one method, which was also a small one.

On average, one small refactoring did an improvement of 0.00000852 in *Maintainability* (measured in the scale of $[0, 1]$), which might not look that much, but refactoring the project regularly can cause a big quality improvement in the long term.

7 Threats to Validity

There is no exact definition for the quality of the source code expressed by a number. The QualityGate and SonarQube tools and the underlying ColumbusQM and SQALE technical debt models are only two of several approaches, with their own advantages and drawbacks. However, both are well-founded, stable, widely adapted models relied upon by industrial and research communities as well. Although we treat this as an external threat, we argue that the bias in their measurement has a limited impact on the presented results.

The sample set of refactorings we examined is quite small. Only a small team worked on producing these patches, thus the generalization of the results is a real threat. However, the refactoring work was carried out during years, thus despite the small number of developers, quite a high amount of effort has been put into it. This mitigates the threat.

We contributed only to the fraction of the OpenStack modules from which analyzed 2 altogether. It might happen that different modules show different

---

[10] https://github.com/openstack/watcher/commit/67455c6.
[11] https://github.com/openstack/watcher/commit/f0b58f8.

results as there are more than 35 modules, thus for the complete generalization of our study, we plan to extend the number of analyzed modules.

It might also happen that the patches we've created are not refactoring patches. This threat can be mitigated as we followed the guidelines of both Refactoring [16] and Clean Code [23]. Another possible threat is that our patches contain poor refactorings that are not really fits into the open-source world. This is mitigated by the fact that at least 2 core members approved our patches before merge. Typically there were at least 5–6 reviewers who reviewed our patches.

8   Conclusions and Future Work

In this study, we investigated 47 refactoring patches in two projects from the worlds leading open source cloud operating system, OpenStack. We analyzed Nova and Watcher modules to find some quality issues which can be fixed. On these problematic parts, we applied various refactoring techniques, e.g. splitting a large method into numerous, smaller methods. The applied refactorings were analyzed in order to investigate whether refactoring really improves code maintainability. We used QualityGate to do the analysis, then results were collected, transformed and analyzed. During the final state of our research, we found out that one particular refactoring is often immensely small (i.e. often affects only a few lines). Out of 47 patches, only 8 produced measurable change in the code quality. The average improvement of all the patches were really small, but it was clearly an improvement and not degradation. Hence, refactoring the code regularly can improve the maintainability of the code in the mid and long-term.

Besides the measurable metrics the human factor is also very important. We got many comments[12,13,14] to our proposed patches that refactoring is always welcome and it is a nice thing that someone pays attention to code quality. In the future, we would like to extend this research by analyzing more patches on many more projects to generalize our results.

Acknowledgment. The project has been supported by the UNKP-17-4 New National Excellence Program of the Ministry of Human Capacities, Hungary.

The authors would also like to express their gratitude to Gergely Ladányi and Béla Vancsics for providing technical support in QualityGate analysis and OpenStack contribution as well as to Balázs Gibizer from Ericsson Hungary for his valuable guidance in the OpenStack development.

---

[12] https://review.openstack.org/349582/.
[13] https://review.openstack.org/247560.
[14] https://review.openstack.org/263343/.

References

1. OpenStack Docs: Hacking: OpenStack Hacking Guideline Enforcement. https://docs.openstack.org/hacking/latest/user/hacking.html
2. User talk: OpenStack Quality Improvement Plan. https://wiki.openstack.org/wiki/User_talk:P%C3%A9ter_Heged%C5%B1s
3. How To Contribute - OpenStack (2018). https://wiki.openstack.org/wiki/How_To_Contribute. Accessed 09 Apr 2018
4. OpenStack Docs: Modules List (2018). https://docs.openstack.org/puppet-openstack-guide/latest/contributor/module-list.html. Accessed 09 Apr 2018
5. Advani, D., Hassoun, Y., Counsell, S.: Extracting refactoring trends from opensource software and a possible solution to the 'related refactoring' conundrum. In: Proceedings of the 2006 ACM Symposium on Applied Computing, SAC 2006, pp. 1713–1720. ACM, New York (2006). http://doi.acm.org/10.1145/1141277.1141685
6. Bakota, T., Hegedűs, P., Siket, I., Ladányi, G., Ferenc, R.: Qualitygate sourceaudit: a tool for assessing the technical quality of software. In: Proceedings of the CSMR-WCRE Software Evolution Week, pp. 440–445. IEEE Computer Society (2014)
7. Bakota, T., Hegedűs, P., Körtvélyesi, P., Ferenc, R., Gyimóthy, T.: A probabilistic software quality model. In: Proceedings of the 27th International Conference on Software Maintenance (ICSM), pp. 243–252. IEEE Computer Society (2011)
8. Bakota, T., Hegedűs, P., Ladányi, G., Körtvélyesi, P., Ferenc, R., Gyimóthy, T.: A cost model based on software maintainability. In: Proceedings of the 28th International Conference on Software Maintenance (ICSM), pp. 316–325. IEEE Computer Society (2012)
9. Baset, S.A., Tang, C., Tak, B.C., Wang, L.: Dissecting open source cloud evolution: an OpenStack case study. In: HotCloud (2013)
10. Demeyer, S.: Refactor conditionals into polymorphism: what's the performance cost of introducing virtual calls? In: Proceedings of the 21st IEEE International Conference on Software Maintenance, ICSM 2005, pp. 627–630. IEEE (2005)
11. Du Bois, B., Demeyer, S., Verelst, J.: Refactoring-improving coupling and cohesion of existing code. In: Proceedings of the 11th Working Conference on Reverse Engineering, pp. 144–151. IEEE (2004)
12. Du Bois, B., Mens, T.: Describing the impact of refactoring on internal program quality. In: Proceedings of the International Workshop on Evolution of Large-Scale Industrial Software Applications, pp. 37–48 (2003)
13. Erl, T., Puttini, R., Mahmood, Z.: Cloud Computing: Concepts Technology & Architecture, 1st edn. Prentice Hall Press, Upper Saddle River (2013)
14. Ubuntu Cloud: OpenStack Wins, Eucalyptus Loses. http://talkincloud.com/ubuntu-cloud-openstack-wins-eucalyptus-loses
15. Fitfield, T.: Introduction to OpenStack. Linux J. **2013**(235) (2013). http://dl.acm.org/citation.cfm?id=2555789.2555793
16. Fowler, M.: Refactoring: Improving the Design of Existing Code. Addison-Wesley Longman Publishing Co., Inc., Boston (1999)
17. Hegedűs, P., Kádár, I., Ferenc, R., Gyimóthy, T.: Empiricalevaluation of software maintainability based on a manually validatedrefactoring dataset. Inf. Softw. Technol. (2017, accepted, to appear). https://doi.org/10.1016/j.infsof.2017.11.012. http://www.sciencedirect.com/science/article/pii/S0950584916303561
18. ISO/IEC: ISO/IEC 9126. Software Engineering - Product quality 6.5. ISO/IEC (2001)

19. ISO/IEC: ISO/IEC 25000:2005. Software Engineering - Software product Quality Requirements and Evaluation (SQuaRE) - Guide to SQuaRE. ISO/IEC (2005)
20. Kemerer, C.F., Paulk, M.C.: The impact of design and code reviews on software quality: an empirical study based on PSP data. IEEE Trans. Software Eng. **35**(4), 534–550 (2009)
21. Kim, M., Gee, M., Loh, A., Rachatasumrit, N.: Ref-finder: a refactoring reconstruction tool based on logic query templates. In: Proceedings of the 18th ACM SIGSOFT International Symposium on Foundations of Software Engineering (FSE 2010), pp. 371–372 (2010)
22. Letouzey, J.L.: The SQALE method for evaluating technical debt. In: Third International Workshop on Managing Technical Debt (MTD), pp. 31–36. IEEE (2012). https://doi.org/10.1109/MTD.2012.6225997
23. Martin, R.C.: Clean Code: A Handbook of Agile Software Craftsmanship. Pearson Education, New York (2009)
24. McIntosh, S., Kamei, Y., Adams, B., Hassan, A.E.: An empirical study of the impact of modern code review practices on software quality. Empir. Softw. Eng. **21**(5), 2146–2189 (2016)
25. Mens, T., Tourwé, T.: A survey of software refactoring. IEEE Trans. Softw. Eng. **30**(2), 126–139 (2004)
26. Mirkalaei, M., Pooya, S.: API Failures in OpenStack Cloud Environments. Ph.D. thesis, École Polytechnique de Montréal (2017)
27. Musavi, P., Adams, B., Khomh, F.: Experience report: an empirical study of API failures in OpenStack cloud environments. In: 2016 IEEE 27th International Symposium on Software Reliability Engineering (ISSRE), pp. 424–434. IEEE (2016)
28. Opdyke, W.F.: Refactoring object-oriented frameworks. Ph.D. thesis, University of Illinois (1992)
29. The OpenStack Foundation. https://www.openstack.org/foundation
30. OpenStack Releases. https://releases.openstack.org/
31. OpenStack Release models. https://releases.openstack.org/reference/release_models.html
32. Ubuntu Cloud Infrastructure. https://help.ubuntu.com/community/UbuntuCloud Infrastructure
33. OpenStack. https://en.wikipedia.org/wiki/OpenStack
34. Sahraoui, H.A., Godin, R., Miceli, T.: Can metrics help to bridge the gap between the improvement of OO design quality and its automation? In: Proceedings of International Conference on Software Maintenance, pp. 154–162. IEEE (2000)
35. Simon, F., Steinbruckner, F., Lewerentz, C.: Metrics based refactoring. In: Proceedings of the Fifth European Conference on Software Maintenance and Reengineering, pp. 30–38. IEEE (2001)
36. Slipetskyy, R.: Security issues in OpenStack. Master's thesis, Institutt for telematikk (2011)
37. Stroulia, E., Kapoor, R.: Metrics of refactoring-based development: an experience report. In: Wang, X., Johnston, R., Patel, S. (eds.) OOIS 2001, pp. 113–122. Springer, Heidelberg (2001). https://doi.org/10.1007/978-1-4471-0719-4_13
38. Szőke, G., Antal, G., Nagy, C., Ferenc, R., Gyimóthy, T.: Empirical study on refactoring large-scale industrial systems and its effects on maintainability. J. Syst. Softw. **129**(C), 107–126 (2017). https://doi.org/10.1016/j.jss.2016.08.071. http://www.sciencedirect.com/science/article/pii/S0164121216301558?via%3Dihub

Teaching Database Design and Analysis in an Effective Way on Digital Platform and Its Effect on Society

Uma Maheswari Sadasivam[1](✉) and Chamundeswari Arumugam[2](✉)

[1] Department of Computer Science and Information Science,
Birla Institute of Technology and Science, Pilani (off campus),
Pilani, Rajasthan, India
umamaheswaris@WILP.BITS-pilani.ac.in
[2] Department of Computer Science and Engineering,
SSN College of Engineering, Kalavakkam, Tamil Nadu, India
chamundeswaria@ssn.edu.in

Abstract. Living in the era of Digital learning where the learners from different culture and diversity ought to be addressed. The quality of teaching that the learner receives matters the most, also that course contents needs to keep pace with the changing nature of organization especially in the IT discipline. The Objective of this paper is to teach database for IT organizations using Digital learning platform and keeping in mind that IT organizations are agile and lean. The paper discusses how the learning platform helps the organization to gear up its employees to keep updated with skills needed to handle DBMS design and analysis to meet the demands of IT sector.

Keywords: SQL · Blended learning · Flipped classroom

1 Introduction

For decades in Software development, the database plays an important part in the form of SQL (Structured Query Language) were the data is stored in relational tables. An application may have a database as backend and sometimes concurrently used by different applications. For example, a banking application or Railways reservation systems use a database management system to provide access to centralized data. In doing so it is equally important that this data is made available on every device across the business. Database system creates backup data copies for disaster recovery and operations restored after a calamity. Many IT organizations today are adapting to such databases for their huge datasets and high scale applications [6]. The paper highlights systematic instructional design technique used to impart knowledge of Designing and Analyzing Database systems for a web or mobile application.

1.1 Work and Change in Nature of Organization

The content, structure and work process keep evolving. Currently work is team-based and collaborative, cognitively complex, depends on social skills and competence in

© Springer International Publishing AG, part of Springer Nature 2018
O. Gervasi et al. (Eds.): ICCSA 2018, LNCS 10964, pp. 481–491, 2018.
https://doi.org/10.1007/978-3-319-95174-4_38

technology. In-addition meeting deadline, going mobile and less dependent on geography is significant [1]. This work differs between organizations as competitive pressures and technological breakthrough varies. These days the organizations are more agile [10], leaner, being customer perspective, meeting dynamic requirements and strategy. The organization's hierarchy in structure-less decision authority, job security which means lifelong careers is less assured and reorganizing the workplace is needed to maintain or gain competitive advantage [1]. So real challenge these days is that organization has-to be more agile, leaner and meet dynamic requirements of customer. The effective method to handle the challenges mentioned can be achieved by gaining the subject knowledge learning database on a digital platform at their convenience and thereby gear up the learners to handle the change in nature of organization.

1.2   Digital Learning Models

It's known that learning is a continuous process and not a onetime event. The early generation of digital learning or web-based learning programs were about physical Classroom-based instructional content over the internet [4]. The experience of using was long sequences of Page-turner content and quizzes. This was a single mode of instructional delivery which did not provide sufficient choices, social contact and context needed to make a successful learning [4]. Then came the next wave of E-learning called blended learning model. Blended learning combines multiple delivery media that are designed to complement each other, promote learning and application-learned behavior. The blended learning model suits agile, leaner nature of organization as it blends learning approaches in their strategies to get the right content in the right format to the right people at the right time [4]. The blended learning programs may include several forms of learning tools such as real time virtual/collaboration software, self-paced web-based courses or video lessons. The blended learning may be mix of event-based activities, face to face classrooms or contact classes, live e-learning and self-paced learning. It's a combination of traditional Instructor-led training, synchronous online conferencing or training, asynchronous Self-paced study and structured training from an expertise or mentor.

1.3   Blended E-Learning Model

The blended E-learning model [4] for teaching any subject can be designed using following decision making as shown in Fig. 1.

The model above says that any Blended learning program can mix and match the following ingredients like content, content delivery method, infrastructure needed, Audience, LO (Learning Outcome) and IT organization support. Using the above model for digital learning, we can design digital learning of database. Using this we can plan, develop, deliver, manage, and evaluate blended learning programs [6]. Many Organizations and universities are collaborating continuously exploring strategies for effective learning and improving performance. While doing so we need to consider a variety of issues to ensure effective delivery of learning and so a high return on investment is achieved. Digital learning model used for teaching database on digital platform is shown in Fig. 2.

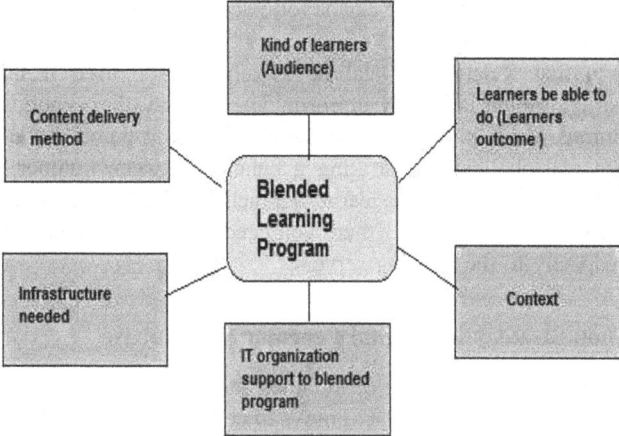

Fig. 1. Blended E-learning model.

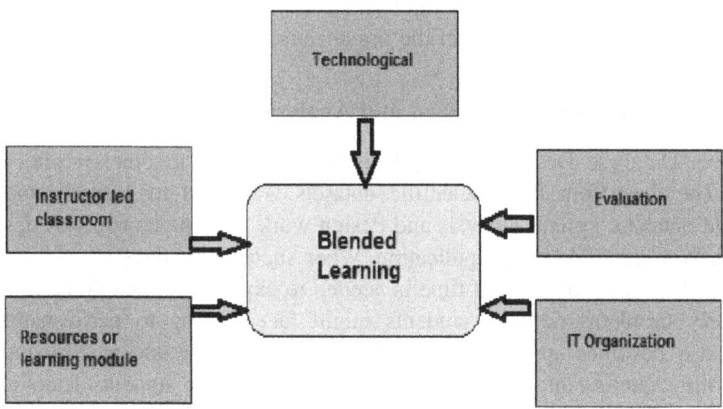

Fig. 2. Blended learning model for database teaching.

2 Blended E-Learning for Teaching Database

2.1 Designing the Digital Learning for Database Course

In case of teaching database this blended learning can be used where a learning program that provides study materials and research resources over the Web. Meanwhile provide instructor-led, classroom training sessions or flipped classrooms with instructions to practice the design problems like Enhanced Entity Relationship/Entity Relationship diagrams, normalization, domain and tuple calculus, Query Optimizer and other topics in database. The collaborative learning which can be used to improve the dynamic communication among many learners that brings about knowledge sharing which promotes better social skills which is essential in most of the organizations. The blending of self-paced and collaborative learning can be followed by moderated, online, peer-to-peer discussion of the topic taught.

It is known that Relational Database system can be used if the data has a well-defined structure and is largely uniform. The schema of an application its properties like columns, types and should be defined Up-front before building the application [5]. The real challenge is striking a balance between number of tables and number of columns in a table can be learnt by practice only. Another important point is that as the data starts to grow larger there is a need to scale the database vertically by adding more capacity to the existing servers.

2.2 Evaluation Strategy for Digital Learning of Database

There is a need for a strict schedule of modules and better assessments methods to be used [2]. And a learner should be able to move to next module only when they meet the specific criteria or score minimum grade to pass so that learning gap is kept to minimum as possible. The course in database may end when learners puts in all the skills learnt and develop a solution for a specified application (project) in a professional way [2]. This evaluation strategy sheds light on how much they learnt and how well they can handle the real time projects in the organization.

2.3 Implemented Database Design and Analysis Course

The course Database Design and Analysis was based on a semester long database project. The data from large scientific datasets was used to prepare students for real-world database system analysis and design work [7]. The course was designed to develop a Web-based database application. When such a large database is used to teach it is that only a small amount of time is needed to explain the data domain. Secondly most likely problems that the students might face leading to performance issues later-on also becomes apparent. This helps with scalability and performance issues when writing queries and application development. Lastly students learn about the scientific data being complex as richly-connected data and in its uses [7].

As mentioned the course was based on problem/project-based teaching method [9]. This method had six expected learning outcomes: (1) Students shall understand conceptual modelling concepts and be able to use Entity Relational model to design database applications. (2) Students shall be familiar with relational data models and be able to design relational database schemas from ER diagrams. (3) Students shall be able to use an industry standard query language (SQL) to query the relational databases. (4) Students shall understand the basic concepts of query optimization and learn simple query optimization techniques. (5) Students shall gain experience in designing and implementing web-based database systems. (6) Students shall improve oral and written communication skills through written and oral presentation of their projects [9].

The whole class was divided into groups of around 4 to 6 (optimal number) and with each group comprising of 5 students (optimal one) were formed. Each group were asked to choose a real-world project and handout as well give a problem description to class and to instructor. Then students were asked to give preliminary and final presentation of their projects. It is during the preliminary presentation each group plays the role of client and other groups ask them question. The class turn in an ER diagram that they heard of and then discuss the solution on the white board.

The students were asked to submit a written document on various stages of DB development for the chosen business problem which is as follows:

- Formulate the ER diagram
- Design the database schema
- Implement the schemas
- Perform normalizations/modifications
- SQL statements to create tables
- Populate and manipulate data (according to use cases) and snapshots of the screen
- Relational algebra for various possible queries
- Verify transaction processing.

Towards the end of semester, each group would present the design of their system and a working demo of the implementation. During this final presentation the class plays role of a client evaluating their colleagues [8]. And students were required to design and implement the DB project while they learn the concepts in flipped classroom mode. As the final touch to the project, all the students fill an evaluation form for each project. The evaluation form requires a good point and one negative feature/point or suggestion for improvement also to be mentioned. These were sent to professor for evaluations. The professor has evaluator (student) name on it removed before being handed over to original group [8]. These help the student to be attentive to the presentations, evaluation skill improves by providing feedback to the presenters as well.

2.4   Case Study: A Systematic Instruction Design Approach to Teach Entity Relationship and Enhanced Entity Relationship Diagrams

It is to be noted that this systematic instruction design on digital learning helps students learn DB design course with ease. This systematic way of learning using the Algorithms which is not in any other online courses so far. The courses from Massive open online courses (MooC) of leading universities or from any online course company like Edx, Udemy, Coursera in database design and Analysis doesn't impart knowledge in a systematic instruction design approach in all topics of Database design course.

To design the ER/EER diagram from the problem statement was foundation needed to analysis and design of database. This was made easy to learn by using a systematic method so that student will be confident with their analysis phase of Database design. This course implemented a systematic method by using the following algorithm:

(a) **For Entity Relationship diagram:**

> *Step 1: Extract the nouns, verbs from the problem statement.*
> *Step 2: Mostly nouns becomes ENTITIES. But only if it has some properties. If it has properties and then those properties become the attributes of the entity.*
> *Step 3: The nouns which doesn't have properties then demote nouns to become attributes.*
> *Step 4: Delete the redundant entities.*
> *Step 5a: Determine the primary keys for each entity.*

Step 5b: The entities which doesn't have a primary key becomes weak entity represented by a Weak relation as well and connected to strong entity.

Step 6: The Verbs extracted becomes the relationship between the entities.

Step 7: Check for redundant relationship and delete them.

Step 8: Find the participation constraint (total or partial) for each relationship between entities.

Step 9: Find the cardinality constraint (1-1, 1-n, n-1 or n-n) for each relationship between entities.

Step 10: Write the role names if unary relationship exists.

Step 11: Never connect one relationship to another relationship. If in need then use Aggregation.

Step 12: Repeat step 2 to step 12 until modelling is agreeable with problem statement.

(b) **For Enhanced Entity Relationship diagram:**

Step 1: Extract the nouns, verbs from the problem statement.

Step 2: Mostly nouns becomes ENTITIES. But only if it has some properties. If it has properties and then those properties become the attributes of the entity.

Step 3: The nouns which doesn't have properties then demote nouns to become attributes.

Step 4: Delete the redundant entities.

Step 5: Determine the primary keys for each entity.

Step 6: Check if Aggregation is needed and use it.

Step 7: An entity type may have additional meaningful subgroupings of its entities called Subclasses and Super classes. Use ISA relationship in such situations.

Step 8: Specify the structural and participation constraints as:

Step 8a: Disjoint Constraint:

- Specifies that the subclasses of the specialization must be disjointed (an entity can a member of at most one of the subclasses of the specialization)
- Specified by d in EER diagram
- If not disjointed, overlap; that is the same entity may be a member of more than one subclass of the specialization
- Specified by o in EER diagram

Step 8b: Completeness Constraint:

- Total specifies that every entity in the superclass must be a member of Some subclass in the specialization/generalization
- Shown in EER diagrams by a double line
- Partial allows an entity not to belong to any of the subclasses
- Shown in EER diagrams by a single line

Step 9: Check for Union types where Super classes represent different entity type such a subclass is called a category or UNION TYPE. Find where we have shared super classes.

Step 10: The Verbs extracted becomes the relationship between the entities.

Step 11: Check for redundant relationship and delete them.

Step 12: Find the participation constraint for each relationship.

Step 13: *Find the cardinality constraint for each relationship.*
Step 14: *Write the role names if unary relationship exists.*
Step 15: *Never connect one relationship to another relationship. If required use aggregation.*
Step 16: *Repeat steps 2 to step 15 until Modelling is agreeable with problem Statement.*

These Algorithms were used by students to learn the ER and EER concepts and they were recording the changes in a table format as in Table 1. Algorithms similarly were developed to learn concepts in normalization, query writing, query optimization, transaction processing and other topics in database course. Algorithms enhanced the quality of instruction delivery and learning. Each group doing a project maintains proper version control for documentation that they submit during various stages of DB development. The groups used the following table (Table 1) to document changes made at every stages of the project.

Table 1. Table documents the changes made in project.

Version Number	Date	Author/Owner	Description of Change

Digital platform there were features which helped the Students to master each module or phase of DB design. Students had self-tests to practice the concepts, assignments, quizzes, glossary and discussion for each stage/module of this course. This reassures that the learning gaps were reduced. They carry out their progress by fulfilling several assessments. The assignments, project documents format, presentations, project discussion and validity are strictly defined. Moodle was used to help with above mentioned features. The projects discussion and demo were done through video conferencing software like Webinar or WebEx.

3   Result

At the end of course, the students were asked to fill an online questionnaire about course as shown in the Fig. 3 which covered all topics or Learning Outcomes of each stages of the course were obtained from the students. Upon this feedback from student's evaluation of courses we could make out that most of the students 80% were able to understand and successfully learnt to design and develop DB from problem statement because a systematic method of teaching strategy in form of algorithm was used.

Questionaire

1. Not satisfied 2. Satisfied with no problems 3. Satisfied with problems 4. Fully satisified

Course Structure:

1. Rate your understanding of the course structure.
2. Constistency of the course content with the objectives?
3. Was the course content relevant?
4. Was the content arranged in clear and logical way?
5. Did the content cover the skills and knowledge or skill presented?
6. Rate the confidence level after completing the course.
7. Links to the external web resources was is it useful?
8. Did the activities in the course help you understand the contents?
9. Do you find case studies help you with understanding of concepts?

ER and EER diagrams:

1. How would rate the amount of material covered?
2. Did the activities help you gain a clearer understanding of Analysis of problem statement?
3. Rate the use of case studies and scenarios help you gain a clearer understanding of the content.
4. Rate the following elements according to how helpful they were to your learning experience (how well these items helped you remember key information scenario based content, quizzes, exams and games.)
5. How was the quality of the examples presented in this part of the course?
6. Was the steps in the algorithm to draw Er and EER was useful in understanding concepts clearly?
7. Did taking the large data sets help you gain a good understanding of this course?
8. Did the Project work help you learn this course with ease in understaning the concepts?
9. Rate the understanding of drawing ER and EER diagrams without the Algorithm?
10. Rate the understanding of drawing ER and EER diagrams with the Algorithms?
11. Rate your Database Analysis skills you gained to be used in real world?

Fig. 3. Questionnaire used by students to evaluate the course.

The Fig. 4 gives feedback obtained from students who learnt ER and EER design and results on the chart shows that using the algorithm the student learnt to design ER and EER with much ease when a systematic way was used to impart the knowledge in learning ER/EER topic.

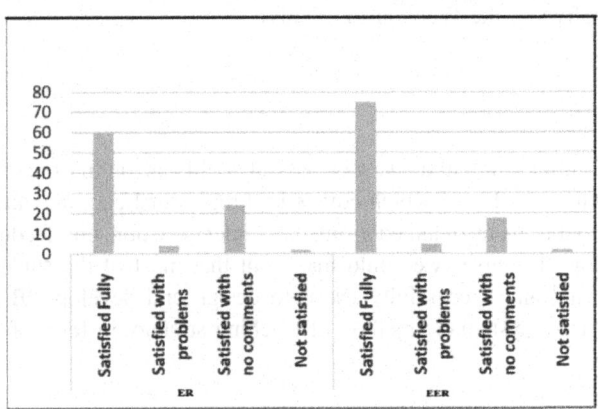

Fig. 4. Student feedback on the topic ER and EER drawing using algorithm.

Similar Algorithms were developed to understand all the topics in database design and analysis phases. The Fig. 5 gives feedback on how the student felt on each topic in DB design and analysis. And obtained results is as in Fig. 6 say that students were satisfied taking this course from the comfort of work place or at home. This result gives the evidence that the digital learning helps students learn DB design course with systematic way of learning using the Algorithms which is not in any other online courses so far. The course can have algorithms extended to support Agile database design as well [10].

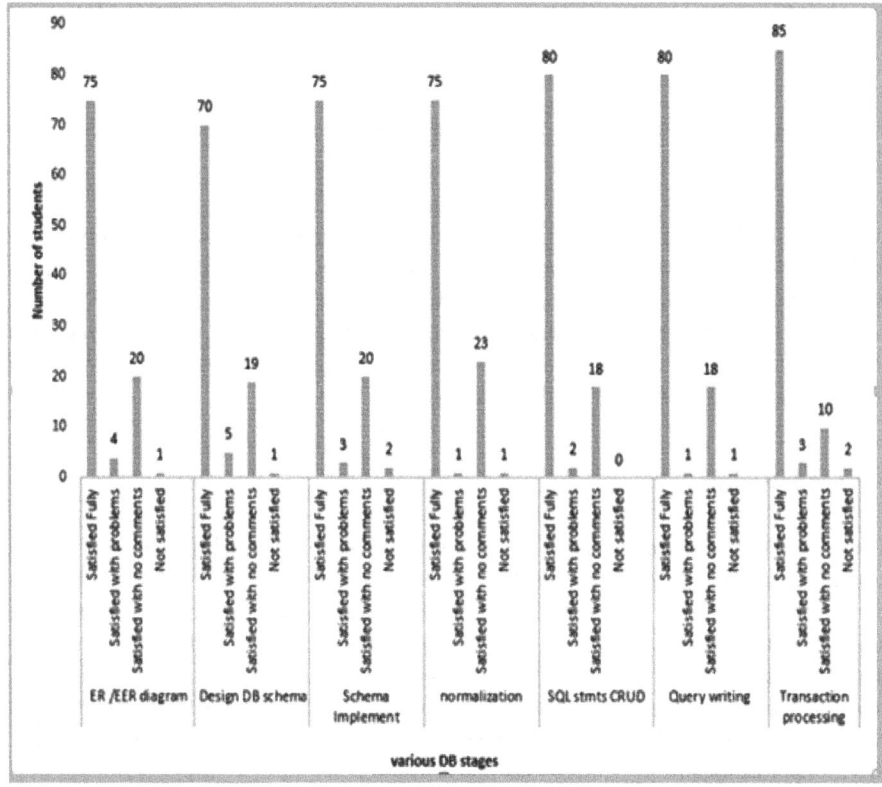

Fig. 5. Students feedback on this course based on learning outcomes or stages in DB design and analysis using the Algorithms developed to teach each topic.

4   Social Benefits of Digital Learning

The Digital learning should be designed as sustainable and be socially responsible one [4]. Social responsibility which says the system should be consistent with the policies of the company and community values with broader view [3]. So be responsible for its own decision/actions and work outcomes [3]. It should also encourage being committed and guide core beliefs and values like integrity and honest. Issues like equal

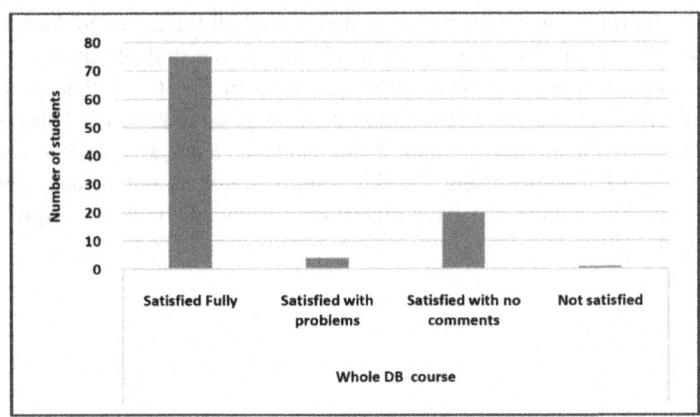

Fig. 6. Students satisfaction of this course being digitized using a systematic instruction design technique.

opportunities, Organizational structure, operations, culture, diversity, nationality should be handled appropriately and adapt to them. And learning on digital platform helps to handle issues like cultural diversity and bring about equal opportunity. Since the organization has moved to Big data products and we can gear up the employees with this database design change. And the organization has skilled employees who can design and develop big data products easily.

5   Conclusion

The learning model for Database designed, which helps in teaching DB design in a structured and integrated way to nurture professionalism in all learners using the digital platform. This kind of system helps in bringing equal opportunities and other social skills essential for the learners to use them at their workplace. It also helps the organization when there is a change in nature of organization migrating from one technology to a new technology. A Blended learning may be used to achieve better results reducing the learning gaps in teaching Database course which plays an important part in IT organizations.

References

1. Judith, H., Kevin, K., Kevin, K.: The Changing Nature of Organizations Work and Workplace. https://www.wbdg.org/resources/changing-natureorganizations-work-and-workplace
2. Dickson, K., Kaider, M.: Designing, developing and delivering work-integrated learning to large student cohorts. In: Proceedings of 2012 Australian Collaborative Education Network National Conference, pp. 61–67. Deakin University, Geelong (2012)

3. Smith, J., Meijer, G., Kielly-Coleman, N.: Assurance of learning: the role of work-integrated learning and industry partners. In: Campbell, M. (ed.) Work-Integrated Learning: Responding to Challenges, pp. 409–419. Australian Collaborative Education Network (ACEN), Perth (2010)
4. Harvey, S.: Building effective blended learning programs. Issue Educ. Tech. **43**(6), 51–54 (2003)
5. Vatika, S., Meenu, D.: SQL and NoSQL databases. Int. J. Adv. Res. Comput. Sci. Softw. Eng. **2**(8), 20–27 (2012)
6. Amir, G., Murtaza, H.: Beyond the hype: big data concepts, methods and analytics. Int. J. Inf. Manage. **35**(2), 137–144 (2015)
7. Paul, J.W., Elizabeth, S., John, V.C.: Using scientific data to teach a database systems course. ACM SIGCSE **35**(1), 224–228 (2003)
8. Guimaraes, M.A.M.: Experience teaching an introduction to DBMS. ACM SIGCSE **31**(4), 48–49 (1999)
9. James, Z.W., Tim, D., Mike, W., Pradip, K.S.: Work in progress - MeTube: a novel way to teach database to undergraduates. In: IEEE International Conference on Frontiers in Education Conference, pp. 685–686 (2009)
10. Scott, W.: Agile/Evolutionary Data Modeling: From Domain Modeling to Physical Modeling. http://agiledata.org/essays/agileDataModeling.html

Study of Various Classifiers
for Identification and Classification
of Non-functional Requirements

László Tóth[1] and László Vidács[1,2(✉)]

[1] Department of Software Engineering, University of Szeged, Szeged, Hungary
{premissa,lac}@inf.u-szeged.hu
[2] MTA-SZTE Research Group of Artificial Intelligence, University of Szeged,
Szeged, Hungary

Abstract. Identification of non-functional requirements in an early phase of software development process is crucial for creating a proper software design. These requirements are often neglected or given in too general forms. However, interviews and other sources of requirements often include important references also to non-functional requirements which are embedded in a bigger textual context. The non-functional requirements have to be extracted from these contexts and should be presented in a formulated and standardized way to support software design. The set of requirements extracted from their textual context have to be classified to formalize them. This task is to be accomplished manually but it can be very demanding and error-prone. Several attempts have been made to support identification and classification tasks using supervised and semi-supervised learning processes. These efforts have achieved remarkable results. Researchers were mainly focused on the performance of classification measured by precision and recall. However, creating a tool which can support business analysts with their requirements elicitation tasks, execution time is also an important factor which has to be taken into account. Knowing the performance and the results of benchmarks can help business analysts to choose a proper method for their classification tasks. Our study presented in this article focuses on both the comparison of performances of the classification processes and their execution time to support the choice among the methods.

Keywords: Non-functional requirements · Requirements elicitation
Classification · Natural language processing

1 Introduction

Non-functional requirements (NFRs) are crucial factors for software design [1]. The lack of a well structured set of non-functional requirements can lead to an inappropriate software design and the failure of the specific project. Security aspects are also a critical part of the software design process which is one of

© Springer International Publishing AG, part of Springer Nature 2018
O. Gervasi et al. (Eds.): ICCSA 2018, LNCS 10964, pp. 492–503, 2018.
https://doi.org/10.1007/978-3-319-95174-4_39

the emphasized concern of the software development these days. These aspects cannot be reviewed completely without security related non-functional requirements. In practice, many NFRs are out of the analysis and even those which are included in specifications are poorly engineered. Incomplete or ambiguous specifications can lead the system into unspecified state [2].

Requirements are originated from memos of interviews and other textual sources like regulations, laws or reports. Regulations and laws are well-structured documents but their structure reflects only the business viewpoints. Memos created during interviews, on the other hand, are very often unstructured or semistructured. Requirements are embedded into these textual contexts and their extraction and classification are ones of the most important duty of business analysts. Identifying and classifying non-functional requirements from this collection of different documents can be demanding and error-prone. Several investigations have been accomplished with remarkable results to support the identification and classification process using natural language processing and machine learning methods [3,4]. Some researchers investigated the use of ontologies which have been created on standards' basis [5,6]. Some researchers like Lu and Liang [7] or Abad et al. [8] utilized supervised learning methods, others utilized semisupervised learning techniques such as Expectation Maximization strategy [9]. Abad et al. applied also clustering techniques to identify the best method for processing requirements sentences. These studies have shown that machine learning processes can be utilized successfully also for requirements engineering if their inputs are prepared for this purpose appropriately. A common representation of the texts containing requirements is the tf-idf model which formulates a sparse matrix containing the measure of the importance of the given word in a given text.

Semi-supervised methods can give better results if there are not enough labeled examples for learning as shown by Casamayor et al. [9]. This is a common issue in requirements engineering that labeled examples can be obtainable with difficulty especially in case of some specific domain. Ontology-based methods can cope with also this issue.

We have compared the performance of classification methods of sklearn library [10] with each other and also with the results of former studies like [7,9] as we will present it in this article later. Because of our experiments are based on sklearn the results of these experiments can show the difference of the performance of different implementation comparing them with the results of former researches. This difference suggests that experiments can be only reproduced if also the implementation of algorithms and methods are the same. Next to the comparison mentioned above, we have measured also the execution time which provides another important factor for business analysts to choose an appropriate classification method for their specific classification tasks.

The main contribution of our work is a broad comparison of processes implemented in sklearn regarding their performance and the execution time. This information together can support a better choice among the tools for requirement classification process. The outcomes of our experiments have also confirmed the results of former researches [7–9].

The paper is organized as follows. The next section introduces our approach and analysis model. In Sect. 3 we introduce the dataset of non-functional requirements and outline the addressed problem. Section 4 provides results of our analysis produced by various classifiers and compares closely related work. The related literature briefly presented in Sect. 5 and we conclude the paper in Sect. 6.

2 Background

The source of requirements are memos of different interviews and regulations, laws and standards. These documents contain texts written in natural languages. In order to these texts be capable of classification they have to be preprocessed. During the preprocessing, texts are transformed into another representation. The most common representation is the tf-idf model which is a measure of the importance of a given word in a given text. The measure of tf-idf is formulated as:

$$tfidf(t, d, D) = tf(t, d) * idf(t, D)$$

where t denotes terms (words in our case), d denotes the document (sentence in our case) and D denotes the collection of documents (the set of sentences in our case). The tf(t, d) is the term frequency in a given document. The idf (inverse document frequency) is formulated as:

$$idf(t, D) = log\frac{|D|}{1 + |\{d \in D : t \in d\}|}$$

Statistical methods often use the bag of words model in which a text or a sentence is represented as the multiset of its words disregarding grammar or modality of the given sentence. In order to these model can be applied sentences have to be preprocessed appropriately. Punctuation characters, stop words are to be removed and words of the sentences are to be stemmed. The most commonly used method for this purpose is the Porter Stemmer. However, using these models some important information will vanish as mentioned above.

Classification of textual information can be performed using classifiers designed for multiclasses and binary classifiers can also be used following the one-versus-all strategy. In this case, classes are classified iteratively, only one class is selected in each step which gets label one, others get label zero. The cumulative result is that class, which produces the highest probability for the given example.

For evaluation, we have used precision and recall. The precision is formulated as:

$$Precision = \frac{tp}{tp + fp}$$

where tp is the true positive which is the number of correct positive classification, fp denotes the false positive which is the case when classifier accepts the example but it has to be rejected. This is called Type I error.

Recall can be formulated as:

$$Recall = \frac{tn}{tn + fn}$$

where tn denotes true negative which is a correct negative classification and fn denotes the false negative which is the case when classifier rejects the example but it has to be accepted. This is called Type II error.

We have used the average of these values to compare the classifiers each other.

3   Experiments

We used TERA Promise NFR dataset for our experiments [11]. This dataset was created by students of DePaul University and it was updated in 2010. This dataset contains requirements sentences of 15 projects which were classified by the students. The statistics about the classification and the related projects is shown in Table 1 and Fig. 1.

Table 1. Requirement labels in the 15 projects of the Promise NFR dataset

Requirement type		Project No															Total
		1	2	3	4	5	6	7	8	9	10	11	12	13	14	15	
Functional	(F)	20	11	47	25	36	27	15	20	16	38	0	0	0	0	0	255
Availability	(A)	1	2	2	0	2	1	0	5	1	1	2	1	1	1	1	21
Fault tolerance	(FT)	0	4	0	0	0	2	0	2	0	0	0	2	0	0	0	10
Legal	(L)	0	0	0	6	3	0	1	3	0	0	0	0	0	0	0	13
Look and feel	(LF)	1	4	0	2	3	2	0	6	0	7	2	2	4	3	2	38
Maintainability	(MN)	0	0	0	0	0	4	0	2	1	0	1	3	2	2	2	17
Operational	(O)	0	0	7	6	10	15	3	9	2	0	0	2	2	3	3	62
Performance	(PE)	2	6	2	2	4	1	2	17	4	4	3	5	0	1	1	54
Portability	(PO)	0	1	0	0	0	0	0	0	0	0	0	0	0	0	0	1
Scalability	(SC)	0	3	4	0	3	4	0	4	0	0	0	1	2	0	0	21
Security	(SE)	1	3	10	10	7	5	2	15	0	1	3	3	2	2	2	66
Usability	(US)	3	6	8	4	5	13	0	10	0	2	2	3	6	4	1	67
Total NFRs		8	29	33	30	37	47	8	73	8	15	13	22	19	16	12	370
Functional		20	11	47	25	36	27	15	20	16	38	0	0	0	0	0	255
Total requirements		28	40	80	55	73	74	23	93	24	53	13	22	19	16	12	625

Regarding class of Portability, the dataset contains only one example so we had removed that example before our experiments were executed.

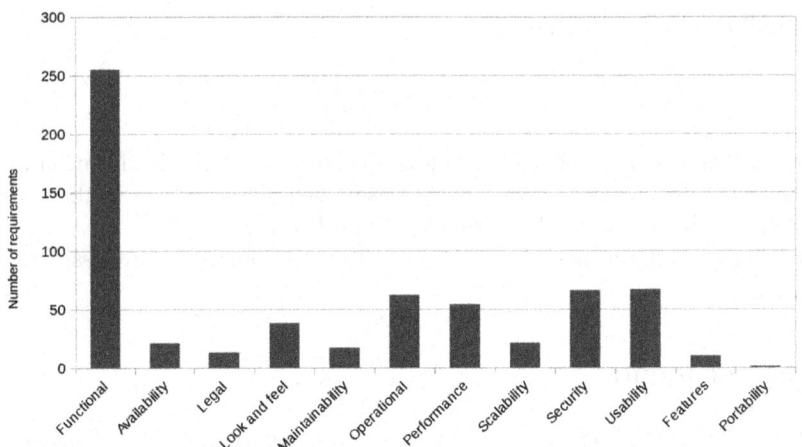

Fig. 1. Requirements classification process

In order to perform classification dataset had been preprocessed: punctuation characters and stop words were removed and the remaining words were stemmed using Porter Stemmer process. The preprocessed dataset was then transformed to tf-idf representation.

We accomplished classification processes using algorithms implemented in sklearn [10] and compared the results each other and the results obtained by Cassamayor et al. in their experiments [9]. The goal of our experiments was determining the best algorithm of classification implemented in sklearn for requirements classification tasks considering precision, recall and F-score, complemented by execution time. For our experiments, we selected those classifiers which had implemented one-vs-all strategy and/or were inherently capable of handling multiclasses. We selected Multinomial-, Gaussian- and Bernoulli Naive Bayes classifiers and also Support Vector Machine with linear kernel, Linear Logistic Regression, Label Propagation, Label Spreading, Decision Tree, Extra Tree, Extra Trees as an ensemble method, K-Nearest Neighbour and Multi Layer Perceptron methods were selected. The selection process was also influenced by classifiers' resource requirements.

The experiments were executed using repeated K-Fold cross-validation method. Both the number of groups and the repetition number were set to 10. Precision, recall and F-measure were calculated both for each test and each class by the corresponding sklearn function and the results were averaged for each classifier. Averaged variance was calculated as well and also the F-score value was computed for every classifier using the averaged precision and recall because the averaged F-score measure does not hold any useful information.

4 Results

In Table 2 the measured average Precision, Recall, F-score is represented such as
their averaged variance. As mentioned in the previous chapter average F-score
does not hold valuable information so F-score was computed using the following
formula:

$$F\text{-}measure = 2 * \frac{Precision * Recall}{Precision + Recall}$$

The average of precision, recall and F-measure values are illustrated in Fig. 3.
The calculated F-measures are plotted in Fig. 2. For comparison purpose, the
results are illustrated using line diagrams. The averaged results and variance
can be studied using Fig. 4.

Table 2. Precision, recall and F-measure of classifiers

Classifier	Average			Comp		Variance	
	P	R	F	F	P	R	F
BernoulliNB	0.43	0.22	0.25	0.29	0.18	0.09	0.06
DT	0.66	0.64	0.62	0.65	0.01	0.03	0.01
ET	0.63	0.62	0.59	0.62	0.01	0.04	0.02
ETs	0.63	0.63	0.59	0.63	0.01	0.04	0.02
GNB	0.72	0.69	0.67	0.70	0.02	0.02	0.02
KNeighbours	0.71	0.52	0.55	0.60	0.08	0.07	0.05
LabelPropagation	0.70	0.68	0.65	0.69	0.02	0.03	0.02
LabelSpread	0.70	0.67	0.65	0.68	0.02	0.03	0.02
Logistic	0.87	0.67	0.72	0.76	0.01	0.05	0.03
MLP	0.38	0.66	0.36	0.48	0.01	0.03	0.01
MultinomialNB	0.84	0.68	0.72	0.75	0.02	0.03	0.02
SVM	0.89	0.65	0.71	0.75	0.01	0.05	0.02

As the results of our experiments present, regarding precision the Multinomial Naive Bayes Classifier, Support Vector Machine with linear kernel and
Linear Logistic Regression has produced the best values. Naive Bayes Classifier was found also in former researches as the best classifier for classification
of requirement sentences comparing it other classifiers such as tf-idf classifier
[9], k-Nearest Neighbour [8,9], Bittern Topic Model (BTM) or Latent Dirichlet
Allocation (LDA) [8]. Lu and Liang have found SVM classifier has performed
best in their research [7].

Analysing the results can be seen that the average precision of other methods
is lower and the worst result was produced by Multilayer Perceptron model. This
outcome could be misleading because both the early stopping was enabled for
that process and the number of layers was reduced for performance purpose.
Therefore the usability of that model for requirements classification needs to

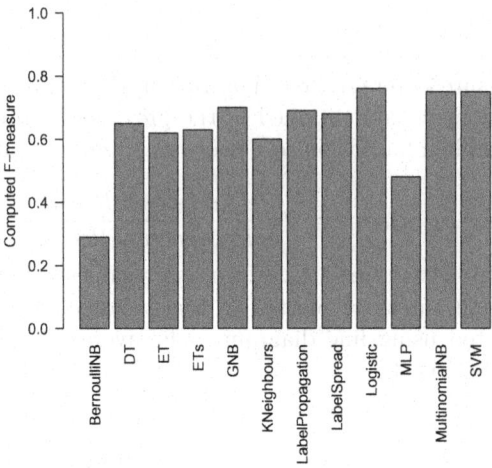

Fig. 2. Computed F-measures of the classifiers

be checked thoroughly. Another classifier which produced weak precision results is the Bernoulli Naive Bayes. This classifier binarizes the feature vector before performs the classification process because its algorithm works on feature vector containing boolean values. Using tf-idf representation this approach has been proved wrong for classification requirement sentences.

Recall is well balanced among the classifiers as shown in Fig. 3. The two exceptions are Bernoulli Naive Bayes and MLP classifiers which have produced also weak precision values.

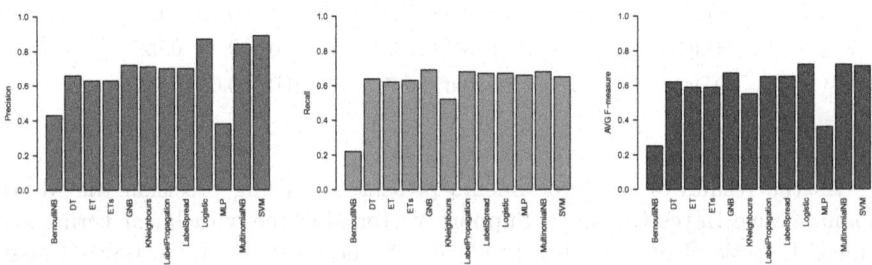

Fig. 3. Average precision, recall and F-measure

The average variance of precision is low (under 5%) in case of the most classifiers except the two mentioned cases. The variance in case of K-Nearest Neighbours is a bit higher (7%) but its performance is also lower than others'.

The size of the training dataset is small, only 625 examples are presented in NFR database. These data are labeled using 12 classes. We have removed the only portability example but the remaining dataset has contained also small

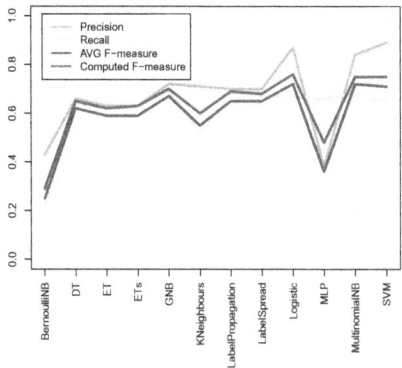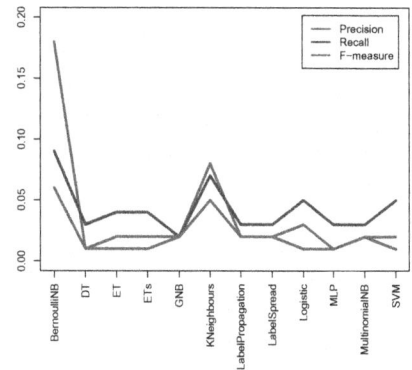

Fig. 4. Classification precision, recall and F-measures (left hand side) and variance statistics (right hand side)

classes as shown in Table 1. Therefore the results presented in this paper are to be validated using a bigger labeled dataset.

As mentioned above the best classifiers identified by our experiences are similar to those that other research has already demonstrated. To choose the best classifier in practice the execution time is to be considered as well. Table 3 and Fig. 5 represents the execution time of classifiers used in our experiments. These values represent the whole execution time of the measurement using the same environment.

According to our experiments, the process based on Multinomial Naive Bayes has produced the best execution time. Based on the precision, recall and the

Table 3. Execution time of classifiers

Classifier	Execution time (s)
BernoulliNB	40.12
DT	455.16
ET	30.80
ETs	284.51
GNB	52.37
KNeighbours	274.66
LabelPropagation	120.67
LabelSpread	150.41
Logistic	353.51
MLP	455.82
MultinomialNB	21.61
SVM	343.68

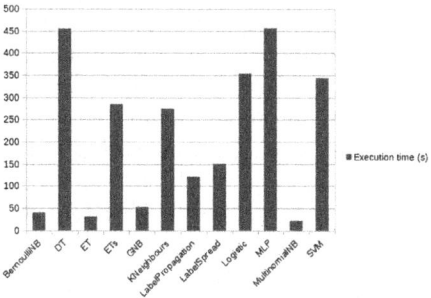

Fig. 5. Execution time of classifiers

execution time the Multinomial Naive Bayes classifier is the best choice in practice for classification of requirement sentences. As mentioned above this classifier was identified as the best based on its performance by some former research [8,9] comparing with some other methods. Our research has complemented the comparison with other popular classifiers implemented by sklearn library. However, classifiers like Logistic Regression or Support Vector Machine has performed a little bit better regarding to their precision and recall but considering the execution time, Multinomial Naive Bayes classifier can be denoted as the best choice for practice.

5   Related Work

The problem of processing requirements documents using natural language processing and machine learning methods has been a research topic for decades [3]. Although non-functional requirements are less dependent on the application domain, it is not a trivial problem to set up a general list of NFR types. The types identified in the literature are widespread, for example Chung et al. [12] identified 156 NFR categories, while Mairiza et al. [13] separated 114 different NFR classes in their work, on the contrary to the 6 high-level categories defined by the ISO standard.

A fundamental study of NFR classification is published relatively lately in 2006 by Cleland et al. [14]. They used 14 NFR categories separated from functional requirements. More than 600 requirements from 15 projects were collected and manually categorized to train and test their categorization methods. Although this is still a valuable dataset today, the requirements were originated from university student projects, not from requirements documents of a production system. Cleland et al. achieved high recall with the tradeoff of really low precision. This experiment was reproduced by several researchers in the past [15,16]. Casamayor et al. [16] employed multinomial naive Bayes classifier coupled with an Expectation Maximization algorithm. Although they improved the precision, the replication of the original study was partial only.

Requirements traceability is a related field, where NLP and information retrieval techniques are frequently applied [17–19]. Hindle et al. [20] used topic modeling to link NFRs to topics found in commit messages. Falessi et al. [21] conducted a large-scale experiment with various NLP techniques including different algebraic models, term weightings and similarity metrics in order to detect identical non-functional requirements.

Sharma et al. [22] addressed the NFR extraction problem with a rule based approach. They implemented a framework for NFR analysis including a DSL language. Sawyer et al. have focused on document archaeology and created an NLP based tool called REVERE to support business analysts in the investigation of different documents containing requirements [23]. This tool has utilized some standard NLP techniques like part-of-speech tagging or semantic tagging and determination of modality.

Denger et al. examined the ambiguity of requirements sentences and investigated the use of language patterns for rewriting these requirements into less ambiguous sentences [24]. The ambiguity of requirements is one of the most prominent issues in requirements engineering which has to be resolved as pointed by Firesmith in his paper [2]. From the perspective of mining software repositories, Paixao et al. [25] investigated the relationship between build results obtained from continuous integration tools with non-functional requirements.

6   Conclusions

Software design and implementation need collected and classified requirements. One of the most important tasks of business analysts is to collect and classify these requirements during elicitation process. The classification process can be a demanding and error-prone task in case of a vast amount of sources. Experiments were conducted to identify appropriate machine learning methods can be used for requirement classification task to support business analysts in their elicitation process. We have compared methods implemented in sklearn library regarding their precision and recall value and also completed this comparison with execution time. As the results of our experiments show the best choice for practice is the Multinomial Naive Bayes classifier. This method has produced very good precision and recall values and the execution time is far the best compared with other processes. This outcome also supports the results of the former researches. We have used the PROMISE dataset which is a small database containing labeled examples. Because of the classification processes depend on strongly the number of learning examples validation have to be performed using a bigger database. Since labeled examples cannot be obtained freely semi-supervised learning methods and also ontology-based methods can be considered. Using topics of Internet forums sentences can be extracted and classified by their topics. This method can produce examples which can be utilized for the learning process of classifiers.

The goal of our future work is to augment the learning examples using sentences extracted from professional topics of the Internet and to find other methods for improving the performance of classifiers.

Acknowledgements. The project has been supported by the European Union, cofinanced by the European Social Fund (EFOP-3.6.3-VEKOP-16-2017-00002).

References

1. Glinz, M.: On non-functional requirements. In: 15th IEEE International Requirements Engineering Conference (RE 2007), pp. 21–26. IEEE, October 2007
2. Firesmith, D.: Common requirements problems, their negative consequences, and the industry best practices to help solve them. J. Object Technol. **6**(1), 17–33 (2007)
3. Ambriola, V., Gervasi, V.: Processing natural language requirements. In: Proceedings 12th IEEE International Conference Automated Software Engineering, pp. 36–45. IEEE Computer Society (1997)
4. Li, Y., Guzman, E., Tsiamoura, K., Schneider, F., Bruegge, B.: Automated requirements extraction for scientific software. Procedia Comput. Sci. **51**, 582–591 (2015)

5. Rashwan, A., Ormandjieva, O., Witte, R.: Ontology-based classification of non-functional requirements in software specifications: a new corpus and SVM-based classifier. In: 2013 IEEE 37th Annual Computer Software and Applications Conference, pp. 381–386. IEEE, July 2013

6. Al Balushi, T.H., Sampaio, P.R.F., Dabhi, D., Loucopoulos, P.: ElicitO: a quality ontology-guided NFR elicitation tool. In: Sawyer, P., Paech, B., Heymans, P. (eds.) REFSQ 2007. LNCS, vol. 4542, pp. 306–319. Springer, Heidelberg (2007). https://doi.org/10.1007/978-3-540-73031-6_23

7. Lu, M., Liang, P.: Automatic classification of non-functional requirements from augmented app user reviews. In: Proceedings of the 21st International Conference on Evaluation and Assessment in Software Engineering - EASE 2017, pp. 344–353. ACM Press, New York (2017)

8. Abad, Z.S.H., Karras, O., Ghazi, P., Glinz, M., Ruhe, G., Schneider, K.: What works better? A study of classifying requirements. In: Proceedings - 2017 IEEE 25th International Requirements Engineering Conference, RE 2017, pp. 496–501, July 2017

9. Casamayor, A., Godoy, D., Campo, M.: Identification of non-functional requirements in textual specifications: a semi-supervised learning approach. Inf. Softw. Technol. 52(4), 436–445 (2010)

10. Pedregosa, F., Varoquaux, G., Gramfort, A., Michel, V., Thirion, B., Grisel, O., Blondel, M., Prettenhofer, P., Weiss, R., Dubourg, V., Vanderplas, J., Passos, A., Cournapeau, D., Brucher, M., Perrot, M., Duchesnay, E.: Scikit-learn: machine learning in Python. J. Mach. Learn. Res. 12, 2825–2830 (2011)

11. Menzies, T., Caglayan, B., Kocaguneli, E., Krall, J., Peters, F., Turhan, B.: The promise repository of empirical software engineering data (2012)

12. Chung, L., Nixon, B.A., Yu, E., Mylopoulos, J.: Non-Functional Requirements in Software Engineering. Kluwer Academic Publishers, Boston/Dordrecht/London (2000)

13. Mairiza, D., Zowghi, D., Nurmuliani, N.: An investigation into the notion of non-functional requirements. In: Proceedings of the 2010 ACM Symposium on Applied Computing - SAC 2010, p. 311. ACM Press (2010)

14. Cleland-Huang, J., Settimi, R., Zou, X., Solc, P.: Automated classification of non-functional requirements. Requir. Eng. 12(2), 103–120 (2007)

15. Slankas, J., Williams, L.: Automated extraction of non-functional requirements in available documentation. In: 2013 1st International Workshop on Natural Language Analysis in Software Engineering (NaturaLiSE), pp. 9–16. IEEE, May 2013

16. Casamayor, A., Godoy, D., Campo, M.: Functional grouping of natural language requirements for assistance in architectural software design. Knowl.-Based Syst. 30, 78–86 (2012)

17. Zou, X., Settimi, R., Cleland-Huang, J.: Improving automated requirements trace retrieval: a study of term-based enhancement methods. Empir. Softw. Eng. 15(2), 119–146 (2010)

18. Mahmoud, A.: An information theoretic approach for extracting and tracing non-functional requirements. In: 2015 IEEE 23rd International Requirements Engineering Conference (RE), pp. 36–45. IEEE, August 2015

19. Mahmoud, A., Williams, G.: Detecting, classifying, and tracing non-functional software requirements. Requir. Eng. 21(3), 357–381 (2016)

20. Hindle, A., Ernst, N.A., Godfrey, M.W., Mylopoulos, J.: Automated topic naming. Empir. Softw. Eng. 18(6), 1125–1155 (2013)

21. Falessi, D., Cantone, G., Canfora, G.: A comprehensive characterization of NLP techniques for identifying equivalent requirements. In: Proceedings of the 2010 ACM-IEEE International Symposium on Empirical Software Engineering and Measurement - ESEM 2010, p. 1. ACM Press (2010)
22. Sharma, V.S., Ramnani, R.R., Sengupta, S.: A framework for identifying and analyzing non-functional requirements from text categories and subject descriptors. In: Proceedings of the 4th International Workshop on Twin Peaks of Requirements and Architecture, pp. 1–8. ACM Press, New York (2014)
23. Sawyer, P., Rayson, P., Garside, R.: REVERE: support for requirements synthesis from documents. Inf. Syst. Front. **4**(3), 343–353 (2002)
24. Denger, C., Berry, D.M., Kamsties, E.: Higher quality requirements specifications through natural language patterns. In: Proceedings - IEEE International Conference on Software- Science, Technology and Engineering, SwSTE 2003, pp. 80–90. IEEE Computer Society (2003)
25. Paixao, K.V., Felicio, C.Z., Delfim, F.M., Maia, M.D.A.: On the interplay between non-functional requirements and builds on continuous integration. In: IEEE International Working Conference on Mining Software Repositories, pp. 479–482. IEEE, May 2017

Workshop Smart Factory Convergence (SFC 2018)

A Hybrid Rule-Based and Fuzzy Logic Model to Diagnostic Financial Area for MSMEs

Germán Méndez Giraldo[1] ⓘ, Eduyn López-Santana[1](✉) ⓘ,
and Carlos Franco[2] ⓘ

[1] Universidad Distrital Francisco José de Caldas, Bogota, Colombia
{gmendez, erlopezs}@udistrital.edu.co
[2] Universidad del Rosario, Bogota, Colombia
carlosa.franco@urosario.edu.co

Abstract. The importance of the micro, small and medium enterprises (MSMEs) in the regional and global economy causes the academic community to worry about its development and growth that is why several institutions publics and privates have advanced studies about problems of these organizations. We present a diagnostic model based on Rules which works together with the fuzzy logic. Our model allows to determine the possible diseases that suffer in financial matters as well as to determine their gravity and to offer alternative solutions.

Keywords: MSME · Financial diagnostics · Fuzzy logic · Rule based system

1 Introduction

The productivity growth of the micro, small and medium enterprises (MSME) sector is not only relevant but crucial in creating employment and development in the Latin-American region. For example, the importance given in each country according to [1] is similar: MSME represent 99.4% of all companies for the case of Argentina, 100% for Bolivia, Chile with 99.9%, 99.9% in Colombia, 98.2% in Costa Rica, 99.9% in El Salvador, Guatemala with 98.6%, in Mexico 99.7%, for Panama, 97.1%, and for Venezuela with 93.6%. In contrast and as a complement to the figure for the Big companies represent 0.6% in Argentina, 0.9% in Chile, Colombia 0.1% and El Salvador with 1%, 8% for Costa Rica, 1.4% for Guatemala, 0.3%, Mexico with 2.9%, 6.4% in Panama and 6.4% for Venezuela. In Colombia it can be stated that the microenterprises existing for 2008 were 596.100 and that they represent 91.9% of all economic units; The small ones of 21,249 with a participation of 6.2%; The medians of 5.365 were 1.5% of all units and finally large companies with 6.083 giving a 0.5% sharing, [2].

In the last census conducted by the National Administrative Department of Statistics (in Spanish DANE) of Colombia in 2005, it indicated that of the 1.442.117 reported establishments, 1.389.698 were MSMEs, i.e., 96.4% and of these 1.336.051 were micro enterprises, 92.6%. These figures alone show the relative importance of these business units for the economic life of the country. Added to this, in the same study it was shown how 80.8% of the personnel employed were given in the MSMEs and in detail it was

© Springer International Publishing AG, part of Springer Nature 2018
O. Gervasi et al. (Eds.): ICCSA 2018, LNCS 10964, pp. 507–519, 2018.
https://doi.org/10.1007/978-3-319-95174-4_40

established that 50.3% corresponded to micro enterprises and 30.5% to small and medium enterprises [3]. These arguments are more than enough to show its importance for the economy but also for way to have a system of full employment.

The main difficulty faced by MSMEs is its short duration and high mortality rate [3], as well as the general insecurity in the country because of the acute internal conflict. In addition, they are affected by three problems: Instability in the rules of the game for private economic activity, corruption in public administration, and limitations of the judicial system. Finally, other obstacles are the restoration of macroeconomic stability, the scarcity and cost of credit, the poor development of the capital market, and the need for more innovation [4], all that indicate that 47.5% of the entrepreneurs were affected by smuggling, and 67.2% suffered by the increase in interest rates.

The main financial problems of the MSMEs originate in the sociocultural and educational level of the owners, because of the reluctant attitude of change of the owners; the companies develop their activities with nonexistent or inadequate management systems. For example, some organizations apply certain financial management strategies that are not compatible with an adequate monitoring and timely correction processes [5]. The lack of follow-up of the financial statements is reflected in the type of immediate decisions without thinking about future projections. This can be reflected in that more than 60% of MSMEs rely on debt funds for their long-term financial needs [6].

The remainder of this paper is organized as follows. Section 2 presents a brief description of the diagnosis of MSMEs. Section 3 introduces the fuzzy logic and rule-based systems. Section 4 describes of proposed model. Section 5 presents some results. Finally, some conclusions are presented in Sect. 6 with future lines of research.

2   Diagnosis of MSME

It was found that in the field of MSMEs there are different difficulties that not only affect them in Colombia but also in the rest of Latin America, and they are recurrent at a global level too. An external factor affecting the financial environment of MSMEs is the difficult access to financing, especially for new entrepreneurs [7]. Consequently, financial institutions will not have special interest in the study of credit applications of newly created small companies, given the high cost that it entails, against an uncertain profitability since it is difficult to qualify credit to the potential client.

We want to review the financial management inside the company to detect that problems in the management of the capital make access difficult to the credit as the banks are fixed in the financial and accounting statements [8, 9] and if they are not correctly presented, banks will have no interest in offering the credit. This management should balance the standardization of the financial planning and control processes, it is necessary to standardize the parameters for long and short-term decision making, additionally it is required the use of financial prediction models, avoiding the error of applying techniques designed in contexts different from those that were designed [10].

All the financial information that is required should be in line with the business reality and is that most studies focus on the detection of obstacles for financing rather than analyzing the internal conditions of the MSMEs, for example, in terms of their management [5].

In the Colombian context, the difficulty of accessing long-term resources (own self or of others) that allow them to finance their investment projects, especially due to the segmentation of credit markets that provoke discrimination towards MSMEs. Banks apply differentials rates of interest on loans according to company size, harming the smallest. It adds to poor business management and poor information systems that provide unreliable information for obtaining new capital [11].

The risk aversion of new entrepreneurs is also evident. They opt for a relatively high initial investment in fixed assets, although the initial costs are higher and only continue to invest in assets based on the operating result of the company, without considering increasing their capital with contributions from new partners [12].

In general, in organizations and especially MSMEs must answer two general financial questions: what investments should the company make? And, how are these investments paid? What is generally observed is that these firms have little assets to do business and cannot access credits due to do not have real sources of guarantee for the loan application. Other MSMEs have management problems such as conflict of interests between shareholders and managers, inadequate levels of inventories or failures in the administration of credit sales [13], managers with little financial preparation in accounting and finance, nonexistent or weakly trained staff that provide inadequate results, absence of financial and accounting information and some incorrect practices with depreciation methods chosen in a "rudimentary" manner or incorrect valuation of assets [14], ignorance of the macroeconomic effects, especially of devaluation and inflation, [15].

From the previous work developed by the Expert Systems and Simulation Research Group (SES) [16], it was possible to define a set of causes and sub causes of the malfunction of the finance area for the MSMEs, these can be summarized in Table 1.

3 Background of Fuzzy Logic and Ruled-Based Systems

3.1 Fuzzy Logic

The fuzzy logic in contrast of classical logic, in which a proposition only admits two values: true or false; It does allow us to approach the way in which the human thinks and where the propositions can be relative [17]. These are represented by concepts such as the intervals between two values. That between the YES and the NO of a question there are also others like the probable or the perhaps. Fuzzy logic is a method to express uncertainties more consistently through fuzzy sets: instead of simply belonging or not belonging, an element may have different degrees of relevance for a set. Fuzzy sets are functions that assign, on a scale of zero to one, this relevance of an element to the set [18].

Some applications have been to identify and evaluate the financial risk of the projects in the case of the duration of the projects due to changes in their times of the execution, these two factors modeled by fuzzy logic allowed to conclude that the project risk depends on the values of activities execution and at the same, time of the duration of their implementation [19]. Another case is developed to recommend to investors about long-term decisions, which measures the decision-maker's aversion given by the investor's age, [20].

Finally, fuzzy logic has been applied to conventional methods of evaluating projects that have been sensitized with the introduction of fuzzy numbers to characterize the behavior of interest rates in such a way that they generate indicators such as net present value (NPV) or the internal rate of return (IRR) of fuzzy characteristics for the evaluation of aquaculture projects, [21].

Table 1. Diagnosis of the financial area of the MSMEs

Diagnosis	Causes	Sub causes
1. The financial market restricts loans to MSMEs, their difficulties are due to mismanagement, inefficient traditional policies, strategic failures, lack of plans and budgets, etc. 2. Poor perception of the sources of financing on the willingness and ability to pay. 3. Market conditions have changed, you cannot increase prices in the same way as costs and expenses and if you do deteriorate the quality of your products. 4. If liquidity is increased, it is possible to improve the activities of the other functional areas to generate more resources and improve their behavior. 5. To exaggerate the use of external financing, they cause collapses in the resources destined to the functional areas. 6. Excessive taxes limit the liquidity of the MSMEs should seek fiscal support from the government.	External Financing	Backup guarantees Debt Level Interest rates
	Liquidity	Profitability External financing Management and control of budgets Reinvestment of profits Rotation of portfolio Internal financing Inventory turnover
	Budget Management and Control	Entrepreneur Profile Validity of Financial Reporting
	Profitability	Level of sales Collections Taxes Costs and expenses Sale price
	Working Capital	Production costs Availability
	Reinvestment Utilities	Percentage of dividends Entrepreneur Profile Profitability
	Inventory turnover	Production Management Market management
	Portfolio Rotation	Credit Policies Collection management

3.2   Rules Based Systems

Gutiérrez [22] defines the rule-based systems (RBS) as one of the methodologies used in expert systems where its use makes the developed system behave as human expert in a knowledge domain, allowing it to make delicate decisions. In these systems, the knowledge base from which it is composed contains the variables and the set of rules that define the problem, and the inference engine which can infer conclusions by applying methods of classical logic [22].

Expert rules-based systems act on two very important elements: data and the knowledge base. The first refer to the evidences, facts or realities known in each situation. The second one is formed by the relationships that exist between a set of objects (data) and which can be represented by a set of rules. The knowledge stored in the knowledge base is of a permanent and static nature, which means that it does not change from one application to another, except that learning elements that are incorporated into the expert system, [23, 24].

The structure of a rule is represented as "If premise, then conclusion". Both the premise and the conclusion can include multiple object - value affirmations within them. Those logical expressions that include only an object-value affirmation are called simple logical expressions; In the case of presenting more affirmations, are called compound logical expressions. Similarly, if a rule contains only simple logical expressions it is called a simple rule; otherwise, composite rule, [23].

Analyzing the learning process, RBS presents certain advantages versus machine learning, for example, RBS is easier to understand, to maintain and to incorporate knowledge domain than machine learning. Additionally, is more economical to track and correct the cause of the mistakes; however, it is more disadvantageous since it is heuristic and requires a lot of manual work than the second one, [25].

The chain of rules is one of the strategies to generate composite conclusions. It is applicable when the premises of some rules correspond to the conclusions of others. That is, facts can be used to give rise to new facts. This is repeated successively until no further conclusions can be drawn, [26]. This means that in the beginning the knowledge base, rules and some initial facts (data) are considered, then the objects are assigned their known values, later each rule of the knowledge base is executed, and new facts are concluded if possible.

Part of this assignment of values can be made by fuzzy logic where rules use the fuzzy concept and are easier to interpret and more flexible to change than the classical rules. In fact, the linguistic values are more understandable than the numerical form. Regarding the structure of these hybrid models, it must be considered that it is necessary to obtain the qualified antecedent and the consequent parts of the rules, to determine the number of rules and to optimize the rules. Also, optimized parameters should be defined for membership functions and for classification systems based on fuzzy rules, the optimized weights of each rule should be calculated [27].

4   Proposed Model

The proposed model is summarized in Fig. 1, in this it is observed how an intelligence model is used in which the Acquisition and Representation of Knowledge phase is worked from the revision of the state of the art not only with specialized literature, but also with knowledge of SES group.

In the development of the bibliographic review and according to expert studies, were stablished twenty diseases as the most relevant. These are: illiquidity; high indebtedness level; Sales of doubtful collection; low profitability; high inventory level; inefficient collection system; insufficient capital; excessive investment in fixed assets; deficient cost estimate; incorrect financial statements; wrong funding; informal loans;

excessive short-term borrowing; poor investments; bad management; bad cash flow; negative equity; canceling debt with debt; leverage financial burden; lack of own resources.

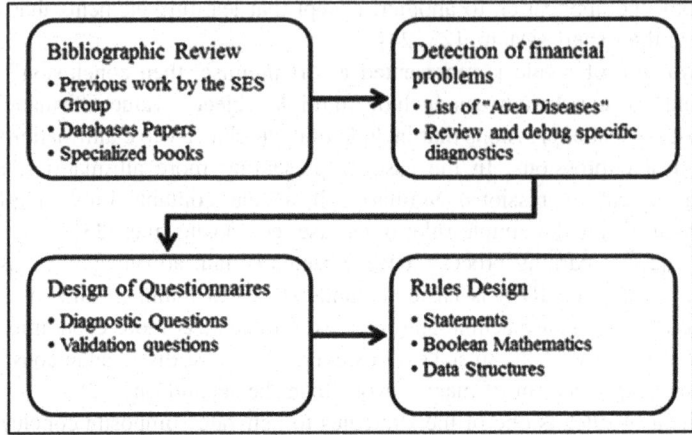

Fig. 1. Methodology used to construct the model.

Each of these diseases was valued by finding a common denominator in relation to what happens to MSMEs at the global, regional and national levels; Of all this a subgroup was formed with the three main diseases: illiquidity, high indebtedness level and insufficient capital. In Table 2, these are described and determine their main causes.

Table 2. Main Diseases of the Financial Area of the MSMEs

Disease	Description	Causes
Illiquidity	There is no enough cash flow to have sufficient guarantee of being able to pay the short-term obligations	Very high accounts receivable Low sales Not having long-term sources to finance the short term Do not match the terms of purchase with the sales Excessive long-term asset investment 6. High Inventory Levels (low rotation)
High indebtedness level	The level of debts that a company can handle depends on the policies and concrete situation of each company. However,	1. Used loans for operating expenses 2. Delayed bank payments 3. Apply for loans without proper support 4. Allocate the money to a different use than was intended

(continued)

Table 2. (*continued*)

Disease	Description	Causes
	there is a limit to that level of indebtedness, if it is very high can reach a point that has to liquidate the organization	5. Business growth based on debt 6. Decapitalization of the company by losses 7. Indiscriminate use of your credit cards 8. Not having a monthly budget of expenses
Insufficient capital	The company begins to have difficulties not only to operate but also to be able to fulfill its obligations with suppliers and banks. Moreover, even if new sources of financing are sought, they do not meet the needs of the company	1. Volume of sales insufficient in relation to the cost to achieve them 2. Excessive price reduction of sales 3. Excessive expense from bad debts 4. Increases in expenses when sales decrease 5. Excessive losses in extraordinary operations 6. Failure to obtain external sources of financing 7. Price increases 8. Poorly planned budgets

In the third stage of the proposed methodology we describe the symptoms and the questions used to evaluate the behavior of the companies, these are listed in Table 3.

Table 3. Questions associated with the main financial area diseases of the MSMEs

Disease	Symptom	Questions
Illiquidity	Delay in payroll payments, taxes, operating expenses or investment in raw material Noncompliance with suppliers Very high short-term accounts payable Frequent loan search Use the own resources to cover its obligations Use advances to cover its obligations	Do you have difficulty to pay your payroll, taxes, operating expenses or raw materials? Do your suppliers complain about the slowness of your payments? Are accounts payable high? How often do you need to make loan requests? Have you used your assets to meet the needs of the company? Do you use credits to cover debts?
High indebtedness level	Accounts payable increase Delay notifications on bank payments	In the financial statements, accounts payable show a high value? Have Banks begin a legal collection process against you?
Insufficient capital	Failure to suppliers' pay Lack of resources to meet obligations payroll and production Inability to respond monetarily to unforeseen situations No money to buy more fixed assets or invest in the long term	Do you have a good payment image with your suppliers? Do you have difficulty in canceling legal and operating obligations? Do you suffer from unforeseen changes? Do you have reserves to make investments?

Once it has the questions, sets the rules system; for this case, only shown a part, specifically for the problem of Illiquidity. The Rules set consists of different statements, see Table 4 and Fig. 2. The associated rules for the transition of the nodes in the search process are defined as:

- Antecedent conditions or propositions: The IF condition is one of the most popular in the programming language since it allows logical comparisons between a value and an expected result.
- Connectors of antecedent propositions: Once defined the antecedent proposition proceeds to determine the connector THEN its function is to link the condition with the consequence
- Condition of consequence or pattern: This is the instruction or result depending on whether the comparison is true or false.

Once the membership functions of the different statements are established, the rules of the diagnostic system are established. An example of these rules for the illiquidity case is as shown in Fig. 3.

Table 4. Definition of statements associated with the main diseases of the financial area for the MSMEs

No[a]	Statement	No	Statement
A1	You frequently apply for loans	A15	You use equity to meet the needs of the company
A2	You use loans to pay off debts	A16	You use equity to increase cash flow or pay short-term obligations
A3	You have many debts on short term	A17	You use credits to cover short-term debts
A4	You have too many difficulties to make your routine payments	A18	You use credits to capitalize on your own resources
A5	You take enough time to make your routine payments	A19	You have too many debts are short term
A6	You cover routine payments with short-term debt	C1	You have liquidity problems
A7	You have formal claims for not paying your obligations	C2	You use loans to make investments
A8	You cover your amounts of the claims with debts on short term	C3	You begin to have problems of liquidity although it still fulfils its commitments
A9	You do not fulfill paying the obligations with its suppliers	C4	You have a culture of non-payment
A10	You cover your default with short-term debts	C5	You have not liquidity problems
A11	The term that your suppliers give you to pay is very short	C6	Your liquidity is good
A12	Suppliers complain about your payment delays	C7	You use wrong your capital to solve illiquidity
A13	Your accounts payable are high in the short term	C8	You use wrong your capital to make investments
A14	You can cover short-term debts quickly	C9	You use wrong credits to make leverage

[a]The prefix A for antecedent statement and prefix C for consequent statement

The application was developed in the Microsoft Excel Software of the Windows Office package, making use of the programming language Visual Basic, which evaluates the way the company is managing its capital and if this is bringing consequences that can affect the normal development of the MSMEs. Some indicators assess the level of indebtedness, the financing of the company, the management of cash flow and financial statements, the management of investments, among others that are necessary to be able to diagnose if the company has a correct way to manage its finances, see Fig. 4.

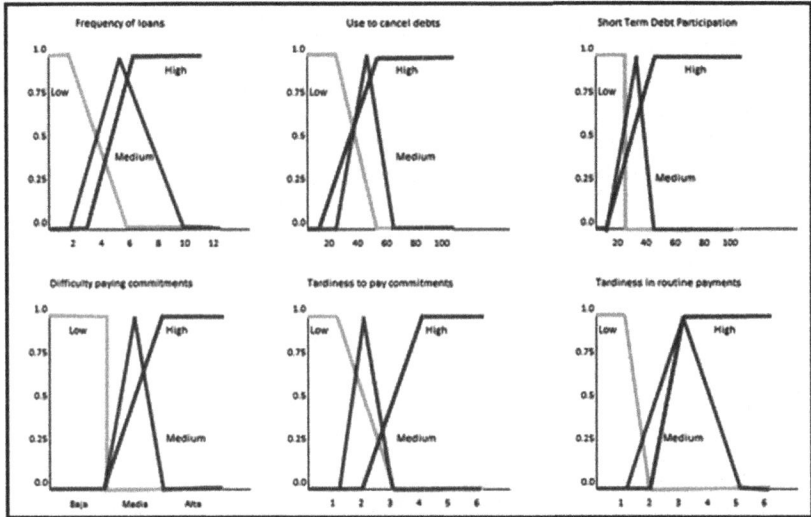

Fig. 2. Function of membership for disease statements.

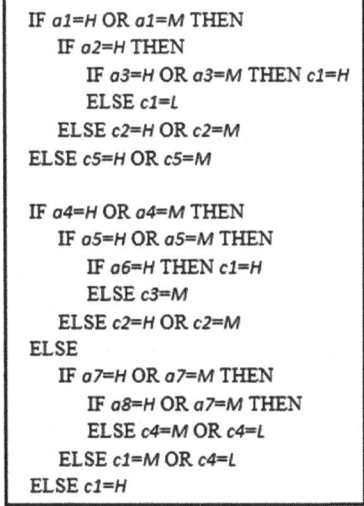

Fig. 3. Diagnostic system rules.

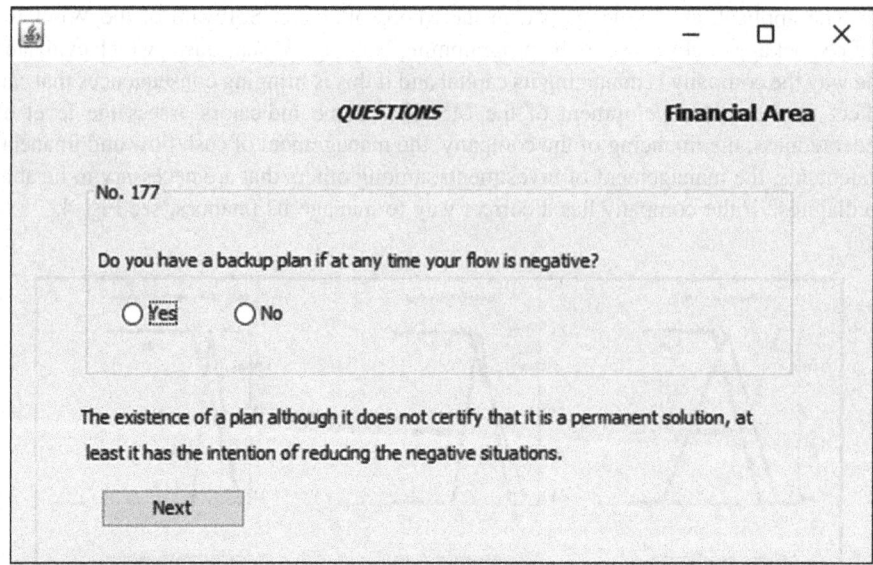

Fig. 4. Prototype of proposed diagnostic system.

5   Results

To validate the functionality of the prototype expert system, extreme cases were simulated in two scenarios. In the first the MSMEs presents all the diseases with a high criticality level. And in the second is the opposite, the company does not suffer from any disease. Finally, the model is run trying to simulate the most probable conditions,

Table 5. Definition of statements associated with the main diseases of the financial area for the MSMEs

Disease	Criticism	Explanation	Treatment
Bad sales	High	The sales presented do not cover the costs	Decrease in cost structure Modify the sale price Improve the strategy of incursion in the market
Illiquidity	Medium	Such loans may be earmarked for investments. Although it suffers to be able to fulfil its obligations, its level of liquidity is enough for the debt term not to increase significantly. The problem is not the lack of liquidity for to cover debts to ST. Could have used own resources to make investments There are liquidity problems	Lightning promotion of the lowest cost products to loyal customers who do not have those products Instant bank loan at the lowest possible interest rate External counselling Collect overdue accounts Negotiate longer terms with suppliers Avoid combining personal accounts with company accounts
High indebtedness	Not suffer		

for this, it is generated a random value for each one of the 211 questions, these results it is evident the correct operation of the application and shown the correct financial management of MSMEs. This is shown in Table 5.

6 Conclusions

The main constraints on the MSMEs are the pursuit of money. Broadly speaking these companies are affected by insufficient capital, the high level of debts they handle and by the inadequate management of money. These three major problems are divided into more specific problems. Because the success or failure of a company is determined by the decisions made and these are directly related to the available capital, the financial aspect becomes a vital element for the company and it must be strictly controlled. If there is poor management or inconsistencies in decision making, they must be identified and corrected as soon as possible.

This diagnostic model is a useful tool to determine the financial status of a company and the solutions proposed for each disease detected. This model covers an analysis from a general perspective, that is, we analyze the common aspects of financial analysis of a company of the type MSMEs, without entering analyzes by each type of business.

If a MSME does not present a problem, this does not mean that it does not require the permanent monitoring of its financial activity, because the problems and their solutions are changing. Just as knowledge in the world is being constantly updated, the knowledge base of the system also must be updated as well, to avoid that as time passes this will not become obsolete.

To be able to perfect the Model for the diagnosis of MSMEs, the inference engine must be worked in a specialized programming language such as CLIPS. Although the module developed in Excel (VBA) works correctly, at the time of expanding the knowledge base probably the ability of the model will not be the best. On the other hand, we must evaluate the quality of the diagnoses by evaluating it in companies and correcting and adjusting the rules of fuzzy logic to the real conditions.

References

1. Zevallos, E.: Panorama de las micro, pequeñas y medianas empresas (Mipymes) en varios países de América Latina. Fundes, San José, Costa Rica (2002)
2. Consejo Privado de Competitividad. Informe Nacional de competitividad 2008–2009 Compes. (2008)
3. Montoya, A., Montoya, I., Castellanos, O.: Situación de la competitividad de las Pyme en Colombia: elementos actuales y retos. Agronomía colombiana 28(1), 107–117 (2010)
4. Restrepo, D.M.: Informe nacional de competitividad 2010–2011: ruta a la prosperidad colectiva: resumen ejecutivo. Compes (2010)
5. Vera-Colina, M.A., Rodríguez-Medina, G., Melgarejo-Molina, Z.: Financial planning and access to financing in small and medium-sized companies in the Venezuelan manufacturing sector. Innovar 21(42), 99–112 (2011)
6. Kulkarni, P., Chirputkar, A.V.: Impact of SME listing on capital structure decisions. In: Proceedings Economics and Finance, vol. 11, pp. 431–444 (2014)

7. Larrán, J., García-Borgoña, A., Manso, G.: Factores determinantes del racionamiento de crédito a las pymes: un estudio empírico en Andalucía. Investigaciones Europeas de Dirección y Economía de la Empresa 16(2), 63–82 (2010)
8. Bartoli, F., Ferri, G., Murro, P., Rotondi, Z.: SME financing and the choice of lending technology in Italy: complementarity or substitutability? J. Bank. Financ. 37(12), 5476–5485 (2013)
9. Florido, J.S., Adame, M.G., Tagle, M.A.: Financial strategies, the professional development of employers and performance of SME's (Aguascalientes case). Procedia-Soc. Behav. Sci. 174, 768–775 (2015)
10. Ferrer, E.V., Campillo, J.P., Serer, G.L.: Validez de la información financiera en los procesos de insolvencia. Un estudio de la pequeña empresa española. Cuadernos de Economía y Dirección de la Empresa 16(1), 29–40 (2013)
11. Vera-Colina, M.A., Melgarejo-Molina, Z.A., Mora-Riapira, E.H.: Acceso a la financiación en Pymes colombianas: una mirada desde sus indicadores financieros. Innovar 24(53), 149–160 (2014)
12. Melgarejo, Z., Vera, M., Mora, E.: Diferencias de desempeño empresarial de pequeñas y medianas empresas clasificadas según la estructura de la propiedad del capital, caso colombiano. Suma de Negocios 5(12), 76–84 (2014)
13. Allen, F., Myers, S., Brealey, R.: Principios de finanzas corporativas. Mc Graw Hill, México (2010)
14. Soriano, M.J., Campos, M.J., Amat, O.: Introducción a la contabilidad y las finanzas: Incluye ejemplos y casos prácticos. Profit Ed (2011)
15. Gitman, L.J., Zutter, C.J., Helfert, E.A., Torres, P.R., Pelufo, E.G.: Principios de administración financiera. Pearson, Argentina (2012)
16. Hurtado, G. Parra, P.: Análisis del Área Funcional de Finanzas para la Estructuración de un Sistema Integral de Diagnóstico para la Pyme mediante Sistemas Dinámicos (tesis pregrado) Bogotá. UDFJC, Colombia (2002)
17. Aristizábal, M., Echeverri, J., Gonzalez, L.: Medición del valor Co-creado por medio de Arquetipos Sistémicos y Lógica Difusa. Politécnica 17, 47–57 (2013)
18. Azeem, M.M., Mohammad, A.A.: An analysis of applications and possibilities of neural networks (fuzzy, logic and genetic algorithm) in finance and accounting. Donnish J. Bus. Financ. Manag. Res. 1(2), 009–018 (2015). http://www.donnishjournals.org/djbfmr
19. Boloş, M.I., Sabău-Popa, D.C., Filip, P., Manolescu, A.: Development of a fuzzy logic system to identify the risk of projects financed from structural funds. Int. J. Comput. Commun. Control 10(4), 480–491 (2015)
20. Zaher, H., Mohamed, N.H.: A control system for long term investor under uncertainty based on fuzzy logic. Int. J. Comput. Appl. 118(9), 47–51 (2015)
21. Palma, M.M., Ochoa, E.A., Espinoza, E.L.M.: La Lógica Difusa para la evaluación económica y financiera de opciones cambiarias: el caso de la producción acuícola. Int. J. Inf. Syst. Softw. Eng. Big Co. (IJISEBC) 3(1), 54–73 (2016)
22. Gutiérrez, J.M.: Sistemas Expertos Basados en Reglas. Departamento de Matemática Aplicada. Universidad de Cantabria (2008)
23. Power, D.J., Sharda, R., Burstein, F.: Decision Support Systems Management Information Systems. Wiley, Hoboken (2015)
24. Martınez-Santiago, F., Cumbreras, M.A.G.: Identificación de formas lógicas en el caso del espanol: propuesta de un modelo basado en reglas y aprendizaje automático. Procesamiento del lenguaje natural 35, 245–252 (2005)

25. Chiticariu, L., Li, Y., Reiss, F.R.: Rule-based information extraction is dead! long live rule-based information extraction systems! In: EMNLP, no. October, pp. 827–832 (2013)
26. Castillo, E., Gutiérrez, M., Hadi, A.: Sistemas expertos y modelos de redes probabilísticas. Universidad de Cantabria (2008). http://computo.fismat.umich.mx/∼htejeda/gutierjm/BookCGH.pdf
27. Ishibuchi, H., Nakashima, T., Morisawa, T.: Voting in fuzzy rule-based systems for pattern classification problems. Fuzzy Sets Syst. **103**(2), 223–238 (1999)

A Novel Cloud-Fog Computing Network Architecture for Big-Data Applications in Smart Factory Environments

Dae Jun Ahn[1], Jongpil Jeong[1(✉)], and Sunpyo Lee[2]

[1] Department of Smart Factory Convergence, Sunkyunkwan University,
Suwon, Gyeonggi-do 16419, Republic of Korea
{djahn92,jpjeong}@skku.edu
[2] Department of Management of Technology,
Hoseo Graduate School of Management of Technology,
Asan, Chungcheongnam-do 31499, Republic of Korea
2017542@vision.hoseo.edu

Abstract. Research on the cloud system is increasing among the various ways to deal with the data generated by the smart factory. In this paper, we propose cloud-based fog computing network architecture that can be efficiently used to store, analyze, and utilize the accumulated data in smart factories. We build and evaluate system modeling and testbed based on the proposed architecture. As a result, the cloud developed in the OpenStack can be used for smart factory operation, analyzing various types of data, and checking the status of real-time processing through a dashboard, making it the most suitable structure for a smart factory environment require processing.

Keywords: OpenStack · Cloud computing · Cloud-fog computing
Smart factory · Big-data

1 Introduction

The need to use the cloud to store, analyze and utilize the big-data generated by a smart factories is increasing, and a cloud platform for smart factories is required. In addition, the need for fog computing is growing in order to overcome the disadvantages of cloud computing. In fog computing, services can be hosted at end devices. The infrastructure of this new distributed computing allows applications to run as close as possible to sensed actionable and massive data, coming out of people, processes and thing [1]. Accordingly, a combination of cloud computing and fog computing is required to construct an architecture for conceptual design and network configuration. At the core of the smart factory is the accumulation of Internet of Things (IoT) sensor data through various facilities and machines (M2M) communication, and big-data will be generated. The data is stored in the cloud and can be used for data analysis.

© Springer International Publishing AG, part of Springer Nature 2018
O. Gervasi et al. (Eds.): ICCSA 2018, LNCS 10964, pp. 520–530, 2018.
https://doi.org/10.1007/978-3-319-95174-4_41

In addition, cloud computing uses data stored in a data center called a cloud server, and data can be processed through faster data collection by using high speed wireless networks [2]. These problem with cloud computing, but is that it is difficult to provide increased latency and location awareness due to the non-proximity between cloud and user. A lot of cloud platforms [3,4] available for smart factories have been researched and we have studied how to configure a cloud platform for smart factories accordingly. In the development of the cloud platform, open source OpenStack will be used to provide various services [5]. Finally, the OpenStack cloud will be used to configure a virtual data repository, and a dashboard will be used to configure the cloud platform for real time monitoring. Fog computing is a new platform introduced by Cisco and extends the cloud computing paradigm to the edge of the networks [6]. Fog computing is a concept designed to solve the problem of not providing delayed response time, location intelligence in the cloud. Accordingly, the fog computing concept in the network configuration reduces the delay time and various service improvements in the cloud computing in storing the data. In addition, as IoT increases, fog computing becomes available to increase network capacity for increasing in data. If cloud computing and fog computing are used together, the latency can be reduced through the distributed effect, and the problem can be solved by dispersing the data concentration phenomenon by concentrating on the nodes necessary for the network bandwidth while dispersing.

By designing a cloud-based fog computing networking architecture, data from smart factories can be processed to enable greater scalability of the big-data processing required at the plant. If cloud based fog computing technology is designed and developed on an open source basis, it will be easy to introduce for future use, and the introduction of an open source based cloud in building a network is a prerequisite. In addition, because it is more scalable than other storage technologies, it has a positive effect on processing, analyzing and storing data at a low cost. Amazon web services (AWS) Cloud [7], which has been developed with the existing compatibility, provides convenient functions and excellent infrastructure, but it needs storage space of data. Because of this, if you design the cloud on an open source basis and build the network at a lower cost, you will be able to reduce initial costs and build smart factories with better services. Fog computing, which addresses the disadvantages of the cloud, such as response time and location awareness, is a concept from Cisco that makes network devices [8]. In processing IoT data, only big-data is transmitted when big-data occurs, so that it does not unnecessarily transmit data to the cloud.

The composition of this paper is as follows; In Sect. 2, we explain the related work for the our proposed. In Sect. 3, we propose the cloud-based fog computing network architecture. Section 4 shows the cloud testbed configuration for big-data collection and cloud storage for smart factory design, and so on. Finally, we explain the conclusion of the idea proposed in Sect. 5.

2 Related Work

2.1 Building a Smart Factory Cloud with OpensStack

The building cloud through the open source OpenStack. IoT, etc, can collect and control information through cloud networking. It will be able to develop and apply cloud for Smart factory, collect information of various APIs in the cloud, collect information necessary for manufacturing, analyze and forecast. Such functionalities can be readily scaled up to cloud robotics in a cyber workspace for hardware in the loop manufacturing [9]. Figure 1 describes the cloud provider and consumer share control of resources in a cloud system that are structured within a classical software stack design: application layer, middleware layer, operating system layer [10]. Architecture configuration through virtualization can be implemented through OpenStack cloud [11].

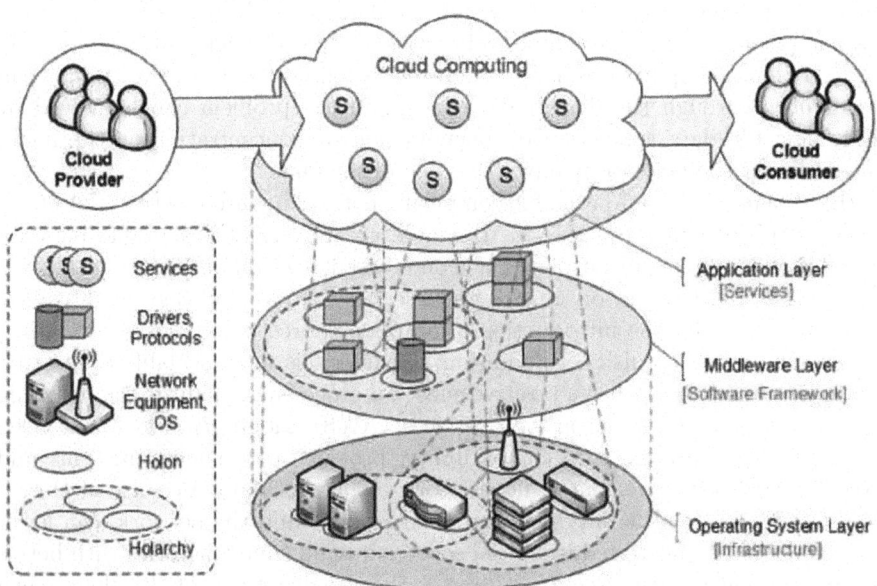

Fig. 1. Holonic cloud computing [10].

2.2 Fog Computing Features

Fog computing is a virtualized platform that is located between the end devices and the data center of cloud computing to provide computing, storage and network services. It is a platform created to support end users and is suitable for applications that require low latency. This places the fog server or node adjacent to the mobile device. The fog server functions as a set-top box, a router, a switch, a resource machine, an AP, etc and can be located close to the cloud server and close to the service. In a single node configuration where you want to be able to evaluate OpenStack, a single network interface card is sufficient. However, using a single network interface in a multi node configuration does not provide enough bandwidth to service a large amount of network traffic in the cloud. If you use a single network interface in your enterprise OpenStack configuration, this can lead to serious performance problems.

Traditional cloud computing has resulted in a high concentration of data centers called the cloud, which has led to increased latency due to bottlenecks. Figure 2 describes the fog computing network which uses local proximity and data caching capabilities. Analyzing data from fog server, it there is content to be used for the first time and it you are forwarding to the requesting user, it is possible to solve the congestion of the terminal. Fog computing can be deployed where network bandwidth is high, which can dissipate this data concentration phenomenon. Distributed processing is supported while cloud computing can be bottlenecked by centralized processing [12].

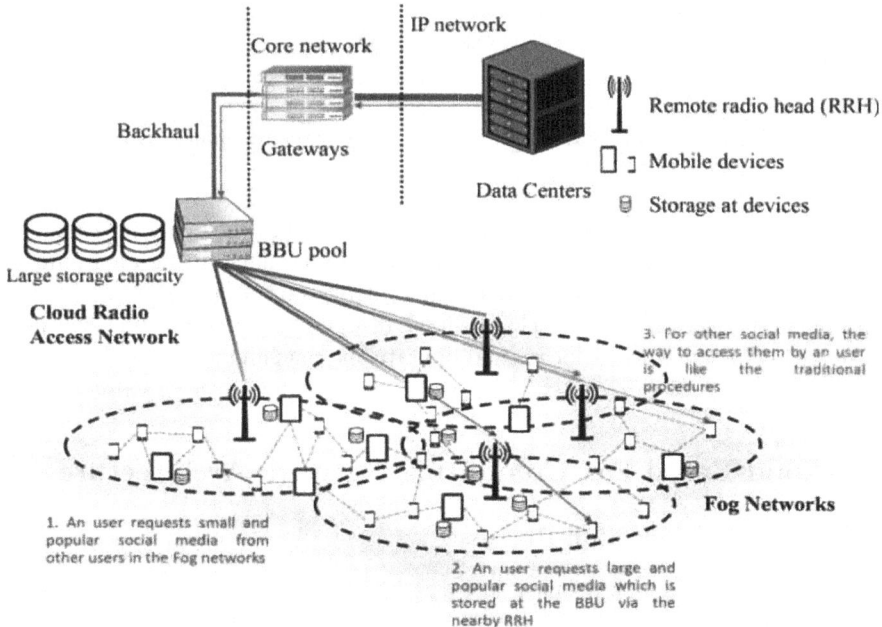

Fig. 2. Fog network operation [12].

2.3   Cloud-Based Virtualizaion Solutions

The runtime sensory data collection from the robot by the application server is accomplished over the TCP connection using a series of 12 floating numbers and one long integer that form one data packet of 52 bytes [13].

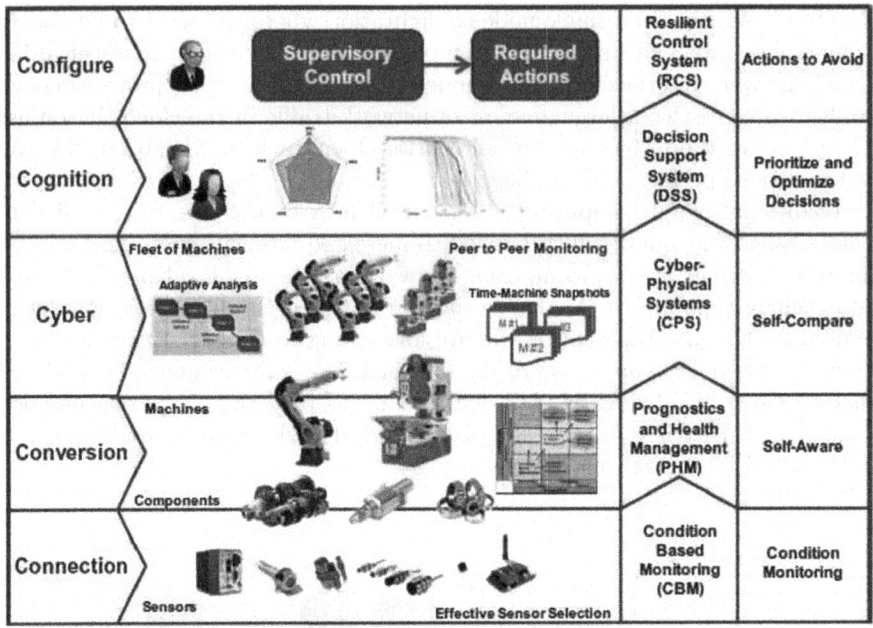

Fig. 3. System configuration in cyber-physical environment [13].

As shown in the above Fig. 3, data can be received in the cyber environment through the cloud server, and devices used in the manufacturing environment such as machine and robot can be remotely controlled from the application server through the dashboard. Using cloud server to operate fog computing will help to reduce response time, it locate and operate the machine made products, and so on.

3   Cloud-Based Fog Computing Network Architecture

3.1   Big-Data Collection Process

The gathering process for smart factorys big-data can be visualized through collecting, processing and analyzing the process of gathering big-data application in cloud-based fog computing network configuration.

The process of analyzing the data is shown in Fig. 4, data sources will be diverse, and informal data generated by IoT, RFID, and device devices can be collected through log servers and cloud servers.

In the process of storing and processing data, it can be stored in a cloud storage space and analyzed in real time, so that data can be configured in various forms. Data analysis will be used through energy efficiency and various management systems. Finally, the real time status of the data is shown through the dashboard and the cloud dedicated dashboard web.

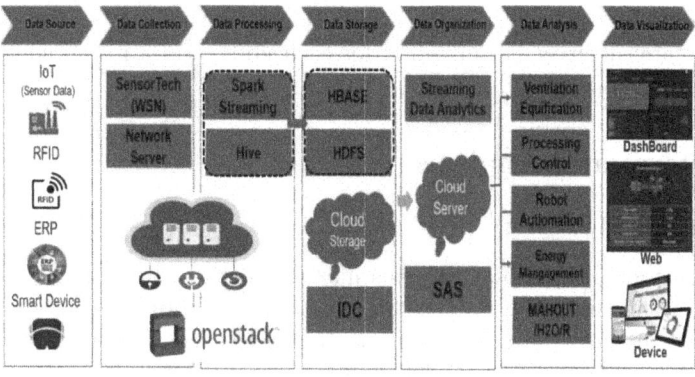

Fig. 4. Big-data collection process.

3.2 Network Architecture

The addition of the concept for the cloud to the smart factory will require a network architecture configuration in Fig. 5. For the architecture that makes up cloud-based fog computing, the network that connects to the cloud must be configured, and there must be an application that responds to the configured network. The cloud server is configured using the OpenStack, and the fog computing is positioned at the edge of the server to configure the cloud-based fog computing. IoT data will also be stored in real time on configured cloud storage. When the necessary gateways and servers are configured between real time storage, they will act as controllers by configuring nodes at the application end. Finally, the IoT sensing data is stored through the gateway and stored

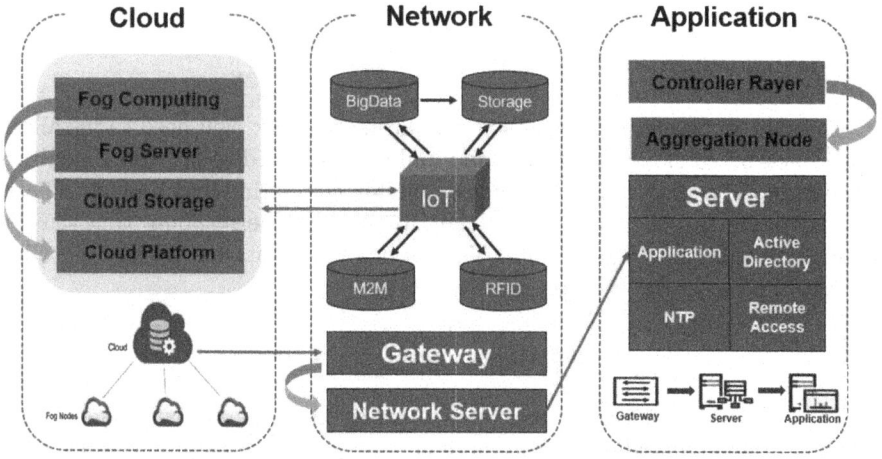

Fig. 5. Cloud-fog smart factory network architecture.

and analyzed by the server. In the application layer that applies the stored and analyzed data, a server is configured for each node, and a real time processing application becomes possible.

4   Performance Analysis

4.1   System Modeling

In an openstack-based cloud, systems management can be managed through a real time dashboard in Fig. 6. Dashboards can manage various services of Open Stack cloud, manage data, and create instances to check response time between cloud data transfers system modeling can be seen through the OpenStack services used, and the OpenStack provisioning technology at the bottom allows real time data to be received and response times confirmed.

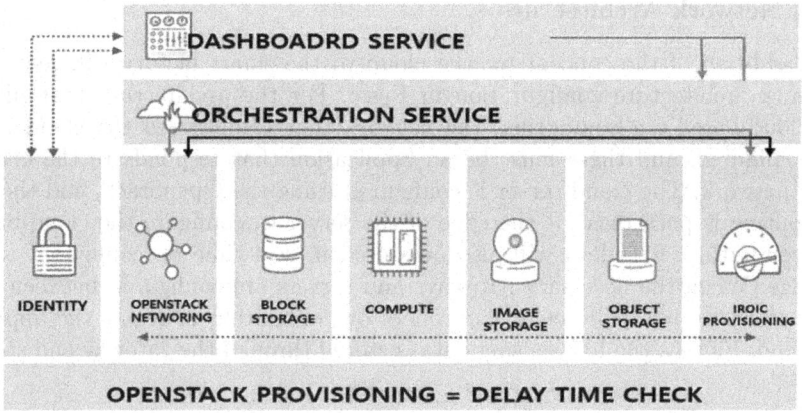

Fig. 6. System management procedure diagram.

To build an OpenStack-based fog computing network, you need to install an OpenStack-based cloud on the VM and build a dashboard to provide a monitoring system. The next step is to connect the fog computing and provide a basis for shortening the response time of the OpenStack. The response time can be known through the available rate. The service represents the service use time and the time represents the processing time.

$$Availability = \frac{Delaytime}{Service} \times 100 \tag{1}$$

The response time can be measured through the available rate. The service will be variable according to the number, and it will measure the time from creating an instance in the OpenStack, measuring the time and storing the data in swift.

$$\frac{dS}{dT} = \frac{\Delta S}{\Delta T} = \frac{S_{(t+1)} - S_i}{T_{t+i} - T_i} = \frac{S}{T} \cdot S^2(T_i) \tag{2}$$

$$dT = S - A \times 100 \tag{3}$$

Big-data can be used simultaneously with storage. An instance is created to measure the response time through provisioning. When you create an instance, it will be stored in swift, which fog computing helps to store data in real time at the edge.

Table 1. TestBed configuration and testing.

Configuration	OpenStack server	Fog computing
Service	OpenStack Newton version	Swift All In One (SAIO)
VM node	VirtualBox VM 2 nodes	VirtualBox VM 1 nodes (app)
System OS	Ubuntu 16.06 LTS version	
Testing	Delay (Response) Time checking	

Accordingly, the response time is numerically reduced. In the VM configuration of Table 1, OpenStack newton version is installed in the cloud, and it is based on cloud and fog computer and each node is configured and operated. As a test method, in order to check the response time, it is possible to check the time by creating an instance through provisioning among the OpenStack cloud services received through fog computing. If you build a testbed environment, you can build a network as shown below. We can build a cloud system for IoT connecting, reduce response time through fog computing of virtual smart factory data, and transfer data to the OpenStack cloud. The fog computing is built on an OpenStack basis and is used as a server for improving the response speed.

4.2   Implementaion and Experimentaion

The server configuration is shown in Fig. 7; SAIO server, OpenStack-based fog server, and OpenStack newton server. The swift server is used as a server to store object storage, and the Newton Server is used to organize the entire OpenStack service and receive DB data.

It create an instance in the OpenStack dashboard and measure the response time rate by selecting flavor on the bare metal node. And it make sure that the network created for bare metal provisioning is selected and create an instance.

In Fig. 8, building a testbed and configuring an OpenStack based cloud solely took 100 (ms), but could reduce response time to 75 (ms) through fog computing. Through the OpenStack provisioning, we created an instance in the dashboard and stored the data. In this process, we used fog computing to store the data

Fig. 7. TestBed network diagram.

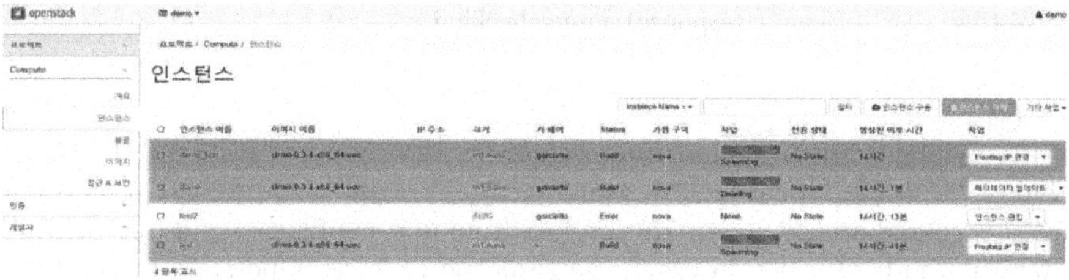

Fig. 8. OpenStack provisioning response time dashboard.

in the OpenStack swift repository. Since the provisioning time of the instance is delayed, the time required will be the response time. This makes it possible to check the response time. And OpenStack based-fog computing delay time is calculated as follows.

$$OpenStackCloud = 100\,(\text{ms}) \tag{4}$$

$$OpenStack + FogComputing = 75\,(\text{ms}) \tag{5}$$

5   Conclusion

In this paper, cloud fog computing network architecture for big-data applications in smart factory environments is proposed. A system architecture that manages various data accumulated in smart factory will be implemented. If cloud-based fog computing is used to collect and store data, response time and data location awareness, etc. can be improved and utilized. It is also used to collect, analyze and utilize the data used in smart factory operation. Unlike conventional cloud computing, Computing devices are not located in a distant center, but are located at the edge of a device close to the terminal device. With the emergence of new data storage methods, the amount of information exponentially grows, it abandons existing data processing methods and attempts to jump to a new dimension. There are increasing researches on cloud systems among various processing methods of data processing in smart factory operation. Accordingly, the cloud can be efficiently used to store, analyze and utilize the accumulated data in the smart factory by using the open source cloud.

Future research will focus on cloud-based fog computing solutions for smart factories, with the aim of collecting data and conducting test operations. Cloud-based fog computing is easy to store and analyze, and has fast response times and can be viewed through real time analysis and dashboards. In the development, we will utilize open source software, and it is based of cloud computing through artificial intelligence (AI) technologies by adding search engine to stored data.

Acknowledgment. This research was supported by Basic Science Research Program through the National Research Foundation of Korea (NRF) funded by the Ministry of Education (NRF-2016R1D1A1B03933828).

References

1. Bonomi, F.: Fog computing and its role the internet of things. In: MCC 12 Proceedings of the First Edition of the MCC Workshop on Mobile Cloud Computing, pp. 13–16 (2012)
2. William, J., Milito, R., Zhu, J., Addepalli, S.: Introduction to cloud and internet of things. Challenges and opportunities. In: Proceedings for the 50th Hawaii International Conference of System Sciences (HICSS), p. 1 (2017)
3. Sefraoul, O., Alssaoul, M., Eleuldj, M.: Cloud computing for internet of things sensing based applications. In: Sixth International Conference on Sensing Technology (ICST), vol. 55, pp. 1–7 (2012)
4. Martin, S., Quoc, H.N.M., Hauswirth, M., Wang, W., Barnaghi, P., Cousin, P.: Open services for IoT Cloud applications in the future internet. In: IEEE WoW-MoM, pp. 1–6 (2013)
5. Titcheu Chekam, T., Zhai, E., Li, Z.: On the synchronization bottleneck of OpenStack swift-like cloud storage systems. In: The 35th Annual IEEE International Conference on Computer Communications, INFOCOM 2016, pp. 1–14 (2018)
6. Datta, S.K., Bonnet, C., Haerri, J.: Fog computing architecture to enable consumer centric internet of things services. In: EURCOM, Biot, France, Conference Paper, vol. 78, pp. 641–658 (2018)
7. Kouchaksaraei, H.R., Karl, H.: Joint orchestration of cloud-based microservices and virtual network functions. Networking and Internet Architecture (cs.NI). Future Generation Computer Systems, vol. 78, pp. 1–2 (2018)
8. Luan, T.H., Gao, L., Li, Z., Xiang, Y., Wei, G., Sun, L.: Fog computing focusing on mobile users at the edge. Netw. Internet Archit. 1–11 (2016)
9. Wang, L.: An overview of internet-enabled Cloud-based cyber manufacturing. Trans. Inst. Meas. Control **39**(4), 388–397 (2017)

10. Morgan, J., O'Donnell, G.E.: Enabling a ubiquitous and cloud manufacturing foundation with field-level service-oriented architecture. Ubiquit. Cloud Enterp. Manuf. **30**, 1–18 (2017)
11. Sefraoui, O., Alssaoui, M., Eleuldj, M.: OpenStack: toward an OpenSource solution for cloud computing. Int. J. Comput. Appl. **55**, 1–5 (2012)
12. Lee, J., Su, N., Park, J., Kim, K., Kim, N.-K., Jung, J.-S., Rae, S.: Fog computing: concept, role. In: 2016 Annual Conference of the Korean Institute of Communication Sciences, vol. 60, pp. 915–916 (2016)
13. Lee, J., Bagheri, B., Kao, H.-A.: A cyber-physical systems architecture for industry 4.0-based manufacturing systems. Manuf. Lett. **3**, 18–23 (2015)

Workshop Theoretical and Computational Chemistry and Its Applications (TCCA 2018)

The ECTN Virtual Education Community Prosumer Model for Promoting and Assessing Chemical Knowledge

Antonio Laganà[1,3](✉) (iD), Osvaldo Gervasi[2] (iD), Sergio Tasso[2] (iD),
Damiano Perri[2] (iD), and Francesco Franciosa[4] (iD)

[1] Dipartimento di Chimica, Biologia e Biotecnologie, Università di Perugia,
06123 Perugia, Italy
lagana05@gmail.com
[2] Dipartimento di Matematica e Informatica, Università di Perugia,
06123 Perugia, Italy
[3] Master-UP srl, 06123 Perugia, Italy
[4] Dipartimento di Economia, Università di Perugia, 06123 Perugia, Italy

Abstract. The dynamism of the learning economies is examined in order to single out the key factors allowing to promote knowledge dissemination and invention developments. The various steps involved in the production and usage of both tacit and explicit technological knowledge as common good are analysed in order to optimize its portability. The role played in this respect by business clusters (especially when adopting the prosumer model) dealing with knowledge is discussed with particular reference to chemical education in Higher Education Institutions. The adoption of the prosumer model for building a European system aimed at promoting and assessing chemical knowledge is examined. The particular case considered in the paper is the one born out of the activities of the Universities member of the European Chemistry Thematic Network association through its Virtual Education Community Committee and the operational support of the former spinoff of the University of Perugia Master-UP s.r.l. Results achieved during the first year of activity are discussed.

Keywords: Prosumer model · E-tests · Assessment of competences

1 Introduction

At present, innovation is one of the main, if not the most important, driver of economic growth (especially in the most developed economies) due to its strong impact on both macro- and micro-economic level. It is, in fact, the key process leading to the creation of new products and/or new productive processes in developed countries, in which the accumulation of capital is insufficient to spur

© Springer International Publishing AG, part of Springer Nature 2018
O. Gervasi et al. (Eds.): ICCSA 2018, LNCS 10964, pp. 533–548, 2018.
https://doi.org/10.1007/978-3-319-95174-4_42

economic growth. Innovation is in general the outcome of one or more learning processes during which new information on the nature, creation, diffusion, transformation and utilization of the existing knowledge is generated. The distinctive feature of knowledge is its increase with no limits both in quantity and in sharing through learning processes. For this reason, modern economies are evolving rapidly towards "learning economies" [1].

The dynamism of learning economies is largely based on the education mechanisms enhancing a fruitful participation of knowledge users to its production according to the so called prosumer model [2,3]. A key player in the European Chemistry Education scenario is the European Chemistry Thematic Network (ECTN) Association[1] a non-profit making association registered in Belgium that is an outcome of six years of network activity (1996–2002) of the Thematic Network funded through the LLLP (Life Long Learning Project) European initiative. The Association, created to provide a sustainable future for ECTN has currently over 120 members coming from 30 different European countries plus various associate members world-wide.

A fundamental activity of the ECTN Association is the promotion of the use of e-learning by formulating and adopting EU harmonized standards and creating appropriate collaborative procedures through the coordination of the Virtual Education Community (VEC) Standing Committee (SC). For this purpose groups of European experts of the member Higher Education Institutions (HEI)s have worked on various topics and produced a series of multi-lingual tests, called EChemTest$^{®}$, that can be used for certification/validation of competences in chemistry at various levels of all citizens, irrespective of their learning path.

At the end of the funded period it was necessary to adopt for EChemTest$^{®}$, as for other ECTN activities, a sustainability model and this paper reports on the background work that led to such decision, describes the solutions adopted and analyzes the main achievements.

Accordingly, in Sect. 2 the economic nature of knowledge is analyzed; in Sect. 3 the foundations of the project launched for making dissemination and assessment of molecular science knowledge sustainable are presented; in Sect. 4 the networked nature of the prosumer model adopted for that purpose is discussed; in Sect. 5 results achieved in 2017 (the first year of implementation of the model) are commented. In Sect. 6 some conclusions are drawn.

2   The Economic Nature of Knowledge

In current economic literature knowledge is considered to be a *common good* because it can be accessed by anyone. Accordingly, it is also usually considered to be (in economic terms) a market-disruptive factor because it does not lead to (either consumer or producer) registration actions. Due to its neutral impact on wealth, knowledge is defined as an externality. Production externalities are

---

[1] http://ectn.eu.

defined positive if they generate benefits to economic agents other than the player and negative (or external diseconomies) if they generate costs. Consumption externalities are the additional satisfaction or utility that a person receives from consuming an additional unit of a good or service. Consumption externalities increase with the closeness of the consumer to the producer and decrease as consumption increases. Public services (and among them knowledge and in particular public education) are usually positive consumption externalities possessing two meaningful characteristics:

- non-rivalry, because they can not be in general substituted;
- non-excludability, because they are available to anyone.

Public education, in particular, has such a high positive externality (with respect to private benefits) that the free market, either perfect or imperfect, in general does not produce it because of its scarce profitability. Its non-excludability makes it highly socially desirable and highly exploited.

2.1   Knowledge Profitability

The most popular way of increasing profitability (i.e. avoid possible market failures) is the adoption of "patents" (or more properly "invention patents") that are legal titles giving the owner an exclusive right to exploit within a territory and for a determined period of time (and at the same time to prevent others to produce, sell or utilize without the inventors consent and the payment of a royalty) the invention. In other words the patent gives the inventor a temporary ownership and an exclusive utilization right on the invention (i.e. a short term monopoly) [4] making the innovation gain a considerable economic value.

Software products are considered a border-line case when dealing with patenting inventions. In recent years softwares have gained an increasing central role in the stimulation of innovation thanks to the increasing importance of automation and networking in production activities. As a result, their status has often changed from writing (like in literature, music, figure arts, architecture, theatre and cinema, elaboration programs and databanks) to technical work. This led to the consequence that the software patenting is allowed if, like any other invention, it has a technical character aiming at solving a specific technical problem through technical effect going beyond the normal, basic, physical interaction between software and machine.

However, as already mentioned, knowledge consumption possesses the qualities of non-rivalry and non-excludability because of its nature of public good. This means that the intrinsic externalities associated to this class of public goods can generate the market failure (say for example that the costs met by the inventor to produce the related innovation might not be returned) and this may deter further activities and make a competitive market system intrinsically scarcely innovative.

For this reason, intellectual copyrights in general (and patents in particular) tackle this problem by attacking the non-appropriability of the knowledge (that causes the market failure). In particular, by allowing the innovators to hold copyrights on their discoveries (such as the patents), a legal means is provided to exclude attributes from a good considered purely public. In other words, protection of the intellectual property makes exclusive the ownership of a good such as knowledge that for its true nature is not appropriable. In this way knowledge transforms itself in a good which is not public anymore eliminating so far the problem of the externalities acquiring benefits and costs related to the nature of the market to which the good is referred.

2.2   Allocation of Resources to Invention

In order to find a solution to problems generated from patenting it was proposed that Policymakers and non-governative and non-profit agencies would support financially research and innovation, leveraging the following assumptions: (a) the knowledge developed from innovation is a public good; (b) innovation reduces costs; (c) innovation is a fundamental change in processes; (d) a patent system pushes only one enterprise to innovate; (e) indivisibility and uncertainty characterize the productive process; (f) there exists a Technological Incentive (TI) defined as the difference between the pre- and post-innovation profit.

On these assumptions three possible cases can be given:

- Monopolistic market: The monopolistic company decides to innovate on the basis of its estimate of the TI. This means that when introducing a radical process-innovation the monopolistic company fixes the price as the lowest post-innovation one and lower than the previous marginal cost.
- Competitive Market: More than one company works on a particular innovation but only one gets the related patent. In this case the TI will be the post-innovation profit. The TI of the competitive company is larger than that of the monopolistic market and the company holding the patent becomes monopolistic.
- Social planning: The innovation is supported by public money (social planner case), prices lower, monopolies do not form and welfare increases. As a result the TI is larger than the one of both the monopolistic and competitive markets.

The pros and cons of the above described monopolistic, competitive and social planning models on the resulting economic and social efficiency (the creation of monopolies versus the improvement of knowledge and the promotion of innovation) were reconsidered by Nordhaus [8] when developing the model of the reward theory of patent. The reward theory of patent states that by introducing (thanks to patenting) a potential monopolistic power a remuneration to successful innovators is given by exclusivity. If the cost to generate an innovation is private, its anticipation and the resulting monopolistic power are a stimulating reward for driving innovation into a market context. If exclusive rights would not be available to the innovator anyone could use related information to duplicate the invention and compete with the inventor thanks to the fact that knowledge is a pure public good. For this reason, the patent system giving exclusive rights protects the innovator and encourages innovation with the length of the protection period being long enough to obtain almost unlimited benefits and sufficiently short to avoid potential losses due to monopolistic effects.

2.3 The Model of Openess of Software and Intellectual Productions

The Free and Libre Open Source Software [5] (FLOSS), released with an open licence, represents an innovative approach for promoting innovation and for spreading knowledge. A similar approach is behind the diffusion of multimedia contents released under the Creative Commons [6] license. We are observing a massive production of software made available with a FLOSS licence and firms prefer quite often to adopt an Open Source program instead of a closed source one, since the availability of the source code allows the deep control against threats and security exposure.

After the initial phase of FLOSS, based on the voluntary work of developers and of the community of users (for bug hunting and triaging, for writing the documentation and for the translation in various idioms of the user interface, web and wiki pages, manuals and books), modern FLOSS is based on the contribution of some companies which include the named software in their top strategies and contribute very actively to the development of the functionalities that better match their goals. Such a very professional approach generates an income in terms of donations both by users (who are very satisfied with the way in which the software project evolves) and by companies that base their revenue on the named software. The software in this way feeds a very large number of companies that carry out training, consultancy and development of functionalities required by the client. LibreOffice [7] represents the most relevant FOSS project that best embodies this model.

3 The Impact of Knowledge on Innovation and Education

Scientific information and technological knowledge are innovation factors. They both act by widening the cognitive capability of individuals. Furthermore information is made of a set of structured data and needs specific knowledge for its articulation through cognitive processes which make it operative. Both information and knowledge have, in general, high generation costs yet with almost no reproduction costs (scale-free property). Unlike other economic inputs, they are both depreciation free (at least in economic terms). This implies that they would both be characterized by an increasing output on their property incompatible with economic balance.

3.1 Knowledge Transfer and Learning

According to the SYS (Stanford-Yale-Sussex Synthesis) [9,10] technological and scientific knowledge have each one of the following important features:

– non-exhaustibility (the permanent capability of reproduction and transfer);

- tacit knowledge (part of knowledge related to a specific firm (including HEIs) or, in any case, places along the production process offer clarification for usability by other people.

The replication cost of information and knowledge is usually, among other economic factors, positive although it tends to vary on different technologies for its degree of tacitness and innovativeness. Knowledge differs from pure information both for its ways and replication costs. As a matter of fact replication costs of the information are confined to the simple physical cost of the copy. On the contrary, its reproduction is a more expensive process, since the cognitive capabilities are hard to be codified and transferred. Then, knowledge reproduction can happen only through a complex learning process.

The tacitness concept refers to the inability of the agent to articulate explicit sequences of procedures about the object. In other words the tacitness is the measure of *what we know more than what we can say* [11]. Higher is the level of tacitness in a technological field higher will be the transfer cost of that knowledge.

An organization creates further knowledge through the interaction between tacit and explicit knowledge. Inside firms the conversion of tacit knowledge in explicit and vice versa, activates a learning process that was called *four-phase learning process* by Nonaka and Takeuchi [12].

3.2   The Four-Phase Learning Process

The four-phase model of the learning process considers the processes leading to the creation and sharing of knowledge and how they may become explicit and self-regenerating.

The studies carried out by Nonaka and Takeuchi suggest that there is an interaction between tacit and explicit knowledge. This interaction is called knowledge conversion. The four phases of the model are:

(1) Socialization: learning as knowledge that transfers itself from one agent to another by creating and sharing tacit knowledge through direct experience (tacit to tacit)
(2) Externalisation: learning as an ability to induce new relevant fragments of knowledge by articulating tacit knowledge through dialogue and reflection (tacit to explicit)
(3) Recombination: learning how to improve knowledge and applying explicit and information (explicit to explicit)
(4) Internalization: learning as absorption capacity acquiring new knowledge during practice (explicit to new explicit).

Explicit knowledge is used and internalized, allowing to develop, identify and create new tacit knowledge. Therefore, through a process of conversion knowledge is made transferable and communicable. Tacit knowledge is the true source of innovation, becoming a strategic value for the company.

As Nonaka and Takeuchi say, an organization must provide the necessary tools to convey and disseminate knowledge in a given context, both individually but also at an aggregate level among several organizations (as we will see with the prosumer model) in order to obtain competitive advantages so to stimulate innovation. The process of creation and sharing can be represented as a succession of individual and social attitudes starting from awareness, interest, implementation, repeated use, personal use, suggested to others, commitment, internalization, institutionalization.

Knowledge, however, does not only reside in individuals or organizations, but it is also localized in hybrid organizational forms like associations (as is the case of the ECTN Association considered in this paper), networks and industrial districts. Among all forms of knowledge, tacitness is the most relevant one as a driver to innovation for all enterprises connected to each other generating a competitive advantage among the companies that are part of it. In fact, in an area of extraordinary concentration of international know-how, it generates productive capacities, encouraging even large companies to concentrate in increasingly specialised and innovative districts, not only to exploit their network economies but also to exploit the intrinsic tacit knowledge that otherwise would not be transferable.

4   The Prosumer Model as a Knowledge Network

The fact that the model of Nonaka and Takeuchi provides that through a collaborative process tacit knowledge can be transformed into an explicit one by activating a cycle generating new knowledge, allows us to state that, although this model is referred to a business context, it can be transferred to other macro economic contexts as it may be the case either of a group of companies collaborate among themselves or even producing and consuming a given set of goods/services as is in a prosumer model.

4.1   Business Clusters

In general, business clusters are a group of companies interacting by generating new knowledge and/or sharing existing one with mutual benefit. According to Porter's definition [13], business clusters are defined as "a geographic concentration of interconnected companies, specialised suppliers, service providers, firms in related sectors, associated institutions, etc. in particular competing/co-operating fields". Clusters have attracted a lot of interest in recent years as they are believed to have significantly improved learning processes. Before analysing the benefits associated with cluster formation, it is necessary to classify them into either horizontal or vertical. The first category concerns companies carrying out the same type of activities (which are, therefore, rival to each other), while the second category concerns companies carrying out different but complementary activities.

– Horizontal dimension: in this dimension, interconnected companies derive a considerable advantage from their ability to monitor, compare and learn from the mistakes made by others when carrying out that same activity.

– Vertical dimension: in this dimension companies are interconnected by input/output interactions, where suppliers and customers contribute to improve the capabilities of companies, thanks to an improvement due to a continuous learning by doing process.

As already said, clusters play a very important role in the process of knowledge diffusion and growth both in a macro and micro economic context. However, there is a further contribution made by Hakansson [14] on the "economics network approach", by integrating the relationships generated among e-learning, innovation and networking. He claims, in fact, that knowledge is multi-layered and this leads to two main consequences:

(1) even if an enterprise specialises in a given sector, it must exceed the limits to acquire knowledge outside its specific field of competence.
(2) because of the heterogeneity of knowledge, each company must consider the contribution of a plurality of actors and institutions (both internal and external) each one of whom has an intrinsic knowledge.

4.2   The Cluster Nature of EChemTest®

Above discussed theories and models exploiting networking in order to enhance innovation processes based on the use of external resources and on the acquisition of new knowledge through clustering with other system players provided a good basis for developing collaborative forms of learning and knowledge dissemination in the Education sector. In particular we discuss here the case of the prosumer model adopted by Master Up s.r.l.[2] in the year 2016 when designing and implementing for the networked use of both the LibreEOL (Exam On Line) [15–17], a knowledge evaluation software tool developed by O. Gervasi and his coworkers, the Chem-Learn portal managing a cluster of Test Centers (TC)s (developed by C. Manuali), and the libraries of Questions and Answers (Q&A) to be used for running Self Evaluation Sessions (SES)s produced by the teams of experts of the Universities members of ECTN.

The e-test machinery, adopted for the ECHEMTEST+ project by ECTN, makes use of EChemTest® procedures developed along several years of LLLPs. EChemTest®, at present a world renowned brand, was a procedure based on the use of individual SESs on e-tests based on subsets of the above mentioned Q&As on Chemical knowledge. The Q&As were randomly selected out of related Libraries designed for assessing at a European University harmonized level for the 3 years (Bachelor) and 2 years (Master) curricular schemes the competences acquired by the students. The SESs were administered for academic purposes under controlled conditions by Test Centers managed by the corresponding host ECTN member Universities using a commercial software. EChemTest® procedures were designed and implemented during a 20 years long series of ECTN projects funded by various European LLLPs starting from 1996.

---

[2] http://www.master-up.it.

Among the initial working groups a strong synergy was established between the EChemTest® working group itself (coordinated by CPE Lyon, FR) and the Core Chemistry (coordinated by the University of Bologna, IT), the Tuning Educational Structures (coordinated by the University of Dortmund, DE) and the Multimedia in Chemistry Education (coordinated by the University of Perugia) working groups. To this end several committees of experts from the different ECTN member HEIs were established in order to develop Q&A Libraries for Schools (General Chemistry GC1) and for University entrance and initial dispersion (General Chemistry GC2), for University Bachelor (level 3 Analytical, Biological, Inorganic, Physical and Organic Chemistry) and for some University Master (level 4 Cultural Heritage, Computational Chemistry and Organic Syntheses) curricula. At the same time, under the coordination of CPE Lyon with the technical support of the University of Perugia (both the Department of Chemistry (DC) and the Department of Mathematics and Informatics (DMI)), a small number of TCs were established and used to maintain Q&A libraries and run EU wide contests and competitions.

4.3   The ECTN Prosumer Model

The EU funded activities of ECTN ended on September 2015 (the expiration date of the EC2E2N2). At that point it became impellent for ECTN to activate for EChemTest® the already mentioned self-sustained ECHEMTEST+ design approach. This was deliberated at the ECTN Association Administrative Council (AC) of April 26, 2015 in Ljublijana (just a few months before the expiration date of EC2E2N2). In that case it was decided to activate, in parallel with the existing Academic EchemTest® SESs, the paid ones offered to private individuals and companies. This was meant to introduce a gradual replacement of the cost covering mechanisms based on network funds and possibly pay for the full maintenance and further evolution of the project.

As from the VEC SC business plan approved at the above mentioned ECTN AC the e-test procedure and related Q&A libraries are the main ECTN Association asset (conservatively estimated to be worth about 2 Meur). Its operational costs (conservatively estimated to be worth about 170 keur per year and leading to a cost per individual SES of 120 euro according to the figures available at that time) were at that time met in money for about 40 keur (25% of the total operating costs) and by in-kind and voluntary work (for the remaining 75%) both provided by the member HEIs. Accordingly, the business plan of ECHEMTEST+ for the following three years was assumed to generate increasing annual income able to match the expected costs of 40 keur a year (an average of approximately 4 keur per TC) thanks to an expected integration of projects and/or Association funds. On this ground the ECTN AC decided to support the ECHEMTEST+ with a special fund of 25 keur to be spent in 5 years.

An important feature of the prosumer model adopted for ECHEMTEST+ was the containment of costs within acceptable limits. The ECHEMTEST+ prosumer scheme leverages the fact that the ECTN member HEIs running e-test SESs (the TCs) for the assessment of the Chemistry competences of their own students already act at the same time as consumers of EChemTest services and as producers of Q&As, assessors of students' competences, designers and developers of e-learning materials (a typical cluster of the horizontal type defined above) for the harmonization at European level of the assessment of Molecular Science competences. This behaviour is quite usual in education in which knowledge is a common good to be at the same time produced and consumed. The only additional action needed to the end of making the prosumer model work was to assign to a company the role of market spinner. For ECHEMTEST⁺ this role was taken by Master-Up srl thanks to its nature of former spinoff of the University of Perugia (born in the year 2004 out of the aggregation of some members of the Chemistry Department and the Mathematics and Informatics Department expert in molecular dynamics simulations and computer science) devoted to the design, production and marketing services for technological innovation as its main goal. As a matter of fact, the mission of Master-Up has been since the very beginning[3] the design and development of e-learning tools for molecular sciences and technologies, the implementation of Open Science and editorial initiatives, the carrying out of computational simulations supporting innovation in chemical applications and on top of that of supporting Virtual organizations and research community activities on Molecular Sciences.

4.4 Learning Objects

In addition to being part of the knowledge cycle of the Nonaka and Takeuchi prosumer model that continuously feeds new knowledge and improves its quality by leveraging the feedbacks obtained from usage of EChemTest®, Master-UP provides the ECTN HEIs also with support for the production of Learning Objects (LO)s. Production, storage and improvement of LOs is provided through the use of the search, retrieval and management functions of the distributed repository GLOREP (Grid Learning Object Repository) [18–27] devoted to educational the progressive evolution of the ECTN educational heritage from tacit to explicit while carrying out research and teaching.

For a scientific-educational environment, the LOs are designed as the basic components for the content of a shared information. The main features of these LOs are: self-consistency, modularity, availability, reusability, interoperability. These features are highly desirable as they give utmost thoroughness to information. So we have stand alone LOs that could also be aggregated with other LOs, usable in several fields, readily available thanks to the use of metadata. The use of metadata allows the cataloging and classification of LOs according to the information content and any other factor it contains. In fact, the metadata allows us to verify the existence of a LO in the GLOREP repository by locating it unambiguously. More in general, the metadata is a set of descriptors, or tags, characterizing the properties and the resources of information themselves.

In GLOREP metadata is used in a hierarchical way (better known as schemas or ontologies) that connects the various components of the resources for an ade-

---

[3] See http://www.master-up.it.

quate and full fruition. This is often performed through the mapping of different metadata schemas. These schemas also provide data for identifying and localizing the resource. In the context of a repositories network, the choice of metadata ensures the interoperability between different types of resources (text, audio, video, etc.) and the integration of various information systems by indexation with a uniform metadata schema. This can be implemented both within and outside of the single repository and makes it crucial the choice of the metadata schema to adopt.

The most important architectural features of GLOREP are the focus on large communities (that implies a complex distributed nature of the repositories), an efficient mechanism of filing and retrieving LOs and related Software Attachments (SA) and the portability on the distribute Infrastructure. The GLOREP distributed repository is made of a central shared database and a distributed federation of local repositories.

5   Present Implementation and Outcomes of ECHEMTEST$^+$

In the first year (2017) of activity of the prosumer model for the ECHEMTEST$^+$ project (just in time to avoid dispersion of competences and momentum of the activities generated during 20 years of ECTN LLLPs funding) the following results were obtained.

5.1   Training Events

Some training events were organized. The typical structure of a training event is

> Day 1: The use of EChemTest$^{®}$ in the post-EC2E2N2 regime; Synchronize the technical management of EchemTest$^{®}$ by TCs; Management of Self evaluation Sessions for TCs; Auxiliary EchemTest$^{®}$ Learning Objects and related distributed repositories of GLOREP; Towards the implementation of EchemTest certificates
> Day 2: EOL: an open source software for certification; Hands on EOL demos and import of libraries.

The main reason for holding training events was to get the personnel managing the TCs familiarized with the e-testing software EOL. EOL (the already mentioned e-testing Open Source software designed and developed at the DMI of the University of Perugia) has the advantage of being of free use (no fees have to be paid, no limits are set for the number of users and SESs, compatibility with the popular Moodle educational software is provided, etc.). On the contrary, the previously used e-test commercial software Question Mark (QM) had fairly high annual fees and severe limits on the number and functionalities of the involved TCs. Furthermore it was using proprietary tools preventing an easy reuse of Q&A

libraries (the opting out of QM was made necessary also because the upgrade from the version used by the EchemTest® SESs running at that time was old and its reinstallation was a rather heavy job). This would have created in any case difficulties to ECTN because people previously in charge for operating centrally QM were not available for the job. At the same time, the exporting of the Q&A libraries into the Open Source EOL environment reconducted them under complete control of ECTN enabling so far an easy and continuous extension and revision of the Q&A libraries, their finalization to more professional use, the implementation of other libraries, a more flexible training of TCs operators, the utilization and development of supplementary learning materials.

5.2   The TC Network of ECHEMTEST+

As commented before, the early part of year 2015 was spent in having all formal decisions taken at the ECTN General Assembly held in Ljubljana in April and to the elaboration of the methodology to follow while the second part of that year was devoted to the design a detailed road map for its implementation. The year 2016 was entirely spent in the demanding effort of making the switching from the EU funding modality to the prosumer one technically feasible with the main tasks being for the Department of DMI Perugia the implementation of the Q&A libraries and for Master-UP the development of the Chem-Learn Portal (at that time the ECTN portal was under restructuring and Master-UP had to build its own in order to interact with the TCs and manage certificates). Finally, the year 2017 was devoted to the launch of the ECHEMTEST+ campaign of SESs.

The TCs actively collaborating in carrying out the ECHEMTEST+ activities by running SES campaigns are: Technical University of Vienna (AT), Aristotle University of Thessaloniki (Greece), Eötvös Lorand University (Hungary), University of Genoa (Italy), University of Naples "Federico II" (Italy), University of Perugia (Italy), University of Siena (Italy), The University of Amsterdam (The Netherlands), Jagiellonian University in Krakow (Poland), Kazan National Research Technological University (Russia), University of Ljubljana (Slovenia), Universidad Mayor de San Andres (Bolivia).

5.3   The Year 2017 SESs and Proficiency Certificates

The number of SESs per Library and TC run in the year 2017 are given in Table 1. Some students have also requested the personal Proficiency Certificate (23 for level 3 and 11 for GC1).

It is interesting to notice that the TCs can be divided in two almost even subsets: one (made of Amsterdam, Kazan, Ljubljana, Naples, Thessaloniki and Vienna) exclusively interested in the use of GC1 and GC2 libraries (Schools and University access and dispersion) and the other (made of Budapest, Genoa, Krakow, Milan, Perugia) mainly (though not exclusively) focused on level 3 ones. Sporadic (statistically marginal) use has been made of level 4 libraries (Computational chemistry, Cultural Heritage).

Table 1. Number of SESs per Library and per TC run in the year 2017. Please notice that Krakow figures include the SESs of the recently established CEL (Chemistry for Everyday Life) Library.

TC	GC1	GC2	AC3	BC3	IC3	OC3	PC3	CEL	TOT
Amsterdam		95							95
Budapest			145	62	126	108	186		627
Genoa		40	41			41	41		163
Kazan	123								123
Krakow	207	117	46		45	55	27	13	510
Ljublijana	1	10							11
Milan	44		133		130	130	133		570
Naples		8							8
Perugia			6		5	27	10		48
Thessaloniki	28	20							48
Vienna		309				1			310

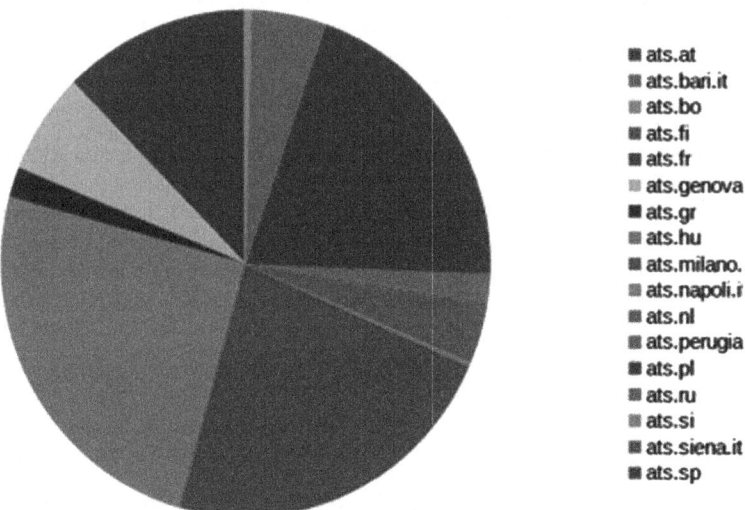

ats.at
ats.bari.it
ats.bo
ats.fi
ats.fr
ats.genova
ats.gr
ats.hu
ats.milano.
ats.napoli.i
ats.nl
ats.perugia
ats.pl
ats.ru
ats.si
ats.siena.it
ats.sp

Fig. 1. A pie chart showing the fraction of SESs run by the different TCs.

A chart showing the SES activities of the different TCs is given in Fig. 1. It shows that the top file ranking HEIs are in the sequence Budapest, Milan, Krakow, Vienna and Genoa.

6   Conclusions and Future Plans

In this paper we have seen how knowledge, both tacit and explicit, and its study is becoming increasingly important as a factor for economic development by generating competitive advantage. This knowledge, if it is conveyed not only to individuals of a particular organisational context but also (at the aggregate level) to a broad audience, generates other knowledge and activates a virtuous circle in which knowledge creates further new knowledge within clusters and networks.

In the paper we show also how such process can be pushed further and national cultural barriers can be broken using ICT technologies and new organizational models. As a concrete example we have discussed here the prosumer model adopted by Master-Up to support the harmonization of Molecular Science skills and knowledge at European level through the formation of a network of University Test Centers running SESs and feeding distributed repositories of Learning Objects. The approach proposed enables the adoption of continuously quality improving mechanisms (thanks to its coordinated and sustainable nature) and supports long-term economic growth.

This is the line along which ECTN will develop. Next year efforts will be devoted to consolidating the process described above by increasing the number of TCs, spreading the use of EchemTest® Proficiency Certificates, enhancing the perception of scientific and teaching advances achieved by the VEC on the open journal system e-magazine VIRT&L-COMM so as to achieve full sustainability within the time spanning of the ECHEMTEST$^+$ project.

Acknowledgments. Support from Master-UP, the ECTN Association and its member HEIs is gratefully acknowledged.

The authors are partially supported by three projects financed by Basic Research Fund, 2015, University of Perugia: G-Lorep and EoL: interfacing between a repository of didactic-scientific material repositories and e-assessment environments (S. Tasso), G-Lorep and Moodle: integration between repository and LCMS (learning content management system) (S. Pallottelli), Computational approaches for the efficient use of General Purpose GPU Computing (O. Gervasi).

References

1. Morone, P., Taylor, R.: Knowledge Diffusion and Innovation: Modelling Complex Entrepreneurial Behaviours. Edward Elgar Publishing, Cheltenham (2010). ISBN 9781847209160
2. Toffler, A.: The Third Wave: The Classic Study of Tomorrow. Bantam, New York (1980)
3. Xie, C., Bagozzi, R.: Trying to prosume: toward a theory of consumers as co-creators of value. J. Acad. Mark. Sci. **36**(1), 109–122 (2008)
4. Arrow, K.: The Economic Welfare and the Allocation of Resources for Invention in The Rate and Direction of Inventive Activity: Economic and Social Factors. Princeton University Press (1962). http://www.nber.org/books/univ62-1. ISBN 0-87014-304-2

5. Fitzgerald, B.: The transformation of open source software. MIS Q. **30**(3), 587–598 (2006). https://doi.org/10.2307/25148740
6. https://mirrors.creativecommons.org/getcreative/. Accessed 8 May 2018
7. Gamalielsson, J., Lundell, B.: Sustainability of open source software communities beyond a fork: how and why has the LibreOffice project evolved? J. Syst. Softw. **89**, 128–145 (2014). https://doi.org/10.1016/j.jss.2013.11.1077S
8. Nordhaus, W.D.: Invention, Growth and Welfare: A Theoretical Treatment of Technical Change. The MIT Press, Cambridge (1969)
9. Freeman, C., Soete, L.: The Economics of Industrial Innovation. Routledge, Abingdon (1997)
10. Frasca, A., Morone, P.: Innovazione, network di imprese e conoscenza: quale ruolo la geographical proximity? J. Public Policy **19**(2), 141–173 (1999)
11. Polany, M.: The Tacit Dimension. University of Chicago Press, Chicago (2009). ISBN 9780226672984
12. Nonaka, I., Takeuchi, H.: The Knowledge-Creating Company. Oxford University Press, Oxford (1995). ISBN 9780195092691
13. Porter, M.E.: Cluster and the new economics of competition. Harv. Bus. Rev. **76**(6), 77–90 (1998)
14. Hakansson, H.: Industrial Technological Development: A Network Approach. Croom Helm Ltd., London (1987)
15. Gervasi, O., Laganà, A.: EoL: a web-based distance assessment system. In: Laganà, A., et al. (eds.) ICCSA 2004. LNCS, vol. 3044, pp. 854–862. Springer, Heidelberg (2004). https://doi.org/10.1007/978-3-540-24709-8_90. ISBN 978-3-540-24709-8
16. Laganà, A., et al.: ELCHEM: a metalaboratory to develop grid e-learning technologies and services for chemistry. In: Gervasi, O., et al. (eds.) ICCSA 2005. LNCS, vol. 3480, pp. 938–946. Springer, Heidelberg (2005). https://doi.org/10.1007/11424758_97. ISBN 978-3-540-32043-2
17. Gervasi, O., Riganelli, A., Pacifici, L., Laganà, A.: VMSLab-G: a virtual laboratory prototype for molecular science on the grid. Future Gener. Comput. Syst. **20**(5), 717–726 (2004). https://doi.org/10.1016/j.future.2003.11.015
18. Vella, F., Neri, I., Gervasi, O., Tasso, S.: A simulation framework for scheduling performance evaluation on CPU-GPU heterogeneous system. In: Murgante, B., et al. (eds.) ICCSA 2012. LNCS, vol. 7336, pp. 457–469. Springer, Heidelberg (2012). https://doi.org/10.1007/978-3-642-31128-4_34. ISBN 978-3-642-31128-4
19. Gervasi, O., Tasso, S., Laganà, A.: Immersive molecular virtual reality based on X3D and web services. In: Gavrilova, M., et al. (eds.) ICCSA 2006. LNCS, vol. 3980, pp. 212–221. Springer, Heidelberg (2006). https://doi.org/10.1007/11751540_23. ISBN 978-3-540-34071-3
20. Costantini, A., Tasso, S., Gervasi, O.: Visualization and web services for studying molecular properties. In: ICCSA 2009, pp. 222–228. IEEE (2009). https://doi.org/10.1109/ICCSA.2009.41. ISBN 978-0-7695-3701-6
21. Tasso, S., Pallottelli, S., Gervasi, O., Tanase, R., Rui, M.: Synchronized content and metadata management in a federation of distributed repositories of chemical learning objects. In: Gervasi, O., et al. (eds.) ICCSA 2017. LNCS, vol. 10406, pp. 14–28. Springer, Cham (2017). https://doi.org/10.1007/978-3-319-62398-6_2. ISBN 978-3-319-62398-6
22. Pallottelli, S., Tasso, S., Pannacci, N., Costantini, A., Lago, N.F.: Distributed and collaborative learning objects repositories on grid networks. In: Taniar, D., Gervasi, O., Murgante, B., Pardede, E., Apduhan, B.O. (eds.) ICCSA 2010. LNCS, vol. 6019, pp. 29–40. Springer, Heidelberg (2010). https://doi.org/10.1007/978-3-642-12189-0_3

23. Tasso, S., Pallottelli, S., Bastianini, R., Laganà, A.: Federation of distributed and collaborative repositories and its application on science learning objects. In: Murgante, B., Gervasi, O., Iglesias, A., Taniar, D., Apduhan, B.O. (eds.) ICCSA 2011. LNCS, vol. 6784, pp. 466–478. Springer, Heidelberg (2011). https://doi.org/10.1007/978-3-642-21931-3_36

24. Tasso, S., Pallottelli, S., Ferroni, M., Bastianini, R., Laganà, A.: Taxonomy management in a federation of distributed repositories: a chemistry use case. In: Murgante, B., et al. (eds.) ICCSA 2012. LNCS, vol. 7333, pp. 358–370. Springer, Heidelberg (2012). https://doi.org/10.1007/978-3-642-31125-3_28

25. Tasso, S., Pallottelli, S., Ciavi, G., Bastianini, R., Laganà, A.: An efficient taxonomy assistant for a federation of science distributed repositories: a chemistry use case. In: Murgante, B., et al. (eds.) ICCSA 2013. LNCS, vol. 7971, pp. 96–109. Springer, Heidelberg (2013). https://doi.org/10.1007/978-3-642-39637-3_8

26. Mariotti, M., Gervasi, O., Vella, F., Cuzzocrea, A., Costantini, A.: Strategies and systems towards grids and clouds integration: a DBMS-based solution. Future Gener. Comput. Syst. https://doi.org/10.1016/j.future.2017.02.047

27. Costantini, A., Gervasi, O., Zollo, F., Caprini, L.: User interaction and data management for large scale grid applications. J. Grid Comput. 12(3), 485497 (2014). https://doi.org/10.1007/s10723-014-9300-0

A Circular Economy Proposal on CO_2 Reuse to Produce Methane Using Energy from Renewable Sources

Antonio Laganà[1,3]([✉]) [iD] and Lorenzo di Giorgio[2,3] [iD]

[1] Dipartimento di Chimica, Biologia e Biotecnologie,
Università di Perugia, 06123 Perugia, Italy
lagana05@gmail.com
[2] Master UP srl, 06123 Perugia, Italy
[3] Dipartimento di Economia, Università di Perugia,
06123 Perugia, Italy

Abstract. The case of a cluster of companies and Public Institutions producing innovation in the field of storing energy obtained from renewable sources and investing in new circular production models is investigated. The role played by externalities in making the production cycle itself a social welfare by minimizing the deadweight losses is examined in detail in the light of the Klepper and Nordhaus models and by performing a Microeconomic Analysis. The study singles out the importance of strategically positioning industrial innovation in the stream of circular economy. As a specific case study the efforts played by Master UP srl in trying to drive such segment of the energy circular economy to success by developing an efficient and fruitful business for carbon neutral methane production is analyzed in terms of production isoquant curves.

Keywords: Circular economy · Computer simulations
Catalytic processes

1 Introduction

At present, increasing efforts are devoted to the development of circular economy initiatives. Recently, the Università degli Studi di Perugia with the support of Master UP srl, a former spin-off of the same University operating in the market of industrial innovation, has submitted the RIA proposal n. 763936 FREE-METHANE to the European Framework Programme Horizon 2020 (H2020) call H2020-LCE-2017-RES-RIA-twoStage under the activity LCE-06-17-Nkt. The goal of that project was to develop new knowledge for the production of carbon neutral methane through chemical catalytic conversion of CO_2 waste flue gases using renewable energies and implement it as validated laboratory technology. To this end advanced computer modeling and research activities of some public institutions were combined with the technological expertise of some private companies.

© Springer International Publishing AG, part of Springer Nature 2018
O. Gervasi et al. (Eds.): ICCSA 2018, LNCS 10964, pp. 549–562, 2018.
https://doi.org/10.1007/978-3-319-95174-4_43

The detailed information on the scientific project are given in Ref. [1] and its partners were the University of the Basque country in Vitoria (Spain), the European Chemistry Thematic Network (ECTN) Association (Belgium), the University of Barcelona (Spain), the National Agency for New Technologies, Energy and the Sustainable Economic Development of Italy (ENEA), Blurock Consulting AB (Sweden), RPC srl (Italy) the National Center for Scientific Research of France (CNRS), the Leuphana University of Luneburg (Germany).

The project was evaluated as "clear, quantified, ambitious and pertinent to the call and its aim to design an integrated system for the production of methane from carbon dioxide, its easy storage, safe transport and efficient use was found to be sound". The methodology was found to be "credible and good". The quoted positive elements are: "production of H_2 will be optimized to enhance the yield/cost ratio and low cost nanomaterials will be used to host redox mediators; CH_4 will be produced through heterogeneous Ni-catalysed reactions already validated in existing apparatus and will be transformed in clathrate hydrates for safe storage and transportation. This is well justified and substantiated. Strategies to mitigate the impact of contaminants from CO_2 streams will be developed. These are clear and appropriate".

However, because of "some shortcoming in documenting the work to reduce costs of electrolitic cells by 70%, the impact of contaminants in CO_2 and the evolution from heterogeneous to homogeneous catalysis", the project did not make it for the second round of the selection. Since then progress has been made, as will be reported in the last section of this paper, on improving on the mentioned shortcoming to get ready for a next H2020 call on CO_2 conversion.

The main focus of the present paper is, indeed, on a revisitation of the project performed during the stage of LdG at Master UP srl [2] in the light of the Klepper [3] and Nordhaus [4] models and on the performing of a microeconomic analysis in order to position the related industrial innovation in the stream of circular economy and, more specifically, to single out the role played by Externalities (Ex) in making the production cycle itself a social welfare. This is aimed at offering to computational modelers of circular economy appropriate examples and ideas on how to handle energetic problems.

Accordingly, the paper is articulated as follows:

In Sect. 2 the key economics and industrial innovation relationships producing significant Exs are discussed;
In Sect. 3 the conditions for increasing marginal Ecological Positive Externalities ($EPEx$s) are discussed;
In Sect. 4 some conclusions are drawn.

2   Economics and Industrial Innovation Relationships

Traditional industrial economic approaches, both classical and neoclassical, have focused on the evaluation of tangible and immediately verifiable economic indicators (e.g. levels of production, prices and quantities, etc.) characterized by simple and rigorous mathematical formalism. For this reason, in the past, the impact of innovation on economy has been largely neglected.

2.1 Process and Product Innovations

In recent years, instead, increasing attention has been put on the role played by innovative industrial processes as a factor of economic growth [5,6]. The turning point of the traditional approach was reached when a differentiation of the concept of invention and innovation was introduced [6] in that the first generates a new product or production process whereas the latter concerns the direct application of the former idea. This differentiation is extremely important and has been adopted by various researchers when separating radical from incremental innovations. In this respect four different kinds of innovative models: (A) Process Innovations, (B) Product Innovations, (C) Exploitation of New Markets (D) Organizational Innovations, were listed.

Process innovations consist of improvements of the industrial production processes related to production costs as follows:

Case a. Process Innovations with lower Fixed Costs (FC) and constant Marginal Costs (MC) in which we have

1. A reduction of FC with an adjustment of Average Costs (AC)
2. A lowering of AC (AC1)
3. A reduction of MES (Minimum Efficient Scale) (i.e: the fraction of the product total quantity (Q) efficiently produced at a minimum AC) with a resulting reduction of Economies of Scale (EoS)

Case b. Process innovations with lower MC and constant FC in which we have:

1. A lowering of both MC and AC curves
2. A reduction of AC and MC
3. An increment of medium level of production
4. A reduction of MC with a resulting increase of MES

Case c. Process innovations with lower MC and incremental FC in which we have:

1. A Labour Intensive (LI) process regime which has a steep slope and intercept with lower FC (and consequent higher MC)
2. A Capital Intensive (CI) process regime which has a less steep slope and intercept with high FC and lower MC

In Case (c) a LI regime leads to maintaining a constant return to scale, with a positioning on a lower production scale, whereas a CI regime leads to a higher exploitation of EoS and a transition to increasing return to scale [7].

This model, as pointed out by Schumpeter [5], would allow a small enterprise to grow thanks to the exploitation of new economies of scale according to the transition from the LI regime to the CI one.

The product innovation, on the other side, is different because it does not lead to a change in production processes but just on the proportions of production factors in the Cobb-Douglas production function defined as:

$$Y = AL^\beta K^\alpha. \tag{1}$$

In the above equation Y is the total production (i.e: the value of all the goods produced intra year of 365.25 days), A is the total productivity factor (TFP) (i.e.: the value of the total quantity of output) formulated as a multi-combination of the L and K factors with L being the Labour given as the Production Factor expressed as the total number of person-hours intra year and K being the Capital given as the Production Factor expressed as the actual value of all machineries, equipments and buildings also for a year. The exponents α and β are the output elasticities of both Capital and Labour factors determined using available technology.

In this case the analysis results more complex because the new product will follow the dynamical industrial and market processes (as we shall further discuss later for the Klepper [3], Nordhaus [4] and Arrow [8] models).

2.2   The Reward Theory of Patents of W. Nordhaus

For innovation within production processes it has to be pointed out that (see Refs. [3,4]) when an innovation is introduced, regardless of whether it is of process or product, it creates distortive effects, not only directly on the user enterprise (allowing an increase in production possibilities) but also on the other companies and economic agents operating in the economy (the already mentioned Externalities).

After all, any kind of innovation that alters the production processes produces as secondary effect that of creating knowledge within the market. This knowledge is then transformed into a public good that in its dual nature of Non-Rivalry and Non-Exclusion can be enjoyed by anyone creating a Free Riding distortion (FR). Because of this it has become necessary to resort to patent protection in order to encourage new innovative processes and resolve the externalities and possible FR phenomena.

In 1969 Nordhaus [4] modeled this effect with his Reward Theory of Patents highlighting how patent protection, as an exclusive right, guarantees a monopoly position to its owner while creating forms of social welfare for the entire economy.

Formally, the innovative Nordhaus model relates the Guaranteed Prize from Surplus (W) to the premium guaranteed to the monopolist based on the price-cost margin or maximum profit (π), the consumer surplus (s) and the deadweight loss of social welfare and disequilibrium due to the monopoly (d) using the following equation $W = \pi + s + d$. Accordingly, the exclusive right involves a trade-off between welfare, which would be created with its positive Exs and profits and monopolistic incentives for the industry.

This stimulates innovations by avoiding dynamic loss of social welfare and at the same time ensuring a flexible creation of knowledge. This leads also to a wise use of the Patent Time Length (PTL) if π is not too large to excessively monopolize the market for long time while still creating a knowledge that can be used by the company. Therefore, π and d will have to be directly proportioned so that the monopolist depending on the PTL loses every year t a π equal to the Discount Rate $X(t)$ estimated as:

$$X(t) = \frac{1 - e^{-rt}}{r} \tag{2}$$

where r is the interest rate. Accordingly one obtains for the company net expected benefits equal to $\overline{W} - dX(t)$ with $dX(t)$ representing the discounted value of the deadweight loss during the t years of the duration of the PTL protection ($\overline{W} - dX(t)$ decreases with increasing t). Therefore, it will be necessary to maximize the expected award W subject to the constraint $c \leq X(t) \cdot \pi$ where c is the cost associated with the introduction of the innovation. In this way, the respect of the price-cost margin π taken as an argument of the function of the deadweight loss $d(\pi)$, will allow the monopolist to keep a correct proportion in $P \wedge MC$ (such as a balance between its Market Power and the benefit to the Society). Accordingly, the creation of innovation results, thanks to the patents as an incentive for the company to achieve monopolistic positions. In this way, the dynamics of the market will also be modified with continuous attempts to innovate by the companies.

2.3   The S. Kleppers Model: The Microeconomic Analysis

The process of monopoly exclusivity can be analyzed either microeconomically (with a focus on entry and exit of companies from the economic and industrial paradigm) or macroeconomically (with a focus on the benefits of innovation on economic growth).

The Klepper's model [3] attempts withintra microeconomic approach the rationalization of the ways in which companies make their entry and exit from highly innovative markets by analysing the regularities of a dynamic system.

In particular, intrany given time period t there is a number K_t of potential new Entrant companies. At the same time, the industry changes intra dynamic way its knowledge and production capacity and sets as well certain technological-productive requirements in order to allow the potential new entrants to access the market. The associated variable s tends, for each company, to a maximum value $SMax$.

Obviously, the probability that such skills will influence the success in introducing a product innovation is given by how these skills will be implemented in the R&D activities of the ith company. In the t period this probability will be given by $s_i + g(rd_{i,t})$ where rd is the cost of the R&D activity and the $g(rd)$ function is the probability of success of R&D in producing innovation.

In this way, any manufacturer will be able to obtain extra profit from the new innovative product, having superior quality and characteristics when compared with the standard product until it becomes the new market standard, making the mono or oligopolistic annuity vanish. This period, characterized by monopoly rents, is called G. Each company will therefore have at G_{t+1} two activities to carry out:

(a) consistently look for new process innovations to produce at lower costs (according to the variable cost-innovation model);
(b) monitor competitors for related innovations at a high fixed cost called F.

As intrany productive activity there will be a given demand for the good denoted by Q_t the market demand function $Q_t = f(p_t)$ that will tend, as time t increases, to make the quantity produced always larger, with time dependent automatic adjustments of price p_t.

From these premises it can be argued that Incumbents (the companies that will remaintractive in the market) and new Entrants will interact at the level of product and process innovation by changing their chances of entering and leaving the industry.

This is formalized in the following equation embodying the model of S. Klepper in its full expression

$$E(\pi_{i,t}) = RD_{i,t} + NP_{i,t} - F \tag{3}$$

where the expected total profit $E(\pi_{i,t})$ is defined in terms of:

- $RD_{i,t} = [s_i + g(rd_{i,t})] \, G - rd_{i,t}$ indicating the company's expected net (with no costs from R&D activity) profit from innovation associated R&D products, with $s_i + g(rd_{i,t})$ being the probability that the ith company develops product innovation (based on its own competences s_i and on the possibility of achieving product innovation $g(rd_{i,t})$ out of the R&D costs $rd_{i,t}$) and G being the monopolistic profit including the R&D costs in the time period t
- $NP_{i,t} = \left[Q_{i,t-1} \wedge \left(\frac{Q_t}{Q_{t-1}} \right) + \Delta q_{i,t} \right] [p_t - c + I(rc_{i,t})] - rc_{i,t} - m\Delta q_{i,t}$ indicating the net profit obtained from the production of a quantity of the pre-innovative standard products (net of both the expenditure in R&D processes and of the adjustments made on the quantity of output adapted to new market demands with bult-in innovations in the production process) with $Q_{i,t}$ being the output of the standard product of the ith company in the time period t, the $\left(\frac{Q_t}{Q_{t-1}} \right)$ ratio being the market request and the expression $Q_{i,t-1} \wedge \left[Q_{i,t-1} \left(\frac{Q_t}{Q_{t-1}} \right) \right]$ being the difference in output of the standard product of the ith company in the time interval $t, t-1$. In the same equation $\Delta q_{i,t}$ is the expansion of the output in period t under the condition $\left[Q_{i,t-1} \left(\frac{Q_t}{Q_{t-1}} \right) \right]$ (with $m\Delta q_{i,t}$ being the related cost adjustment), $I(rc_{i,t})$ is the opportunity of obtaining process innovationfor the ith company in the time period t.
- F indicating the cost of monitoring the innovative processes of competitors.

Through this model S. Klepper rationalizes the dynamics of entry and exit of companies from a more or less innovative industry given the expected profit that they will have net of costs and profits obtained from innovative processes. More specifically the Incumbents (as well as the new entrants) will only be able to do so when $E(\pi_{i,t}) > 0$ (that is when their expected profits will be larger than zero). The new entrants, however, will be subject to an entry constraint given by the limit $E_t = K_t(1 - H(s_i))$ where $H(s)$ is the accumulated competence necessary for entry into the industry at time t. It is therefore obvious to say that as time t increases the system will tend to both require more and more experiences and radical innovations for entry, and to stabilize the average prices imposed by the Incumbents following the marginal innovations and the consequent cost reductions [9].

Then, after a first embryonic phase (named EP or G) and a second growth one, there is a phase of industrial maturity in which the market will be complete with constant output growth (in equilibrium with demand) and market shares stabilized later the old competitions.

In this way the expected profits will tend to reach a value close to or below zero, such that: $E(\pi_{i,t}) < 0$ because the prices too low created by the competition will lead to a difficult entry for the new entrants (regardless of their accumulated competence $H(s)$). The Kleppers model applied to the innovative realities allows to draw, in this way, important conclusions on a possible strategic positioning in the industry, based first on the analysis and then on the knowledge of the phase in which the market itself is operating at a given time.

3 The Increasing Marginal Ecological Positive Externalities and the Deadweight Loss Compensation Effect

The above described models can be applied to the considered activities of Master UP and related patents. In particular, we discuss here the case of the apparatus designed for re-using carbon dioxide (CO_2) to produce methane (CH_4) intra circular economy model.

3.1 The Circular Economic Basic Scheme of the Apparatus

Intra linear economy the following steps (lhs terms) characterize the production of methane

- (A) extraction of a raw gas $\rightarrow$ capture (and storage) of waste CO_2
- (B) refinement and production of CH_4 $\rightarrow$ CO_2 to CH_4 conversion
- (C) distribution of CH_4 to users $\rightarrow$ distribution of CH_4 to users
- (D) consumption and waste CO_2 production $\rightarrow$ combustion and waste CO_2 production

In the scheme adopted in circular economy step A "naturally" chains with step D because its input (CO_2) is the same of the output of D. The specific technology involved in the present project concerns, therefore, step B that is articulated into the following components

- an electrolyzer produces H_2 from water using electric energy generated by renewable sources;
- CH_4 is produced from CO_2 using a reactor based on a solid state catalyser;

The prototype apparatus described in Ref. [1] is, indeed, designed for this and is at the same time robust enough to represent a proper basis for further developments and mature enough to be considered for innovating the present energy storage scenario withintra B2B Circular and Ecological Economic system. Accordingly, it is also well suited to represent a proper application of the above illustrated theories. A circular economy is, in fact, a regenerative system in which differences in resource input, waste emission and related energetic balances are minimized by slowing, closing and narrowing material and energy loops. The concept recognizes the importance of the economy needing to work effectively at all scales for large and small businesses, for organizations and individuals, for global and local market. Transitioning to a circular economy does not only amount to adjustments aimed at reducing the negative impacts of the linear economy. Rather, it represents a systemic shift that builds long-term resilience, generates business and economic opportunities, and provides environmental and social benefits.

Basically we can assume that the methanator and Master UP are a proper example of the meaning and practice of creating a new economic and industrial logic based not just on profits but also on long-term sustainability. In this respect it is only necessary to understand why an enterprise should decide to move from linear to a circular economy model. For this purpose, we decided to work out a suitable production paradigm based on a simplified version of the Nordhaus model in which the expected monopoly profit is guaranteed by the creation of patents. From this assumption one gets a continous innovation stream that guarantees, even for a limited period, a possible dominant position. At the same time, however, it is necessary that the patent form also maximizes social welfare by reducing dynamic deadweight loss. This is possible through the creation of patents conceived on machinery aimed to the creation of a sustainable paradigm of the production cycle. In fact, in this way, patent protection would create a triple benefit:

I. Microeconomic on business: Allowing the creation of maximum profit with monopolistic positions;
II. Microeconomic on the society: Allowing the creation of increasing positive Exs thanks to the reduction and reuse of waste material;
III. Macroeconomic on the environment: Allowing long-term environmental sustainability with the creation of $EPEx$ (see Fig. 1)

This would lead intra dynamic way, as shown by Klepper, to continuous innovative research in these areas by companies in order to ensure their survival in the industry, ensuring, once the patent protection on the new process is over, maintaining a relationship price-cost adjusted to market demand. Every time, however, those companies will seek new innovations and invest in R&D for new circular production models will only produce more positive benefits and Exs that will make the production cycle itself a social welfare minimizing the process of deadweight loss (see Fig. 1).

Now let us assume that $Dl = p_m + Ex^-$ where Dl is the Deadweight loss of the Nordhaus model, p_m is the price set by monopolistic firms (which are always larger than zero) and Ex^- is the negative externality created by the production process. Now let us assume also that all the possible $Ex^- = Wst$ (where Wst is the Waste Flow created by the monopolistic firm). In this way when Wst

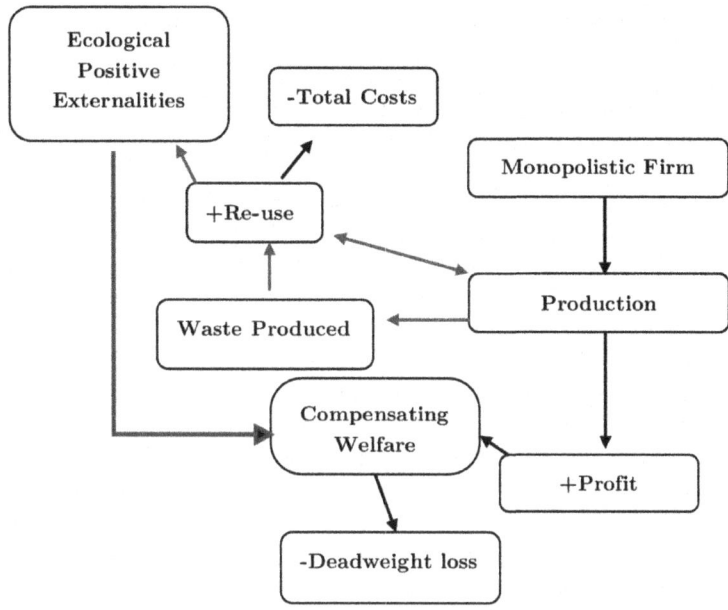

Fig. 1. Positive Exs and compensating effect of Re-use production processes

grows we have an increase of the negative esternalities and at the same time an increase of positive externalities when it decreases according to the following partial derivative expression

$$\frac{\partial Ex^-}{\partial W st} > 0 \wedge \frac{\partial Ex^+}{\partial W st} < 0 \tag{4}$$

In this way all the industrial externalities are created by Wastes Flows of Production processes. For a truly Circular Economic process there should be zero Waste and a total Re-Use of Wasted Production Factors according to the relationship:

if $W st = 0 \rightarrow Ex^- = 0 \rightarrow Dl = p_m$
if $\exists$ Reuse $\rightarrow W st < 0 \rightarrow Ex^- < 0 \rightarrow Ex^+$.

In the last one negative externalities become Positive (Ex^+). This creates a compensation effect with the negative ones due to the prices set by the monopolistic industry in $Welfare/Dl$ ratio. In this way everything becomes dependent just from the patent concession which assure a monopolistic position which induces, according to Klepper model, always new entrant to improve their innovation expenditure $[s_i + g(rd_{i,t})] G - rd_{i,t} \wedge c + I(rc_{i,t})$ trying to enter into the industry or to assume the temporary monopolistic position. In this case assuming the creation of a very simple Circular Model every businesss effort in time $t = i$ (with $i = 1, 2, \ldots, n$) allows the creation of an exponential product and processes innovation for re-use of waste factors guaranting an indirect increasing marginal Ecological Positive Externalities $EPEx$ for the society.

3.2   The Innovative Features of the Free Methane Project

Our project targets a key Chemistry community innovative objective as described in *Energy and Chemistry as an alliance for the Future* document of the German Bunsen Society for Physical Chemistry (2016). The document indicates the key challenges of the society with focus on energy efficiency, low-carbon energy and waste management. In particular, our plans refer to the Clean Energy (CE) Near Zero Emission (NZE) CO_2 call of the H2020 European framework programme [10] aiming at assembling an prototype apparatus for converting waste flues of carbon dioxide into methane (scalable and composable up to the order of MWs).

The first innovative feature of the proposed activity are: The simulation of the CO_2 conversion into methane based on the use of ab initio studies of the elementary chemical processes workflowed within the use of the Grid empowered simulators GEMS [11] that, whenever possible, gathers together in the same workflow the ab initio calculation of the potential energy surface of the involved elementary processes, the fitting of the ab initio values using accurate interpolation functions calibrated on both short and long range regions of the interaction, the integration of (quantum/quasiclassical) dynamical gas-gas and surface-gas equations to calculate rate coefficients together with the most detailed possible assemblage of the components of the overall kinetic scheme. All this is put together for a kinetic study of complex kinetics processes based on the use of the ZACROS package [12] allowing the calculation of detailed yields.

The second innovation element is the collection of data through an open science environment aimed at enhancing clean energy awareness by:

(A) coordinating a EU wide distribution of specific repositories based on the ioChemBD platform [13] managed via cloud access (DataHub/ FedDataPlatform) operating an open instance on top of the EGI cloud for In-silico studies at the service of atomistic simulations aimed at developing more efficient catalysts. This task provides cloud validation of data (parsing, organizing, publishing, analysing and storing information), the planning of new experiments and the design of new calculations;

(B) coordinating a network of (more than 100) European Higher Education Institutions managing e-learning infrastructures for disseminating and assessing molecular science knowledge and for using, as well, distributed LO REPositories (GLOREP) [14].

The third innovation element is the production of innovative technologies for:

(A) the electrolyser producing hydrogen using waste/excess electrical energy produced by renewable energy (wind/solar power) sources optimizing the estimated initial and running ratio yield/cost (patent request 10201700004794 of 18/01/2017 entitled: Electrolyser for the production of H_2);

(B) the methanator optimizing the conversion of CO_2 into CH_4 using an hetero-geneous catalytic reactor based on the P. Sabbatier process (patent 2864524 of 01/07/2016 entitled: Group for the storage of electric energy through methane production);

(C) deferring use of the produced CH_4 for further chemical applications and energy generation either through more traditional means (gasometer, cylinders, pipes, etc.) or innovative solid state or methane clathrate hydrate forming that minimizes safety risks during transportation (patents EP07010346 and WO/2007/122647).

The fourth innovation element is the development of technologies allowing:

(A) the assembling of a pre-commercial industrial device made of the above mentioned components for a user-tailored application. The pre-commercial industrial device will be designed and assembled by a large worldwide oper-ating Italy-based company that will coordinate competences in mechanical, electrical, electronic and automation plants of a certain number of partner companies) and suppliers;

(B) This objective will be pursued by involving world class technological indus-trial operators tackling the problem of transforming laboratory designed apparatuses in industrial ones. For this purpose the management of the electric and electronic components of the apparatus will be optimized in order to minimize electric power usage at critical stages and maximize the coordination of the various components. This will affect the overall efficiency of the system and will allow the possibility of carrying out extended mea-surement campaigns useful for the re-design of the apparatus in view also of composing together several units;

(C) The implementation of a generalizable circular economy demonstrator case of high economic relevance for the systematic re-use of CO_2 as a chemical and fuel feedstock. The demonstrators will produce CH_4 out of the waste by-product of other human activities.

The fifth innovation element is the identification of suitable demo applications:

A typical example of circular economy demo applications are wineries. A winery produces about one cubic meter of CO_2 at normal conditions per liter of wine of such high quality to be directly reduced using electricity gen-erated from renewable sources (wind, sun, etc.) in the same demo installation one can produce and store a quantity of CH_4 sufficient for the internal energy consumption of the whole year.

3.3 An Example of Quantitative Analysis of the Considered Process

The demo application we consider here is the case of a large winery wishing to convert to methane the CO_2 accumulated from the fermentation of wines dur-ing the related season. The particular importance of this demo is the fact that the produced CO_2 is virtually pure and does not require costly filtering tech-nologies. In the following we attempt to estimate whether for a one year period

EPEx conditions are fulfilled. Due to the relatively short period of time considered we assume for the sake of simplicity that we are in the ideal case of constant marginal productivity of the production factors (see Refs. [15,16]) though with the insertion of possible positive externalities at the initial ($t = t0$) time value of our revisited function. Under the mentioned conditions the $t0$ profit function $E(\pi_{t0})$ can be evaluated from Eq. 3 to be

$$E(\pi_{t0}) = TR_{t0} - [(FC_{t0} - \psi_{t0}) + VC_{t0}] \qquad (5)$$

where $TR_{t0} = P_{t0} \cdot Q_{t0}$ and $(FC_{t0} - \psi_{t0}) + VC_{t0}$ are the $t0$ total costs. We then assume that the $t0$ total cost is made of the expenditure associated with the energy used by the production process plus the expenditure associated with the R&D process. In Eq. 5 VC_{t0} corresponds to the R&D expenditure to convert CO_2 to CH_4 (again for simplicity we assume a 1:1 value while the yield of the apparatus is about 1:0.85 at 350° that is easily sustainable due to the exothermic nature of the process), FC_{t0} is the fixed energy cost for producing 1 cubic meter of CO_2 out of 1 liter of wine that turns out to be 0.5 euro and ψ_{t0} is the amount of energy stored per unit of volume when producing CH_4. Given that (at $t = t0$) the normalized price of one liter of wine is 1 euro, the fixed and R&D variable costs are both 0.5 euro per liter and ψ_{t0} is zero one has $E(1_{t0}) \to 0$.

At $t = t1$ ($t1 = 1$ in which the time unit is chosen so as to have 1 cubic meter of CH_4 production) ψ_{t1} is the amount of energy stored per unit of volume when producing CH_4 that from the simplified assumption made above is 1 with the other variables being equal to 1 as in $t0$. As a result at step $t1$ one obtains $E(\pi_{t1}) \to 0.5$. This means that the company shall get positive returns out of the innovation and will be encouraged both to increase the quantity of CO_2 to convert because they increase the production efficiency. The plot of the rhs part of Fig. 2, in fact, shows that, when plotting the production isoquant (the number of liters of wine that can be handled (or in other words the cubic meters of CO_2 that can be converted into CH_4) per Cost/Energy ratio) as a function of the Cost/Energy ratio, an increase of the production efficiency is obtained (in other words the production isoquant of the considered process shifts to lower values of the Cost/Energy ratio when the marginal rate of technical substitution (and equivalently the rate between the marginal productivity of production factor called also the SHIFTER) is constant in time [15] (the corresponding demand and supply curves of the Walrasian equilibrium hypothesis [17,18] plotted in the lhs part of the Figure).

As a result, the process will continue to produce at standard methods (still satisfying the market demand) while investing at the same time on R&D to increase the productivity of the production factors and shift the isoquant to higher efficiency when moving to next steps. The R&D variable cost can be kept inaltered thanks to its positive effect (as shown in step 1) creating a perspective of profit ($E(\pi) > 0$) to increase even further in subsequent steps. Therefore it can be concluded that the circular economy reuse of energy guarantees, through the registering of patents and the consequent temporary monopolistic situations, the fulfilment of the conditions of Positive Ecological Externality also for the societies and clusters of companies.

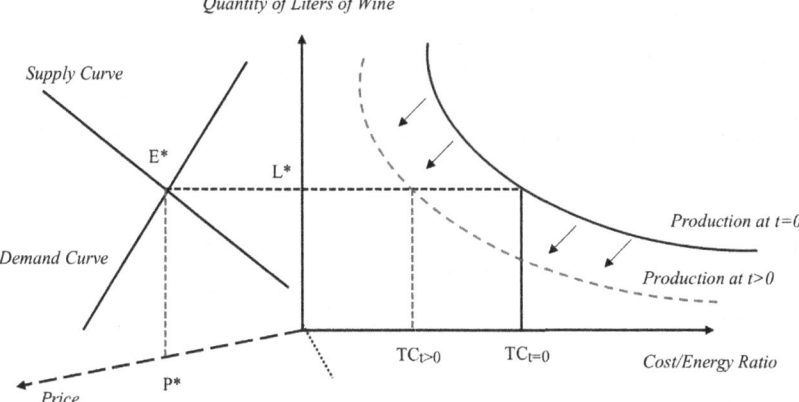

Fig. 2. Rhs part: plot of the SHIFTER of the production isoquant for positive externalities and compensating effect of Re-use production processes; Lhs part: plot of the walrasian general equilibrium

4   Conclusions and Future Plans

From the outcome of our study we can conclude that the joint efforts spent by a cluster of public institutions and private companies in pursuing the winery circular economy project based on an apparatus able to convert electricity generated from renewable sources to produce hydrogen and make it react with carbon dioxide to produce methane is worth to be carried out. For this reason it is adviceable that the partners of the Free Methane proposal reorganize the previous application to the related H2020 call into a more effective Clean Energy (CE) Near Zero Emission (NZE) CO₂ conversion one.

From the analysis reported in the paper we can desume that the Klepper model and in particular the Nordhaus welfare surplus mechanism seen before, are not just theoretical and mathematical formulations useful to understand economics but they are true planning tools for circular industry decisions and investment planning like the one proposed by Master UP, based on the positive effect of Re-use on industrial systems and a new approach to welfare for the entire society.

In particular, it has been shown how knowledge, both tacit and explicit, and its study is becoming increasingly important as a factor for economic development by generating competitive advantage. This knowledge, as shown in the paper, if it is conveyed not only to the individuals of a particular organisational context but also (at the aggregate level) to the market at large, generates other knowledge and activates a virtuous circle in whch knowledge creates further new knowledge within clusters and networks of companies and public institutions.

A particular evidence for that finding is obtained from the Microeconomics analysis illustrated in Sect. 3 that shows how companies get positive returns out of the innovation as particularly well evidenced when plotting the isoquant for the CO_2 to CH_4 conversion. The isoquant of the considered process, in fact, shifts to lower values of the Cost/Energy ratio.

Acknowledgments. Support from Master UP, the ECTN Association and its member HEIs is gratefully acknowledged.

References

1. Falcinelli, S., Capriccioli, A., Pirani, F., Vecchiocattivi, F., Stranges, S., Nicoziani, A., Topini, E., Laganà, A.: Fuel **209**, 802 (2017)
2. Di Giorgio, L.: Report on "Dynamic externalities of circular economy loops: a microeconomics analysis of inter-temporal production systems". VIRT&L-COMM (2018, submitted)
3. Klepper, S.: Entry, exit, growth and innovation over the product life cycle. Am. Econ. Rev. **86**, 3 (1996)
4. Nordhaus, W.D.: Invention, Growth and Welfare: A Theoretical Treatment of Technical Change. The MIT Press, Cambridge (1969)
5. Schumpeter, J.: History of Economic Analysis. Oxford University Press, New York (1954)
6. Fagerberg, J., Mowery, D.C. (ed.): Oxford Handbook of Innovation (OHEI) (2005)
7. Pompei, F.: Economics of Innovation. Department of Economics, University of Perugia (2017)
8. Arrow, K.: The Economic Welfare and the Allocation of Resources for Invention in The Rate and Direction of Inventive Activity: Economic and Social Factors. Princeton University Press (1962). http://www.nber.org/books/univ62-1. ISBN 0-87014-304-2
9. Garavaglia, C.: Determinanti entrata di nuove imprese nei settori industriali: una rassegna. Department of Economics, University of Perugia (2004)
10. Horizon 2020, Work Programme 2018–2020, Secure, Clean and Efficient Energy (European Commission Decision C(2017)7124 of 27 October 2017), Call Building a Low-Carbon, Climate Resilient Future: Secure, Clean and Efficient Energy
11. Laganà, A., Costantini, A., Gervasi, O., Faginas Lago, N., Manuali, C., Rampino, S.: COMPCHEM: progress towards GEMS a Grid Empowered Molecular Simulator and beyond. J. Grid Comput. **8**(4), 571–586 (2010)
12. http://zacros.org/
13. http://www.iochem-bd.org
14. Tasso, S., Pallottelli, S., Rui, M., Laganà, A.: Learning objects efficient handling in a federation of science distributed repositories. In: Murgante, B., et al. (eds.) ICCSA 2014. LNCS, vol. 8579, pp. 615–626. Springer, Cham (2014). https://doi.org/10.1007/978-3-319-09144-0_42
15. Solow, R.M.: A contribution to theory of economic growth. Oxf. J. **70**, 65–94 (1956)
16. Solow, R.M.: Technical changes and the aggregated production function. Rev. Econ. Stat. **39**(3), 312–320 (1957)
17. Scarf, H.: The Computation of Economic Equilibria, New Haven (1973)
18. Arrow, K., Hahn, F.H.: General Competitive Analysis, San Francisco (1971)

Nitrogen Gas on Graphene: Pairwise Interaction Potentials

Jelle Vekeman[1,2] ⓘ, Noelia Faginas-Lago[2(✉)] ⓘ, Inmaculada G. Cuesta[1,3(✉)] ⓘ,
José Sánchez-Marín[1] ⓘ, and Alfredo Sánchez De Merás[1,3(✉)] ⓘ

[1] Instituto de Ciencia Molecular, Universidad de Valencia, Valencia, Spain
{garciain,sanchez}@uv.es
[2] Dipartimento di Chimica, Biologia e Biotecnologie, Università di Perugia,
Perugia, Italy
noelia.faginaslago@unipg.it
[3] Departamento de química física, Universidad de Valencia, Valencia, Spain

Abstract. We investigate different types of potential parameters for the graphene-nitrogen interaction. Interaction energies calculated at DFT level are fitted with the semi-emperical Improved Lennard-Jones potential. Both a pseudo-atom potential and a full atomistic potential are considered. Furthermore, we consider the influence of the electrostatic part on the parameters using different charge schemes found in the literature as well as optimizing the charges ourselves. We have obtained parameters for both the nitrogen dimer and the graphene-nitrogen system. For the former, the four-charges Cracknell scheme reproduces with high precision the CCSD(T) interaction energy as well as the experimental diffusion coefficient in both the pseudo-atom and full atomstic potential. In the second case, the atom-atom model provides an average interaction energy of $2.3\,\mathrm{kcal/mol}$, comparable with the experimental graphene-N_2 interaction of $2.4\,\mathrm{kcal/mol}$.

1 Introduction

N_2 gas is considered a contaminating part of natural gas [1], an energy source believed to be a more environmental friendly alternative for fossil fuels [2]. The efficient use of natural gas requires the separation of, among other components, N_2 from the combustible parts [3]. Furthermore, also in other pre- and post-combustion processes, N_2 needs to be separated from other components [4–6].

Separation of small gases is often achieved via selective adsorption in porous materials exhibiting strong van der Waals interactions [7]. A lot of possible candidates are currently being investigated [8]. At both the theoretical and experimental level, one of the first characterization steps of an adsorbent candidate is the adsorption of N_2 gas at $77\,\mathrm{K}$ [9,10]. Because of its inert properties it is assumed that the pore volume of the material can thus be measured [11]. Ohba et al. have even suggested that the amount of graphene layers in a sheet could be determined via N_2 adsorption [12].

O. Gervasi et al. (Eds.): ICCSA 2018, LNCS 10964, pp. 563–578, 2018.
https://doi.org/10.1007/978-3-319-95174-4_44

Molecular modelling of processes like gas adsorption on different materials has received increasing interest because of the access to as-yet unsynthesized materials and the microscopic view it offers [13]. If modelling wants to be predictive for experimental research, accurate models are needed, giving results that are directly comparable to experiment [14]. It is thus important to obtain accurate models for the N_2 molecule [15].

Graphene and derived materials have shown great promise in the adsorption of small gases, among which N_2, through van der Waals interactions [16,17]. These interactions, because relatively weak, are not easy to determine from an experimental setup and, therefore, the theoretical calculations that can reproduce them play an important role in the determination of the structure and energies of the adsorbed molecules. It is for this reason that we are aiming to provide a set of interaction potentials to model the graphene-N_2 system in a simple yet accurate fashion, suitable for direct implementation in molecular dynamics. The circumcoronene(ccn)-N_2 system has been chosen as a model for quantum chemical study. The potentials have been derived from adequate DFT calculations in order to describe the interactions present in this system, mainly of dispersive origin. These contributions are essentially an effect of the electronic correlation and therefore of quantum mechanical origin. Their precise determination for systems of great size with approximate methods, is still today considered one of the most difficult problems for theoretical chemistry.

The potential we have chosen for the evaluation of the dispersive interactions between molecules is the Improved Lennard-Jones (ILJ) potential [18,19], a modified version of the Lennard-Jones (LJ) potential which has shown to improve the latter without introducing too much complexity [20–23].

In addition to dispersion interactions there are electrostatic contributions to the force field that often play a significant role in the interactions. In this context, we will investigate the influence of different charge schemes in the N_2 molecule. The electrostatic interaction is routinely added to potentials representing the dispersion interaction via the Coulomb summation [24,25]. The charges, which have no true physical meaning, are often chosen more or less arbitrarily as to represent a molecular property of choice, usually the first non-zero multipole present in the molecule [26]. In the case of N_2 this is a quadrupole.

In Sect. 2 we cover the computational details of this work. Section 3 discusses the potential energy models that we considered. The potentials are then tested in Sect. 4 by calculating the diffusion coefficient. Finally in Sect. 5, we draw some conclusions.

2   Computational Details

The N_2 and ccn monomers were optimized at the B3LYP/6-31G** [27,28] level and assumed rigid in further calculations. The bond distance in the N_2 dimer was 1.106 Å, while the average C-C and C-H distances in ccn resulted to be 1.421 Å and 1.088 Å respectively.

All the DFT interaction energy calculations were performed at the B97-D/TZV2P [29,30] level using the Gaussian 09 program [52]. The counter-poise correction was used in all cases to diminish the basis set superposition error [31]. The B97-D functional recovers the attractive forces of dispersion through a correction of empirical nature designed to adequately describe the correlation of long-range origin. The representation of non-covalent systems, including many van der Waals pure complexes, is good, reaching on average the CCSD(T) precision [20,29,32–34], and, unlike the latter, allows the theoretical character-ization of large molecular systems. The combination of a small computational cost and reasonable precision makes it an efficient quantum chemical method for the study of systems involving polycyclic aromatic hydrocarbons (PAHs). Similarly, the use of the split-valence triple-zeta basis supplemented with two polarization functions TZV2P has also been found sufficient to represent the polarization effects in similar systems.

For the N_2 dimer, 99 different relative configurations were generated at ran-dom and for each of those a scan over the distance was done between 3.4 Å and 20 Å. Close to the equilibrium distance, more points were sampled, while at longer distances, less points were included. This led to a total of 44 distances that were calculated for all of the 99 relative orientations.

Since graphene is virtually an infinite system, ccn ($C_{54}H_{18}$), was used as a model for DFT calculations. Ten different N_2 orientations were generated with respect to the ccn molecule at random positions above the ccn plane whereby the N_2 was not allowed to take positions above the outer benzene rings to avoid edge effects. For these geometries a scan was done over distances between 2.4 Å and 20 Å. Again, care was taken to include more points in the equilibrium region than at large distances. A total of 30 distances were included. Three of the ran-domly generated N_2 molecule orientations are shown in Fig. 1 together with a ccn molecule. This approach has proven its worth previously [20,34]. To optimize the parameters specifying the potentials for the N_2-N_2 and the ccn-N_2 interactions, we fitted them to the respective interaction energies at DFT level.

The molecular dynamics simulations were done using the DL_POLY v.2.2 [35] program in the microcanonical (NVE) ensemble using periodic boundary conditions in the x, y and z-direction at standard conditions (273 K and 1 atm). All simulations were run for 5 000 000 time steps with 3 000 000 equilibration steps and a time step of 1 fs. This implies a total run time of 5 ns. Equilibration was verified via monitoring of relevant properties through time, such as energy and temperature. Van der Waals and Coulombic cutoffs were set to 18 Å. As a starting position 100 N_2, were randomly positioned in a cubic cell with sides of 159.82 Å to ensure a density of 1.139 kg/m^3, the density of N_2 at standard conditions.

The diffusion coefficient, D, for a single particle is defined by the Einstein equation

$$D = \frac{1}{2d} \lim_{\tau \to \infty} \frac{d}{d\tau} \langle [\overrightarrow{r}(\tau) - \overrightarrow{r}(0)]^2 \rangle \tag{1}$$

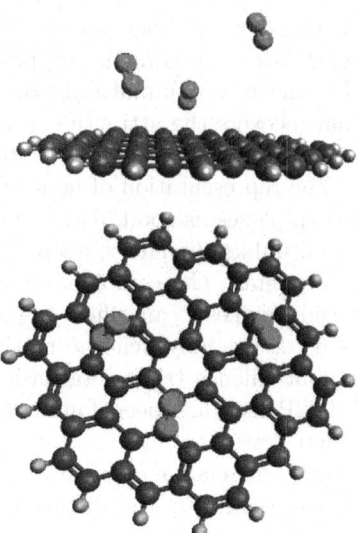

Fig. 1. Side- and top-view of a ccn molecule with three of the randomly generated positions for the N_2 molecule.

where d is the dimension of the system, $\overrightarrow{r}(\tau)$ is the position of the particle at time τ and the angle brackets denote the average over time origins. The quantity $\langle[\overrightarrow{r}(\tau) - \overrightarrow{r}(0)]^2\rangle$ is denoted as the mean squared displacement (MSD) of the particle and is obtained from the output of DL_POLY v.2.2. Plotting this MSD against time gives a linear relation from which the slope gives the diffusion coefficient after dividing by twice the dimension of the system as shown in (1).

To ensure good statistics, it is important to get a sufficient amount of ensembles to average the diffusion coefficient [36]. Different ensembles can either be taken over time or over space. We have chosen a procedure where the production run is divided in half. A time average is then taken from step 1 to the time step halfway the production run. A second time average is taken from step two to the time step halfway the production run + 1 and so on. This way, we ensure an ensemble of 1 000 000 time-averaged MSD values that we plot as a function of the timestep. We repeated this procedure five times, starting from different initial configurations to ensure averaging over space as well.

3   Interaction Potential Models

To describe the total interaction potential energy, we assume it can be divided into a nonelectrostatic part and an electrostatic contribution. The non electrostatic part is represented by the semi-empirical ILJ potential developed by Pirani et al. [18] while the electrostatic part is calculated as a simple Coulombic sum

$$V_{\text{tot}}(R) = V_{\text{nelec}}(R) + V_{\text{elec}}(R) = V_{\text{ILJ}}(R) + V_{\text{Coul}}(R). \tag{2}$$

It is known that the Lennard-Jones potential performs well in the equilibrium region, but suffers from shortcomings in both the short- and longe range-part of the potential. The Improved Lennard-Jones potential has shown extensively to lower these problems via the introduction of an extra parameter controlling the R-dependence of the repulsive term [19,37–39]. The ILJ potential has the following form

$$
V_{\text{ILJ}}(R) = \epsilon \left[\frac{m}{n(R) - m} \left(\frac{r_0}{R} \right)^{n(R)} - \frac{n(R)}{n(R) - m} \left(\frac{r_0}{R} \right)^m \right] \tag{3}
$$

with

$$
n(R) = \beta + 4 \left(\frac{R}{r_0} \right). \tag{4}
$$

Here m takes the value of 6 for neutral systems. ϵ represents the well depth, while r_0 represents its location. Both are directly related to the polarizability of the molecules of interest. β is a dimensionless parameter usually restricted between 7 and 9 that allows for fine tuning of the potential, especially in the long range attractive region. It is related to the hardness of the interacting partners and allows overcoming possible deficiencies of the electrostatic part of the potential.

The ILJ potential is a site to site pairwise interaction potential and thus needs the allocation of dispersion centres within the system of interest. In the case of the N_2 molecule it is possible to place one interaction centre in the centre of mass of the N_2, thus reducing the molecule to a pseudo-atom based on the total molecular polarizability. We will refer to this type of potential as CM-CM potential from now on. A second possibility is to consider an interaction centre on each N-atom, thus taking into account the effects of atomic polarizabilities by means of separate atom-atom ILJ terms. In that case the dispersion energy of the N_2 dimer is described as a 4-term potential

$$
V_{\text{nelec}}(R_{\text{AB}}) = \sum_{i,j=1}^{2} V_{\text{ILJ}}(R_{ij}) \tag{5}
$$
$$
= V_{\text{ILJ}}(R_{11}) + V_{\text{ILJ}}(R_{21}) + V_{\text{ILJ}}(R_{12}) + V_{\text{ILJ}}(R_{22})
$$

where i and j indicate the nitrogen atoms of N_2 molecules A and B respectively within the dimer. This type of potential will be referred to as atom-atom potential.

For the simulation of small gases, often partial charges are introduced in the system to calculate the electrostatic interaction. Although they do not have an actual physical meaning, they are usually chosen such as to represent a molecular property relevant for the interaction; often the lowest non-zero multipole is chosen. We optimize the parameters for the ILJ potential using different charge schemes found in the literature and try to further optimize the charges ourselves.

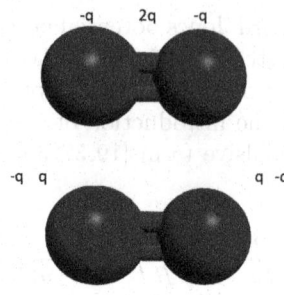

Fig. 2. Representation of the three and four site charge schemes showing the location of the respective charges in the N_2 molecule

For the N_2 gas, usually a three site or a four site charge system is proposed [15]. The three-charge system has negative charges on the N atoms and a balancing charge on the centre of mass of double the magnitude to get a neutrally charged molecule. Although this contradicts the chemical structure of the N_2 molecule—where the negative charge is concentrated in the triple bond— this model reproduces the quadrupole of the molecule if the charges are chosen appropriately. The four site charge system, on the other hand, positions a positive and negative charge on either side of the N-atoms. The positive charges are positioned at a distance of 1.694 Å of each other, while the negative charges are separated by a distance of 2.088 Å. Schematic representations are shown in Fig. 2.

An electrostatic energy contribution is then calculated as the Coulombic sum

$$V_{\text{Coul}}(R) = \sum_{i,j} \frac{q_i q_j}{R_{ij}} \tag{6}$$

where i and j are the respective point charges present in the N_2 dimer and follow the order rule stated before (see (5)).

Various charge schemes found in the literature were used. For the three-charge model, we have used values proposed by Stone [40], the charge scheme proposed by Murthy et al. (MOM) [41], and the TraPPE scheme proposed by Potoff and Siepmann [42]. For the four-charge model, we have used the charges proposed by Cracknell et al. [43]. Aside from using previously defined charge schemes, we have also refitted the charges ourselves within the three-charge model. The negative charge was then considered as an extra parameter within the fitting. The value for the positive charge followed naturally from the negative one to assure a neutral N_2 molecule.

For the ccn molecule, we always consider an ILJ interaction centre on every C atom, to make sure the N_2 molecule interacts strongest with the closest carbon atoms. Furthermore the electrostatic interactions are considered negligible for the graphene-N_2 interaction. This means that for the ccn-N_2 system, after placing an interaction centre on both N atoms, we can write the potential as

$$V_{\text{nelec}}(R_{\text{ccn-N}_2}) = \sum_{i=1}^{54} \sum_{j=1}^{2} V_{\text{ILJ}}(R_{ij}) \qquad (7)$$

where i runs over the 54 carbon atoms within the ccn molecule and j runs over the 2 nitrogen atoms within the N_2 molecule.

It matters to point out that each of the aforementioned charge schemes belongs to a force field that carries its own parameters for a standard Lennard-Jones potential. Here, however, we use the charges of each force field and then refit all the other parameters of the ILJ potential to obtain new force fields.

We have fitted the models described in this section for both the N_2 and ccn-N_2 systems to a set of interaction energies calculated at the DFT level by optimizing the parameters of the ILJ potential and, in specific cases, the partial charges in the Coulombic sum.

3.1 N_2 Dimer

Firstly we are considering the case of a single interaction centre on the centre of mass of the N_2 molecule. The interaction parameters can be found in Table 1 with their respective partial charges. It is clear from the table that explicitly including the electrostatic part by means of the Coulombic sum only affects the ILJ parameters when large charges are used. This observation applies for both the three- and four-charge model.

Table 1. Interaction parameters for the N_2 dimer using a CM-CM model.

Charge scheme	ϵ (kcal/mol)	r_0 (Å)	β	q^- (e)
No charges				
No charges	0.193	4.314	8.431	/
Three-charge model				
MOM	0.198	4.307	8.391	−0.405
TraPPE	0.200	4.305	8.374	−0.482
Stone	0.200	4.304	8.368	−0.510
Optimized	0.211	4.289	8.281	−0.788
Four-charge model				
Cracknell	0.189	4.322	8.465	−0.373

In the three-charge model, increasing the charges, increases the ϵ while decreasing r_0 and β. Reversed trends are seen for the four-charge model. Increasing the charge, induces a decrease in ϵ and an increase in r_0 and β. For the three-charge model, the optimized charges are higher than the ones found in the literature.

We can compare the ϵ and r_0 values for the Improved Lennard-Jones potential to the respective values of the Lennard-Jones potential since the equilibrium regions of both behave equally. Ravikovitch et al. have reported values of

0.202 kcal/mol for ϵ and 4.058 Å for r_0 for a LJ CM-CM model without charges [44]. The ϵ is higher than ours, while the r_0 is smaller, but in reasonable agreement taking into account that they were acquired via very different methods.

Table 2. Interaction parameters for the N_2 dimer using an atom-atom model.

Charge scheme	ϵ (kcal/mol)	r_0 (Å)	β	q^-(e)
No charges				
No charges	0.074	3.893	8.033	/
Three charge model				
MOM	0.077	3.895	7.869	−0.405
TraPPE	0.078	3.896	7.802	−0.482
Stone	0.078	3.897	7.775	−0.510
Optimized	0.079	3.897	7.720	−0.564
Four charge model				
Cracknell	0.072	3.902	8.051	−0.373

Atom-atom potential parameters can be found in Table 2. Introduction of the electrostatic part changes the parameters to a smaller extent than in the CM-CM model. For the three-charge model, the ϵ and r_0 increase slightly with increasing charges, while β decreases. The optimized charges are again slightly higher than the ones from the literature. For the four-charge model, ϵ decreases, while r_0 and β increase.

Again we can compare the ϵ and r_0 parameters of the atom-atom model directly to the TraPPE and MOM Lennard-Jones alternatives for the three-charge model [41,42]. The ϵ and r_0 for both the MOM and the TraPPE potential are 0.072 kcal/mol and 3.730 Å respectively which compares reasonably well with our values. Furthermore, we can compare to ILJ parameters using a three-charge model proposed by Bramastya et al. [45]. They propose values of 0.081 kcal/mol, 3.770 Å and 9.000 for ϵ, r_0 and β respectively while using a charge of −0.515 e on the N atom. The LJ ϵ and r_0 proposed by Cracknell using a four-charge model are 0.075 kcal/mol and 3.724 Å respectively, again well comparable with our parameters.

In order to examine the performances of the different approaches, the interaction energies of some highly symmetrical configurations of the N_2-dimer have been calculated with the different interaction potentials fitted. The values are presented in Table 3. Three representative configurations, in T-shape, parallel and linear, were taken into account and were compared with the interaction energies computed at the CCSD(T)/CBS [46] level, which is a well-recognized standard for evaluating the accuracy of other computational methods.

From Table 3 it can be seen that the interaction energies of N_2-dimers calculated with the different fittings are in general in good agreement with the CCSD(T) results for the considered noncovalent interaction. Indeed, the proposed potentials correctly reproduce the stability sequence for N_2 dimer,

Table 3. Interaction energies (D_e) and centre-to-centre bond distance (r_0), of the representative configurations of the N_2 dimer calculated by potential energy functions derived from B97-D/TZV2P calculations.

	Linear		Parallel		T-shape	
	D_e(kcal/mol)	r_0(Å)	D_e(kcal/mol)	r_0(Å)	D_e(kcal/mol)	r_0(Å)
CM-CM model						
no charges[a]			0.199	4.270		
three charge model						
MOM	0.119	4.46	0.174	4.360	0.253	4.210
Stone	0.077	4.57	0.160	4.38	0.284	4.18
TraPPE	0.088	4.54	0.164	4.38	0.276	4.19
Opt	-	–	0.111	4.46	0.417	4.08
four charge model						
Cracknell	0.052	4.75	0.169	4.32	0.256	4.21
Atom-atom model						
no charges	0.140	4.76	0.293	3.78	0.206	4.27
three charge model						
MOM	0.103	4.88	0.263	3.87	0.263	4.23
Stone	0.077	4.95	0.238	3.91	0.295	4.20
TraPPE	0.084	4.93	0.246	3.90	0.286	4.21
Opt	0.063	4.99	0.222	3.94	0.315	4.19
four charge model						
Cracknell	0.057	5.01	0.245	3.89	0.261	4.22
CCSD(T) [46]	0.006	4.74	0.205	3.57	0.277	4.03

[a] The CM-CM no-charge model does not allow to differentiate the different conformations. It provides an average over all configurations.

T-shape > parallel > linear. However, they are not able to accurately reproduce the very small interaction energy of the linear configuration. Still, the fittings of B97-D results predict the dimer to be bound in this geometry, unlike M11, ω B97X-D or B3LYP-D3 among others [46].

In the CM-CM model the charge schemes giving in average the best results are those using four charges, with absolute errors of 0.004–0.008 kcal/mol. The three-charge system and no-charge model perform worse. For the atom-atom potential, a similar trend is seen so that the four-charge model is to be preferred over the schemes with three or zero charges. The quantitative error in interaction energies relative to CCSD(T) is a little bigger but is in tolerable range. As for the bond distances, the proposed potentials give higher values than those calculated with CCSD(T), with differences around 0.25 Å.

3.2   ccn-N_2 System

In Table 4 the interaction parameters can be found for the ccn-N_2 system using the CM and one site per atom model for N_2. In the literature parameters of

Table 4. Interaction parameters for the N_2-ccn system comparing the atom-CM and atom-atom models.

Model	ϵ (kcal/mol)	r_0 (Å)	β
C-CM(N_2)	0.123	4.133	6.470
C-N	0.087	3.808	7.861

Table 5. Interaction energies (D_e) and centre-to-centre bond distance (r_0), of the representative configurations of the N_2-ccn and N_2-Bz calculated by potential energy functions derived from B97-D/TZV2P calculations.

ccn-N_2	D_e (kcal/mol)	r_0 (Å)	Bz-N_2	D_e (kcal/mol)	r_0 (Å)
C-CM (N_2)	2.189	3.630	C-CM (N_2)	0.741	3.888
C-N/perpendicular	1.980	3.769	C-N/perpendicular	0.735	3.984
C-N/parallel	2.593	3.391	C-N/parallel	1.024	3.554
exp (graph-N_2) [47,48]	**2.398**	3.340	RBDMC [49]	1.154	–
			exp [50]	0.92 ± 0.07	–

this type are usually obtained via the Berthelot mixing rules from the separate parameters for the N_2 molecule and the C atom within the surface, graphene in this case. This makes a direct comparison with our parameters difficult. Consequently, to validate our fitted potentials for the ccn-N_2 system, a study similar to that of the N_2 dimer has been carried out. Furthermore, we also considered the interaction of N_2 with benzene (Bz), although our parameterization of the ILJ potential is specifically designed for larger molecules. We have, then, evaluated the equilibrium distance and binding energy for both ccn-N_2 and Bz-N_2 complexes by means of the ILJ potentials fitted to reproduce B97-D/TZV2P numbers. The obtained results are collected in Table 5.

From the analysis of data in Table 5, it can be seen that the CM-model consistently underestimates the binding energies with respect to experimental values. Just by construction, this model is not able to reproduce the influence of orientation of N_2 over the aromatic surface on the computed energies, so giving too much weight to less bonded contributions and, consequently, providing too low interactions.

This problem does not appear in the atom-atom model and, in fact, this model can give account of the different stability of different conformations. The obtained interaction energies represent lower and upper limits containing the experimental value and providing an arithmetic mean value of 2.3 kcal/mol. Nevertheless, since the probability of the parallel conformation is larger than that of the perpendicular one, the experimental value of 2.398 kcal/mol is closer to the upper limit. A good agreement is also encountered for the equilibrium distances.

Notably, despite the limitations introduced by its own design, a good agreement between experimental and theoretical results is also found in the Bz-N_2 interaction. Again, the CM model gives too low binding energies and the experimental value is closer to the upper limit. Finally, there is also a reasonable agreement between our values and those computed by the rigid-body diffusion Monte Carlo (RBDMC) method [49].

4 Diffusion Coefficients

The force fields described above were used to calculate the diffusion coefficients of N_2 gas at standard conditions (273 K and 1 atm). 100 molecules were simulated in a simulation box with a size coinciding with the gas density of N_2 at standard conditions.

The calculated diffusion coefficients can be seen in Table 6 along with the experimental value. Neither the CM-CM model nor the atom-atom model perform consistently better than the other over all the different charge schemes.

Table 6. Diffusion coefficients calculated using the respective force fields compared to the experimental value.

| Model | No charges | Three charge model | | | | Four charge model | Exp. [51] |
		MOM	TraPPE	Stone	Optimized	Cracknell	
CM-CM $10^5 \cdot D \,(\mathrm{m^2/s})$	1.527	1.209	0.946	0.809	0.339	1.631	1.55
atom-atom $10^5 \cdot D \,(\mathrm{m^2/s})$	1.766	1.246	0.910	0.899	0.750	1.658	

For the CM-CM model, the three-charge model performs worse upon increasing the charges. The smallest charges of the MOM scheme, give already an absolute error (E_a) of $0.341 \cdot 10^{-5} \,\mathrm{m^2/s}$ compared to the experimental value. The four-charge model performs better, with an E_a of $-0.081 \cdot 10^{-5} \,\mathrm{m^2/s}$ for the Cracknell charges. Again, the E_a becomes larger upon increasing the charges. For the CM-CM model, it seems better not to include charges at all which gives rise to an E_a of only $0.023 \cdot 10^{-5} \,\mathrm{m^2/s}$. This result matters because for massive calculations, simplicity in the potential can lead to significant production time savings.

For the atom-atom potential, a similar trend is seen. Increasing the charges worsens the performance. However in this case, the four-charge model of Cracknell ($E_a = -0.108 \cdot 10^{-5} \,\mathrm{m^2/s}$) is to be preferred over a model without charges ($E_a = -0.216 \cdot 10^{-5} \,\mathrm{m^2/s}$). However, in case of large simulations, leaving out the Coulombic sum altogether seems justified to save computing time. The difference in performance between the no-charge model and the best performing three-charge model (MOM) is a lot smaller than for the CM-CM case, an E_a of $-0.216 \cdot 10^{-5} \,\mathrm{m^2/s}$ versus $0.304 \cdot 10^{-5} \,\mathrm{m^2/s}$.

As a comparison we calculated the diffusion coefficient using the parameters proposed by Bramastya et al. [45], to obtain a result of $0.900 \cdot 10^{-5} \,\mathrm{m^2/s}$, leading to an E_a of $0.650 \cdot 10^{-5} \,\mathrm{m^2/s}$.

5 Conclusions

In this work we have fitted the Improved Lennard-Jones potential to interaction energies at DFT level for the N_2 dimer and the ccn-N_2 system. We have considered the N_2 molecule as a pseudo-atom, but we also obtained parameters for the N atoms within the molecule. No systematic performance difference was found between the centre of mass or the atom representation.

The influence of adding the Coulombic sum to this potential was investigated for the N_2 dimer by use of different charge schemes found in the literature. Both three- and four-charge models were used. It was shown that raising the charges within the charge schemes, has a progressive influence on the other parameters. The specific trends depend on the model used. The potentials that we have constructed have shown to reproduce well the interaction energies and equilibrium distances found experimentally. It is worth to note that the Cracknell scheme provides a very accurate interaction energy compared to the CCSD(T) reference values [39]. Furthermore, for the graphene-N_2 system, the atom-atom potential predicts an average interaction energy of ca 2.3 kcal/mol, only 0.1 kcal/mol below the experimental determination [40,41].

We have tested the developed force field by calculating the diffusion coefficient for the N_2 gas. Generally speaking, it was observed that increasing the charges within a certain model, worsens the results. Furthermore, we found that the Cracknell four-charge model gives very good results overall, although the CM-CM model without charges performs the best of all the considered models.

Acknowledgment. The project leading to this application has received funding from the European Unions Horizon 2020 research and innovation programme under the Marie Sklodowska-Curie grant agreement No. 642294. N. F.-L. acknowledges financial support from the "Fondazione Cassa di Risparmio di Perugia" (Project code: 2015.0331.021 Scientific and Technological research).

References

1. Cristancho, D., Akkutlu, I.Y., Criscenti, L.J., Wang, Y.: Gas storage in model kerogen pores with surface heterogeneities. In: SPE Europec featured at 78th EAGE Conference and Exhibition (2016)
2. Chen, J.J., Li, W.W., Li, X.L., Yu, H.Q.: Improving biogas separation and methane storage with multilayer graphene nanostructure via layer spacing optimization and lithium doping: a molecular simulation investigation. Environ. Sci. Technol. **46**, 10341 (2012)
3. Cavenati, S., Grande, C.A., Rodrigues, A.E.: Adsorption equilibrium of methane, carbon dioxide, and nitrogen on zeolite 13X at high pressures. J. Chem. Eng. Data **49**(4), 1095–1101 (2004)
4. Bahamon, D., Vega, L.F.: Systematic evaluation of materials for post-combustion CO_2 capture in a Temperature Swing Adsorption process. Chem. Eng. J. **284**, 438–447 (2016)

5. Lombardi, A., Pirani, F., Laganà, A., Bartolomei, M.: Energy transfer dynamics and kinetics of elementary processes (promoted) by gas-phase CO_2-N_2 collisions: selectivity control by the anisotropy of the interaction. J. Comput. Chem. **37**(16), 1463–1475 (2016)
6. Lombardi, A., Faginas-Lago, N., Gaia, G., Federico, P., Aquilanti, V.: Collisional energy exchange in CO_2-N_2 gaseous mixtures. In: Gervasi, O., et al. (eds.) ICCSA 2016. LNCS, vol. 9786, pp. 246–257. Springer, Cham (2016). https://doi.org/10.1007/978-3-319-42085-1_19
7. Gómez-Gualdrón, D.A., Wilmer, C.E., Farha, O.K., Hupp, J.T., Snurr, R.Q.: Exploring the limits of methane storage and delivery in nanoporous materials. J. Phys. Chem. C **118**(13), 6941–6951 (2014)
8. Morris, R.E., Wheatley, P.S.: Gas storage in nanoporous materials. Angew. Chem. - Int. Ed. **47**(27), 4966–4981 (2008)
9. Do, D.D., Do, H.D., Nicholson, D.: Effects of surface structure and temperature on the surface mediation, layer concentration and molecular projection area: adsorption of argon and nitrogen onto graphitized thermal carbon black. Adsorpt. Sci. Technol. **25**(6), 347–364 (2007)
10. Peng, Y., Krungleviciute, V., Eryazici, I., Hupp, J.T., Farha, O.K., Yildirim, T.: Methane storage in metal-organic frameworks: current records, surprise findings, and challenges. J. Am. Chem. Soc. **135**(32), 11887–11894 (2013)
11. Prosenjak, C., Nabais, J.M.V., Laginhas, C.E., Carrott, P.J.M., Carrott, M.M.L.R.: Simulations of phenol adsorption onto activated carbon and carbon black. Adsorpt. Sci. Technol. **28**(8–9), 797–806 (2010)
12. Ohba, T., Takase, A., Ohyama, Y., Kanoh, H.: Grand canonical Monte Carlo simulations of nitrogen adsorption on graphene materials with varying layer number. Carbon N. Y. **61**, 40–46 (2013)
13. Ohno, H., Mukae, Y.: Machine learning approach for prediction and search: application to methane storage in a metalorganic framework. J. Phys. Chem. C **120**(42), 23968 (2016)
14. Wongkoblap, A., Intomya, W., Somrup, W., Charoensuk, S., Junpirom, S., Tangsathitkulchai, C.: Pore size distribution of carbon with different probe molecules. Eng. J. **14**(3), 45–56 (2010)
15. Makrodimitris, K., Papadopoulos, G.K., Theodorou, D.N.: Prediction of permeation properties of CO_2 and N_2 through silicalite via molecular simulations. J. Phys. Chem. B **105**, 777–788 (2001)
16. Gadipelli, S., Guo, Z.X.: Graphene-based materials: synthesis and gas sorption, storage and separation. Prog. Mater Sci. **69**, 1–60 (2015)
17. Szczęśniak, B., Choma, J., Jaroniec, M.: Gas adsorption properties of graphene-based materials. Adv. Colloid Interface Sci. **243**, 46–59 (2017)
18. Pirani, F., Brizi, S., Roncaratti, L.F., Casavecchia, P., Cappelletti, D., Vecchiocattivi, F.: Beyond the Lennard-Jones model: a simple and accurate potential function probed by high resolution scattering data useful for molecular dynamics simulations. Phys. Chem. Chem. Phys. **10**(36), 5489–5503 (2008)
19. Faginas-Lago, N., Lombardi, A., Albertí, M., Grossi, G.: Accurate analytic intermolecular potential for the simulation of Na^+ and K^+ ion hydration in liquid water. J. Mol. Liq. **204**, 192–197 (2015)
20. Yeamin, M.B., Faginas-Lago, N., Alberti, M., Cuesta, I.G., Sanchez-Marin, J., Sanchez de Meras, A.M.J.: Multi-scale theoretical investigation of molecular hydrogen adsorption over graphene: coronene as a case study. RSC Adv. **4**(97), 54447–54453 (2014)

21. Bartolomei, M., Carmona-Novillo, E., Hernández, M.I., Campos-Martínez, J., Pirani, F.: Global potentials for the interaction between rare gases and graphene-based surfaces: an atom-bond pairwise additive representation. J. Phys. Chem. C **117**(20), 10512–10522 (2013)

22. Faginas-Lago, N., Yeamin, M.B., Sánchez-Marín, J., Cuesta, I.G., Albertí, M., Sánchez de Merás, A.: Modelization of the H_2 adsorption on graphene and molecular dynamics simulation. Theoret. Chem. Acc. **136**(8), 91 (2017)

23. Faginas-Lago, N., Yeni, D., Huarte, F., Wang, Y., Alcamí, M., Martin, F.: Adsorption of hydrogen molecules on carbon nanotubes using quantum chemistry and molecular dynamics. J. Phys. Chem. A **120**(32), 6451–6458 (2016)

24. Getman, R.B., Bae, Y.S., Wilmer, C.E., Snurr, R.Q.: Review and analysis of molecular simulations of methane, hydrogen, and acetylene storage in metal-organic frameworks. Chem. Rev. **112**(2), 703–723 (2012)

25. Eggimann, B.L., Sunnarborg, A.J., Stern, H.D., Bliss, A.P., Siepmann, J.I.: An online parameter and property database for the TraPPE force field. Mol. Simul. **40**(1–3), 101–105 (2013)

26. Albertí, M., Pirani, F., Laganá, A.: Carbon dioxide clathrate hydrates: selective role of intermolecular interactions and action of the SDS catalyst. J. Phys. Chem. A **117**(32), 6991–7000 (2013)

27. Becke, A.D.: Density-functional thermochemistry. III. The role of exact exchange. J. Chem. Phys. **98**(7), 5648 (1993)

28. Hehre, W.J., Ditchfield, R., Pople, J.A.: Self-consistent molecular orbital methods. XII. Further extensions of Gaussian-type basis sets for use in molecular orbital studies of organic molecules. J. Chem. Phys. **56**(5), 2257–2261 (1972)

29. Grimme, S.: Semiempirical GGA-type density functional constructed with a long-range dispersion correction. J. Comput. Chem. **27**, 1787 (2006)

30. Schäfer, A., Huber, C., Ahlrichs, R.: Fully optimized contracted Gaussian basis sets of triple zeta valence quality for atoms Li to Kr. J. Chem. Phys. **100**(8), 5829 (1994)

31. Boys, S., Bernardi, F.: The calculation of small molecular interactions by the differences of separate total energies. Some procedures with reduced errors. Mol. Phys. **19**(4), 553–566 (1970)

32. Grimme, S.: Accurate description of van der Waals complexes by density functional theory including empirical corrections. J. Comput. Chem. **25**(12), 1463–1473 (2004)

33. Peverati, R., Baldridge, K.K.: Implementation and performance of DFT-D with respect to basis set and functional for study of dispersion interactions in nanoscale aromatic hydrocarbons implementation and performance of DFT-D with respect to basis set and functional for study of dispersi. J. Chem. Theory Comput. **4**, 2030–2048 (2008)

34. Wilson, J., Faginas-Lago, N., Vekeman, J., Cuesta, I.G., Sánchez-Marín, J., SánchezdeMerás, A.: Modeling the interaction of carbon monoxide with flexible graphene: from coupled cluster calculations to molecular-dynamics simulations. ChemPhysChem **19**, 774–783 (2018)

35. Smith, W., Forester, T.R.: DL_POLY_2.0: a general-purpose parallel molecular dynamics simulation package. J. Mol. Graph. **14**(3), 136–141 (1996)

36. Pranami, G., Lamm, M.H.: Estimating error in diffusion coefficients derived from molecular dynamics simulations. J. Chem. Theory Comput. **11**, 4586–4592 (2015)

37. Bartolomei, M., Pirani, F., Marques, J.M.: Modeling coronene nanostructures: analytical potential, stable configurations and Ab Initio energies. J. Phys. Chem. C **121**(26), 14330–14338 (2017)

38. Faginas Lago, N., Huarte Larranaga, F., Alberti, M.: On the suitability of the ILJ function to match different formulations of the electrostatic potential for water-water interactions. Eur. Phys. J. D **55**(1), 75–85 (2009)

39. Alberti, M., Faginas Lago, N.: Ion size influence on the Ar solvation shells of M^+-C_6F_6 clusters (M = Na, K, Rb, Cs). J. Phys. Chem. A **116**(12), 3094–3102 (2012)

40. Stone, A.: The Theory of Intermolecular Forces, vol. 1. Oxford University Press, Oxford (2013)

41. Murthy, C.S., Singer, K., Klein, M.L., Mcdonald, I.R.: Pairwise additive effective potentials for nitrogen. Mol. Phys. **41**(6), 1387–1399 (1980)

42. Potoff, J.J., Siepmann, J.I.: Vapor-liquid equilibria of mixtures containing alkanes, carbon dioxide, and nitrogen. AIChE J. **47**(7), 1676–1682 (2001)

43. Cracknell, R.F., Nicholson, D., Tennison, S.R., Bromhead, J.: Adsorption and selectivity of carbon dioxide with methane and nitrogen in slit-shaped carbonaceous micropores: simulation and experiment. Adsorption **2**(3), 193–203 (1996)

44. Ravikovitch, P.I., Vishnyakov, A., Neimark, A.V.: Density functional theories and molecular simulations of adsorption and phase transitions in nanopores. Phys. Rev. E **64**(1), 20 (2001)

45. Bramastya, Y., Faginas-Lago, N., Lombardi, A., Evangelisti, S.: Carbon dioxide and nitrogen separation by multilayer graphtriyne membranes: a molecular dynamics study. Carbon N. Y. (2018, in Press)

46. Lu, T., Chen, F.: Revealing the nature of intermolecular interaction and configurational preference of the nonpolar molecular dimers $(H_2)_2$, $(N_2)_2$, and $(H_2)(N_2)$. J. Mol. Model. **19**(12), 5387–5395 (2013)

47. Vidali, G., Ihm, G., Kim, H.Y., Cole, M.W.: Potentials of physical adsorption. Surf. Sci. Rep. **12**(4), 135–181 (1991)

48. Zhao, J., Buldum, A., Han, J., Lu, J.P.: Gas molecule adsorption in carbon nanotubes and nanotube bundles. Nanotechnology **13**(2), 195–200 (2002)

49. Buch, V.: Treatment of rigid bodies by diffusion Monte Carlo: application to the para-H_2-H_2O and ortho-H_2-H_2O clusters. J. Chem. Phys. **97**(1), 726–729 (1992)

50. Ernstberger, B., Krause, H., Neusser, H.J.: Atoms, molecules metastable decay and binding energies of van der Waals cluster ions. Zeitschrift für Phys. D **20**, 189–192 (1991)

51. Mostinsky, I.: https://doi.org/10.1615/AtoZ.d.diffusion_coefficient (2011)

52. Frisch, M.J., Trucks, G.W., Schlegel, H.B., Scuseria, G.E., Robb, M.A., Cheeseman, J.R., Scalmani, V., Barone, V., Mennucci, B., Petersson, G.A., Nakatsuji, H., Caricato, M., Li, X., Hratchian, H.P., Izmaylov, A.F., Bloino, J., Zheng, G., Sonnenberg, J.L., Hada, M., Ehara, M., Toyota, K., Fukuda, R., Hasegawa, J., Ishida, M., Nakajima, T., Honda, Y., Kitao, O., Nakai, H., Vreven, T., Montgomery, J.A., Peralta, J.J.E., Ogliaro, F., Bearpark, M., Heyd, J.J., Brothers, E., Kudin, K.N., Staroverov, V.N., Kobayashi, R., Normand, J., Raghavachari, K., Rendell, A., Burant, J.C., Iyengar, S.S., Tomasi, J., Cossi, M., Rega, N., Millam, J.M., Klene, M., Knox, J.E., Cross, J.B., Bakken, V., Adamo, C., Jaramillo, J., Gomperts, R., Stratmann, R.E., Yazyev, O., Austin, A.J., Cammi, R., Pomelli, C., Ochterski, J.W., Martin, R.L., Morokuma, K., Zakrzewski, V.G., Voth, G.A., Salvador, P., Dannenberg, J.J., Dapprich, S., Daniels, A.D., Farkas, Ö., Foresman, J.B., Ortiz, J.V., Cioslowski, J., Fox, D.J.: Gaussian-09 Revision D.01, Wallingford CT (2009)

Confinement of the Pentanitrogen Cation Inside Carbon Nanotubes

Stefano Battaglia[1,2] (ID), Stefano Evangelisti[1] (ID), Thierry Leininger[1] (ID), and Noelia Faginas-Lago[2(✉)] (ID)

[1] Laboratoire de Chimie et Physique Quantiques, IRSAMC, Université de Toulouse et CNRS, 118 Route de Narbonne, 31062 Toulouse Cedex, France
{stefano.battaglia,stefano,Thierry.Leininger}@irsamc.ups-tlse.fr
[2] Dipartimento di Chimica, Biologia e Biotecnologie, Università degli Studi di Perugia, Vie Else di Sotto 8, 06123 Perugia, Italy
noelia.faginaslago@unipg.it

Abstract. In recent years, the field of polynitrogen chemistry has seen a sparking activity, with new outstanding theoretical and experimental results. Polynitrogen clusters are excellent candidates for high-energy density materials, but their intrinsic instability poses great challenges for the synthesis and the subsequent storage. In this work, we explore by means of quantum chemical calculations the confinement of the pentanitrogen cation, N_5^+, inside carbon nanotubes of different diameters. The interaction of the two fragments is such that a charge transfer from the nanotube to the nitrogen cation occurs and leads to the subsequent decomposition of N_5^+, thus resulting in an overall unstable system. Nonetheless, preliminary results on the confinement of the neutral N_8 chain (as the product of an $N_5^+ + N_3^-$ addition) are presented, where it is shown that the encapsulation decreases the overall energy of the complex system. Two stable N_8 isomers are discussed and a first investigation on possible decomposition pathways is carried out.

Keywords: Carbon nanotubes · HEDM · Molecular confinement · Polynitrogen · Pentanitrogen cation

1 Introduction

Probably the most peculiar property of nitrogen is the incredible energy difference between single, double and triple bond [1]. Three times the energy of a single bond corresponds to less than half of the energy of a triple bond; thus it should not come as a surprise that nitrogen exists naturally only in its molecular form. Single- and double-bonded polynitrogen (PN) clusters contain a huge amount of energy and have been proposed as possible high-energy density materials (HEDM)[1,2]. Additionally to their potential to store energy, they have an innocuous effect on the environment, since decomposition of pure nitrogen clusters usually leads to the release of N_2 only.

© Springer International Publishing AG, part of Springer Nature 2018
O. Gervasi et al. (Eds.): ICCSA 2018, LNCS 10964, pp. 579–592, 2018.
https://doi.org/10.1007/978-3-319-95174-4_45

The N_3^- azide anion was the first pure nitrogen molecule experimentally synthesized in a lab [3] and after this achievement in 1890, it took more than a century before the pentanitrogen cation N_5^+ was successfully isolated in 1999 by Christe and coworkers [4]. Since then, an incredible amount of work has been done trying to predict new stable species entirely composed by nitrogen as HEDM candidates.

Many theoretical and partly experimental investigations focused on possible pure nitrogen salts composed by the ions N_3^-, N_5^+ and N_5^- [5–10]. Other groups focused more on the possibility to either synthesize new PN molecular crystals or identify novel molecular nitrogen phases [11,12], both of which are often attainable only under extreme conditions. Most notably, the cubic gauche polymeric nitrogen form was successfully synthesized a few years ago under very high temperature and pressure [13].

In recent years, different PN clusters and molecular crystals were theoretically predicted and some were experimentally obtained [14–20]. In 2017, two main achievements renovated once again the interest in the field, namely the isolation and characterization of *cyclo*-N_5^- pentazolate [21] and the synthesis of the cubic gauche form of nitrogen under near-ambient conditions [22].

Despite the recent successes, other ways to stabilize (and hopefully store) single- and double-bonded PN clusters were proposed too, in particular molecular confinement. For the latter approach, carbon nanomaterials such as fullerenes, carbon nanotubes (CNTs) and graphene layers appear as ideal candidates. By spatially confining PN clusters inside the cavity of such materials, thanks to less geometrical freedom as well as non-bonded interactions with the hosting system, the guest fragments may be favorably stabilized and stored. First investigations in this direction have proposed the encapsulation of nitrogen chains inside carbon nanotubes and have theoretically predicted, as well as later experimentally observed, the feasibility of this approach [22–27]. Besides carbon nanotubes, other types of carbon nanostructures as well as other nanomaterials have been proposed as valid alternatives [28–32].

In this work, we extend our previous contribution [33] in which we studied the confinement inside carbon nanotubes of the simplest PN cluster, the azide anion, by investigating the second-longest experimentally accessible PN compound, the pentanitrogen cation. Furthermore, we discuss preliminary results on a more challenging system: an encapsulated molecular N_8 chain confined inside a $(5,5)$ CNT.

The article is organized as follows: the next Section lists the computational details of the calculations carried out in this study. In the Results Section, we firstly present and discuss the main findings regarding the pentanitrogen cation, and secondly, we include some preliminary results regarding the encapsulation of N_8. Finally, in the Conclusions Section, we highlight the main achievements of this work and briefly outline the aim of this research.

2   Computational Details

Carbon nanotubes used in this work were treated as finite-size systems, with addition of hydrogen atoms at the two ends in order to saturate the dangling carbon atoms. Two classes were considered, namely zigzag nanotubes with helical indices $(n, 0)$ and armchair nanotubes with helical indices (m, m). In the case of $(n, 0)$ CNTs, n was chosen equal to 8, 10 or 12, while for armchair nanotubes, the values of m considered were 4, 5 or 6. This choice of indices provided CNTs with a diameter in the range comprised between 6.26 Å and 9.40 Å. The length of the nanotubes was ≈ 13.57 Å for zigzag and ≈ 15.43 Å for armchair CNTs, respectively.

The fragment geometries used in the unrelaxed interaction energies calculations were optimized using density functional theory (DFT), employing the Becke exchange energy functional [34,35] and the Lee-Yang-Parr correlation energy functional [36] (B3LYP). The CNTs were optimized for the lowest electronic state at this level of theory, namely the triplet and singlet state for zigzag and armchair nanotubes, respectively. The polynitrogen molecules were minimized for the closed-shell singlet state.

On the other hand, calculations involving N_8 as well as the relaxation of any complex systems, were carried out using the APFD density functional [37], which will be discussed directly in the Results section.

In all calculations, the double-ζ 6-31G basis set [38] was used for hydrogen and carbon, while diffuse and polarization functions were added for nitrogen (6-31+G*). Interaction energies presented in this work were corrected for the basis set superposition error using the counterpoise correction scheme introduced by Boys and Bernardi [39]. The single point energies involving the pentanitrogen cation were calculated either by second-order Møller-Plesset perturbation theory (MP2) or second-order n-electron valence perturbation theory (NEVPT2) [40–42], while the preliminary study on N_8 was carried out entirely using DFT. The need for multireference perturbation theory (NEVPT2) resulted necessary for zigzag nanotubes, which similarly to other low-dimensional zigzag hydrocarbons have a ground state of open-shell character. Reference wavefunctions for calculating NEVPT2 energies were obtained using the complete active space self-consistent field (CASSCF) method [43]. The active space used was that of 10 electrons in 10 molecular orbitals, all belonging to the carbon nanotube.

All calculations in this contribution were carried out using either the 2015.1 version of the MOLPRO program package [44,45] or the Gaussian09 software, version D01 [46]. Natural population analyses (NPA) [47] were performed using the NBO program version 3.1 [48] bundled in the Gaussian09 software, while all figures including molecular structures were generated using the Avogadro program [49].

3   Results

The first approach of this study consisted in the calculation of unrelaxed interaction energies between the N_5^+ cation confined inside different carbon nanotubes, where the N_5^+ was placed in the middle of the nanotubes, from both the edges and the wall. The computed values are plotted in Fig. 1 as a function of the CNTs diameter. For all nanotubes except the smallest $(4, 4)$ one, the energy is negative, thus suggesting a favorable interaction between the two fragments. The magnitude of the interaction appears to be independent from the helicity of the CNT and to relate only to the diameter of the latter. This is due to the distance of the confined species from the nanotube wall. The small bump observed for nanotubes $(10, 0)$ and $(6, 6)$ is most likely due to the different methodologies applied to obtain the energies.

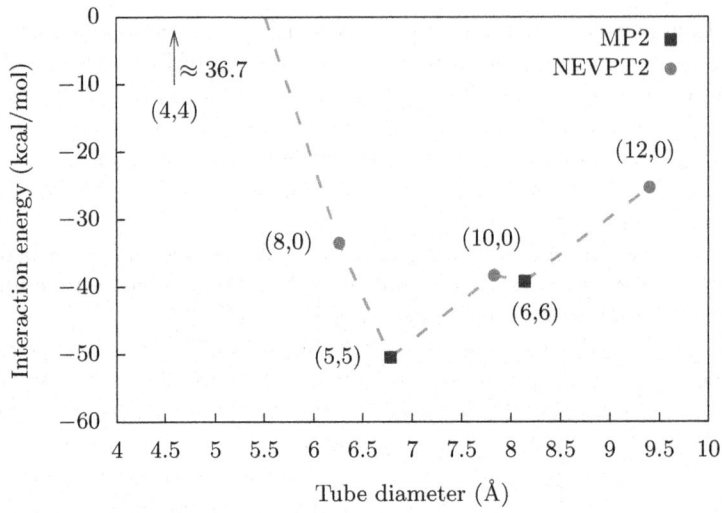

Fig. 1. Unrelaxed interaction energies as a function of the CNT diameter

In the case of armchair nanotubes, the ground state of the complex system is a closed-shell singlet state, thus allowing the account of relaxation effects by performing a geometry optimization using restricted DFT. This is not the case for zigzag nanotubes, where a multireference approach is strictly required, since broken-symmetry DFT fails to accurately describe the electronic structure of the ground state. Luckily, the most favorable interaction is observed for the $(5, 5)$ CNT, with a value of -50.44 kcal/mol. Thus, we have relaxed the N_5^+@CNT$(5, 5)$ system using DFT in combination with the APFD exchange and correlation functional [37]. One of the shortcomings of DFT is the inability of accurately describing long-range dispersion effects by means of standard GGA or hybrid density functionals. In recent years, different schemes to solve these problems have been devised and the APFD functional was designed with this goal in mind. In particular, dispersion effects are accounted for from an empirical dispersion scheme based on spherical atom dispersion terms. In our previous study, we have observed a good performance of the APFD functional, especially the ability to accurately reproduce MP2 interaction energies [33].

Surprisingly, the relaxation process led to the breaking of the N_5^+ compound confined in the nanotube. The decomposition process happens barrierless, as can be seen from Fig. 2, where the relative energies and a few intermediate geometries of the PN species are depicted. In order to ensure the bond breaking was not an artifact due to the choice of functional, the optimization was repeated with the B3LYP density functional with inclusion of the D3 dispersion scheme [50]. Also in this case however, the result was the same with the breaking of the confined guest system happening barrierless.

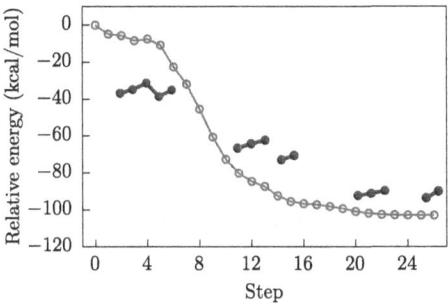

Fig. 2. Relative energies w.r.t. step zero during the relaxation process. Geometries at steps 7, 11 and 26 are depicted along the curve without the surrounding nanotube for better representation.

Additional to the system N_5^+@CNT(5,5), the relaxation using the APFD functional was performed on the smaller (4, 4) and larger (6, 6) CNTs, respectively. In both cases, the confined cation breaks again after a few optimization cycles, leading to final conformations exemplified by Fig. 3 for one of the two nanotubes.

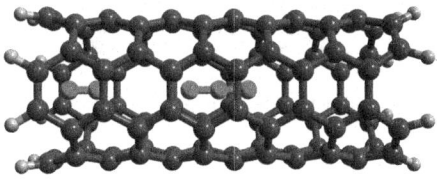

Fig. 3. Final structure of N_5^+@CNT(4, 4)

In order to investigate the nature of the bond breaking, we performed a series of natural population analyses of the APFD electron density. The analysis of the N_5^+ cation in gas phase assigned the partial atomic charges according to Fig. 4. The molecule is symmetric and belongs to the C_{2v} molecular point group and thus its charge distribution is symmetric with respect to the central nitrogen

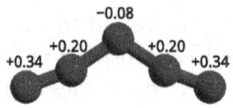

Fig. 4. Partial atomic charges of the N_5^+ cation in gas phase

atom. By repeating the NPA on the nitrogen cation confined inside the $(5,5)$ CNT before the geometry relaxation, a significantly different charge distribution appears, as can be seen in Fig. 5. Note how only the partial charges of the two external atoms as well as the central one are affected, because of their vicinity to the nanotube wall. The total sum of the partial charges on the N_5^+ is 0.57, implying a (partial) charge transfer from the nanotube to the cation.

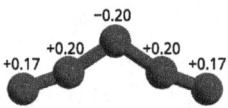

Fig. 5. Partial atomic charges of the N_5^+ cation confined inside the cavity of a $(5,5)$ CNT

A third and last NPA on the fully relaxed geometry revealed that after bond breaking, an even larger charge transfer occurred and a total of two electrons were given by the nanotube to the nitrogen species. Figure 6 shows the partial charge distribution of the two (nitrogen) fragments, where the total charge on the N_3 fragment is virtually minus one, while that of N_2 is approximately zero. The double electron transfer is most likely the trigger of the dissociation happening inside the cavity.

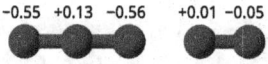

Fig. 6. Partial atomic charges of the decomposed fragments after relaxation inside the cavity of a $(5,5)$ CNT

It was shown in a previous work [10] that the $N_5^\bullet$ radical species dissociates barrierless into the products $N_3^\bullet$ radical and neutral N_2. In order to be sure that this decomposition is described correctly by our methodological approach, we successfully reproduced the dissociation using the APFD functional.

For the first electron transfer from the CNT to the N_5^+ to occur, the electron affinity (EA) of the pentanitrogen cation has to be larger than the ionization potential (IP) of the carbon nanotube. The IP of a hydrogen-terminated $(5,5)$ CNT was studied by Buonocore et al. [51] and estimated to be between 4.2 and

5.2 eV depending on the approach used to compute it. The (vertical) electron affinity of N_5^+ on the other hand, is obtained in this work according to the formula EA $= E(N) - E(N + 1)$, where N stands for the number of electrons and $E(N)$ and $E(N + 1)$ are total electronic energies computed at the geometry of the system with N electrons. The value calculated for N_5^+ using the APFD functional is 6.37 eV, thus resulting in an estimated difference between the EA of N_5^+ and the IP of CNT $(5, 5)$ in the range $\approx$ 2.17–3.17 eV. Although this is just a qualitative result, it proves how it is energetically favorable for the nanotube to transfer an electron to the cation, triggering the decomposition reaction. Therefore, we argue that there would not even be the necessity for the second electron transfer in order for the bond breaking to occur. Note that the charge transfer could be in principle influenced by the finite-size model of the CNT used in this work, since the IP depends on the length of the system. However, in Ref. [51] it is shown that the CNT IP decreases as a function of the length of the tube, thus in the limit of an infinite nanotube, the transfer would be even more favored by the smaller IP. Consequently, we argue that by modeling the CNT using periodic boundary conditions, the first electron transfer would be observed as well, initiating the decomposition of N_5^+. Finally, to understand the second charge transfer process, an argument based on EA and IP is certainly harder to make as it is not known a priori at which moment of the reaction the transfer occurs and it would require a more detailed study which goes beyond the scope of this investigation.

A possible way to avoid the electron transfer process and the subsequent decomposition, is the encapsulation into the cavity of a counterion together with N_5^+, such that the interaction between the two confined species is stronger than that of the cation with the CNT. A possible candidate is the azide anion, which is proven to be favorably confined inside carbon nanotubes [33]. Moreover, the reaction $N_5^+ + N_3^- \rightarrow N_8$ was extensively studied by Fau and Bartlett showing all possible reaction patways in gas phase [7].

In that work, the authors have come to the conclusion that linear isomers of molecular N_8 are not stable at ambient conditions due to low activation barriers leading to dissociation. In particular they suggested that the lattice energy of a crystal made by N_5^+ and N_3^- ion pairs could increase sufficiently the barriers and make N_8 stable. In 2014, a crystal structure for the N_8 molecule was theoretically predicted by DFT calculations to be stable at ambient conditions, although not composed by the ion pair, but instead by a combination of the linear isomers [14].

Here, we present some preliminary results on the confinement of two N_8 linear isomers inside the cavity of a $(5, 5)$ carbon nanotube. From the different stable isomers identified in Ref. [7], we consider in the following only the EEE and EZE conformers (adopting the same nomenclature of Ref. [7]) represented in Fig. 7, as they appear particularly suited for confinement inside CNTs due to their linear structure.

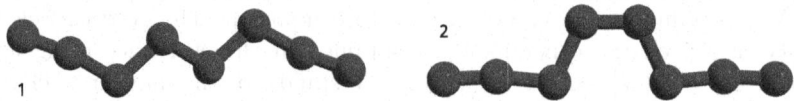

Fig. 7. Two stable N_8 isomers, (1) the EEE conformation and (2) the EZE conformation

For both isomers, there are two possible decomposition pathways: in one case a terminal N_2 molecule detaches from the chain and produces $N_6 + N_2$, while in the second case, both external N_3 fragments simultaneously break away from the central nitrogen atoms, resulting in $2N_3 + N_2$. The scheme in Fig. 8 graphically depicts the relative electronic energies of the various conformers calculated in gas phase using the APFD functional. The structures depicted correspond to the EZE isomer only, but are representative for the EEE conformer too. The electronic energy difference between the two stable isomers is within 1 kcal/mol and, as can be seen from Fig. 8, the activation energies for the decomposition reactions are similar for both the EZE and the EEE conformations (numbers in parenthesis).

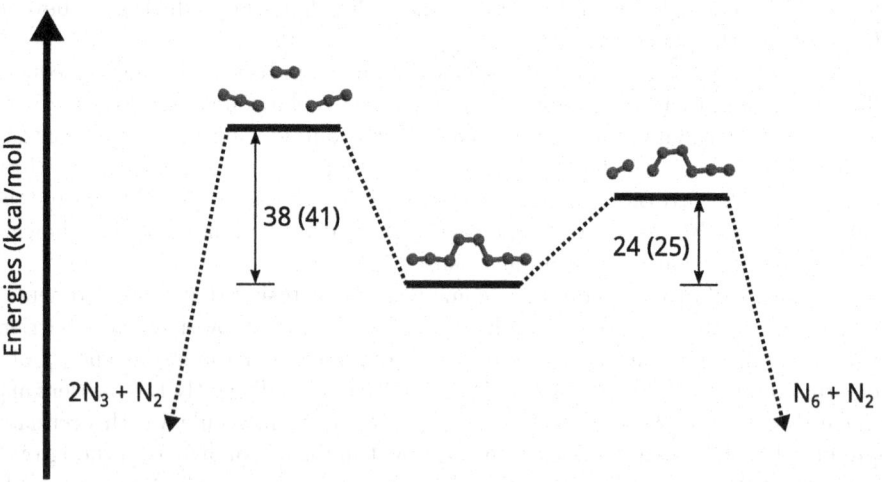

Fig. 8. Potential energy surface of the N_8 decomposition pathways in gas phase. Molecules and numbers depicted correspond to the EZE conformer, while the values in parenthesis refer to the EEE conformer.

Proceeding as in the first part of this contribution, we computed the interaction energies of both isomers confined inside a $(5,5)$ CNT, after a geometry relaxation of the entire system. The computed energies for the EEE and the EZE isomers are -42.48 kcal/mol and -37.34 kcal/mol, respectively, both showing a clear favorable interaction. Subsequent frequency calculations ensured that both structures are true minima of the potential energy surface and thus stable states. A notable effect of the nanotube on N_8 can be appreciated by the energy difference of the two isomers when confined in the cavity. From a difference of less than 1 kcal/mol, the EEE conformation is now more stable than the EZE conformation by 5.27 kcal/mol.

For both stable conformations, the transition state structures (Fig. 9) of the two known decomposition pathways in gas phase (as illustrated for EZE in Fig. 8) were confined inside the carbon nanotube wih the aim to investigate if the gas phase transitions states remain such when confined in the CNT. If that is the case, we are interested in the activation energies to undergo decomposition.

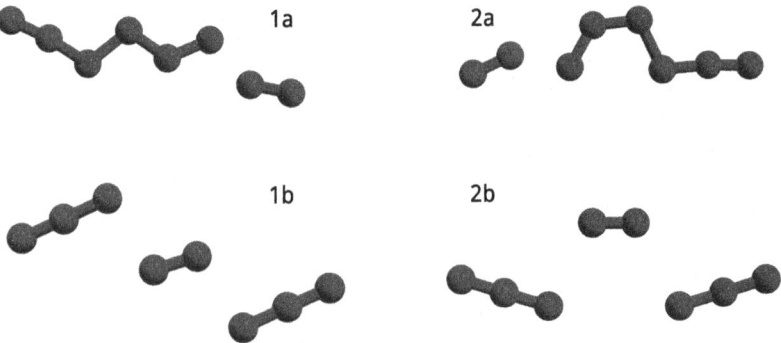

Fig. 9. Transition state structures of the decomposition reactions in gas phase for (1) the EEE conformer and (2) the EZE conformer

Preliminary results suggest that not all the transition states depicted in Fig. 9 are still valid inside a $(5, 5)$ CNT. Of the four structures shown in Fig. 9, only (1a) appears to be a transition state. This is probably due to the more linear conformation (with respect to the other three geometries) which might "fit" better in the cavity, such that the molecule does not undergo a large distortion. Such an interpretation is valid also for the stable isomers, as the EEE conformer, being slightly more "linear" than the EZE one, is favored by approximately 5 kcal/mol over the EZE structure. We argue that steric effects are likely to play a crucial role in favoring certain isomers over others, selectively closing certain reaction pathways and possibly giving rise to new stable and metastable structures otherwise not existing in gas phase.

Nonetheless, on the base of these preliminary results only, it is yet not possible to make definitive conclusions, and a full exploration of the potential energy surface for the different reactions inside carbon nanotubes still has to be carried out.

4   Conclusions

In the present contribution we studied the confinement of the pentanitrogen cation inside carbon nanotubes by means of high level quantum chemical calculations. A combination of wave function methods and density functional theory was used to obtain interaction energies, relaxation effects and allowed for a charge distribution analysis, based on natural bond orbitals. It is shown that, despite favorable unrelaxed interaction energies between N_5^+ and carbon nanotubes, a charge transfer from the host system to the guest cation is responsible for triggering the decomposition of the latter into the azide anion and molecular nitrogen. As previously shown in the literature [10] and confirmed here, a single electron is enough to initiate the barrierless decomposition of the pentanitrogen cation. Such a transfer initially occurs because the electron affinity of N_5^+ is larger than the ionization potential of the carbon nanotube. This process eventually leads to a second charge transfer, in which the intermediate N_3 radical gains a second electron from the nanotube, resulting in $N_3^- + N_2$.

A possible way to circumvent the decomposition, is the addition of a counterion in the cavity, which might stabilize N_5^+. To this end, we presented preliminary results of the encapsulation of N_8 inside a $(5,5)$ CNT, as a possible result of the reaction $N_3^- + N_5^+ \rightarrow N_8$. We have not yet explicitly considered the reaction, but instead have investigated if the possible N_8 product is favorably hosted in the cavity of the carbon nanotube.

Preliminary results show that two linear isomers of N_8 stable in gas phase are stable inside the nanotube too, with favorable interaction energy. Moreover, the relative energy difference between the two isomers is slightly increased by few kcal/mol. The transition states of two decomposition pathways existing in gas phase were considered, suggesting that not all of them remain valid when confined. The results so far obtained for N_8 appear to be explicable in terms of geometric effects, where the "more" linear EEE isomer is more stable than the EZE isomer. A similar argument is valid for the transition states too.

Despite being still an ongoing research, these findings suggest that steric effects due to the restricted space available in the cavity can close certain reaction pathways and favor certain isomers over others. The diameter of the nanotube could be used as a tunable parameter providing fine control on the encapsulated molecule. In particular, the aim is to either increase the activation energy or even close the reaction pathways leading to decomposition of N_8, thus favoring selected isomers inside the cavity. The final goal of this research is to propose alternative ways to store polynitrogen molecules without recurring to extreme conditions. Still, one has to face the problem of producing the stable PN system in the first place, but also in this case, CNTs can serve the purpose and perform as a nanoreactor.

Acknowledgments. The results included in this publication have received funding from the European Union's Horizon 2020 research and innovation programme under the Marie Skłodowska-Curie grant agreement n°642294. S. E. and T. L. acknowledge the "Programme Investissements d'Avenir" ANR-11-IDEX-0002-02, reference ANR-10-LABX-0037-NEXT for financial support. N. F.-L. acknowledges Fondazione Cassa di

Risparmio di Perugia (P 2014/1255, ACT 2014/6167) for funding. The calculations of this work have been partly performed using the resources of the HPC center CALMIP, under the grant 2016-p1048. S. B. wishes to thank Dr. Oriana Brea for insightful discussions.

References

1. Samartzis, P.C., Wodtke, A.M.: All-nitrogen chemistry: how far are we from N_{60}? Int. Rev. Phys. Chem. **25**(4), 527–552 (2006)
2. Zarko, V.E.: Searching for ways to create energetic materials based on polynitrogen compounds (review). Combust. Explos. Shock Waves **46**(2), 121–131 (2010)
3. Curtius, T.: Ueber stickstoffwasserstoffsäure (azoimid) N_3H. Berichte der Dtsch. Chem. Ges. **23**(2), 3023–3033 (1890)
4. Christe, K.O., Wilson, W.W., Sheehy, J.A., Boatz, J.A.: N_5^+: a novel homoleptic polynitrogen ion as a high energy density material. Angew. Chem. Int. Ed. **38**(13/14), 2004–2009 (1999)
5. Wang, X., Hu, H., Tian, A., Wong, N., Chien, S.H., Li, W.K.: An isomeric study of N_5^+, N_5, and N_5^-: a Gaussian-3 investigation. Chem. Phys. Lett. **329**(5–6), 483–489 (2000)
6. Gagliardi, L., Orlandi, G., Evangelisti, S., Roos, B.O.: A theoretical study of the nitrogen clusters formed from the ions N_3^-, N_5^+, and N_5^-. J. Chem. Phys. **114**(24), 10733–10737 (2001)
7. Fau, S., Bartlett, R.J.: Possible products of the end-on addition of N_3^- to N_5^+ and their stability. J. Phys. Chem. A **105**(16), 4096–4106 (2001)
8. Evangelisti, S., Leininger, T.: Ionic nitrogen clusters. J. Mol. Struct. THEOCHEM **621**(1–2), 43–50 (2003)
9. Fau, S., Wilson, K.J., Bartlett, R.J.: On the stability of $N_5^+N_5^-$. J. Phys. Chem. A **106**(18), 4639–4644 (2002)
10. Dixon, D.A., Feller, D., Christe, K.O., Wilson, W.W., Vij, A., Vij, V., Jenkins, H.D.B., Olson, R.M., Gordon, M.S.: Enthalpies of formation of gas-phase N_3, N_3^-, N_5^+, and N_5^- from ab initio molecular orbital theory, stability predictions for $n_5^+n_3^-$ and $n_5^+n_5^-$, and experimental evidence for the instability of $N_5^+N_3^-$. J. Am. Chem. Soc. **126**(3), 834–843 (2004)
11. Tomasino, D., Kim, M., Smith, J., Yoo, C.S.: Pressure-induced symmetry-lowering transition in dense nitrogen to layered polymeric nitrogen (LP-N) with colossal raman intensity. Phys. Rev. Lett. **113**(20), 205502 (2014)
12. Frost, M., Howie, R.T., Dalladay-Simpson, P., Goncharov, A.F., Gregoryanz, E.: Novel high-pressure nitrogen phase formed by compression at low temperature. Phys. Rev. B **93**(2), 024113 (2016)
13. Eremets, M.I., Gavriliuk, A.G., Trojan, I.A., Dzivenko, D.A., Boehler, R.: Single-bonded cubic form of nitrogen. Nat. Mater. **3**(8), 558–563 (2004)
14. Hirshberg, B., Gerber, R.B., Krylov, A.I.: Calculations predict a stable molecular crystal of N_8. Nat. Chem. **6**(1), 52–56 (2014)
15. Greschner, M.J., Zhang, M., Majumdar, A., Liu, H., Peng, F., Tse, J.S., Yao, Y.: A new allotrope of nitrogen as high-energy density material. J. Phys. Chem. A **120**(18), 2920–2925 (2016)
16. Steele, B.A., Oleynik, I.I.: Sodium pentazolate: a nitrogen rich high energy density material. Chem. Phys. Lett. **643**, 21–26 (2016)

17. Adeleke, A.A., Greschner, M.J., Majumdar, A., Wan, B., Liu, H., Li, Z., Gou, H., Yao, Y.: Single-bonded allotrope of nitrogen predicted at high pressure. Phys. Rev. B **96**(22), 224104 (2017)

18. Bondarchuk, S.V., Minaev, B.F.: Super high-energy density single-bonded trigonal nitrogen allotropea chemical twin of the cubic gauche form of nitrogen. Phys. Chem. Chem. Phys. **19**(9), 6698–6706 (2017)

19. Steele, B.A., Stavrou, E., Crowhurst, J.C., Zaug, J.M., Prakapenka, V.B., Oleynik, I.I.: High-pressure synthesis of a pentazolate salt. Chem. Mater. **29**(2), 735–741 (2017)

20. Yu, S., Huang, B., Zeng, Q., Oganov, A.R., Zhang, L., Frapper, G.: Emergence of novel polynitrogen molecule-like species, covalent chains, and layers in magnesium-nitrogen Mg_xN_y phases under high pressure. J. Phys. Chem. C **121**(21), 11037–11046 (2017)

21. Zhang, C., Sun, C., Hu, B., Yu, C., Lu, M.: Synthesis and characterization of the pentazolate anion cyclo-N_5^- in $(N_5)_6(H_3O)_3(NH_4)_4Cl$. Science **355**(6323), 374–376 (2017)

22. Benchafia, E.M., Yao, Z., Yuan, G., Chou, T., Piao, H., Wang, X., Iqbal, Z.: Cubic gauche polymeric nitrogen under ambient conditions. Nat. Commun. **8**(1), 930 (2017)

23. Abou-Rachid, H., Hu, A., Timoshevskii, V., Song, Y., Lussier, L.S.: Nanoscale high energetic materials: a polymeric nitrogen chain N_8 confined inside a carbon nanotube. Phys. Rev. Lett. **100**(19), 196401 (2008)

24. Ji, W., Timoshevskii, V., Guo, H., Abou-Rachid, H., Lussier, L.: Thermal stability and formation barrier of a high-energetic material N_8 polymer nitrogen encapsulated in (5,5) carbon nanotube. Appl. Phys. Lett. **95**(2), 021904 (2009)

25. Zheng, F., Yang, Y., Zhang, P.: Polymeric nitrogen chains confined in carbon nanotube bundle. Int. J. Mod. Phys. B **26**(18), 1250047 (2012)

26. Benchafia, E.M., Yu, C., Sosnowski, M., Ravindra, N.M., Iqbal, Z.: Plasma synthesis of nitrogen clusters on carbon nanotube sheets. JOM **66**(4), 608–615 (2014)

27. Wu, Z., Benchafia, E.M., Iqbal, Z., Wang, X.: N_8^- polynitrogen stabilized on multi-wall carbon nanotubes for oxygen-reduction reactions at ambient conditions. Angew. Chem. Int. Ed. **126**, 12763–12767 (2014)

28. Timoshevskii, V., Ji, W., Abou-Rachid, H., Lussier, L.S., Guo, H.: Polymeric nitrogen in a graphene matrix: an ab initio study. Phys. Rev. B **80**(11), 115409 (2009)

29. Sharma, H., Garg, I., Dharamvir, K., Jindal, V.K.: Structure of polynitrogen clusters encapsulated in C_{60}: a density functional study. J. Phys. Chem. C **114**(19), 9153–9160 (2010)

30. Zheng, F., Wang, C., Zhang, P.: Polymeric nitrogen chain confined inside a silicon carbide nanotube. J. Comput. Theor. Nanosci. **9**(8), 1129–1133 (2012)

31. Liu, S., Yao, M., Ma, F., Liu, B., Yao, Z., Liu, R., Cui, T., Liu, B.: High energetic polymeric nitrogen stabilized in the confinement of boron nitride nanotube at ambient conditions. J. Phys. Chem. C **120**(30), 16412–16417 (2016)

32. Faginas-Lago, N., Yeni, D., Huarte, F., Wang, Y., Alcamí, M., Martin, F.: Adsorption of hydrogen molecules on carbon nanotubes using quantum chemistry and molecular dynamics. J. Phys. Chem. A **120**(32), 6451–6458 (2016)

33. Battaglia, S., Evangelisti, S., Faginas-Lago, N., Leininger, T.: N_3^- azide anion confined inside finite-size carbon nanotubes. J. Mol. Model. **23**(10), 294 (2017)

34. Becke, A.D.: Density-functional exchange-energy approximation with correct asymptotic behavior. Phys. Rev. A **38**(6), 3098–3100 (1988)

35. Becke, A.D.: Density-functional thermochemistry. III. The role of exact exchange. J. Chem. Phys. **98**(7), 5648–5652 (1993)

36. Lee, C., Yang, W., Parr, R.G.: Development of the Colle-Salvetti correlation-energy formula into a functional of the electron density. Phys. Rev. B **37**(2), 785–789 (1988)
37. Austin, A., Petersson, G.A., Frisch, M.J., Dobek, F.J., Scalmani, G., Throssell, K.: A density functional with spherical atom dispersion terms. J. Chem. Theory Comput. **8**(12), 4989–5007 (2012)
38. Hehre, W.J., Ditchfield, R., Stewart, R.F., Pople, J.A.: Self-consistent molecular-orbital methods. I. Use of Gaussian expansions of Slater-type atomic orbitals. J. Chem. Phys. **51**(6), 2657–2664 (1969)
39. Boys, S.F., Bernardi, F.: The calculation of small molecular interactions by the differences of separate total energies. Some procedures with reduced errors. Mol. Phys. **19**(4), 553–566 (1970)
40. Angeli, C., Cimiraglia, R., Evangelisti, S., Leininger, T., Malrieu, J.P.: Introduction of n-electron valence states for multireference perturbation theory. J. Chem. Phys. **114**(23), 10252–10264 (2001)
41. Angeli, C., Cimiraglia, R., Malrieu, J.P.: n-electron valence state perturbation theory: a spinless formulation and an efficient implementation of the strongly contracted and of the partially contracted variants. J. Chem. Phys. **117**(20), 9138–9153 (2002)
42. Angeli, C., Pastore, M., Cimiraglia, R.: New perspectives in multireference perturbation theory: the n-electron valence state approach. Theor. Chem. Acc. **117**(5–6), 743–754 (2007)
43. Roos, B.O., Taylor, P.R., Siegbahn, P.E.M.: A complete active space SCF method (CASSCF) using a density matrix formulated super-CI approach. Chem. Phys. **48**(2), 157–173 (1980)
44. Werner, H.J., Knowles, P.J., Knizia, G., Manby, F.R., Schütz, M., Celani, P., Győrffy, W., Kats, D., Korona, T., Lindh, R., Mitrushenkov, A.O., Rauhut, G., Shamasundar, K.R., Adler, T.B., Amos, R.D., Bernhardsson, A., Berning, A., Cooper, D.L., Deegan, M.J.O., Dobbyn, A.J., Eckert, F., Goll, E., Hampel, C., Hesselmann, A., Hetzer, G., Hrenar, T., Jansen, G., Köppl, C., Liu, Y., Lloyd, A.W., Mata, R.A., May, A.J., McNicholas, S.J., Meyer, W., Mura, M.E., Nicklass, A., O'Neill, D.P., Palmieri, P., Peng, D., Pflüger, K., Pitzer, R., Reiher, M., Shiozaki, T., Stoll, H., Stone, A.J., Tarroni, R., Thorsteinsson, T., Wang, M.: MOLPRO, version 2015.1, a package of ab initio programs (2015)
45. Werner, H.J., Knowles, P.J., Knizia, G., Manby, F.R., Schütz, M.: Molpro: a general-purpose quantum chemistry program package. Wiley Interdiscip. Rev. Comput. Mol. Sci. **2**(2), 242–253 (2012)
46. Frisch, M.J., Trucks, G.W., Schlegel, H.B., Scuseria, G.E., Robb, M.A., Cheeseman, J.R., Scalmani, G., Barone, V., Mennucci, B., Petersson, G.A., Nakatsuji, H., Caricato, M., Li, X., Hratchian, H.P., Izmaylov, A.F., Bloino, J., Zheng, G., Sonnenberg, J.L., Hada, M., Ehara, M., Toyota, K., Fukuda, R., Hasegawa, J., Ishida, M., Nakajima, T., Honda, Y., Kitao, O., Nakai, H., Vreven, T., Montgomery Jr., J.A., Peralta, J.E., Ogliaro, F., Bearpark, M., Heyd, J.J., Brothers, E., Kudin, K.N., Staroverov, V.N., Kobayashi, R., Normand, J., Raghavachari, K., Rendell, A., Burant, J.C., Iyengar, S.S., Tomasi, J., Cossi, M., Rega, N., Millam, J.M., Klene, M., Knox, J.E., Cross, J.B., Bakken, V., Adamo, C., Jaramillo, J., Gomperts, R., Stratmann, R.E., Yazyev, O., Austin, A.J., Cammi, R., Pomelli, C., Ochterski, J.W., Martin, R.L., Morokuma, K., Zakrzewski, V.G., Voth, G.A., Salvador, P., Dannenberg, J.J., Dapprich, S., Daniels, A.D., Farkas, Ö., Foresman, J.B., Ortiz, J.V., Cioslowski, J., Fox, D.J.: Gaussian 09 Revision D.01

47. Reed, A.E., Weinstock, R.B., Weinhold, F.: Natural population analysis. J. Chem. Phys. **83**(2), 735–746 (1985)
48. Glendening, E.D., Badenhoop, J.K., Reed, A.D., Carpenter, J.E., Weinhold, F.: NBO version 3.1
49. Hanwell, M.D., Curtis, D.E., Lonie, D.C., Vandermeersch, T., Zurek, E., Hutchison, G.R.: Avogadro: an advanced semantic chemical editor, visualization, and analysis platform. J. Cheminf. **4**(1), 17 (2012)
50. Grimme, S., Antony, J., Ehrlich, S., Krieg, H.: A consistent and accurate ab initio parametrization of density functional dispersion correction (DFT-D) for the 94 elements H-Pu. J. Chem. Phys. **132**(15), 154104 (2010)
51. Buonocore, F., Trani, F., Ninno, D., Di Matteo, A., Cantele, G., Iadonisi, G.: Ab initio calculations of electron affinity and ionization potential of carbon nanotubes. Nanotechnology **19**(2), 025711 (2008)

Potential Energy Surface for the Interaction of Helium with the Chiral Molecule Propylene Oxide

Patricia R. P. Barreto[1], Alessandra F. Albernaz[2], Vincenzo Aquilanti[3,4] (iD),
Noelia Faginas-Lago[3] (iD), Gaia Grossi[3], Andrea Lombardi[3], Federico Palazzetti[3(✉)] (iD),
and Fernando Pirani[3]

[1] Laboratòrio Associado de Plasma, Instituto Nacional de Pesquisas Espaciais,
São José dos Campos, São Paulo 12247-970, Brazil
[2] Instituto de Fìsica, Universidade de Brasilia, Brasilia, Distrito Federal 70919-970, Brazil
[3] Dipartimento di Chimica, Biologia e Biotecnologie, Università degli Studi di Perugia,
06123 Perugia, Italy
federico.palazzetti@unipg.it
[4] Istituto di Struttura della Materia, Consiglio Nazionale delle Ricerche, 00133 Rome, Italy

Abstract. The discovery of propylene oxide in the interstellar medium has raised considerable interest about this molecule, which represents one of the simplest cases of chiral systems. In this paper, we present a quantum chemical study and a phenomenological approach, through the Pirani potential function, of the system He – propylene oxide in fourteen different configurations. Comparison of the optimized molecular structure at various level of theory, as well as a discussion on the two approaches is reported. The analytical form of the Pirani potential function permits future applications of classical simulations of molecular-beam collision experiments, especially to those related to chirality discrimination phenomena, in progress in our laboratory.

Keywords: van der Waals cluster · Chiral molecule · Quantum chemistry

1 Introduction

Propylene oxide has been extensively studied both from a theoretical and experimental point of view. Its recent discovery in the interstellar space [1] has provided additional motivation by the scientific community about this molecule [2], especially for the issues related to the evolution of life and origin of chiral discrimination in nature [3–7]. Previous studies concerned the characterization of the isomerization paths and chirality exchange paths [8, 9], and determination of spectroscopical properties [10–15]. Propylene oxide presents the important feature to be in a rigid conformation, excluding the rotation of the methyl group. This is a rare property in common chiral molecules and simplifies considerably the study of the dynamics, avoiding multiple calculations for different conformers. (For studies on prototypical chiral molecules such as peroxides and persulphydes see also Refs. [16–19]). Propylene oxide is an ideal candidate in scattering experiments for investigation of manifestation of chirality in gas phase, being commercially available both in racemic and the two enantiomeric forms, possessing

© Springer International Publishing AG, part of Springer Nature 2018
O. Gervasi et al. (Eds.): ICCSA 2018, LNCS 10964, pp. 593–604, 2018.
https://doi.org/10.1007/978-3-319-95174-4_46

good stability and vapor pressure. Supersonic molecular beams of propylene oxide and their alignment [20] have been characterized through the electrostatic hexapolar technique. For hexapolar orientation technique see [21, 22, 60–62], for single photon excitation technique see [23], for brute-force technique see [24] for natural technique, *i.e.* without the use of external fields, see [25–30]. For the manifestation of chirality in photodissociation and collisional processes see Refs. [31–37].

In this paper, we report the single point energies of fourteen configurations of the system He – propylene oxide, calculated by *ab initio* methods. The choice of these configurations relies upon geometric and symmetric configurations and can be used in future for applications similar to the harmonics expansion, already seen for simpler systems [38, 39]. The *ab initio* energy points are compared with the recently developed Pirani potential function [40, 41]. This latter is particularly suitable for reproducing the van der Waals part of the interaction and anisotropies caused by charge-transfer, permanent dipole and quadrupole moment perturbations. Combination with explicit electrostatic terms, permits the treatment of pronounced anisotropic effects.

The paper is organized as follows: in Sect. 2, we give information on the *ab initio* calculations; in Sect. 3, we report the results and discussions; in Sect. 4, we illustrate the Pirani function potential; conclusions are given in Sect. 5.

2 *Ab Initio* Calculations

The *ab initio* calculations for the He – propylene oxide system (Fig. 1) were performed by the Molpro package program [42]. The optimized structure of propylene oxide has been calculated by the CBS-Q3B method (in Table 1, we report the geometry calculated at various levels of theory). The single point energy values have been determined by using the ccsd(t) method, with the aug-cc-pvdz basis set. We have calculated 100 energy points for each configuration. The configurations define the direction through which the helium moves with respect to the center-of-mass of the molecule, their choice is important in view of comparisons with other methods and for future implementations in methods to generate analytical potential functions (see for example [43, 44]). We consider fourteen configurations identified by the letters V, E and F. To define the configurations, we consider a distorted tetrahedron, whose vertices are the C atoms of the groups CH_3 and CH_2 (called C3 and C2, respectively), the O, and the H connected to the asymmetric carbon (Fig. 2a). The group V is composed by four configurations, characterized by passing through the center-of-mass of the molecule and the vertices of the tetrahedron: V1 passes through C3, V2 through C2, V3 through O, and V4 through H. The group E is given by the directions connecting the center-of-mass of the molecule and the center-of-mass of the edge of the tetrahedron, *i.e.* the center-of-mass between two vertices of two groups that represent the vertices of the tetrahedron. In order to calculate the centers-of-mass of the edges involving C3 and C2, we considered the whole masses of the groups CH_3 and CH_2. As such, we indicated by E1, the configuration passing through the center-of-mass of the edge C3-C2; E2 through C3-O, E3 through C3-H, E4 through C2-O, E5 through C2-H, finally, and E6 through the center-of-mass of O-H. The group F refers to the directions passing through the centers-of-mass of the faces of the tetrahedron and the center-of-mass of the molecule: F1 passes through the center-of-mass of C3-C2-H, F2 through C3-C2-H, F3 through C3-O-H, and F4 through C2-O-H.

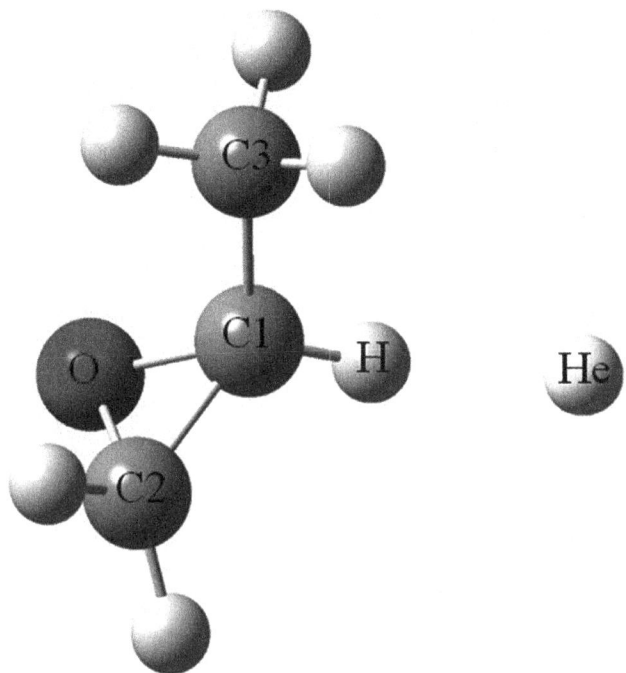

Fig. 1. The system propylene oxide – He. We indicate, in grey the carbon atoms, in white the hydrogens, in red the oxygen and in light blue the helium (indicated by the related chemical symbol). The carbon atoms are labeled by C1, C2 and C3; the hydrogen, bound to the asymmetric carbon (C1), is indicated by H. (Color figure online)

Table 1. The electric dipole moment (in Debye) and geometrical properties calculated at various levels of theory, compared with experimental reference data [59]. The bond distances (see Fig. 1 for the carbon atom labels) are in Å and the bond angle in degrees.

Method	Dipole moment (Debye)	Distance C1-C2 (Å)	Distance C2-C3 (Å)	Distance C1-O (Å)	Distance C2-O (Å)	Distance C3-H (Å)	Angle C1-C2-C3 (degrees)
CBS-Q3B	2.32	1.47	1.51	1.43	1.43	1.09	122.4°
G2	2.34	1.46	1.50	1.43	1.44	1.09	121.9°
G2MP2	2.34	1.47	1.50	1.44	1.44	1.09	121.9°
G3B3	2.32	1.46	1.51	1.43	1.44	1.10	122.4°
Exp. [59]	2.01	1.47	1.51		1.44	1.09	120.9°

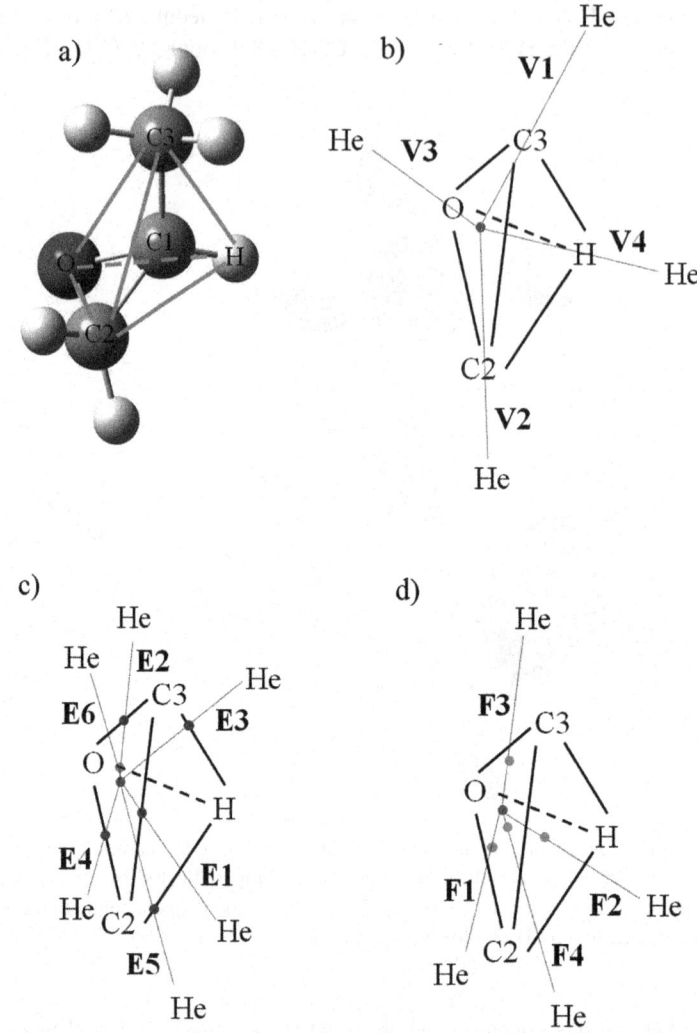

Fig. 2. (a) The propylene oxide inscribed in a distorted tetrahedron, whose vertices are C1, C3, O and H. (b) The configurations identified by the He directed along a straight line running from the center-of-mass of the molecule to the four vertices of the tetrahedron: V1, V2, V3, and V4. (c) The configurations corresponding to the semi-lines connecting the center-of-mass of the molecule and the centers-of-mass of a couple of atoms (or groups), *i.e.* the edge of the distorted tetrahedron: E1, E2, E3, E4, E5, and E6. (d) The configurations defined by the straight lines directed from the center-of-mass of the molecules and a triad of atoms (or groups), *i.e.* the centers-of-mass of the faces of the distorted tetrahedron: F1, F2, F3, and F4.

3   Pirani Potential Function

The Pirani potential function is a potential model that describes the weak interactions of a pair of atoms (or group of atoms) as a sum of two contributions: a repulsive component of the potential and an attractive component. It represents a generalization of the well-known Lennard-Jones (12-6) and Maitland and Smith models [40]. The Pirani potential function reads as follows:

$$V(R) = D_e \left[\frac{m}{n(x) - m} \left(\frac{1}{x} \right)^{n(x)} - \frac{n(x)}{n(x) - m} \left(\frac{1}{x} \right)^6 \right] \tag{1}$$

where $n(x) = \beta + 4x^2$, being β a dimensionless parameter. For a broad class of systems β depends on the hardness of the interacting atoms or molecules. More precisely, β in the range 7–10 can be used to describe systems involving atoms and molecules that are highly or not very polarizable and where electrostatic forces, such as ion-permanent dipole and ion–ion interactions, are present at long-range [45, 46]. The parameter m assumes a value of 6 for two neutral partners, 4 for ion-induced dipole interactions, 2 for ion-permanent dipole interactions, and 1 for ion–ion systems.

It has been demonstrated that differently from the classical Lennard-Jones model the Pirani function correctly reproduces the long-range behavior of the potential for a wide variety of systems [47–49]. The function in Eq. 1 is versatile due to the relationship of the parameters D_e, R_{eq}, m, and β with the molecular polarizability [40]. For this reason, it can be applied to more complex molecular systems, exploiting the additivity of the polarizabilities in building the interactions as a result of a collection of interacting centers. This particularly interesting feature of such an approach has been applied to small molecules and aggregates, [50–52], to liquid state systems [53–56] and has been widely used in the modeling of the interactions in plasma kinetics applications [57, 58]. In the present case, the interaction potential is given as a sum of the binary interactions of He with CH_3, CH_2 (both considered structureless), O, H, and C (the asymmetric carbon, also identified by C1). In Table 2, we report the parameters adopted in Eq. 1.

Table 2. The parameters of the Pirani potential for each interacting pair He – atom or He – group (for all the group (or atom)-He pair, $m = 6$ and $\beta = 8$).

Group (atom)-He pair	D_e	R_{eq}
CH_3-He	18.6	3.69
CH_2-He	17.6	3.61
O-He	17.0	3.22
H-He	10.9	2.97
C-He	15.5	3.40

4   Results and Discussion

Table 1 reports the geometry properties of the propylene oxide molecule calculated with various methods and compared with the data reported in Ref. [59]. The energy points have been calculated on the geometry optimized by the CBS-Q3B method that presents the following bond distances: C1-C2 1.47 Å, C2-C3 1.51 Å, C1-O 1.43 Å, C2-O 1.43 Å, C3-H 1.09 Å and the bond angle C1-C2-C3 122.4°.

Figure 3 reports the potential energy as a function of the distance between the He atom and the center-of-mass of the molecule of the four V configurations of the system He – propylene oxide. The two methods show a good agreement for V1 and V2 configurations; the *ab initio* approach tends to underestimate the energy minimum of V3 and V4, and for this latter presents a higher equilibrium distance, with respect the Pirani potential.

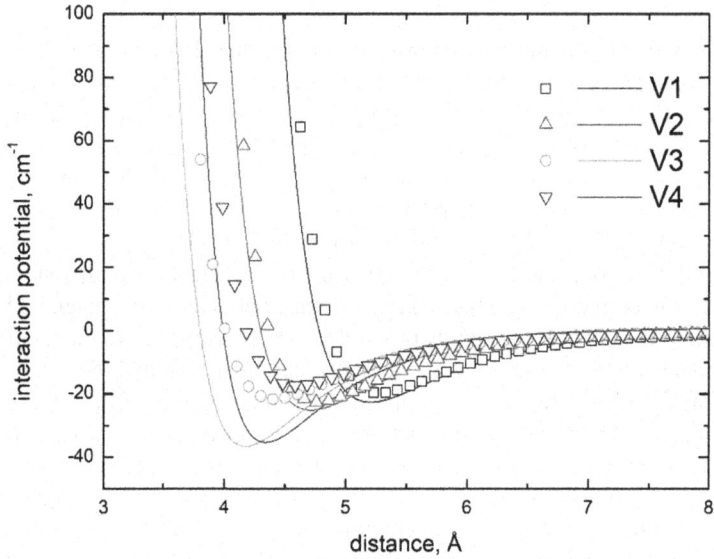

Fig. 3. The potential energy profiles of the four V configurations of the propylene oxide – He system. The energy points calculated *ab initio* are indicated by symbols, while the potential determined by the Pirani potential is indicated by lines.

In Fig. 4, we report the potential profiles of the six E configurations. The best agreement is given by E3, while there is a substantial underestimation of the minimum energy calculated by the *ab initio* method, except for E2. For all the configurations there is an acceptable agreement for what concern the equilibrium distances.

In Fig. 5, we present the interaction potentials of the four F configurations. There is also in this case a good agreement between the two methods, confirming, as seen for the previous cases an underestimation of the energies calculated by the *ab initio* method with respect to those calculated by the phenomenological model.

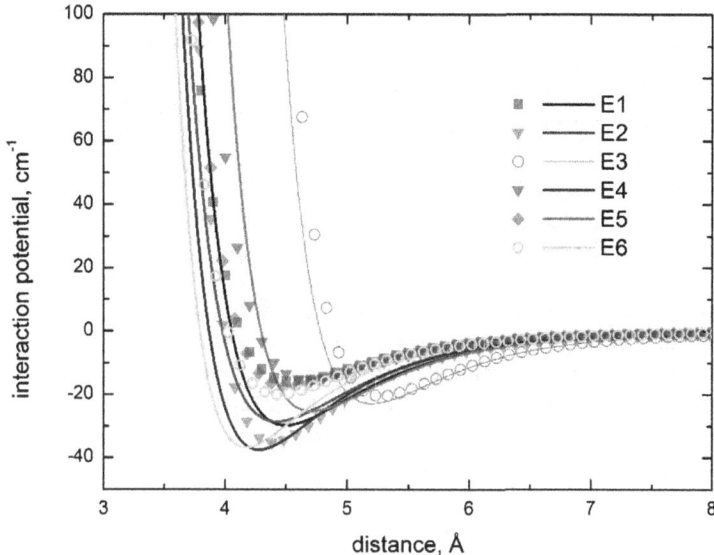

Fig. 4. The potential energy profiles of the six E configurations of the propylene oxide – He system. The energy points calculated *ab initio* are indicated by symbols, while the potential determined by the Pirani potential is indicated by lines.

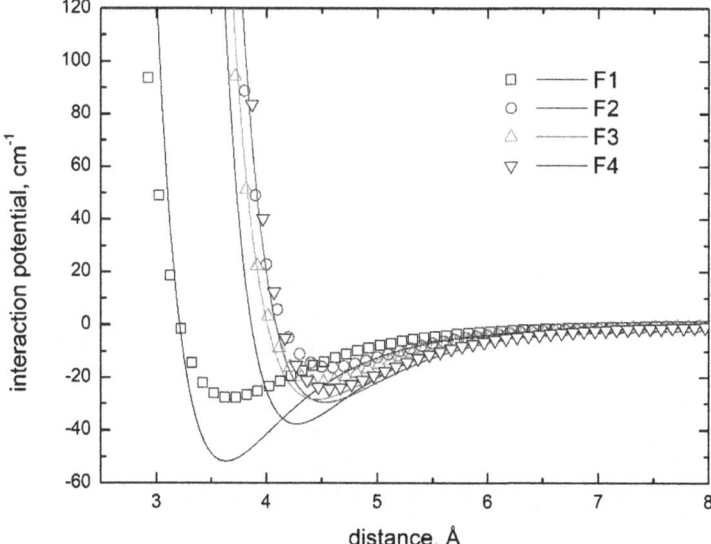

Fig. 5. The potential energy profiles of the four F configurations of the propylene oxide – He system. The energy points calculated *ab initio* are indicated by symbols, while the potential determined by the Pirani potential is indicated by lines.

5   Conclusions

The single point energies of fourteen configurations of the He – propylene oxide system have been calculated by *ab initio* methods, the optimization of the molecular structure has been performed by CBS-Q3B, while the energy points have been calculated at the ccsd(t) level of theory, using the aug-cc-pvdz basis set. The interaction potentials of the same configurations have been calculated by the phenomenological model Pirani potential function that represents a generalized method of the well-known Lennard – Jones (12-6) and Maitland and Smith potentials. Comparisons present a substantial agreement, although *ab initio* methods tend to underestimate the well-depths (*ca.* 15–20 cm^{-1}). Collision experiments are necessary to establish the nature of the interactions. The Pirani potential reveals to be a powerful method, useful for the implementation in molecular dynamics simulation codes. Future developments will concern studies of chiral discrimination through molecular dynamics simulations and molecular-beam collision experiments of helium with aligned propylene oxide.

Acknowledgments. Noelia Faginas Lago, Gaia Grossi and Federico Palazzetti acknowledge Fondo Ricerca di Base 2015 del Dipartimento di Chimica, Biologia e Biotecnologie dell'Università di Perugia for financial support. The authors acknowledge the Italian Ministry for Education, University and Research, MIUR, for financial supporting through SIR 2014 "Scientific Independence for young Researchers" (RBSI14U3VF) and the AMIS project through the program "Dipartimenti di Eccellenza". Andrea Lombardi acknowledges financial support from MIUR PRIN 2015 (contract 2015F59J3R_002).

References

1. McGuire, B.A., Carroll, P.B., Loomis, R.A., Finneran, I.A., Jewell, P.R., Remijan, A.J., Blake, G.A.: Discovery of the interstellar chiral molecule propylene oxide (CH$_3$CHCH$_2$O). Science **2**(5), 99–110 (2017)
2. Su, Z., Borho, N., Yunjie, X.: Chiral self-recognition: direct spectroscopic detection of the homochiral and heterochiral dimers of propylene oxide in the gas phase. J. Am. Chem. Soc. **128**, 17126–17131 (2006)
3. Aquilanti, V., Maciel, G.S.: Observed molecular alignment in gaseous streams and possible chiral effects in vortices and surface scattering. Orig. Life Evol. Biosph. **36**, 435–441 (2006)
4. Aquilanti, V., Grossi, G., Lombardi, A., Maciel, G.S., Palazzetti, F.: The origin of chiral discrimination: supersonic molecular beam experiments and molecular dynamics simulations of collisional mechanisms. Physica Scr. **78**(5), 7 p. (2008). Article no. 058119
5. Palazzetti, F., Maciel, G.S., Lombardi, A., Grossi, G., Aquilanti, V.: The astrochemical observatory: molecules in the laboratory and in the cosmos. J. Chin. Chem. Soc. **59**(9), 1045–1052 (2012)
6. Lombardi, A., Palazzetti, F., Aquilanti, V., Pirani, F., Casavecchia, P.: The astrochemical observatory: experimental and computational focus on the chiral molecule propylene oxide as a case study. In: Gervasi, O., et al. (eds.) ICCSA 2017. LNCS, vol. 10408, pp. 267–280. Springer, Cham (2017). https://doi.org/10.1007/978-3-319-62404-4_20

7. Aquilanti, V., Caglioti, C., Casavecchia, P., Grossi, G., Lombardi, A., Palazzetti, F., Pirani, F.: The astrochemical observatory: computational and theoretical focus on molecular chirality changing torsions around O - O and S - S bonds. In: 1906 AIP Conference Proceedings (2017). Article no. 030010

8. Elango, M., MacIel, G.S., Palazzetti, F., Lombardi, A., Aquilanti, V.: Quantum chemistry of C_3H_6O molecules: structure and stability, isomerization pathways, and chirality changing mechanisms. J. Phys. Chem. A **114**(36), 9864–9874 (2010)

9. Elango, M., Maciel, G.S., Lombardi, A., Cavalli, S., Aquilanti, V.: Quantum chemical and dynamical approaches to intra and intermolecular kinetics: the $CnH_2nO(n = 1, 2, 3)$ molecules. Int. J. Quantum Chem. **111**, 1784–1791 (2011)

10. Turchini, S., Zena, N., Contini, G., Alberti, G., Alagia, M., Stranges, S., Fronzono, G., Stener, M., Decleva, P., Prosperi, T.: Circular dichroism in photoelectron spectroscopy of free chiral molecules: experiment and theory on methyl-oxirane. Phys. Rev. A **70**, 014502 (2004)

11. Stranges, S., Turchini, S., Alagia, M., Alberti, G., Contini, G., Decleva, P., Fronzoni, G., Stener, M.: Valence photoionization dynamics in circular dichroism of chiral free molecules: the methyl-oxirane. J. Chem. Phys. **122**, 244303 (2005)

12. Gerbi, A., Vattuone, L., Rocca, M., Valbusa, U., Pirani, F., Cappelletti, D., Vecchiocattivi, F.: Stereodynamic effects in the adsorption of propylene molecules on Ag(001). J. Phys. Chem. B **109**, 22884–22889 (2005)

13. Merten, C., Bloino, J., Barone, V., Yunjie, X.: Anharmonicity effects in the vibrational CD spectra of propylene oxide. J. Phys. Chem. Lett. **4**, 3424–3428 (2013)

14. Falcinelli, S., Vecchiocattivi, F., Alagia, M., Schio, L., Richter, R., Stranges, S., Catone, D., Arruda, M.S., Mendes, L.A.V., Palazzetti, F., Aquilanti, V., Pirani, F.: Double photoionization of propylene oxide: a coincidence study of the ejection of a pair of valence-shell electrons. J. Chem. Phys. **148**, 114302 (2018)

15. Blanco, S., Melandri, S., Maris, A., Caminati, W., Velino, B., Kisiel, Z.: Free jet rotational spectrum of propylene oxide-krypton and modelling and *ab initio* calculations for propylene oxide-rare gas dimers. Phys. Chem. Chem. Phys. **5**, 1359–1364 (2003)

16. Barreto, P.R.P., Vilela, A.F.A., Lombardi, A., Maciel, G.S., Palazzetti, F., Aquilanti, V.: The hydrogen peroxide-rare gas systems: quantum chemical calculations and hyperspherical harmonic representation of the potential energy surface for atom-floppy molecule interactions. J. Phys. Chem. A **111**(49), 12754–12762 (2007)

17. Maciel, G.S., Barreto, P.R.P., Palazzetti, F., Lombardi, A., Aquilanti, V.: A quantum chemical study of H2S2: intramolecular torsional mode and intermolecular interactions with rare gases. J. Chem. Phys. **129**(16), 10 p. (2008). Article no. 164302

18. Barreto, P.R.P., Palazzetti, F., Grossi, G., Lombardi, A., Maciel, G.S., Vilela, A.F.A.: Range and strength of intermolecular forces for van der waals complexes of the type H_2Xn-Rg, with X = O, S and n = 1, 2. Int. J. Quan. Chem. **110**(3), 777–786 (2010)

19. Aquilanti, V., Caglioti, C., Lombardi, A., Maciel, G.S., Palazzetti, F.: Screens for displaying chirality changing mechanisms of a series of peroxides and persulfides from conformational structures computed by quantum chemistry. In: Gervasi, O., et al. (eds.) ICCSA 2017. LNCS, vol. 10408, pp. 354–368. Springer, Cham (2017). https://doi.org/10.1007/978-3-319-62404-4_26

20. Aquilanti, V., Bartolomei, M., Pirani, F., Cappelletti, D., Vecchiocattivi, F., Shimizu, Y., Kasai, T.: Orienting and aligning molecules for stereochemistry and photodynamics. Phys. Chem. Chem. Phys. **5**, 291–300 (2005)

21. Che, D.-C., Palazzetti, F., Okuno, Y., Aquilanti, V., Kasai, T.: Electrostatic hexapole state-selection of the asymmetric-top molecule propylene oxide. J. Phys. Chem. A **114**(9), 3280–3286 (2010)

22. Che, D.-C., Kanda, K., Palazzetti, F., Aquilanti, V., Kasai, T.: Electrostatic hexapole state-selection of the asymmetric-top molecule propylene oxide: rotational and orientational distributions. Chem. Phys. **399**, 180–192 (2012)

23. Weida, M.J., Parmenter, C.A.: Aligning symmetric and asymmetric top molecules via single photon excitation. J. Chem. Phys. **107**, 7138–7147 (1997)

24. Bulthuis, J., Moeller, J., Loesch, H.J.: Brute force orientation of asymmetric top molecules. J. Phys. Chem. A **101**, 7684–7690 (1997)

25. Aquilanti, V., Ascenzi, D., Cappelletti, D., Pirani, F.: Velocity dependence of collisional alignment of oxygen molecules in gaseous expansions. Nature **371**, 399–402 (1994)

26. Aquilanti, V., Ascenzi, D., deCastro Vitores, M., Pirani, F., Cappelletti, D.: A quantum mechanical view of molecular alignment and cooling in seeded supersonic expansion. J. Chem. Phys. **111**, 2620–2632 (1999)

27. Pirani, F., Cappelletti, D., Bartolomei, M., Aquilanti, V., Scotoni, M., Vescovi, M., Ascenzi, D., Bassi, D.: Orientation of benzene in supersonic expansions, probed by IR-laser absorption and by molecular beam scattering. Phys. Rev. Lett. **86**, 5038–5053 (2001)

28. Pirani, F., Bartolomei, M., Aquilanti, V., Scotoni, M., Vescovi, M., Ascenzi, D., Bassi, D., Cappelletti, D.: Collisional orientation of the benzene molecular plane in supersonic seeded expansions, probed by infrared polarized laser absorption spectroscopy and by molecular beam scattering. J. Chem. Phys. **119**, 265–276 (2003)

29. Pirani, F., Maciel, G.S., Cappelletti, D., Aquilanti, V.: Experimental benchmarks and phenomenology of interatomic forces: open shell and electronic anisotropy effect. Int. Rev. Phys. Chem. **25**, 165–199 (2006)

30. Pirani, F., Cappelletti, D., Bartolomei, M., Aquilanti, V., Demarchi, G., Tosi, P., Scotoni, M.: The collisional alignment of acetylene molecules in supersonic seeded expansions probed by infrared absorption and molecular beam scattering. Chem. Phys. Lett. **437**, 176–182 (2007)

31. Nakamura, M., Yang, S.-J., Tsai, P.-Y., Kasai, T., Lin, K.-C., Che, D.-C., Lombardi, A., Palazzetti, F., Aquilanti, V.: Hexapole-oriented asymmetric-top molecules and their stereodirectional photodissociation dynamics. J. Phys. Chem. A **120**(27), 5389–5398 (2016)

32. Lombardi, A., Palazzetti, F.: Chirality in molecular collision dynamics J. Phys. Cond. Mat. **30**(6), 19 p. (2018). Article no. 063003

33. Lombardi, A., Palazzetti, F., Aquilanti, V., Grossi, G.: Chirality in molecular collisions. In: 1906 AIP Conference Proceedings (2017). Article no. 030012

34. Su, T.-M., Palazzetti, F., Lombardi, A., Grossi, G., Aquilanti, V.: Molecular alignment and chirality in gaseous streams and vortices. Rendiconti Lincei **24**(3), 291–297 (2013)

35. Palazzetti, F., Tsai, P.-Y., Lombardi, A., Nakamura, M., Che, D.-C., Kasai, T., Lin, K.-C., Aquilanti, V.: Aligned molecules: chirality discrimination in photodissociation and in molecular dynamics. Rendiconti Lincei **24**(3), 299–308 (2013)

36. Aquilanti, V., Grossi, G., Lombardi, A., Maciel, G.S., Palazzetti, F.: Aligned molecular collisions and a stereodynamical mechanism for selective chirality. Rendiconti Lincei **22**(2), 125–135 (2011)

37. Lombardi, A., Maciel, G.S., Palazzetti, F., Grossi, G., Aquilanti, V.: Alignment and chirality in gaseous flows. J. Vac. Soc. Jpn. **53**(11), 645–653 (2010)

38. Palazzetti, F., Munusamy, E., Lombardi, A., Grossi, G., Aquilanti, V.: Spherical and hyperspherical representation of potential energy surfaces for intermolecular interactions. Int. J. Quan. Chem. **111**(2), 318–332 (2011)

39. Barreto, P.R.P., Ribas, V.W., Palazzetti, F.: Potential energy surface for the H_2O-H_2 system. J. Phys. Chem. A **113**(52), 15047–15054 (2009)

40. Albernaz, A.F., Aquilanti, V., Barreto, P.R.P., Caglioti, C., Cruz, A.C.P.S., Grossi, G., Lombardi, A., Palazzetti, F.: Interactions of hydrogen molecules with halogen-containing diatomics from *ab initio* calculations: spherical-harmonics representation and characterization of the intermolecular potentials. J. Phys. Chem. A **120**(27), 5315–5324 (2016)

41. Falcinelli, S., Rosi, M., Candori, P., Vecchiocattivi, F., Bartocci, A., Lombardi, A., Faginas-Lago, N., Pirani, F.: Modeling the intermolecular interactions and characterization of the dynamics of collisional autoionization processes. In: Murgante, B., et al. (eds.) ICCSA 2013. LNCS, vol. 7971, pp. 69–83. Springer, Heidelberg (2013). https://doi.org/10.1007/978-3-642-39637-3_6

42. Werner, H.J., Knowles, P.J., Knizia, G., Manby, F.R., Schütz, M.: Molpro: a general-purpose quantum chemistry program package. WIREs Comput. Mol. Sci. **2**, 242–253 (2012)

43. Lombardi, A., Faginas-Lago, N., Gaia, G., Federico, P., Aquilanti, V.: Collisional energy exchange in CO_2–N_2 gaseous mixtures. In: Gervasi, O., et al. (eds.) ICCSA 2016. LNCS, vol. 9786, pp. 246–257. Springer, Cham (2016). https://doi.org/10.1007/978-3-319-42085-1_19

44. Lombardi, A., Palazzetti, F., Maciel, G.S., Aquilanti, V., Sevryuk, M.B.: Simulation of oriented collision dynamics of simple chiral molecules. Int. J. Quan. Chem. **111**(7–8), 1651–1658 (2011)

45. Lombardi, A., Palazzetti, F.: A comparison of interatomic potentials for rare gas nanoaggregates. J. Mol. Struct.: THEOCHEM **852**(1–3), 22–29 (2008)

46. Lago, N.F., Albertí, M., Laganà, A., Lombardi, A.: Water $(H_2O)_m$ or Benzene $(C_6H_6)_n$ Aggregates to Solvate the K^+? In: Murgante, B., et al. (eds.) ICCSA 2013. LNCS, vol. 7971, pp. 1–15. Springer, Heidelberg (2013). https://doi.org/10.1007/978-3-642-39637-3_1

47. Faginas-Lago, N., et al.: An innovative synergistic grid approach to the computational study of protein aggregation mechanisms. J. Mol. Model. **20**(7), 2226 (2014). https://doi.org/10.1007/s00894-014-2226-4

48. Lombardi, A., Lago, N.F., Laganà, A., Pirani, F., Falcinelli, S.: A bond-bond portable approach to intermolecular interactions: simulations for n-methylacetamide and carbon dioxide dimers. In: Murgante, B., et al. (eds.) ICCSA 2012. LNCS, vol. 7333, pp. 387–400. Springer, Heidelberg (2012). https://doi.org/10.1007/978-3-642-31125-3_30

49. Faginas-Lago, N., Bin Yeamin, Md., Sanchez-Martin, J., Cuesta, I.G., Albertì, M., Sanchez de Meras, A.: Modelization of the H_2 adsorption on graphene and molecular dynamics simulation. Theor. Chem. Acc. **136**(8), 91 (2017). https://doi.org/10.1007/s00214-017-2110-2

50. Albertí, M., Lago, N.F.: Competitive solvation of K^+ by C_6H_6 and H_2O in the K^+-$(C_6H_6)_n$-$(H_2O)_m$ (n = 1–4; m = 1–6) aggregates. Eur. Phys. J. D **67**(4) (2013). https://doi.org/10.1140/epjd/e2013-30753-x

51. Albertí, M., Lago, N.F., Pirani, F.: Ar solvation shells in K+-HFBz: from cluster rearrangement to solvation dynamics. J. Phys. Chem. **115**(40), 10871–10879 (2011). https://doi.org/10.1021/jp206601m

52. Faginas-Lago, N., Albertí, M., Lombardi, A., Palazzetti, F.: Acetone-water mixtures: molecular dynamics using a semiempirical intermolecular potential. In: Gervasi, O., et al. (eds.) ICCSA 2017. LNCS, vol. 10406, pp. 3–13. Springer, Cham (2017). https://doi.org/10.1007/978-3-319-62398-6_1

53. Faginas-Lago, N., Lombardi, A., Albertí, M., Grossi, G.: Accurate analytic intermolecular potential for the simulation of Na^+ and K^+ ion hydration in liquid water. J. Mol. Liq. **204**, 192–197 (2015). https://doi.org/10.1016/j.molliq.2015.01.029

54. Faginas-Lago, N., Lombardi, A., Albertí, M.: Aqueous N-methylacetamide: new analytic potentials and a molecular dynamics study. J. Mol. Liq. **224**, 792–800 (2016). https://doi.org/10.1016/j.molliq.2016.10.077

55. Faginas Lago, N., Albertí, M., Lombardi, A., Pirani, F.: A force field for acetone: the transition from small clusters to liquid phase investigated by molecular dynamics simulations. Theor. Chem. Acc. **135**(7), 161 (2016). https://doi.org/10.1007/s00214-016-1914-9

56. Faginas-Lago, N., Albertí, M., Lombardi, A.: Acetone clusters molecular dynamics using a semiempirical intermolecular potential. In: Gervasi, O., et al. (eds.) ICCSA 2016. LNCS, vol. 9786, pp. 129–140. Springer, Cham (2016). https://doi.org/10.1007/978-3-319-42085-1_10

57. Lombardi, A., Laganà, A., Pirani, F., Palazzetti, F., Lago, N.F.: Carbon oxides in gas flows and earth and planetary atmospheres: state-to-state simulations of energy transfer and dissociation reactions. In: Murgante, B., et al. (eds.) ICCSA 2013. LNCS, vol. 7972, pp. 17–31. Springer, Heidelberg (2013). https://doi.org/10.1007/978-3-642-39643-4_2

58. Lombardi, A., Faginas-Lago, N., Pacifici, L., Costantini, A.: Modeling of energy transfer from vibrationally excited CO_2 molecules: cross sections and probabilities for kinetic modeling of atmospheres, flows, and plasmas. J. Phys. Chem. **117**(45), 11430–11440 (2013). https://doi.org/10.1021/jp408522m

59. Hellwege, K.H., Hellwege, A.M. (eds.): Structure Data of Free Polyatomic Molecules. Landolt-Bornstein: Group II: Atomic and Molecular Physics, vol. 7. Springer, Berlin (1976)

60. Palazzetti, F., Maciel, G.S., Kanda, K., Nakamura, M., Che, D.-C., Kasai, T., Aquilanti, V.: Control of conformers combining cooling by supersonic expansion of seeded molecular beams with hexapole selection and alignment: experiment and theory on 2-butanol. Phys. Chem. Chem. Phys. **16**(21), 9866–9875 (2014)

61. Nakamura, M., Yang Jr., S.-J., Lin, K.-C., Kasai, T., Che, D.-C., Lombardi, A., Palazzetti, F., Aquilanti, V.: Stereodirectional images of molecules oriented by a variable-voltage hexapolar field: fragmentation channels of 2-bromobutane electronically excited at two photolysis wavelengths. J. Chem. Phys. **147**(1), 7 p. (2017). Article no. 013917

62. Kasai, T., Che, D.-C., Okada, M., Tsai, P.-Y., Lin, K.-C., Palazzetti, F., Aquilanti, V.: Directions of chemical change: experimental characterization of the stereodynamics of photodissociation and reactive processes. Phys. Chem. Chem. Phys. **16**(21), 9776–9790 (2014)

First-Principles Molecular Dynamics and Computed Rate Constants for the Series of OH-HX Reactions (X = H or the Halogens): Non-Arrhenius Kinetics, Stereodynamics and Quantum Tunnel

Nayara D. Coutinho[1], Vincenzo Aquilanti[2,3],
Flávio O. Sanches-Neto[1], Eduardo C. Vaz[4],
and Valter H. Carvalho-Silva[4(✉)]

[1] Institute of Chemistry, University of Brasília,
Campus Darcy Ribeiro, Brasília, Brazil
[2] Dipartimento di Chimica, Biologia e Biotecnologie,
Università di Perugia, Via Elce di Sotto 8, 06123 Perugia, Italy
[3] Istituto di Struttura della Materia,
Consiglio Nazionale delle Ricerche, 00185 Rome, Italy
[4] Grupo de Química Teórica e Estrutural de Anápolis,
Ciências Exatas e Tecnológicas, Universidade Estadual de Goiás,
CP 459, Anápolis, GO 75001-970, Brazil
fatioleg@gmail.com

Abstract. This paper is part of a series aiming at elucidating the mechanisms involved in the *non*-Arrhenius behavior of the four-body OH + HX (X = H, F, Cl, Br and I) reactions. These reactions are very important in atmospheric chemistry. Additionally, these four-body reactions are also of basic relevance for chemical kinetics. Their kinetics has manifested *non*-Arrhenius behavior: the experimental rate constants for the OH + HCl and OH + H$_2$ reactions, when extended to low temperatures, show a concave curvature in the Arrhenius plot, a phenomenon designated as *sub*-Arrhenius behavior, while reactions with HBr and HI are considered as typical processes that exhibit negative temperature dependence of the rate constants (*anti*-Arrhenius behavior). From a theoretical point of view, these reactions have been studied in order to obtain the potential energy surface and to reproduce these complex rate constants using the Transition State Theory. Here, in order to understand the *non*-Arrhenius mechanism, we exploit recent information from *ab initio* molecular dynamics. For OH + HI and OH + HBr, the visualizations of rearrangements of bonds along trajectories has shown how molecular reorientation occurs in order that the reactants encounter a mutual angle of approach favorable for them to proceed to reaction. Besides the demonstration of the crucial role of stereodynamics, additional documentation was also provided on the interesting manifestation of the roaming phenomenon, both regarding the search for reactive configurations sterically favorable to reaction and the subsequent departure of products involving their vibrational excitation. Under moderate tunneling regime, the OH + H$_2$ reaction was satisfactory described by *deformed*-Transition-State

© Springer International Publishing AG, part of Springer Nature 2018
O. Gervasi et al. (Eds.): ICCSA 2018, LNCS 10964, pp. 605–623, 2018.
https://doi.org/10.1007/978-3-319-95174-4_47

Theory. In the same reaction, the catalytic effect of water can be assessed by path integral molecular dynamics. For the OH + HCl reaction, the theoretical rate coefficients calculated with Bell tunneling correction were in good agreement with experimental data in the entire temperature range 200–2000 K, with minimal effort compared to much more elaborate treatments. Furthermore, the Born-Oppenheimer molecular dynamics simulation showed that the orientation process was less effective than for HBr and HI reactions, emphasizing the role of the quantum tunneling effect of penetration of an energy barrier in the reaction path along the potential energy surface. These results can shed light on the clarification of the different *non*-Arrhenius mechanisms involved in four-body reaction, providing rate constants and their temperature dependence of relevance for pure and applied chemical kinetics.

1 Introduction

The OH + HX → H$_2$O + X (X = H or halogen) reactions contribute to fundamental processes in atmospheric chemistry. The reaction of hydrogen halide and hydroxyl radical are of interest regarding mechanisms for the depletion of ozone and the OH + H$_2$ reaction promotes balance of the concentration of hydroxyl radical. Further understanding of these reactions is important from the technological point of view, for example, in the kinetic study of the role of iodine in light water reactor accidents, where volatile fission products such as iodine can be released from fuel into an atmosphere of hydrogen and vapor [1].

Additionally, these four-body reactions are of basic relevance for both experimental and theoretical chemical kinetics. The rate constants for most rate processes depend on absolute temperature according to the Arrhenius law: however, for these reactions, when extended to low temperatures, deviations are observed: the kinetics data available for the reaction with HCl [2, 3] and H$_2$ [4–7], show a concave curvature for low temperatures, a phenomenon described as *sub*-Arrhenius behavior, while reactions with HBr [8–14] and HI [15–19] are considered as typical processes that exhibit negative temperature dependence of the reaction rate (*anti*-Arrhenius behavior).

Although important in the technological and atmospheric context, the experimental studies for hydroxyl radical and hydrogen iodine are limited: just a few values are available for rate constants near 300 K [15–18]. Takacs and Glass [15], using fast flow system found for a temperature of 295 K, the rate constant equal to 1.3 · 10^{-11}cm^3 molecule^{-1}s^{-1}. Mac Leod et al. [16], using a laser photolysis-resonance fluorescence (LP-RF) apparatus, measured the rate constant at 298 K and found $k = 2.7 · 10^{-11}$cm^3 molecule^{-1}s^{-1}. In 1990, Lancar et al. [17] experimentally measured the rate constant at 298 K using discharge-flow reactors coupled to electron paragmagnetic resonance (EPR) and mass spectrometry for analysis and found that the rate constant was 3.3($\pm$0.2) · 10^{-11}cm^3 molecule^{-1}s^{-1}. In 1999, Jost Campuzano-Crowley [19] measured the rate constants at room temperature and, in order to solve the discrepancies in the literature, extended the study to a small temperature range between 246 and 353 K. Under these conditions, the authors showed that the rate constants had a negative dependence on temperature, the same *anti*-Arrhenius behavior observed for the reaction between OH and

HBr. As a result, this study produced the following adjustment for the rate constants:

$$k\left(246 - 353\text{K}\right) = 7.0 \cdot 10^{-11} \left(T/_{298}\right)^{-1.5\pm0.5} \text{cm}^3 \text{ molecule}^{-1}\text{s}^{-1}.$$

In a contribution to the understanding of the detailed microscopic dynamics of the OH + HI reaction, Moise et al. used crossed molecular beam experiments to measure relative state-to-state cross-section and steric asymmetries, and a comparison was made with the previously studied systems OH-HCl and OH-HBr [20]. They discussed the relevance of the potential energy surface of these molecular systems in the reactive process. From a theoretical perspective, the direct and reverse reactions have been of interest for some time. In 1997, Inada and Akagane [21] predicted the activation energy for the $I + H_2O \rightarrow OH + HI$ reaction using the quadratic configuration interaction method with single and double substitutions (QCISD) [21]. Canneaux et al. [22] obtained a potential energy profile of the $I + H_2O$ reaction, showing that the relative energy of products is lower than that of the transition state, and they determined the quantitative rate constants for the reactions involving iodine-containing species, using the canonical transition state theory with a simple Wigner tunneling correction. Very recently, the stationary points and zero-point vibrational energies for the $I + H_2O$ potential energy surface have been predicted at high-level *ab initio* CCSD(T) method, with spin–orbit coupling corrections [23]. However, all previous works neglect the understanding of *anti*-Arrhenius behavior.

The direct and inverse reactions $OH + HBr \rightarrow H_2O + Br$ and their isotopic variants have been exhaustively studied in recent years, both from a theoretical and an experimental point of view, by different research groups. The kinetic data obtained from the reaction between the hydroxyl radical and hydrogen bromide have shown that a strong negative temperature dependence for values below 200 K. The first kinetic data obtained for range of temperature were measured by Ravishankara et al. [8] for the range from 249 to 416 K. The authors found that the rate constant was temperature independent and equal to $k = 1.19(\pm0.14) \cdot 10^{-11} \text{cm}^3\text{s}^{-1}$. Before the work of Ravishankara et al. [8], some other authors had obtained the rate constant value for isolated temperatures: Takacs and Glass (298 K) [24], Smith and Zellner (298 K) [25] and Wilson et al. (1925 K) [26].

However, the first kinetic study that was able to identify the negative dependence on temperature was developed by Sims *et al.* [9] for the temperature range from 23 to 295 K. This same behavior was observed by Atkinson *et al.* [10] for the range of temperature from 76 to 242 K. The only discrepancy between these last two studies was whether the rate constant really was dependent on temperature for above 150 K. In order to solve this uncertainty, in 2002 the experimental groups of Rowe and Smith made new measurements for the rate constants in the temperature range between 23 and 416 K [12]. This study produced as a final result [14]: $k(T) = 1.11 \cdot 10^{-11} \left(T/_{298}\right)^{-0.91} \text{cm}^3 \text{ molecules}^{-1}\text{s}^{-1}$ and $k(T) = 1.06 \cdot 10^{-11} \left(T/_{298}\right)^{-1.09} \cdot \exp\left(-10.5K/_T\right) \text{cm}^3 \text{ molecules}^{-1}\text{s}^{-1}$. The authors demonstrated that both of which accurately describe the negative temperature dependence for OH + HBr reaction.

Concomitantly, several other papers have been published with the objective of understanding the isotopic effect on the rate constant of the OH + HBr reaction. In the study of Bedjanian et al. [11] (230–360 K), primary kinetics isotopic effects (KIE) are found near 1.8. In 2001, Jaramillo and Smith [12] proposed to study the KIE for a different temperature range. The authors observed that for the temperature of 120 K the deuterated reactants reacted as fast or faster than the neutral hydrogen isotope. Mullen and Smith [13] selected the temperature range between 53 and 135 K and found that the primary KIE was temperature independent within experimental error.

Another important phenomenon in this reaction, the stereodynamic aspect had been convincingly revealed in experiments, where in order to understand orientational effects, the Osaka group [27–30] studied the OH + HBr reaction using crossed molecular beams for higher than thermal energy (0.05–0.026 eV). The results indicated that the cross-section decreased increasing the collision energy and suggested that reorientation effects of the reagents strongly favor the reactivity. That is, if reorientation effects are present in the OH + HBr reaction, they are probably more pronounced for small values of the collision energy, since reagents have more time to reorient before the reactive process.

More recently, in 2010 Tsai et al. [27] continued the experimental studies for the OH + HBr reaction in order to prove the energy dependence of reorientation effects and to extract information on the ratio of the O-end, H-end and sideways collisions. The Osaka group used an orientating hexapole electrostatic field. Regarding the relative importance of the reactive sites, it was found that the O-end attack is most favored for this reaction than the H-end attack by a factor of 3.4 ± 2.3; they also suggested a cone of acceptance with a limiting angle [27] of $\alpha = 117 \pm 13$ degrees for the reaction to occur. The authors also suggested that the orientation effect may be related to the spatial distribution of the HOMO electron of the OH radical.

From a theoretical point of view, the OH + HBr reaction has been studied under a focus on the calculation of the rate constants and on the interpretation of the *anti*-Arrhenius behavior [31–35]. Recently, de Oliveira-Filho et al. [34, 35] calculated an accurate potential energy surface using high-level electronic structure calculations. The authors found a saddle point with less energy than the reactants and the presence of a van der Waals well, which they suggested as being responsible for the negative activation energy observed in experimental kinetic data. The same authors performed quasi-classical trajectories (QCT), obtained information about the cross-section and found a good description of the rate constants for the range of temperature 5–500 K [35]. Simultaneously, Zhang et al. [36] studied five stationary points on the potential energy surface that included entrance and exit complexes, as well as the transition state using the CCSD(T)/cc-pV5Z-PP calculation level. Even using a different methodology, the values for energy and geometric parameters were consistent with those obtained by de Oliveira-Filho et al. [34, 35]. However, none of these authors discussed the importance of the favored stereodynamic effect at low temperatures observed in the Osaka experiments [27–30].

The rate constant for the OH + HCl [25, 37–45] shows a phenomenon designated as *sub*-Arrhenius behavior [47, 48]. Generally, there is a consensus in the literature that processes exhibiting this behavior are intrinsically dominated by the quantum tunneling effect of penetration of an energy barrier along the reaction path on the potential energy surface [49, 50]. From a theoretical perspective, much effort has been dedicated to obtaining the potential energy surface (PES) and rate constants for OH + HCl reaction. Recently, the Schaefer group obtained a potential energy profile of the OH + HCl reaction by the CCSD(T) method with correlation consistent basis sets through cc-pVQZ, showing energy, geometry and frequencies for five stationary points along the reaction path [51]. The Guo group calculated a full-dimensional global PES generated by fitting ca. 25,000 multi-reference configuration interaction points using a permutation invariant polynomial method [52]. Later, they calculated the thermal rate constant for a wide range of temperatures using ring-polymer molecular dynamics and observed the deviations in the rate constant with available experimental data for low temperatures [53].

In order to improve the more accurate full-dimensional global PES, the Guo group fitted a new set of *ab initio* points obtained by (UCCSD(T)-F12b/AVTZ), and the rate constant was calculated by canonical variational transition state theory. The authors found a lower barrier for forward reaction than that of previous PES [53], and the rate constant had a better agreement with experimental values, however, for low temperatures the disagreement was still significant [3]. More recently, the Guo group [54] presented a study using ring polymer molecular dynamics for the title reaction and its deuterium analogue. The calculated RPMD rate constants are in excellent agreement with experimental data confirming the accuracy of the potential energy surface. Recently, the investigation of the catalytic effect of NH_3 and HCOOH on the reaction between OH and HCl found both *sub*-Arrhenius and anti-Arrhenius plots of rate constants, depending on the reactive channel analyzed [55].

From a quasi-classical trajectory method, the Guo group showed that for the OH + HCl reaction, the vibrational excitation of the HCl reactant greatly increased the reactivity, while the OH vibrational mode acts essentially as a spectator [56]. This result was assessed as contradicting Polanyi's rule, which suggests that the translational energy is more efficient than vibrational energy in enhancing an early barrier reaction. However, they explained that this violation can be elucidated by a sudden vector projection model, which attributes the promotional effect of the HCl vibration to its strong coupling with the coordinate in the transition state [56, 57].

Relevant from our view point are the quasi-classical trajectory calculations by Bonnet et al. [58] who demonstrated unexpected reaction pathways involving strong reorientation of the reagents, and showed that the most important channels were far from the reaction path, using a dynamical extension of the notion of cone of acceptance to rationalize the stereodynamic effects [58].

An alternative source of important information comes from molecular beam scattering experiments with oriented reactants. Only a non-reactive experiments is available: Cireasa and collaborators [59] report stereodynamical features in the inelastic collisions between OH and HCl molecule, showing that H-end attack is favored for the inelastic collision system. They define a "steric asymmetry factor" and found it negative, in contrast with the analogous four-body reaction, OH + HBr, for which the O-end attack is more favorable by a factor three over that at the H-end [27, 28].

The OH + H_2 reaction plays a fundamental role in atmospheric chemistry, astrochemistry and combustion processes. There are several experimental and theoretical kinetic works about this reaction. In a more recent work, Kästner estimate the reaction rate constants in the range from 150 to 1000 K obtaining excellent agreement with experimental values. Instanton theory and canonical variational theory with micro-canonical optimized multidimensional tunneling were applied using a fitted potential energy surface [7]. Considering the importance of the reaction of the hydroxyl with molecular hydrogen, a variety of PES have been proposed and the more recent is a global potential energy surface fitted by a neural network to UCCSD(T)-F12a/AVTZ data [60]. A scattering study using a quantum-classical method [61] showed that H_2 reactive dynamics depends on the vibrational excitation, while the non reactive one is mainly vibrationally adiabatic and that OH reactive dynamics is not affected by its vibrational excitation.

In 1975, the first molecular hydrogen (H_2) studies focused in medical applications were reported [62–64]. However, only after 32 years Ohsawa demonstrated the applicability of this gas, gaining notoriety due to the presented results [65]. He and coworkers showed a significant decrease of cerebral infarction in rats exposed to a 2% to 4% v/v of molecular hydrogen. Ohsawa et al. [65] provided a new possibility for medicine and between 2007 and 2015 was 63 types of diseases was reported as the treated using H_2 gas [65, 66]. The possibility of treatment is suggested due to the specific activity of H_2 in neutralizing hydroxyl radicals, an antioxidant agent [62, 65]. Studies have shown that this neutralization reaction has a high isotopic effect. The possibility of tunneling reactions, especially when involving low mass atoms, such as hydrogen, can be directly related to this effect [67].

Potential Energy Surfaces for the OH – Hydrogen Halides. In Fig. 1, a schematic view of the potential energy surface for $OH + HX \rightarrow H_2O + X$ (X = halogen) can been seen. The reactions with hydroxyl radical and hydrogen iodine, hydrogen bromide and hydrogen chloride are highly exothermic, with ΔH^0 equal to -47.70, -31.43 and -15.82 kcal/mol, respectively, while the reaction with hydrogen fluoride is endothermic ($\Delta H^0 = 17.6$ kcal/mol). These differences are due to the fact that the energy of dissociation of HF is much greater than that for the other hydrogen halides. As seen for four reactions, there is an entrance complex, followed by a saddle-point barrier and exit complex in the product channel; however, as expected, the energies of stationary points change in function of the hydrogen halide. The transition-state barrier has a positive energy for the OH + HF and OH + HCl reaction, while for the other two reactions the transition state is energetically lower than the entrance channel (apparent negative activation energy).

The anisotropic forces generated by electrostatic and dispersion interactions promote the formation of the wells in the reactant in the PES. However, differently from the entrance complex (HO—HX), the origin of stability of the exit complex (X—H_2O) cannot be explained by electrostatic or dispersion interaction, since neither the geometry nor the energy encodes with this type of interaction. The Guo group [69] showed strong evidence that the interactions between halogens and water have a covalent origin due to the two-center-electron bond formed between an unpaired electron of the halogen atom and a lone pair of H_2O.

Rates for the OH – Hydrogen Halides Reactions: Figure 2 shows the comparison among the rate constants OH + HI, OH + HBr and OH + Cl reactions (for the endothermic

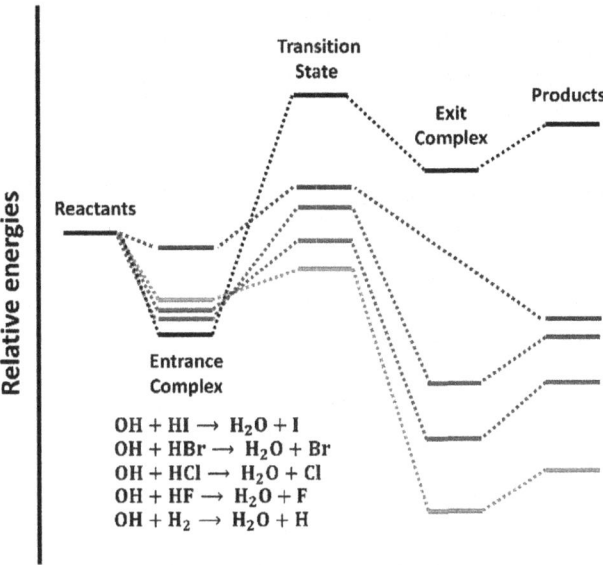

Fig. 1. Pictorial view comparing the stationary points on the potential energy surfaces for the OH + HX → H$_2$O + X (H or Halogens) reaction, adapted from Refs. [46, 68].

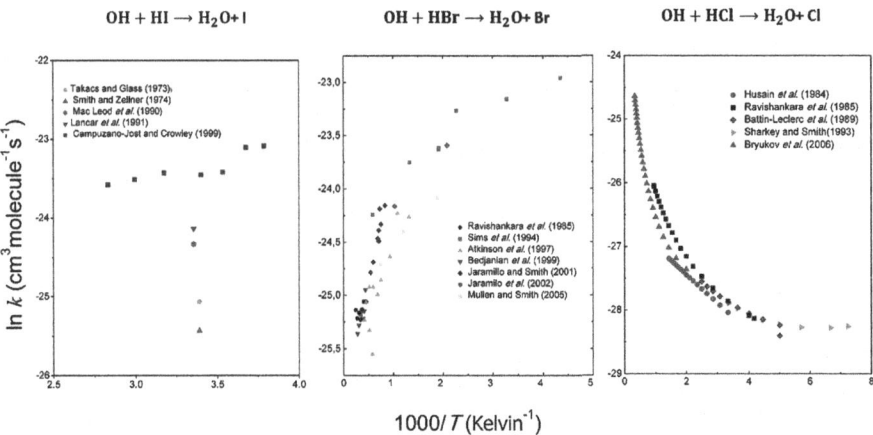

Fig. 2. Temperature dependence of the rate constants for the OH + HI, OH + HBr and OH + HCl reactions.

OH + HF reaction there are no kinetic data available). As can be seen, among the three reactions, the HI molecules were found to have the highest rate constant for the range of temperature available, and the HCl molecule had the smallest reactive reaction in almost the entire temperature range. Additionally, as already mentioned, the reaction between HCl and OH has a *sub*-Arrhenius behavior, while the other two reactions show an *anti*-Arrhenius behavior.

In this paper we focus on the origin of *non*-Arrhenis kinetics for the tetraatomic hydrogen reaction of OH with HCl, HBr and HI, exploiting recent information from *ab initio* molecular dynamic studies with the aim of understanding the role of tunneling, stereodynamics and roaming for each of these systems.

2   Ab Initio Molecular Dynamics for the OH + HX Reaction

Molecular Dynamics Simulations. The aim of disentangling the basic questions concerning the peculiar kinetics of these reaction is approached by molecular dynamics simulations. The technique of choice, the Born-Oppenheimer molecular dynamics BOMD [70–72], is suited to follow the evolution of the reaction and provide a full explanation of its apparently unusual features. The dynamical relevance of this feature is adequately scrutinized under the microscope of the present canonical trajectory simulations and very relevant appeared to us the additional specific goal to provide a link with the overlooked experimental stereodynamical studies [20, 21, 55, 61].

Electronic structure calculations are essential in molecular dynamics simulations and the reliability of intermolecular forces depends on the quality of the employed quantum chemistry methods and of the computational effort involved. Since a chemical process involves the adjustment of the electronic structure according to the evolution of the nuclear positions, reaction mechanisms emerge with no need of computationally prohibitive explorations to find reaction pathways. On the contrary, the exploit of the automatic focusing of trajectories on regions actually sampled during the reaction [75], provides information on parts of the multidimensional potential energy surface which demand more accuracy for improving the realistic simulations of the dynamics. Randomly generated initial conditions and procedures for equilibration with respect to a thermal bath (see the following subsection), permit to efficiently bypass the often severe bottlenecks of computational dynamics, such as both the impact parameter integration to provide total cross sections, and their Boltzmann kinetic energy averaging, allowing the direct specification of the temperature.

Computational Methods: The *ab initio* Born-Oppenheimer Molecular Dynamics (BOMD) simulations were carried out using the Car-Parrinello MD 3.17.1 package [76]. The reactions were modelled as occurring in periodically repeated cubic cells of each of side-length 6 Å, where one HX (X = I, Br and Cl) molecule and one OH radical were added. The electronic structure was treated within the generalized gradient approximation to density functional theory (DFT), through the Perdew-Burke-Ernzerhofn (PBE) exchange-correlation functional [77]. Vanderbilt ultrasoft pseudopotentials were employed to represent core-valence electron interactions [78]. A plane-wave basis set was used to expand the valence electronic wave function with an energy cutoff of 25 Ry. The equations of motion were integrated using the Verlet scheme with a time step of 4 au (0.121 fs) and a total time of 2 ps. The temperatures of the system were controlled by the Nosé-Hoover Thermostat scheme [79] at 50, 200, 350 and 500 K. At each temperature, 60 trajectories were simulated with different initial configurations.

3 Representation of Stereodirectional and Roaming Dynamics

Figure 3 illustrates the coordinate choice for this discussion of the $OH + HX \rightarrow H_2O + X$ ($X = I, Br$ and Cl) reactions [75, 80–82]. In a four-body system, the configuration is fixed by six coordinates, two of them are those utilized here for exhibiting the stereodirectional effect on the molecular dynamics: they are the bond length r_1 and the angle θ. Their values are fixed when starting the simulations and serve to identify the trajectories in the following presentation. The initial settings have been selected according to the following criteria: r_1^0 ranging from 1.7 to 3.2 Å with steps of 0.3 Å and θ_0 ranging from 0 to 180° with a 20° increment; all other coordinates were obtained randomly, within limits that guaranteed realistic initial configurations of the system. In the initial configurations, two other variables are held fixed for all cases, the HX bond length at 1.61, 1.47, 1.27 Å for HI, HBr and HCl, respectively and the OH^2 bond length at 1.0 Å. More details of the 60 initial configurations can be obtained in our previous papers [63, 68–70].

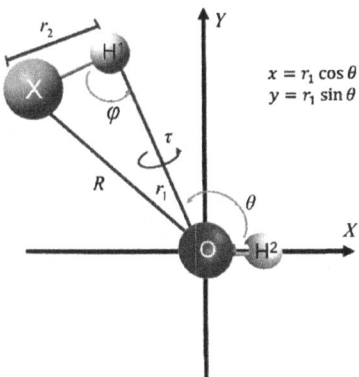

$$x = r_1 \cos \theta$$
$$y = r_1 \sin \theta$$

Fig. 3. Definitions of geometrical parameters for the configuration of the four-atom process suited to extract stereodynamical information on the role of the mutual direction between approaching reactants. The origin is on the oxygen atom, the OH bond, lies in the X axis, while Y is the axis perpendicular to X in the XOH^2 plane oriented as in the figure.

The coordinate s, appropriate to simply describe the evolution of the reactive event is the difference between lengths of bonds being broken and formed, respectively ($s = r_2 - r_1$, see Fig. 1). Negative values of s correspond to the configuration of reagents, positive values to those of the products. The "exchange rate" for the reaction is conveniently defined as the inverse of the "switching" time, defined by the time when either $r_2 = r_1$ or $s = 0$.

The analysis of the correlation between the initial configuration and the exchange rate for the OH + HBr and OH + HI has shown that for low temperature the reactivity of the systems is sensitive to the initial condition, however as the temperature increases the initial configuration appears to be partially lost during the reactive process, arguably because of the manifestation of the roaming effect. Additionality, for the OH + HI reaction the number of reactive trajectories (17, 18, 17 and 21, for 50, 200, 350 and 500 K, respectively) and the time required for the mutual reactant orientations for the hydrogen exchange was less than for the OH + HBr reaction (23, 25, 32 and 38, for 50, 200, 350 and 500 K, respectively). These values are taken to suggest that the stereo-dynamic effect is more pronounced for the OH + HI reaction. In contradiction to these reactions, the OH + HCl reaction shows temperature independence and the initial configurations do not seem to be very important for reactive process: much larger number of trajectories led to water product (31, 45, 44 and 43 for 50, 200, 350 and 500 K, respectively). Thus, the dependence of reactivity on the stereodirectionality is markedly lower than observed for HBr and HI, and concomitantly, the roaming effect was more pronounced here [75, 80, 81].

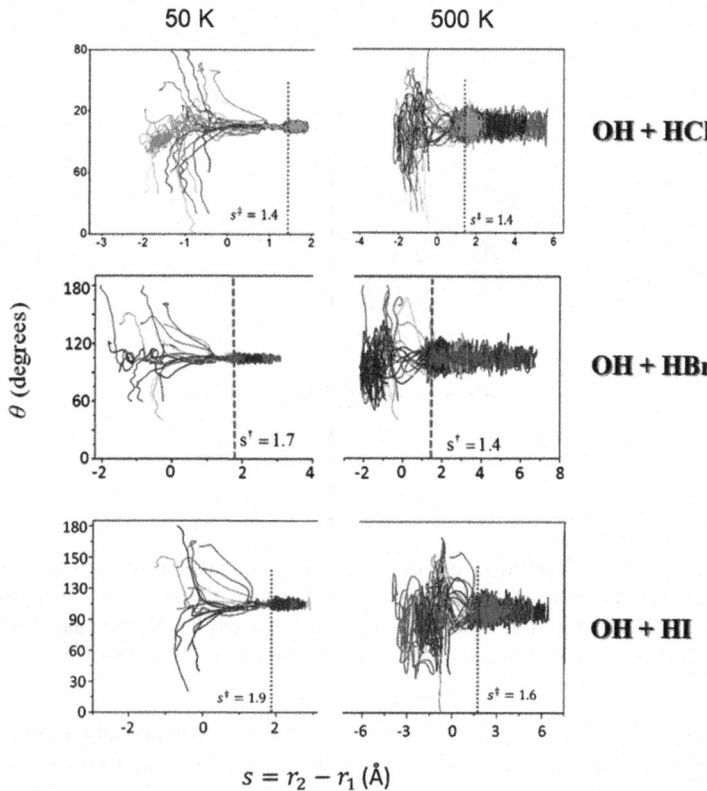

Fig. 4. Evolution at two extreme temperatures (50 and 500 K) of the stereodynamical angle of approach θ (Fig. 1) for "canonical" trajectories *versus* the reaction coordinate $s = r_2 - r_1$, conveniently defined as the difference between the lengths of the bond which is broken, r_2 and of the bond which is formed, r_1, the for OH + HCl, OH + HBr and OH + HI reactions. The trajectories are distinguished by different colours. Indicated by arrows is the value of $s^{\ddagger}$, identified by averaging for all trajectories of a given temperature the values of the reaction coordinate $s = r_2 - r_1$ for which a water molecule can be considered as formed. (Color figure online)

The origin of roaming effect as a rearrangement between weakly bound reactants is connected to high-lying regions of the ground state potential energy surfaces [83, 84] and indicated in Refs. [85–87]. Typically, these regions involve molecular configurations far from the transition state geometry and are propitiated by pronounced bond elongations, such as manifested when, on the way to reaction, the systems are emerging from nonadiabatic paths involving conical intersections. In all three reactions, we observe analogously that in our case "roaming" is favored by starting trajectories at elongated r_1.

More information about the role of the stereodynamic and roaming effect appears in the analysis of the stereodynamical angle of approach θ_0 versus the reaction coordinate $s = r_2 - r_1$. Figure 4 compares the evolution at two extreme temperature (50 and 500 K) of the stereodynamical angle of approach for OH + HCl [82], OH + HBr [75, 80] and OH + HI [81] reactions.

For the *anti*-Arrhenius reactions, when the dynamics is started with those values of θ_0 close to that leading to the formation of the bond angle of water $\theta_0 \sim 104°$, the system finds an easier way to products, but this adjustment is progressively less effective for higher temperatures. The reactive microscopic dynamics for OH + HCl was different, most of the trajectories experience difficulty in finding the favorable approaching angle for reactivity, evidencing again the preponderant "roaming" effect. Additionally, it has to be noted how the final energy appears to dispose as excitation in the bending mode of the product water, as is visually clear to a much greater extent again for the higher temperatures (see Ref. [84] for experimental comparisons for an analogous case study).

4 Rate Constant and Tunnel

Born-Oppenheimer Molecular Dynamics Rate Constant. The molecular-dynamics work reported here has been devoted mostly to the mechanistic aspects featuring as most relevant in the change of kinetics behavior of these reaction. In general, the extraction of quantitative information on rate constants from molecular dynamics simulations is an important issue, but a very difficult one to be tackled. In previous papers we suggested and tested a direct approach to estimate rate constants [75, 80–82], based on the rate of formation of product, water in these cases; being the bimolecular process OH + HX of the second order, the general formula for the rate constant can be written:

$$k = \frac{d[H_2O]}{dt} ([OH][HX])^{-1}$$

as the ratio of the rate of formation of water and the product of the initial concentrations of the two reactants. In our numerical experiments, the concentration for each reactant is $[C] \sim 5 \times 10^{21}$ molecules.cm^{-3}. The formation of water is "observed" in our first-principles nanoreactor as the appearance of one product molecule in the volume of the box, i.e. $[C]$ times the fraction f of reactive versus total trajectories and emerging at the 'transition time', $t^{\ddagger}$:

$$\frac{d[H_2O]}{dt} = \frac{f[C]}{t^{\ddagger}}.$$

The comparison between the Born-Oppenheimer molecular dynamics rate constant with experiments for OH-hydrogen halides reactions shows that was necessary to calibrate the "nanoreactor" against experimental results. After calibration of the nanoreactor, the calculated rate constants were in good agreement with experimental data for these reactions. Indeed, these results are indicative that this methodology provides at least a semi-quantitative route to the extraction of rate constants from *first-principles* molecular dynamics numerical experiments. Additionally, we observed that the best results were obtained for systems with higher reactivities, such as the OH + HI reaction. In this way, we conclude that the slower the reactive encounters, the greater the need for calibration of the reactor.

Theoretical Rate Constants. In order to account for the tunneling effect in the OH + HCl reaction, the quantitative information on the rate constants, in our previous papers was obtained performing a high-level Transition-State-Theory, modified to account for tunneling conditions. In this work we employ the *deformed*-Transition State Theory (*d*-TST) and both the Bell-1935, and Bell-1958 formulas to calculate the kinetic rate constants for the OH + HCl reaction in a wide range of temperatures (200–2000 K) at the MP2/6-311 ++G(d,p) level of calculation. A comparison between the calculated rate constants with experiments and previous theoretical works is shown in Fig. 5. More details about this treatment can be found in Refs. [49, 50]. A code to compute the

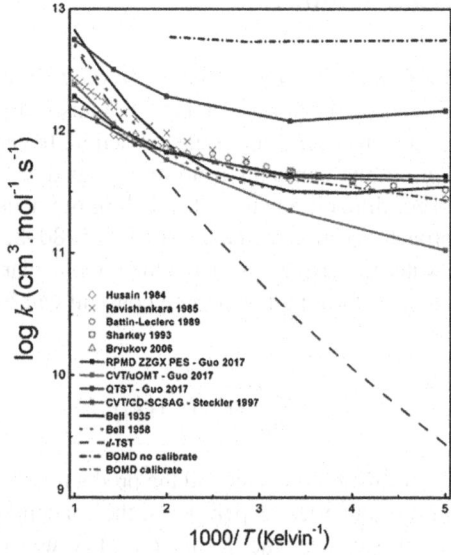

Fig. 5. Arrhenius plot for the OH + HCl → H₂O + Cl reaction and comparison between de *d*-TST, Bell-1935, and Bell-1958 rate constants computed at the MP2/6-311 ++G(d,p) level and theoretical [3, 53, 54] and experimental [41, 43, 44, 88, 89] values available in the literature.

kinetic rate constants with tunneling corrections has been developed in script-shell language and can be requested from the authors.

No major differences were found using either the Bell-1935 or Bell-1958 formulas: also, it can be seen that both formulations, involving minimal effort with respect to much more elaborated treatments, can estimate with satisfactory agreement the rate constants of the reaction for the whole wide range of investigated temperatures. On the other hand, as expected, the *d*-TST does not describe the range of experimental data for low temperature, where tunneling effects become more dominant, because its validity is limited to weak tunneling [50, 90].

In order to analyze OH + H_2 reaction under moderate tunneling regime, we performed Path-Integral Molecular Dynamics and could observe the reaction both in gas phase and in the presence of water [91]. Subsequently, we calculated the rate constants with *deformed*-Transition-State Theory and Bell-58 corrections [50, 92] at the QCISD (T)/aug-cc-pVDZ level of calculation. We gradually added water molecules to the system, in view of the fact that the system has relevance for human body conditions: we observe an increase in the reaction rate constant at the body temperature mediated by water. These results are partial, and we will soon present elsewhere.

5 Additional Remarks and Conclusions

In retrospect, the reactions between the hydroxyl radical and hydrogen halide are among the most studied elementary reactions, both from an experimental and theoretical point of view. The rate constants for these reactions evidence a *non*-Arrhenius behavior. While the reaction with HCl and H_2 is characterized by *sub*-Arrhenius behavior, the reactions with HBr and HI are prototypes of reactions with *anti*-Arrhenius behavior and therefore have apparent negative activation energy. Thus, in order to provide an interpretation of non-Arrhenius behavior we here put into perspective the reaction with three different halogens (Cl, Br and I).

Firstly, using Born-Oppenheimer molecular dynamics, this study was able to provide an interpretation of the negative dependence of the rate constant on temperature for the OH + HBr and OH + HI reactions, confirming the suggestion obtained experimentally that this phenomenon has stereodynamical origin, which until now has been neglected by theoretical studies. For the OH + HBr reaction, the analysis of simulations showed that for low temperature, the reactants reorient to find the propitious alignment leading to reaction; however, this adjustment is progressively less effective for higher temperatures. The wandering paths observed mainly for high temperature, evidence the "roaming" effect, which becomes more preponderant for higher r_1^0 (lengths of the bond that is formed) values. Additionally, we propose a new methodology to extract the thermal rate constants from molecular dynamics. The smaller number of reactive trajectories for and the time required for the mutual reactant orientations for the hydrogen exchange for the OH + HI suggest a greater role of stereodynamics here.

More specifically, for the OH + HCl reaction, the Born-Oppenheimer molecular dynamics simulation showed that the orientation process is important, but it is less so than for OH + HBr and OH + HI reactions. The initial configurations of the system do not seem to have significant weight in the reactive process. Regardless of the simulated temperature, many initial configurations led to reactive trajectories. When making a connection between the potential energy surface and the reaction dynamics of this process, we observed that unlike the *anti*-Arrhenius reactions, in this system there is an energy barrier, and the fact that there is the effective orientation of reagents does not influence significantly the reactive process. For low temperatures, the long-range interaction forces provide the orientation of reactants for the formation of the OH—HCl complex. It was expected that the complex formation delayed the reactive process, since there is an energy barrier limiting the reaction, and the reactants would take time to acquire the energy needed to promote the reaction. However, this complex is generally born with an excess of internal energy, which may be used to overcome the reaction barrier. Additionally, if this internal energy is not enough to overcome the barrier, it is increasing the probability of quantum tunneling and consequently, the probability of effective collisions increases. Thus, quantum tunneling can explain the fact that below the cross-over temperature, the rate constants remain constant as temperature decreases.

In this study we also calculated the rate constants for the OH + HCl reaction using high-level Transition-State-Theory modified to account for tunneling conditions. The Bell tunneling correction was in good agreement with experimental data in the entire temperature range of 200–2000 K, with minimal effort compared to much more elaborate treatments. After calibration, the Born-Oppenheimer molecular dynamics rate constants were also in close agreement with experimental data. Indeed, these results are indicative that this methodology provides at least a semi-quantitative route to the extraction of rate constants from first-principles molecular dynamics numerical experiments. Additionally, we observed that the best results were obtained for systems with higher reactivities, such as the OH + HI reaction. In this way, we conclude that the slower the reactive encounters, the greater the need for calibration of the reactor.

Considering the limitations imposed by a *non*-adiabatic process and the lack of kinetic experimental values in the reaction between OH and HF, we adopted precautions to connect the *non*-Arrhenius behavior with the methodology used in this study and in previous ones. However, the understanding obtained with the analogous reaction strongly suggests a *sub*-Arrhenius behavior under moderate quantum tunneling. Situation is similar to the reaction of the OH with H_2, much studied experimentally and theoretically because of its simplicity: in a sence it can be included in this series of OH + HX reaction. As expected, we have verified using the presented techniques that tunneling it the main mechanism for low temperature reactivity.

Finally, we can conclude that the *non*-Arrhenius behaviors for reaction between OH radical and hydrogen halide came from the combination of stereodynamics, roaming and quantum tunneling effects. For all reactions we observed that the orientation effect is very important; however, the role of this effect has a different contribution in each system, since the kinetics of reactions is highly influenced by the potential energy surface profile.

Acknowledgements. The authors are grateful for the support given by CAPES and CNPq. Valter H. Carvalho-Silva thanks PrP/UEG for research funding programs through PROBIP and PRÓ-PROJETOS programs. This research is also supported by the High Performance Computing Center at the Universidade Estadual de Goiás (UEG).

References

1. Lilington, J.: Light Water Reactor Safety (1994)
2. Zuo, J., Zhao, B., Guo, H., Xie, D.: Rate coefficients of the HCl + OH → Cl + H_2O reaction from ring polymer molecular dynamics. J. Phys. Chem. A **120**, 3433–3440 (2016)
3. Zuo, J., Zhao, B., Guo, H., Xie, D.: A global coupled cluster potential energy surface for HCl + OH ↔ Cl + H_2O. Phys. Chem. Chem. Phys. **15**, 9770–9777 (2017)
4. Kaufman, F., Del Greco, F.P.: Fast reactions of OH radicals. Symp. Combust. **9**, 659–668 (1963)
5. Orkin, V.L., Kozlov, S.N., Poskrebyshev, G.A., Kurylo, M.J.: Rate constant for the reaction of OH with H_2 between 200 and 480 K. J. Phys. Chem. A **110**, 6978–6985 (2006)
6. Lam, K.Y., Davidson, D.F., Hanson, R.K.: A shock tube study of H_2 + OH → H_2O + H using OH laser absorption. Int. J. Chem. Kinet. **45**, 363–373 (2013)
7. Meisner, J., Kästner, J.: Reaction rates and kinetic isotope effects of H_2 + OH → H_2O + H. J. Chem. Phys. **144**, 174303 (2016)
8. Ravishankara, A.R., Wine, P.H., Wells, J.R.: The OH + HBr reaction revisited **447**, 83–85 (1985)
9. Sims, I.R., Smith, I.W.M., Clary, D.C., Bocherel, P., Rowe, B.R.: Ultra-low temperature kinetics of neutral-neutral reactions - new experimental and theoretical results for OH + HBr between 295 K and 23 K. J. Chem. Phys. **101**, 1748–1751 (1994)
10. Atkinson, D.B., Jaramillo, V.I., Smith, M.A.: Low-temperature kinetic behavior of the bimolecular reaction OH + HBr (76 − 242 K). J. Phys. Chem. A **101**, 3356–3359 (1997)
11. Bedjanian, Y., Riffault, V., Le Bras, G., Poulet, G.: Kinetic study of the reactions of OH and OD with HBr and DBr. J. Photochem. Photobiol. A Chem. **128**, 15–25 (1999)
12. Jaramillo, V.I., Smith, M.A.: Temperature-dependent kinetic isotope effects in the gas-phase reaction: OH + HBr. J. Phys. Chem. A **105**, 5854–5859 (2001)
13. Mullen, C., Smith, M.A.: Temperature dependence and kinetic isotope effects for the OH + HBr reaction and H/D isotopic variants at low temperatures (53–135 K) measured using a pulsed supersonic Laval nozzle flow reactor. J. Phys. Chem. A **109**, 3893–3902 (2005)
14. Jaramillo, V.I., Gougeon, S., Le Picard, S.D., Canosa, A., Smith, M.A., Rowe, B.R.: A consensus view of the temperature dependence of the gas phase reaction: OH + HBr → H_2O + Br. Int. J. Chem. Kinet. **34**, 339–344 (2002)
15. Takacs, G.A., Glass, G.P.: Reactions of hydroxyl radicals with some hydrogen halides. J. Phys. Chem. **77**, 1948–1951 (1973)
16. Mac Leod, H., Balestra, C., Jourdain, J.L., Laverdet, G., Bras, G.L.E.: Kinetic study of the reaction OH + HI by laser photolysis-resonance fluorescence. Int. J. Chem. Kinet. **22**, 1167–1176 (1990)
17. Lancar, I.T., Mellouki, A., Poulet, G.: Kinetics of the reactions of hydrogen iodide with hydroxyl and nitrate radicals. Chem. Phys. Lett. **177**, 554–558 (1991)
18. Butkovskaya, N.I., Setser, D.W.: Dynamics of OH and OD radical reactions with HI and GeH4 studied by infrared chemiluminescence of the H_2O and HDO products. J. Chem. Phys. **106**, 5028–5042 (1997)
19. Campuzano-Jost, P., Crowley, J.N.: Kinetics of the reaction of OH with HI between 246 and 353 K. J. Phys. Chem. A **103**, 2712–2719 (1999)
20. Moise, A., Parker, D.H., Ter Meulen, J.J.: State-to-state inelastic scattering of OH by HI: a comparison with OH-HCl and OH-HBr. J. Chem. Phys. **126**, 124302 (2007)

21. Inada, Y., Akagane, K.: Non-empirical analysis of the chemical reactions of iodine with steam; $I + H_2O \rightarrow HI + OH$ and $I + H_2O \rightarrow IOH + H$, in severe light water reactor accidents. J. Nucl. Sci. Technol. **34**, 217–221 (1997)

22. Canneaux, S., Xerri, B., Louis, F., Cantrel, L.: Theoretical study of the gas-phase reactions of iodine atoms (2P3/2) with H_2, H_2O, HI, and OH. J. Phys. Chem. A **114**, 9270–9288 (2010)

23. Hao, Y., Gu, J., Guo, Y., Zhang, M., Xie, Y., Schaefer III, H.F.: Spin-orbit corrected potential energy surface features for the I (2P3/2) + $H_2O \rightarrow HI + OH$ forward and reverse reactions. Phys. Chem. Chem. Phys. **16**, 2641–2646 (2014)

24. Takacs, G.A., Glass, G.P.: Reactions of hydrogen atoms and hydroxyl radicals with hydrogen bromide. J. Phys. Chem. **77**, 1060–1064 (1973)

25. Smith, I.W.M., Zellner, R.: Rate measurements of reaction of OH by resonance absorption. J. Chem. Soc., Faraday Trans. **8**, 1045–1056 (1973)

26. Wilson, W.E., O'Donovan, J.T., Fristrom, R.M.: Flame inhibition by halogen compounds. In: 12th Symposium on Combustion (1969)

27. Tsai, P., Che, D., Nakamura, M., Lin, K., Kasai, T.: Orientation dependence in the four-atom reaction of OH + HBr using the single-state oriented OH radical beam. Phys. Chem. Chem. Phys. **12**, 2532–2534 (2010)

28. Tsai, P.-Y., Che, D., Nakamura, M., Lin, K., Kasai, T.: Orientation dependence for Br formation in the reaction of oriented OH radical with HBr molecule. Phys. Chem. Chem. Phys. **13**, 1419–1423 (2011)

29. Che, D.-C., Matsuo, T., Yano, Y., Bonnet, L., Kasai, T.: Negative collision energy dependence of Br formation in the OH + HBr reaction. Phys. Chem. Chem. Phys. **10**, 1419–1423 (2008)

30. Che, D.-C., Doi, A., Yamamoto, Y., Okuno, Y., Kasai, T.: Collision energy dependence for the Br formation in the reaction of OD + HBr. Phys. Scr. **80**, 48110 (2009)

31. Clary, D.C., Stoecklint, T.S., Wickham, A.G., Stoecklin, T.S., Wickham, A.G.: Rate constants for chemical reactions of radicals at low temperatures. J. Chem. Soc., Faraday Trans. **89**, 2185–2191 (1993)

32. Clary, D.C., Nyman, G., Hernandez, R.: Mode selective chemistry in the reactions of OH with HBr and HCl. J. Chem. Phys. **101**, 3704–3714 (1994)

33. Nizamov, B., Setser, D.W., Wang, H., Peslherbe, G.H., Hase, W.L., Nizamov, B., Setser, D. W.: Quasiclassical trajectory calculations for the OH (X2Π) and OD (X2Π) + HBr reactions: energy partitioning and rate constants. J. Chem. Phys. **105**, 9897–9911 (1996)

34. de Oliveira-Filho, A.G.S., Ornellas, F.R., Bowman, J.M.: Quasiclassical trajectory calculations of the rate constant of the OH + HBr $\rightarrow$ Br + H_2O reaction using a full-dimensional Ab initio potential energy surface over the temperature range 5 to 500 K. J. Phys. Chem. Lett. **5**, 706–712 (2014)

35. de Oliveira-Filho, A.G.S., Ornellas, F.R., Bowman, J.M.: Energy disposal and thermal rate constants for the OH + HBr and OH + DBr reactions: quasiclassical trajectory calculations on an accurate potential energy surface. J. Phys. Chem. A **118**, 12080 (2014)

36. Zhang, M., Hao, Y., Guo, Y., Xie, Y., Schaefer, H.F.: Anchoring the potential energy surface for the Br + $H_2O \rightarrow HBr + OH$ reaction. Theor. Chem. Acc. **133**, 1513 (2014)

37. Zahniser, M.S., Kaufman, F.: Kinetics of the reaction of OH with HCl. Chem. Phys. Lett. **27**, 507–510 (1974)

38. Keyser, L.F.: High-pressure flow kinetics. A study of the hydroxyl + hydrogen chloride reaction from 2 to 100 torr. J. Phys. Chem. **88**, 4750–4758 (1984)

39. Molina, M., Molina, L., Smith, C.: The rate of the reaction of OH with HCl. Int. J. Chem. Kinet. **16**, 1151–1160 (1984)

40. Husain, D., Plane, J.M.C., Slater, N.K.H.: Kinetic investigation of the reactions of OH(X2Π) with the hydrogen halides, HCl, DCl, HBr and DBr by time-resolved resonance fluorescence (A2∑ + −X2Π). J. Chem. Soc. Faraday Trans. 2 **77**, 1949 (1981)
41. Ravishankara, A.R., Wine, P.H., Wells, J.R., Thompson, R.L.: Kinetic study of the reaction of OH with HCl from 240 to 1055 K. Chem. Phys. Lett. **17**, 1281–1297 (1985)
42. Smith, I.W.M., Williams, M.D.: Effects of isotopic substitution and vibrational excitation on reaction rates. J. Chem. Soc., Faraday Trans. **2**(80), 1043–1055 (1986)
43. Sharkey, P., Smith, I.W.M.: Kinetics of elementary reactions at low temperatures: rate. J. Chem. Soc., Faraday Trans. **89**, 631–638 (1993)
44. Battin-Leclerc, F., Kim, I.K., Talukdar, R.K., Portmann, R.W., Ravishankara, A.R., Steckler, R., Brown, D.: Rate coefficients for the reactions of OH and OD with HCl and DCl between 200 and 400 K. J. Phys. Chem. A **103**, 3237–3244 (1999)
45. Bryukov, M.G., Dellinger, B.: Kinetics of the Gas-Phase Reaction of OH with HCl, 936–943 (2006)
46. Meisner, J., Kästner, J.: Reaction rates and kinetic isotope effects of H_2 + OH → H_2O + H, 174303 (2016)
47. Aquilanti, V., Mundim, K.C., Cavalli, S., Fazio, D., Aguilar, A., Lucas, J.M.: Exact activation energies and phenomenological description of quantum tunneling for model potential energy surfaces. The F + H2 reaction at low temperature. Chem. Phys. **398**, 186–191 (2012)
48. Cavalli, S., Aquilanti, V., Mundim, K.C., De Fazio, D.: Theoretical reaction kinetics astride the transition between moderate and deep tunneling regimes: the F + HD case. J. Phys. Chem. A **118**, 6632–6641 (2014)
49. Silva, V.H.C., Aquilanti, V., de Oliveira, H.C.B., Mundim, K.C.: Uniform description of non-Arrhenius temperature dependence of reaction rates, and a heuristic criterion for quantum tunneling vs classical non-extensive distribution. Chem. Phys. Lett. **590**, 201–207 (2013)
50. Carvalho-Silva, V.H., Aquilanti, V., de Oliveira, H.C.B., Mundim, K.C.: Deformed transition-state theory: deviation from Arrhenius behavior and application to bimolecular hydrogen transfer reaction rates in the tunneling regime. J. Comput. Chem. **38**, 178–188 (2017)
51. Guo, Y., Zhang, M., Xie, Y., Schaefer, H.F.: Communication: some critical features of the potential energy surface for the Cl + H_2O → HCl + OH forward and reverse reactions. J. Chem. Phys. **139**, 10–14 (2013)
52. Li, J., Dawes, R., Guo, H.: Kinetic and dynamic studies of the Cl(2Pu) + $H_2O(X^~1A$ 1) → HCl($X^~1\Sigma$ +) + OH($X^~2\Pi$) reaction on an ab initio based full-dimensional global potential energy surface of the ground electronic state of ClH2O. J. Chem. Phys. **139**, (2013)
53. Zuo, J., Li, Y., Guo, H., Xie, D.: Rate coefficients of the HCl + OH → Cl + H_2O reaction from ring polymer molecular dynamics. J. Phys. Chem. A **120**, 3433–3440 (2016)
54. Zuo, J., Xie, C., Guo, H., Xie, D.: Accurate determination of tunneling affected rate coefficients : theory assessing experiment. J. Phys. Chem. Lett. **8**, 3392–3397 (2017)
55. Mallick, S., Sarkar, S., Bandyopadhyay, B., Kumar, P.: Effect of ammonia and formic acid on the OH• + HCl reaction in the troposphere: competition between single and double hydrogen atom transfer pathways. J. Phys. Chem. A **122**, 350–363 (2018)
56. Li, J., Corchado, J.C., Espinosa-Garcia, J., Guo, H.: Final state-resolved mode specificity in HX + OH → X + H_2O (X = F and Cl) reactions: a quasi-classical trajectory study. J. Chem. Phys. **142**, 84314 (2015)
57. Song, H., Guo, H.: Mode specificity in the HCl + OH → Cl + H_2O reaction: Polanyi's rules vs sudden vector projection model. J. Phys. Chem. A **119**, 826–831 (2015)

58. Bonnet, L., Larrégaray, P., Duguay, B., Rayes, J.-C., Che, D.-C., Kasai, T.: Stereoselectivity as a probe of unexpected reaction pathways. Chem. Soc. Jpn. **80**, 707–710 (2007)
59. Cireasa, R., Beek, M.C., Van, Moise, A., Meulen, J.J.: Inelastic state-to-state scattering of OH (, J = 3/2, f) by HCl. 74319 (2005)
60. Chen, J., Xu, X., Xu, X., Zhang, D.H.: A global potential energy surface for the H_2 + OH ↔ H_2O + H reaction using neural networks. J. Chem. Phys. **138**, 154301 (2013)
61. Martí, C., Pacifici, L., Laganà, A., Coletti, C.: A quantum-classical study of the OH + H_2 reactive and inelastic collisions. Chem. Phys. Lett. **674**, 103–108 (2017)
62. Ohno, K., Ito, M., Ichihara, M., Ito, M.: Molecular hydrogen as an emerging therapeutic medical gas for neurodegenerative and other diseases. Oxid. Med. Cell. Longev. (2012)
63. Dole, M., Wilson, F.R., Fife, W.P.: Hyperbaric hydrogen therapy: a possible treatment for cancer. Science **190**, 152–154 (1975)
64. Ostojic, S.M.: Molecular hydrogen: an inert gas turns clinically effective. Ann. Med. **47**, 301–304 (2015)
65. Ohsawa, I., Ishikawa, M., Takahashi, K., Watanabe, M., Nishimaki, K., Yamagata, K., Katsura, K., Katayama, Y., Asoh, S., Ohta, S.: Hydrogen acts as a therapeutic antioxidant by selectively reducing cytotoxic oxygen radicals. Nat. Med. **13**, 688–694 (2007)
66. Ichihara, M., Sobue, S., Ito, M., Ito, M., Hirayama, M., Ohno, K.: Beneficial biological effects and the underlying mechanisms of molecular hydrogen - comprehensive review of 321 original articles. Med. Gas Res. **5**, 1–21 (2015)
67. Bhattacharya, S., Panda, A.N., Meyer, H.D.: Multiconfiguration time-dependent Hartree approach to study the OH + H_2 reaction. J. Chem. Phys. **132**, 8 (2010)
68. Hao, Y., Gu, J., Guo, Y., Zhang, M., Xie, Y., Schaefer III, H.F.: Spin–orbit corrected potential energy surface features for the I (2P3/2) + H_2O → HI + OH forward and reverse reactions. Phys. Chem. Chem. Phys. **16**, 2641 (2014)
69. Li, J., Li, Y., Guo, H.: Communication: covalent nature of XH_2O (X F, Cl, and Br) interactions. J. Chem. Phys. **138** (2013)
70. Marx, D., Hutter, J.: Ab initio molecular dynamics: Theory and implementation. Mod. Methods Algorithms Quantum Chem. **1**, 301–449 (2000)
71. Paranjothy, M., Sun, R., Zhuang, Y., Hase, W.L.: Direct chemical dynamics simulations: coupling of classical and quasiclassical trajectories with electronic structure theory. WIRE Comput. Mol. Sci. **3**, 296–316 (2013)
72. Marx, D., Hutter, J.: Ab Initio Molecular Dynamics: Basic Theory and Advanced Methods. Cambridge University Press, New York (2009)
73. Kasai, T., Che, D.-C., Okada, M., Tsai, P.-Y., Lin, K.-C., Palazzetti, F., Aquilanti, V.: Directions of chemical change: experimental characterization of the stereodynamics of photodissociation and reactive processes. Phys. Chem. Chem. Phys. **16**, 9776 (2014)
74. Cireasa, R., Moise, A., Ter Meulen, J.J.: Steric effects in state-to-state scattering of OH (2Π3/2, J = 3/2, f) by HCl. J. Chem. Phys. **123**, 8 (2005)
75. Coutinho, N.D., Silva, V.H.C., de Oliveira, H.C.B., Camargo, A.J., Mundim, K.C., Aquilanti, V.: Stereodynamical origin of anti-arrhenius kinetics: negative activation energy and roaming for a four-atom reaction. J. Phys. Chem. Lett. **6**, 1553–1558 (2015)
76. CPMDversion 3.17.1: Copyright IBM (2012)
77. Perdew, J.P., Burke, K., Ernzerhof, M.: Generalized gradient approximation made simple. Phys. Rev. Lett. **78**, 1396 (1997). [Phys. Rev. Lett. 77, 3865 (1996)]
78. Vanderbilt, D.: Soft self-consistent pseudopotentials in a generalized eigenvalue formalism. Phys. Rev. B **41**, 7892–7895 (1990)
79. Martyna, G.J., Klein, M.L., Tuckerman, M.: Nose-Hoover chains: the canonical ensemble via continuous dynamics. J. Chem. Phys. **97**, 2635–2643 (1992)

80. Coutinho, N.D., Aquilanti, V., Silva, V.H.C., Camargo, A.J., Mundim, K.C., de Oliveira, H. C.B.: Stereodirectional origin of anti-arrhenius kinetics for a tetraatomic hydrogen exchange reaction: born-oppenheimer molecular dynamics for OH + HBr. J. Phys. Chem. A **120**, 5408–5417 (2016)

81. Coutinho, N.D., Carvalho-Silva, V.H., de Oliveira, H.C.B., Aquilanti, V.: The HI + OH $H_2O + I$ reaction by first-principles molecular dynamics: stereodirectional and anti-Arrhenius kinetics. In: Gervasi, O., et al. (eds.) ICCSA 2017. LNCS, vol. 10408, pp. 297–313. Springer, Cham (2017). https://doi.org/10.1007/978-3-319-62404-4_22

82. Coutinho, N.D., Sanches-Neto, F.O., Carvalho-Silva, V.H., de Oliveira, H.C.B., Ribeiro, L. A., Aquilanti, V.: Kinetics of the OH + HCl → H_2O + Cl reaction: rate determining roles of stereodynamics and roaming, and the of quantum tunnelling. Submitted (2018)

83. Hause, M.L., Herath, N., Zhu, R., Lin, M.C., Suits, A.G.: Roaming-mediated isomerization in the photodissociation of nitrobenzene. Nat. Chem. **3**, 932–937 (2011)

84. Herath, N., Suits, A.G.: Roaming radical reactions. J. Phys. Chem. Lett. **2**, 642–647 (2011)

85. Tsai, P.-Y., Chao, M.-H., Kasai, T., Lin, K.-C., Lombardi, A., Palazzetti, F., Aquilanti, V.: Roads leading to roam. Role of triple fragmentation and of conical intersections in photochemical reactions: experiments and theory on methyl formate. Phys. Chem. Chem. Phys. **16**, 2854–2865 (2014)

86. Lombardi, A., Palazzetti, F., Aquilanti, V., Li, H.-K., Tsai, P.-Y., Kasai, T., Lin, K.-C.: Rovibrationally excited molecules on the verge of a triple breakdown: molecular and roaming mechanisms in the photodecomposition of methyl formate. J. Phys. Chem. A **120**, 5155–5162 (2016)

87. Nakamura, M., Tsai, P.-Y., Kasai, T., Lin, K.-C., Palazzetti, F., Lombardi, A., Aquilanti, V.: Dynamical, spectroscopic and computational imaging of bond breaking in photodissociation: roaming and role of conical intersections. Faraday Discuss. **177**, 77–98 (2015)

88. Husain, D., Plane, J.M.C., Xiang, C.C.: Kinetic studies of the reactions of $OH(X^2\Pi)$ with hydrogen chloride and deuterium chloride at elevated temperatures by time-resolved resonance fluorescence $(A^2\sum^+ - X^2\Pi)$. J. Chem. Soc., Faraday Trans. 2(80), 713–728 (1984)

89. Bryukov, M.G., Dellinger, B., Knyazev, V.D.: Kinetics of the gas-phase reaction of OH with HCl. J. Phys. Chem. A **110**, 936–943 (2006)

90. Sanches-Neto, F.O., Coutinho, N.D., Carvalho-Silva, V.H.: A novel assessment of the role of the methyl radical and water formation channel in the CH3OH + H reaction. Phys. Chem. Chem. Phys. Submit

91. Marx, D., Parrinello, M.: *Ab initio* path integral molecular dynamics: basic ideas. J. Chem. Phys. **104**, 4077–4082 (1996)

92. Bell, R.P.: The Tunnel Effect in Chemistry. Chapman and Hall, London (1980)

Workshop Parallel and Distributed Data Mining (WPDM 2018)

Parallel Mining of Correlated Heavy Hitters

Marco Pulimeno[1], Italo Epicoco[1,2], Massimo Cafaro[1,2(✉)], Catiuscia Melle[1], and Giovanni Aloisio[1,2]

[1] University of Salento, 73100 Lecce, Italy
{marco.pulimeno,italo.epicoco,massimo.cafaro,catiuscia.melle, giovanni.aloisio}@unisalento.it
[2] Euro-Mediterranean Center on Climate Changes Foundation, 73100 Lecce, Italy

Abstract. We present a message-passing based parallel algorithm for mining Correlated Heavy Hitters from a two-dimensional data stream. To the best of our knowledge, this is the first parallel algorithm solving the problem. We show, through experimental results, that our algorithm provides very good scalability, whilst retaining the accuracy of its sequential counterpart.

Keywords: Correlated Heavy Hitters · Message-passing

1 Introduction

Mining of Correlated Heavy Hitters (CHH) is a problem which has been recently proposed by [22]. Determining CHHs is a data mining task which commonly arises in the context of network monitoring and management, as well as anomaly and intrusion detection.

When considering the stream of pairs (source address, destination address) consisting of IP packets passing through a router, it is useful and important being able to identify the nodes responsible for the majority of the traffic passing through that router (i.e., the frequent items over a single dimension); however, for each given frequent source, we are also interested to discover the target destinations receiving the majority of connections by the same source.

Therefore, the mining process works as follows: initially the most important sources are detected as frequent items over the first dimension, then we mine the frequent destinations in the context of each identified source, i.e., the stream's correlated heavy hitters. We recall here preliminary notations and definitions, that shall be used in order to formally state the problem we solve in this paper through a message-passing based parallel algorithm. Let σ be a stream of tuples (x, y) of length n: $\sigma = < (x_1, y_1), (x_2, y_2), \ldots, (x_n, y_n) >$. The frequency f_{xy} of the tuple (x, y) is defined as follows.

Definition 1. *The frequency f_{xy} of the tuple (x, y) in the stream σ is given by* $f_{xy} = |\{i : (x = x_i) \land (y = y_i)\}|$.

© Springer International Publishing AG, part of Springer Nature 2018
O. Gervasi et al. (Eds.): ICCSA 2018, LNCS 10964, pp. 627–641, 2018.
https://doi.org/10.1007/978-3-319-95174-4_48

If we consider the sub-stream induced by the projection of the tuples of the stream σ on its first dimension, also referred to as the *primary dimension*, we can define the frequency f_x of an item appearing as first element in a tuple (x, y).

Definition 2. *The frequency f_x of an item x which appears as first element in a tuple (x, y) in the stream σ is given by $f_x = |\{i : (x = x_i)\}|$.*

The items x appearing in the primary dimension of the stream σ are referred to as *primary items*. Similarly, the items y appearing in the *secondary dimension* are referred to as *secondary items* or as *correlated items*.

The Exact Correlated Heavy Hitters problem can not be solved using limited space and only one pass through the input stream, hence the Approximate Correlated Heavy Hitters problem (ACHH) is introduced [22]. We state the problem as follows.

Problem 1. Approximate Correlated Heavy Hitters problem (ACHH problem).

Given a data stream σ of length n consisting of (x, y) tuples in which the item x is drawn from a universe set $\mathcal{U}_1 = \{1, \ldots, m_1\}$ and the item y is drawn from a universe set $\mathcal{U}_2 = \{1, \ldots, m_2\}$, two user-defined thresholds ϕ_1 and ϕ_2 such that $0 < \phi_1 < 1$ and $0 < \phi_2 < 1$ and two error bounds ϵ_1 and ϵ_2 such that $0 < \epsilon_1 < \phi_1$ and $0 < \epsilon_2 < \phi_2$, the Approximate Correlated Heavy Hitters (ACHH) problem requires determining all of the primary items x such that

$$f_x > \phi_1 n \tag{1}$$

and no items with

$$f_x \leq (\phi_1 - \epsilon_1)n \tag{2}$$

should be reported; moreover, we are required to determine for each frequent primary candidate x, all of the tuples (x, y) such that

$$f_{xy} > \phi_2 f_x \tag{3}$$

and no tuple (x, y) such that

$$f_{xy} \leq (\phi_2 - \epsilon_2)f_x \tag{4}$$

should be reported.

In this paper, we propose a parallel algorithm for solving the Approximate Correlated Heavy Hitters problem. The paper is organized as follows. In Sect. 2 we recall related work. We present our parallel algorithm in Sect. 3, and thoroughly analyze it in Sect. 4. Extensive experimental results are provided in Sect. 5. Finally, we draw our conclusions in Sect. 6.

2   Related Work

Mining frequent items is one of the most important topics in data mining. As such, it has attracted a number of researchers, who have published extensively on this subject. Here, we recall the most important work.

Misra and Gries [25] generalized the seminal work of Boyer and Moore [1,2] (the so called MJRTY algorithm). Their algorithm behaves exactly as MJRTY, but uses multiple counters, i.e. pairs (item, frequency), to keep track of the frequent items in the input stream. Interestingly, this algorithm, has been forgotten for about twenty years, and later rediscovered and slightly improved with regard to speed (by using a clever summary data structure) by Demaine et al. [16] (the so-called *Frequent* algorithm) and Karp et al. [21].

Counters are also used in many other algorithms, including *Sticky Sampling*, *Lossy Counting* [23], and *Space Saving* [24]. It is worth noting here that Space Saving is still the most accurate algorithm for mining frequent items.

A different class of algorithms is based on the use of a sketch data structure, which is usually a bi-dimensional array of counters. Items are mapped, through a set of hash functions (one for each row of the sketch), to corresponding sketch cells. Each cell holds a counter, whose values is then updated as required by the algorithm. Sketch–based algorithms include *CountSketch* [11], *Group Test* [14], *Count-Min* [13] and *hCount* [20].

Parallel algorithms for frequent items include message-passing, shared-memory and accelerators based algorithms. Almost all of the proposed algorithms are parallel versions of Frequent and Space Saving. Among message-passing algorithms, we recall here [9,10] (slightly improved in [5]). With regard to shared-memory architectures, it is worth citing [15,26,29,30]. Recently, [27] proposed novel shared-memory algorithms. Accelerator based algorithms for frequent items exploiting a GPU (Graphics Processing Unit) or the Intel Phi processor include [3,8,18,19].

Mining time faded frequent items has been investigated in [4,7,12,28]. A parallel message-passing based algorithm has been recently proposed in [6].

Regarding CHHs, an algorithm based on the nested application of Frequent has been recently presented in [22]. The outermost application mines the primary dimension, whilst the innermost one mines correlated secondary items. The main drawbacks of this algorithm, being based on Frequent, are the accuracy (which is very low), the huge amount of space required and the rather slow speed (owing to the nested summaries).

In [17], we proposed a fast and accurate algorithm for mining CHHs. Our Cascading Space Saving Correlated Heavy Hitters (CSSCHH) algorithm exploits the basic ideas of Space Saving, combining two summaries for tracking the primary item frequencies and the tuple frequencies. We refer to our algorithm as Cascading Space Saving since it is based on the use of two distinct and independent applications of Space Saving.

A stream summary $\mathcal{S}$ with k counters is the data structure used by Space Saving in order to monitor up to k distinct items. Space Saving processes one item at a time. When the item is already monitored by a counter, its estimated frequency is incremented by one. When it is not monitored, there are two possibilities. If a counter is available, it will be in charge of monitoring the item and its estimated frequency is set to one. Otherwise, if all of the counters are already occupied (their frequencies are different from zero), the counter storing the item with minimum frequency is incremented by one, then the monitored item is replaced by the new item. It can be proved that Space Saving correctly reports in its summary all of the ϕ-frequent items of the processed input stream with $\phi > \frac{1}{k}$ [24].

Therefore, we use two independent Space Saving stream summaries as data structures. The first, denoted by $\mathcal{S}^p$, and referred to as the primary stream summary, monitors a subset of primary items which appears in the stream through the use of k_1 distinct counters. The second, denoted by $\mathcal{S}^t$, includes k_2 counters and monitors a subset of the tuples which appear in the stream.

We proved that CSSCHH is correct and outperforms the algorithm proposed in [22] with regard to speed, accuracy and space required; we also showed how to select the values of k_1 and k_2 in order to minimize the space required. Full details can be found in [17]. In this work we design a parallel version of CSSCHH which we call PCSSCHH. To the best of our knowledge, this is the first parallel algorithm for message-passing architectures solving the ACHH problem.

3   A Parallel Algorithm for the ACHH Problem

In this paper we assume an offline setting, in which the stream tuples have been stored as a static dataset. This is not restrictive, since we shall show that our algorithm can also work in the streaming (online) setting as well. In the offline setting, we partition the input dataset by using a simple 1D block-based domain decomposition among the available p processes; then, in parallel, each process updates its local summaries with the items belonging to its own block. Once the blocks have been processed, one of the processes is in charge of determining the CHHs. The processes engage in a parallel reduction in which their summaries are merged into global summaries preserving all of the information stored in the original local summaries. These summaries can then be queried to return the CHHs.

The streaming (online) setting is related to a distributed scenario in which there are p distributed sites, each handling a different stream $\sigma_i, i = 1, \ldots, p$. One of the p sites may act as a centralized coordinator, or there can be another different site taking this responsibility. The coordinator broadcasts, when required, a "query" message to the p sites, which then temporarily stop processing their sub-streams, and engage in the merge procedure. The distributed sites can be thought as being multi-threaded processes, in which one thread processing the stream temporarily stops when a query message is received from the coordinator, creates a copy of its local summaries and then resumes stream processing whilst another thread engages in the distributed merging using the copies of the summaries.

Our PCSSCHH algorithm starts by initializing the $\mathcal{S}^p$ primary stream summary data structure allocating k_1 counters and the correlated $\mathcal{S}^t$ stream summary allocating k_2 counters. Algorithm 1 presents the pseudocode related to the initialization phase of PCSSCHH.

Algorithm 1. PCSSCHH Init

Require: Threshold for primary items ϕ_1; threshold for correlated items ϕ_2; tolerance for primary items ϵ_1; tolerance for correlated items ϵ_2.
Ensure: Properly initialized $\mathcal{S}^p$ and $\mathcal{S}^t$ stream summaries
1: **procedure** PCSSCHH-INIT($\phi_1, \phi_2, \epsilon_1, \epsilon_2$)
2: $\quad \beta \leftarrow \frac{1}{\epsilon_2 \phi_1}$
3: $\quad \gamma \leftarrow \frac{\epsilon_2 + \phi_2}{\epsilon_2 \phi_1}$
4: $\quad k_1 \leftarrow \max \left\{ \frac{1}{\epsilon_1}, \gamma + \sqrt{\beta \gamma} \right\}$
5: $\quad k_2 \leftarrow \beta \frac{k_1}{k_1 - \gamma}$
6: $\quad$ Allocate k_1 counters for $\mathcal{S}^p$
7: $\quad$ Allocate k_2 counters for $\mathcal{S}^t$
8: $\quad$ **return** $\mathcal{S}^p$ and $\mathcal{S}^t$
9: **end procedure**

Once a processor has initialized its summaries, it can begin processing the stream's tuples. The n tuples of the stream σ are distributed, through domain decomposition, to the p processors so that each one is responsible for either $\lfloor n/p \rfloor$ or $\lceil n/p \rceil$ tuples; let $left$ and $right$ be respectively the indices of the first and last tuple handled by the process with rank id (ranks are numbered from 0 to $p - 1$), then:

$$left = \lfloor (id - 1)\, n/p \rfloor ; \tag{5}$$

$$right = \lfloor id\, n/p \rfloor - 1. \tag{6}$$

PCSSCHH is presented in pseudocode as Algorithms 2 and 3. Each processor starts processing its own substream, which consists of all of the tuples from $left$ to $right$. In particular, items belonging to the primary dimension are mined using the $\mathcal{S}^p$ summary, whilst tuples are mined using the $\mathcal{S}^t$ summary. Next, parallel reductions based on the COMBINE user's defined reduction operator provide

---

Algorithm 2. PCSSCHH

Require: σ: a stream consisting of tuples (x, y); $\mathcal{S}^p$ and $\mathcal{S}^t$: stream summaries;
Ensure: $\mathcal{S}_g^p$ and $\mathcal{S}_g^t$ stream summaries.
1: **procedure** PCSSCHH-UPDATE($\mathcal{S}^p, \mathcal{S}^t, \sigma$)
2: $\quad$ SPACESAVING($\mathcal{S}^p, left, right$)
3: $\quad$ SPACESAVING($\mathcal{S}^t, left, right$)
4: $\quad \mathcal{S}_g^p \leftarrow$ PARALLELREDUCTION($\mathcal{S}^p, k_1$, COMBINE)
5: $\quad \mathcal{S}_g^t \leftarrow$ PARALLELREDUCTION($\mathcal{S}^t, k_2$, COMBINE)
6: **end procedure**

Algorithm 3. COMBINE

Require: $\mathcal{S}_1, \mathcal{S}_2$: summaries ordered by counters' frequency; k, number of counters in each summary
Ensure: the *combined summary* $\mathcal{S}_C$
1: **procedure** COMBINE($\mathcal{S}_1, \mathcal{S}_2, k$)
2:     $m_1 \leftarrow \mathcal{S}_1[0].\hat{f}$ ▷ minimum of all of the frequencies in $\mathcal{S}_1$
3:     $m_2 \leftarrow \mathcal{S}_2[0].\hat{f}$ ▷ minimum of all of the frequencies in $\mathcal{S}_2$
4:     let $\mathcal{S}_C$ be an empty summary
5:     **for each** counter $\mathcal{S}_1[j]$ in $\mathcal{S}_1$ **do**
6:         $new\_counter.i \leftarrow \mathcal{S}_1[j].i$
7:         $counter_{\mathcal{S}_2} \leftarrow \mathcal{S}_2.\text{FIND}(\mathcal{S}_1[j].i)$
8:         **if** $counter_{\mathcal{S}_2}$ **then**
9:             $new\_counter.\hat{f} \leftarrow \mathcal{S}_1[j].\hat{f} + counter_{\mathcal{S}_2}.\hat{f}$
10:            $\mathcal{S}_2.\text{REMOVE}(counter_{\mathcal{S}_2})$
11:        **else**
12:            $new\_counter.\hat{f} \leftarrow \mathcal{S}_1[j].\hat{f} + m_2$
13:        **end if**
14:        $\mathcal{S}_C.\text{PUT}(new\_counter)$
15:    **end for**
16:    **for each** counter $\mathcal{S}_2[j]$ in $\mathcal{S}_2$ **do**
17:        $new\_counter.i \leftarrow \mathcal{S}_2[j].i$
18:        $new\_counter.\hat{f} \leftarrow \mathcal{S}_2[j].\hat{f} + m_1$
19:        $\mathcal{S}_C.\text{PUT}(new\_counter)$
20:    **end for**
21:    $\mathcal{S}_C.\text{PRUNE}(k)$ ▷ Select k counters with the greatest frequencies and delete the others
22:    **return** $\mathcal{S}_C$
23: **end procedure**

---

the final $\mathcal{S}_g^p$ and $\mathcal{S}_g^t$ summaries (the subscript g stands for "global"), that can be used for answering queries related to CHHs.

The parallel reduction operator (COMBINE) works as follows. We denote by $\mathcal{S}[j].i$ and $\mathcal{S}[j].\hat{f}$ respectively the item monitored by the jth counter of a summary $\mathcal{S}$ and its corresponding estimated frequency. Let $\mathcal{S}_1$ and $\mathcal{S}_2$ be the two summaries to be merged and k their number of counters. We begin determining m_1 and m_2, the minimum frequencies respectively in the input summary $\mathcal{S}_1$ and $\mathcal{S}_2$. After initializing an empty summary $\mathcal{S}_C$, we scan the counters of $\mathcal{S}_1$. For each counter monitoring an item, we search $\mathcal{S}_2$ for a corresponding counter monitoring the same item. If we find it, we initialize a new counter with this item setting as frequency of the item the sum of the frequencies in the corresponding counters of $\mathcal{S}_1$ and $\mathcal{S}_2$ and delete the counter in $\mathcal{S}_2$. Otherwise, we let the frequency be the sum of the frequency of the item in $\mathcal{S}_1$ and m_2. The new counter is then inserted in $\mathcal{S}_C$. Next, we scan the remaining counters in $\mathcal{S}_2$. Since the counters in $\mathcal{S}_2$ corresponding to items in $\mathcal{S}_1$ have been deleted, for each counter in $\mathcal{S}_2$ we prepare a new counter monitoring that item and set its frequency to the sum of the item's frequency in $\mathcal{S}_2$ and m_1. Finally, if the $\mathcal{S}_C$ summary holds more than k counters, we retain the first k counters with the greatest frequencies and delete the others.

We have proved in [9] that the above reduction correctly merges two Space Saving summaries, and that the resulting $\mathcal{S}_C$ merged summary is affected by an error which is within the error bound of the original input summaries $\mathcal{S}_1$ and $\mathcal{S}_2$.

The final $\mathcal{S}_g^p$ and $\mathcal{S}_g^t$ stream summaries can be queried for CHHs as follows. The query procedure internally uses two lists, F and C. The former stores primary items and their estimated frequencies $(r, \hat{f}_r)$. The latter stores CHHs $(r, s, \hat{f}_{rs})$ in which r is a primary frequent item candidate, s the correlated frequent item candidate and $\hat{f}_{rs}$ the estimated frequency of the tuple (r, s).

The query algorithm inspects all of the k_1 counters in the $\mathcal{S}_g^p$ stream summary. If the frequency of the jth monitored item is greater than the selection criterion (i.e., $\mathcal{S}_g^p[j].\hat{f} > \phi_1 n$), then we add the monitored item $r = \mathcal{S}_g^p[j].i$ and its estimated frequency $\hat{f}_r = \mathcal{S}_g^p[j].\hat{f}$ to F.

The algorithm inspects now all of the k_2 counters of the $\mathcal{S}_g^t$ stream summary. The monitored items in $\mathcal{S}_g^t$ are the tuples (r, s). We check if the primary item r is a primary frequent item candidate (i.e., if $r \in F$); if this condition is true and the estimated frequency of the jth tuple is greater than the selection criterion (i.e., $\mathcal{S}_g^t[j].\hat{f} > \phi_2(\hat{f}_r - \frac{n}{k_1}))$, then the triplet $(r, s, \hat{f}_{rs})$ is added to C.

Taking into account the result in [9] related to the correctness of the merge procedure, it still holds what we proved in [17] and restated in Theorems (1) and (2) with reference to PCSSCHH. Thus the reported sets F and C correctly solve the ACHH problem.

Theorem 1. *The PCSSCHH algorithm reports in the outputted set F all of the primary items x whose exact frequency f_x is greater than the threshold, i.e., $f_x > \phi_1 N$ and no items whose exact frequency is such that $f_x \leq (\phi_1 - \frac{1}{k_1})N$.*

Theorem 2. *All of the tuples (x, y) with the item x reported as primary frequent candidate and with exact frequency f_{xy} greater than the threshold $(f_{xy} > \phi_2 f_x)$ are reported in the outputted set C as correlated heavy hitter candidates. No tuple with a primary item x reported as frequent primary candidate and with exact frequency less than $f_{xy} \leq (\phi_2 - \frac{k_2\phi_2 + k_1}{k_2(k_1\phi_1 - 1)})f_x$ is reported as correlated heavy hitter candidate.*

The Query procedure is presented as Algorithm 4.

4   Analysis

Regarding the parallel complexity of the algorithm, its worst case complexity is analyzed as follows. The initialization done in Algorithm 1 requires $O(1)$ constant time. Determining the initial domain decomposition requires $O(1)$ time as well. Algorithm 2 requires $O(n/p)$ time to process, using Space Saving, the tuples in the input block (the primary dimension with the $\mathcal{S}^p$ summary, and tuples with the $\mathcal{S}^t$ summary). Indeed, a block consists of $O(n/p)$ tuples, and Space Saving complexity is linear in the length of the input.

Algorithm 4. PCSSCHH Query

Require: $\mathcal{S}_g^p$ and $\mathcal{S}_g^t$ stream summaries.
Ensure: Set of correlated frequent items C
1: **procedure** PCSSCHH-QUERY($\mathcal{S}_g^p$, $\mathcal{S}_g^t$)
2:     $F \leftarrow \emptyset$
3:     **for each** counter $\mathcal{S}_g^p[j]$ in $\mathcal{S}_g^p$ **do**
4:         $r \leftarrow \mathcal{S}_g^p[j].i;\ \hat{f}_r \leftarrow \mathcal{S}_g^p[j].\hat{f}$
5:         **if** $\hat{f}_r > \phi_1 n$ **then**
6:             $F \leftarrow F \cup \{(r, \hat{f}_r)\}$
7:         **end if**
8:     **end for**
9:     **for each** $\mathcal{S}_g^t[j] \in \mathcal{S}_g^t$ **do**
10:         $(r, s) \leftarrow \mathcal{S}_g^t[j].i;\ \hat{f}_{rs} \leftarrow \mathcal{S}_g^t[j].\hat{f}$
11:         **if** $r \in F \wedge (\hat{f}_{rs} > \phi_2(\hat{f}_r - \frac{n}{k_1}))$ **then**
12:             $C \leftarrow C \cup \{(r, s, \hat{f}_{rs})\}$
13:         **end if**
14:     **end for**
15:     **return** C
16: **end procedure**

Finally, two parallel reductions determine the output. These two reductions require $O((k_1 + k_2)\log p)$ time, since the user's defined reduction operator COMBINE (Algorithm 3) requires $O(k \log p)$ time to merge two summaries of k counters. Indeed, the input summaries can be combined in $O(k)$ time, by using the hash tables in the implementation of the summaries.

For each item in $\mathcal{S}_1$, a corresponding item in $\mathcal{S}_2$ can be found in $O(1)$ time. The entry for the item can be inserted in $\mathcal{S}_C$ in $O(1)$ time and, if the item has been found in the other summary, the corresponding entry can be deleted from $\mathcal{S}_2$ again in $O(1)$ time. Since there are at most k entries in a summary, scanning and processing the first summary requires $O(k)$.

Next, the entries in $\mathcal{S}_2$ are scanned (note that there can be at most k entries in $\mathcal{S}_2$: this may happen only when the items in the two summaries are all distinct, otherwise there will be less than k entries because corresponding items are removed from $\mathcal{S}_2$ each time a match is found). For each entry in $\mathcal{S}_2$, the corresponding item is inserted in $\mathcal{S}_C$ in $O(1)$ time. Therefore, processing $\mathcal{S}_2$ requires in the worst case $O(k)$ time.

The combined summary $\mathcal{S}_C$ is returned as is if its total number of entries is less than or equal to k, otherwise only the last k entries (i.e., those entries corresponding to the items with greatest frequencies) are returned. The time required is $O(k)$.

Therefore, at most $O(k)$ work is done in each step of the parallel reduction, and there are $O(\log p)$ such steps. It follows that a parallel reduction can be done in $O(k \log p)$ time in the worst case.

The parallel complexity of our algorithm is therefore

$$T_p = O(n/p + (k_1 + k_2) \log p) \qquad (7)$$

in the worst case. Finally, the complexity of a query (Algorithm 4) is simply $O(k_1 + k_2)$, owing to the fact that we simply need to perform a linear scan of both summaries, and the work done processing each entry is $O(1)$ in the worst case.

We now analyze, from a theoretical perspective, our algorithm. Since the sequential algorithm requires $T_1 = O(n)$ time in the worst case [17], the parallel overhead is $T_o = pT_p - T_1 = p(k_1 + k_2) \log p$. The isoefficiency is then given by

$$n \geq Cp(k_1 + k_2) \log p \qquad (8)$$

where C is a constant. If we consider k_1 and k_2 to be constants as well, then the isoefficiency function is given by $p \log p$. Even though the algorithm is not perfectly scalable, it is only a small factor $(\log p)$ away from optimality.

5   Experimental Results

In order to evaluate the parallel algorithm for mining CHHs, we have implemented PCSSCHH in C++. The source code has been compiled using the Intel C++ compiler v15.0.3 and the Intel MPI library v5.0.3 on Linux CentOS distribution with the following flags: -O3 -xHost -std=c++11. The tests have been carried out on "Athena" parallel cluster kindly provided by the Euro-Mediterranean Center on Climate Changes, Foundation (CMCC) in Italy. The cluster is made of 482 computational nodes, each one equipped with 64 GB of RAM and two Intel 2.60 GHz octa-core Xeon E5-2670 processors. The source code is freely available for inspection and for reproducibility of results contacting the authors by email.

The synthetic datasets used in our experiments are distributed according to the Zipf distribution. In each one of the experiments, the execution has been repeated 5 times using a different seed for the pseudo-random number generator used for creating the input data stream. For each input distribution generated, the results have been averaged over all of the runs. The input items are tuples of two 32 bits unsigned integers.

The experiments are aimed at evaluating the parallel algorithm behavior in terms of performance and accuracy. We used the parallel speedup, efficiency and scaled speedup metrics to measure the computational performance and the *precision* and *recall* to evaluate the impact of the parallelization on the algorithm's accuracy. In the experiments, we vary the following input parameters: length of the data stream (ni), skewness of the zipfian distribution (ρ), number of counters (k_1, k_2) used in the primary and secondary summaries and the number of processes (p). For the scaled speedup measurement we used three different values of *grain size*, i.e., the number of tuples assigned to a process; in the scaled speedup analysis (also known as weak scalability) the grain size is kept constant while the number of processes increases.

Table 1. Experiments carried out.

Parameter	Values	Default
Stream size (ni, billions)	1, 3, 6	1
Skew (ρ)	1.0, 1.4, 1.8	1.4
Counters (k_1, k_2)	$k_1 = 833, k_2 = 2633$	$k_1 = 3050, k_2 = 12450$
	$k_1 = 1033, k_2 = 3500$	
	$k_1 = 1673, k_2 = 6323$	
	$k_1 = 3050, k_2 = 12450$	
Grain Size (ni, millions)	100, 500, 750	-
Num. Procs. (p)	1, 16, 32, 64, 128, 256, 512	-

Table 1 reports all of the parameters used in our experiments.

We begin our analysis discussing the computational performance of the algorithm. Figures 1 and 2 show the parallel speedup and efficiency measured varying respectively the stream size and the skew of the input distribution, while Fig. 3 shows the corresponding elapsed times (the plots of Figs. 1a, 2a, 3a and b use a log-log scale, whilst Figs. 1b and 2b use a log scale on the x axis, related to the number of processes).

According to the Amdahl's law, when the problem size increases, the parallel algorithm performs better (the so-called Amdahl's effect), and shows very good scalability up to 64 processes. In order to use a greater number of processes, owing to the isoefficiency analysis reported in the previous Section, we need to increase the problem size.

For low skew values, the time required to update a summary increases owing to the higher number of cache misses due to a greater number of distinct items, which also increases the hash table's access time. Since the update time increases but the communication time remains the same, the speedup improves.

In Fig. 4 the scaled speedup is reported, using a log-log scale. The results clearly show that the algorithm performs well when the grain size is increased.

Regarding the accuracy of the algorithm, we measured *recall* and *precision*. The recall is the total number of true frequent items reported over the number of frequent items given by an exact algorithm. Therefore, an algorithm is correct iff its recall is equal to one. Since in all of the experiments we used a number of counters k_1, k_2 that guarantees the correctness of the algorithm, we observed a recall equal to one in each experiment. For this reason, the corresponding plots have not been reported.

Since precision is defined as the total number of true frequent items reported over the total number of items reported, this metric quantifies the number of false positives outputted by an algorithm. The accuracy of the sequential algorithm has been already well analyzed in [17]; here, the goal is to prove that the parallelization does not impact on the accuracy. Figure 5 reports, using a log scale for the x axis, the precision obtained varying the number of counters. As

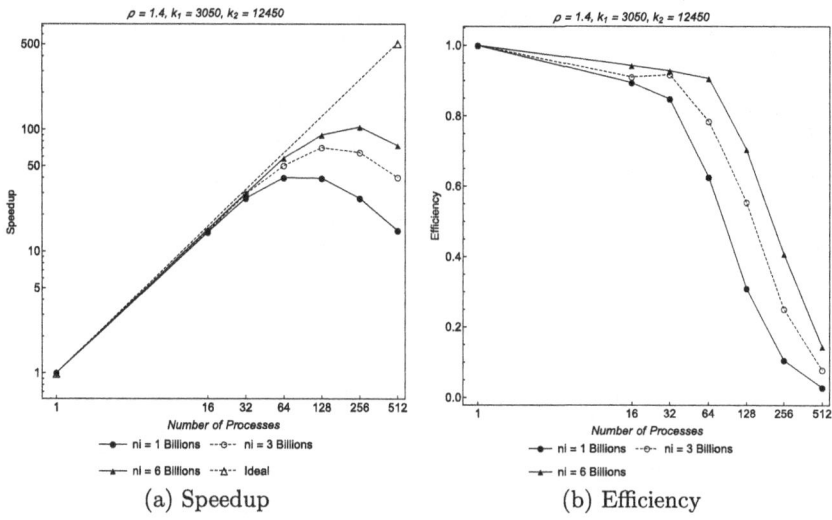

Fig. 1. Speedup and efficiency varying the input stream size.

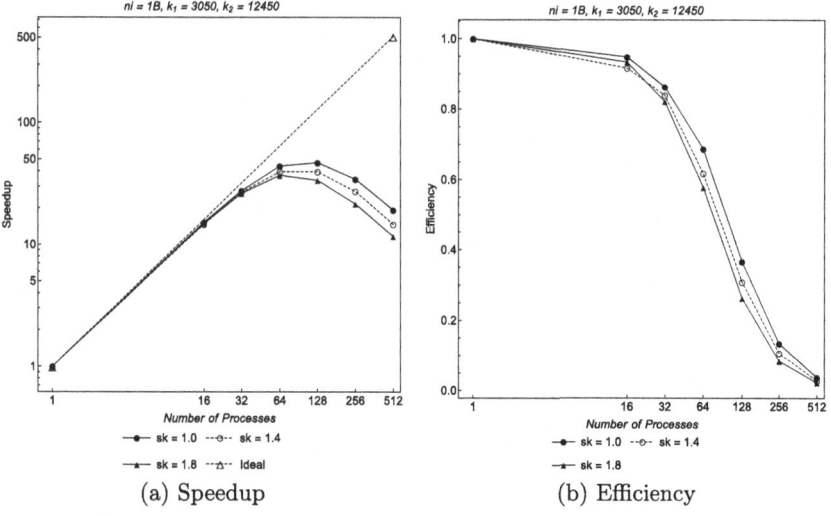

Fig. 2. Speedup and efficiency varying the skew of the distribution.

expected, when we use a few counters the algorithm is less accurate. The results also show that the parallelization, and in particular the reduction in which we merge the summaries, does not introduce any significant estimation error, indeed the precision does not change varying the number of processes.

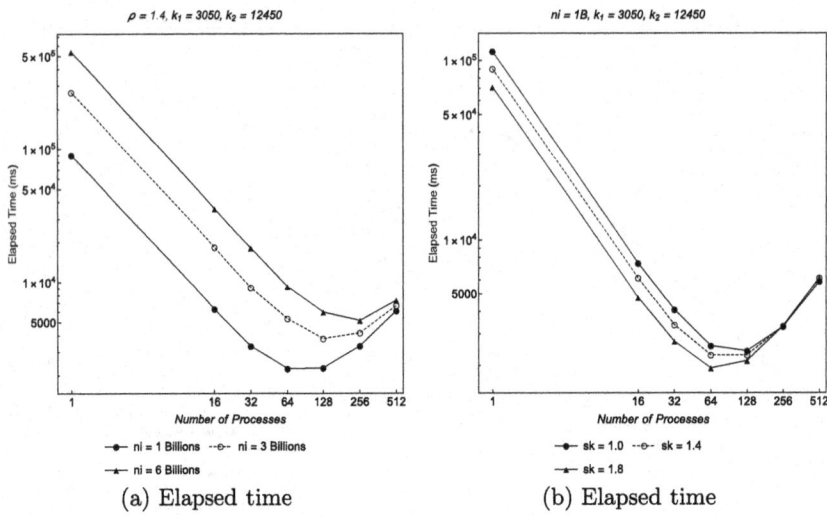

Fig. 3. Elapsed time varying the stream size and the skew of the distribution.

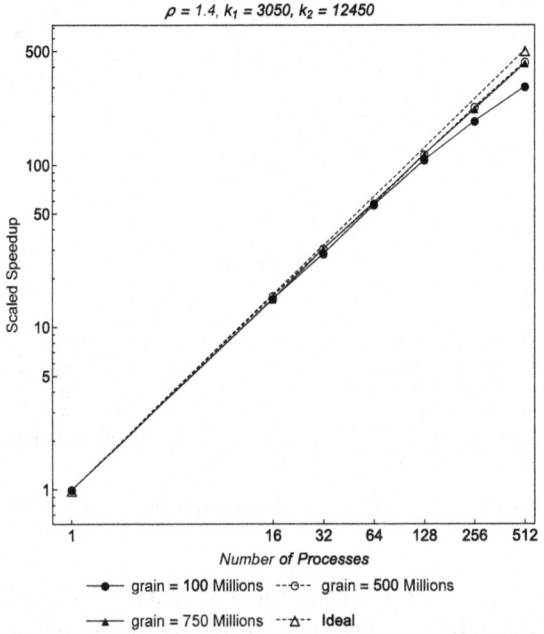

Fig. 4. Scaled speedup varying the grain size.

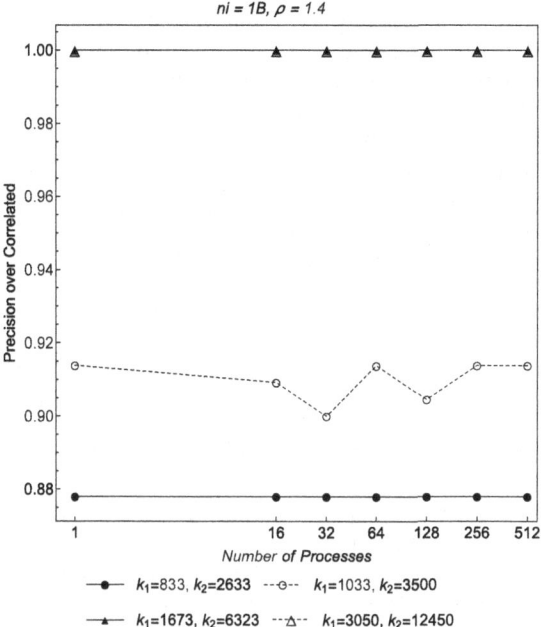

Fig. 5. Precision varying the number of processes and the number of counters in the primary and secondary stream summaries.

6   Conclusions

In this paper we have presented a message-passing based parallel algorithm for mining Correlated Heavy Hitters from a two-dimensional data stream. We have shown, through extensive experimental results, that our algorithm solves the ACHH problem and provides very good scalability, whilst retaining the accuracy of its sequential counterpart. To the best of our knowledge, this is the first parallel algorithm solving the problem.

Acknowledgements. The authors would like to thank the Supercomputing Center of the Euro-Mediterranean Center on Climate Changes, Foundation for granting the access to the Athena supercomputer machine.

References

1. Boyer, R., Moore, J.: MJRTY - a fast majority vote algorithm. Technical report 32, Institute for Computing Science, University of Texas, Austin (1981)
2. Boyer, R., Moore, J.S.: MJRTY - a fast majority vote algorithm. In: Boyer, R.S. (ed.) Automated Reasoning: Essays in Honor of Woody Bledsoe. Automated Reasoning Series, pp. 105–117. Kluwer Academic Publishers, Dordrecht (1991)

3. Cafaro, M., Epicoco, I., Aloisio, G., Pulimeno, M.: CUDA based parallel implementations of space-saving on a GPU. In: 2017 International Conference on High Performance Computing Simulation (HPCS), pp. 707–714, July 2017. https://doi.org/10.1109/HPCS.2017.108

4. Cafaro, M., Epicoco, I., Pulimeno, M., Aloisio, G.: On frequency estimation and detection of frequent items in time faded streams. IEEE Access 5, 24078–24093 (2017). https://doi.org/10.1109/ACCESS.2017.2757238

5. Cafaro, M., Pulimeno, M.: Merging frequent summaries. In: Proceedings of the 17th Italian Conference on Theoretical Computer Science (ICTCS 2016), vol. 1720. pp. 280–285. CEUR Proceedings (2016)

6. Cafaro, M., Pulimeno, M., Epicoco, I.: Parallel mining of time-faded heavy hitters. Expert Syst. Appl. 96, 115–128 (2018). https://doi.org/10.1016/j.eswa.2017.11.021, http://www.sciencedirect.com/science/article/pii/S0957417417307777

7. Cafaro, M., Pulimeno, M., Epicoco, I., Aloisio, G.: Mining frequent items in the time fading model. Inf. Sci. 370–371, 221–238 (2016). https://doi.org/10.1016/j.ins.2016.07.077

8. Cafaro, M., Pulimeno, M., Epicoco, I., Aloisio, G.: Parallel space saving on multi- and many-core processors. Concurr. Comput.: Pract. Exp. 30(7), e4160-n/a (2017). https://doi.org/10.1002/cpe.4160

9. Cafaro, M., Pulimeno, M., Tempesta, P.: A parallel space saving algorithm for frequent items and the hurwitz zeta distribution. Inf. Sci. 329, 1–19 (2016). https://doi.org/10.1016/j.ins.2015.09.003, http://www.sciencedirect.com/science/article/pii/S002002551500657X

10. Cafaro, M., Tempesta, P.: Finding frequent items in parallel. Concurr. Comput.: Pract. Exp. 23(15), 1774–1788 (2011). https://doi.org/10.1002/cpe.1761

11. Charikar, M., Chen, K., Farach-Colton, M.: Finding frequent items in data streams. In: Widmayer, P., et al. (eds.) ICALP 2002. LNCS, vol. 2380, pp. 693–703. Springer, Heidelberg (2002). https://doi.org/10.1007/3-540-45465-9_59

12. Chen, L., Mei, Q.: Mining frequent items in data stream using time fading model. Inf. Sci. 257, 54–69 (2014). https://doi.org/10.1016/j.ins.2013.09.007, http://www.sciencedirect.com/science/article/pii/S0020025513006403

13. Cormode, G., Muthukrishnan, S.: An improved data stream summary: the count-min sketch and its applications. J. Algorithms 55(1), 58–75 (2005). https://doi.org/10.1016/j.jalgor.2003.12.001

14. Cormode, G., Muthukrishnan, S.: What's hot and what's not: tracking most frequent items dynamically. ACM Trans. Database Syst. 30(1), 249–278 (2005). https://doi.org/10.1145/1061318.1061325

15. Das, S., Antony, S., Agrawal, D., El Abbadi, A.: Thread cooperation in multicore architectures for frequency counting over multiple data streams. Proc. VLDB Endow. 2(1), 217–228 (2009). https://doi.org/10.14778/1687627.1687653

16. Demaine, E.D., López-Ortiz, A., Munro, J.I.: Frequency estimation of internet packet streams with limited space. In: Möhring, R., Raman, R. (eds.) ESA 2002. LNCS, vol. 2461, pp. 348–360. Springer, Heidelberg (2002). https://doi.org/10.1007/3-540-45749-6_33

17. Epicoco, I., Cafaro, M., Pulimeno, M.: Fast and accurate mining of correlated heavy hitters. Data Min. Knowl. Discov. 32(1), 162–186 (2018). https://doi.org/10.1007/s10618-017-0526-x

18. Erra, U., Frola, B.: Frequent items mining acceleration exploiting fast parallel sorting on the GPU. Proc. Comput. Sci. **9**, 86–95 (2012). https://doi.org/ 10.1016/j.procs.2012.04.010, http://www.sciencedirect.com/science/article/pii/ S1877050912001317. Proceedings of the International Conference on Computational Science, ICCS 2012

19. Govindaraju, N.K., Raghuvanshi, N., Manocha, D.: Fast and approximate stream mining of quantiles and frequencies using graphics processors. In: Proceedings of the 2005 ACM SIGMOD International Conference on Management of Data, SIGMOD 2005, pp. 611–622. ACM (2005). https://doi.org/10.1145/1066157.1066227

20. Jin, C., Qian, W., Sha, C., Yu, J.X., Zhou, A.: Dynamically maintaining frequent items over a data stream. In: Proceedings Of CIKM, pp. 287–294. ACM Press (2003)

21. Karp, R.M., Shenker, S., Papadimitriou, C.H.: A simple algorithm for finding frequent elements in streams and bags. ACM Trans. Database Syst. **28**(1), 51–55 (2003). https://doi.org/10.1145/762471.762473

22. Lahiri, B., Mukherjee, A.P., Tirthapura, S.: Identifying correlated heavy-hitters in a two-dimensional data stream. Data Min. Knowl. Disc. **30**(4), 797–818 (2016). https://doi.org/10.1007/s10618-015-0438-6

23. Manku, G.S., Motwani, R.: Approximate frequency counts over data streams. In: VLDB, pp. 346–357 (2002)

24. Metwally, A., Agrawal, D., Abbadi, A.E.: An integrated efficient solution for computing frequent and top-k elements in data streams. ACM Trans. Database Syst. **31**(3), 1095–1133 (2006). https://doi.org/10.1145/1166074.1166084

25. Misra, J., Gries, D.: Finding repeated elements. Sci. Comput. Program. **2**(2), 143–152 (1982)

26. Roy, P., Teubner, J., Alonso, G.: Efficient frequent item counting in multi-core hardware. In: Proceedings of the 18th ACM SIGKDD International Conference on Knowledge Discovery and Data Mining, KDD 2012, pp. 1451–1459. ACM (2012). https://doi.org/10.1145/2339530.2339757

27. Tangwongsan, K., Tirthapura, S., Wu, K.L.: Parallel streaming frequency-based aggregates. In: Proceedings of the 26th ACM Symposium on Parallelism in Algorithms and Architectures, SPAA 2014, pp. 236–245. ACM (2014). https://doi.org/ 10.1145/2612669.2612695

28. Wu, S., Lin, H., Gao, Y., Lu, D.: Novel structures for counting frequent items in time decayed streams. World Wide Web **20**(5), 1111–1133 (2017). https://doi.org/ 10.1007/s11280-017-0433-5

29. Zhang, Y.: Parallelizing the weighted lossy counting algorithm in high-speed network monitoring. In: Second International Conference on Instrumentation, Measurement, Computer, Communication and Control (IMCCC), pp. 757–761 (2012). https://doi.org/10.1109/IMCCC.2012.183

30. Zhang, Y., Sun, Y., Zhang, J., Xu, J., Wu, Y.: An efficient framework for parallel and continuous frequent item monitoring. Concurr. Comput.: Pract. Exp. **26**(18), 2856–2879 (2014). https://doi.org/10.1002/cpe.3182

An Innovative Framework for Supporting Frequent Pattern Mining Problems in IoT Environments

Peter Braun[1], Alfredo Cuzzocrea[2(✉)], Carson K. Leung[1],
Adam G. M. Pazdor[1], Syed K. Tanbeer[1], and Giorgio Mario Grasso[3]

[1] University of Manitoba, Winnipeg, Canada
kleung@cs.unimanitoba.ca
[2] University of Trieste and ICAR-CNR, Trieste, Italy
alfredo.cuzzocrea@dia.units.it
[3] University of Messina, Messina, Italy
gmgrasso@unime.it

Abstract. In the current era of big data, high volumes of a wide variety of data of different veracity can be easily generated or collected at a high velocity from rich sources of data include devices from the Internet of Things (IoT). Embedded in these big data are useful information and valuable knowledge. Hence, frequent pattern mining and its related research problem of association rule mining, which aim to discover implicit, previously unknown and potentially useful information and knowledge—in the form of sets of frequently co-occurring items or rules revealing relationships between these frequent sets—from these big data have drawn attention of many researchers. For instance, since introduction of the research problems of association rule mining or frequent pattern mining, numerous information system and engineering approaches have been developed. These include the development of serial algorithms, distributed and parallel algorithms, as well as MapReduce-based big data mining algorithms. These algorithms can be run in local computers, distributed and parallel environments, as well as clusters, grids and clouds. In this paper, we describe some of these algorithms and discuss how to mine frequent patterns or association rules in fogs—i.e., edges of the computing network.

Keywords: Frequent patterns · Frequent sets of items · Association rules
Big data · Distributed computing · Parallel computing
High performance computing · Cloud computing · Fog computing
Edge computing

1 Introduction

With advances in technology, high volumes of a wide variety of data of different veracity can be easily generated or collected at a high velocity from rich sources of data —such as devices from the Internet of Things (IoT) like sensors—in various real-life applications such as bioinformatics, social networks, sensor and stream systems, smart worlds, as well as the Web. Embedded in these big data—such as banking records,

© Springer International Publishing AG, part of Springer Nature 2018
O. Gervasi et al. (Eds.): ICCSA 2018, LNCS 10964, pp. 642–657, 2018.
https://doi.org/10.1007/978-3-319-95174-4_49

business transactions, documents, financial reports, marketing advertisements, medical images, patient charts, surveillance videos, telecommunication logs, texts, web logs, as well as streams of biological, life science and social media data—are useful information and valuable knowledge. Hence, *data mining* techniques [1]—which help to discover implicit, previously unknown and potentially useful information and knowledge from these big data—are in demand.

As a popular data mining task, association rule mining aims to discover interesting association rules of the form A $\Rightarrow$ C revealing relationships between frequent patterns A and C. The resulting rules help data analysts to understand consumer behavior, know the web surfing patterns, and get an insight about popular events.

In general, the mining process for association rules [2, 3] consists of two key steps:

1. *Mining of frequent patterns* [4, 5]: Given a dataset and a user-specified minimum frequency threshold, this first key step finds all frequent patterns (i.e., sets of items that frequently co-occur together). A pattern is considered *frequent* if the frequency of its occurrences in transactions of the dataset meets or exceeds the user-specified minimum frequency threshold.

2. *Formation of interesting association rules*: Given the mined frequent patterns from the first key step and a user-specified minimum interestingness threshold, this second key step finds all association rules of the form A $\Rightarrow$ C, where A and C are mined frequent patterns. An association rule is considered *interesting* if its interestingness metric (e.g., confidence, correlation, lift) meets or exceeds the user-specified minimum interestingness threshold.

Between these two key steps, the first step of frequent pattern mining is more computationally intensive. Hence, it has drawn attention to many researchers in developing numerous efficient frequent pattern mining algorithms.

Many of the early frequent pattern mining algorithms were Apriori-based [4], which depend on a generate-and-test paradigm to mine frequent patterns from transaction datasets by first generating candidates and then checking their actual frequency (i.e., occurrences) against the dataset. To improve algorithmic efficiency, other serial frequent pattern mining algorithms—such as tree-based frequent pattern mining algorithms (e.g., FP-growth [6]), hyperlinked array based frequent pattern mining algorithms (e.g., H-mine [7]), and bitwise-based frequent pattern mining algorithms (e.g., B-mine [8])—have been developed. Besides these transaction-centric algorithms that mine the datasets "horizontally", there are also item-centric algorithms (e.g., Eclat [9], dEclat [10], VIPER [11]) that mine the datasets "vertically".

Many of these serial frequent pattern mining algorithms have been extended to handle other related data mining tasks. The following are some instances of these extensions:

1. *Sequential pattern mining* [12–14], which adds the temporal dimension to frequent pattern mining so that data analysts can find frequently occurring sequences of events or sequences of frequently purchased merchandise items.

2. *Stream mining* [15, 16], which handles situations where data are generated or collected continuously at a high velocity. Stream mining algorithms usually use the landmark, sliding window, or time-fading model to process the dynamic streaming data (cf. static transaction databases) as follows:

    a. For instance, landmark based mining algorithms usually consider all data from a landmark.

    b. In contrast, sliding-window based algorithms usually focus on data that fall within the sliding window. When the window slides, older data are ignored in order leave space for newer data.

    c. Algorithms with the time-fading model, on the other hand, usually put more emphasis (i.e., heavier weight) on recent data than older data. The weight on older data gradually faded out when time goes by.

3. *Contrast pattern mining* [17, 18], which compares two or more sets of frequent patterns so that data analysts can spot the spatial or temporal differences between the different sets.

4. *Uncertain data mining* [19–21], which handles situations where data are riddled with uncertainty [22] (cf. precise data in transaction databases) that partially caused by inherent measurement inaccuracies, sampling and duration errors, network latencies, and intentional blurring of data to preserve anonymity. It also handles situations with uncertain objects for sensor devices and noisy data management technologies. Uncertain data mining algorithms usually captures data uncertainty in order to handle data of different veracity.

While there are some other extensions in terms of functionality or types of patterns to be mined, to avoid distraction, we focus on *frequent pattern mining* (but not its extensions) from static precise data in this paper.

In addition to the aforementioned algorithms for the discovery of frequent patterns in serial, there are also distributed and parallel frequent pattern mining algorithms [23, 24]. Examples include the Count Distribution, Data Distribution, and Candidate Distribution algorithms [25]. Many of these distributed and parallel algorithms mine frequent patterns using distributed or parallel computing, in which frequent patterns are found by multiple processors that either

1. have access to a shared memory with which information is exchanged among processors, or

2. have their own private memory (i.e., distributed memory) with which for information is exchanged via message passing among the processors.

Many of these distributed and parallel frequent pattern mining algorithms are implemented using

1. *Open Multi-Processing (OpenMP)* [26, 27], or
2. *Message Passing Interface (MPI)* [26, 27],

and run in computer clusters or grids. *Cluster computing* [28] usually involves a group of distributed or parallel computers that are interconnected through high-speed networks such as local area networks. These computers work together as a single computing group to manage, query and process data. *Grid computing* [29], on the other hand, can be considered as a form of distributed or parallel computing that coordinates heterogeneous networked loosely coupled computers. Each computer in the grid may perform a different task.

As technology advances, a wide variety of data of different veracity can be easily generated or collected at a high velocity from rich sources of data such as devices from the Internet of Things (IoT). Volumes of these big data [30, 31] can go beyond the ability of commonly-used software to capture, manage, and process within a tolerable elapsed time. Hence, new forms of processing, mining and analyzing data are needed to enable enhanced decision making, insight, knowledge discovery, and process optimization. This leads to the development of MapReduce-based frequent pattern mining algorithms [32, 33]. As implied by its name, MapReduce [34, 35] involves two key functions:

1. the "map" function, and
2. the "reduce" function.

Specifically, the input data are read, divided into several partitions (sub-problems), and assigned to different processors. Each processor executes the "map" function on each partition (sub-problem). The "map" function takes a pair of $\langle key_1, value_1 \rangle$ and returns a list of $\langle key_2, value_2 \rangle$-pairs as an intermediate result, where key_1 & key_2 are keys in the same or different domains, and $value_1$ & $value_2$ are the corresponding values in some domains. Afterwards, these pairs are shuffled and sorted. Each processor then executes the "reduce" function on a single key key_2 from this intermediate result key_2, list of $value_2$ together with the list of all values that appear with this key in the intermediate result. The "reduce" function combines, aggregates, summarizes, filters, and/or transforms the list of values associated with a given key key_2 (for all k keys) and returns a single (aggregated or summarized) value $value_3$ (where key_2 is a key in some domains, and $value_2$ & $value_3$ are the corresponding values in some domains). Many of these algorithms are run in clouds. *Cloud computing* [36] can be considered as another form of distributed or parallel computing. Public, private or hybrid cloud involves a group of interconnected and virtualized computers to provide on-demand services such as infrastructure-as-a-service (IaaS), platform-as-a-service (PaaS), software-as-a-service (SaaS), and mining-as-a-service (MaaS) [37], based on several consolidated research results (e.g., [52–54]).

Frequent pattern mining with cloud computing are efficient in many practical real-life situations. However, with exponentially growing volumes of big data, can we mine frequent patterns more efficiently and effectively? In this paper, we consider *fog computing*, which is also known as *edge computing* or *fogging*. A key difference between cloud and fog computing is that cloud computing makes good use of a network of remote servers hosted on the Internet to store, manage, and process data. Fog computing, on the other hand, makes good use of the edge of the network. It supports the Internet of Things (IoT) concepts by facilitating the computation in proximity to end-users. In other words, it stores, manages, and processes data either on IoT devices or networking services between these end devices and data centers.

Our *key contributions* of this paper—on the topic of mining frequent patterns from IoT devices with fog computing—include the following:

1. a review of notable frequent pattern mining algorithms (e.g., serial algorithms, distributed and parallel algorithms, MapReduce-based algorithms) for finding frequent patterns from very large dataset or big data, and
2. a feasibility study on frequent pattern mining with fog computing.

The remainder of this paper is organized as follows. Next section describes some notable serial frequent pattern mining algorithms. Section 3 describes some distributed and parallel frequent pattern mining algorithms, and Sect. 4 describes some MapReduce-based frequent pattern mining algorithms. Section 5 discusses how to mine frequent patterns with fog computing. Finally, conclusions are given in Sect. 6.

2 Serial Algorithms

A classical serial frequent pattern mining is the Apriori algorithm [4], which applies a generate-and-test paradigm in mining frequent patterns in a level-wise bottom-up fashion. Specifically, the algorithm first generates candidate patterns of cardinality k (i.e., candidate k-itemset) and tests if each of them is frequent (i.e., tests if its frequency meets or exceeds the user-specified minimum frequency threshold). Based on these frequent patterns of cardinality k (i.e., frequent k-itemsets), the algorithm then generates candidate patterns of cardinality $k + 1$ (i.e., candidate $(k + 1)$-itemsets). This process is applied repeatedly to discover frequent patterns of all cardinalities. A disadvantage of the Apriori algorithm is that it requires K_{max} scans of the database to discover all frequent patterns (where K_{max} is the maximum cardinality of discovered patterns).

To address this disadvantage of the Apriori algorithm, variants of the Apriori algorithm [4] reduces the number of scans of the database by applying the *pass bundling* technique in each when generating candidate itemsets (for cardinality/Pass $k \geq 3$). For instance:

1. a variant of the Apriori algorithm statistically bundles a fixed number of passes (e.g., three passes) to generate all candidate k-, $(k + 1)$-, and $(k + 2)$-itemsets from frequent $(k - 1)$-itemsets;
2. another variant of the Apriori algorithm dynamically bundles several passes (depending on the number of generated candidates in these bundled passes).

On the one hand, the use of the pass bundling technique reduces the number of passes/database scans. On the other hand, these two variants of the Apriori algorithm still require multiple passes/database scans when mining frequent patterns. In contrast, a third variant of the Apriori algorithm—namely, the Partition algorithm [38]—requires only two passes/database scans. Specifically, the Partition algorithm first reads and divides the database into partitions. The algorithm then finds patterns that are locally frequent in each partition. Taking the union of these locally frequent patterns forms global candidate patterns. Afterwards, the Partition algorithm scans the database a second time to check every global candidate pattern if it is globally frequent in the database.

To further address the disadvantage of the Apriori algorithm & its variants, the FP-growth algorithm [6] improves efficiency by using an extended prefix-tree structure called Frequent Pattern tree (FP-tree) to capture the content of the transaction database. Unlike the Apriori algorithm, FP-growth scans the database twice. The key idea of FP-growth is recursively extract relevant paths from the FP-tree to form projected databases (i.e., collection of transactions containing some items), from which subtrees (i.e., smaller FP-trees) capturing the content of relevant transactions are built. While FP-growth avoids the generate-and-test paradigm of Apriori (because FP-growth uses the divide-and-conquer paradigm), a disadvantage of FP-growth is that many smaller FP-trees (e.g., for $\{a\}$-projected database, $\{a, b\}$-projected database, $\{a, b, c\}$-projected database, etc.) need to be built during the mining process. In other words, FP-growth requires lots of memory space.

To avoid building and keeping multiple FP-trees at the same time during the mining process, algorithms like TD-FP-Growth [39] and H-mine [7] have been developed. Unlike the FP-growth (which mines frequent patterns by traversing the global FP-tree and subtrees in a bottom-up fashion), the TD-FP-Growth algorithm traverses only the global FP-tree and in a top-down fashion. During the mining process, instead of recursively building sub-trees, TD-FP-Growth keeps updating the global FP-tree by adjusting tree pointers. A disadvantage of TD-FP-Growth is that many of the pointers need to be updated during the mining process.

Along this direction, the H-mine algorithm [7] uses a new data structure—namely, a hyperlinked-array structure called H-struct. Like FP-growth and TD-FP-Growth, the H-mine algorithm also scans the database twice, but it captures the content of the transaction database in the hyperlinked-array structure (instead of the tree structure). During the mining process, the H-mine algorithm also recursively updates links in the H-struct. During the mining process, some array entries in the H-struct may contain K_{max} hyperlinks (where K_{max} is the maximum cardinality of discovered patterns). Like TD-FP-Growth (which may need to update many pointers during the mining process), a disadvantage of H-mine is that many of the hyperlinks need to be updated during the mining process.

Besides these well-known algorithms—such as Apriori, FP-growth, TD-FP-Growth, and H-mine—that mine frequent patterns "horizontally" (i.e., using a transaction-centric approach to find what k-itemset is supported by or contained in a transaction), frequent patterns can also be mined "vertically" (i.e., using an item-centric approach to count the number of transactions supporting or containing the patterns). Three notable vertical frequent pattern mining algorithms are Eclat [9], dEclat [10], and VIPER [11]. Like the Apriori algorithm, Eclat also uses a level-wise bottom-up paradigm. With Eclat, the database is treated as a collection of item lists. Each list for an item x keeps IDs of transactions containing x. The length of the list for x gives the frequency of 1-itemset $\{x\}$. By taking the intersection of lists for two frequent itemsets α and β, we get the IDs of transactions containing $(\alpha \cup \beta)$. Again, the length of the resulting (intersected) list gives the frequency of the pattern $(\alpha \cup \beta)$. Eclat works well when the database is sparse. However, when the database is dense, these item lists can be long.

As an extension to the Eclat algorithm, dEclat [10] also uses a level-wise bottom-up paradigm. Unlike Eclat (which uses keeps sets of IDs of transactions containing itemsets, i.e., tidsets), dEclat uses diffset which is the set difference between tidsets of two related itemsets. Specifically, the diffset of a k-itemset $\alpha = \gamma \cup \{a\}$, where γ is its $(k - 1)$-prefix, is defined as the difference between the tidset of α and the tidset of γ. To start the mining process, dEclat computes the diffset of 1-itemset $\{x\}$ by taking the complement of the tidset of $\{x\}$, i.e.:

$$\text{diffset}(\{x\}) = \text{tidset}(TDB) - \text{tidset}(\{x\}) \tag{1}$$

$$= \{t_j | x \notin t_j \subseteq \text{TDB}\} \tag{2}$$

where t_j represents the j-th transactions in the transaction database TDB. The diffset of $\{x\}$ then captures those transactions that do not contain $\{x\}$. For a transaction database TDB containing n transactions, the frequency of 1-itemset $\{x\}$ can then be computed by $n - |\text{diffset}(\{x\})|$, where $|\text{diffset}(\{x\})|$ represents the length of diffset$(\{x\})$. Afterwards, let k-itemsets $\alpha = \gamma \cup \{a\}$ and $\beta = \gamma \cup \{b\}$ sharing a common $(k - 1)$-prefix γ such that $(\alpha \cup \beta) = \gamma \cup \{a, b\}$. Then, taking the set difference between diffset(β) and diffset(α) gives the diffset of the resulting $(\alpha \cup \beta)$. The frequency of $(\alpha \cup \beta)$ can be computed by subtracting the length of diffset$(\alpha \cup \beta)$ from the frequency of α. dEclat works well when the database is dense. However, when the database is sparse, these diffsets can be long.

Alternatively, VIPER [11] represents the item lists in the form of bit vectors. Each bit in a vector for a domain item x indicates the presence (bit "1") or absence (bit "0") of transaction containing x. The number of "1" bits for x gives the support of 1-itemset $\{x\}$. By computing the dot product of vectors for two frequent itemsets α and β, we get the vector indicating the presence of transactions containing $(\alpha \cup \beta)$. Again, the number of "1" bits of this vector gives the frequency of the resulting pattern $(\alpha \cup \beta)$. VIPER works well when the database is dense. However, when the database is sparse, lots of space may be wasted because the vector contains lots of 0s.

3   Distributed and Parallel Algorithms

To speed up the frequent pattern mining process, distributed and parallel algorithms that apply high performance computing techniques (e.g., distributed and/or parallel computing) have been developed. For instance, with distributed computing, many of these distributed algorithms mine frequent patterns by using multiple processors that have their own private memory (i.e., distributed memory). The processors exchange information by message passing, which is supported by systems like Message Passing Interface (MPI).

As another instance, with parallel computing, many of these parallel algorithms mine frequent patterns by using multiple processors that have access to a shared memory. Exchange of information among processors is supported by systems like Open Multi-Processing (OpenMP).

Among many distributed and parallel frequent pattern mining algorithms, notable ones include Count Distribution, Data Distribution, and Candidate Distribution algorithms [25]. As a parallelization of the Apriori algorithm, Count Distribution partitions transactional database and assigns them to parallel processors. Each processor first generates local candidate 1-itemsets. As these local candidate 1-itemsets from one processor may overlap with those from other processer, each processor exchanges this information about candidates with other processors. Consequently, these local candidate 1-itemsets are merged to form global candidate 1-itemsets. Each processor then counts the local frequency (or occurrences) of candidate k-itemsets (for $k \geq 1$), synchronizes and exchanges this local frequency information with other processors to find globally frequent k-itemsets, from which candidate $(k + 1)$-itemsets can be formed. This process is applied repeatedly to discover frequent patterns of all cardinalities. While Count Distribution minimizes communication costs by exchanging only frequency information, it requires redundant computations by summing the frequency information of the same candidate from different processors to determine if such a candidate is frequent.

As another parallelization of the Apriori algorithm, Data Distribution [25] partitions candidate itemsets, divides transactional database, and assigns them to parallel processors. Unlike the Count Distribution algorithm (in which candidate itemsets from different processors may overlap), candidate itemsets from each processor in Data Distribution is mutually exclusive (i.e., disjoint). Hence, each processor counts the frequency of candidate k-itemsets (for $k \geq 1$) based on local and remote database partitions (exchanged from other processors) to find globally frequent k-itemsets, from which candidate $(k + 1)$-itemsets can be formed and synchronized. This process is applied repeatedly to discover frequent patterns of all cardinalities. While Data Distribution utilizes aggregate memory by exploiting mutually exclusive candidate itemsets, it requires the broadcast of local data to other processors.

As a third parallelization of the Apriori algorithm, Candidate Distribution [25] eliminates synchronization at the price of data replication. Specifically, Candidate Distribution starts with Count Distribution or Data Distribution for early passes of the mining process. At some Pass P, Candidate Distribution partitions and redistribute frequent P-itemsets among processors such that candidate $(P + 1)$-itemsets can be formed locally without the need of information (i.e., candidate itemsets) from other processors. It does so by putting frequent itemsets from an equivalence class to the same processor. Candidate Distribution also divides the database among processors in such a way that frequency (i.e., occurrence) can be counted independently without the need of information (i.e., frequency information) from other processors. Although such a division of the database may result in some data replication, a benefit is that the algorithm does not need to broadcast local data to other processor. In subsequent passes, each processor counts the frequency of candidate k-itemsets (for $k > P$) based on only local database partitions to find globally frequent k-itemsets, from which candidate $(k + 1)$-itemsets can be formed without synchronization. This process is applied repeatedly to discover frequent patterns of all cardinalities.

Inspired by the performance gain of the serial tree-based algorithms (e.g., FP-growth) over the serial Apriori-based algorithms, researchers exploited the FP-tree-based distributed and parallel tree-based frequent pattern mining techniques. Most of the resulting algorithms partition the database, assign each part to each processor, and then individually construct local FP-tree in parallel.

Some other tree-based algorithms build a global FP-tree for the entire database by parallelizing the tree construction technique. Even though the local or the global FP-trees can be constructed with less inter-processor communication, many of these algorithms suffer from excessive communications overhead during the mining process. For instance, algorithms like MLPT [40] and the LFP-tree [41] broadcast the itemset-based prefix-trees to all processors multiple times among processors.

Instead of constructing several local FP-trees, some tree-based algorithms [42] use a tree partition-based technique to build only one FP-tree and divide it into several independent partitions to mine frequent patterns by assigning one partition to each processor. However, these algorithms may suffer from memory constraint and inter-processor communication cost.

4 MapReduce-Based Algorithms

Along directions of mining frequent patterns from very large databases in distributed and parallel computing environments, algorithms that use the MapReduce model [34, 35] for handling big data have been gaining momentum. In general, characteristics of these big data can be described by the well-known 5V's:

1. *value*, which focuses on the usefulness of data (e.g., knowledge that can be discovered from the big data);
2. *variety*, which focuses on differences in types, contents, or formats of data;
3. *velocity*, which focuses on the speed at which data are collected or generated;
4. *veracity*, which focuses on the quality of data (e.g., precise data, uncertain and imprecise data); and
5. *volume*, which focuses on the quantity of data.

Embedded in these big data are rich sets of useful information and knowledge to be mined by MapReduce-based frequent pattern mining algorithms.

MapReduce is a high-level programming model, which consists of a master node and multiple worker nodes, for handling big data. As implied by its name, MapReduce involves two key functions: "map" and "reduce" functions commonly used in functional programming languages such as LISP for list processing:

- the mapper applies a mapping function to each value in the list of values and returns the resulting list;
- the reducer applies a reducing function to combine all the values in the list of values and returns the combined result.

An advantage of using the MapReduce model is that users only need to focus on specifying these "map" and "reduce" functions—without worrying about implementation details for the following tasks:

- handling machine failures,
- managing inter-machine communication,
- partitioning the input data, or
- scheduling and executing the program across multiple machines.

The Single Pass Counting (SPC), Fixed Passes Combined-counting (FPC), and Dynamic Passes Combined-counting (DPC) algorithms [43] are some notable algorithms that use MapReduce to mine frequent patterns from big data. These three algorithms are based on both the Apriori and the Count Distribution algorithms. SPC first divides the big data into partitions, and then executes "map" and "reduce" functions in each pass k to generate candidate k-itemsets (i.e., candidate patterns each consisting of k items) and count their frequency. More specifically, SPC executes the following "map" and "reduce" functions in Pass 1:

- map_1: $\langle$ID of transaction $t_j \in$ partition P_i, contents of $t_j\rangle \mapsto$ list of $\langle$item $x \in t_j, 1\rangle$, and
- $reduce_1$: $\langle x$, list of 1's$\rangle \mapsto$ list of $\langle$frequent 1-itemset $\{x\}$, frequency($\{x\}$)$\rangle$.

Here, the worker node corresponding to each partition P_i of the big data executes the "map" function by outputting $\langle x, 1\rangle$ (which represents the frequency of candidate 1-itemset $\{x\}$ in t_j to be 1) for every item x in transaction $t_j \in P_i$. The "reduce" function is then executed by summing all the 1's for each x to compute its frequency, and outputting $\langle\{x\}$, frequency($\{x\}$)$\rangle$ for each frequent 1-itemset $\{x\}$. In each subsequent pass $k \geq 2$, SPC generates candidate k-itemsets from frequent $(k-1)$-itemsets. The worker node corresponding to each partition P_i then outputs $\langle X, 1\rangle$ for every candidate k-itemset X that exists in some transaction $t_j \in P_i$. Afterwards, the "reduce" function sums all the 1's for each X to compute its frequency, and output $\langle X$, frequency(X)$\rangle$ for each frequent itemset X. In other words, SPC executes the following map and "reduce" functions in Pass k (for every $k \geq 2$):

- $map_{k \geq 2}$: $\langle$ID of $t_j \in P_i$, contents of $t_j\rangle \mapsto$ list of $\langle$candidate k-itemset $X \subseteq t_j, 1\rangle$, and
- $reduce_{k \geq 2}$: $\langle X$, list of 1's$\rangle \mapsto$ list of $\langle$frequent k-itemset X, frequency(X)$\rangle$.

The three algorithms (SPC, FPC and DPC) are similar except that both FPC and DPC apply the *pass bundling* technique to reduce the number of passes/data scans in each P_i when generating candidate itemsets (for Pass $k \geq 3$). Between them, FPC statistically bundles a fixed number of passes (e.g., three passes) to generate all candidate k-, $(k + 1)$-, and $(k + 2)$-itemsets from frequent $(k - 1)$-itemsets. In contrast, DPC dynamically bundles several passes (depending on the number of generated candidates in these bundled passes).

On the one hand, the use of the pass bundling technique reduces the number of passes/data scans in each partition P_i. On the other hand, the Apriori-based SPC, FPC and DPC algorithms still require multiple passes/data scans when mining frequent patterns from big data. In contrast, the MapReduce version of the Partition algorithm [44] requires only two passes/data scans. Hence, the Partition-based MapReduce algorithm uses two sets of "map" and "reduce" functions. Specifically, by executing the first "map" function, the master node reads and divides big data into partitions. The worker node corresponding to each partition P_i then outputs $\langle X, 1\rangle$ for every candidate pattern X (of any cardinality) that exists in some transaction $t_j \in P_i$. The first "reduce" function then sums all the 1's for each X to find patterns that are locally frequent in P_i. Taking the union of these locally frequent patterns forms global candidate patterns:

- map_1: $\langle$ID of transaction $t_j \in P_i$, contents of $t_j\rangle \mapsto$ list of $\langle$itemset $X \subseteq t_j, 1\rangle$, and
- $reduce_1$: $\langle X$, list of 1's$\rangle \mapsto$ list of $\langle$locally frequent itemset X, NULL$\rangle$.

Afterwards, by executing the second "map" function, the worker node corresponding to each partition P_i outputs $\langle X, 1\rangle$ for every global candidate pattern X that exists in some transaction $t_j \in P_i$. Then, the "reduce" function sums all the 1's for each X to compute its frequency, and outputs $\langle X$, frequency(X)$\rangle$ for each frequent itemset X:

- map_2: $\langle$ID of $t_j \in P_i$, contents of $t_j\rangle \mapsto$ list of $\langle$global candidate pattern $X \subseteq t_j, 1\rangle$, and

- reduce$_2$: $\langle X$, list of 1's$\rangle \mapsto$ list of $\langle$globally frequent pattern X, frequency$(X)\rangle$.

Besides these Apriori-based algorithms, a tree-based algorithm—called Parallel FP-growth (PFP) algorithm [45]—also uses MapReduce to parallelize the tree-based FP-growth algorithm for mining frequent patterns and query recommendation. PFP executes a "map" function to read and divide big data into several partitions. The worker node corresponding to each partition P_i then outputs $\langle\{x\}, 1\rangle$ for every item x in transaction $t_j \in P_i$. The "reduce" function then sums all the 1's for each x to compute its frequency, and outputs $\langle\{x\}$, frequency$(\{x\})\rangle$ for frequent $\{x\}$:

- map$_1$: $\langle$ID of transaction $t_j \in P_i$, contents of $t_j\rangle \mapsto$ list of $\langle$item $x \in t_j$, 1$\rangle$, and
- reduce$_1$: $\langle x$, list of 1's$\rangle \mapsto$ list of $\langle$frequent 1-itemset $\{x\}$, frequency$(\{x\})\rangle$.

Afterwards, PFP executes a second "map" function to read the big data a second time to form an $\{x\}$-projected database (i.e., a collection of transactions containing x) for each item x in the list produced from the first "reduce" function (i.e., for each frequent 1-itemset $\{x\}$). The worker node corresponding to each projected database then builds appropriate local FP-trees (based on the projected database assigned to the node) to mine frequent k-itemsets (for $k \geq 2$). The second "reduce" function outputs $\langle X$, frequency$(X)\rangle$ for frequent X. To summarize, PFP executes two sets of "map" and "reduce" functions (cf. SPC executes K sets of "map" and "reduce" functions, whereas FPC and DPC execute at most K sets of "map" and "reduce" functions due to the pass bundling technique, where K is maximum cardinality of discovered patterns):

- map$_2$: $\langle$ID of transaction $t_j \in P_i$, contents of $t_j\rangle \mapsto$ list of $\langle\{x\}$, $\{x\}$-projected database$\rangle$, and
- reduce$_2$: $\langle\{x\}$, $\{x\}$-projected database$\rangle \mapsto$ list of $\langle$frequent itemset X, frequency$(X)\rangle$.

As PFP was designed for query recommendation, it usually takes a third set of "map" and "reduce" functions to aggregate and rank the list of frequent itemsets for the top-K frequent patterns to facilitate recommendations.

Similarly, MREclat [46] and Dist-Eclat [47] can be considered as MapReduce versions of the vertical frequent pattern mining algorithms Eclat and dEclat, respectively. BigFIM [47] can be considered as MapReduce versions of a hybrid of the Apriori and dEclat algorithms.

To handle big data, most of these MapReduce-based algorithms mine big data efficiently with *cloud computing*, which makes good use of a network of remote servers hosted on the Internet—such as Amazon Web Services (AWS) or cloud data center—to store, manage, process, and analyze data.

5   Fog-Computing-Based Frequent Pattern Mining

Nowadays, big data grow exponentially, especially in volume. This is partially due to the availability, accessibility and popularity of IoT devices. With these devices, high volumes of a wide variety of valuable data of different veracity can be easily generated or collected at a high velocity. For instance, big data can be collected on merchandise items that have been purchased by consumers through their mobile phones or watches.

Mining on these big purchasing data helps reveal interesting patterns such as consumer behavior, popularity of merchandise items, and/or effectiveness of mobile ads. Similarly, big data can also be generated on web pages surfed by the IoT device users on their mobile phones or watches. Mining on these big web data (big web logs) helps reveal interesting patterns such as collections of popular web pages with rich contents.

When applying cloud computing to mine frequent patterns from data generated or collected on these devices, these high volumes of data are usually transmitted to data centers in the cloud. Once data are in the cloud, they are partitioned and distributed among several worker nodes so that sets of "map" and "reduce" functions can be applied and data mining process can be executed in parallel.

A logical question is: Can we mine frequent patterns from these devices more efficiently and effectively? In response to this question, we exploit another high-performance computing concept—namely, *fog computing* [48–50], which is also known as *edge computing* or *fogging*.

In general, fog computing supports the Internet of Things (IoT) concepts by making good use of the edge of the network, i.e., by facilitating the computation in proximity to end-users. In other words, it stores, manages, processes, and analyzes data either on IoT devices or networking services between these end devices and data centers.

5.1   Approach #1: Mining Frequent Patterns on Local IoT Devices

One of our approaches of mining frequent patterns from IoT devices with fog computing can be described as follows. Instead of transmitting local data to data centers where data are then partitioned and redistributed among several worker nodes, we keep local data on the IoT devices, from which patterns that are frequent locally on these devices can be found. Then, inspired by (the serial or MapReduce version of) the Partition algorithm, we take the union of these locally frequent patterns to form global candidate patterns. Afterwards, by counting the frequency of these global candidates on each device, transmitting their frequency count to other devices (or a master node), and summing the frequency counts to discover globally frequent patterns in the network.

Our study on this approach shows the feasibility of mining frequent patterns from IoT devices with fog computing. Moreover, mining with this approach appears to be more efficient and practical than that with cloud computing because computations (i.e., mining and analysis) are performed closer to end-users.

5.2   Approach #2: Mining Frequent Patterns Through Local Networking Services that Lie Between IoT Devices and Data Cloud Centers

Understanding that some IoT devices may not necessary be too powerful for mining locally frequent patterns, we suggest an alternative approach of mining frequent patterns from IoT devices with fog computing. Specifically, instead of mining frequent patterns on local IoT devices, we transmit local data from the IoT devices to their local networking services that lie between the IoT devices and the usual data centers (used in cloud computing). The local networking services then mine for locally frequent patterns (i.e., patterns that are frequent with respect to the data collected from one or more IoT devices served by the local networking services). Afterwards, we take the union of these locally frequent patterns to form global candidate patterns. By counting the frequency of these global candidates on the local networking services, transmitting the frequency counts of these candidates to other devices (or a master node) and summing the frequency counts, we discover globally frequent patterns in the network.

Similar to our study on the first approach of mining frequent patterns on local IoT devices, our study on this second approach of mining frequent patterns through local networking services also shows the feasibility of frequent pattern mining with fog computing. Moreover, mining with this approach also appears to be more efficient and practical than that with cloud computing because computations (i.e., mining and analysis) are performed closer to end-users.

Mining with either of these two approaches reduces the latency and network bandwidth, enables geographic focus, and increases reliability and security.

6 Conclusions

In the current era of big data, high volumes of a wide variety of data of different veracity can be easily generated or collected at a high velocity from rich sources of data include devices from the Internet of Things (IoT). Embedded in these big data are useful information and valuable knowledge. Data mining aims to discover implicit, previously unknown and potentially useful information and knowledge from these data. Among different data mining tasks, association rule mining focuses on finding interesting rules that reveal associations or relationships between frequent patterns on the antecedents and consequences of rules. Association rule mining process consists of two key steps: Frequent pattern mining and rule formation. Over the past two decades, numerous frequent pattern mining algorithms have been proposed. In this paper, we reviewed several notable serial, distributed and parallel, as well as MapReduce-based algorithms for mining frequent patterns on local computers, in distributed and parallel environments, and/or using computer clusters, grids and clouds. Moreover, we also discussed how to mine big data—which are generated or collected from IoT devices—for frequent patterns using fog computing, with which computations are performed on edges of the network, perhaps by even incorporating adaptive metaphors (e.g., [51]).

References

1. Frawley, W.J., Piatetsky-Shapiro, G., Matheus, C.J.: Knowledge discovery in databases: an overview. AI Mag. 13(3), 57–70 (1992)
2. Agrawal, R., Imieliński, T., Swami, A.: Mining association rules between sets of items in large databases. In: Proceedings of ACM SIGMOD 1993, pp. 207–216 (1993)
3. Leung, C.K., Jiang, F., Cruz, E.M.D., Elango, V.S.: Association rule mining in collaborative filtering. In: Collaborative Filtering Using Data Mining and Analysis, pp. 159–179 (2017)
4. Agrawal, R., Srikant, R.: Fast algorithms for mining association rules in large databases. In: Proceedings of VLDB 1994, pp. 487–499 (1994)
5. Leung, C.K.: Frequent itemset mining with constraints. In: Encyclopedia of Database Systems, 2nd edn (2018). https://doi.org/10.1007/978-0-387-39940-9_170

6. Han, J., Pei, J., Yin, Y.: Mining frequent patterns without candidate generation. In: Proceedings of ACM SIGMOD 2000, pp. 1–12 (2000)
7. Pei, J., Han, J., Lu, H., Nishio, S., Tang, S., Yang, D.: H-mine: hyper-structure mining of frequent patterns in large databases. In: Proceedings of IEEE ICDM 2001, pp. 441–448 (2001)
8. Jiang, F., Leung, C.K., Zhang, H.: B-mine: frequent pattern mining and its application to knowledge discovery from social networks. In: Li, F., Shim, K., Zheng, K., Liu, G. (eds.) APWeb 2016. LNCS, vol. 9931, pp. 316–328. Springer, Cham (2016). https://doi.org/10.1007/978-3-319-45814-4_26
9. Zaki, M.J.: Scalable algorithms for association mining. IEEE TKDE **12**(3), 372–390 (2000)
10. Zaki, M.J.: Fast vertical mining using diffsets. In: Proceedings of ACM KDD 2003, pp. 326–335 (2003)
11. Shenoy, P., Bhalotia, J.R., Bawa, M., Shah, D.: Turbo-charging vertical mining of large databases. In: Proceedings of ACM SIGMOD 2000, pp. 22–33 (2000)
12. Agrawal, R., Srikant, R.: Mining sequential patterns. In: Proceedings of IEEE ICDE 1995, pp. 3–14 (1995)
13. Jiang, F., Leung, C.K., Sarumi, O.A., Zhang, C.Y.: Mining sequential patterns from uncertain big DNA data in the spark framework. In: Proceedings of IEEE BIBM 2016, pp. 874–881 (2016)
14. Chanda, A.K., Ahmed, C.F., Samiullah, M., Leung, C.K.: A new framework for mining weighted periodic patterns in time series databases. Expert Syst. Appl. **79**, 207–224 (2017)
15. Leung, C.K., Khan, Q.I.: DSTree: a tree structure for the mining of frequent sets from data streams. In: Proceedings of IEEE ICDM 2006, pp. 928–932 (2006)
16. Shajib, M.B., Samiullah, M., Ahmed, C.F., Leung, C.K., Pazdor, A.G.M.: An efficient approach for mining frequent patterns over uncertain data streams. In: Proceedings of IEEE ICTAI 2016, pp. 980–984 (2016)
17. Ramamohanarao, K.: Contrast pattern mining and its applications. In: Proceedings of ADC 2010, pp. 5–8 (2010)
18. Carmichael, C.L., Hayduk, Y., Leung, C.K.: Visually contrast two collections of frequent patterns. In: Proceedings of IEEE ICDM Workshops 2011, pp. 1128–1135 (2011)
19. Leung, C.K.-S., Mateo, M.A.F., Brajczuk, D.A.: A tree-based approach for frequent pattern mining from uncertain data. In: Washio, T., Suzuki, E., Ting, K.M., Inokuchi, A. (eds.) PAKDD 2008. LNCS, vol. 5012, pp. 653–661. Springer, Heidelberg (2008). https://doi.org/10.1007/978-3-540-68125-0_61
20. Leung, C.K.-S.: Uncertain frequent pattern mining. In: Aggarwal, C.C., Han, J. (eds.) Frequent Pattern Mining, pp. 339–367. Springer, Cham (2014). https://doi.org/10.1007/978-3-319-07821-2_14
21. Leung, C.K., MacKinnon, R.K., Jiang, F.: Finding efficiencies in frequent pattern mining from big uncertain data. World Wide Web (WWW) **20**(3), 571–594 (2017)
22. Li, Y., Bailey, J., Kulik, L., Pei, J.: Mining probabilistic frequent spatio-temporal sequential patterns with gap constraints from uncertain databases. In: Proceedings of IEEE ICDM 2013, pp. 448–457 (2013)
23. Zaki, M.J.: Parallel and distributed association mining: a survey. IEEE Concurr. **7**(4), 14–25 (1999)
24. Tanbeer, S.K., Ahmed, C.F., Jeong, B.: Parallel and distributed frequent pattern mining in large databases. In: Proceedings of IEEE HPCC 2009, pp. 407–414 (2009)
25. Agrawal, R., Shafer, J.C.: Parallel mining of association rules. IEEE TKDE **8**(6), 962–969 (1996)
26. Chandru, V., Mueller, F.: Hybrid MPI/OpenMP programming on the Tilera manycore architecture. In: Proceedings of HPCS 2016, pp. 326–333 (2016)

27. Utrera, G., Gil, M., Martorell, X.: In search of the best MPI-OpenMP distribution for optimum Intel-MIC cluster performance. In: Proceedings of HPCS 2015, pp. 429–435 (2015)

28. Rosa, A., Chen, L.Y., Binder, W.: Predicting and mitigating jobs failures in big data clusters. In: Proceedings of IEEE/ACM CCGrid 2015, pp. 221–230 (2015)

29. Ertl, B., Stevanovic, U., Hayrapetyan, A., Wegh, B., Hardt, M.: Identity harmonization for federated HPC, grid and cloud services. In: Proceedings of HPCS 2016, pp. 621–627 (2016)

30. Cuzzocrea, A., Leung, C.K., Jiang, F., MacKinnon, R.K.: Complex mining from uncertain big data in distributed environments: problems, definitions and two effective and efficient algorithms. In: Big Data Management and Processing, pp. 297–332 (2017)

31. Leung, C.K.: Big data analysis and mining, Chap. 30. In: Encyclopedia of Information Science and Technology, 4th edn (2017)

32. Leung, C.K.-S., Hayduk, Y.: Mining frequent patterns from uncertain data with MapReduce for big data analytics. In: Meng, W., Feng, L., Bressan, S., Winiwarter, W., Song, W. (eds.) DASFAA 2013. LNCS, vol. 7825, pp. 440–455. Springer, Heidelberg (2013). https://doi.org/10.1007/978-3-642-37487-6_33

33. Fumarola, F., Malerba, D.: A parallel algorithm for approximate frequent itemset mining using MapReduce. In: Proceedings of HPCS 2014, pp. 335–342 (2014)

34. Dean, J., Ghemawat, S.: MapReduce: simplified data processing on large clusters. In: Proceedings of OSDI 2004, pp. 137–150 (2004)

35. Noor, S., Uddin, V.: MapReduce for multi-view object recognition. In: Proceedings of HPCS 2016, pp. 575–582 (2016)

36. Buyya, R., Yeo, C.S., Venugopal, S., Broberg, J., Brandic, I.: Cloud computing and emerging IT platforms: vision, hype, and reality for delivering computing as the 5th utility. FGCS 25(6), 599–616 (2009)

37. Han, Z., Leung, C.K.: FIMaaS: scalable frequent itemset mining-as-a-service on cloud for non-expert miners. In: Proceedings of BigDAS 2015, pp. 84–91 (2015)

38. Savasere, A., Omiecinski, E., Navathe, S.: An efficient algorithm for mining association rules in large databases. In: Proceedings of VLDB 1995, pp. 432–444 (1995)

39. Wang, K., Tang, L., Han, J., Liu, J.: Top down FP-Growth for association rule mining. In: Chen, M.-S., Yu, P.S., Liu, B. (eds.) PAKDD 2002. LNCS (LNAI), vol. 2336, pp. 334–340. Springer, Heidelberg (2002). https://doi.org/10.1007/3-540-47887-6_34

40. Zaiane, O.R., El-Hajj, M., Lu, P.: Fast parallel association rule mining without candidacy generation. In: Proceedings of IEEE ICDM 2001, pp. 665–668 (2001)

41. Yu, K.-M., Zhou, J., Hsiao, W.C.: Load balancing approach parallel algorithm for frequent pattern mining. In: Malyshkin, V. (ed.) PaCT 2007. LNCS, vol. 4671, pp. 623–631. Springer, Heidelberg (2007). https://doi.org/10.1007/978-3-540-73940-1_63

42. Chen, D., Lai, C., Hu, W., Chen, W.G., Zhang, Y., Zheng, W.: Tree partition based parallel frequent pattern mining on shared memory systems. In: Proceedings of IEEE IPDPS 2006 (2006)

43. Lin, M., Lee, P., Hsueh, S.: Apriori-based frequent itemset mining algorithms on MapReduce. In: Proceedings of ICUIMC 2012 (2012). Article no. 76

44. Rajaraman, A., Ullman, J.D.: Mining of Massive Datasets. Cambridge University Press, Cambridge (2011)

45. Li, H., Wang, Y., Zhang, D., Zhang, M., Chang, E.Y.: PFP: parallel FP-growth for query recommendation. In: Proceedings of ACM RecSys 2008, pp. 107–114 (2008)

46. Zhang, Z., Ji, G., Tang, M.: MREclat: an algorithm for parallel mining frequent itemsets. In: Proceedings of CBD 2013, pp. 177–180 (2013)

47. Snady, M., Emin, A., Bart, G.: Frequent itemset mining for big data. In: Proceedings of IEEE BigData 2013, pp. 111–118 (2013)

48. Bonomi, F., Milito, R., Natarajan, P., Zhu, J.: Fog computing: a platform for Internet of Things and analytics. In: Bessis, N., Dobre, C. (eds.) Big Data and Internet of Things: A Roadmap for Smart Environments. SCI, vol. 546, pp. 169–186. Springer, Cham (2014). https://doi.org/10.1007/978-3-319-05029-4_7
49. Dastjerdi, A.V., Buyya, R.: Fog computing: helping the Internet of Things realize its potential. IEEE Comput. **49**(8), 112–116 (2016)
50. Linthicum, D.S.: Connecting fog and cloud computing. IEEE Cloud Comput. **4**(2), 18–20 (2017)
51. Cannataro, M., Cuzzocrea, A., Pugliese, A.: A probabilistic approach to model adaptive hypermedia systems. In: Proceedings of WebDyn 2001, pp. 12–30 (2001)
52. Cuzzocrea, A., Furfaro, F., Saccà, D.: Enabling OLAP in mobile environments via intelligent data cube compression techniques. J. Intell. Inf. Syst. **33**(2), 95–143 (2009)
53. Cuzzocrea, A.: Accuracy control in compressed multidimensional data cubes for quality of answer-based OLAP tools. In: Proceedings of SSDBM 2006, pp. 301–310 (2006)
54. Cuzzocrea, A., Fortino, G., Rana, O.F.: Managing data and processes in cloud-enabled large-scale sensor networks: state-of-the-art and future research directions. In: Proceedings of IEEE/ACM CCGrid 2013, pp. 583–588 (2013)

An Innovative Architecture for Supporting Cyber-Physical Security Systems

Alfredo Cuzzocrea[1,2]([✉]), Massimiliano Nolich[1], and Walter Ukovich[1]

[1] DIA Department, University of Trieste, Trieste, Italy
{alfredo.cuzzocrea,walter.ukovich}@dia.units.it, mnolich@units.it
[2] ICAR-CNR, Rende, Italy

Abstract. Physical and cybersecurity is an important topic to be managed in complex communication systems. Specialized equipments and devices help human operators in managing security issues. The security manager of such system shall be capable to correctly decode all the incoming inputs from perceiving subsystems, that can be of different types, and that shall be aggregated and interpreted in the actual environments in order to generate alarms and countermeasures. This paper presents the design of a Decision and Control Unit (DCU) for such systems. The DCU aims at helping the security manager of the system to take informed decision in real-time reducing him/her workload. The general requirements, the architecture and the design of this decision support and decision making system are presented. An example of alarm detection is finally outlined.

Keywords: Cybersecurity · Physical security
Decision support systems

1 Introduction

Communication systems are complex systems of fundamental importance in modern society. A wide set of attacks can be conducted to block the communication capabilities of such systems. Such attacks can affect physical subsystems or can be cyber, i.e. they can affect the software running on the communication system reducing, modifying or blocking its communication capabilities. The system administrator of a communication system usually operates as security manager: it shall be informed if an attack occurs, and shall decide whether a countermeasure can preserve the communication capabilities of the system. Such decision shall be taken in real-time and shall consider a wide range of equipment capable of perceive physical and cyber-attacks. The adoption of a decision support system (DSS) can help the security manager to be accurately informed on the status of the attacks and can suggest the best countermeasure to apply in that conditions.

For managing complex systems and to operate in real-time, a modern DSS typically includes these advanced features:

- it can integrate an expert system;
- it can aggregate data and perform data fusion;
- it can integrate soft computing, data mining and machine learning systems;
- it can integrate other artificial intelligence (AI) tools.

One important property that a modern DSS shall implement is the adaptation to the effective environment (like in related research efforts – e.g., [1]): the so called Situation Awareness (SA) supports a decision-maker to perceive the inputs taking into account the environmental context of the in order to make improved decisions [2]. Many definitions of SA have been developed, some of which are quite general, whilst others are closely tied with applications. SA can be analyzed from different points of view: technical and cognitive. The former relates to aggregates, fusing and processing data, the latter concerns the human capacity to understand the implications and draw conclusions to perform decisions.

In this paper we present the design of a Decision and Control Unit (DCU) suited for such systems. The proposed DSS has an hybrid structure: on the basis of a model-driven structure, we have integrated a soft computing based decision component; this component integrates learning capabilities and is capable of performing adaptation to the effective environment. The DCU aims at helping the security manager of the system to take informed decision in real-time reducing him/her workload. The general requirements, the architecture and the design of this decision support and decision making system are outlined.

2 Physical Security Use Case

In this Section, an overview of the DCU requirements for physical security of complex Communication Systems (CS) is presented. To this aim, the Unified Modeling Language (UML) formalism is applied. In particular, first, a *use-case diagram* is developed in order to show the interactions between the DCU and a set of external entities (i.e., the *actors*). Then, a *sequence diagram* is introduced is order to model a typical usage scenario for the DCU.

2.1 DCU Requirements for Physical Requirements

Figure 1 depicts the use-case diagram showing the DCU requirements for the physical security.

Three actors interact with the DCU: PHYSICAL DETECTION (PD), RISK ASSESSMENT and the SECURITY MANAGER (SM). In particular:

1. PD is a scalable distributed multi-sensor network for protection against physical attack [3–6]. We assume that it is composed only by low or null emitted power sensors, specifically passive sensors (passive radar, infra-red camera, radiometric SAR, RFID) and low emission radars (noise radar based sensors).

2. RISK ASSESSMENT is a risk analysis tool in charge of identifying the level of risk associated with the potential threats.
3. the SM is the person responsible to take operational decisions when any accident occurs in the GS.

The defined actors trigger the following use cases for the DCU:

1. PD
   (a) *Communicate detected target.* Whenever a target is detected inside the GS perimeter, the multi-sensor network provides the DCU all the information needed for the protection against the possible physical attack, i.e.: the date and time of the detection; an ID conveying spatial information associated to the sensor that has acquired the considered data; the sensor range and position; the target position, speed, dimensions and typology (i.e., person, animal, car, bicycle, and so on); the altitude of the acquisition.
   (b) *Get threat notification.* Once the DCU has determined if the detected target is a threat to be defeated, the PD has to receive a feedback about it.
2. RISK ASSESSMENT
   (a) *Provide risk map.* The RISK ASSESSMENT tool provides to the DCU the risk maps for all the CS infrastructure assets, i.e., the cumulative risk value of the assets and the individual value associated with each specific threat. This information is combined by the DCU with the information about the detected target in order to determine if some countermeasures have to be applied.
   (b) *Receive data about new attacks.* The risk maps provided by the RISK ASSESSMENT tool have to be continuously actualized with the new information about the discovery of new threats, threats materialization and impacts, existence of effective countermeasures and critical assets modification. Such information is supplied by the DCU and is essential to keep the infrastructure security under control.
3. SM
   (a) *Get alarm notification.* Whenever the DCU identifies a new threat, the SM has to receive a notification about it in order to be constantly aware about the CS state.
   (b) *Receive suggestions.* Whenever a new threat is identified by the DCU, a list of possible countermeasures has to be provided to the SM. More in detail, depending on the type of the specific decision and the context within which it must be taken, two operative settings are possible:
      – if the alarm detected has a safe recovery operation associated to it, a Decision Making Systems (DMS) attitude is considered and, once identified, the best decision alternative is automatically implemented by the DCU (*autonomous operations*), and only a notification is given to the SM;

- when the countermeasures to be applied can affect the integrity of the communication system and, therefore, an external authorization from a human operator is needed, a DSS attitude is considered. In this case, a set of different alternatives is identified and presented to the SM, who will then choose which one to implement (human-driven operations).

(c) *Apply countermeasure.* As specified above, if a DSS operative setting is considered, the SM has to choose which countermeasure to apply against the detected attack.

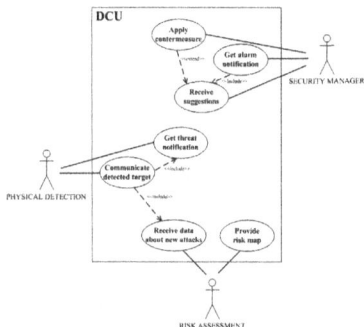

Fig. 1. Use-case diagram for physical security.

2.2   Typical DCU Usage Scenario for Physical Security

The sequence diagram of Fig. 2 depicts a typical DCU usage scenario for physical security.

Assume that an attacker (for example, a car) is moving inside the perimeter area of the infrastructure hosting the CS hardware (*1: Move*), thus altering the state of the CS (*2: Perceive*).

One (or more) sensor(s) of PD detects the target (*3: Reveal*) and sends the related information to the DCU. At this point, the DCU sends a notification about the new detection to the RISK ASSESSMENT (*4: Notify new detection*), which provides the appropriate risk map (*5: Provide risk map*). The DCU has now at its disposal all the information necessary to determine the current alarm class characterizing the state of the CS and to identify the possible countermeasures to be applied. An alarm is sent by the DCU to the SM (*6: Alarm*), who evaluates the received suggestions and applies the selected countermeasure (*7: Apply countermeasures*).

3   Cybersecurity Use Case

Analogously to the previous Section, Fig. 3 depicts the use-case diagram showing the DCU requirements for the cybersecurity.

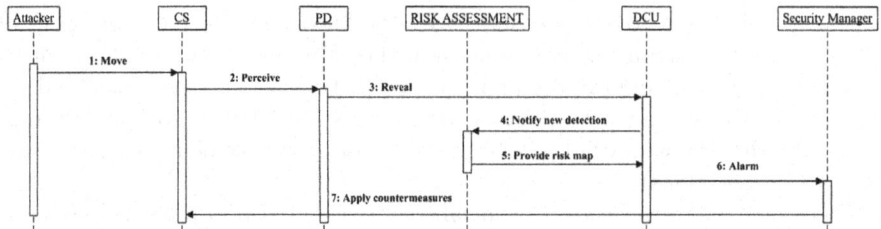

Fig. 2. DCU usage scenario for physical security.

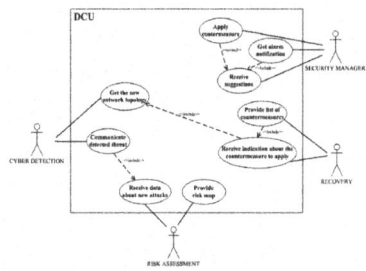

Fig. 3. Use-case diagram for cybersecurity.

Four actors interact with the DCU: CYBER DETECTION (CD), RECOVER, RISK ASSESSMENT and the SM. RISK ASSESSMENT and SM have the same meaning of the physical security case, while:

1. PD is a scalable distributed sensor network for protection against cyber-attacks. Data are collected from both network-based sources (network probes installed in positions that allow the monitoring of the whole traffic-purpose specific machines installed in the network) and host-based sources (host probes, i.e., software in charge of picking logs and gathering traffic in the ground station machines) [7–9].
2. RECOVER is a management network system for the automatic restoration and the intelligent reconfiguration of the CS network in case of attack [10–12].

The defined actors trigger the following use cases for the DCU:

1. CD
   (a) *Communicate detected target.* Whenever an anomaly is detected, the sensor network provides the DCU all the information needed for the protection against the possible cyber-attack, i.e.: the date and time of the detection; an ID conveying spatial information associated to the sensor that has acquired the considered data; the cyber-threat classification (e.g., anomaly, attack, DoS, etc.; the attacker IP).
   (b) *Get the new network topology.* Once the DCU has determined the current alarm class characterizing the state of the CS network and has suggested

to RECOVER which action to apply, the new network topology has to be communicated to CD.

2. RECOVER

   (a) *Provide list of countermeasures.* The RECOVER unit can perform one of the following actions: drop anomalous traffic flows; reroute anomalous (suspicious) traffic flows; reroute traffic flows over a congested link; isolate a portion of the network under attack; calculate and install recovery path.

   (b) *Receive indication about the countermeasure to apply.* RECOVERY has to receive indications from the DCU about the countermeasure to apply on the basis of the detected threat and the specific contingency.

The use cases associated to RISK ASSESSMENT and to the SM have the same meaning of the physical security case.

3.1 Typical DCU Usage Scenario for Cybersecurity

The sequence diagram of Fig. 4 depicts a typical DCU usage scenario for cybersecurity.

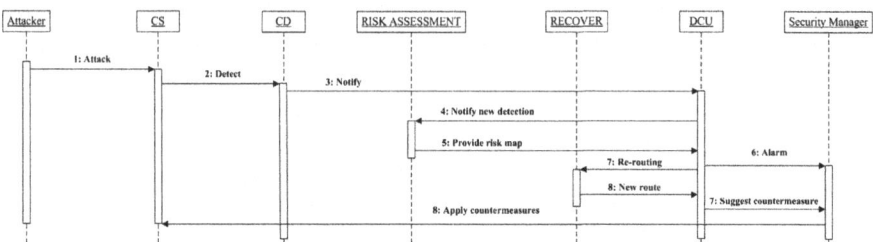

Fig. 4. DCU usage scenario for cybersecurity.

Assume that an attacker is trying to manipulate a software in one of the nodes of the CS (*1: Attack*), thus affecting its normal functionalities (*2: Detect*). One (or more) sensor(s) of CD detects the attack (*3: Notify*) and sends the related information to the DCU. At this point, the DCU sends a notification about the new detection to the RISK ASSESSMENT (*4: Notify new detection*), which provides the appropriate risk map (*5: Provide risk map*). The DCU has now at its disposal all the information necessary to classify the detected cyberthreat and, therefore, to determine the best countermeasure among the actions that can be performed by RECOVER. In particular, for the software manipulation at a node, a request of rerouting the anomalous traffic flows is sent to RECOVER by the DCU (*7: Re-routing*) and, simultaneously, an alarm is notified to the SM (*6: Alarm*). RECOVER then suggest the new route (*6: New route*), which has to be validated by the SM (*7: Suggest countermeasure*) and, then, applied (*8: Apply countermeasures*).

4   Decision and Control Unit Structure

The Decision and Control Unit (DCU) is the high level part of the DSS has the following elements:

Decision Component. It is the main part of the DCU: on the basis of risk assessment inputs, saliency analysis, historical data analysis and best practices it alerts the security manager and computes the best action to be performed to preserve the communication. This component is able to be trained incrementally as new security alerts and corresponding countermeasures adopted have considered valuable by the security manager;

Data Component. It contains the data on the environment and on the configuration of the devices available in each subsystems;

Model Component. It performs simulation to generate valuable data to be used to validate the rules performed by the decision component.

Knowledge Management Component. It gathers all the historical data of past attacks and successful countermeasures and the set of best practices gathered from the experience of security experts.

In Fig. 5 the internal structure of the DCU is depicted, with details on the internal structure of the Decision Component, the core element of the unit. The experts knowledge is gather in the different elements of the DCU:

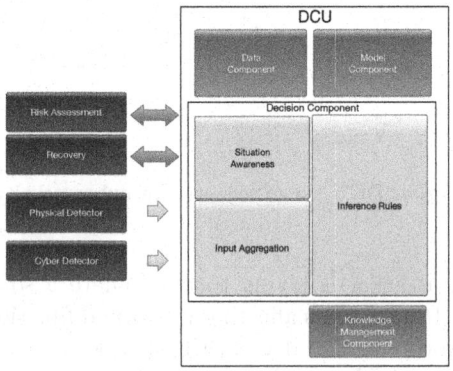

Fig. 5. Internal structure of the DCU.

– Data Component collects all the data concerning the physical and topological structure of the communication station. For what concerns physical security, it shall contain all the details regarding physical maps of the system, persons and vehicles allowed to access the system, route on the street, etc. Considering cybersecurity, detail on services implemented and required in each node, together with the topology and the communication characteristics of the network shall be detailed.

- Model Component contains the mathematical model of both physical and cyber-attacks. These models are built on the basis of general knowledge of such attacks and are used to initially train the inference rule system inside the Decision Component so that it can operate even if no previous experiences are given to the Decision Component.
- Knowledge Management Component gathers all the expert rules available for a given situation, and can log all the actions and countermeasures that are successfully performed on the system under operation.

The DCU can operate as an hybrid system: it can operate as a classical model driven DSS if no specific on-site specific knowledge is available, and it uses expert rules and good performed operations to adapt the decision to the specific environment using incremental learning.

The Decision Component has three functional blocks inside:

- Input Aggregation: the incoming inputs are collected and aggregated using a data fusion algorithm.
- Situation Awareness: this is a function that
- Inference Rules: it is formed by a set of linguistic rules that translate the risk assessment principles into alarm actions.

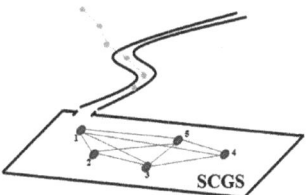

Fig. 6. Example of alarm detection. (Color figure online)

5   Practical Application Scenario: Space Control Ground Station

With the aim of showing an example of alarm detection, the Space Control Ground Station (SCGS) of Fig. 6 is considered. In order to act correctly, the DCU has to have at its disposal information regarding both the physical structure of the SCGS (i.e., the perimeter area, the buildings, the possible accesses to the station, and so on) and the topology of the communication network. In the Scenario represented in Fig. 6, PD communicates to the DCU the behavior of a target detected inside the surveillance area, i.e., PD provides the tracking of the subsequent positions of the target (red dots in the Figure) and its velocity. Starting from this information and considering the risk maps provided by RISK ASSESSMENT, the DCU perform a contingency analysis, classifying the current behavior of the target as suspicious and, thus, sending an alarm to the SM. At this point, both physical and cyber-countermeasures can be suggested by the DCU. For example, the physical access to the perimeter area of the SCGS can be blocked by a human operator, while the communication nodes 1 and 2 (i.e., the portion of the communication network possibly affected by the physical attack) can be isolated, thus asking to RECOVERY to re-route the traffic flows considering only the secure nodes.

6   Conclusions and Future Work

Cyber-Physical security is an emerging topic in all the communication and infrastructural systems. The issue to be taken into account involve different competencies in different fields and a Decision Support System can help the humans responsible of the security to provide a better and faster control of the problem, while reducing their workload. The system architecture presented in this paper help the reconfiguration of the system in different application contexts.

Future work is oriented towards several goals: (*i*) devising more advanced case studies that can be developed on top of our general architecture, like in recent research proposals (e.g., [13–15]); (*ii*) connoting our architecture by means of emerging *big data features* (e.g., [16–18]); (*iii*) coupling our architecture with emerging scenarios such as social networks (e.g., [19,20]).

References

1. Cannataro, M., Cuzzocrea, A., Pugliese, A.: A probabilistic approach to model adaptive hypermedia systems. In: Proceedings of the International Workshop for Web Dynamics, pp. 12–30 (2001)
2. Hall, M.J., Hansen, D.D., Jones, K.: Cross-domain situational awareness and collaborative working for cyber security. In: 2015 International Conference on Cyber Situational Awareness, Data Analytics and Assessment (CyberSA), pp. 1–8. IEEE (2015)
3. Boulmakoul, A., Karim, L., Elbouziri, A., Lbath, A.: A system architecture for heterogeneous moving-object trajectory metamodel using generic sensors: tracking airport security case study. IEEE Syst. J. 9(1), 283–291 (2015)
4. Gould, D., Pollard, R., Sarno, C., Tittensor, P.: Developments to a multiband passive radar demonstrator system. In: 2007 IET International Conference on Radar Systems, pp. 1–5. IET (2007)
5. Capria, A., Petri, D., Martorella, M., Conti, M., DalleMese, E., Berizzi, F.: DVB-T passive radar for vehicles detection in urban environment. In: 2010 IEEE International Geoscience and Remote Sensing Symposium (IGARSS), pp. 3917–3920. IEEE (2010)
6. Lukin, K., Mogyla, A., Palamarchuk, V., Vyplavin, P., Zemlyaniy, O., Shiyan, Y., Zaets, M.: Ka-band bistatic ground-based noise waveform sar for short-range applications. IET Radar Sonar Navig. 2(4), 233–243 (2008)
7. Callegari, C., Gazzarrini, L., Giordano, S., Pagano, M., Pepe, T.: A novel PCA-based network anomaly detection. In: 2011 IEEE International Conference on Communications (ICC), pp. 1–5. IEEE (2011)

8. Callegari, C., Giordano, S., Pagano, M.: On the combined use of sketches and CUSUM for anomaly detection. In: 2015 International Conference on Computing and Network Communications (CoCoNet), pp. 157–162. IEEE (2015)
9. Callegari, C., Pietro, A.D., Giordano, S., Pepe, T., Procissi, G.: The LogLog counting reversible sketch: a distributed architecture for detecting anomalies in backbone networks. In: 2012 IEEE International Conference on Communications (ICC), pp. 1287–1291. IEEE (2012)
10. Chierichetti, F., Epasto, A., Kumar, R., Lattanzi, S., Mirrokni, V.: Efficient algorithms for public-private social networks. In: Proceedings of the 21th ACM SIGKDD International Conference on Knowledge Discovery and Data Mining, pp. 139–148. ACM (2015)
11. Chowdhury, N.M.K., Boutaba, R.: A survey of network virtualization. Comput. Netw. **54**(5), 862–876 (2010)
12. Tootoonchian, A., Gorbunov, S., Ganjali, Y., Casado, M., Sherwood, R.: On controller performance in software-defined networks. Hot-ICE **12**, 1–6 (2012)
13. Choo, K.R., Bishop, M., Glisson, W.B., Nance, K.L.: Internet- and cloud-of-things cybersecurity research challenges and advances. Comput. Secur. **74**, 275–276 (2018)
14. Leszczyna, R.: Cybersecurity and privacy in standards for smart grids - a comprehensive survey. Comput. Stand. Interfaces **56**, 62–73 (2018)
15. Takahashi, T., Panta, B., Kadobayashi, Y., Nakao, K.: Web of cybersecurity: linking, locating, and discovering structured cybersecurity information. Int. J. Commun. Syst. **31**(3) (2018)
16. Cuzzocrea, A., Furfaro, F., Saccà, D.: Enabling OLAP in mobile environments via intelligent data cube compression techniques. J. Intell. Inf. Syst. **33**(2), 95–143 (2009)
17. Cuzzocrea, A.: Accuracy control in compressed multidimensional data cubes for quality of answer-based OLAP tools. In: Proceedings of the 18th International Conference on Scientific and Statistical Database Management, SSDBM 2006, 3–5 July 2006, Vienna, Austria, pp. 301–310 (2006)
18. Cuzzocrea, A., Fortino, G., Rana, O.F.: Managing data and processes in cloud-enabled large-scale sensor networks: state-of-the-art and future research directions. In: 13th IEEE/ACM International Symposium on Cluster, Cloud, and Grid Computing, CCGrid 2013, Delft, Netherlands, 13–16 May 2013, pp. 583–588 (2013)
19. Das, S.: Social cybersecurity: understanding and leveraging social influence to increase security sensitivity. IT - Inf. Technol. **58**(5), 237–245 (2016)
20. Hatfield, J.M.: Social engineering in cybersecurity: the evolution of a concept. Comput. Secur. **73**, 102–113 (2018)

Workshop Sustainability Performance Assessment: Models, Approaches and Applications Toward Interdisciplinary and Integrated Solutions (SPA 2018)

Integrated SDSS for Environmental Risk Analysis in Sustainable Coastal Area Planning

Michele Greco[1,4(✉)] ⓘ, Giovanni Martino[1], Annibale Guariglia[2], Lucia Trivigno[3], Vito Sansanelli[2], Angela Losurdo[2], and Giovanni Mussuto[4]

[1] Engineering School, University of Basilicata, Via dell'Ateneo Lucano10, Potenza, Italy
michele.greco@unibas.it
[2] Geocart Srl, Viale del Basento 120, Potenza, Italy
[3] Centre of Integrated Geomorphology in Mediterranean Area, Via F. Baracca 175, Potenza, Italy
[4] Regional Environmental Observatory Research Foundation, Corso Vittorio Emanuele II n. 3, 85052 Marsico Nuovo, PZ, Italy

Abstract. The work deals with the development and implementation of a Spatial Decision Support System (SDSS) platform for coastal environmental risk analysis through the integration of multisource satellite data (Sentinel-1 and 2 and COSMOSkyMed) coupled with open source coastal hydrodynamic model addressed to flooding, erosion and pollution. The processing results allow us to cope with longshore pollutant dynamics connected to bathing use, to derive the shoreline changes and back-dune vegetation mapping, rocky coast movements detection as well as coastal area changes derived through advanced images segmentation techniques, multi-band change-detection and Persistent Scattered Interferometric Synthetic Aperture Radar technologies (PSInSAR). The SDSS provides cyclical production and updating in phase with satellite data acquisition frequency of the coastal scenarios for flooding risk analysis. All of these issues well enable operative products to be employed in the knowledge chain for sustainable coastal area planning activities. Moreover, self-consistent applicative tools, provided with proper graphical interface developed in IDL and integrated in SDSS, lead displaying and automatic extraction of the coastline sequence from Sentinel-1 data. Thus the comparison of two or more shorelines, even if multi-sources, provides the computation of coastal erosion and aggradation as well as the areas prone to coastal flooding. Finally, some interoperable tools for morpho-hydrodynamic modelling assimilation have been developed and implemented to reproduce flooding and pollution risk scenarios as well as coastal resilience assessment at different return time.

Keywords: SDSS · SAR · Change-detection · Coastal risk
Hydrodynamic modelling

1 Introduction

The increasing of coastal population density and the progressive growth of economic and touristic pressures, related to the exploitation and over-exploitation of marine and coastal resources, are some of the issues threatening the delicate natural framework of

© Springer International Publishing AG, part of Springer Nature 2018
O. Gervasi et al. (Eds.): ICCSA 2018, LNCS 10964, pp. 671–684, 2018.
https://doi.org/10.1007/978-3-319-95174-4_51

sea-side areas and in-shore coasts as well as the objective issues related to the management of coastal risks mainly concerning natural hazards and human activities.

In Basilicata (Southern Italy), with about 75 km of littoral (rocky and cliffs, sandy and stony), the coastal system is a precious and fragile resource of highly natural and landscaping significance to be protected and promoted through an economic and social natural-friendly development.

Coastal erosion occurs over the years mainly induced by drastic reduction of river sediment supply due to relevant and distributed interventions both all over the basins and along rivers [1–3] as well as increasing human pressure due to touristic and productive settlements [4]. The real spreading of such a phenomena have sensitively augmented public awareness to the opportunity to allocate resources for structural and not structural interventions addressed to risk prevention rather than emergency management. Such a smart governance approach might be based on an all-embracing and systematic analysis of coastal area vulnerability and resilience to identify appropriate mitigation and contrast measures and structural priorities to cope with sea aggression and seriously compromising the Lucanian coast [5]. In such a sensitive and vulnerable context appropriate resources to improve and implement conventional and innovative monitoring systems as well as modelling procedures able to continuously support management activities must be employed.

The paper proposes the results of the operative projects MATER and COMUIN-MARE addressed to the development of a general methodology of environmental and territorial analysis for the exploitation of natural resources. That is, the first operational results in terms of definition and implementation of a Spatial Decision Support System for hydraulic and environmental coastal risk forecast and prevention [6] are proposed. The main frame deals with the integration and use of ground and remote earth observation data, with particular reference to new satellite missions, such as Sentinel-1 and 2 [7, 8] as well as COSMOSkyMed. That is, among the operative products, the project shapes the structuring and implementation of an expandable SDSS based on open-data catalogues, enabling management and displaying of both basic information, including the relative metadata, and post-processing results obtained through open-source change-detecting codes and hydro-morphological modelling. The SDSS allows the development of integrative methodologies for systematic coastal monitoring and might be interfaced in an open source WebGIS environment dialoguing with the Regional Spatial Data Infrastructure. The SDSS provides the integration of ground and remotely sensed data with Open Source Information technologies for advanced analyses and web publishing geo-data for providing a simple and intuitive end-user consultation. The interoperability WMS (Web Map Service) standards, by the OGC (Open Geospatial Consortium) based on PSInSAR and Change Detection methodologies are used for geo-data analyses [9].

Finally, data processing validation for the developed procedures has been provided comparing the products to the ground data acquired by aerial surveys, carried on with a multi-sensor platform such as metric camera, thermal camera, hyperspectral systems and Laser. Such validated information are data input of morpho-hydrodynamic and pollutant dynamics numerical models in order to create several critical risk scenarios for coastal areas.

2   GIS and Spatial DSS Implementation

Decision Support Systems (DSS) are a specific class of computerized information tools and systems, which allow decision-making activities.

In general, DSS are interactive computer-based systems and subsystems proposed to help decision makers on communication technologies, data, documents, knowledge and/or models to identify and solve problems and make choices [10]. They should assist in formulating alternatives, accessing data, running numerical and/or conceptual assessment models, displaying and interpreting results [11].

A wide range of spatially distributed information on characteristic coastal areas, such as shoreline, beach morphology, land use/cover, topography, etc., are available enabling the Spatial Decision Support Systems (SDSS).

In such a view, the Geographic Information System (GIS) is generator for SDSS due to its high performing functions to store, retrieve, analyze, manipulate as well as display large volumes of spatial digital data and create thematic maps or logical frameworks.

The analysis of functional and architectural system requirements, supported by the research and identification of the reference solutions within the engineering software led to the design of a scalable and modular architecture.

The architecture modelling of the proposed system, highlighting its modularity through the robustness of software components and internal and external interfaces of the system identified, like SERVER FTP, CATALOGER, WEBGIS and DSS.

In a general view, the SDSS are new web-based software systems providing a series of functions of data and model analyses enabled in an simple interactive and expeditive way, increasing the efficiency and robustness of the decision-making through the creation of real-time or near-real-time alternative scenarios in the time-space domain [12, 13]. Comparing both systems, traditional computer based SDSS and web-based SDSS, the last ones present several advantages [11–19], such as:

– global, quick and user-friendly accessibility;
– high efficiency in real-time for model improvement and data update;
– independent platform compliant to virtual machine;
– centralized control coping with lower costs for hardware, software, distribution, maintenance and training.

These issues facilitate a wide community of stakeholders to access and participate in the public planning and decision-making processes, which can fruitfully impact the quality of their work even improving public awareness of the existence of spatial digital data and scientific models. In such a framework, a DSS evolution is made up of SDSS having the added value of the explicit consideration of the spatial dimension of decision-making problems which are intrinsic features to take into account in territorial system management and transformation. Thus, the proposed GIS-DSS platform is set up as a SDSS and deliberately implemented on the basis of open-source solutions extending its functionality.

Therefore, previous study and analysis of the state-of-the-art of available open-source solutions in GIS environment have been carried on addressing QGIS.

QGIS is an open-source system released under GNU General Public License and it is an official project of the Open Source Geospatial Foundation (OSGeo). The software is available for Linux, Unix, Mac OSX, Windows and Android platforms and supports several formats of spatial data. Furthermore, it allows us to process on spatial databases offering vector analysis tools, geoprocessing and database management. Finally, it is possible to adapt QGIS to specific needs due to the extensible architecture of plug-ins that can be created through specific libraries.

The SDSS module has been developed in Python (ver. 2.7) and set up as plug-in of QGIS (ver. 2.10 Pisa) on OS Windows 7 pro 64 bit.

3   Data Layers, Tools and Plug-in

The proposed QGIS project has been implemented with several informative layers, namely of new acquisition and so updatable by the user, and such implemented information layers are related to the multisource data as reported in Table 1.

Table 1.   Currently implemented information layers

Information layers	Contents
Framework	All the information layers are raster type, except those of satellite data, and complain with official formats of the cartography released by the Military Geographical Institute (IGM)
Bathymetry	Archive data relative to the bathymetric campaigns in 2012 and 2015
Cartography	Historical data in raster format of the official IGM cartography at 25.000 edition 1949
DTM	Digital terrain models in raster format derived from aerial Lidar scans of archive and new acquisition refer to 2006, 2008, 2011, 2012, 2013 and 2015, all of them have been pre-loaded
Shoreline	Shoreline, in vector format produced by multisource data, both of archive and new acquisition. In particular, they have been extracted according to data availability in the following order of priority: laser data, digital orthophoto and historical cartography and relative to 1947, 1949, 1988, 2001, 2005, 2006, 2008, 2011, 2012, 2013, 2015
Orthophoto	Information layers refer to historical and of archive orthophotos, B/W and coloured ones, obtained with analogue technologies and orthophotos of latest production obtained with high-resolution digital cameras. The pre-loaded layers are relative to 1947, 1998, 2001, 2006, 2008, 2011, 2012, 2013 and 2015
Thermography	Aerial survey across the coastal strip performed with digital thermal camera
Satellite images	Sample catalogue containing some satellite images and related shorelines extracted from the same data. Radar Sentinel 1 and Optical Sentinel 2 data have been inserted. On the satellite data no cropping operation were performed but they have been included in the full coverage of the scanned images
Topographic survey	Ground survey 2015 available in the form of row measured points and coastline derived from the acquired points
Lidar data	Laser data of archive and new campaigns are available, after a careful clipping work and geographic homogenization

The system is able to process data through specific tools designated for such a purpose. That is, the Lidar Data were not directly pre-loaded into the system, because QGIS does not allow direct displaying in the native format and so, within the project, an ad hoc plug-in has been designated. The plug-in, named LAStoDEMCompare, manages the work-flow that, from the data in Lidar format, led to create the DEM in Raster format as well as the management and query of the extracted data.

3.1 Management of Geographic Datum

As one of the GIS system features is the management of information layers in different coordinate systems. The project enforces the management and processing procedure of the coordinates in QGIS environment in order to ensure the download and management of available, namely future, multisource data as specifically as possible.

The management of geographic datum in QGIS environment is entrusted to an "*on-the-fly*" testing algorithm (OTF) which automatically manages the datum conversions and geographic projections among information layers in different coordinate systems adopting some specific libraries produced and distributed by OSGeo.

These libraries contain, for almost all the reference systems, global and local, the geodetic parameters such as projection, ellipsoid, false origins and scale factors, etc., useful for the automatic re-screening of the associated geographic data.

This enhances the user to use geographic information coherently to several reference systems.

However, the precision on which data are re-developed, and thus overlapped, depends on the source data accuracy, moving from rigorous transformations for the most widespread global systems to approximate transformations for some local systems.

Considering that the most common systems in Italy are the Gauss-Boaga and ETRF89/ETRF2000 projections/ETRF2000, several GIS software including QGIS use simplified algorithms based on 7-parameters-Helmert transformation, and provide approximate transformation values with several meters of error according to altimetry.

Therefore, a new library has been published by recalculating these parameters in order to improve the precision of transformations at a regional level. The application of recalculated parameters on a sample of transformed points has led to average deviations in position of about 30 cm on the converted points referring to the grids of the Military Geographical Institute.

3.2 Self-extraction of the Coastline

The processing results include the coastline mapping, the back-dune vegetation mapping, the detection of rocky coast movements as well as new landfills, new buildings and spills. They have been produced by applying innovative images segmentation techniques, multi-band change-detection and PSInSAR (Persistent Scattered Interferometric Synthetic Aperture Radar) typologies, having the significant advantage of cyclical production and/or update with the same acquisition frequency of satellite data.

Through self-consistent applicative tools, provided with proper graphical interface developed in IDL and integrated in SDSS, and appropriate change-detection techniques, it is possible to display and automatically extract the coastline from Sentinel-1 data. Moreover, the system is able to compare two acquisitions, also multi-sources, e.g. by highlighting and calculating the eroding areas and those progressively emerged on the beach as shown in Figs. 1 and 2. The plots report the multi-source coastlines relative to the acquisitions in 1947-1949-1998-2001-2005-2006-2008-2011-2012-2013 and 2015 referring to the 2015 orthophoto base.

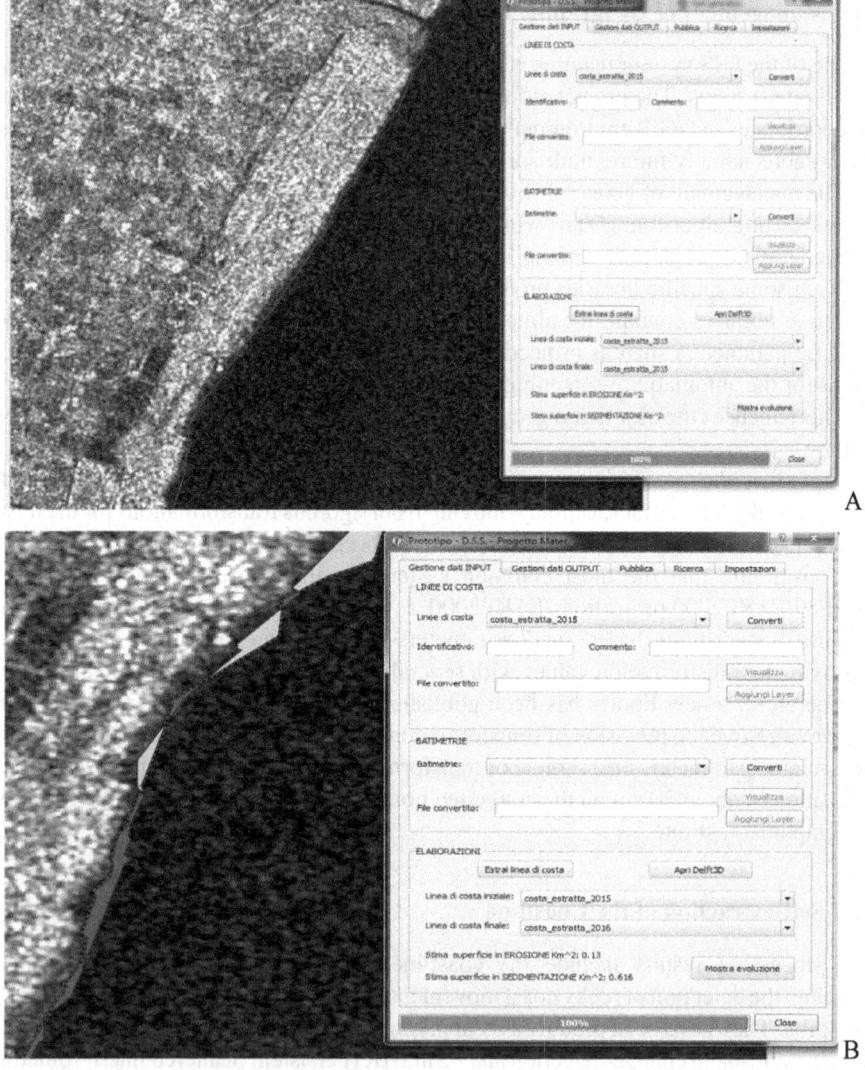

Fig. 1. Coastline extraction from Sentinel-1 data (A); Comparison between two available dataset (B).

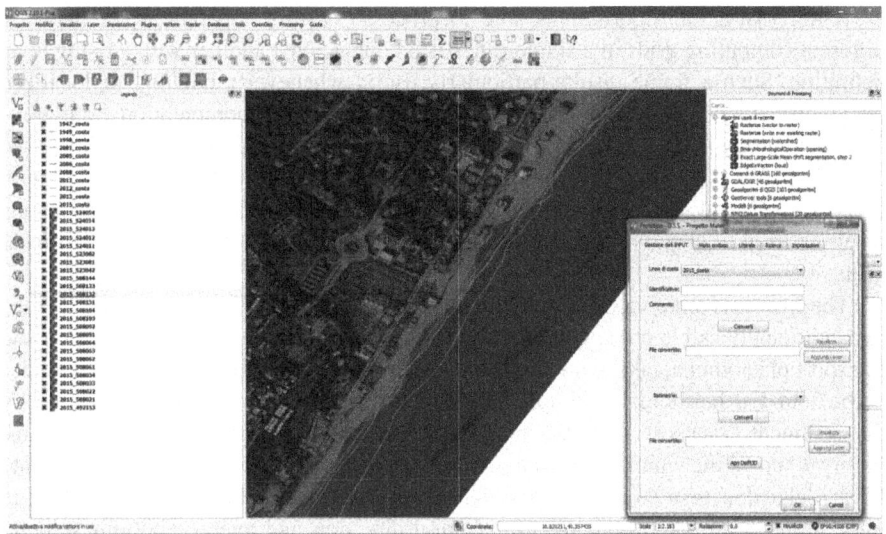

Fig. 2. Graphic comparison between two multi-source coastlines on orthophoto basis.

3.3 Morpho-Hydrodynamic and Water Bathing Quality Modelling

In order to reproduce possible alternative scenarios, to simulate the coastal system response at different natural and anthropic stresses, as well as to provide a valuable qualitative-quantitative support for decision-making, some tools able to make the SDSS interoperable by a morpho-hydrodynamic modelling software have been developed and implemented. For such a purpose, in the start-up phase, Delft3D (Deltares- NL) [20] was employed.

The Delft3D software (http://oss.deltares.nl/web/opendelft3d/home), produced and distributed by the Research Institute Deltares (NL), is available both in pre-compiled mode and open source, and is based on consolidated calculation algorithms resulting primarily from activities carried out by the Environmental Fluid Mechanics Section of the Faculty of Civil Engineering and Geosciences at Delft University of Technology (TUDelft-NL). The system is mainly composed of three modules grouping hydrodynamic simulation models, morphological and wave motion models as well as pre- and post-processing tools. The module relative to wave energy (Delft3d-WAVE) uses the SWAN (Simulating WAves Nearshore) [21] as a core processing code. This represents the state-of-the-art of so-called third-generation phase-averaged models, able to simulate, in steady or unsteady conditions the following issues:

- time-space propagation of wave motion
- shoaling and refraction for bathymetric variation and induced by currents
- wave generation, even considering the non-linear effects due to the overlapping of waves of different height and period
- energy dissipation due to the interaction between waves and seabed
- wave breaking and vegetation
- diffraction and reflection phenomena.

If necessary, the algorithm is able to process "*nesting*" operations, or may use different computing grids in a single run, nested one against another with a rising level definition. Such a frame results particularly useful whenever modelling of localized phenomena whenever detailed scales are required with a high computational outlay.

The hydrodynamic module, Delft3D-FLOW, is a multi-dimensional program based on Navier-Stokes equations for an incompressible fluid, under the Boussinesq assumptions for shallow water. It calculates steady or unsteady flows and transport phenomena, resulting from tidal and/or weather forcing, on a rectilinear and uniform or curvilinear grid.

The hydrodynamic module is able to simulate, with a highly accurate and defined unconditionally stable procedure, both in 2DH and 3D modes, even with diffusion and transport phenomena, taking into account the time variation of physical characteristics of the fluid. Furthermore, it is coupled to the transport module which allow us to identify the sediment transport induced by coastal currents, in time and space domains. Figure 3 shows the simulated effects in terms of bathymetric evolution of the Basento River delta due to a storm surge which event occurred in January 2015, while in Figs. 4 and 5 the average wave propagation direction and average bottom velocity distribution are reported respectively.

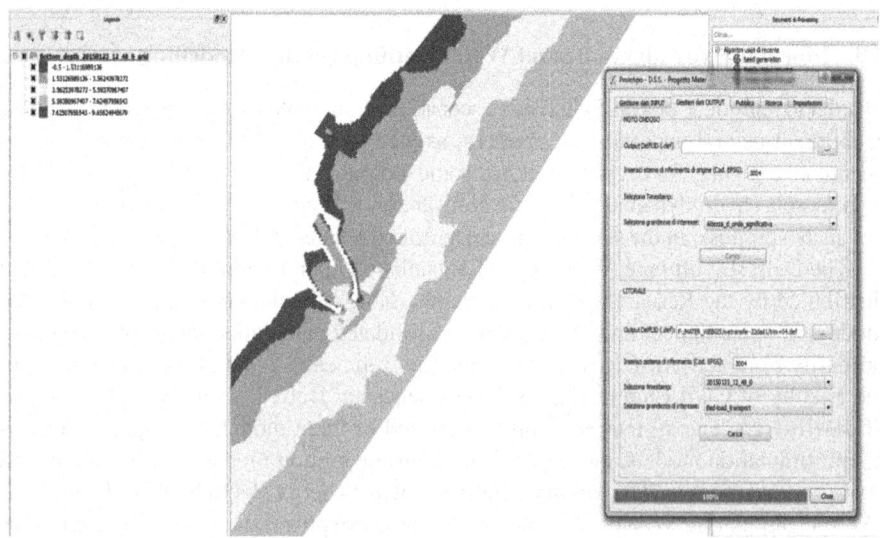

Fig. 3. Time representation of bathymetry.

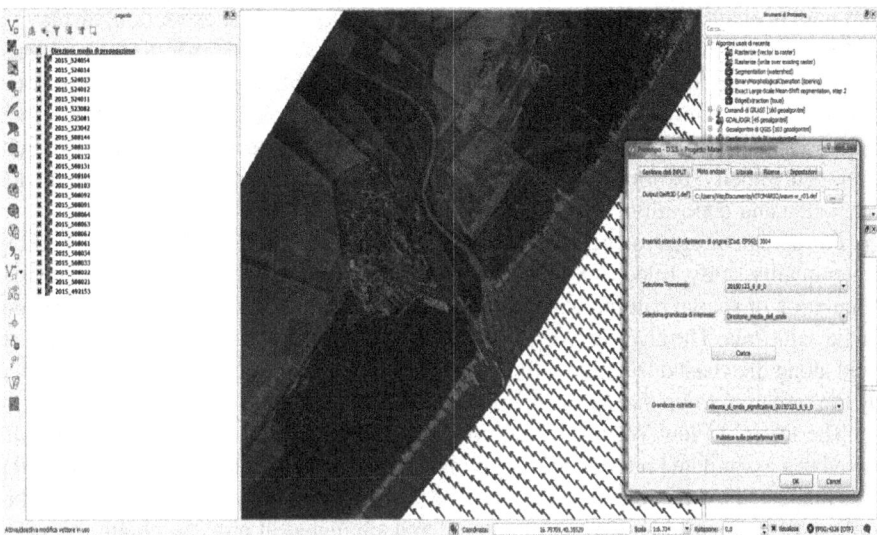

Fig. 4. Time representation of the average direction of wave propagation.

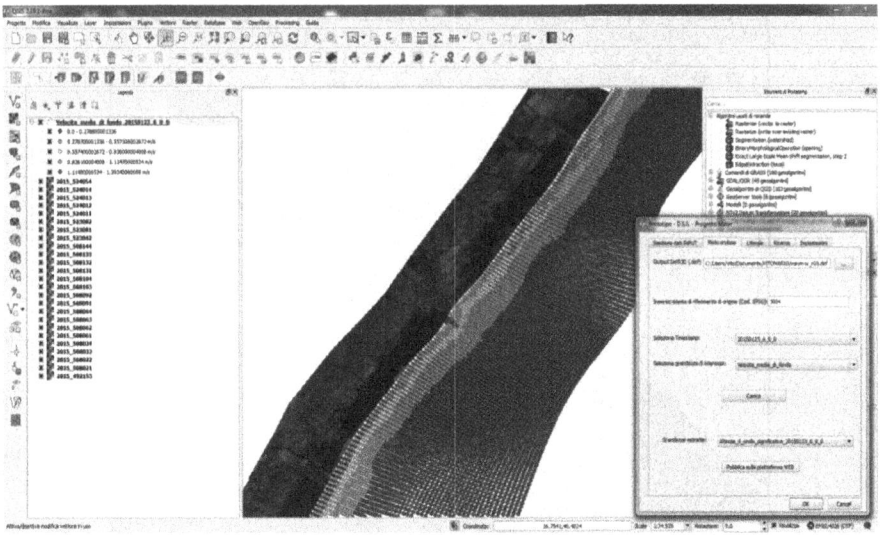

Fig. 5. Time representation of the average bottom velocity.

The main architecture of the implemented system switches on the SDSS to communicate with Delft3D code, both in terms of input for numerical computation and collecting the corresponding output for further analysis in QGIS environment. Indeed, the coastline can automatically be extracted and forwarded to pre- and post-processing data tools available in the Delft3D package. Although, the Delft3D code has a structured and complex output format which cannot be directly managed by QGIS, the developed and implemented set-up tool working in the SDSS allows us the extraction, displaying and multi-time management of the Delft3D output data. In reference to the sea wave propagation, the SDSS deals with significant wave height, significant period, average direction of wave motion and bottom velocity, as well as some data related to the coastal processes such as bottom sediment transport, suspended sediment transport, height averaged velocity, bottom shear stress and bathymetry variation in the time domain due to erosion and deposition.

Further, an integration between the Operative Project MATER and a coastal bathing water quality study, titled COMUNINMARE, has been proposed in terms of numerical simulation of spatial bathing water quality evolution due to the river discharge flowing in the delta area. The analyses have been carried on referring to the observed data measured along the coast during the ordinary water quality monitoring campaign performed by the research group during the bathing season 2017 (April–September 2017).

The Delft3d-Flow-Wave–D-Waq coupled model has been applied and the results have been assimilated into the SDSS giving detailed and suitable information about the area interested by the pollutant dynamics. More in details, both parameters Escherichia Coli and Enterococci have been monitored and simulated in order to obtain the space pollutant propagation in delta area. Figures 6 and 7 report the computation mesh and the space E.C. pollutant propagation in the area of delta Basento river.

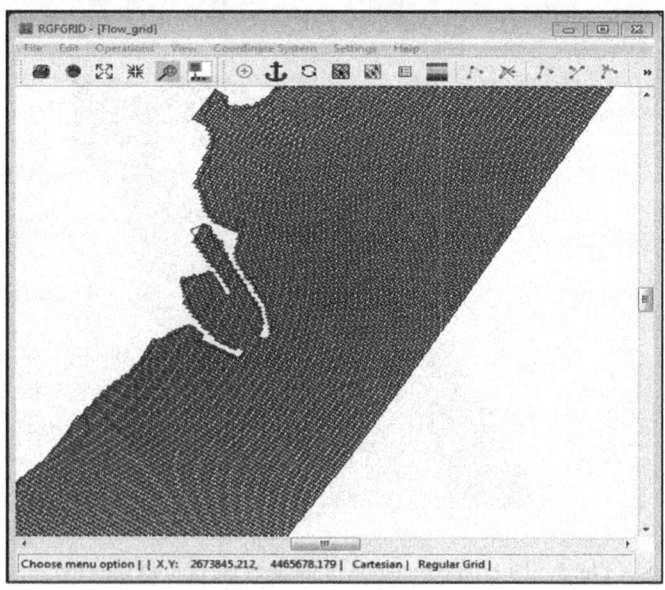

Fig. 6. Delft3D-flow computational mesh detail of Basento delta river

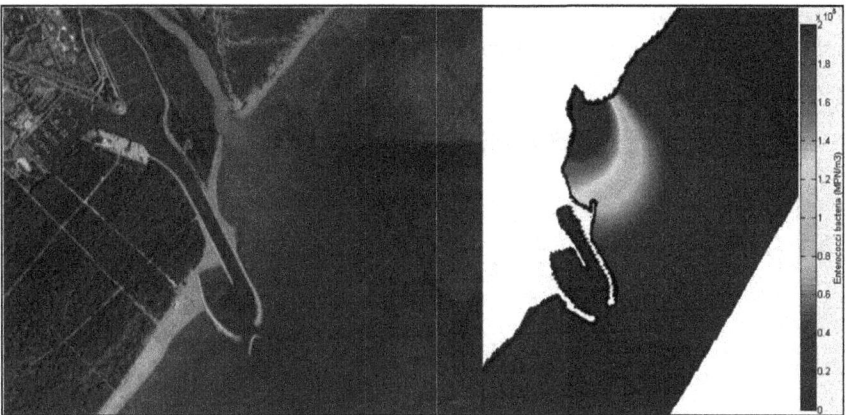

Fig. 7. Delft3d-Flow-Wave–D-Waq coupled modelling for Escherichia C. concentration space evolution in delta Basento river

3.4   WEB-GIS and Geo-Portal

The INSPIRE directive 2007/2/EC (INfrastructure for Spatial Information in Europe) aimed at harmonizing the organisation, accessibility and sharing methodologies of environmental spatial information among the EU Member States in order to support the EU environmental policies. Furthermore, according to such a directive, the information infrastructure might enable and ensure that spatial data obtained/collected from different sources should be supplied, stored and shared between users and applications. In such a context, the geo-portal represents the access point to the collection, management and distribution services of geo-referenced data for territorial analyses and/or down-streaming application domains. It does generally comprise a "Data Catalogue" for information download in local cockpit, providing a WebGIS tool with operational sections devoted to data publication, navigation and query. Such a WebGIS service is a geographic information system published online, which allows a mapping service of available data on the web. In such a way, it is indeed the extension into the net of specific applications designed and developed for digital cartography management. Thus, WebGIS leads the possibility of real-time interaction and the management of the access profile to the information at different levels (developer, simple user etc.). Furthermore, the access and consultation by the user is ensured even at low-level profiles without high technological upgrades.

The WebGIS-MATER platform, in such a scenario, is a Geoportal enabling publication, cataloguing, viewing and querying of information layers produced by the algorithms developed within the MATER operative project. In the framework of the INSPIRE directive, the platform should be used as SDSS and data-showing on interactive maps providing services for several integrated technologies (GeoServer for WMS/WFS/WFS-T/WCS, pycsw and CSW).

Figure 8 proposes the overlap between the DTM 2015 of the Cavone delta river area and the multi-source coastlines acquired in 1998-2005-2006-2008-2011-2012 supplying general and detailed information about the delta dynamics and beach evolution for further analyses: i.e. on delta migration velocity and local induced morphological changes.

Fig. 8. DTM e multi-source coastlines for the Cavone delta river.

Furthermore, due to the high acquisition frequency of Sentinel-1 images, it is possible to perform interesting comparative analysis of multi-source data related to the coastline relief as shown in Fig. 9. In such a figure the overlap between the Sentinel-1 image acquired on February 13th 2016 and the shorelines collected on August 29th 2015,

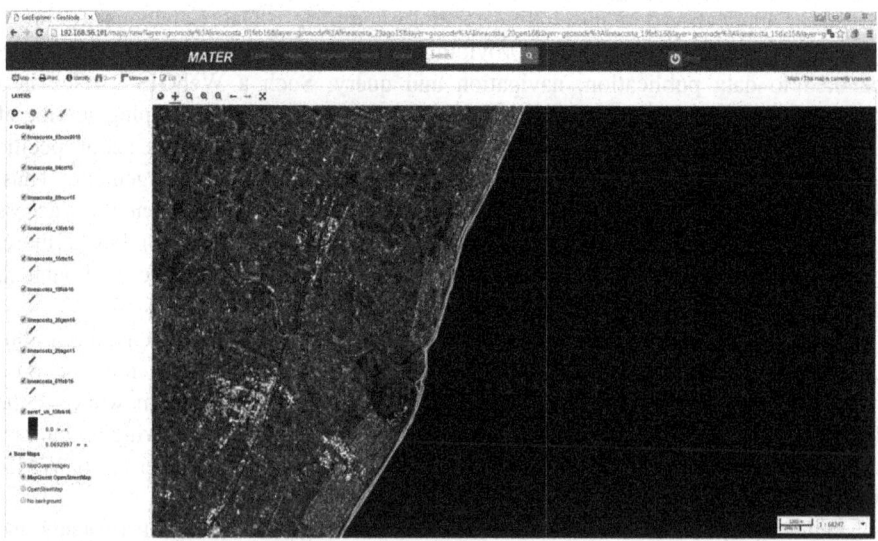

Fig. 9. Sentinel-1 data and multi-source coastlines around the Agri delta river.

October 4th 2015, March 11th 2015, November 3rd and 9th 2015, December 15th 2015, January 20th 2016, February 1st, 13th and 19th 2016 is reported.

Finally, the system also enables the viewing of maps produced by other organizations, even on their respective servers, via WMS (Web Map Service). In this way, the application is fully interoperable, ensuring both the publication of its own information layers, through OGC standards, and the integration and use of information layers derived from other sources with the same publishing standards defined by OGC as well.

4   Conclusions

The paper presents the preliminary results of the operative projects MATER and COMUINMARE, aimed at developing a methodology of environmental and territorial analysis for the exploitation of natural resources and supplying the first operational products for the definition and implementation of a Spatial Decision Support System for hydraulic-coastal risk forecast and prevention. The main issue deals with the integration and use of ground and remote earth observation data, with particular reference to the new satellite missions Sentinel-1 and 2 as well as COSMOSkyMed constellation data.

Among the operative products, the project provides the structuring and implementation of an expandable SDSS based on open-data catalogues, able to manage and display both the basic information, including the relative metadata, and post-processing results with open-source change-detecting codes and hydro-morphological modelling. The SDSS includes the development of integrative methodologies for systematic and continuous coastal monitoring, interfaced in an open source WebGIS environment dialoguing with the Regional Spatial Data Infrastructure in compliance with INSPIRE Directive. The SDSS also supplies the integration of ground and remotely sensed data with open-source information technologies, for the basic and advanced analyses, and web publishing of geographic data for a simple and intuitive end-user consultation.

References

1. Greco, M., Mauro, A., Mirauda, D., Sole, A., Vita, M.: Integrated monitoring system of littoral and fluvial sediment transport in Basilicata. In: Brebbia, C.A., Saval Perez, J.M., Garcia Andion, L. (eds.) Costal Environment V, incorporating Oil Spill Studies. Environmental Studies Series Fifth International Conference on Environmental Problems in Coastal Regions 2004, vol. 10, pp. 199–207. WIT Press, Alicante (2004). SSN 1462-6098, ISBN 1-85312-710-8
2. Carone, M.T., Greco, M., Molino, B.: A sediment-filter ecosystem for reservoir rehabilitation. Ecol. Eng. **26**(2), 182–189 (2006). https://doi.org/10.1016/j.ecoleng.2005.09.002. ISSN 09258574
3. Greco, M., Martino, G.: Assessment of maritime erosion index for Ionian-Lucanian coast. In: Lollino, G., Manconi, A., Locat, J., Huang, Yu., Canals Artigas, M. (eds.) Engineering Geology for Society and Territory - Volume 4, pp. 41–44. Springer, Cham (2014). https://doi.org/10.1007/978-3-319-08660-6_8. ISBN 978-3-319-08659-0, ISBN 978-3-319-08660-6

4. Greco, M., Martino, G.: Modelling of coastal infrastructure and delta river interaction on ionic Lucanian littoral. Proc. Eng. **70**, 763–772 (2014). https://doi.org/10.1016/j.proeng. 2014.02.083. ISSN 1877-7058, WOS 000341500600083 EID 2-s2.0-84899675420

5. Greco, M., Martino, G.: Vulnerability assessment or preliminary flood risk mapping and management in coastal areas. Nat. Hazards **82**(1), 7–26 (2016). https://doi.org/10.1007/s11069-016-2293-1. ISSN 0921-030X, EID 2-s2.0-84961839721

6. Greco, M., Martino, G., Guariglia, A., Trivigno, L.I., Sansanelli, V., Losurdo, A.: Development of an integrated SDSS for coastal risks monitoring and assessment. J. Coast. Zone Manage. **20**, 446 (2017). https://doi.org/10.4172/2473-3350.1000446

7. Hajduch, G., Bourbigot, M., Johnsen, H., Piantanida, R., Poullaouec, J.: Sentinel-1 Product Specification. S1-RS-MDA-52-7441 (2015)

8. European Spatial Agency (ESA): Sentinel-1 User Handbook, Sentinel-1 Team GMES-S10P-EOPG-TN-13-0001 (2013)

9. Losurdo, A., Marzo, C., Guariglia, A.: New change detection technique applied to COSMO-SkyMed stripmap himage data. In: Proceeding of "Fringe 2015 Workshop", Frascati, Italia, ESA SP-731, Marzo 2015 (2015)

10. Power, J.D.: Building web-based decision support systems. Stud. Inf. Control **11**(4), 291–302 (2002)

11. Paz, J.O., Batchelor, W.D., Pedersen, P.: WebGro: a web-based soybean management decision support system. Agron. J. **96**, 1771–1779 (2004). https://doi.org/10.2134/agronj2004.1771

12. Peng, Z.R., Tsou, M.H.: Internet GIS: Distributed Geographic Information Services for the Internet and Wireless Networks. Wiley, Hoboken (2003). s2.0-84958758546

13. Wang, L., Cheng, Q.: Web-based collaborative decision support services: concept, challenges and application. In: Proceedings of the ISPRS Vienna 2006 Symposium, Vienna, 12–14 July 2006

14. Miller, R., Guertin, D.P., Heilman, P.: An internet-based spatial decision support system for rangeland watershed management. In: Proceedings of the 1st Interagency Conference on Research in the Watersheds, Benson, pp. 725–730, 27–30 October 2003

15. Rinner, C.: Web-based spatial decision support: status and research directions. J. Geograph. Inf. Decis. Anal. **7**(1), 14–31 (2003)

16. Dymond, R.L., Regmi, B., Lohani, V.K., Dietz, R.: Interdisciplinary web-enabled spatial decision support system for watershed management. J. Water Resour. Plan. Manage. **130**(4), 290–300 (2004). https://doi.org/10.1061/(ASCE)0733-9496(2004)130:4(290)

17. Choi, J.B., Engel, A., Farnsworth, R.L.: Web-based GIS and spatial decision support system for watershed management. J. Hydroinf. **7**(3), 165–174 (2005)

18. Sugumaran, R., Meyer, J., Davis, J.: A web-based environmental decision support system (WEDSS) for environmental planning and watershed management. J. Geograph. Systems **6**, 1–16 (2004). https://doi.org/10.1007/s10109-004-0137-0

19. Zhang, Y., Sugumaran, R., McBroom, M., DeGroote, J., Kauten, R.L., Barten, P.K.: Web-based spatial decision support system and watershed management with a case study. Int. J. Geosci. **2**, 195–203 (2011). https://doi.org/10.4236/ijg.2011.23021

20. Deltares: Delft3D-FLOW User Manual. Deltares ver. 3.15.30932 (2013)

21. Booij, N., Ris, R.C., Holthuijsen, L.H.: A third-generation wave model for coastal regions, part I, model description and validation. J. Geophys. Res. **104**(C4), 7649–7666 (1999)

A Review of Residential Water Consumption Determinants

Nguyen Bich-Ngoc[(⊠)] and Jacques Teller

LEMA, Urban and Environmental Engineering Department, University of Liège,
4000 Liège, Belgium
{BichNgoc.Nguyen, Jacques.Teller}@uliege.be

Abstract. Water supply sectors are facing higher uncertainty in both resource availability and consumer demand. Future conservation programs require a full understanding of underlying factors of residential water consumption. However, previous studies have only considered one or several groups of factors without putting them all together in a bigger picture. This study was developed to provide a comprehensive view on these determinants and their relationships, as well as to discuss current gaps and possible directions. Determinants are categorized into six groups: (1) Economic; (2) Socio-demographic; (3) Physical properties; (4) Technological; (5) Climatic; and (6) Spatial drivers. All these determinants produce a very complex picture with many possible interrelationships. This nature, in one hand, poses challenges in selecting suitable technique to avoid autocorrelation, but on the other hand, provides chances to substitute unavailable important data with proxy variables. We have emphasized the lack of regional and cultural diversity in current studies, as most of them were carried out in developed and arid areas. Hence, a wider range of country specific and local-based studies is needed to better reflect the determinants and their relationships in diverse contexts. In future studies, a broader assessment scope taking into account effects such as feedback loop, spillover, and rebound should also be considered. In addition, these studies must deal with modern issues such as balancing between smart monitoring device utilization and consumer privacy.

Keywords: Residential water consumption · Determinant · Review
End-use · Smart meter

1 Introduction

Water supply sectors are facing higher uncertainty in both resource availability and consumer demand. Climate change patterns including higher temperatures and alterations in precipitation patterns are likely to impact the inflow to drinking water reservoirs and to cause higher uncertainty in water availability [1]. On the other hand, both increase and decrease in water demand, especially in urban area, have been observed around the world [2–5]. Ongoing population growth, urbanization, and higher living standards are among the common identified drivers behind the upsurge in water consumption [2, 6, 7], while technology development and mandatory water restrictions are considered the reasons behind the reduction in water use [4]. These uncertain

© Springer International Publishing AG, part of Springer Nature 2018
O. Gervasi et al. (Eds.): ICCSA 2018, LNCS 10964, pp. 685–696, 2018.
https://doi.org/10.1007/978-3-319-95174-4_52

fluctuations in water demand create difficulties for many cities around the world to provide a safe, steady, and affordable drinking water supply [1]. Hence, a full understanding of underlying factors of residential water consumption is vital for the development of a more sustainable water management system.

Determinants of household water consumption have been studied since the late 1960s at different aggregation levels (city, municipal, census tract, household) [8]. At the beginning, price and other socio-economic factors were the dominant focus [8–12]. Besides, physical characteristics of properties such as lot size, size of outdoor space, housing typology, *etc.* were also often found in water demand modelling literature [13–15]. Technological development including (1) implementation of high water efficiency fixtures and appliance [16–19], (2) providing real-time feedback using smart technology [20] is constantly gaining the interest of water conservation researchers. Climatic effect is also an important factor in water demand modelling, especially when significant amount of water was used externally [21–23]. Not until the beginning of 21st century, spatial dimension started to be considered in water demand literature [6, 8, 15].

Even though there have been many publications on determinants of water consumption. Previous studies have only considered one or several groups of factors without putting them all together in a bigger picture. This study was developed to provide a comprehensive view on determinants of residential water consumption and their interrelationships. We also discuss the gaps in current literature and possible directions for future researches.

2 Economic Determinants

Price was one of the first and most studied factors in the water demand management literature [7, 9–12, 24]. Interest in pricing and other economic instruments was backed up by the logic that higher water prices lead to lower consumption. However, that is only true if water behaves as a normal economic goods. Savenije argued that since most water uses are essential and irreplaceable, market theory could not be simply applied for water demand management [25]. Empirical evidence has generally supported that residential water demand is relatively price-inelastic, *i.e.* large increase in water price generally leads to small or no change in water consumption [10, 11]. However, when zooming in, the price elasticity of water demand varies among different end-uses. Whilst price mechanisms would not make great differences in essential uses, it can significantly affect water-related leisure activities such as gardening or filling swimming pools [7, 26]. Using water consumption data from Seville (Spain) as a case study, Martínez-Espiñeira and Nauges discussed the existence of water demand threshold which is the essential amount of water for basic need. When the threshold is approached, increment in price would barely affect demand [27]. Additionally, the impact of price on water consumption also differs among socio-demographic groups. Inman and Jeffrey hypothesized that water use in low income families was just for basic need and could not be reduced even with higher water price [17]. On the other hand, other studies suggested very little or no effect of price on well-off individuals [26] since price signal is not strong enough to curb their consumption [7]. Renwick and Green also observed that water consumption is more responsive to price change during summertime [28]. These understandings are critical for setting price schemes which can target savings in high consumption group whilst not posing the conservation burden on indispensable uses.

Different water pricing structures were also proven to influence domestic water consumption [9, 12, 29–31]. There has been evidence for effect of increasing block tariffs (IBT) on water demand control [17, 31]. Though IBT is gaining popularity worldwide [32], there are several drawbacks of this pricing scheme. Firstly, it increases revenue instability which in turn leads to affordability problems for the utility companies [26]. A fixed fee independent of the water consumed was suggested to overcome this problem [7, 33]. Secondly, IBT might also fail to promote social equity. Since households with more members are expected to consume more water, they will more likely to be charged higher prices. Moreover, such households often include more vulnerable members such as children and the elderly [34]. In 2003, Liu et al. proposed an increasing block price scheme based on per capita consumption instead of per connection. This scheme is proven to meet both equity and efficiency [30]. Martins et al. demonstrated that, by introducing social subsidies, the burden of water conservation can be alleviated from large family [34].

3   Socio-Demographic Determinants

Beside price, other socio-demographic determinants often included in literature are household size [11, 16, 35, 36], income [37–39], age structure [11, 16, 39, 40], education, and immigration [11, 41, 42].

Whilst studies using aggregate data have generally included average household size as independent variable for water consumption estimation [15, 36], household-based studies often considered the number of adults, number of teenagers, and/or number of children in their analyses [16, 30, 43]. Bigger households tend to consume more water in total but less per person [18]. This "economies of scale" effect tends to vanish if the household size is too small [44]. Nevertheless, the Western world has been undergoing a demographic transition [7] with the downsizing of household size and the growth of one-person household [45]. This common phenomenon occurring throughout urban regions of the developed world intensifies the effect of "inefficient" water use in small household [7, 45].

The positive effect of income on water use was widely accepted and empirically demonstrated [7, 37, 38]. Families with higher income tend to have higher total water consumption [39] as well as water consumption per capita [7]. However, Willis et al. observed that the water demand is not significantly different between high- and middle-income groups. Low income group shows similar indoor water consumption but much less external water use [18].

Though previous studies showed consistent results of income and household size effects on water consumption, there has been no agreement on how age structure influences water use. Using data from South East Queensland (Australia), Bennett et al. concluded that children generally use less water than adults [16]. Using the same dataset, Beal et al. also noticed that pensioners tend to use more water than average [40]. Willis et al. argued that retired people tend to spend a relatively great proportion of their time at home, hence, consume more water [46]. Residential water demand data from Aurora, Colorado (US) during a turbulent drought period (2000–2005) also supports a positive correlation between average age and water consumption [39]. On the other hand, Nauges and Reynaud using water expenditure data from Grironde (France) suggested the negative effect of age on water consumption. They argued that older people show more saving attitude and generally use less water [11]. It should be noted that different ways of age classification and/or statistical models might lead to dissimilar conclusions. However, since both Nauges and Reynaud's and Beal et al. researches made comparison between average water consumption in pensioner group and the global average water consumption, it should be safe to assume that contradictory results were more likely caused by the cultural differences. Whilst data in Nauges and Reynaud's study (2001) was collected during the early 1990s in France, later studies used data from the beginning of 21st century in the US and Australia.

Even though education level was included in several water consumption studies [8, 16, 47], others decided to exclude it due to its high correlation with income [48]. Positive influence of education on environmental awareness in general and water conservation attitude in particular was confirmed by Gilg and Barr [49]. Still, other studies observed the gap between people intention and their actual conservation behavior [50]. In fact, House-Peters et al. noticed that household with higher percentage of well-educated residents in Hillsboro, Oregon (US) had higher water consumption [41]. Similarly, Makki et al. found that household group with higher educational level consumed more shower water per person than group with lower educational level [43]. Other studies suggested insignificant effect of education on different water end-uses [16].

Other socio-demographic variables such as immigration and religion were not often considered by American and Australian scholars. Using water consumption data in UK, Smith and Ali made a connection between water use patterns and districts' ethnically and religiously characteristics. The authors argued that since patterns are so tightly related to religious practices, it is expected that religion is also an important factor in water volumes estimation [42]. Nauges and Reynaud reasoned that immigrants from developing countries often face with water scarcity, hence, they may present more prudent attitudes towards the use of water [11].

4 Physical Property Determinants

House typology was proven to be significantly connected with water use both indoor and outdoor [13–15]. Fox et al. classified properties based on number of bedrooms, house type (e.g. flat, terrace, cluster home, or detached), and the presence of garden. Higher water consumption was observed for properties with more bedrooms. However, the authors also noted that the linear relation between property size and number of occupants could not be assumed. This could explain the higher variation in water use of properties with five bedrooms and more [14].

Beside size, house age was also included in several studies as an independent variable. Harlan et al. expected that newer homes in Phoenix (U.S) would consume less water since they were required by law to install high water efficiency fixture. However, only small to non-significant effect was found. It could be explained by the fact that new houses are often bigger and have more bathrooms. Percentage of homes with three or more bathrooms in the US has increased from nearly 0 to 24% between 1997 and 2004 [51]. House-Peters *et al.* also linked higher water consumption in Hillsboro (U.S) households with newer, larger, and higher value properties [41].

External water use is usually related to leisure activities; thus, it is more susceptible to seasonal and price effects [7]. Presence of swimming pool was identified as the strongest determinant of external use. Families with swimming pool, on average, use twice as much water outdoors as homes without swimming pools [15]. Proportion of properties with swimming pool is positively correlated with average lot size and negatively correlated with urban density [36]. On the other hand, garden irrigation has also been seen as a major component of external water consumption [14]. Beside the size of outdoor space, lifestyle and household attitude toward gardening are significant determinants for outdoor water use [13]. Interestingly, Syme *et al.* observed that ownership of sophisticated lawn reticulation system does not lead to lower water consumption [13].

Further than being powerful predictors for water demand on their own, characteristics of physical properties can also serve as proxy variables to study the relationship between socio-demographic factors with water demand due to their high correlation. For example, Seyranian *et al.* included house size (square feet) and the number of bedrooms as rough proxies for the number of residents in their study [52]. Size, age, and values of properties could also be used as indicators for family income [44].

5 Technological Determinants

Applying technology in water conservation has been received much research attention in recent years [19]. Several studies were carried out to assess the effect of water efficient devices on water consumption behavior and water saving [18, 24]. Recently, technology advancement was also used to give people real-time feedback on the volume and end uses of consumed water [20, 32]. This application is expected to raise people awareness and through that inspire water conservation behavior [20].

High efficiency fixtures and appliances have been advocated as a low cost solution for sustainable water management [18]. The majority of previous studies suggested that retrofitting high indoor efficiency fixtures could result in a relative savings between 9–12% [17], whilst comprehensive replacement of household appliance with high water efficiency appliances could reduce indoor water consumption by 35 to 50% [17]. Reducing water demand also induces positive effect on the whole life cycle cost of drinking water treatment and distribution, and ultimately reduce the ecological footprint of the city or region [18]. Despite the positive results from other studies, Campbell *et al.* raised concern about offsetting behavior. Their study showed that giving people water saving devices caused very small decreases or fairly large increases in water consumption [24]. Their example of offsetting behavior is when people know that their showerhead is low-flow, they tend to feel free to take longer shower.

Another application of new technology in water conservation is real-time feedback using smart meter, data logger, and in-home display [20, 32, 53]. Despite the fact that smart meter implementation in water sector is still in its infancy, some positive results were delivered by several studies in Australia. Britton *et al.* used smart meter as a mean to detect possible post meter leakage [53]. The obtained information was then delivered to targeted household with different communication strategies. Most of the household then fixed the leak which led to 89% reduction of hourly water loss [53]. Instead of leakage, Willis *et al.* chose to target shower end-use. The research group provided 151 families in the Gold Coast (Australia) with alarming visual display monitors which were set to alarm after 40L of consumed water. The results revealed reductions in both shower duration as well as volume of water used. Also, some participants chose to reduce the flowrate to have longer shower whilst still saving water [20].

On the contrary, a study was conducted in Aurora, Colorado (US) showed that group with water smart reader consumed more water than the control group [32]. It should be noted that an increase block rate system was employed. Hence, when people were aware of their real-time consumption, they tried to stay in their targeted block to save money but not to save water in general [32].

6 Climatic Determinants

The proportion of external water use varies from place to place and can be up to 60% of total household water consumption during summer time [41]. Whilst indoor use is rather independent of climate, external use is affected by prevailing weather conditions such as temperature, evaporation, and rainfall [13, 22]. Most studies considered average household water consumption during winter months as the base use which generally is not affected by either temperature or rainfall [22, 41]. The occurrence of rainfall would cause an immediately drop in seasonal use or average water consumption during summer month followed by a gradual increase [23]. Gato *et al.*, using daily water use data in East Doncaster water supply distribution zone (Australia), confirmed a non-linear relationship between temperature and water use in the summer which was previously hypothesized in Maidment *et al.* study (1985) [22, 23]. The ratio of summer-to-winter water usage varies highly among locations. Balling *et al.* reported that the greatest sensitivity to season was found in census tracts with large lots, high occurrence of pools, a large proportion of non-native vegetation, and a high percentage of wealthy residents [21].

Currently, there is an imbalance in water demand literature regarding climatic effect. The majority of these studies were focused on arid and semi-arid climate [39, 41]. Using the case of Oregon (US), House-Peters *et al.* reasoned that outdoor use, which is sensitive to variation in climate, also significantly influence residential water consumption in maritime temperate climate [41].

7 Spatial Determinants

Knowing how people will settle across space is a key to understand the changes in the urban metabolism of water [38]. As said, geographical effect on water demand has not been studied until the early 2000s. Most of these studies have used aggregate data at municipal or census tract level [4, 6, 36].

Higher urban density reduces domestic water demand through smaller lot size and outdoor space is the common conclusion from literature [14, 36]. March and Saurí recognized that net population density, which is expressed as number of residentials per a unit of residential plot area (excluding collector road and commune space), is the most critical variable to explain water consumption [38]. Although high urban density displays a better water efficiency, Hummel and Lux noticed a trend of lower population density in urban core area due to urban sprawl [45, 54]. Domene and Saurí suggested several explanations for this trend including: comparatively cheaper housing in peri-urbanization area, increase the preferences of citizens to be 'closer to nature', and improvements in commuting networks [54].

Moreover, effects of socio-demographic and other factors on water consumption also display spatial variation. Households tend to use water at a level comparable to their neighbors, irrespective of their demographic and economic characteristics [4, 15]. Wentz and Gober used geographically-weighted regression to model water consumption of Phoenix, Arizona (US) at census tract level. Their model – including percent of home with pool, average lot size, percent of residential area of mesic landscaping, and average household size – showed varied explanatory power over water use across census tracts. Effects of the average household size and percent of home with pool on water use were proven to be spatial dependent. In other words, an increase in household size of one person increased water use by more than 100,000L in some tracts and less than 40,000L in others [15]. House-Peters et al. advocated the importance of identifying the most water sensitive census blocks and their physical as well as socioeconomic characteristics, as it determines effective targets for conservation efforts [41].

8 Discussion and Possible Topics for Further Researches

As noted by Corbella and Pujol, all these determinants produce a very complex picture with many possible interrelationships [7]. Effect of one variable is hardly independent from those of others. For example, income often positively correlates with age [16, 39]. Bennett et al. (2013) observed that with age, people move to higher income group and often have more children. However, it could be argued that in other cultural contexts, the correlation between income and number of children might be very different. Another example could be taken from Millock and Nauges' study in 2010. Their results suggested that socio-economic variables influence people's choices of adopting water efficiency equipment [48]. This intercorrelation nature of water demand drivers, in one hand, poses challenges for researchers in choosing suitable modeling technique as well as selecting factors to avoid autocorrelation. On the other hand, when important explanatory variables are not available, proxy variables might be considered to provide the needed information. For instance, building structure variables from tax assessor's record can be used as proxies for income and household size [6].

As discussed in Sect. 6, current knowledge about domestic water demand determinants is rather limited in developed countries, with Australia and the US as the two most studied countries [6, 18, 33, 41]. Several studies have been carried out in Germany [45], France [11], and Spain [36, 54]. With dramatic demographic growth in many urban areas, cities in developing countries are facing challenges to provide adequate services including clean water for their citizen [55]. There is a requirement for specific country and location based research [56] because of the differences in: (1) cultural, community norm, religious custom; (2) climate and environmental conditions; (3) technology advancement (at both individual and network levels); (4) water pricing structures and legislation, and (5) environmental education.

Traditional researches often considered the effects of explanatory factors on water consumption as one-way. In reality, it is more complicated with possibilities of feedback loop, spillover [45], as well as rebound effects [57]. An example of rebound effect which was discussed in Sect. 5 is when people rely completely on the saving effects of water efficiency fixtures, they tend to change their behaviors in the direction which causing more water consumption [17]. Another complexity of the water demand management is the balancing among environmental, economic, and social sustainability. Whilst the observed trend of lower consumption in the Meuse basin is positive for natural resource conservation [56], it reduced utility companies' revenue and threatened the companies' ability to maintain their infrastructures. Grafton and Ward also revealed the welfare losses of mandatory water restriction in Sydney (Australia) [58]. Hence, future studies should consider water demand determinants in a holistic approach with attention to feedback, spillover, and rebound effects.

Empirical results supported that effects of water use predictors change with different end-uses. Whilst household size is important to explain indoor water use, it has almost no effect on external water use [41]. Several studies agreed on the insignificant effect of educational level on total water consumption [16, 48]. When segregating water consumption for each end-use, education level is a significant determinant for shower/bath and dishwasher end-use categories [16, 59]. Willis *et al.* advocated the use of smart meter coupled with data logger for end-use analysis and real-time feedback provision [20]. Even though broadly installation of smart meter could provide researchers with valuable information, concern about individual's privacy has been raised in energy sector [60]. Further investigation should be carried out to find the balance between consumer privacy and legitimate application of smart meter in water management.

References

1. Kristvik, E., Muthanna, T.M., Alfredsen, K.: Assessment of future water availability under climate change, considering scenarios for population growth and ageing infrastructure. J. Water Clim. Chang. (2018). https://doi.org/10.2166/wcc.2018.096
2. Brears, R.C.: Urban Water Security. Wiley, Hoboken (2017)

3. Fan, L., Gai, L., Tong, Y., Li, R.: Urban water consumption and its influencing factors in China: evidence from 286 cities. J. Clean. Prod. **166**, 124–133 (2017). https://doi.org/10.1016/j.jclepro.2017.08.044

4. Franczyk, J., Chang, H.: Spatial analysis of water use in Oregon, USA, 1985-2005. Water Resour. Manag. **23**, 755–774 (2009). https://doi.org/10.1007/s11269-008-9298-9

5. Bartoszczuk, P.: Basics of water pricing and necessity to model municipal water pricing. In: Proceedings Environment Informatics Industrial Environmental Protection, Methods Tools (EnviroInfo 2009), Berlin, Germany, pp. 215–222 (2009)

6. Chang, H., Parandvash, G.H., Shandas, V.: Spatial variations of single-family residential water consumption in Portland, Oregon. Urban Geogr. **31**, 953–972 (2010). https://doi.org/10.2747/0272-3638.31.7.953

7. Corbella, H.M., Pujol, D.S.: What lies behind domestic water use? A review essay on the drivers of domestic water consumption. Boletín la A.G.E. **50**, 297–314 (2009)

8. House-Peters, L.A., Chang, H.: Urban water demand modeling: review of concepts, methods, and organizing principles. Water Resour. Res. **47**, (2011). https://doi.org/10.1029/2010wr009624

9. Howe, C.W., Linaweaver, F.P.: The impact of price on residential water demand and its relation to system design and price structure. Water Resour. Res. **3**, 13–32 (1967). https://doi.org/10.1029/WR003i001p00013

10. Espey, M., Espey, J., Shaw, W.D.D.: Price elasticity of residential demand for water: a meta-analysis. Water Resour. Res. **33**, 1369–1374 (1997). https://doi.org/10.1029/97WR00571

11. Nauges, C., Reynaud, A.: Estimation de la demande domestique d'eau potable en France. Rev. Économique **52**, 167 (2001). https://doi.org/10.3917/reco.521.0167

12. Arbués, F., Barberán, R., Villanúa, I.: Price impact on urban residential water demand: a dynamic panel data approach. Water Resour. Res. **40**, 1–9 (2004). https://doi.org/10.1029/2004WR003092

13. Syme, G.J., Shao, Q., Po, M., Campbell, E.: Predicting and understanding home garden water use. Landsc. Urban Plan. **68**, 121–128 (2004). https://doi.org/10.1016/j.landurbplan.2003.08.002

14. Fox, C., McIntosh, B.S., Jeffrey, P.: Classifying households for water demand forecasting using physical property characteristics. Land Policy **26**, 558–568 (2009). https://doi.org/10.1016/j.landusepol.2008.08.004

15. Wentz, E.A., Gober, P.: Determinants of small-area water consumption for the city of Phoenix, Arizona. Water Resour. Manag. **21**, 1849–1863 (2007). https://doi.org/10.1007/s11269-006-9133-0

16. Bennett, C., Stewart, R.A., Beal, C.D.: ANN-based residential water end-use demand forecasting model. Expert Syst. Appl. **40**, 1014–1023 (2013). https://doi.org/10.1016/j.eswa.2012.08.012

17. Inman, D., Jeffrey, P.: A review of residential water conservation tool performance and influences on implementation effectiveness. Urban Water J. **3**, 127–143 (2006). https://doi.org/10.1080/15730620600961288

18. Willis, R.M., Stewart, R.A., Giurco, D.P., Talebpour, M.R., Mousavinejad, A.: End use water consumption in households: impact of socio-demographic factors and efficient devices. J. Clean. Prod. **60**, 107–115 (2013). https://doi.org/10.1016/j.jclepro.2011.08.006

19. Carragher, B.J., Stewart, R.A., Beal, C.D.: Quantifying the influence of residential water appliance efficiency on average day diurnal demand patterns at an end use level: a precursor to optimised water service infrastructure planning. Resour. Conserv. Recycl. **62**, 81–90 (2012). https://doi.org/10.1016/j.resconrec.2012.02.008

20. Willis, R.M., Stewarta, R.A., Panuwatwanich, K., Jones, S., Kyriakides, A.: Alarming visual display monitors affecting shower end use water and energy conservation in Australian residential households. Resour. Conserv. Recycl. **54**, 1117–1127 (2010). https://doi.org/10. 1016/j.resconrec.2010.03.004

21. Balling Jr., R.C., Gober, P.: Climate variability and residential water use in the city of Phoenix, Arizona. J. Appl. Meteorol. Climatol. **46**, 1130–1137 (2007). https://doi.org/10. 1175/JAM2518.1

22. Gato, S., Jayasuriya, N., Roberts, P.: Temperature and rainfall thresholds for base use urban water demand modelling. J. Hydrol. **337**, 364–376 (2007). https://doi.org/10.1016/j.jhydrol. 2007.02.014

23. Maidment, D.R., Miaou, S.-P., Crawford, M.M.: Transfer function models of daily urban water use. Water Resour. Res. **21**, 425–432 (1985)

24. Campbell, H.E., Johnson, R.M., Larson, E.H.: Prices, devices, people, or rules: The relative effectiveness of policy instruments in water conservation. Rev. Policy Res. **21**, 637–662 (2004). https://doi.org/10.1111/j.1541-1338.2004.00099.x

25. Savenije, H.H.G.: Why water is not an ordinary economic good, or why the girl is special. Phys. Chem. Earth **27**, 741–744 (2002). https://doi.org/10.1016/S1474-7065(02)00060-8

26. Renwick, M.E., Archibald, S.O.: Demand side management policies for residential water use: who bears the conservation burden? Land Econ. **74**, 343–359 (1998). https://doi.org/10. 2307/3147117

27. Martínez-Espiñeira, R., Nauges, C.: Is all domestic water consumption sensitive to price control? Appl. Econ. **36**, 1697–1703 (2004). https://doi.org/10.1080/0003684042000218570

28. Renwick, M.E., Green, R.D.: Do residential water demand side management policies measure up? An analysis of eight California water agencies. J. Environ. Econ. Manag. **40**, 37–55 (2000). https://doi.org/10.1006/jeem.1999.1102

29. Olmstead, S.M., Michael Hanemann, W., Stavins, R.N.: Water demand under alternative price structures. J. Environ. Econ. Manag. **54**, 181–198 (2007). https://doi.org/10.1016/j. jeem.2007.03.002

30. Liu, J., Savenije, H.H.G., Xu, J.: Water as an economic good and water tariff design: comparison between IBT-con and IRT-cap. Phys. Chem. Earth **28**, 209–217 (2003). https:// doi.org/10.1016/S1474-7065(03)00027-5

31. Olmstead, S.M., Hanemann, W.M., Stavins, R.N.: Does price structure matter? Household water demand under increasing-block and uniform prices (2003)

32. Strong, A., Goemans, C.: The impact of real-time quantity information on residential water demand. Water Resour. Econ. **10**, 1–13 (2015). https://doi.org/10.1016/j.wre.2015.02.002

33. Hoffmann, M., Worthington, A., Higgs, H.: Urban water demand with fixed volumetric charging in a large municipality: the case of Brisbane, Australia. Aust. J. Agric. Resour. Econ. **50**, 347–359 (2006). https://doi.org/10.1111/j.1467-8489.2006.00339.x

34. Martins, R., Cruz, L., Barata, E.: Water price regulation: a review of Portuguese tariff recommendations. Public Organ. Rev. **13**, 197–205 (2013). https://doi.org/10.1007/s11115-013-0230-2

35. Gregory, G.D., Leo, M.D.: Repeated behavior and environmental psychology: the role of personal involvement and habit formation in explaining water consumption. J. Appl. Soc. Psychol. **33**, 1261–1296 (2003). https://doi.org/10.1111/j.1559-1816.2003.tb01949.x

36. Villar-Navascués, R.A., Pérez-Morales, A.: Factors affecting domestic water consumption on the Spanish Mediterranean coastline. Prof. Geogr. **0124**, 1–13 (2018). https://doi.org/10. 1080/00330124.2017.1416302

37. Dalhuisen, J.M., Florax, R.J.G.M., de Groot, H.L.F., Nijkamp, P.: Price and income elasticities of residential water demand: why empirical estimates differ. Land Econ. **79**, 292–308 (2001). https://doi.org/10.2307/3146872

38. March, H., Saurí, D.: The suburbanization of water scarcity in the Barcelona metropolitan region: sociodemographic and urban changes influencing domestic water consumption. Prof. Geogr. **62**, 32–45 (2010). https://doi.org/10.1080/00330120903375860
39. Kenney, D.S., Goemans, C., Klein, R., Lowrey, J., Reidy, K.: Residential water demand management: lessons from Aurora, Colorado. J. Am. Water Resour. Assoc. **44**, 192–207 (2008). https://doi.org/10.1111/j.1752-1688.2007.00147.x
40. Beal, C.D., Stewart, R.A., Huang, T., Rey, E.: SEQ residential end use study. Smart Water Syst. Metering 80–84 (2011). https://doi.org/10.1111/jawr.12036
41. House-Peters, L., Pratt, B., Chang, H.: Effects of urban spatial structure, sociodemographics, and climate on residential water consumption in Hillsboro, Oregon. J. Am. Water Resour. Assoc. **46**, 461–472 (2010). https://doi.org/10.1111/j.1752-1688.2009.00415.x
42. Smith, A., Ali, M.: Understanding the impact of cultural and religious water use. Water Environ. J. **20**, 203–209 (2006). https://doi.org/10.1111/j.1747-6593.2006.00037.x
43. Makki, A.A., Stewart, R.A., Panuwatwanich, K., Beal, C.: Revealing the determinants of shower water end use consumption: enabling better targeted urban water conservation strategies. J. Clean. Prod. **60**, 129–146 (2013). https://doi.org/10.1016/j.jclepro.2011.08.007
44. Arbués, F., García-Valiñas, M.Á., Martínez-Espiñeira, R.: Estimation of residential water demand: a state-of-the-art review. J. Soc. Econ. **32**, 81–102 (2003). https://doi.org/10.1016/S1053-5357(03)00005-2
45. Hummel, D., Lux, A.: Population decline and infrastructure: the case of the German water supply system. Vienna Yearb. Popul. Res. 167–191 (2007). https://doi.org/10.1553/populationyearbook2007s167
46. Willis, R.M., Stewart, R.A., Panuwatwanich, K., Capati, B., Giurco, D.: Gold coast domestic water end use study. Water J. Aust. Water Assoc. **36**, 79–85 (2009)
47. Arbués, F., Villanúa, I.: Potential for pricing policies in water resource management: estimation of urban residential water demand in Zaragoza, Spain. Urban Stud. **43**, 2421–2442 (2006)
48. Millock, K., Nauges, C.: Household adoption of water-efficient equipment: the role of socio-economic factors, environmental attitudes and policy. Environ. Resour. Econ. **46**, 539–565 (2010). https://doi.org/10.1007/s10640-010-9360-y
49. Gilg, A., Barr, S.: Behavioural attitudes towards water saving? Evidence from a study of environmental actions. Ecol. Econ. **57**, 400–414 (2006). https://doi.org/10.1016/j.ecolecon.2005.04.010
50. Vermeir, I., Verbeke, W.: Sustainable food consumption: exploring the consumer "attitude - behavioral intention" gap. J. Agric. Environ. Ethics **19**, 169–194 (2006). https://doi.org/10.1007/s10806-005-5485-3
51. Harlan, S.L., Yabiku, S.T., Larsen, L., Brazel, A.J.: Household water consumption in an arid city: affluence, affordance, and attitudes. Soc. Nat. Resour. **22**, 691–709 (2009). https://doi.org/10.1080/08941920802064679
52. Seyranian, V., Sinatra, G.M., Polikoff, M.S.: Comparing communication strategies for reducing residential water consumption. J. Environ. Psychol. **41**, 81–90 (2015). https://doi.org/10.1016/j.jenvp.2014.11.009
53. Britton, T.C., Stewart, R.A., O'Halloran, K.R.: Smart metering: enabler for rapid and effective post meter leakage identification and water loss management. J. Clean. Prod. **54**, 166–176 (2013). https://doi.org/10.1016/j.jclepro.2013.05.018
54. Domene, E., Saurı, D.: Urbanisation and water consumption: influencing factors in the metropolitan region of Barcelona urbanisation and water consumption: influencing factors in the metropolitan region of Barcelona. Urban Stud. **43**, 1605–1623 (2006). https://doi.org/10.1080/00420980600749969

55. Cohen, B.: Urbanization in developing countries: current trends, future projections, and key challenges for sustainability. Technol. Soc. **28**, 63–80 (2006). https://doi.org/10.1016/j.techsoc.2005.10.005

56. Westhoff, M., Dewals, B., Archambeau, P., Dewals, B., Erpicum, S., Pirotton, M.: Towards enhanced estimates of future drinking water demand in the Meuse basin (2015)

57. Cominola, A., Giuliani, M., Castelletti, A., Rosenberg, D.E., Abdallah, A.M.: Implications of data sampling resolution on water use simulation, end-use disaggregation, and demand management. Environ. Model Softw. **102**, 199–212 (2018). https://doi.org/10.1016/j.envsoft.2017.11.022

58. Grafton, Q., Chu, L., Kompas, T., Ward, M.: Understanding and Managing Urban Water in Transition 15. Springer, Heidelberg (2015). https://doi.org/10.1007/978-94-017-9801-3

59. Makki, A.A., Stewart, R.A., Beal, C.D., Panuwatwanich, K.: Novel bottom-up urban water demand forecasting model: revealing the determinants, drivers and predictors of residential indoor end-use consumption. Resour. Conserv. Recycl. **95**, 15–37 (2015). https://doi.org/10.1016/j.resconrec.2014.11.009

60. McKenna, E., Richardson, I., Thomson, M.: Smart meter data: balancing consumer privacy concerns with legitimate applications. Energy Policy **41**, 807–814 (2012). https://doi.org/10.1016/j.enpol.2011.11.049

Carbon Stock as an Indicator for the Estimation of Anthropic Pressure on Territorial Components

Arianna Mazzariello[1], Angela Pilogallo[1], Francesco Scorza[1(✉)] (iD),
Beniamino Murgante[1,2] (iD), and Giuseppe Las Casas[1] (iD)

[1] School of Engineering, Laboratory of Urban and Regional Systems
Engineering, University of Basilicata, 10, Viale dell'Ateneo Lucano,
85100 Potenza, Italy
{arianna.mazzariello,angela.pilogallo,
francesco.scorza,beniamino.murgante,
giuseppe.lascasas}@unibas.it
[2] Environmental Observatory Foundation of Basilicata Region (FARBAS),
Corso Vittorio Emanuele II n. 3, 85052 Marsico Nuovo, PZ, Italy

Abstract. Since the beginning of the industrial era, humans have been modifying the chemical composition and physical properties of the atmosphere, favoring an increase in the concentration of gases such as carbon dioxide (CO_2), methane (CH_4) and nitrogen oxide (N_2O) well beyond the limits never previously exceeded [1]. If there is still uncertainty in the world and in some cases scepticism about the real extent of environmental or climate change, the increase in the concentration of these gases shows that humans are actually changing, heavily, the environment [2]. Growing disquiet of the scientific community about phenomena linked to climate modification and land use changes, to which they are often due or at least related, has led to the need to strengthen the levels of information and develop methodologies capable of constituting an adequate framework to support policies for territorial planning and land transformation that can boast a holistic view of services and functions that are indispensable and/or desirable for human wellbeing. It is precisely in this context that this work is aimed at providing an estimate of the amount of carbon stored within the boundaries of the Basilicata region, no longer referring to it as an estimated quantity for its own sake, but as an assessment of a service provided by ecosystems for the regulation of the global climate that has gained increasing strength over the last 50 years [3].

Keywords: Carbon storage · Ecosystem services · Regional planning
Sustainable development

1 Introduction

Reducing greenhouse gas (GHG) emissions is one of the core components of all the actions related to avoiding, adapting or coping with climate change [4]. Limiting global warming to any level means that the total amount of carbon dioxide (CO_2) in the

© Springer International Publishing AG, part of Springer Nature 2018
O. Gervasi et al. (Eds.): ICCSA 2018, LNCS 10964, pp. 697–711, 2018.
https://doi.org/10.1007/978-3-319-95174-4_53

atmosphere must be limited and this objective can be pursued through two main "decarbonisation" strategies:

1. the gradual elimination of CO_2 generation, for example by abandoning fossil fuels in favour of low-carbon energy sources or by increasing transport sector efficiency;
2. upscaling CO_2 sequestration and preserving all the areas in which it is currently stored to a significant extent.

The second option in the past has not been applied nearly at all [4]. Therefore, although it has not contributed to past experience, it can be seen as an important opportunity in the current scenario (Fig. 1).

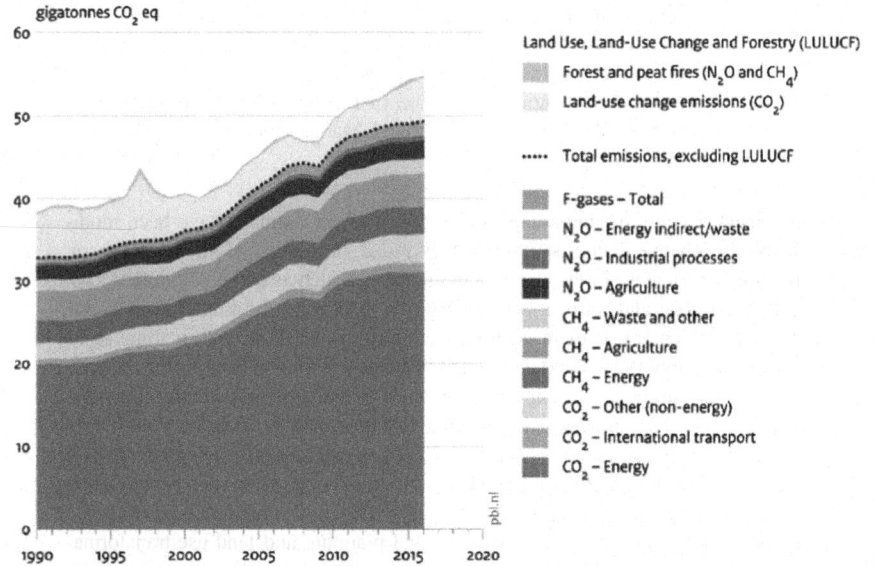

Fig. 1. Global greenhouse gas emissions, per type of gas and source, including LULUCF (Source: EDGAR v4.3.2 (EC-JRC/PBL 2017))

In order for the planner to be able to support this complex and articulated process, it is necessary to make available adequate data and models.

A globally integrated carbon observation and analysis system is indeed needed to improve the fundamental understanding of the global carbon cycle, to improve our ability to project future changes, and to verify the effectiveness of policies aiming to reduce greenhouse gas emissions and increase carbon sequestration [5].

Only in the light of a clear and complete cognitive framework, it is possible to propose effective strategies for sustainable development and specifically aimed at reducing the concentration of CO_2 in the atmosphere assessing, on a case-by-case basis, which of the two options described above should be chosen or how and according to which criteria they should be mutually integrated.

Such approaches have already been undertaken with the aim of understanding how the dynamics of land use change have affected CO_2 emissions [6] using different models and data sets that often lead to different results. Some authors also commented on these discrepancies, stating that spatial distributing method is secondary to the quality of the data, and that the need for standardized spatial distributing methods is less important than the need for high quality databases [7]. Interesting direction in involving citizens in CO_2 emission reduction processes are under several cooperation projects [8, 9] enhancing user behavior role [10].

The aim of this work is to provide a methodological basis for the evaluation of territorial policies directly related to land use change by integrating the wide range of selection and evaluation criteria with a useful tool to estimate the effects of each change in terms of carbon storage, sequestration or emissions.

As explained in detail below, our findings show a great criticality in the retrieval of basic data which inevitably reflects on the accuracy of the results obtained. This is partly due to the complexity of the phenomena that contribute to carbon storage within the soil horizons and to the large number of variables involved. Probably if regional systematic studies aimed at acquiring and categorizing all the necessary data have never been carried out, it is also because there was a lack of a methodological approach capable of integrating them into a tool effectively useful both in terms of decision support and in supporting the planning phase of interventions to be undertaken in a sustainable development perspective. In this we feel we have made our contribution.

2 Methodology

The vision of the Millennium Ecosystem Assessment (MA) is a world in which people and institutions appreciate natural systems as vital assets, recognize the central roles these assets play in supporting human well-being, and routinely incorporate their material and intangible values into decision making [11]. The accomplishment of this global project depends on the commitment that the scientific community is putting into the portrayal and communication of ecosystem services provided by the territory at various levels, as well as into providing decision makers and administrators with methodologies and tools that are effective and efficient without losing the perception of all the details that in any way help to define the peculiarities of an area. As indeed, several attempts have been made to make the assessment and mapping of ecosystem services a useful tool to support territorial planning, overcoming the common conception of a mere representation of a topic belonging almost exclusively to the world of academic research [12, 13].

According with Bagstad et al. [14], criteria to consider for evaluating ES tools so that they can actually be supportive to decision-makers and they make ecosystem service assessments quantifiable, replicable, credible, flexible, and affordable [15] are:

1. Quantification and uncertainty. A qualitative evaluation may be useful in such processes like screening, scoping or ranking; on the other hand, some models return a numerical output, which is indispensable for the evaluation of ES trade-offs. In the

latter case uncertainty estimates constitute an added value since providing a single output value may omit important information regarding certainty of results;

2. Time requirements. Rapidity in tool's implementation affects the widespread extent to which it is used;

3. Capacity for independent application. The opportunity to have a software license that makes tool independently runnable or to apply the tool directly in a public domain is obviously more attractive to both academics and private decision-maker;

4. Level of development and documentation. Tool's credibility and authoritativeness closely depend on the availability of documents about its methods, key algorithms, assumptions as well as peer reviewed journal articles describing its application;

5. Scalability. Being able to use a single analysis tool at all scales is certainly more practical even if it is always advisable to check the accuracy of the results; hardly a tool is designed to work well at every level of territorial detail;

6. Generalizability. A lot of tools currently available are place-specific although many others allow to customize the analysis context and to run the application in different eco-regional and socioeconomic settings;

7. Non-monetary and cultural perspective. A challenge for ES evaluation tools is running analysis and providing results from different point of view both in terms of valuation system (monetary or not) and in perspective (for example by being able to distinguish between the perspective of local populations and that of tourists),

8. Affordability, insights, integration with existing environmental assessment. ES evaluation tools are all the more appreciated when they integrate with established management and planning processes.

Among the technological solutions available to produce territorial assessment of ES we used inVEST - Integrated Valuation of Ecosystem Services and Tradeoffs - [16] that, within the evaluation framework described above, is placed as an open source ecosystem service mapping and valuation model that can be independently applied and tested and has to be accessed through a GIS software. It consists in a quantitative tool that provide spatially explicit ecosystem service trade-off maps and results, whose uncertainty through varying inputs is reported in an output table, and it can be performed at different levels, making it possible to execute the analysis consistent with the discretization of the available data as well as the dynamic characteristics of the system. Examples of ecosystem services and commodity production that inVEST can model include water quality, water provision for irrigation and hydropower, storm peak mitigation, soil conservation, carbon sequestration, pollination, cultural and spiritual values, recreation and tourism, timber and non-timber forest products, agricultural products, and residential property values [17].

With regard to the ecosystem service relative to carbon storage, inVEST propose a model that estimates the net amount of carbon stored in a land parcel over time and, optionally, the market values of the carbon sequestered in remaining stock according to the land use maps and classifications produced by the user.

Using maps of land use and land cover types (LULC), this model aggregates the amount of carbon stored in what it considers to be the 4 main "pools":

- aboveground biomass, including all living plant material above the soil (e.g., bark, trunks, branches, leaves)

- belowground biomass, encompasses the living root systems of aboveground biomass
- soil the organic component of soil, and represents the largest terrestrial carbon pool
- dead organic matter, includes litter as well as lying and standing dead wood.

Data required basically consist of a land-use or land-cover raster and a table in *.csv format containing for each of the LULC classes present, the values of carbon density for each pool expressed in Mg/Ha. For each LULC type, the model requires an estimate of the amount of carbon in at least one of the four fundamental pools described; obviously the more the input table will be complete, the more the result of the model will be accurate and complete.

At the end of execution the model returns to output a raster showing the amount of carbon currently stored in Mg of carbon in each grid cell. It is a sum of all of the carbon pools provided by the biophysical table.

The model simplifies the carbon cycle which allows it to run with relatively little information, but also leads to important limitations, including an oversimplified carbon cycle, an assumed linear change in carbon sequestration over time, and potentially inaccurate discounting rates. Biophysical conditions important for carbon sequestration such as photosynthesis rates and the presence of active soil organisms are also not included in the model.

To improve the results from the implementation of this model, it would be useful to resort to land use maps suitably detailed according to all the variables that influence processes associated with carbon storage. A slightly more sophisticated LULC classification could involve, for example, broad age categories (e.g., forest of age 0–10 years, 11–20, 21–40, etc.) or could stratify LULC types by variables known to affect carbon storage such as rainfall, temperature, and elevation that typically influence carbon storage and sequestration [18–20]. If this kind of data could be available model should result substantially more accurate.

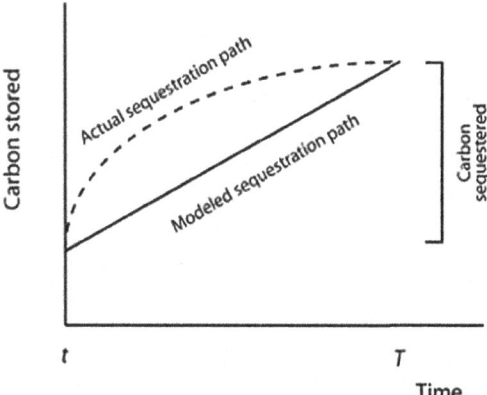

Fig. 2. inVest model assumes a linear trend over time for the carbon sequestration (the solid line) while the actual path may be non-linear (like the dotted line) [16]

Another simplification of the model is not to include the mutual carbon shift between pools: in the case of the death of a tree, for example, the carbon is immediately dispersed into the atmosphere without considering any intermediate passage.

Finally the last approximation is assuming a linear trend over time for the carbon sequestration while it is widely recognized that carbon is sequestered at a higher rate in the first few years and a lower rate in subsequent years (Fig. 2).

If there are several scenarios available, i.e. two land use maps covering the same territory but corresponding to different time periods, the "Carbon Storage and Sequestration: Climate Regulation" model can be used to calculate the net change in carbon storage over time in terms of sequestration and loss map unit by map unit.

Additionally inVEST can be used to assess the effectiveness of policies related to a framework of Reducing Emissions from Forest Degradation and Deforestation (REDD) or REDD+. To perform this analysis, three LULC maps are required: two for the current and a future baseline scenario, and one for a future setting under a REDD policy.

The second one is used to compute a reference level of emissions against which the REDD scenario can be compared. Based on these three LULC maps, the carbon biophysical model produces three rasters for total carbon storage for each of them and two sequestration rasters for future and REDD settings.

3   Data Search

As already mentioned in the description of the model employed, data to be input for estimating the carbon stock are a raster map of land use and a table containing, for each class of land cover, the values of carbon stored within the four components of the system.

In order to implement the software it is essential to insert at least one of the four values although, given the high uncertainty of the estimate made considering the simplifications and limitations already described and embedded in the model, it is advisable to provide an input table as complete as possible. In this regard, it is useful to remember that the developers of the program themselves recommend in order to obtain a more accurate assessment, the further subdivision of each land use class using as parameters additional quantities not considered in inVEST whose influence on the phenomenon of carbon storage is, however, established.

The raster of the land-cover classes was derived from a shapefile available on the regional website and containing the Corine Land Cover classification available at the third level of detail and on a scale of 1:5 000.

The use of GIS software allowed the raster rendering of the original vector file.

The other data requested were more difficult to obtain because, at present, the only systematic study carried out at national level concerns only soils covered by forest vegetation for which, in the context of the National Inventory of Forests and Forest Tanks (INFC), data on organic carbon are provided for the alive component of the topsoil, for the necromass, for regeneration and finally for soil and litter. This study, carried out by direct sampling of forest stands, was replicated in 1985, 2005 and 2015, producing three inventories at ten-year frequency, the last of which, however, has not yet been made available.

If, in relation to carbon stored as necromass, epigean biomass and organic component present in litter and soil, we can take the values provided by INFC as they are, the deduction of hypogean biomass should be derived on the basis of experimental relationships obtained and present in the literature. In particular, CAIRNS et al. (1997) [21] showed that the root biomass in forest stands is linearly dependent on the epigeous one ($R^2 = 0.83$), representing on average a percentage that ranges between 25 and 26%, without significant differences between conifers and deciduous [22].

The same authors also argue that epigeal biomass represents the single variable with greater explanatory power of the variations of root biomass followed by the trees population age, the basimetric area and the density [22]. Assuming a mean value of the ratio equal to 0.26, it was therefore possible to deduce the hypogean biomass starting from the epigean one.

As regards other land cover, unfortunately there is no national study. The SIAS (Development of Soil Environmental Indicators) project, carried out by the Higher Institute for Environmental Protection and Research (ISPRA) with the aim of harmonising regional data already independently processed, has not yet published the results for the entire national territory. The ultimate aim was to provide a map of the organic carbon content within the first 30 cm of soil as land cover varies and considering the variability of the carbon component as a function of a variety of other parameters such as altitude and climate (Fig. 3).

As can be seen from the representation of the results available, the organic carbon amount is generally lower in lowland areas, especially if highly urbanized or exposed to intensive agriculture, while on average higher values characterize mountain areas.

A further trend is recognizable according to the latitude, so for the same coverage, the percentage of carbon is lower in southern areas because the influence of climate factor is greater (Fig. 4).

In order to find required data, a review of regional projects from which to draw reasonable data was therefore carried out, even being aware that they are subject to approximations, given the complex nature of the phenomenon of carbon storage within soils, strongly influenced by many other variables.

From the Italian regions only Abruzzo, Sardinia and Emilia Romagna have made the data accessible. First of all, the study conducted by the Abruzzo Region was taken into consideration, since the reference territory is morphologically and climatically more similar to that of Basilicata. However, ISPRA was critical of the results of this study as some of the data were strongly overestimated compared to national distributions.

The Sardinia Region, also within the framework of the SIAS project carried out by ISPRA, made the points at which the sampling was carried out and deduced public and, on the basis of the data acquired, proposed a formula for calculating organic carbon dependent not only on the type of horizon, but also on the precise characteristics of the local layers. Although of considerable accuracy, this methodology is not applicable within the Basilicata region as data necessary for the estimation according to the proposed formula are almost unavailable.

CLC_DEF	DESCRIZIONE
141	AREE VERDI URBANE
211	SEMINATIVO IN AREE NON IRRIGUE
212	SEMINATIVO IN AREE IRRIGUE
221	VIGNETI
222	FRUTTETI
223	OLIVETI
231	PRATI STABILI
241	COLTURE TEMPORANEE ASSOCIATE A COLTURE PERMANENTI
242	SISTEMI COLTURALI E PARTICELLARI COMPLESSI
243	AREE OCCUPATE DA COLTURE AGRARIE E VERDE NATURALE
321	AREE A PASCOLO NATURALE, PRATERIE
331	SPIAGGE,DUNE,SABBIE
332	ROCCE, RUPI, AFFIORAMENTI
333	AREE A VEGETAZIONE RADA
411	PALUDI INTERNE
511	CANALI, IDROVIE, CORSI D'ACQUA
512	BACINI D'ACQUA

Fig. 3. Land use classes according to CLC-III level in Basilicata

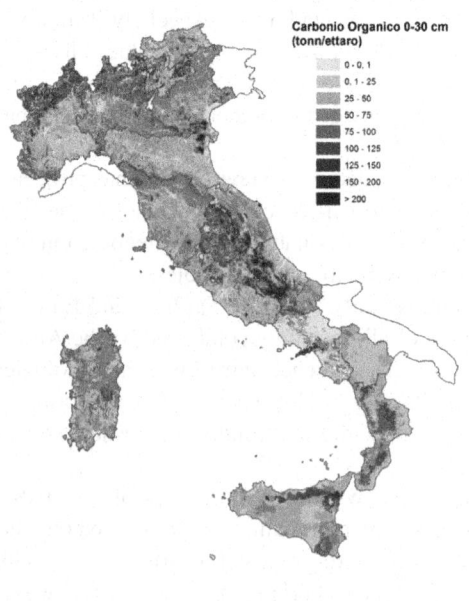

Fig. 4. Amount in tonnes per hectare of organic carbon in the Italian soil surface horizons.

It was therefore decided to derive the necessary data from the elaborations carried out in Emilia Romagna where, in order to properly take into account the variability of the processes that contribute to carbon storage, two different maps were produced: the first relating to mountain areas, which represents the average carbon content in the first 100 cm of soil and in the organic surface horizons in the case of forest soils; the second relating to plains, which exclusively reports the value of carbon stored within the first metre of depth. The substantial difference lies in the fact that on the first map it is possible to read an aggregate value of hypogean biomass and, in the case of forest soils, also of a part of the epigean biomass, unlike what happens on the map of the plains, where only the value of hypogean biomass is reported. Given the difficulty of disaggregating data related to the mountain environment, although aware of the approximation induced, it was decided to refer only to the data available for lowland areas.

Since the Emilia Romagna model does not provide a database but only a raster in which the percentages of organic carbon vary not only according to the type of land cover, the use of statistics has allowed to obtain for each class a single value of hypogeal biomass to be included in inVEST and on the basis of which to calculate other values required.

The values of hypogeal biomass deduced from the raster map of Emilia Romagna were thus submitted to an adaptation test in order to verify their distribution according to the hypothesized probability function. This assessment was made using a normal probabilistic paper. For the normally distributed populations, the average value was assumed as representative of the entire class; for those not distributed according to a Gaussian, the Box-Cox transform was applied in order to normalise their distribution and assume the median value as representative of the kind of coverage.

Once the data for the hypogeal biomass had been obtained, the values to be included in remaining pools were calculated by applying the equation previously exposed for the estimation of epigeous biomass again, and by obtaining stored carbon in the necromass and litter+soil systems by a linear regression.

4   Results

Once all the data necessary for the implementation of the Carbon Storage and Sequestration: Climate Regulation module had been obtained, the software was implemented and returned a representative map of the carbon contents (Mg) stored inside each of the cells in which the entire regional territory was discretized.

Although the input data are affected by an uncertainty due to the lack of official sources and to some simplifications adopted in the procedure, within the representation of the stored carbon contents it is possible to find correspondence with what was expected. Rather than estimating the actual content, it may prove useful in identifying how concentrations vary across the region (Fig. 5).

As can be seen, the highest values of organic carbon are found in protected areas such as EUAP, SIC, ZPS, ZSC. In particular, high values in the main regional forests are found: the Forest of Gallipoli-Cognato (ZPS), Monte Paratiello, the Forest of

Pierfaone, Monte Li Foi, the Dolomites of Pietrapertosa and the Forest of Montepiano. Instead, there is a greater variability within the Pollino National Park, as well as in that of the Lucanian Apennines, Val d'Agri and Lagonegrese and in the Park of Murgia Materana (Fig. 6).

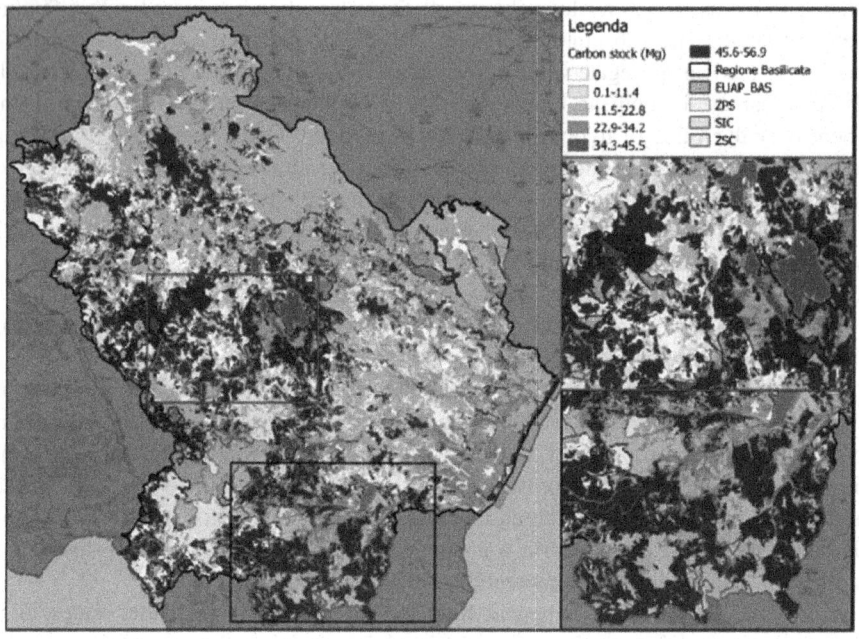

Fig. 6. Overlapping obtained results with the perimeters of regional protected areas

However, there are areas of high carbon concentration which do not fall within the above-mentioned protected areas, but which should be safeguarded because they have a primary ecosystem function. This also corresponds to the normative indications of the Legge Galasso[1], which provides for protection regimes for the territories covered by forests and woods, even if run through or damaged by fire, and those subject to reforestation restrictions.

By summing values obtained for each cell, it is possible to determine total stocked carbon amount in Basilicata of 732.73 million tons, corresponding to a value per unit area of about 733 Mg/Ha.

---

[1] 431/1985 Law, known as the Galasso Law, introduced a series of restrictions aimed at safeguarding landscape and environmental heritage and was then integrated into the still in force "Code of Cultural Heritage and Landscape".

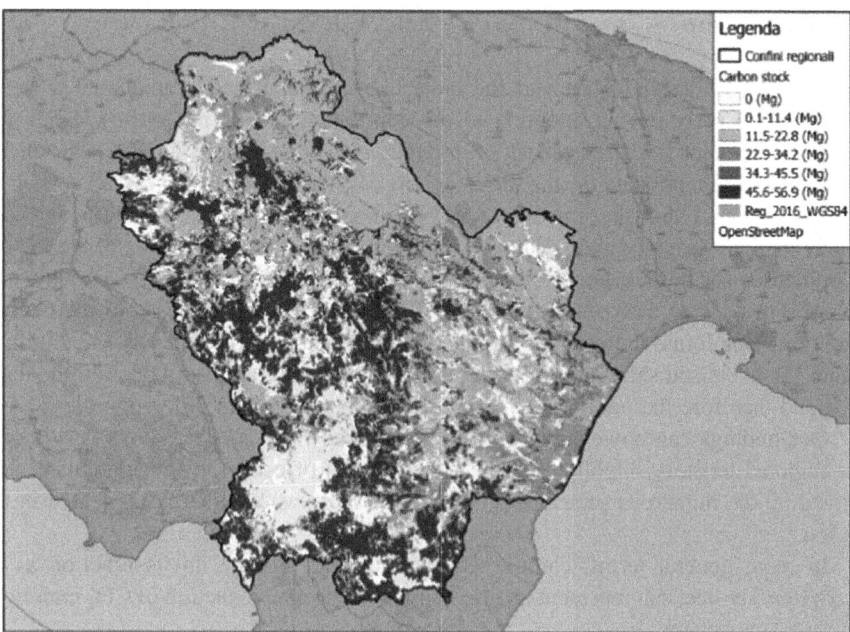

Fig. 5. Representation of carbon contents (Mg) stored within the area of Basilicata region

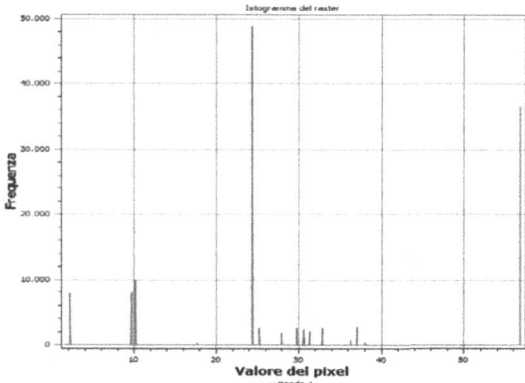

Fig. 7. Histogram of stored carbon values obtained for the Basilicata Region

These numbers correspond to about 2689 million tonnes of CO_2[2] equal to 2690.4 Mg/Ha which, being stored underground, avoid impacting on the sadly well-known phenomenon of the greenhouse effect (Fig. 7).

---

[2] Considering molecular weights of oxygen and carbon, respectively equal to 15,999 and 12,011, it results that to one ton of carbon corresponds about 3,67 tons of carbon dioxide.

5 Conclusion

Carbon stored assessment has been the subject of many analyses on a national scale but almost exclusively paying attention to the contribution made by forest species (ref. CarboItaly project[3]). There is a lack of in-depth analysis at a more detailed scale and of accurate and reliable data on the different soil cover typologies.

It was found that the amount of carbon monoxide varies significantly between different climate regions and soil cover. With reference to the publication of the ISTAT 2000 census for homogeneous areas, total carbon stored in Italian soils amounts to a quantity that varies between 490.0 ± 121.7 million tonnes. This leads to the conclusion that value found in this study for the only Basilicata region, equal to 732.7 million tonnes, is oversized showing the strong dependence of the applied model on the input data and therefore the poor comparability with other studies at different scales.

Our findings can however be used to identify how the concentrations vary within the regional territory, highlighting the role in terms of ecosystem regulation service, played by the numerous protected areas and the large wooded surfaces located in the region.

In more general terms, carbon sequestration and storage, in its function as an ecosystem service, can represent an alternative form for the reduction of CO_2 emissions into the atmosphere.

Enhancing territorial carbon stock could represent, for example, an alternative to investment in renewable energy and this could lead to a paradigm shift in the management of territorial processes of adaptation to climate change and relative policies at national, regional and local level. It could be said that carbon stocks are an alternative technology for reducing CO_2 in the atmosphere.

This study has shown the weakness of the cognitive structure necessary for such assessments: there are no detailed studies in Basilicata for the classification of carbon pools in relation to land uses characteristic of the territory. New instruments and territorial analyses are therefore necessary and represent a research domain to be developed with the contribution of local authorities.

A further development hypothesis for the present study could be represented by a monetization of impacts able to evaluate compensation measures through new institutional tools (norms and procedures). Results would be a completely renewed territorial management system in which the transformation, in any sector of human activity, is not only subject to the traditional system of charges, but should include "sustainability" charges that can also be monetized through the model proposed in this research work, as long as reliable territorial data and products on an adequate scale are made available.

This is an applied research domain typical of spatial planning in which the demand for effective planning tools, able to ensure adequate levels of sustainability in territorial

---

[3] CARBOITALY is a research project funded by the Italian Ministry of Education, University and Research within the framework of the Special Supplementary Fund for Research (FISR), the Strategic Programme for Sustainable Development and Climate Change, with the main objective of quantifying the extent of net carbon sequestration by forest and agricultural ecosystems at national level.

transformations, is contrasted with the need to spread the use of technologies for the production of renewable energy as a fight against climate change, without accompanying these processes with appropriate tools to assess the effects.

In a wider view of this research, our position refers to the wider methodological framework we appeal "rationality in planning" [23–25]. This work helps to extend territorial knowledge and interpretation opportunity referring to the sustainable planning toolkit [26]. Overlapping recent achievements on land take [27–29], ecosystem services [12, 13, 30], antifragile planning [31] and territorial resilience [32], we may recognize a contribution in decision making for territorial development and in particular the increased robustness of knowledge management tools [33, 34] for a new planning agenda [35].

Acknowledgements. This research has been supported by the Environmental Observatory Foundation of Basilicata Region (FARBAS).

References

1. Petit, J., Jouzel, J., Raynaud, D., Barkov, N., Barnola, J., Basile-Doelsch, I., Bender, M., Chappellaz, J., Davis, M., Delaygue, G., Delmotte, M., Kotlyakov, V., Legrand, M., Lipenkov, V., Lorius, C., Pepin, L., Ritz, C., Saltzman, E., Stievenard, M.: Climate and atmospheric history of the past 420,000 years from the Vostok ice core, Antarctica. Nature **399**(6735), 429–436 (1999)
2. Alberti, G., Barbati, A., Bianchi, M., Colangelo, G., Corona, P., De Fililippis, D., Fioravanti, M., Guerci, L., Gasparini, P., Lafortezza, R., Leronni, V., Matteucci, G., Minotta, G., Minunno, F., Nolè, A., Notarangelo, G., Notarnicola, G., Peressotti, A., Pettenella, D., Sanesi, G., Scarascia Mugnozza, G., Tabacchi, G.: Foreste e ciclo del carbonio in Italia: come mitigare il cambiamento climatico. Fondazione Gas Natural, p. 240 (2010)
3. Millennium Ecosystem Assessment: Ecosystems and Human Well-Being: Synthesis. Island Press, Washington, DC (2005)
4. Rogelj, J., den Elzen, M., Höhne, N., Fransen, T., Fekete, H., Winkler, H., Schaeffer, R., Sha, F., Riahi, K., Meinshausen, M.: Paris agreement climate proposals need a boost to keep warming well below 2 °C. Nature **534**, 631–639 (2016)
5. Ciais, P., Dolman, A.J., Bombelli, A., Duren, R., Peregon, A., Rayner, P.J., et al.: Current systematic carbon-cycle observations and the need for implementing a policy-relevant carbon observing system. Biogeosciences **11**, 3547–3602 (2014)
6. Zuoji, D.O.N.G.: The territorial planning under the concept of low-carbon. Urban Stud. **7** (2010)
7. Liebens, J., VanMolle, M.: Infuence of estimation procedure on soil organic carbon stock assessment in Flanders, Belgium. Soil Use Manag. **19**, 364–371 (2003)
8. Attolico, A., et al.: Engaged communities for low carbon development process. In: Gervasi, O., et al. (eds.) ICCSA 2017. LNCS, vol. 10409, pp. 573–584. Springer, Cham (2017). https://doi.org/10.1007/978-3-319-62407-5_41
9. Scorza, F., et al.: Growing sustainable behaviors in local communities through smart monitoring systems for energy efficiency: RENERGY outcomes. In: Murgante, B., et al. (eds.) ICCSA 2014. LNCS, vol. 8580, pp. 787–793. Springer, Cham (2014). https://doi.org/10.1007/978-3-319-09129-7_57

10. Scorza, F.: Towards self energy-management and sustainable citizens' engagement in local energy efficiency agenda. Int. J. Agric. Environ. Inf. Syst. (IJAEIS) **7**(1), 44–53 (2016)
11. Daily, G.C., Polasky, S., Goldstein, J., Kareiva, P.M., Mooney, H.A., Pejchar, L., Ricketts, T.H., Salzman, J., Shallenberger, R.: Ecosystem services in decision making: time to deliver. Ecol. Soc. Am. Front. Ecol. Environ. **7**, 21–28 (2009)
12. Pilogallo, A., Scorza, F., Las Casas, G.: Tourism attractiveness: main components for a spacial appraisal of major destinations according with ecosystem services approach. In: Gervasi, O., et al. (eds.) ICCSA 2018. LNCS, vol. 10964, pp. 726–738 (2018)
13. Scorza, F., Pilogallo, A., Las Casas, G.: Investigating tourism attractiveness in inland areas: ecosystem services, open data and smart specializations. In: Calabrò, F., Della Spina, L., Bevilacqua, C. (eds.) New Metropolitan Perspectives, pp. 30–38. Springer, Cham (2018). https://doi.org/10.1007/978-3-319-92099-3_4
14. Bagstad, K.J., Semmens, D.J., Waage, S., Winthrop, R.: A comparative assessment of decision-support tools for ecosystem services quantification and valuation. Ecosyst. Serv. **5**, 27–39 (2013)
15. Scorza, F., Murgante, B., Las Casas, G., Fortino, Y., Pilogallo, A.: Investigating territorial specialization in tourism sector by ecosystem services approach. In: Stratigea, A., Kavroudakis, D. (eds.) Paving the Way for Smart, Inclusive and Resilient Cities and Island Communities in the Mediterranean: Current Research Paths and Experience-Based Evidence. Springer, Heidelberg (2018)
16. Natural Capital Project (NCP): InVEST User Guide (2015)
17. Nelson, E., Mendoza, G., Regetz, J., Polasky, S., Tallis, H., Cameron, D.R., Chan, K.M., Daily, G.C., Goldstein, J., Kareiva, P.M., Lonsdorf, E., Naidoo, R., Ricketts, T.H., Shaw, R.: Modeling multiple ecosystem services, biodiversity conservation, commodity production, and tradeoffs at landscape scales. Ecol. Soc. Am. Front. Ecol. Environ. **7**, 4–11 (2009)
18. Raich, J.W., Russell, A.E., Kitayama, K., Parton, W.J., Vitousek, P.M.: Temperature influences carbon accumulation in moist tropical forests. Ecology **87**, 76–87 (2006)
19. Jenny, H.: The Soil Resource. Springer, New York (1980). https://doi.org/10.1007/978-1-4612-6112-4
20. Coomes, D.A., Allen, R.B., Scott, N.A., Goulding, C., Beets, P.: Designing systems to monitor carbon stocks in forests and shrublands. Forest Ecol. Manag. **164**, 89–108 (2002)
21. Cairns, M.A., Brown, S., Helmer, E.H., Baumgardner, G.A.: Root biomass allocation in the world's upland forests. Oecologia **111**, 1–11 (1997)
22. Galvagni, D., Gregori, E., Zorn, G.: Modelli di valutazione della biomassa radicale di popolamenti forestali. L'Italia forestale e montana (2006)
23. Las Casas, G.B.: L'etica della Razionalità. In: Urbanistica e Informazioni, vol. 144 (1995)
24. Las Casas, G.B., Scorza, F.: Un approccio "context-based" e "valutazione integrata" per il futuro della programmazione operativa regionale in Europa. In: Bramanti Salone (a cura di) Lo Sviluppo Territoriale Nell'economia Della Conoscenza: Teorie, Attori Strategie, Collana Scienze Regionali, 41, FrancoAngeli, MilanoCasas (2009)
25. Las Casas, G.B., Tilio, L., Tsoukiàs, A.: Public decision processes: the interaction space supporting planner's activity. In: Murgante, B., et al. (eds.) ICCSA 2012. LNCS, vol. 7334, pp. 466–480. Springer, Heidelberg (2012). https://doi.org/10.1007/978-3-642-31075-1_35
26. Las Casas, G., Scorza, F.: Sustainable planning: a methodological toolkit. In: Gervasi, O., et al. (eds.) ICCSA 2016. LNCS, vol. 9786, pp. 627–635. Springer, Cham (2016). https://doi.org/10.1007/978-3-319-42085-1_53
27. Martellozzo, F., et al.: Modelling the impact of urban growth on agriculture and natural land in Italy to 2030. Appl. Geogr. **91**, 156–167 (2018)
28. Amato, F., et al.: Fuzzy definition of rural urban interface: an application based on land use change scenarios in Portugal. Environ. Model Softw. **104**, 171–187 (2018)

29. Amato, F., et al.: The effects of urban policies on the development of urban areas. Sustainability **8**, 297 (2016)

30. Scorza, F., Fortino, Y., Giuzio, B., Murgante, B., Las Casas, G.: Measuring territorial specialization in tourism sector: the Basilicata region case study. In: Gervasi, O., et al. (eds.) ICCSA 2017. LNCS, vol. 10409, pp. 540–553. Springer, Cham (2017). https://doi.org/10.1007/978-3-319-62407-5_38

31. Las Casas, G., Scorza, F.: A renewed rational approach from liquid society towards anti-fragile planning. In: Gervasi, O., et al. (eds.) ICCSA 2017. LNCS, vol. 10409, pp. 517–526. Springer, Cham (2017). https://doi.org/10.1007/978-3-319-62407-5_36

32. Lombardini, G., Scorza, F.: Resilience and smartness of coastal regions. a tool for spatial evaluation. In: Gervasi, O., et al. (eds.) ICCSA 2016. LNCS, vol. 9788, pp. 530–541. Springer, Cham (2016). https://doi.org/10.1007/978-3-319-42111-7_42

33. Scorza, F., Las Casas, G.B., Murgante, B.: That's ReDO: ontologies and regional development planning. In: Murgante, B., et al. (eds.) ICCSA 2012. LNCS, vol. 7334, pp. 640–652. Springer, Heidelberg (2012). https://doi.org/10.1007/978-3-642-31075-1_48

34. Scorza, F., Casas, G.L., Murgante, B.: Overcoming interoperability weaknesses in e-government processes: organizing and sharing knowledge in regional development programs using ontologies. In: Lytras, M.D., et al. (eds.) WSKS 2010. CCIS, vol. 112, pp. 243–253. Springer, Heidelberg (2010). https://doi.org/10.1007/978-3-642-16324-1_26

35. Las Casas, G., Scorza, F., Murgante, B.: New urban agenda and open challenges for urban and regional planning. In: Calabrò, F., Della Spina, L., Bevilacqua, C. (eds.) New Metropolitan Perspectives, pp. 282–288. Springer, Cham (2018). https://doi.org/10.1007/978-3-319-92099-3_33

Tourism Attractiveness: Main Components for a Spacial Appraisal of Major Destinations According with Ecosystem Services Approach

Angela Pilogallo, Lucia Saganeiti, Francesco Scorza[(✉)],
and Giuseppe Las Casas

School of Engineering, Laboratory of Urban and Regional Systems Engineering,
University of Basilicata, 10, Viale dell'Ateneo Lucano, 85100 Potenza, Italy
{angela.pilogallo, lucia.saganeiti, francesco.scorza,
giuseppe.lascasas}@unibas.it

Abstract. It is widely recognized that tourism sector plays an important role in territorial analysis both because of its economic and employment potential and its environmental and social implications. Investigating dynamics that influence tourist attractiveness and receptivity is fundamental in territorial planning sector in order to monitor regional and sustainable development policies, above all with a view to pursuing the 17 Sustainable Development Goals (SDGs) defined by the 2030 Agenda for Sustainable Development [1].

Within the methodological framework established by the Millenium Ecosystem Assessment [2], the evaluation of tourism specialization degree was carried out following the ecosystem services approach and relying on inVEST, a spatially-explicit model developed with the aim of providing a decision support system able to quantify the set of goods and services profitable for human well-being and provided by ecosystems.

The study area, located in the Southern Italy and including regional territories of Basilicata and Puglia regions, was chosen because in recent years it has been characterized by a steadily growing flow of arrivals and presence which a significant impetus was given by the designation of Matera as the Capital of European Culture for 2019. The work is completed by the contextualization of the results obtained within the framework of tourist attractiveness and accessibility of the examined area, which presents strong differences as much as it includes Basilicata, a region poorly infrastructuralized and only recently emerging in the tourism market, and Puglia considered instead a very sought-after Italian destinations.

Keywords: Tourism · Ecosystem services · Regional planning
Sustainable development

1 Introduction

Despite the economic crisis of recent years, the uncertainty due to the instability of international political scene and the increasing number of terrorist attacks, the frequency of natural disasters and the health pandemics that often occur as a consequence,

© Springer International Publishing AG, part of Springer Nature 2018
O. Gervasi et al. (Eds.): ICCSA 2018, LNCS 10964, pp. 712–724, 2018.
https://doi.org/10.1007/978-3-319-95174-4_54

the tourism sector shows an enviable resilience compared to other sectors of world economy. Accounting for one tenth of global GDP and representing 1 out of every 10 jobs in the world [3], tourism has been recognized as a relevant tool to drive sustainable development and a key instrument to pursue the implementation of the SDGs [4]. Indeed, although it is explicitly mentioned in three objectives, namely SDG 8 on 'Decent Work and Economic Growth', SDG 12 on 'Responsible Consumption and Production' and SDG 14 on 'Life below Water', it is clearly evident that it has a direct impact on efforts to achieve other goals such as protecting the environment, eradicating poverty and advancing gender equality.

On the other hand, however, if it's not properly supported by policies of sustainability and an appropriate regional planning and programming, its rapid development could constitute a significant threat, especially where ecosystems with a strong tourist appeal interface with ecosystems characterized by high naturalness or peculiar landscape emergencies, sometimes already sufficiently vulnerable. To these must be added all the tourism's global environmental impacts whose evaluation increasingly find its place in scientific research and literature. Gossling et al. [5], for example, estimated that tourism sector during the year 2000 was responsible for 5% of global fossil energy consumption and associated emissions of CO_2, as well as the use of 0.5% of the world's biologically productive lands.

These results, only partly confirmed by United Nations and World Meteorological Organization, highlight the need for more reliable data for the assessment of direct and indirect impacts of tourism such as effects on food consumption to be added to existing considerable data for example on water use in tourism [6].

In the light of the above, it is clear that effectiveness and efficiency of careful regional planning in terms of sustainability must inevitably pass from an accurate cognitive framework in terms of territorial specialization degree. Furthermore, omission of cultural ecosystem services within this cognitive framework may lead to policies, plans or activities being ineffectual or even counterproductive [7] and the sociocultural values can be key determinants of the success or failure of conservation strategies [8].

This report illustrates methodology and data used to assess tourist attractiveness of the territories of Basilicata and Puglia and interprets the results in the light of recent dynamics of tourism sector's fast development that has invested these areas in the last decade and that considerable vigor have acquired following the designation of Matera as Capital of Culture 2019.

As evidenced by studies carried out by the regional administration [9], the Puglia region is affected by territorial planning problems in terms of governance of both municipal and extra-municipal areas which become more and more evident along coastal areas where anthropic pressure and over-exploitation of resources cause widespread degradation phenomena [10] partly attributable to tourist flows in respect of which Puglia is the second favorite region of Southern Italy [11].

Basilicata, on the other hand, is one of the last places in Italy in terms of tourist attractiveness although in recent years the trend for flows arriving in Matera has been strongly growing and the destination is listed among the Southern Italy cities with the greatest connotation oriented towards international customers together with renowned locations such as Naples and Capri [11].

2   Assessment of "Recreation and Tourism" as a Cultural Ecosystem Service

The concept of ecosystem services dates back at least to the 1970s but gained momentum within scientific literature in the 1990s and was then mainstreamed by the Millennium Ecosystem Assessment [2, 12].

Since then efforts to put it into practice have increased strongly [13] and despite the widespread recognition that integrating ES into spatial planning might be a promising approach towards sustainable development because it supports making such services explicit [14], a critical challenge persists: how to move from scientific knowledge to real-world decision making [15].

Several attempts have been made to make the assessment and mapping of ecosystem services a useful tool to support territorial planning, overcoming the common conception of a mere representation of a topic belonging almost exclusively to the world of academic research. However, many of these studies highlighted an objective difficulty in selecting the most appropriate scale for assessing (and eventually monetising) ecosystem services, since they often form dynamically in complex chains of ecosystem functions at different spatial levels. So, a relatively fixed-scale approach will miss some of the ES dynamics, especially regulation services typically relevant and observable at larger scales [16]. This complication is less evident in estimating some of the ES, such as cultural services related to recreation which can be identified and monetised in a relatively straightforward manner [16].

Since, unfortunately, land-use transformation policies are often linked to an increase in anthropized surfaces with all that this implies, some studies specifically focussed in assessing the degree of ecosystem services supply in relation to biodiversity loss have been conducted, though very frequently neglecting the highly dynamic nature of ecosystem services [12] (Fig. 1).

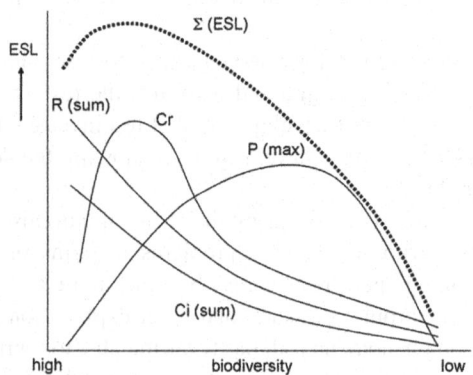

Fig. 1. Generalized functional relationships between the levels of Regulating (R), Provisioning (P), Cultural – recreation (Cr) and Cultural – information (Ci) ecosystem services and the degree of loss of biodiversity related to different land use intensities [12].

The purpose of this work has been precisely to evaluate and represent the temporal evolutions of ecosystem services linked to tourist receptiveness and recreation in a territory that during the last decade has undergone a significant transformation boost, due to an increase in the visibility of Matera actually sparked in 1945 with the publication of *Cristo si è fermato a Eboli*, well before the explosion of all the phenomena and dynamics related to so-called "mass tourism".

The ultimate goal is precisely to meet the challenge of including dynamics of transformation also described through the mapping of ES, in order to build a complex model of interpretation of the territory able to support planners and administrators in formulating the most appropriate sustainability policies without setting limits to the economic development of the areas involved.

Since we agree with Fish et al. [17] in defining Cultural Ecosystem Services as "ecosystems' contribution to the non-material benefits (capabilities and experiences) that arise from human–ecosystem relationships" we looked for the model with better account taken of the social value that we attribute to this ES.

Really, a wide variety of methods to capture the many facets of tourism and recreation sectors have been proposed considering different variables and factors as input parameters significant for the frequency and intensity of use of the ES in question. Some of them can also quantify specific contributions of setting characteristics, such as the beauty of landscapes, the probability of wildlife encounters, the degree of infrastructure development. Many of these take a comprehensive approach by providing methods of data collection based on in-depth interviews, tape recordings, on-site measurements experiences via questionnaires or make use of virtual and interactive technologies such as, for example, through computer-animated choice experiments.

According with Bagstad et al. [18], criteria to consider for evaluating ES tools so that they can actually be supportive to decision-makers and they make ecosystem service assessments quantifiable, replicable, credible, flexible, and affordable are:

1. Quantification and uncertainty. A qualitative evaluation may be useful in such processes like screening, scoping or ranking; on the other hand, some models return a numerical output, which is indispensable for the evaluation of ES trade-offs. In the latter case uncertainty estimates constitute an added value since providing a single output value may omit important information regarding certainty of results;
2. Time requirements. Rapidity in tool's implementation affects the widespread extent to which it is used;
3. Capacity for independent application. The opportunity to have a software license that makes tool independently runnable or to apply the tool directly in a public domain is obviously more attractive to both academics and private decision-maker;
4. Level of development and documentation. Tool's credibility and authoritativeness closely depend on the availability of documents about its methods, key algorithms, assumptions as well as peer reviewed journal articles describing its application;
5. Scalability. Being able to use a single analysis tool at all scales is certainly more practical even if it is always advisable to check the accuracy of the results; hardly a tool is designed to work well at every level of territorial detail;

6. Generalizability. A lot of tools currently available are place-specific although many others allow to customize the analysis context and to run the application in different eco-regional and socioeconomic settings;
7. Non-monetary and cultural perspective. A challenge for ES evaluation tools is running analysis and providing results from different point of view both in terms of valuation system (monetary or not) and in perspective (for example by being able to distinguish between the perspective of local populations and that of tourists);
8. Affordability, insights, integration with existing environmental assessment. ES evaluation tools are all the more appreciated when they integrate with established management and planning processes.

Among the technological solutions available to produce territorial assessment of ES we used inVEST - Integrated Valuation of Ecosystem Services and Tradeoffs - [19] that, within the evaluation framework described above, is placed as an open source ecosystem service mapping and valuation model that can be independently applied and tested and has to be accessed through a GIS software. It consists in a quantitative tool that provide spatially explicit ecosystem service trade-off maps and results, whose uncertainty through varying inputs is reported in an output table, and it can be performed at different levels, making it possible to execute the analysis consistent with the discretization of the available data as well as the dynamic characteristics of the system. Examples of ecosystem services and commodity production that inVEST can model include water quality, water provision for irrigation and hydropower, storm peak mitigation, soil conservation, carbon sequestration, pollination, cultural and spiritual values, recreation and tourism, timber and non-timber forest products, agricultural products, and residential property values [20].

Concerning the module Recreation and Tourism, the software, after having discretised the study area in a number of cells, depends on the chosen size, elaborates a multiple linear regression model that includes geospatial functions on a complex system of input variables.

The tool outputs maps show current patterns of recreational use parameterizing the model and using a proxy for visitation: geotagged photographs posted to the website Flickr in the decade 2005–2014 [19]. The model starts to run by computing the number of photos available on the social network for each cell in which the territory has been discretized. Then, a simple linear regression is performed to estimate the effect of each attribute within the study region, returning for each of them the coefficient of linear regression.

For the present case, a hexagonal cell structure was chosen for the spatial database over a typical rectangular grid due to its better ability to represent and account for certain spatial continuities and connectivity in the rather complex landscape features [16].

Since the purpose of the analysis was to evaluate temporal evolution of the tourist attractiveness of the territory between Basilicata and Puglia regions, paying particular attention to the role played by Matera in acting as a development driver, the assessment was made considering the two domains in which the area of the Murgia Materana is most likely to make greater its influence: natural heritage and cultural heritage.

The first domain includes all the areas, places and forms of the territory included within the naturalistic heritage of the study region. Each of them constitutes one of the geometric and geo-referenced variables inserted into inVEST model and in regard of which predictive parameters on the basis of the best correspondence of their spatial distribution with respect to the phenomenon to be described were identified.

A total of four kind of elements were considered:

- the system of protected areas and all the sites to which, even in the absence of a real binding regime, significant value from the point of view of local naturality and biodiversity, is attributed. This category includes EUAP, i.e. areas included in the official list of protected natural areas drawn up by the Ministry of the Environment and Protection of Land and Sea, Important Birds Area (IBA), wetlands listed in the Ramsar Convention and sites belonging to the Natura 2000 ecological network;
- the network of nature trails and all the historical routes, including all the sheep-tracks system which often links remote areas to each other and to those once were the main routes for transhumance;
- the totality of geosites represented by landforms with a specific shape, which alone or in collaboration with other bioecological or anthropic elements can become objects of heritage [21] officially recognised and categorised by ISPRA which keeps their National Register;
- the hydrographic network of rivers and streams as classified within the layer available on the national cartographic portal [22].

In addition to the above-mentioned information layers that constitute the actual natural heritage, it was deemed appropriate to consider within the variables that certainly affect the availability degree of the resources system the state pertinence road network consisting of highways and national roads currently in charge of the ANAS, the National Road Administration. The issue of accessibility as a variable that can significantly weigh on the resources availability has already been explored by other authors [23] who in some cases have estimated a real comfort distance in correspondence to which the greatest recreational potential has been registered.

With reference to the second domain, the cultural heritage, we have tried to consider not only places and physical structures that play an important role by hosting events and exhibitions of cultural importance, but also the set of historic centers that, in addition to being focal aggregation sites, illustrate the whole stratification of populations and events that over time have contributed to the development and transformation of the territory, giving the material heritage a unique and unavoidable identity value.

To the cultural heritage belong:

- all the attractions and points of interest generically defined as cultural goods and that constitute a heterogeneous class in terms of type, size, relevance and distribution. This category includes, for example, natural caves with rock paintings from the Iron Age, aqueduct systems dating back to the Roman era, the numerous fountains and drinkers that testify to the importance of peasant culture in the history of the area, cellars which are natural or semi-natural cavities that have always been used by man for the storage of food or land products to be preserved, a lot of fortified farms that, although belonging to different eras, testify the degree of garrison of the territory even in the most remote areas. This also includes a whole series of elements related to industrial archaeology, such as steel bridges and other transport and connection infrastructures, the numerous water mills serving the textile or cereal industry depending on the location, mills that are significantly linked to the landscape characterized by the widespread presence of secular olive groves;

- the archaeological sites within the two regions whose vectorial layers have been extracted from the geodatabases created within the framework of the respective regional landscape plans;
- theatres and museums as places of culture in which representations from past eras are revived as well as demonstrations and exchanges in the field of modern art;
- all the polygons representative of the historical centres and extracted from the territorial geodatabase of the National Statistical Institute (ISTAT) as a type 1 'population centre';
- all the 'tratturi', sheep-tracks and historical routes that are fully part of the cultural heritage of local communities within which there is still a very strong link with the land and rural culture that for centuries have been undisputed protagonists of economic and social development of these areas.

As for the naturalistic-environmental heritage, it was considered indispensable to consider the issue of accessibility by adding to the layers described, that of state-run roads.

3   Results

The analysis was initially aimed at visualizing the areas within the two most attractive regions according to the data that inVEST implements within its model on the basis of geo-referenced photos taken and uploaded to Flickr considering the entire period available that is the decade 2005–2014 (Fig. 2).

The results averaged over the entire decade gives a picture in which it is possible to distinctly recognize areas that record a greater degree of attractiveness, namely the Gargano and the Salento peninsula. Among the most highlighted localities there are Matera (MT), Alberobello (BA), Lecce (LE) and, to a lesser extent, Potenza (PZ), Bari (BA) and Foggia (FG).

Since the purpose of the work was actually to evaluate the evolution of preferences over time in terms of destination of tourist flows, the analysis was repeated considering only the first and last two years of the available period.

From the comparison between the two figures (Fig. 3) it clearly emerges that tourist attractiveness of the entire area has increased both in terms of extension of the areas affected by significant tourist flows and in terms of strengthening appeal of the localities which were already destinations of a remarkable tourism.

Moreover, overlapping results obtained with the input layers, a fundamental role played by the accessibility of the sites emerges since the highest growth trends are recorded along the main road lines (Fig. 4).

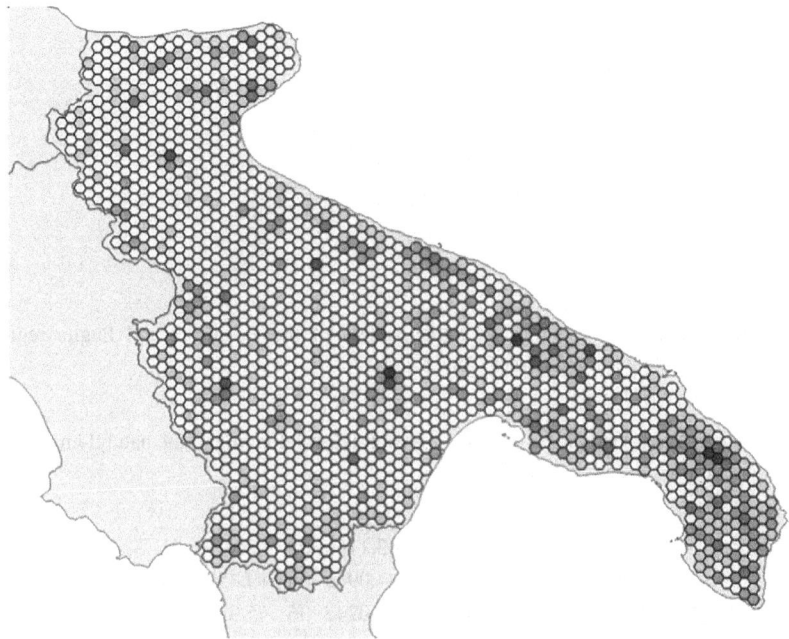

Fig. 2. Tourism attractiveness of the Basilicata and Puglia regions considering the decade 2005–2014.

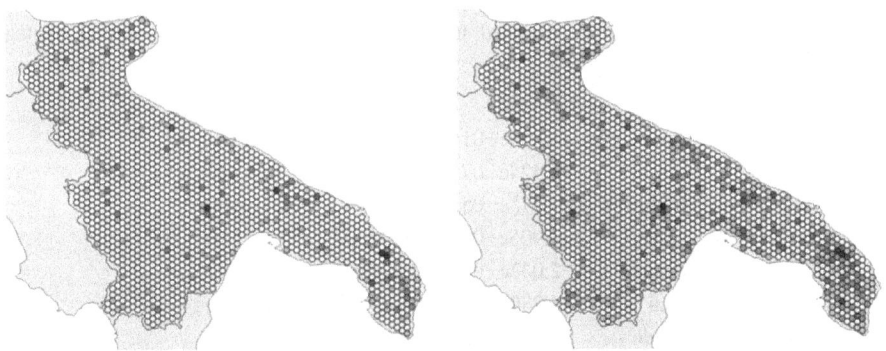

Fig. 3. Comparison between tourism attractiveness of the Basilicata and Puglia regions considering the years 2005–2006 (a) and 2013–2014 (b).

Further considerations can be made by analyzing coefficients of linear regression, provided in output by inVEST for both domains considered (Tables 1, 2 and 3).

As it is possible to verify from data collected in the tables, for both domains the influence of accessibility shows values comparable and of the same order of magnitude. However, it should be noted that the value of R-squared for the regression carried out for the cultural heritage domain is significantly higher.

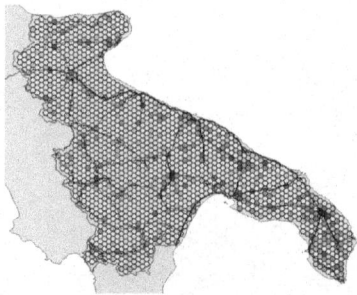

Fig. 4. Overlapping between tourism attractiveness of the Basilicata and Puglia regions in 2013–2014 and state pertinence road's layer.

Table 1. Regression coefficients obtained for each layer belonging to the natural-environmental heritage domain for the period 2005–2014

	estimate	stderr	t value
(Intercept)	+7.507e−01	+3.116e−02	+2.409e+01
strade	+3.874e−05	+4.096e−06	+9.459e+00
acque	−4.197e−05	+7.074e−06	−5.933e+00
geositii	+2.048e−06	+1.979e−07	+1.035e+01
protette	−1.042e−08	+3.085e−09	−3.379e+00
sentieri	+2.724e−06	+2.280e−06	+1.195e+00

Table 2. Regression coefficients obtained for each layer belonging to the cultural heritage domain for the period 2005–2014

	estimate	stderr	t value
(Intercept)	+6.439e−01	+3.140e−02	+2.051e+01
cstorici	+5.424e−07	+1.698e−08	+3.195e+01
tratturi	−1.275e−05	+3.099e−06	−4.114e+00
archeo	−6.905e−08	+1.229e−07	−5.618e−01
teamus	−2.037e−05	+4.067e−06	−5.008e+00
beni	−1.230e−04	+2.610e−05	−4.711e+00
strade	+1.693e−05	+3.438e−06	+4.925e+00

Table 3. R-squared values obtained for natural-environmental and cultural heritage

	Natural-environmental heritage	Cultural heritage
Multiple R-squared	0.1477	0.4848
Adjusted R-squared	0.1450	0.4829

This leads us to conclude that the conducted linear regression is much more significant in the field of cultural heritage. Moreover, as it was easy to imagine, an important role in the degree of tourist attractiveness is fulfilled by accessibility to places and points of interest. The comparison between the images allows in fact a clear observation that the areas in which the growth trend is more evident are located along the main communication and transport routes.

4 Conclusion

The purpose of this work was to evaluate the temporal evolution in the decade between 2005 and 2014 of the tourist attractiveness of the regions of Basilicata and Puglia. The main focus was on determining whether and how the candidature and designation of Matera as European Capital of Culture for 2019 had played a role within the framework of visibility and attractiveness of the two regions.

The analysis was conducted through an approach based on ecosystem services.

It has been used inVEST, a geographically explicit tool that calculates an attractiveness index based on georeferenced photos uploaded to social media Flickr.

Many studies on the level of attractiveness are present in the scientific literature but most of them have been traditionally carried out by conducting surveys at entrances to major attractions such as national parks. This method is expensive and provides limited spatial and temporal coverage [24].

Online data shared on social networks, instead, are becoming an increasingly attractive source of information about cultural ecosystem services [25] and an important database both for regional studies and for more detailed scale assessments such as the identification of visit patterns of urban parks and the assessment of factors influencing their use [26].

Landscape photographs tell about the significance of human relationships with landscapes, human practices in landscapes and the landscape features that might possess value in terms of cultural ecosystem services [25] and, moreover, as has already been established in previous studies carried out on a regional scale [27], it allows destinations which, although not part of the traditional tourist circuits, have a strong power of attraction for visitor flows, to emerge.

In order to allow a more holistic planning of natural resources and land use [28], the assessment of tourist attractiveness through the approach of ecosystem services and the consequent monetization of these services could be an even more useful tool considering the need to pursue at international level shared sustainable development objectives and performances [29, 30].

Moreover, our position refers to the wider methodological framework we appeal rationality in planning [31–34]. This work helps to add a tile to the mosaic of the tools (tool kit [35]) of territorial analysis and evaluation. Overlapping recent achievements on land take [36–38], ecosystem services [27, 39, 40], antifragile planning [40] and territorial resilience [41], we may recognize a contribution in decision making for territorial development and in particular the increased robustness of knowledge management tools [42, 43] for a new planning agenda [40].

References

1. United Nations: Transforming Our World: The 2030 Agenda for Sustainable Development, New York (2015)
2. Millennium Ecosystem Assessment: Ecosystems and Human Well-Being: Synthesis. Island Press, Washington, DC (2005)
3. World Travel & Tourism Council (WTTC): Travel and Tourism Global Economic Impact and Issues, London, UK (2017)
4. United Nations World Tourism Organization (UNWTO): Tourism and the sustainable development goals – journey to 2030. In: World Tourism Organization and United Nations Development Programme, Madrid (2017)
5. Gossling, S., Borgstrom-Hansson, C., Horstmeier, O., Saggel, S.: Ecological footprint analysis as a tool to assess tourism sustainability. Ecol. Econ. **43**, 199–211 (2002)
6. Gössling, S., Peeters, P.: Assessing tourism's global environmental impact 1900–2050. J. Sustain. Tour. **23**(5), 639–659 (2015)
7. Chan, K.M.A., Satterfield, T., Goldstein, J.: Rethinking ecosystem services to better address and navigate cultural values. Ecol. Econ. **74**, 8–18 (2012)
8. Mascia, M.B., Brosius, J.P., Dobson, T.A., Forbes, B.C., Horowitz, L., McKean, M.A., Turner, N.J.: Conservation and the social sciences. Conserv. Biol. **17**, 649–650 (2003)
9. Regione Puglia – Assessorati Assetto del Territorio ed Ecologia: Definizione del Documento strategico della regione Puglia per il periodo 2006–2013 (2006)
10. Romano, G., Dal Sasso, P., Trisorio Liuzzi, G., Gentile, F.: Multi-criteria decision analysis for land suitability mapping in a rural area of Southern Italy. Land Use Policy **48**, 131–143 (2015)
11. ISTAT: Movimento turistico in Italia. Anno 2016. Statistiche report (2017)
12. De Groot, R.S., Alkemade, R., Braat, L., Hein, L., Willemen, L.: Challenges in integrating the concept of ecosystem services and values in landscape planning, management and decision making. Ecol. Complex. **7**, 260–272 (2010)
13. Daily, G.C., Matson, P.A.: Ecosystem services: from theory to implementation. Proc. Natl. Acad. Sci. **105**(28), 9455–9456 (2008)
14. Grêt-Regameya, A., Altwegg, J., Sirén, E.A., van Strien, M.J., Weibel, B.: Integrating ecosystem services into spatial planning - a spatial decision support tool. Landsc. Urban Plan. **165**, 206–219 (2017)
15. Ruckelshaus, M., McKenzie, E., Tallis, H., Guerry, A., Daily, G., Kareiva, P., Polasky, S., Ricketts, T., Bhagabati, N., Wood, S.A., Bernhardt, J.: Notes from the field: lessons learned from using ecosystem service approaches to inform real-world decisions. Ecol. Econ. **115**, 11–21 (2015)
16. Tammi, I., Mustajärvi, K., Rasinmäki, J.: Integrating spatial valuation of ecosystem services into regional planning and development. Ecosyst. Serv. **26**, 329–344 (2017)
17. Fish, R., Church, A., Winter, M.: Conceptualising cultural ecosystem services: a novel framework for research and critical engagement. Ecosyst. Serv. **21**, 208–217 (2016)
18. Bagstad, K.J., Darius, J., Semmens, D.J., Waage, S., Winthrop, R.: A comparative assessment of decision-support tools for ecosystem services quantification and valuation. Ecosyst. Serv. **5**, 27–39 (2013)
19. Natural Capital Project (NCP): InVEST User Guide (2015)
20. Nelson, E., Mendoza, G., Regetz, J., Polasky, S., Tallis, H., Cameron, D.R., Chan, K.M., Daily, G.C., Goldstein, J., Kareiva, P.M., Lonsdorf, E., Naidoo, R., Ricketts, T.H., Shaw, R.: Modeling multiple ecosystem services, biodiversity conservation, commodity production, and tradeoffs at landscape scales. Ecol. Soc. Am. Front. Ecol. Environ. **7**, 4–11 (2009)

21. Ilieş, D.C., Josan, N.: Geosites-geomorphosites and relief. GeoJ. Tour. Geosites Year II **3**(1), 78–85 (2009)
22. NATIONAL CARTOGRAPHIC PORTAL Homepage. http://www.pcn.minambiente.it/mattm/. Accessed 03 Apr 2018
23. Nahuelhual, L., Carmona, A., Lozada, P., Jaramillo, A., Aguayo, M.: Mapping recreation and ecotourism as a cultural ecosystem service: an application at the local level in Southern Chile. Appl. Geogr. **40**, 71–82 (2013)
24. Wood, S.A., Gurry, A.D., Silver, J.M., Lacayo, M.: Using social media to quantify nature-based tourism and recreation. Sci. Rep. **3**, (2013). https://doi.org/10.1038/srep02976
25. Oteros-Rozas, E., Martín-López, B., Fagerholm, N., Bieling, C., Plieninger, T.: Using social media photos to explore the relation between cultural ecosystem services and landscape features across five European sites. Ecol. Indic. (2017)
26. Donahue, M.L., Keeler, B.L., Wood, S.A., Fisher, D.M., Hamstead, Z.A., Mc Phearson, T.: Using social media to understand drivers of urban park visitation in the Twin Cities, MN. Landsc. Urban Plan. **175**, 1–10 (2018)
27. Scorza, F., Murgante, B., Las Casas, G., Fortino, Y., Pilogallo, A.: Investigating territorial specialization in tourism sector by ecosystem services approach. In: Stratigea, A., Kavroudakis, D. (eds.) Paving the Way for Smart, Inclusive and Resilient Cities and Island Communities in the Mediterranean: Current Research Paths and Experience-based Evidence. Springer (2018)
28. Jäppinen, J.-P., Heliölä, J.: Towards a sustainable and genuinely green economy. The value and social significance of ecosystem services in Finland (TEEB for Finland). In: Jäppinen, J.-P., Heliölä, J. (eds.) Synthesis and Roadmap. The Finnish Environment 1en/2015. The Finnish Ministry of Environment, Helsinki (2015)
29. Scorza, F., Grecu, V.: Assessing sustainability: research directions and relevant issues. In: Gervasi, O., et al. (eds.) ICCSA 2016. LNCS, vol. 9786, pp. 642–647. Springer, Cham (2016). https://doi.org/10.1007/978-3-319-42085-1_55
30. Dvarioniene, J., Grecu, V., Lai, S., Scorza, F.: Four perspectives of applied sustainability: research implications and possible integrations. In: Gervasi, O., et al. (eds.) ICCSA 2017. LNCS, vol. 10409, pp. 554–563. Springer, Cham (2017). https://doi.org/10.1007/978-3-319-62407-5_39
31. Las Casas, G.B.: L'etica della Razionalità. In: Urbanistica e Informazioni, vol. 144 (1995)
32. Las Casas, G.B., Scorza, F.: Un approccio "context-based" e "valutazione integrata" per il futuro della programmazione operativa regionale in Europa. In: Salone, B. (a cura di) Lo Sviluppo Territoriale Nell'economia Della Conoscenza: Teorie, Attori Strategie, Collana Scienze Regionali, vol. 41, FrancoAngeli, Milano (2009)
33. Las Casas, G.B., Tilio, L., Tsoukiàs, A.: Public decision processes: the interaction space supporting planner's activity. In: Murgante, B., et al. (eds.) ICCSA 2012. LNCS, vol. 7334, pp. 466–480. Springer, Heidelberg (2012). https://doi.org/10.1007/978-3-642-31075-1_35
34. Casas, G.L., Scorza, F.: Sustainable planning: a methodological toolkit. In: Gervasi, O., et al. (eds.) ICCSA 2016. LNCS, vol. 9786, pp. 627–635. Springer, Cham (2016). https://doi.org/10.1007/978-3-319-42085-1_53
35. Martellozzo, F., et al.: Modelling the impact of urban growth on agriculture and natural land in Italy to 2030. Appl. Geogr. **91**, 156–167 (2018)
36. Amato, F., et al.: Fuzzy definition of Rural Urban Interface: an application based on land use change scenarios in Portugal. Environ. Model Softw. **104**, 171–187 (2018)
37. Amato, F., et al.: The effects of urban policies on the development of urban areas. Sustainability **8**, 297 (2016)

38. Scorza, F., Fortino, Y., Giuzio, B., Murgante, B., Las Casas, G.: Measuring territorial specialization in tourism sector: the Basilicata region case study. In: Gervasi, O., et al. (eds.) ICCSA 2017. LNCS, vol. 10409, pp. 540–553. Springer, Cham (2017). https://doi.org/10.1007/978-3-319-62407-5_38

39. Las Casas, G., Scorza, F.: A renewed rational approach from liquid society towards anti-fragile planning. In: Gervasi, O., et al. (eds.) ICCSA 2017. LNCS, vol. 10409, pp. 517–526. Springer, Cham (2017). https://doi.org/10.1007/978-3-319-62407-5_36

40. Scorza, F., Pilogallo, A., Las Casas, G.: Investigating tourism attractiveness in inland areas: ecosystem services, open data and smart specializations. In: Calabrò, F., Della Spina, L., Bevilacqua, C. (eds.) ISHT 2018. SIST, vol. 100, pp. 30–38. Springer, Cham (2019). https://doi.org/10.1007/978-3-319-92099-3_4

41. Lombardini, G., Scorza, F.: Resilience and smartness of coastal regions. A tool for spatial evaluation. In: Gervasi, O., et al. (eds.) ICCSA 2016. LNCS, vol. 9788, pp. 530–541. Springer, Cham (2016). https://doi.org/10.1007/978-3-319-42111-7_42

42. Scorza, F., Las Casas, G.B., Murgante, B.: That's ReDO: ontologies and regional development planning. In: Murgante, B., et al. (eds.) ICCSA 2012. LNCS, vol. 7334, pp. 640–652. Springer, Heidelberg (2012). https://doi.org/10.1007/978-3-642-31075-1_48

43. Scorza, F., Casas, G.L., Murgante, B.: Overcoming interoperability weaknesses in e-government processes: organizing and sharing knowledge in regional development programs using ontologies. In: Lytras, M.D., et al. (eds.) WSKS 2010. CCIS, vol. 112, pp. 243–253. Springer, Heidelberg (2010). https://doi.org/10.1007/978-3-642-16324-1_26

Using Open Data and Open Tools in Defining Strategies for the Enhancement of Basilicata Region

Raffaella Carbone[2], Giovanni Fortunato[2], Giovanna Pace[2],
Emanuele Pastore[2], Luciana Pietragalla[2], Lydia Postiglione[2],
and Francesco Scorza[1(✉)] 🆔

[1] School of Engineering, University of Basilicata,
Viale dell' Ateneo Lucano 10, 85100 Potenza, Italy
francesco.scorza@unibas.it
[2] Postgraduate School of Smart Basilicata Project,
Educational Objective Three (OF3) "Smart Mobility and Urban Services",
University of Basilicata, Viale dell' Ateneo Lucano 10, 85100 Potenza, Italy
rafcar88@gmail.com, giovanni.fortunato88@libero.it,
giovanna89.pace@tiscali.it,
pastore.emanuele@gmail.com,
lucy.pietragalla@gmail.com, lydia.postiglione@yahoo.it

Abstract. Open data availability, participation and knowledge sharing are becoming increasingly important in planning processes aimed at protecting and enhancing the territory. This paper presents an application of Volunteered Geographic Information (VGI) for the creation of an open database for the enhancement of Basilicata region territory. The work was carried out during the Smart Basilicata training project and led to the definition of a map of the services of the regional territory, starting from open source tools and data available online and processed through geographic information systems.

Keywords: Smart city · Smart communities · Urban planning
Open data · Volunteered Geographic Information · Citizens as sensors
Governance

1 Introduction

Nowadays it is increasingly evident that data availability, open access to datasets in "near real-time", participation and knowledge sharing have importance within the planning process [1].

This concept is based on a more participative method to government where citizen's ideas and activities have to be considered and collected in a sort of a continuous flow.

Consequently, public involvement, getting ideas, suggestions or simply data\information production, is a daily activity aiming to have a wider inspiration in decision making.

© Springer International Publishing AG, part of Springer Nature 2018
O. Gervasi et al. (Eds.): ICCSA 2018, LNCS 10964, pp. 725–733, 2018.
https://doi.org/10.1007/978-3-319-95174-4_55

In recent times a lot of activities have been developed with the support of mass cooperation. This tendency often adopted in public agencies and local authorities, is based on an open government approach.

This approach leads to "Crowdsourcing" [15], where a lot of activities or decisions have been realized using a mass collaboration, or to "Volunteered Geographic Information" [14], where distributed masses create, manage and disseminate spatial data [13].

Open data play a central role in helping to communicate actions and data for territorial governance in a transparent and accessible way.

They are defined as one of the pillars of smart cities [9, 18] because they are public or public interest data that allow the development of innovative solutions and the interaction between users/citizens and the city, adopting an approach based on the transition from the concept of government to the concept of governance [2, 3].

Murgante and Borruso [5] defined a set of indicators able to identify the smartness level in cities:

1. adoption of OpenData and OCG Standard;
2. free wifi;
3. projects implementation of augmented reality for tourism;
4. crowdfunding initiatives;
5. decisions taken by crowdsourcing;
6. implementation of INSPIRE Directive;
7. quantity of public services achievable through App.

This openness of the public data represents a simplification of administrative processes [12] with impacts on economic and business system, cartographic and geographical information [4], transport [8, 10, 11], tourism [19], cultural heritage [20], planning and programming activities [16, 17].

The increase of data availability and accessibility allows to define different levels of knowledge to understand the dynamism and the territorial metamorphoses.

In this work it is shown how it is possible to use the existing public information to develop territorial analysis based on updated and updatable data useful in defining development policies.

2   An Open Database for Territory Enhancement

The research activity presented in this article was carried out during the training of Smart Basilicata Project [7] "*Educational Objective Three (OF3) "Smart Mobility and Urban Services"* (project promoted by the Italian ministry of education, university and research) and it had the objective of creating the basis for the creation of an open database for the enhancement of the territory of the Basilicata region.

The work was focused on the distribution of activities and services present on the regional territory and it was divided into three phases:

1. data collection through google My Maps;
2. data georeferencing used the QGIS software;
3. data analysis.

The final result of the work was the drafting of a "Charter of services of the Basilicata Region".

2.1 The Implementation Context of the Workshop

In the first phase of the work the services and activities to be found were defined, subdividing them into ten macro-categories. To each category was assigned an identification code. The macro categories identified are:

- Education and training
- Business and commerce
- Services
- Public services
- Tourism
- Culture, art publishing
- Sport and leisure
- Health
- Security and safety
- Financial services.

Using Google My Maps, it was possible to identify and to map the activities listed above, searched by consulting various sources: databases of various institutions that can be consulted online, websites of the activities, available lists by associations or public authority.

Table 1 and Fig. 1 show an excerpt from the table containing the sources consulted for the education and training category.

My Maps by *Google* is a free platform that allowed to create maps in an interactive and collaborative way and it allows to integrate the activities and services already located on maps with those identified through the sources mentioned above.

My Maps could be defined as an interactive way to build an Open Government, which guarantees a widespread control on the management of public things by citizens, as a form of co-planning/planning that makes a service really useful and strategically linked to a single objective: community welfare through transparency, participation and collaboration.

Putting the citizen in the condition of having certain knowledge and using intuitive tools means to adopt the assumptions of Open Data [6].

During this data collection phase, approximately 17000 activities and services were identified throughout the Basilicata region (Table 2).

2.2 Georeferencing Data

Google My Maps allowed us to export the maps created during the data collection phase in kmz format. Then, these maps were reported in Q-GIS software for further processing (Fig. 2).

Table 1. Sources of "Education and training" category.

Category	Sources
IF01-primary school	MIUR website:
IF02-elementary school	cercalatuascuola.istruzione.it
IF03-middle school	
IF04-high school	
IF05-nursery	Websites of the municipalities
IF06-university	MIUR website:
	albolaboratori.miur.it/Regione.aspx?LabCat=304
	Website of the University of Basilicata:
	portale.unibas.it/site/home/ateneo/dipartimenti-e-scuole.html
	Website of "Università della Terza Età":
	unitre.net/unitre/Basilicata.html
	Website of ASP:
	aspbasilicata.it/non-assegnata/corsi-di-laurea
IF08-music conservatory	Websites of music conservatories in Potenza and Matera:
	conservatoriopotenza.it/content/contatti-e-invio-mail
	conservatoriomatera.it
IF09-private training institution	Basilicatagiovani.eu
	Websites of the private training institutions
IF10-research Center	MIUR website:
	albolaboratori.miur.it/Regione.aspx?LabCat=304
IF11-study Center	Websites of the study centers
IF12-technological park	Website of technological park in Val Basento:
	tecnoparco-vba.it/contatti.html
IF13-driving school	Website of Ministry of Infrastructure and Transport:
	https://www.ilportaledellautomobilista.it/gms/organizzazione/65
IF14-language school	Websites of language schools

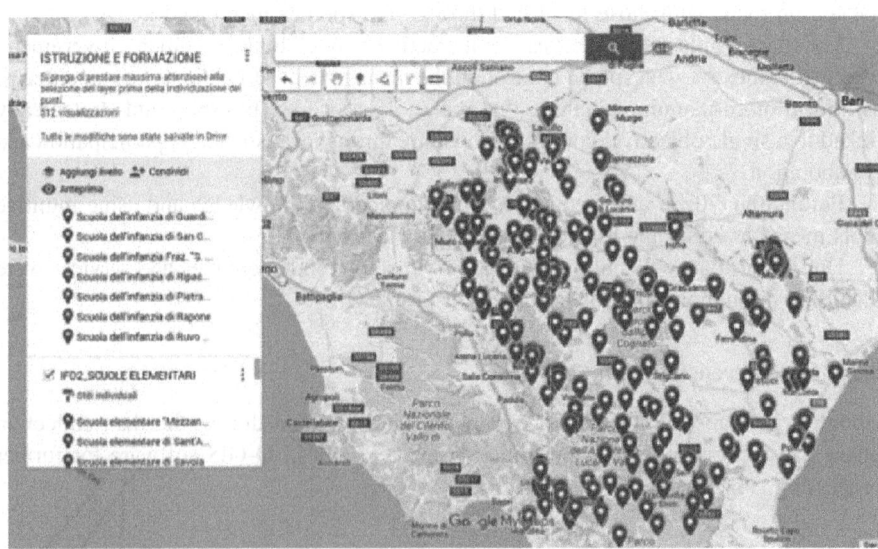

Fig. 1. Map of the "Education and training" category made on Google My Maps.

Table 2. Number of activities identified during the data collection phase.

Category	n° activities
Education and training	944
Business and commerce	3.790
Services	3.565
Public services	437
Tourism	1.595
Culture, art publishing	1.574
Sport and leisure	1.991
Health	1.708
Security and safety	540
Financial services	738

My Maps adopts a geographic coordinates system, so the maps have been exported with the coordinates system EPSG 4326. For a correct processing on the software Q-GIS, it was necessary to reproject the data in a flat coordinates system, in particular for the Basilicata it has adopted the coordinates system EPSG 32633. Therefore, the kmz files were imported into Q-GIS, reprojected in the correct system and saved as shape files. For each shape, an attribute table has been created containing the fields shown below (Table 3).

Table 3. Attribute table fields.

Field name	Type	Length	Description
Denominazione	String	254	Name of the activity/service
L1_CODE	String	10	Macro-category code
L1_CAT	String	254	Macro category name
L2_CODE	Integer	4	Sub-category code
L2_CAT	String	254	Subcategory name
x_coord	Real	23	Latitude
Y_coord	Real	23	Longitude

Making uniform the attribute tables was necessary in order to be able to join the various vectors and obtain an overall shape containing all the categories of services and activities of the Basilicata region.

2.3   Data Analysis

The georeferenced data were used to process analysis using the QGIS software. The final result was the production of the "Charter of Services of the Basilicata region" divided into the various categories mentioned above. It is a useful tool for assessing the current distribution of services in Basilicata, to identify the most served and lacking municipalities.

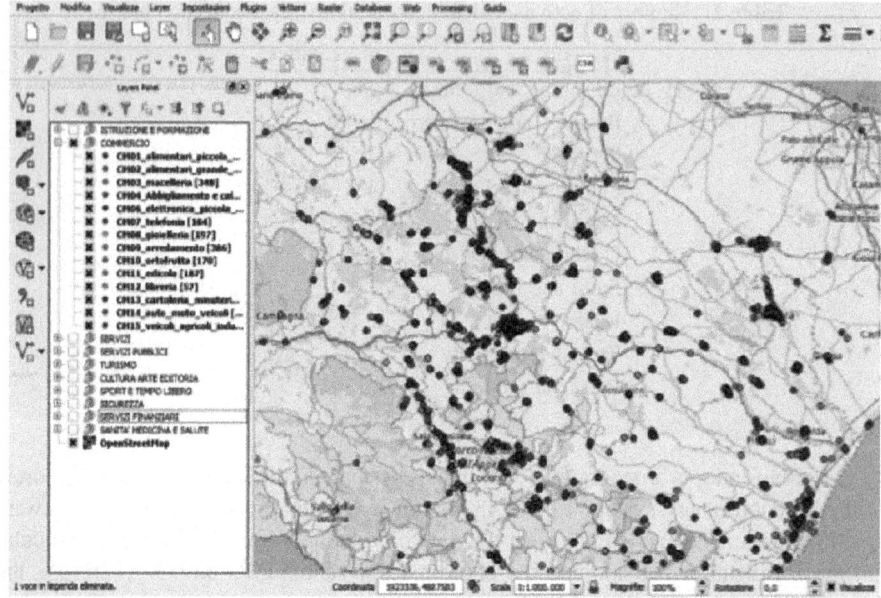

Fig. 2. Map of the "Business and commerce" category imported on QGIS.

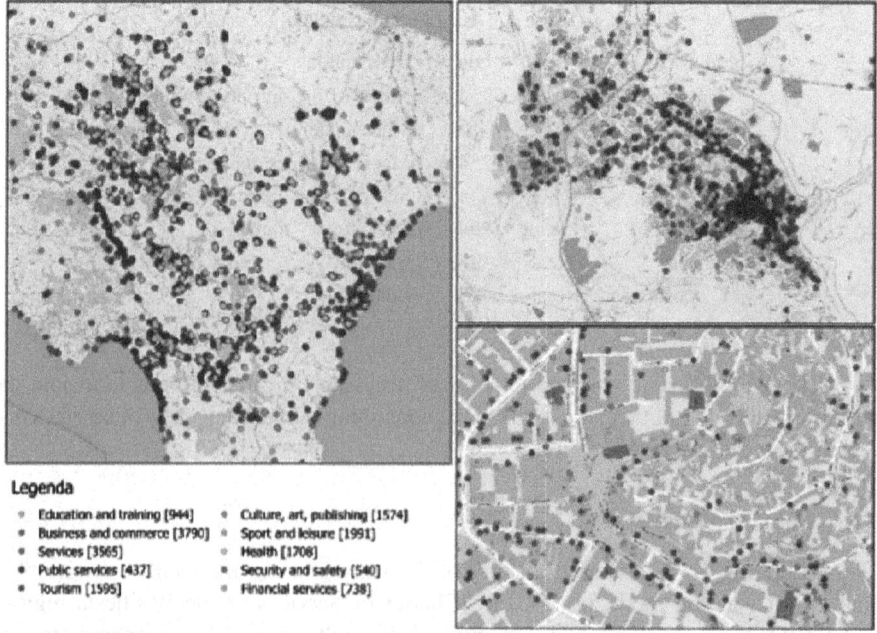

Fig. 3. Charter of services of Basilicata: distribution on the regional territory and on the municipality of Matera.

The produced data have been published in HTML format on the online platform of the Engineering Laboratory of Urban and Territorial Systems (LISUT) of the University of Basilicata (Figs. 3 and 4).

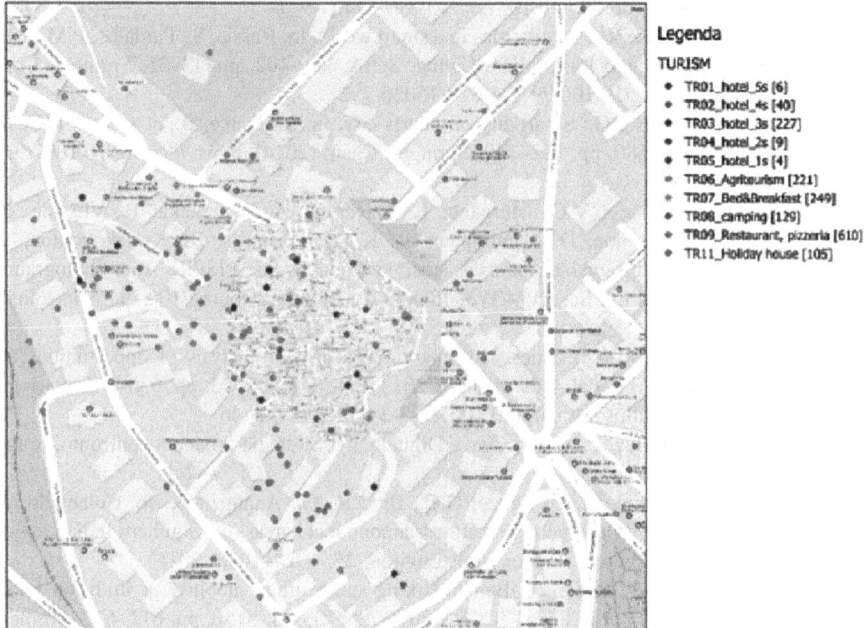

Fig. 4. Charter of the tourism: distribution in the municipality of Matera.

3 Conclusions

The work presented in this paper shows how using online tools it is possible to create an open database that allows the assessment of the status of a territory respect to some issues and then create a starting point for the definition of strategies for the enhancement of the territory.

The procedural approach was completely based on Open Data analysis through Open Tools (software and web services) and it demonstrate that the integration of such resources overcomes the dependence from proprietary data formats and proprietary software towards interoperability and open information [1].

Acknowledgements. This research has been supported by the University of Basilicata, more particularly the activities developed by Raffaella Carbone are part of Smart Basilicata Project (Bando "Smart Cities and Communities and Social Innovation" Avviso MIUR n.84/Ric2012, PON 2007–2013 del 2 marzo 2012) Educational Objective Three (OF3) "Smart Mobility and Urban Services".

References

1. Las Casas, G., Murgante, B., Scorza, F.: Regional local development strategies benefiting from open data and open tools and an outlook on the renewable energy sources contribution. In: Papa, R., Fistola, R. (eds.) Smart Energy in the Smart City. GET, pp. 275–290. Springer, Cham (2016). https://doi.org/10.1007/978-3-319-31157-9_14
2. Murgante, B., Borruso, G.: Smart cities in a smart world. In: Rassia, S., Pardalos, P.M. (eds.) Future City Architecture for Optimal Living. SOIA, vol. 102, pp. 13–35. Springer, Cham (2015). https://doi.org/10.1007/978-3-319-15030-7_2
3. Murgante, B., Borruso, G.: Smart city or smurfs city. In: Murgante, B., et al. (eds.) ICCSA 2014. LNCS, vol. 8580, pp. 738–749. Springer, Cham (2014). https://doi.org/10.1007/978-3-319-09129-7_53
4. Pantazis, D.N., Moussas, V.C., Murgante, B., Daverona, A.C., Stratakis, P., Vlissidis, N., Kavadias, A., Economou, D., Santimpantakis, K., Karathanasis, B., Kyriakopoulou, V., Gadolou, E.: Smart sustainable islands vs smart sustainable cities. ISPRS Ann. Photogramm. Remote Sens. Spatial Inf. Sci. **IV-4/W3**, 45–53 (2017). https://doi.org/10.5194/isprs-annals-iv-4-w3-45-2017
5. Murgante, B., Borruso, G.: Cities and smartness: a critical analysis of opportunities and risks. In: Murgante, B., et al. (eds.) ICCSA 2013. LNCS, vol. 7973, pp. 630–642. Springer, Heidelberg (2013). https://doi.org/10.1007/978-3-642-39646-5_46
6. Dameri, R., Giovanacci, L.: Smart City e Digital City. Strategie urbane a confronto, Franco Angeli (2015)
7. Salvia, M., Cornacchia, C., Di Renzo, G.C., Braccio, G., Annunziato, M., Colangelo, A., Orifici, L., Lapenna, V.: Promoting smartness among local areas in a Southern Italian region: the smart Basilicata project. Indoor Built Environ. **25**, 1024–1038 (2016)
8. Garau, C., Masala, F., Pinna, F.: Benchmarking smart urban mobility: a study on Italian cities. In: Gervasi, O., et al. (eds.) ICCSA 2015. LNCS, vol. 9156, pp. 612–623. Springer, Cham (2015). https://doi.org/10.1007/978-3-319-21407-8_43
9. Albino, V., Berardi, U., Dangelico, R.M.: Smart cities: definitions, dimensions, performance, and initiatives. J. Urban Technol. **22**, 3–21 (2015)
10. Pinna, F., Masala, F., Garau, C.: Urban policies and mobility trends in Italian smart cities. Sustainability **9**, 494 (2017)
11. Garau, C., Masala, F., Pinna, F.: Cagliari and smart urban mobility: analysis and comparison. Cities **56**, 35–46 (2016)
12. Belisario, E., Cogo, G., Epifani, S., Forghieri, C.: Come si fa Open Data? Istruzioni per l'uso per Enti e Amministrazioni Pubbliche vers. 2.0, e-gov. Maggioli Editore (2011)
13. Sui, D.S.: The wikification of GIS and its consequences: or Angelina Jolie's new tattoo and the future of GIS. Comput. Environ. Urban Syst. **32**(1), 1–5 (2008)
14. Goodchild, M.F.: Citizens as voluntary sensors: spatial data infrastructure in the world of Web 2.0. Int. J. Spat. Data Infrastruct. Res. **2**, 24–32 (2007)
15. Goodchild, M.F.: NeoGeography and the nature of geographic expertise. J. Locat. Based Serv. **3**, 82–96 (2009)
16. Murgante, B., Tilio, L., Lanza, V., Scorza, F.: Using participative GIS and e-tools for involving citizens of Marmo Platano – Melandro area in European programming activities. J. Balk. Near East. Stud. **13**(1), 97–115 (2011). https://doi.org/10.1080/19448953.2011.550809. ISSN 1944-8953
17. Forte, F., Girard, L.F., Nijkamp, P.: Smart policy, creative strategy and urban development - studies in regional. Science **35**(4), 947–963 (2005)

18. Batty, M., Axhausen, K.W., Giannotti, F., Pozdnoukhov, A., Bazzani, A., Wachowicz, M., Ouzounis, G., Portugali, Y.: Smart cities of the future. Eur. Phys. J. Spec. Top. **214**(1), 481–518 (2012)
19. Murgante, B., Tilio, L., Scorza, F., Lanza, V.: Crowd-cloud tourism, new approaches to territorial marketing. In: Murgante, B., Gervasi, O., Iglesias, A., Taniar, D., Apduhan, B.O. (eds.) ICCSA 2011. LNCS, vol. 6783, pp. 265–276. Springer, Heidelberg (2011). https://doi.org/10.1007/978-3-642-21887-3_21
20. Gizzi, F.T., Murgante, B., Biscione, M., Danese, M., Sileo, M., Potenza, M.R., Masini, N.: Mobile technology to contribute operatively to the safeguard of cultural heritage. In: Schiuma, G., Carlucci, D. (eds.) Big Data in the Arts and Humanities Theory and Practice, Chapter 14, pp. 171–185. CRC Press, Taylor & Francis Group (2018). ISBN: 978-1-4987-6585-5

From the UN New Urban Agenda to the Local Experiences of Urban Development: The Case of Potenza

Giuseppe Las Casas and Francesco Scorza[✉]

School of Engineering, Laboratory of Urban and Regional Systems Engineering,
University of Basilicata, 10, Viale dell'Ateneo Lucano, 85100 Potenza, Italy
{giuseppe.lascasas,francesco.scorza}@unibas.it

Abstract. The references that United Nations New Urban Agenda (UN HABITAT, 2015 and 2016, 2017) draw to the attention of disciplinary debate could represent a strong innovation for urban governance instruments and procedures. Especially in this period when European cities are defining the operational framework of development strategies 2014–2020 within the complex system of programming and management of European resources.

Tools that the New Cohesion Policy proposes for the definition of local urban agendas are based on a procedural innovation that makes cities protagonists in a complex process of resources planning and managing (huge but never sufficient) for the regeneration and development of cities.

In this work we propose an evaluation of the ITI of the Municipality of Potenza, approved in 2017, as it represents an approach that looks at strategic visions of urban development born in a context of fragility of local government and financial contingency for the municipal finances. A representative situation of a large number of medium-sized cities that are called upon to perform functions of 'Managing Authority' within the management of resources of Regional Operational Programmes without a structured process of technical/administrative 'empowerment' that defines skills, functions and scenarios of sustainability within an urban planning careful to the three principles: equity, efficiency, conservation of resources.

In the proposed case study, a framework of isolated interventions emerges which implement parts of a strategy consistent with the guidelines of the urban planning instrument and which require an integrated vision of the main priority intervention areas of local context (mobility, urban parks, historical-cultural resources, services to citizens).

Keywords: Urban development · Integrated programming · Rational planning

1 New Urban Agenda Inspiring Disciplinary Renewal

The research for effective forms of disciplinary renewal, beyond the many pressures that come from the contemporary practice of territorial government - which we will discuss later - leads us to consider the recent production of the United Nations as a key reference for determining a new season for urban policies that can achieve the

© Springer International Publishing AG, part of Springer Nature 2018
O. Gervasi et al. (Eds.): ICCSA 2018, LNCS 10964, pp. 734–743, 2018.
https://doi.org/10.1007/978-3-319-95174-4_56

expectations of utility required by local communities. These are territorial issues that characterize the current programming season, which is marked by a wealth of uncertainties that derive from suffering caused by the recent global economic crisis - which many consider 'outdated' -, from widespread demand for infrastructure upgrading - which will probably be disregarded - the urgent need to qualify services and public facilities in those marginal territorial contexts where the real challenge is to counteract abandonment, favoring forms of anti-fragile development [1–4] because they are self-centered.

The New Urban Agenda (NUA) of the United Nations [5–7] proposes an essential framework of performative references that address a territorial government practice in which inter-scalarity, disciplinary integration, an inclusive approach of citizens' demands (with particular attention to those of the weaker sections of the community) and attention to the sustainable use of territorial resources become pillars on which to base urban and territorial policies.

NUA then highlights the performative dimension of plans, compared to the traditional forms of conformative planning, linking the concreteness of tools to the local demanding framework (context based [8] or place based [9]) that must guide the transformation actions and urban development.

In this direction, according to the United Nations [5] lesson, among the key elements of the shared vision public decision places the attention to the reduction and management of anthropogenic and natural risks, the safeguard of resources and "ecosystem services" and the promotion of "civic engagement" as participation and inclusion in a system of territorial governance that relaunches the role of planning within an integrated system of tools and resources.

NUA also explicitly refers to the plan as a rational tool in which to adopt approaches to urban and territorial development that have to be sustainable, meet inclusive gender criteria and address the needs of the elderly, through the implementation of policies, strategies, and capacity building in actions at all levels based on fundamental drivers of change that include:

- development and implementation of urban policies at an appropriate level, including partnerships at local and national scale, building integrated systems of cities and human settlements and promoting cooperation between all the tiers of government in order to implement integrated and sustainable urban development;
- strengthening urban governance, through virtuous institutions and mechanisms that empower and involve relevant urban stakeholders, adequate control and monitoring systems and budgets that provide for coherence between resources and urban development plans to enable sustainable, inclusive and sustainable economic growth;
- actions to relaunch long-term integrated planning and design at the urban and territorial scales in order to optimise spatial dimension of the urban form and guarantee the benefits of the urbanisation process;
- support for effective, innovative and sustainable frameworks and financing instruments to strengthen municipal financial capacities and related tax systems to create, support and share in an inclusive way the added value generated by sustainable urban development.

In comparing these references with the actuality of urban application in Italy, it emerges how, to put things in order with respect to the national context, it is possible to affirm that the Italian response to this demand for innovation can be effectively sought in the new instruments of Community origin that are emerging in the programming of urban development: strategy for metropolitan areas, strategy for internal areas, urban agenda connected with the implementation of the instruments of the 2014–2020 Cohesion Policy, on condition that we follow the roads of an approach strongly oriented to the pursuit of the NUA policies.

With regard to the "Strategy for Internal Areas", we can say that they seek to identify models of territorial organization that implement the production paradigm of green economy and become emblematic of a new model of sustainable economic development. In this context many authors look at the analysis of experiences to transfer effective models of participation and co-design [10].

Metro PON is the tool that at national level implements and supports the development strategies of metropolitan areas by integrating European and national policy paths on urban development, including:

- the centrality of cities in the European agenda for sustainable development and social cohesion, supported by the European Parliament, the Committee of the Regions and the European Commission;
- the concentration of urgent development and cohesion issues in large urban areas;
- the plan for constitutional and administrative reform for the establishment of metropolitan cities, which assigns an increasingly important role to the large municipalities mayors;
- the need to strengthen the urban governance institutions role as key actors in investment strategies and inter-institutional dialogue.

The urban dimension centrality in the 2014–2020 cohesion policy is testified by the allocation of at least 5% of FESR resources to urban areas through Integrated Actions for Sustainable Urban Development. The fundamental reference that has guided European and national policies is represented by the Amsterdam Pact (EU, 2016) that establishes the European Union Urban Agenda.

The 12 priorities promoted by the Amsterdam Pact are: (1) Migrants and refugees inclusion, (2) Air quality, (3) Urban poverty, (4) Housing, (5) Circular economy, (6) Adaptation to climate change, (7) Energy transition, (8) Urban mobility, (9) Digital transition, (10) Public procurement, (11) Jobs and skills in local economy, (12) Sustainable land use and eco-based solutions.

This document sets out areas for action consistent with the priority areas set out by the United Nations in the New Urban Agenda (Habitat III), the Agenda for Sustainable Development (SDGs, 2030 Agenda on Sustainable Development) and the Paris Accord (December 2015).

Within the implementation of the Regional Operational Programmes, cities have been called upon to define integrated urban development interventions according to a negotiating approach with the regional authorities that - at least on a procedural level - enhances the strategic role of the development actions self-determined by each beneficiary.

The result is "new" strategic plans for cities within which heterogeneous projects (infrastructure, urban regeneration, economic, social, cultural development, etc.) can be financed.

This work aims at discussing the case of the City of Potenza which, within the programmatic framework described above, adopted in 2017 a strategic document: "Integrated Territorial Investment (ITI) for the Urban Development of the City of Potenza".

After having underlined in the second chapter, the strong framework of investment program based on a well articulated and demanding context, in the third chapter, on the basis of an application developed within the course of Territorial Engineering, we try to demonstrate how such program has found an implementation based on important but isolated interventions, reproducing a diffused approach in the last ones which, on the one hand, adheres to the well-founded instances of an integrated vision of needs of a territorial system, and, on the other, clashes with a financing mechanism that does not allow to realize such an integrated vision.

2 Potenza Application: From a Strong Vision to a Weak Selection

The ITI of Potenza is representative of the development plans generated at local level by the complex policy framework that has determined a new focus on cities in the 2014–2020 programming period.

We can consider two contrasting but illustrative evaluations of the general experience of ITI in Italy:

1. an opportunity to re-launch the role of strategic urban planning
2. a redundant tool that adds to the numerous plan documents with the result of making more burdensome the city governance.

Both of them highlight an instance of integration between plans that refers to the criteria of flexibility and adaptability to contexts that the UN guidelines reaffirm as the keys to overcoming the tradition of conformative urban and territorial plans.

The strategic part of the document of Potenza City of includes a detailed analysis of the context that allows to identify "ambitions" of urban development that start from needs closely related to urban life and those that the role of regional capital requires as territorial functions that the city must express.

The elements that are assumed by the ITI as strategic areas of intervention [11] are:

- A resilient city, not only in its infrastructure and built space, which knows how to regenerate and strengthen itself in difficult times, drawing lessons from the reasons of the crisis and developing the ability to plan its development path with greater awareness and with the contribution of all social components: the concept of urban resilience involves the transition from the model of mere redevelopment to a model of urban regeneration, which actively involves the community, environmentally aware and resource-conserving, aimed at reducing the impact of human activity.

- A sustainable city, where activities take place with attention to the respect of environmental resources, where citizens assume life habits based on waste reduction, with the support of a correct organization of public environmental services, promotion of circular economy and fight against climate change: the concept of urban sustainability must converge the programming of urban space towards specific priority objectives, such as functionality and sustainable mobility, high environmental quality, social and intergenerational cohesion, welfare, careful cost management.
- An integrated city: in its structural components, with a system of interconnection between urban area and suburbs that can enhance the specific vocations of places; in economic components, where young people can revitalize the entrepreneurial fabric thanks to their exciting innovative contribution of acquired skills and creativity; in social components, where no one feels excluded, where knowing how to do and know how to be individual and collective is the social network of protection of the disadvantaged, overcoming difficult conditions, even temporary.
- An accessible city, where is guaranteed access to quality places and services, that a capital city is and must be able to provide.
- A city projected to consolidate its role as a pole of attraction for the various areas of reference, through the structuring of sectoral dynamics with variable geometry that know how to fit the needs of communities, intercepting their requirements and accompanying them in the realization of expectations.
- A city aware of its own historical, cultural, environmental, social, economic value, and that on this recognized worth lays foundations for its future development, creating the right synergies so that each component integrates with the others to produce significant opportunities for the growth of the territory.
- A participatory city, based on a consensus on the idea of a sustainable city, with the triggering of participatory processes that allow to assess with greater awareness the needs of inhabitants and, more generally, of all users of the city: the urban system must offer citizens the opportunity to actively participate in processes, encouraging identification with their living space and sharing of urban space.

We quote this extract from the document as it is representative of an integrated approach oriented to addressing the priorities that both the UN's New Urban Agenda and the Amsterdam Pact affirm to be essential.

The strategic structure summarised above is divided within the document into five areas of intervention within which the projects and the 33 funded projects are divided:

1. Enterprise and innovation
2. Enhancement of buildings and public spaces
3. Mobility
4. Waste
5. Social inclusion and support for education.

The proposal of the Municipality of Potenza collects a total of 33 project profiles for a total investment of € 47,800,000.00, of which € 45,431,723.26 will be financed by FESR.

The project sheets compose a fragmented framework of interventions that in an a-systematic way, probably, seem to respond to the aims of consensus building on the part of political and technical decisional components that have generated the ITI programming process.

We base this statement on the fact that it is difficult, both in terms of the strategic framework and the areas of intervention, to reconstruct the infrastructure, services and investment chains that will enable the stated objectives to be fully achieved.

Therefore, an approach not oriented towards fully addressing priority issues identified in line with the framework of "ambitions" of the city prevails but rather a use of funding that helps to complete portions of sectoral projects that belong to a portfolio of projects and actions on the city that the Administration draws on when it is called to package integrated proposals in response to funding opportunities, but not built in the perspective of integration to which it declares to want to adhere. This would lead to a loss of the overall picture that should be clearly determined by the planning tool.

The need arises, therefore, to bring back the consideration on the discipline as a process that defines systematic scenarios of knowledge which allow decision-makers to identify priorities to be finalized with respect to resources and achievements on the urban context.

This process may seem obvious to those who operate and carry out research in the field of town planning and programming. Equally, however, we are not surprised that this is systematically disregarded in practice. So, then? A proposal: to draw a more complete picture around each of the areas of intervention proposed by the Potenza Municipality based on the procedure of the Logical Framework Approach that makes the link between problems, objectives and the programme of actions explicit.

This work was the subject of the exercise of the Engineering Course of the Territory of the a.y. 2017/2018 by the students of the School of Engineering of the University of Basilicata.

Below you will find an extract of a work developed within the course of "Territorial Engineering", which, starting from the investment project on the building structures of the F. Stabile Theatre of Potenza, deals with the theme of cultural policies for the enhancement of spaces for culture and leisure in Potenza, connecting with a framework of aspirations particularly felt within the significant proportion of students outside the University of Basilicata.

3   For a Cultural Policy of the Municipality of Potenza

The city of Potenza is characterized by the presence of numerous cultural attractions that, with their activities, represent a living part of the identity of the place.

The intervention sheets number 8 and number 9 of the ITI, related to the F. Stabile Theatre and that propose building and restoration works, have led to develop an evaluation of the cultural system of the city.

The theater is a unique structure of its kind in the territory and, according to art. 12 of Regional Law no. 37 of December 12, 2014 "Promotion and development of the performing arts", it has been recognized as a regional artistic excellence, and called "Historical Theatre of Basilicata".

To this end, as for all the other cards of the ITI of Potenza, one of the city entire system of offer and its merits and critical issues related to the ability to develop synergies has been elaborated. Cultural sites - in fact - must be conceived as assets to be safeguarded and valorised and, if well managed, they can strengthen local economy.

More than 55 centres active in the promotion of cultural activities have been identified and classified according to their location:

- Management (cultural centres are managed by different institutions);
- Use Destinations, which classifies centers into:
  - Theatres and Cinemas;
  - Schools;
  - University;
  - Religious structures;
  - Cultural associations;
  - Museums and Art Galleries;
  - Public buildings;
  - Libraries and Archives;
  - Spaces for outdoor activities;
- Location on the territory, with reference to the district in which structures are located.

Starting from weaknesses and strengths identified with a SWOT analysis, a problems hierarchy has been built, which converges on the de facto poor enhancement of the cultural offer system and on its effects (Fig. 1).

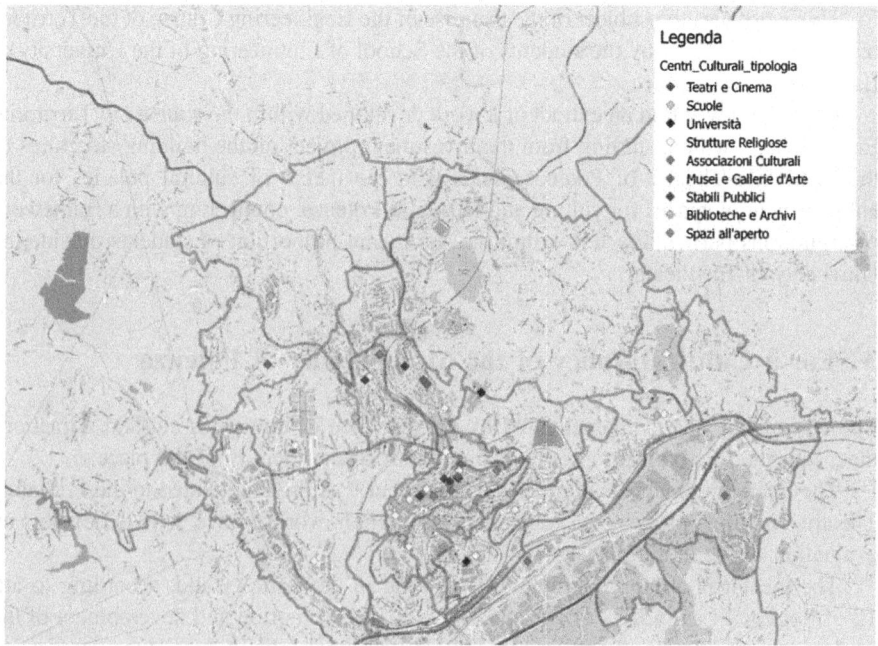

Fig. 1. Mapping of cultural centres in Potenza

It emerges that the territory is characterized by an heterogeneous or dispersed distribution of cultural centers and is affected by the inadequacy of public transport that generates a widespread problem of accessibility and use.

Difficulties related to mobility lead to low participation in cultural activities and do not contribute to their exploitation.

This inevitably leads, together with a lack of active collaboration between the various operators working in the cultural sector of Potenza, in fact, the various cultural centers are managed by different operators who do not seek synergies, to determine a clear weakness and lack of effectiveness of the Municipality of Potenza cultural policy and, consequently, the offer that presents itself to the citizen and a tourist is fragmented and difficult to understand.

The lack of cooperation, and therefore the impossibility of submitting larger projects together, makes it difficult to access funding. In addition, the lack of cooperation is compounded by the impossibility of implementing municipal, national and European initiatives related to promoting and enhancing cultural heritage, such as the "Youth Card" at municipal level or GEP (European Heritage Days).

On the whole, cultural sector has plenty of opportunities for growth, if enhancement policies are implemented to solve the problems of lack of event planning, inadequate promotional actions and limited use of spaces.

In response to this demanding situation, ITI proposes actions for energy efficiency and maintenance of the frescoes of the F. Stabile Theatre, but no action is oriented to address critical issues of the city cultural system.

It ensures that all the functions defined by Regional Law n.37 "Promotion and development of the performing arts" of December 12, 2014 remain necessarily unanswered, apart from the management and conservation of places intended for the performing arts owned by them or entrusted to them, as for the structures that suffer from significant thermic dispersion:

- the management and enhancement of entertainment activities;
- the formation of cultural activities for tourism purposes;
- cooperation with cultural institutions and associations.

It would be possible to contribute, instead, to the removal of the main critical points, even if only with a further modest investment and to structuring an integrated approach, by actions of:

- coordination of cultural activities in a single programme and integrated communication of events;
- promotion of active participation of cultural operators in the Cultural Policy of the Municipality of Potenza;
- enhancement of the capacity of cultural operators to apply to calls for proposals and calls for access to FUS, Regional and European funding.

Introduction of the "Culture Charter" service charter for young people, students and disadvantaged groups.

4 Research Perspectives

The research and use of additional funds in a programming perspective as proposed by L.R. 37/2014 appears to be a useful perspective as long as we consider the infrastructure system for cultural activities as part of a system of enhancement of the city with a view to improving its attractiveness.

Prospects for this research are therefore two-sided:

- The valorisation of Integrated Territorial Investment programmes as a trigger for further public and mixed investment policies with the aim of adhering to what the strategic document calls "ambitions of the City".
- The attractiveness that is seen not only with reference to the potential for hotel and extra-hotel hospitality, but as the search for synergies between the services that the City offers as a whole and as a center of dissemination initiatives in the territory of Basilicata, especially throughout the Apennines that results to be the weakest one.

Both these two directions look at the need to deliberate: the formulation of the Structural Plan and the Strategic Plan, two figures of the vast (too) toolkit that, although in the precariousness of their definitions, could serve as a guide for the achievement of investments in the territory that were: shared and "concentrated, place-context based" [12] and, therefore, able to activate effects in the direction of growth that enhances the "assets" of a land that, despite the wounds inflicted on the open territory, still has significant potentials.

To this end, starting from the strategic document of the ITI [11], it will be possible to define a structured framework of goals, connected to each other and converging to the definition of the desired role for the city and consequent innovative knowledge management tools (among others we focus urban development Ontologies [13]).

On the basis of methodological research that aims to oppose the "liquefaction" of forms of territorial government Bauman [14], consolidating a propensity towards shared and participated "anti-fragile planning" [4, 15] and pushing towards an appropriate form of resilience [16].

A continuation of the research work that is placed towards the pursuit of that rationality of the public decision to which the citizens are entitled [17, 18].

Acknowledgements. The work represents a joint reflection of the authors (Sects. 1, 2 and 4). Section 3 is an extract from a wider study by Cristina Guglielmi and Margherita Magnante, currently in the process of being published.

References

1. Las Casas, G.B., Scorza, F., Murgante, B.: Razionalità A-Priori: una proposta verso una pianificazione antifragile, Ital. J. Reg. Sci. (2018, in printing)
2. Las Casas, G.B., Scorza, F.: I conflitti fra lo sviluppo economico e l'ambiente: strumenti di controllo. In: Atti della XIX Conferenza nazionale SIU, Cambiamenti, Responsabilità e strumenti per l'urbanistica a servizio del paese, Catania, 16–18 Giugno 2016. Planum Publisher, Roma-Milano (2017)

3. Las Casas, G., Scorza, F., Murgante, B.: New urban agenda and open challenges for urban and regional planning. In: Calabrò, F., Della Spina, L., Bevilacqua, C. (eds.) ISHT 2018. SIST, vol. 100, pp. 282–288. Springer, Cham (2018). https://doi.org/10.1007/978-3-319-92099-3_33

4. Las Casas, G., Scorza, F.: A renewed rational approach from liquid society towards anti-fragile planning. In: Gervasi, O., et al. (eds.) ICCSA 2017. LNCS, vol. 10409, pp. 517–526. Springer, Cham (2017). https://doi.org/10.1007/978-3-319-62407-5_36

5. UN HABITAT: International Guidelines on Urban and Territorial Planning, UN-Habitat (2015)

6. UN HABITAT: New Urban Agenda, UN-Habitat (2016)

7. UN HABITAT: Action Framework for Implementation of the New Urban Agenda UN UN-Habitat (2017)

8. Las Casas, G.B., Scorza, F.: Un approccio "context-based" e "valutazione integrata" per il futuro della programmazione operativa regionale in Europa. In: Bramanti, A., Salone, C. (a cura di) Lo Sviluppo Territoriale Nell'economia Della Conoscenza: Teorie, Attori Strategie, Collana Scienze Regionali, FrancoAngeli, Milano, vol. 41 (2009)

9. Barca, F.: An agenda for a reformed cohesion policy: a place-based approach to meeting European union challenges and expectations. In: Independent Report Prepared at the Request of the European Commissioner for Regional Policy, Danuta Hübner, European Commission, Brussels (2009)

10. Francini, M., Viapiana, M.F., Palermo, A.: Aree interne: un'importante inclinazione territoriale per integrate politiche di coesione. In: Territorio: 80, 1, Franco Angeli, Milano (2017). https://doi.org/10.3280/tr2017-080018

11. Città di Potenza: Investimento territoriale integrato per lo sviluppo urbano della Città di Potenza - Documento Strategico (2017)

12. Leone, F., Zoppi, C.: Participatory Processes and Spatial Planning: The Regional Landscape Plan Of Sardinia. Territorio geovernance e sostenibilità, Milano (2016). Franco Angeli. ISBN 9788891740984

13. Scorza, F., Las Casas, G.B., Murgante, B.: That's ReDO: ontologies and regional development planning. In: Murgante, B., et al. (eds.) ICCSA 2012. LNCS, vol. 7334, pp. 640–652. Springer, Heidelberg (2012). https://doi.org/10.1007/978-3-642-31075-1_48

14. Bauman, Z.: Liquid Modernity. John Wiley & Sons, Hoboken (2013)

15. Blečić, I., Cecchini, A.: Verso una pianificazione antifragile, F. Angeli (2016)

16. Davoudi, S.: Resilience: a bridging concept or a dead end? Plann. Theor. Pract. 13(2), 299–307 (2012)

17. Las Casas, G.B.: L'etica della Razionalità. In: Urbanistica e Informazioni, vol. 144 (1995)

18. Casas, G.L., Scorza, F.: Sustainable planning: a methodological toolkit. In: Gervasi, O., et al. (eds.) ICCSA 2016. LNCS, vol. 9786, pp. 627–635. Springer, Cham (2016). https://doi.org/10.1007/978-3-319-42085-1_53

The Role of Intermediate Territories for New Sustainable Planning and Governance Approaches. Criteria and Requirements for Determining Multi-municipal Dimension: South Italy Case

Piergiuseppe Pontrandolfi[(✉)] and Antonella Cartolano

University of Basilicata DICEM, Matera, Italy
piergiuseppe.pontrandolfi@gmail.com, anto.cartolano@gmail.com

Abstract. In a context like the Italian one, in which the pulverization of Municipalities, the hyper-territorialization and the inadequacy of the current administrative network are the cause of ineffective and inefficient public policies, the paper investigates the close relationship between institutional and economic-territorial policies, through a comprehensive re-reading of the system of the organization of local authorities in Italy aimed, on the basis of some reading and interpretation criteria adopted, to identify more relevant territorial morphologies to ensure more advanced and effective forms of representation and government. The aim is to experiment with a possible methodology for reading the territories able to respond to the need to adapt the territorial structure of local authorities to the new challenges of modernity and economic-productive innovation and to the rescaling induced by globalization. A contribution to the process, still in progress, on the rules and principles according to which municipalities should join in functional, areas or networks, able to govern territories and promote conditions of greater sustainability in local development processes (1).

Keywords: Planning · Governance · Territory

1 Introduction

In a national regulatory scenario that is increasingly pushing towards the promotion of aggregative and centralizing logics, the contribution asks about the possible effects of this legislative trend on territorial governance and, in particular, on the planning and development policies of territories in the absence of guiding criteria that may accompany this now irreversible process. A process that cannot be driven by the need to rationalise public spending alone and cannot be anchored in purely quantitative terms, given that public policies are not indifferent to the "geographical perimeter" to which they refer, even more so if the theme of comparison is the government of the territory.

On the one hand the "pulverization of Municipalities" and on the other the phenomenon of "hyper-territorialization" [2], produce a "geographical short-circuit" that hinders the effectiveness of actions and functions, direct or indirect, placed on the local authorities [3], with an increase in the economic/territorial imbalances, aggravated by

© Springer International Publishing AG, part of Springer Nature 2018
O. Gervasi et al. (Eds.): ICCSA 2018, LNCS 10964, pp. 744–762, 2018.
https://doi.org/10.1007/978-3-319-95174-4_57

the existence of multiple and diversified models of organization of the geographical space [4].

Hence the need for a comprehensive redesign of the institutional architecture that moves in the direction of accompanying current territorial and urban dynamics towards institutional forms and instruments of territorial government that are more responsive to the new challenges to which public action must respond, imagining therefore, new forms of organization and extension of various territorial entities and most appropriate instruments of governance.

However, it should be noted that a certain mismatch between territorial dynamics and political-administrative partitions is inevitable. In fact, the territory is articulated in institutional regions, and it means however to claim to contain within a defined boundaries a complex, dynamic and evolving system of spatial relations. Despite this it is also true that political-administrative action gains in effectiveness when its territorial "cut-out" corresponds to that of functional regions; just as it is also true that the latter, in turn, to some extent are modelled also with references to the spatial distribution of the network of collective services, infrastructures and other structuring factors that depend on the decisions and funding of the public administration [1].

It is a matter of configuring a more appropriate institutional framework that represents the "hard core" of policies and projects, capable of producing sedimentations and cumulative processes [5], even in the recognition of "variable geometry" strategies, policies and actions [6, 7].

It is obvious how the affirmation of new spaces of government has a direct impact on the operational instruments of planning, programming [8] and the management of territories at all levels, thus representing further key elements of reflection.

It is a matter of crossing boundaries with respect to their limited operativeness, in order to establish network relationships with other territorial interlocutors, through the search for new crystals for the interpretation of regional and sub-regional areas, more suitable to respond to the peculiarities of the territories and to the strategies and policies implemented.

It is demonstrated, in fact, how today's "administrative cropping" differs significantly from the actual economic-political geography of the country [3].

Experimentation of new territorial organizations, t proliferation of soft spaces resulting from past planning seasons and sectoral policies, obligation of the associated management of services - even though they are manifestations of awareness of the importance and need to act on a more coherent scale to that of territorial and urban dynamics coinciding with the multi-communal dimension in its different configurations - highlight strong operational limits that hinder the effective recognition of optimal relevant areas, both for an effective and efficient reorganization of local services and for the promotion of credible local development policies and programmes.

Indeed, understanding necessary prerequisites for policies to take shape in a stable way in territories is itself a strategic step. Spatial organization of the Italian territory - characterized by a preponderance of small centres that, in many cases, suffer from limited accessibility to services - is a strategic key to the priority intervention for the relaunch of the entire country.

Therefore, starting from this close link between territorial and political spheres, an important part of the work focuses on the research of possible criteria to be adopted for the identification of multi-municipal areas, functional to the management and implementation of development strategies and territorial rebalancing.

2 Criteria and Requirements for Determining Multimunicipal Dimension

As already observed in previous studies [8, 9], rather than methodologies in the strict sense, it seems more correct to speak of "analytical strategies" that - starting from some initial premises and based on subsequent steps - outline an operational path of identification of "pertinent" spatial areas starting from clear objectives.

"Multi-step" strategies that involve a more "selective" treatment of informations, in relation to characteristics of examined territory and leaving a relatively wide border to interpretative interventions of the analyst.

The identification of possible "relevant" multi-municipal geographies took place through a series of criteria that accompanied, in successive steps, the reading of the territories. On the basis of the performance objectives for the multi-municipal morphologies to be identified and their functioning, a minimum set of criteria has been identified for the identification of different kinds of multi-municipal morphologies which, in the first instance, represent the areas in which the territories, through a voluntary process shared from below, must recognize their own identity and functional unity.

Multi-municipal morphologies are identified on the basis of the recognition of characters and conditions capable, theoretically at least, of meeting following objectives:

- to offer an adequate quality of life or guarantee the presence of a minimum endowment of services to person such that any development policy is not frustrated and that human permanence in the area is maintained;
- to harmonize transformation choices of the physical assets of the territories in a perspective that favours local development processes (assuming physical dimension of uses and transformations of the territory as an aspect not secondary to development policies);
- to represent a stable organizational and institutional structure with respect to development policies, without prejudicing possible opening up to multiple and variable geometries which flexible and adaptable planning and management tools can be connected to.

On the basis of these objectives, readings and interpretations of the elements that structure and characterize territories or which represent the main economic and territorial dynamics were made to carry out an applicative experimentation aimed at identifying different inter-municipal morphologies.

First reading concerned the presence of services (to individuals and companies) within the territory and their level of accessibility. The diversity of territories, in terms of equipment and infrastructure, requires a preliminary survey of the location of existing services and equipment, in order to preserve fixed assets where they exist and to enhance their value to make them functional in responding to the demands and needs of less well-equipped neighbouring territories.

A second reading referred to the reconstruction of " planning territories" referring to past programming seasons and to the community in particular. This aspect, as reiterated for example in recent experimentation of Local Territorial Systems [6] and of the Urban Bioregions [10] is fundamental for the interpretation of the most recent territorial and economic dynamics. The network of actors, protagonists in various ways of promoting local strategies and projects, is a crucial aspect for understanding functioning of territories and for the implementation of development policies. The ability of territories to work together and experiences that have taken on a wider vision than the limited municipal dimension, refer, in the first instance, to the seasons of community planning (Territorial Pacts, PIT, PSL, Internal Areas strategy, etc.). These experiences help in understanding the heritage of existing relationships to consolidate/recover, develop, implement and eventually build shared visions of territorial development.

Furthermore, reading of physical characteristics of the territories, with reference to that set of "invariants" [10] that restore physiognomy of the territory and contribute to defining its identity.

In this sense, reading landscapes - as perceived by insular populations and whose character derives from the action of natural and/or human factors and their interrelations (European Landscape Convention Art. 1, letter a) - in addition to influencing the functionality of multi-municipal morphologies (think of the issue of accessibility), general rules of settlement and those of possible transformation of the physical assets of the territory, help to define sustainable and competitive territorial development models [11] and this is why they represent central elements in identification of entities at a pluri-municipal scale.

Each of the readings made has found operative support in the construction of cognitive and analytical frameworks specifically imagined in research or in consideration of studies, researches, analyses and elaborations already existing, considered and evaluated, within the work, according to the objectives set.

The readings made and subsequent interpretations and simulations were based on general interpretative rules defined upstream and during the process of experimental and gradual "identification" of groupings and aggregations.

Rules defined are the following:

1. groupings must present a certain degree of homogeneity;
2. groupings shall ensure that an appropriate level of spatial and functional interdependence is recognised;
3. groupings cannot overlap;
4. groupings may not present continuity solutions (they must be spatially contiguous);
5. the number of groupings must be limited;
6. the size of the groupings must reach (not exceed) an appropriate size threshold;
7. the internal accessibility of the groupings must meet certain requirements;
8. groupings must show a certain stability over time [5].

The interpretation work was based on a step-to-step reading that progressively crosses the different thematic readings made, trying to give a summary of the subsequent results achieved.

Before going into the operational description of the simulations performed, some further clarifications are necessary.

Criteria and rules applied and step-to-step methodology adopted were conceived for a possible operational experimentation in local contexts considered; hence need for a simple approach that could accompany the self-recognition process without, for this reason, giving up considering the complexity of the situations and contexts examined.

Proposed and tested methodology seeks to preserve a right balance between the operational immediacy of reading context and the complexity and number of variables to be considered, filling, at least in part, the data availability gap that is still recorded (with reference to example services, economic activities, internet coverage, etc…).

Experimentation area includes the southern peninsular regions, and in particular Campania, Puglia and Basilicata; Calabria was not considered for the objective difficulties in the recognition of data that prevented production of the same analyzes carried out for the other Regions.

The field of study is considerable interesting for several reasons. These include the presence of border areas in which interesting inter-regional dynamics are observed. Precisely the territory of Basilicata Region is representative of a reality in which internal dynamics are strongly conditioned by relations with other realities outside regional boundaries and in which there are consolidated processes of gravitations that currently do not find any administrative representativeness.

Another interesting element is represented by the diversity of the territorial contexts under study; we move from the metropolitan area of Naples, in the opinion of many the only true Italian metropolis, to several "internal areas" present in each region. Physical and structural characteristics of these three regions, in fact, implicate the need for a polycentric-reticular rebalancing of the territories.

Finally, the condition of peninsularity facilitates the definition of boundaries and stimulates its reading transversely to the Tyrrhenian and Ionian/Adriatic coastal roads.

3 Proposed Multi-municipal Reading for Campania, Puglia and Basilicata

First reading refers to the presence within considered territories of service supply, of mobility infrastructures and productive system, all strategic variables that characterize their structure and organization.

Spatial analysis of these facilities is aimed at identifying a territorial articulation capable of maximizing accessibility conditions for local population to use these services and consume goods; therefore, reference is made to policies for allocating resources, locating supply, organizing and developing communications [5].

Analytical reading of these different situations was preceded by a preliminary and essential survey of existing services and equipment, in order to identify areas with the highest concentration and those, on the contrary, less densely served.

The main objective was to identify Municipalities or groups of Municipalities that, due to the equipment and services offered and not having the characteristics of metropolitan centres or medium-sized cities, potentially lend themselves to being poly-attracts towards the adjacent Municipalities less gifted, or complementary poles. In this case, it is a question of identifying the specific group of Municipalities which, even if not territorially contiguous, generally have a certain amount of functional services for a larger territory.

Analysis carried out develops in following phases:

- selection and classification of main services;
- data recognition;
- data preparation;
- geolocation of services;
- elaboration of the concentration maps functional to territorial readings;
- identification of the poles.

In absence of a national inventory from which information about the presence of equipment and services could be obtained, a preliminary survey of the main existing services was carried out.

A fundamental first step was the discretization of essential services of citizenship or of the patrimony of services that must necessarily be offered to the local populations in order to guarantee a good quality of life and the permanency throughout them.

There are three questions and elements analysed functional to the identification of poles (of services): the presence of services to the population, the infrastructural facilities for mobility, the basic economic-productive system.

Each of three aspects has been described through a detailed survey and organization of available data, processed in order to obtain initial indications on the potential of territories in terms of services, infrastructures and production facilities.

The recognition of heritage of services has not been limited to the identification, within a municipality, of the presence of a specific equipment or service, but has gone so far as to geologise acquired data.

In absence of a univocal database it was not possible to proceed with identification of all types of existing services (and which would deserve to be registered), just as it was not possible to proceed with a precise localization of services for entire national context (Fig. 1). Above services listed represent only those for which it was possible to make a survey through open-data banks and/or specific processing.

For this reason, for each category listed above, an in-depth analysis was carried out on web to identify official databases that present geolocalized data of services to be registered.

In other cases - that is, when the official portal of a specific service made available the list, in various forms, of addresses - addresses were extrapolated and processed before proceeding to next geolocation of the elements of interest.

Specifically, free bathgeo service was used to map and geolocate address lists.

Numerous difficulties encountered in acquisition and processing data did not particularly affect result. Scale of reference, suitable for analysis referring to a vast area, and the nature of analyses, which do not go into qualitative considerations, have involved

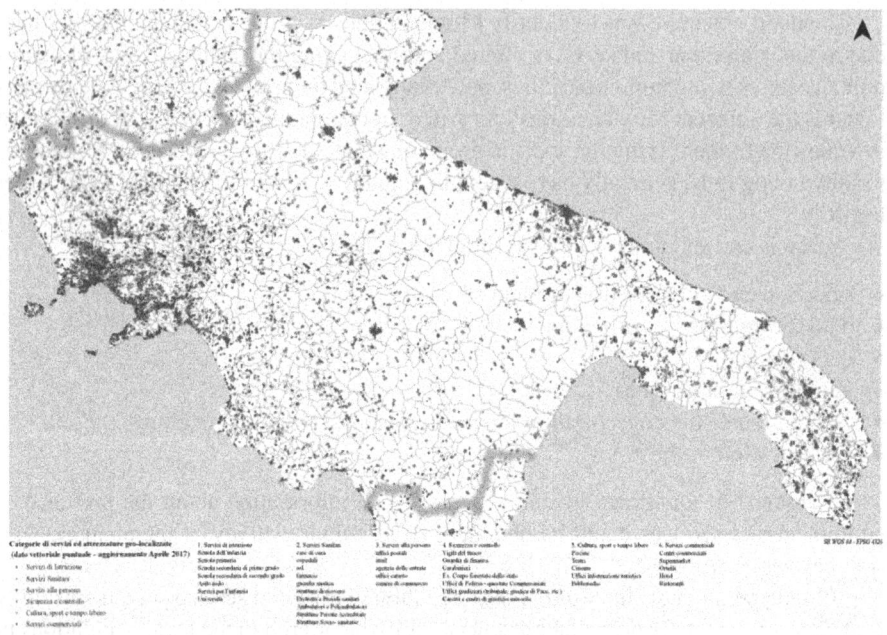

Fig. 1. Geolocation of services and equipment.

the fact that simple geolocation of services, together with a suitably evaluated classification, could represent a solid and valid starting point for conducting an analysis with a high degree of accuracy, useful for achieving significant results.

Subsequent to the operation of returning to map, and as these are point data, we proceeded to draw up a map of concentrations using the IT tools available in GIS environment (Fig. 2).

The objective was to identify the areas with the greatest concentration of services, starting from geolocalized data, in order to identify areas most equipped. The function used is that of "Kernel density" with a research radius of about 10 km.

Raster of personal and mobility services concentrations and of enterprises and production companies have been elaborated (Fig. 3), problem has been identified of the so-called "intermediate poles" represented by one or more municipalities in which there is a greater concentration of services and of mobility equipment and which have a greater liveliness in economic terms (in terms of significant presence of production facilities).

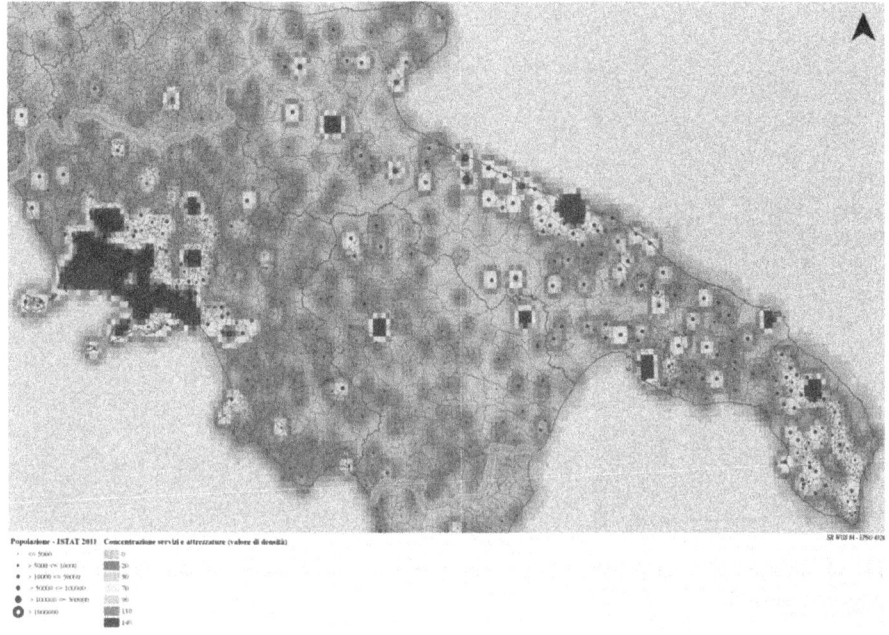

Fig. 2. Map of concentration services and equipment.

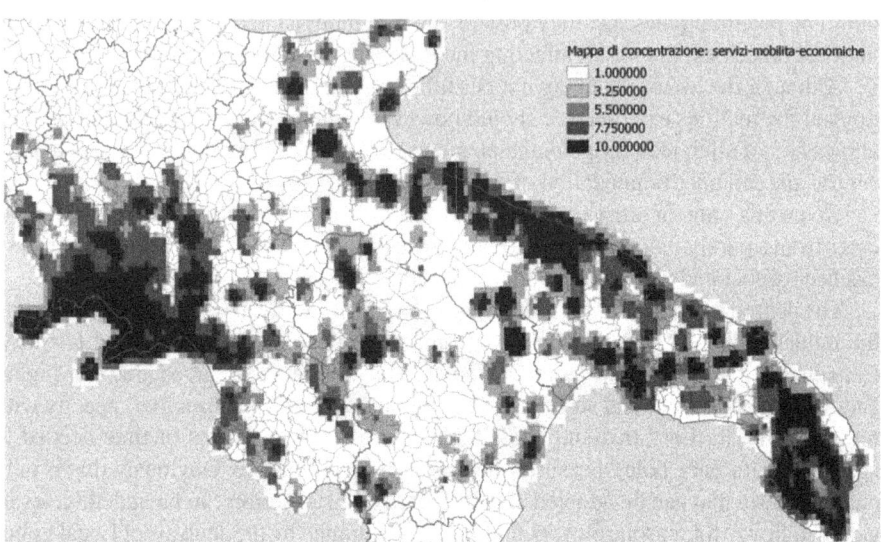

Fig. 3. Map of concentration of summary services - mobility - economic activities.

At this point, to determine the potential poles around which to construct multi-municipal morphologies, a threshold value was considered and established in 5 (mean value) (Fig. 4).

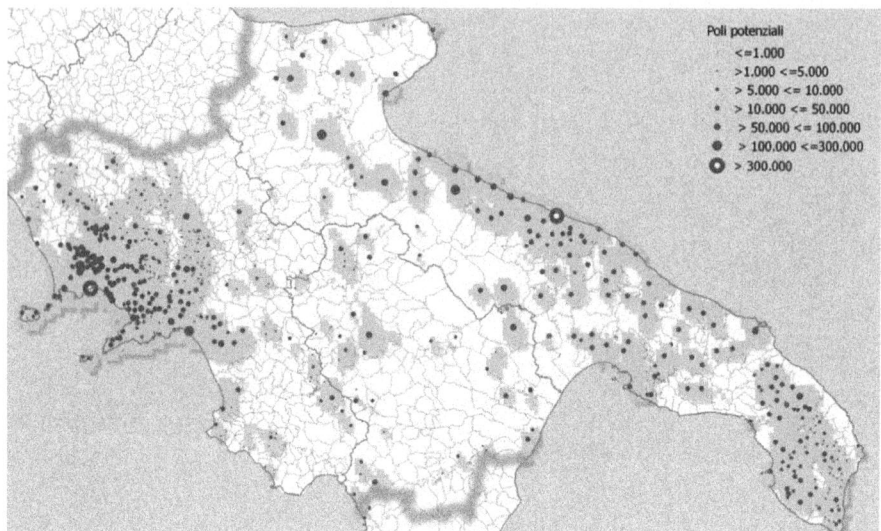

Fig. 4. Identification of potential poles with services concentration greater than the average placed value of 5.

Following elaborations carried out, there is a preliminary indication of areas that, for endowments of services, infrastructures for mobility and economic activities turn out to be potential poles, i.e. they possess the minimum characteristics to trigger gravitational processes, first of all affecting the less gifted neighbouring territorial realities.

Although the use of data may not be sufficiently representative of the actual conditions of the realities examined, it should however be noted that this method of reading allows first of all to identify potential elements that can be strengthened towards a polycentric and reticular organization of the territory [12].

Given this - and in order to define a first identification of multi-municipal morphologies from a purely functional point of view - theme of services, as previously discussed, has been associated with theme of accessibility.

The degree of accessibility, in fact, is one of the most effective criteria for assessing the influence that a "potential pole" has on a more or less vast surrounding territory. Considering therefore that "potential poles", by definition assumed, have a higher endowment of services and such as to exert an influence and an attractive capacity with respect to the territory that surrounds them, accessibility, in terms of time needed to access the reference pole, measures the extent of this influence. Obviously this is only one of criteria that can be adopted and applied. To this criterion can be added the evaluation of flows, for reasons of work and study, as assumed by the analysis of Local Labor Systems developed in the follow-up of the research work.

The gravity areas of thus identified range from metropolitan areas to smaller centers, assuming, therefore, that each multi-municipal morphology has within it one or more main centers around which areas of influence and/or gravitation are generated [1].

On the basis of these considerations "poles", as previously identified, have been preliminarily classified into 7 ranges, which identify their descending functional rank.

For each typology of poles accessibility isochrons have been calculated, divided into 10 min intervals and within the maximum limit of 40 min.

As already mentioned, just to take into account conditions of spatial proximity, a pole of lower rank - included in an area of influence in the maximum limit of 20 min - was not considered as a pole for the calculation of isochrons, considering it absorbed by area of influence of the potential pole of higher rank in whose limit isochron falls.

Furthermore, in areas where there is a high concentration of poles, belonging to the same rank, selection took place considering the most populous centre.

5 levels of isochrones were identified by maps elaborated with reference to poles of two metropolitan cities, the first level poles, the second level poles, the third level poles and finally the fourth level poles.

From representation of the isochrones immediately emerge as north of Campania, in addition to registering a high number of potential poles, it is also characterized by a favourable accessibility to them. An opposite situation is recorded in the north of Puglia, and in particular in the Gargano, where, in addition to registering a limited number of potential poles, a reduced accessibility to them is also noticeable, given the limited extent of the areas reached within 10 to 20 min (Fig. 5).

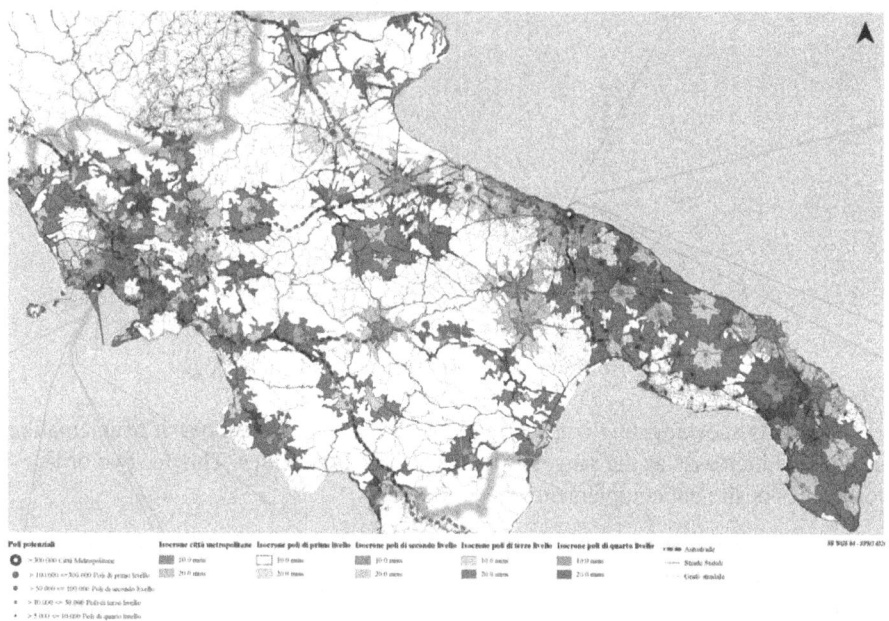

Fig. 5. Isochrons of potential poles.

Central and southern parts of Puglia are characterized by an easy accessibility with respect to the poles - as can be detected by large areas reachable within ten and twenty minutes - with a prevalence of third level poles, i.e. with a population between 10,000 and the 50,000 inhabitants.

Observing Basilicata Region and the south of Campania, it is immediately evident how limited the number of potential poles is, with an accessibility that is not always optimal. Starting from preliminary identification of areas of influence of the potential poles, we proceeded to the evaluation of possible pluri-municipal morphologies (Fig. 6). Deliberately, during the evaluation activity, regional and provincial limits were not taken into account, assuming single Municipality as the basic unit. Evaluation took place for subsequent cross-readings.

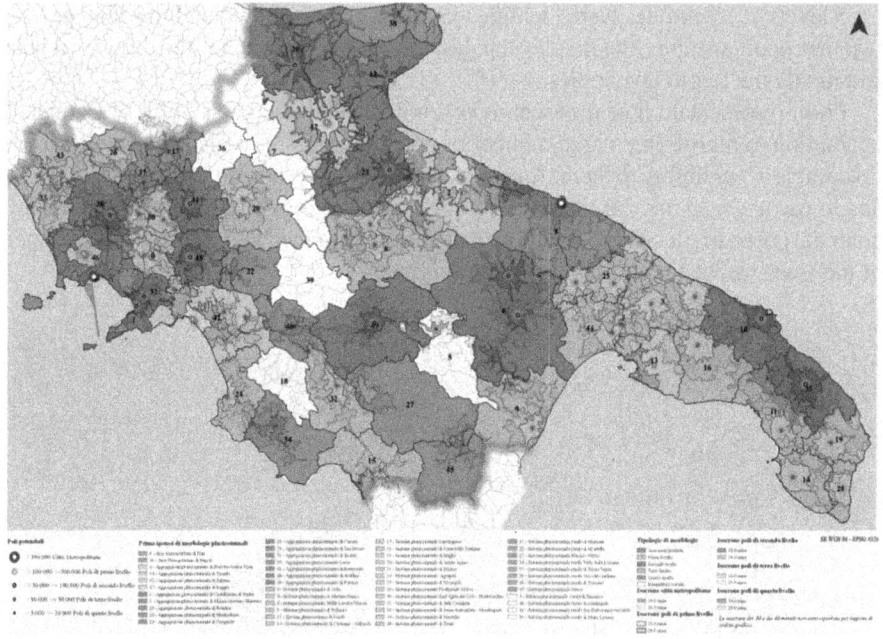

Fig. 6. First identification of pluri-municipal morphologies.

Generally speaking, and considering due exceptions, the number of Municipalities considered increases as the range of pole considered decreases. This for two orders of reasons, opposite but complementary:

- on the one hand, not to further streamline flows on already densely populated urban and/or metropolitan areas;
- on the other, aim to increase the critical mass (in terms above all of resident population) to increase efficiency in management of services as well as development opportunities in less densely populated areas.

Therefore, there are two objectives pursued in this preliminary perimeter: to lighten weight of metropolitan/urban areas by strengthening the innermost areas and imagining more structured and consolidated urban systems (as proposed by Archibugi in the definition of urban ecosystems).

Completed checks on the perimetrations of different morphologies, starting from poles and relative isochrones, we have found ourselves faced with areas without potential poles and not included in any area of influence of major centres. These areas, named as rebalancing of services, are those in which, presumably, condition of the absence of services and accessibility is more dramatic. These are border areas between Campania and Puglia, in the northern part of two regions, border areas between the Potentino and the Avellinese, areas of internal Cilento of Campania and those, finally, of a hinge between two provinces of Basilicata.

It should be noted that the main limit of the comparisons made is represented by the fact that various territorial readings, from time to time considered, are contained and limited, generally, within existing administrative, provincial and regional limits, not taking into account the particularity of border areas.

Conscious of this condition (institutionally imposed) we proceeded to cross-reading with:

- perimeters of Local Labor Systems to 2011 in order to take into account the commuting flows for work and study purposes contained within each SSL (Figs. 7 and 8);

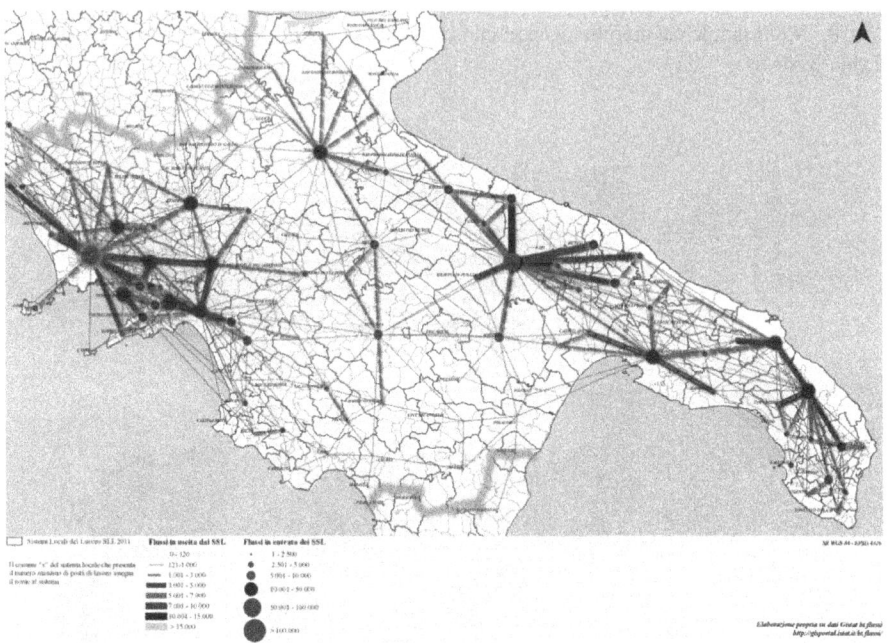

Fig. 7. Commuting flows for work and study purposes.

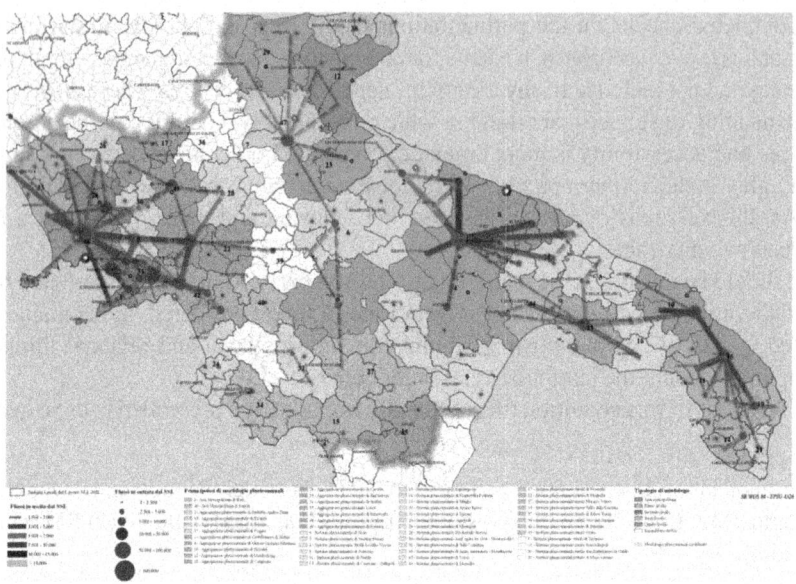

Fig. 8. Multi-municipal morphologies, commuting flows for work and study purposes and Local Labor Systems.

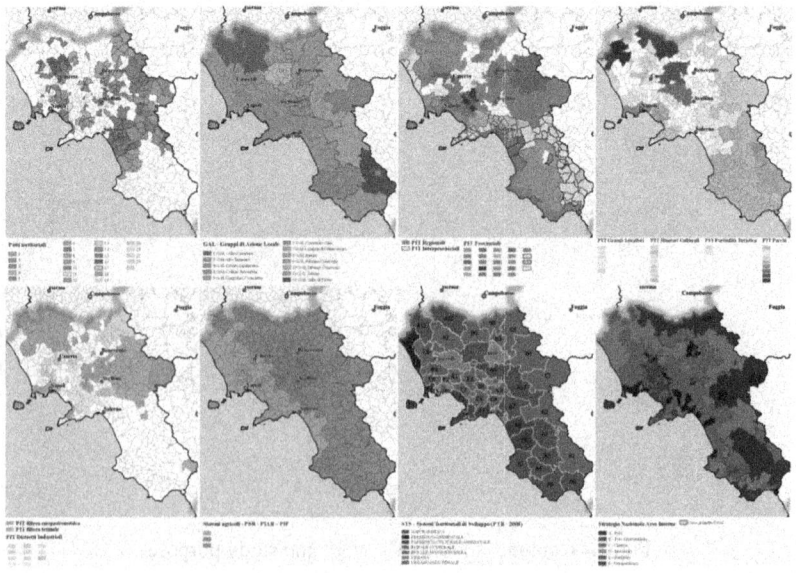

Fig. 9. Planning framework for the campania region.

- reading of territorial perimeters defined in the past programming seasons and of the multi-city scale configurations stratified over time, which help to intercept network of local actors as learned in the SLOT experience and to highlight the ability of territories to work together (Figs. 9 and 10);

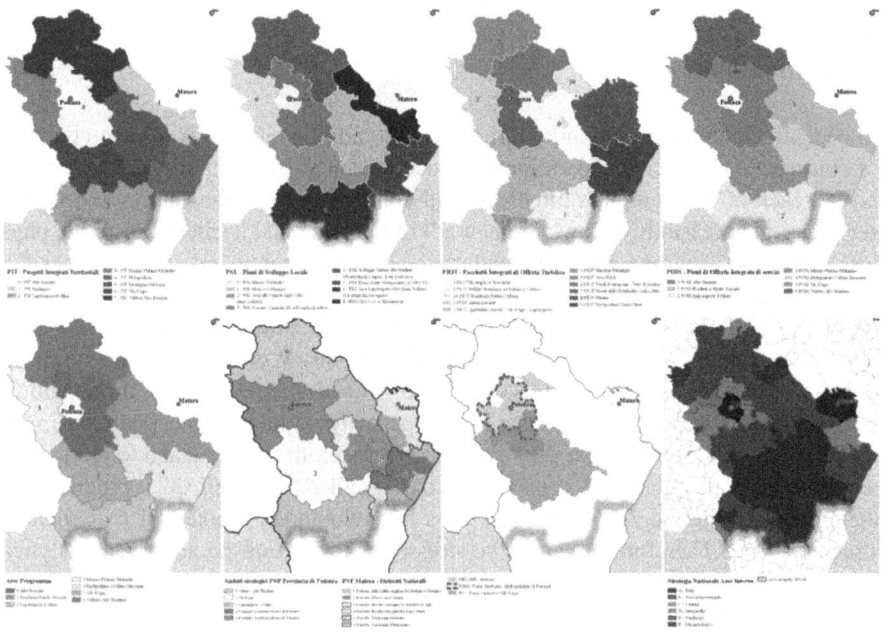

Fig. 10. Planning framework for the Basilicata region.

- physical-morphological aspects, functional to understand on the one hand the physical barriers that hinder consolidation of solid and stable cooperation relationships over time between various Municipalities belonging to multi-municipal entities and, on the other, any homogeneous landscape;

Finally, the map has been subjected to a series of subjects (deliberately not experts) residing in the territories of the three Regions to verify if the perimeter correspondence with perception of real relationships of gravity and influence, as perceived by people who they live, for reasons of residence or work, territories in question. With reference to this last aspect, it should be noted how the comparison is only an example and how perception of these aspects, by the real actors of the territories, is an important issue in recognition of territorial morphologies. This comparison, by way of example, has been used to refine morphologies according to real dynamics as perceived locally.

It is interesting to note - from the cross between pluri-municipal morphologies as configured in the last hypothesis with the SLLs and the planning frameworks reconstructed for the three regions - as high heterogeneity of the territorial perimeters defined during various programming seasons render difficult to identify stable morphologies to take into account in defining possible new configurations.

In fact, especially for older experiences, perimeters linked to planning and/or planning strategies and policies have a high variability that prevents a summary reading to be taken as an element of consistency and stability consolidated over time.

4 Conclusion

The identification of preliminary pluri-municipal morphologies took place on the basis of construction of a cognitive framework accompanied by a plurality of information layers (each of which returns often very different territorial organizations and forms): services and accessibility, flows, framework of planning and territorial districts, physical, ecological-environmental and land use readings, perceptual/identity readings.

On a large scale, identification of pluri-municipal morphologies took place primarily on the basis of essential prerequisites that regulate human life and permanency in the territories, or presence of essential services of citizens. Without doubt the system of organization of goods supply and services, whose functioning determines the conditions of life quality, can be assessed, even if only partially, in terms of accessibility [5]. In fact, services, and in particular the "advanced" ones, both to person and to production, represent the main polarities through which the so-called "urban effect" is produced and therefore the same degree of attractiveness and evolutionary potential of settlement structures [12]. Therefore, it cannot be stressed that most of the advanced analytical proposals are essentially based on the concepts of "functional or nodal system" (5) and on the area of influence [1]. Preliminary evaluations and proposals (of "basic" we could say) followed a series of successive adjustments, as described above, functional to the multiplicity of elements that must be based on the recognition and interpretation of territories. Starting from these assumptions, identification of pluri-municipal morphologies has come about with the specific purpose of recognizing territories that can represent a design and management reference that is stable over time.

The framework of morphologies, thus constituted, represents the background with respect to which different subjects and different actions are placed and interact.

Analysis identifies six profiles of pluri-municipal morphologies, for a total of 49, namely:

- monocentric structures in which there is a centre with a strong attractiveness and in which there is a large concentration of activities and people, high levels of mobility for work, study and use of services, polarization of innovative and strategic activities. These are the large urban areas, meaning, for urban areas, not only the administrative boundaries of cities but also territory surrounding them, within which the functions that city is no longer able to contain and within which the dynamics typical of metropolitan areas are verified. These are therefore metropolitan areas.
- pluri-municipal morphologies of first level structures articulated, again, around a centre with strong attractiveness, but smaller than metropolitan area. These are typically provincial capitals with a population of more than 100,000 and less than 300,000 inhabitants.
- Second level pluri-municipal morphologies. These include poles with populations over 50,000 and less than 100,000, which, together with poles of previous structure,

largely coincide with the classification of medium-sized cities Anci-IFEL 2013. The limit of 50,000 inhabitants is taken as a threshold minimum to identify poles, or urban centres, able to offer essential services. These are cities that, although often presenting high quality conditions of life, do not reach a more advanced threshold of "urbanity" [13].

These cities can play an important role not only for the welfare of inhabitants, but also for surrounding rural populations. Their presence serves to prevent depopulation of rural areas and exodus towards cities and to promote a balanced territory development [14].

– Third-level multi-municipal morphologies. In these we can find one or more poles with dimensions between 10,000 and 20,000 inhabitants (third level poles ap-point).

These morphologies are characterized by the presence of centres of small-medium size, with a low density of services. Generally, these structures include Municipalities classified as internal. Despite the certainly not optimal conditions, the presence of the poles, even if of lower rank for dimensional characteristics and for services, represents a potential on which to invest, from which to imagine and build a polycentric and more balanced development of the whole territory.

– Four-tier plurinominal morphologies. Unlike previous ones, in this category poles assume even smaller dimensions, including between 5,000 and 10,000 inhabitants. Weaker provision of services and more marked levels of rurality of municipalities included in these areas.

The sixth and last morphology refers to classified areas of "rebalancing of services" and coincides with internal areas of the country, classified as peripheral and ultra-peripheral in the SNAI and with those classified as rural areas with complex development problems. Within these, no pole is present and, therefore, their configuration presupposes and requires, as a priority, policies to enhance services and mobility infrastructures to be implemented on multi-municipal scale.

This last group of morphologies identifies complex and articulated structures in several urban centres that have weak functional relationships between them [15]. In particular, urban centres, with a population below a critical threshold, should integrate with each other in "city systems" in order to reach, together, the so-called city effect, overturning existing and traditional dependency condition and of gravitation with respect to centres of higher rank, often distant, functionally overloaded and hypertrophic. It is what is called a "strategy of integration and polarization" [13].

These profiles can be traced back to a network model [16] in which the role of a centre does not necessarily depend on its size but also and above all on its ability to integrate itself in the exchange circuits - not just economic ones - bringing into play its environmental and cultural specificities [12].

In these morphologies, therefore, verified mutual accessibility between various centres within the maximum limit of 40 min, polycentric models to be built starting from existing potentials in terms of services and equipment.

Looking more closely at Basilicata, in the region there are 9 multi-municipal morphologies, 4 of which are interregional. Lucan territory, hinge between the two

Tyrrhenian and Ionian/Adriatic coastal routes, is characterized by having only two urban poles, coinciding with the two provincial capitals of Potenza and Matera, around which two second level morphologies develop. Furthermore, reading of the Lucan context returns a particular condition for on-board areas, i.e. those areas in which processes of gravitation and relationships, even historically consolidated, between different centers represent territorial morphologies that do not find any representativeness in current administrative limits.

One thinks, for example, of the reality of Matera that stands in close contact with important centres of the Puglia Region, with respect to which substantial gravitational flows are generated (think of the Matera-Altamura relations); in this sense, there is an area of mutual influence between urban centres (in addition to Altamura certainly also Gravina in Puglia) that looks beyond current regional limits and is characterized by the presence of Bradanica infrastructure.

Identified criteria (territorial readings addressed to services, accessibility, economic dimension, flows, planning) and step-to-step methodology adopted are conceived to have a possible operational application in local realities; hence the need for a simple approach that can accompany the self-recognition process, without oversimplifying complexity of the issues to be considered.

It should be stressed that we speak of "self-recognition" within a methodological frame of reference in which each reality, starting from its specificity, can bring out aspects of greater identity. In fact, it is not possible to impose solutions evaluated only in the abstract and hetero-direct to very different local and regional situations.

Evaluations and solutions must necessarily come from the bottom and with the widest possible participation of public and private subjects, configuring reading criteria proposed in the research work, as possible guide criteria in the accompaniment of local actors (public and private) in a self-recognition of the territories, inspired by the logic of interdependence and complementarity mentioned in the work.

In order to avoid that interest in new territorial readings on pluri-municipal scale may be conditioned by rigid regional (and clearly provincial) administrative boundaries, a reconsideration of the role and the same geographical extension and morphology of regions is proposed, to model them on the networks of cities and territories and adapt them as much as possible to a new functional articulation of the national territory and the European one [1].

Moreover, having noted that cities are no longer functional realities limited to the areas of single municipality, it will be necessary to recognize that this is no longer valid only for the few large metropolitan aggregates, but also for medium and small-sized cities. Therefore, policies should be referred to general category of the 'urban and territorial system' consisting of aggregations of municipalities. Such pluri-municipal aggregations could also be realized - and preferably - on the basis of voluntary accessions; certainly, however, such a process of institutional reorganization can not only be left to spontaneous and to extemporaneousness of initiatives [1].

A similar approach is also promoted by the European Union in the economic planning for the period 2014–2020. The EU urged Member States to strengthen their "institutional capacity" in the sense of taking a coordinated set of reform actions aimed at making public institutions, including decentralized ones, capable of tackling challenges of territorial competitiveness at global level, promoting smart, sustainable and inclusive growth, which is the purpose of new and well-known "Europe 2020" strategy [17].

Starting from the SSSE (European Space Development Scheme) of 1999, the principle of "polycentric and balanced spatial development" was enunciated, aimed at satisfying two mutually synergistic objectives: the competitive integration of Europe into world economy and the multiplication development engines on European territory.

To answer to the demand of effective development policies according with a rational planning approach [18, 19] and an efficient redefinition of organizational structure of the territories, it is necessary first of all a change of cultural paradigm that can not be founded only on the logic of spending cuts, which can only be pursued in presence of processes and adequate organizational models, through fight against waste and realization of economies of scale; in fact, it is not possible any automatism between the type of management chosen and the attainment of benefits and savings.

The process of institutional reorganization and stabilization of public finances - aimed at simplifying, rationalizing and reorganizing local self-esteem system - invests primarily organizational structure of the Municipalities, specifically those of smaller demographic size, for which it is urgent find new and more effective solutions [20].

In this perspective, a very challenging path from an institutional standpoint emerges, during which not only aspects relating to new perimeters of institutional and administrative areas should be carefully assessed, but also those relating to the precise definition of functions and possible new territorial entities that will be established, also in reference to local specificities and to substantial patrimony of experiences and infra-communal relations diffused in different contexts.

On the other hand, however, "liquidity" and speed of economic and territorial dynamics and processes require adequate margins of flexibility both in the organization of processes and in the definition of territorial areas of reference, apparently opposite conditions with respect to necessary stability of institutional arrangements, as argued and proposed in the present research work.

In this sense, it is necessary to imagine, above all, flexible instruments and procedures in the territories governance, capable of adapting to "variable geometries" of different configurations of questions and territorial dynamics, while recognizing a "hard core" of administrative organization on to invest human and financial resources, in order to promote an overall rebalancing of current structure of local institutions in our country.

References

1. Dematteis, G.: L'Italia e le sue Regioni. Regioni come reti di sistemi urbani. Abramo printing s.p.a., vol. 19, pp. 197–216 (2014)
2. Ferlaino, F., Molinari, P.: Neofederalismo, neoregionalismo e intercomunalità: il governo regionale e provinciale del territorio. Atti della XXX Conferenza Italiana di Scienze Regionali "Federalismo, integrazione europea e crescita regionale", Firenze (2009)
3. Società Geografica Italiana Onlus: Il riordino territoriale dello Stato, Scenari Italiani 2014. Rapporto annuale della Società Geografica Italiana (2014)
4. Rapporto Istat Sistemi Locali del Lavoro 2011: La nuova geografia dei Sistemi Locali, Roma (2015)

5. Preto, G., Occelli, S.: Zonizzazione territoriale ed ambiti spaziali delle politiche, Considerazioni teorico-metodologiche. In: Working Paper n. 105, IRES (1994)
6. Dematteis, G.: SLoT (Sistema locale territoriale). Uno strumento per rappresentare, leggere e trasformare il territorio. Documento del Convegno: Per un patto di sostenibilitá. Sviluppo locale e sostenibilità tra teoria e pratica, Pinerolo (2003)
7. Celata, F.: L'individuazione di partizioni del territorio nelle politiche di sviluppo locale in Italia. Ipotesi interpretative. Rivista Geografica Italiana **115**, 1–25 (2008)
8. Sforzi, F.: La regionalizzazione dei flussi come base spaziale per la pianificazione dei trasporti: alcune valutazioni empiriche delle principali tecniche. In: Reggiani, A. (a cura di) Territorio e trasporti. Modelli matematici per l'analisi e la pianificazione, F. Angeli, pp. 188–213 (1985)
9. Ires: L'organizzazione territoriale del Piemonte. In: Quaderni di ricerca Ires, n. 56, Torino: Ires (1988)
10. Magnaghi, A.: Il progetto locale. Verso la coscienza di luogo. Bollati Boringhieri Editore (2000)
11. Altieri, G.: Il paesaggio come elemento identitario e fonte di riconoscibilità nei processi di pianificazione territoriale della Provincia Autonoma di Trento. In: Planum. The Journal of Urbanism n° 25, vol. 2 (2012)
12. Fanfano, D.: La descrizione delle reti territoriali per il progetto di sviluppo locale autosostenibile. In: Magnaghi, A. (a cura di), Rappresentare i luoghi, metodi e tecniche. Alinea, Firenze (2001)
13. Archibugi, F.: La Città Ecologica. Urbanistica e sostenibilità. In: Bollati Boringhieri (2002)
14. ANCI-IFEL. "Quaderno n° 4", MMXIII (2013)
15. Parr, J.B.: The polycentric urban region: a closer inspection. Reg. Stud. **38**, 231–240 (2004)
16. Camagni, R., Salone, C.: Network urban structures in Northern Italy: elements for a theoretical frame-work. Urban Stud. **306**, 1053–1064 (1993)
17. Bruzzo, A.: Riferimenti teorici per la delimitazione territoriale delle Regioni. In: Argomenti, terza serie, n° 3 (2016)
18. Casas, G.L., Scorza, F.: Sustainable planning: a methodological toolkit. In: Gervasi, O., et al. (eds.) ICCSA 2016. LNCS, vol. 9786, pp. 627–635. Springer, Cham (2016). https://doi.org/10.1007/978-3-319-42085-1_53
19. Las Casas, G., Scorza, F.: A renewed rational approach from liquid society towards anti-fragile planning. In: Gervasi, O., et al. (eds.) ICCSA 2017. LNCS, vol. 10409, pp. 517–526. Springer, Cham (2017). https://doi.org/10.1007/978-3-319-62407-5_36
20. Casas, G.L., Scorza, F.: Discrete spatial assessment of multi-parameter phenomena in low density region: the Val D'Agri case. In: Gervasi, O., et al. (eds.) ICCSA 2015. LNCS, vol. 9157, pp. 813–824. Springer, Cham (2015). https://doi.org/10.1007/978-3-319-21470-2_59

Investigating Good Practices for Low Carbon Development Perspectives in Basilicata

Alessandro Attolico[1], Rosalia Smaldone[1], Francesco Scorza[2(✉)],
Emanuela De Marco[3], and Angela Pilogallo[2]

[1] Province of Potenza, Department of Territorial Planning and Development,
Environment and Civil Protection, Potenza, Italy
{alessandro.attolico,
rosalia.smaldone}@provinciapotenza.it
[2] LISUT - School of Engineering, University of Basilicata, Potenza, Italy
francesco.scorza@unibas.it, angela.pilogallo@libero.it
[3] SMART BASILICATA - School of Engineering,
University of Basilicata, Potenza, Italy
emanuelademarco83@gmail.com

Abstract. The Good Practices selected by the province of Potenza within the LOCARBO project, which are part of the Three Thematic Pillars of the project described below fully testify the experimentation of new cooperation practices in low-density contexts, where the results are positive when virtuous collaborations have been activated, linking energy policies objectives with citizens awareness, sustainable energy themes and new local entrepreneurial actions able to provide positive externalities from the economic point of view and the exploitation of local resources. This work re-classify the Good Practices presented in the LOCARBO project, according to different criteria constructed looking at the peculiar characteristics of the territorial context of reference. Low density contexts, implementation of integrated projects, inter-institutional cooperation models, collaborative approaches between institution and community and valorization of communities skills and local resources are the new criteria built after reading the local peculiarities, through to review projects and development strategies in Energy efficiency programs.

Keywords: Energy efficiency · Best practices · Context based policy

1 Introduction

The issue tackled by LOCARBO project, financed by the INTERREG EUROPE Program, fully fits *Priority Axis 3 Low Carbon Economy of the Interreg Europe Program*, which seeks change in improved implementation of regional development policies that incorporate actions to increase levels of energy efficiency including public buildings and the housing sector. Reduction of energy consumption by businesses and households is presented as a key field of action just as the introduction of ICT based solutions (through increasing the energy performance of public buildings or public awareness strategies).

© Springer International Publishing AG, part of Springer Nature 2018
O. Gervasi et al. (Eds.): ICCSA 2018, LNCS 10964, pp. 763–775, 2018.
https://doi.org/10.1007/978-3-319-95174-4_58

The province of Potenza leads the partnership reinforcing a former effective experience in transnational cooperation.

In this work, the Good Practices selected by the province of Potenza within the LOCARBO project, which are part of the Three Thematic Pillars of the project described below, are re-classified according to different criteria constructed according to the peculiar characteristics of the territories concerned and of relevance regarding the territorial context of reference.

In fact, issues related to the low density of the territories, social and economic problems, infrastructural deficiencies and the presence of significant environmental values emerge.

These issues strongly influenced the interaction with stakeholders and strategies in the sustainable development policies implementation, dictating a new classification that takes into account these aspects.

Conclusions underline the importance of experiences of international cooperation as an opportunity to compare different territorial realities, empowering technical capacity of the staff involved in project implementation and bringing added values for local experiences and actors participating in an effective networking process.

2 Three Thematic Pillars Structuring Institutional Innovations for Low Carbon Economy

The project approaches the 3 thematic pillars (TPs) in a fully integrated way. Partners are aware that only by bringing pieces of the puzzle together (services, organizational structures and technological solutions) regional policies on EE can be successful.

These three pillars structure is characterizing the project. Each TP represents a domain of interactions and operative application for the partners:

- TP1: Supplementary services and products offered by authorities
- TP2: Innovative cooperation models
- TP3: Innovative smart technologies.

The first TP represents the issues coming from role and responsibilities by the local authorities. Local authorities can play an active role in providing services and products in addressing energy issues that affect their local communities and are often looked to by local businesses and local residents for guidance and support on energy related issues. By identifying the energy products and supplementary services currently being offered by the local authority, and where practicable, making them more widely available, simple interventions and technologies can be introduced that have a great influence in behavioral change that contributes effectively towards a constantly improving 'energy aware' community.

Dramatic savings can be made from simple internal or consultant lead energy awareness campaigns that can not only reduce energy consumption and cost, but prove significant in encouraging behavioral change in management and staff. The identification of these services can be transferred and implemented into local policies and grouped into cost and manageability sectors by partners in such a way that best fits their organization.

The second TP fits whit the identification of innovative cooperation models to be implemented in concrete projects based on a primary role of local communities and citizens. Penetration of smart technologies and requirements of energy efficiency could be the leading factors when implementing the policy instruments in particular region. The current state and future trends on smart technologies penetration in the everyday life requires for the new cooperation models in order to empower those technologies in managing energy flows in order to increase energy efficiency. The proactive role of energy consumers is based on the energy awareness of local communities' and the ability to influence the way of policy instruments' implementation to the demand oriented direction. Therefore, the role of local authorities and all the stakeholders of energy sector should be oriented to finding the most appropriate cooperation models, which would be based on sustainability principles: economic, social and environmental ones through the whole value chain of energy supply. Sustainable value chain management is driven by the values of the final consumers.

The third TP regards the effective application of smart technologies in energy saving. In a general view the concept of "innovative technologies" in the sector of Energy Efficiency concern with a huge variety of technological solutions, equipment, procedures delivered both at hard (i.e. plants and infrastructure) and soft (i.e. software, web, and "smart" application) level of application. Therefore, the technology should be considered as a driver to enhance citizens' and communities' commitment in EE shared strategy.

The LOCARBO focus will be on "perceived benefits", "availability of risk sharing", "trust building process among stakeholders and local actors", "users' empowerment" considered as expected impact deriving from the adoption of technological plants or solutions.

The Province of Potenza looks at the implementation of the Territorial Master Plan as a way of concrete application of LOCARBO results especially in the weakest underdeveloped areas.

To look at inclusive energy policy making represents a form of innovation in governance models, practices and needs for new effective procedures to be integrated in the traditional administrative structure concerning territorial planning.

Apart from the technological innovation representing one of the most exploited issues in transnational cooperation project operating in the sector of energy efficiency, one of the main output of LOCARBO is the Local Implementation Plan: a strategic document affirming the route for transferring Learned Best Practices in the local policy framework, promoting investments and ensuring sustainable performance for the local communities.

3   Good Practices from Territory

Some of the good practices presented in this work fully testify the experimentation of new cooperation practices in low-density contexts, where the results are positive when virtuous collaborations have been activated, linking energy policies objectives with citizens awareness, sustainable energy themes and new local entrepreneurial actions able to provide positive externalities from the economic point of view and the exploitation of local resources.

For instance, the San Chirico Raparo biomass energy production plant, oriented to ensure electricity and heating supplies or public buildings, represents a driving factor to improve the wood chips industry in the municipality. Therefore it is relevant because it affects the local community not only in terms of energy savings but also as a local economy driver.

Starting from efficiency issues and from the need to convert energy production in a sustainable way, investments alternatives should be strongly connected with endogenous territorial resources (natural, cultural, human, financial etc.).

In the same way, the municipality of Calvello as well as Balvano with *At school for energy efficiency* project, testify how the citizens involvement and young population in particular in energy renewal processes, represents the winning strategy, necessary to take action of profound technological and scientific renewal of local contexts.

School has the opportunity to quality teaching approaches and training experiences putting in practice effective design activities for students; local administration could receive effective contribution allowing the identification of local interventions hypothesis in energy efficiency sector.

The development of a new class of smart technologies, make the sector and service extremely challenging and attractive from the scientific, technological, energetic, economic and social point of view as well as potentially very powerful.

Other GP are aimed at *monitoring* the efficiency of energy renewal initiatives undertaken, in order to demonstrate the positive effects on the environment and the economic benefits deriving from the use of new energy from renewable sources (Table 1).

Table 1. Classification of BP of the LOCARBO project based on the three TPs.

	Title	Synthetic description of the good practice
TP-1	**The Regional Energy Company** (SEL) energetic services	The Public Company SEL promotes interventions for the rationalization and reduction of energy consumption and related costs of public authorities of the regional/provincial territory, promoting also planning activities
	Province of Potenza as Covenant Coordinator for the Covenant of Mayors for Climate and Energy	The Province as a public authority provides strategic guidance and technical support to Covenant of Mayors signatories and municipalities willing to sign up to it. Main objective of the Province is to promote decarbonised and resilient territories, where citizens have access to secure, sustainable and affordable energy
	San Chirico Raparo Municipality biomass heating system	The Municipality of San Chirico Raparo (The Municipality is in the territory and under the jurisdiction of the Province of Potenza) commissioned an ESCO to realized biomass heating systems at the service of some public buildings. The Biomass comes from the forestry resources of the Municipality

(*continued*)

Table 1. (*continued*)

	Title	Synthetic description of the good practice
TP-2	Province of Potenza **Resilient Municipalities** and Communities' NetworK-WeResilient	The Province of Potenza, capitalizing on the strategic and positive experiences made in the past decade (especially through the Provincial Territorial Coordination Master Plan (TCP)) has constituted A WIDE TERRITORIAL NETWORK including all the 100 Municipalities of its territory through a statement of commitment aiming at developing a common territorial development strategy covering the combination of the three main components of territorial development: sustainable development, territorial safety and climate change contrasting policies
	Calvello Energetic Village	The municipality of Calvello (The Municipality is in the territory and under the jurisdiction of the Province of Potenza) has activated a strategy, also on the basis of its Sustainable Energy Action Plan (SEAP), with a strong community involvement, in the field of EE and RES actions in some strategic areas: - Public lighting, - Public and private buildings, - Transport, - Waste collection and recycling
	Melfi Sustainable Energy Strategy	The municipality of Melfi (The Municipality is in the territory and under the jurisdiction of the Province of Potenza) has activated a strategy, also on the basis of its Sustainable Energy Action Plan (SEAP), with a strong community involvement, in the field of EE and RES actions in some strategic areas: - Public lighting, - Public and private buildings, - Transport, - Waste collection and recycling
TP-3	**EE-SMS:** Energy Efficiency Smart Monitoring System	The Province of Potenza promoted the development of EE-SMS Pilot Application. It is based on a ICT Platform, connected with local sensors network, allowing new approach and model for monitoring energy consumption and energy performance in public building; in particular in schools. Such system pursued the objective to increase the awareness of operators and local communities interested in management/use of public buildings concerning energy consumption through 'real-time data' allowing experiment and evaluation of energy saving and energy consumption rationalization. Actually the system works on 6 sample buildings: 3 in the Province of Potenza and in the Municipality of Avrig (Romania)

(continued)

Table 1. (*continued*)

Title	Synthetic description of the good practice
ATER (Territorial agency for residential buildings) Sustainable Public Housing	The GP represents a model of design promoted by the public Entity ATER for the social housing. It is oriented to energy saving promoting the use of innovative materials with a low environmental impact, and RES technologies
At school for energy efficiency: A project of Energy Efficiency for the Public Lighting Networks of the industrial area of the Municipality of Balvano (PZ)	A project of Energy Efficiency for the Public Lighting Networks of the industrial area of the Municipality of Balvano (PZ), awarded with the second place at National competition ENEL of 2013. The Project has been realized by the teachers and students of the High School "Ten. Remo Righetti" in Melfi (PZ)

4   An Alternative "Context Based" Classification

The BP presented refers to a particular context, the province of Potenza, in which some phenomena must be explained in order to contextualize in a comprehensive manner the interventions and projects presented.

In particular we must consider some distinctive characteristics of the provincial territory that strongly connote its structure and dynamics.

The provincial territory includes 100 municipalities of which 82 with a population of less than 5,000 inhabitants. It has a population of about 377,258 residents with a population density (ab for sq km) of 57.21, lower than regional (59.4 ab/kmq.) (URBES 2015). This is a context in which there is a low population density and the territorial structure consists mainly of small municipalities in which there is an evident condition of settlement discomfort due to various factors.

First of all the persistence of a fragile economic development, expressed by an average income per inhabitant below the national average (10,519 € in 2015), and a lack of public and private services both to citizens and businesses. Moreover, the orographic conditions and extreme fragmentation of land ownership have strongly influenced the development of extensive agriculture.

In addition, a lack in infrastructures and services affects the ability of small and medium sized enterprises to form an economically relevant production sector, above all for the obvious difficulties related to road transport and the sale of products.

This has contributed to a gradual decline of many municipalities in the province of Potenza and especially those of small size with the triggering of progressive hydro-logical instability dynamics, exacerbated by the lack of adequate tools for town and country planning.

The lack of interest in the investments concentration, due both to a delayed infrastructural upgrading together with the progressive territory marginalization from the strategic decision-making processes, result in an area depopulation trend (−4.00% of resident population from 2001 to 2011, ISTAT).

This condition has a strong impact on the labour market as shown by the employment figures which, according to ISTAT surveys, show an unemployment rate of 20%, with a youth unemployment rate of nearly 34.2% in 2016.

The subtraction of human resources reduce economy growth prospects and deplete social and cultural fabric.

Moreover, aging of the population, witch in Potenza province is 187.2 elder people every 100 young people in 2017, testifies the presence of a large segment of over 65 year populations, not decisive in providing significant impulses to social and economic growth.

In this context, specific development strategies are needed, strongly linked to the local dimension where critical factors and resources must be identified.

Indeed, territory peculiarities and endogenous resources identification, is the support of a "place based" policy [3], oriented towards the implementation of development strategies that respond to the objectives and local needs in a dimension where cooperation with the actors, entrepreneurs and citizens takes on a fundamental role.

On the basis of these considerations it is possible to re-read the good practices of the LOCARBO project by making a reclassification based on new criteria and in particular:

– Low density contexts_development approaches in small communities;
– Integrated projects;
– Inter-institutional cooperation models;
– Collaborative approaches between institution and community;
– Valorization of communities skills and local resources.

4.1 Low Density Contexts_Development Approaches in Small Communities

Small local communities are often penalized because they do not have adequate economic and administrative resources to activate renewal processes.

Local Municipalities must activate local investments and promote development policies, implementing targeted renewal actions and demonstration investments that support a low carbon development strategy.

It is in this sense that the good practices of Calvello (TP-2) and San Chirico Raparo (TP-1), respectively 1,940 and 1,120 inhabitants in the Province of Potenza, turn out to be virtuous examples of activation in small local contexts in which the involvement of local communities is fundamental for the diffusion of sustainable behaviors, based on a formal 'green' agreement between users, local administrations and business/services operators.

In particular, pilot investments in the energy sector that have primarily affected public buildings and local services demonstrate that the adoption of low-carbon energy sources generates significant benefits from the economic and environmental point of view, allowing the population to get in touch with the new opportunities and benefits resulting from a smarter use of existing resources.

These type of policies stimulate the interest in conversion to the renewable energy use for private buildings, triggering a renewal of private buildings and the growth of local businesses.

The municipality of Calvello has recognized the importance to develop a new policy in the energy sector fully recognizing the proactive role of energy consumers in the renovation process. In fact, many interventions have been financed for private buildings renovation through the activation of reward mechanisms that have encouraged private individuals to catch up with energy innovations, encouraging virtuous cooperation processes towards common and shared objectives. In addiction the municipality has carried out a series of actions that, by exploiting the oil royalties as a source of funding, has allowed the start of a process of "democratization of energy". The process of financing energy renewal actions is a virtuous process that gives back to the community the greatest benefits both in terms of energy saving and the possibility of renewing the building stock. The renewal process has also triggered virtuous investment mechanisms in which local entrepreneurs could play a key role in the construction of alternative and clean energy production plants.

San Chirico Raparo municipality has achieved a biomass heating system at the service of some public buildings. The biomass comes from the forestry resources of the Municipality. So a process of local entrepreneurship involvement will start in order to stimulate biomass market and processing, to scale up biomass energy production for private energy consumption also. The local municipality is working to have a relevant representative role in reducing CO_2 emissions and being an experimental promoter for innovative energy production in a small local context. In particular it means:

- A significant reduction in energy consumption costs for municipal building and public buildings and services;
- Local economy implementation and development with new occupational scenarios;
- Local natural resources exploitation;

Technological innovation and the valorisation of local resources are two aspects that together constitute success factors for the development of local communities.

4.2 Integrated Projects

The good practices proposed in this paper are virtuous examples of integrated projects in which a series of actions contribute to implement a common development objective on sustainable energy and the intelligent use of resources.

In fact, on the basis of the Sustainable Energy Action Plan, some municipalities, such as Calvello (TP-2) and Melfi (TP-2), have activated a series of interventions in some strategic sectors such as redevelopment of public lighting systems, energy re-qualification interventions on municipal buildings and on existing building stock, actions in the transport and waste sectors, providing innovative and ecologically oriented technological solutions. Integrated interventions, together with an active stakeholders involvement and a set of tangible and intangible practices, aim at the energy transformation of the municipalities involved, evolving from energy consumers to self-sufficient entities.

4.3 Inter-institutional Cooperation Models

An important aspect according to which a classification of best practices is to be carried out is that of recognizing important inter-institutional cooperation initiatives aimed at facilitating and promoting relations among institutions, the experiences exchange, the creation of inter-institutional comparison tables in which to converge towards common and shared priorities, favoring down-scaling processes of community policies in local contexts and creating the ideal conditions for actively involving the potentially interested parties.

The Province of Potenza, capitalizing the strategic and positive experiences made in the past decade (especially through the Provincial Territorial Coordination Master Plan (TCP)) has constituted a wide territorial nework including all the 100 Municipalities of its territory through a statement of commitment aiming at developing a common territorial development strategy covering the combination of the three main components of territorial development: sustainable development, territorial safety and climate change contrasting policies.

The implementation methodology is based on the active involvement of stakeholders, communities and civil society.

The Province, with the adoption of the Strategic Framework for the Contrast to Climate Change (2015) as a thematic study of the Provincial Structural Plan, is coordinating the active involvement of Municipalities and Communities on the topic of climate protection, through a strong action of propulsion and support also on the themes of renewable energy, energy efficiency and the conscious use of resources (Resilience). From 1 April 2016 the Province of Potenza is the leader of #we resilient (TP-2), a prestigious international cooperation project.

The overall objective is to improve policy-making tools to increase energy efficiency linked to the built environment. This will have to be achieved by experimenting with innovative ways by regional/local authorities that support the change in behavior of energy consumers.

Moreover The Province is strengthening the resilience implementation through an increasingly devolved "integrated territorial governance" coordination role and down-scaling the experience to the urban context by performing and coordinating participatory urban planning paths.

Until now many results have been reached. Promoting comprehensive resilience across the provincial territory, engaging local communities and indigenous culture in resilience implementation, permanent networking with Cities, stakeholders and major groups for a comprehensive sustainable territorial development, performing supportive actions to Cities with a subsidiary and wide-area approach, performing programs and actions for including communities and people in relevant institutional decision making processes, building capacities, developing capabilities, raising awareness, increasing political will and public support in local disaster risk reduction, building local to trans-national partnerships for sharing cooperation and best practices exchanges.

4.4 Collaborative Approaches Between Institution and Community

The Municipality of Melfi (TP-2) is representative of an effective approach in the design and implementation of the SEAP based on a broad integrated approach involving local institutions and communities. In particular the actions oriented to the energy and structural renovation of school buildings combined with technical and technological investments also the involvement of the users (teachers and students) as promoter of innovation. They delivered training activities on energy retrofits of the building also including the development of monitoring systems based on open technologies. This approach reinforced the commitment and the awareness of local community connecting citizens point of view on energy renovations with the dimension of investments procurements under the responsibility of local municipality.

The first step of implementation will be to monitor actions taken, through the measurement of their progress, of the budget spent for the activation and the tons of CO_2 reduced.

This is very important to activate the community's interest in the issues of energy saving and the use of sustainable sources in order to share the development objectives. In fact, the possibility of providing data that tangibly testifies to the benefits produced by this type of action helps to motivate the efforts undertaken.

This is the case of EE-SMS (TP-3) Pilot Application promoted by Province of Potenza. It is based on a ICT Platform, connected with local sensors network, allowing new approach and model for monitoring energy consumption and energy performance in public building; in particular in schools. Such system pursued the objective to increase the awareness of operators and local communities interested in management/use of public buildings concerning energy consumption through 'real-time data' allowing experiment and evaluation of energy saving and energy consumption rationalization.

The GP also represents a positive process of users capacity empowerment in energy management. In particular ICT sensors for energy consumption analysis was an enabling support to demonstrate how daily behaviors could contribute in global achievement in energy sector.

The process of technological implementation was connected with a process of local community engagement. Real data concerning specific energy consumption was the basic information for:

– Improving buildings energy management;
– Promoting/demonstrating users awareness in energy management.

4.5 Valorization of Communities Skills and Local Resources

This category of BP includes several projects that focus on the promotion and optimization of local resources, both in terms of professional development and skills in the sustainable energy sectors, and in terms of exploitation of renewable resources in the area.

Two good practices have been selected that fully respect these characteristics.

The first is "At school for energy efficiency_Energy Efficiency of Public Lighting Networks of the Industrial Zone of Balvano (PZ)" (TP-3) project that represents how local school community (teachers and students) could contribute to develop technical contribution of specific issues concerning energy renovation.

A winn-winn approach could be identified: school has the opportunity to quality teaching approaches and training experiences putting in practice effective design activities for students; local administration could receive effective contribution allowing the identification of local interventions hypothesis in energy efficiency sector.

In particular, local administrations need a growing need for support on a sensitive theme such as public lighting, and considering the confusion and the lack of valid, clear and standardized tools it is considered that GPs can favor sustainable and continuous development of skills and professionalism to support local administrations in the management of public lighting systems and the realization of effective planning of energy redevelopment and efficiency improvement programs.

The study was carried out in school and essentially focused on students with the aim of promoting, raising awareness and encouraging education and knowledge on energy saving, environmental pollution and technological innovation.

The second BP in this category refers to exploitation of local resources. San Chirico Raparo's biomass heating system (TP-1) is based on wood chips coming from municipal forests. This is a strongly contextualized project with respect to the site and local territorial characteristics. The plant represents a driving factor to improve the wood chips industry in the municipality. Therefore it is relevant because it affects the local community not only in terms of energy savings but also as a local economy driver.

The table below shows the new classification of GP according to the new criteria that arise from the reading of the place peculiarities (Table 2):

Table 2. Re-classification of GP according to the new criteria.

New classification criteria	BP proposed
Low density contexts_development approaches in small communities	**Calvello** Energetic Village (TP-2); **San Chirico Raparo** Municipality biomass heating system (TP-1)
Integrated projects	**Calvello** Energetic Village (TP-2); **Melfi** Sustainable Energy Strategy (TP-2)
Inter-institutional **cooperation models**	#**WeResilient**_Province of Potenza Resilient Municipalities and Communities' NetworK (TP-2); **The Regional Energy Company (SEL)** energetic services (TP-1); **ATER** (Territorial agency for residential buildings) Sustainable Public Housing (TP-3); **Province of Potenza as Covenant Coordinator** for the Covenant of Mayors for Climate and Energy (TP-1)
Collaborative approaches between institution and community	**EE-SMS**:Energy Efficiency Smart Monitoring System (TP3); **Melfi** Sustainable Energy Strategy (TP-2)
Valorization of **communities skills and local resources**	**At school for energy efficiency:** A project of Energy Efficiency for the Public Lighting Networks of the industrial area of the Municipality of Balvano (PZ) (TP-3); **San Chirico Raparo** Municipality biomass heating system (TP-1)

5 Conclusions

The aim is to bring out the highlights of the new policies affecting the development processes of the territory, providing important insights on aspects related to institutional interaction but also on the involvement of the population and endogenous resources activation.

The main idea of the LOCARBO project is to improve Policy Instruments in such way, that it would reflect the real need of the energy consumers.

This is to be achieved by finding innovative ways for regional/local authorities to support energy consumers' behaviour change (see also [16]). The challenge to involve and motivate stakeholders (especially energy consumers) is perceived broadly as a major problem for public authorities. Motivation and awareness of consumers are of high significance to influence their behaviour and support more conscious energy decisions.

In this view is recommended to pot emphasis on stakeholder involvement during Action Plan design and implementation [11]. As it is addressed in LOCARBO project [2], stakeholders are essential for the project, as most of the time national and regional policy makers (as a main stakeholder group) have the means to implement project results, thus their involvement is essential for long term success and result sustainability. According to those preliminary results and recommendations the LOCARBO experience will be traced as a good practice on applied sustainability in energy efficiency policy domain [17, 18].

Acknowledgement. This research was developed in the framework of the Project "Novel roles of regional and local authorities in supporting energy consumers' behaviour change towards a low carbon economy – LOCARBO" led by the Province of Potenza (Italy) and funded by the EU's European Regional Development fund through the INTERREG EUROPE, 2014–2020.

Emanuela De Marco contributed to this work in the frameworks of SMART BASILICATA training activities she attended at the Urban and Regional Engineering Laboratory (LISUT) at University of Basilicata.

References

1. Angelini, A., Bruno, A.: Place-based. Sviluppo locale e programmazione 2014–2020, Franco Angeli, Milano (2016)
2. Attolico, A., Scorza, F.: A transnational cooperation perspective for "low carbon economy". In: Gervasi, O., et al. (eds.) ICCSA 2016. LNCS, vol. 9786, pp. 636–641. Springer, Cham (2016). https://doi.org/10.1007/978-3-319-42085-1_54
3. Barca, F.: Un'agenda per la riforma della politica di coesione. Una politica di sviluppo rivolta ai luoghi per rispondere alle sfide e alle aspettative dell'Unione Europea. Rapporto indipendente (2009). www.dps.tesoro.it/documentazione/comunicati/2010/rapporto%20barca%20(capitoli %201%20e%205)_ita%2001_07_2010.pdf
4. Covenant of Mayors: How to develop a Sustainable Energy Action Plan (SEAP) – guidebook (2010). www.eumayors.eu/IMG/pdf/seap_guidelines_en.pdf
5. European Commission: First Report on Economic and Social Cohesion (1996). www.ec. europa.eu/regional_policy/sources/docoffic/official/repor_en.htm

6. European Commission: Second Report on Economic and Social Cohesion (2001). www.ec. europa.eu/regional_policy/sources/docoffic/offi/reports/contentpdf_it.htm
7. European Commission: Europa 2020. Una strategia per una crescita intelligente, sostenibile e inclusiva. Comunicazione della Commissione (2010). www.ec.europa.eu/eu2020/pdf/ COMPLET%20IT%20BARROSO%20-%20Europ%202020%20-%20IT%20version.pdf
8. European Commission: Integrated Territorial Investment (2013). www.ec.europa.eu/ regional_policy/sources/docgener/informat/2014/iti_en.pdf
9. Grossman, G.M., Helpman, E.: Innovation and Growth in the Global Economy. MIT Press, Cambridge (1991)
10. Las Casas, G., Scorza, F.: A renewed rational approach from liquid society towards anti-fragile planning. In: Gervasi, O., et al. (eds.) ICCSA 2017. LNCS, vol. 10409, pp. 517–526. Springer, Cham (2017). https://doi.org/10.1007/978-3-319-62407-5_36
11. Casas, G.L., Scorza, F.: Sustainable planning: a methodological toolkit. In: Gervasi, O., et al. (eds.) ICCSA 2016. LNCS, vol. 9786, pp. 627–635. Springer, Cham (2016). https://doi.org/ 10.1007/978-3-319-42085-1_53
12. Legambiente: Rapporto Comuni rinovabili 2016 (2016). www.legambiente.it/sites/default/ files/docs/rapporto_comuni_rinnovabili_2016.pdf
13. Ministero della coesione territoriale: Metodi e obiettivi per un uso effi cace dei Fondi Comunitari 2014–2020, Documento di apertura del confronto al pubblico (2012). www.coesioneterritoriale. gov.it/wp-content/uploads/2012/12/Metodi-e-obiettivi-per-unuso-efficace-dei-fondi-comuni tari-2014-20.pdf
14. Scorza, F., Attolico, A.: Innovations in promoting sustainable development: the local implementation plan designed by the province of Potenza. In: Gervasi, O., et al. (eds.) ICCSA 2015. LNCS, vol. 9156, pp. 756–766. Springer, Cham (2015). https://doi.org/10. 1007/978-3-319-21407-8_54
15. Scorza, F., et al.: Growing sustainable behaviors in local communities through smart monitoring systems for energy efficiency: RENERGY outcomes. In: Murgante, B., et al. (eds.) ICCSA 2014. LNCS, vol. 8580, pp. 787–793. Springer, Cham (2014). https://doi.org/ 10.1007/978-3-319-09129-7_57
16. Scorza, F.: Towards self energy-management and sustainable citizens' engagement in local energy efficiency agenda. Int. J. Agric. Environ. Inf. Syst. (IJAEIS) 7(1), 44–53 (2016)
17. Dvarioniene, J., Grecu, V., Lai, S., Scorza, F.: Four perspectives of applied sustainability: research implications and possible integrations. In: Gervasi, O., et al. (eds.) ICCSA 2017. LNCS, vol. 10409, pp. 554–563. Springer, Cham (2017). https://doi.org/10.1007/978-3-319-62407-5_39
18. Scorza, F., Grecu, V.: Assessing sustainability: research directions and relevant issues. In: Gervasi, O., et al. (eds.) ICCSA 2016. LNCS, vol. 9786, pp. 642–647. Springer, Cham (2016). https://doi.org/10.1007/978-3-319-42085-1_55

Author Index

Printed in the United States
By Bookmasters